SHELLY CASHMAN SERIES®

Microsoft® Office 365™
OFFICE 2016

ADVANCED

SHELLY CASHMAN SERIES®

Microsoft® Office 365™
OFFICE 2016

ADVANCED

Corinne L. Hoisington

Mary Z. Last

Philip J. Pratt

Eric J. Schmieder

Susan L. Sebok

Joy L. Starks

Misty E. Vermaat

CENGAGE
Learning·

Australia • Brazil • Japan • Korea • Mexico • Singapore • Spain • United Kingdom • United States

Microsoft® Office 2016: Advanced
Corinne L. Hoisington, Mary Z. Last, Philip J. Pratt, Eric J. Schmieder, Susan L. Sebok, Joy L. Starks, Misty E. Vermaat

SVP, General Manager: Balraj S. Kalsi

Product Director: Kathleen McMahon

Senior Product Team Manager: Lauren Murphy

Product Team Manager: Andrea Topping

Senior Director, Development: Julia Caballero

Product Development Manager: Leigh Hefferon

Managing Content Developer: Emma F. Newsom

Developmental Editors: Amanda Brodkin, Deb Kaufmann, Lyn Markowicz, Lisa Ruffolo, Karen Stevens

Product Assistant: Erica Chapman

Manuscript Quality Assurance: Jeffrey Schwartz, John Freitas, Serge Palladino, Susan Pedicini, Danielle Shaw, Chris Scriver

Production Director: Patty Stephan

Senior Content Project Manager: Stacey Lamodi

Manufacturing Planner: Julio Esperas

Designer: Diana Graham

Text Designer: Joel Sadagursky

Cover Template Designer: Diana Graham

Cover image(s): karawan/Shutterstock.com; Mrs. Opossum/Shutterstock.com

Compositor: Lumina Datamatics, Inc.

Vice President, Marketing: Brian Joyner

Marketing Director: Michele McTighe

Marketing Manager: Stephanie Albracht

The material in this book was written using Microsoft Office 2016 and was Quality Assurance tested before the publication date. As Microsoft continually updates Office 2016 and Office 365, your software experience may vary slightly from what is seen in the printed text.

Mac users: If you're working through this product using a Mac, some of the steps may vary. Additional information for Mac users is included with the data files for this product.

For product information and technology assistance, contact us at
Cengage Learning Customer & Sales Support, 1-800-354-9706

For permission to use material from this text or product, submit all requests online at **www.cengage.com/permissions**. Further permissions questions can be e-mailed to **permissionrequest@cengage.com**

Library of Congress Control Number: 2016943101

Soft-cover Edition ISBN: 978-1-305-87040-6

Loose-leaf Edition ISBN: 978-1-337-25135-8

Cengage Learning
20 Channel Center Street
Boston, MA 02210
USA

Cengage Learning is a leading provider of customized learning solutions with employees residing in nearly 40 different countries and sales in more than 125 countries around the world. Find your local representative at **www.cengage.com**.

Cengage Learning products are represented in Canada by Nelson Education, Ltd.

To learn more about Cengage Learning, visit **www.cengage.com**

Purchase any of our products at your local college store or at our preferred online store **www.cengagebrain.com**

Printed at CLDPC, USA, 04-18

Microsoft® Office 365™
OFFICE 2016
ADVANCED

Contents

Microsoft **PowerPoint 2016**

Microsoft **Access 2016**

Microsoft Outlook 2016

Productivity Apps for School and Work

Corinne Hoisington

OneNote
Sway
Office Mix
Edge

Lochlan keeps track of his class notes, football plays, and internship meetings with OneNote.

Zoe is using the annotation features of Microsoft Edge to take and save web notes for her research paper.

Nori is creating a Sway site to highlight this year's activities for the Student Government Association.

Hunter is adding interactive videos and screen recordings to his PowerPoint resume.

© Rawpixel/Shutterstock.com

Being computer literate no longer means mastery of only Word, Excel, PowerPoint, Outlook, and Access. To become technology power users, Hunter, Nori, Zoe, and Lochlan are exploring Microsoft OneNote, Sway, Mix, and Edge in Office 2016 and Windows 10.

In this Module

Learn to use productivity apps!
Links to companion **Sways**, featuring **videos** with hands-on instructions, are located on www.cengagebrain.com.

Introduction to OneNote 2016

notebook | section tab | To Do tag | screen clipping | note | template | Microsoft OneNote Mobile app | sync | drawing canvas | inked handwriting | Ink to Text

Bottom Line
- OneNote is a note-taking app for your academic and professional life.
- Use OneNote to get organized by gathering your ideas, sketches, webpages, photos, videos, and notes in one place.

As you glance around any classroom, you invariably see paper notebooks and notepads on each desk. Because deciphering and sharing handwritten notes can be a challenge, Microsoft OneNote 2016 replaces physical notebooks, binders, and paper notes with a searchable, digital notebook. OneNote captures your ideas and schoolwork on any device so you can stay organized, share notes, and work with others on projects. Whether you are a student taking class notes as shown in **Figure 1** or an employee taking notes in company meetings, OneNote is the one place to keep notes for all of your projects.

Figure 1: OneNote 2016 notebook

Each **notebook** is divided into sections, also called **section tabs**, by subject or topic.

Use **To Do tags**, icons that help you keep track of your assignments and other tasks.

Type on a page to add a **note**, a small window that contains text or other types of information.

Personalize a page with a **template**, or stationery.

Write or draw directly on the page using drawing tools.

Pages can include pictures such as **screen clippings**, images from any part of a computer screen.

Attach files and enter equations so you have everything you need in one place.

Creating a OneNote Notebook

OneNote is divided into sections similar to those in a spiral-bound notebook. Each OneNote notebook contains sections, pages, and other notebooks. You can use One-Note for school, business, and personal projects. Store information for each type of project in different notebooks to keep your tasks separate, or use any other organization that suits you. OneNote is flexible enough to adapt to the way you want to work.

When you create a notebook, it contains a blank page with a plain white background by default, though you can use templates, or stationery, to apply designs in categories such as Academic, Business, Decorative, and Planners. Start typing or use the buttons on the Insert tab to insert notes, which are small resizable windows that can contain text, equations, tables, on-screen writing, images, audio and video recordings, to-do lists, file attachments, and file printouts. Add as many notes as you need to each page.

Learn to use OneNote!

Links to companion **Sways**, featuring **videos** with hands-on instructions, are located on www.cengagebrain.com.

Syncing a Notebook to the Cloud

OneNote saves your notes every time you make a change in a notebook. To make sure you can access your notebooks with a laptop, tablet, or smartphone wherever you are, OneNote uses cloud-based storage, such as OneDrive or SharePoint. **Microsoft OneNote Mobile app**, a lightweight version of OneNote 2016 shown in **Figure 2**, is available for free in the Windows Store, Google Play for Android devices, and the AppStore for iOS devices.

If you have a Microsoft account, OneNote saves your notes on OneDrive automatically for all your mobile devices and computers, which is called **syncing**. For example, you can use OneNote to take notes on your laptop during class, and then open OneNote on your phone to study later. To use a notebook stored on your computer with your OneNote Mobile app, move the notebook to OneDrive. You can quickly share notebook content with other people using OneDrive.

Figure 2: Microsoft OneNote Mobile app

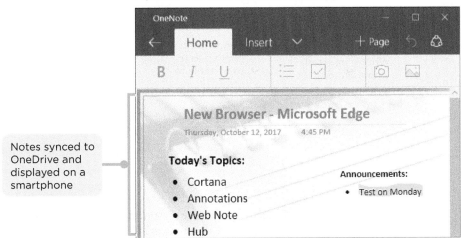

Notes synced to OneDrive and displayed on a smartphone

Taking Notes

Use OneNote pages to organize your notes by class and topic or lecture. Beyond simple typed notes, OneNote stores drawings, converts handwriting to searchable text and mathematical sketches to equations, and records audio and video.

OneNote includes drawing tools that let you sketch freehand drawings such as biological cell diagrams and financial supply-and-demand charts. As shown in **Figure 3**, the Draw tab on the ribbon provides these drawing tools along with shapes so you can insert diagrams and other illustrations to represent your ideas. When you draw on a page, One-Note creates a **drawing canvas**, which is a container for shapes and lines.

On the Job Now

OneNote is ideal for taking notes during meetings, whether you are recording minutes, documenting a discussion, sketching product diagrams, or listing follow-up items. Use a meeting template to add pages with content appropriate for meetings.

Figure 3: Tools on the Draw tab

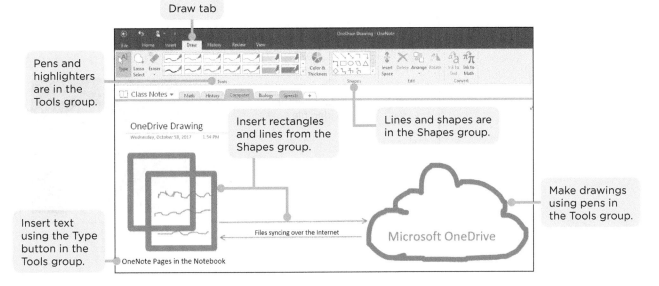

Draw tab

Pens and highlighters are in the Tools group.

Insert rectangles and lines from the Shapes group.

Lines and shapes are in the Shapes group.

Make drawings using pens in the Tools group.

Insert text using the Type button in the Tools group.

Converting Handwriting to Text

When you use a pen tool to write on a notebook page, the text you enter is called **inked handwriting**. OneNote can convert inked handwriting to typed text when you use the **Ink to Text** button in the Convert group on the Draw tab, as shown in **Figure 4**. After OneNote converts the handwriting to text, you can use the Search box to find terms in the converted text or any other note in your notebooks.

Figure 4: Converting handwriting to text

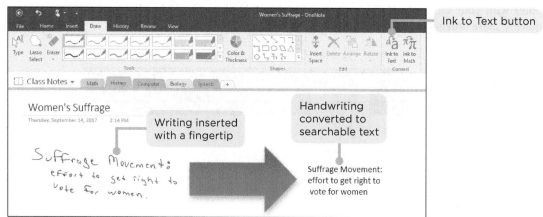

Ink to Text button

On the Job Now

Use OneNote as a place to brainstorm ongoing work projects. If a notebook contains sensitive material, you can password-protect some or all of the notebook so that only certain people can open it.

Recording a Lecture

If your computer or mobile device has a microphone or camera, OneNote can record the audio or video from a lecture or business meeting as shown in **Figure 5**. When you record a lecture (with your instructor's permission), you can follow along, take regular notes at your own pace, and review the video recording later. You can control the start, pause, and stop motions of the recording when you play back the recording of your notes.

Figure 5: Video inserted in a notebook

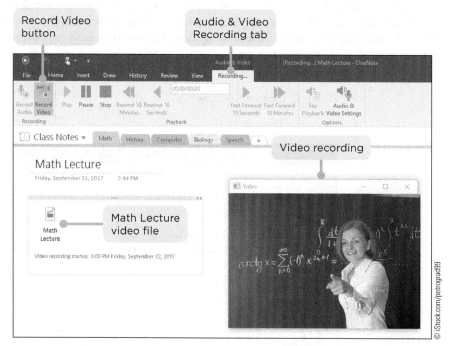

Try This Now

Learn to use OneNote!

Links to companion **Sways**, featuring **videos** with hands-on instructions, are located on www.cengagebrain.com.

1: Taking Notes for a Week

As a student, you can get organized by using OneNote to take detailed notes in your classes. Perform the following tasks:

    a. Create a new OneNote notebook on your Microsoft OneDrive account (the default location for new notebooks). Name the notebook with your first name followed by "Notes," as in **Caleb Notes**.

    b. Create four section tabs, each with a different class name.

    c. Take detailed notes in those classes for one week. Be sure to include notes, drawings, and other types of content.

    d. Sync your notes with your OneDrive. Submit your assignment in the format specified by your instructor.

2: Using OneNote to Organize a Research Paper

You have a research paper due on the topic of three habits of successful students. Use OneNote to organize your research. Perform the following tasks:

    a. Create a new OneNote notebook on your Microsoft OneDrive account. Name the notebook **Success Research**.

    b. Create three section tabs with the following names:

- **Take Detailed Notes**
- **Be Respectful in Class**
- **Come to Class Prepared**

    c. On the web, research the topics and find three sources for each section. Copy a sentence from each source and paste the sentence into the appropriate section. When you paste the sentence, OneNote inserts it in a note with a link to the source.

    d. Sync your notes with your OneDrive. Submit your assignment in the format specified by your instructor.

3: Planning Your Career

Note: This activity requires a webcam or built-in video camera on any type of device.

Consider an occupation that interests you. Using OneNote, examine the responsibilities, education requirements, potential salary, and employment outlook of a specific career. Perform the following tasks:

    a. Create a new OneNote notebook on your Microsoft OneDrive account. Name the notebook with your first name followed by a career title, such as **Kara - App Developer**.

    b. Create four section tabs with the names **Responsibilities, Education Requirements, Median Salary**, and **Employment Outlook**.

    c. Research the responsibilities of your career path. Using OneNote, record a short video (approximately 30 seconds) of yourself explaining the responsibilities of your career path. Place the video in the Responsibilities section.

    d. On the web, research the educational requirements for your career path and find two appropriate sources. Copy a paragraph from each source and paste them into the appropriate section. When you paste a paragraph, OneNote inserts it in a note with a link to the source.

    e. Research the median salary for a single year for this career. Create a mathematical equation in the Median Salary section that multiplies the amount of the median salary times 20 years to calculate how much you will possibly earn.

    f. For the Employment Outlook section, research the outlook for your career path. Take at least four notes about what you find when researching the topic.

    g. Sync your notes with your OneDrive. Submit your assignment in the format specified by your instructor.

Introduction to Sway

Sway site | responsive design | Storyline | card | Creative Commons license | animation emphasis effects | Docs.com

Bottom Line

- Drag photos, videos, and files from your computer and content from Facebook and Twitter directly to your Sway presentation.
- Run Sway in a web browser or as an app on your smartphone, and save presentations as webpages.

Expressing your ideas in a presentation typically means creating PowerPoint slides or a Word document. Microsoft Sway gives you another way to engage an audience. Sway is a free Microsoft tool available at Sway.com or as an app in Office 365. Using Sway, you can combine text, images, videos, and social media in a website called a **Sway site** that you can share and display on any device. To get started, you create a digital story on a web-based canvas without borders, slides, cells, or page breaks. A Sway site organizes the text, images, and video into a **responsive design**, which means your content adapts perfectly to any screen size as shown in **Figure 6**. You store a Sway site in the cloud on OneDrive using a free Microsoft account.

Figure 6: Sway site with responsive design

You can display a Sway presentation in a web browser.

Sway uses responsive design to make sure pages fit perfectly on any device.

© iStock.com/marinello, © iStock.com/marekuliasz

Learn to use Sway!

Links to companion **Sways**, featuring **videos** with hands-on instructions, are located on www.cengagebrain.com.

Creating a Sway Presentation

You can use Sway to build a digital flyer, a club newsletter, a vacation blog, an informational site, a digital art portfolio, or a new product rollout. After you select your topic and sign into Sway with your Microsoft account, a **Storyline** opens, providing tools and a work area for composing your digital story. See **Figure 7**. Each story can include text, images, and videos. You create a Sway by adding text and media content into a Storyline section, or **card**. To add pictures, videos, or documents, select a card in the left pane and then select the Insert Content button. The first card in a Sway presentation contains a title and background image.

Figure 7: Creating a Sway site

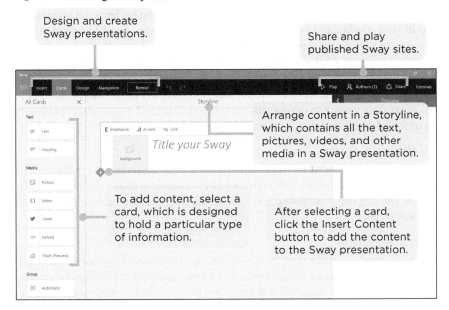

Design and create Sway presentations.

Share and play published Sway sites.

Arrange content in a Storyline, which contains all the text, pictures, videos, and other media in a Sway presentation.

To add content, select a card, which is designed to hold a particular type of information.

After selecting a card, click the Insert Content button to add the content to the Sway presentation.

Adding Content to Build a Story

As you work, Sway searches the Internet to help you find relevant images, videos, tweets, and other content from online sources such as Bing, YouTube, Twitter, and Facebook. You can drag content from the search results right into the Storyline. In addition, you can upload your own images and videos directly in the presentation. For example, if you are creating a Sway presentation about the market for commercial drones, Sway suggests content to incorporate into the presentation by displaying it in the left pane as search results. The search results include drone images tagged with a **Creative Commons license** at online sources as shown in **Figure 8**. A Creative Commons license is a public copyright license that allows the free distribution of an otherwise copyrighted work. In addition, you can specify the source of the media. For example, you can add your own Facebook or OneNote pictures and videos in Sway without leaving the app.

On the Job Now

If you have a Microsoft Word document containing an outline of your business content, drag the outline into Sway to create a card for each topic.

Figure 8: Images in Sway search results

Select the source of media objects

Information about Creative Commons licenses

Storyline title

The Market for Commercial Drones

Drag an image to the picture placeholder box

Suggested images in the search results

On the Job Now

If your project team wants to collaborate on a Sway presentation, click the Authors button on the navigation bar to invite others to edit the presentation.

Designing a Sway

Sway professionally designs your Storyline content by resizing background images and fonts to fit your display, and by floating text, animating media, embedding video, and removing images as a page scrolls out of view. Sway also evaluates the images in your Storyline and suggests a color palette based on colors that appear in your photos. Use the Design button to display tools including color palettes, font choices, **animation emphasis effects**, and style templates to provide a personality for a Sway presentation. Instead of creating your own design, you can click the Remix button, which randomly selects unique designs for your Sway site.

Publishing a Sway

Use the Play button to display your finished Sway presentation as a website. The Address bar includes a unique web address where others can view your Sway site. As the author, you can edit a published Sway site by clicking the Edit button (pencil icon) on the Sway toolbar.

Sharing a Sway

When you are ready to share your Sway website, you have several options as shown in **Figure 9**. Use the Share slider button to share the Sway site publically or keep it private. If you add the Sway site to the Microsoft **Docs.com** public gallery, anyone worldwide can use Bing, Google, or other search engines to find, view, and share your Sway site. You can also share your Sway site using Facebook, Twitter, Google+, Yammer, and other social media sites. Link your presentation to any webpage or email the link to your audience. Sway can also generate a code for embedding the link within another webpage.

Figure 9: Sharing a Sway site

Share button

Post the Sway site on Docs.com

Send friends a link to the Sway site

Drag the slider button to Just me to keep the Sway site private

Options differ depending on your Microsoft account

| ▷ Play | 유 Authors (1) | ⌂ Share |

Share ⬤ Just me

Share with the world

D Docs.com - Your public gallery

Share with friends

f 🐦 g+ Y⟨ ⟨ ···

https://sway.com/JQDFrUaxmg4IEbbk

◢ More options

☑ Viewers can duplicate this Sway

Stop sharing

Try This Now

1: Creating a Sway Resume

Sway is a digital storytelling app. Create a Sway resume to share the skills, job experiences, and achievements you have that match the requirements of a future job interest. Perform the following tasks:

    a. Create a new presentation in Sway to use as a digital resume. Title the Sway Storyline with your full name and then select a background image.

    b. Create three separate sections titled **Academic Background, Work Experience**, and **Skills**, and insert text, a picture, and a paragraph or bulleted points in each section. Be sure to include your own picture.

    c. Add a fourth section that includes a video about your school that you find online.

    d. Customize the design of your presentation.

    e. Submit your assignment link in the format specified by your instructor.

2: Creating an Online Sway Newsletter

Newsletters are designed to capture the attention of their target audience. Using Sway, create a newsletter for a club, organization, or your favorite music group. Perform the following tasks:

    a. Create a new presentation in Sway to use as a digital newsletter for a club, organization, or your favorite music group. Provide a title for the Sway Storyline and select an appropriate background image.

    b. Select three separate sections with appropriate titles, such as Upcoming Events. In each section, insert text, a picture, and a paragraph or bulleted points.

    c. Add a fourth section that includes a video about your selected topic.

    d. Customize the design of your presentation.

    e. Submit your assignment link in the format specified by your instructor.

3: Creating and Sharing a Technology Presentation

To place a Sway presentation in the hands of your entire audience, you can share a link to the Sway presentation. Create a Sway presentation on a new technology and share it with your class. Perform the following tasks:

    a. Create a new presentation in Sway about a cutting-edge technology topic. Provide a title for the Sway Storyline and select a background image.

    b. Create four separate sections about your topic, and include text, a picture, and a paragraph in each section.

    c. Add a fifth section that includes a video about your topic.

    d. Customize the design of your presentation.

    e. Share the link to your Sway with your classmates and submit your assignment link in the format specified by your instructor.

Introduction to Office Mix

add-in | clip | slide recording | Slide Notes | screen recording | free-response quiz

To enliven business meetings and lectures, Microsoft adds a new dimension to presentations with a powerful toolset called Office Mix, a free add-in for PowerPoint. (An **add-in** is software that works with an installed app to extend its features.) Using Office Mix, you can record yourself on video, capture still and moving images on your desktop, and insert interactive elements such as quizzes and live webpages directly into PowerPoint slides. When you post the finished presentation to OneDrive, Office Mix provides a link you can share with friends and colleagues. Anyone with an Internet connection and a web browser can watch a published Office Mix presentation, such as the one in **Figure 10**, on a computer or mobile device.

Figure 10: Office Mix presentation

Adding Office Mix to PowerPoint
To get started, you create an Office Mix account at the website mix.office.com using an email address or a Facebook or Google account. Next, you download and install the Office Mix add-in (see **Figure 11**). Office Mix appears as a new tab named Mix on the PowerPoint ribbon in versions of Office 2013 and Office 2016 running on personal computers (PCs).

Figure 11: Getting started with Office Mix

Capturing Video Clips

A **clip** is a short segment of audio, such as music, or video. After finishing the content on a PowerPoint slide, you can use Office Mix to add a video clip to animate or illustrate the content. Office Mix creates video clips in two ways: by recording live action on a webcam and by capturing screen images and movements. If your computer has a webcam, you can record yourself and annotate the slide to create a **slide recording** as shown in **Figure 12**.

Figure 12: Making a slide recording

Record your voice; also record video if your computer has a camera.

Use the Slide Notes button to display notes for your narration.

For best results, look directly at your webcam while recording video.

Choose a video and audio device to record images and sound.

Use inking tools to write and draw on the slide as you record.

When you are making a slide recording, you can record your spoken narration at the same time. The **Slide Notes** feature works like a teleprompter to help you focus on your presentation content instead of memorizing your narration. Use the Inking tools to make annotations or add highlighting using different pen types and colors. After finishing a recording, edit the video in PowerPoint to trim the length or set playback options.

The second way to create a video is to capture on-screen images and actions with or without a voiceover. This method is ideal if you want to show how to use your favorite website or demonstrate an app such as OneNote. To share your screen with an audience, select the part of the screen you want to show in the video. Office Mix captures everything that happens in that area to create a **screen recording**, as shown in **Figure 13**. Office Mix inserts the screen recording as a video in the slide.

Figure 13: Making a screen recording

Record the action on the screen within the red dashed outline.

Record audio while capturing your on-screen actions.

Select Area button

Inserting Quizzes, Live Webpages, and Apps

To enhance and assess audience understanding, make your slides interactive by adding quizzes, live webpages, and apps. Quizzes give immediate feedback to the user as shown in **Figure 14**. Office Mix supports several quiz formats, including a **free-response quiz** similar to a short answer quiz, and true/false, multiple-choice, and multiple-response formats.

Figure 14: Creating an interactive quiz

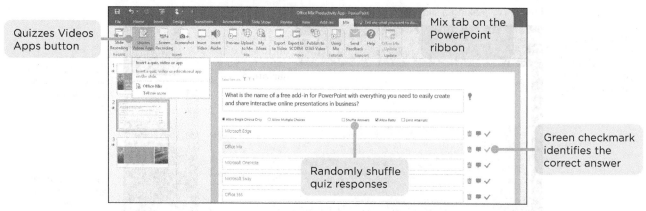

Quizzes Videos Apps button

Mix tab on the PowerPoint ribbon

Green checkmark identifies the correct answer

Randomly shuffle quiz responses

Sharing an Office Mix Presentation

When you complete your work with Office Mix, upload the presentation to your personal Office Mix dashboard as shown in **Figure 15**. Users of PCs, Macs, iOS devices, and Android devices can access and play Office Mix presentations. The Office Mix dashboard displays built-in analytics that include the quiz results and how much time viewers spent on each slide. You can play completed Office Mix presentations online or download them as movies.

Figure 15: Sharing an Office Mix presentation

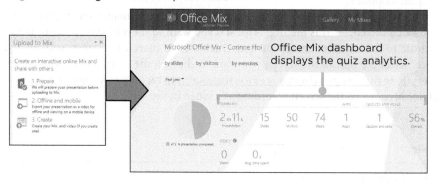

Office Mix dashboard displays the quiz analytics.

Try This Now

Learn to use Office Mix!
Links to companion **Sways**, featuring **videos** with hands-on instructions, are located on www.cengagebrain.com.

1: Creating an Office Mix Tutorial for OneNote

Note: This activity requires a microphone on your computer.

Office Mix makes it easy to record screens and their contents. Create PowerPoint slides with an Office Mix screen recording to show OneNote 2016 features. Perform the following tasks:

   a. Create a PowerPoint presentation with the Ion Boardroom template. Create an opening slide with the title **My Favorite OneNote Features** and enter your name in the subtitle.
   b. Create three additional slides, each titled with a new feature of OneNote. Open OneNote and use the Mix tab in PowerPoint to capture three separate screen recordings that teach your favorite features.
   c. Add a fifth slide that quizzes the user with a multiple-choice question about OneNote and includes four responses. Be sure to insert a checkmark indicating the correct response.
   d. Upload the completed presentation to your Office Mix dashboard and share the link with your instructor.
   e. Submit your assignment link in the format specified by your instructor.

2: Teaching Augmented Reality with Office Mix

Note: This activity requires a webcam or built-in video camera on your computer.

A local elementary school has asked you to teach augmented reality to its students using Office Mix. Perform the following tasks:

   a. Research augmented reality using your favorite online search tools.
   b. Create a PowerPoint presentation with the Frame template. Create an opening slide with the title **Augmented Reality** and enter your name in the subtitle.
   c. Create a slide with four bullets summarizing your research of augmented reality. Create a 20-second slide recording of yourself providing a quick overview of augmented reality.
   d. Create another slide with a 30-second screen recording of a video about augmented reality from a site such as YouTube or another video-sharing site.
   e. Add a final slide that quizzes the user with a true/false question about augmented reality. Be sure to insert a checkmark indicating the correct response.
   f. Upload the completed presentation to your Office Mix dashboard and share the link with your instructor.
   g. Submit your assignment link in the format specified by your instructor.

3: Marketing a Travel Destination with Office Mix

Note: This activity requires a webcam or built-in video camera on your computer.

To convince your audience to travel to a particular city, create a slide presentation marketing any city in the world using a slide recording, screen recording, and a quiz. Perform the following tasks:

   a. Create a PowerPoint presentation with any template. Create an opening slide with the title of the city you are marketing as a travel destination and your name in the subtitle.
   b. Create a slide with four bullets about the featured city. Create a 30-second slide recording of yourself explaining why this city is the perfect vacation destination.
   c. Create another slide with a 20-second screen recording of a travel video about the city from a site such as YouTube or another video-sharing site.
   d. Add a final slide that quizzes the user with a multiple-choice question about the featured city with five responses. Be sure to include a checkmark indicating the correct response.
   e. Upload the completed presentation to your Office Mix dashboard and share your link with your instructor.
   f. Submit your assignment link in the format specified by your instructor.

Introduction to Microsoft Edge

Reading view | Hub | Cortana | Web Note | Inking | sandbox

Microsoft Edge is the default web browser developed for the Windows 10 operating system as a replacement for Internet Explorer. Unlike its predecessor, Edge lets you write on webpages, read webpages without advertisements and other distractions, and search for information using a virtual personal assistant. The Edge interface is clean and basic, as shown in **Figure 16**, meaning you can pay more attention to the webpage content.

Figure 16: Microsoft Edge tools

Browsing the Web with Microsoft Edge

One of the fastest browsers available, Edge allows you to type search text directly in the Address bar. As you view the resulting webpage, you can switch to **Reading view**, which is available for most news and research sites, to eliminate distracting advertisements. For example, if you are catching up on technology news online, the webpage might be difficult to read due to a busy layout cluttered with ads. Switch to Reading view to refresh the page and remove the original page formatting, ads, and menu sidebars to read the article distraction-free.

Consider the **Hub** in Microsoft Edge as providing one-stop access to all the things you collect on the web, such as your favorite websites, reading list, surfing history, and downloaded files.

Locating Information with Cortana

Cortana, the Windows 10 virtual assistant, plays an important role in Microsoft Edge. After you turn on Cortana, it appears as an animated circle in the Address bar when you might need assistance, as shown in the restaurant website in **Figure 17**. When you click the Cortana icon, a pane slides in from the right of the browser window to display detailed information about the restaurant, including maps and reviews. Cortana can also assist you in defining words, finding the weather, suggesting coupons for shopping, updating stock market information, and calculating math.

Figure 17: Cortana providing restaurant information

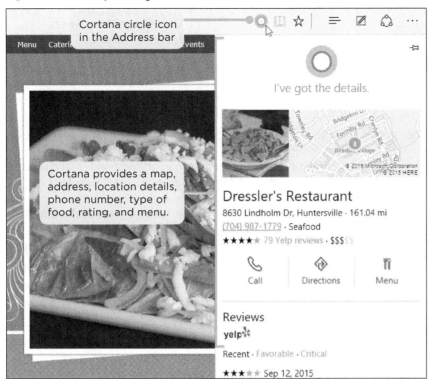

Annotating Webpages

One of the most impressive Microsoft Edge features are the **Web Note** tools, which you use to write on a webpage or to highlight text. When you click the Make a Web Note button, an **Inking** toolbar appears, as shown in **Figure 18**, that provides writing and drawing tools. These tools include an eraser, a pen, and a highlighter with different colors. You can also insert a typed note and copy a screen image (called a screen clipping). You can draw with a pointing device, fingertip, or stylus using different pen colors. Whether you add notes to a recipe, annotate sources for a research paper, or select a product while shopping online, the Web Note tools can enhance your productivity. After you complete your notes, click the Save button to save the annotations to OneNote, your Favorites list, or your Reading list. You can share the inked page with others using the Share Web Note button.

On the Job Now

To enhance security, Microsoft Edge runs in a partial sandbox, an arrangement that prevents attackers from gaining control of your computer. Browsing within the **sandbox** protects computer resources and information from hackers.

Figure 18: Web Note tools in Microsoft Edge

Inking toolbar with Web Note tools for making annotations

Writing and drawing created with the Pen tool

Highlighted text

Save a copy of the webpage with annotations

Typed note

Try This Now

1: Using Cortana in Microsoft Edge

Note: This activity requires using Microsoft Edge on a Windows 10 computer.

Cortana can assist you in finding information on a webpage in Microsoft Edge. Perform the following tasks:

a. Create a Word document using the Word Screen Clipping tool to capture the following screenshots.

- Screenshot A—Using Microsoft Edge, open a webpage with a technology news article. Right-click a term in the article and ask Cortana to define it.
- Screenshot B—Using Microsoft Edge, open the website of a fancy restaurant in a city near you. Make sure the Cortana circle icon is displayed in the Address bar. (If it's not displayed, find a different restaurant website.) Click the Cortana circle icon to display a pane with information about the restaurant.
- Screenshot C—Using Microsoft Edge, type **10 USD to Euros** in the Address bar without pressing the Enter key. Cortana converts the U.S. dollars to Euros.
- Screenshot D—Using Microsoft Edge, type **Apple stock** in the Address bar without pressing the Enter key. Cortana displays the current stock quote.

b. Submit your assignment in the format specified by your instructor.

2: Viewing Online News with Reading View

Note: This activity requires using Microsoft Edge on a Windows 10 computer.

Reading view in Microsoft Edge can make a webpage less cluttered with ads and other distractions. Perform the following tasks:

a. Create a Word document using the Word Screen Clipping tool to capture the following screenshots.

- Screenshot A—Using Microsoft Edge, open the website **mashable.com**. Open a technology article. Click the Reading view button to display an ad-free page that uses only basic text formatting.
- Screenshot B—Using Microsoft Edge, open the website **bbc.com**. Open any news article. Click the Reading view button to display an ad-free page that uses only basic text formatting.
- Screenshot C—Make three types of annotations (Pen, Highlighter, and Add a typed note) on the BBC article page displayed in Reading view.

b. Submit your assignment in the format specified by your instructor.

3: Inking with Microsoft Edge

Note: This activity requires using Microsoft Edge on a Windows 10 computer.

Microsoft Edge provides many annotation options to record your ideas. Perform the following tasks:

a. Open the website **wolframalpha.com** in the Microsoft Edge browser. Wolfram Alpha is a well-respected academic search engine. Type **US$100 1965 dollars in 2015** in the Wolfram Alpha search text box and press the Enter key.

b. Click the Make a Web Note button to display the Web Note tools. Using the Pen tool, draw a circle around the result on the webpage. Save the page to OneNote.

c. In the Wolfram Alpha search text box, type the name of the city closest to where you live and press the Enter key. Using the Highlighter tool, highlight at least three interesting results. Add a note and then type a sentence about what you learned about this city. Save the page to OneNote. Share your OneNote notebook with your instructor.

d. Submit your assignment link in the format specified by your instructor.

8 | Using Document Collaboration, Integration, and Charting Tools

Objectives

You will have mastered the material in this module when you can:

- Insert, edit, view, and delete comments
- Track changes
- Review tracked changes
- Compare documents
- Combine documents
- Link an Excel worksheet to a Word document
- Break a link
- Create a chart in Word
- Format a Word chart
- View and scroll through side-by-side documents
- Create a new document for a blog post
- Insert a quick table
- Publish a blog post

Introduction

Word provides the capability for users to work with other users, or **collaborate**, on a document. For example, you can show edits made to a document so that others can review the edits. You also can merge edits from multiple users or compare two documents to determine the differences between them.

From Word, you can interact with other programs and incorporate the data and objects from those programs in a Word document. For example, you can link an Excel worksheet in a Word document or publish a blog post from Word. You also can use the charting features of Microsoft Office 2016 in Word.

Project — Memo with Chart

A memo is an informal document that businesses use to correspond with others. Memos often are internal to an organization, for example, to employees or coworkers.

The project in this module uses Word to produce the memo shown in Figure 8–1. First, you open an existing document that contains the memo and the Word table. Next, you insert comments and edit the document, showing the changes so that other users can review the changes. The changes appear on the screen with options that allow the author of the document to accept or reject the changes and delete the comments. Then, you chart the Word table using charting features available in several Microsoft Office applications. In this module, you also learn how to link an Excel worksheet to a Word document and create a document for a blog post.

INTEROFFICE MEMORANDUM

TO: ALL EMPLOEES
FROM: TIMO PEREZ
SUBJECT: QUARTERLY REVENUE COMPARISON
DATE: OCTOBER 20, 2017

Revenue figures for the third quarter have been compiled. I would like to thank everyone for helping our fitness center realize an increase in revenue during the third quarter. Below are a table and chart that show a revenue comparison for the last two quarters. In the next few days, you will see a post on our blog, indicating upcoming dates associated with our appreciation events.

Second and Third Quarter Revenue Comparison

Revenue Category	Third Quarter	Second Quarter
Athletic Instruction	$4,689.25	$4,140.25
Guest Admission Fees	$987.32	$897.65
Membership Fees	$31,975.99	$28,676.47
Merchandise Sales	$9,547.22	$8,569.14
Personal Training Services	$9,876.32	$8,762.77
Snack Bar	$6,842.75	$6,157.50
Supplement Sales	$3,021.22	$2,729.42

Word table

chart created from Word table

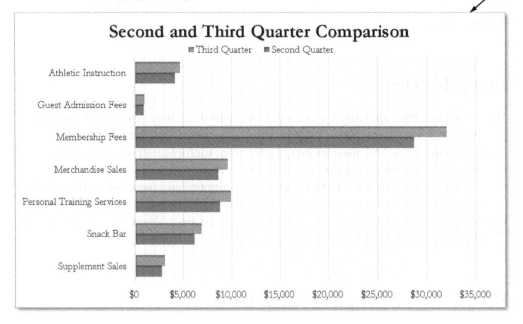

Figure 8–1

In this module, you will learn how to create the document shown in Figure 8–1. The following roadmap identifies general activities you will perform as you progress through this module:

1. INSERT COMMENTS AND TRACK CHANGES in the memo with the table.

2. REVIEW the COMMENTS AND TRACKED CHANGES.

3. LINK an EXCEL WORKSHEET TO a WORD DOCUMENT.

4. CHART a WORD TABLE using Word's Chart Tools tab.

5. CREATE AND PUBLISH a BLOG POST.

To Run Word and Change Word Settings

If you are using a computer to step through the project in this module and you want your screens to match the figures in this book, you should change your screen's resolution to 1366 × 768. The following steps run Word, display formatting marks, and change the zoom to page width.

1 Run Word and create a blank document in the Word window. If necessary, maximize the Word window.

2 If the Print Layout button on the status bar is not selected, click it so that your screen is in Print Layout view.

3 If the 'Show/Hide ¶' button (Home tab | Paragraph group) is not selected already, click it to display formatting marks on the screen.

4 To display the page the same width as the document window, if necessary, click the Page Width button (View tab | Zoom group).

Reviewing a Document

Word provides many tools that allow users to collaborate on a document. One set of collaboration tools within Word allows you to track changes in a document and review the changes. That is, one computer user can create a document and another user(s) can make changes and insert comments in the same document. Those changes then appear on the screen with options that allow the originator (author) to accept or reject the changes and delete the comments. With another collaboration tool, you can compare and/or merge two or more documents to determine the differences between them.

To illustrate Word collaboration tools, this section follows these general steps:

1. Open a document to be reviewed.

2. Insert comments in the document for the originator (author).

3. Track changes in the document.

4. View and delete the comments.

5. Accept and reject the tracked changes. For illustration purposes, you assume the role of originator (author) of the document in this step.

6. Compare the reviewed document to the original to view the differences.

7. Combine the original document with the reviewed document and with another reviewer's suggestions.

To Open a Document and Save It with a New File Name

Assume your coworker has created a draft of a memo and is sending it to you for review. The file, called Fitness Center Revenue Comparison Memo Draft, is located on the Data Files. Please contact your instructor for information about accessing the Data Files. To preserve the original memo, you save the open document with a new file name. The following steps save an open document with a new file name.

1 Navigate to the location of the Data Files on your hard drive, OneDrive, or other storage location.

2 Open the file Fitness Center Revenue Comparison Memo Draft.

If requested by your instructor, change the name Timo Perez at the top of the memo to your name.

3 Navigate to the desired save location on your hard drive, OneDrive, or other storage location.

4 Save the file just opened on your hard drive, OneDrive, or other storage location using Fitness Center Revenue Comparison Memo with Comments and Tracked Changes as the file name.

BTW

The Ribbon and Screen Resolution
Word may change how the groups and buttons within the groups appear on the ribbon, depending on the computer's screen resolution. Thus, your ribbon may look different from the ones in this book if you are using a screen resolution other than 1366 x 768.

To Insert a Comment

1 INSERT COMMENTS & TRACK CHANGES | 2 REVIEW COMMENTS & TRACKED CHANGES
3 LINK EXCEL WORKSHEET TO WORD DOCUMENT | 4 CHART WORD TABLE | 5 CREATE & PUBLISH BLOG POST

Reviewers often use comments to communicate suggestions, tips, and other messages to the author of a document. A **comment** is a note inserted in a document. Comments do not affect the text of the document.

After reading through the memo, you have two comments for the originator (author) of the document. The following steps insert a comment in the document. *Why? You insert a comment that requests that the author insert a graph in the document.*

• Position the insertion point at the location where the comment should be located (in this case, in the third sentence of the memo immediately to the left of the t in the word, table).

• Display the Review tab.

• If the 'Display for Review' box (Review tab | Tracking group) does not show All Markup, click the 'Display for Review' arrow (Review tab | Tracking group) and then click All Markup on the Display for Review menu to instruct Word to display the document with all proposed edits shown as markup (Figure 8–2).

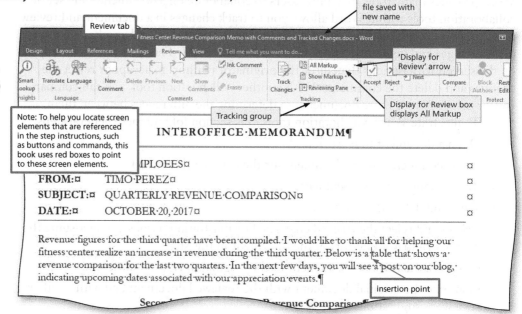

Figure 8–2

Q&A What are the other Display for Review options?

If you click the 'Display for Review' arrow, several options appear. Simple Markup means Word incorporates proposed changes in the document and places a vertical line near the margin of the line containing the proposed change or a comment balloon at the location of a user comment. All Markup means that all proposed changes are highlighted and all comments appear in full. No Markup shows the proposed edits as part of the final document, instead of as markup. Original shows the document before changes.

②

- Click the 'Insert a Comment' button (Review tab | Comments group) to display a comment balloon in the markup area in the document window and place comment marks around the commented text in the document window.

- Change the zoom so that the entire document and markup area are visible in the document window (Figure 8–3).

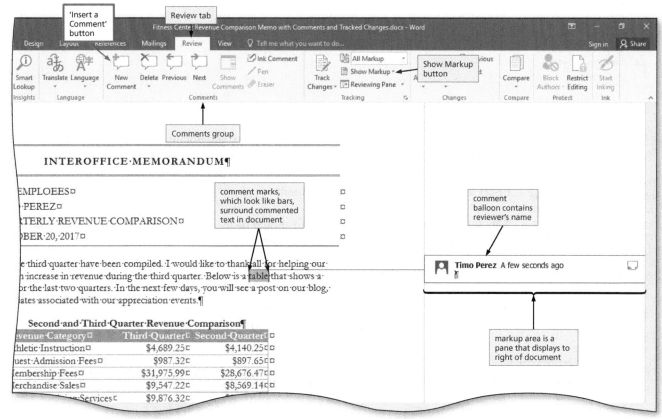

Figure 8–3

Q&A What if the markup area does not appear with the comment balloon?

The balloons setting has been turned off. Click the Show Markup button (Review tab | Tracking group) and then, if a check mark does not appear to the left of Comments on the Show Markup menu, click Comments. If comments still do not appear, click the Show Markup button again, point to Balloons on the Show Markup menu, and then click 'Show Only Comments and Formatting in Balloons' on the Balloons submenu, which is the default setting.

Why do comment marks surround selected text?

A comment is associated with text. If you do not select text on which you wish to comment, Word automatically selects the text to the right or left of the insertion point for the comment.

❸
- In the comment balloon, type the following comment text: **Add a graph of the data below the table.**
- If necessary, scroll to the right so that the entire comment is visible on the screen (Figure 8–4).

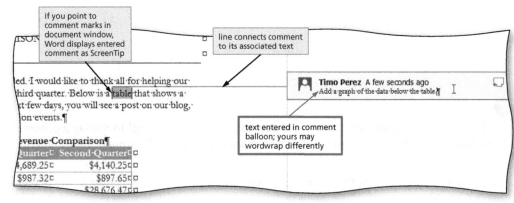

Figure 8–4

Other Ways

1. Press CTRL+ALT+M

To Insert Another Comment

BTW
Touch Screen Differences
The Office and Windows interfaces may vary if you are using a touch screen. For this reason, you might notice that the function or appearance of your touch screen differs slightly from this module's presentation.

The second comment you want to insert in the document is to request that the blog post also contain a calendar. Because you want the comment associated with several words, you select the text before inserting the comment. The following steps insert another comment in the document.

❶ Select the text where the comment should be located (in this case, the text, post on our blog, in the last sentence of the memo).

❷ Click the 'Insert a Comment' button (Review tab | Comments group) to display another comment balloon in the markup area in the document window.

❸ In the new comment balloon, type the following comment text: **Suggest posting a calendar on the blog.** (Figure 8–5).

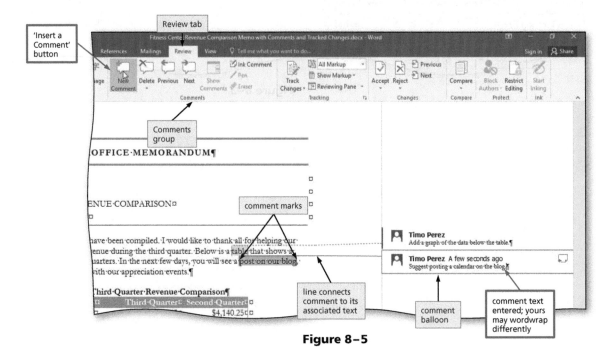

Figure 8–5

To Change Reviewer Information

Word uses predefined settings for the reviewer's initials and/or name that appears in the document window, the comment balloon, and the Reviewing task pane. If the reviewer's name or initials are not correct, you would change them by performing the following steps.

1a. Click the Change Tracking Options Dialog Box Launcher (Review tab | Tracking group) to display the Track Changes Options dialog box. Click the 'Change User Name' button (Track Changes Options dialog box) to display the Word Options dialog box.

or

1b. Open the Backstage view and then click the Options tab to display the Word Options dialog box. If necessary, click General in the left pane.

2. Enter the correct name in the User name text box (Word Options dialog box), and enter the correct initials in the Initials text box.

3. Click the OK button to change the reviewer information. If necessary, click the OK button in the Track Changes Options dialog box.

To Edit a Comment in a Comment Balloon

You modify comments in a comment balloon by clicking inside the comment balloon and editing the same way you edit text in the document window. In this project, you change the word, graph, to the word, chart, in the first comment. The following steps edit a comment in a balloon.

1 Click the first comment balloon to select it.

Q&A How can I tell if a comment is selected?
A selected comment appears surrounded by a rectangle and contains a Reply button to the right of the comment.

2 Position the insertion point at the location of the text to edit (in this case, to the left of the g in graph in the first comment) (Figure 8–6).

3 Replace the word, graph, with the word, chart, to edit the comment (shown in Figure 8–7).

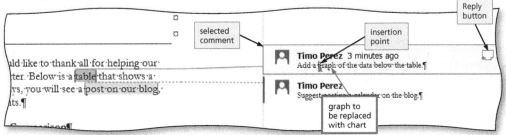

Figure 8–6

To Reply to a Comment

1 INSERT COMMENTS & TRACK CHANGES | 2 REVIEW COMMENTS & TRACKED CHANGES
3 LINK EXCEL WORKSHEET TO WORD DOCUMENT | 4 CHART WORD TABLE | 5 CREATE & PUBLISH BLOG POST

Sometimes, you want to reply to an existing comment. *Why? You may want to respond to a question by another reviewer or provide additional information to a previous comment you inserted.* The following steps reply to the first comment you inserted in the document.

1

- If necessary, click the comment to which you wish to reply so that the comment is selected (in this case, the first comment).

2

- Click the Reply button in the selected comment to display a reply comment for the selected comment.

3

- In the new indented comment, type the following comment text: **Suggest using horizontal bars to plot the categories.** (Figure 8–7).

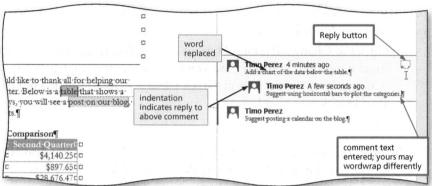

Figure 8–7

Other Ways
1. Click 'Insert a Comment' button (Review tab | Comments group) 2. Press CTRL+ALT+M

To Customize the Status Bar

1 INSERT COMMENTS & TRACK CHANGES | 2 REVIEW COMMENTS & TRACKED CHANGES
3 LINK EXCEL WORKSHEET TO WORD DOCUMENT | 4 CHART WORD TABLE | 5 CREATE & PUBLISH BLOG POST

You can customize the items that appear on the status bar. Recall that the status bar presents information about a document, the progress of current tasks, the status of certain commands and keys, and controls for viewing. Some indicators and buttons appear and disappear as you type text or perform certain commands. Others remain on the status bar at all times.

The following steps customize the status bar to show the Track Changes indicator. *Why? The Track Changes indicator does not appear by default on the status bar.*

1

- If the status bar does not show a desired item (in this case, the Track Changes indicator), right-click anywhere on the status bar to display the Customize Status Bar menu.

2

- Click the item on the Customize Status Bar menu that you want to show (in this case, Track Changes) to place a check mark beside the item, which also immediately may show as an indicator on the status bar (Figure 8–8).

Q&A Can I show or hide any of the items listed on the Customize Status Bar menu?
Yes, click the item to display or remove its check mark.

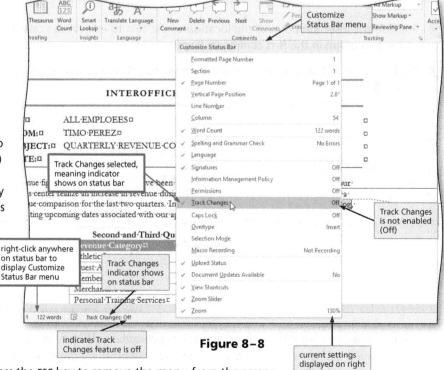

Figure 8–8

3

- Click anywhere outside of the Customize Status Bar menu or press the ESC key to remove the menu from the screen.

To Enable Tracked Changes

When you edit a document that has the track changes feature enabled, Word marks all text or graphics that you insert, delete, or modify and refers to the revisions as **markups** or **revision marks**. An author can identify the changes a reviewer has made by looking at the markups in a document. The author also has the ability to accept or reject any change that a reviewer has made to a document.

The following step enables tracked changes. **Why?** *To track changes in a document, you must enable (turn on) the track changes feature.*

1

- If the Track Changes indicator on the status bar shows that the track changes feature is off, click the Track Changes indicator on the status bar to enable the track changes feature (Figure 8–9).

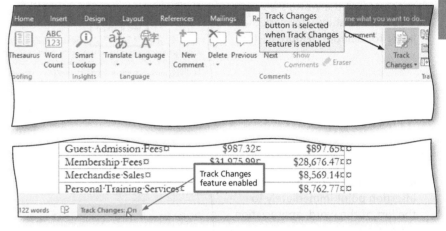

Figure 8–9

Other Ways

1. Click Track Changes button (Review tab | Tracking group)

2. Click Track Changes arrow (Review tab | Tracking group), click Track Changes

3. Press CTRL+SHIFT+E

To Track Changes

You have four suggested changes for the current document:

1. Insert the words, and chart, after the word, table, in the third sentence so that it reads: ... a table and chart that ...

2. Delete the letter, s, at the end of the word, shows.

3. Insert the word, upcoming, before the word, appreciation, in the last sentence so that it reads: ... our upcoming appreciation events.

4. Change the word, all, to the word, everyone, in the first sentence so that it reads: ... thank everyone for....

The following steps track these changes as you enter them in the document. **Why?** *You want edits you make to the document to show so that others can review the edits.*

- Position the insertion point immediately to the left of the word, that, in the third sentence of the memo to position the insertion point at the location for the tracked change.

- Type **and chart** and then press the SPACEBAR to insert the typed text as a tracked change (Figure 8–10).

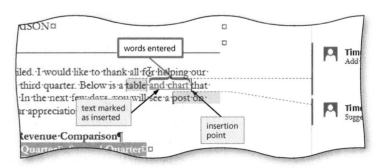

Figure 8–10

Why is the inserted text in color and underlined?

When the track changes feature is enabled, Word marks (signals) all text inserts by underlining them and changing their color, and marks all deletions by striking through them and changing their color.

When I scroll left, I see a vertical bar in the margin. What is the bar?

The bar is called a changed line (shown in Figure 8–16), which indicates a tracked change is on the line to the right of the bar.

2

- In the same sentence, delete the s at the end of the word, shows (so that it reads, show), to mark the letter for deletion (Figure 8–11).

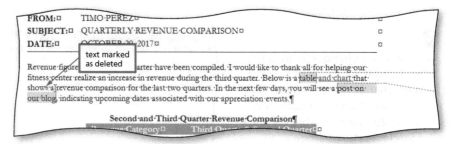

Figure 8–11

3

- In the next sentence, position the insertion point immediately to the left of the word, appreciation. Type **upcoming** and then press the SPACEBAR to insert the typed text as a tracked change.

- In the second sentence, double-click the word, all, to select it.

- Type **everyone** as the replacement text, which tracks a deletion and an insertion change (Figure 8–12).

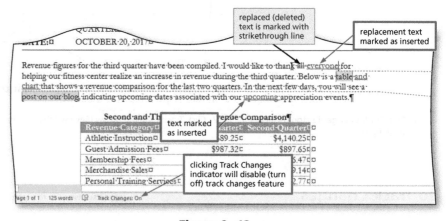

Figure 8–12

Can I see the name of the person who tracked a change?

You can point to a tracked change in the document window; Word then will display a ScreenTip that identifies the reviewer's name and the type of change made by that reviewer.

TO CHANGE HOW MARKUPS AND COMMENTS ARE DISPLAYED

The tracked changes entered in the previous steps appeared inline instead of in markup balloons. Inline means that the inserts are underlined and the deletions are shown as strikethroughs. The default Word setting displays comments and formatting changes in balloons and all other changes inline. If you wanted all changes and comments to appear in balloons or all changes and comments to appear inline, you would perform the following steps.

1. Click the Show Markup button (Review tab | Tracking group) to display the Show Markup menu and then point to Balloons on the Show Markup menu.

2. If you want all revisions and comments to appear in balloons, click 'Show Revisions in Balloons' on the Balloons submenu. If you want all revisions and comments to appear inline, click 'Show All Revisions Inline' on the Balloons submenu. If you want to use the default Word setting, click 'Show Only Comments and Formatting in Balloons' on the Balloons submenu.

To Disable Tracked Changes

When you have finished tracking changes, you should disable (turn off) the track changes feature so that Word stops marking your revisions. You follow the same steps to disable tracked changes as you did to enable them; that is, the indicator or button or keyboard shortcut functions as a toggle, turning the track changes feature on or off each time the command is issued. The following step disables tracked changes.

1 To turn the track changes feature off, click the Track Changes indicator on the status bar (shown in Figure 8–12), or click the Track Changes button (Review tab | Tracking group), or press CTRL+SHIFT+E.

To Use the Reviewing Task Pane

1 INSERT COMMENTS & TRACK CHANGES | 2 REVIEW COMMENTS & TRACKED CHANGES
3 LINK EXCEL WORKSHEET TO WORD DOCUMENT | 4 CHART WORD TABLE | 5 CREATE & PUBLISH BLOG POST

Word provides a Reviewing task pane that can be displayed either at the left edge (vertically) or the bottom (horizontally) of the screen. *Why? As an alternative to reading through tracked changes in the document window and comment balloons in the markup area, some users prefer to view tracked changes and comments in the Reviewing task pane.* The following steps display the Reviewing task pane on the screen.

1
- Click the Reviewing Pane arrow (Review tab | Tracking group) to display the Reviewing Pane menu (Figure 8–13).

2
- Click 'Reviewing Pane Vertical' on the Reviewing Pane menu to display the Reviewing task pane on the left side of the Word window.

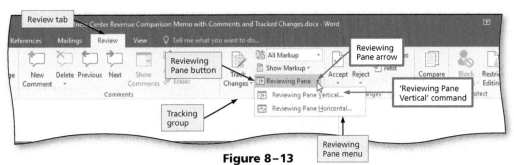

Figure 8–13

Q&A What if I click the Reviewing Pane button instead of the button arrow?
Word displays the Reviewing task pane in its most recent location, that is, either vertically on the left side of the screen or horizontally on the bottom of the screen.

3
- Click the Show Markup button (Review tab | Tracking group) to display the Show Markup menu.
- Point to Balloons on the Show Markup menu to display the Balloons submenu (Figure 8–14).

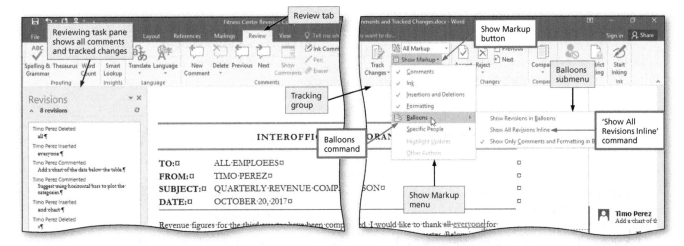

Figure 8–14

Why display the Balloons submenu?

Because the Reviewing task pane shows all comments, you do not need the markup area to display comment balloons. Thus, you will display all revisions inline.

4

• Click 'Show All Revisions Inline' on the Balloons submenu to remove the markup area from the Word window and place all markups inline (Figure 8–15).

 Can I edit revisions in the Reviewing task pane?

Yes. Simply click in the Reviewing task pane and edit the text the same way you edit in the document window.

5

• Click the Close button in the Reviewing task pane to close the task pane.

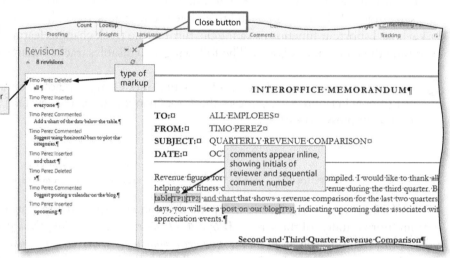

Figure 8–15

 Can I also click the Reviewing Pane button on the ribbon to close the task pane?

Yes.

To Display Tracked Changes and Comments as Simple Markup

1 INSERT COMMENTS & TRACK CHANGES | 2 REVIEW COMMENTS & TRACKED CHANGES

3 LINK EXCEL WORKSHEET TO WORD DOCUMENT | 4 CHART WORD TABLE | 5 CREATE & PUBLISH BLOG POST

Word provides a Simple Markup option instead of the All Markup option for viewing tracked changes and comments. *Why? Some users feel the All Markup option clutters the screen and prefer the cleaner look of the Simple Markup option.* The following step displays tracked changes using the Simple Markup option.

1

• Click the 'Display for Review' arrow (Review tab | Tracking group) to display the Display for Review menu.

• Click Simple Markup on the Display for Review menu to show a simple markup instead of all markups in the document window (Figure 8–16).

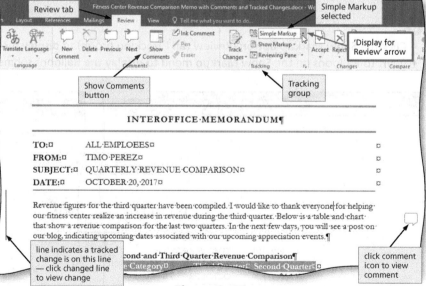

What if the comments appear in the markup area instead of as icons in the document?

Be sure the Show Comments button (Review tab | Comments group) is not selected. When the Show Comments button is selected, the comments appear in the markup area to the right of the document.

🅟 **Experiment**

• Click the comment icon to display the comments. Click the comment icon again to hide the comments.

Click one of the changed lines to display the tracked changes. Click one of the changed lines to hide the tracked changes.

Figure 8–16

To Show All Markup

You prefer to show all markup where comments appear in the markup area and have tracked changes visible in the document window. The following steps show all markup and comments in balloons.

1 Click the 'Display for Review' arrow (Review tab | Tracking group) and then click All Markup on the Display for Review menu to instruct Word to display the document with all proposed edits shown as markup.

2 Click the Show Markup button (Review tab | Tracking group) to display the Show Markup menu, point to Balloons on the Show Markup menu, and then click 'Show Only Comments and Formatting in Balloons', so that the markup area reappears with the comment balloons.

3 Save the memo again on the same storage location with the same file name.

TO PRINT MARKUPS

When you print a document with comments and tracked changes, Word chooses the zoom percentage and page orientation that will best show the comments on the printed document. You can print the document with its markups, which looks similar to how the Word window shows the markups on the screen, or you can print just the list of the markups. If you wanted to print markups, you would perform the following steps.

1. Open the Backstage view and then click the Print tab in the Backstage view to display the Print gallery.

2. Click the first button in the Settings area to display a list of options specifying what you can print. To print the document with the markups, if necessary, place a check mark to the left of Print Markup. To print just the markups (without printing the document), click 'List of Markup' in the Document Info area.

3. Click the Print button.

Reviewing Tracked Changes and Comments

After tracking changes and entering comments in a document, you send the document to the originator for his or her review. For demonstration purposes in this module, you assume the role of originator and review the tracked changes and comments in the document.

To do this, be sure the markups are displayed on the screen. Click the Show Markup button (Review tab | Tracking group) and verify that the Comments, 'Insertions and Deletions', and Formatting check boxes each contain a check mark. Ensure the 'Display for Review' box (Review tab | Tracking group) shows All Markup; if it does not, click the 'Display for Review' arrow (Review tab | Tracking group) and then click All Markup on the Display for Review menu. This option shows the final document with tracked changes.

If you wanted to see how a document would look if you accepted all the changes, without actually accepting them, click the 'Display for Review' arrow (Review tab | Tracking group) and then click No Markup on the Display for Review menu. If you print this view of the document, it will print how the document will look if you accept all the changes. If you wanted to see how the document looked before any changes were made, click the 'Display for Review' arrow (Review tab | Tracking group) and then click Original on the Display for Review menu. When you have finished reviewing the various options, if necessary, click the 'Display for Review' arrow (Review tab | Tracking group) and then click All Markup on the Display for Review menu.

To View Comments

1 INSERT COMMENTS & TRACK CHANGES | 2 REVIEW COMMENTS & TRACKED CHANGES
3 LINK EXCEL WORKSHEET TO WORD DOCUMENT | 4 CHART WORD TABLE | 5 CREATE & PUBLISH BLOG POST

The next step is to read the comments in the marked-up document using the Review tab. *Why? You could scroll through the document and read each comment that appears in the markup area, but you might overlook one or more comments using this technique. Thus, it is more efficient to use the Review tab.* The following step views comments in the document.

- Position the insertion point at the beginning of the document, so that Word begins searching for comments from the top of the document.

- Click the Next Comment button (Review tab | Comments group), which causes Word to locate and select the first comment in the document (Figure 8–17).

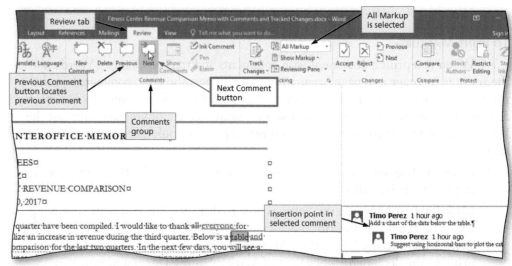

Figure 8–17

To Delete a Comment

1 INSERT COMMENTS & TRACK CHANGES | 2 REVIEW COMMENTS & TRACKED CHANGES
3 LINK EXCEL WORKSHEET TO WORD DOCUMENT | 4 CHART WORD TABLE | 5 CREATE & PUBLISH BLOG POST

The following step deletes a comment. *Why? You have read the comment and want to remove it from the document.*

- Click the Delete Comment button (Review tab | Comments group) to remove the comment balloon from the markup area (Figure 8–18).

Q&A
What if I accidentally click the Delete Comment arrow?
Click Delete on the Delete Comment menu.

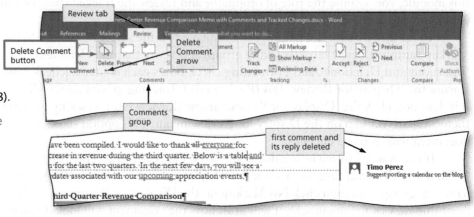

Figure 8–18

Other Ways

1. Right-click comment (or, if using touch, tap 'Show Context Menu' button on mini toolbar), click Delete Comment on shortcut menu

To Mark Comments as Done

Instead of deleting comments, some users prefer to leave them in the document but mark them as done. When you mark a comment as done, it changes color. If you wanted to mark a comment as done, you would perform the following steps.

1. Right-click the comment to display a shortcut menu.
2. Click 'Mark Comment Done' on the shortcut menu.

To Delete All Comments

1 INSERT COMMENTS & TRACK CHANGES | 2 REVIEW COMMENTS & TRACKED CHANGES
3 LINK EXCEL WORKSHEET TO WORD DOCUMENT | 4 CHART WORD TABLE | 5 CREATE & PUBLISH BLOG POST

The following steps delete all comments at once. ***Why?*** *Assume you now want to delete all the comments in the document at once because you have read them all.*

- Click the Delete Comment arrow (Review tab | Comments group) to display the Delete Comment menu (Figure 8–19).

- Click 'Delete All Comments in Document' on the Delete Comment menu to remove all comments from the document, which also closes the markup area (shown in Figure 8–20).

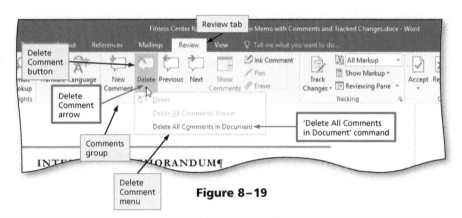

Figure 8–19

To Review Tracked Changes

1 INSERT COMMENTS & TRACK CHANGES | 2 REVIEW COMMENTS & TRACKED CHANGES
3 LINK EXCEL WORKSHEET TO WORD DOCUMENT | 4 CHART WORD TABLE | 5 CREATE & PUBLISH BLOG POST

The next step is to review the tracked changes in the marked-up document using the Review tab. ***Why?*** *As with the comments, you could scroll through the document and point to each markup to read it, but you might overlook one or more changes using this technique. A more efficient method is to use the Review tab to review the changes one at a time, deciding whether to accept, modify, or delete each change.* The following steps review the changes in the document.

- Position the insertion point at the beginning of the document, so that Word begins the review of tracked changes from the top of the document.

- Click the Next Change button (Review tab | Changes group), which causes Word to locate and select the first markup in the document (in this case, the deleted word, all) (Figure 8–20).

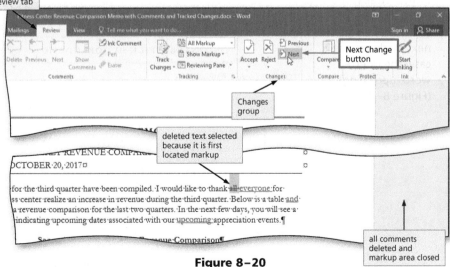

Figure 8–20

Q&A What if my document also had contained comments?

When you click the Next Change button (Review tab | Changes group), Word locates the next tracked change or comment, whichever appears first.

● Because you agree with this change, click the 'Accept and Move to Next' button (Review tab | Changes group) to accept the deletion of the word, all, and instruct Word to locate and select the next markup (in this case, the inserted word, everyone) (Figure 8–21).

Q&A

What if I accidentally click the 'Accept and Move to Next' arrow (Review tab | Changes group)?
Click 'Accept and Move to Next' on the Accept and Move to Next menu.

What if I wanted to accept the change but not search for the next tracked change?
You would click the 'Accept and Move to Next' arrow and then click 'Accept This Change' on the Accept and Move to Next menu.

Figure 8–21

3

● Click the 'Accept and Move to Next' button (Review tab | Changes group) to accept the insertion of the word, everyone, and instruct Word to locate and select the next markup (in this case, the inserted words, and chart).

● Click the 'Accept and Move to Next' button (Review tab | Changes group) to accept the insertion of the words, and chart, and instruct Word to locate and select the next markup (in this case, the deleted letter s).

● Click the 'Accept and Move to Next' button (Review tab | Changes group) to accept the deletion of the letter s, and instruct Word to locate and select the next markup (in this case, the inserted word, upcoming) (Figure 8–22).

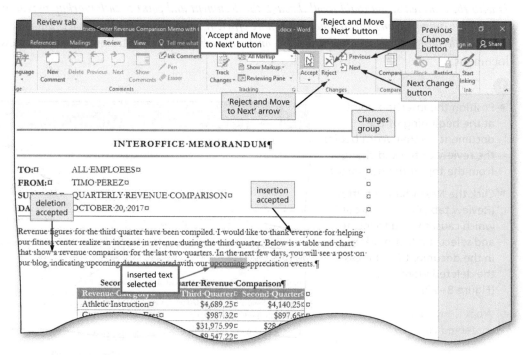

Figure 8–22

- Because you do not agree with this change, click the 'Reject and Move to Next' button (Review tab | Changes group) to reject the marked deletion, and instruct Word to locate and select the next markup.

Q&A

What if I accidentally click the 'Reject and Move to Next' arrow (Review tab | Changes group)?
Click 'Reject and Move to Next' on the Reject and Move to Next menu.

What if I wanted to reject the change but not search for the next tracked change?
You would click the 'Reject and Move to Next' arrow (Review tab | Changes group) and then click Reject Change on the Reject and Move to Next menu.

What if I did not want to accept or reject a change but wanted to locate the next tracked change?
You would click the Next Change button (Review tab | Changes group) to locate the next tracked change or comment. Likewise, to locate the previous tracked change or comment, you would click the Previous Change button (Review tab | Changes group).

- Click the OK button in the dialog box that appears, which indicates the document contains no more comments or tracked changes.

- Save the reviewed file on your hard drive, OneDrive, or other storage location using Fitness Center Revenue Comparison Memo Reviewed as the file name.

Other Ways

1. Right-click comment or tracked change (or, if using touch, tap 'Show Context Menu' button on mini toolbar), click desired command on shortcut menu

TO ACCEPT OR REJECT ALL TRACKED CHANGES

If you wanted to accept or reject all tracked changes in a document at once, you would perform the following step.

1. To accept all tracked changes, click the 'Accept and Move to Next' arrow (Review tab | Changes group) to display the Accept and Move to Next menu and then click 'Accept All Changes' on the menu to accept all changes in the document and continue tracking changes or click 'Accept All Changes and Stop Tracking' to accept all changes in the document and stop tracking changes.

or

1. To reject all tracked changes, click the 'Reject and Move to Next' arrow (Review tab | Changes group) to display the Reject and Move to Next menu and then click 'Reject All Changes' on the menu to reject all changes in the document and continue tracking changes or click 'Reject All Changes and Stop Tracking' to reject all changes in the document and stop tracking changes.

BTW

Document Inspector
If you wanted to ensure that all comments were removed from a document, you could use the document inspector. Open the Backstage view, display the Info gallery, click the 'Check for Issues' button, and then click Inspect Document. Place a check mark in the 'Comments, Revisions, Versions, and Annotations' check box and then click the Inspect button (Document Inspector dialog box). If any comments are located, click the Remove All button.

Changing Tracking Options

If you wanted to change the color and markings reviewers use for tracked changes and comments or change how balloons are displayed, use the Advanced Track Changes Options dialog box (Figure 8–23). To display the Advanced Track Changes Options dialog box, click the Change Tracking Options Dialog Box Launcher (Review tab | Tracking group) and then click the Advanced Options button (Track Changes Options dialog box).

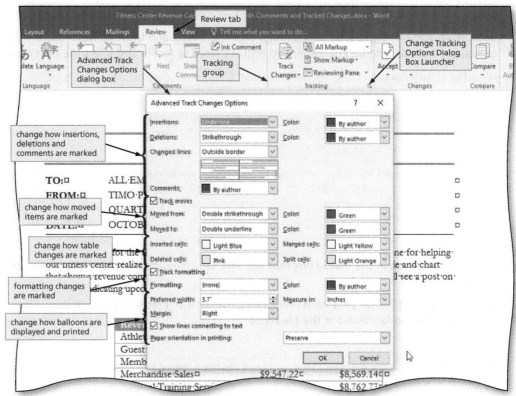

Figure 8–23

Compare and Merge
If you wanted to compare two documents and merge the changes into an existing document instead of into a new document, you would click the Original document option button (Compare Documents dialog box) to merge into the original document or click the Revised document option button (Compare Documents dialog box) to merge into the revised document (shown in Figure 8–25), and then click the OK button.

To Compare Documents

1 INSERT COMMENTS & TRACK CHANGES | 2 REVIEW COMMENTS & TRACKED CHANGES
3 LINK EXCEL WORKSHEET TO WORD DOCUMENT | 4 CHART WORD TABLE | 5 CREATE & PUBLISH BLOG POST

With Word, you can compare two documents to each other. *Why? Comparing documents allows you easily to identify any differences between two files because Word displays the differences between the documents as tracked changes for your review. By comparing files, you can verify that two separate files have the same or different content. If no tracked changes are found, then the two documents are identical.*

Assume you want to compare the original Fitness Center Revenue Comparison Memo Draft document with the Fitness Center Revenue Comparison Memo Reviewed document so that you can identify the changes made to the document. The following steps compare two documents.

- If necessary, display the Review tab.

- Click the Compare button (Review tab | Compare group) to display the Compare menu (Figure 8–24).

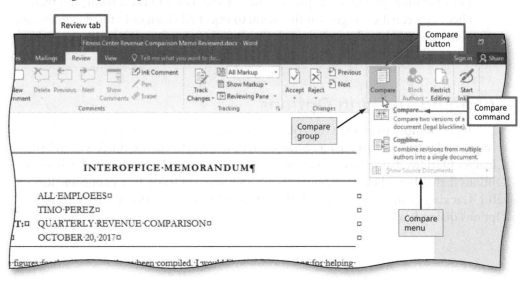

Figure 8–24

- Click Compare on the Compare menu to display the Compare Documents dialog box.

- Click the Original document arrow (Compare Documents dialog box) and then click the file, Fitness Center Revenue Comparison Memo Draft, in the Original document list to select the first file to compare and place the file name in the Original document box.

Q&A What if the file is not in the Original document list?
Click the Open button to the right of the Original document arrow, locate the file, and then click the Open button (Open dialog box).

- Click the Revised document arrow (Compare Documents dialog box) and then click the file, Fitness Center Revenue Comparison Memo Reviewed, in the Revised document list to select the second file to compare and place the file name in the Revised document box. If necessary, change the name in the 'Label changes with' box to Timo Perez.

Q&A What if the file is not in the Revised document list?
Click the Open button to the right of the Revised document arrow, locate the file, and then click the Open button (Open dialog box).

- If a More button appears in the dialog box, click it to expand the dialog box, which changes the More button to a Less button.

- If necessary, in the Show changes in area, click New document so that tracked changes are marked in a new document. Ensure that all your settings in the expanded dialog box (below the Less button) match those in Figure 8–25.

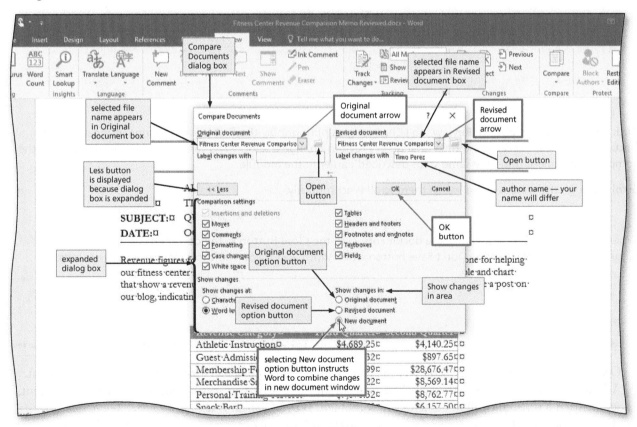

Figure 8–25

- Click the OK button to open a new document window and display the differences between the two documents as tracked changes in a new document window; if the Reviewing task pane appears on the screen, click its Close button (Figure 8–26). Note that, depending on settings, your compare results may differ from Figure 8–26.

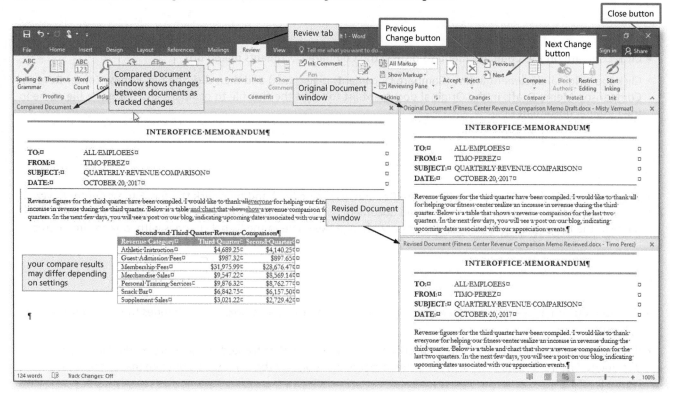

Figure 8–26

Q&A

What if the original and source documents do not appear on the screen with the compared document?
Click the Compare button (Review tab | Compare group) to display the Compare menu, point to 'Show Source Documents' on the Compare menu, and then click Show Both on the Show Source Documents submenu.

Experiment

- Click the Next Change button (Review tab | Changes group) to display the first tracked change in the compared document. Continue clicking the Next Change or Previous Change buttons. You can accept or reject changes in the compared document using the same steps described earlier in the module.

- Scroll through the windows and watch them scroll synchronously.

4

- When you have finished comparing the documents, click the Close button in the document window (shown in Figure 8–26) and then click the Don't Save button when Word asks if you want to save the compare results.

To Combine Revisions from Multiple Authors

1 INSERT COMMENTS & TRACK CHANGES | 2 REVIEW COMMENTS & TRACKED CHANGES
3 LINK EXCEL WORKSHEET TO WORD DOCUMENT | 4 CHART WORD TABLE | 5 CREATE & PUBLISH BLOG POST

Often, multiple reviewers will send you their markups (tracked changes) for the same original document. Using Word, you can combine the tracked changes from multiple reviewers' documents into a single document, two documents at a time, until all documents are combined. *Why? Combining documents allows you to review all markups from a single document, from which you can accept and reject changes and read comments. Each reviewer's markups are shaded in a different color to help you visually differentiate among multiple reviewers' markups.*

Assume you want to combine the original Fitness Center Revenue Comparison Memo Draft document with the Fitness Center Revenue Comparison Memo with Comments and Tracked Changes document and also with a document called Fitness Center Revenue Comparison Memo Reviewed by W Evans. The file by W Evans identifies another grammar error in the memo. The following steps combine these three documents, two at a time.

- Click the Compare button (Review tab | Compare group) to display the Compare menu (Figure 8–27).

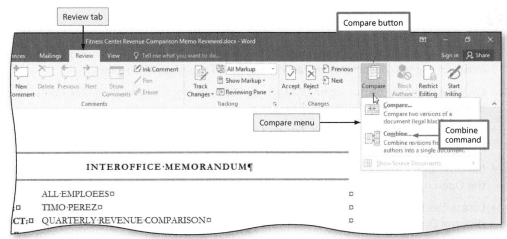

Figure 8–27

- Click Combine on the Compare menu to display the Combine Documents dialog box.

- Click the Original document arrow (Combine Documents dialog box) and then click the file, Fitness Center Revenue Comparison Memo Draft, in the Original document list to select the first file to combine and place the file name in the Original document box.

Q&A | What if the file is not in the Original document list?
Click the Open button to the right of the Original document arrow, locate the file, and then click the Open button (Open dialog box).

- Click the Revised document arrow (Combine Documents dialog box) and then click the file, Fitness Center Revenue Comparison Memo with Comments and Tracked Changes, in the Revised document list to select the second file to combine and place the file name in the Revised document box.

Q&A | What if the file is not in the Revised document list?
Click the Open button to the right of the Revised document arrow, locate the file, and then click the Open button (Open dialog box).

- If a More button appears in the dialog box, click it to expand the dialog box, which changes the More button to a Less button.

- In the Show changes in area, if necessary, click Original document so that tracked changes are marked in the original document (Fitness Center Revenue Comparison Memo Draft). Ensure that all your settings in the expanded dialog box (below the Less button) match those in Figure 8–28.

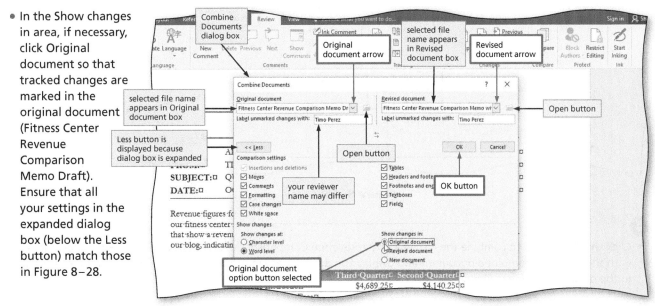

Figure 8–28

- Click the OK button to combine the Fitness Center Revenue Comparison Memo Draft document with the Fitness Center Revenue Comparison Memo with Comments and Tracked Changes document and display the differences between the two documents as tracked changes in the original document.

- Click the Compare button again (Review tab | Compare group) and then click Combine on the Compare menu to display the Combine Documents dialog box.

- Locate and display the file name, Fitness Center Revenue Comparison Memo Draft, in the Original document text box (Combine Documents dialog box) to select the first file and place the file name in the Original document box.

- Click the Open button to the right of the Revised document box arrow (Combine Documents dialog box) to display the Open dialog box.

- Locate the file name, Fitness Center Revenue Comparison Memo Reviewed by W Evans, in the Data Files and then click the Open button (Open dialog box) to display the selected file name in the Revised document box (Combine Documents dialog box).

- If a More button appears in the Combine Documents dialog box, click it to expand the dialog box.

- If necessary, in the 'Show changes in' area, click Original document so that tracked changes are marked in the original document (Fitness Center Revenue Comparison Memo Draft). Ensure that all your settings in the expanded dialog box (below the Less button) match those in Figure 8–29.

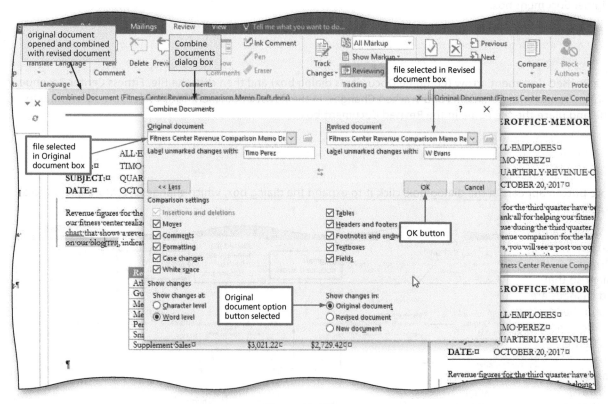

Figure 8–29

- Click the OK button to combine the Fitness Center Revenue Comparison Memo Reviewed by W Evans document with the currently combined document and display the differences among the three documents as tracked changes in the original document (Figure 8–30).

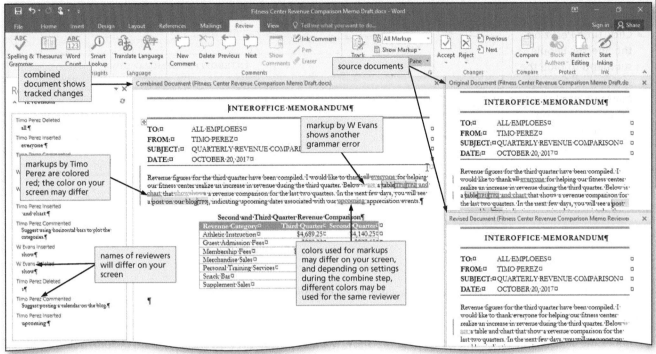

Figure 8–30

Q&A What if my screen does not display the original and source documents?
Click the Compare button (Review tab | Compare group) to display the Compare menu, point to 'Show Source Documents' on the Compare menu, and then click Show Both on the Show Source Documents submenu.

Experiment

- Click the Next Change button (Review tab | Changes group) to display the first tracked change in the combined document. Continue clicking the Next Change or Previous Change buttons. You can accept or reject changes in the combined document using the same steps described earlier in the module.

To Show Tracked Changes and Comments by a Single Reviewer

1 INSERT COMMENTS & TRACK CHANGES | 2 REVIEW COMMENTS & TRACKED CHANGES
3 LINK EXCEL WORKSHEET TO WORD DOCUMENT | 4 CHART WORD TABLE | 5 CREATE & PUBLISH BLOG POST

Why? Instead of looking through a document for a particular reviewer's markups, you can show markups by reviewer. The following steps show the markups by the reviewer named W Evans.

1

- Click the Show Markup button (Review tab | Tracking group) to display the Show Markup menu and then point to Specific People on the Show Markup menu to display the Specific People submenu (Figure 8–31).

Q&A What if my Specific People submenu differs?
Your submenu may have additional, different, or duplicate reviewer names or colors, depending on your Word settings.

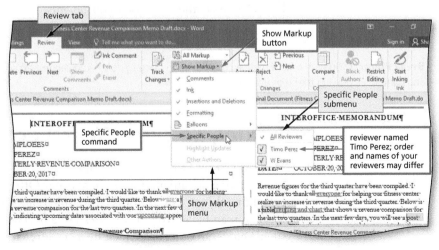

Figure 8–31

● Click Timo Perez on the Specific People submenu to hide the selected reviewer's markups and leave other markups on the screen (Figure 8–32).

Q&A Are the Timo Perez reviewer markups deleted?
No. They are hidden from view.

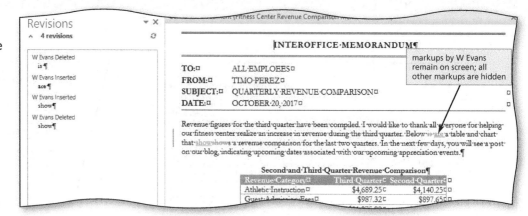

Figure 8–32

 **Experiment**

● Practice hiding and showing reviewer markups in this document.

● Redisplay all reviewer comments by clicking the Show Markup button (Review tab | Tracking group), pointing to Specific People, and then clicking All Reviewers on the Specific People submenu.

To Customize the Status Bar and Close the Document

You are finished working with tracked changes in this module. The following steps remove the Track Changes indicator from the status bar and close the combined document without saving it.

1 Right-click anywhere on the status bar to display the Customize Status Bar menu.

2 Remove the check mark to the left of Track Changes on the Customize Status Bar menu, which removes the Track Changes indicator from the status bar.

3 Click anywhere outside of the Customize Status Bar menu, or press the ESCAPE key, to remove the Customize Status Bar menu from the screen.

4 Close the Word window containing the combined document. When Word displays the dialog box, click the Don't Save button.

5 Close any other open Word documents.

Break Point: If you wish to take a break, this is a good place to do so. You can exit Word now. To resume at a later time, run Word and continue following the steps from this location forward.

Linking an Excel Worksheet to a Word Document

With Microsoft Office, you can copy part or all of a document created in one Office program to a document created in another Office program. The item being copied is called the **object**. For example, you could copy an Excel worksheet (the object) that is located in an Excel workbook (the source file) to a Word document (the destination file). That is, an object is copied from a source to a destination.

You can use one of three techniques to copy objects from one program to another: copy and paste, embed, or link.

- **Copy and paste**: When you copy an object and then paste it, the object becomes part of the destination document. You edit a pasted object using editing features of the destination program. For example, when you select an Excel worksheet in an Excel workbook, click the Copy button (Home tab | Clipboard group) in Excel, and then click the Paste button (Home tab | Clipboard group) in Word, the Excel worksheet becomes a Word table.

- **Embed:** When you embed an object, like a pasted object, it becomes part of the destination document. The difference between an embedded object and a pasted object is that you edit the contents of an embedded object using the editing features of the source program. The embedded object, however, contains static data; that is, any changes made to the object in the source program are not reflected in the destination document. If you embed an Excel worksheet in a Word document, the Excel worksheet remains as an Excel worksheet in the Word document. When you edit the Excel worksheet from within the Word document, you will use Excel editing features.

- **Link:** A linked object, by contrast, does not become a part of the destination document even though it appears to be a part of it. Rather, a connection is established between the source and destination documents so that when you open the destination document, the linked object appears as part of it. When you edit a linked object, the source program runs and opens the source document that contains the linked object. For example, when you edit a linked worksheet, Excel runs and displays the Excel workbook that contains the worksheet; you then edit the worksheet in Excel. Unlike an embedded object, if you open the Excel workbook that contains the Excel worksheet and then edit the Excel worksheet, the linked object will be updated in the Word document, too.

How do I determine which method to use: copy/paste, embed, or link?

- If you simply want to use the object's data and have no desire to use the object in the source program, then copy and paste the object.

- If you want to use the object in the source program but you want the object's data to remain static if it changes in the source file, then embed the object.

- If you want to ensure that the most current version of the object appears in the destination file, then link the object. If the source file is large, such as a video clip or a sound clip, link the object to keep the size of the destination file smaller.

The steps in this section show how to link an Excel worksheet (the object), which is located in an Excel workbook (the source file), to a Word document (the destination file). The Word document is similar to the same memo used in the previous section, except that all grammar errors are fixed and it does not contain the table. To link the worksheet to the memo, you will follow these general steps:

1. Run Excel and open the Excel workbook that contains the object (worksheet) you want to link to the Word document.

2. Select the object (worksheet) in Excel and then copy the selected object to the Clipboard.

3. Switch to Word and then link the copied object to the Word document.

Note: The steps in this section assume you have Microsoft Excel 2016 installed on your computer. If you do not have Excel 2016, read the steps in this section without performing them.

To Open a Word Document, Run Excel, and Open an Excel Workbook

The first step in this section is to open the memo that is to contain the link to the Excel worksheet object. The memo file, named Fund-Raising Memo without Table, is located on the Data Files. The Excel worksheet to be linked to the memo is in an Excel workbook called Fitness Center Revenue Comparison in Excel, which also is located on the Data Files. Please contact your instructor for information about accessing the Data Files. The following steps open a Word document, run Excel, and open an Excel workbook. (Do not exit Word or close the open Word document during these steps.)

1 In Word, open the file called Fitness Center Revenue Comparison Memo without Table located on the Data Files.

2 Run Excel and open a blank workbook.

3 In Excel, open the file called Fitness Center Revenue Comparison on the Data Files.

BTW
Linked Objects
When you open a document that contains linked objects, Word displays a dialog box asking if you want to update the Word document with data from the linked file. Click the Yes button only if you are certain the linked file is from a trusted source; that is, you should be confident that the source file does not contain a virus or other potentially harmful program before you instruct Word to link the source file to the destination document.

Excel Basics

The Excel window contains a rectangular grid that consists of columns and rows. A column letter above the grid identifies each column. A row number on the left side of the grid identifies each row. The intersection of each column and row is a cell. A cell is referred to by its unique address, which is the coordinates of the intersection of a column and a row. To identify a cell, specify the column letter first, followed by the row number. For example, cell reference A1 refers to the cell located at the intersection of column A and row 1 (Figure 8–33).

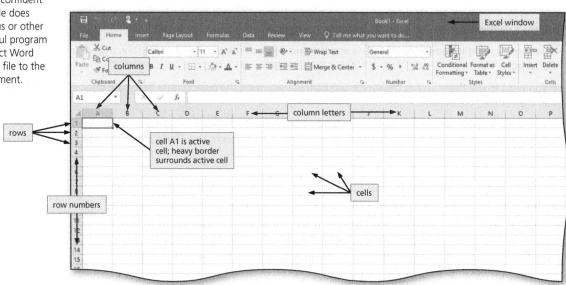

Figure 8–33

To Link an Excel Worksheet to a Word Document

1 INSERT COMMENTS & TRACK CHANGES | 2 REVIEW COMMENTS & TRACKED CHANGES
3 LINK EXCEL WORKSHEET TO WORD DOCUMENT | 4 CHART WORD TABLE | 5 CREATE & PUBLISH BLOG POST

The following steps link an Excel worksheet to a Word document. *Why? You want to copy the Excel worksheet to the Clipboard and then link the Excel worksheet to the Word document.*

1

- In the Excel window, drag through the cells in the range A1 through C8 to select them.

- In the Excel window, click the Copy button (Home tab | Clipboard group) to copy the selected cells to the Clipboard (Figure 8–34).

Q&A What if I click the Copy arrow by mistake?
Click Copy on the Copy menu.

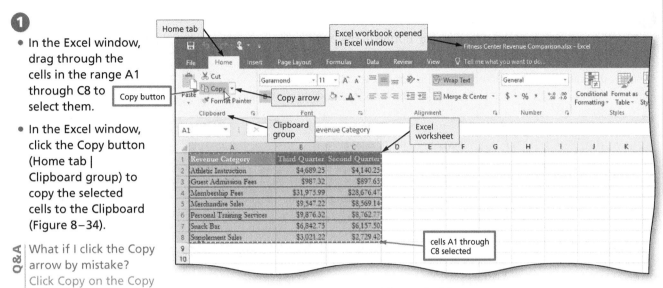

Figure 8–34

What is the dotted line around the selected cells?
Excel surrounds copied cells with a moving marquee to help you visually identify the copied cells.

2

- Click the Word app button on the taskbar to switch to Word and display the open document in the Word window.

- Position the insertion point on the paragraph mark below the table title.

- In Word, click the Paste arrow (Home tab | Clipboard group) to display the Paste gallery.

Q&A What if I accidentally click the Paste button instead of the Paste arrow?
Click the Undo button on the Quick Access Toolbar and then click the Paste arrow.

- Point to the 'Link & Keep Source Formatting' button in the Paste gallery to display a live preview of that paste option (Figure 8–35).

Experiment

- Point to the various buttons in the Paste gallery to display a live preview of each paste option.

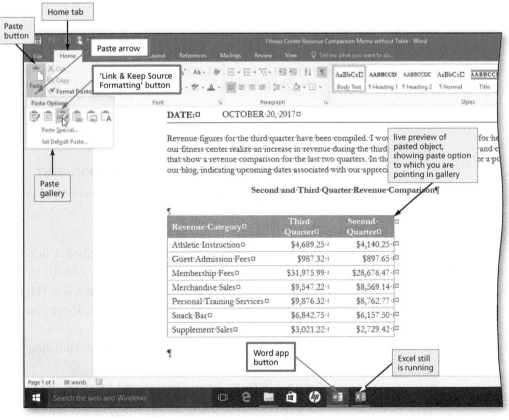

Figure 8–35

3

- Click the 'Link & Keep Source Formatting' button in the Paste gallery to paste and link the object at the location of the insertion point in the document.

◄ Q&A What if I wanted to copy an object instead of link it?

To copy an object, you would click the 'Keep Source Formatting' button in the Paste gallery. To convert the object to a picture so that you can use tools on Word's Picture Tools Format tab to format it, you would click the Picture button in the Paste gallery.

- Select and then center the linked Excel table using the same technique you use to select and center a Word table.

- Resize the linked Excel table until the table is approximately the same size as Figure 8–36.

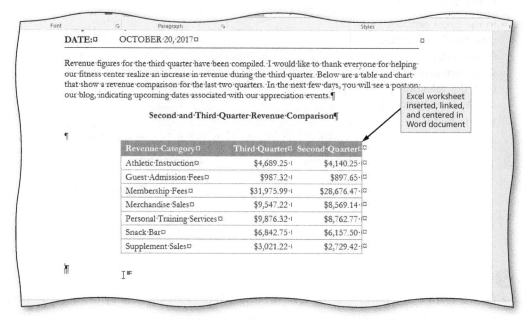

Figure 8–36

◄ Q&A What if I wanted to delete the linked worksheet?

You would select the linked worksheet and then press the DELETE key.

Other Ways

1. Click Paste arrow (Home tab | Clipboard group), click Paste Special, click Paste link (Paste Special dialog box), click 'Microsoft Excel Worksheet Object' in As list, click OK button

2. To link an entire source file, click Object button (Insert tab | Text group), click Create from File tab (Object dialog box), locate file, click 'Link to file' check box, click OK button

---

BTW

Editing Embedded Objects

If you wanted to edit an embedded object in the Word document, you would double-click the object to display the source program's interface in the destination program. For example, double-clicking an embedded Excel worksheet in a Word document displays the Excel ribbon in the Word window. To redisplay the Word ribbon in the Word window, double-click outside of the embedded object.

TO EMBED AN EXCEL WORKSHEET IN A WORD DOCUMENT

If you wanted to embed an Excel worksheet in a Word document, instead of link it, you would perform the following steps.

1. Run Excel.

2. In Excel, select the worksheet cells to embed. Click the Copy button (Home tab | Clipboard group) to copy the selected cells to the Clipboard.

3. Switch to Word. In Word, click the Paste arrow (Home tab | Clipboard group) to display the Paste gallery and then click Paste Special in the Paste gallery to display the Paste Special dialog box.

4. Select the Paste option button (Paste Special dialog box), which indicates the object will be embedded.

5. Select 'Microsoft Excel Worksheet Object' as the type of object to embed.

6. Click the OK button to embed the contents of the Clipboard in the Word document at the location of the insertion point.

To Edit a Linked Object

At a later time, you may find it necessary to change the data in the Excel worksheet. Any changes you make to the Excel worksheet while in Excel will be reflected in the Excel worksheet in the Word document because the objects are linked to the Word document. If you wanted to edit a linked object, such as an Excel worksheet, you would perform these steps.

1. In the Word document, right-click the linked Excel worksheet, point to 'Linked Worksheet Object' on the shortcut menu, and then click Edit Link on the Linked Worksheet Object submenu to run Excel and open the source file that contains the linked worksheet.
2. In Excel, make changes to the Excel worksheet.
3. Click the Save button on the Quick Access Toolbar to save the changes.
4. Exit Excel.
5. If necessary, redisplay the Word window.
6. If necessary, to update the worksheet with the edited Excel data, click the Excel worksheet in the Word document and then press the F9 key, or right-click the linked object and then click Update Link on the shortcut menu to update the linked object with the revisions made to the source file.

BTW

Opening Word Documents with Links

When you open a document that contains a linked object, Word attempts to locate the source file associated with the link. If Word cannot find the source file, open the Backstage view, display the Info tab, then click 'Edit Links to Files' in the Related Documents area at the bottom of the right pane to display the Links dialog box. Next, select the appropriate source file in the list (Links dialog box), click the Change Source button, locate the source file, and then click the OK button.

To Break a Link

1 INSERT COMMENTS & TRACK CHANGES | 2 REVIEW COMMENTS & TRACKED CHANGES
3 LINK EXCEL WORKSHEET TO WORD DOCUMENT | 4 CHART WORD TABLE | 5 CREATE & PUBLISH BLOG POST

Why? *You can convert a linked or embedded object to a Word object by breaking the link. That is, you break the connection between the source file and the destination file.* When you break a linked object, such as an Excel worksheet, the linked object becomes a Word object, a Word table in this case. The following steps break the link to the Excel worksheet.

- Right-click the linked object (the linked Excel worksheet, in this case) to display a shortcut menu.
- Point to 'Linked Worksheet Object' on the shortcut menu to display the Linked Worksheet Object submenu (Figure 8–37).

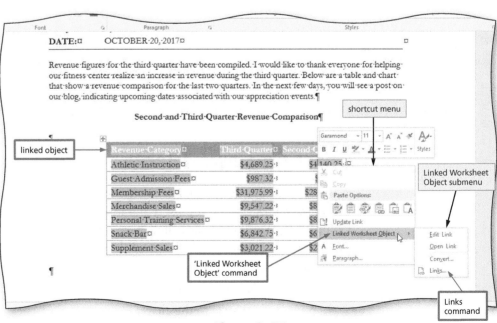

Figure 8–37

- Click Links on the Linked Worksheet Object submenu to display the Links dialog box.

- If necessary, click the source file listed in the dialog box to select it (Links dialog box).

- Click the Break Link button, which displays a dialog box asking if you are sure you want to break the selected links (Figure 8–38).

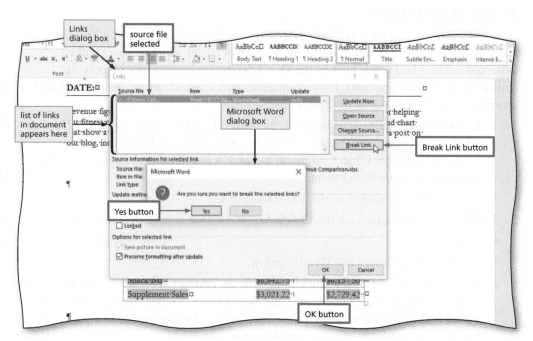

Figure 8–38

- Click the Yes button in the dialog box to remove the source file from the list (break the link).

Q&A

How can I verify the link is broken?

Right-click the table in the Word document to display a shortcut menu. If the shortcut menu does not contain a 'Linked Worksheet Object' command, a link does not exist for the object. Or, when you double-click the table, Excel should not open an associated workbook.

- Close the Word document without saving it.

- Exit Excel without saving changes to the workbook.

Other Ways

1. Select link, press CTRL+SHIFT+F9

Why would I break a link?

If you share a Word document that contains a linked object, such as an Excel worksheet, users will be asked by Word if they want to update the links when they open the Word document. If users are unfamiliar with links, they will not know how to answer the question. Further, if they do not have the source program, such as Excel, they may not be able to open the Word document. When sharing documents, it is recommended you convert links to a regular Word object; that is, break the link.

Charting a Word Table

Several Office applications, including Word, enable you to create charts from data. In the following pages, you will insert and format a chart of the Fitness Center Revenue Comparison Word table using the Chart Tools tab in Word. You will follow these general steps to insert and then format the chart:

1. Create a chart of the table.
2. Remove a data series from the chart.
3. Apply a chart style to the chart.
4. Change the colors of the chart.
5. Add a chart element.
6. Edit a chart element.

7. Format chart elements.

8. Add an outline to the chart.

To Open a Document

The next step is to open the Fitness Center Revenue Comparison Memo file that contains the final wording so that you can create a chart of its Word table. This file, called Fitness Center Revenue Comparison Memo with Table, is located on the Data Files. Please contact your instructor for information about accessing the Data Files. The following step opens a document.

1 Navigate to the Data Files and then open the file called Fitness Center Revenue Comparison Memo with Table.

To Chart a Table

1 INSERT COMMENTS & TRACK CHANGES | 2 REVIEW COMMENTS & TRACKED CHANGES
3 LINK EXCEL WORKSHEET TO WORD DOCUMENT | 4 CHART WORD TABLE | 5 CREATE & PUBLISH BLOG POST

The following steps insert a default chart and then copy the data to be charted from the Word table in the Word document to a chart spreadsheet. *Why? To chart a table, you fill in or copy the data into a chart spreadsheet that automatically opens after you insert the chart.*

1

- Center the paragraph mark below the table so that the inserted chart will be centered. Leave the insertion point on this paragraph mark because the chart will be inserted at the location of the insertion point.

- Display the Insert tab.

- Click the 'Add a Chart' button (Insert tab | Illustrations group) to display the Insert Chart dialog box.

- Click Bar in the left pane (Insert Chart dialog box) to display the available types of bar charts in the right pane.

Experiment

- Click the various types of charts in the left pane and watch the subtypes appear in the right pane. When finished experimenting, click Bar in the left pane.

- If necessary, click Clustered Bar in the right pane to select the chart type (Figure 8–39).

Experiment

- Click the various types of bar charts in the right pane and watch the graphic change in the right pane. When finished experimenting, click Clustered Bar in the right pane.

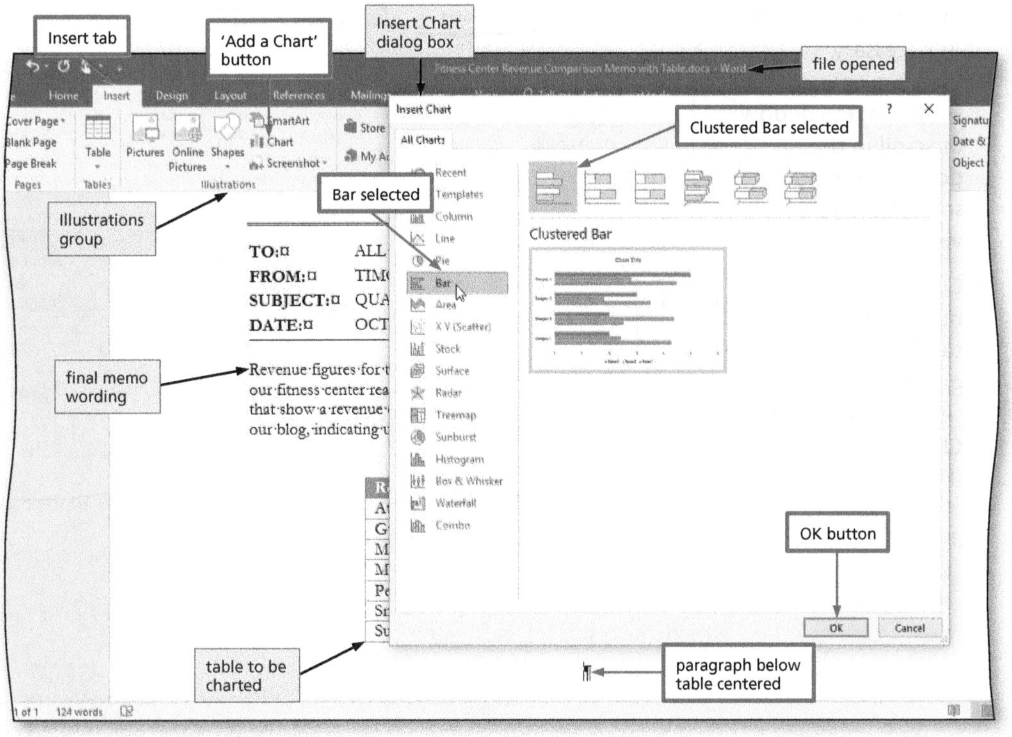

Figure 8–39

2

- Click the OK button so that Word creates a default clustered bar chart in the Word document at the location of the insertion point (Figure 8–40).

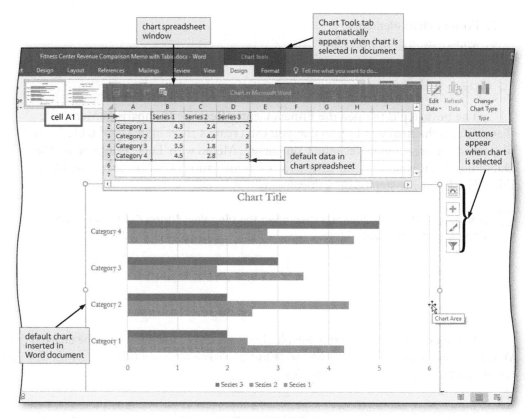

What are the requirements for the format of a table that can be charted? The chart spreadsheet window shows the layout for the selected chart type. In this case, the categories are in the rows and the series are in the columns. Notice the categories appear in the chart in reverse order.

Figure 8–40

3

- In the Word document, select the table to be charted. (If necessary, drag the chart spreadsheet window or scroll in the document window so that the table is visible.)

- Click the Copy button (Home tab | Clipboard group) to copy the selected table to the Clipboard (Figure 8–41).

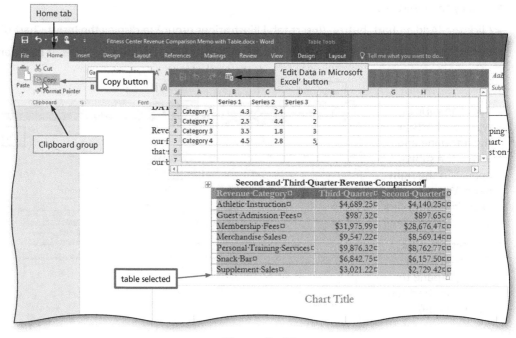

Figure 8–41

Instead of copying table data to the chart spreadsheet, could I type the data directly into the spreadsheet?

Yes. If the chart spreadsheet window does not appear, click the Edit Data arrow (Chart Tools Design tab | Data group) and then click Edit Data on the menu. You also can click the 'Edit Data in Microsoft Excel' button to use Excel to enter the data (if Excel is installed on your computer), or click the Edit Data arrow (Chart Tools Design tab | Data group) and then click 'Edit Data in Excel' on the Edit Data menu.

- In the chart spreadsheet window, click the Select All button (upper-left corner of worksheet) to select the entire worksheet.

- Right-click the selected worksheet to display a mini toolbar or shortcut menu (Figure 8–42).

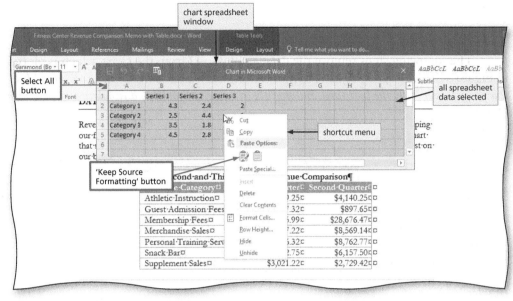

Figure 8–42

5

- Click the 'Keep Source Formatting' button on the shortcut menu to paste the contents of the Clipboard starting in the upper-left corner of the worksheet.

- When Word displays a dialog box indicating that the pasted contents are a different size from the selection, click the OK button.

Q&A Why did Word display this dialog box?

The source table contains three columns, and the target worksheet has four columns. In the next section, you will delete the fourth column from the chart spreadsheet.

- Resize the chart worksheet window by dragging its window edges, move it by dragging its title bar, and resize the columns by dragging the borders of the column headings so the worksheet window appears as shown in Figure 8–43. Notice that the chart in the Word window automatically changes to reflect the new data in the chart worksheet (Figure 8–43).

Q&A Why did some of the cells have the # symbol in them before I resized the columns?

Excel places a # symbol in cells whose value is too wide to fit in a cell.

Figure 8–43

To Remove a Data Series from the Chart

The following steps remove the data in column D from the chart, which is plotted as Series 3 (shown in Figure 8–43). *Why? By default, Word selects the first four columns in the chart spreadsheet window. The chart in this project covers only the first three columns: the revenue categories and two data series — Third Quarter and Second Quarter.*

- Ensure the chart is selected in the Word document and then drag the sizing handle in cell D8 of the chart spreadsheet leftward so that the selection ends at cell C8; that is, the selection should encompass cells A1 through C8 (Figure 8–44).

Q&A
How would I add a data series?
Add a column of data to the chart spreadsheet. Drag the sizing handle outward to include the series, or you could click the Select Data button (Chart Tools Design tab | Data group), click the Add button (Select Data Source dialog box), click the Select Range button (Edit Series dialog box), drag through the data range in the worksheet, and then click the OK button.

How would I add or remove data categories?
Follow the same steps to add or remove data series, except work with spreadsheet rows instead of columns.

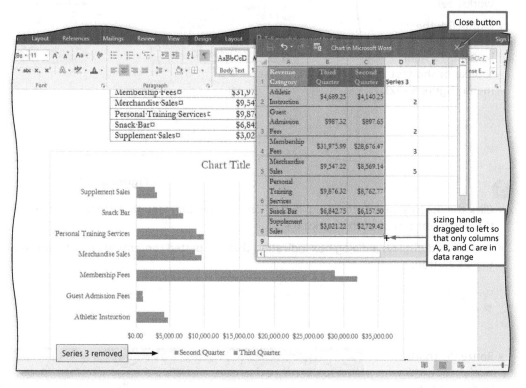

Figure 8–44

- Close the chart spreadsheet window by clicking its Close button.

Other Ways

1. Click Select Data button (Chart Tools Design tab | Data group), click series to remove (Select Data Source dialog box), click Remove button, click OK button

To Apply a Chart Style

The next step is to apply a chart style to the chart. *Why? Word provides a Chart Styles gallery, allowing you to change the chart's format to a more visually appealing style.* The following steps apply a chart style to a chart.

1

- Display the Chart Tools Design tab.

- If necessary, click the chart to select it.

- Point to Style 5 in the Chart Styles gallery (Chart Tools Design tab | Chart Styles group) to display a live preview of that style applied to the graphic in the document (Figure 8–45).

Experiment

- Point to various styles in the Chart Styles gallery and watch the style of the chart change in the document window.

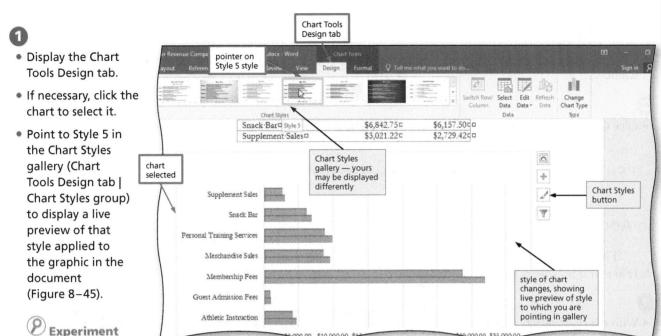

Figure 8–45

2

- Click Style 5 in the Chart Styles gallery (Chart Tools Design tab | Chart Styles group) to apply the selected style to the chart.

Other Ways

1. Click Chart Styles button attached to chart, click Style tab, click desired style

To Change Colors of a Chart

1 INSERT COMMENTS & TRACK CHANGES | 2 REVIEW COMMENTS & TRACKED CHANGES
3 LINK EXCEL WORKSHEET TO WORD DOCUMENT | 4 CHART WORD TABLE | 5 CREATE & PUBLISH BLOG POST

The following steps change the colors of the chart. **Why?** *Word provides a predefined variety of colors for charts. You select one that best matches the colors already used in the letter.*

1

- With the chart selected, click the 'Chart Quick Colors' button (Chart Tools Design tab | Chart Styles group) to display the Chart Quick Colors gallery.

Q&A

What if the chart is not selected?
Click the chart to select it.

- Point to Color 2 in the Chart Quick Colors gallery to display a live preview of the selected color applied to the chart in the document (Figure 8–46).

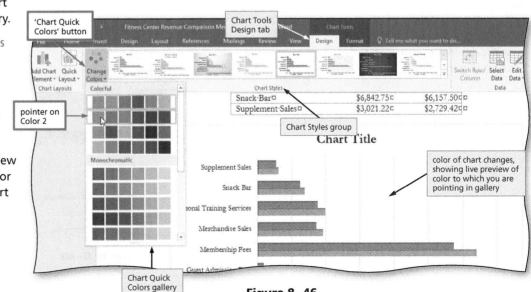

Figure 8–46

Experiment

- Point to various colors in the Chart Quick Colors gallery and watch the colors of the chart change in the document window.

- Click Color 2 in the Chart Quick Colors gallery to apply the selected color to the chart.

Other Ways

1. Click Chart Styles button attached to chart, click Color tab, click desired style

To Add a Chart Element

1 INSERT COMMENTS & TRACK CHANGES │ 2 REVIEW COMMENTS & TRACKED CHANGES
3 LINK EXCEL WORKSHEET TO WORD DOCUMENT │ 4 CHART WORD TABLE │ 5 CREATE & PUBLISH BLOG POST

The following steps add minor vertical gridlines to the chart. *Why? You want to add more vertical lines to the chart so that it is easier to see the dollar values associated with each bar length.*

- With the chart selected, click the 'Add Chart Element' button (Chart Tools Design tab | Chart Layouts group) to display the Add Chart Element gallery and then point to Gridlines to display the Gridlines submenu (Figure 8–47).

Experiment

- Point to various elements in the Add Chart Element gallery so that you can see the other types of elements you can add to a chart. When finished, point to Gridlines.

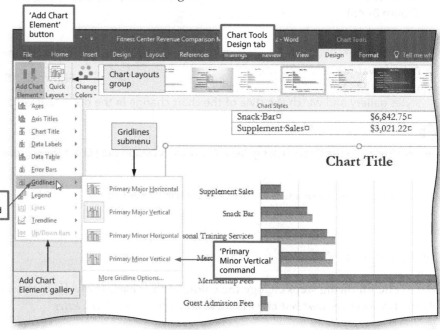

Figure 8–47

- Click 'Primary Minor Vertical' on the Gridline submenu to add vertical minor gridlines to the chart (Figure 8–48).

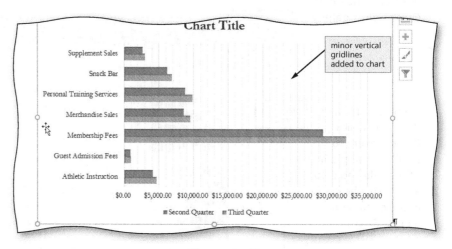

Figure 8–48

To Select a Chart Element and Edit It

The following steps change the chart title. *Why? You want to change the title from the default to a more meaningful name.*

- Display the Chart Tools Format tab.

- With the chart selected, click the Chart Elements arrow (Chart Tools Format tab | Current Selection group) to display the Chart Elements list (Figure 8–49).

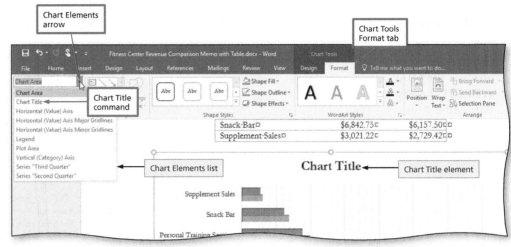

Figure 8–49

- Click Chart Title in the Chart Elements list to select the chart's title.

- Type **Second and Third Quarter Comparison** as the new title (Figure 8–50).

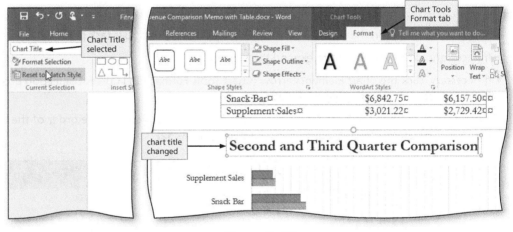

Figure 8–50

Other Ways

1. Click chart element in chart to select element

To Format Chart Elements

Currently, the category names on the vertical axis are in reverse order of the row labels in the table; that is, category names are in alphabetical order from bottom to top and the row labels in the table are in alphabetical order from top to bottom. Also, the numbers across the bottom display with two decimal places following the dollar values. The following steps format axis elements. *Why? You want the categories to display in the same order as the table, the numbers to display as whole numbers, and the legend to appear at the top of the chart.*

- If necessary, select the chart by clicking it.

- With the chart selected, click the Chart Elements arrow (Chart Tools Format tab | Current Selection group) to display the Chart Elements list and then click 'Vertical (Category) Axis'.

- Click the Chart Elements button attached to the right of the chart to display the CHART ELEMENTS gallery.

- Point to and then click the Axes arrow in the CHART ELEMENTS gallery to display the Axes fly-out menu (Figure 8–51).

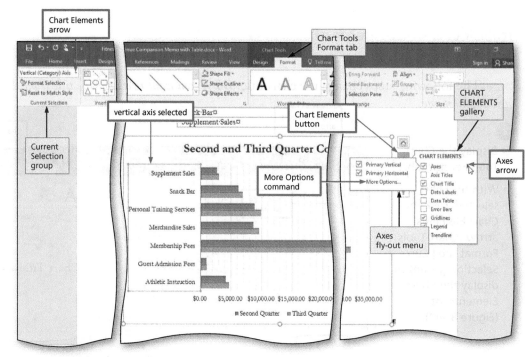

Figure 8–51

2

- Click More Options on the Axes fly-out menu to open the Format Axis task pane.

- If necessary, click Axis Options to expand the section.

- If necessary, click the Chart Elements arrow (Chart Tools Format tab | Current Selection group) to display the Chart Elements list and then click 'Vertical (Category) Axis'.

- Place a check mark in the 'Categories in reverse order' check box so that the order of the categories in the chart matches the order of the categories in the table (Figure 8–52).

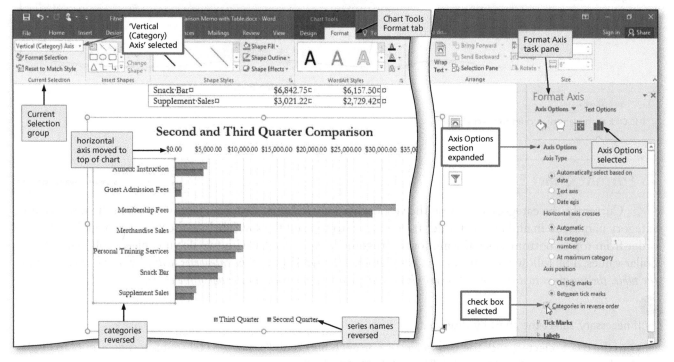

Figure 8–52

Q&A Why did the horizontal axis move from the bottom of the chart to the top?

When you reverse the categories, the horizontal axis automatically moves from the bottom of the chart to the top of the chart. Notice that the series names below the chart also are reversed.

3

- With the chart selected, click the Chart Elements arrow (Chart Tools Format tab | Current Selection group) to display the Chart Elements list and then click 'Horizontal (Value) Axis'.

- If necessary, click Labels and click Number at the bottom of the Format Axis task pane to expand these two sections in the task pane.

- If necessary, scroll the task pane to display the entire Labels and Number sections.

- In the Labels section, click the Label Position arrow and then click High to move the axis to the bottom of the chart.

- In the Number section, change the value in the Decimal places text box to 0 (the number zero) and then press the ENTER key (Figure 8–53).

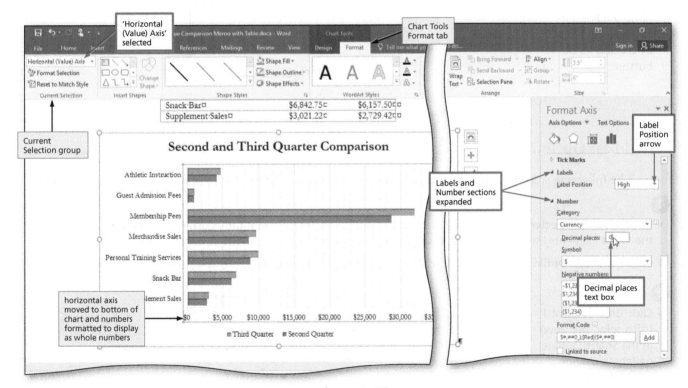

Figure 8–53

4

- With the chart selected, click the Chart Elements arrow (Chart Tools Format tab | Current Selection group) to display the Chart Elements list and then click Legend.

Q&A What happened to the Format Axis task pane?

It now is the Format Legend task pane. The task pane title and options change, depending on the element you are using or formatting.

- If necessary, click Legend Options to expand the section in the Format Legend task pane.

- Click Top to select the option button.

- Remove the check mark from the 'Show the legend without overlapping the chart' check box so that the legend drops down into the chart a bit (Figure 8–54).

5

- Drag the legend up slightly so that it rests on top of the vertical lines in the chart.

- Close the Format Legend task pane by clicking its close button.

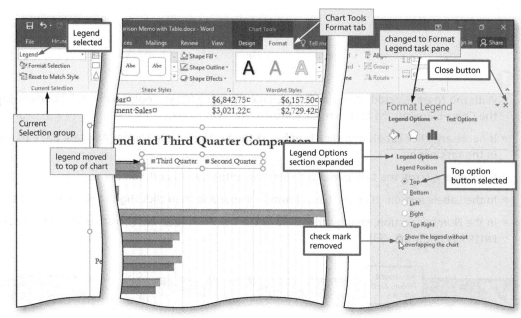

Figure 8–54

To Add an Outline to a Chart

1 INSERT COMMENTS & TRACK CHANGES | 2 REVIEW COMMENTS & TRACKED CHANGES
3 LINK EXCEL WORKSHEET TO WORD DOCUMENT | 4 CHART WORD TABLE | 5 CREATE & PUBLISH BLOG POST

The following steps add an outline to the chart with a shadow. *Why? You want a border surrounding the chart.*

1

- With the chart selected, click the Chart Elements arrow (Chart Tools Format tab | Current Selection group) to display the Chart Elements list and then, if necessary, click Chart Area.

- Click the Shape Outline arrow (Chart Tools Format tab | Shape Styles group) to display the Shape Outline gallery.

2

- Click 'Green, Accent 1' (fifth color, first row) in the Shape Outline gallery to change the outline color.

- Click the Shape Outline arrow (Chart Tools Format tab | Shape Styles group) again and then point to Weight in the Shape Outline gallery to display the Weight gallery (Figure 8–55).

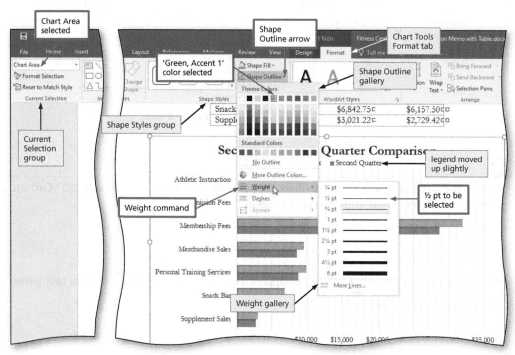

Figure 8–55

- Click ½ pt in the Weight gallery to apply the selected weight to the outline.

- Click the Shape Effects button (Chart Tools Format tab | Shape Styles group) and then point to Shadow in the Shape Effects gallery to display the Shadow gallery (Figure 8–56).

- Click 'Offset Diagonal Bottom Right' in the Shadow gallery to apply the selected shadow to the outline.

- Save the modified memo on your hard drive, OneDrive, or other storage location using Fitness Center Revenue Comparison Memo with Table and Clustered Chart as the file name.

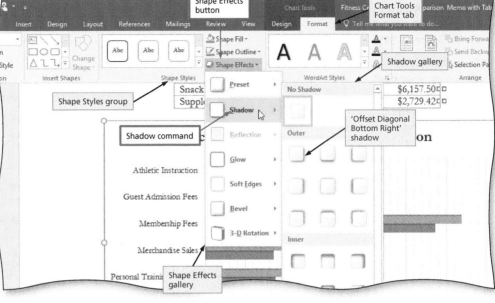

Figure 8–56

To Change a Chart Type

1 INSERT COMMENTS & TRACK CHANGES | 2 REVIEW COMMENTS & TRACKED CHANGES
3 LINK EXCEL WORKSHEET TO WORD DOCUMENT | 4 CHART WORD TABLE | 5 CREATE & PUBLISH BLOG POST

The following steps change the chart type. *Why? After reviewing the document, you would like to see how the chart looks as a 3-D clustered bar chart.*

- Display the Chart Tools Design tab.

- Click the 'Change Chart Type' button (Chart Tools Design tab | Type group) to display the Change Chart Type dialog box.

- Click '3-D Clustered Bar' (Change Chart Type dialog box) in the right pane to change the chart type (Figure 8–57).

 **Experiment**

- Point to the chart preview in the dialog box to see in more detail how the chart will look in the document.

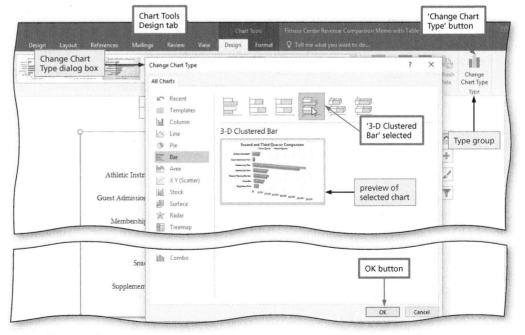

Figure 8–57

- Click the OK button to change the chart type (Figure 8–58).

- Save the revised memo on your hard drive, OneDrive, or other storage location using Fitness Center Revenue Comparison Memo with Table and 3-D Clustered Chart as the file name.

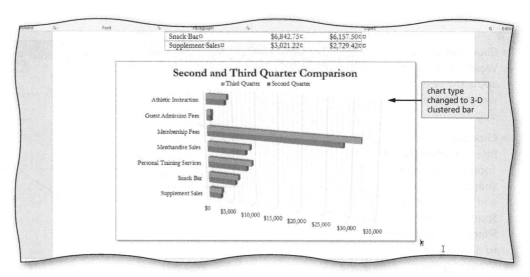

Figure 8–58

BTW

Conserving Ink and Toner

If you want to conserve ink or toner, you can instruct Word to print draft quality documents by clicking File on the ribbon to open the Backstage view, clicking the Options tab in the Backstage view to display the Word Options dialog box, clicking Advanced in the left pane (Word Options dialog box), scrolling to the Print area in the right pane, placing a check mark in the 'Use draft quality' check box, and then clicking the OK button. Then, use the Backstage view to print the document as usual.

TO CHART A WORD TABLE USING MICROSOFT GRAPH

In previous versions of Word, you charted Word tables using an embedded program called Microsoft Graph, or simply Graph. When working with the chart, Graph has its own menus and commands because it is a program embedded in Word. Using Graph commands, you can modify the appearance of the chart after you create it. If you wanted to create a chart using the legacy Graph program, you would perform these steps.

1. Select the rows and columns or table to be charted.

2. Display the Insert tab.

3. Click the Object button (Insert tab | Text group) to display the Object dialog box.

4. If necessary, click the Create New tab (Object dialog box).

5. Scroll to and then select 'Microsoft Graph Chart' in the Object type list to specify the object being inserted.

6. Click the OK button to run the Microsoft Graph program, which creates a chart of the selected table or selected rows and columns.

To View and Scroll through Documents Side by Side

1 INSERT COMMENTS & TRACK CHANGES | 2 REVIEW COMMENTS & TRACKED CHANGES
3 LINK EXCEL WORKSHEET TO WORD DOCUMENT | **4 CHART WORD TABLE** | 5 CREATE & PUBLISH BLOG POST

Word provides a way to display two documents side by side, each in a separate window. By default, the two documents scroll synchronously, that is, together. If necessary, you can turn off synchronous scrolling so that you can scroll through each document individually. The following steps display documents side by side. *Why? You would like to see the how the document with the clustered chart looks alongside the document with the 3-D clustered bar chart.*

- Position the insertion point at the top of the document because you want to begin viewing side by side from the top of the documents.

- Open the file called Fitness Center Revenue Comparison Memo with Table and Clustered Chart so that both documents are open in Word.

- Display the View tab (Figure 8–59).

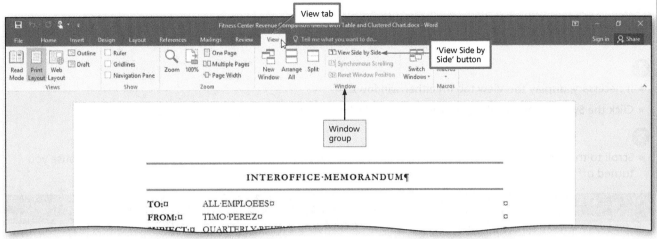

Figure 8–59

2

- Click the 'View Side by Side' button (View tab | Window group) to display each open window side by side (Figure 8–60).

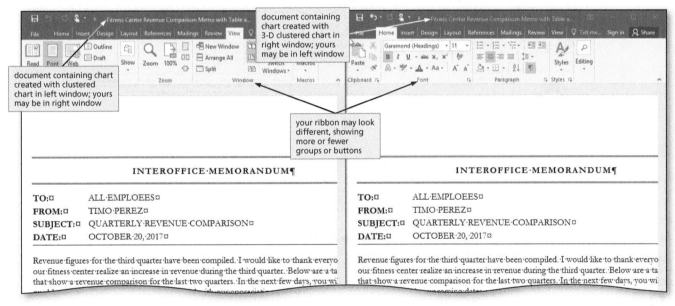

Figure 8–60

3

- If necessary, adjust the zoom to fit the memo contents in each window.

- Scroll to the bottom of one of the windows and notice how both windows (documents) scroll together (Figure 8–61).

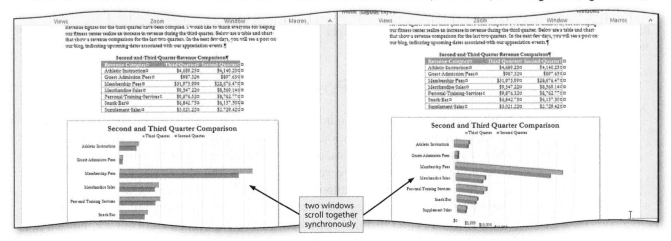

Figure 8–61

Q&A
Can I scroll through one window separately from the other?

By default, synchronous scrolling is active when you display windows side by side. If you want to scroll separately through the windows, simply turn off synchronous scrolling.

4

- If necessary, display the View tab (in either window).

- Click the Synchronous Scrolling button (View tab | Window group) to turn off synchronous scrolling.

5

- Scroll to the top of the window on the right and notice that the window on the left does not scroll because you turned off synchronous scrolling (Figure 8–62).

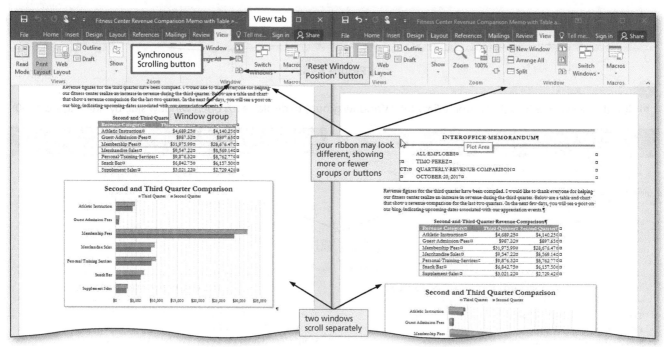

Figure 8–62

Q&A
What is the purpose of the 'Reset Window Position' button?

It repositions the side-by-side windows so that each consumes the same amount of screen space.

6

- In either window, click the 'View Side by Side' button (View tab | Window group) to turn off side-by-side viewing and display each window in the full screen.

- Close each open Word document, saving them if prompted.

Break Point: If you wish to take a break, this is a good place to do so. You can exit Word now. To resume at a later time, run Word and continue following the steps from this location forward

Creating a Blog Post

A **blog**, short for **weblog**, is an informal website consisting of date- or time-stamped articles, or **posts**, in a diary or journal format, usually listed in reverse chronological order. Blogs reflect the interests, opinions, and personalities of the author, called the **blogger**, and sometimes of the website visitors as well.

Blogs have become an important means of worldwide communications. Businesses create blogs to communicate with employees, customers, and vendors. Teachers create blogs to collaborate with other teachers and students, and home users create blogs to share aspects of their personal life with family, friends, and others.

This section of the module creates a blog post and then publishes it to a registered blog account at WordPress, which is a blogging service on the web. The blog relays current events for the Yellville Fitness Center employees. This specific blog post is a communication about the upcoming events.

What should you consider when creating and posting on a blog?

When creating a blog post, you should follow these general guidelines:

1. **Create a blog account on the web.** Many websites exist that allow users to set up a blog free or for a fee. Blogging services that work with Word 2016 include Blogger, SharePoint blog, Telligent Community, TypePad, and WordPress. For illustration purposes in this module, a free blog account was created at WordPress.com.

2. **Register your blog account in Word.** Before you can use Word to publish a blog post, you must register your blog account in Word. This step establishes a connection between Word and your blog account. The first time you create a new blog post, Word will ask if you want to register a blog account. You can click the Register Later button if you want to learn how to create a blog post without registering a blog account.

3. **Create a blog post.** Use Word to enter the text and any graphics in your blog post. Some blogging services accept graphics directly from a Word blog post. Others require that you use a picture hosting service to store pictures you use in a blog post.

4. **Publish a blog post.** When you publish a blog post, the blog post in the Word document is copied to your account at the blogging service. Once the post is published, it appears at the top of the blog webpage. You may need to click the Refresh button in the browser window to display the new post.

TO REGISTER A BLOG ACCOUNT

Once you set up a blog account with a blog provider, you must register it in Word so that you can publish your Word post on the blog account. If you wanted to register a blog account, with WordPress for example, you would perform the following steps.

1. Click the Manage Accounts button (Blog Post tab | Blog group) to display the Blog Accounts dialog box.

2. Click the New button (Blog Accounts dialog box) to display the New Blog Account dialog box.

3. Click the Blog arrow (New Blog Account dialog box) to display a list of blog providers and then select your provider in the list.

4. Click the Next button to display the New [Provider] Account dialog box (i.e., a New WordPress Account dialog box would appear if you selected WordPress as the provider).

5. In the Blog Post URL text box, replace the <Enter your blog URL here> text with the web address for your blog account. (Note that your dialog box may differ, depending on the provider you select.)

Q&A | What is a URL?

A URL (Uniform Resource Locator), often called a web address, is the unique address for a webpage. For example, the web address for a WordPress blog account might be smith.wordpress.com; in that case, the complete blog post URL would read as http://smith.wordpress.com/xhlrpc.php in the text box.

6. In the Enter account information area, enter the user name and password you use to access your blog account.

Q&A | Should I click the Remember Password check box?

If you do not select this check box, Word will prompt you for a password each time you publish to the blog account.

7. If your blog provider does not allow pictures to be stored, click the Picture Options button, select the correct option for storing your posted pictures, and then click the OK button (Picture Options dialog box).

8. Click the OK button to register the blog account.

9. When Word displays a dialog box indicating the account registration was successful, click the OK button.

To Create a Blank Document for a Blog Post

1 INSERT COMMENTS & TRACK CHANGES | 2 REVIEW COMMENTS & TRACKED CHANGES
3 LINK EXCEL WORKSHEET TO WORD DOCUMENT | 4 CHART WORD TABLE | **5 CREATE & PUBLISH BLOG POST**

The following steps create a new blank Word document for a blog post. ***Why?*** *Word provides a blog post template you can use to create a blank blog post document.*

- Open the Backstage view.

- Click the New tab in the Backstage view to display the New gallery.

- Click the Blog post thumbnail to select the template and display it in a preview window (Figure 8–63).

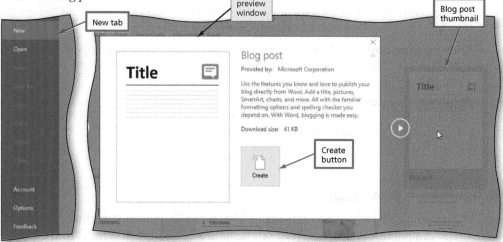

Figure 8–63

- Click the Create button in the preview window to create a new document based on the selected template (Figure 8–64). If necessary, adjust the zoom so that the text is readable on the screen.

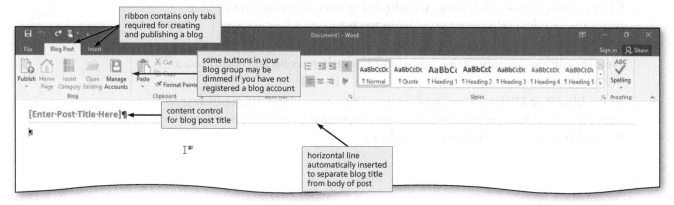

Figure 8–64

Q&A

What if a Register a Blog Account dialog box appears?
Click the Register Later button to skip the registration process at this time. Or, if you have a blog account, you can click the Register Now button and follow the instructions to register your account.

Why did the ribbon change?
When creating a blog post, the ribbon in Word changes to display only the tabs required to create and publish a blog post.

To Enter Text

The next step is to enter the blog post title and text in the blog post. The following steps enter text in the blog post.

1 Click the 'Enter Post Title Here' content control and then type **Appreciation Events** as the blog title.

2 Position the insertion point below the horizontal line and then type these two lines of text, pressing the ENTER key at end of each sentence (Figure 8–65):

Thank you to everyone for helping our fitness center realize an increase in revenue during the third quarter!

See the following calendar for key dates, including appreciation events!

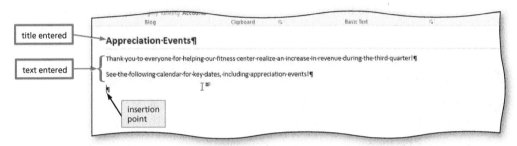

Figure 8–65

Q&A
Can I format text in the blog post?
Yes, you can use the Basic Text and other groups on the ribbon to format the post. You also can check spelling using the Proofing group.

To Insert a Quick Table

1 INSERT COMMENTS & TRACK CHANGES | 2 REVIEW COMMENTS & TRACKED CHANGES
3 LINK EXCEL WORKSHEET TO WORD DOCUMENT | 4 CHART WORD TABLE | 5 CREATE & PUBLISH BLOG POST

Word provides several quick tables, which are preformatted table styles that you can customize. Calendar formats are one type of quick table. The following steps insert a calendar in the blog. *Why? You will post the upcoming key dates in the calendar.*

1

- Display the Insert tab.

- With the insertion point positioned as shown in Figure 8–65, click the 'Add a Table' button (Insert tab | Tables group) to display the Add a Table gallery.

- Point to Quick Tables in the Add a Table gallery to display the Quick Tables gallery (Figure 8–66).

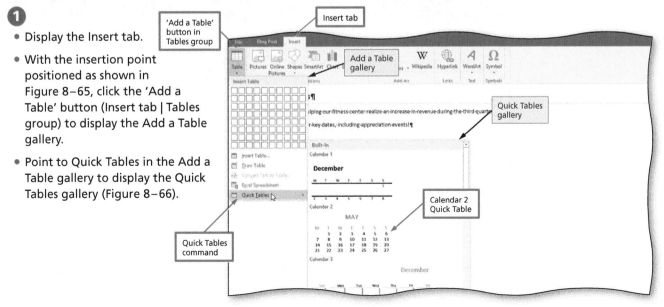

Figure 8–66

2

- Click Calendar 2 in the Quick Tables gallery to insert the selected Quick Table in the document at the location of the insertion point (Figure 8–67).

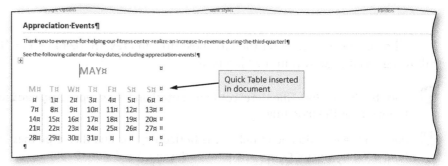

Figure 8–67

To Edit and Format a Table

The calendar in the blog post should show the month of November with a first day of the month starting on Wednesday. The following steps edit the table and apply a quick style.

1 Change the month in the first cell of the table from May to November.

2 Edit the contents of the cells in the table so that the first day of the month starts on a Wednesday and the 30 (the last day of the month) is on a Thursday.

3 Enter the text in the appropriate cells for November 1, 7, 16, and 22, as shown in Figure 8–68.

4 If necessary, display the Table Tools Design tab.

5 Remove the check mark from the First Column check box (Table Tools Design tab | Table Style Options group) because you do not want the first column in the table formatted differently.

6 Apply the 'Grid Table 1 Light - Accent 6' table style to the table.

7 If necessary, left-align the heading and resize the table column widths to 1".

8 Make any other necessary adjustments so that the table appears as shown in Figure 8–68.

9 Save the blog on your hard drive, OneDrive, or other storage location using Fitness Center Blog as the file name.

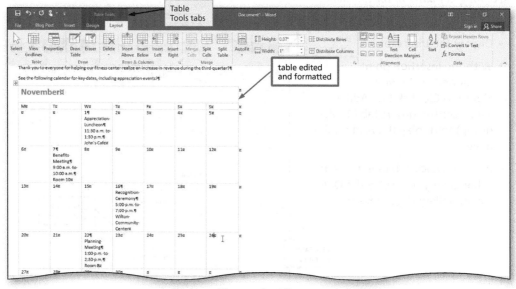

Figure 8–68

Note: If you have not registered a blog account, read the next series of steps without performing them.

To Publish a Blog Post

The following step publishes the blog post. *Why? Publishing the blog post places the post at the top of the webpage associated with this blog account.*

- Display the Blog Post tab.
- Click the Publish button (Blog Post tab | Blog group), which causes Word to display a brief message that it is contacting the blog provider and then display a message on the screen that the post was published (Figure 8–69).

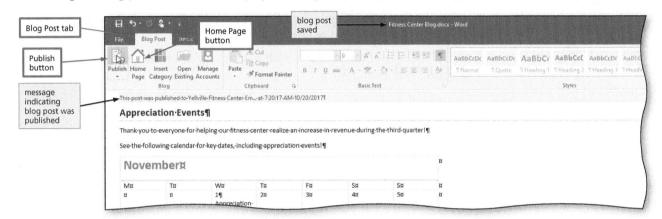

Figure 8–69

To Display a Blog Webpage in a Browser Window

The following steps display the current blog account's webpage in a browser window. *Why? You can view a blog account associated with Word if you want to verify a post was successful.*

- Click the Home Page button (Blog Post tab | Blog group) (shown in Figure 8–69), which runs the default browser (Microsoft Edge, in this case) and displays the webpage associated with the registered blog account in the browser window. You may need to click the Refresh button in your browser window to display the most current webpage contents (Figure 8–70).

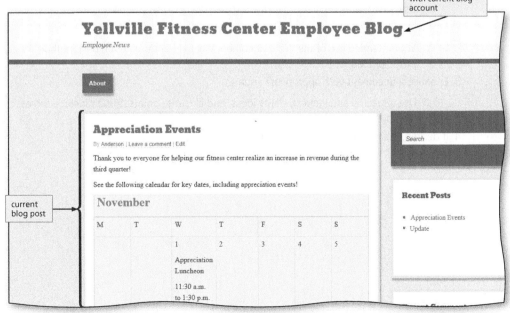

Figure 8–70

What if the wrong webpage is displayed?

You may have multiple blog accounts registered with Word. To select a different blog account registered with Word, switch back to Word, click the Manage Accounts button (Blog Post tab | Blog group), click the desired account (Blog Accounts dialog box), and then click the Close button. Then, repeat Step 1.

2

- Exit both the browser and Word.

TO OPEN AN EXISTING BLOG POST

If you wanted to open an existing blog post to modify or view it in Word, you would perform the following steps.

1. Click the Open Existing button (Blog Post tab | Blog group) to display the Open Existing Post dialog box.
2. Select the title of the post you wish to open and then click the OK button (Open Existing Post dialog box).

Summary

In this module, you have learned how to insert comments, track changes, review tracked changes, compare documents and combine documents, link or embed an Excel worksheet to a Word document, chart a table and format the chart, and create and publish a blog post.

CONSIDER THIS: PLAN AHEAD

What decisions will you need to make when creating documents to share or publish?

Use these guidelines as you complete the assignments in this module and create your own shared documents outside of this class.

1. If sharing documents, be certain received files and copied objects are virus free.

   a) Do not open files created by others until you are certain they do not contain a virus or other malicious program (malware).

   b) Use an antivirus program to verify that any files you use are free of viruses and other potentially harmful programs.

2. If necessary, determine how to copy an object.

   a) Your intended use of the Word document will help determine the best method for copying the object: copy and paste, embed, or link.

3. Enhance a document with appropriate visuals.

   a) Use visuals to add interest, clarify ideas, and illustrate points. Visuals include tables, charts, and graphical images (i.e., pictures).

4. If desired, post communications on a blog.

Apply Your Knowledge

Reinforce the skills and apply the concepts you learned in this module.

Working with Comments and Tracked Changes

Note: To complete this assignment, you will be required to use the Data Files. Please contact your instructor for information about accessing the Data Files.

Instructions: Run Word. Open the file named Apply 8–1 Social Engineering Draft from the Data Files. The document includes two paragraphs of text that contain tracked changes and comments. You are to insert additional tracked changes and comments, accept and reject tracked changes, and delete comments.

Perform the following tasks:

1. If necessary, customize the status bar so that it displays the Track Changes indicator.
2. Enable (turn on) tracked changes.
3. If requested by your instructor, change the user name and initials so that your name and initials are displayed in the tracked changes and comments.
4. Use the Review tab to navigate to the first comment. Follow the instruction in the comment. Be sure tracked changes are on when you add the required text to the document.
5. When you have finished making the change, reply to the comment with a new comment that includes a message stating you completed the requested task. Mark the comment as done. How does a comment marked as done differ from the other comments? What color are the WU markups? What color are your markups?
6. Insert the following comment for the word, naivety, at the end of the first sentence in the first paragraph: Is this word spelled correctly?
7. With tracked changes on, change the word, that, in the fourth sentence to the word, who.
8. Reply to the comment entered in Step 6 to add this sentence: Be sure to look it up in the dictionary or a dictionary app.
9. Navigate to the remaining comments and read through each one.
10. Print the document with tracked changes.
11. Print only the tracked changes.
12. Save the document with the file name, Apply 8–1 Social Engineering Reviewed (Figure 8–71).
13. Show only your tracked changes in the document. Show all users' tracked changes in the document.
14. Reject the insertion of the words, that are, in the last sentence in the first paragraph.
15. If necessary, delete the comment that begins with the words, Reject the tracked change….
16. Insert the word, social, as a tracked change at the beginning of the second paragraph as instructed in the comment.
17. Accept all the remaining edits in the document.
18. Delete all the remaining comments.
19. Disable (turn off) tracked changes. Remove the Track Changes indicator from the status bar.
20. If requested by your instructor, add your name on a line below the bulleted list.
21. Save the modified file with the file name, Apply 8–1 Social Engineering Final. Submit the documents in the format specified by your instructor.
22. ✳ Answer the questions posed in #5. How would you change the color of your tracked changes?

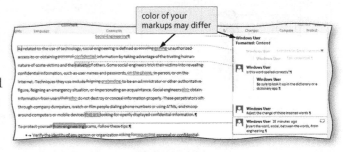

Figure 8–71

Extend Your Knowledge

Extend the skills you learned in this module and experiment with new skills. You may need to use Help to complete the assignment.

Using Microsoft Graph to Create a Chart

Note: To complete this assignment, you will be required to use the Data Files. Please contact your instructor for information about accessing the Data Files.

Instructions: Run Word. Open the file named Extend 8–1 Workshop Registrations Memo Draft from the Data Files. You will use Microsoft Graph to chart the table in the memo.

Perform the following tasks:

1. Search the web to learn about Microsoft Graph. What is Microsoft Graph?
2. Select the table in the memo to be charted and then insert a Microsoft Graph chart (Figure 8–72) (refer to the section in this module titled To Chart a Word Table Using Microsoft Graph). Close the Datasheet window.
3. Click Help on the menu bar in the Graph window and then click 'Microsoft Graph Help' to open the Graph Help window. Browse through the help information to learn how to use Graph.
4. Click the By Column button on the Standard toolbar to plot the data by column instead of by row. What text appears along the horizontal axis now?
5. Move the legend to the bottom of the chart.
6. Change the chart type to a bar chart.
7. Display the categories on the category axis in reverse order, leaving the value axis at the bottom. *Hint*: Select the Scale tab in Format Axis dialog box and then place check marks in all three check boxes. If necessary, also change the number of tick marks between items to show all classes.
8. Resize the table so that workshop titles appear on a single line.
9. Change the color of the chart area.
10. Change the color of the series named Registrations, which changes the color of the bars.

11. If they are not displayed already, display value axis major gridlines.
12. Center the chart below the table.
13. If requested by your instructor, change the name at the top of the memo to your name.
14. Save the modified file with the file name, Apply 8–1 Workshop Registrations Memo Final. Submit the document in the format specified by your instructor.
15. ☀ Answer the question posed in #4. Do you prefer using Microsoft Graph or the Chart Tools tab to create a chart in Word? Why?

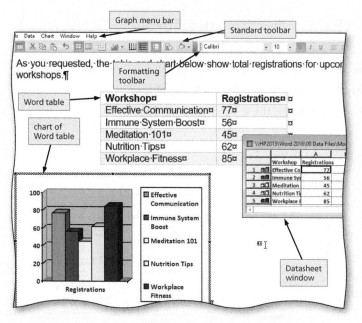

Figure 8–72

Expand Your World

Create a solution that uses cloud or web technologies by learning and investigating on your own from general guidance.

Creating a Blog Account Using a Blogger Service

Instructions: You would like to create a blog account so that you can use Word for blog posts. You research a variety of blogging services and select one for use.

Note: You will use a blog account, many of which you can create at no cost, to complete this assignment. If you do not want to create a blog account, read this assignment without performing the instructions.

Perform the following tasks:
1. Run a browser. Research these blogging services: Blogger, SharePoint blog, Telligent Community, TypePad, and WordPress.
2. Navigate to the blogger service with which you want to set up an account and then follow the instructions to set up an account.
3. Set up your blog in the blogger service.
4. In Word, register your blog account (refer to the section in this module titled To Register a Blog Account).
5. Create a blog post in Word and then publish your blog post to your account.
6. ⊛ Which blogger service did you select and why? Would you recommend this blogger service? Why or why not?

In the Labs

Design, create, modify, and/or use a document following the guidelines, concepts, and skills presented in this module. Labs 1 and 2, which increase in difficulty, require you to create solutions based on what you learned in the module; Lab 3 requires you to apply your creative thinking and problem-solving skills to design and implement a solution.

Lab 1: Creating a Memo with an Excel Table and Chart

Note: To complete this assignment, you will be required to use the Data Files. Please contact your instructor for information about accessing the Data Files.

Problem: Your supervisor has asked you to prepare a memo that contains an Excel table and a chart comparing current and projected subscriber enrollments. (*Note:* If you do not have Excel on your computer, create the table using Word instead of importing it from Excel.) You prepare the document shown in Figure 8–73.

Perform the following tasks:
1. Use the Memo (elegant) template to create a new memo and then enter all text in the memo, as shown in the figure. (If you cannot locate this template, open the file called Memo (elegant) from the Data Files.) Delete the row containing the cc in the header. Remove the first line indent from the paragraphs below the header. *Hint*: Use the Paragraph Settings Dialog Box Launcher.
2. Run Excel and open the Lab 8–1 Subscriber Breakdown in Excel workbook, which is located on the Data Files. Below the paragraph in the memo, link the worksheet in the Lab 8–1

Continued >

STUDENT ASSIGNMENTS

In the Labs *continued*

Subscriber Breakdown in Excel workbook to the Word memo. (If you do not have Excel on your computer, create the table in Word.)

3. Break the link between the Excel table in the Word document and the Excel worksheet in the Excel workbook. Center the table. If necessary, resize the table so that it looks like the one in Figure 8–73.

4. Insert a line with markers chart, centered below the table.

   a. Copy the rows from the table to the chart spreadsheet window. Remove the Series 3 data series from the chart spreadsheet.

   b. Apply the Style 11 chart style to the chart.

   c. Change the colors to Color 3.

   d. Add a vertical axis title, NUMBER OF SUBSCRIBERS. *Hint:* Use the Chart Elements gallery.

   e. Change the chart title to SUBSCRIBER PROJECTIONS.

   f. Move the legend so that it appears in the upper-right portion of the chart. Remove the check mark from the 'Show the legend without overlapping the chart' check box. If necessary, position the legend as shown in the figure.

   g. Format the vertical axis so that its minimum value (starting point) is 5000 and the maximum is 100000. Add primary major horizontal gridlines to the chart.

   h. Add an "Inside Left Shadow" effect to the chart.

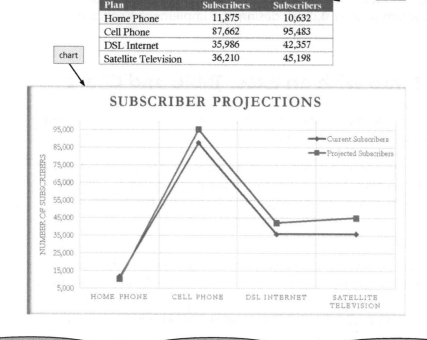

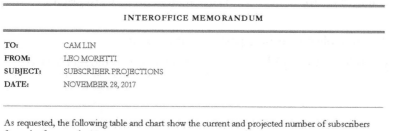

Communication World Subscribers table:

Plan	Current Subscribers	Projected Subscribers
Home Phone	11,875	10,632
Cell Phone	87,662	95,483
DSL Internet	35,986	42,357
Satellite Television	36,210	45,198

Figure 8–73

5. Adjust spacing above and below paragraphs as necessary so that all of the memo contents fit on a single page.

6. If requested by your instructor, change the name at the top of the memo from Leo Moretti to your name.

7. Save the document with Lab 8–1 Subscriber Projections as the file name and then submit it in the format specified by your instructor.

8. ✸ This lab instructed you to remove the first line indent from the paragraphs in the memo. Why do you think this was requested?

Lab 2: **Working with Comments and Tracked Changes**

Note: To complete this assignment, you will be required to use the Data Files. Please contact your instructor for information about accessing the Data Files.

Problem: Your supervisor has asked you to prepare a draft of a document, showing all tracked changes and comments. You mark up the document shown in Figure 8–74.

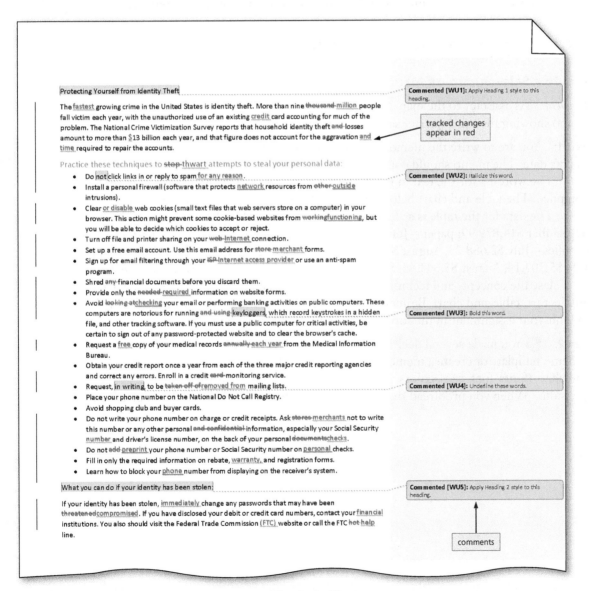

Figure 8–74

Continued >

In the Labs *continued*

Perform the following tasks:

1. Open the file named Lab 8–2 Preventing Identity Theft Draft from the Data Files.

2. Insert the comments and track all changes shown in Figure 8–74.

3. Save the document with the file name, Lab 8–2 Preventing Identity Theft Draft with Markups.

4. Make the changes indicated in the comments and then delete the comments in the document.

5. Accept all tracked changes in the document.

6. Save the document with the file name, Lab 8–2 Preventing Identity Theft Final.

7. Compare the Lab 8–2 Preventing Identity Theft Draft file (original document) with the Lab 8–2 Preventing Identity Theft Final file (revised document). Save the compare result with the file name, Lab 8–2 Preventing Identity Theft Compared.

8. Close all windows and then open the Lab 8–2 Preventing Identity Theft Compared file. Print the document with markups. Use the Review tab to review each change. Close the document without saving.

9. ✳ How could you determine if two documents contained the same content?

Lab 3: **Consider This: Your Turn**

Create a Sales Summary Memo with a Table and Chart

Problem: As assistant to the manager of an office supply store, you have been asked to create a memo showing the third quarter sales figures by category.

Part 1: You are to write the memo to Carlos Mendez with a subject of Third Quarter Sales. Use today's date. The memo should contain a table and chart as specified below.

The wording for the text in the memo is as follows: Third quarter sales figures have been compiled. The table and chart below show sales by category for the third quarter.

The data for the table is as follows: technology – July $15,210.10, August $13,298.11, September $14,879.99; paper – July $3,546.29, August $4,687.19, September $4,983.21; office supplies – July $2,688.23, August $3,021.25, September $2,234.66; and breakroom supplies – July $5,302.14, August $5,843.54, September $6,001.03. Create a chart of all table data.

Use the concepts and techniques presented in this module to create and format the memo and its text, table, and chart. Be sure to check the spelling and grammar of the finished memo. Submit your assignment in the format specified by your instructor.

Part 2: ✳ You made several decisions while creating the memo in this assignment: whether to use a memo template or create a memo from scratch, and how to organize and format the memo, table, and chart (fonts, font sizes, colors, shading, styles, etc.). What was the rationale behind each of these decisions? When you proofread the document, what further revisions did you make and why?

9 Creating a Reference Document with a Table of Contents and an Index

Objectives

You will have mastered the material in this module when you can:

- Insert a screenshot
- Add and modify a caption
- Create a cross-reference
- Insert and link text boxes
- Compress pictures
- Work in Outline view
- Work with a master document and subdocuments

- Insert a cover page
- Create and modify a table of contents
- Use the Navigation Pane
- Create and update a table of figures
- Build, modify, and update an index
- Create alternating footers
- Add bookmarks

Introduction

During the course of your academic studies and professional activities, you may find it necessary to compose a document that is many pages or even hundreds of pages in length. When composing a long document, you must ensure that the document is organized so that a reader easily can locate material in that document. Sometimes a document of this nature is called a **reference document**.

Project — Reference Document

A **reference document** is any multipage document organized so that users easily can locate material and navigate through the document. Examples of reference documents include user guides, term papers, pamphlets, manuals, proposals, and plans.

The project in this module uses Word to produce the reference document shown in Figure 9–1. This reference document, titled *Using Microsoft Word 2016*, is a

Microsoft Word 2016

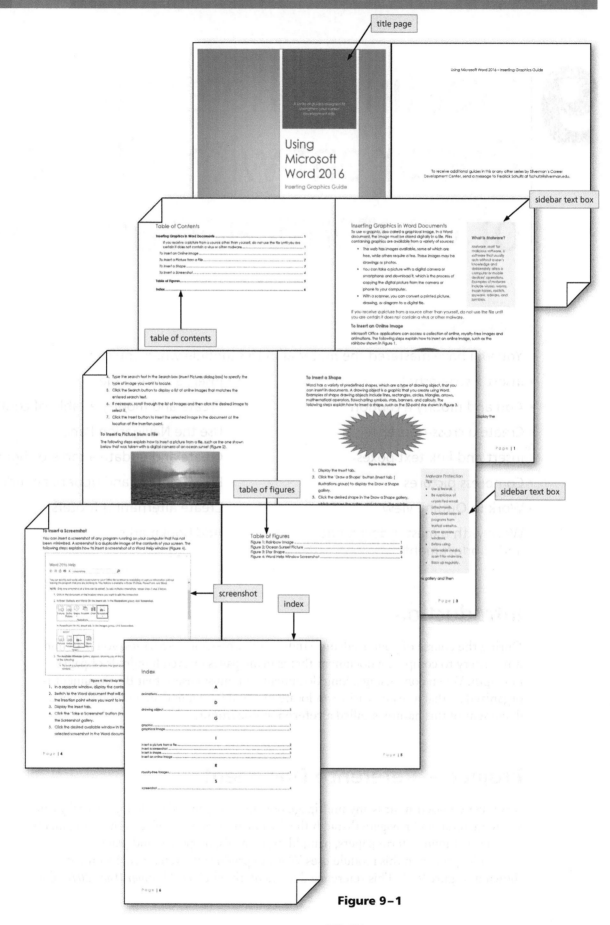

Figure 9–1

multipage guide that is distributed by Silverman College to students and staff. Notice that the inner margin between facing pages has extra space to allow duplicated copies of the document to be bound (i.e., stapled or fastened in some manner) — without the binding covering the words.

The *Using Microsoft Word 2016* reference document begins with a title page designed to entice the target audience to open the document and read it. Next is the copyright page, followed by the table of contents. The document then describes how to insert four types of graphics in a Word document: online image, picture from a file, shape, and screenshot. The end of this reference document has a table of figures and an index to assist readers in locating information contained within the document. A miniature version of the *Using Microsoft Word 2016* reference document is shown in Figure 9–1.

The section of the *Using Microsoft Word 2016* reference document that is titled Inserting Graphics in Word Documents is a draft document that you will modify. The draft document is located on the Data Files. Please contact your instructor for information about accessing the Data Files. After editing content in the draft document, you will incorporate a final version in the reference document.

In this module, you will learn how to create the document shown in Figure 9–1. The following roadmap identifies general activities you will perform as you progress through this module:

1. MODIFY a draft of a REFERENCE DOCUMENT.

2. CREATE a MASTER DOCUMENT for the reference document.

3. ORGANIZE the REFERENCE DOCUMENT.

To Run Word and Change Word Settings

If you are using a computer to step through the project in this module and you want your screens to match the figures in this book, you should change your screen's resolution to 1366 × 768. The following steps run Word, display formatting marks, and change the zoom to page width.

1 Run Word and create a blank document in the Word window. If necessary, maximize the Word window.

2 If the Print Layout button on the status bar is not selected, click it so that your screen is in Print Layout view.

3 To display the page the same width as the document window, if necessary, click the Page Width button (View tab | Zoom group).

BTW
The Ribbon and Screen Resolution
Word may change how the groups and buttons within the groups appear on the ribbon, depending on the computer's screen resolution. Thus, your ribbon may look different from the ones in this book if you are using a screen resolution other than 1366 x 768.

Preparing a Document to Be Included in a Reference Document

Before including the Inserting Graphics Draft document in a longer document, you will make several modifications to the document:

1. Insert a screenshot.

2. Add captions to the images in the document.

3. Insert references to the figures in the text.

4. Mark an index entry.

5. Insert text boxes that contain information about malware.

6. Compress the pictures.

7. Change the bullet symbol.

The following pages outline these changes.

CONSIDER THIS

How should you prepare a document to be included in a longer document?

Ensure that reference elements in a document, such as captions and index entries, are formatted properly and entered consistently.

• **Captions:** A **caption** is text that appears outside of an illustration, usually below it. If the illustration is identified with a number, the caption may include the word, Figure, along with the illustration number (i.e., Figure 1). In the caption, separate the figure number from the text of the figure by a space or punctuation mark, such as a period or colon (Figure 1: Rainbow Image).

• **Index Entries:** If your document will include an index, read through the document and mark any terms or headings that you want to appear in the index. Include any term that the reader may want to locate quickly. Omit figures from index entries if the document will have a table of figures; otherwise, include figures in the index if appropriate.

BTW

Protected View

To keep your computer safe from potentially dangerous files, Word may automatically open certain files in a restricted mode, called Protected View. To see the Protected View settings, click File on the ribbon to open the Backstage view, click the Options tab to display the Word Options dialog box, click Trust Center in the left pane (Word Options dialog box), click the 'Trust Center Settings' button in the right pane to display the Trust Center dialog box, and then click Protected View in the left pane to show the current Protected View settings.

To Open a Document and Save It with a New File Name

The draft document that you will insert in the reference document is named Inserting Graphics Draft. The draft document is located on the Data Files. Please contact your instructor for information about accessing the Data Files. To preserve the contents of the original draft, you save it with a new file name. The following steps open the draft file and then save it with a new file name.

1 Navigate to the location of the Data Files on your hard drive, OneDrive, or other storage location.

2 Open the file named Inserting Graphics Draft.

3 Navigate to the desired save location on your hard drive, OneDrive, or other storage location.

4 Save the file just opened on your hard drive, OneDrive, or other storage location using Inserting Graphics Final as the file name.

5 If the 'Show/Hide ¶' button (Home tab | Paragraph group) is selected, click it to hide formatting marks.

Q&A What if some formatting marks still appear after clicking the 'Show/Hide ¶' button? Open the Backstage view, click the Options tab to display the Word Options dialog box, click Display in the left pane (Word Options dialog box), remove the check mark from the Hidden text check box, and then click the OK button.

6 Display the View tab and then click the Multiple Pages button (View tab | Zoom group) so that you can see all three pages of the document at once (Figure 9–2).

7 When you have finished viewing the document, click the Page Width button (View tab | Zoom group) to display the document as wide as possible in the document window.

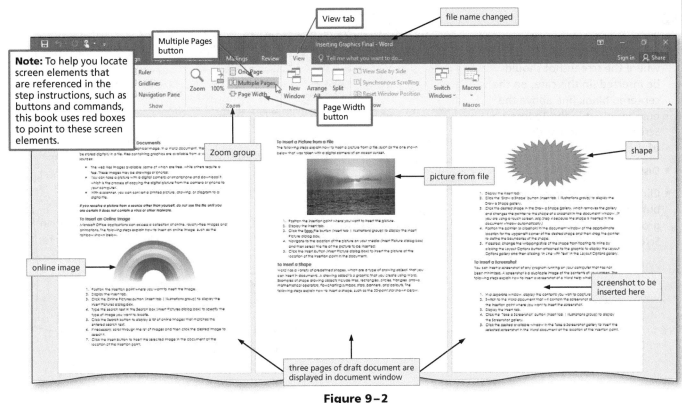

Figure 9–2

To Insert a Screenshot

1 MODIFY REFERENCE DOCUMENT | 2 CREATE MASTER DOCUMENT | 3 ORGANIZE REFERENCE DOCUMENT

A **screenshot** is a duplicate image of the contents of your computer or mobile device's screen. The current document is missing a screenshot of a Word Help window. To insert a screenshot, you first must display the screen for which you want a screenshot in a window on your computer or mobile device. *Why? From within Word, you can insert a screenshot of any app running on your computer, provided the app has not been minimized.* The following steps insert a screenshot in a document.

• Display the contents you want to capture in a screenshot (in this case, type **screenshots** in the 'Tell me what you want to do' text box, click 'Get Help on "screenshots"' on the menu to open a Word 2016 Help window, and then click the 'Insert a screenshot or clipping - Office Support' link to display the associated Help information. If necessary, scroll through, reposition and resize the Word Help window so that it matches Figure 9–3.

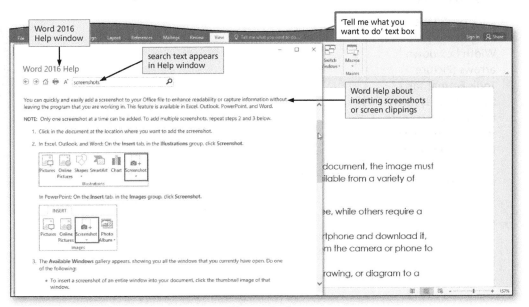

Figure 9–3

2

- In the Word window, position the insertion point in the document where the screenshot should be inserted (in this case, on the centered blank line above the numbered list in the To Insert a Screenshot section at the bottom of the document).

- Display the Insert tab.

- Click the 'Take a Screenshot' button (Insert tab | Illustrations group) to display the Take a Screenshot gallery (Figure 9–4).

Q&A

What is a screen clipping?
A screen clipping is a section of a window. When you select Screen Clipping in the Take a Screenshot gallery, the window turns opaque so that you can drag through the part of the window to be included in the document.

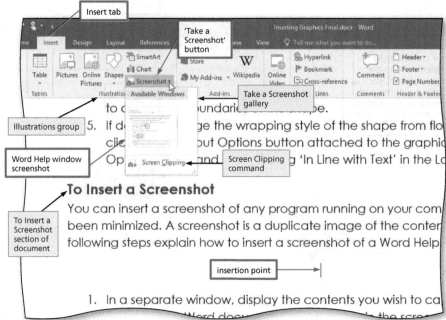

Figure 9–4

Why does my Take a Screenshot gallery show more windows?
You have additional programs running on your desktop, and their windows are not minimized.

3

- Click the Word Help window screenshot in the Take a Screenshot gallery to insert the selected screenshot in the Word document at the location of the insertion point.

- Click the Shape Height and Shape Width box down arrows (Picture Tools Format tab | Size group) as many times as necessary to resize the screenshot to approximately 5.1" tall by 6.28" wide (Figure 9–5).

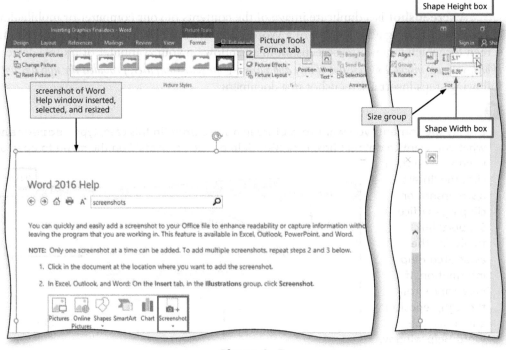

Figure 9–5

Q&A

Why can I not set the exact measurements shown above?
You may need to click the Advanced Layout: Size Dialog Box Launcher (Picture Tools Format tab | Size group) to display the Size sheet in the Layout dialog box and then remove the checkmark from the 'Lock aspect ratio' check box.

Why did the screenshot appear on a new page?
The screenshot is too tall to fit at the bottom of page 3.

To Add a Caption

In Word, you can add a caption to an equation, a figure, and a table. If you move, delete, or add captions in a document, Word renumbers remaining captions in the document automatically. In this reference document, the captions contain the word, Figure, followed by the figure number, a colon, and a figure description. The following steps add a caption to a graphic, specifically, the screenshot. *Why? The current document contains four images: an image from an online source, a picture from a file, a shape, and a screenshot. All of these images should have captions.*

- If the screenshot is not selected already, click it to select the graphic for which you want a caption.

- Display the References tab.

- Click the Insert Caption button (References tab | Captions group) to display the Caption dialog box with a figure number automatically assigned to the selected graphic (Figure 9–6).

Q&A

Why is the figure number a 1?
No other captions have been assigned in this document yet. When you insert a new caption, or move or delete items containing captions, Word automatically updates caption numbers throughout the document.

What if the Caption text box has the label Table or Equation instead of Figure?
Click the Label arrow (Caption dialog box) and then click Figure in the Label list.

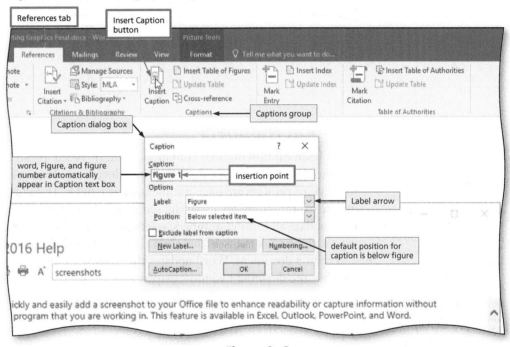

Figure 9–6

- Press the COLON key (:) and then press the SPACEBAR in the Caption text box (Caption dialog box) to place separating characters between the figure number and description.

- Type **Help Window Screenshot** as the figure description (Figure 9–7).

Q&A

Can I change the format of the caption number?
Yes, click the Numbering button (Caption dialog box), adjust the format as desired, and then click the OK button.

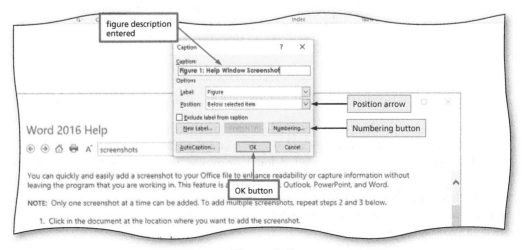

Figure 9–7

3

- Click the OK button to insert the caption below the selected graphic.
- If necessary, scroll to display the caption in the document window (Figure 9–8).

Q&A

How do I change the position of a caption?

Click the Position arrow (Caption dialog box) and then select the desired position of the caption.

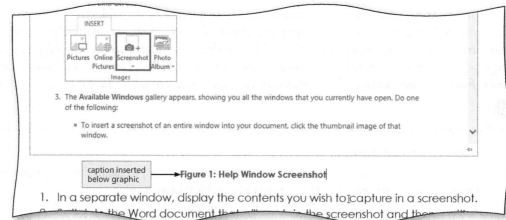

Figure 1: Help Window Screenshot

1. In a separate window, display the contents you wish to capture in a screenshot.

Figure 9–8

BTW

Captions

If a caption appears with extra characters inside curly braces ({ }), Word is displaying field codes instead of field results. Press ALT+F9 to display captions correctly as field results. If Word prints fields codes for captions, click File on the ribbon to open the Backstage view, click the Options tab in the Backstage view to display the Word Options dialog box, click Advanced in the left pane (Word Options dialog box), scroll to the Print section in the right pane, remove the check mark from the 'Print field codes instead of their values' check box, click the OK button, and then print the document again.

Caption Numbers

Each caption number contains a field. In Word, recall that a **field** is a placeholder for data that can change in a document. Examples of fields you have used in previous projects are page numbers, merge fields, IF fields, and the current date. You update caption numbers using the same technique used to update any other field. That is, to update all caption numbers, select the entire document and then press the F9 key, or right-click the field and then click Update Field on the shortcut menu. When you print a document, Word updates the caption numbers automatically, regardless of whether the document window displays the updated caption numbers.

To Hide White Space

White space is the space displayed in the margins at the top and bottom of pages (including any headers and footers) and also space between pages. To make it easier to see the text in this document as you scroll through it, the following step hides white space.

1 Position the pointer in the document window in the space between the pages or below the last page in the document and then double-click when the pointer changes to a 'Hide White Space' button to hide white space.

To Create a Cross-Reference

1 MODIFY REFERENCE DOCUMENT | 2 CREATE MASTER DOCUMENT | 3 ORGANIZE REFERENCE DOCUMENT

The next step in this project is to add a reference to the new figure. *Why? In reference documents, the text should reference each figure specifically and, if appropriate, explain the contents of the figure.*

Because figures may be inserted, deleted, or moved, you may not know the actual figure number in the final document. For this reason, Word provides a method of creating a **cross-reference**, which is a link to an item, such as a heading, caption, or footnote in a document. By creating a cross-reference to the caption, the text that mentions the figure will be updated whenever the caption to the figure is updated. The following steps create a cross-reference.

1

- At the end of the last sentence below the To Insert a Screenshot heading, position the insertion point to the left of the period, press the SPACEBAR, and then press the LEFT PARENTHESIS (( ) key.
- Display the Insert tab.
- Click the 'Insert Cross-reference' button (Insert tab | Links group) to display the Cross-reference dialog box (Figure 9–9).

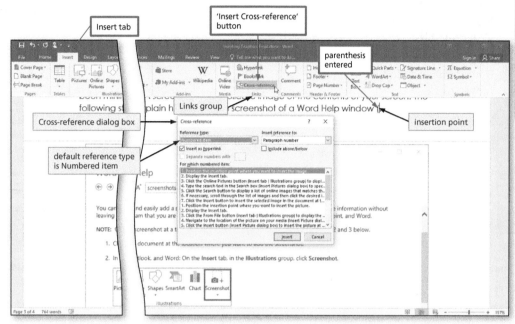

Figure 9–9

2

- Click the Reference type arrow (Cross-reference dialog box) to display the Reference type list; scroll to and then click Figure, which displays a list of figures from the document in the For which caption list (which, at this point, is only one figure).
- If necessary, click 'Figure 1: Help Window Screenshot' in the For which caption list to select the caption to reference.
- Click the 'Insert reference to' arrow and then click 'Only label and number' to instruct Word that the cross-reference in the document should list just the label, Figure, followed by the figure number (Figure 9–10).

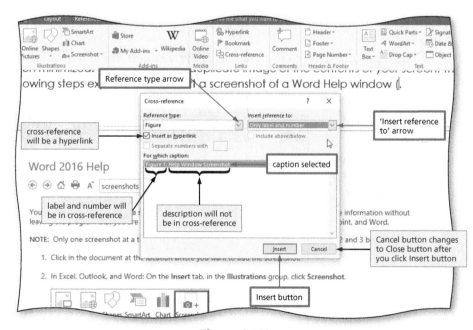

Figure 9–10

3

- Click the Insert button to insert the cross-reference in the document at the location of the insertion point.

Q&A What if my cross-reference is shaded in gray?

The cross-reference is a field. Depending on your Word settings, fields may appear shaded in gray to help you identify them on the screen.

4

- Click the Close button (Cross-reference dialog box).

- Press the RIGHT PARENTHESIS ( )) key to close off the cross-reference (Figure 9–11).

Q&A

How do I update a cross-reference if a caption is added, deleted, or moved?

In many cases, Word automatically updates a cross-reference in a document if the item to which it refers changes. To update a cross-reference manually, select the cross-reference and then press the F9 key, or right-click the cross-reference and then click Update Field on the shortcut menu.

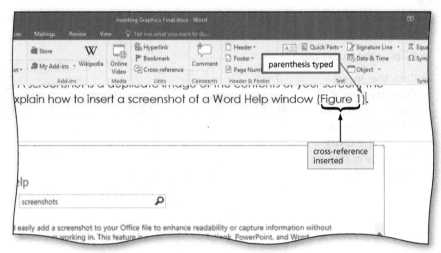

Figure 9–11

Other Ways

1. Click 'Insert Cross-reference' button (References tab | Captions group)

To Go to an Object

1 MODIFY REFERENCE DOCUMENT | **2 CREATE MASTER DOCUMENT** | **3 ORGANIZE REFERENCE DOCUMENT**

Often, you would like to bring a certain page, graphic, or other part of a document into view in the document window. Although you could scroll through the document to find a desired page, graphic, or part of the document, Word enables you to go to a specific location via the Go To sheet in the Find and Replace dialog box.

The following steps go to a graphic. *Why? The next step in this module is to add a caption to another graphic in the document, so you want to display the graphic in the document window.*

1

- Display the Home tab.

- Click the Find arrow (Home tab | Editing group) to display the Find menu (Figure 9–12).

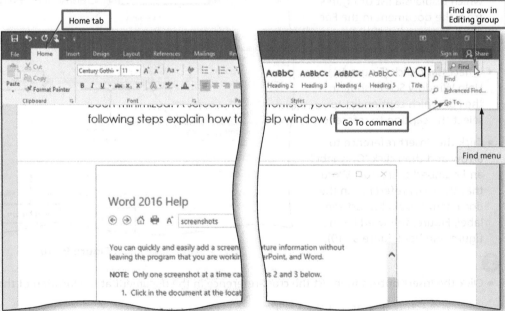

Figure 9–12

- Click Go To on the Find menu to display the Find and Replace dialog box.

- Scroll through the Go to what list and then click Graphic to select it.

- Click the Previous button to display the previous graphic in the document window (which is the star shape, in this case) (Figure 9–13).

- Click Close button to close the dialog box.

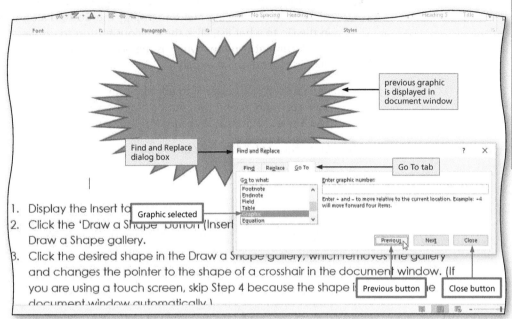

Figure 9–13

Other Ways

1. Press CTRL+G

To Add Captions and Create Cross-References

The previous steps added a caption to the screenshot graphic and then created a cross-reference to that caption. The following steps add captions to the remaining three graphics in the document (that is, the star shape, the picture, and the online image).

① Click the star shape to select the graphic for which you want to add a caption.

② Click the Insert Caption button (References tab | Captions group) to display the Caption dialog box with a figure number automatically assigned to the selected graphic.

③ Press the COLON (:) key and then press the SPACEBAR in the Caption text box (Caption dialog box) to place separating characters between the figure number and description.

④ Type **Star Shape** as the figure description and then click the OK button to insert the caption below the selected graphic.

⑤ At the end of the last sentence above the graphic, change the word, below, to the word, in, and then press the SPACEBAR.

⑥ Click the 'Insert Cross-reference' button (Insert or References tab | Links or Captions group) to display the Cross-reference dialog box, if necessary, click 'Figure 1: Star Shape' in the For which caption list to select the caption to reference, click the Insert button to insert the cross-reference at the location of the insertion point, and then click the Close button in the Cross-reference dialog box.

Q&A | Why did I not need to change the settings for the reference type and reference to in the dialog box?
Word retains the previous settings in the dialog box.

BTW
Touch Screen Differences
The Office and Windows interfaces may vary if you are using a touch screen. For this reason, you might notice that the function or appearance of your touch screen differs slightly from this module's presentation.

7 Click the Find arrow (Home tab | Editing group) to display the Find menu and then click Go To on the Find menu to display the Go To dialog box. With Graphic selected in the Go to what list, click the Previous button to display the previous graphic in the document window (which is the ocean sunset picture in this case). Click the Close button to close the dialog box.

8 Repeat Steps 1 through 7 to add the caption, Ocean Sunset Picture, to the picture of the ocean sunset and the caption, Rainbow Image, to the image of the rainbow. Also add a cross-reference at the end of the sentences above each image (Figure 9–14).

9 Close the Cross-reference dialog box.

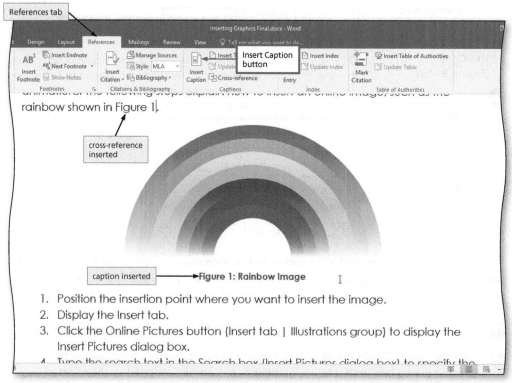

Figure 9–14

To Mark an Index Entry

1 MODIFY REFERENCE DOCUMENT | 2 CREATE MASTER DOCUMENT | 3 ORGANIZE REFERENCE DOCUMENT

The last page of the reference document in this project is an index, which lists important terms discussed in the document along with each term's corresponding page number. For Word to generate the index, you first must mark any text you wish to appear in the index. *Why? When you mark an index entry, Word creates a field that it uses to build the index.* Index entry fields are hidden and are displayed on the screen only when you show formatting marks, that is, when the 'Show/Hide ¶' button (Home tab | Paragraph group) is selected.

In this document, you want the word, animations, in the first sentence below the To Insert an Online Image heading to be marked as an index entry. The following steps mark an index entry.

1

- Select the text you wish to appear in the index (the word, animations, in the first sentence of the document in this case).

- Click the Mark Entry button (References tab | Index group) to display the Mark Index Entry dialog box (Figure 9–15).

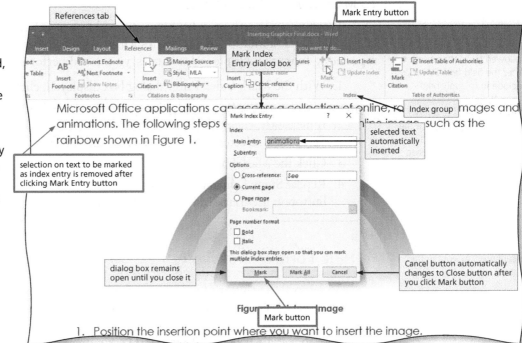

Figure 9–15

2

- Click the Mark button (Mark Index Entry dialog box) to mark the selected text in the document as an index entry.

Q&A Why do formatting marks now appear on the screen?
When you mark an index entry, Word automatically shows formatting marks (if they are not showing already) so that you can see the index entry field. Notice that the marked index entry begins with the letters, XE.

- Click the Close button in the Mark Index Entry dialog box to close the dialog box (Figure 9–16).

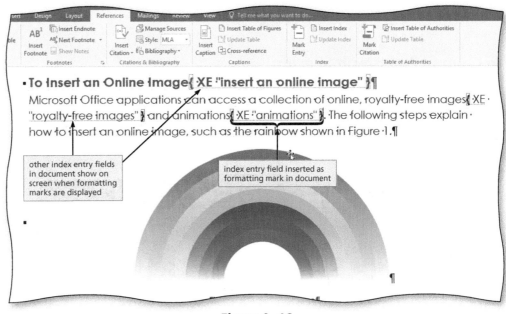

Figure 9–16

Q&A How could I see all index entries marked in a document?
With formatting marks displaying, you could scroll through the document, scanning for all occurrences of XE, or you could use the Navigation Pane (that is, place a check mark in the 'Open the Navigation Pane' check box (View tab | Show group)) to find all occurrences of XE.

Other Ways

1. Select text, press ALT+SHIFT+X

To Mark Multiple Index Entries

Word leaves the Mark Index Entry dialog box open until you close it, which allows you to mark multiple index entries without having to reopen the dialog box repeatedly. To mark multiple index entries, you would perform the following steps.

1. With the Mark Index Entry dialog box displayed, click in the document window; scroll to and then select the next index entry.
2. If necessary, click the Main entry text box (Mark Index Entry dialog box) to display the selected text in the Main entry text box.
3. Click the Mark button.
4. Repeat Steps 1 through 3 for all entries. When finished, click the Close button in the Mark Index Entry dialog box.

To Hide Formatting Marks

To remove the clutter of index entry fields from the document, you should hide formatting marks. The following step hides formatting marks.

1 If the 'Show/Hide ¶' button (Home tab | Paragraph group) is selected, click it to hide formatting marks.

Q&A What if the index entries still appear after clicking the 'Show/Hide ¶' button?
Open the Backstage view, click the Options tab to display the Word Options dialog box, click Display in the left pane (Word Options dialog box), remove the check mark from the Hidden text check box, and then click the OK button.

To Change Paragraph Spacing in a Document

1 MODIFY REFERENCE DOCUMENT | 2 CREATE MASTER DOCUMENT | 3 ORGANIZE REFERENCE DOCUMENT

In Word, you easily can expand or condense the amount of space between lines in all paragraphs in a document. The following steps expand paragraph spacing. *Why? You feel the document text would be easier to read if the paragraphs were more open.*

- Display the Design tab.
- Click the Paragraph Spacing button (Design tab | Document Formatting group) to display the Paragraph Spacing gallery (Figure 9–17).

Experiment

- Point to various spacing commands in the Paragraph Spacing gallery and watch the paragraphs conform to that spacing.

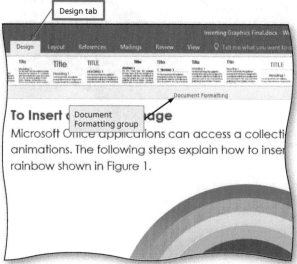
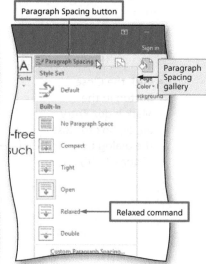

Figure 9–17

2
- Click Relaxed in the Paragraph Spacing gallery to expand the spacing of paragraphs in the document.

To Show White Space

For the remainder of creating this project, you would like to see headers, footers, and margins. Thus, you should show white space. The following step shows white space.

 Position the pointer in the document window on the page break and then double-click when the pointer changes to a 'Show White Space' button to show white space.

To Insert a Sidebar Text Box

1 MODIFY REFERENCE DOCUMENT | **2 CREATE MASTER DOCUMENT** | 3 ORGANIZE REFERENCE DOCUMENT

A **sidebar text box** is a text box that runs across the top or bottom of a page or along the right or left edge of a page. The following steps insert a built-in sidebar text box. ***Why?*** *Sidebar text boxes take up less space on the page than text boxes positioned in the middle of the page.*

- Be sure the insertion point is near the top of page 1 of the document, as shown in Figure 9–18.

Q&A Does the insertion point need to be at the top of the page?
The insertion point should be close to where you want to insert the text box.

- Display the Insert tab.
- Click the 'Choose a Text Box' button (Insert tab | Text group) to display the Choose a Text Box gallery.

Experiment

- Scroll through the Choose a Text Box gallery to see the variety of available text box styles.
- Scroll to display Grid Sidebar in the Choose a Text Box gallery (Figure 9–18).

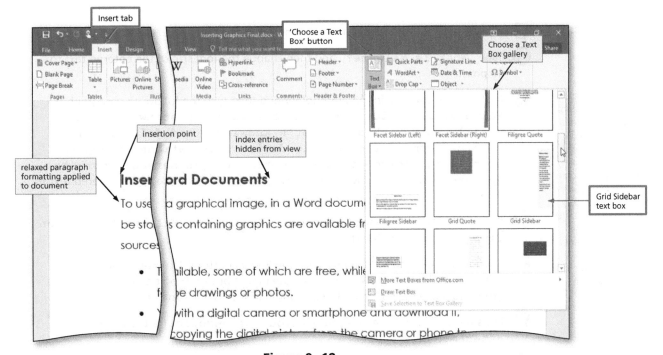

Figure 9–18

● Click Grid Sidebar in the Choose a Text Box gallery to insert that text box style in the document (Figure 9–19).

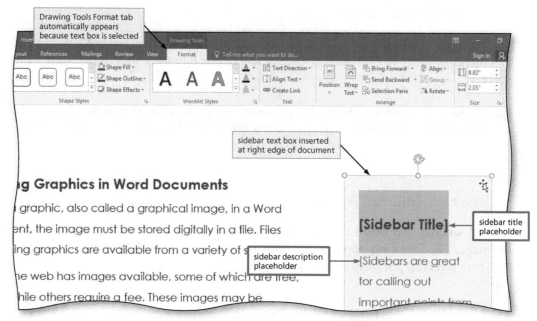

Figure 9–19

Other Ways

1. Click 'Explore Quick Parts' button (Insert tab | Text group), click 'Building Blocks Organizer' on Explore Quick Parts menu, select desired text box name in Building blocks list, click Insert button

To Enter and Format Text in the Sidebar Text Box

The next step is to enter the text in the sidebar text box. The following steps enter text in the text box.

① If necessary, click the sidebar title placeholder in the text box to select it.

② Type **What Is Malware?** and then change the font size of the entered text to 12 point.

③ Click the sidebar description placeholder and then type the following paragraph: **Malware, short for malicious software, is software that usually acts without a user's knowledge and deliberately alters a computer or mobile device's operations. Examples of malware include viruses, worms, trojan horses, rootkits, spyware, adware, and zombies.** Change the font size of the entered text to 10 point.

④ Press the ENTER key. Change the font size to 12 point. Type **Malware Protection Tips** and then press the ENTER key.

⑤ Change the font size to 10 point. Click the Bullets button (Home tab | Paragraph group) to bullet the list. Click the Decrease Indent button (Home tab | Paragraph group) to move the bullet symbol left one-half inch. Type **Use a firewall.**

⑥ Press the ENTER key. Type **Be suspicious of unsolicited email attachments.**

⑦ Press the ENTER key. Type **Download apps or programs from trusted websites.**

8 Press the ENTER key. Type **Close spyware windows.**

9 Press the ENTER key. Type **Before using removable media, scan it for malware.** If necessary, drag the bottom of the text box down to make it longer so that all of the entered text is visible.

10 Press the ENTER key. Type **Back up regularly.**

11 Click the One Page button (View tab | Zoom group) so that you can see all of the entered text at once (Figure 9–20).

12 Change the zoom to page width.

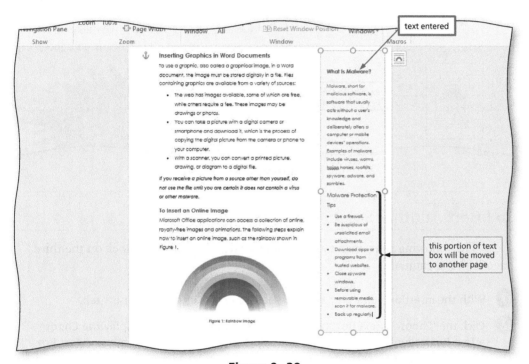

Figure 9–20

To Use the Navigation Pane to Go to a Page

Instead of one long text box, this project splits the text box across the top of two pages, specifically, the first and third pages of this document. The following steps use the Navigation Pane to display page 3 in the document window so that you can insert another text box on that page.

1 If necessary, display the View tab. Place a check mark in the 'Open the Navigation Pane' check box (View tab | Show group) to open the Navigation Pane at the left edge of the Word window.

2 Click the Pages tab in the Navigation Pane to display thumbnail images of the pages in the document.

3 Scroll to and then click the thumbnail of the third page in the Navigation Pane to display the top of the selected page in the top of the document window (Figure 9–21).

4 Leave the Navigation Pane open for use in the next several steps.

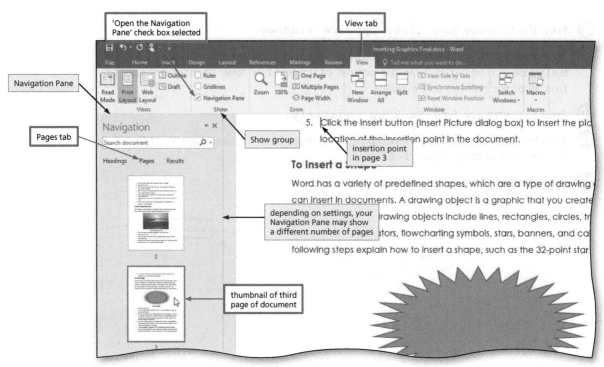

Figure 9–21

BTW
Deleting Building Blocks
To delete an existing building block, click the 'Explore Quick Parts' button (Insert tab | Text group) to display the Explore Quick Parts menu, click 'Building Blocks Organizer' on the Explore Quick Parts menu to display the Building Blocks Organizer dialog box, select the building block to delete (Building Blocks Organizer dialog box), click the Delete button, click the Yes button in the dialog box that appears, and then close the Building Blocks Organizer dialog box.

To Insert Another Sidebar Text Box

The following steps insert a Grid Sidebar text box building block on the third page in the document.

1 With the insertion point on page 3 in the document, display the Insert tab.

2 Click the 'Choose a Text Box' button (Insert tab | Text group) to display the Choose a Text Box gallery and then locate and select Grid Sidebar in the Choose a Text Box gallery to insert that text box style in the document.

3 Press the DELETE key four times to delete the current contents from the text box (Figure 9–22).

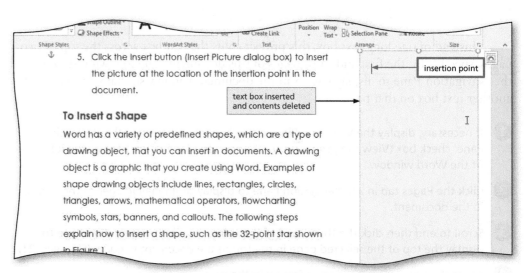

Figure 9–22

To Link Text Boxes

Word allows you to link two separate text boxes. *Why? You can flow text from one text box into the other.* To link text boxes, the second text box must be empty, which is why you deleted the contents of the text box in the previous steps. The following steps link text boxes.

- Click the thumbnail of the first page in the Navigation Pane to display the top of the selected page in the document window.

- Click the text box on the first page to select it.

- If necessary, display the Drawing Tools Format tab.

- Click the Create Link button (Drawing Tools Format tab | Text group), which changes the pointer to the shape of a cup.

- Move the pointer in the document window to see its new shape (Figure 9–23).

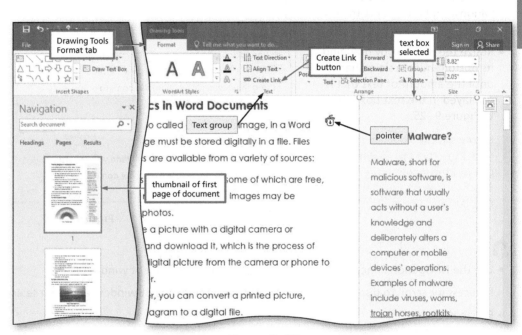

Figure 9–23

②

- Scroll through the document to display the second text box, which is located on the third page, in the document window.

Q&A

Can I use the Navigation Pane to go to the second text box?
No. If you click in the Navigation Pane, the link process will stop and the pointer will return to its default shape.

- Position the pointer in the empty text box, so that the pointer shape changes to a pouring cup (Figure 9–24).

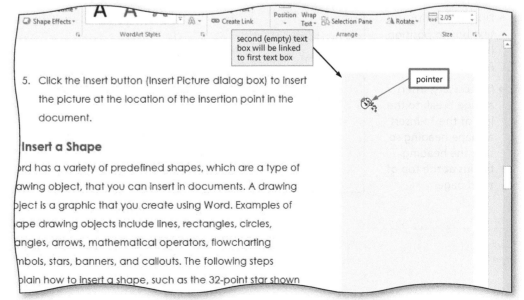

Figure 9–24

3

- Click the empty text box to link it to the first text box (or, if using a touch screen, you will need to use a stylus to tap the empty text box).

- If necessary, scroll to display the first text box in the document window and then select the text box.

- Resize the text box by dragging its bottom-middle sizing handle until the amount of text that is displayed in the text box is similar to Figure 9–25.

Q&A
How would I remove a link?
Select the text box in which you created the link and then click the Break Link button (Drawing Tools Format tab | Text group).

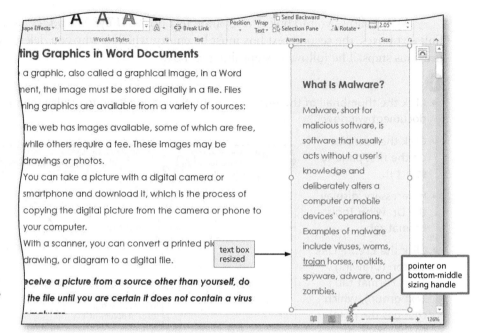

Figure 9–25

4

- Use the Navigation Pane to display the third page in the document window.

- If necessary, scroll to display the second text box in the document window and then select the text box.

- Resize the text box by dragging its bottom-middle sizing handle until the amount of text that is displayed in the text box is similar to Figure 9–26.

- Drag the entire text box to position it as shown in Figure 9–26.

- If necessary, insert a page break to the left of the To Insert a Shape heading so that the heading begins at the top of third page.

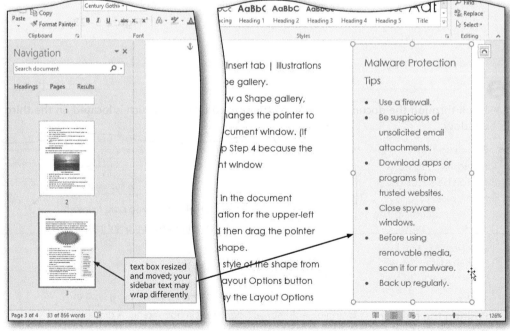

Figure 9–26

To Compress Pictures

If you plan to use email to send a Word document that contains pictures or graphics or post it for downloading, you may want to reduce its file size to speed up file transmission time. ***Why? Pictures and other graphics in Word documents can increase the size of these files.*** In Word, you can compress pictures, which reduces the size of the Word document. Compressing the pictures in Word does not cause any loss in their original quality. The following steps compress pictures in a document.

- Click a picture in the document to select it, such as the ocean sunset, and then display the Picture Tools Format tab.

- Click the Compress Pictures button (Picture Tools Format tab | Adjust group) to display the Compress Pictures dialog box.

- If the 'Apply only to this picture' check box (Compress Pictures dialog box) contains a check mark, remove the check mark so that all pictures in the document are compressed.

- If necessary, click 'Print (220 ppi): excellent quality on most printers and screens' in the Target output area to specify how images should be compressed (Figure 9–27).

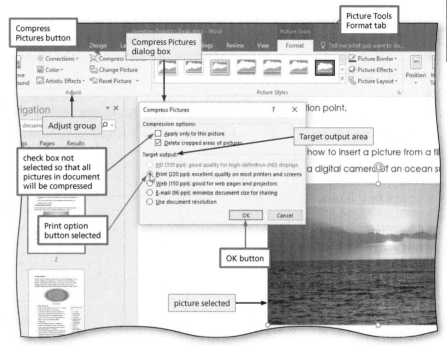

Figure 9–27

- Click the OK button to compress all pictures in the document.

◁ Can I compress a single picture?
Q&A Yes. Select the picture and then place a check mark in the 'Apply only to this picture' check box (Compress Pictures dialog box).

Other Ways

1. Click the Tools button in Save As dialog box, click Compress Pictures on Tools menu, select options (Compress Pictures dialog box), click OK button

To Save Pictures in Other Formats

You can save any graphic in a document as a picture file for use in other documents or apps. If you wanted to save a graphic in a Word document, you would perform the following steps.

1. Right-click the graphic to display a shortcut menu.

2. Click 'Save as Picture' on the shortcut menu to display the File Save dialog box.

3. Navigate to the location you want to save the graphic.

BTW
Compressing Pictures
Selecting a lower ppi (pixels per inch) in the Target output area (Compress Picture dialog box) creates a smaller document file, but also lowers the quality of the images.

4. Click the 'Save as type' arrow (File Save dialog box) and then select the graphic type for the saved graphic.

5. Click the Save button (File Save dialog box) to save the graphic in the specified location using the specified graphic type.

To Change the Symbol Format in a Bulleted List

The following steps change the symbol in a bulleted list. *Why? The project in this module uses a square bullet symbol for the bulleted list instead of the default round bullet symbol.* Word provides several predefined bullet symbols for use in bulleted lists.

- Navigate to the first page and then select the bulleted list for which you want to change the bullet symbol (in this case, the three bulleted paragraphs on the first page).

- Click the Bullets arrow (Home tab | Paragraph group) to display the Bullets gallery (Figure 9–28).

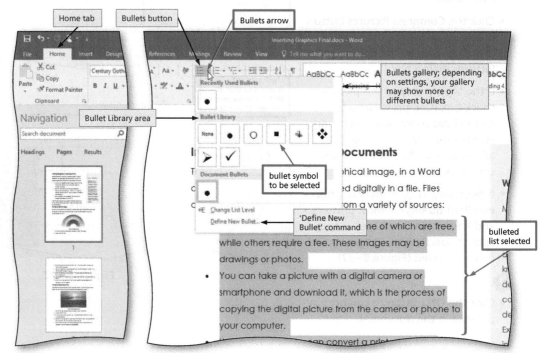

Figure 9–28

- Click the desired bullet symbol in the Bullet Library area to change the bullet symbol on the selected bulleted list (Figure 9–29).

Q&A
Can I select any bullet symbol in the Bullet Library area? Yes. You also can click 'Define New Bullet' in the Bullets gallery if the bullet symbol you desire is not shown in the Bullet Library area.

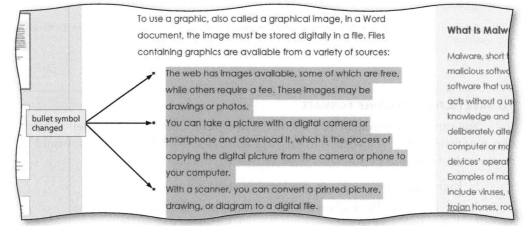

Figure 9–29

3

- Click anywhere to remove the selection from the text.

- Save the document again on the same storage location with the same file name.

To Close Open Panes, Documents, and Windows

The following steps close the open Word document and the Word Help window.

1 Close the Navigation Pane.

2 Close the open document (leave Word running).

3 If necessary, display the Word Help window and close it.

TO RECOVER UNSAVED DOCUMENTS (DRAFT VERSIONS)

If you accidently exit Word without saving a document, you may be able to recover the unsaved document, called a **draft version**, in Word. If you wanted to recover an unsaved document, you would perform these steps.

1. Run Word and create a blank document in the Word window.
2. Open the Backstage view and then, if necessary, click the Open tab to display the Open gallery. Scroll to the bottom of the Recent Documents list. Click the 'Recover Unsaved Documents' button to display an Open dialog box that lists unsaved files retained by Word.

   or

   Open the Backstage view and then, if necessary, click the Info tab to display the Info gallery. Click the Manage Document button to display the Manage Document menu. Click 'Recover Unsaved Documents' on the Manage Document menu to display an Open dialog box that lists unsaved files retained by Word.
3. Select the file to recover and then click the Open button to display the unsaved file in the Word window.
4. To save the document, click the Save As button on the Message Bar.

TO DELETE ALL UNSAVED DOCUMENTS (DRAFT VERSIONS)

If you wanted to delete all unsaved documents, you would perform these steps.

1. Run Word and create a blank document in the Word window.
2. Open the Backstage view and then, if necessary, click the Info tab to display the Info gallery.
3. Click the Manage Document button to display the Manage Document menu.
4. If available, click 'Delete All Unsaved Documents' on the Manage Document menu.
5. When Word displays a dialog box asking if you are sure you want to delete all copies of unsaved files, click the Yes button to delete all unsaved documents.

Break Point: If you wish to take a break, this is a good place to do so. You can exit Word now. To resume at a later time, run Word and continue following the steps from this location forward.

BTW
Bullets
You can select from a variety of other bullet symbols or change the font attributes of a bullet by clicking 'Define New Bullet' in the Bullets gallery and then clicking the Symbol button or Font button in the Define New Bullet dialog box. You also can change the level of a bullet by clicking 'Change List Level' in the Bullets gallery.

BTW
Distributing a Document
Instead of printing and distributing a hard copy of a document, you can distribute the document electronically. Options include sending the document via email; posting it on cloud storage (such as OneDrive) and sharing the file with others; posting it on social media, a blog, or other website; and sharing a link associated with an online location of the document. You also can create and share a PDF or XPS image of the document, so that users can view the file in Adobe Reader or XPS Viewer instead of in Word.

Working with a Master Document

When you are creating a document that includes other files, you may want to create a master document to organize the documents. A **master document** is simply a document that contains links to one or more other documents, each of which is called a **subdocument**. In addition to subdocuments, a master document can contain its own text and graphics.

In this project, the master document file is named Using Microsoft Word 2016 - Inserting Graphics Guide. This master document file contains a link to one subdocument: Inserting Graphics Final. The master document also contains other items: a title page, a copyright page, a table of contents, a table of figures, and an index. The following sections create this master document and insert the necessary elements in the document to create the finished Using Microsoft Word 2016 – Inserting Graphics Guide document.

To Change the Document Theme

The first step in creating this master document is to change its document theme to Slice. The following steps change the document theme.

1 If necessary, run Word and create a new blank document.

2 Click Design on the ribbon to display the Design tab.

3 Click the Themes button (Design tab | Document Formatting group) to display the Themes gallery.

4 Click Slice in the Themes gallery to change the document theme to the selected theme.

Outlines

To create a master document, Word must be in Outline view. You then enter the headings of the document as an outline using Word's built-in heading styles. In an outline, the major heading is displayed at the left margin with each subordinate, or lower-level, heading indented. In Word, the built-in Heading 1 style is displayed at the left margin in Outline view. Heading 2 style is indented below Heading 1 style, Heading 3 style is indented further, and so on. (Outline view works similarly to multilevel lists.)

You do not want to use a built-in heading style for the paragraphs of text within the document, because when you create a table of contents, Word places all lines formatted using the built-in heading styles in the table of contents. Thus, the text below each heading is formatted using the Body Text style.

Each heading should print at the top of a new page. Because you might want to format the pages within a heading differently from those pages in other headings, you insert next page section breaks between each heading.

To Switch to Outline View

The following steps switch to Outline view. ***Why?*** *To create a master document, Word must be in Outline view.*

- Display the View tab (Figure 9–30).

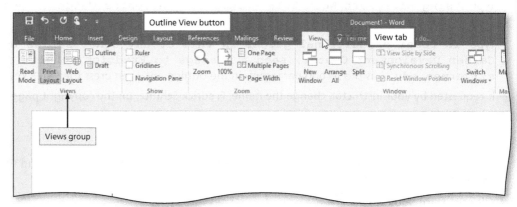

Figure 9–30

- Click the Outline View button (View tab | Views group), which displays the Outlining tab on the ribbon and switches to Outline view.

- Be sure the 'Show Text Formatting' check box is selected and the 'Show First Line Only' check box is not selected (Outlining tab | Outline Tools group) (Figure 9–31).

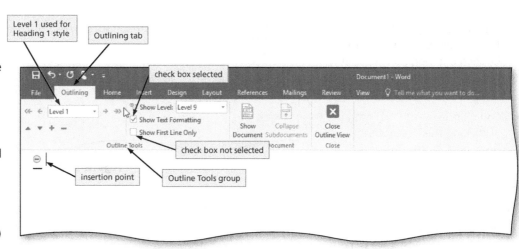

Figure 9–31

To Add Entries in Outline View

The Using Microsoft Word 2016 – Inserting Graphics Guide document contains these three major headings: Inserting Graphics in Word Documents, Table of Figures, and Index. The heading, Inserting Graphics in Word Documents, is not entered in the outline. ***Why not?*** *It is part of the subdocument inserted in the master document.*

The first page of the outline (the copyright page) does not contain a heading; instead it contains three paragraphs of body text, which you enter directly in the outline. The Inserting Graphics in Word Documents content is inserted from the subdocument. You will instruct Word to create the content for the Table of Figures and Index later in this module. The following steps create an outline that contains headings and body text to be used in the master document.

- Click the 'Demote to Body Text' button (Outlining tab | Outline Tools group), so that you can enter the paragraphs of text for the copyright page.
- Type `Using Microsoft Word 2016 - Inserting Graphics Guide` as the first paragraph in the outline and then press the ENTER key.
- Type `To receive additional guides in this or any other series by Silverman's Career Development Center, send a message to Fredrick Schultz at fschultz@ silverman.edu.` as the second paragraph in the outline and then press the ENTER key.

  If requested by your instructor, change the name, Fredrick Schultz, on the copyright page to your name.

Q&A Why is only my first line of text in the paragraph displayed?
Remove the check mark from the 'Show First Line Only' check box (Outlining tab | Outline Tools group).

- Right-click the hyperlink (in this case, the email address) to display a shortcut menu and then click Remove Hyperlink on the shortcut menu.
- Click the third Body Text style bullet and then type `Copyright 2017` as the third paragraph and then press the ENTER key.
- Click the 'Promote to Heading 1' button (Outlining tab | Outline Tools group) because you are finished entering body text and will enter the remaining headings in the outline next (Figure 9–32).

Q&A Could I press SHIFT+TAB instead of clicking the 'Promote to Heading 1' button?
Yes.

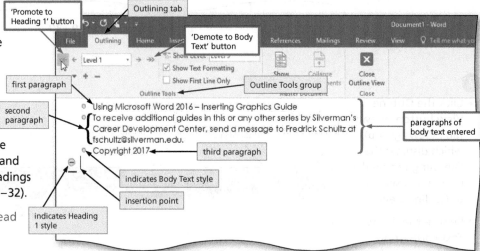

Figure 9–32

- Display the Layout tab.
- Click the 'Insert Page and Section Breaks' button (Layout tab | Page Setup group) and then click Next Page in the Section Breaks area in the Insert Page and Section Breaks gallery because you want to enter a next page section break before the next heading.

- Type `Table of Figures` and then press the ENTER key.
- Repeat Step 2.
- Type `Index` as the last entry (Figure 9–33).

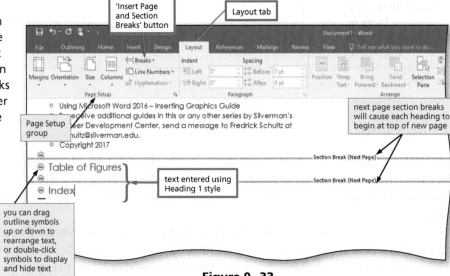

Figure 9–33

Q&A Why do the outline symbols contain a minus sign?
The minus sign means the outline level does not have any subordinate levels. If an outline symbol contains a plus sign, it means the outline level has subordinate levels.

To Show First Line Only

Users often instruct Word to display just the first line of each paragraph of body text. *Why? When only the first line of each paragraph is displayed, the outline often is more readable.* The following step displays only the first line of body text paragraphs.

- Display the Outlining tab.

- Place a check mark in the 'Show First Line Only' check box (Outlining tab | Outline Tools group), so that Word displays only the first line of each paragraph (Figure 9–34).

Q&A How would I redisplay all lines of the paragraphs of body text? Remove the check mark from the 'Show First Line Only' check box (Outlining tab | Outline Tools group).

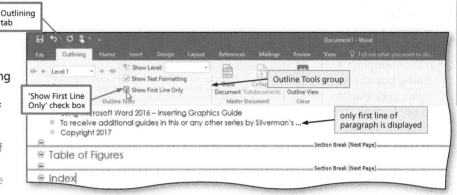

Figure 9–34

- Save this master document on your hard drive, OneDrive, or other storage location using the file name, Using Microsoft Word 2016 - Inserting Graphics Guide.

Other Ways

1. Press CTRL+SHIFT+L

To Insert a Subdocument

The next step is to insert a subdocument in the master document. The subdocument to be inserted is the Inserting Graphics Final file, which you created earlier in the module. Word places the first line of text in the subdocument at the first heading level in the master document. *Why? The first line in the subdocument was defined using the Heading 1 style.* The following steps insert a subdocument in a master document.

- Display the Home tab. If formatting marks do not appear, click the 'Show/Hide ¶' button (Home tab | Paragraph group).

- Position the insertion point where you want to insert the subdocument (on the section break above the Table of Figures heading).

- Display the Outlining tab. Click the Show Document button (Outlining tab | Master Document group) so that all commands in the Master Document group appear.

- Click the Insert Subdocument button (Outlining tab | Master Document group) to display the Insert Subdocument dialog box.

- Locate and select the Inserting Graphics Final file (Insert Subdocument dialog box) (Figure 9–35).

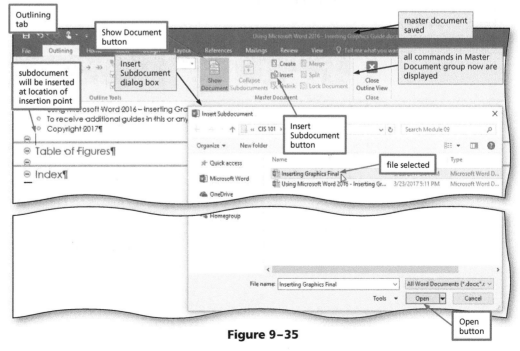

Figure 9–35

- Click the Open button (Insert Subdocument dialog box) to insert the selected file as a subdocument.
- If Word displays a dialog box about styles, click the 'No to All' button.
- Press CTRL+HOME to position the insertion point at the top of the document (Figure 9–36).

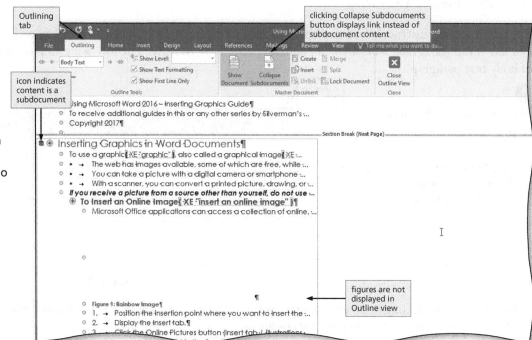

Figure 9–36

Master Documents and Subdocuments

When you open the master document, the subdocuments initially are collapsed; that is, they are displayed as hyperlinks (Figure 9–37). To work with the contents of a master document after you open it, switch to Outline view and then expand the subdocuments by clicking the Expand Subdocuments button (Outlining tab | Master Document group).

You can open a subdocument in a separate document window and modify it. To open a collapsed subdocument, click the hyperlink. To open an expanded subdocument, double-click the subdocument icon to the left of the document heading (shown in Figure 9–37).

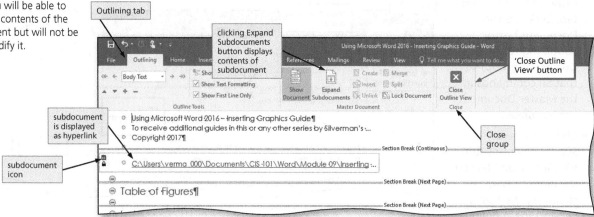

Figure 9–37

If, for some reason, you wanted to remove a subdocument from a master document, you would expand the subdocuments, click the subdocument icon to the left of the subdocument's first heading, and then press the DELETE key. Although Word removes the subdocument from the master document, the subdocument file remains on the storage media.

Occasionally, you may want to convert a subdocument to part of the master document — breaking the connection between the text in the master document and the subdocument. To do this, expand the subdocuments, click the subdocument icon, and then click the Remove Subdocument button (Outlining tab | Master Document group).

To Hide Formatting Marks

To remove the clutter of index entry fields from the document, you should hide formatting marks. The following step hides formatting marks.

1 Display the Home tab. If the 'Show/Hide ¶' button (Home tab | Paragraph group) is selected, click it to hide formatting marks.

To Exit Outline View

1 MODIFY REFERENCE DOCUMENT | 2 CREATE MASTER DOCUMENT | 3 ORGANIZE REFERENCE DOCUMENT

The following step exits Outline View. ***Why?*** *You are finished organizing the master document.*

1

- Display the Outlining tab.

- Click the 'Close Outline View' button (shown in Figure 9–37) (Outlining tab | Close group) to redisplay the document in Print Layout view, which selects the Print Layout button on the status bar.

- If necessary, press CTRL+HOME to display the top of the document (Figure 9–38).

Experiment

- Scroll through the document to familiarize yourself with the sections. When finished, display the top of the subdocument in the document window.

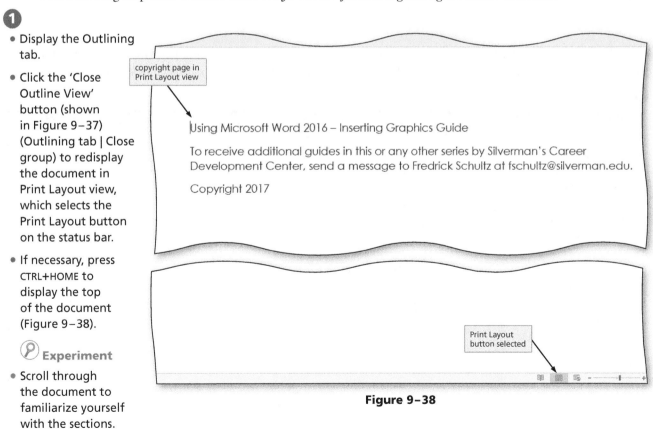

Figure 9–38

- Save the document again on the same storage location with the same file name.

Organizing a Reference Document

Reference documents are organized and formatted so that users easily can navigate through and read the document. The reference document in this module includes the following elements: a copyright page, a title page, a table of contents, a table of figures, an index, alternating footers, and a gutter margin. This section illustrates the tasks required to include these elements.

CONSIDER THIS

What elements are common to reference documents?

Reference documents often include a title page, a table of contents, a table of figures or list of tables (if one exists), and an index.

- **Title Page.** A title page should contain, at a minimum, the title of the document. Some also contain the author, a subtitle, an edition or volume number, and the date written.

- **Table of Contents.** The table of contents should list the title (heading) of each chapter or section and the starting page number of the chapter or section. You may use a leader character, such as a dot or hyphen, to fill the space between the heading and the page number. Sections preceding the table of contents are not listed in it — list only material that follows the table of contents.

- **Table of Figures or List of Tables.** If you have multiple figures or tables in a document, consider identifying all of them in a table of figures or a list of tables. The format of the table of figures or list of tables should match the table of contents.

- **Index.** The index usually is set in two columns or one column. The index can contain any item a reader might want to look up, such as a heading or a key term. If the document does not have a table of figures or list of tables, also include figures and tables in the index.

To Insert a Cover Page

1 MODIFY REFERENCE DOCUMENT | 2 CREATE MASTER DOCUMENT | **3 ORGANIZE REFERENCE DOCUMENT**

Word has many predefined cover page formats that you can use for the title page in a document. The following steps insert a cover page. *Why? The reference document in this module includes a title page.*

1

- Display the Insert tab.

- Click the 'Add a Cover Page' button (Insert tab | Pages group) to display the Add a Cover Page gallery (Figure 9–39).

Experiment

- Scroll through the Add a Cover Page gallery to see the variety of available predefined cover pages.

Q&A

Does it matter where I position the insertion point before inserting a cover page?

No. By default, Word inserts the cover page as the first page in a document.

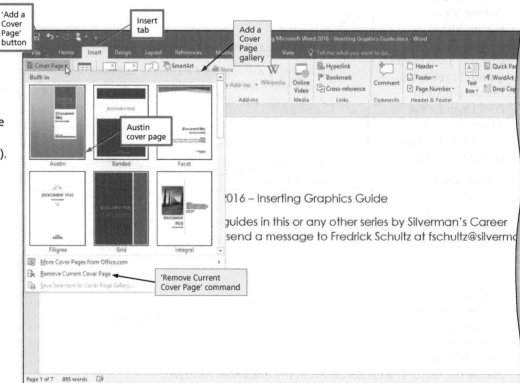

Figure 9–39

2

- Click Austin in the Add a Cover Page gallery to insert the selected cover page as the first page in the current document.

- Display the View tab. Click the One Page button (View tab | Zoom group) to display the entire cover page in the document window (Figure 9–40).

Q&A Does the cover page have to be the first page?
No. You can right-click the desired cover page and then click the desired location on the submenu.

How would I delete a cover page?
You would click the 'Add a Cover Page' button (Insert tab | Pages group) and then click 'Remove Current Cover Page' in the Add a Cover Page gallery (shown in Figure 9–39).

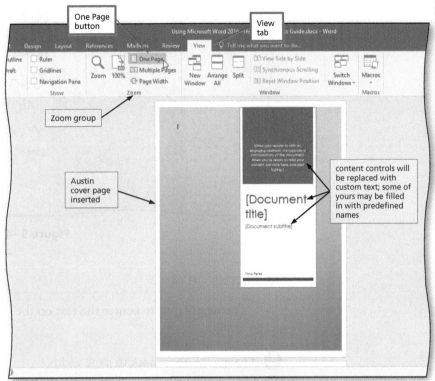

Figure 9–40

Other Ways

1. Click 'Explore Quick Parts' button (Insert tab | Text group), click 'Building Blocks Organizer', select desired cover page building block (Building Blocks Organizer dialog box), click Insert button, click Close button

To Enter Text in Content Controls

The next step is to select content controls on the cover page and replace their instructions or text with the title page information. Keep in mind that the content controls present suggested text. Depending on settings on your computer or mobile device, some content controls already may contain customized text, which you will change. You can enter any appropriate text in any content control. The following steps enter title page text on the cover page.

1 Click the content control that begins with the instruction, [Draw your reader in with an engaging abstract…] and then type **A series of guides designed to strengthen your career development skills.**

2 Click the [Document title] content control and then type **Using Microsoft Word 2016** as the title.

3 Click the [Document subtitle] content control and then type **Inserting Graphics Guide** as the subtitle.

4 Click the author content control and then type **Fredrick Schultz** as the name (Figure 9–41).

Q&A Why is my author content control filled in?
Depending on settings, your content control already may display an author name.

If requested by your instructor, change the name, Fredrick Schultz, to your name.

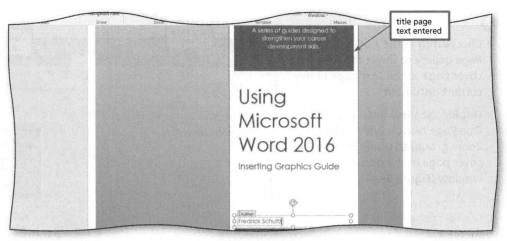

Figure 9–41

To Center Text

The next step is to center the text on the copyright page. The following steps center text.

1 Change the zoom back to page width.

2 Scroll to display the copyright page text in the document window.

3 Select the text on the copyright page and then center it.

4 Deselect the text.

To Insert a Continuous Section Break and Change the Margins in the Section

The margins on the copyright page are wider than the rest of the document. To change margins for a page, the page must be in a separate section. The next steps insert a continuous section break and then change the margins.

1 Position the insertion point at the location for the section break, in this case, to the left U in Using on the copyright page.

2 Display the Layout tab. Click the 'Insert Page and Section Breaks' button (Layout tab | Page Setup group) to display the Insert Page and Section Breaks gallery.

3 Click Continuous in the Insert Page and Section Breaks gallery to insert a continuous section break to the left of the insertion point.

4 Click the Adjust Margins button (Layout tab | Page Setup group) to display the Adjust Margins gallery and then click Wide in the Adjust Margins gallery to change the margins on the copyright page to the selected settings (Figure 9–42).

Figure 9–42

To Adjust Vertical Alignment on a Page

1 MODIFY REFERENCE DOCUMENT | 2 CREATE MASTER DOCUMENT | **3 ORGANIZE REFERENCE DOCUMENT**

You can instruct Word to center the contents of a page vertically using one of two options: place an equal amount of space above and below the text on the page, or evenly space each paragraph between the top and bottom margins. The following steps vertically center text on a page. *Why? The copyright page in this project evenly spaces each paragraph on a page between the top and bottom margins, which is called justified vertical alignment.*

- Click the Page Setup Dialog Box Launcher (Layout tab | Page Setup group) to display the Page Setup dialog box.

- Click the Layout tab (Page Setup dialog box) to display the Layout sheet.

- Click the Vertical alignment arrow and then click Justified (Figure 9–43).

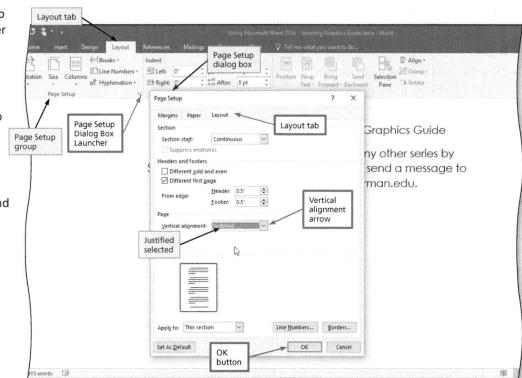

Figure 9–43

- Click the OK button to justify the text in the current section.

- To see the entire justified page, display the View tab and then click the One Page button (View tab | Zoom group) (Figure 9–44).

- Change the zoom back to page width.

Q&A

What are the other vertical alignments?

Top, the default, aligns contents starting at the top margin on the page. Center places all contents centered vertically on the page, and Bottom places contents at the bottom of the page.

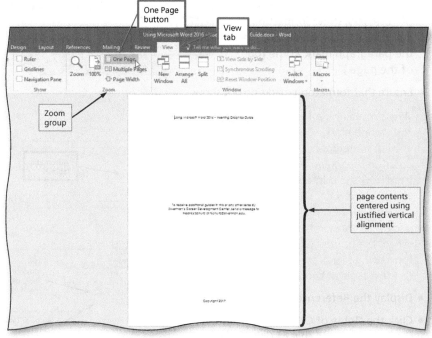

Figure 9–44

To Insert a Blank Page

The following step inserts a blank page. *Why? In the reference document in this module, the table of contents is on a page between the copyright page and the first page of the subdocument.*

1

• Position the insertion point to the left of the word, Inserting, on the first page of the subdocument (as shown in Figure 9–45).

• Display the Insert tab.

• Click the 'Add a Blank Page' button (Insert tab | Pages group) to insert a blank page at the location of the insertion point.

• If necessary, scroll to display the blank page in the document window (Figure 9–45).

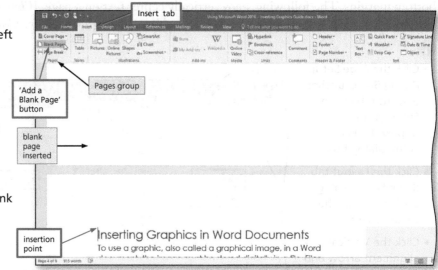

Figure 9–45

To Create a Table of Contents

A table of contents lists all headings in a document and their associated page numbers. When you use Word's built-in heading styles (for example, Heading 1, Heading 2, and so on), you can instruct Word to create a table of contents from these headings. In the reference document in this module, the heading of each section uses the Heading 1 style, and subheadings use the Heading 2 style.

The following steps use a predefined building block to create a table of contents. *Why? Using Word's predefined table of contents formats can be more efficient than creating a table of contents from scratch.*

1

• Position the insertion point at the top of the blank page 3, which is the location for the table of contents. (If necessary, show formatting marks so that you easily can see the paragraph mark at the top of the page.)

• Ensure that formatting marks do not show.

Q&A
Why should I hide formatting marks?
Formatting marks, especially those for index entries, sometimes can cause wrapping to occur on the screen that will be different from how the printed document will wrap. These differences could cause a heading to move to the next page. To ensure that the page references in the table of contents reflect the printed pages, be sure that formatting marks are hidden when you create a table of contents.

• Display the References tab.

• Click the 'Table of Contents' button (References tab | Table of Contents group) to display the Table of Contents gallery (Figure 9–46).

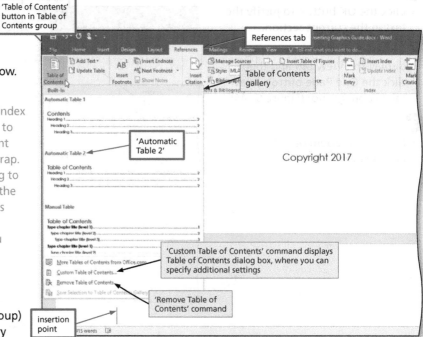

Figure 9–46

2

- Click 'Automatic Table 2' in the Table of Contents gallery to insert the table of contents at the location of the insertion point (Figure 9–47). If necessary, scroll to see the table of contents.

Q&A
How would I delete a table of contents?
You would click the 'Table of Contents' button (References tab | Table of Contents group) and then click 'Remove Table of Contents' in the Table of Contents gallery (shown in Figure 9-46).

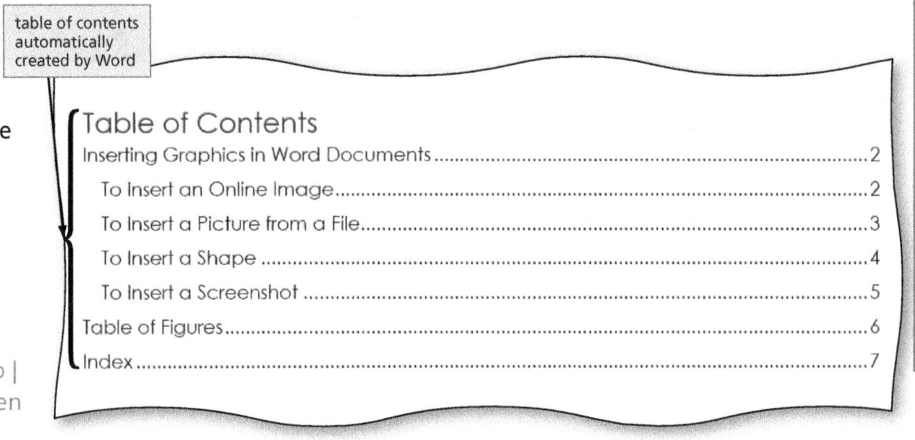

table of contents automatically created by Word

Table of Contents

Figure 9–47

Other Ways

1. Click 'Table of Contents' button (References tab | Table of Contents group), click 'Custom Table of Contents', select table of contents options (Table of Contents dialog box), click OK button

2. Click 'Explore Quick Parts' button (Insert tab | Text group), click 'Building Blocks Organizer', select desired table of contents building block (Building Blocks Organizer dialog box), click Insert button, click Close button

To Insert a Continuous Section Break and Change the Starting Page Number in the Section

The table of contents should not be the starting page number; instead, the subdocument should be the starting page number in the document. To change the starting page number, the page must be in a separate section. The following steps insert a continuous section break and then change the starting page number for the table of contents.

1 Position the insertion point at the location for the section break, in this case, to the left of I in Inserting Graphics in Word Documents on page 4 of the document.

2 Display the Layout tab. Click the 'Insert Page and Section Breaks' button (Layout tab | Page Setup group) to display the Insert Page and Section Breaks gallery.

3 Click Continuous in the Insert Page and Section Breaks gallery to insert a continuous section break to the left of the insertion point.

4 Position the insertion point in the table of contents.

5 Display the Insert tab. Click the 'Add Page Numbers' button (Insert tab | Header & Footer group) to display the Add Page Numbers menu and then click 'Format Page Numbers' on the Add Page Numbers menu to display the Page Number Format dialog box.

6 Click the Start at down arrow (Page Number Format dialog box) until 0 is displayed in the Start at box (Figure 9–48).

7 Click the OK button to change the starting page for the current section.

BTW
Advanced Layout Options
You can adjust Word's advanced layout options by clicking File on the ribbon to open the Backstage View, clicking the Options tab in the Backstage View to display the Word Options dialog box, clicking Advanced in the left pane (Word Options dialog box), scrolling to the Layout options for area in the right pane, placing a check mark in the desired settings, and then clicking the OK button.

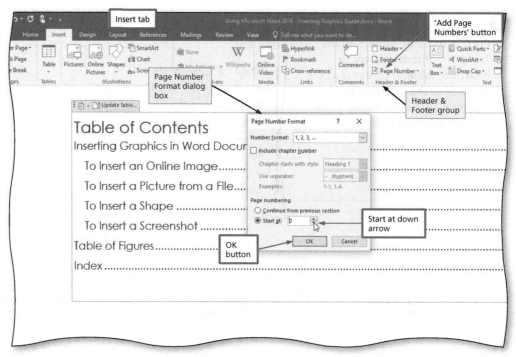

Figure 9–48

To Update Page Numbers in a Table of Contents

1 MODIFY REFERENCE DOCUMENT | 2 CREATE MASTER DOCUMENT | **3 ORGANIZE REFERENCE DOCUMENT**

When you change a document, you should update the associated table of contents. The following steps update the page numbers in the table of contents. *Why? The starting page number change will affect the page numbers in the table of contents.*

- If necessary, click the table of contents to select it.

Q&A Why does the ScreenTip say 'CTRL+Click to follow link'?
Each entry in the table of contents is a link. If you hold down the CTRL key while clicking an entry in the table of contents, Word will display the associated heading in the document window.

❷

- Click the Update Table button that is attached to the table of contents to display the Update Table of Contents dialog box.

- Ensure the 'Update page numbers only' option button is selected because you want to update only the page numbers in the table of contents (Figure 9–49).

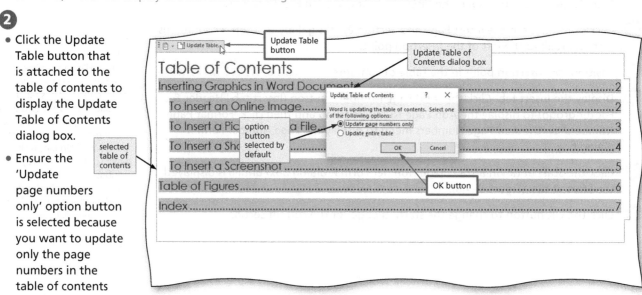

Figure 9–49

- Click the OK button (Update Table of Contents dialog box) to update the page numbers in the table of contents.

- Click outside the table of contents to remove the selection from the table (Figure 9–50).

page numbers updated; your page numbers will differ if your document layout does not match Figure 9-1 at beginning of module exactly

Table of Contents

Figure 9–50

Other Ways

1. Select table, click Update Table button (References tab | Table of Contents group)

2. Select table, press F9 key

To Find a Format

1 MODIFY REFERENCE DOCUMENT | 2 CREATE MASTER DOCUMENT | **3 ORGANIZE REFERENCE DOCUMENT**

The subdocument contains a sentence of text formatted as bold italic. To find this text in the document, you could scroll through the document until it is displayed on the screen. A more efficient way is to find the bold, italic format using the Find and Replace dialog box. The following steps find a format. ***Why? You want to add the text to the table of contents.***

- If necessary, display the Home tab.

- Click the Find arrow (Home tab | Editing group) to display the Find menu (Figure 9–51).

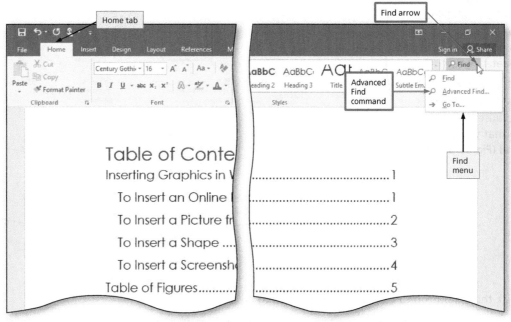

Figure 9–51

2

- Click Advanced Find on the Find menu to display the Find and Replace dialog box.

- If Word displays a More button in the Find and Replace dialog box, click it so that it changes to a Less button and expands the dialog box.

- Click the Format button (Find and Replace dialog box) to display the Format menu (Figure 9–52).

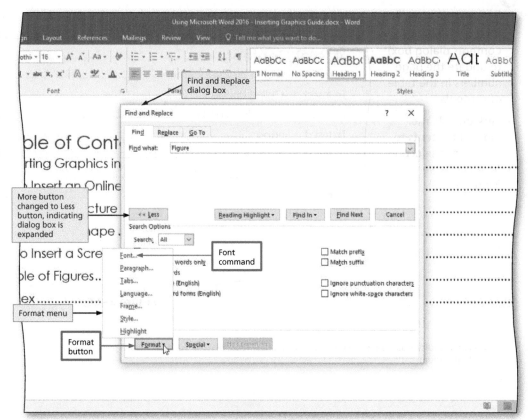

Figure 9–52

3

- Click Font on the Format menu to display the Find Font dialog box. If necessary, click the Font tab (Find Font dialog box) to display the Font sheet.

- Click Bold Italic in the Font style list because that is the format you want to find (Figure 9–53).

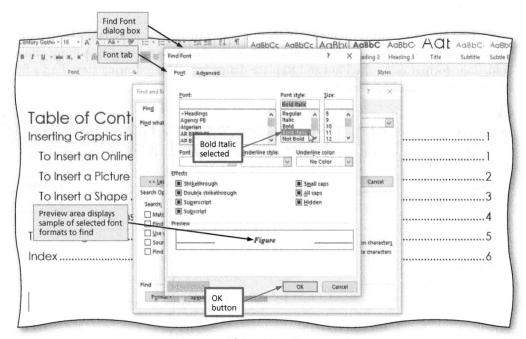

Figure 9–53

4

- Click the OK button to close the Find Font dialog box.

- Be sure no text is in the Find what text box (or click the Find what arrow and then click [Formatting Only]).

- Be sure all check boxes in the Search Options area are cleared.

- When the Find and Replace dialog box is active again, click its Find Next button to locate and highlight in the document the first occurrence of the specified format (Figure 9–54).

Q&A How do I remove a find format?
You would click the No Formatting button in the Find and Replace dialog box.

 ⑤

- Click the Cancel button (Find and Replace dialog box) because the located occurrence is the one you wanted to find.

Q&A Can I search for (find) special characters, such as page breaks?
Yes. To find special characters, you would click the Special button in the Find and Replace dialog box.

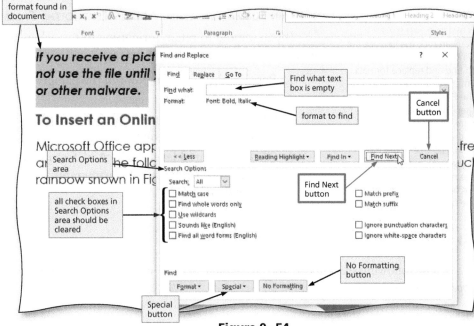

Figure 9–54

Other Ways

1. Press CTRL+F

To Format Text as a Heading

The following steps format a paragraph of text as a Heading 3 style. Occasionally, you may want to add a paragraph of text, which normally is not formatted using a heading style, to a table of contents. One way to add the text is to format it as a heading style.

① With the formatted paragraph still selected (shown in Figure 9–54), if necessary, display the Home tab.

② Click Heading 3 in the Styles gallery to apply the selected style to the current paragraph in the document. Click outside the paragraph to deselect it (Figure 9–55).

③ If necessary, drag the bottom of the sidebar text box up so that it ends after the word 'zombies'.

BTW

Find and Replace
The expanded Find and Replace dialog box allows you to specify how Word locates search text. For example, selecting the Match case check box instructs Word to find the text exactly as you typed it, and selecting the 'Find whole words only' check box instructs Word to ignore text that contains the search text (i.e., the word, then, contains the word, the). If you select the Use wildcard check box, you can use wildcard characters in a search. For example, with this check box selected, the search text of *ing would search for all words that end with the characters, ing.

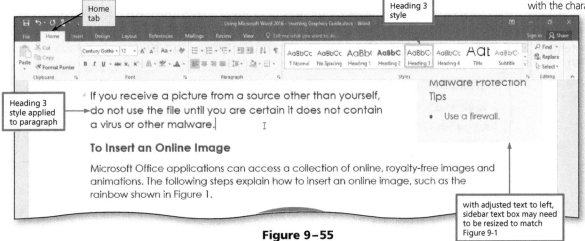

Figure 9–55

BTW

Replace Formats
You can click the Replace tab (Find and Replace dialog box) to find and replace formats. Enter the format to find in the Find what text box and then follow the same steps to enter the format to replace in the Replace with text box. Next, click the Replace or Replace All button to replace the next occurrence of the format or all occurrences of the format in the document.

TO RETAIN FORMATTING WHEN ADDING TEXT TO THE TABLE OF CONTENTS

If you wanted to retain formatting of text when adding it to the table of contents, you would perform the following steps.

1. Position the insertion point in the paragraph of text that you want to add to the table of contents.
2. Click the Add Text button (References tab | Table of Contents group) to display the Add Text menu.
3. Click the desired level on the Add Text menu, which adds the format of the selected style to the selected paragraph and adds the paragraph of text to the table of contents.

To Update the Entire Table of Contents   1 MODIFY REFERENCE DOCUMENT | 2 CREATE MASTER DOCUMENT | **3 ORGANIZE REFERENCE DOCUMENT**

The following steps update the entire table of contents. *Why? The text changed to the Heading 3 style should appear in the table of contents.*

- Display the table of contents in the document window.
- Click the table of contents to select it.
- Click the Update Table button that is attached to the table of contents to display the Update Table of Contents dialog box.
- Click the 'Update entire table' option button (Update Table of Contents dialog box) because you want to update the entire table of contents (Figure 9–56).

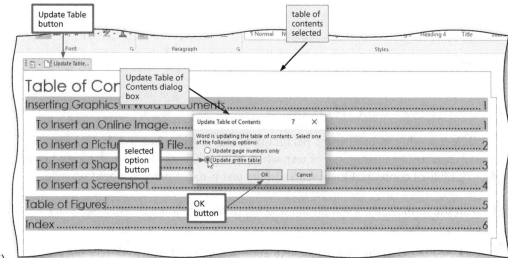

Figure 9–56

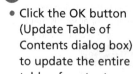

- Click the OK button (Update Table of Contents dialog box) to update the entire table of contents (Figure 9–57).

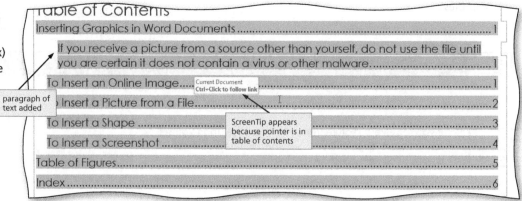

Figure 9–57

Other Ways

1. Select table, click Update Table button (References tab | Table of Contents group)

2. Select table, press F9 key

To Change the Format of a Table of Contents

You can change the format of the table of contents to any of the predefined table of contents styles or to custom settings. The following steps change the table of contents format. *Why? In this table of contents, you specify the format, page number alignment, and tab leader character.*

1

- Display the References tab.

- Click the 'Table of Contents' button (References tab | Table of Contents group) to display the Table of Contents gallery (Figure 9–58).

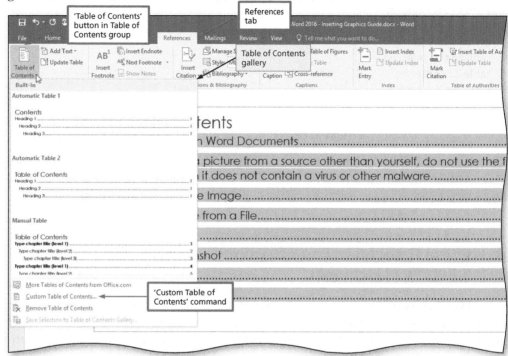

Figure 9–58

2

- Click 'Custom Table of Contents' in the Table of Contents gallery to display the Table of Contents dialog box.

- Click the Formats arrow (Table of Contents dialog box) and then click Simple to change the format style for the table of contents.

- Place a check mark in the 'Right align page numbers' check box so that the page numbers appear at the right margin in the table of contents.

- If necessary, click the Tab leader arrow and then click the first leader type in the list so that the selected leader characters appear between the heading name and the page numbers in the table of contents (Figure 9–59).

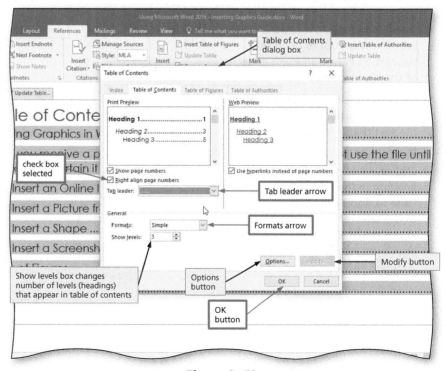

Figure 9–59

- Click the OK button to modify the table of contents according to the specified settings. When Word displays a dialog box asking if you want to replace the selected table of contents, click the Yes button (Figure 9–60).

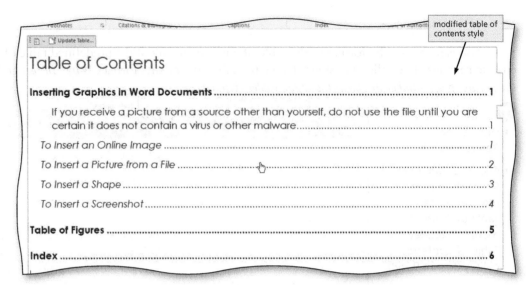

Figure 9–60

To Use the Navigation Pane to Go to a Heading in a Document

1 MODIFY REFERENCE DOCUMENT | 2 CREATE MASTER DOCUMENT | **3 ORGANIZE REFERENCE DOCUMENT**

When you use Word's built-in heading styles in a document, you can use the Navigation Pane to go to headings in a document quickly. *Why? When you click a heading in the Navigation Pane, Word displays the page associated with that heading in the document window.* The following step uses the Navigation Pane to display an associated heading in the document window.

- Display the View tab. Place a check mark in the 'Open the Navigation Pane' check box (View tab | Show group) to open the Navigation Pane at the left edge of the Word window.

- If necessary, click the Headings tab in the Navigation Pane to display the text that is formatted using Heading styles.

- Click the Table of Figures heading in the Navigation Pane to display the top of the selected page in the top of the document window (Figure 9–61).

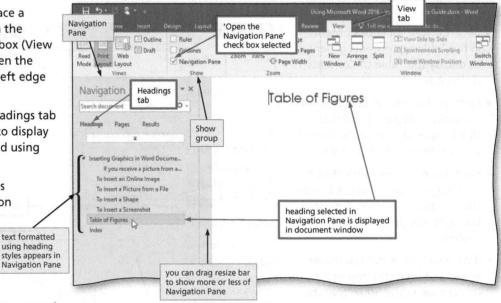

Figure 9–61

Q&A

What if all of the headings are not displayed?

Right-click a heading in the Navigation Pane and then click Expand All on the shortcut menu to ensure that all headings are displayed. If a heading still is not displayed, verify that the heading is formatted with a heading style. To display or hide subheadings below a heading in the Navigation Pane, click the triangle to the left of the heading. If a heading is too wide for the Navigation Pane, you can point to the heading to display a ScreenTip that shows the complete title.

To Create a Table of Figures

The following steps create a table of figures. *Why? At the end of the reference document is a table of figures, which lists all figures and their corresponding page numbers. Word generates this table of figures from the captions in the document.*

- Ensure that formatting marks are not displayed.

- Position the insertion point at the end of the Table of Figures heading and then press the ENTER key, so that the insertion point is on the line below the heading.

- Display the References tab.

- Click the 'Table of Figures Dialog' button (References tab | Captions group) to display the Table of Figures dialog box.

- Be sure that all settings in your dialog box match those in Figure 9–62.

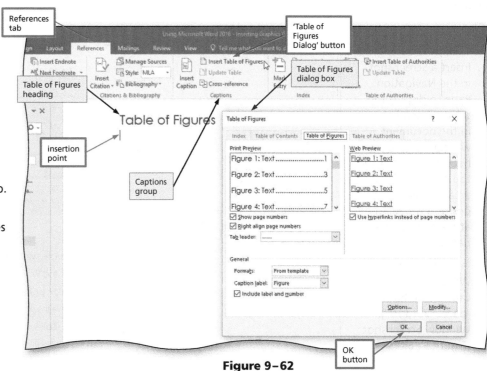

Figure 9–62

- Click the OK button (Table of Figures dialog box) to create a table of figures at the location of the insertion point (Figure 9–63).

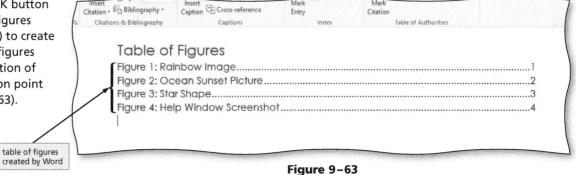

Figure 9–63

To Change the Format of the Table of Figures

If you wanted to change the format of the table of figures, you would perform the following steps.

1. Click the table of figures to select it.

2. Click the 'Table of Figures Dialog' button (References tab | Captions group) to display the Table of Figures dialog box.

3. Change settings in the dialog box as desired.

4. Click the OK button (Table of Figures dialog box) to apply the changed settings.

5. Click the OK button when Word asks if you want to replace the selected table of figures.

BTW

Table of Contents Styles

If you wanted to change the level associated with each style used in a table of contents, click the Options button in the Table of Contents dialog box (shown in Figure 9–59), enter the desired level number in the text box beside the appropriate heading or other styled item, and then click the OK button. To change the formatting associated with a style, click the Modify button in the Table of Contents dialog box.

To Edit a Caption and Update the Table of Figures

The following steps change the Figure 4 caption and then update the table of figures. *Why? When you modify captions in a document or move illustrations to a different location in the document, you will have to update the table of figures.*

- Click the heading, To Insert a Screenshot, in the Navigation Pane to display the selected heading in the document window. (If this heading is not at the top of page 7, insert a page break to position the heading at the top of a new page.)

- Insert the text, Word, in the Figure 4 caption so that it reads: Word Help Window Screenshot (Figure 9–64).

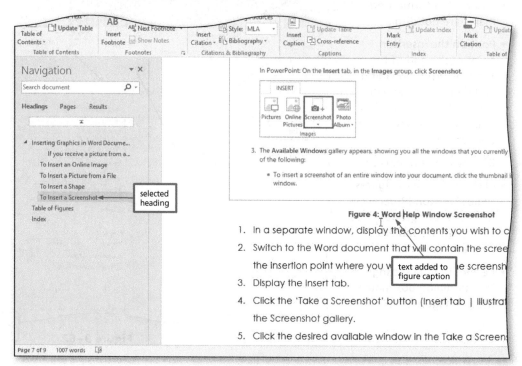

Figure 9–64

- Click the heading, Table of Figures, in the Navigation Pane to display the Table of Figures heading in the document window.

- Click the table of figures to select it.

- Click the 'Update Table of Figures' button (References tab | Captions group) to display the Update Table of Figures dialog box.

- Click 'Update entire table' (Update Table of Figures dialog box), so that Word updates the contents of the entire table of figures instead of updating only the page numbers (Figure 9–65).

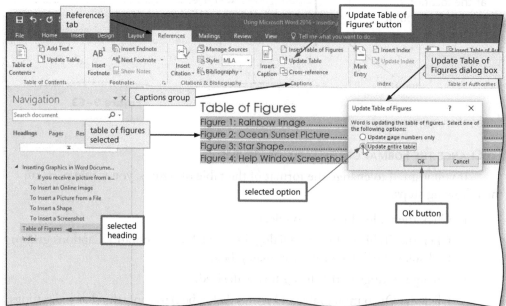

Figure 9–65

- Click the OK button to update the table of figures and then click outside the table to deselect it (Figure 9–66).

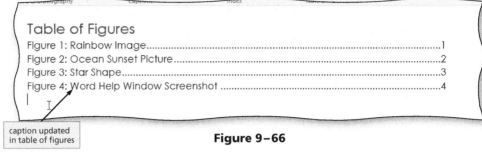

Table of Figures
Figure 1: Rainbow Image...1
Figure 2: Ocean Sunset Picture..2
Figure 3: Star Shape...3
Figure 4: Word Help Window Screenshot 4

caption updated in table of figures

Figure 9–66

Q&A

Are the entries in the table of figures links?
Yes. As with the table of contents, you can CTRL+click any entry in the table of figures and Word will display the associated figure in the document window.

Other Ways

1. Select table of figures, press F9 key

To Build an Index

1 MODIFY REFERENCE DOCUMENT | 2 CREATE MASTER DOCUMENT | **3 ORGANIZE REFERENCE DOCUMENT**

The reference document in this module ends with an index. Earlier, this module showed how to mark index entries. **Why?** *For Word to generate the index, you first must mark any text you wish to appear in the index.*

Once all index entries are marked, Word can build the index from the index entry fields in the document. Recall that index entry fields begin with XE, which appears on the screen when formatting marks are displayed. When index entry fields show on the screen, the document's pagination probably will be altered because of the extra text in the index entries. Thus, be sure to hide formatting marks before building an index. The following steps build an index.

- Click the heading, Index, in the Navigation Pane to display the Index heading in the document window.

- Click to the right of the Index heading and then press the ENTER key, so that the insertion point is on the line below the heading.

- Ensure that formatting marks are not displayed.

- Click the Insert Index button (References tab | Index group) to display the Index dialog box.

- If necessary, click the Formats arrow in the dialog box and then click Classic in the Formats list to change the index format.

- Place a check mark in the 'Right align page numbers' check box.

- Click the Tab leader arrow and then click the first leader character in the list to specify the leader character to be displayed between the index entry and the page number.

- Click the Columns down arrow until the number of columns is 1 to change the number of columns in the index (Figure 9–67).

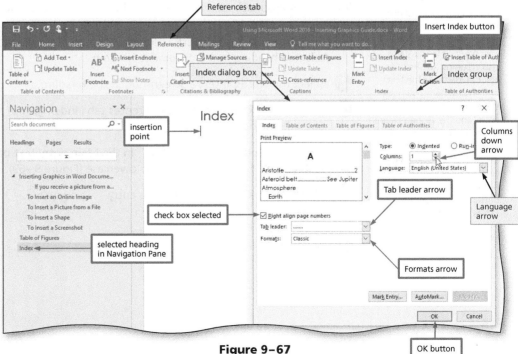

Figure 9–67

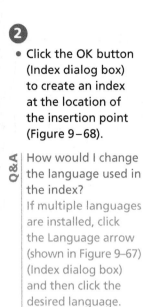

2

- Click the OK button (Index dialog box) to create an index at the location of the insertion point (Figure 9–68).

Q&A How would I change the language used in the index?
If multiple languages are installed, click the Language arrow (shown in Figure 9–67) (Index dialog box) and then click the desired language.

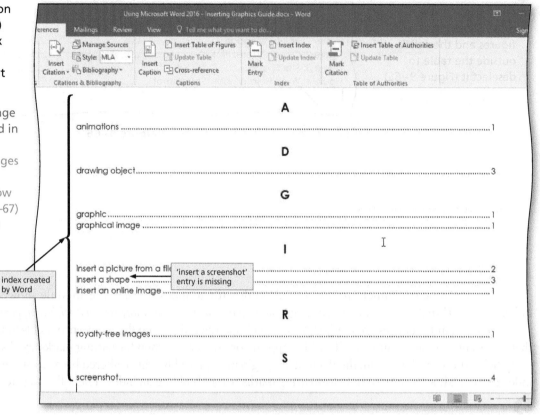

Figure 9–68

BTW

Index Files

Instead of marking index entries in a document, you can create a concordance file that contains all index entries you wish to mark. A concordance file contains two columns: the first column identifies the text in the document you want Word to mark as an index entry, and the second column lists the index entries to be generated from the text in the first column. To mark entries in the concordance file, click the AutoMark button in the Index and Tables dialog box.

To Mark Another Index Entry

Notice in Figure 9–68 that the 'insert a screenshot' index entry is missing. The following steps mark an index entry in the Insert a Screenshot section.

1 Click the heading, To Insert a Screenshot, in the Navigation Pane to display the selected heading in the document window.

2 Select the words, Insert a Screenshot, in the heading.

3 Click the Mark Entry button (References tab | Index group) to display the Mark Index Entry dialog box.

4 Type **insert a screenshot** in the Main entry text box (Mark Index Entry dialog box) so that the entry is all lowercase (Figure 9–69).

5 Click the Mark button to mark the entry.

6 Close the dialog box.

7 Hide formatting marks.

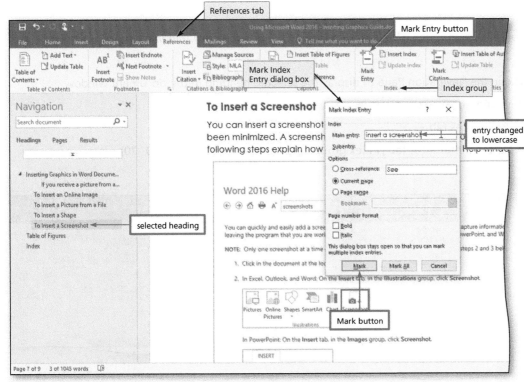

Figure 9–69

BTW
Navigation Pane
You can drag any heading in the Navigation Pane to reorganize document content. For example, you could drag the To Insert a Screenshot heading upward in the Navigation Pane so that its content appears earlier in the document.

TO EDIT AN INDEX ENTRY

At some time, you may want to change an index entry after you have marked it. For example, you may forget to lowercase the entry for the headings. If you wanted to change an index entry, you would perform the following steps.

1. Display formatting marks.
2. Locate the XE field for the index entry you wish to change (i.e., { XE "Insert a Screenshot" }).
3. Change the text inside the quotation marks (i.e., { XE "insert a screenshot" }).
4. Update the index as described in the steps in the upcoming steps titled To Update an Index.

TO DELETE AN INDEX ENTRY

If you wanted to delete an index entry, you would perform the following steps.

1. Display formatting marks.
2. Select the XE field for the index entry you wish to delete (i.e., { XE "insert a screenshot" }).
3. Press the DELETE key.
4. Update the index as described in the steps in the next set of steps.

BTW
Field Codes
If your index, table of contents, or table of figures displays odd characters inside curly braces ({ }), then Word is displaying field codes instead of field results. Press ALT+F9 to display the index or table correctly.

To Update an Index

The following step updates an index. *Why? After marking a new index entry, you must update the index.*

- Click the heading, Index, in the Navigation Pane to display the selected heading in the document window.
- In the document window, click the index to select it.
- If necessary, display the References tab.
- Click the Update Index button (References tab | Index group) to update the index (Figure 9–70).

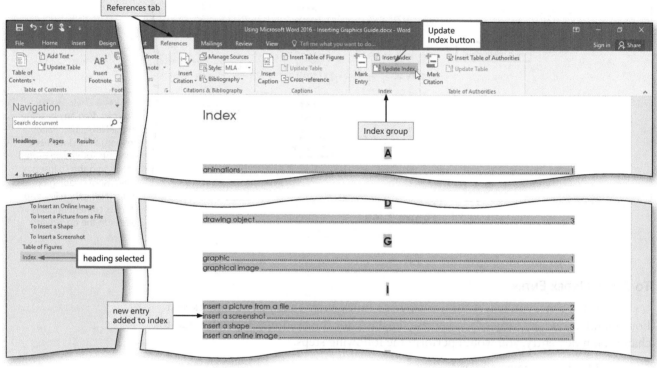

Figure 9–70

Other Ways

1. Select index, press F9 key

TO CHANGE THE FORMAT OF THE INDEX

If you wanted to change the format of the index, you would perform the following steps.

1. Click the index to select it.
2. Click the Insert Index button (References tab | Index group) to display the Index dialog box.
3. Change settings in the dialog box as desired. If you want to modify the style used for the index, click the Modify button.
4. Click the OK button (Index dialog box) to apply the changed settings.
5. Click the OK button when Word asks if you want to replace the selected index.

To Delete an Entire Index

If you wanted to delete an index, you would perform the following steps.

1. Click the index to select it.
2. Press SHIFT+F9 to display field codes.
3. Drag through the entire field code, including the braces, and then press the DELETE key.

Table of Authorities

In addition to creating an index, table of figures, and table of contents, you can use Word to create a table of authorities. Legal documents often include a **table of authorities** to list references to cases, rules, statutes, etc. To create a table of authorities, mark the citations first and then build the table of authorities.

The procedures for marking citations, editing citations, creating the table of authorities, changing the format of the table of authorities, and updating the table of authorities are the same as those for indexes. The only difference is you use the buttons in the Table of Authorities group on the References tab instead of the buttons in the Index group.

BTW

Table of Authorities
See the Supplementary Word Tasks section in Module 11 for additional instructions related to creating a table of authorities.

To Create Alternating Footers Using a Footer Building Block

1 MODIFY REFERENCE DOCUMENT | 2 CREATE MASTER DOCUMENT | 3 ORGANIZE REFERENCE DOCUMENT

The *Using Microsoft Word 2016* document is designed so that it can be duplicated back-to-back. That is, the document prints on nine separate pages. When it is duplicated, however, pages are printed on opposite sides of the same sheet of paper. *Why? Back-to-back duplicating saves resources because it enables the nine-page document to use only five sheets of paper.*

In many books and documents that have facing pages, the page number is always on the same side of the page — often on the outside edge. In Word, you accomplish this task by specifying one type of header or footer for even-numbered pages and another type of header or footer for odd-numbered pages. The following steps create alternating footers beginning on the fourth page of the document (the beginning of the subdocument).

- If necessary, hide formatting marks.
- Use the Navigation Pane to display the page with the heading, Inserting Graphics in Word Documents.
- Display the Insert tab.
- Click the 'Add a Footer' button (Insert tab | Header & Footer group) and then click Edit Footer to display the footer area.
- Be sure the 'Link to Previous' button (Header & Footer Tools Design tab | Navigation group) is not selected.
- Place a check mark in the 'Different Odd & Even Pages' check box (Header & Footer Tools Design tab | Options group), so that you can enter a different footer for odd and even pages.
- If necessary, click the Show Next button (Header & Footer Tools Design tab | Navigation group) to display the desired footer page (in this case, the Odd Page Footer -Section 4-).

2

- Click the 'Insert Alignment Tab' button (Header & Footer Tools Design tab | Position group) to display the Alignment Tab dialog box.

- Click Right (Alignment Tab dialog box) because you want to place a right-aligned tab stop in the footer (Figure 9–71).

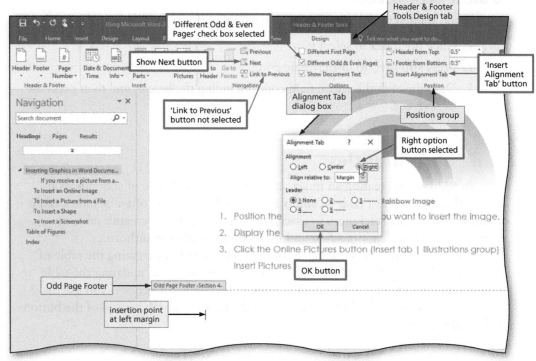

Figure 9–71

3

- Click the OK button to align the paragraph and insertion point in the footer at the right margin.

- Click the 'Add Page Numbers' button (Header & Footer Tools Design tab | Header & Footer group) to display the Add Page Numbers gallery.

- Point to Current Position in the Add Page Numbers gallery to display the Current Position gallery (Figure 9–72).

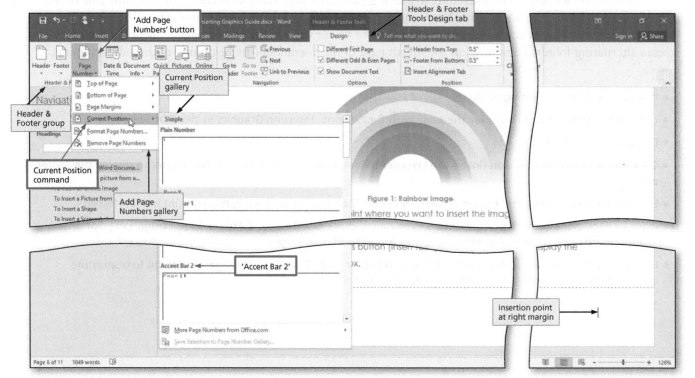

Figure 9–72

- Click 'Accent Bar 2' in the Current Position gallery to insert the selected page number in the footer (Figure 9–73).

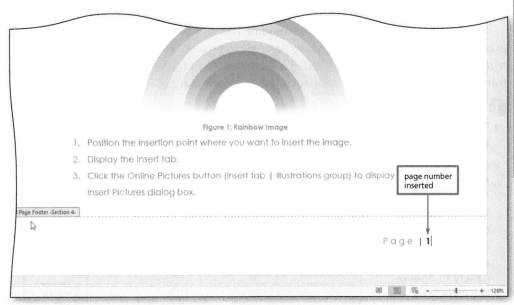

Figure 9–73

- Click the Show Next button (Header & Footer Tools Design tab | Navigation group) to display the next footer, in this case, Even Page Footer -Section 4-.
- Be sure the 'Link to Previous' button (Header & Footer Tools Design tab | Navigation group) is not selected.

- Click the 'Add Page Numbers' button (Header & Footer Tools Design tab | Header & Footer group) to display the Add Page Numbers gallery.

- Point to Current Position in the Add Page Numbers gallery to display the Current Position gallery and the click 'Accent Bar 2' in the Current Position gallery to insert the selected page number in the footer (Figure 9–74).

Q&A Can I create alternating headers?
Yes. Follow the same basic procedure, except insert a header building block or header text.

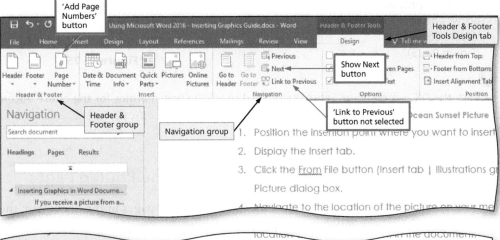

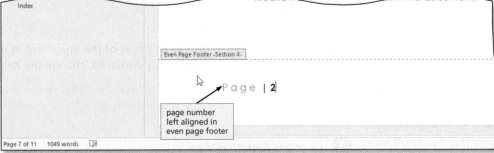

Figure 9–74

To Set a Gutter Margin

The reference document in this module is designed so that the inner margin between facing pages has extra space. **Why?** *Extra space on facing pages allows printed versions of the documents to be bound (such as stapled) — without the binding covering the words.* This extra space in the inner margin is called the **gutter margin**. The following steps set a three-quarter-inch left and right margin and a one-half-inch gutter margin.

- Display the Layout tab.

- Click the Adjust Margins button (Layout tab | Page Setup group) and then click Custom Margins in the Adjust Margins gallery to display the Page Setup dialog box.

- Type .75 in the Left box, .75 in the Right box, and .5 in the Gutter box (Page Setup dialog box).

- Click the Apply to arrow and then click Whole document (Figure 9–75).

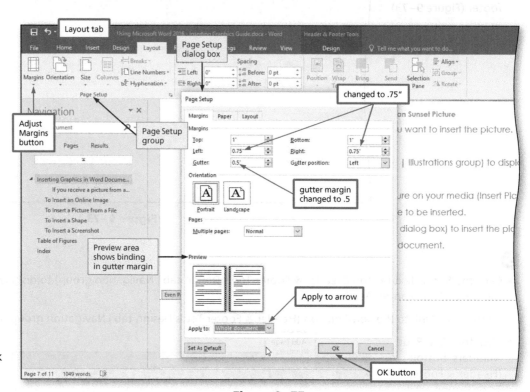

Figure 9–75

2

- Click the OK button (Page Setup dialog box) to set the new margins for the entire document.

To Check the Layout of the Printed Pages

To view the layout of all the pages in the document, the following steps display all the pages as they will print.

1 Open the Backstage view.

2 Click the Print tab to display all pages of the document in the right pane, as shown in Figure 9–76. (If all pages are not displayed, change the Zoom level to 10%.)

Q&A Why do blank pages appear in the middle of the document?
When you insert even and odd headers or footers, Word may add pages to fill the gaps.

3 Close the Backstage view.

Word Module 9

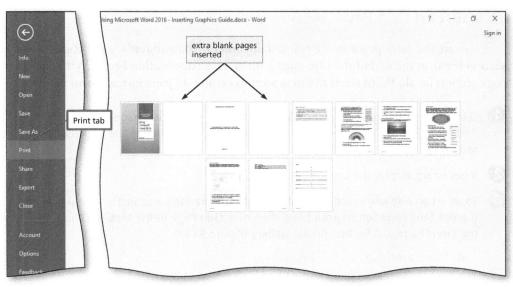

Figure 9–76

BTW
Set Print Scaling
If you wanted to ensure a document prints on a certain paper size, you can scale the document by opening the Backstage view, clicking the Print tab to display the Print gallery, clicking the bottom option in the Settings area (Print gallery), pointing to 'Scale to Paper Size', and then clicking the desired paper size before printing the document.

To Switch to Draft View

1 MODIFY REFERENCE DOCUMENT | 2 CREATE MASTER DOCUMENT | 3 ORGANIZE REFERENCE DOCUMENT

To adjust the blank pages automatically inserted in the printed document by Word, you change the continuous section break at the top of the document to an odd page section break. The following step switches to Draft view. *Why? Section breaks are easy to see in Draft view.*

1

- Display the View tab. Click the Draft View button (View tab | Views group) to switch to Draft view.

- Scroll to the top of the document and notice how different the document looks in Draft view (Figure 9–77).

Q&A
What happened to the graphics, footers, and other items?
They do not appear in Draft view because Draft view is designed to make editing text in a document easier.

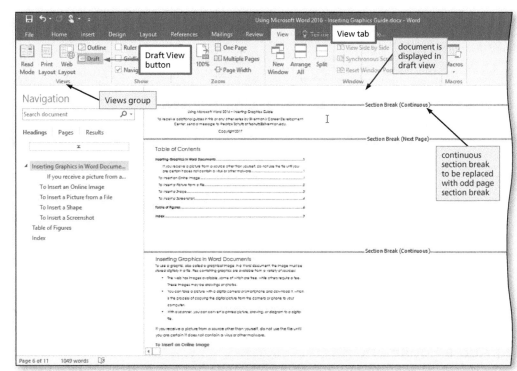

Figure 9–77

BTW
Different First Page
If you wanted only the first page of a document to have a different header or footer, you could place a check mark in the 'Different First Page' check box (Header & Footer Tools Design tab | Options group). Doing so instructs Word to create a first page header or first page footer that can contain content that differs from the rest of the headers or footers.

To Insert an Odd Page Section Break

To fix the extra pages in the printed document, you will replace the continuous section break at the end of the title page with an odd page section break. With an odd page section break, Word starts the next section on an odd page instead of an even page.

1 Select the continuous section break at the bottom of the title page (or top of the document in Draft view) and then press the DELETE key to delete the selected section break.

2 If necessary, display the Layout tab.

3 To insert an odd page section break, click the 'Insert Page and Section Breaks' button (Layout tab | Page Setup group) and then click Odd Page in the Section Breaks area in the Insert Page and Section Breaks gallery (Figure 9–78).

Q&A Can I insert even page section breaks?
Yes. To instruct Word to start the next section on an even page, click Even Page in the Insert Page and Section Breaks gallery.

4 Click the Print Layout button on the status bar to switch to Print Layout view.

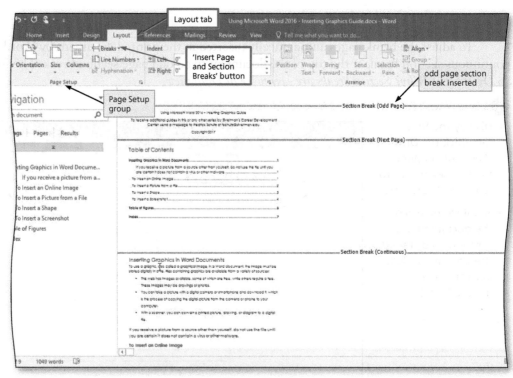

Figure 9–78

To Add a Bookmark

1 MODIFY REFERENCE DOCUMENT | 2 CREATE MASTER DOCUMENT | **3 ORGANIZE REFERENCE DOCUMENT**

A **bookmark** is an item in a document that you name for future reference. The following steps add bookmarks. *Why? Bookmarks assist users in navigating through a document online. For example, you could bookmark the headings in the document, so that users easily could jump to these areas of the document.*

- Use the Navigation Pane to display the To Insert an Online Image heading in the document window and then select the heading in the document.

- Display the Insert tab.

- Click the 'Insert a Bookmark' button (Insert tab | Links group) to display the Bookmark dialog box.

- Type **OnlineImage** in the Bookmark name text box (Figure 9–79).

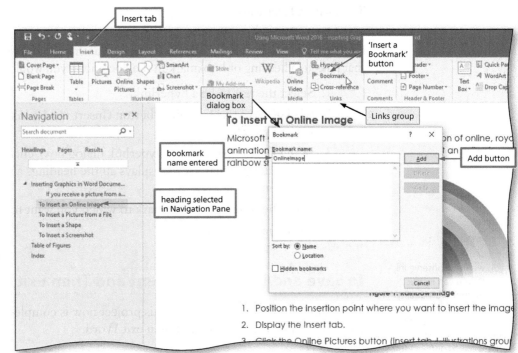

Figure 9–79

Q&A What are the rules for bookmark names?

Bookmark names can contain only letters, numbers, and the underscore character (_). They also must begin with a letter and cannot contain spaces.

- Click the Add button (Bookmark dialog box) to add the bookmark name to the list of existing bookmarks in the document.

- Repeat Steps 1 and 2 for these headings in the document: To Insert a Picture from a File, To Insert a Shape, and To Insert a Screenshot (use bookmark names PictureFromFile, Shape, and Screenshot).

TO GO TO A BOOKMARK

Once you have added bookmarks, you can jump to them. If you wanted to go to a bookmark, you would perform the following steps.

1. Click the 'Insert a Bookmark' button (Insert tab | Links group) to display the Bookmark dialog box (shown in Figure 9–79).

2. Click the bookmark name in the Bookmark name list (Bookmark dialog box) and then click the Go To button.

or

1. Press the F5 key to display the Go To sheet in the Find and Replace dialog box.

2. Click Bookmark in the list (Find and Replace dialog box), select the bookmark name, and then click the Go To button.

BTW

Link to Graphic
If you wanted to link a graphic in a document to a webpage, you would click the 'Add a Hyperlink' button (Insert tab | Links group), enter the web address in the Address text box (Insert Hyperlink dialog box), and then click the OK button. To display the webpage associated with the graphic, tap or CTRL+click the graphic.

TO INSERT A HYPERLINK

Instead of or in addition to bookmarks in online documents, you can insert hyperlinks that link one part of a document to another. If you wanted to insert a hyperlink that links to a heading or bookmark in the document, you would follow these steps.

1. Select the text to be a hyperlink.
2. Click the 'Add a Hyperlink' button (Insert tab | Links group) to display the Insert Hyperlink dialog box.
3. In the Link to bar (Insert Hyperlink dialog box), click 'Place in This Document', so that Word displays all the headings and bookmarks in the document.
4. Click the heading or bookmark to which you want to link.
5. Click the OK button.

BTW
Conserving Ink and Toner
If you want to conserve ink or toner, you can instruct Word to print draft quality documents by clicking File on the ribbon to open the Backstage view, clicking the Options tab to display the Word Options dialog box, clicking Advanced in the left pane (Word Options dialog box), scrolling to the Print area in the right pane, placing a check mark in the 'Use draft quality' check box, and then clicking the OK button. Then, use the Backstage view to print the document as usual.

To Save and Print a Document and Then Exit Word

The reference document for this project now is complete. The following steps save and print the document and then exit Word.

1 Save the document again on the same storage location with the same file name.

2 If requested by your instructor, print the finished document (shown in Figure 9–1 at the beginning of this module).

3 Save the document as a PDF file and submit the PDF in the format requested by your instructor.

4 Exit Word.

Summary

In this module, you have learned how to insert a screenshot, add captions, create cross-references, insert a sidebar text box, link text boxes, compress pictures, use Outline view, work with master documents and subdocuments, and create a table of contents, a table of figures, and an index.

CONSIDER THIS: PLAN AHEAD

What decisions will you need to make when creating reference documents?
Use these guidelines as you complete the assignments in this module and create your own reference documents outside of this class.

1. Prepare a document to be included in a longer document.
   a) If a document contains multiple illustrations (figures), each figure should have a caption and be referenced from within the text.
   b) All terms in the document that should be included in the index should be marked as an index entry.
2. Include elements common to a reference document, such as a title page, a table of contents, and an index.
   a) The title page entices passersby to take a copy of the document.
   b) A table of contents at the beginning of the document and an index at the end helps a reader locate topics within the document.
   c) If a document contains several illustrations, you also should include a table of figures.
3. Prepare the document for distribution, including page numbers, gutter margins for binding, bookmarks, and hyperlinks as appropriate.

Apply Your Knowledge

Reinforce the skills and apply the concepts you learned in this module.

Working with Outline View

Note: To complete this assignment, you will be required to use the Data Files. Please contact your instructor for information about accessing the Data Files.

Instructions: Run Word. Open the document, Apply 9-1 Communications Outline Draft, from the Data Files. The document is an outline for a paper. You are to modify the outline in Outline view. The final outline is shown in Figure 9–80.

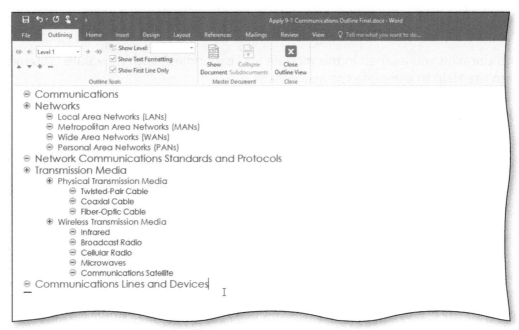

Figure 9–80

Perform the following tasks:

1. If necessary, switch to Outline view.
2. Move the item on the fourth line, Communications, up four lines so that it is at the top of the outline.
3. Promote the item, PANs, so that it is Level 2 instead of Level 3.
4. In the Physical Transmission Media section, move the item, Coaxial Cable, down one line.
5. Practice collapsing and expanding by collapsing the Physical Transmission Media item and then expanding the Physical Transmission Media item.
6. Change the word, Links, in the Communications Links and Devices item to the word, Lines, so that it reads: Communications Lines and Devices.
7. Promote the item, Communications Lines and Devices, to Heading 1 (Level 1).
8. Demote the five items in the outline below the item, Wireless Transmission Media (Infrared, Broadcast Radio, Cellular Radio, Microwaves, and Communications Satellite) so that they are Level 3 instead of Level 2.
9. Insert an item, called Metropolitan Area Networks (MANs), as a Level 2 item below the Local Area Networks (LANs) item.
10. Delete the item called Monitoring Network Traffic.

Continued >

Apply Your Knowledge *continued*

11. Remove the check mark in the 'Show Text Formatting' check box (Outlining tab | Outline Tools group). Place the check mark in the check box again. What is the purpose of this check box?

12. Close Outline View. How does the document differ when displayed in Print Layout view?

13. If requested by your instructor, add your name at the end of the first line of the outline. Save the modified file with the new file name, Apply 9-1 Communications Outline Final. Submit the document in the format specified by your instructor.

14. ✳ Answer the questions posed in #11 and #12. What are two different ways to expand and collapse items in an outline, to move items up and down an outline, and to demote and promote items in an outline?

Extend Your Knowledge

Extend the skills you learned in this module and experiment with new skills. You may need to use Help to complete the assignment.

Working with Screenshots

Note: To complete this assignment, you will be required to use the Data Files. Please contact your instructor for information about accessing the Data Files.

Instructions: Run Word. Open the document, Extend 9-1 Word 2016 Screenshots Draft, from the Data Files. You will insert a screenshot and a screen clipping in the document.

Perform the following tasks:

1. Use Help to expand your knowledge about screenshots, screen clippings, saving images, and print scaling.

2. Change the page from portrait to landscape orientation. Change the margins to Narrow.

3. From Word, create a blank document so that you have two separate Word windows open. Switch to the Word window with the Extend 9-1 Word 2016 Screenshots Draft file open. Insert a screenshot, centered on the blank line below the first paragraph. If necessary, crop the bottom of the screenshot so that it ends at the status bar.

4. Insert a screen clipping of the ribbon, centered on the blank line below the second paragraph.

5. Save the Word screenshot as a JPEG file with the name, Extend 9-1 Word 2016 Screenshot.

6. Save the screen clipping of the ribbon as a JPEG file with the file name, Extend 9-1 Word 2016 Ribbon Screen Clipping.

7. Add a border, shadow, or glow effect to the screenshot and the screen clipping.

8. Add these callouts to the screenshot: Quick Access Toolbar, ribbon, status bar. Change the callout lines to arrows. Format the callouts as necessary for readability.

9. Add these callouts to the screen clipping: tab, group, button. Change the callout lines to arrows. Format the callouts as necessary for readability (Figure 9–81).

10. Print the document so that it fits on a single page; that is, make sure it is scaled to the paper size.

11. Locate the saved JPEG files and then double-click them. In what program did they open?

12. If requested by your instructor, add a text box to the Word screen with your name in it. Save the modified file with the new file name, Extend 9-1 Word Screenshots Final. Submit the documents in the format specified by your instructor.

13. ✳ Answer the question posed in #11. How did you print the document so that it fits on a single page? What changes could you make to the document so that it all fits on a single page when you view it on the screen?

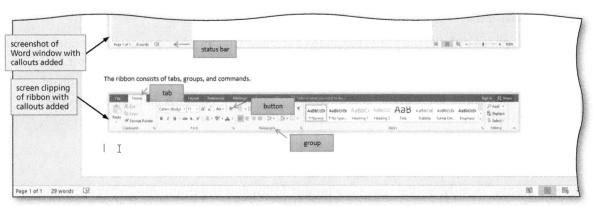

screenshot of Word window with callouts added

screen clipping of ribbon with callouts added

Figure 9–81

Expand Your World

Create a solution that uses cloud or web technologies by learning and investigating on your own from general guidance.

Using an Online Photo Editor

Note: To complete this assignment, you will be required to use the Data Files. Please contact your instructor for information about accessing the Data Files.

Instructions: Assume you have a digital photo that you want to edit before including it in a Word document.

Perform the following tasks:
1. Run a browser. Search for the text, online photo editor, using a search engine. Visit several of the online photo editors and determine which you would like to use to edit a photo. Navigate to the desired online photo editor.
2. In the photo editor, open the image called Dog.JPG from the Data Files (Figure 9–82). Use the photo editor to enhance the image. Apply at least five enhancements. Which enhancements did you apply?
3. If requested by your instructor, add your name as a text element to the photo.

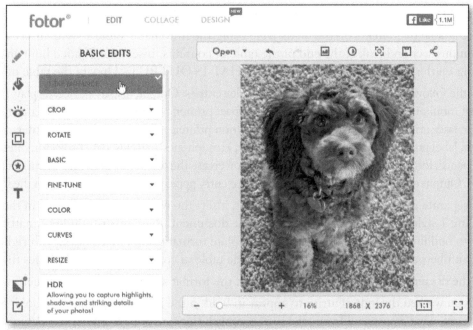

Figure 9–82

Continued >

Expand Your World *continued*

4. Save the photo with the file name, Expand 9-1 Revised Dog. In what format did the online photo editor save the file? Submit the photo in the format specified by your instructor.

5. ✺ Answer the questions posed in #2 and #4. Which online photo editors did you evaluate? Which one did you select to use, and why? Do you prefer using the online photo editor or Word to enhance images?

In the Labs

Design, create, modify, and/or use a document following the guidelines, concepts, and skills presented in this module. Labs 1 and 2, which increase in difficulty, require you to create solutions based on what you learned in the module; Lab 3 requires you to apply your creative thinking and problem-solving skills to design and implement a solution.

Lab 1: Creating a Reference Document with a Cover Page, a Table of Contents, and an Index

Note: To complete this assignment, you will be required to use the Data Files. Please contact your instructor for information about accessing the Data Files.

Problem: As a part-time assistant in the Technology Center at Baxter County Library, you have been asked to prepare a guide briefly describing types of output. A miniature version of this document is shown in Figure 9–83. A draft of the body of the document is on the Data Files.

Perform the following tasks:

1. Open the document, Lab 9-1 Output Draft, from the Data Files. Save the document with a new file name, Lab 9-1 Output Final.

2. Create a title page by inserting the Ion (Dark) style cover page. Use the following information on the title page: year - 2017; title – Learning Technology; subtitle – Output; author – Technology Center; company name - Baxter County Library; company address - 10 Center Street, Baxter, UT 20189.

3. If requested by your instructor, use your name as the author instead of Technology Center.

4. Insert a blank page between the title page and the WHAT IS OUTPUT? heading.

5. Create a table of contents on the blank page using the Automatic Table 1 style. Insert a continuous section break at the end of the table of contents. Insert the Banded built-in footer starting on the page with the section titled WHAT IS OUTPUT? Update the table of contents.

6. Mark the following terms in the document as index entries: Output, display device, display, flat-panel display, monitor, liquid crystal display, printer, impact printer, nonimpact printer, ink-jet printer, photo printer, laser printer, all-in-one printer, multifunction printer, 3-D printer, thermal printer, mobile printer, label printer, plotter, large-format printer, Headphones, earbuds, data projector, interactive whiteboard, force feedback, and tactile output. Lowercase the first letter in the index entries for the words, Output and Headphones, so that the entire entry appears in lowercase letters in the index.

7. On a separate page at the end of the document, insert the word, Index, formatted in the Heading 1 style and then build an index for the document. Remember to hide formatting marks prior to building the index. Use the From template format using one column, with right-aligned page numbers and leader characters. Update the table of contents so that it includes the index.

8. Save the document again and then submit it in the format specified by your instructor.

9. ✺ If you wanted the index entries to appear in bold in the index but remain not bold in the document, what steps would you take to accomplish this?

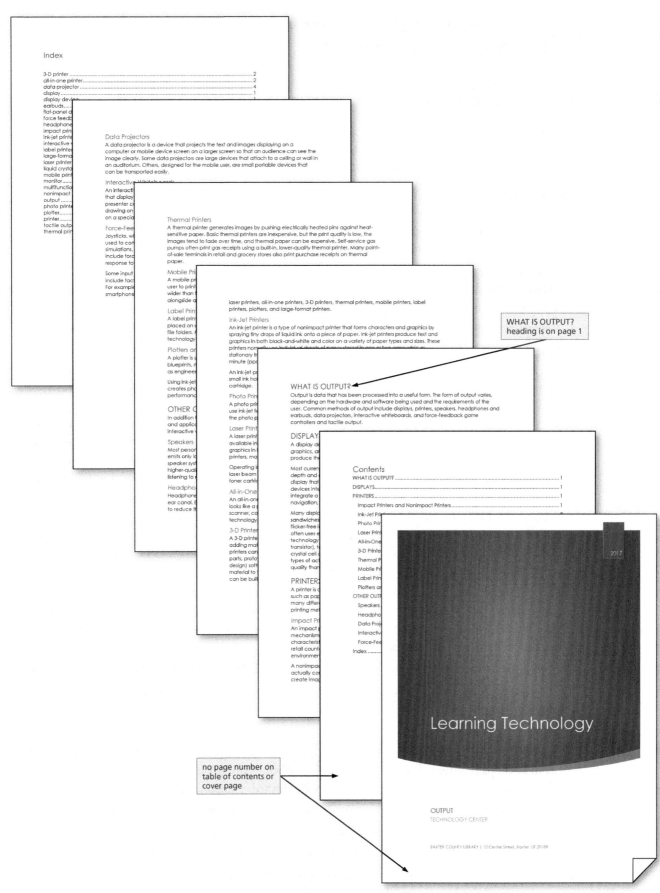

Index

Data Projectors

A data projector is a device that projects the text and images displaying on a computer or mobile device screen on a larger screen so that an audience can see the image clearly. Some data projectors are large devices that attach to a ceiling or wall in an auditorium. Others, designed for the mobile user, are small portable devices that can be transported easily.

Interactive Whiteboards

An interacti
that display
presenter c
drawing on
on a specia

Force-Fee
Joysticks, w
used to co
simulations,
include forc
response to

Some input
include tact
For example
smartphone

Thermal Printers

A thermal printer generates images by pushing electrically heated pins against heat-sensitive paper. Basic thermal printers are inexpensive, but the print quality is low, the images tend to fade over time, and thermal paper can be expensive. Self-service gas pumps often print gas receipts using a built-in, lower-quality thermal printer. Many point-of-sale terminals in retail and grocery stores also print purchase receipts on thermal paper.

Mobile Pri
A mobile pr
user to print
wider than
alongside a

Label Prin
A label prin
placed on
file folders.
technolog

Plotters ar
A plotter is
blueprints, r
as engineer

Using ink-jet
creates pho
performanc

OTHER C
In addition
and applica
interactive

Speakers
Most person
emits only la
speaker syst
higher-quali
listening to

Headpho
Headphone
ear canal. E
to reduce th

laser printers, all-in-one printers, 3-D printers, thermal printers, mobile printers, label printers, plotters, and large-format printers.

Ink-Jet Printers

An ink-jet printer is a type of nonimpact printer that forms characters and graphics by spraying tiny drops of liquid ink onto a piece of paper. Ink-jet printers produce text and graphics in both black-and-white and color on a variety of paper types and sizes. These printers normally use individual sheets of paper stored in one or two removable or stationary tr
minute (ppr

An ink-jet pr
small ink hol
cartridge.

Photo Prin
A photo prir
use ink-jet f
the photo p

Laser Printi
A laser printi
available in
graphics in
printers, ma

Operating i
laser beam
toner cartrid

All-in-One
An all-in-on
looks like a
scanner, co
technology

3-D Printer
A 3-D printe
adding mat
printers can
parts, proto
design) soft
material to
can be buil

PRINTERS
A printer is
such as pap
many differ
printing met

Impact Pr
An impact
mechanism
characterist
retail counte
environmer

A nonimpac
actually cor
create imag

WHAT IS OUTPUT?
heading is on page 1

WHAT IS OUTPUT?

Output is data that has been processed into a useful form. The form of output varies, depending on the hardware and software being used and the requirements of the user. Common methods of output include displays, printers, speakers, headphones and earbuds, data projectors, interactive whiteboards, and force-feedback game controllers and tactile output.

DISPLAY
A display d
graphics, a
produce th

Most curren
depth and
display that
devices inte
integrate a
navigation,

Many displa
sandwiches
flicker-free i
often uses e
technology
transistor), t
crystal cell
types of act
quality than

Contents

2017

Learning Technology

OUTPUT
TECHNOLOGY CENTER

BAXTER COUNTY LIBRARY | 10 Center Street, Baxter, UT 20189

no page number on
table of contents or
cover page

Figure 9–83

Continued >

In the Labs *continued*

Lab 2: **Using a Master Document and Subdocument for a Reference Document**

Note: To complete this assignment, you will be required to use the Data Files. Please contact your instructor for information about accessing the Data Files.

Problem: Your supervisor at your part-time job has asked you to prepare a guide about transmission media. A miniature version of this document is shown in Figure 9–84. The document is a master document with one subdocument. The subdocument is on the Data Files.

Perform the following tasks:

1. Open the file named Lab 9-2 Transmission Media Draft from the Data Files. Save the document with the file name, Lab 9-2 Transmission Media Subdocument Final, so that any changes you make are saved in a new file.

2. Add the following captions to the figures: first figure – Figure 1: Transfer Rates for Physical Transmission Media Used in LANs; second figure – Figure 2: Wireless Transmission Media Transfer Rates; third figure – Figure 3: Communication Satellites.

3. Replace the occurrences of XX in the document with cross-references to the figure captions.

4. Insert a Retrospect Sidebar text box on the first page. Enter this text in the text box: `What is bandwidth?` Select the description placeholder and then type: `Bandwidth is the amount of data that can travel over transmission media. Higher bandwidths can transmit more data.` Press the ENTER key. Type: `What is a GPS?` Press the ENTER key. Type: `A GPS (global positioning system) is a navigation system that consists of one or more earth-based receivers that accept and analyze signals sent by satellites in order to determine the receiver's geographic location.` Format the second question the same as the first.

5. On the last page, insert another Retrospect Sidebar text box and then delete the contents of the second text box. Link the two text boxes together. Resize each text box so that each one contains just one question and answer. Move the first text box to the top of the first page and the second text box to the middle of the second page to the right of the Communications Satellite heading. Save and close the document.

6. Create a new document. Change the document theme to Facet. In Outline View, type `Copyright 2017` as the first line formatted as Body Text, and the remaining lines containing the Table of Figures and Index headings, each formatted as Heading 1/Level 1. Insert a next page section break between each line.

7. Save the master document with the file name, Lab 9-2 Transmission Media Master Document.

8. Between the Copyright line and Table of Figures headings, insert the subdocument named Lab 9-2 Transmission Media Subdocument Final.

9. Switch to Print Layout view.

10. Create a cover page by inserting the Banded style cover page. Use the following information on the title page: title – Transmission Media; author – Silvia Mendez; company name – Banner Electronics; company address – 403 Payton Boulevard, Hanson, MO 30393.

11. If requested by your instructor, use your name as the author instead of Silvia Mendez.

12. Format the copyright page with a vertical alignment of Bottom.

13. Insert a blank page between the copyright page and the heading, Transmission Media.

14. Create a table of contents on the blank page using the Distinctive style, right-aligned page numbers, and dots for leader characters.

Index

buildings or mountains, microwave stations often sit on the tops of buildings, towers, or mountains.

Microwave transmission typically is used in environments where installing physical transmission media is difficult or impossible and where line-of-sight transmission is available. For example, microwave transmission is used in wide-open areas, such as deserts or lakes, between buildings in a close geographic area, or to communicate with a satellite.

Communications Satellite
A communications satellite is a space station that receives microwave signals from an earth-based station, amplifies (strengthens) the signals, and broadcasts the signals back over a wide area to any number of earth-based stations (Figure 3). These earth-based stations often are microwave stations. Other devices, such as smartphones and GPS receivers, also can function as earth-based stations. Transmission from an earth-based station to a satellite is an uplink. Transmission from a satellite to an earth-based station is a downlink.

Applications such as air navigation, television and radio broadcasts, weather forecasting, videoconferencing, paging, GPS, and Internet connections use communications satellites. With the proper satellite dish and a satellite modem, consumers can access the Internet using satellite technology. With satellite Internet connections, however, uplink transmissions usually are slower than downlink transmissions. This difference in speeds usually is acceptable to most Internet satellite users because they download much more data than they upload.

What is a GPS?
A GPS (global positioning system) is a navigation system that consists of one or more earth-based receivers that accept and analyze signals sent by satellite in order to determine the receiver's geographic location.

Table of Figures

linked sidebar text boxes

Coaxial Cable
Coaxial cable, often referred to as coax (pronounced KO-ax), consists of a single copper wire surrounded by at least three layers: (1) an insulating material, (2) a woven or braided metal, and (3) a plastic outer coating. CATV network wiring often uses coaxial cable because it can be cabled over longer distances than twisted-pair cable. Most of today's computer networks, however, do not use coaxial cable because other transmission media, such as fiber-optic cable, transmit signals at faster rates.

Fiber-Optic Cable
The core of a fiber-optic cable consists of dozens or hundreds of thin strands of glass or plastic that use light to transmit signals. Each strand, called an optical fiber, is as thin as a human hair. Inside the fiber-optic cable, an insulating glass cladding and a protective coating surround each optical fiber.

Fiber-optic cables have the several advantages over cables that use wire. For example, fiber-optic cables can carry significantly more signals than wire cables, have faster data transmission, are less susceptible to noise (interference) from other devices, have better security for signals during transmission, and typically are much thinner and lighter weight. Disadvantages of fiber-optic cable are it costs more than twisted-pair or coaxial cable and can be difficult to install and modify.

WIRELESS TRANSMISSION MEDIA
Wireless transmission media send communications signals through the air or s... opt for wireless transmission media because it is more convenient than install... addition to convenience, businesses use wireless transmission media in locatio... impossible to install cables. Types of wireless transmission media used in co... include infrared, broadcast radio, cellular radio, microwaves, and communica... Figure 2 lists transfer rates of various wireless transmission media.

cross-references added

Medium		Maximum Transfer Rate
Infrared		115 Kbps to 4 Mbps
Broadcast radio	• Bluetooth	1 Mbps to 24 Mbps
	• 802.11b	11 Mbps
	• 802.11a	54 Mbps
	• 802.11g	54 Mbps
	• 802.11n	300 Mbps
	• 802.11ac	500 Mbps to 1 Gbps
	• 802.11ad	up to 7 Gbps
	• UWB	110 Mbps to 480 Mbps
Cellular radio	• 2G	9.6 Kbps to 144 Kbps
	• 3G	144 Kbps to 3.84 Mbps
	• 4G	3p to 100 Mbps
Microwave radio		10 Gbps
Communications satellite		7.56 Tbps

Figure 2: Wireless Transmission Media Transfer Rates

Infrared
Infrared (IR) is a wireless transmission medium that sends signals using infrared light waves. Mobile computers and devices, such as a mouse, printer, and smartphone, may have an IrDA port that enables the transfer of data from one device to another using infrared light waves.

Broadcast Radio
Broadcast radio is a wireless transmission medium that distributes radio signals through the air over long distances, such as between cities, regions, and countries, and short distances, such as within an office or home.

For radio transmissions, you need a transmitter to send the broadcast radio signal and a receiver to accept it. To receive the broadcast radio signal, the receiver has an antenna that is located in the range of the signal. Some networks use a transceiver, which both sends and receives signals from wireless devices. Broadcast radio is slower and more susceptible to noise than physical transmission media, but it provides flexibility and portability.

Cellular Radio
Cellular radio is a form of broadcast radio that is in wide use for mobile communications, specifically wireless modems and mobile phones. A mobile phone uses high-frequency radio waves to transmit voice and digital data messages. Because only a limited number of radio frequencies exist, mobile service providers reuse frequencies so that they can accommodate the large number of users. Some users install an amplifier or booster to improve the signal

Table of Contents

TRANSMISSION MEDIA
Transmission media consist of materials or substances capable of carrying one or more communications signals. When you send data from a computer or mobile device, the signal that carries the data may travel over various transmission media. This is especially true when the transmission spans a long distance. Although many media and devices are involved, the entire communications process could take less than one second.

What is bandwidth?
Bandwidth is the amount of data that can travel over transmission media. Higher bandwidths can transmit more data.

PHYSICAL TRANSMISSION MEDIA
Physical transmission media use wire, cable, and other tangible materials to send communications signals. These wires and cables typically are used underground or within or between buildings. Ethernet and token ring LANs often use physical transmission media. Figure 1 lists the transfer rates of LANs using various physical transmission media.

Type of Cable and LAN	Maximum Transfer Rate
Twisted-Pair Cable	
• 10Base-T (Ethernet)	10 Mbps
• 100Base-T (Fast Ethernet)	100 Mbps
• 1000Base-T (Gigabit Ethernet)	1 Gbps
• Token ring	4 Mbps to 16 Mbps
Coaxial Cable	
• 10Base2 (ThinWire Ethernet)	10 Mbps
• 10Base5 (ThickWire Ethernet)	10 Mbps
Fiber-Optic Cable	
• 10Base-F (Ethernet)	10 Mbps
• 100Base-FX (Fast Ethernet)	100 Mbps
• FDDI (Fiber Distributed Data Interface) token ring	100 Mbps
• Gigabit Ethernet	1 Gbps
• 10-Gigabit Ethernet	10 Gbps
• 40-Gigabit Ethernet	40 Gbps
• 100 Gigabit Ethernet	100 Gbps

Figure 1: Transfer Rates for Physical Transmission Media Used in LANs

captions added to figures

...-Pair Cable
...e more widely used transmission media for network cabling and landline phone ... twisted-pair cable. Twisted-pair cable consists of one or more twisted-pair wires ...ogether. Each twisted-pair wire consists of two separate insulated copper wires that ...ed together. The wires are twisted together to reduce noise, which is an electrical ...r that can degrade communications.

footer added

TRANSMISSION MEDIA

Sabria Morales

ELKMORE ELECTRONICS • 461 Payson Boulevard • Hannover, MD 36390

vertical alignment set to Bottom

Copyright 2017

Figure 9–84

Continued >

In the Labs continued

15. At the end of the document, if necessary, format the Table of Figures heading using the Heading 1 style. Then, add a table of figures below the heading using the Formal format with right-aligned page numbers and a tab leader character.

16. Build an index for the document. Remember to hide formatting marks prior to building the index. Use the Formal format in two columns with right-aligned page numbers.

17. Insert a continuous section break at the bottom of the table of contents page. Format the page number on the table of contents page to begin on page 0. Beginning on the fourth page (with the heading, Transmission Media), create alternating footers. Insert a right tab for the even page footer. Align left the odd page footer. Insert the Accent Bar 2 page number style. The cover page, copyright page, or table of contents should not contain the footer.

18. If necessary, resize Figure 1 so that the Twisted-Pair Cable text fits on Page 1, resize Figure 2 so that it fits at the bottom of page 2, and resize Figure 3 so that it fits at the bottom of page 4.

19. From the copyright page forward, set the left and right margins to .75" and set a gutter margin of .5". You may need to fix extra pages inserted by replacing next page section breaks with odd or even page section breaks.

20. Insert a bookmark for each Heading 1 and Heading 2 in the document.

21. Compress the pictures in the document.

22. Update the table of contents, table of figures, and index.

23. Make any additional adjustments so that the document looks like Figure 9–84.

24. Save the document again. Also save the document as a PDF file. Submit the Word documents or the PDF file in the format specified by your instructor. If requested by your instructor, print the document back to back.

25. ⊛ If you added a figure in the Broadcast Radio section, how would you renumber the remaining figures in the document?

Lab 3: **Consider This: Your Turn**

Create a Reference Document about Graphics and Media Apps

Note: To complete this assignment, you will be required to use the Data Files. Please contact your instructor for information about accessing the Data Files.

Problem: In your Introduction to Computers class, you have been asked to create a reference document that discusses various graphics and media apps.

Part 1: You decide to use master documents and subdocuments for this reference document. The subdocument you created is a file named Lab 9-3 Graphics and Media Apps Draft located on the Data Files. In this subdocument, mark at least 10 terms as index entries. Insert at least two screenshots of various graphics and media apps on your computer or mobile device and then add captions to the screenshot images. Compress the images and then save the subdocument file using a different file name. Create a master document that contains the subdocument file. The master document also should have a title page (cover page), a table of contents, a table of figures, and an index. Format the document with a footer that contains a page number. Use the concepts and techniques presented in this module to organize and format the document. Submit your assignment in the format specified by your instructor.

Part 2: ⊛ You made several decisions while creating the reference document in this assignment: which terms to mark as index entries, which screenshot images to include, what text to use for captions, and how to organize and format the subdocument and master document (table of contents, table of figures, index, gutter margins, etc.). What was the rationale behind each of these decisions? When you proofread the document, what further revisions did you make and why?

10 | Creating a Template for an Online Form

Objectives

You will have mastered the material in this module when you can:

- Save a document as a template
- Change paper size
- Change page color
- Insert a borderless table in a form
- Show the Developer tab
- Insert plain text, drop-down list, check box, rich text, combo box, and date picker content controls
- Edit placeholder text

- Change properties of content controls
- Insert and format a rectangle shape
- Customize a theme
- Protect a form
- Open a new document based on a template
- Fill in a form

Introduction

During your personal and professional life, you undoubtedly have filled in countless forms. Whether a federal tax form, a time card, a job application, an order, a deposit slip, a request, or a survey, a form is designed to collect information. In the past, forms were printed; that is, you received the form on a piece of paper, filled it in with a pen or pencil, and then returned it manually. With an **online form**, you use a computer or mobile device to access, fill in, and then return the form. In Word, you easily can create an online form for electronic distribution; you also can fill in that same form using Word.

Project — Online Form

Today, people are concerned with using resources efficiently. To minimize paper waste, protect the environment, enhance office efficiency, and improve access to data, many businesses have moved toward a paperless office. Thus, online forms have replaced many paper forms. You access online forms on a website, on your company's intranet, or from your inbox if you receive the form via email.

The project in this module uses Word to produce the online form shown in Figure 10–1. Ellie's Coffee Stop is a coffeehouse interested in customer feedback. Instead of sending a survey via the postal service, Ellie's Coffee Stop will send the

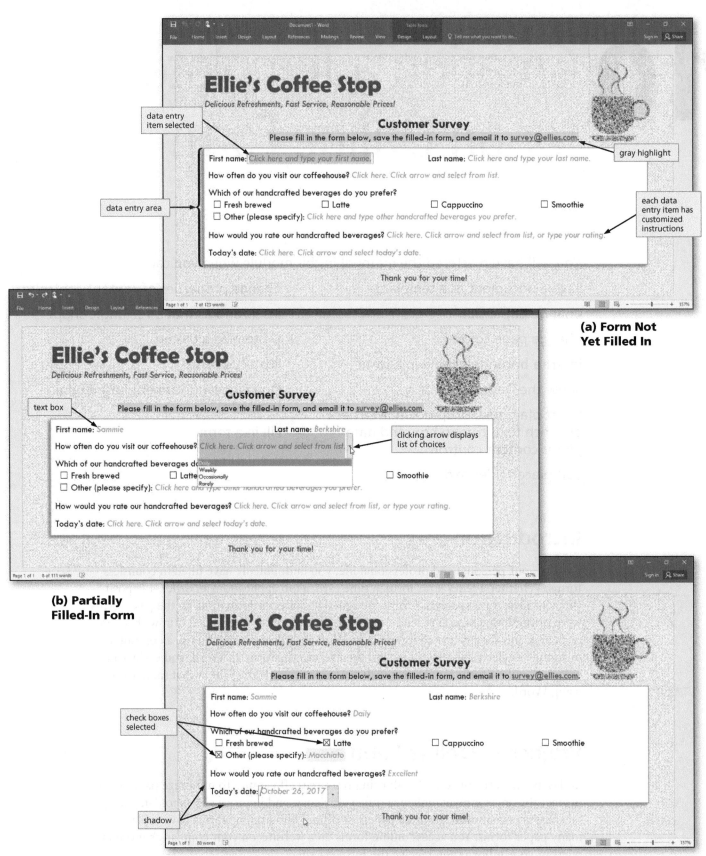

(a) Form Not Yet Filled In

(b) Partially Filled-In Form

(c) Filled-In Form

Figure 10–1

survey via email to customers for whom it has email addresses. Upon receipt of the online form (a survey), the customer fills in the form, saves it, and then sends it back via email to Ellie's Coffee Stop.

Figure 10–1a shows how the form is displayed on a user's screen initially, Figure 10–1b shows the form partially filled in by one user, and Figure 10–1c shows how this user filled in the entire form.

The data entry area of the form contains three text boxes (named First Name, Last Name, and Other Beverages), one drop-down list box (named Frequency of Visits), five check boxes (named Fresh Brewed, Latte, Cappuccino, Smoothie, and Other Beverages), a combination text box/drop-down list box (named Beverage Rating), and a date picker (named Today's Date).

The form is designed so that it fits completely within a Word window that is set at a page width zoom and has the ribbon collapsed, which reduces the chance a user will have to scroll the window while filling in the form. The data entry area of the form is enclosed by a rectangle that has a shadow on its left and bottom edges. The line of text above the data entry area is covered with the color gray, giving it the look of text that has been marked with a gray highlighter pen.

In this module, you will learn how to create the form shown in Figure 10–1. The following roadmap identifies general activities you will perform as you progress through this module:

1. SAVE a DOCUMENT as a TEMPLATE.
2. SET FORM FORMATS FOR the TEMPLATE.
3. ENTER TEXT, GRAPHICS, AND CONTENT CONTROLS in the form.
4. PROTECT the FORM.
5. USE the FORM.

To Run Word and Change Word Settings

If you are using a computer to step through the project in this module and you want your screens to match the figures in this book, you should change your screen's resolution to 1366 × 768. The following steps run Word, display formatting marks, and change the zoom to page width.

1. Run Word and create a blank document in the Word window. If necessary, maximize the Word window.

2. If the Print Layout button on the status bar is not selected, click it so that your screen is in Print Layout view.

3. To display the page the same width as the document window, if necessary, click the Page Width button (View tab | Zoom group).

4. If the 'Show/Hide ¶' button (Home tab | Paragraph group) is not selected already, click it to display formatting marks on the screen.

5. If the rulers are displayed on the screen, click the View Ruler check box (View tab | Show group) to remove the rulers from the Word window.

Saving a Document as a Template

A **template** is a file that contains the definition of the appearance of a Word document, including items such as default font, font size, margin settings, and line spacing; available styles; and even placement of text. Every Word document you create is based on a template. When you select the Blank document thumbnail on the Word start screen or in the New gallery of the Backstage view, Word creates a document based on the Normal template. Word also provides other templates for more specific types of documents, such as memos, letters, and resumes, some of which you have used in previous modules. Creating a document based on these templates can improve your productivity because Word has defined much of the document's appearance for you.

In this module, you create an online form. If you create and save an online form as a Word document, users will be required to open that Word document to display the form on the screen. Next, they will fill in the form. Then, to preserve the content of the original form, they will have to save the form with a new file name. If they accidentally click the Save button on the Quick Access Toolbar during the process of filling in the form, Word will replace the original blank form with a filled-in form.

If you create and save the online form as a template instead, users will open a new document window that is based on that template. This displays the form on the screen as a brand new Word document; that is, the document does not have a file name. Thus, the user fills in the form and then clicks the Save button on the Quick Access Toolbar to save his or her filled-in form. By creating a Word template for the form, instead of a Word document, the original template for the form remains intact when the user clicks the Save button.

BTW
The Ribbon and Screen Resolution
Word may change how the groups and buttons within the groups appear on the ribbon, depending on the computer's screen resolution. Thus, your ribbon may look different from the ones in this book if you are using a screen resolution other than 1366 x 768.

To Save a Document as a Template

1 SAVE DOCUMENT TEMPLATE | 2 SET FORM FORMATS FOR TEMPLATE
3 ENTER TEXT, GRAPHICS, & CONTENT CONTROLS | 4 PROTECT FORM | 5 USE FORM

The following steps save a new blank document as a template. *Why? The template will be used to create the online form shown in Figure 10–1.*

1

- With a new blank document in the Word window, open the Backstage view and then click the Export tab in the left pane of the Backstage view to display the Export gallery.

- Click 'Change File Type' in the Export gallery to display information in the right pane about various file types that can be opened in Word.

- Click Template in the right pane to specify the file type for the current document (Figure 10–2).

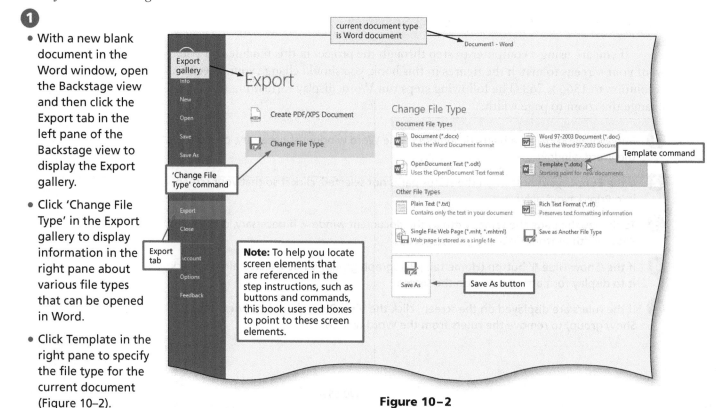

Note: To help you locate screen elements that are referenced in the step instructions, such as buttons and commands, this book uses red boxes to point to these screen elements.

Figure 10–2

2

- Click the Save As button to display the Save As dialog box with the file type automatically changed to Word Template.

Q&A How does Word differentiate between a saved Word template and a saved Word document?
Files typically have a file name and a file extension. The file extension identifies the file type. The source program often assigns a file type to a file. A Word document has an extension of .docx, whereas a Word template has an extension of .dotx. Thus, a file named July Report.docx is a Word document, and a file named Fitness Form.dotx is a Word template.

- Type **Coffeehouse Customer Survey** in the File name box to change the file name and then navigate to the desired save location (Figure 10–3).

Q&A Why is my save location the Custom Office Templates folder?
The default save location for your templates may be the Custom Office Templates folder. If you are using a home computer, you can save your template in that folder. If you are using a public computer, you should change the save location to your local storage location.

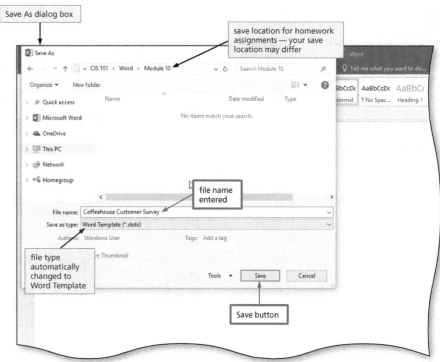

Figure 10–3

3

- Click the Save button (Save As dialog box) to save the document as a Word template with the entered file name in the specified location.

Other Ways	
1. Press F12, change document type to Word Template	2. Open Backstage view, click Save As, change document type to Word Template

Changing Document Settings

To enhance the look of the form, you change several default settings in Word:

1. Display the page as wide as possible in the document window to maximize the amount of space for text and graphics on the form, called page width zoom.
2. Change the size of the paper so that it fits completely within the document window.
3. Adjust the margins so that as much text as possible will fit in the document.
4. Change the document theme to Headlines and the theme fonts to the Tw Cen MT font set.
5. Change the page color to a shade of gold with a pattern.

The first item was completed earlier in the module. The following sections make the remaining changes to the document.

BTW
Touch Screen Differences
The Office and Windows interfaces may vary if you are using a touch screen. For this reason, you might notice that the function or appearance of your touch screen differs slightly from this module's presentation.

To Change Paper Size

For the online form in this module, all edges of the page appear in the document window. Currently, only the top, left, and right edges are displayed in the document window. The following steps change paper size. *Why? To display all edges of the document in the document window in the current resolution, change the height of the paper from 11 inches to 4 inches.*

1

• Display the Layout tab.

• Click the 'Choose Page Size' button (Layout tab | Page Setup group) to display the Choose Page Size gallery (Figure 10–4).

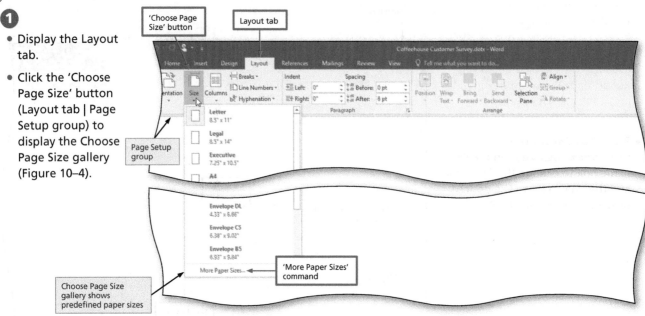

Figure 10–4

2

• Click 'More Paper Sizes' in the Choose Page Size gallery to display the Paper sheet in the Page Setup dialog box.

• In the Height box (Page Setup dialog box), type **4** as the new height (Figure 10–5).

3

• Click the OK button to change the paper size to the entered measurements, which, in this case, are 8.5 inches wide by 4 inches tall.

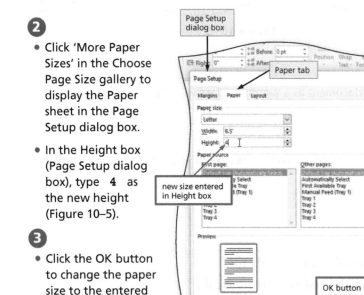

Figure 10–5

To Collapse the Ribbon

To display more of a document or other item in the Word window, you can collapse the ribbon, which hides the groups on the ribbon and displays only the main tabs. For the online form to fit entirely in the Word window, you collapse the ribbon. The following step collapses the ribbon so that you can see how the form fits in the document window.

1 Click the 'Collapse the Ribbon' button on the ribbon (shown in Figure 10–5) to collapse the ribbon (Figure 10–6).

Q&A What happened to the 'Collapse the Ribbon' button?
The 'Pin the ribbon' button replaces the 'Collapse the Ribbon' button when the ribbon is collapsed. You will see the 'Pin the ribbon' button only when you expand a ribbon by clicking a tab.

What if the height of my document does not match the figure?
You may need to show white space. To do this, position the pointer above the top of the page below the ribbon and then double-click when the pointer changes to a 'Show White Space' button (or, if using touch, double-tap below the page). Or, your screen resolution may be different; if so, you may need to adjust the page height or width values.

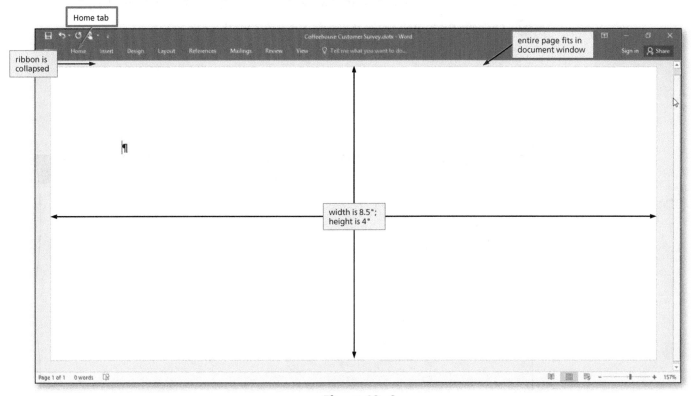

Figure 10–6

To Expand the Ribbon

After you verify that the entire form will fit in the document window, you should expand the ribbon so that you can see the groups while creating the online form. The following steps expand the ribbon.

1 Click Home on the collapsed ribbon to expand the Home tab.

2 Click the 'Pin the ribbon' button on the expanded Home tab to restore the ribbon.

To Set Custom Margins

Recall that Word is preset to use 1-inch top, bottom, left, and right margins. To maximize the space for the contents of the form, this module sets the left and right margins to .5 inches, the top margin to .25 inches, and the bottom margin to 0 inches. The following steps set custom margins.

1 Display the Layout tab. Click the Adjust Margins button (Layout tab | Page Setup group) to display the Adjust Margins gallery.

2 Click Custom Margins in the Adjust Margins gallery to display the Margins sheet in the Page Setup dialog box.

3 Type **.25** in the Top box (Page Setup dialog box) to change the top margin setting.

4 Type **0** (zero) in the Bottom box to change the bottom margin setting.

Q&A | Why set the bottom margin to zero?
This allows you to place form contents at the bottom of the page, if necessary.

5 Type **.5** in the Left box to change the left margin setting.

6 Type **.5** in the Right box to change the right margin setting (Figure 10–7).

7 Click the OK button to set the custom margins for this document.

Q&A | What if Word displays a dialog box indicating margins are outside the printable area?
Click the Ignore button because this is an online form that is not intended for printing.

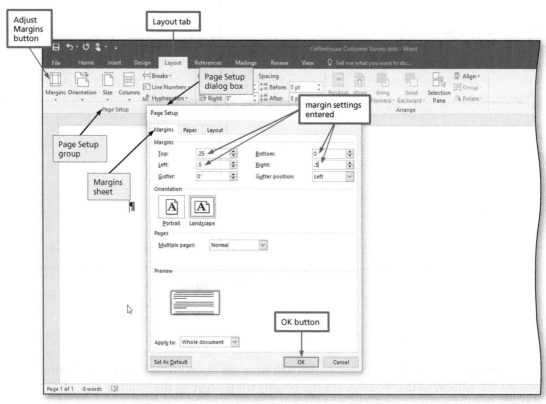

Figure 10–7

To Change the Document Theme and Theme Fonts

The following steps change the document theme colors to Headlines and the theme fonts to Tw Cen MT.

1 Display the Design tab. Click the Themes button (Design tab | Document Formatting group) and then click Headlines in the Themes gallery to change the document theme.

2 Click the Theme Fonts button (Design tab | Document Formatting group) and then scroll through the Theme Fonts gallery to display the Tw Cen MT font set (Figure 10–8).

3 Click 'Tw Cen MT' in the Theme Fonts gallery to change the font set.

BTW

Set a Theme as the Default
If you wanted to change the default theme, you would select the theme you want to be the default theme, or select the color scheme, font set, and theme effects you would like to use as the default. Then, click the 'Set as Default' button (Design tab | Document Formatting group), which uses the current settings as the new default.

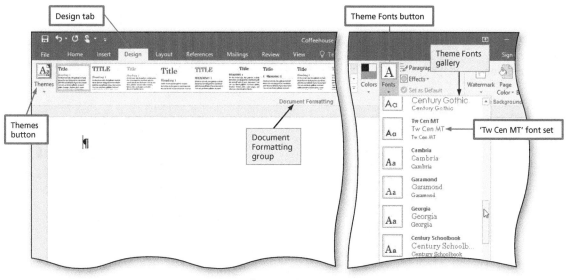

Figure 10–8

To Add a Page Color

1 SAVE DOCUMENT TEMPLATE | 2 SET FORM FORMATS FOR TEMPLATE
3 ENTER TEXT, GRAPHICS, & CONTENT CONTROLS | 4 PROTECT FORM | 5 USE FORM

The following steps change the page color. *Why? This online form uses a shade of gold for the page color (background color) so that the form is more visually appealing.*

1

• Click the Page Color button (Design tab | Page Background group) to display the Page Color gallery.

• Point to 'Gold, Accent 3' (seventh color in the first row) in the Page Color gallery to display a live preview of the selected background color (Figure 10–9).

Experiment

• Point to various colors in the Page Color gallery and watch the page color change in the document window.

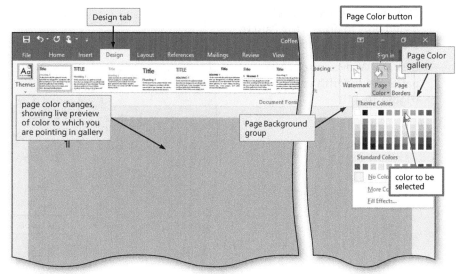

Figure 10–9

2

- Click 'Gold, Accent 3' to change the page color to the selected color.

Q&A Do page colors print?
When you change the page color, it appears only on the screen. Changing the page color does not affect a printed document.

To Add a Pattern Fill Effect to a Page Color

When you changed the page color in the previous steps, Word placed a solid color on the screen. The following steps add a pattern to the page color. **Why?** *For this online form, the solid background color is a little too bold. To soften the color, you can add a pattern to it.*

1

- Click the Page Color button (Design tab | Page Background group) to display the Page Color gallery (Figure 10–10).

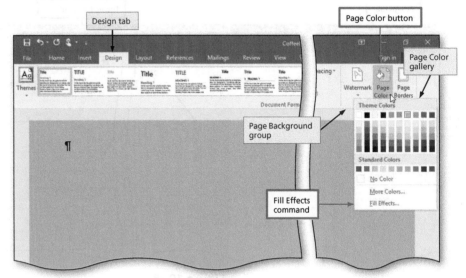

Figure 10–10

2

- Click Fill Effects in the Page Color gallery to display the Fill Effects dialog box.

- Click the Pattern tab (Fill Effects dialog box) to display the Pattern sheet in the dialog box.

- Click the Weave pattern (sixth pattern in the fifth row) to select it (Figure 10–11).

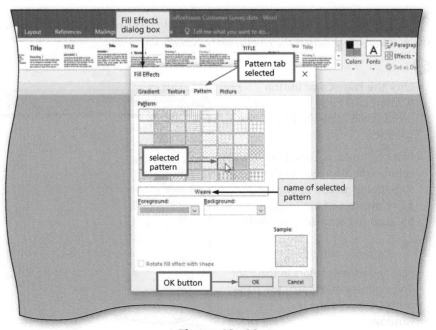

Figure 10–11

3
- Click the OK button to add the selected pattern to the current page color (Figure 10–12).

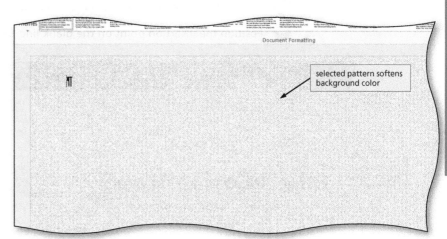

selected pattern softens background color

Figure 10–12

Enter Content in the Online Form

The next step in creating the online form in this module is to enter the text, graphics, and content controls in the document. The following sections describe this process.

To Enter and Format Text

The following steps enter the text at the top of the online form.

1 Type **Ellie's Coffee Stop** and then press the ENTER key.

2 Type **Delicious Refreshments, Fast Service, Reasonable Prices!** and then press the ENTER key.

3 Type **Customer Survey** and then press the ENTER key.

4 Type **Please fill in the form below, save the filled-in form, and email it to survey@ellies.com.** and then press the ENTER key.

If requested by your instructor, change the name, ellies, in the email address to your name.

Q&A | Why did the email address change color?
In this document theme, the color for a hyperlink is a shade of aqua. When you pressed the ENTER key, Word automatically formatted the hyperlink in this color. Later in this module, you will change the color of the hyperlink.

5 Format the characters on the first line to 28-point Berlin Sans FB Demi font with the color of Orange, Accent 2, Darker 50% and then remove space after the paragraph (spacing after should be 0 pt).

6 Format the characters on the second line to italic with the color of Purple, Accent 5, Darker 25%.

7 Format the characters on the third line to 16-point bold font with the color of Brown, Accent 6, Darker 50% and center the text on the line. Remove space before and after this paragraph (spacing before and after should be 0 pt).

8 Center the text on the fourth line and increase the spacing after this line to 12 point.

9 Position the insertion point on the blank line below the text (Figure 10–13).

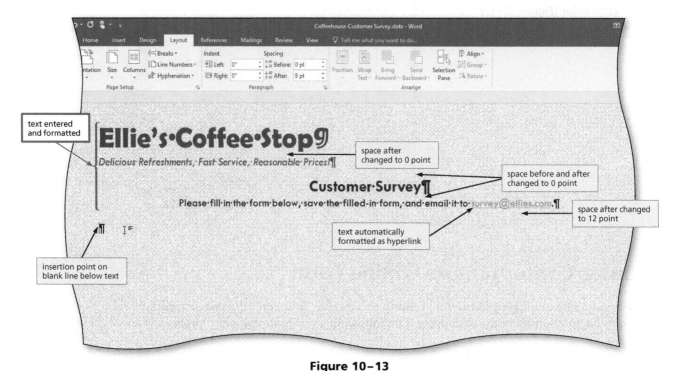

Figure 10–13

BTW
Ordering Graphics
If you have multiple graphics displaying on the screen and would like them to overlap, you can change their stacking order by using the Bring Forward and Send Backward arrows (Picture Tools Format tab | Arrange group). The 'Bring to Front' command on the Bring Forward menu displays the selected object at the top of the stack, and the 'Send to Back' command on the Send Backward menu displays the selected object at the bottom of the stack. The Bring Forward and Send Backward commands each move the graphic forward or backward one layer in the stack. These commands also are available through the shortcut menu that is displayed when you right-click a graphic.

To Insert an Image and Scale It

The next step is to insert an image of a coffee cup in the form. Because the graphic's original size is too large, you will reduce its size. The following steps insert and scale a graphic.

1 Display the Insert tab. Click the Online Pictures button (Insert tab | Illustrations group) to display the Insert Pictures dialog box.

2 Type **coffee cup** in the Search box (Insert Pictures dialog box) and then click the Search button to display a list of images that matches the entered search text.

3 Click the coffee cup image that matches the one in Figure 10–14 (or a similar image) and then click the Insert button to download the image, close the dialog box, and insert the graphic in the document at the location of the insertion point.

Q&A What if I cannot locate the same image?
Click the Cancel button and then close the Insert Pictures dialog box. Click the From File button (Insert tab | Illustrations group) to display the Insert Picture dialog box, navigate to the Colorful-Coffee-Circles-6-2400px.png file on the Data Files (Insert Picture dialog box), and click the Insert button to insert the picture.

4 With the graphic still selected, use the Shape Height and Shape Width boxes (Picture Tools Format tab | Size group) to change the graphic height to approximately 1.3" and width to 1.03", respectively (shown in Figure 10–14).

Q&A What if the Picture Tools Format tab is not the active tab on my ribbon?
Double-click the graphic, or click the Picture Tools Format tab on the ribbon.

To Format a Graphic's Text Wrapping

Word inserted the coffee cup image as an inline graphic, that is, as part of the current paragraph. In this online form, the graphic should be positioned to the right of the company name (shown in Figure 10–1 at the beginning of this module). Thus, the graphic should be a floating graphic instead of an inline graphic. The text in the online form should not wrap around the graphic. Thus, the graphic should float in front of the text. The following steps change the graphic's text wrapping to In Front of Text.

1 With the graphic selected, click the Layout Options button attached to the graphic to display the LAYOUT OPTIONS gallery (Figure 10–14).

2 Click 'In Front of Text' in the LAYOUT OPTIONS gallery to change the graphic from inline to floating with the selected wrapping style.

3 Click the Close button in the LAYOUT OPTIONS gallery to close the gallery.

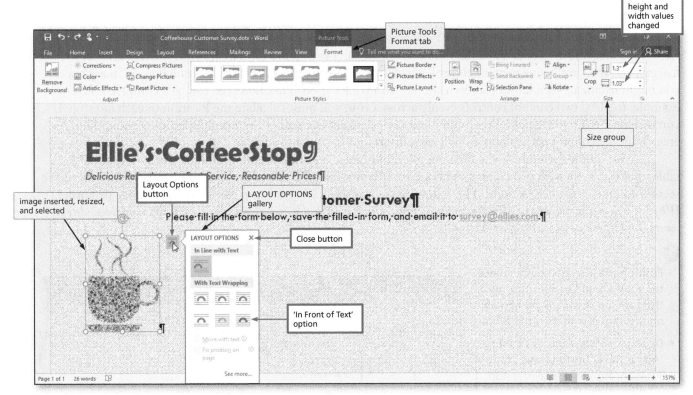

Figure 10–14

To Move a Graphic

The final step associated with the graphic is to move it so that it is positioned on the right side of the online form. The following steps move a graphic.

1 If necessary, scroll to display the top of the form in the document window.

2 Drag the graphic to the location shown in Figure 10–15.

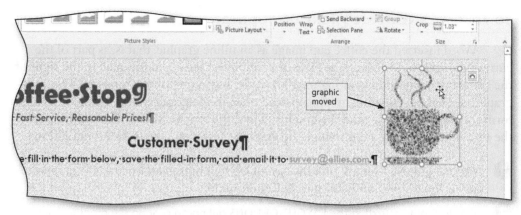

Figure 10–15

To Use a Table to Control Layout

The first line of data entry in the form consists of the First Name content control, which begins at the left margin, and the Last Name content control, which begins at the center point of the same line. At first glance, you might decide to set a tab stop at each content control location. This, however, can be a complex task. For example, to place two content controls evenly across a row, you must calculate the location of each tab stop. If you insert a 2 × 1 table instead, Word automatically calculates the size of two evenly spaced columns. Thus, to enter multiple content controls on a single line, insert a table to control layout.

In this online form, the line containing the First Name and Last Name content controls will be a 2 × 1 table, that is, a table with two columns and one row. By inserting a 2 × 1 table, Word automatically positions the second column at the center point. The following steps insert a 2 × 1 table in the form and remove its border. **Why?** *When you insert a table, Word automatically surrounds it with a border. Because you are using the tables solely to control layout, you do not want the table borders visible.*

1
- Position the insertion point where the table should be inserted, in this case, on the blank paragraph mark below the text on the form.
- Display the Insert tab. Click the 'Add a Table' button (Insert tab | Tables group) to display the Add a Table gallery (Figure 10–16).

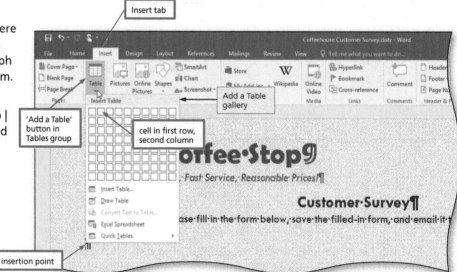

Figure 10–16

2
- Click the cell in the first row and second column of the grid to insert an empty 2 × 1 table at the location of the insertion point.
- Select the table.

Q&A

How do I select a table?
Point somewhere in the table and then click the table move handle that appears in the upper-left corner of the table (or, if using touch, tap the Select Table button (Table Tools Layout tab | Table group) and then tap Select Table on the Select Table menu).

- If necessary, display the Table Tools Design tab.

- Click the Borders arrow (Table Tools Design tab | Borders group) to display the Borders gallery (Figure 10–17).

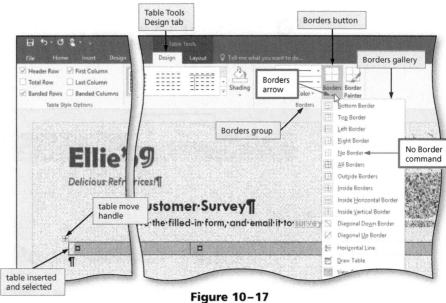

Figure 10–17

3

- Click No Border in the Borders gallery to remove the borders from the table.

4

- Click the first cell of the table to remove the selection (Figure 10–18).

Q&A

My screen does not display the end-of-cell marks. Why not?
Display formatting marks by clicking the 'Show/Hide ¶' button (Home tab | Paragraph group).

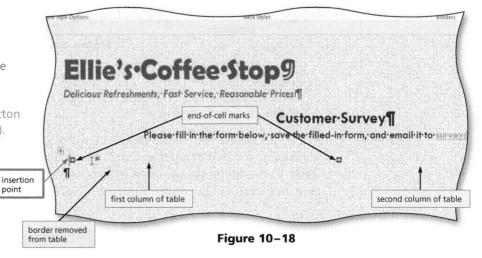

Figure 10–18

Other Ways

1. Click 'Add a Table' button (Insert tab | Tables group), click Insert Table in Add a Table gallery, enter number of columns and rows, click OK button (Insert Table dialog box)

To Show Table Gridlines

When you remove the borders from a table, you no longer can see the individual cells in the table. To help identify the location of cells, you can display **gridlines**, which show cell outlines on the screen. The following steps show gridlines.

1 If necessary, position the insertion point in a table cell.

2 Display the Table Tools Layout tab.

3   If gridlines do not show already, click the 'View Table Gridlines' button (Table Tools Layout tab | Table group) to show table gridlines on the screen (Figure 10–19).

Q&A   Do table gridlines print?
No. Gridlines are formatting marks that show only on the screen. Gridlines help users easily identify cells, rows, and columns in borderless tables.

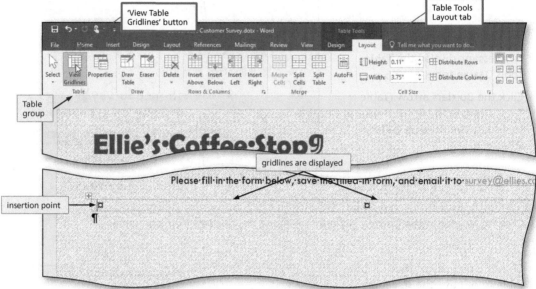

Figure 10–19

Content Controls

To add data entry fields in a Word form, you insert content controls. Word includes nine different content controls you can insert in your online forms. Table 10–1 outlines the use of each of these controls. The following sections insert content controls in the online form for the project in this module.

Table 10–1 Content Controls		
Type	**Icon**	**Use**
Building Block Gallery		User selects a built-in building block from the gallery.
Check Box		User selects or deselects a check box.
Combo Box		User types text entry or selects one item from a list of choices.
Date Picker		User interacts with a calendar to select a date or types a date in the placeholder.
Drop-Down List		User selects one item from a list of choices.
Picture		User inserts a drawing, a shape, a picture, image, or a SmartArt graphic.
Plain Text	Aa	User enters text, which may not be formatted.
Repeating Section		Users can instruct Word to create a duplicate of the content control.
Rich Text	Aa	User enters text and, if desired, may format the entered text.

How do you determine the correct content control to use for each data entry field?

For each data entry field, decide which content control best maps to the type of data the field will contain. The field specifications for the fields in this module's online form are listed below:

- The First Name, Last Name, and Other Beverages data entry fields will contain text. The first two will be plain text content controls and the last will be a rich text content control.

- The Frequency of Visits data entry field must contain one of these four values: Daily, Weekly, Occasionally, Rarely. This field will be a drop-down list content control.

- The Fresh Brewed, Latte, Cappuccino, Smoothie, and Other Beverage data entry fields will be check boxes that the user can select or deselect.

- The Beverage Rating data entry field can contain one of these four values: Excellent, Good, Fair, and Poor. In addition, users should be able to enter their own value in this data entry field if none of these four values is applicable. A combo box content control will be used for this field.

- The Today's Date data entry field should contain only a valid date value. Thus, this field will be a date picker content control.

To Show the Developer Tab

1 SAVE DOCUMENT TEMPLATE | 2 SET FORM FORMATS FOR TEMPLATE
3 ENTER TEXT, GRAPHICS, & CONTENT CONTROLS | 4 PROTECT FORM | 5 USE FORM

To create a form in Word, you use buttons on the Developer tab. The following steps display the Developer tab on the ribbon. *Why? Because it allows you to perform more advanced tasks not required by everyday Word users, the Developer tab does not appear on the ribbon by default.*

- Open the Backstage view (Figure 10–20).

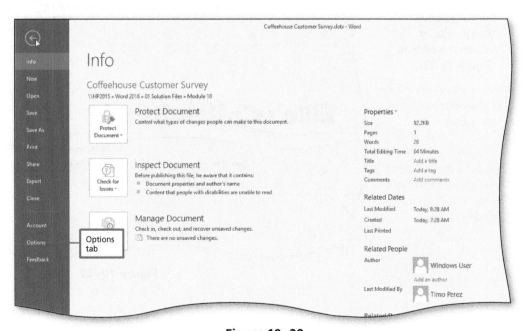

Figure 10–20

2

- Click the Options tab in the left pane of the Backstage view to display the Word Options dialog box.

- Click Customize Ribbon in the left pane (Word Options dialog box) to display associated options in the right pane.

- Place a check mark in the Developer check box in the Main Tabs list (Figure 10–21).

Q&A What are the plus symbols to the left of each tab name?
Clicking the plus symbol expands to show the groups.

Can I show or hide any tab in this list?
Yes. Place a check mark in the check box to show the tab, or remove the check mark to hide the tab.

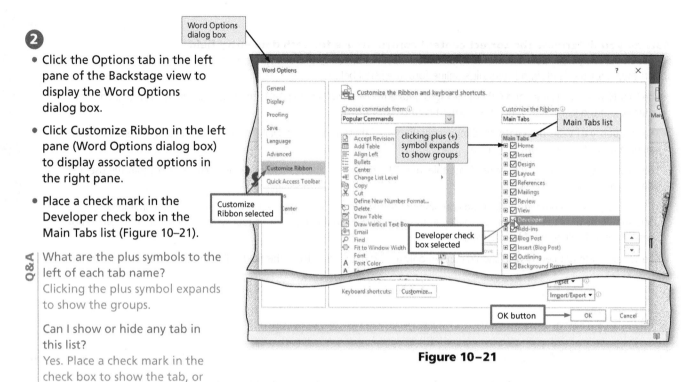

Figure 10–21

3

- Click the OK button to show the Developer tab on the ribbon (Figure 10–22).

Q&A How do I remove the Developer tab from the ribbon?
Follow these same steps, except remove the check mark from the Developer check box (Word Options dialog box).

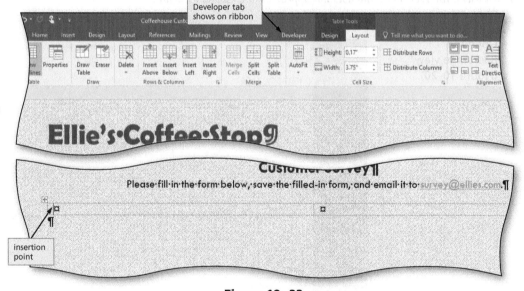

Figure 10–22

To Insert a Plain Text Content Control

1 SAVE DOCUMENT TEMPLATE | 2 SET FORM FORMATS FOR TEMPLATE
3 ENTER TEXT, GRAPHICS, & CONTENT CONTROLS | **4 PROTECT FORM** | **5 USE FORM**

The first item that a user enters in the Customer Survey is his or her first name. Because the first name entry contains text that the user should not format, this online form uses a plain text content control for the First Name data entry field. The following steps enter the label, First name:, followed by a plain text content control. *Why? The label, First name:, is displayed to the left of the plain text content control. To improve readability, a colon or some other character often separates a label from the content control.*

- With the insertion point in the first cell of the table as shown in Figure 10–22, type **First name:** as the label for the content control.
- Press the SPACEBAR (Figure 10–23).

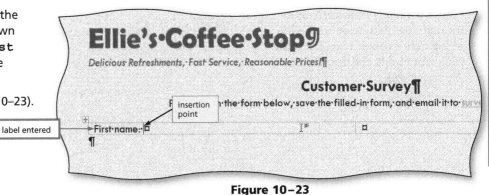

Figure 10–23

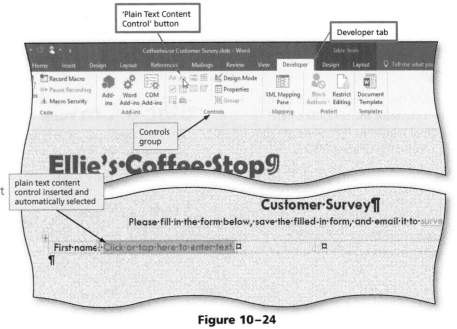

Figure 10–24

- Display the Developer tab.
- Click the 'Plain Text Content Control' button (Developer tab | Controls group) to insert a plain text content control at the location of the insertion point (Figure 10–24).

Q&A

Is the plain text content control similar to the content controls that I have used in templates installed with Word, such as in the letter, memo, and resume templates? Yes. The content controls you insert through the Developer tab have the same functionality as the content controls in the templates installed with Word.

To Edit Placeholder Text

1 SAVE DOCUMENT TEMPLATE | 2 SET FORM FORMATS FOR TEMPLATE
3 ENTER TEXT, GRAPHICS, & CONTENT CONTROLS | 4 PROTECT FORM | 5 USE FORM

A content control displays **placeholder text**, which instructs the user how to enter values in the content control. The default placeholder text for a plain text content control is the instruction, Click or tap here to enter text. The following steps edit the placeholder text for the plain text content control just entered. *Why? You can change the wording in the placeholder text so that it is more instructional or applicable to the current form.*

- With the plain text content control selected (shown in Figure 10–24), click the Design Mode button (Developer tab | Controls group) to turn on Design mode, which displays tags at the beginning and ending of the placeholder text (Figure 10–25).

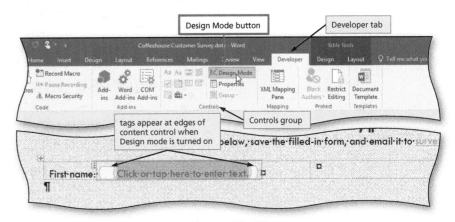

Figure 10–25

• Even if it already is selected, drag through the placeholder text, Click or tap here to enter text., because you want to edit the instruction (Figure 10–26).

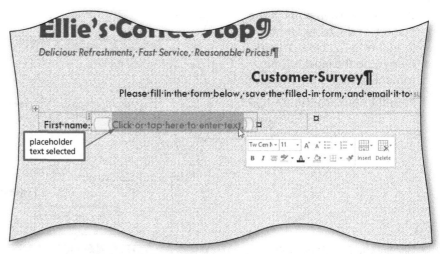

Figure 10–26

• Edit the placeholder text so that it contains the text, Click here and type your first name., as the instruction (Figure 10–27).

Q&A What if the placeholder text wraps to the next line?
Because of the tags at each edge of the placeholder text, the entered text may wrap in the table cell. Once you turn off Design mode, the placeholder text should fit on a single line. If it does not, you can adjust the font size of the placeholder text to fit.

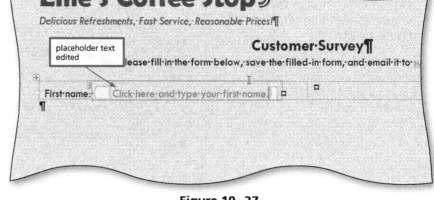

Figure 10–27

4

• Click the Design Mode button (Developer tab | Controls group) to turn off Design mode (Figure 10–28).

Q&A What if I notice an error in the placeholder text?
Follow these steps to turn on Design mode, correct the error, and then turn off Design mode.

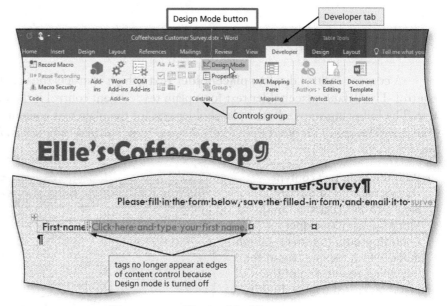

Figure 10–28

To Change the Properties of a Plain Text Content Control

You can change a variety of properties to customize content controls. The following steps change the properties of a plain text content control. *Why? In this form, you assign a tag name to a content control for later identification. You also apply a style to the content control to define how text will look as a user types data or makes selections, and you lock the content control so that a user cannot delete the content control during the data entry process.*

1

- With the content control selected, click the Control Properties button (Developer tab | Controls group) to display the Content Control Properties dialog box (Figure 10–29).

Q&A How do I know the content control is selected?
A selected content control is surrounded by an outline. It also may be shaded.

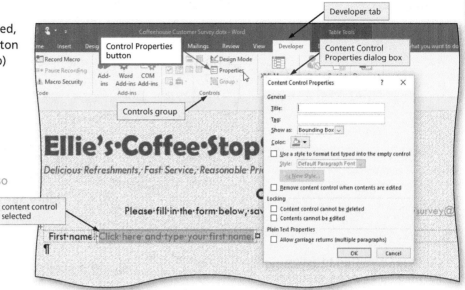

Figure 10–29

2

- Type **First Name** in the Tag text box (Content Control Properties dialog box).

- Place a check mark in the 'Use a style to format text typed into the empty control' check box so that the Style box becomes active.

- Click the Style arrow to display the Style list (Figure 10–30).

Q&A Why leave the Title text box empty?
When you click a content control in a preexisting Word template, the content control may display an identifier in its top-left corner. For templates that you create, you can instruct Word to display this identifier, called the Title, by changing the properties of the content control. In this form, you do not want the identifier to appear.

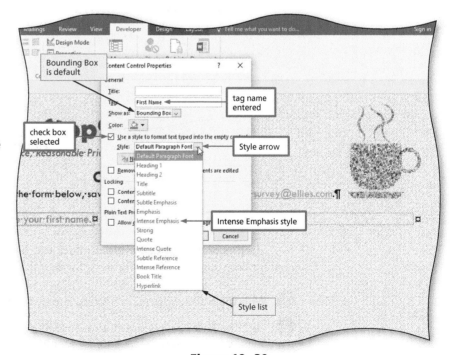

Figure 10–30

What is a bounding box?
A bounding box is a rectangle that surrounds the content control on the form. You can show content controls with a bounding box, with tags, or with no visible markings.

- Click Intense Emphasis to select the style for the content control.

- Place a check mark in the 'Content control cannot be deleted' check box so that the user cannot delete the content control (Figure 10–31).

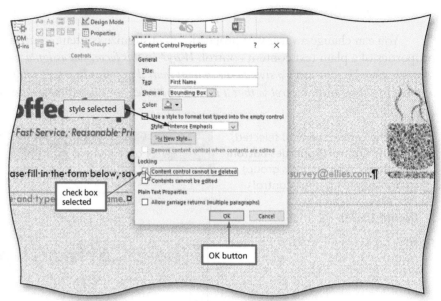

Figure 10–31

- Click the OK button to assign the modified properties to the content control (Figure 10–32).

Q&A

Why is the placeholder text not formatted to the selected style, Intense Emphasis, in this case? When you apply a style to a content control, as described in these steps, the style is applied to the text the user types during the data entry process. To change the appearance of the placeholder text, apply a style using the Home tab as described in the next steps.

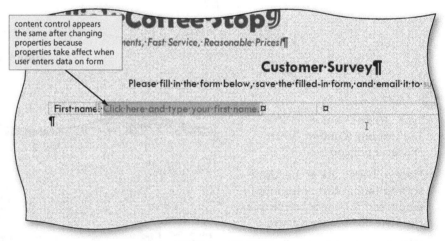

Figure 10–32

To Format Placeholder Text

In this online form, the placeholder text has the same style applied to it as the content control. The following steps format placeholder text.

1. With the placeholder text selected, display the Home tab.

2. Click the Styles gallery down arrow (Home tab | Styles group) to scroll through the Styles gallery to display the Intense Emphasis style or click the More button (Home tab | Styles group).

3. Click Intense Emphasis in the Styles gallery (even if it is selected already) to apply the selected style to the selected placeholder text (Figure 10–33).

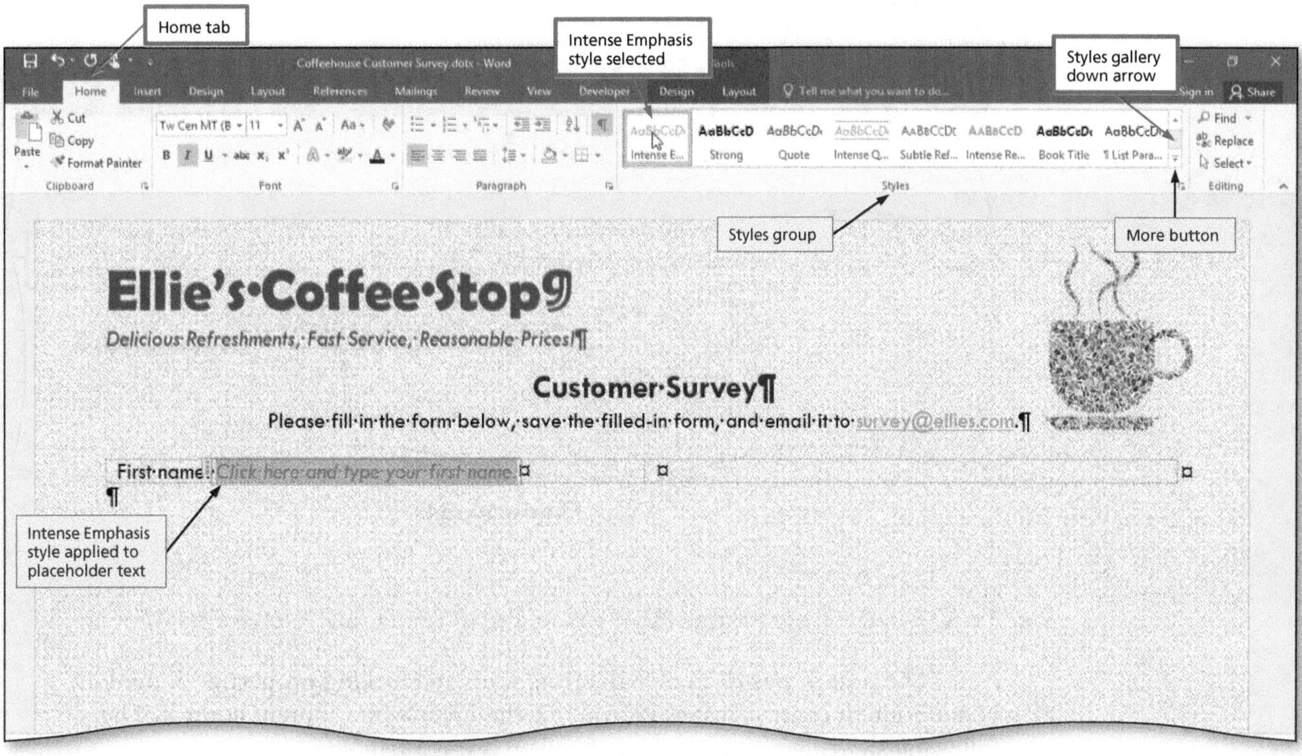

Figure 10–33

To Insert Another Plain Text Content Control and Edit Its Placeholder Text

The second item that a user enters in the Customer Survey is his or her last name. The steps for entering the last name content control are similar to those for the first name, because the last name also is a plain text content control. The following steps enter the label, Last Name:, and then insert a plain text content control and edit its placeholder text.

1 Position the insertion point in the second cell (column) in the table.

2 With the insertion point in the second cell of the table, type **Last name:** as the label for the content control and then press the SPACEBAR.

3 Display the Developer tab. Click the 'Plain Text Content Control' button (Developer tab | Controls group) to insert a plain text content control at the location of the insertion point.

4 With the plain text content control selected, click the Design Mode button (Developer tab | Controls group) to turn on Design mode (Figure 10–34).

5 Select the placeholder text to be changed.

6 Edit the placeholder text so that it contains the text, Click here and type your last name., as the instruction.

7 Click the Design Mode button (Developer tab | Controls group) to turn off Design mode.

BTW
Deleting Content Controls
To delete a content control, right-click it and then click 'Remove Content Control' on the shortcut menu.

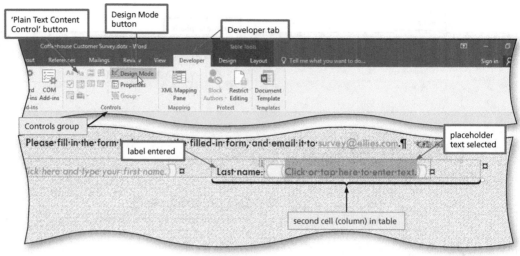

Figure 10–34

To Change the Properties of a Plain Text Content Control

The next step is to change the title, style, and locking properties of the Last Name content control, just as you did for the First Name content control. The following steps change properties of a plain text content control.

1 With the content control selected, click the Control Properties button (Developer tab | Controls group) to display the Content Control Properties dialog box.

2 Type `Last Name` in the Tag text box (Content Control Properties dialog box).

3 Place a check mark in the 'Use a style to format text typed into the empty control' check box to activate the Style box.

4 Click the Style arrow and then select Intense Emphasis in the list to specify the style for the content control.

5 Place a check mark in the 'Content control cannot be deleted' check box (Figure 10–35).

6 Click the OK button to assign the properties to the content control.

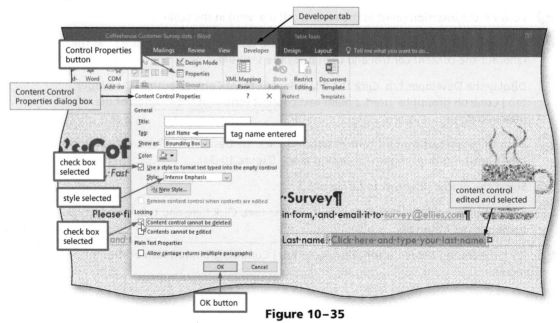

Figure 10–35

To Format Placeholder Text

As with the placeholder text for the first name, the placeholder text for the last name should use the Intense Emphasis style. The following steps format placeholder text.

1 With the last name placeholder text selected, display the Home tab.

2 Locate and select the Intense Emphasis style in the Styles gallery (Home tab | Styles group) to apply the selected style to the selected placeholder text.

To Increase Space before a Paragraph

The next step in creating this online form is to increase space before a paragraph so that the space below the table is consistent with the space between other elements on the form. The following steps increase space before a paragraph.

1 Position the insertion point on the blank line below the table.

2 Display the Layout tab.

3 Change the value in the Spacing Before box (Layout tab | Paragraph group) to 8 pt to increase the space between the table and the paragraph (shown in Figure 10–36).

To Insert a Drop-Down List Content Control

1 SAVE DOCUMENT TEMPLATE | 2 SET FORM FORMATS FOR TEMPLATE
3 ENTER TEXT, GRAPHICS, & CONTENT CONTROLS | 4 PROTECT FORM | 5 USE FORM

In the online form in this module, the user selects from one of these four choices for the Frequency of Visits content control: Daily, Weekly, Occasionally, or Rarely. The following steps insert a drop-down list content control. **Why?** *To present a set of choices to a user in the form of a drop-down list, from which the user selects one, insert a drop-down list content control. To view the set of choices, the user clicks the arrow at the right edge of the content control.*

1
- With the insertion point positioned on the blank paragraph mark below the First Name content control, using either the ruler or the Layout tab, change the left indent to 0.06" so that the entered text aligns with the text immediately above it (that is, the F in First).
- Type **How often do you visit our coffeehouse?** and then press the SPACEBAR.

2
- Display the Developer tab.
- Click the 'Drop-Down List Content Control' button (Developer tab | Controls group) to insert a drop-down list content control at the location of the insertion point (Figure 10–36).

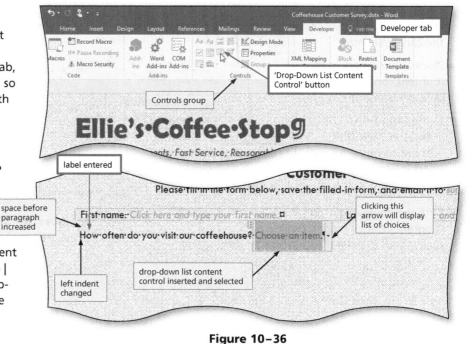

Figure 10–36

To Edit Placeholder Text

The following steps edit the placeholder text for the drop-down list content control.

1 If necessary, display the Developer tab. With the drop-down list content control selected, click the Design Mode button (Developer tab | Controls group) to turn on Design mode.

2 Edit the placeholder text so that it contains this instruction, which contains two separate sentences: Click here. Click arrow and select from list.

3 Click the Design Mode button (Developer tab | Controls group) to turn off Design mode.

To Change the Properties of a Drop-Down List Content Control

1 SAVE DOCUMENT TEMPLATE | 2 SET FORM FORMATS FOR TEMPLATE
3 ENTER TEXT, GRAPHICS, & CONTENT CONTROLS | **4 PROTECT FORM** | **5 USE FORM**

The following steps change the properties of a drop-down list content control. *Why? In addition to identifying a tag, selecting a style, and locking the drop-down list content control, you can specify the choices that will be displayed when a user clicks the arrow to the right of the content control.*

- With the drop-down list content control selected, click the Control Properties button (Developer tab | Controls group) to display the Content Control Properties dialog box.

- Type **Frequency of Visits** in the Tag text box (Content Control Properties dialog box).

- Place a check mark in the 'Use a style to format text typed into the empty control' check box to activate the Style box.

- Click the Style arrow and then select Intense Emphasis in the list to specify the style for the content control.

- Place a check mark in the 'Content control cannot be deleted' check box.

- In the Drop-Down List Properties area, click 'Choose an item.' to select it (Figure 10–37).

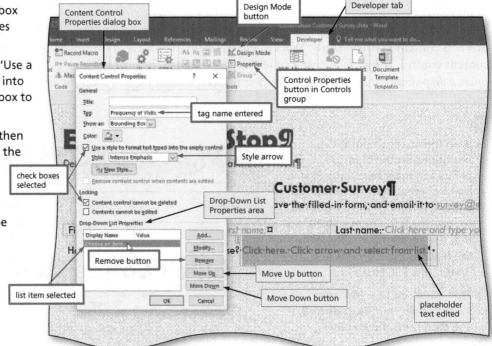

Figure 10–37

- Click the Remove button (Content Control Properties dialog box) to delete the 'Choose an item.' entry.

Q&A Why delete the 'Choose an item.' entry?
If you leave it in the list, it will appear as the first item in the list when the user clicks the content control arrow. You do not want it in the list, so you delete it.

Can I delete any entry in a drop-down list using the Remove button?
Yes, select the entry in this dialog box and then click the Remove button. You also can rearrange the order of entries in a list by selecting the entry and then clicking the Move Up or Move Down buttons.

- Click the Add button to display the Add Choice dialog box.

- Type **Daily** in the Display Name text box (Add Choice dialog box), and notice that Word automatically enters the same text in the Value text box (Figure 10–38).

Q&A What is the difference between a display name and a value?
Often, they are the same, which is why when you type the display name, Word automatically enters the same text in the Value text box. Sometimes, however, you may want to store a shorter or different value. If the display name is long, entering shorter values makes it easier for separate programs to analyze and interpret entered data.

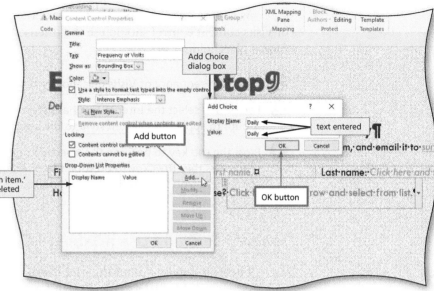

Figure 10–38

- Click the OK button (Add Choice dialog box) to add the entered display name and value to the list of choices in the Drop-Down List Properties area (Content Control Properties dialog box).

- Click the Add button to display the Add Choice dialog box.

- Type **Weekly** in the Display Name text box.

- Click the OK button to add the entry to the list.

- Click the Add button to display the Add Choice dialog box.

- Type **Occasionally** in the Display Name text box.

- Click the OK button to add the entry to the list.

- Click the Add button to display the Add Choice dialog box.

- Type **Rarely** in the Display Name text box.

- Click the OK button to add the entry to the list (Figure 10–39).

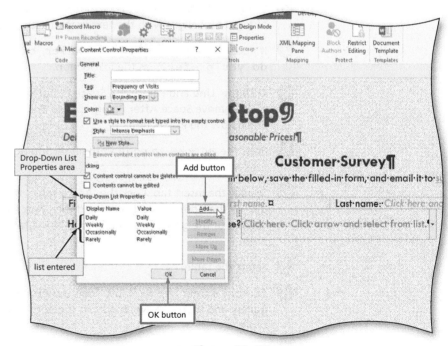

Figure 10–39

- Click the OK button (Content Control Properties dialog box) to change the content control properties.

Q&A What if I want to change an entry in the drop-down list?
You would select the drop-down list content control, click the Control Properties button (Developer tab | Controls group) to display the Content Control Properties dialog box, select the entry to change, click the Modify button, adjust the entry, and then click the OK button.

To Format Placeholder Text

As with the previous placeholder text, the placeholder text for the Frequency of Visits content control should use the Intense Emphasis style. The following steps format placeholder text.

1 With the Frequency of Visits placeholder text selected, display the Home tab.

2 Locate and select the Intense Emphasis style in the Styles gallery (Home tab | Styles group) to apply the selected style to the selected placeholder text.

3 Press the END key to position the insertion point at the end of the current line and then press the ENTER key to position the insertion point below the Frequency of Visits content control. If necessary, turn off italics.

To Enter Text and Use a Table to Control Layout

The next step is to enter the user instructions for the check box content controls and insert a 4 × 1 borderless table so that four evenly spaced check boxes can be displayed horizontally below the check box instructions. The following steps enter text and insert a borderless table.

1 With the insertion point positioned on the paragraph below the Frequency of Visits content control, click Normal in the Styles gallery (Home tab | Styles group) to format the current paragraph to the Normal style.

2 Using either the ruler or the Layout tab, change the left indent to 0.06" so that the entered text aligns with the text immediately above it (that is, the H in How).

3 If necessary, turn off italics. Type **Which of our handcrafted beverages do you prefer?** as the instruction.

4 Click the 'Line and Paragraph Spacing' button (Home tab | Paragraph group) and then click 'Remove Space After Paragraph' so that the check boxes will appear one physical line below the instructions.

5 Press the ENTER key to position the insertion point on the line below the check box instructions.

6 Display the Insert tab. Click the 'Add a Table' button (Insert tab | Tables group) to display the Add a Table gallery and then click the cell in the first row and fourth column of the grid to insert an empty 4 × 1 table at the location of the insertion point.

7 Select the table.

8 Click the Borders arrow (Table Tools Design tab | Borders group) to display the Borders gallery and then click No Border in the Borders gallery to remove the borders from the table.

9 Click the first cell of the table to remove the selection (shown in Figure 10–40).

To Insert a Check Box Content Control

The following step inserts the first check box content control. *Why? In the online form in this module, the user can select up to five check boxes: Fresh brewed, Latte, Cappuccino, Smoothie, and Other.*

1

- Position the insertion point at the location for the check box content control, in this case, the leftmost cell in the 4 × 1 table.

- Display the Developer tab.

- Click the 'Check Box Content Control' button (Developer tab | Controls group) to insert a check box content control at the location of the insertion point (Figure 10–40).

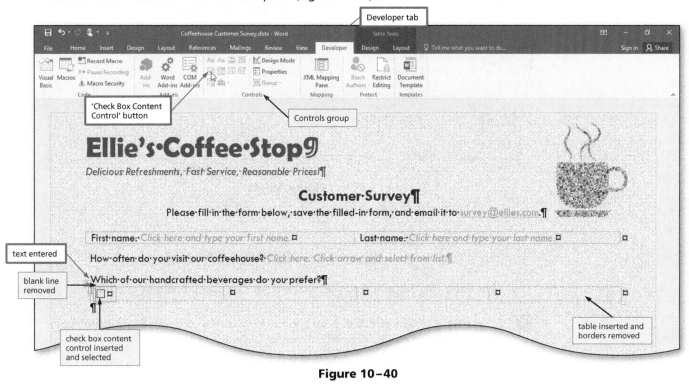

Figure 10–40

To Change the Properties of a Check Box Content Control

The next step is to change the title and locking properties of the content control. The following steps change properties of a check box content control.

1 With the content control selected, click the Control Properties button (Developer tab | Controls group) to display the Content Control Properties dialog box.

2 Type **Fresh Brewed** in the Tag text box (Content Control Properties dialog box).

3 Click the Show as arrow and then select None in the list, because you do not want a border surrounding the check box content control.

4 Place a check mark in the 'Content control cannot be deleted' check box (Figure 10–41).

5 Click the OK button to assign the properties to the selected content control.

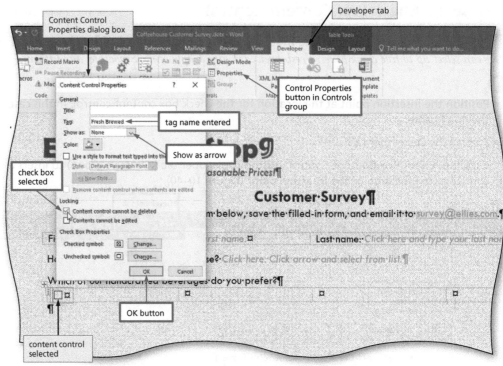

Figure 10–41

To Add a Label to a Check Box Content Control

The following steps add a label to the right of a check box content control.

1 With content control selected, press the END key twice to position the insertion point after the inserted check box content control.

2 Press the SPACEBAR and then type **Fresh brewed** as the check box label (Figure 10–42).

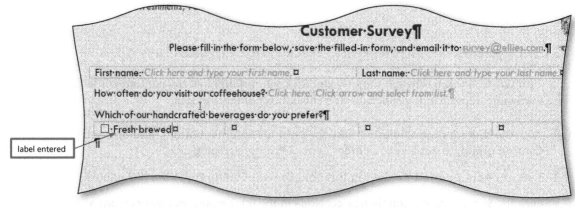

Figure 10–42

To Insert Additional Check Box Content Controls

The following steps insert the remaining check box content controls and their labels.

1 Press the TAB key to position the insertion point in the next cell, which is the location for the next check box content control.

2 Click the 'Check Box Content Control' button (Developer tab | Controls group) to insert a check box content control at the location of the insertion point.

3 With the content control selected, click the Control Properties button (Developer tab | Controls group) to display the Content Control Properties dialog box.

4 Type **Latte** in the Tag text box (Content Control Properties dialog box).

5 Click the Show as arrow and then select None in the list because you do not want a border surrounding the check box content control.

6 Place a check mark in the 'Content control cannot be deleted' check box and then click the OK button to assign the properties to the selected content control.

7 With content control selected, press the END key twice to position the insertion point after the inserted check box content control.

8 Press the SPACEBAR and then type **Latte** as the check box label.

9 Repeat Steps 1 through 8 for the Cappuccino and Smoothie check box content controls.

10 Position the insertion point on the blank line below the 4 × 1 table and then repeat Steps 1 through 8 for the Other Beverage check box content control, which has the label, Other (please specify):, followed by the SPACEBAR. If necessary, using either the ruler or the Layout tab, change the left indent so that check box above is aligned with the check box below (Figure 10–43).

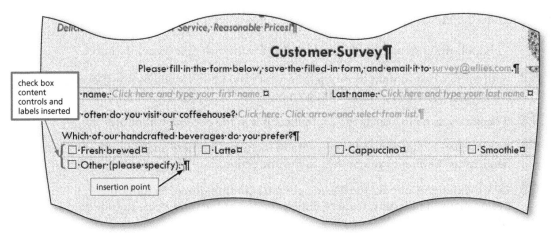

Figure 10–43

To Insert a Rich Text Content Control

The next step is to insert the content control that enables users to type in any other beverages they prefer. The difference between a plain text and rich text content control is that the users can format text as they enter it in the rich text content control. The following step inserts a rich text content control. *Why? Because you want to allow users to format the text they enter in the Other Beverage content control, you use the rich text content control.*

- If necessary, position the insertion point at the location for the rich text content control (shown in Figure 10–43).

- If necessary, display the Developer tab.

- Click the 'Rich Text Content Control' button (Developer tab | Controls group) to insert a rich text content control at the location of the insertion point (Figure 10–44).

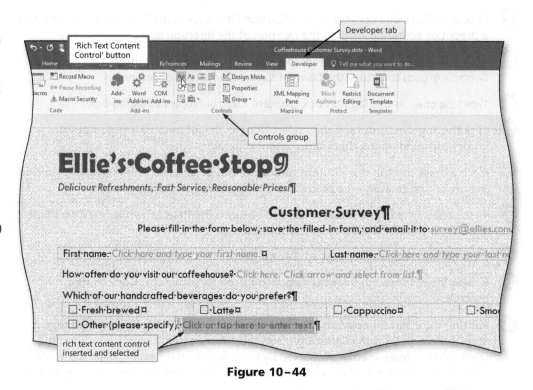

Figure 10–44

To Edit Placeholder Text

The following steps edit placeholder text for the rich text content control.

1 With the rich text content control selected, click the Design Mode button (Developer tab | Controls group) to turn on Design mode.

2 If necessary, scroll to display the content control in the document window.

3 Edit the placeholder text so that it contains the text, Click here and type other handcrafted beverages you prefer., as the instruction.

4 Click the Design Mode button (Developer tab | Controls group) to turn off Design mode. If necessary, scroll to display the top of the form in the document window.

To Change the Properties of a Rich Text Content Control

In the online form in this module, you change the same three properties for the rich text content control as for the plain text content control. That is, you enter a tag name, specify the style, and lock the content control. The following steps change the properties of the rich text content control.

1 With the content control selected, click the Control Properties button (Developer tab | Controls group) to display the Content Control Properties dialog box.

2 Type **Other Beverages** in the Tag text box (Content Control Properties dialog box).

3 Place a check mark in the 'Use a style to format text typed into the empty control' check box to activate the Style box.

4 Click the Style arrow and then select Intense Emphasis in the list to specify the style for the content control.

5 Place a check mark in the 'Content control cannot be deleted' check box (Figure 10–45).

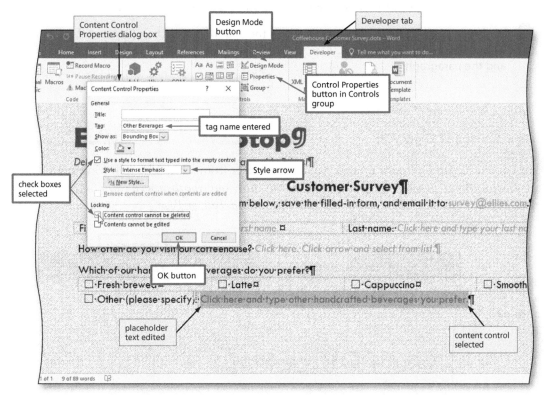

Figure 10–45

6 Click the OK button to assign the properties to the content control.

To Format Placeholder Text and Add Space before a Paragraph

The placeholder text for the Other Beverage text entry should use the Intense Emphasis style, and the space below the check boxes should be consistent with the space between other elements on the form. The next steps format placeholder text and increase space before a paragraph.

1 With the Other Beverage placeholder text selected, display the Home tab.

2 Locate and select the Intense Emphasis style in the Styles gallery (Home tab | Styles group) to apply the selected style to the selected placeholder text.

3 Press the END key to position the insertion point on the paragraph mark after the Other Beverage content control and then press the ENTER key to position the insertion point below the Other Beverage content control.

4 If necessary, display the Home tab. With the insertion point positioned on the paragraph below the Other Beverage content control, click Normal in the Styles gallery (Home tab | Styles group) to format the current paragraph to the Normal style.

5 Using either the ruler or the Layout tab, change the left indent to 0.06" so that the entered text aligns with the text two lines above it (that is, the W in Which).

6 Display the Layout tab. Change the value in the Spacing Before box (Layout tab | Paragraph group) to 8 pt to increase the space between the Other Beverage check box and the paragraph.

To Insert a Combo Box Content Control

1 SAVE DOCUMENT TEMPLATE | 2 SET FORM FORMATS FOR TEMPLATE
3 ENTER TEXT, GRAPHICS, & CONTENT CONTROLS | 4 PROTECT FORM | 5 USE FORM

In Word, a combo box content control allows a user to type text or select from a list. The following steps insert a combo box content control. *Why? In the online form in this module, users can type their own entry in the Beverage Rating content control or select from one of these four choices: Excellent, Good, Fair, or Poor.*

1
- With the insertion point positioned on the blank paragraph mark, type **How would you rate our handcrafted beverages?** and then press the SPACEBAR.

2
- Display the Developer tab.
- Click the 'Combo Box Content Control' button (Developer tab | Controls group) to insert a combo box content control at the location of the insertion point (Figure 10–46).

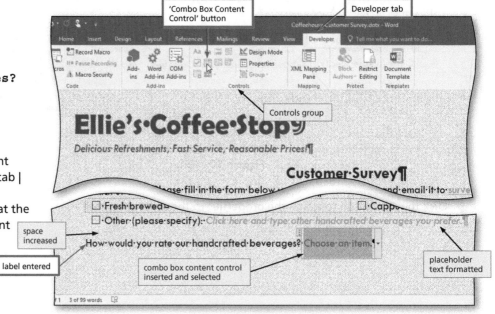

Figure 10–46

To Edit Placeholder Text

The following steps edit the placeholder text for the combo box content control.

1 With the combo box content control selected, click the Design Mode button (Developer tab | Controls group) to turn on Design mode.

2 If necessary, scroll to page 2 to display the combo box content control.

Q&A | What if the content control moves to another page?
Because Design mode displays tags, the content controls and placeholder text are not displayed in their proper positions on the screen. When you turn off Design mode, the content controls will return to their original locations and the extra page should disappear.

3 Edit the placeholder text so that it contains this instruction, which contains two sentences (Figure 10–47): Click here. Click arrow and select from list, or type your rating.

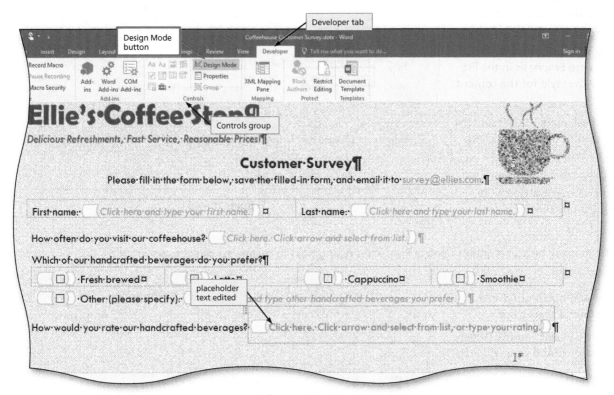

Figure 10–47

4 Click the Design Mode button (Developer tab | Controls group) to turn off Design mode.

To Change the Properties of a Combo Box Content Control

You follow similar steps to enter the list for a combo box content control as you do for the drop-down list content control. The following steps change the properties of a combo box content control. *Why? You enter the tag name, specify the style for typed text, and enter the choices for the drop-down list.*

1

- With the content control selected, click the Control Properties button (Developer tab | Controls group) to display the Content Control Properties dialog box.

- Type **Beverage Rating** in the Tag text box (Content Control Properties dialog box).

- Place a check mark in the 'Use a style to format text typed into the empty control' check box to activate the Style box.

- Click the Style arrow and then select Intense Emphasis in the list to specify the style for the content control.

- Place a check mark in the 'Content control cannot be deleted' check box.

- In the Drop-Down List Properties area, click 'Choose an item.' to select it (Figure 10–48).

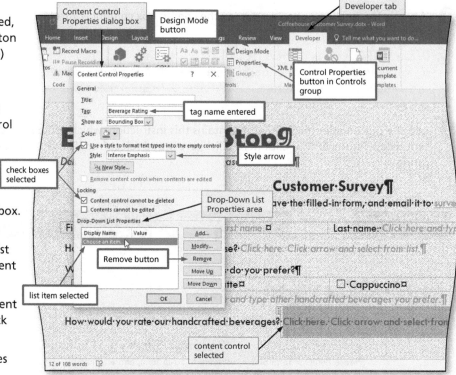

Figure 10–48

2

- Click the Remove button (Content Control Properties dialog box) to delete the selected entry.

3

- Click the Add button to display the Add Choice dialog box.

- Type **Excellent** in the Display Name text box (Add Choice dialog box).

- Click the OK button to add the entered display name to the list of choices in the Drop-Down List Properties area (Content Control Properties dialog box).

- Click the Add button and add **Good** to the list.

- Click the Add button and add **Fair** to the list.

- Click the Add button and add **Poor** to the list (Figure 10–49).

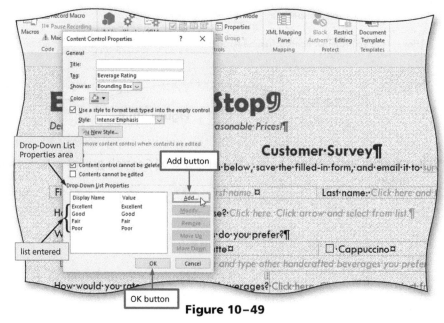

Figure 10–49

④

• Click the OK button (Content Control Properties dialog box) to change the content control properties.

◁ | How do I make adjustments to entries in the list?
Q&A | Follow the same procedures as you use to make adjustments to entries in a drop-down list content control.

To Format Placeholder Text

As with the previous placeholder text, the placeholder text for the Beverage Rating should use the Intense Emphasis style. The following steps format placeholder text.

① With the Beverage Rating placeholder text selected, display the Home tab.

② Locate and select the Intense Emphasis style in the Styles gallery (Home tab | Styles group) to apply the selected style to the selected placeholder text.

③ Press the END key to position the insertion point at the end of the current line and then press the ENTER key to position the insertion point below the Beverage Rating content control.

④ Click Normal in the Styles list (Home tab | Styles group) to format the current paragraph to the Normal style.

⑤ Using either the ruler or the Layout tab, change the left indent to 0.06" so that the entered text aligns with the text above it (that is, the H in How).

To Insert a Date Picker Content Control

1 SAVE DOCUMENT TEMPLATE | 2 SET FORM FORMATS FOR TEMPLATE
3 ENTER TEXT, GRAPHICS, & CONTENT CONTROLS | 4 **PROTECT FORM** | 5 **USE FORM**

To assist users with entering dates, Word provides a date picker content control, which displays a calendar when the user clicks the arrow to the right of the content control. Users also can enter a date directly in the content control without using the calendar. The following steps enter the label, Today's date:, and a date picker content control. *Why? The last item that users enter in the Coffeehouse Customer Survey is today's date.*

①

• With the insertion point below the Beverage Rating content control, type **Today's date:** as the label for the content control and then press the SPACEBAR.

②

• Display the Developer tab.

• Click the 'Date Picker Content Control' button (Developer tab | Controls group) to insert a date picker content control at the location of the insertion point (Figure 10–50).

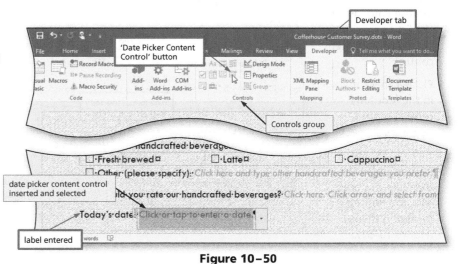

Figure 10–50

To Edit Placeholder Text

The following steps edit the placeholder text for the date picker content control.

1 With the date picker content control selected, click the Design Mode button (Developer tab | Controls group) to turn on Design mode.

2 If necessary, scroll to display the date picker content control.

3 Edit the placeholder text so that it contains this instruction, which contains two sentences: Click here. Click arrow and select today's date.

4 Click the Design Mode button (Developer tab | Controls group) to turn off Design mode.

5 If necessary, scroll to display the top of the form in the document window.

To Change the Properties of a Date Picker Content Control

1 SAVE DOCUMENT TEMPLATE | 2 SET FORM FORMATS FOR TEMPLATE
3 ENTER TEXT, GRAPHICS, & CONTENT CONTROLS | 4 PROTECT FORM | 5 USE FORM

The following steps change the properties of a date picker content control. *Why? In addition to identifying a tag name for a date picker content control, specifying a style, and locking the control, you will specify how the date will be displayed when the user selects it from the calendar.*

- With the content control selected, click the Control Properties button (Developer tab | Controls group) to display the Content Control Properties dialog box.

- Type **Today's Date** in the Tag text box.

- Place a check mark in the 'Use a style to format text typed into the empty control' check box to activate the Style box.

- Click the Style arrow and then select Intense Emphasis in the list to specify the style for the content control.

- Place a check mark in the 'Content control cannot be deleted' check box.

- In the Display the date like this area, click the desired format in the list (Figure 10–51).

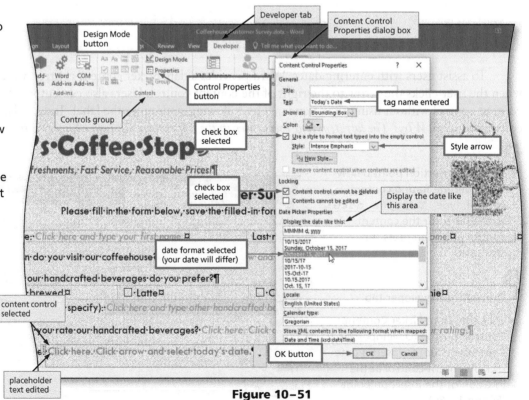

Figure 10–51

2

- Click the OK button to change the content control properties.

To Format Placeholder Text

As with the previous placeholder text, the placeholder text for today's date should use the Intense Emphasis style. The following steps format placeholder text.

1 With the today's date placeholder text selected, display the Home tab.

2 Locate and select the Intense Emphasis style in the Styles gallery (Home tab | Styles group) to apply the selected style to the selected placeholder text.

3 Press the END key to position the insertion point at the end of the current line and then press the ENTER key to position the insertion point below the Today's Date content control.

4 Click Normal in the Styles gallery (Home tab | Styles group) to format the current paragraph to the Normal style.

To Enter and Format Text

The following steps enter and format the line of text at the bottom of the online form.

1 Be sure the insertion point is on the line below the Today's Date content control.

2 Center the paragraph mark.

3 Format the text to be typed with the color of Orange, Accent 2, Darker 50%.

4 Type **Thank you for your time!**

5 Change the space before the paragraph to 18 point (Figure 10–52).

6 If the text flows to a second page, reduce spacing before paragraphs in the form so that all lines fit on a single page.

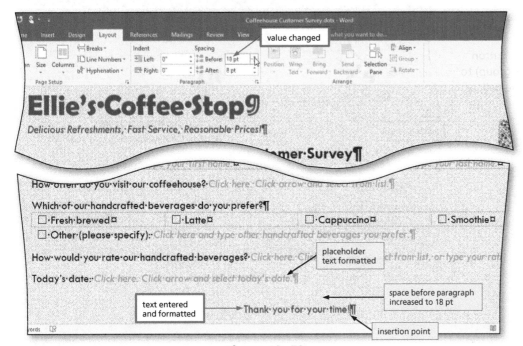

Figure 10–52

To Hide Gridlines and Formatting Marks

Because you are finished with the tables in this form and will not enter any additional tables, you will hide the gridlines. You also are finished with entering and formatting text on the screen. To make the form easier to view, you hide the formatting marks, which can clutter the screen. The following steps hide gridlines and formatting marks.

1 If necessary, position the insertion point in a table cell.

2 Display the Table Tools Layout tab. If gridlines are showing, click the 'View Table Gridlines' button (Table Tools Layout tab | Table group) to hide table gridlines.

3 Display the Home tab. If the 'Show/Hide ¶' button (Home tab | Paragraph group) is selected, click it to remove formatting marks from the screen.

4 Save the template again on the same storage location with the same file name.

Break Point: If you wish to take a break, this is a good place to do so. You can exit Word now. To resume at a later time, run Word, open the file called Coffeehouse Customer Survey, and continue following the steps from this location forward.

To Draw a Rectangle

1 SAVE DOCUMENT TEMPLATE | 2 SET FORM FORMATS FOR TEMPLATE
3 ENTER TEXT, GRAPHICS, & CONTENT CONTROLS | 4 PROTECT FORM | 5 USE FORM

The next step is to emphasize the data entry area of the form. The data entry area includes all the content controls in which a user enters data. The following steps draw a rectangle around the data entry area, and subsequent steps format the rectangle. *Why? To call attention to the data entry area of the form, this module places a rectangle around the data entry area, changes the style of the rectangle, and then adds a shadow to the rectangle.*

1

- Position the insertion point on the last line in the document (shown in Figure 10–52).

- Display the Insert tab.

- Click the 'Draw a Shape' button (Insert tab | Illustrations group) to display the Draw a Shape gallery (Figure 10–53).

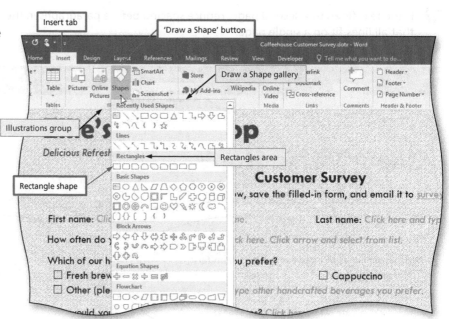

Figure 10–53

2

- Click the Rectangle shape in the Rectangles area of the Draw a Shape gallery, which removes the gallery and changes the pointer to the shape of a crosshair in the document window.

Q&A What if I am using a touch screen? Proceed to Step 5 because the shape is inserted in the document window after you tap the rectangle shape in the Draw a Shape gallery.

- Position the pointer (a crosshair) in the approximate location for the upper-left corner of the desired shape (Figure 10–54).

Figure 10–54

3

- Drag the pointer downward and rightward to form a rectangle around the data entry area, as shown in Figure 10–55.

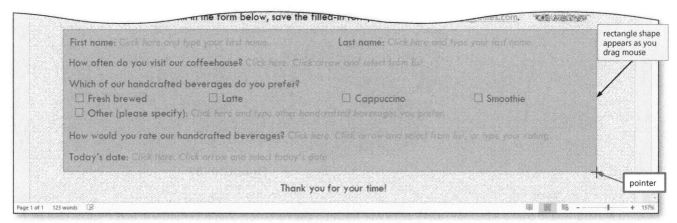

Figure 10–55

4

- Release the mouse button to draw the rectangle shape on top of the data entry area (Figure 10–56).

Q&A What happened to all the text in the data entry area?
When you draw a shape in a document, Word initially places the shape in front of, or on top of, any text in the same area. You can change the stacking order of the shape so that it is displayed behind the text. Thus, the next steps move the shape behind the text.

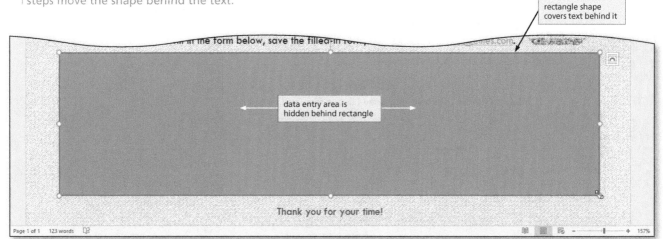

Figure 10–56

⑤

- If necessary, change the values in the Shape Height and Shape Width boxes (Drawing Tools Format tab | Size group) to 1.95" and 7.58" (shown in Figure 10–59).

To Send a Graphic behind Text

1 SAVE DOCUMENT TEMPLATE | 2 SET FORM FORMATS FOR TEMPLATE

3 ENTER TEXT, GRAPHICS, & CONTENT CONTROLS | **4 PROTECT FORM** | **5 USE FORM**

The following steps send a graphic behind text. **Why?** *You want the rectangle shape graphic to be positioned behind the data entry area text, so that you can see the text in the data entry area along with the shape.*

①

- If necessary, display the Drawing Tools Format tab.

- With the rectangle shape selected, click the Layout Options button attached to the graphic to display the LAYOUT OPTIONS gallery (Figure 10–57).

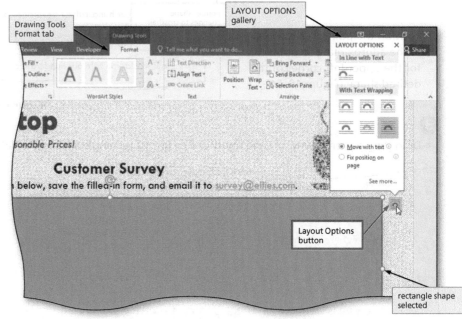

Figure 10–57

②

- Click Behind Text in the LAYOUT OPTIONS gallery to position the rectangle shape behind the text (Figure 10–58).

Q&A What if I want a shape to cover text?

You would click 'In Front of Text' in the LAYOUT OPTIONS gallery.

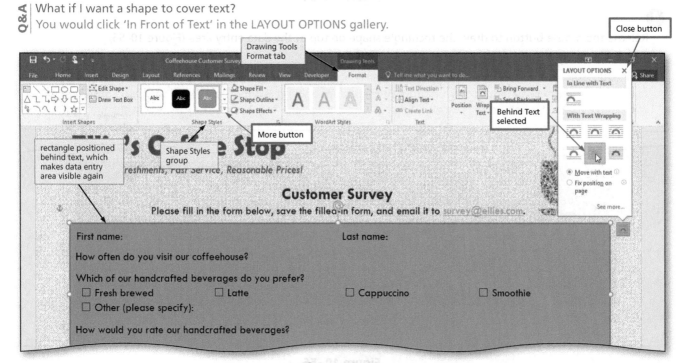

Figure 10–58

3
• Click the Close button in the LAYOUT OPTIONS gallery to close the gallery.

Other Ways	
1. Click Wrap Text button (Drawing Tools Format tab | Arrange group), click desired option	2. Right-click object (or, if using touch, tap 'Show Context Menu' button on mini toolbar), point to Wrap Text on shortcut menu, click desired option

To Apply a Shape Style

The next step is to apply a shape style to the rectangle, so that the text in the data entry area is easier to read. The following steps apply a style to the rectangle shape.

1 With the shape still selected, click the More button in the Shape Styles gallery (Drawing Tools Format tab | Shape Styles group) (shown in Figure 10–58) to expand the Shape Styles gallery.

2 Point to 'Colored Outline - Aqua, Accent 1' in the Shape Styles gallery (second effect in first row) to display a live preview of that style applied to the rectangle shape in the form (Figure 10–59).

3 Click 'Colored Outline - Aqua, Accent 1' in the Shape Styles gallery to apply the selected style to the selected shape.

BTW

Formatting Shapes
Like other drawing objects or pictures, shapes can be formatted or have styles applied. You can change the fill in a shape by clicking the Shape Fill arrow (Drawing Tools Format tab | Shape Styles group), add an outline or border to a shape by clicking the Shape Outline arrow (Drawing Tools Format tab | Shape Styles group), and apply an effect (such as shadow or 3-D effects) by clicking the Shape Effects arrow (Drawing Tools Format tab | Shape Styles group).

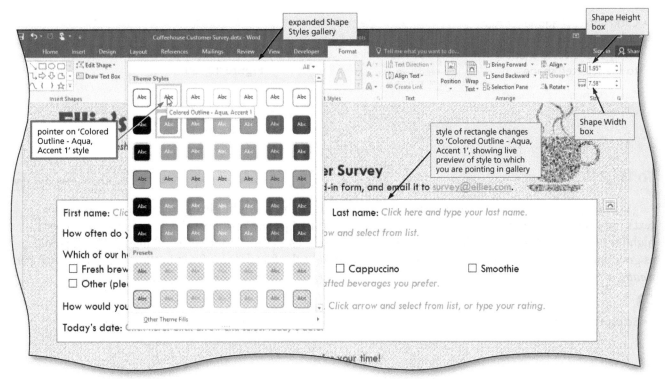

Figure 10–59

To Add a Shadow to a Shape

The following steps add a shadow to the rectangle shape. ***Why?*** *To further offset the data entry area of the form, this online form has a shadow on the outside bottom and left edges of the rectangle shape.*

1

• With the shape still selected, click the Shape Effects button (Drawing Tools Format tab | Shape Styles group) to display the Shape Effects menu.

2

• Point to Shadow on the Shape Effects menu to display the Shadow gallery.

• Point to 'Offset Diagonal Bottom Left' in the Outer area in the Shadow gallery to display a live preview of that shadow effect applied to the selected shape in the document (Figure 10–60).

🄿 **Experiment**

• Point to various shadows in the Shadow gallery and watch the shadow on the selected shape change.

3

• Click 'Offset Diagonal Bottom Left' in the Shadow gallery to apply the selected shadow to the selected shape.

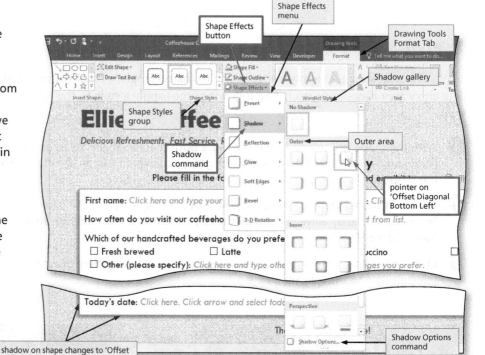

Figure 10–60

Q&A | Can I change the color of a shadow?
Yes. Click Shadow Options (shown in Figure 10–60) in the Shadow gallery.

To Highlight Text

To emphasize text in an online document, you can highlight it. **Highlighting** alerts a reader to online text's importance, much like a highlighter pen does on a printed page. Word provides 15 colors you can use to highlight text, including the traditional yellow and green, as well as some nontraditional highlight colors, such as gray, dark blue, and dark red. The following steps highlight the fourth line of text in the color gray. ***Why?*** *You want to emphasize the line of text on the form that contains instructions related to completing the form.*

1

• Select the text to be highlighted, which, in this case, is the fourth line of text.

Q&A | Why is the selection taller than usual?
Earlier in this project you increased the space after this paragraph. The selection includes this vertical space.

• If necessary, display the Home tab.

• Click the 'Text Highlight Color' arrow (Home tab | Font group) to display the Text Highlight Color gallery.

Q&A | The Text Highlight Color gallery did not appear. Why not?
You clicked the 'Text Highlight Color' button instead of the 'Text Highlight Color' arrow. Click the Undo button on the Quick Access Toolbar and then repeat Step 1.

What if the icon on the 'Text Highlight Color' button already displays the color I want to use?
You can click the 'Text Highlight Color' button instead of the arrow.

2

- Point to Gray-25% in the Text Highlight Color gallery to display a live preview of this highlight color applied to the selected text (Figure 10–61).

🔍 **Experiment**

- Point to various colors in the Text Highlight Color gallery and watch the highlight color on the selected text change.

3

- Click Gray-25% in the Text Highlight Color gallery to highlight the selected text in the selected highlight color.

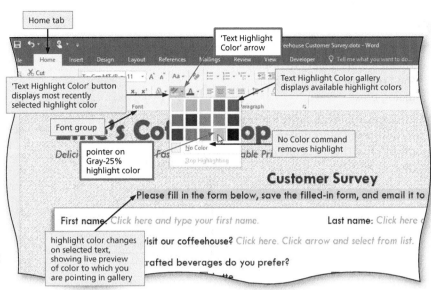

Figure 10–61

Q&A | How would I remove a highlight from text?
Select the highlighted text, click the 'Text Highlight Color' arrow, and then click No Color in the Text Highlight Color gallery.

Other Ways

1. Click 'Text Highlight Color' arrow (Home tab | Font group), select desired color, select text to be highlighted in document, select any additional text to be highlighted, click 'Text Highlight Color' button to turn off highlighting

To Customize a Theme Color and Save It with a New Theme Name

1 SAVE DOCUMENT TEMPLATE | 2 SET FORM FORMATS FOR TEMPLATE
3 ENTER TEXT, GRAPHICS, & CONTENT CONTROLS | 4 PROTECT FORM | 5 USE FORM

The final step in formatting the online form in this module is to change the color of the hyperlink. A document theme has 12 predefined colors for various on-screen objects, including text, backgrounds, and hyperlinks. You can change any of the theme colors. The following steps customize the Headlines theme, changing its designated theme color for hyperlinks. **Why?** *You would like the hyperlink to be dark orange, to match other text on the form.*

1

- Display the Design tab.

- Click the Theme Colors button (Design tab | Document Formatting group) to display the Theme Colors gallery (Figure 10–62).

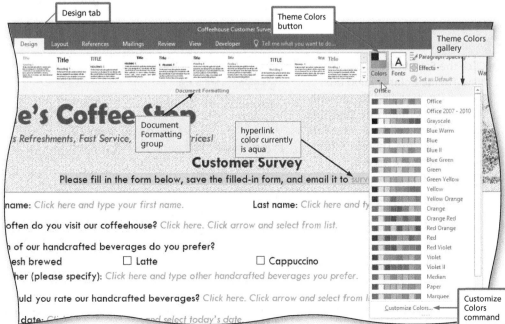

Figure 10–62

2

- Click Customize Colors in the Theme Colors gallery to display the Create New Theme Colors dialog box.

- Click the Hyperlink button (Create New Theme Colors dialog box) to display the Theme Colors gallery (Figure 10–63).

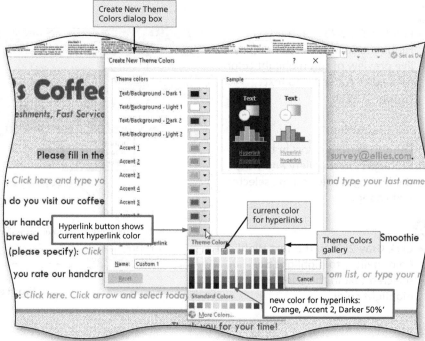

Figure 10–63

3

- Click 'Orange, Accent 2, Darker 50%' in the Hyperlink column (sixth color in bottom row) as the new hyperlink color.

- Type **Coffeehouse Customer Survey** in the Name text box (Figure 10–64).

Q&A What if I wanted to reset all the original theme colors?
You would click the Reset button (Create New Theme Colors dialog box) before Clicking the Save button.

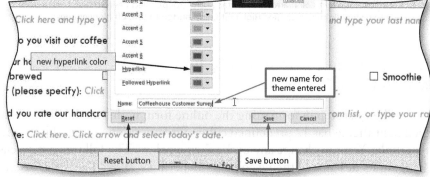

Figure 10–64

4

- Click the Save button (Create New Theme Colors dialog box) to save the modified theme with the name, Coffeehouse Customer Survey, which will be positioned at the top of the Theme Colors gallery for future access (Figure 10–65).

Q&A What if I do not enter a name for the modified theme?
Word assigns a name that begins with the letters, Custom, followed by a number (i.e., Custom8).

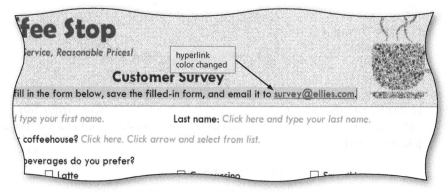

Figure 10–65

Other Ways

1. Make changes to theme colors, fonts, and/or effects; click Themes button (Design tab | Document Formatting group), click 'Save Current Theme' in Themes gallery

To Protect a Form

When you **protect a form**, you are allowing users to enter data only in designated areas — specifically, the content controls. The following steps protect the online form. *Why? To prevent unwanted changes and edits to the form, it is crucial that you protect a form before making it available to users.*

- Display the Developer tab.

- Click the Restrict Editing button (Developer tab | Protect group) to open the Restrict Editing task pane (Figure 10–66).

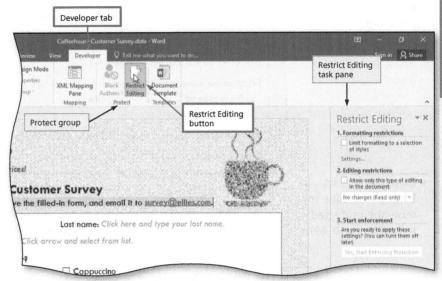

Figure 10–66

- In the Editing restrictions area, place a check mark in the 'Allow only this type of editing in the document' check box and then click its arrow to display a list of the types of allowed restrictions (Figure 10–67).

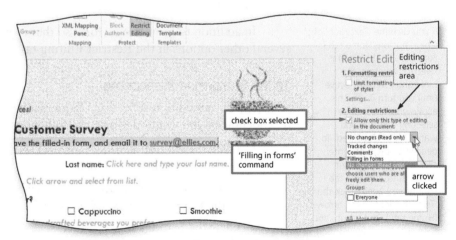

Figure 10–67

- Click 'Filling in forms' in the list to instruct Word that the only editing allowed in this document is to the content controls.

- In the Start enforcement area, click the 'Yes, Start Enforcing Protection' button, which displays the Start Enforcing Protection dialog box (Figure 10–68).

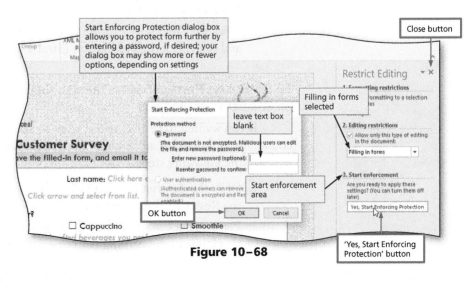

Figure 10–68

4

- Click the OK button (Start Enforcing Protection dialog box) to protect the document without a password.

Q&A

What if I enter a password?

If you enter a password, only a user who knows the password will be able to unprotect the document.

- Close the Restrict Editing task pane to show the protected form (Figure 10–69).

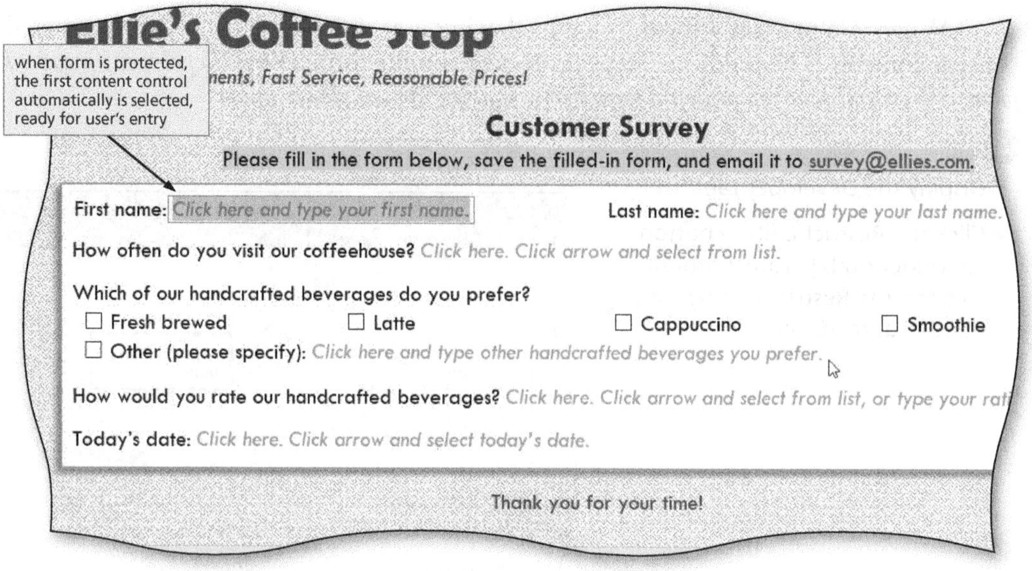

Figure 10–69

Other Ways

1. Open Backstage view, click Info tab, click Protect Document button, click Restrict Editing on Protect Document menu

BTW

Highlighter

If you click the 'Text Highlight Color' button (Home tab | Font group) without first selecting any text, the highlighter remains active until you turn it off. This allows you to continue selecting text that you want to be highlighted. To deactivate the highlighter, click the 'Text Highlight Color' button (Home tab | Font group) again, click the 'Text Highlight Color' arrow (Home tab | Font group) and then click Stop Highlighting on the Text Highlight Color menu, or press the ESC key.

Protecting Documents

In addition to protecting a form so that it only can be filled in, Word provides several other options in the Restrict Editing task pane.

TO SET FORMATTING RESTRICTIONS

If you wanted to restrict users from making certain types of formatting changes to a document, you would perform the following steps.

1. Click the Restrict Editing button (Developer tab | Protect group) to display the Restrict Editing task pane.
2. Place a check mark in the 'Limit formatting to a selection of styles' check box in the Formatting restrictions area.
3. Click the Settings link and then select the types of formatting you want to allow (Formatting Restrictions dialog box).
4. Click the OK button.
5. Click the 'Yes, Start Enforcing Protection' button, enter a password if desired, and then click the OK button (Start Enforcing Protection dialog box).

TO SET EDITING RESTRICTIONS TO TRACKED CHANGES OR COMMENTS OR NO EDITS

If you wanted to restrict users' edits to allow only tracked changes, allow only comments, or not allow any edits (that is, make the document read only), you would perform the following steps.

1. Click the Restrict Editing button (Developer tab | Protect group) to display the Restrict Editing task pane.
2. Place a check mark in the 'Allow only this type of editing in the document' check box in the Editing restrictions area, click the arrow, and then click the

desired option — that is, Tracked changes, Comments, or No changes (Read only) — to specify the types of edits allowed in the document.
3. Click the 'Yes, Start Enforcing Protection' button, enter a password if desired, and then click the OK button (Start Enforcing Protection dialog box).

To Hide the Developer Tab

You are finished using the commands on the Developer tab. Thus, the following steps hide the Developer tab from the ribbon.

1 Open the Backstage view and then click the Options tab in the left pane of the Backstage view to display the Word Options dialog box.

2 Click Customize Ribbon in the left pane (Word Options dialog box).

3 Remove the check mark from the Developer check box in the Main Tabs list.

4 Click the OK button to hide the Developer tab from the ribbon.

To Hide the Ruler, Collapse the Ribbon, Save the Template, and Exit Word

If the ruler is displayed on the screen, you want to hide it. You also want to collapse the ribbon so that when you test the form in the next steps, the ribbon is collapsed. Finally, the online form template for this project now is complete, so you can save the template again and exit Word. The following steps perform these tasks.

1 If the ruler is displayed on the screen, remove the check mark from the View Ruler check box (View tab | Show group).

2 Click the 'Collapse the Ribbon' button on the ribbon (shown in Figure 10–5 earlier in this module) to collapse the ribbon.

3 Save the template again on the same storage location with the same file name.

4 Exit Word.

Working with an Online Form

When you create a template, you use the Open tab in the Backstage view to open the template so that you can modify it. After you have created a template, you then can make it available to users. Users do not open templates with the Open command in Word. Instead, a user creates a new Word document that is *based* on the template, which means the title bar displays the default file name, Document1 (or a similar name) rather than the template name. When Word creates a new document that is based on a template, the document window contains any text and formatting associated with the template. If a user accesses a letter template, for example, Word displays the contents of a basic letter in a new document window.

BTW
Password-Protecting Documents
You can save documents with a password to keep unauthorized users from accessing files. To do this, type the password in the Start Enforcing Protection dialog box (shown in Figure 10–68); or open the Backstage view, click Save As, display the Save As dialog box, click the Tools button (Save As dialog box), click General Options on the Tools menu, type the password in the appropriate text box (General Options dialog box), type the password again (Confirm Password dialog box), and then click the OK button and Save button (Save As dialog box). As you type a password in the text box, Word displays a series of dots instead of the actual characters so that others cannot see your password as you type it.
  Be sure to keep the password confidential. Choose a password that is easy to remember and that no one can guess. Do not use any part of your first or last name, Social Security number, birthday, and so on. Use a password that is at least six characters long, and if possible, use a mixture of numbers and letters.

To Use File Explorer to Create a New Document That Is Based on a Template

When you save a template on storage media, as instructed earlier in this module, a user can create a new document that is based on the template through File Explorer. *Why? This allows the user to work with a new document instead of risking the chance of altering the original template.* The following steps create a new Word document that is based on the Coffeehouse Customer Survey template.

- Click the File Explorer button on the Windows taskbar to open a File Explorer window.
- Navigate to the location of the saved template (Figure 10–70).

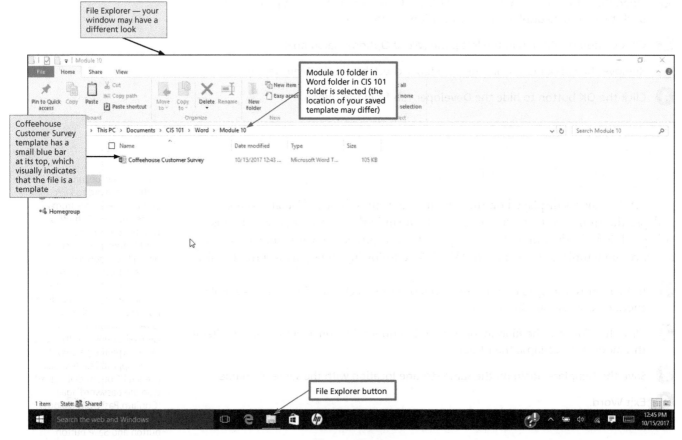

Figure 10–70

- Double-click the Coffeehouse Customer Survey file in the File Explorer window, which runs Word and creates a new document that is based on the contents of the selected template (Figure 10–71).

Q&A

Why did my background page color disappear?

If the background page color does not appear, open the Backstage view, click the Options tab to display the Word Options dialog box, click Advanced in the left pane (Word Options dialog box), scroll to the Show document content section, place a check mark in the 'Show background colors and images in Print Layout view' check box, and then click the OK button.

Why does my ribbon show only three tabs: File, Tools, and View?

Your screen is in Read mode. Click the View tab and then click Edit Document to switch to Print Layout view.

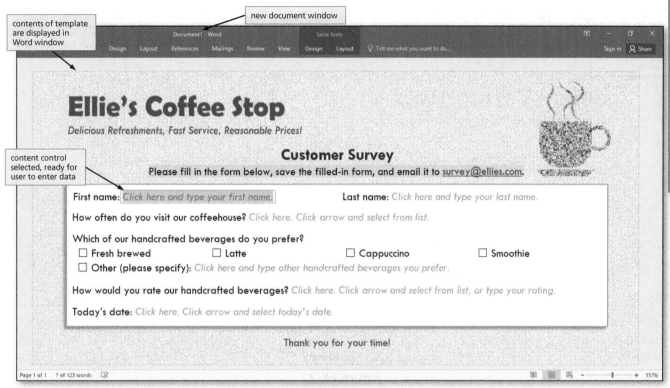

Figure 10–71

To Fill In a Form and Save It

1 SAVE DOCUMENT TEMPLATE | 2 SET FORM FORMATS FOR TEMPLATE
3 ENTER TEXT, GRAPHICS, & CONTENT CONTROLS | 4 PROTECT FORM | 5 USE FORM

The next step is to enter data in the form. To advance from one content control to the next, a user can click the content control or press the TAB key. To move to a previous content control, a user can click it or press SHIFT+TAB. The following steps fill in the Coffeehouse Customer Survey form. *Why? You want to test the form to be sure it works as you intended.*

- With the First Name content control selected, type **Sammie** and then press the TAB key.

- Type **Berkshire** in the Last Name content control.

    If requested by your instructor, use your first and last name instead of the name, Sammie Berkshire.

- Press the TAB key to select the Frequency of Visits content control and then click its arrow to display the list of choices (shown in Figure 10–1b at the beginning of this module).

- Click Weekly in the list.

- Click the Latte and Other Beverage check boxes to select them.

- Type **Macchiato** in the Other Beverage content control.

- Click the Beverage Rating content control and then click its arrow to display the list of choices (Figure 10–72).

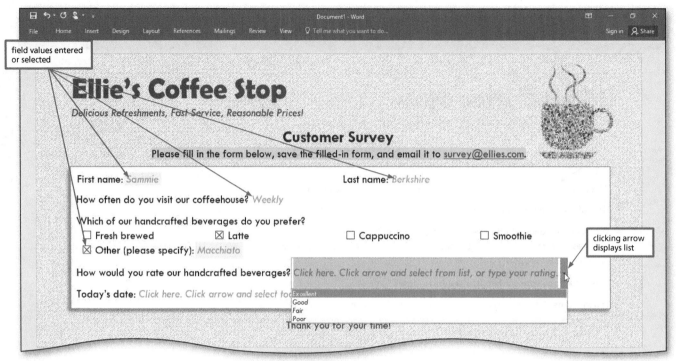

Figure 10–72

2

- Select Excellent in the list.

- Click the Today's Date content control and then click its arrow to display a calendar (Figure 10–73).

3

- Click October 26, 2017 in the calendar to complete the data entry (shown in Figure 10–1c at the beginning of this module).

4

- Save the file on your storage location with the file name, Berkshire Survey. If Word asks if you want to also save changes to the document template, click the No button.

  If requested by your instructor, use your last name in the file name instead of the name, Berkshire.

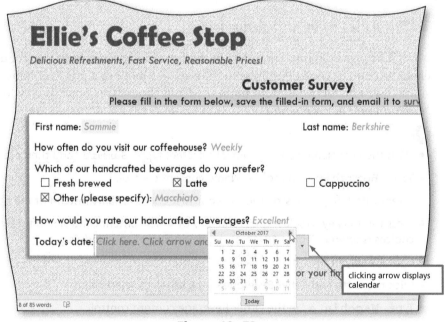

Figure 10–73

Q&A
Can I print the form?
You can print the document as you print any other document. Keep in mind, however, that the colors used were designed for viewing online. Thus, different color schemes would have been selected if the form had been designed for a printout.

- Exit Word. (If Word asks if you want to save the modified styles, click the Don't Save button.)

- If the File Explorer window still is open, close it.

Working with Templates

If you want to modify the template, open it by clicking the Open tab in the Backstage view, clicking the template name, and then clicking the Open button in the dialog box. Then, you must **unprotect the form** by clicking the Restrict Editing button (Developer tab | Protect group) and then clicking the Stop Protection button in the Restrict Editing task pane.

When you created the template in this module, you saved it on your local storage location. In environments other than an academic setting, you would not save the template on your own storage location; instead, you would save the file in the Custom Office Templates folder. When you save a template in the Custom Office Templates folder, you can locate the template by opening the Backstage view, clicking the New tab to display the New gallery, and then clicking the PERSONAL tab in the New gallery, which displays the template in the New gallery (Figure 10–74).

BTW
Protected Documents
If you open an existing form that has been protected, Word will not allow you to modify the form's appearance until you unprotect it. To unprotect a form (or any protected document), open the Restrict Formatting and Editing task pane by clicking the Restrict Editing button (Developer tab | Protect group) or opening the Backstage view, displaying the Info gallery, clicking the Protect Document button, and clicking Restrict Editing on the Protect Document menu. Then, click the Stop Protection button in the Restrict Editing task pane and close the task pane. If a document has been protected with a password, you will be asked to enter the password when you attempt to unprotect the document.

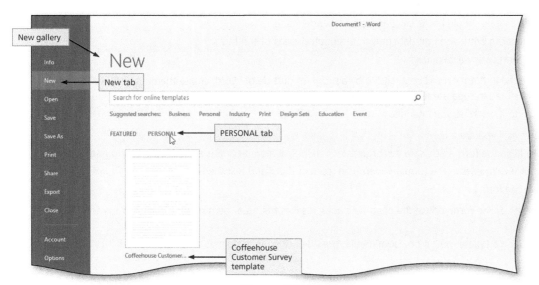

Figure 10–74

BTW
Linking a Form to a Database
If you want to use or analyze the data that a user enters into a form in an Access database or an Excel worksheet, you could save the form data in a comma-delimited text file. This file separates each data item with a comma and places quotation marks around text data items. Then, you can use Access or Excel to import the comma-delimited text file for use in the respective program. To save form data, open the Backstage view, click Save As in the Backstage view, and then display the Save As dialog box. Click the Tools button (Save As dialog box) and then click Save Options on the Tools menu to display the Word Options dialog box. Click Advanced in the left pane (Word Options dialog box), scroll to the Preserve fidelity when sharing this document area in the right pane, place a check mark in the 'Save form data as delimited text file' check box, and then click the OK button. Next, be sure the file type is Plain Text (Save As dialog box) and then click the Save button to save the file as a comma-delimited text file. You can import the resulting comma-delimited file in an Access database or an Excel worksheet. To convert successfully, you should use the legacy controls (i.e., text form field, check box form field, etc.), which are available through the Legacy Tools button (Developer tab | Controls group). To use Word 2016 content controls, use the 'XML Mapping Pane' button (Developer tab | Mapping group) and refer to the Supplementary Word Tasks section in Module 11 for instructions about working with XML.

Summary

In this module, you have learned how to create an online form. Topics covered included saving a document as a template, changing paper size, using a table to control layout, showing the Developer tab, inserting content controls, editing placeholder text, changing properties of content controls, and protecting a form.

STUDENT ASSIGNMENTS

CONSIDER THIS: PLAN AHEAD

What decisions will you need to make when creating online forms?

Use these guidelines as you complete the assignments in this module and create your own online forms outside of this class.

1. Design the form.

    a) To minimize the time spent creating a form while using a computer or mobile device, consider sketching the form on a piece of paper first.

    b) Design a well-thought-out draft of the form — being sure to include all essential form elements, including the form's title, text and graphics, data entry fields, and data entry instructions.

2. For each data entry field, determine its field type and/or list of possible values that it can contain.

3. Save the form as a template, instead of as a Word document, to simplify the data entry process for users of the form.

4. Create a functional and visually appealing form.

    a) Use colors that complement one another.

    b) Draw the user's attention to important sections.

    c) Arrange data entry fields in logical groups on the form and in an order that users would expect.

    d) Data entry instructions should be succinct and easy to understand.

    e) Ensure that users can enter and edit data only in designated areas of the form.

5. Determine how the form data will be analyzed.

    a) If the data entered in the form will be analyzed by a program outside of Word, create the data entry fields so that the entries are stored in separate fields that can be shared with other programs.

6. Test the form, ensuring it works as you intended.

    a) Fill in the form as if you are a user.

    b) Ask others to fill in the form to be sure it is organized in a logical manner and is easy to understand and complete.

    c) If any errors or weaknesses in the form are identified, correct them and test the form again.

7. Publish or distribute the form.

    a) Not only does an online form reduce the need for paper, it saves the time spent making copies of the form and distributing it.

    b) When the form is complete, post it on social media, the web, or your company's intranet, or email it to targeted recipients.

Apply Your Knowledge

Reinforce the skills and apply the concepts you learned in this module.

Filling In an Online Form

Note: To complete this assignment, you will be required to use the Data Files. Please contact your instructor for information about accessing the Data Files.

Instructions: In this assignment, you access a template through File Explorer. The template is located on the Data Files. The template contains an online form (Figure 10–75). You are to fill in the form.

document created
based on template

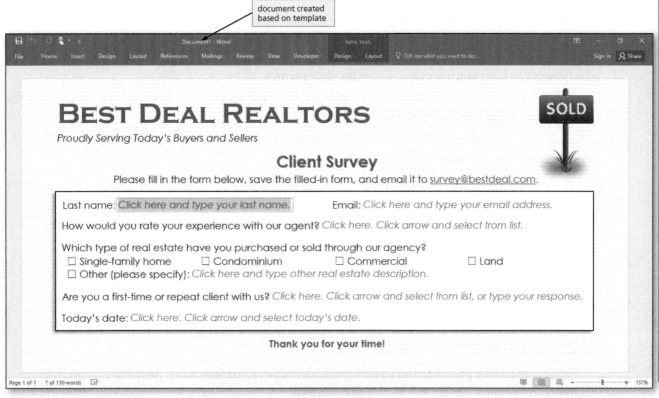

Figure 10–75

Perform the following tasks:

1. Run File Explorer. Double-click the Apply 10-1 Realtor Client Survey template in File Explorer to create a new document based on the template.

2. When Word displays a new document based on the template, if necessary, collapse the ribbon, hide formatting marks, and change the zoom to page width. Your screen should look like Figure 10–75 and display Document1 on the title bar instead of the file name.

3. With the Last Name content control selected, type **Janda** as the last name, or if requested by your instructor, enter your last name.

4. Click the Email content control selected, type **janda@world.net** or, if requested by your instructor, enter your email address.

5. Click the Agent Rating content control and then click its arrow. Click Excellent in the list.

6. Click the Land check box to select it.

7. Click the Other check box. If necessary, click the Other text box and then type **Multi-family home** in the text box.

8. Click the Client Type content control to select it. Click the Client Type arrow and then review the list. Press the ESC key because none of these choices answers the question. Type **Repeat buyer and seller** as the response.

9. Click the Today's Date content control and then click the arrow to display a calendar. If necessary, scroll to display the calendar for November 2017. Click 'November 2, 2017', (or today's date, if requested by your instructor) in the calendar.

Continued >

Apply Your Knowledge *continued*

10. Save the modified file with a new file name, Apply 10-1 Janda Survey (or, if requested by your instructor, replace the name, Janda, with your last name). Submit the document in the format specified by your instructor. Close the document.

11. Use Word to open the Apply 10-1 Realtor Client Survey template from the Data Files (click the Open tab in the Backstage view).

12. Save the template with a new name, Apply 10-1 Realtor Client Survey Modified.

13. Unprotect the template.

14. Change the Today's Date content control to the format d-MMM-yy (i.e., 12-Nov-17).

15. Protect the modified template.

16. Save the modified template. Submit the revised template in the format specified by your instructor.

17. ✳ In this form, what are the options in the Agent Rating and Client Type lists? What items might you add to the Client Type list? How would you add those items?

Extend Your Knowledge

Extend the skills you learned in this module and experiment with new skills. You may need to use Help to complete the assignment.

Working with Picture Content Controls, Grouping Objects, Themes, and Passwords

Note: To complete this assignment, you will be required to use the Data Files. Please contact your instructor for information about accessing the Data Files.

Instructions: Run Word. Open the document, Extend 10-1 Contest Entry Form Draft, from the Data Files. You will add a picture content control in a text box and then format the text box, group the graphical images, change the text highlight color, change the shadow color, change the shape fill effect to a texture, change theme colors, reset theme colors, save a modified theme, and protect a form with a password.

Perform the following tasks:
1. Use Help to review and expand your knowledge about these topics: picture content controls, text boxes, grouping objects, shadows, shape fill effects, changing theme colors, and protecting forms with passwords.

2. Add a simple text box to the empty space in the right side of the data entry area. Remove space after the paragraph. Resize the text box so that it fits completely in the data entry area.

3. In the text box, type the label, Recipe Photo:, and then below the label, insert a picture content control. Resize the picture content control so that it fits in the text box and then center both the picture and label in the text box (Figure 10–76). Remove the border from the text box.

4. Change the fill effect in the rectangle shape to a texture of your choice. If necessary, change the font color or style of text in the data entry area so that it is readable on the texture.

5. Group the three graphics at the top of the form together. Move the grouped graphics. Return them to their original location.

6. Change the text highlight color of the third line of text to a color other than yellow. If necessary, change the text color so that you can read the text in the new highlight color.

7. Add a shadow to the rectangle and then change the color of the shadow on the rectangle to a color other than the default.

8. Customize the theme colors for Accent 3 (Customize Colors command in Theme Colors gallery). Reset the theme colors before closing the dialog box. Customize the theme colors for Accent 1 and Hyperlink. Customize theme colors for other items as desired. Save the modified theme colors.

9. Make any necessary formatting changes to the form.

10. If requested by your instructor, change the email address to your email address.

11. Protect the form using the word, fun, as the password.

12. Save the revised document with the file name, Extend 10-1 Contest Entry Form Modified.

13. Test the form. When filling in the form, use your own recipe photo or the picture called Beef Stew on the Data Files for the picture content control. Submit the online form in the format specified by your instructor.

14. ✲ Which texture did you select and why? What is the advantage of grouping graphics? Besides changing the color of the shadow, what other shadow settings can you adjust?

Figure 10–76

Expand Your World

Create a solution that uses cloud or web technologies by learning and investigating on your own from general guidance.

Inserting Online Videos

Note: To complete this assignment, you will be required to use the Data Files. Please contact your instructor for information about accessing the Data Files.

Instructions: You have created an online form for a pool opening and would like to add to the form an online video that shows a pool being vacuumed.

Perform the following tasks:

1. Use Help to learn about inserting online videos.
2. Open the document named Expand 10-1 Pool Opening Form Draft from the Data Files.
3. If requested by your instructor, replace Junior's in the company name with your first name.
4. Display the Insert tab and then click the Online Video button (Insert tab | Media group) to display the Insert Video dialog box (Figure 10–77). Type **pool vacuuming** in the one of the search boxes to display a list of videos that match your search criteria.
5. Scroll through the list of videos, clicking several to see their name, length, and source. Click the View Larger button in the lower-right corner of the video so that you can watch the video. Select an appropriate video and then click the Insert button to insert it on the form. Change the layout to In Front of Text, position the video on the right side of the data entry form, and resize the video border if necessary.

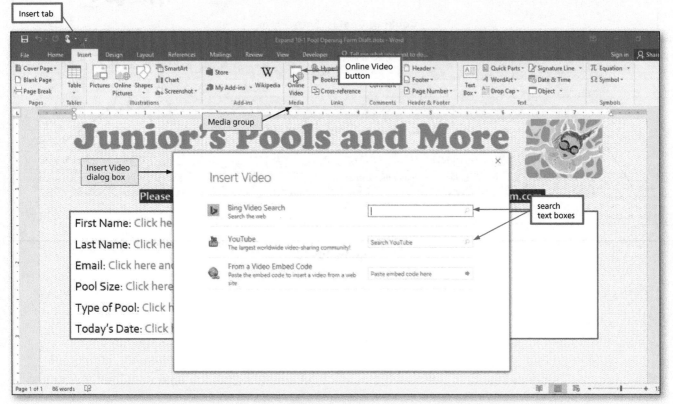

Figure 10–77

6. Protect the form. Save the form again and then submit it in the format specified by your instructor.

7. Access the template through File Explorer. Test the video.

8. ✹ What options are available in the search results dialog box while you are watching a video? What are some of the sources for the videos in the dialog box? Which video did you insert in the form, and why? How do you play the video inserted on the form? Does the video play where you inserted it on the form? If not, where does it play?

In the Labs

Design, create, modify, and/or use a document following the guidelines, concepts, and skills presented in this module. Labs 1 and 2, which increase in difficulty, require you to create solutions based on what you learned in the module; Lab 3 requires you to apply your creative thinking and problem-solving skills to design and implement a solution.

Lab 1: Creating an Online Form with Plain Text and Drop-Down List Content Controls

Problem: Your aunt owns Dee's Dog Grooming and has asked you to prepare an online survey, shown in Figure 10–78.

Perform the following tasks:

1. Save a blank document as a template, called Lab 10-1 Dog Grooming Request Form, for the online form.

2. If necessary, change the view to page width.

3. Change the paper size to a width of 8.5 inches and a height of 4 inches.

4. Change the margins as follows: top – 0.25", bottom – 0", left – 0.5", and right – 0.5".

5. Change the document theme to Celestial.

6. Change the page color to Dark Blue, Text 2, Lighter 60%. Change the fill effect to the 30% pattern.

7. Enter and format the company name, message, and form title as shown in Figure 10–78 (or with similar fonts). If requested by your instructor, change the business name from Dee's to your first name. Insert the image shown (or a similar image) using the term, dog bath, as the search text (the exact image is located on the Data Files). Change the wrapping style of the graphics to In Front of Text. If necessary, resize the graphic and position it in the location shown.

8. Enter the instructions above the data entry area and highlight the line in Gray-50%.

9. Customize the colors so that the hyperlink color is Blue, Accent 2, Darker 50%. Save the modified theme.

Continued >

In the Labs *continued*

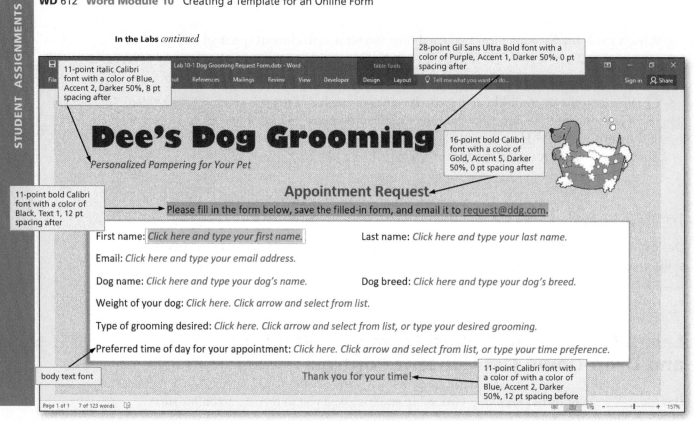

Figure 10–78

10. In the data entry area, enter the labels as shown in Figure 10–78 and the content controls as follows: First Name, Last Name, Email, Dog Name, and Dog Breed are plain text content controls. Dog Weight is a drop-down list content control with these choices: Less than 10 pounds, 10 to 25 pounds, 26 to 45 pounds, 46 to 65 pounds, More than 65 pounds. Grooming Type is a combo box content control with these choices: Bath and brush; Bath and haircut; Bath and shed treatment; Bath, shed treatment, and haircut. Preferred Time is a combo box content control with these choices: Weekday mornings, Weekday afternoons, Weekend mornings, Weekend afternoons.

11. Format the placeholder text to the Intense Emphasis style. Edit the placeholder text of all content controls to match Figure 10–78. Change the properties of the content controls so that each contains a tag name, uses the Intense Emphasis style, and has locking set so that the content control cannot be deleted.

12. Enter the line below the data entry area as shown in Figure 10–78.

13. Adjust spacing above and below paragraphs as necessary so that all contents fit on a single screen.

14. Draw a rectangle around the data entry area and send it behind the text. Change the shape style of the rectangle to Colored Outline - Gold, Accent 5. Apply the Offset Diagonal Bottom Left shadow to the rectangle.

15. Protect the form.

16. Save the form again and then submit it in the format specified by your instructor.

17. Access the template through File Explorer. Fill in the form using personal data and then submit the filled-in form in the format specified by your instructor.

18. ✳ If the dog groomer wanted the owner's middle name on the same line as the first and last names, how would you evenly space the three items across the line?

Lab 2: Creating an Online Form with Plain Text, Drop-Down List, Combo Box, Rich Text, Check Box, and Date Picker Content Controls

Problem: You work part-time for Antwon's DJ Service. Your supervisor has asked you to prepare a customer survey (Figure 10–79).

Perform the following tasks:

1. Save a blank document as a template for the online form and name it Lab 10-2 DJ Customer Survey.

2. If necessary, change the view to page width.

3. Change the paper size to a width of 8.5 inches and a height of 4 inches.

4. Change the margins as follows: top – 0.25", bottom – 0", left – 0.5", and right – 0.5".

5. Change the document theme to Berlin.

6. Change the page color to Brown, Accent 1. Change the fill effect to the dotted diamond pattern.

7. Enter and format the company name, business tag line, and form title as shown in Figure 10–79 (or with similar fonts). If requested by your instructor, change the business name from Antwon's to your first name. Insert the image using the text, music note, as the search text (the exact image is located on the Data Files). Change the wrapping style of the graphic to In Front of Text. If necessary, resize the graphic and move it to the location shown.

8. Enter the instructions above the data entry area and highlight the line Dark Yellow.

9. In the data entry area, enter the labels as shown in Figure 10–79 and the content controls as follows: First Name and Last Name are plain text content controls. Event Type is a combo box content control with these choices: Birthday, Corporate, Fundraiser, Graduation, Prom, Reunion, Wedding. Event Date is a date picker content control. Ballads, Country, Dance, Ethnic, Hip-Hop, Jazz, Oldies, Rock, and Other Genre are check boxes. Other Genre is a rich text content control. Rating is a drop-down list content control with these choices: Excellent, Good, Fair, Poor.

10. Format the placeholder text to Intense Emphasis. Edit the placeholder text of all content controls to match Figure 10–79. Change the properties of the content controls so that each contains a tag name, uses the Intense Emphasis style, and has locking specified so that the content control cannot be deleted.

11. Customize the colors so that the hyperlink color is White, Hyperlink. Save the modified theme.

12. Enter the line below the data entry area as shown in Figure 10–79.

Continued >

STUDENT ASSIGNMENTS

In the Labs *continued*

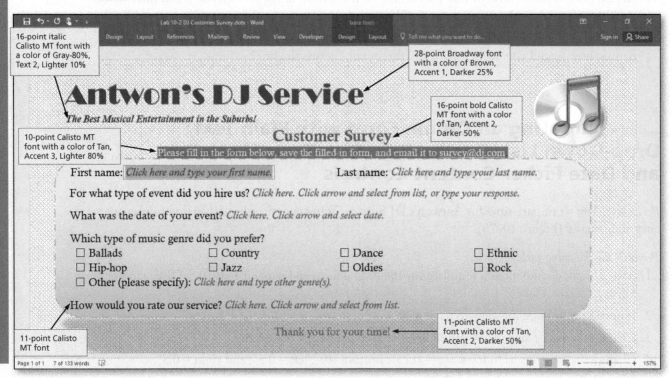

16-point italic Calisto MT font with a color of Gray-80%, Text 2, Lighter 10%

28-point Broadway font with a color of Brown, Accent 1, Darker 25%

16-point bold Calisto MT font with a color of Tan, Accent 2, Darker 50%

10-point Calisto MT font with a color of Tan, Accent 3, Lighter 80%

11-point Calisto MT font with a color of Tan, Accent 2, Darker 50%

11-point Calisto MT font

Figure 10–79

13. Change the color of labels in the data entry area as shown in the figure.

14. Adjust spacing above and below paragraphs as necessary so that all contents fit on the screen.

15. Draw a Rounded Rectangle around the data entry area. Change the shape style of the rectangle to Subtle Effect - Tan, Accent 2. Change the shape outline to Long Dash Dot. Add a Perspective Diagonal Lower Right shadow.

16. Protect the form.

17. Save the form again and then submit it in the format specified by your instructor.

18. Access the template through File Explorer. Fill in the form using personal data and submit the filled-in form in the format specified by your instructor.

19. ✳ What other question might a DJ service ask its customers? If you were to add this question to the form, how would you fit it so that the form still displays in its entirety on a single page?

Lab 3: **Consider This: Your Turn**

Create an Online Form for a Deli

Problem: As a part-time employee at your local deli, you have been asked to create an online customer survey.

Part 1: Create a template that contains the deli name (Rick's Deli), the deli's tag line (Fresh Ingredients Everyday!), and an appropriate image. The third line should have the text, Customer Survey. The fourth line should be highlighted and should read: Please fill in the form below, save the filled-in form, and then email it to survey@ricksdeli.com. The data entry area should contain the following. First Name and Last Name are plain text content controls within a table.

A combo box content control with the label, How do you usually place your order?, has these choices: Counter, Phone, Online, Text. The following instruction should appear above these check boxes: What foods do you like at our deli (check all that apply)?; the check boxes are Sandwiches, Soups, Salads, Sides, Desserts, and Other. A rich text content control has the label, Other (please specify), where customers can enter their own response. A drop-down list content control with the label, How would you rate our food?, has these choices: Excellent, Good, Fair, and Poor. A rich text content control has the label, Would you like to see any items added to our menu?, where customers can enter their own response. A date picker content control with the label, What date were you last in our deli? On the last line, include the text: Thank you for your business!

Use the concepts and techniques presented in this module to create and format the online form. Use meaningful placeholder text for all content controls. (For example, the placeholder text for the First Name plain text content control could be as follows: Click here and type your first name.) Draw a rectangle around the data entry area of the form. Add a shadow to the rectangle. Apply a style to the placeholder text. Assign names, styles, and locking to each content control. Protect the form, test it, and submit it in the format specified by your instructor.

Part 2: ❄ You made several decisions while creating the online form in this assignment: placeholder text to use, graphics to use, and how to organize and format the online form (fonts, font sizes, styles, colors, etc.). What was the rationale behind each of these decisions? When you proofread and tested the online form, what further revisions did you make, and why?

11 | Enhancing an Online Form and Using Macros

Objectives

You will have mastered the material in this module when you can:

- Unprotect a document
- Specify macro settings
- Convert a table to text
- Insert and edit a field
- Create a character style
- Apply and modify fill effects
- Change a shape

- Remove a background from a graphic
- Apply an artistic effect to a graphic
- Insert and format a text box
- Group objects
- Record and execute a macro
- Customize the Quick Access Toolbar
- Edit a macro's VBA code

Introduction

Word provides many tools that allow you to improve the appearance, functionality, and security of your documents. This module discusses tools used to perform the following tasks:

- Modify text and content controls.
- Enhance with color, shapes, effects, and graphics.
- Automate a series of tasks with a macro.

Project — Online Form Revised

This module uses Word to improve the visual appearance of and add macros to the online form created in Module 10, producing the online form shown in Figure 11–1a. This project begins with the Coffeehouse Customer Survey online form created in Module 10. Thus, you will need the online form template created in Module 10 to complete this project. (If you did not create the template, see your instructor for a copy.)

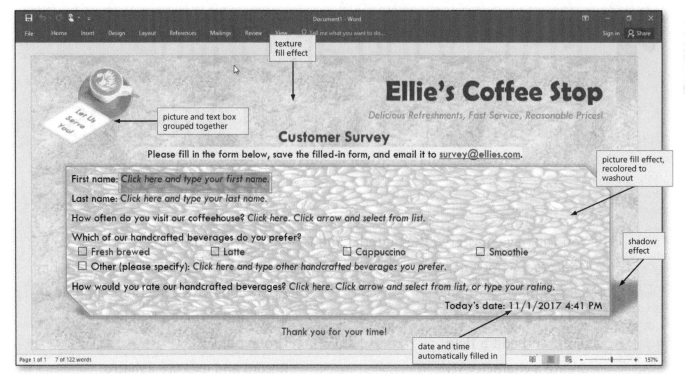

(a) Modified and Enhanced Online Form

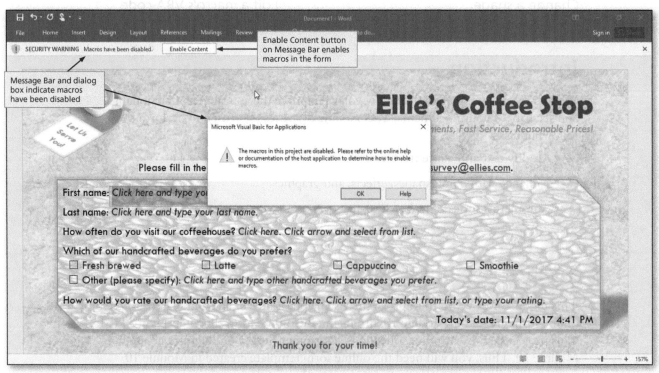

(b) Macros in Online Form Generate Security Warning

Figure 11–1

This project modifies the fonts and font colors of the text in the Coffeehouse Customer Survey online form and enhances the contents of the form to include a texture fill effect, a picture fill effect, and a text box and picture grouped together. The date in the form automatically displays the computer or mobile device's system date, instead of requiring the user to enter the date.

This form also includes macros to automate tasks. A **macro** is a set of commands and instructions grouped together to allow a user to accomplish a task automatically. One macro allows the user to hide formatting marks and the ruler by pressing a keyboard shortcut (sometimes called a shortcut key) or clicking a button on the Quick Access Toolbar. Another macro specifies how the form is displayed initially on a user's Word screen. As shown in Figure 11–1b, when a document contains macros, Word may generate a security warning. If you are sure the macros are from a trusted source and free of viruses, then enable the content. Otherwise, do not enable the content, which protects your computer from potentially harmful viruses or other malicious software.

In this module, you will learn how to create the form shown in Figure 11–1. The following roadmap identifies general activities you will perform as you progress through this module:

1. SAVE a DOCUMENT AS a MACRO-ENABLED TEMPLATE.
2. MODIFY the TEXT AND FORM CONTENT CONTROLS.
3. ENHANCE the FORM'S VISUAL APPEAL.
4. CREATE MACROS TO AUTOMATE TASKS in the form.

To Run Word and Change Word Settings

If you are using a computer to step through the project in this module and you want your screens to match the figures in this book, you should change your screen's resolution to 1366 × 768. The following steps run Word, hide formatting marks, and change the zoom to page width.

1. Run Word and create a blank document in the Word window. If necessary, maximize the Word window.

2. If the Print Layout button on the status bar is not selected, click it so that your screen is in Print Layout view.

3. If the 'Show/Hide ¶' button (Home tab | Paragraph group) is selected, click it to hide formatting marks because you will not use them in this project.

4. If the rulers are displayed on the screen, click the View Ruler check box (View tab | Show group) to remove the rulers from the Word window because you will not use the rulers in this project.

5. If the edges of the page do not extend to the edge of the document window, display the View tab and then click the Page Width button (View tab | Zoom group).

BTW
The Ribbon and Screen Resolution
Word may change how the groups and buttons within the groups appear on the ribbon, depending on the computer's screen resolution. Thus, your ribbon may look different from the ones in this book if you are using a screen resolution other than 1366 x 768.

To Save a Macro-Enabled Template

The project in this module contains macros. Thus, the first step in this module is to open the Coffeehouse Customer Survey template created in Module 10 (see your instructor for a copy if you did not create the template) and then save the template as a macro-enabled template. *Why? To provide added security to templates, a basic Word template cannot store macros. Word instead provides a specific type of template, called a **macro-enabled template**, in which you can store macros.*

- Open the template named Coffeehouse Customer Survey created in Module 10.

- Open the Backstage view, click the Save As tab to display the Save As gallery, navigate to the desired save location, and display the Save As dialog box.

- Type **Coffeehouse Customer Survey Modified** in the File name text box (Save As dialog box) to change the file name.

- Click the 'Save as type' arrow to display the list of available file types and then click 'Word Macro-Enabled Template' in the list to change the file type (Figure 11–2).

- Click the Save button (Save As dialog box) to save the file using the entered file name as a macro-enabled template.

Q&A

How does Word differentiate between a Word template and a Word macro-enabled template?

A Word template has an extension of .dotx, whereas a Word macro-enabled template has an extension of .dotm. Also, the icon for a macro-enabled template contains an exclamation point.

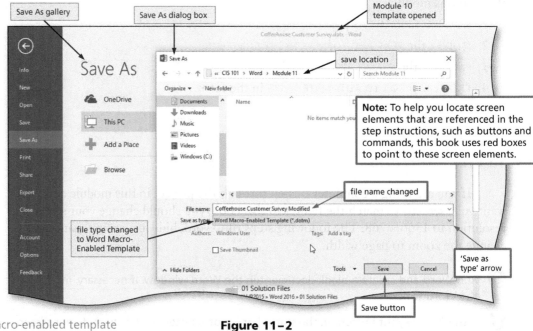

Figure 11–2

BTW
Macro-Enabled Documents
The previous set of steps showed how to create a macro-enabled template. If you wanted to create a macro-enabled document, you would click the 'Save as type' arrow (Save As dialog box), click 'Word Macro-Enabled Document', and then click the Save button.

To Show the Developer Tab

Many of the tasks you will perform in this module use commands on the Developer tab. Thus, the following steps show the Developer tab on the ribbon.

1 Open the Backstage view and then click the Options tab in the left pane of the Backstage view to display the Word Options dialog box.

2 Click Customize Ribbon in the left pane (Word Options dialog box) to display associated options in the right pane.

3 If it is not selected already, place a check mark in the Developer check box in the Main Tabs list.

4 Click the OK button to show the Developer tab on the ribbon.

To Unprotect a Document

The Coffeehouse Customer Survey Modified template is protected. Recall that Module 10 showed how to protect a form so that users could enter data only in designated areas, specifically, the content controls. The following steps unprotect a document. *Why? Before this form can be modified, it must be unprotected. Later in this project, after you have completed the modifications, you will protect it again.*

1

- Display the Developer tab.

- Click the Restrict Editing button (Developer tab | Protect group) to open the Restrict Editing task pane (Figure 11–3).

2

- Click the Stop Protection button in the Restrict Editing task pane to unprotect the form.

- Click the Close button in the Restrict Editing task pane to close the task pane.

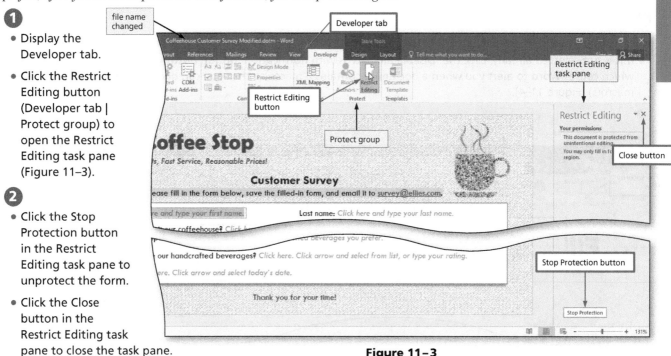

Figure 11–3

Other Ways

1. Click File on ribbon, if necessary, click Info tab in Backstage view, click Protect Document button, click Restrict Editing on Protect Document menu, click Stop Protection button in Restrict Editing task pane

---

How do you protect a computer from macro viruses?

A **computer virus** is a type of malicious software, or malware, which is a potentially damaging computer program that affects, or infects, a computer or mobile device negatively by altering the way the computer or mobile device works, usually without the user's knowledge or permission. Millions of known viruses and other malicious programs exist. The increased use of networks, the Internet, and email has accelerated the spread of computer viruses and other malicious programs.

- To combat these threats, most computer users run an **antivirus program** that searches for viruses and other malware and destroys the malicious programs before they infect a computer or mobile device. Macros are known carriers of viruses and other malware. For this reason, you can specify a macro setting in Word to reduce the chance your computer or mobile device will be infected with a macro virus. These macro settings allow you to enable or disable macros. An **enabled macro** is a macro that Word will execute, and a **disabled macro** is a macro that is unavailable to Word.

- As shown in Figure 11–1b at the beginning of this module, you can instruct Word to display a security warning on a Message Bar if it opens a document that contains a macro(s). If you are confident of the source (author) of the document and macros, enable the macros. If you are uncertain about the reliability of the source of the document and macros, then do not enable the macros.

To Specify Macro Settings in Word

Why? *When you open the online form in this module, you want the macros enabled. At the same time, your computer or mobile device should be protected from potentially harmful macros. Thus, you will specify a macro setting that allows you to enable macros each time you open this module's online form or any document that contains a macro from an unknown source.* The following steps specify macro settings.

- Click the Macro Security button (Developer tab | Code group) to display the Trust Center dialog box.

- If it is not selected already, click the 'Disable all macros with notification' option button (Trust Center dialog box), which causes Word to alert you when a document contains a macro so that you can decide whether to enable the macro(s) (Figure 11–4).

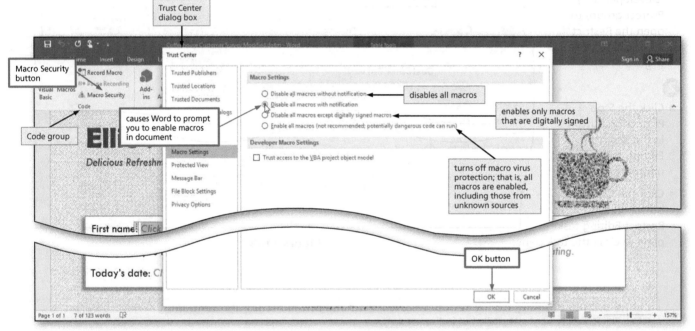

Figure 11–4

- Click the OK button to close the dialog box.

Other Ways

1. Click File on ribbon, click Options tab in Backstage view, click Trust Center in left pane (Word Options dialog box), click 'Trust Center Settings' button in right pane, if necessary, click Macro Settings in left pane (Trust Center dialog box), select desired setting, click OK button in each dialog box

---

BTW
Touch Screen Differences
The Office and Windows interfaces may vary if you are using a touch screen. For this reason, you might notice that the function or appearance of your touch screen differs slightly from this module's presentation.

Modifying Text and Form Content Controls

The form created in Module 10 is enhanced in this module by performing these steps:

1. Delete the current image.
2. Change the fonts, colors, and alignments of the first four lines of text and the last line.
3. Convert the 2 × 1 table containing the First Name and Last Name content controls to text so that each of these content controls is on a separate line.
4. Delete the date picker content control and replace it with a date field.
5. Modify the color of the hyperlink and the first row of check box labels.

The following pages apply these changes to the form.

To Delete a Graphic, Format Text, and Change Paragraph Alignment

The online form in this module contains a different image. It also has different formats for the company name, business tag line, form name, form instructions, date line, and thank you line. The following steps delete the image, format text, and change paragraph alignment.

1 Click the coffee cup image to select it and then press the DELETE key to delete the selected image.

2 Change the color of the first line of text, Ellie's Coffee Stop, third line of text, Customer Survey, and the last line of text, Thank you for your time!, to 'Purple, Accent 5, Darker 25%' (ninth color in fifth row).

3 Change the color of the business tag line to Aqua, Accent 1 (fifth color in first row).

4 Right-align the first and second lines of text (company name and business tag line).

5 Change the highlight color on the fourth line of text to Yellow.

6 Right-align the line of text containing the Today's date content control.

7 If necessary, widen the text box surrounding the data entry area to include the entire date placeholder (Figure 11–5).

If requested by your instructor, change the name, ellies, in the email address to your name.

BTW
Saving and Resetting Themes
If you have changed the color scheme and font set and want to save this combination for future use, save it as a new theme by clicking the Themes button (Design tab | Themes group), clicking 'Save Current Theme' in the Themes gallery, entering a theme name in the File name box (Save Current Theme dialog box), and then clicking the Save button. If you want to reset the theme template to the default, you would click the Themes button (Design tab | Themes group) and then click 'Reset to Theme from Template' in the Themes gallery.

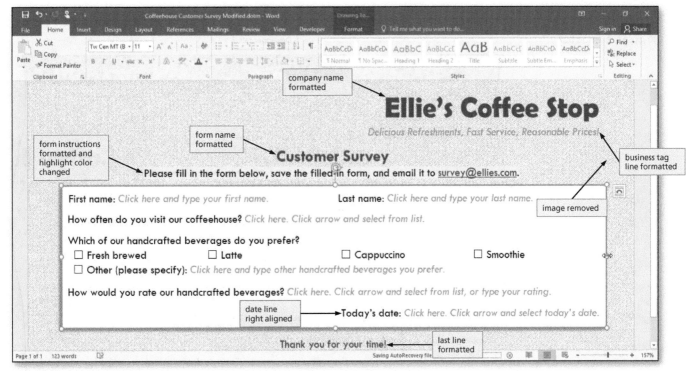

Figure 11–5

BTW
Document Properties
If you wanted to insert document properties into a document, you would click the 'Explore Quick Parts' button (Insert tab | Text group) to display the Explore Quick Parts menu, Point to Document Property on the Explore Quick Parts menu, and then click the property you want to insert on the Document Property menu. To create custom document properties for a document, open the Backstage view, if necessary, click the Info tab to display the Info gallery, click the Properties button in the far right pane to display the Properties menu, click Advanced Properties on the Properties menu to display the Document Properties dialog box, click the Custom tab (Document Properties dialog box) to display the Custom sheet, enter the name of the new property in the Name text box, select its type and value in the dialog box, click the Add button to add the property to the document, and then click the OK button to close the dialog box.

To Change the Properties of a Plain Text Content Control

In this online form, the First Name and Last Name content controls are on separate lines. In Module 10, you selected the 'Content control cannot be deleted' check box in the Content Control Properties dialog box so that users could not delete the content control accidentally while filling in the form. With this check box selected, however, you cannot move a content control from one location to another on the form. Thus, the following steps change the locking properties of the First Name and Last Name content controls so that you can rearrange them.

1 Display the Developer tab.

2 Click the First Name content control to select it.

3 Click the Control Properties button (Developer tab | Controls group) to display the Content Control Properties dialog box.

4 Remove the check mark from the 'Content control cannot be deleted' check box (Content Control Properties dialog box) (Figure 11–6).

5 Click the OK button to assign the modified properties to the content control.

6 Click the Last Name content control to select it and then click the Control Properties button (Developer tab | Controls group) to display the Content Control Properties dialog box.

7 Remove the check mark from the 'Content control cannot be deleted' check box (Content Control Properties dialog box) and then click the OK button to assign the modified properties to the content control.

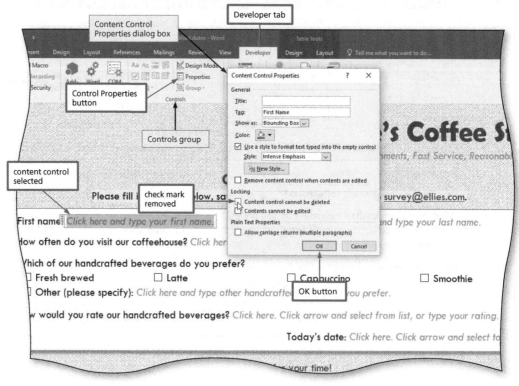

Figure 11–6

To Convert a Table to Text

The First Name and Last Name content controls currently are in a 2 × 1 table. The following steps convert the table to regular text, placing a paragraph break at the location of the second column. *Why? In this online form, these content controls are on separate lines, one below the other. That is, they are not in a table.*

- Position the insertion point somewhere in the table.
- Display the Table Tools Layout tab.
- Click the 'Convert to Text' button (Table Tools Layout tab | Data group) to display the Convert Table To Text dialog box.
- Click Paragraph marks (Convert Table To Text dialog box), which will place a paragraph mark at the location of each new column in the table (Figure 11–7).

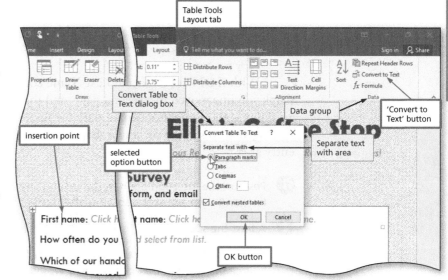

- Click the OK button to convert the table to text, separating each column with the specified character, a paragraph mark in this case.

Figure 11–7

Q&A Why did the Last Name content control move below the First Name content control?
The Separate text with area (Convert Table To Text dialog box) controls how the table is converted to text. The Paragraph marks setting converts each column in the table to a line of text below the previous line. The Tabs setting places a tab character where each column was located, and the Commas setting places a comma where each column was located.

- With the First Name and Last Name lines selected, using either the ruler or the Layout tab, change the left indent to 0.06" so that the text aligns with the text immediately below it (that is, the H in How), as shown in Figure 11–8.

- Click anywhere to remove the selection from the text.

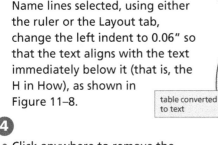

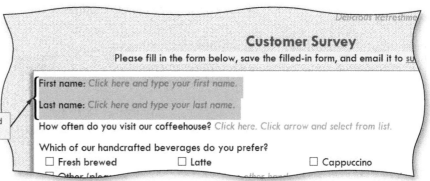

Figure 11–8

To Change the Properties of a Plain Text Content Control

You are finished moving the First Name and Last Name content controls. The following steps reset the locking properties of these content controls.

1. Display the Developer tab.

2. Click the First Name content control to select it and then click the Control Properties button (Developer tab | Controls group) to display the Content Control Properties dialog box.

3 Place a check mark in the 'Content control cannot be deleted' check box (Content Control Properties dialog box) and then click the OK button to assign the modified properties to the content control.

4 Repeat Steps 2 and 3 for the Last Name content control.

To Adjust Paragraph Spacing and Resize the Rectangle Shape

With the First Name and Last Name content controls on separate lines, the thank you line moved to a second page, and the rectangle outline in the data entry area now is too short to accommodate the text. The following steps adjust paragraph spacing and extend the rectangle shape downward so that it surrounds the entire data entry area.

1 Position the insertion point in the second line of text on the form (the business tag line) and then adjust the spacing after to 6 pt (Layout tab | Paragraph group).

2 Adjust the spacing after to 6 pt for the First Name and Last Name lines.

3 Adjust the spacing before and after to 6 pt for the line that begins, How often do you visit..., and the line that begins, How would you rate...

4 Adjust the spacing before to 12 pt for the thank you line.

5 Scroll to display the entire form in the document window. If necessary, reduce spacing after other paragraphs so that the entire form fits in a single document window.

6 Click the rectangle shape to select it.

7 Position the pointer on the bottom-middle sizing handle of the rectangle shape.

8 Drag the bottom-middle sizing handle downward so that the shape includes the bottom content control, in this case, the Today's Date content control (Figure 11–9). If necessary, resize the other edges of the shape to fit the text.

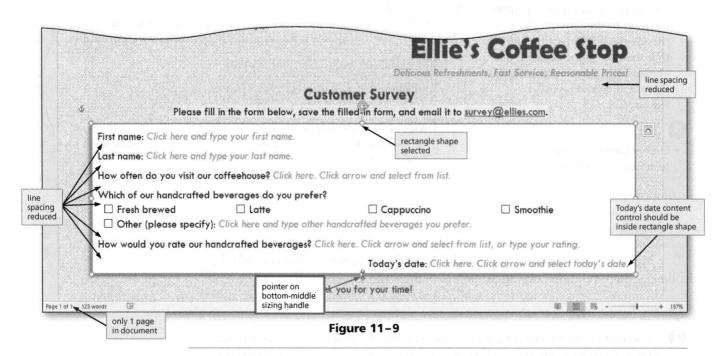

Figure 11–9

To Change the Properties of a Date Picker Content Control

In this online form, instead of the user entering the current date, the computer or mobile device's system date will be filled in automatically by Word. Thus, the Today's Date content control is not needed and can be deleted. To delete the content control, you first will need to remove the check mark from the 'Content control cannot be deleted' check box in the Content Control Properties dialog box. The following steps change the locking properties of the Today's Date content control and then delete the content control.

1 Display the Developer tab.

2 Click the Today's Date content control to select it.

3 Click the Control Properties button (Developer tab | Controls group) to display the Content Control Properties dialog box.

4 Remove the check mark from the 'Content control cannot be deleted' check box (Content Control Properties dialog box) (Figure 11–10).

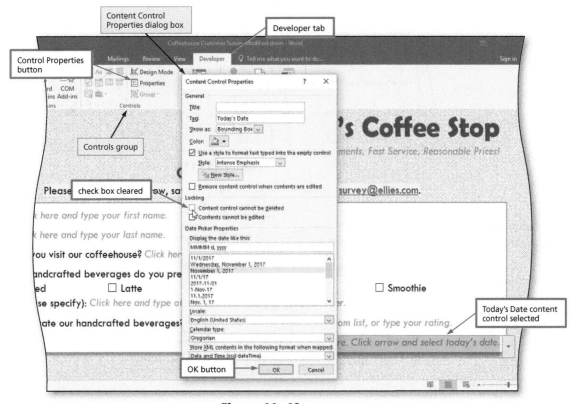

Figure 11–10

5 Click the OK button to assign the modified properties to the content control.

6 Right-click the Today's Date content control to display a shortcut menu and then click 'Remove Content Control' on the shortcut menu to delete the selected content control.

To Insert a Date Field

The following steps insert the date and time as a field in the form at the location of the insertion point. *Why? The current date and time is a field so that the form automatically displays the current date and time. Recall that a field is a set of codes that instructs Word to perform a certain action.*

- Display the Insert tab.
- With the insertion point positioned as shown in Figure 11–11, which is the location for the date and time, click the 'Explore Quick Parts' button (Insert tab | Text group) to display the Explore Quick Parts menu.

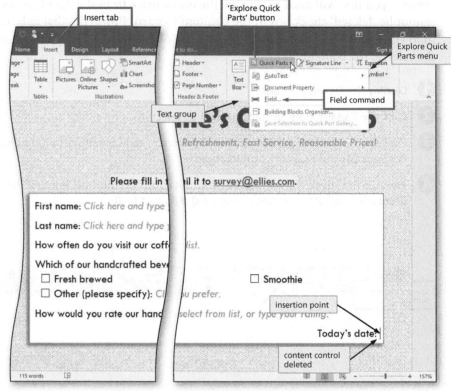

Figure 11–11

- Click Field on the Explore Quick Parts menu to display the Field dialog box.
- Scroll through the Field names list (Field dialog box) and then click Date, which displays the Date formats list in the Field properties area.
- Click the date in the format of 11/1/2017 1:29:14 PM in the Date formats list to select a date format — your date and time will differ (Figure 11–12).

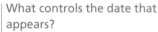

Q&A

What controls the date that appears?

Your current computer or mobile device date appears in this dialog box. The format for the selected date shows in the Date formats box. In this case, the format for the selected date is M/d/yyyy h:mm:ss am/pm, which displays the date as month/day/ year hours:minutes:seconds AM/PM.

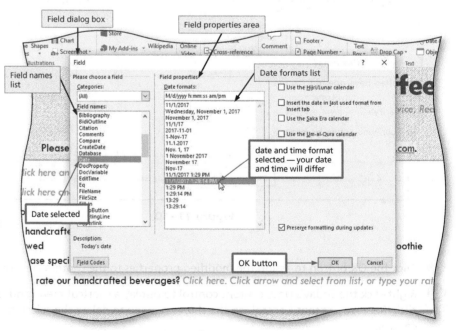

Figure 11–12

- Click the OK button to insert the current date and time at the location of the insertion point (Figure 11–13).

Q&A
How do I delete a field?
Select it and then press the DELETE key or click the Cut button (Home tab | Clipboard group), or right-click the field and then click Cut on the shortcut menu or mini toolbar.

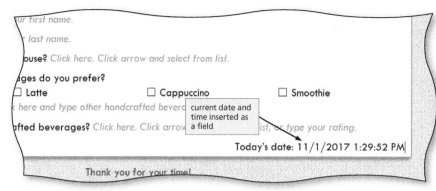

Figure 11–13

Other Ways

1. Click 'Insert Date and Time' button (Insert tab | Text group), select date format (Date and Time dialog box), place check mark in Update automatically check box, click OK button

To Edit a Field

1 SAVE DOCUMENT AS MACRO-ENABLED TEMPLATE | 2 MODIFY TEXT & FORM CONTENT CONTROLS
3 ENHANCE FORM'S VISUAL APPEAL | 4 CREATE MACROS TO AUTOMATE TASKS

The following steps edit the field. *Why? After you see the date and time in the form, you decide not to include the seconds in the time. That is, you want just the hours and minutes to be displayed.*

- Right-click the date field to display a shortcut menu (Figure 11–14).

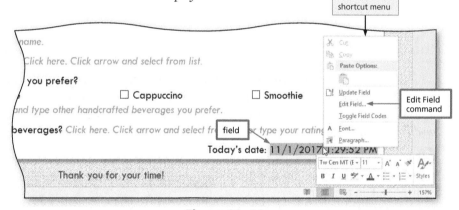

Figure 11–14

- Click Edit Field on the shortcut menu to display the Field dialog box.

- If necessary, scroll through the Field names list (Field dialog box) and then click Date to display the Date formats list in the Field properties area.

- Select the desired date format, in this case 11/1/2017 1:31 PM (Figure 11–15).

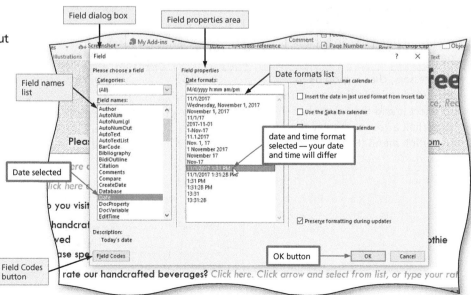

Figure 11–15

3
- Click the OK button to insert the edited field at the location of the insertion point (Figure 11–16).

BTW
Field Formats
If you wanted to create custom field formats, you would click the Field Codes button (Field dialog box) (shown in Figure 11-15) to display advanced field properties in the right pane in the dialog box, click the Options button to display the Field Options dialog box, select the format to apply in the Formatting list, click the 'Add to Field' button, and then click the OK button in each open dialog box.

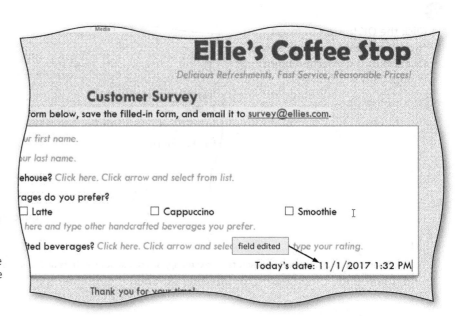

Figure 11–16

To Modify a Style Using the Styles Task Pane

1 SAVE DOCUMENT AS MACRO-ENABLED TEMPLATE | 2 MODIFY TEXT & FORM CONTENT CONTROLS
3 ENHANCE FORM'S VISUAL APPEAL | 4 CREATE MACROS TO AUTOMATE TASKS

The new text highlight color of the form instructions makes it difficult to see the hyperlink. In this online form, the hyperlink should be the same color as the company name so that the hyperlink is noticeable. The following steps modify a style using the Styles task pane. *Why? The Hyperlink style is not in the Styles gallery. To modify a style that is not in the Styles gallery, you can use the Styles task pane.*

1
- Position the insertion point in the hyperlink in the form.
- Display the Home tab.
- Click the Styles Dialog Box Launcher (Home tab | Styles group) to open the Styles task pane.
- If necessary, click Hyperlink in the list of styles in the task pane to select it and then click the Hyperlink arrow to display the Hyperlink menu (Figure 11–17).

Q&A What if the style I want to modify is not in the list?
Click the Manage Styles button at the bottom of the task pane (shown in Figure 11–18), locate the style, and then click the Modify button in the dialog box.

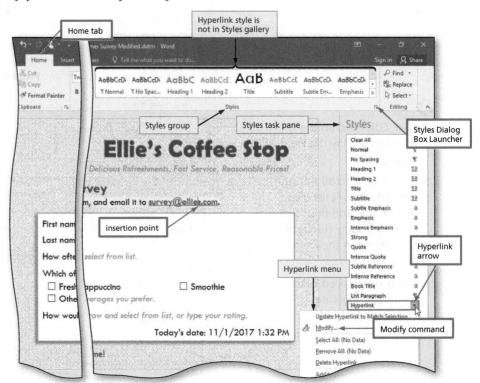

Figure 11–17

- Click Modify on the Hyperlink menu to display the Modify Style dialog box.
- Click the Font Color arrow (Modify Style dialog box) to display the Font Color gallery (Figure 11–18).

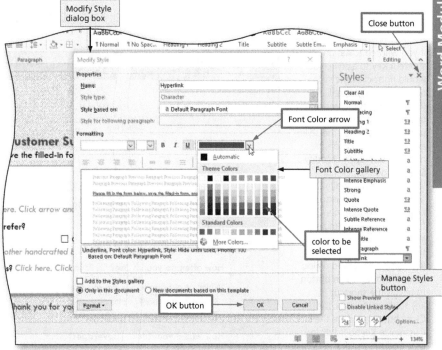

Figure 11–18

- Click 'Purple, Accent 5, Darker 25%' (ninth color in fifth row) as the new hyperlink color.
- Click the OK button to close the dialog box. Close the Styles task pane (Figure 11–19).

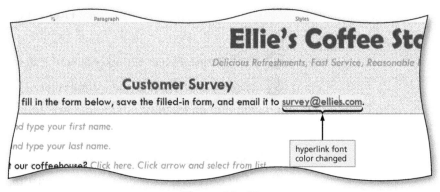

Figure 11–19

To Modify a Style

In this online form, the placeholder text is to be one shade darker than the company name. Currently, the placeholder text is formatted using the Intense Emphasis style, which uses a shade of aqua as the font color. Thus, the following steps modify the color of the Intense Emphasis style to the darkest shade of purple.

1 Scroll through the Styles gallery (Home tab | Styles group) to locate the Intense Emphasis style.

2 Right-click Intense Emphasis in the Styles gallery to display a shortcut menu and then click Modify on the shortcut menu to display the Modify Style dialog box.

3 Click the Font Color arrow (Modify Style dialog box) to display the Font Color gallery (Figure 11–20).

BTW
Hidden Styles
Some styles are hidden, which means they do not appear in the Styles task pane. You can display all styles, including hidden styles, by clicking the Manage Styles button in the Styles task pane (Figure 11–18), which displays the Manage Styles dialog box. Click the Edit tab, if necessary, and then locate the style name in the Select a style to edit list.

BTW

Assign a Shortcut Key to a Style
If you wanted to assign a shortcut key to a style, you would right-click the style name in the Styles gallery (Home tab | Styles group) or display the Styles task pane and then click the style arrow, click Modify on the menu to display the Modify Style dialog box, click the Format button (Modify Style dialog box), click Shortcut key on the Format menu to display the Customize Keyboard dialog box, press the desired shortcut key(s) (Customize Keyboard dialog box), click the Assign button to assign the shortcut key to the style, click the Close button to close the Customize Keyboard dialog box, and then click the OK button to close the Modify Style dialog box.

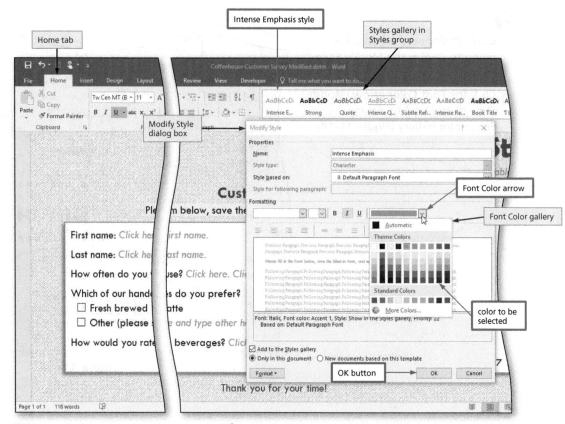

Figure 11–20

4. Click 'Purple, Accent 5, Darker 50%' (ninth color in last row) as the new color.

5. Click the OK button to change the color of the style, which automatically changes the color of every item formatted using this style in the document.

To Modify the Default Font Settings

You can change the default font so that the current document and all future documents use the new font settings. That is, if you exit Word, restart the computer or mobile device, and run Word again, documents you create will use the new default font. If you wanted to change the default font from 11-point Calibri to another font, font style, font size, font color, and/or font effects, you would perform the following steps.

1. Click the Font Dialog Box Launcher (Home tab | Font group) to display the Font dialog box.

2. Make desired changes to the font settings in the Font dialog box.

3. Click the 'Set As Default' button to change the default settings to those specified in Step 2.

4. When the Microsoft Word dialog box is displayed, select the desired option button and then click the OK button.

BTW

Advanced Character Attributes
If you wanted to set advanced character attributes, you would click the Font Dialog Box Launcher (Home tab | Font group) to display the Font dialog box, click the Advanced tab (Font dialog box) to display the Advanced sheet, select the desired Character Spacing or OpenType Features settings, and then click the OK button.

TO RESET THE DEFAULT FONT SETTINGS

To change the font settings back to the default, you would follow the steps in the previous section, using the default font settings when performing Step 2. If you do not remember the default settings, you would perform the following steps to restore the original Normal style settings.

1. Exit Word.
2. Use File Explorer to locate the Normal.dotm file (be sure that hidden files and folders are displayed and include system and hidden files in your search), which is the file that contains default font and other settings.
3. Rename the Normal.dotm file to oldnormal.dotm file so that the Normal.dotm file no longer exists.
4. Run Word, which will recreate a Normal.dotm file using the original default settings.

BTW
Character vs. Paragraph Styles
In the Styles task pane, character styles display a lowercase letter a to the right of the style name, and paragraph styles show a paragraph mark. With a character style, Word applies the formats to the selected text. With a paragraph style, Word applies the formats to the entire paragraph.

To Create a Character Style

1 SAVE DOCUMENT AS MACRO-ENABLED TEMPLATE | 2 MODIFY TEXT & FORM CONTENT CONTROLS
3 ENHANCE FORM'S VISUAL APPEAL | 4 CREATE MACROS TO AUTOMATE TASKS

In this online form, the first row of check box labels are to be the same color as the placeholder text. The following steps create a character style called Check Box Labels. **Why?** *Although you could select each of the check box labels and then format them, a more efficient technique is to create a character style.* If you decide to modify the formats of the check box labels at a later time, you simply change the formats assigned to the style to automatically change all characters in the document based on that style.

- Position the insertion point in one of the check box labels.
- Click the Styles Dialog Box Launcher (Home tab | Styles group) to open the Styles task pane.
- Click the Manage Styles button in the Styles task pane to display the Manage Styles dialog box (Figure 11–21).

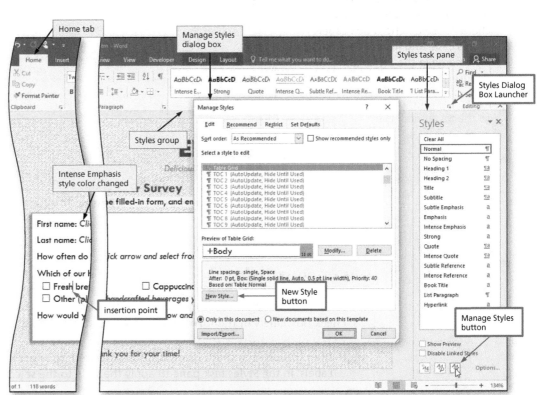

Figure 11–21

2

- Click the New Style button (Manage Styles dialog box) to display the Create New Style from Formatting dialog box.

- Type **Check Box Labels** in the Name text box (Create New Style from Formatting dialog box) as the name of the new style.

- Click the Style type arrow and then click Character so that the new style does not contain any paragraph formats.

- Click the Font Color arrow to display the Font Color gallery and then click 'Purple, Accent 5, Darker 50%' (ninth color in last row) as the new color (Figure 11–22).

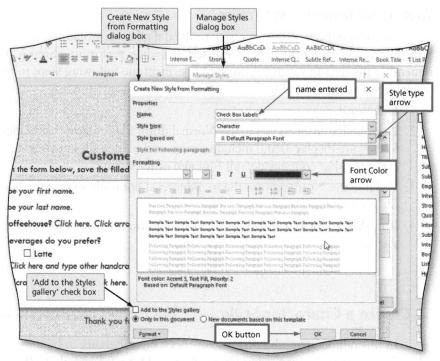

Figure 11–22

3

- Click the OK button in each open dialog box to create the new character style, Check Box Labels in this case, and insert the new style name in the Styles task pane (Figure 11–23).

Q&A

What if I wanted the style added to the Styles gallery?

You would place a check mark in the 'Add to the Styles gallery' check box (Create New Style from Formatting dialog box), shown in Figure 11–22.

Figure 11–23

To Apply a Style

The next step is to apply the Check Box Labels style just created to the first row of check box labels in the form. The following steps apply a style.

1 Drag through the check box label, Fresh brewed, to select it and then click 'Check Box Labels' in the Styles task pane to apply the style to the selected text.

2 Repeat Step 1 for these check box labels (Figure 11–24): Latte, Cappuccino, and Smoothie.

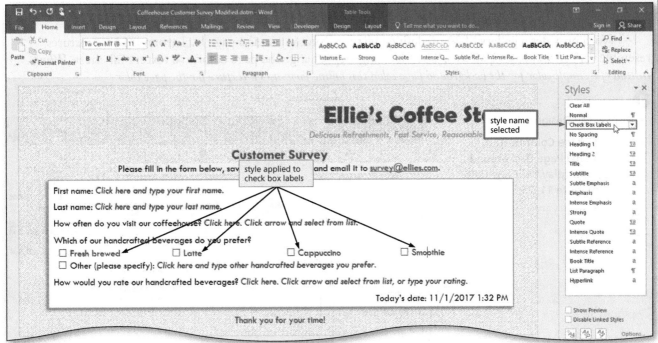

Figure 11–24

Q&A Do I have to drag through one word labels to apply a style?
No. You simply can position the insertion point in the word before clicking the desired style to apply.

③ Close the Styles task pane.

④ If necessary, click anywhere to remove the selection from the check box label.

⑤ Save the template again on the same storage location with the same file name.

BTW
Saving Templates
When you save a template that contains building blocks, the building blocks are available to all users who access the template.

Break Point: If you wish to take a break, this is a good place to do so. You can exit Word now. To resume at a later time, run Word, open the file called Coffeehouse Customer Survey Modified, and continue following the steps from this location forward.

Enhancing with Color, Shapes, Effects, and Graphics

You will enhance the form created in Module 10 by performing these steps:

1. Apply a texture fill effect for the page color.
2. Change the appearance of the shape.
3. Change the color of a shadow on the shape.
4. Fill a shape with a picture.
5. Insert a picture, remove its background, and apply an artistic effect.
6. Insert and format a text box.
7. Group the picture and the text box together.

The following pages apply these changes to the form.

To Use a Fill Effect for the Page Color

Word provides a gallery of 24 predefined textures you can use as a page background. These textures resemble various wallpaper patterns. The following steps change the page color to a texture fill effect. *Why?* *Instead of a simple color for the background page color, this online form uses a texture for the page color.*

1

- Display the Design tab.

- Click the Page Color button (Design tab | Page Background group) to display the Page Color gallery (Figure 11–25).

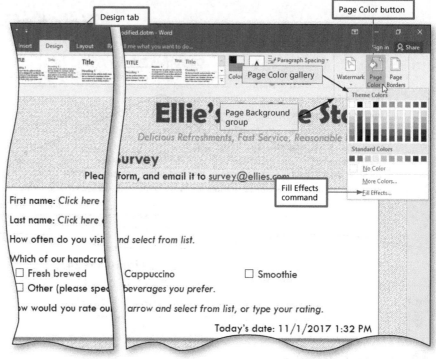

Figure 11–25

2

- Click Fill Effects in the Page Color gallery to display the Fill Effects dialog box.

- Click the Texture tab (Fill Effects dialog box) to display the Texture sheet.

- Scroll to, if necessary, and then click the Stationery texture in the Texture gallery to select the texture (Figure 11–26).

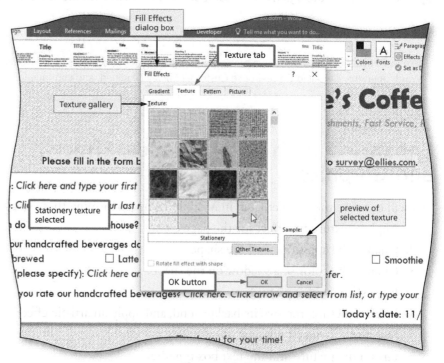

Figure 11–26

3

- Click the OK button to apply the selected texture as the page color in the document (Figure 11–27).

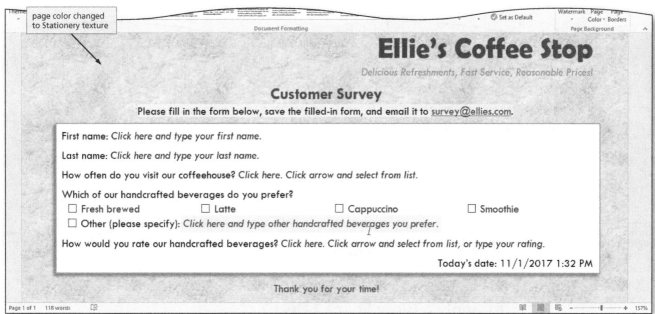

Figure 11–27

How would I remove a texture page color?
You would click the Page Color button (Design tab | Page Background group) and then click No Color in the Page Color gallery.

To Change a Shape

The following steps change a shape. *Why? This online form uses a variation of the standard rectangle shape.*

1

- Click the rectangle shape to select it.
- Display the Drawing Tools Format tab.
- Click the Edit Shape button (Drawing Tools Format tab | Insert Shapes group) to display the Edit Shape menu.
- Point to Change Shape on the Edit Shape menu to display the Change Shape gallery (Figure 11–28).

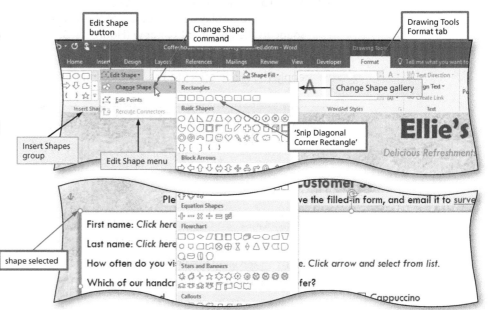

Figure 11–28

2
- Click 'Snip Diagonal Corner Rectangle' in the Rectangles area in the Change Shape gallery to change the selected shape (Figure 11–29).

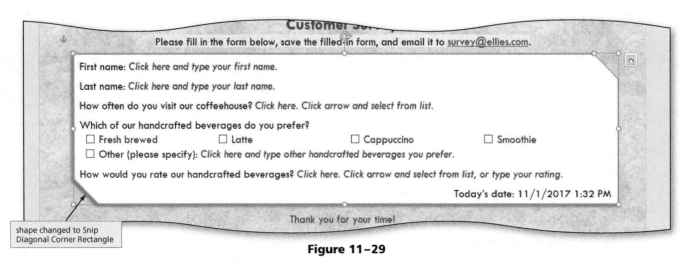

shape changed to Snip
Diagonal Corner Rectangle

Figure 11–29

To Apply a Glow Shape Effect

The next step is to apply a glow effect to the rectangle shape. You can apply the same effects to shapes as to pictures. That is, you can apply shadows, reflections, glows, soft edges, bevels, and 3-D rotations to pictures and shapes. The following steps apply a shape effect.

1 With the rectangle shape selected, click the Shape Effects button (Drawing Tools Format tab | Shape Styles group) to display the Shape Effects menu.

2 Point to Glow on the Shape Effects menu to display the Glow gallery.

3 Point to 'Aqua, 5 pt glow, Accent color 1' in the Glow Variations area (first glow in first row) to display a live preview of the selected glow effect applied to the selected shape in the document window (Figure 11–30).

4 Click 'Aqua, 5 pt glow, Accent color 1' in the Glow gallery (first glow in first row) to apply the shape effect to the selected shape.

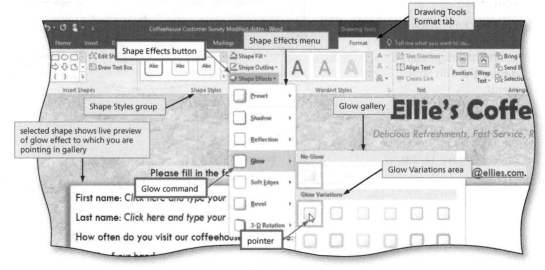

Figure 11–30

To Apply a Shadow Shape Effect

The following steps apply a shadow effect and change its color. *Why? The rectangle in this online form has a shadow with a similar color to the placeholder text.*

1

- With the rectangle shape still selected, click the Shape Effects button (Drawing Tools Format tab | Shape Styles group) again to display the Shape Effects menu.

- Point to Shadow on the Shape Effects menu to display the Shadow gallery.

- Point to 'Perspective Diagonal Upper Right' in the Perspective area at the bottom of the Shadow gallery to display a live preview of that shadow applied to the shape in the document (Figure 11–31).

 **Experiment**

- Point to various shadows in the Shadow gallery and watch the shadow on the selected shape change.

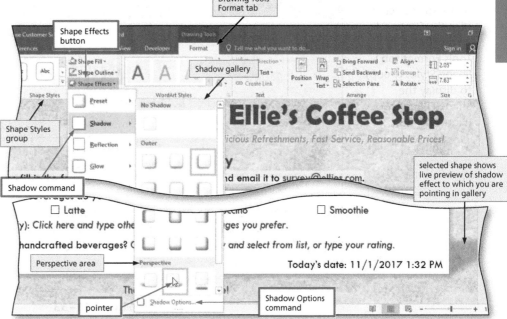

Figure 11–31

2

- Click 'Perspective Diagonal Upper Right' in the Shadow gallery to apply the selected shadow to the selected shape.

- Click the Shape Effects button (Drawing Tools Format tab | Shape Styles group) again to display the Shape Effects menu.

- Point to Shadow in the Shape Effects menu to display the Shadow gallery.

- Click Shadow Options in the Shadow gallery to open the Format Shape task pane.

- Click the Shadow Color button (Format Shape task pane) and then click 'Purple, Accent 5, Darker 50%' (ninth color in last row) in the Shadow Color gallery to change the shadow color.

- Click the Transparency down arrow as many times as necessary until the Transparency box displays 60% to change the amount of transparency in the shadow (Figure 11–32).

3

- Click the Close button to close the Format Shape task pane.

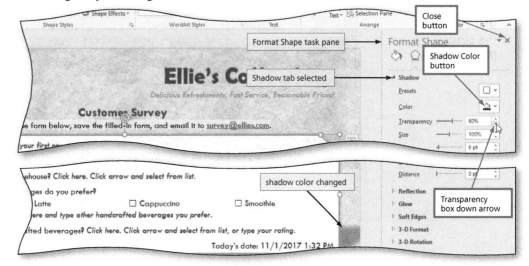

Figure 11–32

To Fill a Shape with a Picture

The following steps fill a shape with a picture. **Why?** *The rectangle in this online form contains a picture of coffee beans. The picture, called Coffee Beans, is located on the Data Files. Please contact your instructor for information about accessing the Data Files.*

1

- With the rectangle shape still selected, click the Shape Fill arrow (Drawing Tools Format tab | Shape Styles group) to display the Shape Fill gallery (Figure 11–33).

Q&A My Shape Fill gallery did not appear. Why not?
You clicked the Shape Fill button instead of the Shape Fill arrow. Repeat Step 1.

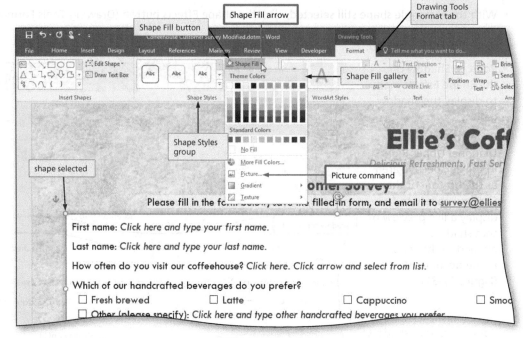

Figure 11–33

2

- Click Picture in the Shape Fill gallery to display the Insert Pictures dialog box.

- Click the Browse button (Insert Pictures dialog box) to display the Insert Picture dialog box. Locate and then select the file called Coffee Beans (Insert Picture dialog box).

- Click the Insert button (Insert Picture dialog box) to fill the rectangle shape with the picture (Figure 11–34).

Figure 11–34

To Change the Color of a Picture

The text in the rectangle shape is difficult to read because the picture just inserted is too dark. You can experiment with adjusting the brightness, contrast, and color of a picture so that the text is readable. In this project, the color is changed to the washout setting so that the text is easier to read. The following steps change the color of the picture to washout.

1 Display the Picture Tools Format tab.

2 With the rectangle shape still selected, click the Color button (Picture Tools Format tab | Adjust group) to display the Color gallery.

3 Point to Washout in the Recolor area in the Color gallery to display a live preview of the selected color applied to the selected picture (Figure 11–35).

4 Click Washout in the Color gallery to apply the selected color to the selected picture.

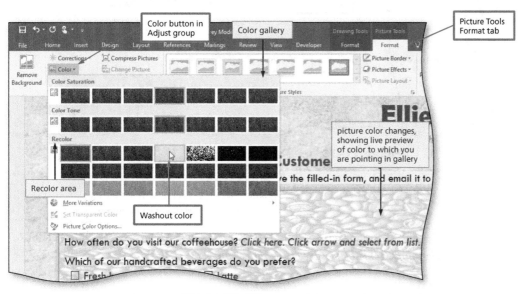

Figure 11–35

To Insert, Change Wrapping Style, and Resize a Picture

The top of the online form in this module contains a picture of a coffee cup on a saucer with a spoon on the saucer. The picture, called Coffee Cup, is located on the Data Files. Please contact your instructor for information about accessing the Data Files.

You will change the wrapping style of the inserted picture so that it can be positioned in front of the text. Because the graphic's original size is too large, you also will resize it. The following steps insert a picture, change its wrapping style, and resize it.

1 Position the insertion point in a location near where the picture will be inserted, in this case, near the top of the online form.

2 Display the Insert tab. Click the From File button (Insert tab | Illustrations group) to display the Insert Picture dialog box.

3 Locate and then click the file called Coffee Cup (Insert Picture dialog box) to select the file.

BTW

Drawing Canvas
Some users prefer inserting graphics on a drawing canvas, which is a rectangular boundary between a shape and the rest of the document; it also is a container that helps you resize and arrange shapes on the page. To insert a drawing canvas, click the 'Draw a Shape' button (Insert tab | Illustrations group) and then click 'New Drawing Canvas' in the Draw a Shape gallery. You can use the Drawing Tools Format tab to insert objects in the drawing canvas or format the appearance of the drawing canvas.

④ Click the Insert button to insert the picture at the location of the insertion point.

⑤ With the picture selected, click the Wrap Text button (Picture Tools Format tab | Arrange group) and then click 'In Front of Text' so that the graphic can be positioned on top of text.

⑥ Change the value in the Shape Height box (Picture Tools Format tab | Size group) to 1" and the value in the Shape Width box (Picture Tools Format tab | Size group) to 1.78".

⑦ If necessary, scroll to display the online form in the document window (Figure 11–36).

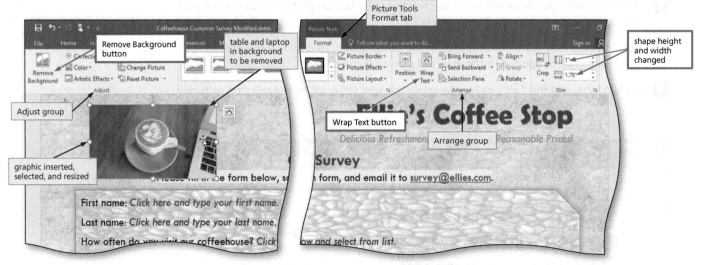

Figure 11–36

To Remove a Background

In Word, you can remove a background from a picture. The following steps remove a background. *Why? You remove the table and laptop in the background from the picture of the coffee cup.*

①

• With the coffee cup picture selected, click the Remove Background button (Picture Tools Format tab | Adjust group) (shown in Figure 11–36), to display the Background Removal tab and show the proposed area to be deleted in purple (Figure 11–37).

Q&A What is the Background Removal tab?

You can draw around areas to keep or areas to remove by clicking the respective buttons on the Background Removal tab. If you mistakenly mark too much, use the Delete Mark button. You also can drag the proposed rectangle to adjust the proposed removal area. When finished marking, click the 'Close Background Removal and Keep Changes' button, or to start over, click the 'Close Background Removal and Discard Changes' button.

Figure 11–37

2

- Drag the proposed marking lines downward slightly, as shown in Figure 11–38, so that the entire saucer shows and the entire table and laptop in the background is shaded purple. If necessary, drag the marking lines a few times.

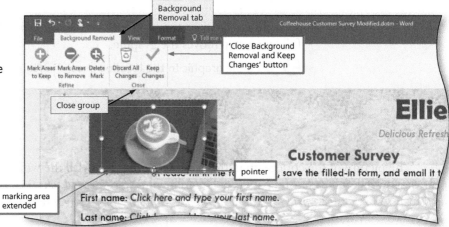

Figure 11–38

3

- Click the 'Close Background Removal and Keep Changes' button (Background Removal tab | Close group) to remove the area shaded purple to close the Background Removal tab (Figure 11–39).

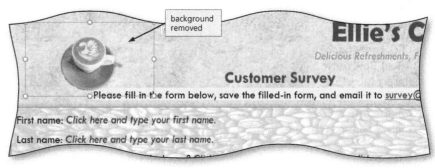

Figure 11–39

To Apply an Artistic Effect

1 SAVE DOCUMENT AS MACRO-ENABLED TEMPLATE | 2 MODIFY TEXT & FORM CONTENT CONTROLS
3 ENHANCE FORM'S VISUAL APPEAL | **4 CREATE MACROS TO AUTOMATE TASKS**

Word provides several different artistic effects, such as blur, line drawing, and paint brush, that alter the appearance of a picture. The following steps apply an artistic effect to the picture. *Why? You want to soften the look of the picture a bit.*

1

- With the picture still selected, click the Artistic Effects button (Picture Tools Format tab | Adjust group) to display the Artistic Effects gallery.

- Point to Crisscross Etching (third effect in fourth row) in the Artistic Effects gallery to display a live preview of the effect applied to the selected picture in the document window (Figure 11–40).

2

- Click Crisscross Etching in the Artistic Effects gallery to apply the selected effect to the selected picture.

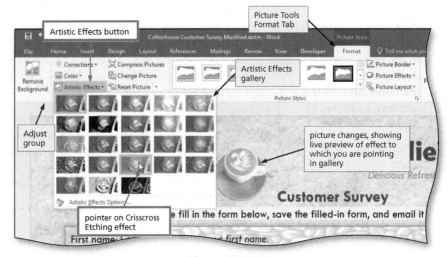

Figure 11–40

To Move the Graphic

In this project, the graphic is to be positioned on the left edge of the form. The following step moves the graphic.

 Drag the graphic to the location shown in Figure 11–41.

To Draw a Text Box

1 SAVE DOCUMENT AS MACRO-ENABLED TEMPLATE | 2 MODIFY TEXT & FORM CONTENT CONTROLS
3 ENHANCE FORM'S VISUAL APPEAL | **4 CREATE MACROS TO AUTOMATE TASKS**

The picture of the coffee cup in this form has a text box with the words, Let Us Serve You!, positioned near the lower-left corner of the saucer. The following steps draw a text box. **Why?** *The first step in creating the text box is to draw its perimeter. You draw a text box using the same procedure as you do to draw a shape.*

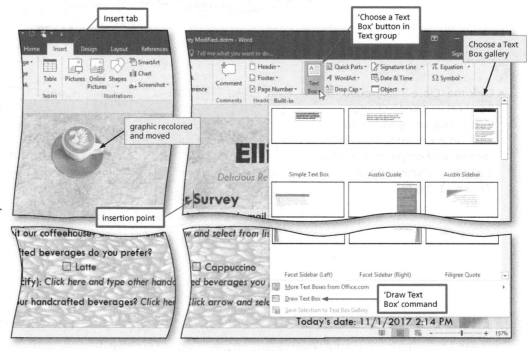

①

- Position the insertion point somewhere in the top of the online form.
- Display the Insert tab.
- Click the 'Choose a Text Box' button (Insert tab | Text group) to display the Choose a Text Box gallery (Figure 11–41).

Figure 11–41

②

- Click 'Draw Text Box' in the Text Box gallery, which removes the gallery and changes the shape of the pointer to a crosshair.
- Drag the pointer to the right and downward to form the boundaries of the text box, as shown in Figure 11–42.

Q&A What if I am using a touch screen?
A text box is inserted in the document window. Proceed to Step 4.

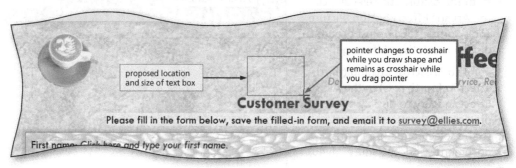

Figure 11–42

③

- Release the mouse button so that Word draws the text box according to your drawing in the document window.

• Verify your shape is the same approximate height and width as the one in this project by changing the values in the Shape Height and Shape Width boxes (Drawing Tools Format tab | Size group) to 0.68" and 0.8", respectively (Figure 11–43).

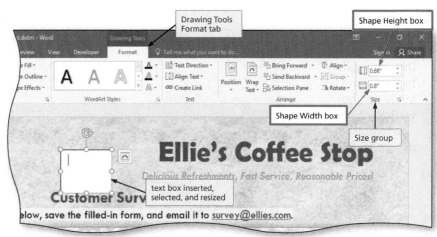

Figure 11–43

To Add Text to a Text Box and Format the Text

The next step is to add the phrase, Let Us Serve You!, centered in the text box using a text effect. You add text to a text box using the same procedure you do when adding text to a shape. The following steps add text to a text box.

1 Display the Home tab. With the text box selected, click the Center button (Home tab | Paragraph group) so that the text you enter is centered in the text box.

2 With the text box selected, click the 'Text Effects and Typography' button (Home tab | Font group) and then click 'Fill - Aqua, Accent 1, Shadow' (second effect in first row) in the Text Effects gallery to specify the format for the text in the text box.

3 If your insertion point is not positioned in the text box (shape), right-click the shape to display a shortcut menu and the mini toolbar and then click Edit Text on the shortcut menu or mini toolbar to place an insertion point centered in the text box.

4 Type `Let Us Serve You!` as the text for the text box (shown in Figure 11–44). (If necessary, adjust the height of the text box to fit the text.)

To Change Text Direction in a Text Box

1 SAVE DOCUMENT AS MACRO-ENABLED TEMPLATE | 2 MODIFY TEXT & FORM CONTENT CONTROLS
3 ENHANCE FORM'S VISUAL APPEAL | 4 CREATE MACROS TO AUTOMATE TASKS

The following steps change text direction in a text box. **Why?** *The direction of the text in the text box should be vertical instead of horizontal.*

1

• Display the Drawing Tools Format tab.

• With the shape still selected, click the Text Direction button (Drawing Tools Format tab | Text group) to display the Text Direction gallery (Figure 11–44).

Q&A What if my text box no longer is selected?
Click the text box to select it.

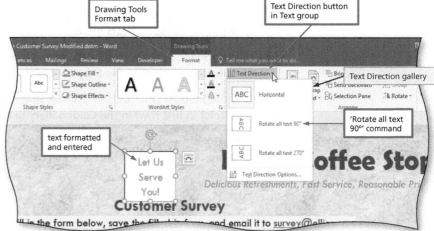

Figure 11–44

2

● Click 'Rotate all text 90°' in the Text Direction gallery to display the text in the text box vertically from top to bottom (Figure 11–45).

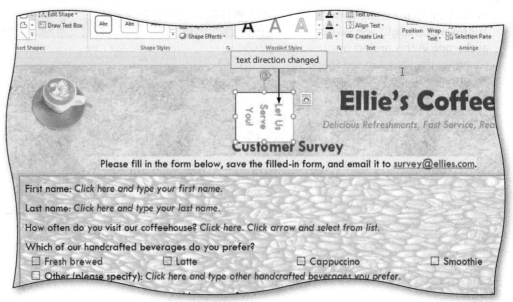

Figure 11–45

Other Ways

1. Right-click text box, click Format Shape on shortcut menu, click Text Options tab (Format Shape task pane), click Layout & Properties button, expand Text Box section, click Text direction box, select desired direction, click Close button

---

To Apply a Shadow Shape Effect to a Text Box

The text box in this online form has an inside shadow that is in the same color as the business tag line. The following steps apply a shadow effect and change its color.

1 Move the text box to the left so that it is visible when you change the shadows and colors.

2 With the text box still selected, click the Shape Effects button (Drawing Tools Format tab | Shape Styles group) to display the Shape Effects menu.

3 Point to Shadow in the Shape Effects menu to display the Shadow gallery and then click Inside Center in the Inner area of the Shadow gallery to apply the selected shadow to the selected shape.

4 Click the Shape Effects button (Drawing Tools Format tab | Shape Styles group) again to display the Shape Effects menu.

5 Point to Shadow in the Shape Effects menu to display the Shadow gallery and then click Shadow Options in the Shadow gallery to display the Format Shape task pane.

6 Click the Shadow Color button (Format Shape task pane) and then click 'Aqua, Accent 1' (fifth color in first row) in the Color gallery to change the shadow color (shown in Figure 11–46).

7 Click the Close button to close the Format Shape task pane.

To Change a Shape Outline of a Text Box

You change an outline on a text box (shape) using the same procedure as you do with a picture. The following steps remove the shape outline on the text box. *Why? The text box in this form has no outline.*

- With the text box still selected, click the Shape Outline arrow (Drawing Tools Format tab | Shape Styles group) to display the Shape Outline gallery (Figure 11–46).

 The Shape Outline gallery did not display. Why not?
You clicked the Shape Outline button instead of the Shape Outline arrow. Repeat Step 1.

Experiment

- Point to various colors in the Shape Outline gallery and watch the color of the outline on the text box change in the document.

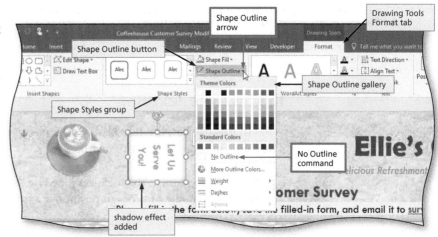

Figure 11–46

- Click No Outline in the Shape Outline gallery to remove the outline from the selected shape.

Other Ways

1. Click Format Shape Dialog Box Launcher (Drawing Tools Format tab | Shape Styles group); expand Line section (Format Shape task pane); click No line to remove line, or click Solid line, click Outline color button, and select desired color to change line color; click Close button

2. Right-click text box (or, if using touch, tap 'Show Context Menu' button on mini toolbar), click Format Shape on shortcut menu, expand Line section (Format Shape task pane), click No line to remove line, or click Solid line, click Outline color button, and select desired color to change line color; click Close button

To Apply a 3-D Effect to a Text Box

Word provides 3-D effects for shapes (such as text boxes) that are similar to those it provides for pictures. The following steps apply a 3-D rotation effect to a text box. *Why? In this form, the text box is rotated using a 3-D rotation effect.*

- With the text box selected, click the Shape Effects button (Drawing Tools Format tab | Shape Styles group) to display the Shape Effects gallery.

- Point to '3-D Rotation' in the Shape Effects gallery to display the 3-D Rotation gallery.

- Point to 'Isometric Top Up' in the Parallel area (third rotation in first row) to display a live preview of the selected 3-D effect applied to the text box in the document window (Figure 11–47).

Experiment

- Point to various 3-D rotation effects in the 3-D Rotation gallery and watch the text box change in the document window.

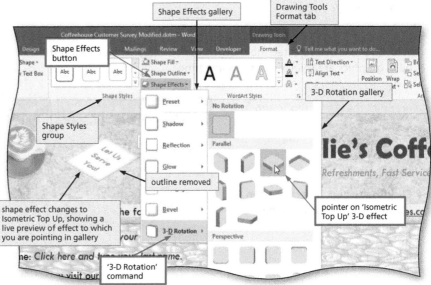

Figure 11–47

• Click 'Isometric Top Up' in the 3-D Rotation gallery to apply the selected 3-D effect.

Other Ways
1. Click Format Shape Dialog Box Launcher (Drawing Tools Format tab | Shape Styles group), click Text Options tab (Format Shape task pane), click Text Effects button, if necessary expand 3-D Rotation Section, select desired options, click Close button	2. Right-click text box (or, if using touch, tap 'Show Context Menu' button on mini toolbar), click Format Shape on shortcut menu, click Text Options tab (Format Shape task pane), click Text Effects button, if necessary expand 3-D Rotation Section, select desired options, click Close button

To Move the Text Box

In this project, the text box is to be positioned near the lower-left of the graphic. The following step moves the text box.

1 Drag the text box to the location shown in Figure 11–48. (You may need to drag the text box a couple of times to position it as shown in the figure.)

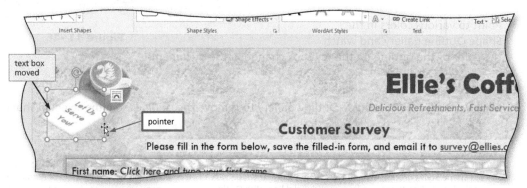

Figure 11–48

To Group Objects

1 SAVE DOCUMENT AS MACRO-ENABLED TEMPLATE | 2 MODIFY TEXT & FORM CONTENT CONTROLS
3 ENHANCE FORM'S VISUAL APPEAL | 4 CREATE MACROS TO AUTOMATE TASKS

When you have multiple graphics, such as pictures, shapes, and text boxes, positioned on a page, you can group them so that they are a single graphic instead of separate graphics. The following steps group the coffee cup graphic and the text box together. *Why? Grouping the graphics makes it easier to move them because they all move together as a single graphic.*

• With the text box selected, hold down the CTRL key while clicking the coffee cup picture (that is, CTRL+click), so that both graphics are selected at the same time.

Q&A What if I had more than two graphics that I wanted to group? For each subsequent graphic to select, CTRL+click the graphic, which enables you to select multiple objects at the same time.

• Click the Group Objects button (Drawing Tools Format tab | Arrange group) to display the Group Objects menu (Figure 11–49).

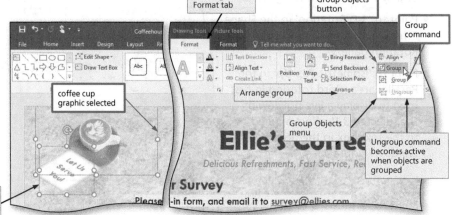

Figure 11–49

- Click Group on the Group Objects menu to group the selected objects into a single selected object (Figure 11–50).

Q&A

What if I wanted to ungroup grouped objects?

Select the object to ungroup, click the Group Objects button (Drawing Tools Format tab | Arrange group), and then click Ungroup on the Group Objects menu.

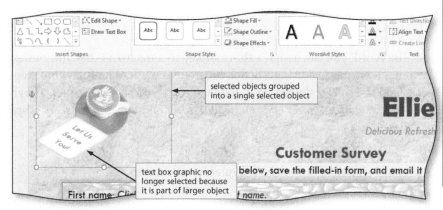

Figure 11–50

❸

- Click outside of the graphic to position the insertion point in the document and deselect the graphic.

- Save the template again on the same storage location with the same file name.

Break Point: If you wish to take a break, this is a good place to do so. You can exit Word now. To resume at a later time, run Word, open the file called Coffeehouse Customer Survey Modified, and continue following the steps from this location forward.

Using a Macro to Automate a Task

A **macro** consists of a series of Word commands or instructions that are grouped together as a single command. This single command is a convenient way to automate a difficult or lengthy task. Macros often are used to simplify formatting or editing activities, to combine multiple commands into a single command, or to select an option in a dialog box using a shortcut key.

To create a macro, you can use the macro recorder or the Visual Basic Editor. With the macro recorder, Word generates the VBA instructions associated with the macro automatically as you perform actions in Word. If you wanted to write the VBA instructions yourself, you would use the Visual Basic Editor. This module uses the macro recorder to create a macro and the Visual Basic Editor to modify it.

The **macro recorder** creates a macro based on a series of actions you perform while the macro recorder is recording. The macro recorder is similar to a video camera: after you start the macro recorder, it records all actions you perform while working in a document and stops recording when you stop the macro recorder. To record a macro, you follow this sequence of steps:

1. Start the macro recorder and specify options about the macro.

2. Execute the actions you want recorded.

3. Stop the macro recorder.

After you record a macro, you can execute the macro, or play it, any time you want to perform the same set of actions.

BTW

Naming Macros
If you give a new macro the same name as an existing built-in command in Microsoft Word, the new macro's actions will replace the existing actions. Thus, you should be careful not to assign a macro a name reserved for automatic macros (see Table 11–1 later in this module) or after any Word commands. To view a list of built-in macros in Word, click the View Macros button (View tab | Macros group) to display the Macros dialog box. Click the Macros in arrow and then click Word commands.

To Record a Macro and Assign It a Shortcut Key

In Word, you can assign a shortcut key to a macro so that you can execute the macro by pressing the shortcut key instead of using a dialog box to execute it. The following steps record a macro that hides formatting marks and the rulers; the macro is assigned the shortcut key, ALT+H. *Why? Assume you find that you are repeatedly hiding the formatting marks and rulers while designing the online form. To simplify this task, the macro in this project hides these screen elements.*

- Display formatting marks and the rulers on the screen.
- Display the Developer tab.
- Click the Record Macro button (Developer tab | Code group) to display the Record Macro dialog box.
- Type **HideScreenElements** in the Macro name text box (Record Macro dialog box).

Q&A
Do I have to name a macro?
If you do not enter a name for the macro, Word assigns a default name. Macro names can be up to 255 characters in length and can contain only numbers, letters, and the underscore character. A macro name cannot contain spaces or other punctuation.

- Click the 'Store macro in' arrow and then click 'Documents Based On Coffeehouse Customer Survey Modified'.

Q&A
What is the difference between storing a macro with the document template versus the Normal template?
Macros saved in the Normal template are available to all future documents; macros saved with the document template are available only with a document based on the template.

- In the Description text box, type this sentence (Figure 11–51): **Hide formatting marks and the rulers.**

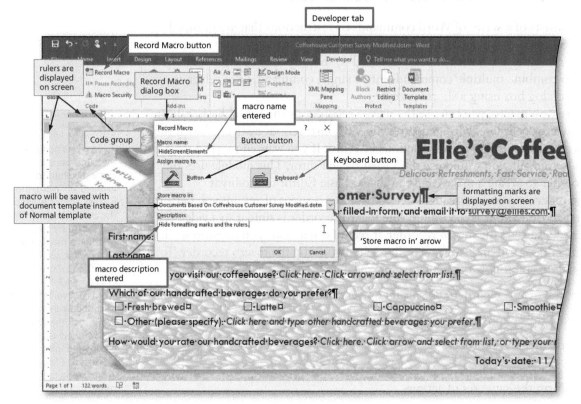

Figure 11–51

- Click the Keyboard button to display the Customize Keyboard dialog box.

- Press ALT+H to display the characters, Alt+H, in the 'Press new shortcut key' text box (Customize Keyboard dialog box) (Figure 11–52).

Q&A Can I type the letters in the shortcut key (ALT+H) in the text box instead of pressing them? No. Although typing the letters places them in the text box, the shortcut key is valid only if you press the shortcut key combination itself.

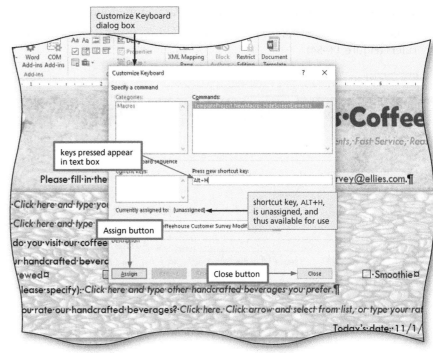

Figure 11–52

- Click the Assign button (Customize Keyboard dialog box) to assign the shortcut key, ALT+H, to the macro named HideScreenElements.

- Click the Close button (Customize Keyboard dialog box), which closes the dialog box, displays a Macro Recording button on the status bar, and starts the macro recorder (Figure 11–53).

Q&A How do I record the macro? While the macro recorder is running, any action you perform in Word will be part of the macro — until you stop or pause the macro.

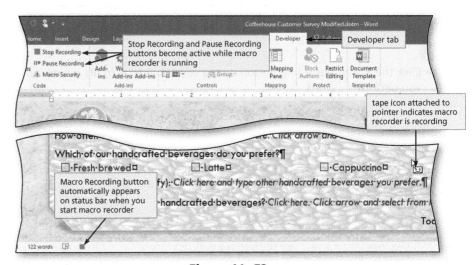

Figure 11–53

What is the purpose of the Pause Recording button (Developer tab | Code group)?
If, while recording a macro, you want to perform some actions that should not be part of the macro, click the Pause Recording button to suspend the macro recorder. The Pause Recording button changes to a Resume Recorder button that you click when you want to continue recording.

- Display the Home tab.

Q&A What happened to the tape icon? While recording a macro, the tape icon might disappear from the pointer when the pointer is in a menu, on the ribbon, or in a dialog box.

- Click the 'Show/Hide ¶' button (Home tab | Paragraph group) to hide formatting marks.

- Display the View tab. Remove the check mark from the View Ruler check box (View tab | Show group) to hide the rulers (Figure 11–54).

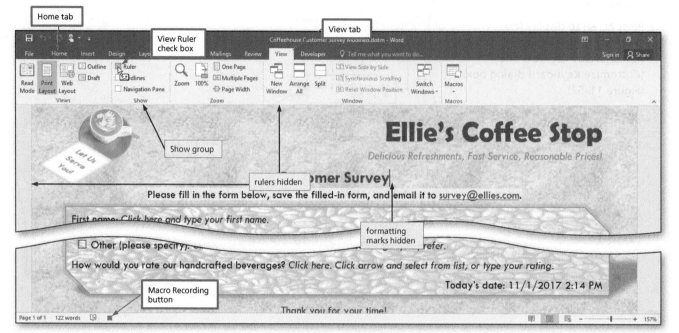

Figure 11–54

- Click the Macro Recording button on the status bar to turn off the macro recorder, that is, to stop recording actions you perform in Word.

Q&A

What if I made a mistake while recording the macro?

Delete the macro and record it again. To delete a macro, click the View Macros button (Developer tab | Code group), select the macro name in the list (Macros dialog box), click the Delete button, and then click the Yes button.

What if I wanted to assign the macro to a button instead of a shortcut key?

You would click the Button button in the Record Macro dialog box (shown in Figure 11–51) and then follow Steps 4 and 5 in this section.

Other Ways

1. Click View Macros arrow (View tab | Macros group), click Record Macro on View Macros menu

2. Press ALT+F8, click Create button (Macros dialog box)

To Run a Macro

BTW

Running Macros
You can run a macro by clicking the View Macros button (Developer tab | Code group or View tab | Macros group) or by pressing ALT+F8 to display the Macros dialog box, selecting the macro name in the list, and then clicking the Run button (Macros dialog box).

The next step is to execute, or run, the macro to ensure that it works. Recall that this macro hides formatting marks and the rulers, which means you must be sure the formatting marks and rulers are displayed on the screen before running the macro. Because you created a shortcut key for the macro in this project, the following steps show formatting marks and the rulers so that you can run the HideScreenElements macro using the shortcut key, ALT+H.

1 Display formatting marks on the screen.

2 Display rulers on the screen.

3 Press ALT+H, which causes Word to perform the instructions stored in the HideScreenElements macro, that is, to hide formatting marks and rulers.

Word Module 11

To Add a Command and a Macro as Buttons on the Quick Access Toolbar

1 SAVE DOCUMENT AS MACRO-ENABLED TEMPLATE | 2 MODIFY TEXT & FORM CONTENT CONTROLS
3 ENHANCE FORM'S VISUAL APPEAL | 4 CREATE MACROS TO AUTOMATE TASKS

Word allows you to add buttons to and delete buttons from the Quick Access Toolbar. You also can assign a command, such as a macro, to a button on the Quick Access Toolbar. The following steps add an existing command to the Quick Access Toolbar and assign a macro to a new button on the Quick Access Toolbar. *Why? This module shows how to add the New File command to the Quick Access Toolbar and also shows how to create a button for the HideScreenElements macro so that instead of pressing the shortcut keys, you can click the button to hide formatting marks and the rulers.*

1

- Click the 'Customize Quick Access Toolbar' button on the Quick Access Toolbar to display the Customize Quick Access Toolbar menu (Figure 11–55).

Q&A
What happens if I click the commands listed on the Customize Quick Access Toolbar menu?
If the command does not have a check mark beside it and you click it, Word places the button associated with the command on the Quick Access Toolbar. If the command has a check mark beside it and you click (deselect) it, Word removes the command from the Quick Access Toolbar.

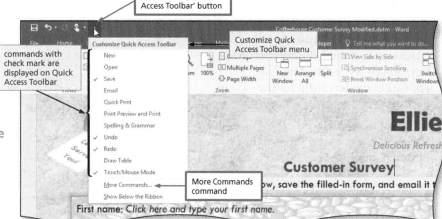

Figure 11–55

2

- Click More Commands on the Customize Quick Access Toolbar menu to display the Word Options dialog box with Quick Access Toolbar selected in the left pane.
- Scroll through the list of popular commands (Word Options dialog box) and then click New File to select the command.
- Click the Add button to add the selected command (New File, in this case) to the Customize Quick Access Toolbar list (Figure 11–56).

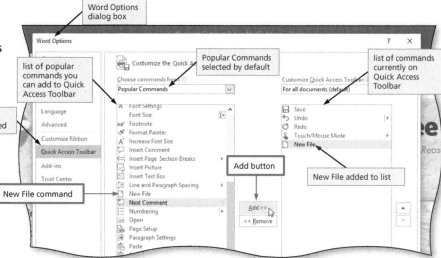

Figure 11–56

3

- Click the 'Choose commands from' arrow to display a list of categories of commands (Figure 11–57).

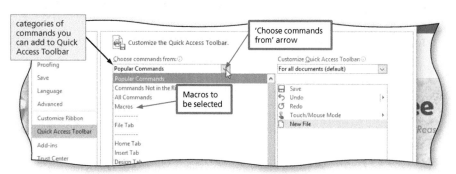

Figure 11–57

4

- Click Macros in the Choose commands from list to display the macro in this document.

- If necessary, click the macro to select it.

- Click the Add button (Word Options dialog box) to display the selected macro in the Customize Quick Access Toolbar list.

- Click the Modify button to display the Modify Button dialog box.

- Change the name in the Display name text box to **Hide Screen Elements** (Modify Button dialog box), which will be the text that appears in the ScreenTip for the button.

- In the list of symbols, click the screen icon as the new face for the button (Figure 11–58).

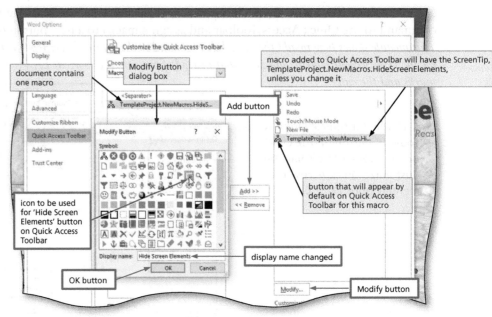

Figure 11–58

5

- Click the OK button (Modify Button dialog box) to change the button characteristics in the Customize Quick Access Toolbar list (Figure 11–59).

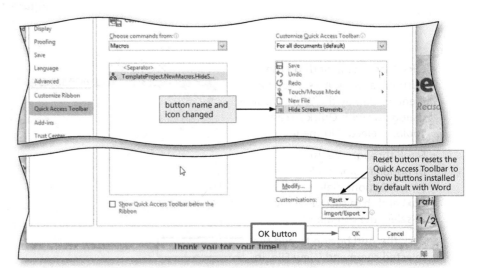

Figure 11–59

6

- Click the OK button (Word Options dialog box) to add the buttons to the Quick Access Toolbar (Figure 11–60).

Figure 11–60

Other Ways

1. Right-click Quick Access Toolbar, click 'Customize Quick Access Toolbar' on shortcut menu

To Use the New Buttons on the Quick Access Toolbar

The next step is to test the new buttons on the Quick Access Toolbar, that is, the New button and the 'Hide Screen Elements' button, which will execute, or run, the macro that hides formatting marks and the rulers. The following steps use buttons on the Quick Access Toolbar.

1 Click the New button on the Quick Access Toolbar to display a new blank document window. Close the new blank document window.

2 Display formatting marks on the screen.

3 Display rulers on the screen.

4 Click the 'Hide Screen Elements' button on the Quick Access Toolbar, which causes Word to perform the instructions stored in the HideScreenElements macro, that is, to hide formatting marks and the rulers.

To Delete Buttons from the Quick Access Toolbar

1 SAVE DOCUMENT AS MACRO-ENABLED TEMPLATE | 2 MODIFY TEXT & FORM CONTENT CONTROLS
3 ENHANCE FORM'S VISUAL APPEAL | 4 CREATE MACROS TO AUTOMATE TASKS

The following steps delete the New button and the 'Hide Screen Elements' button from the Quick Access Toolbar. *Why? If you no longer plan to use a button on the Quick Access Toolbar, you can delete it.*

1
- Right-click the button to be deleted from the Quick Access Toolbar, in this case the 'Hide Screen Elements' button, to display a shortcut menu (Figure 11–61).

2
- Click 'Remove from Quick Access Toolbar' on the shortcut menu to remove the button from the Quick Access Toolbar.

3
- Repeat Steps 1 and 2 for the New File button on the Quick Access Toolbar.

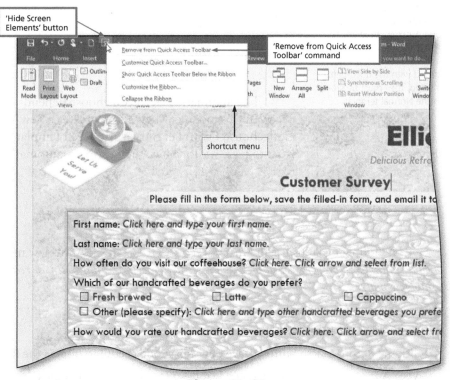

Figure 11–61

To Delete a Macro

If you wanted to delete a macro, you would perform the following steps.

1. Click the View Macros button (Developer tab | Code group) to display the Macros dialog box.
2. Click the macro to delete and then click the Delete button (Macros dialog box) to display a dialog box asking if you are sure you want to delete the macro. Click the Yes button in the dialog box.
3. Close the Macros dialog box.

Automatic Macros

The previous section showed how to create a macro, assign it a unique name (HideScreenElements) and a shortcut key, and then add a button that executes the macro on the Quick Access Toolbar. This section creates an **automatic macro**, which is a macro that executes automatically when a certain event occurs. Word has five prenamed automatic macros. Table 11–1 lists the name and function of these automatic macros.

BTW

Automatic Macros
A document can contain only one AutoClose macro, one AutoNew macro, and one AutoOpen macro. The AutoExec and AutoExit macros, however, are not stored with the document; instead, they must be stored in the Normal template. Thus, only one AutoExec macro and only one AutoExit macro can exist for all Word documents.

Table 11–1 Automatic Macros	
Macro Name	**Event That Causes Macro to Run**
AutoClose	Closing a document that contains the macro
AutoExec	Running Word
AutoExit	Exiting Word
AutoNew	Creating a new document based on a template that contains the macro
AutoOpen	Opening a document that contains the macro

The automatic macro you choose depends on when you want certain actions to occur. In this module, when a user creates a new Word document that is based on the Coffeehouse Customer Survey Modified template, you want to be sure that the zoom is set to page width. Thus, the AutoNew automatic macro is used in this online form.

To Create an Automatic Macro

1 SAVE DOCUMENT AS MACRO-ENABLED TEMPLATE | 2 MODIFY TEXT & FORM CONTENT CONTROLS
3 ENHANCE FORM'S VISUAL APPEAL | **4 CREATE MACROS TO AUTOMATE TASKS**

The following steps use the macro recorder to create an AutoNew macro. *Why? The online form in this module is displayed properly when the zoom is set to page width. Thus, you will record the steps to zoom to page width in the AutoNew macro.*

• Display the Developer tab.

• Click the Record Macro button (Developer tab | Code group) to display the Record Macro dialog box.

• Type **AutoNew** in the Macro name text box (Record Macro dialog box).

• Click the 'Store macro in' arrow and then click 'Documents Based On Coffeehouse Customer Survey Modified'.

• In the Description text box, type this sentence (Figure 11–62): **Specifies how the form initially is displayed.**

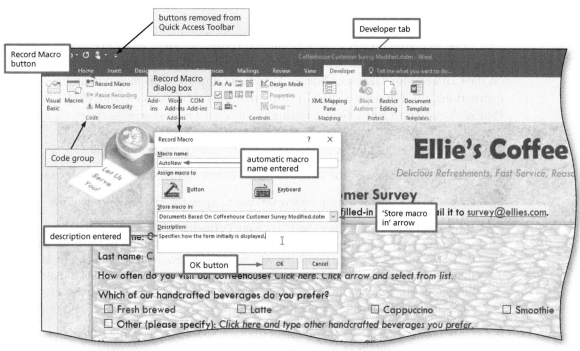

Figure 11–62

2

- Click the OK button to close the Record Macro dialog box and start the macro recorder.
- Display the View tab.
- Click the Page Width button (View tab | Zoom group) to zoom page width (Figure 11–63).

3

- Click the Macro Recording button on the status bar to turn off the macro recorder, that is, stop recording actions you perform in Word.

How do I test an automatic macro?

Activate the event that causes the macro to execute. For example, the AutoNew macro runs whenever you create a new Word document that is based on the template.

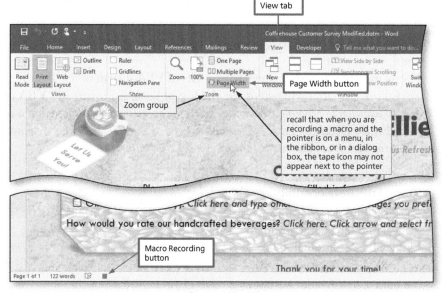

Figure 11–63

To Run the AutoNew Macro

The next step is to execute, or run, the AutoNew macro to ensure that it works. To run the AutoNew macro, you need to create a new Word document that is based on the Coffeehouse Customer Survey Modified template. This macro contains instructions to zoom page width. To verify that the macro works as intended, you will change the zoom to 100% before testing the macro. The following steps run a macro.

1 Use the Zoom Out button on the status bar to change the zoom to 100%.

2 Save the template with the same file name, Coffeehouse Customer Survey Modified.

3 Click the File Explorer button on the taskbar to open the File Explorer window.

4 Locate and then double-click the file named Coffeehouse Customer Survey Modified to display a new document window that is based on the contents of the Coffeehouse Customer Survey Modified template, which should be zoomed to page width as shown in Figure 11–1a at the beginning of this module. (If Word displays a dialog box about disabling macros, click its OK button. If the Message Bar displays a security warning, click the Enable Content button.)

5 Close the new document that displays the form in the Word window. Click the Don't Save button when Word asks if you want to save the changes to the new document.

6 Close the File Explorer window.

7 Change the zoom back to page width.

BTW

VBA

VBA includes many more statements than those presented in this module. You may need a background in programming if you plan to write VBA code instructions in macros you develop and if the VBA code instructions are beyond the scope of those instructions presented in this module.

To Edit a Macro's VBA Code

1 SAVE DOCUMENT AS MACRO-ENABLED TEMPLATE | 2 MODIFY TEXT & FORM CONTENT CONTROLS
3 ENHANCE FORM'S VISUAL APPEAL | **4 CREATE MACROS TO AUTOMATE TASKS**

As mentioned earlier, a macro consists of VBA instructions. To edit a recorded macro, you use the Visual Basic Editor. The following steps use the Visual Basic Editor to add VBA instructions to the AutoNew macro. *Why? In addition to zooming page width when the online form is displayed in a new document window, you would like to be sure that the Developer tab is hidden and the ribbon is collapsed. These steps are designed to show the basic composition of a VBA procedure and illustrate the power of VBA code statements.*

- Display the Developer tab.

- Click the View Macros button (Developer tab | Code group) to display the Macros dialog box.

- If necessary, select the macro to be edited, in this case, AutoNew (Figure 11–64).

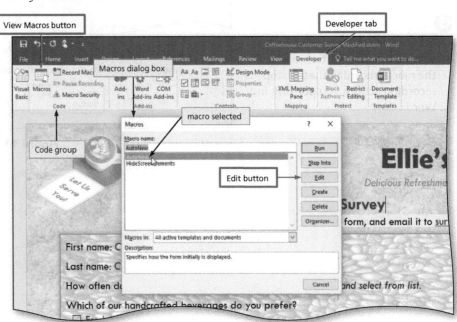

Figure 11–64

2

- Click the Edit button (Macros dialog box) to run the Visual Basic Editor and display the VBA code for the AutoNew macro in the Code window — your screen may look different depending on previous Visual Basic Editor settings (Figure 11–65).

What if the Code window does not appear in the Visual Basic Editor?
In the Visual Basic Editor, click View on the menu bar and then click Code. If it still does not appear and you are in a network environment, this feature may be disabled for some users.

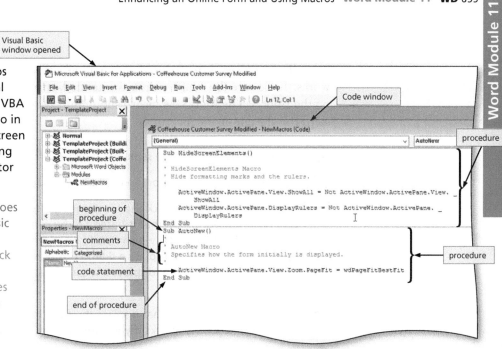

Figure 11–65

What are the lines of text (instructions) in the Code window?
The named set of instructions associated with a macro is called a **procedure**. It is this set of instructions — beginning with the word, Sub, and continuing sequentially to the line with the words, End Sub — that executes when you run the macro. The instructions within a procedure are called **code statements**.

3

- Position the insertion point at the end of the second-to-last line in the AutoNew macro and then press the ENTER key to insert a blank line for a new code statement.

- On a single line, type `Options.ShowDevTools = False` and then press the ENTER key, which enters the VBA code statement that hides the Developer tab.

What are the lists that appear in the Visual Basic Editor as I enter code statements?
The lists present valid statement elements to assist you with entering code statements. Because they are beyond the scope of this module, ignore them.

- On a single line, type `If Application.CommandBars.Item("Ribbon").Height > 100 Then` and then press the ENTER key, which enters the beginning VBA if statement that determines whether to collapse the ribbon.

- On a single line, press the TAB key, type `ActiveWindow.ToggleRibbon` and then press the ENTER key, which enters the beginning VBA code statement that collapses the ribbon.

- On a single line, press SHIFT+TAB and then type `End If` to enter the ending VBA code statement that determines whether to collapse the ribbon (Figure 11–66).

4

- Click the Close button on the right edge of the Microsoft Visual Basic window title bar.

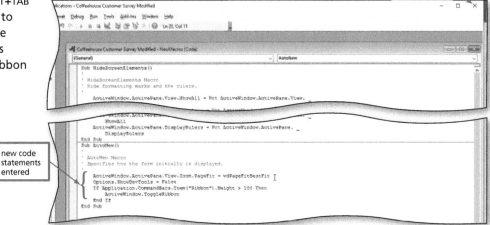

Figure 11–66

To Run the AutoNew Macro

The next step is to execute, or run, the AutoNew macro again to ensure that it works. To be sure the macro works as intended, ensure the Developer tab is displayed on the ribbon. The AutoNew macro should hide the Developer tab. The following steps run the automatic macro.

1 Save the template with the same file name, Coffeehouse Customer Survey Modified.

2 Click the File Explorer button on the taskbar to open the File Explorer window.

3 Locate and then double-click the file named Coffeehouse Customer Survey Modified to open a new document that is based on the contents of the Coffeehouse Customer Survey Modified template, which should be zoomed to page width and display no Developer tab. (If Word displays a dialog box about disabling macros, click its OK button. If the Message Bar displays a security warning, click the Enable Content button.)

4 Close the new document that displays the form in the Word window. Click the Don't Save button when Word asks if you want to save the changes to the new document.

5 Close the File Explorer window.

VBA

As shown in the previous steps, a VBA procedure begins with a Sub statement and ends with an End Sub statement. The Sub statement is followed by the name of the procedure, which is the macro name (AutoNew). The parentheses following the macro name in the Sub statement are required. They indicate that arguments can be passed from one procedure to another. Passing arguments is beyond the scope of this module, but the parentheses still are required. The End Sub statement signifies the end of the procedure and returns control to Word.

Comments often are added to a procedure to help you remember the purpose of the macro and its code statements at a later date. Comments begin with an apostrophe (') and appear in green in the Code window. The macro recorder, for example, placed four comment lines below the Sub statement. These comments display the name of the macro and its description, as entered in the Record Macro dialog box. Comments have no effect on the execution of a procedure; they simply provide information about the procedure, such as its name and description, to the Developer of the macro.

For readability, code statement lines are indented four spaces. Table 11–2 explains the function of each element of a code statement.

Table 11–2 Elements of a Code Statement		
Code Statement		
Element	**Definition**	**Examples**
Keyword	Recognized by Visual Basic as part of its programming language; keywords appear in blue in the Code window	Sub End Sub
Variable	An item whose value can be modified during program execution	ActiveWindow.ActivePane.View.Zoom.PageFit
Constant	An item whose value remains unchanged during program execution	False
Operator	A symbol that indicates a specific action	=

To Protect a Form Using the Backstage View and Exit Word

You now are finished enhancing the online form and adding macros to it. Because the last macro hid the Developer tab on the ribbon, you will use the Backstage view to protect the form. The following steps use the Backstage view to protect the online form so that users are restricted to entering data only in content controls.

1 Open the Backstage view and then, if necessary, display the Info gallery.

2 Click the Protect Document button to display the Protect Document menu.

3 Click Restrict Editing on the Protect Document menu to open the Restrict Editing task pane.

4 In the Editing restrictions area, if necessary, place a check mark in the 'Allow only this type of editing in the document' check box, click its arrow, and then select 'Filling in forms' in the list.

5 Click the 'Yes, Start Enforcing Protection' button and then click the OK button (Start Enforcing Protection dialog box) to protect the document without a password.

6 Close the Restrict Editing task pane.

7 Save the template again on the same storage location with the same file name.

8 Exit Word.

9 If the File Explorer window still is open, close it.

Supplementary Word Tasks

If you plan to take the certification exam, you should be familiar with the skills in the following sections.

Adding a Digital Signature to a Document

Some users attach a **digital signature** to a document to verify its authenticity. A digital signature is an electronic, encrypted, and secure stamp of authentication on a document. This signature confirms that the file originated from the signer (file creator) and that it has not been altered.

A digital signature references a digital certificate. A **digital certificate** is an attachment to a file, macro project, email message, or other digital content that vouches for its authenticity, provides secure encryption, or supplies a verifiable signature. Many users who receive online forms enable the macros based on whether they are digitally signed by a developer on the user's list of trusted sources. You can obtain a digital certificate from a commercial certification authority or from your network administrator.

Once a digital signature is added, the document becomes a read-only document, which means that modifications cannot be made to it. Thus, you should create a digital signature only when the document is final. In Word, you can add two types of digital signatures to a document: (1) an invisible digital signature or (2) a signature line.

TO ADD AN INVISIBLE DIGITAL SIGNATURE TO A DOCUMENT

An invisible digital signature does not appear as a tangible signature in the document. If the status bar displays a Signatures button, the document has an invisible digital signature. If you wanted to add an invisible digital signature to a document, you would perform the following steps.

1. Open the Backstage view and then, if necessary, display the Info gallery.
2. Click the Protect Document button to display the Protect Document menu and then click 'Add a Digital Signature' on the Protect Document menu to display the Sign dialog box. (If a dialog box appears indicating you need a digital ID, click the Yes button and then follow the on-screen instructions. If a dialog box about signature services appears, click its OK button.)
3. Type the purpose of the digital signature in the Purpose for signing this document text box.
4. Click the Sign button to add the digital signature, show the Signatures button on the status bar, and display Marked as Final on a Message Bar.

Q&A How can I view or remove the digital signatures in a document?
Open the Backstage view, if necessary, display the Info tab, and then click the View Signatures button to display the Signatures task pane. To remove a digital signature, click the arrow beside the signature name, click Remove Signature on the menu, and then click the Yes button in the dialog box.

TO ADD A SIGNATURE LINE TO A DOCUMENT

A **digital signature line**, which resembles a printed signature placeholder, allows a recipient of the electronic file to type a signature, include an image of his or her signature, or write a signature using the ink feature on a mobile computer or device. Digital signature lines enable organizations to use paperless methods of obtaining signatures on official documents, such as contracts. If you wanted to add a digital signature line to a document, you would perform the following steps.

1. Position the insertion point at the location for the digital signature.
2. Display the Insert tab. Click the 'Add a Signature Line' button (Insert tab | Text group) to display the Signature Setup dialog box. (If a dialog box appears about signature services, click its OK button.)
3. Type the name of the person who should sign the document in the appropriate text box.
4. If available, type the signer's title and email address in the appropriate text boxes.
5. Place a checkmark in the 'Allow the signer to add comments in the Sign dialog' check box so that the recipient can send a response back to you.
6. Click the OK button (Signature Setup dialog box) to insert a signature line in the document at the location of the insertion point.

Q&A How does a recipient insert his or her digital signature?
When the recipient opens the document, a Message Bar appears that contains a View Signatures button. The recipient can click the View Signatures button to display the Signatures task pane, click the requested signature arrow, and then click Sign on the menu (or double-click the signature line in the document) to display a dialog box that the recipient then completes.

BTW

Lock Tracking
If you wanted to require a password to turn off tracked changes, you would click the Track Changes button (Review tab | Tracking group), click Lock Tracking on the Track Changes menu, enter the password in each text box, and then click the OK button. To enter the password to turn off tracked changes, follow the same steps, entering the password when prompted.

Copying and Renaming Styles and Macros

If you have created a style or macro in one document or template, you can copy the style or a macro to another so that you can use it in a second document or template.

TO COPY A STYLE FROM ONE TEMPLATE OR DOCUMENT TO ANOTHER

If you wanted to copy a style from one template or document to another, you would perform the following steps.

1. Open the document or template into which you want to copy the style.

2. If necessary, click the Styles Dialog Box Launcher (Home tab | Styles group) to open the Styles task pane, click the Manage Styles button at the bottom of the Styles task pane to display the Manage Styles dialog box, and then click the Import/Export button (Manage Styles dialog box) to display Styles sheet in the Organizer dialog box. Or, click the Document Template button (Developer tab | Templates group) to display the Templates and Add-ins dialog box, click the Organizer button (Templates and Add-ins dialog box) to display the Organizer dialog box, and then, if necessary, click the Styles tab to display the Styles sheet in the dialog box. Notice that the left side of the dialog box displays the style names in the currently open document or template.

3. Click the Close File button (Organizer dialog box) to clear the right side of the dialog box.

Q&A What happened to the Close File button?
It changed to an Open File button.

4. Click the Open File button (Organizer dialog box) and then locate the file that contains the style you wish to copy. Notice that the styles in the located document or template appear on the right side of the dialog box.

5. On the ride side of the dialog box, select the style you wish to copy and then click the Copy button to copy the selected style to the document or template on the left. You can continue to copy as many styles as necessary.

6. When finished copying styles, click the Close button to close the dialog box.

TO RENAME A STYLE

If you wanted to rename a style, you would perform the following steps.

1. Open the document or template that contains the style to rename.

2. If necessary, click the Styles Dialog Box Launcher (Home tab | Styles group) to display the Styles task pane, click the Manage Styles button at the bottom of the Styles task pane to display the Manage Styles dialog box, and then click the Import/Export button (Manage Styles dialog box) to display the Styles sheet in the Organizer dialog box. Or, click the Document Template button (Developer tab | Templates group) to display the Templates and Add-ins dialog box, click the Organizer button (Templates and Add-ins dialog box) to display the Organizer dialog box, and then, if necessary, click the Styles tab to display the Styles sheet in the dialog box. Notice that the left side of the dialog box displays the style names in the currently open document or template.

BTW
Building Blocks
If you wanted to make building blocks available in other documents and templates, instead of just the current document or template, you would save them in the Normal.dotm file instead of the Building Blocks.dotx file. To do this, click the 'Explore Quick Parts' button (Insert tab | Text group), click Building Blocks Organizer on the Explore Quick Parts menu, click the building block for which you want to change the save location, click the Edit Properties button (Building Blocks Organizer dialog box), click the Save in button (Modify Building Block dialog box), select Normal in the list, click the OK button (Modify Building Block dialog box), and then click the Close button (Building Blocks Organizer dialog box).

3. Select the style you wish to rename and then click the Rename button (Organizer dialog box) to display the Rename dialog box.

4. Type the new name of the style in the text box and then click the OK button (Rename dialog box).

Q&A Can I delete styles too?

Yes, click the Delete button (Organizer dialog box) to delete any selected styles.

5. When finished renaming styles, click the Close button (Organizer dialog box) to close the dialog box.

TO COPY A MACRO FROM ONE TEMPLATE OR DOCUMENT TO ANOTHER

If you wanted to copy a macro from one template or document to another, you would perform the following steps.

1. Open the document or template into which you want to copy the macro.

2. If necessary, click the View Macros button (Developer tab | Code group or View tab | Macros group) to display the Macros dialog box, click the Organizer button (Macros dialog box) to display Macro Project Items sheet in the Organizer dialog box. Or, click the Document Template button (Developer tab | Templates group) to display the Templates and Add-ins dialog box, click the Organizer button (Templates and Add-ins dialog box) to display the Organizer dialog box, and then, if necessary, click the Macro Project Items tab to display the Macro Project Items sheet in the dialog box. Notice that the left side of the dialog box displays the macro names in the currently open document or template.

3. Click the Close File button (Organizer dialog box) to clear the right side of the dialog box.

Q&A What happened to the Close File button?

It changed to an Open File button.

4. Click the Open File button (Organizer dialog box) and then locate the file that contains the macro you wish to copy. Notice that the macros in the located document or template appear on the right side of the dialog box.

5. On the ride side of the dialog box, select the macro you wish to copy and then click the Copy button to copy the selected macro to the document or template on the left. You can continue to copy as many macros as necessary.

6. When finished copying macros, click the Close button (Organizer dialog box) to close the dialog box.

TO RENAME A MACRO

If you wanted to rename a macro, you would perform the following steps.

1. Open the document that contains the macro to rename.

2. If necessary, click the View Macros button (Developer tab | Code group or View tab | Macros group) to display the Macros dialog box and then click the Organizer button (Macros dialog box) to display Macro Project Items sheet in the Organizer dialog box. Or, click the Document Template button (Developer tab | Templates group) to display the Templates and Add-ins dialog box, click the

Organizer button (Templates and Add-ins dialog box) to display the Organizer dialog box, and then, if necessary, click the Macro Project Items tab to display the Macro Project Items sheet in the dialog box. Notice that the left side of the dialog box displays the macro names in the currently open document or template.

3. Select the macro you wish to rename and then click the Rename button (Organizer dialog box) to display the Rename dialog box.

4. Type the new name of the macro in the text box and then click the OK button (Rename dialog box).

Q&A Can I delete macros, too?
Yes, click the Delete button (Organizer dialog box) to delete any selected macros.

5. When finished renaming macros, click the Close button to close the dialog box.

Preparing a Document for Internationalization

Word provides internationalization features you can use when creating documents and templates. Use of features should be determined based on the intended audience of the document or template. By default, Word uses formatting consistent with the country or region selected when installing Windows. In addition to inserting symbols, such as those for currency, and using date and time formats that are recognized internationally or in other countries, you can set the language used for proofing tools and other language preferences.

TO SET THE LANGUAGE FOR PROOFING TOOLS

If you wanted to change the language that Word uses to proof documents or templates, you would perform the following steps.

1. Click the Language button (Review tab | Language group) to display the Language menu.

2. Click 'Set Proofing Language' on the Language menu to display the Language dialog box. (If you want to set this language as the default, click the 'Set As Default' button.)

3. Select the desired language to use for proofing tools and then click the OK button.

TO SET LANGUAGE PREFERENCES

If you wanted to change the language that Word uses for editing, display, Help, and ScreenTips, you would perform the following steps.

1. Click the Language button (Review tab | Language group) to display the Language menu and then click Language Preferences on the Language menu to display the language settings in the Word Options dialog box. Or, open the Backstage view, click the Options tab in the left pane to display the Word Options dialog box, and then click Language in the left pane (Word Options dialog box) to display the language settings.

2. Select preferences for the editing language, display language, and Help language, and then click the OK button.

BTW
Advanced Paragraph Options
A widow is when the last line of a paragraph appears by itself at the top of a page, and an orphan is when the first line of a paragraph appears by itself at the bottom of a page. To prevent widows and orphans, click the Paragraph Settings Dialog Box Launcher (Home tab | Paragraph group), click the Line and Page Breaks tab (Paragraph dialog box), place a check mark in the 'Widow/Orphan control' check box, and then click the OK button. Similarly, you can select the 'Keep with next' check box to keep selected paragraphs together, the 'Keep lines together' check box to keep selected lines together, and the 'Page break before' check box to insert a page break before the selected paragraph.

Enhancing a Document's Accessibility

Word provides several options for enhancing the accessibility of documents for individuals who have difficulty reading. Some previously discussed tasks you can perform to assist users include increasing zoom and font size, customizing the ribbon, ensuring tab/reading order in tables is logical, and using Read mode. You also can use the accessibility checker to locate and address problematic issues, and you can add alternative text to graphics and tables.

TO USE THE ACCESSIBILITY CHECKER

The accessibility checker scans a document and identifies issues that could affect a person's ability to read the content. Once identified, you can address each individual issue in the document. If you wanted to check accessibility of a document, you would perform the following steps.

1. Open the Backstage view and then, if necessary, display the Info gallery.
2. Click the 'Check for Issues' button to display the Check for Issues menu.
3. Click Check Accessibility on the Check for Issues menu, which scans the document and then displays accessibility issues in the Accessibility Checker task pane.
4. Address the errors and warnings in the Accessibility Checker task pane and then close the task pane.

TO ADD ALTERNATIVE TEXT TO GRAPHICS

For users who have difficulty seeing images on the screen, you can include **alternate text**, also called **alt text**, to your graphics so that these users can see or hear the alternate text when working with your document. Graphics you can add alt text to include pictures, shapes, text boxes, SmartArt graphics, and charts. If you wanted to add alternative text to graphics, you would perform the following steps.

1. Click the Format Shape Dialog Box Launcher (Picture Tools Format tab | Picture Styles group or Drawing Tools Format tab or SmartArt Tools Format tab or Chart Tools Format tab | Shape Styles group); right-click the object and then click Format Picture, Format Shape, Format Object, or Format Chart Area on the shortcut menu to open the Format Picture, Format Shape, or Format Chart Area task pane.
2. Click the 'Layout & Properties' button (Format Picture, Format Shape, or Format Chart Area task pane) and then, if necessary, expand the Alt Text section.
3. Type a brief title and then type a narrative description of the picture in the respective text boxes.
4. Close the task pane.

TO ADD ALTERNATIVE TEXT TO TABLES

For users who have difficulty seeing tables on the screen, you can include alternative text to your tables so that these users can see or hear the alternative text when working with your document. If you wanted to add alternative text to a table, sometimes called a table title, you would perform the following steps.

1. Click the Table Properties button (Table Tools Layout tab | Table group), or right-click the table and then click Table Properties on the shortcut menu to display the Table Properties dialog box.
2. Click the Alt Text tab (Table Properties dialog box) to display the Alt Text sheet.
3. Type a brief title and then type a narrative description of the table in the respective text boxes.
4. Click the OK button to close the dialog box.

Table of Authorities

Legal documents often include a **table of authorities** to list references to cases, rules, statutes, etc., along with the page number(s) on which the references appear. To create a table of authorities, mark the citations first and then build the table of authorities. The procedures for marking citations, editing citations, creating the table of authorities, changing the format of the table of authorities, and updating the table of authorities are the same as those for indexes. The only difference is that you use the buttons in the Table of Authorities group on the References tab instead of the buttons in the Index group.

TO MARK A CITATION

If you wanted to mark a citation, creating a citation entry, you would perform the following steps.

1. Select the long, full citation that you wish to appear in the table of authorities (for example, State v. Smith 220 J.3d 167 (UT, 1997)).
2. Click the Mark Citation button (References tab | Table of Authorities group) or press ALT+SHIFT+I to display the Mark Citation dialog box.
3. If necessary, click the Category arrow (Mark Citation dialog box) and then select a new category type.
4. If desired, enter a short version of the citation in the Short citation text box.
5. Click the Mark button to mark the selected text in the document as citation.

Q&A Why do formatting marks now appear on the screen?
When you mark a citation, Word automatically shows formatting marks (if they are not showing already) so that you can see the citation field. The citation entry begins with the letters, TA.

6. Click the Close button in the Mark Citation dialog box.

Q&A How could I see all marked citation entries in a document?
With formatting marks displaying, you could scroll through the document, scanning for all occurrences of TA, or you could use the Navigation Pane (that is, place a check mark in the 'Open the Navigation Pane' check box (View tab | Show group)) to find all occurrences of TA.

BTW
Working with Lists
In a numbered list, if you wanted to restart numbering, you would click the Numbering arrow, click 'Set Numbering Value' in the Numbering Library gallery to display the Set Numbering Value dialog box, click 'Start new list' (Set Numbering Value dialog box), and then click the OK button. To continue list numbering in a subsequent list, you would click 'Continue from previous list' in the Set Numbering Value dialog box. You also can specify a starting number in a list by entering the value in the 'Set value to' box (Set Numbering Value dialog box).

BTW
Line Numbers
If you wanted to insert line numbers in a document, click the 'Show Line Numbers' button (Layout tab | Page Setup group) and then click the desired line number setting on the Show Line Numbers menu.

To Mark Multiple Citations

Word leaves the Mark Citation dialog box open until you close it, which allows you to mark multiple citations without having to redisplay the dialog box repeatedly. To mark multiple citations, you would perform the following steps.

1. With the Mark Citation dialog box displayed, click in the document window; scroll to and then select the next citation.
2. If necessary, click the Selected text text box (Mark Citation dialog box) to display the selected text in the Selected text text box.
3. Click the Mark button.
4. Repeat Steps 1 through 3 for all citations you wish to mark. When finished, click the Close button in the dialog box.

To Edit a Citation Entry

At some time, you may want to change a citation entry after you have marked it. For example, you may need to change the case of a letter. If you wanted to change a citation entry, you would perform the following steps.

1. Display formatting marks.
2. Locate the TA field for the citation entry you wish to change.
3. Change the text inside the quotation marks.
4. Update the table of authorities as described in the steps at the end of this section.

To Delete a Citation Entry

If you wanted to delete a citation entry, you would perform the following steps.

1. Display formatting marks.
2. Select the TA field for the citation entry you wish to delete.
3. Press the DELETE key, or click the Cut button (Home tab | Clipboard group), or right-click the field and then click Cut on the mini toolbar or shortcut menu.
4. Update the table of authorities as described in the steps at the end of this section.

To Build a Table of Authorities

Once all citations are marked, Word can build a table of authorities from the citation entries in the document. Recall that citation entries begin with TA, and they appear on the screen when formatting marks are displayed. When citation entries show on the screen, the document's pagination probably will be altered because of the extra text in the citation entries. Thus, be sure to hide formatting marks before building a table of authorities. To build a table of authorities, you would perform the following steps.

1. Position the insertion point at the location for the table of authorities.
2. Ensure that formatting marks are not displayed.

3. Click the 'Insert Table of Authorities' button (References tab | Table of Authorities group) to display the Table of Authorities dialog box.

4. If necessary, select the category to appear in the table of authorities by clicking the desired option in the Category list, or leave the default selection of All so that all categories will be displayed in the table of authorities.

5. If necessary, click the Formats arrow (Table of Authorities dialog box) and then select the desired format for the table of authorities.

6. If necessary, click the Tab leader arrow and then select the desired leader character in the list to specify the leader character to be displayed between the marked citation and the page number.

7. If you wish to display the word, passim, instead of page numbers for citations with more than four page references, select the Use passim check box.

Q&A   What does the word, passim, mean?
Here and there.

8. Click the OK button (Table of Authorities dialog box) to create a table of authorities using the specified settings at the location of the insertion point.

TO UPDATE A TABLE OF AUTHORITIES

If you add, delete, or modify citation entries, you must update the table of authorities to display the new or modified citation entries. If you wanted to update a table of authorities, you would perform the following steps.

1. In the document window, click the table of authorities to select it.

2. Click the 'Update Table of Authorities' button (References tab | Table of Authorities group) or press the F9 key to update the table of authorities.

TO CHANGE THE FORMAT OF THE TABLE OF AUTHORITIES

If you wanted to change the format of the table of authorities, you would perform the following steps.

1. Click the table of authorities to select it.

2. Click the 'Insert Table of Authorities' button (References tab | Table of Authorities group) to display the Table of Authorities dialog box.

3. Change settings in the dialog box as desired. To change the style of headings, alignment, etc., click the Formats arrow and then click From template; next, click the Modify button to display the Style dialog box, make necessary changes, and then click the OK button (Style dialog box).

4. Click the OK button (Table of Authorities dialog box) to apply the changed settings.

5. Click the OK button when Word asks if you want to replace the selected category of the table of authorities.

To Delete a Table of Authorities

If you wanted to delete a table of authorities, you would perform the following steps.

1. Click the table of authorities to select it.

2. Press SHIFT+F9 to display field codes.

3. Drag through the entire field code, including the braces, and then press the DELETE key, or click the Cut button (Home tab | Clipboard group), or right-click the field and then click Cut on the mini toolbar or shortcut menu.

Working with XML

You can convert an online form to the XML format so that the data in the form can be shared with other programs, such as Microsoft Access. XML is a popular format for structuring data, which allows the data to be reused and shared. **XML**, which stands for Extensible Markup Language, is a language used to encapsulate data and a description of the data in a single text file, the **XML file**. XML uses **tags** to describe data items. Each data item is called an **element**. Businesses often create standard XML file layouts and tags to describe commonly used types of data.

In Word, you can save a file in a default XML format, in which Word parses the document into individual components that can be used by other programs. Or, you can identify specific sections of the document as XML elements; the elements then can be used in other programs, such as Access. This feature may not be available in all versions of Word.

To Save a Document in the Default XML Format

If you wanted to save a document in the XML format, you would perform the following steps.

1. Open the file to be saved in the XML format (for example, a form containing content controls).

2. Open the Backstage view and then click Save As to display the Save As gallery.

3. Navigate to the desired save location and then display the Save As dialog box.

4. Click the 'Save as type' arrow (Save As dialog box), click 'Word XML Document' in the list, and then click the Save button to save the template as an XML document.

Q&A How can I identify an XML document?

XML documents typically have an .xml extension.

BTW
Linking to External Content
If you wanted to link to external document content, you could click the Object button (Insert tab | Text group), click the Create from File tab (Object dialog box), locate the external file, place a check mark in the 'Link to file' check box, and then click the OK button.

To Attach a Schema File

To identify sections of a document as XML elements, you first attach an XML schema to the document, usually one that contains content controls. An **XML schema** is a special type of XML file that describes the layout of elements in other XML files. Word users typically do not create XML schema files. Software developers or other technical personnel create an XML schema file and provide it to Word users. XML schema files, often simply called **schema files**, usually have an extension of .xsd. Once the schema is attached, you can use the XML Mapping Pane (Developer tab |

Mapping group) to insert controls from the schema into the document. If you wanted to attach a schema file to a document, such as an online form, you would perform the following steps.

1. Open the file to which you wish to attach the schema, such as an online form that contains content controls.

2. Open the Backstage view and then use the Save As command to save the file with a new file name, to preserve the contents of the original file.

3. Click the Document Template button (Developer tab | Templates group) to display the Templates and Add-ins dialog box.

4. Click the XML Schema tab (Templates and Add-ins dialog box) to display the XML Schema sheet and then click the Add Schema button to display the Add Schema dialog box.

5. Locate and select the schema file (Add Schema dialog box) and then click the Open button to display the Schema Settings dialog box.

6. Enter the URI and alias in the appropriate text boxes (Schema Settings dialog box) and then click the OK button to add the schema to the Schema Library and to add the namespace alias to the list of available schemas in the XML Schema sheet (Templates and Add-ins dialog box).

Q&A

What is a URI and an alias?

Word uses the URI, also called a **namespace**, to refer to the schema. Because these names are difficult to remember, you can define a namespace alias. In a setting outside of an academic environment, a computer administrator would provide you with the appropriate namespace entry.

7. If necessary, place a check mark in the desired schema's check box.

8. Click the OK button, which causes Word to attach the selected schema to the open document and open the XML Structure task pane in the Word window.

TO DELETE A SCHEMA FROM THE SCHEMA LIBRARY

To delete a schema from a document, you would remove the check mark from the schema name's check box in the XML Schema sheet in the Templates and Add-ins dialog box. If you wanted to delete a schema altogether from the Schema Library, you would do the following.

1. Click the Document Template button (Developer tab | Templates group) to display the Templates and Add-ins dialog box.

2. Click the XML Schema tab (Templates and Add-ins dialog box) to display the XML Schema sheet and then click the Schema Library button to display the Schema Library dialog box.

3. Click the schema you want to delete in the Select a schema list (Schema Library dialog box) and then click the Delete Schema button.

4. When Word displays the Schema Library dialog box asking if you are sure you wish to delete the schema, click the Yes button.

5. Click the OK button (Schema Library dialog box) and then click the Cancel button (Templates and Add-ins dialog box).

BTW

Opening Files
In addition to current and previous versions of Word documents and templates, XML and PDF files, and webpage files, all discussed previously, you can open a variety of other types of documents through the Open dialog box, including rich text format, text files, OpenDocument text, WordPerfect files, and Works files. To open these documents, open the Backstage view, click the Open tab to display the Open gallery, click the Browse button to display the Open dialog box, click the file type arrow (Open dialog box), click the desired file type to open, locate the file, and then click the Open button to open the file and display its contents in a Word window. Through the Save dialog box, you can save these open files in their native format or save them as a Word document or template.

Summary

In this module, you learned how to enhance the look of text and graphics and automate a series of tasks with a macro. You also learned about several supplementary tasks that you should know if you plan to take the certification exam.

CONSIDER THIS: PLAN AHEAD

What decisions will you need to make when creating macro-enabled and enhanced online forms?

Use these guidelines as you complete the assignments in this module and create your own online forms outside of this class.

1. Save the form to be modified as a macro-enabled template, if you plan to include macros in the template for the form.

2. Enhance the visual appeal of a form.

   a) Arrange data entry fields in logical groups on the form and in an order that users would expect.
   b) Draw the user's attention to important sections.
   c) Use colors and images that complement one another.

3. Add macros to automate tasks.

   a) Record macros, if possible.
   b) If you are familiar with computer programming, write VBA code to extend capabilities of recorded macros.

4. Determine how the form data will be analyzed.

   a) If the data entered in the form will be analyzed by a program outside of Word, create the data entry fields so that the entries are stored in a format that can be shared with other programs.

Apply Your Knowledge

Reinforce the skills and apply the concepts you learned in this module.

Working with Graphics, Shapes, and Fields

Note: To complete this assignment, you will be required to use the Data Files. Please contact your instructor for information about accessing the Data Files.

Instructions: Run Word. Open the template, Apply 11-1 Realtor Client Survey, from the Data Files. In this assignment, you add an artistic effect to pictures, group images, change a shape, use a texture fill effect, and insert a date field (Figure 11–67).

Perform the following tasks:
1. Unprotect the template.
2. Apply the Glow Diffused artistic effect to the sale sign image (the image to the right in the Data File). Change the color saturation of the same image (the sale sign) to 400%. Apply the following glow effect to the SOLD stamp image: Orange, 5 pt glow, Accent color 2. *Hint:* Picture Effects button (Picture Tools Format tab | Picture Styles group).
3. Move the SOLD stamp image on top of the sale sign image as shown in Figure 11–67. Group the two sale sign and SOLD stamp images together. Move the grouped images down so that the base of the sign post is even with the instruction line.
4. Change the page color to the Recycled paper texture fill effect.
5. Change the shape around the data entry area from Rectangle to Snip Single Corner Rectangle.

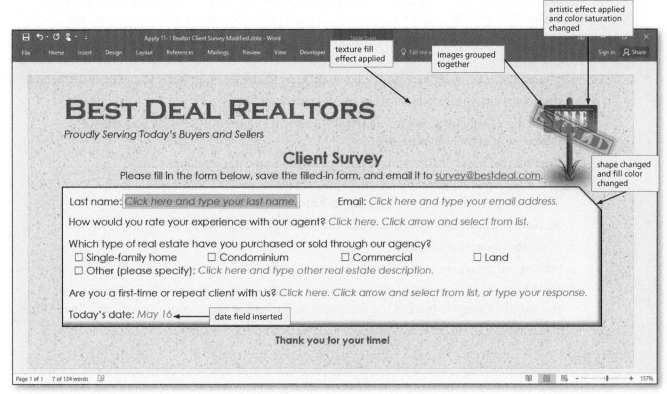

Figure 11–67

Continued >

Apply Your Knowledge *continued*

6. Change the fill color of the rectangle shape to Lime, Accent 4, Lighter 80%.

7. Apply the Inside Diagonal Bottom Right shadow to the rectangle shape.

8. Display the Developer tab. Change the properties of the date picker content control so that its contents can be deleted and then delete the content control. Insert a date field after the Today's Date: label in the format month day (i.e., September 13). Change the format of the displayed date field to Intense Emphasis. Hide the Developer tab.

9. If requested by your instructor, change the email address on the form to your email address.

10. Protect the form. Save the modified form using the file name, Apply 11-1 Realtor Client Survey Modified. Submit the revised template in the format specified by your instructor.

11. ✳ If you wanted to change the picture on the form, you could delete the current pictures and then insert new ones, or you could use the Change Picture button (Picture Tools Format tab | Adjust group). Which technique would you use and why?

Extend Your Knowledge

Extend the skills you learned in this module and experiment with new skills. You may need to use Help to complete the assignment.

Working with Document Security

Note: To complete this assignment, you will be required to use the Data Files. Please contact your instructor for information about accessing the Data Files.

Instructions: Run Word. Open the document, Extend 11-1 Billing Issue Letter Draft, from the Data Files. You will add a digital signature line, encrypt the document with a password, remove the password, and mark the document as final.

Perform the following tasks:

1. Use Help to review and expand your knowledge about these topics: signature lines, passwords, document encryption, and marking the document as final.

2. Add a digital signature line to end of the document (Figure 11–68). Use your personal information in the signature line.

3. Encrypt the document. Be sure to use a password you will remember.

4. Save the revised document with a new file name, Extend 11-1 Billing Issue Letter Modified. Then, close the document and reopen it. Enter the password when prompted.

5. Remove the password from the document.

6. Mark the document as final.

7. Submit the document in the format specified by your instructor.

8. ✳ When you encrypted the document, what password did you use? Why did you choose that password? When you marked the document as final, what text appeared on the title bar? What text appeared in the Message Bar? What appeared on the status bar?

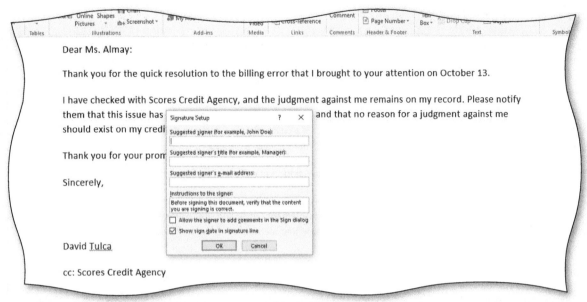

Figure 11–68

Expand Your World

Create a solution that uses cloud or web technologies by learning and investigating on your own from general guidance.

Obtaining Digital IDs

Instructions: You are interested in obtaining a digital ID so that you can digitally sign your documents in Word. You plan to research various digital ID services to determine the one best suited to your needs.

Perform the following tasks:

1. Run Word. Open the Backstage view and then, if necessary, display the Info tab. Click the Protect Document button and then click 'Add a Digital Signature' on the Protect Document menu.

2. When Word displays the Get a Digital ID dialog box, click the Yes button, which runs a browser and displays an Office Help window with a list of services that issue digital IDs (Figure 11–69).

3. Click the link beside each service to learn more about each one.

4. Use a search engine to read reviews about these services.

5. Compose a Word document comparing and contrasting the digital ID services suggested by Microsoft. Be sure to cite your sources. In your report, recommend the service you feel best suits your needs.

6. ⊛ Which digital ID services did you evaluate? When you read the reviews, were there other services not listed on the Office website? If so, what were their names? Which digital ID service would you recommend? Why?

Continued >

STUDENT ASSIGNMENTS

Expand Your World *continued*

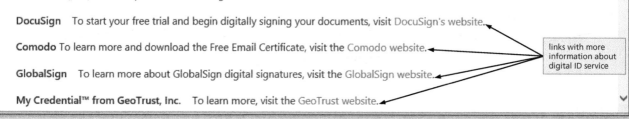

signature. A digitally signed message proves to the recipient that you, not an imposter, signed the contents of the message, and that the contents haven't been altered in transit. To learn more about using digital IDs in Outlook, see Get a digital ID. To learn more about digitally signing documents, see Digital signatures and certificates.

NOTES:

- A digital signature isn't the same as a message signature, which is a customizable salutation. A digital signature adds unique code to a message which only comes from the digital ID held by the true sender.

- Your organization may have its own policies and procedures for using digital IDs and certificates. See your network administrator for more information.

To find services that issue digital IDs for your use, or services that complement Office and use digital IDs, check out the following websites. It's up to you which one you choose, and others are available that are not in this list, but these are some certificate authorities (CAs) that are qualified to issue digital certificates.

DocuSign To start your free trial and begin digitally signing your documents, visit DocuSign's website.

Comodo To learn more and download the Free Email Certificate, visit the Comodo website.

GlobalSign To learn more about GlobalSign digital signatures, visit the GlobalSign website.

My Credential™ from GeoTrust, Inc. To learn more, visit the GeoTrust website.

links with more information about digital ID service

Figure 11–69

In the Labs

Design, create, modify, and/or use a document following the guidelines, concepts, and skills presented in this module. Labs 1 and 2, which increase in difficulty, require you to create solutions based on what you learned in the module; Lab 3 requires you to apply your creative thinking and problem-solving skills to design and implement a solution.

Lab 1: Enhancing the Graphics, Shapes, and Text Boxes on an Online Form

Problem: You created the Dee's Dog Grooming online form shown in Figure 10–78 in the Student Assignments for Module 10. Your aunt has asked you to change the form's appearance and add a text box. You modify the form so that it looks like the one shown in Figure 11–70.

Perform the following tasks:

1. Open the template called Lab 10-1 Dog Grooming Request Form that you created in the Lab 1 Student Assignment in Module 10. Save the template with a new file name of Lab 11-1 Dog Grooming Request Form Modified. If you did not complete the lab in Module 10, see your instructor for a copy. Unprotect the template.

2. Use the Water droplets texture fill effect for the page color.

3. Modify the formats of the company name, business tag line, form title, user instruction, and thank you lines as shown in Figure 11–70 (or with similar fonts). If requested by your instructor, change the first word in the business name from Dee's to your first name.

4. Use the picture fill effect to place a picture in the rectangle shape. Use the picture called Paw-Prints-Heart from the Data Files. Change the color of the picture in the rectangle to Washout.

5. Create a character style, with the name Data Entry Labels, for all labels in the data entry that starts with the current format and uses 11-point bold Calibri font, and a color of Gold, Accent 5.

6. Change the shape of the rectangle to Snip and Round Single Corner Rectangle. If necessary, change the shape outline color (border) to Gold, Accent 5, Darker 50%.

7. Apply the Offset Right shadow effect to the rectangle shape. Change the shadow color to Gold, Accent 5, Darker 25%. Change the transparency of the shadow to 20%.

8. Modify the Intense Emphasis style to the color Purple, Accent 1, Darker 25% and apply the bold and italic formats.

9. Change the image on the right to the picture called Dog from the Data Files. Resize the image as shown. Remove the background, as shown in the figure. Change the Color Tone to Temperature: 11200 K. Save the modified image with the file name, Dog Modified.

10. Draw a text box that is approximately 0.5" × 1.1" that contains the text, Your Dog Will Love Us!, centered in the text box. Apply the Colored Outline - Gold, Accent 5 shape style to the text box. Apply the Off Axis 2 Left 3-D rotation to the text box. Add an Offset Diagonal Bottom Right shadow to this text box. Position the text box as shown in the figure.

11. Adjust spacing above and below paragraphs as necessary so that all contents fit on a single screen. Protect the form. Save the form again and submit it in the format specified by your instructor.

12. Access the template through File Explorer. Fill in the form using personal data and submit the filled-in form in the format specified by your instructor.

13. ✳ What is the advantage of creating a style for the data entry labels?

Figure 11–70

Continued >

STUDENT ASSIGNMENTS

In the Labs *continued*

Lab 2: Enhancing the Look of an Online Form and Adding Macros to the Form

Problem: You created the Antwon's DJ Service online form shown in Figure 10–79 in the Student Assignments in Module 10. Your supervisor has asked you to change the form's appearance, add a field, and add some macros. You modify the form so that it looks like the one shown in Figure 11–71.

Perform the following tasks:

1. Open the template called Lab 10-2 DJ Customer Survey that you created in Lab 2 of Module 10. Save the template as a macro-enabled template with a new file name of Lab 11-2 DJ Customer Survey Modified. If you did not complete the lab in Module 10, see your instructor for a copy. Unprotect the template.

2. Change the document theme to Circuit.

3. Use the Newsprint texture fill effect for the page color.

4. Change the fill color in the rectangle shape to Red, Accent 3, Lighter 80%. Change the shape outline to small dots. Change the outline color to Red, Accent 3, Darker 25%. Change the shape shadow to Inside Center.

5. Modify the formats of the company name, business tag line, form title, user instruction, and thank you line as shown in Figure 11–71 (or with similar fonts).

6. Convert the table to text for the 2 × 1 table containing the First Name and Last Name content controls. Change the left indent to 0.06" on these two lines.

Figure 11–71

7. Modify the Intense Emphasis style to Red, Accent 3, Darker 25%.

8. Adjust spacing above and below paragraphs as necessary so that all contents fit on a single screen. If necessary, adjust the rectangle so that it covers the entire data entry area.

9. Change the current image to the one shown in the figure (or a similar image). The image in the figure is called Music-Notes on the Data Files. Resize the image and position it as shown.

10. Record a macro that hides the formatting marks and the rulers. Name it HideScreenElements. Store it in Documents Based On Lab 11-2 DJ Customer Survey Modified template. Assign it the shortcut key, ALT+H. Run the macro to test it.

11. Add a button to the Quick Access Toolbar for the macro created in Step 10. Test the button and then delete the button from the Quick Access Toolbar.

12. Create an automatic macro called AutoNew using the macro recorder. Store it in Documents Based On Lab 11-2 DJ Customer Survey Modified template. The macro should change the view to page width.

13. Edit the AutoNew macro so that it also hides the Developer tab and the ribbon.

14. Protect the form. Save the form again and submit it in the format specified by your instructor.

15. Access the template through File Explorer. Fill in the form and submit the filled-in form in the format specified by your instructor.

16. ✺ If a recorded macro does not work as intended when you test it, how would you fix it?

Lab 3: **Consider This: Your Turn**

Modify an Online Form for a Deli

Problem: You created the deli customer survey online form that was defined in the Lab 3: Consider This: Your Turn assignment in Module 10. Your supervisor was pleased with the initial design. You and your supervisor, however, believe the form can be improved by enhancing its appearance.

Part 1: Make the following modifications to the deli customer survey form that you created in Module 10. (If you did not complete the lab in Module 10, see your instructor for a copy.) Change the font and color of the deli name, tag line, and form title; change the page color to a texture; change the highlight color; and change the font and color of the last line. Change the rectangle shape around the data entry area. In the rectangle, add a picture fill effect using an image of a submarine sandwich (one is available on the Data Files for use, if desired) and recolor it as necessary. Change the color of the shadow in the rectangle. Delete the existing image on the form, replace it with an image of vegetables (one is available on the Data Files for use, if desired), and apply an artistic effect to the image. Draw a text box with the text, Mmm…Mmm…Good!, and apply a 3-D effect to the text box.

Specify the appropriate macro security level. Record a macro that hides screen elements and then assign the macro to a button on the Quick Access Toolbar. Record another macro for a task you would like to automate. Add another button to the Quick Access Toolbar for any Word command not on the ribbon.

Use the concepts and techniques presented in this module to modify the online form. Be sure to save it as a macro-enabled template. Protect the form, test it, and submit it in the format specified by your instructor.

Part 2: ✺ You made several decisions while creating the online form in this assignment: formats to use (i.e., fonts, font sizes, colors, styles, etc.), graphics to use, which task to automate, and which button to add to the Quick Access Toolbar. What was the rationale behind each of these decisions? When you proofread and tested the online form, what further revisions did you make, and why?

8 | Customizing a Template and Handouts Using Masters

Objectives

You will have mastered the material in this module when you can:

- Apply slide and font themes to a slide master
- Change a slide master background
- Add a background style and graphic to a slide master
- Insert a placeholder into a slide layout
- Apply a Quick Style to a placeholder
- Change text direction and character spacing
- Hide background graphics on individual slides

- Apply a fill to a text box and change transparency
- Rename a slide master
- Save a slide master as a template
- Create handouts using the handout master
- Create speaker notes using the notes master

Introduction

PowerPoint provides a variety of designs and layouts to meet most presenters' needs. At times, however, you may need a different set of colors, fonts, placeholders, or graphics to display throughout a presentation. PowerPoint allows you to customize the master layouts for slides, handouts, and speaker notes. These masters specify the precise locations and styles of placeholders, pictures, text boxes, and other slide and handout elements.

Once you determine your custom specifications in these masters, you can save the file as a template so that you can reuse these key elements as a starting point for multiple presentations. This unique **template** is a set of special slides you create and then use to create similar presentations. A template consists of a general master slide layout that has elements common to all the slide layouts. One efficient way to create similar presentations is to create a template, save the template, open the template, and then save the slides as a different PowerPoint presentation each time a new presentation is required.

Templates help speed and simplify the process of creating a presentation, so many PowerPoint designers create a template for common presentations they develop frequently. Templates can have a variable number of slide layouts depending upon the complexity of the presentation. A simple presentation can have a few slide layouts; for example, the Zip Line presentation will have three slide layouts. A more complex template can have many slide masters and layouts.

Project — Presentation with Customized Slide, Handout, and Notes Masters

BTW
Multiple Slide Masters
You can insert additional slide masters in one file so that one presentation can have two or more different styles. Each slide master has a related set of layout masters. In contrast, however, one presentation can have only one handout master and one notes master.

Zip lining has grown in popularity in recent years as a tourist and recreational activity throughout the world. Guests are suspended on a cable strung along a slope and propelled downward while gripping a free-moving pulley. Zip lines have been used since the1800s as a method of transporting people and goods over rugged terrain. Facilities offer a wide variety of courses that vary in length and height and are appropriate for people of all ages. The project in this module (Figure 8–1) showcases the amenities at Tree Top Adventures, a park featuring four zip line courses. All three slides are created by starting with a template file that contains two basic slide elements: the park's name on a formatted placeholder and an illustration of a family zip lining. The overall template, called the **slide master** (Figure 8–1a), is formatted with a theme, customized title and text fonts, and customized footer placeholders for the slide layouts. The title slide layout (Figure 8–1b) is used to create Slide 1 (Figure 8–1c), which introduces audiences to the zip line experience. Similarly, the blank slide layout (Figure 8–1d) is used for Slide 2 (Figure 8–1e), which promotes the fun that various groups can share in the park's natural setting. The title and content layout (Figure 8–1f) is used to develop the text describing the four courses and the graphics on Slide 3 (Figure 8–1g). In addition, the custom handout master (Figure 8–1h) is used to create a handout with an illustration of a female zip lining and header and footer text (Figure 8–1i). Likewise, the custom notes master (Figure 8–1j) is used to create speaker notes pages (Figures 8–1k–m).

In this module, you will learn how to create the slides shown in Figure 8–1. The following roadmap identifies general activities you will perform as you progress through this module:

1. CUSTOMIZE SLIDE MASTERS by changing the theme fonts and background.

2. FORMAT and ARRANGE slide master FOOTERS.

3. INSERT and FORMAT GRAPHICS and TEXT BOXES.

4. RENAME and DELETE SLIDE LAYOUTS.

5. CUSTOMIZE HANDOUT and NOTES MASTERS.

6. USE a CUSTOM TEMPLATE to create a new presentation.

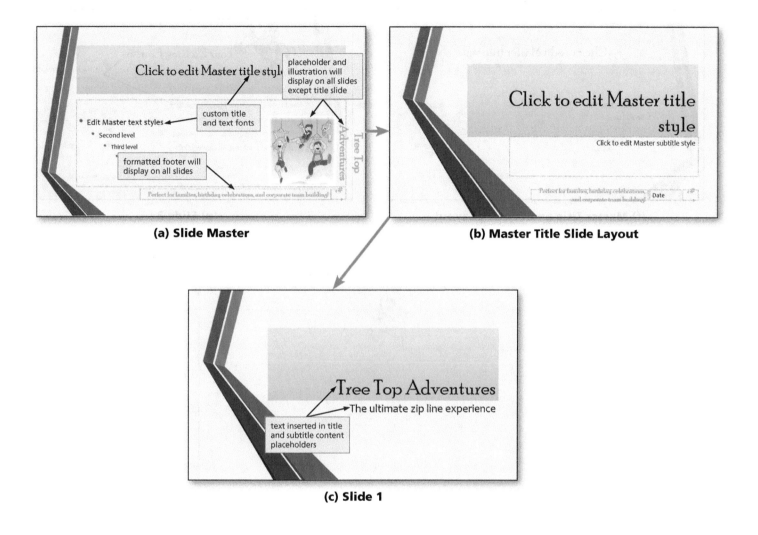

(a) Slide Master

(b) Master Title Slide Layout

(c) Slide 1

(d) Master Blank Layout

(e) Slide 2

Figure 8–1 (Continued)

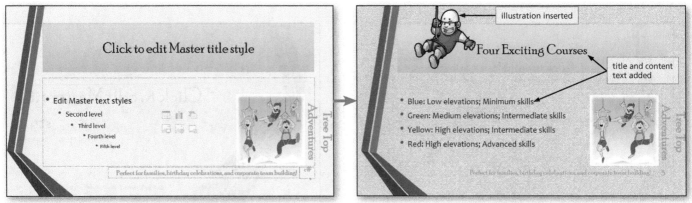

(f) Master Title and Content Layout   **(g) Slide 3**

(h) Handout Master

(i) Handout

Figure 8–1 (Continued)

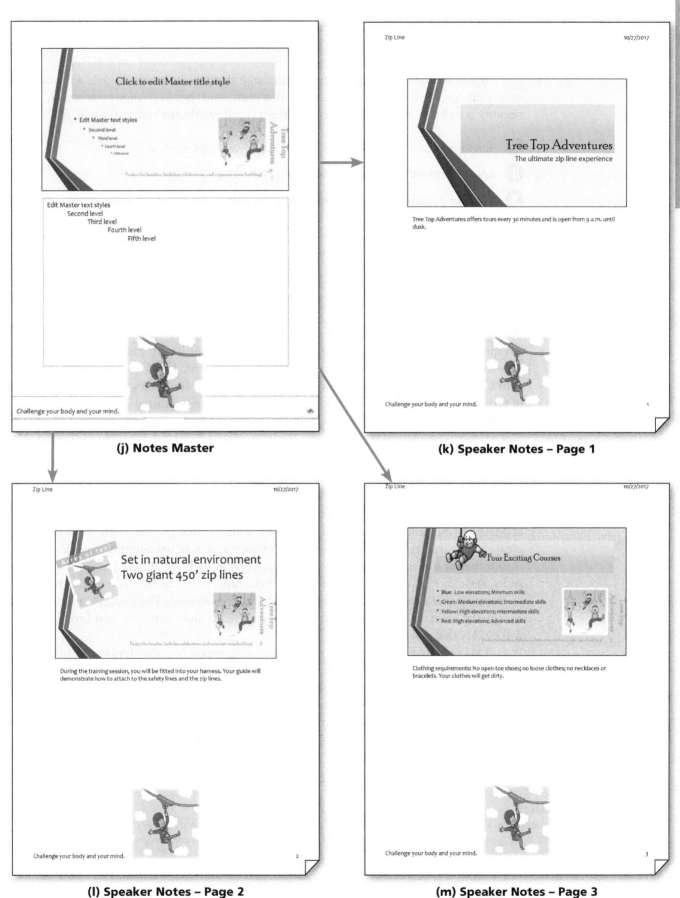

(j) Notes Master

(k) Speaker Notes – Page 1

(l) Speaker Notes – Page 2

(m) Speaker Notes – Page 3

Figure 8–1

To Run PowerPoint and Save a Presentation with a New File Name

If you are using a computer to step through the project in this module and you want your screens to match the figures in this book, you should change your screen's resolution to 1366 × 768. The following steps run PowerPoint and save a new file.

1 Run PowerPoint. If necessary, maximize the PowerPoint window.

2 Apply the Blank Presentation theme.

3 Save the presentation on your hard drive, OneDrive, or other storage location using the file name, Zip Line.

BTW
The Ribbon and Screen Resolution
PowerPoint may change how the groups and buttons within the groups appear on the ribbon, depending on the computer or mobile device's screen resolution. Thus, your ribbon may look different from the ones in this book if you are using a screen resolution other than 1366 x 768.

Customizing Presentation Slide Master Backgrounds and Fonts

PowerPoint has many template files with the file extension .potx. Each template file has three masters: slide, handout, and notes. A slide master has at least one layout; you have used many of these layouts, such as Title and Content, Two Content, and Picture with Caption, to create presentations. A **handout master** designates the placement of text, such as page numbers, on a sheet of paper intended to distribute to audience members. A **notes master** defines the formatting for speaker's notes.

Slide Master

If you select a document theme and want to change one of its components on every slide, you can override that component by changing the slide master. In addition, if you want your presentation to have a unique design, you might want to create a slide master rather than attempt to modify a current presentation theme. A slide master indicates the size and position of text and object placeholders, font styles, slide backgrounds, transitions, and effects. Any change to the slide master results in changing that component on every slide in the presentation. For example, if you change the second-level bullet on the slide master, each slide with a second-level bullet will display this new bullet format.

One presentation can have more than one slide master. You may find two or more slide masters are necessary when your presentation reuses special slide layouts. In this Zip Line presentation, for example, one slide will have the title slide to introduce the overall concept, another will have a blank slide to showcase the adventure park, and a third slide will have a title and a bulleted list to give specific information about the zip line courses. All slides except the title slide, which has background graphics hidden by default, will have an illustration of a family zip lining and the words, Tree Top Adventures, on the slide master.

BTW
Touch Screen Differences
The Office and Windows interfaces may vary if you are using a touch screen. For this reason, you might notice that the function or appearance of your touch screen differs slightly from this module's presentation.

CONSIDER THIS

Plan the slide master.

Using a new slide master gives you the freedom to specify every slide element. Like an artist with a new canvas or a musician with blank sheet music, your imagination permits you to create an appealing master that conveys the overall look of your presentation.

Before you start developing the master, give your overall plan some careful thought. The decisions you make at this point should be reflected on every slide. A presentation can have several master layouts, but you should change these layouts only if you have a compelling need to change them. Use the concepts you have learned throughout the modules in this book to guide your decisions about fonts, colors, backgrounds, art, and other essential slide elements.

To Display a Slide Master

To begin developing the Zip Line slides, you need to display the slide master. *Why? The slide master allows you to customize the slide components and create a unique design.* The following steps display the slide master.

1

- Click View on the ribbon to display the View tab (Figure 8–2).

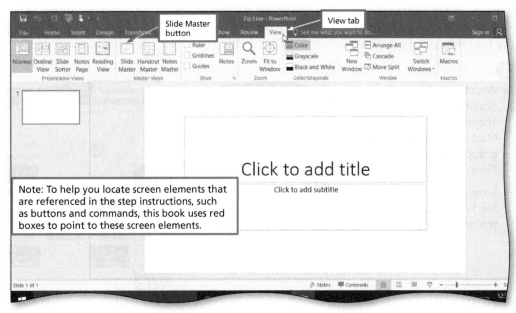

Figure 8–2

2

- Click the Slide Master button (View tab | Master Views group) to display the Slide Master tab and the slide thumbnails in the Thumbnail pane.

- If necessary, scroll up and then click the Office Theme Slide Master layout (Figure 8–3).

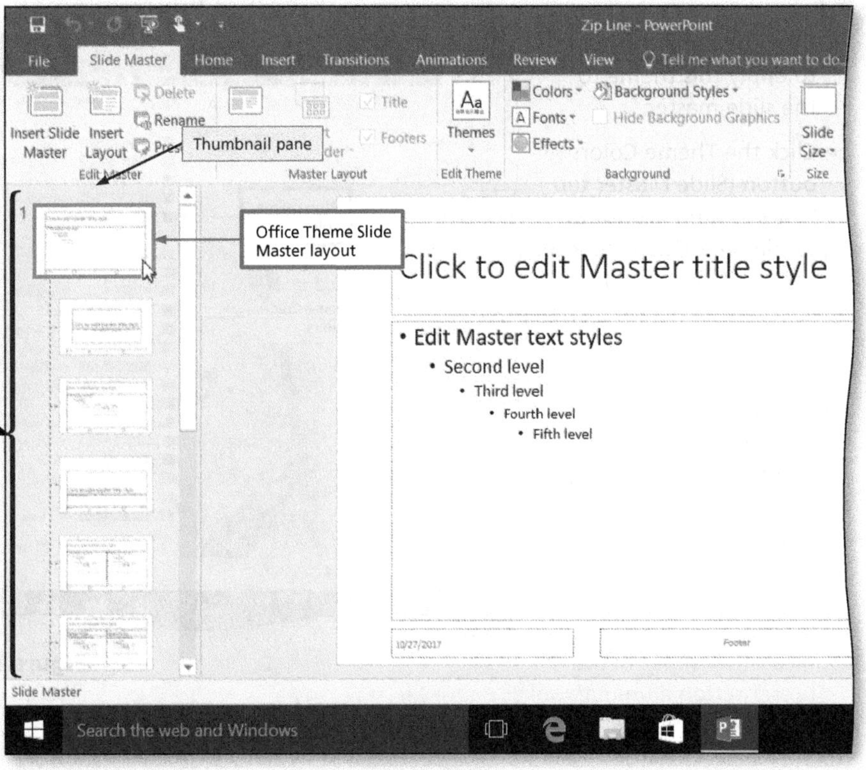

Q&A

What are all the other thumbnails in the left pane below the slide master?

They are all the slide layouts associated with this slide master. You have used many of these layouts in the presentations you have developed in the exercises in this book.

Why is the layout given this name?

The slide layout names begin with the theme applied to the slides. In this case, the default Office Theme is applied. The first slide layout in the list is called the master because it controls the colors, fonts, and objects that are displayed on all the other slides in the presentation.

Figure 8–3

To Apply Slide and Font Themes to a Slide Master

You can change the look of an entire presentation by applying formats to the slide master in the same manner that you apply these formats to individual slides. In this presentation, you will change the slide theme to Parallax and the font colors to blue and green. *Why? The Parallax theme features two lines, which are similar to the zip line cables, along the left edges and colors that match the blue sky.* The following steps apply a theme and change the font theme colors.

1

- With the slide master displaying, click the Themes button (Slide Master tab | Edit Theme group) to display the Themes gallery.

- Scroll down to display the Parallax theme in the gallery (Figure 8–4).

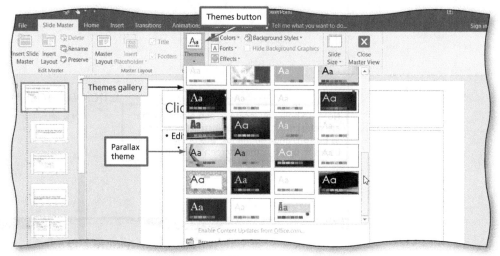

Figure 8–4

2

- Click the Parallax theme to apply this theme to the slide master.

- Click the Theme Colors button (Slide Master tab | Background group) to display the Theme Colors gallery (Figure 8–5).

3

- Click the Blue color scheme in the Theme Colors gallery to change the slide master colors to Blue.

Q&A Can I insert another set of slide masters to give other slides in the presentation a unique look?

Yes. PowerPoint allows you to insert multiple masters into an existing presentation.

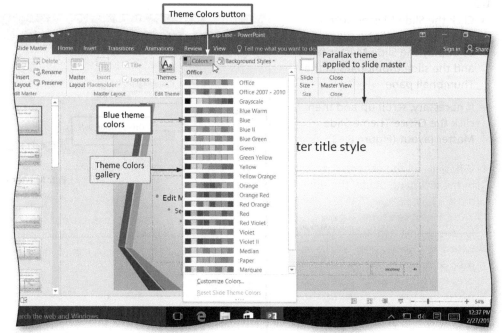

Figure 8–5

To Customize Theme Fonts

Each theme has a heading font and a body font applied to it. At times both fonts are the same, and other times, the heading font differs from the body font, but both fonts coordinate with each other. You can customize theme fonts by selecting your own combination of heading and body font and then giving the new theme font set a unique name. ***Why?*** *A particular font may match the tone of the presentation and help convey the message you are presenting.* The following steps apply a new heading font and body font to the Parallax theme.

- Click the Theme Fonts button (Slide Master tab | Background group) to display the Theme Fonts gallery (Figure 8–6).

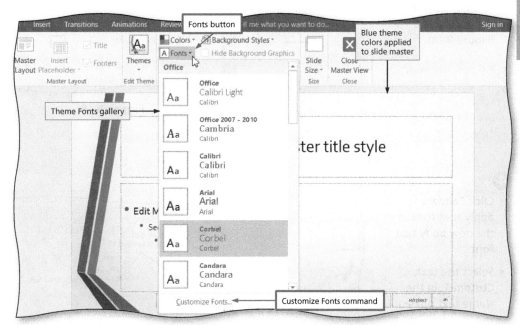

Figure 8–6

- Click Customize Fonts in the Theme Fonts gallery to display the Create New Theme Fonts dialog box.

- Click the Heading font arrow and then scroll down to display Poor Richard in the list (Figure 8–7).

Q&A Can I preview the fonts to see how they are displayed on the slide master?

No preview is available when using the Create New Theme Fonts dialog box. Once you select the font, however, PowerPoint will display text in the Sample box.

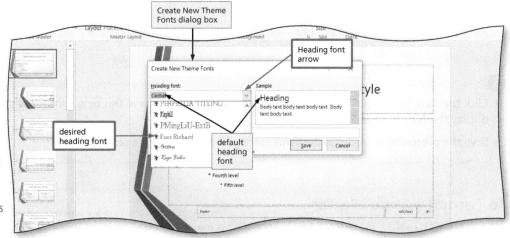

Figure 8–7

❸

• Click Poor Richard to apply that font as the new heading text font.

• Click the Body font arrow and then scroll up to display Candara in the list (Figure 8–8).

Q&A What if the Poor Richard or Candara fonts are not in my list of fonts?
Select fonts that resemble the fonts shown in Figure 8–8.

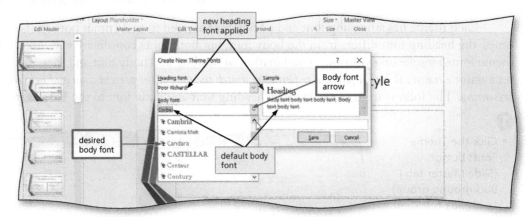

Figure 8–8

❹

• Click Candara to apply that font as the new body text font.

• Select the text, Custom 1, in the Name text box and then type `Zip` to name the new font set (Figure 8–9).

Q&A Must I name this font set I just created?
No. If you name the set, however, you easily will recognize this combination in your font set if you want to use it in new presentations. It will display in the Custom area of the Fonts gallery.

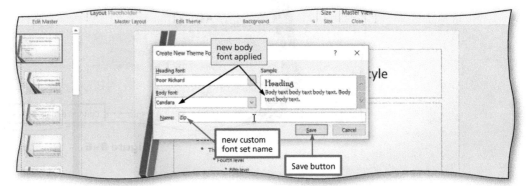

Figure 8–9

❺

• Click the Save button (Create New Theme Fonts dialog box) to save this new font set with the name, Zip, and to display the font changes in the slide master.

• Save the presentation again in the same storage location with the same file name.

To Format a Slide Master Background and Apply a Quick Style

1 CUSTOMIZE SLIDE MASTERS | 2 FORMAT & ARRANGE FOOTERS | 3 INSERT & FORMAT GRAPHICS & TEXT BOXES
4 RENAME & DELETE SLIDE LAYOUTS | 5 CUSTOMIZE HANDOUTS & NOTES MASTERS | 6 USE CUSTOM TEMPLATE

Once you have applied a theme to the slide master and determined the fonts for the presentation, you can further customize the slide master. *Why? Adding a unique background and customizing the colors can give your presentation a unique look that matches the message you are conveying.* The following steps format the slide master background and then apply a Quick Style.

1

- Click the Background Styles button (Slide Master tab | Background group) to display the Background Styles gallery (Figure 8–10).

🔎 **Experiment**

- Point to various styles in the Background Styles gallery and watch the backgrounds change on the slide master.

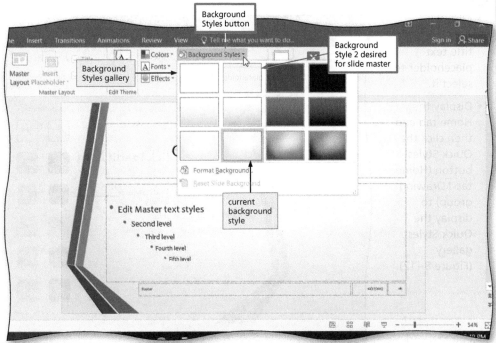

Figure 8–10

2

- Click Background Style 2 (second style in first row) to apply this background to the slide master (Figure 8–11).

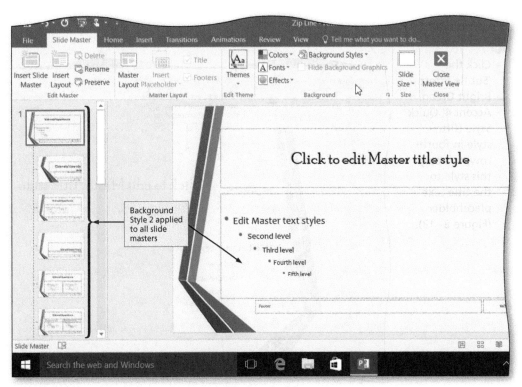

Figure 8–11

- Click the slide master title text placeholder to select it.

- Display the Home tab and then click the Quick Styles button (Home tab | Drawing group) to display the Quick Styles gallery (Figure 8–12).

Experiment

- Point to various styles in the Quick Styles gallery and watch the background and borders change on the slide master title text placeholder.

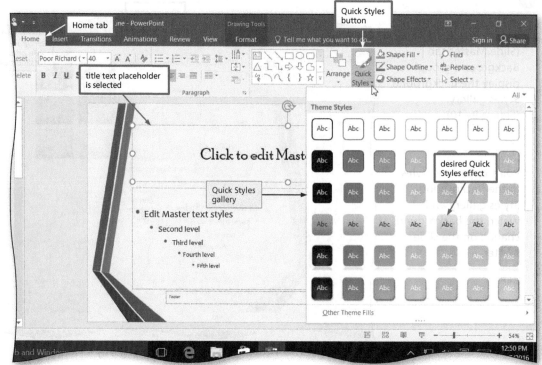

Figure 8–12

- Click the 'Subtle Effect – Bright Green, Accent 4' Quick Style (fifth style in fourth row) to apply this style to the title text placeholder (Figure 8–13).

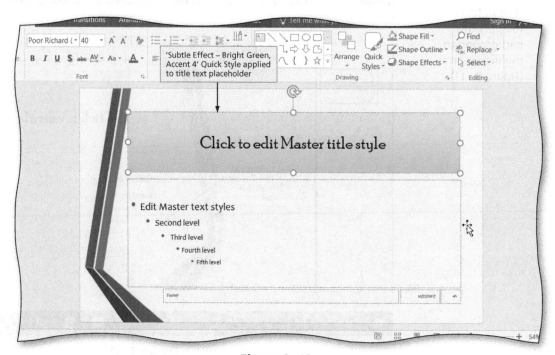

Figure 8–13

To Delete, Move, and Add Text to a Slide Master Footer

Slide numbers, the date and time, and footer text can be displayed anywhere on a slide, not just in the default footer placeholder locations. At times you may want to rearrange or delete these slide elements. *Why?* *These placeholders might interfere with other slide content, or you might not want to display information, such as a page number or the date.* The following steps delete one footer placeholder, move the footer placeholders, and then add footer text on the slide master.

- With the slide master displaying, click the border of the date footer placeholder to select it (Figure 8–14).

- Press the DELETE key to delete the date placeholder.

Q&A What should I do if the placeholder still is showing on the slide? Be certain you clicked the placeholder border and not just the text. The border must display as a solid line before you can delete it.

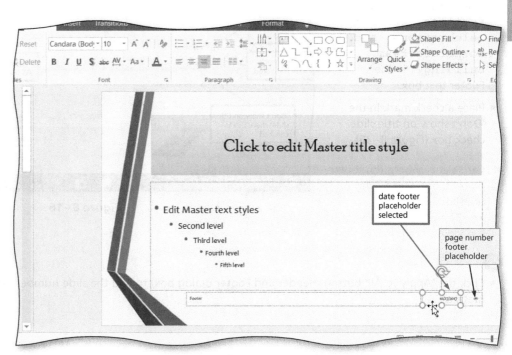

Figure 8–14

- Click the content footer placeholder and then drag it to the location where the date placeholder originally appeared (Figure 8–15).

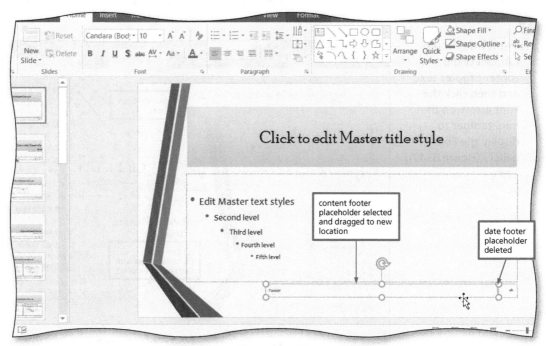

Figure 8–15

- Display the Insert tab, click the Header & Footer button (Insert tab | Text group), and then place a check mark in the Slide number check box.

- Place a check mark in the Footer check box and then type **Perfect for families, birthday celebrations, and corporate team building!** in the Footer text box.

- Place a check mark in the 'Don't show on title slide' check box (Figure 8–16).

Q&A Can I verify where the footer placeholders will display on the slide layout?
Yes. The black boxes in the bottom of the Preview area indicate the footer placeholders' locations.

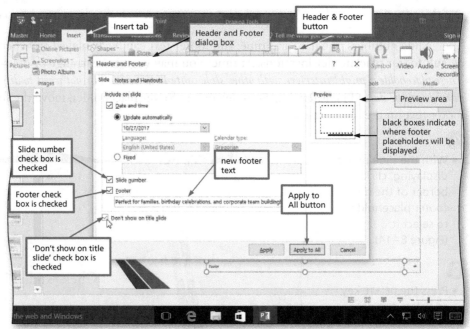

Figure 8–16

- Click the 'Apply to All' button (Header and Footer dialog box) to add the slide number and footer text to the slide master.

To Format Slide Master Footer Text

1 CUSTOMIZE SLIDE MASTERS | 2 FORMAT & ARRANGE FOOTERS | 3 INSERT & FORMAT GRAPHICS & TEXT BOXES
4 RENAME & DELETE SLIDE LAYOUTS | 5 CUSTOMIZE HANDOUTS & NOTES MASTERS | 6 USE CUSTOM TEMPLATE

You can format slide master footer text using the same font styles and text attributes available to title and subtitle text. *Why? Using the same font ensures continuity among the slide elements.* The following steps format the footer text.

- Display the Home tab, select the content footer text, and then click the Font arrow on the mini toolbar to display the Font gallery (Figure 8–17).

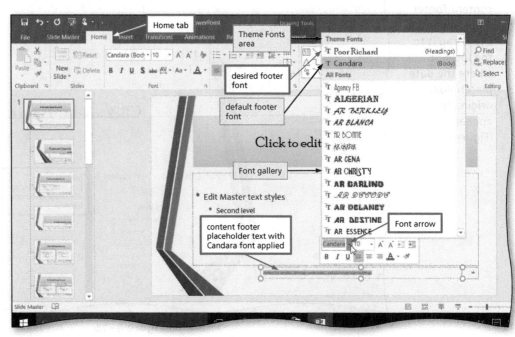

Figure 8–17

2

- Click Poor Richard in the Theme Fonts section of the Font gallery to change the footer font.
- Click the Increase Font Size button several times to increase the font size to 20 point.
- Change the font color to Green (sixth color in Standard Colors row).
- Click the Bold button to bold the text.
- Click the Align Right button to move the footer text alignment to the right border of the placeholder.
- Use the Format Painter to apply the content footer placeholder formatting to the page number placeholder (Figure 8–18).

Q&A Why does the page number placeholder now display on two lines?
The increased font size split the placeholder. The page number itself will display on only one line on the slides.

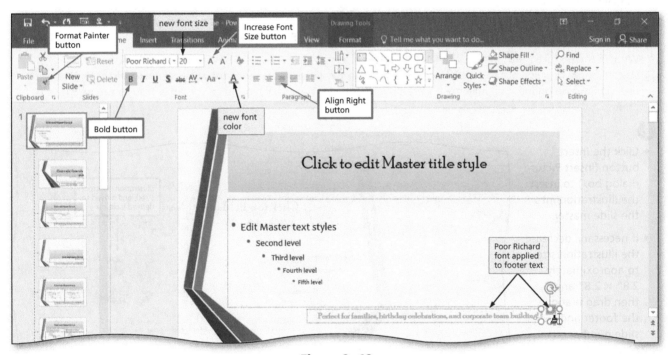

Figure 8–18

To Insert a Background Graphic into a Slide Master

1 CUSTOMIZE SLIDE MASTERS | 2 FORMAT & ARRANGE FOOTERS | 3 INSERT & FORMAT GRAPHICS & TEXT BOXES
4 RENAME & DELETE SLIDE LAYOUTS | 5 CUSTOMIZE HANDOUTS & NOTES MASTERS | 6 USE CUSTOM TEMPLATE

The theme, fonts, footer, and background colors of the slide master are set. The next step is to draw the viewers' attention to the presentation by placing the Family illustration, located in the Data Files, in the same location on every slide. **Why?** *The repetition of this picture creates consistency and helps reinforce the message.* The following steps insert an illustration of a family zip lining into the slide master.

- With the slide master displaying, click the Insert tab and then click the Pictures button (Insert tab | Images group) to display the Insert Picture dialog box.

- Navigate to the location where your data files are stored and then if necessary, scroll down and click Family to select the file (Figure 8–19).

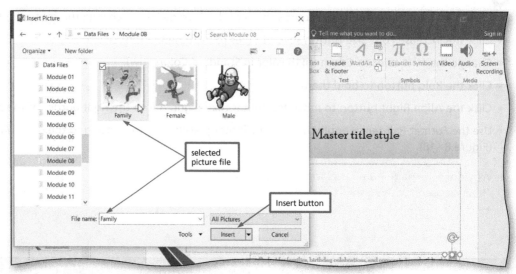

Figure 8–19

Q&A What if the picture is not in my Data Files folder?

Use the same process, but select the device containing the illustration. Another option is to locate this illustration or a similar one online. You may need to remove the illustration background to call attention to the people zip lining.

- Click the Insert button (Insert Picture dialog box) to insert the illustration into the slide master.

- If necessary, decrease the illustration size to approximately 2.8″ × 2.8″ and then drag it above the footer and slide number placeholders, as shown in Figure 8–20.

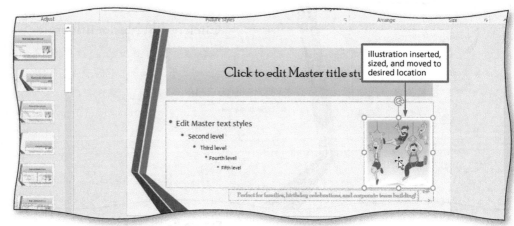

Figure 8–20

Break Point: If you wish to take a break, this is a good place to do so. Be sure to save the Zip Line file again and then you can exit PowerPoint. To resume at a later time, run PowerPoint, open the file called Zip Line, open Slide Master view, and continue following the steps from this location forward.

Adding and Formatting Placeholders

Each design theme determines where placeholders appear on individual layouts. The slide master has placeholders for bulleted lists, title text, pictures, and other graphical elements. At times, you may find that you need a specific placeholder for a design element not found on any of the slide master layouts. You can add a placeholder in Slide Master view for text, SmartArt, charts, tables, and other graphical elements.

To Insert a Placeholder into a Blank Layout

The words, Tree Top Adventures, will appear on the title slide, but you may desire to add these words to every text slide. *Why? Displaying this text in the same location on all slides helps emphasize the name and also provides a consistent, uniform look to the presentation.* One efficient method of adding this text is to insert a placeholder, type the words, and, if necessary, format the characters. The following steps insert a placeholder into the Blank Layout.

- In the Thumbnail pane, scroll down and then click the Blank Layout to display this layout.

- If necessary, display the Slide Master tab and then click the Insert Placeholder arrow (Slide Master tab | Master Layout group) to display the Insert Placeholder gallery (Figure 8–21).

Q&A Why does the Insert Placeholder button on my screen differ from the button shown in Figure 8–21? The image on the button changes based on the type of placeholder content that was last inserted. A placeholder can hold any content, including text, pictures, and tables. If the last type of placeholder inserted was for SmartArt, for example, the Insert Placeholder button would display the SmartArt icon.

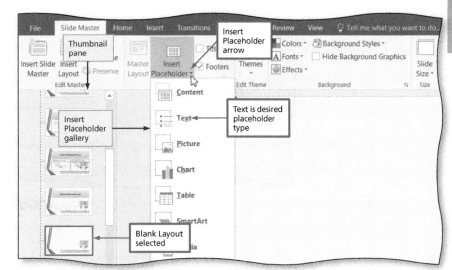

Figure 8–21

- Click Text in the gallery.

Q&A Could I have inserted a Content placeholder rather than a Text placeholder? Yes. The Content placeholder is used for any of the seven types of slide content: text, table, chart, SmartArt, picture, clip art, or media. In this project, you will insert text in the placeholder. If you know the specific kind of content you want to place in the placeholder, it is best to select that placeholder type.

- Position the pointer, which is a crosshair, at the upper-right area of the layout (Figure 8–22).

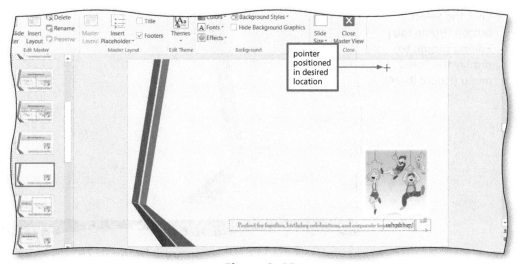

Figure 8–22

4

- Click to insert the new placeholder into the Blank Layout (Figure 8–23).

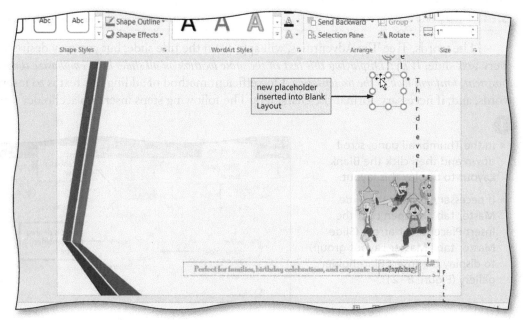

Figure 8–23

To Add and Format Placeholder Text

Now that the text placeholder is positioned, you can add the desired text and then format the characters. You will need to delete the second-, third-, fourth-, and fifth-level bullets in this placeholder. *Why? The placeholders are not used in this presentation.* The following steps add and format the words in the new Blank Layout placeholder.

1

- Display the Home tab and then click inside the new placeholder.
- Click the Select button (Home tab | Editing group) to display the Select menu (Figure 8–24).

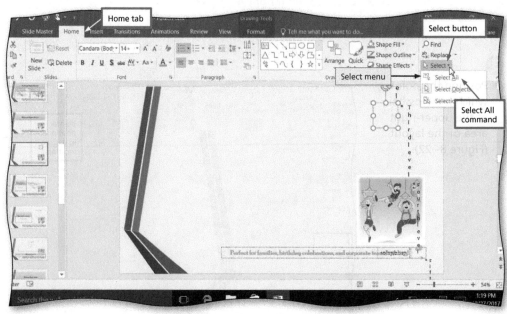

Figure 8–24

2

- Click Select All in the Select menu to select all the text in the placeholder (Figure 8–25).

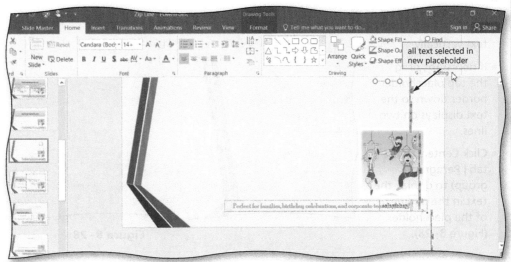

Figure 8–25

3

- Press the DELETE key to delete all the selected text in the placeholder.
- Click the Bullets button (Home tab | Paragraph group) to remove the bullet from the placeholder.
- Type **Tree Top Adventures** in the placeholder.
- Drag the bottom sizing handle down until it is above the Family illustration, as shown in Figure 8–26.

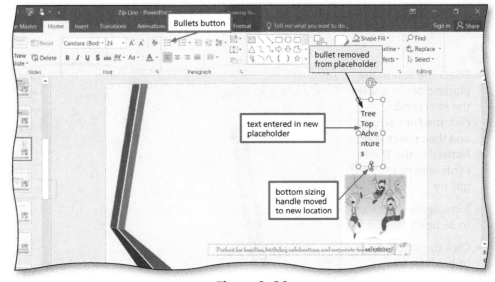

Figure 8–26

4

- Click the Text Direction button (Home tab | Paragraph group) to display the Text Direction gallery (Figure 8–27).

🔎 **Experiment**

- Point to various directions in the Text Direction gallery and watch the words in the placeholder change direction on the layout.

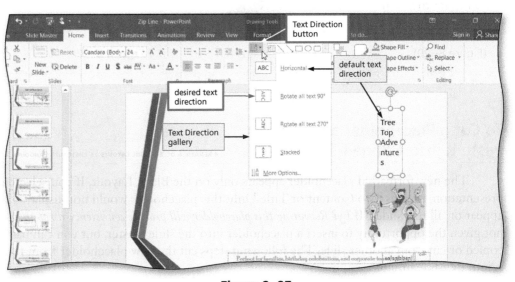

Figure 8–27

- Click 'Rotate all text 90°' to display the text vertically.

- If necessary, drag the top placeholder border down so the text displays on two lines.

- Click Center (Home tab | Paragraph group) to display the text in the middle of the placeholder (Figure 8–28).

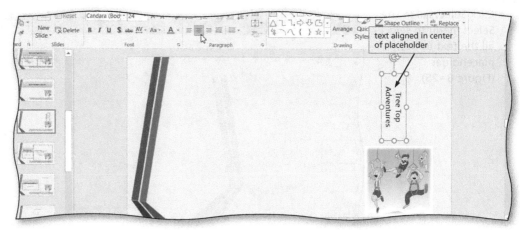

Figure 8–28

Q&A What is the difference between the Center button in the Align gallery and the Center button in the Paragraph group?

The Center button in the Paragraph group centers the text between the left and right borders. The Center button in the Align gallery positions the text between the top and bottom borders of the placeholder.

- Select the text in the placeholder to display the mini toolbar, click the Font arrow, and then select Poor Richard in the Theme Fonts area of the Font gallery.

- Increase the font size to 36 point.

- Click the Bold button to bold the text.

- Click the Font Color button to change the font color to Green (sixth color in Standard Colors row) (Figure 8–29).

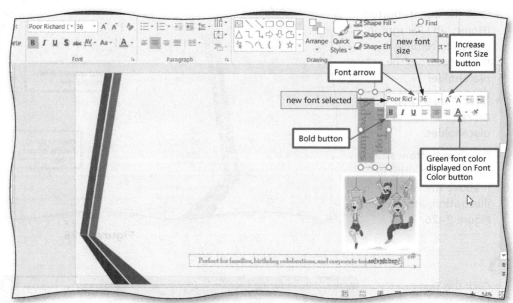

Figure 8–29

To Cut a Placeholder and Paste It into a Slide Master

1 CUSTOMIZE SLIDE MASTERS | 2 FORMAT & ARRANGE FOOTERS | 3 INSERT & FORMAT GRAPHICS & TEXT BOXES
4 RENAME & DELETE SLIDE LAYOUTS | 5 CUSTOMIZE HANDOUTS & NOTES MASTERS | 6 USE CUSTOM TEMPLATE

The new formatted placeholder appears only on the Blank Layout. If you selected any other layout in your presentation, such as Two Content or Title Only, this placeholder would not display. This placeholder should appear on all text slides. *Why? Repeating this placeholder will provide consistency throughout the presentation.* You are not given the opportunity to insert a placeholder into the slide master, but you can paste a placeholder that you copied or cut from another slide. The following steps cut the new placeholder from the Blank Layout and paste it into the slide master.

1

- With the Home tab displaying, click the new placeholder border and then click the Cut button (Home tab | Clipboard group) to delete the placeholder from the layout and copy it to the Clipboard (Figure 8–30).

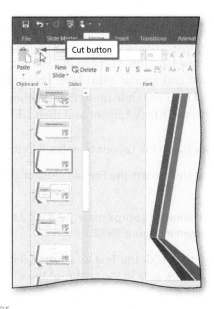
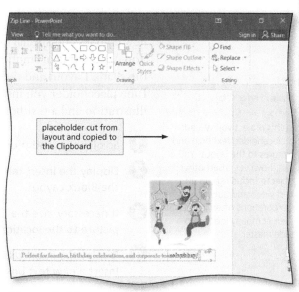

Q&A Why did I click the Cut button instead of the Copy button? Tapping or clicking the Cut button deletes the placeholder. Tapping or clicking the Copy button keeps the original placeholder on the slide, so if you paste the placeholder on the slide master, a second, identical placeholder would display on the Blank Layout.

Figure 8–30

2

- Scroll up and then click the Parallax Slide Master thumbnail in the Thumbnail pane to display the slide master.

- Click the Paste button (Home tab | Clipboard group) to copy the placeholder from the Clipboard to the slide master.

- Drag the placeholder to the location shown in Figure 8–31 and then move the Family illustration slightly to the left so that the text does not overlap this picture.

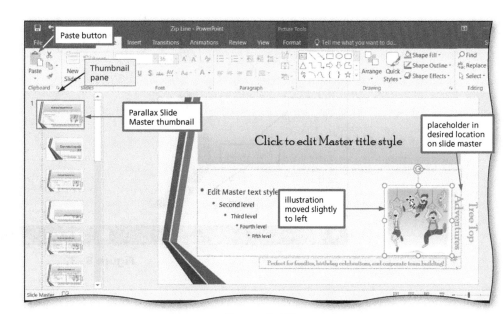

Figure 8–31

Break Point: If you wish to take a break, this is a good place to do so. Be sure to save the Zip Line file again and then you can exit PowerPoint. To resume at a later time, run PowerPoint, open the file called Zip Line, open Slide Master view, and continue following the steps from this location forward.

To Insert an Illustration and a Text Box into a Blank Layout

BTW

Inserting Objects into the Slide Master
In this project you will add a placeholder, text box, and pictures to the layout. You can, however, insert other objects, including clip art and video and audio files. Corporations often insert their company logos into a slide master.

One slide in the completed presentation will feature Tree Top Adventures' new courses and special events. To ensure continuity when publicizing the Tree Top Adventures promotions and facilities, you can insert another illustration into the Blank Layout and then add and format a text box. This layout includes the Zip Line placeholder you inserted into the slide master. The following steps insert an illustration and a text box into the Blank Layout and then add text in the text box.

1 Scroll down and then click the Blank Layout thumbnail in the Thumbnail pane.

2 Display the Insert tab, and then insert the Female illustration from the Data Files into the Blank Layout.

3 If necessary, size the illustration to approximately 2.8" × 2.8" and then drag the picture to the location shown in Figure 8–32.

4 Display the Insert tab and then click the Text Box button (Insert tab | Text group). Insert a new text box in a blank area in the center of the slide layout.

5 Type **Acres of fun!** as the text box text (Figure 8–32).

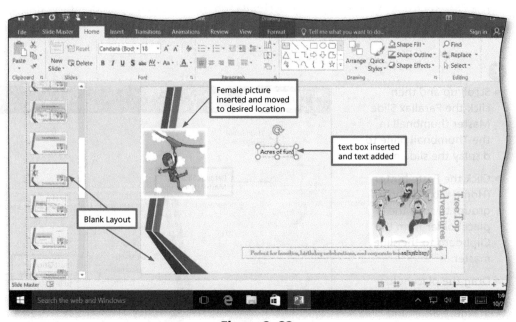

Figure 8–32

To Apply a Fill to a Text Box and Increase Transparency

1 CUSTOMIZE SLIDE MASTERS | 2 FORMAT & ARRANGE FOOTERS | **3 INSERT & FORMAT GRAPHICS & TEXT BOXES**
4 RENAME & DELETE SLIDE LAYOUTS | 5 CUSTOMIZE HANDOUTS & NOTES MASTERS | 6 USE CUSTOM TEMPLATE

Now that the text is added, you can format the text box. A **fill** refers to the formatting of the interior of a shape. The fill can be a color, picture, texture, pattern, or the presentation background. If a color fill is desired, you can increase the transparency so that some of the background color or pattern mixes with the fill color. The following steps apply a green fill to the text box on the Blank Layout and increase the transparency. *Why? The green color is part of the Blue theme colors and also coordinates well with the green text.*

- Click the Shape Fill arrow (Home tab | Drawing group) to display the Shape Fill gallery.

Experiment

- Point to various colors in the Shape Fill gallery and watch the placeholder background change.

- Click Green (sixth color in Standard Colors row) to fill the text box.

- Click the Drawing dialog box launcher (Home tab | Drawing group) to display the Format Shape pane (Figure 8–33).

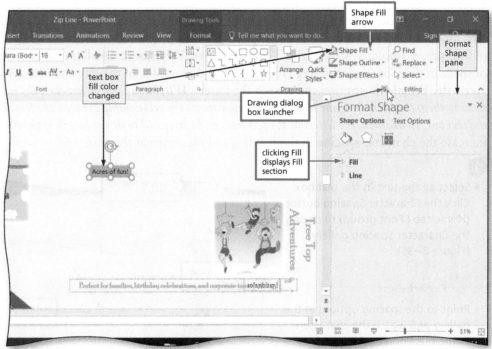

Figure 8–33

- If necessary, click Fill to display the Fill section.

- Click the Transparency slider in the Fill section and drag it to the right until 50% is displayed in the Transparency text box (Figure 8–34).

Experiment

- Drag the Transparency slider to the left and right, and watch the text box background change.

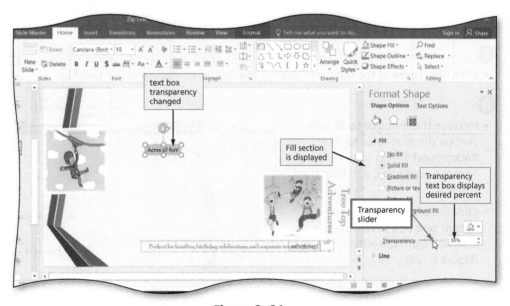

Figure 8–34

Other Ways

1. Enter percentage in Transparency text box

2. Click Transparency up or down arrow

To Change Character Spacing

Now that the text is added and the text box is formatted, you can change the spacing between the letters. The amount of space, called **character spacing**, can be increased or decreased from the Normal default in one of four preset amounts: Very Tight, Tight, Loose, or Very Loose. In addition, you can specify a precise amount of space in the Character Spacing tab of the Font dialog box. In this presentation, you will move the text box above the Female illustration and stretch the letters. *Why? You want to associate the text box with the illustration, so moving them together along the left side of the slide shows the relationship between the female zip liner and the words in the text box. In addition, the letters in the text box can be stretched to fit the length of the illustration.* The following steps increase the character spacing in the text box and then format the text.

1

- Select all the text in the text box. Click the Character Spacing button (Home tab | Font group) to display the Character Spacing gallery (Figure 8–35).

Experiment

- Point to the spacing options in the gallery and watch the characters in the placeholder change.

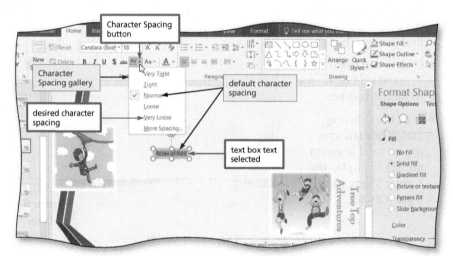

Figure 8–35

2

- Click Very Loose in the gallery to change the character spacing in the text box.

3

- Increase the font size to 28 point, change the font color to White, Background 1 (first color in first Theme Colors row), and then bold this text.

- Click the text inside the Acres of fun! text box to remove the selection from the letters (Figure 8–36).

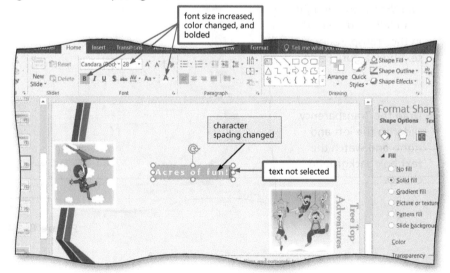

Figure 8–36

Other Ways

1. Click Font dialog box launcher (Home tab | Font group), click Character Spacing tab (Font dialog box), select Expanded or Condensed in Spacing box and point size in By box

2. Right-click text, click Font on shortcut menu, click Character Spacing tab (Font dialog box), select Expanded or Condensed in Spacing box and point size in By box

To Change a Text Box Internal Margin

Each placeholder and text box has preset internal margins, which are the spaces between the border and the contents of the box. The default left and right margins are 0.1", and the default top and bottom margins are 0.05". In this project, you will drag the text box above the Female illustration, so you want to change the margins. *Why? You want the text to align as closely as possible against the top and bottom borders of the box and the left and right margins to have a slight space between the border and the first and last letters.* The following steps change all four text box margins.

- In the Format Shape pane, click the 'Size & Properties' Shape Option (Format Shape pane).

- If necessary, click Text Box to display the Text Box section.

- Increase the Left margin setting to 0.3".

- Increase the Right margin setting to 0.3".

- Decrease the Top margin setting to 0".

- Decrease the Bottom margin setting to 0" (Figure 8–37).

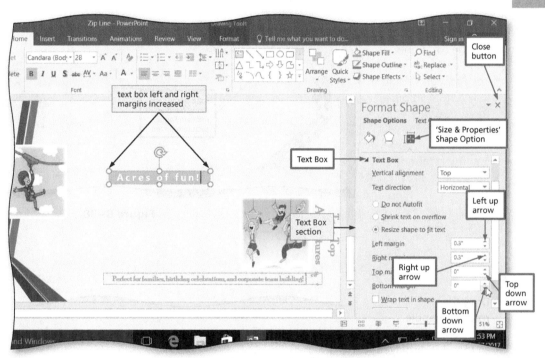

Figure 8–37

Q&A

Must I change all the margins?

No. You can change one, two, three, or all four internal margins depending upon the placeholder shape and the amount of text entered.

- Click the Close button (Format Shape pane).

To Rotate a Picture and a Text Box

Why? To balance the pictures on the slide, you can move the Female illustration and the Acres of fun! text box. For a dramatic effect, you can change the orientation of the picture and the placeholder on the slide by rotating them. Dragging the circular rotation handle above a selected object allows you to rotate an object in any direction. The following steps move and rotate the Female picture and the Acres of fun! text box.

1

- Click the Female illustration to select it.

- Position the pointer over the rotation handle so that it changes to a Free Rotate pointer (Figure 8–38).

Q&A

I selected the picture, but I cannot see the rotation handle. Why?
The rotation handle may not be visible at the top of the slide layout. Drag the picture downward, and the rotation handle will appear.

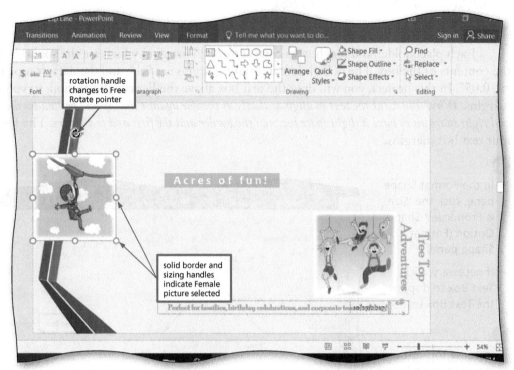

Figure 8–38

2

- Drag the rotation handle counterclockwise so that it is displayed as shown in Figure 8–39.

Q&A

I am using a touch screen and am having difficulty moving the rotation handle. What can I do?
When moving small items on a slide, it may be easier to use a mouse or a stylus instead of attempting to make adjustments using your fingers.

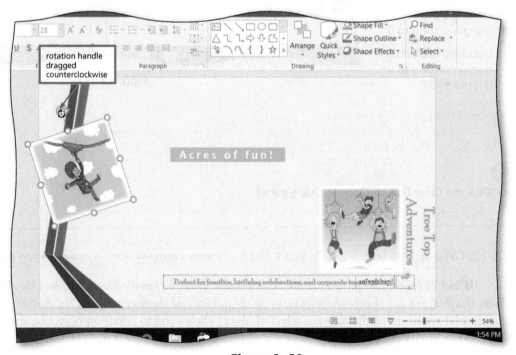

Figure 8–39

③

- Drag the illustration to position it as shown in Figure 8–40.

Q&A Can I move the picture in small increments?
Yes. To move or nudge the picture in very small increments, hold down the CTRL key with the picture selected while pressing the UP ARROW, DOWN ARROW, RIGHT ARROW, or LEFT ARROW keys. You cannot perform this action using a touch screen.

④

- Click the Acres of fun! text box to select it. Position the pointer over the rotation handle so that it changes to a Free Rotate pointer.

- Rotate the text box so that it is at the same angle as the Female illustration.

- Drag the text box above the Female illustration, as shown in Figure 8–40.

Figure 8–40

Other Ways

| 1. For text box, click Rotate button (Drawing Tools Format tab | Arrange group), choose desired rotation | 2. For picture, click Rotate button (Picture Tools Format tab | Arrange group), choose desired rotation | 3. For picture, right-click picture, click Format Picture on shortcut menu, click Effects icon (Format Picture pane), click 3-D Rotation, set rotation to desired angle | 4. For text box, right-click text box, click Format Shape on shortcut menu, click Effects icon (Format Shape pane), click 3-D Rotation, set rotation to desired angle |

To Hide and Unhide Background Graphics

The placeholder, text box, pictures, and other graphical elements are displayed on some slide master layouts and are hidden on others. You have the ability to change the default setting by choosing to hide or unhide the background graphics. The Hide Background Graphics check box is a toggle that displays and conceals the graphics. To hide background graphics on a layout, you would perform the following steps.

1. Display the Slide Master tab, select the desired layout, and then click the Hide Background Graphics check box (Slide Master tab | Background group) to insert a check mark in it.

2. To unhide the graphics, click the same check box to make them appear.

To Rename a Slide Master and a Slide Layout

Once all the changes are made to a slide master and a slide layout, you may want to rename them with meaningful names that describe their functions or features. The new slide master name will be displayed on the status bar; the new layout name will be displayed in the Slide Layout gallery. The following steps rename the Parallax Slide Master, the Title Slide Layout, the Blank Layout, and the Title and Content Layout. *Why? Renaming the layouts gives meaningful names that reflect the purpose of the design.*

1

- Display the Slide Master tab, click the Parallax Slide Master, and then click the Rename button (Slide Master tab | Edit Master group) to display the Rename Layout dialog box.

- Delete the text in the Layout name text box and then type **Zip Line** in the text box (Rename Layout dialog box) (Figure 8–41).

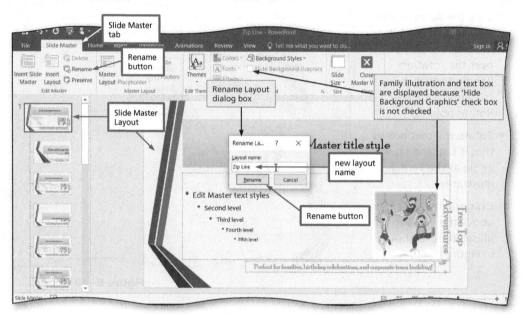

Figure 8–41

2

- Click the Rename button (Rename Layout dialog box) to give the layout the new name, Zip Line Slide Master.

3

- Display the Title Slide Layout, click the Rename button, delete the text in the Layout name text box, and then type **Zip Title** as the new layout name (Figure 8–42).

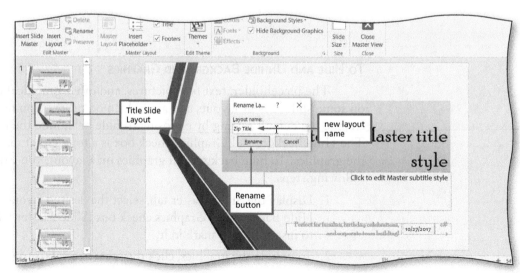

Figure 8–42

- Click the Rename button (Rename Layout dialog box) to rename the Title Slide layout.
- Scroll down and then click the Blank Layout to display it, click the Rename button, delete the text in the Layout name text box, and then type **Acres** as the new layout name (Figure 8–43).

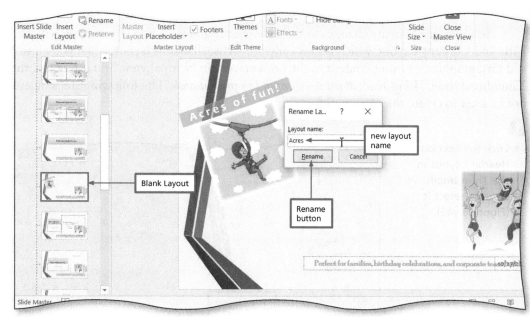

Figure 8–43

- Click the Rename button (Rename Layout dialog box).
- Scroll up to display the Title and Content Layout, click the Rename button, delete the text in the Layout name text box, and then type **Miscellaneous** as the new layout name (Figure 8–44).

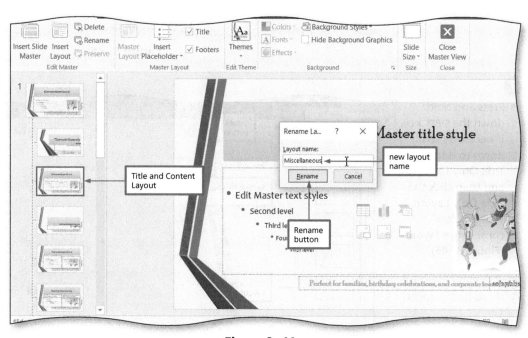

Figure 8–44

- Click the Rename button (Rename Layout dialog box).

To Delete a Slide Layout

You have made many changes to the slide master and two slide layouts. You will use these layouts and the Title and Content Layout, which is now called the Miscellaneous layout, when you close Master view and then add text, graphics, or other content to the presentation in Normal view. You can delete the other layouts in the Thumbnail pane. *Why? You will not use them in this presentation.* The following steps delete slide layouts that will not be used to create the presentation.

- Click the Section Header Layout in the Thumbnail pane to select it (Figure 8–45).

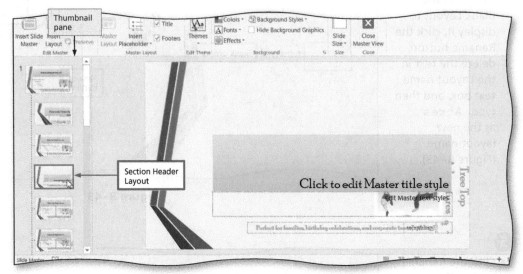

Figure 8–45

❷
- Press and hold down the SHIFT key, if necessary scroll down to display the Title Only Layout, and then click the Title Only Layout to select four consecutive layouts (Figure 8–46).

Q&A Why did I select only these four layouts? The layout below the Title Only Layout is the Acres layout, and you will use that layout when you create Slide 2 in your presentation.

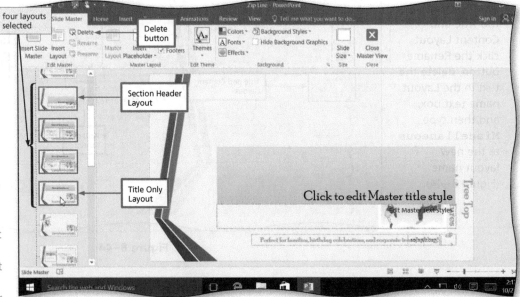

Figure 8–46

3

- Click the Delete button (Slide Master tab | Edit Master group) to delete the four layouts.
- Click the Content with Caption Layout (the layout below the Acres layout) and then select all layouts below it including the last layout, which is the Vertical Title and Text Layout, in the Thumbnail pane (Figure 8–47).

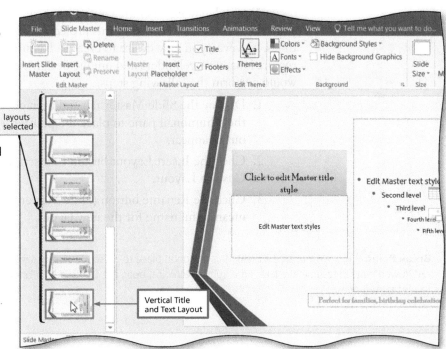

Figure 8–47

4

- Click the Delete button (Slide Master tab | Edit Master group) to delete the 10 layouts (Figure 8–48).

 Now that I have created this slide master, can I ensure that it will not be changed when I create future presentations?
Yes. Normally a slide master is deleted when a new design template is selected. To keep the original master as part of your presentation, you can preserve it by selecting the thumbnail and then clicking the Preserve button in the Edit Master group. An icon in the shape of a pushpin is displayed below the slide number to indicate the master is preserved. If you decide to unpreserve a slide master, select this thumbnail and then click the Preserve button.

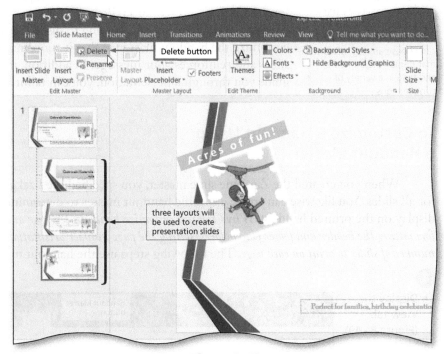

Figure 8–48

Other Ways

1. Click Delete button (Home tab | Slides group)
2. Right-click selected slide, click Delete Layout on shortcut menu
3. Press DELETE key on keyboard

To Add a New Slide Layout

The slide layouts included within each slide master are practical and varied. As you have learned in completing this project, editing these layouts is easy and useful. At times, however, you may desire to create a layout from scratch, especially if your design requires many placeholders and unique design elements. To add a new slide layout, you would perform the following steps.

1. Display the Slide Master tab and then click between the layout thumbnails in the Thumbnail pane to place the pointer where you desire the new slide layout to appear.
2. Click the Insert Layout button to insert a new slide layout with the name, Custom Layout.
3. Click the Rename button (Slide Master tab | Edit Master group) and type a meaningful name for the new layout.

Break Point: If you wish to take a break, this is a good place to do so. Be sure to save the Zip Line file again and then you can exit PowerPoint. To resume at a later time, run PowerPoint, open the file called Zip Line, and continue following the steps from this location forward.

Customizing Handout and Notes Masters

You have used PowerPoint's slide master template file to create unique slide layouts for the Zip Line presentation. PowerPoint also has master template files to create handouts and notes. If you are going to distribute handouts to your audience, you can customize the handout master so that it coordinates visually with the presentation slides and reinforces your message. In addition, if you are going to use speaker notes to guide you through a presentation, you can tailor the notes master to fit your needs.

To Customize a Handout Using a Handout Master

1 CUSTOMIZE SLIDE MASTERS | 2 FORMAT & ARRANGE FOOTERS | 3 INSERT & FORMAT GRAPHICS & TEXT BOXES
4 RENAME & DELETE SLIDE LAYOUTS | **5 CUSTOMIZE HANDOUTS & NOTES MASTERS** | **6 USE CUSTOM TEMPLATE**

When you created the Zip Line slide master, you specified the background, fonts, theme, and pictures for all slides. You likewise can create a specific handout master to determine the layout and graphics that will display on the printed handout. *Why? You can customize handouts for your audience's needs by moving, restoring, and formatting the header and footer placeholders; setting the page number orientation; adding graphics; and specifying the number of slides to print on each page.* The following steps use the handout master to create a custom handout.

- Display the View tab (Figure 8–49).

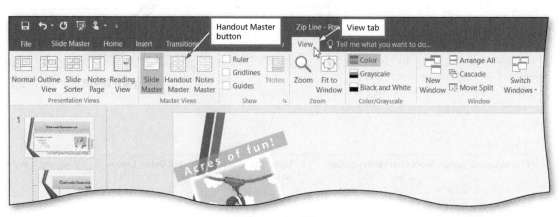

Figure 8–49

2

- Click the Handout Master button (View tab | Master Views group) to display the Handout Master tab.

- If a Microsoft PowerPoint dialog box is displayed, click the Check Out button to close the dialog box.

- Click the 'Slides Per Page' button (Handout Master tab | Page Setup group) to display the Slides Per Page gallery (Figure 8–50).

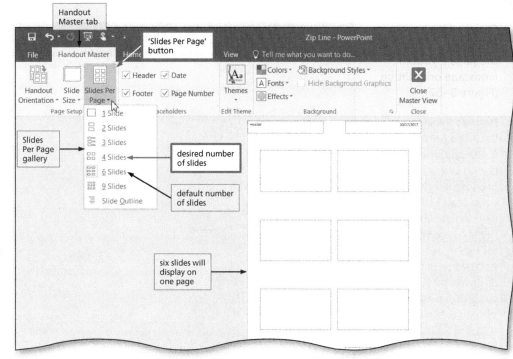

Figure 8–50

 Is 6 Slides the default layout for all themes?

Yes. If you have fewer than six slides in your presentation or want to display slide details, then choose a handout layout with 1, 2, 3, or 4 slides per sheet of paper.

3

- Click 4 Slides in the list to change the layout from 6 slides to 4 slides.

- Click the Handout Orientation button (Handout Master tab | Page Setup group) to display the Handout Orientation gallery (Figure 8–51).

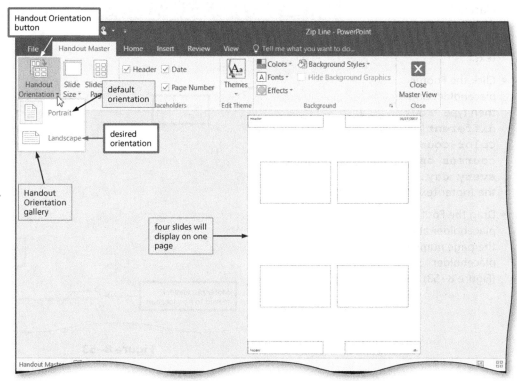

Figure 8–51

- Click Landscape in the gallery to display the page layout in landscape orientation (Figure 8–52).

Q&A How do I decide between portrait and landscape orientation? If your slide content is predominantly vertical, such as an athlete running or a skyscraper in a major city, consider using the default portrait orientation. If, however, your slide content has long lines of text or pictures of four-legged animals, landscape orientation may be a more appropriate layout.

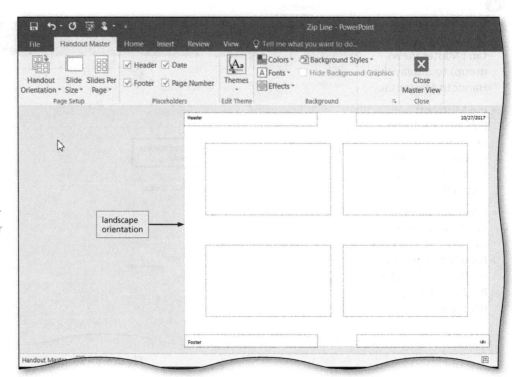

Figure 8–52

- Click the Header placeholder and then type **Zip Line** as the header text.

- Click the Footer placeholder and then type **Four different color-coded courses open every day.** as the footer text.

- Drag the Footer placeholder above the page number placeholder (Figure 8–53).

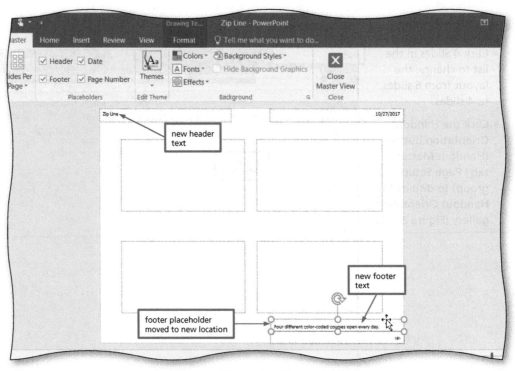

Figure 8–53

PowerPoint Module 8

6

- Click the Theme Fonts button (Handout Master tab | Background group) to display the Theme Fonts gallery (Figure 8–54).

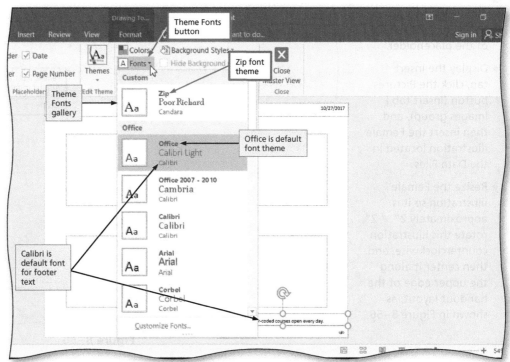

Figure 8–54

7

- Click Zip in the Custom area of the gallery to apply the Candara font to the text in the placeholders.

- Select the footer text, display the Home tab and then click the Align Text button (Home tab | Paragraph group) to display the Align Text gallery (Figure 8–55).

Experiment

- Point to the Top and Middle icons in the Align Text gallery and watch the words in the placeholder change alignment on the layout.

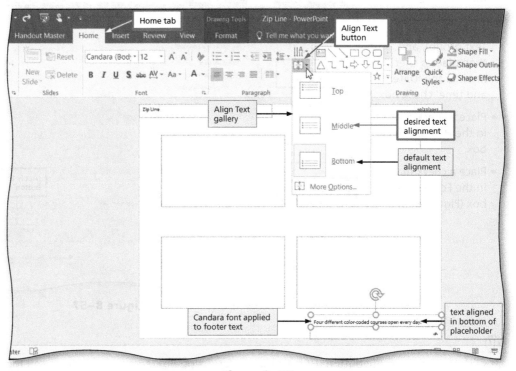

Figure 8–55

- Click Middle to display the text in the middle of the placeholder.

- Display the Insert tab, click the Pictures button (Insert tab | Images group), and then insert the Female illustration located in the Data Files.

- Resize the Female illustration so it is approximately 2″ × 2″, rotate this illustration counterclockwise, and then center it along the upper edge of the handout layout, as shown in Figure 8–56.

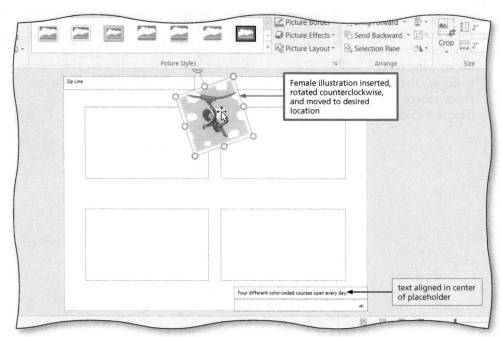

Figure 8–56

- Display the Insert tab, click the 'Header & Footer' button (Insert tab | Text group), and then place a check mark in the 'Date and time' check box.

- Place a check mark in the Header check box.

- Place a check mark in the Footer check box (Figure 8–57).

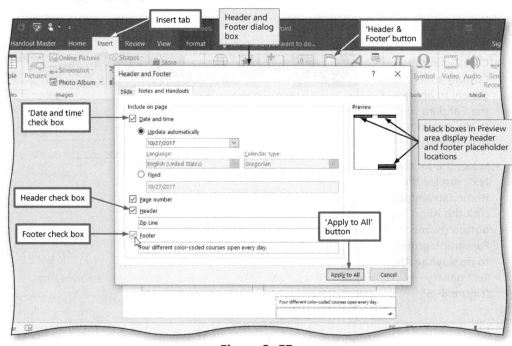

Figure 8–57

- Click the 'Apply to All' button (Header and Footer dialog box) to add the header and footer text and date to the handout master.

◄ | Where will the header and footer display on the handout?
Q&A | The black boxes in the preview area show where these placeholders are located.

To Customize a Notes Page Using a Notes Master

If you type notes in the Notes pane, you can print them for yourself or for your audience. The basic format found in the Backstage view generally suffices for handouts, but you may desire to alter the layout using the notes master. *Why? You may desire to add graphics and rearrange and format the header, footer, and page number placeholders.* The following steps use the notes master to create a custom handout.

1
- Display the View tab (Figure 8–58).

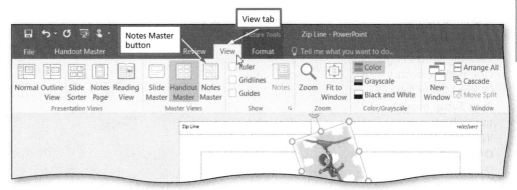

Figure 8–58

2
- Click the Notes Master button (View tab | Master Views group) to display the Notes Master tab.
- If a Microsoft PowerPoint dialog box is displayed, click the Check Out button to close the dialog box.
- Click the Footer placeholder, delete the text, and then type **Challenge your body and your mind.** as the new footer text.

3
- Click the Theme Fonts button to display the Theme Fonts gallery (Figure 8–59).

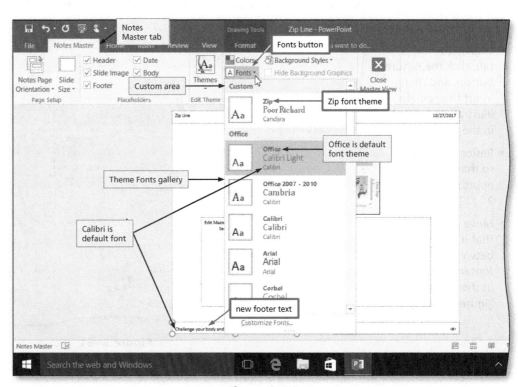

Figure 8–59

4

- Click Zip in the Custom area of the Theme Fonts gallery to apply the Candara font to the text in the header, footer, date, and page number placeholders.

- Click the 'Notes Page Orientation' button (Notes Master tab | Page Setup group) to display the 'Notes Page Orientation' gallery (Figure 8–60).

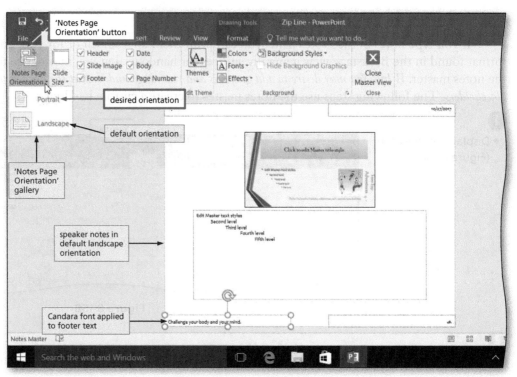

Figure 8–60

5

- Click Portrait in the gallery to display the page layout in portrait orientation.

- Display the Insert tab, click the Pictures button, and then insert the Female illustration located in the Data Files.

- Resize the picture so that it is approximately 2″ × 2″.

- Move the picture so that it is centered between the two footer placeholders, as shown in Figure 8–61.

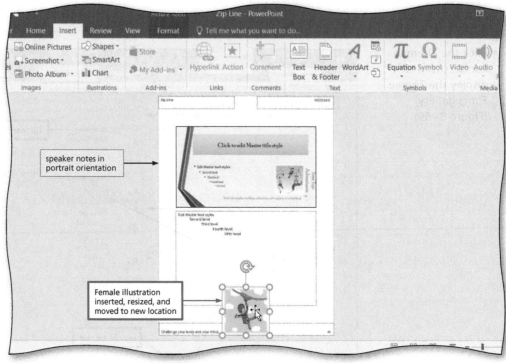

Figure 8–61

To Close Master View

You now can exit Master view and return to Normal view. *Why? All the changes to the slide master, handout master, and notes master are complete.* The following steps close Master view.

- Display the Notes Master tab (Figure 8–62).

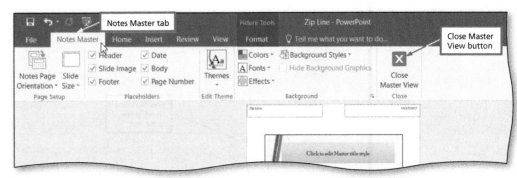

Figure 8–62

- Click the 'Close Master View' button (Notes Master tab | Close group) to exit Master view and return to Normal view.

To Save a Master as a Template

The changes and enhancements you have made to the Zip Line slide master, handout master, and notes master are excellent starting points for future presentations. The background text and graphics allow users to add text boxes, pictures, SmartArt, tables, and other elements depending upon the specific message that needs to be communicated to an audience. Saving a slide master as a template is convenient when you often reuse and modify presentations. *Why? You can save your slide layouts as a template to use for a new presentation and use the revised handout and notes masters to print unique pages.* The following steps save the Zip Line master as a template.

- Display the Save As dialog box.

- Click the 'Save as type' arrow to display the 'Save as type' list (Figure 8–63).

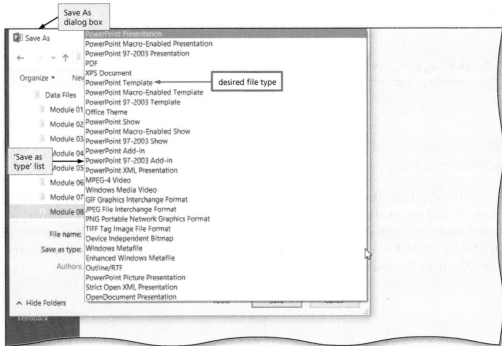

Figure 8–63

- Click 'PowerPoint Template' in the 'Save as type' list to change the save as type.

Q&A

Why do the file name extensions, such as (*.potx), display after the file type in my 'Save as type' list?
These letters identify the file format or type. You can configure Windows to show or hide all common file extensions by opening File Explorer, displaying the View tab, clicking the Options button, clicking the View tab in the Folder Options dialog box, and then either checking or unchecking 'Hide extensions for known file types' in the Advanced settings area.

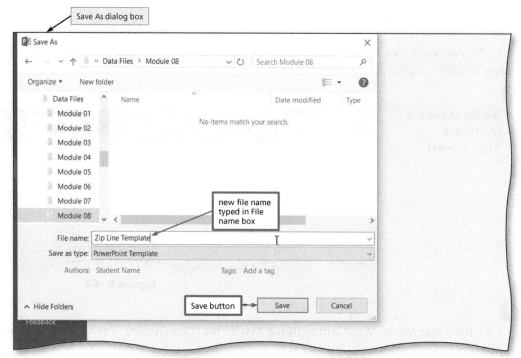

Figure 8–64

- Type **Zip Line Template** in the File name box and then navigate to the desired save location (in this case, the Module 08 folder in the Data Files folder) (Figure 8–64).

- Click the Save button (Save As dialog box) to save the Zip Line presentation as a template.

- Close the Zip Line Template file.

Break Point: If you wish to take a break, this is a good place to do so. You can exit PowerPoint now. To resume at a later time, run PowerPoint and continue following the steps from this location forward.

To Open a Template and Save a Presentation

1 CUSTOMIZE SLIDE MASTERS | 2 FORMAT & ARRANGE FOOTERS | 3 INSERT & FORMAT GRAPHICS & TEXT BOXES
4 RENAME & DELETE SLIDE LAYOUTS | 5 CUSTOMIZE HANDOUTS & NOTES MASTERS | **6 USE CUSTOM TEMPLATE**

The Zip Line Template file you created is a convenient start to a new presentation. The graphical elements and essential slide content are in place; you then can customize the layouts for a specific need, such as a new event or special program. Unless users specify a different location, PowerPoint saves templates they create in a folder called 'Custom Office Templates' in the Documents folder. The steps on the next page open the Zip Line Template file and save the presentation with the Zip Line name.

- In Backstage view, click the Open tab to display the Open dialog box (Figure 8–65).

- If necessary, navigate to the save location and then select the file, Zip Line Template.

Q&A If I did not change the default save location, can I select the Zip Line Template from the list of Recent Presentations or by opening the Custom Office Templates folder?
Yes. Either technique will locate the desired template.

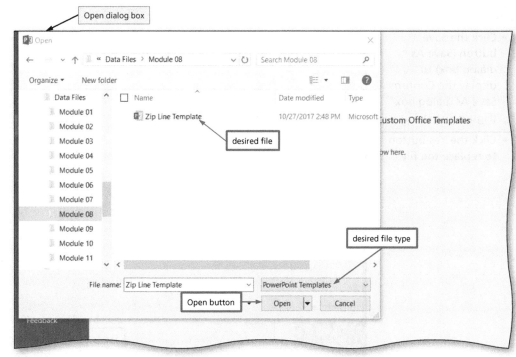

Figure 8–65

- Click the Open button to open the file, Zip Line Template.

- In Backstage view, click the Save As tab to display the Save As dialog box.

- Navigate to the location where your files are saved.

- Click the 'Save as type' arrow to display the 'Save as type' list, and then click PowerPoint Presentation in the 'Save as type' list to change the save as type.

- Click Zip Line in the Save As dialog box to select the file (Figure 8–66).

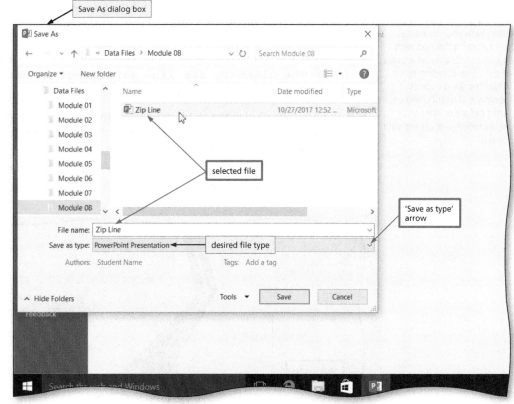

Figure 8–66

- Click the Save button (Save As dialog box) to display the Confirm Save As dialog box (Figure 8–67).

- Click the Yes button to replace the file.

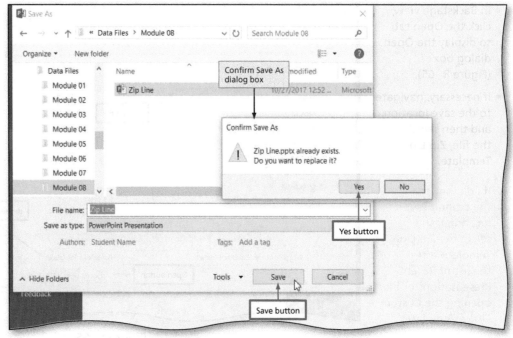

Figure 8–67

To Add Text and Notes to the Title Slide

By default, the title slide layout, which was renamed Zip Line Title, is applied to the first slide. The following steps add text and speaker notes to Slide 1.

1 With the title slide displaying, type **Tree Top Adventures** as the title text and **The ultimate zip line experience** as the subtitle text. Increase the subtitle text font size to 32 point.

2 If necessary, display the Notes pane. Click the Notes pane and then type **Tree Top Adventures offers tours every 30 minutes and is open from 9 a.m. until dusk.** (Figure 8–68).

If requested by your instructor, change the time in the Notes pane from 9 a.m. to the time of day you were born.

Figure 8–68

To Add Text and Notes to the Blank Layout

The second slide in your presentation will highlight important features. The Acres slide layout, which is the new name for the Blank Layout, is designed so that you can add variable slide content above the Female illustration in the upper-left corner. The following steps add a text box and speaker notes to Slide 2. *Why? The text box will call attention to the features at the Tree Top Adventures, and the speaker notes contain ideas that a presenter may want to discuss during a presentation.*

1 Insert a slide with the Acres layout and then insert a text box between the two illustrations. Type `Set in natural environment` as the first line of text box text and then press the ENTER key. Type `Two giant 450' zip lines` as the second line of text.

2 Increase the text box font size to 54 point. Size the text box as shown in Figure 8–69 and then drag it to the location shown in the figure.

3 In the Notes pane, type `During the training session, you will be fitted into your harness. Your guide will demonstrate how to attach to the safety lines and the zip lines.` (Figure 8–69).

Figure 8–69

To Add Text, Notes, and an Illustration to the Title and Content Layout

The third slide in your presentation will list details about the four courses. In addition, the Notes pane will contain information about clothing requirements. The Miscellaneous layout, which is the new name for the Title and Content slide layout, will allow you to insert text into the content placeholder. The following steps insert a slide and add text and a picture to the title and content placeholder.

1 Insert a slide with the Miscellaneous layout and then type `Four Exciting Courses` as the title text.

2 Type `Blue: Low elevations; Minimum skills` as the first content placeholder paragraph.

3 Type `Green: Medium elevations; Intermediate skills` as the second paragraph.

4 Type `Yellow: High elevations; Intermediate skills` as the third paragraph.

5 Type `Red: High elevations; Advanced skills` as the fourth paragraph.

6 In the Notes pane, type `Clothing requirements: No open-toe shoes; no loose clothes; no necklaces or bracelets. Your clothes will get dirty.`

7 Click anywhere on the blue background without a text box or illustration and then insert the illustration with the file name, Male, located in the Data Files. If necessary, decrease its size to approximately 2.5″ × 2.5″, and then move the illustration to the upper-left of the slide (Figure 8–70).

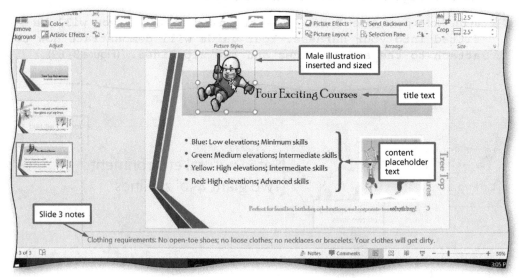

Figure 8–70

To Apply a Fill Color to a Slide

1 CUSTOMIZE SLIDE MASTERS | 2 FORMAT & ARRANGE FOOTERS | 3 INSERT & FORMAT GRAPHICS & TEXT BOXES
4 RENAME & DELETE SLIDE LAYOUTS | 5 CUSTOMIZE HANDOUTS & NOTES MASTERS | 6 USE CUSTOM TEMPLATE

Earlier in this project, you formatted the interior of the Acres text box by applying a fill. In a similar manner, you can apply a fill to an entire slide by selecting a color from the Shape Fill gallery. If desired, you can increase the transparency to soften the color. The following steps apply a fill to Slide 3 and increase the transparency. ***Why?*** *Because the text boxes on Slide 3 have a green font color and the title text placeholder has a green background, you can coordinate the Slide 3 fill color by changing the Slide 3 background to turquoise and decrease the transparency so the letters can be read easily.*

1

• With Slide 3 displaying, right-click anywhere on the blue background without a text box or illustration to display the shortcut menu (Figure 8–71).

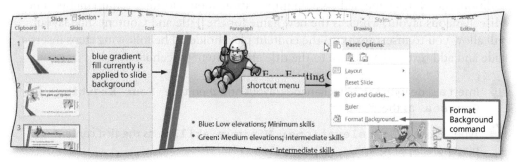

Figure 8–71

2

- Click Format Background on the shortcut menu to display the Format Background pane.

- With the Fill section displaying and the Solid fill option selected, click the Color button to display the Fill Color gallery (Figure 8–72).

Q&A Can I experiment with previewing the background colors?
No live preview feature is available.

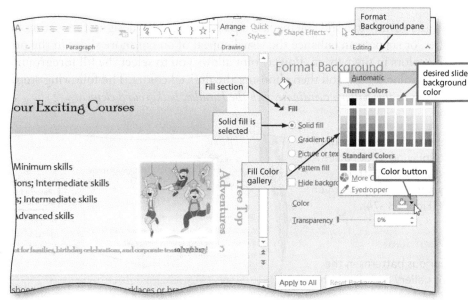

Figure 8–72

 3

- Click 'Turquoise, Accent 3' (seventh color in first Theme Colors row) to change the slide background color.

- Click the Transparency slider in the Fill Color area and drag it to the right until 50% is displayed in the Transparency text box (Figure 8–73).

Experiment

- Drag the Transparency slider to the left and right and watch the text box background change.

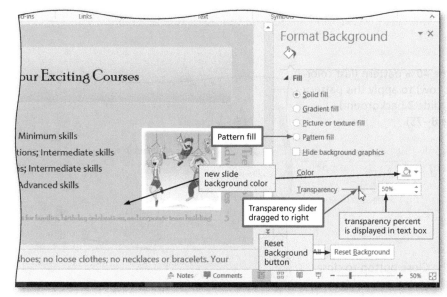

Figure 8–73

Q&A How can I delete a fill color if I decide not to apply one to my slide?
Any fill effect in the Format Background dialog box is applied immediately. If this dialog box is displayed, click the Reset Background button. If you already have applied the fill color, you must click the Undo button on the Quick Access Toolbar.

Other Ways

1. Enter percentage in Transparency text box

2. Click Transparency up or down arrow

To Apply a Pattern to a Slide

You add variety to a slide by making a **pattern fill**. This design of repeating horizontal or vertical lines, dots, dashes, or stripes can enhance the visual appeal of one or more slides in the presentation. If you desire to change the colors in the pattern, PowerPoint allows you to select the fill foreground and background colors by clicking the Color button and then choosing the desired colors. The following steps apply a pattern to Slide 3. *Why? The dots in this pattern coordinate with the Parallax background elements.*

- With the Format Background pane displaying, click Pattern fill to display the Pattern gallery and the 5% pattern on Slide 3 (Figure 8–74).

 **Experiment**

- Click various patterns in the Pattern gallery and watch the Slide 3 background change.

Q&A How can I delete a pattern if I decide not to apply one to my slide?
If the Format Background pane is displayed, click the Reset Background button. If you already have applied the pattern, you must click the Undo button on the Quick Access Toolbar.

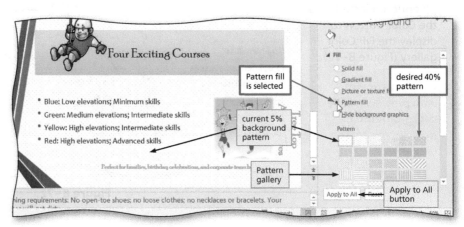

Figure 8–74

- Click the 40% pattern (last color in first row) to apply this pattern to the Slide 3 background (Figure 8–75).

Q&A Can I apply this pattern to all the slides in the presentation?
Yes. You would click the 'Apply to All' button in the Format Background pane.

3

- Click the Close button to close the Format Background task pane.

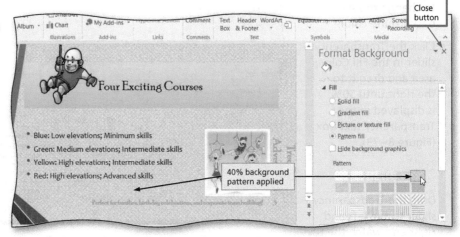

Figure 8–75

To Add a Slide Transition

A final enhancement you will make in this presentation is to apply the Fly Through transition to all slides and then change the transition speed and effect option. The following steps apply a transition and effect to the presentation.

1 Display the Transitions tab and then apply the Fly Through transition in the Dynamic Content category to all three slides in the presentation.

2 Change the duration from 00.80 to 02.00.

3 Change the Effect Option from In to 'Out with Bounce'.

To Print a Handout Using the Handout Master

The handout master you created has header and footer text using the Candara font, a revised location for the Footer placeholder, and the Family illustration in the lower-left corner. The following steps print a handout using the handout master.

1
- Open the Backstage view and then display the Print gallery.

2
- Click the 'Full Page Slides' button in the Settings area to display the gallery (Figure 8–76).

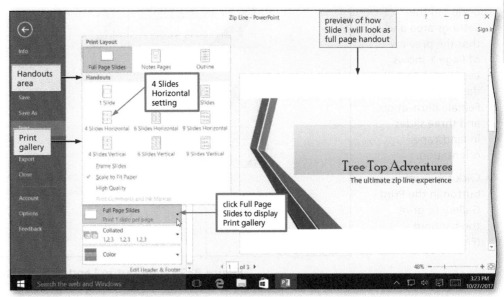

Figure 8–76

3
- Click '4 Slides Horizontal' in the Handouts area.
- Click Portrait Orientation in the Settings area to display the Orientation gallery (Figure 8–77).

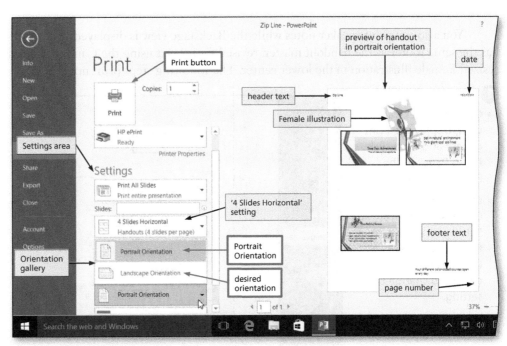

Figure 8–77

- Click Landscape Orientation to change the setting.

- Verify that '4 Slides Horizontal' is selected as the option in the Settings area and that the preview of Page 1 shows the header text, date, footer text, Female illustration, and three slides in landscape orientation.

- Click the Print button in the Print Gallery to print the handout (Figure 8–78).

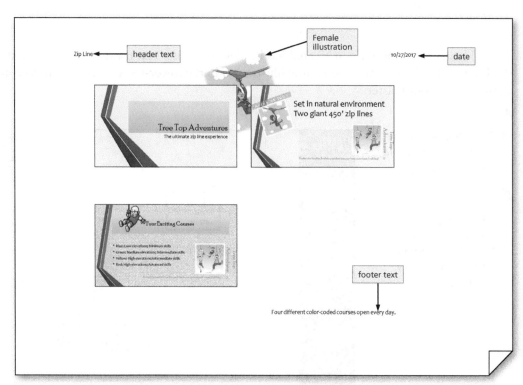

Figure 8–78 Handout in Landscape Orientation

To Print Speaker Notes Using the Notes Master

1 CUSTOMIZE SLIDE MASTERS | 2 FORMAT & ARRANGE FOOTERS | 3 INSERT & FORMAT GRAPHICS & TEXT BOXES
4 RENAME & DELETE SLIDE LAYOUTS | 5 CUSTOMIZE HANDOUTS & NOTES MASTERS | 6 USE CUSTOM TEMPLATE

You also can print speaker notes while the Backstage view is displayed. The custom notes master you created has the same footer as the handout master, revised footer text using the Candara font, the current date, and the resized Female illustration in the lower center. The following steps print notes pages using the notes master.

- Open the Backstage view, display the Print gallery and then click Notes Pages in the Print Layout area.

- Click Landscape Orientation in the Settings area and then click Portrait Orientation in the gallery to change the setting.

- If necessary, click the Previous Page button to preview Slide 1.

- Verify that the page preview shows the header text, date, speaker notes, revised footer text, Female illustration, and page number in portrait orientation (Figure 8–79).

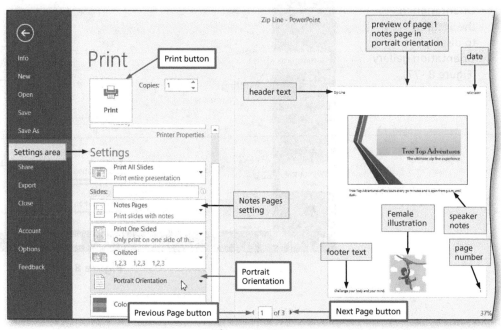

Figure 8–79

2

- Click the Previous Page and Next Page buttons to display previews of the other pages.
- Click the Print button in the Print gallery to print the notes (Figure 8–80).

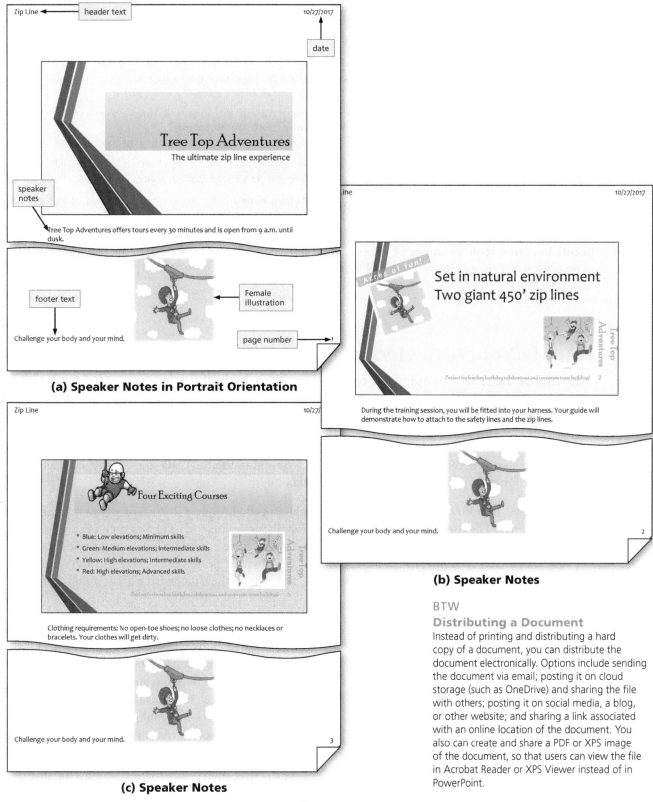

(a) Speaker Notes in Portrait Orientation

(b) Speaker Notes

(c) Speaker Notes

BTW

Distributing a Document
Instead of printing and distributing a hard copy of a document, you can distribute the document electronically. Options include sending the document via email; posting it on cloud storage (such as OneDrive) and sharing the file with others; posting it on social media, a blog, or other website; and sharing a link associated with an online location of the document. You also can create and share a PDF or XPS image of the document, so that users can view the file in Acrobat Reader or XPS Viewer instead of in PowerPoint.

Figure 8–80

3

- Because the project now is complete, you can save the presentation and exit PowerPoint.

Summary

In this module, you learned how to customize master slide layouts by changing the slide and font themes, formatting the background and footers, and adding background graphics. You then inserted a placeholder, added and formatted text, applied a fill, and changed the internal margins. Also, you rotated a picture and a placeholder, displayed the background graphics, and renamed and deleted slide layouts. Then you customized the handout and notes masters by adding a picture and changing the layout orientation. You then saved the slide master as a template, opened this template, added slide content, and printed a handout and speaker notes pages.

What decisions will you need to make when creating your next presentation?
Use these guidelines as you complete the assignments in this module and create your own slide show decks outside of this class.

1. **Plan the slide master.** Using a new slide master gives you the freedom to plan every aspect of your slide. Take care to think about the overall message you are trying to convey before you start PowerPoint and select elements for this master.

2. **Develop the slide master prior to creating presentation slides.** You can save time and create consistency when you design and build your master at the start of your PowerPoint session rather than after you have created individual slides.

3. **Decide how to distribute copies of slides.** Some audience members will desire printed copies of your slides. To conserve paper and ink, you may decide to limit the number of copies you print or to post the presentation electronically in a shared location for users to print the presentation if they so choose.

Apply Your Knowledge

Reinforce the skills and apply the concepts you learned in this module.

Applying a Slide Theme to a Slide Master, Creating a New Theme Font, and Changing the Title Layout

Note: To complete this assignment, you will be required to use the Data Files. Please contact your instructor for information about accessing the Data Files.

Instructions: Run PowerPoint. Open the presentation called Apply 8-1 Pottery, which is located in the Data Files. The three slides in this presentation discuss pottery classes. Instructors at a local art studio will teach you techniques in working with clay to create a ceramic bowl or to paint a molded pottery piece. The document you open is a partially formatted presentation. You will apply a slide theme to a slide master, create a new theme font, and change the slide master background. Your slides should look like Figure 8–81.

Perform the following tasks:

1. Display the Office Theme Slide Master and then apply the Crop theme. Change the theme colors to Blue Warm and then create a customized theme font named Clay using Baskerville Old Face for the heading font and Book Antiqua for the body font. Create a background on all slides by inserting the photo called Pottery, which is located in the Data Files, and then change the transparency to 75%. Make sure the 'Hide background graphics' check box in the Fill section of the Format Background task pane is not checked so that the theme graphics are displayed.

2. Display the Title Slide layout and then decrease the font size of the title text to 60 point and change the color to Dark Red (first color in Standard Colors row). Increase the font size of the subtitle text to 36 point and then apply the Quick Style 'Colored Fill - Teal, Accent 5' Quick Style (sixth style in second row).

3. Display the Two Content Layout and then change the font color of the title text to Dark Red. Display the Picture with Caption Layout and change the font color of the title text also to Dark Red. Close Master view.

4. On Slide 1 (Figure 8–81b), type **Creative Pottery Art Studio** as the title text and **Clay Classes or Pick and Paint** as the subtitle text, as shown in the figure.

5. On Slide 2 (Figure 8–81c), change the layout to Two Content. Increase the size of the hands and clay picture to approximately 2.8" × 4.2" and then apply the Rotated, White picture style. Increase the size of the orange pot illustration to approximately 4" × 4". Move both pictures to the locations shown in the figure.

6. On Slide 3 (Figure 8–81d), change the layout to Picture with Caption. Increase the size of the text in the four paragraphs to 20 point and add the Star Bullets to this text. Decrease the size of the picture to approximately 5" × 4.86", apply the Bevel Perspective picture style, and then move the picture to the location shown in the figure.

7. If requested by your instructor, add the name of your high school mascot as the fifth bulleted paragraph on Slide 3.

8. Apply the Checkerboard transition (Exciting category) and then change the duration to 3.00 for all slides.

9. Run the presentation and then save the file using the file name, Apply 8-1 Creative Pottery.

10. Submit the revised document in the format specified by your instructor.

11. ✻ In this presentation, you created a new theme font in the Slide Master and named it Clay. Is this name appropriate? You also changed the theme colors to Blue Warm. Was this a good choice of theme colors? Would another set of colors been a better complement for the Pottery picture background?

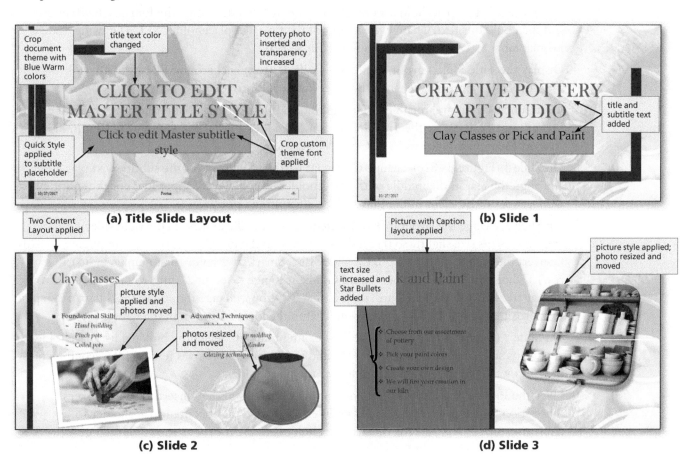

(a) Title Slide Layout

(b) Slide 1

(c) Slide 2

(d) Slide 3

Figure 8–81

Extend Your Knowledge

Extend the skills you learned in this module and experiment with new skills. You may need to use Help to complete the assignment.

Adding a Background to a Slide Master, Hiding a Background Graphic on a Slide, Adjusting Footer Content and Placeholders, Inserting and Renaming a Layout

Note: To complete this assignment, you will be required to use the Data Files. Please contact your instructor for information about accessing the Data Files.

Instructions: Run PowerPoint. Open the presentation called Extend 8-1 Tree, which is located in the Data Files. You will add a background graphic to the slide master, insert a fixed date, adjust content and placeholders, and insert and rename a layout, as shown in Figure 8–82.

Perform the following tasks:

1. Display the Wisp Slide Master. Display the Header and Footer dialog box, click the 'Date and time' check box, click Fixed, and then enter 11/8/17 in the Fixed text box. Apply this fixed date to all slides. Format the date by increasing the font size to 12 point and the font color to 'Black, Text 1' (second color in first Theme Colors row). Insert the illustration called Potted Tree, which is located in the Data Files, in the lower-right corner of the slide near the date, as shown in Figure 8–82a.

2. Display the Two Content Layout. Hide the background graphics. (*Hint:* Click the 'Hide Background Graphics' check box (Slide Master tab | Background group).) Create a background by inserting the illustration called Tree, which is located in the Data Files. Change the transparency to 85%.

3. Select the title text placeholder in the Two Content Layout, change the font size to 40 point and then bold this text. Change the height of the title text placeholder to 1" (Drawing Tools Format tab | Size group), as shown in Figure 8–82b.

4. Display the Title Slide Layout. Apply the Trellis Pattern background fill (fifth pattern in seventh row). If necessary, change the foreground color to 'Orange, Accent 1'.

5. Insert a new layout and rename it Closing Slide. Hide the background graphics. Create a background by inserting the Tree illustration you added to the Two Content Layout in Step 2. Change the transparency to 10%. Close Master view.

6. On Slide 1 (Figure 8–82c), change the layout to Title Slide. Select the subtitle text placeholder and align the text in the middle of the placeholder. Use the eyedropper to color the subtitle text with a dark orange color in the Potted Tree illustration's pot.

7. On Slide 2, change the layout to Two Content. Move the illustration to the right side of the slide and decrease its size slightly so that it does not overlap the placeholder or the date (Figure 8–82d). Convert the bulleted text to the 'Basic Block List' SmartArt graphic (first graphic in first List row). Change the colors to 'Transparent Gradient Range - Accent 2' (fifth color in Accent 2 row), change the style to Powder (fourth style in first 3-D row), change the size of the SmartArt graphic to approximately 5" × 4.72", and then move it to the location shown in the figure.

8. On Slide 3 (Figure 8–82e), apply the Two Content layout. Select the bulleted list placeholder, change its size to approximately 5" × 3", and then apply the Canvas texture fill (second texture in first row). Align the text in the middle of the placeholder.

9. Click the Pictures icon in the right content placeholder and then insert the Three Trees illustration, which is located in the Data Files. Resize the right content placeholder to approximately 5" × 8.75". Move both placeholders to the locations shown in the figure.

10. On Slide 4 (Figure 8–82f), change the layout to Two Content. Select the bulleted list placeholder and then apply Green, Accent 6, Lighter 60% fill (last color in third Theme Colors row). Select the bulleted list and change the bullets to a numbered list with the 1) 2) 3) style. Align the numbered list in the middle of the placeholder. Adjust the size of this placeholder to approximately 4.5" × 5.5" and then move it to the location shown in the figure.

11. Select the photo on Slide 4, adjust the size to approximately 4" × 6.26", change the border color to 'Orange, Accent 1, Lighter 60%' (fifth color in third Theme Colors row), and then move the picture to the location shown.

12. Insert a new slide as Slide 5 and then apply the Closing Slide layout (Figure 8–82g). Copy the subtitle text placeholder from Slide 1 and paste it in Slide 5. Remove the bullet in the subtitle text placeholder and then move the placeholder to the location shown in Figure 8–82g. Delete the title text placeholder.

13. If requested by your instructor, add a sixth bullet with the name of your high school mascot in the bulleted list on Slide 3.

14. Apply the Rotate transition in the Dynamic Content category to all slides and then change the duration to 3.00 seconds.

15. Run the presentation and then save the file using the file name, Extend 8–1 Plant a Tree.

16. Submit the revised document in the format specified by your instructor.

17. ✸ In this presentation, you changed the background of some slides to a tree illustration. Was this a good choice? Why? In the Slide Master, you inserted a layout, named it Closing Slide, and added the tree illustration as a background. Was this a good choice for a closing slide?

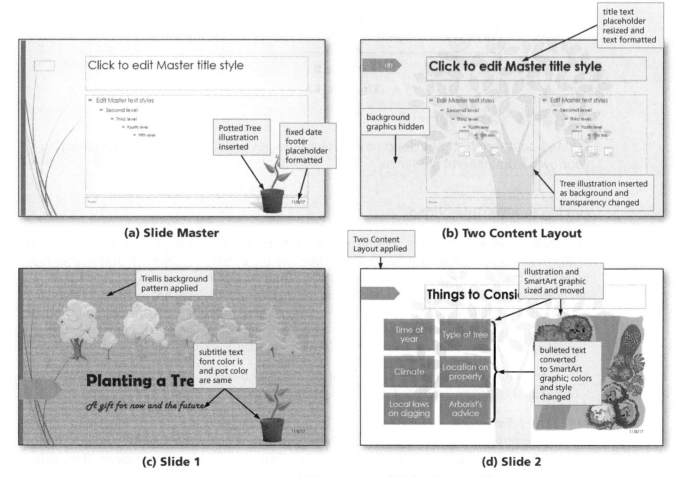

(a) Slide Master

(b) Two Content Layout

(c) Slide 1

(d) Slide 2

Figure 8–82 (Continued)

Continued >

Extend Your Knowledge *continued*

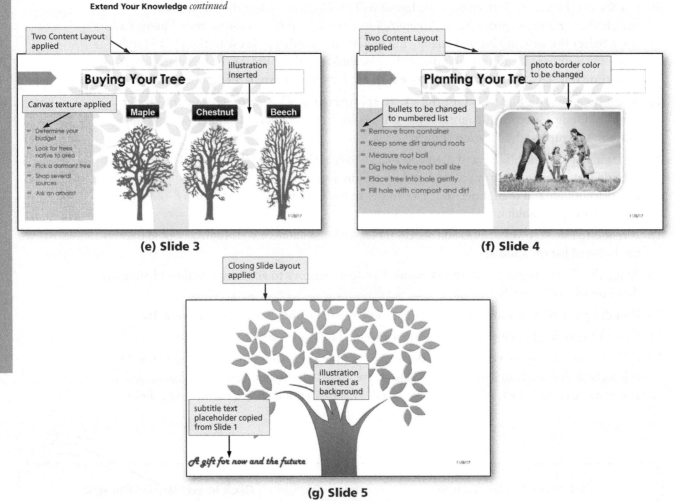

(e) Slide 3   (f) Slide 4

(g) Slide 5

Figure 8–82

Expand Your World

Create a solution that uses cloud or web technologies by learning and investigating on your own from general guidance.

Linking to a YouTube Video

Instructions: You have created a presentation and want to play a video from an online website, such as YouTube or a news or sports organization, while running a slide show. Some websites encourage users to share video clips, while others restrict users from performing this process. The videos are not downloaded and inserted, or **embedded**, in the file; instead, they are **linked** to the presentation so that when the slide show is running and an Internet connection is present, the user can click the Play button to begin watching the video. PowerPoint includes commands on the Insert Video dialog box to insert a video clip from YouTube and from other websites.

Note: You will need Internet access to complete this assignment. If you do not have Internet access, read this assignment without performing the instructions.

Perform the following tasks:
1. Run PowerPoint and then open the Zip Line presentation you created in this module. At the end of the presentation, insert one slide using the Miscellaneous layout and then add the title text, **Zip Lining Experiences** on Slide 4.

2. With Slide 4 displaying, click the Insert Video icon in the content placeholder to display the Insert Video dialog box.

3. If necessary, click the YouTube icon in the 'Also insert from' area to display the YouTube search box. Click the YouTube search text box, type `zip lining` as the search text, and then click the Search button (the magnifying glass) or press the ENTER key. Watch several videos on the website and then select one you desire to link to your PowerPoint presentation.

4. Click the Insert button (Insert Video dialog box) to display the selected clip on Slide 4. Increase the clip size, and then add a border and an effect. Click the 'Header & Footer' button (Insert tab | Text group) to display the Header and Footer dialog box, click the Footer check box to remove the check mark, and then click the Apply button to hide the footer on this slide. Move the video to the left side of the slide.

5. If requested by your instructor, enter the name of the city or county in which you were born in the Notes pane.

6. Run the presentation and then save the file with the new file name, Expand 8-1 Zip Line with Video.

7. ✸ Do videos add to the audience's ability to retain information presented during a presentation? Do they increase interest in the topic? Why did you select this specific video to display on Slide 4?

In the Labs

Design, create, modify, and/or use a presentation following the guidelines, concepts, and skills presented in this module. Labs 1 and 2, which increase in difficulty, require you to create solutions based on what you learned in the module; Lab 3 requires you to apply your creative thinking and problem-solving skills to design and implement a solution.

Lab 1: Deleting Slide Layouts, Adding a Placeholder, Renaming a Slide Master, and Saving a Slide Master as a Template

Note: To complete this assignment, you will be required to use the Data Files. Please contact your instructor for information about accessing the Data Files.

Problem: You are the president of your bicycle club. Your club plans many events every year for special bike rides. You decide to design a template that can be used for each month's activities. You create the slide master template shown in Figure 8–83a, the title slide layout in Figure 8–83b, and the three slides in Figures 8–83c–e.

Perform the following tasks:
1. Run PowerPoint. Open the presentation, Lab 8-1 Bike Club, which is located in the Data Files.
2. Display Slide Master view. Delete all layouts except the Title Slide Layout and the Blank Layout.
3. Display the Damask Slide Master. Insert the Spokes Logo picture, which is located in the Data Files, and then move it to the upper-left corner. Add the text, `April Events` in the footer placeholder, change the font color to Yellow (fourth color in Standard Colors row), increase the font size to 40 point, and apply the footer to all slides (Figure 8–83a). Delete the date and slide number placeholders. Rename the Slide Master as Spokes Slide Master.

Continued >

In the Labs *continued*

4. Display the Title Slide Layout (Figure 8–83b), insert the photo called Cyclist, which is located in the Data Files, as the new background fill, and then change the transparency to 10%. To display the footer, click the Footers check box (Slide Master | Master Layout group). Delete the title text and subtitle text placeholders.

5. Insert a Right Triangle shape on the left side of the slide. Change the size of the shape to approximately 6" × 6" and then move it to the lower-left area of the slide. Copy this triangle shape, paste it in the slide, and then click the Rotate button (Drawing Tools Format tab | Arrange group) to display the Rotate gallery. Click Flip Horizontal and then move the shape to the lower-right area of the slide.

6. Insert a Text placeholder in the left triangle shape, delete all the sample text, remove the bullet, change the size to approximately 4" × 2", change the font size to 32 point, change the font color to Dark Red (first color in Standard Colors), and then move the text box near the top of the triangle. Copy the Text placeholder, paste it in the right triangle, change the font size to 24 point, and then right align the text. Rename this layout Spokes Title Slide. Close Master view.

7. Save the file as a template with the file name, Lab 8–1 Spokes Spring Events Template.

8. On Slide 1 (Figure 8–83c), reapply the Spokes Title Slide layout to display the changes that were made in the previous steps. Type **First Saturday** in the left triangle Text placeholder and **Sunrise ride along the lake** in the right triangle Text placeholder.

9. Insert the photo called Bikes on Pier, which is located in the Data Files. Resize the photo to approximately 3" × 4.5". Apply the Soft Edge Oval picture style, add the Watercolor Sponge artistic effect (second effect in third row), and then move the photo below the right triangle text box.

10. Insert a new slide (Figure 8–83d) and apply the Spokes Title Slide layout. Type **Second Sunday** in the left triangle Text placeholder and **Ride the resurfaced 24-mile bike path** in the right Text placeholder. Insert the photo called Bike Path, which is located in the Data Files. Change the size of the photo to approximately 2.3" × 3.65", apply the Bevel Rectangle picture style, and then move the photo below the right triangle text box.

11. Insert a new slide (Figure 8–83e) with the Blank layout. Insert the photo called Group of Cyclists, which is located in the Data Files. Adjust the size of the photo to approximately 5" × 7.5" and then apply the Center Shadow Rectangle picture style. Rotate the photo counter-clockwise and then move it to the location shown in the figure.

12. On Slide 3, insert a text box and then type **Last Saturday: New members' meet and greet** in the text box. Change the font size to 32 point and the font color to Dark Red, size the text box to approximately 2" × 3.44", and then apply the Stationery texture fill (fourth texture in fourth row). Rotate the text box counter-clockwise and move it to the location shown in the figure.

13. If requested by your instructor, type the number of bones you have broken in place of the number, 24, in the right text box on Slide 2.

14. Apply the Split transition in the Subtle category to all slides and then change the duration to 2.50 seconds.

15. Run the presentation and then save the template file as a presentation using the file name, Lab 8-1 Spokes Spring Events.

16. Submit the document in the format specified by your instructor.

17. ❀ In Step 7, you saved the presentation as a template. How does creating a template help facilitate updating slides on a monthly or weekly basis? How did adding the triangle shapes and text boxes to the title slide layout enhance your presentation?

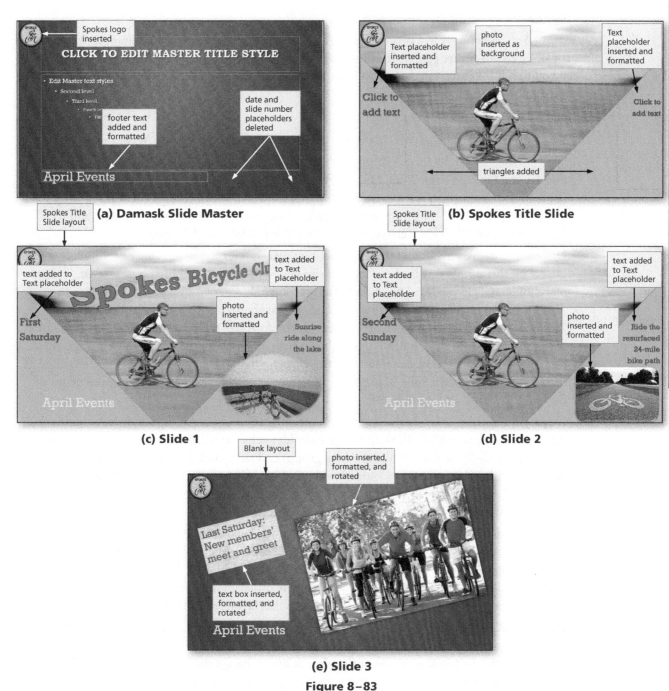

(a) Damask Slide Master

(b) Spokes Title Slide

(c) Slide 1

(d) Slide 2

(e) Slide 3

Figure 8–83

Lab 2: Formatting Slide Master Layouts, Inserting Placeholders, and Creating Handouts Using the Handout and Notes Masters

Note: To complete this assignment, you will be required to use the Data Files. Please contact your instructor for information about accessing the Data Files.

Continued >

Problem: You and your coworkers will be participating in a one-day team-building event at a nearby outdoor adventure center. Your manager made all the arrangements, gave you the details and asked you to put together a presentation for all the employees who will be attending the program. Create the five slides shown in Figure 8–84.

Perform the following tasks:

1. Run PowerPoint and apply the Blank Presentation theme. Display Slide Master view. Delete all layouts except the Title Slide Layout, Title and Content Layout, and Blank Layout.

2. Display the Office Theme Slide Master. Format the Background using a Solid fill, select the color Light Green (fifth color in Standard Colors row), and then change the transparency to 35%. Apply the Wind transition in the Exciting category and then change the duration to 3.25 seconds for all slides. Rename this slide master to Outdoor Adventure.

3. Display the Blank Layout and then insert a Text placeholder in the left side of the slide. Delete all the sample text in the placeholder, remove the bullet, and then type **TEAM** in the placeholder. Click the Text Direction button (Home tab | Paragraph group) to display the Text Direction gallery and then click Stacked. Adjust the size of the text placeholder to 7.5" × 2", change the font to Georgia, increase the font size to 96 point, change the font color to 'Green, Accent 6, Darker 25%' (last color in fifth Theme Colors row), and then align this text in the center of the placeholder. Cut this placeholder and then paste it into the left edge of the Outdoor Adventure Slide Master and then align it with the top, left, and bottom edges of the slide, as shown in Figure 8–84a.

4. Display the Blank Layout again. Insert a Picture placeholder on the slide and then change the placeholder size to 6.5" × 9". With this placeholder selected, click the Shape Outline arrow (Drawing Tools Format tab | Shape Styles group) and then click 'Green, Accent 6, Darker 50%' (last color in last Theme Colors row) to add a border. Click the Shape Effects button (Drawing Tools Format tab | Shape Styles group), point to Glow, and then click 'Green, 18 pt glow, Accent color 6' (last color in last Glow Variations row).

5. Insert a Text placeholder in the right side of the slide, delete all the sample text (but not the bullet), change the size to approximately 6.5" × 2", change the font to Georgia, change the font size to 36 point, change the font color to 'Green, Accent 6, Darker 25%', and then change the Text Direction to 'Rotate all text 90°'. Move the Text placeholder and the Picture placeholders to the locations shown in Figure 8–84b. Rename this layout to Team Picture.

6. Display the Title Slide Layout. Change the title text font to Georgia and then change the font size to 54 point. Apply the 'Subtle Effect - Green, Accent 6' Quick Style (last style in fourth row). Align this text in the middle of the placeholder. Change the subtitle text font to Bradley Hand ITC and then change the font size to 36 point. Align this text in the bottom of the placeholder, as shown in Figure 8–84c. Rename this layout to Team Title.

7. Display the Title and Content Layout. Change the title text font to Georgia, change the font size to 54 point, and then right-align this text. Select the content placeholder and then drag the left-center sizing handle slightly to the right so that the placeholder's new size is approximately 4.76" × 10.5" and it does not overlap the TEAM placeholder, as shown in the Figure 8–84d. Select the five levels of text styles in the content placeholder and then change the font to Bradley Hand ITC. Align the text in the Middle of the placeholder.

8. With the Content placeholder selected, click the Shape Outline arrow (Drawing Tools Format tab | Shape Styles group) and then click 'Green, Accent 6, Darker 50%' (last color in last Theme Colors row) to add a border. Click the Shape Effects button (Drawing Tools Format tab | Shape Styles group), point to Glow, and then click 'Green, 18 pt glow, Accent color 6' (last color in last Glow Variations row). Rename this layout to Team Title and Picture.

9. Display the Handout Master and then change the orientation to Landscape. Type `Outdoor Adventure Day` as the header text. Click the Date check box (Handout Master tab | Placeholders group) to remove the check mark so that the date does not display. Insert the picture called Ant Team, which is located in the Data Files, change the size to approximately 1.3" × 1.61", and then move it to the upper-right area of the handout master, as shown in Figure 8–84e.

10. Display the Notes Master. Type `Outdoor Adventure Day` as the header text, change the font to Bradley Hand ITC, and then increase the font size to 20 point. Delete the Date placeholder. Center the Header placeholder at the top of the page and then align the text in the center and the middle of the placeholder. Display the Header and Footer dialog box and then place a check mark in the Header check box. Insert the picture called Climbing Tower, which is located in the Data Files, change the size to approximately 3" × 2", and then move it between the Footer and Slide Number text boxes, as shown in Figure 8–84f. Select the five master text styles and then change the font to Bradley Hand ITC. Close Master view.

11. With Slide 1 displaying with the Team Title Layout, type `Outdoor Adventure Day` as the title text and then type, `We'll build cohesiveness, restore group morale, and renew workplace energy` as the subtitle text, as shown in Figure 8–84g. Display the Notes pane and then type `Challenging teamwork situations help focus the mind and body.` as the Notes text.

12. Insert a slide with the Team Picture Layout. Insert the picture called Team, which is located in the Data Files. Type `Gain confidence while connecting to and respecting the environment` in the text box, as shown in Figure 8–84h. Type `We'll preserve the natural environment while having fun and staying healthy.` in the Notes pane.

13. Insert a slide with the Team Title and Picture Layout. Type `Event Schedule` as the title text. In the content placeholder, type `Meet Saturday morning at Sandridge Nature Center` as the first paragraph, `Orientation meeting at 8 a.m.` as the second paragraph, `Activities begin at 9 a.m.` as the third paragraph, `Lunch served at noon` as the fourth paragraph, and `Debriefing starts at 4 p.m.` as the last paragraph, as shown in Figure 8–84i. If requested by your instructor, type the name of the last TV program you watched as the sixth bulleted paragraph. Type `Participation in a short program can inspire a substantial, lasting change in attitude and behavior.` in the Notes pane.

14. Insert a slide with the Team Title and Picture Layout. Type `High Ropes Obstacle Course` as the title text. Insert the High Ropes photo, which is located in the Data Files, in the Content placeholder. Increase the photo size to approximately 5.5" × 9.5" and then move it to the location shown in Figure 8–84j. Type `The course has three levels with eight activities each. It starts at 2' above ground and ends at a height of 20'.` in the Notes pane.

15. Insert a slide with the Team Picture Layout. Insert the picture called Tug of War, which is located in the Data Files, in the content placeholder. Type `We saved the best for last!` in the text box (Figure 8–84k). Type `This popular team-building exercise requires brute strength from each side.` in the Notes pane.

16. Run the presentation and then save the file using the file name, Lab 8–2 Team Building.

17. Submit the presentation in the format specified by your instructor.

18. Print the handout (Figure 8–84l) and speaker notes (Figure 8–84m–q).

19. ✺ What are the benefits of creating slide layout masters? Did inserting and formatting Text placeholders and adding the word TEAM and bulleted text add interest to the presentation? Why?

Continued >

In the Labs *continued*

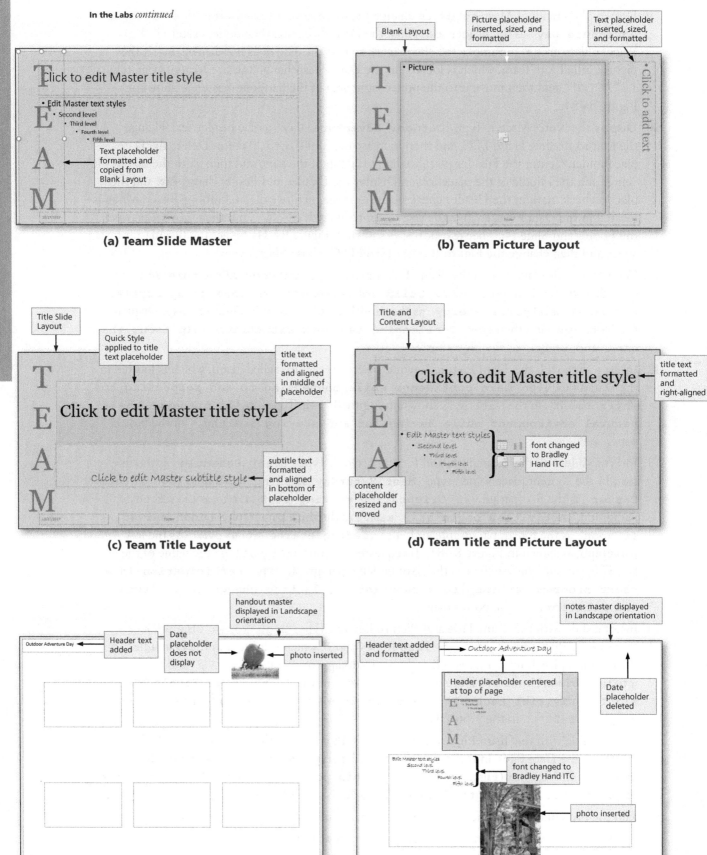

(a) Team Slide Master

(b) Team Picture Layout

(c) Team Title Layout

(d) Team Title and Picture Layout

(e) Handout Master

(f) Notes Master

Figure 8–84 (Continued)

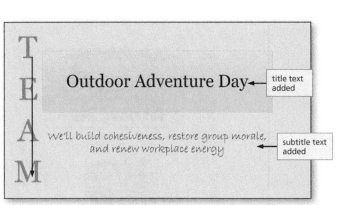

(g) Slide 1

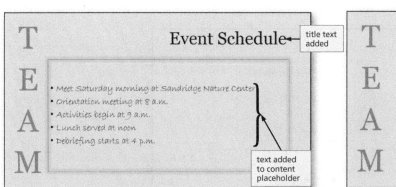

(i) Slide 3

(j) Slide 4

(k) Slide 5

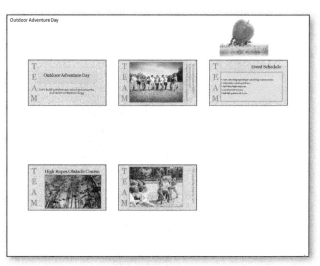

(l) Handout

Figure 8–84 (Continued)

In the Labs *continued*

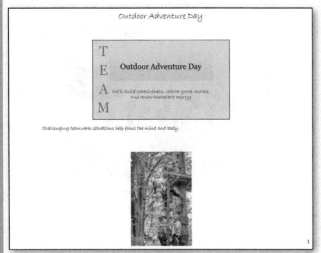

(m) Notes Page 1

(n) Notes Page 2

(o) Notes Page 3

(p) Notes Page 4

(q) Notes Page 5

Figure 8–84

Lab 3: **Consider This: Your Turn**

Design and Create a Presentation about Alligators

Part 1:   Alligators are reptiles found primarily in the southeastern areas of the United States and in China. They can weigh more than 1,000 pounds and live approximately 50 years in freshwater swamps, rivers, marshes, and lakes. Males have an average length of 11.2 feet, and females average 8.2 feet. Review some websites to learn about alligators, including their habitat, diet, and anatomy. Use the concepts and techniques presented in this module to create a presentation about this reptile. Develop at least two slide master layouts that include an inserted placeholder, a formatted text box, and picture that displays on all slides, and then rename these layouts. Delete the layouts you do not use. Change the theme colors. Customize the theme fonts. Create a handout master and a notes master with inserted pictures. Three pictures are available in the Data Files: Alligator Drawing, Alligator Head, and Green Alligator. Include information about alligators in the Notes pane. Review and revise your presentation as needed and then save the file using the file name, Lab 8-3 Alligators. Submit your assignment in the format specified by your instructor.

Part 2:   You made several decisions while creating the presentation in this assignment: where to move the inserted placeholder and formatted text box, which layout masters to use, and where to place the pictures in the slides, notes, and handouts. What was the rationale behind each of these decisions? When you reviewed the document, what further revisions did you make and why?

9 Modifying a Presentation Using Graphical Elements

Objectives

You will have mastered the material in this module when you can:

- Change a text box outline color, weight, and style
- Set text box formatting as the default for new text boxes
- Apply a gradient, texture, pattern, and effects to a text box
- Convert WordArt to SmartArt
- Reorder SmartArt shapes
- Promote and demote SmartArt text

- Add and remove SmartArt shapes
- Convert a SmartArt graphic to text
- Insert and modify shapes to create custom artwork
- Customize and reset the ribbon
- Create a handout by exporting a file to Microsoft Word
- Save the presentation as a picture presentation

BTW
Identifying Shapes
Most objects in our world are composed of shapes: a circle, square, and triangle. Artists see objects as combinations of these shapes and begin their drawings by sketching these basic forms in proportion to each other. For example, a tree has the form of a circle for the branches and a rectangle for the trunk. A car has the form of a rectangle for the body, a smaller rectangle for the passenger compartment, and four circles for the wheels. Become observant of the relationships between objects in your world as you learn to use PowerPoint's drawing tools.

Introduction

PowerPoint's themes determine the default characteristics of slide objects. Colors, border weights and styles, fills, effects, and other formatting options give the slides a unique character. You can create your own designs for text boxes, shapes, lines, and other slide content, and then reuse these graphical objects throughout the presentation. Once you learn to format one type of object, such as a text box, you can use similar techniques to format other slide objects, such as SmartArt and shapes. One efficient way to create consistent graphical elements is to save your settings as the default. Then, when you insert the same objects later during the presentation design process, they will have the same characteristics as the initial element.

SmartArt graphics have individual layouts, styles, and color schemes. If one of these designs does not meet the specific needs of your slide content, you can modify the graphic by adding shapes, reordering the current shapes, and changing each element's size and location. You also can convert the SmartArt to text or to a shape if SmartArt is not the best method of conveying your ideas to an audience. PowerPoint's myriad formatting options allow you to tailor graphical elements to best fit your unique design needs.

Project — Presentation with Customized Text Boxes, SmartArt, and Shapes

The lure of sailing in tranquil waters near white sandy beaches and tropical paradises has stirred the imagination of experienced sailors and landlubbers alike. The American Sailing Association (ASA) accredits schools that provide training for people to sail safely and confidently, with eight levels of certification. Some schools offer one-week programs where students learn how to maneuver the vessel, communicate with crewmates, navigate, and other skills.

The presentation you create in this module (Figure 9–1) would be useful to show at travel shows and boating stores to promote these classes. All four slides are created by modifying a starting file that has a variety of content. The title slide (Figure 9–1a) contains a colorful picture and a text box that is formatted with an outline style, a weight, and a color. These modifications are saved as the default settings for all other text boxes inserted into other slides. The second slide (Figure 9–1b) features a new picture and a formatted text box. The text on Slide 3 (Figure 9–1c) is converted from WordArt to a SmartArt graphic. The layout, style, color, and shapes are changed and enhanced. The final slide (Figure 9–1d) has bulleted text converted from a SmartArt graphic; it also has a sailboat composed of formatted shapes. After the slides are created, you export the file to Microsoft Word to create a handout (Figure 9–1e, f) and then save the presentation as a picture presentation.

In this module, you will learn how to create the slides shown in Figure 9–1. The following roadmap identifies general activities you will perform as you progress through this module:

1. INSERT and CUSTOMIZE TEXT BOXES by changing the weight, color, and style and by adding an effect, pattern, and fill.

2. CONVERT WORDART TO SMARTART and then FORMAT by changing bullet levels, the layout, and the shape.

3. INSERT and FORMAT SHAPES.

4. DRAW and FORMAT LINES.

5. CUSTOMIZE THE RIBBON by adding a new group and buttons.

6. EXPORT a FILE to Microsoft Word and CREATE a PICTURE PRESENTATION.

(a) Slide 1

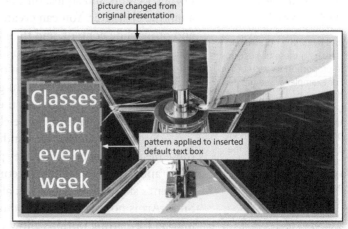

(b) Slide 2

Figure 9–1 (Continued)

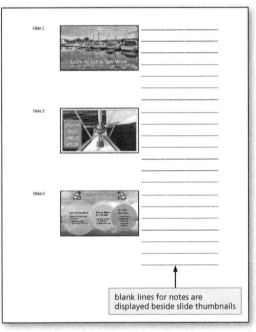

formatted SmartArt graphic

picture inserted into text box

gradient applied to inserted text box

picture flipped

Class Highlights

Learn Sailing Basics
• Maneuver, trim sails, navigate
• No prior sailing experience required

Course Begins on Monday
• Anchor at night in local bays
• Limited class size

Earn ASA Certificate
• Three levels of certification
• Instructor covers all material

(c) Slide 3

text from converted SmartArt graphic

sailboat created from inserted and formatted shapes

Mainsail

Jib

Hull

• **Inspect the boat**
 • Check the rigging (cables and ropes)
 • Remove lines from winches and cleats
• **Hoist sails**
 • Attach and raise mainsail and jib
 • Trim sails to adjust for wind direction
• **Sail safely**
 • Constantly watch for wind shifts
 • Beware of boom suddenly changing sides

(d) Slide 4

Slide 1

Learn to Sail in One Week

Slide 2

Slide 3

blank lines for notes are displayed beside slide thumbnails

(e) Microsoft Word Handout – Page 1

Slide 4

(f) Microsoft Word Handout – Page 2

Figure 9–1

To Run PowerPoint and Save a File

If you are using a computer to step through the project in this module and you want your screens to match the figures in this book, you should change your screen's resolution to 1366 × 768. The following steps run PowerPoint and then save a file.

1 Run PowerPoint. If necessary, maximize the PowerPoint window.

2 Open the presentation, Sailing, located in the Data Files.

3 Save the presentation using the file name, Sailing Lessons.

Choose colors wisely.
Color can create interest in the material on your slides, so you need to think about which colors best support the message you want to share with your audience. The color you add to text boxes signals that the viewer should pay attention to the contents. Orange, red, and yellow are considered warm colors and will be among the first colors your viewers perceive on your slide. Blue and green are considered cool colors, and they often blend into a background and are less obvious than the warm colors.

Formatting Text Boxes

Text boxes can be formatted in a variety of ways to draw attention to slide content. You can apply formatting, such as fill color, gradient, texture, and pattern. You can add a picture; change the outline color, weight, and style; and then set margins and alignment. Once you determine the desired effects for a text box, you can save these settings as a default to achieve consistency and save time. Then, each time you insert another text box, the same settings will be applied.

In the following pages, you will perform these tasks on Slide 1:

1. Insert a text box into Slide 1.
2. Type text into the text box.
3. Change the text box outline weight.
4. Change the text box outline color.
5. Change the text box outline style.
6. Apply a glow effect to the text box.
7. Set the text box formatting as the default for new text boxes.

Once the text box formatting is complete on Slide 1, you then will perform these tasks on Slide 2:

1. Insert a text box and enter text.
2. Apply a pattern to the text box.
3. Change the text box pattern foreground and background colors.

You also will perform these tasks on Slide 3:

1. Insert a text box and enter text.
2. Apply a gradient fill to the text box.
3. Align the text box in the center of the slide.
4. Change the Slide 3 picture.

To Insert a Text Box and Text

The default text box for the Office Theme is displayed with the Calibri font and has no border, fill, or effects. To begin customizing the Sailing Lessons presentation, you will insert a text box and then type the text that serves as the title to your presentation. The following steps insert a text box and enter text into the text box.

1 Display the Insert tab, click the Text Box button (Insert tab | Text group), position the pointer in the lower-left corner of Slide 1, and then click to insert the new text box.

2 Type **Learn to Sail in One Week** as the text box text (Figure 9–2).

Figure 9–2

Q&A

Do I need to position the text box in the precise location indicated in Figure 9–2?
No. You will reposition the text box later in this module after you have made the formatting changes.

Can I change the shape of the text box?
Yes. By default, a rectangular text box is inserted. If you want to use a different shape, select the text box, display the Drawing Tools Format tab, click the Edit Shape button (Drawing Tools Format tab | Insert Shapes group), point to Change Shape in the list, and then click the desired new shape.

To Format Text Box Text

You now can choose a font and font size that complement the Slide 1 photo. A WordArt style can add visual interest to the text box. The following steps change the text box text to WordArt, change the font size, and center the text in the text box.

1 Select all the text box text, display the Drawing Tools Format tab, click the WordArt Styles More button (Drawing Tools Format tab | WordArt Styles group) to expand the gallery, and then click 'Fill - White, Outline - Accent 2, Hard Shadow - Accent 2' (fourth style in third row) to apply this style.

2 Increase the font size to 66 point.

3 Center the text in the text box. If necessary, drag the text box to the location shown in Figure 9–3.

BTW
Line Spacing Measurements
The lower part of each letter rests on an imaginary line called the baseline. The space between the baseline of one row of type and the baseline of the row beneath it is called line spacing. Typically, the line spacing is 120 percent of the font size. For example, if the font size is 10 point, the line spacing is 12 point so that two points of space are displayed between the lines.

Figure 9–3

To Change a Text Box Outline Weight

The first graphical change you will make to the text box border is to increase the thickness, which is called the outline. *Why? This thicker line is a graphical element that helps to call attention to the box.* The weight, or thickness, of the text box border is measured in points. The following steps increase the outline weight.

- With the text box still selected, if necessary display the Home tab, and then click the Shape Outline arrow (Home tab | Drawing group) to display the Shape Outline gallery.

- Click Weight in the Shape Outline gallery to display the Weight list (Figure 9–4).

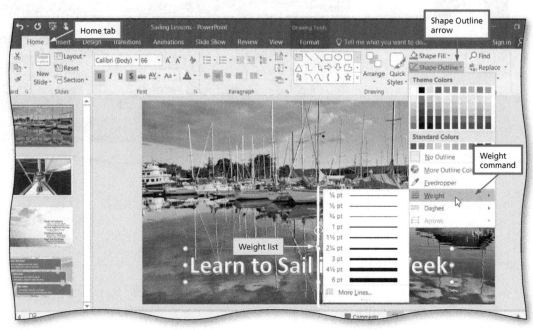

Figure 9–4

- Point to 6 pt to display a live preview of this outline line weight (Figure 9–5).

 **Experiment**

- Point to various line weights on the Weight list and watch the border weights on the text box change.

Figure 9–5

- Click 6 pt to add an outline around the text box.

Other Ways

1. Click Shape Outline arrow (Drawing Tools Format tab | Shape Styles group), click Weight

2. Right-click text box, click Outline below shortcut menu, click Weight

To Change a Text Box Outline Color

1 INSERT & CUSTOMIZE TEXT BOXES | 2 CONVERT WORDART TO SMARTART & FORMAT | 3 INSERT & FORMAT SHAPES | 4 DRAW & FORMAT LINES | 5 CUSTOMIZE THE RIBBON | 6 EXPORT FILE & CREATE PICTURE PRESENTATION

The default outline color in the Office Theme is black. In this project, you will change the outline color to orange. *Why? Orange matches the WordArt text color and contrasts well with the blue water.* The following steps change the text box outline color.

- With the text box still selected, click the Shape Outline arrow again to display the Shape Outline gallery.

- Point to Orange (third color in Standard Colors row) to display a live preview of that outline color on the text box (Figure 9–6).

Experiment

- Point to various colors in the Shape Outline gallery and watch the border colors on the text box change.

- Click Orange to change the text box border color.

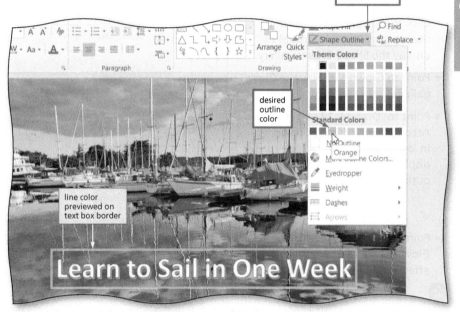

Figure 9–6

To Change a Text Box Outline Style

1 INSERT & CUSTOMIZE TEXT BOXES | 2 CONVERT WORDART TO SMARTART & FORMAT | 3 INSERT & FORMAT SHAPES | 4 DRAW & FORMAT LINES | 5 CUSTOMIZE THE RIBBON | 6 EXPORT FILE & CREATE PICTURE PRESENTATION

The default outline style is a solid line. You can add interest by changing the style to dashes, dots, or a combination of dashes and dots. The following steps change the text box outline style to Long Dash Dot. *Why? The dashes and dots in this pattern resemble the ripples in the water.*

- Display the Shape Outline gallery and then point to Dashes to display the Dashes list.

- Point to 'Long Dash Dot' to display a live preview of this outline style (Figure 9–7).

Experiment

- Point to various styles in the Shape Outline gallery and watch the borders on the text box change.

- Click 'Long Dash Dot' to change the text box border style.

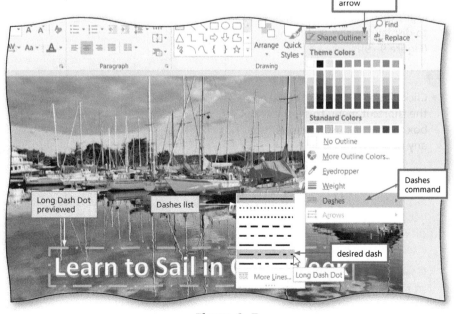

Figure 9–7

To Apply an Effect to a Text Box

PowerPoint provides a variety of visual effects to add to the text box. They include shadow, glow, reflection, and 3-D rotation. The following steps apply a glow effect to the text box. **Why?** *The water in the background photo has a soft texture, so you can coordinate with this soft effect by adding a glow effect to the text box.*

1

- Click the Shape Effects button (Home tab | Drawing group) to display the Shape Effects gallery.

- Point to Glow to display the Glow gallery.

- Point to 'Orange, 18 pt glow, Accent color 2' (second color in last Glow Variations row) to display a live preview of this outline effect (Figure 9–8).

🔎 **Experiment**

- Point to various effects in the Glow gallery and watch the glow effects change on the text box.

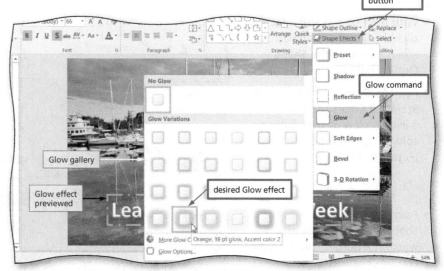

Figure 9–8

2

- Click the 'Orange, 18 pt glow, Accent color 2' variation to apply the glow effect.

To Set Text Box Formatting as the Default

The text box you inserted and formatted has a variety of visual elements that work well with the sailboat picture and overall theme. You can insert text boxes with the same formatting into other slides in the presentation. **Why?** *To save time and ensure all the formatting changes are applied consistently, you can set the formatting of one text box as the default for all other text boxes you insert into the presentation.* The following steps set the text box on Slide 1 as the default.

1

- Right-click the text box outline to display the shortcut menu (Figure 9–9).

2

- Click 'Set as Default Text Box' on the shortcut menu to set the text box formatting as the default for any new text boxes.

Q&A What should I do if the 'Set as Default Text Box' command is not displayed on the shortcut menu? Repeat Step 1 and be certain to click the text box border, not the interior of the box.

Does setting the default text box affect all presentations or just the current one? Only the current presentation is affected.

Figure 9–9

To Insert a Formatted Text Box and Enter Text

Any new text boxes you insert will have the same formatting you applied to the Slide 1 text box. You want to emphasize to your presentation viewers that sailing lessons are available all year, so a text box on Slide 2 is a good place to state this information. The following steps insert a formatted text box into Slide 2 and enter text.

1 Display Slide 2, display the Insert tab, and then click the Text Box button.

2 Insert the text box into the left side of the slide and then type `Classes` as the first line of the text box text.

3 Press SHIFT+ENTER to insert a line break and then type `held` as the second text box line.

4 Press SHIFT+ENTER to insert a line break and then type `every` as the third text box line.

5 Press SHIFT+ENTER to insert a line break and then type `week` as the fourth text box line.

6 If necessary, drag the text box to the location shown in Figure 9–10.

BTW

Adding Contrast for Energy
The samples in the Pattern and Color gallery rows and columns range from light to dark. If you want your graphic to have a high level of energy, consider using colors at opposite ends of the rows and columns to add a dramatic effect. The greater the contrast, the higher the energy. In contrast, if your goal is to give your graphic a peaceful feeling, use colors in the same rows and columns that have the same levels of intensity.

text entered in inserted text box

Figure 9–10

To Apply a Pattern to a Text Box

1 INSERT & CUSTOMIZE TEXT BOXES | 2 CONVERT WORDART TO SMARTART & FORMAT | 3 INSERT & FORMAT SHAPES
4 DRAW & FORMAT LINES | 5 CUSTOMIZE THE RIBBON | 6 EXPORT FILE & CREATE PICTURE PRESENTATION

Why? *A pattern fill can call attention to a text box.* PowerPoint provides a Pattern gallery, allowing you to change the appearance of the text box with a variety of horizontal and vertical lines, dots, dashes, and stripes. If desired, you can change the default fill foreground and background colors. The following steps apply a pattern to the Slide 2 text box and change the foreground and background colors.

1

- Right-click anywhere on the Slide 2 text box to display the shortcut menu (Figure 9–11).

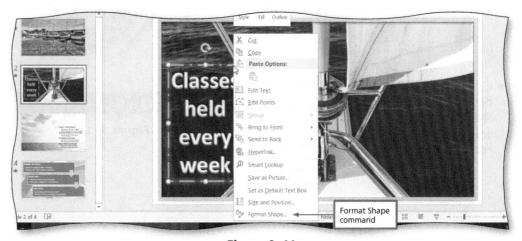

Format Shape command

Figure 9–11

2

- Click Format Shape on the shortcut menu to display the Format Shape pane.

- If necessary, click Fill to expand the Fill section. Click Pattern fill to display the Pattern gallery and the 5% pattern on the text box (Figure 9–12).

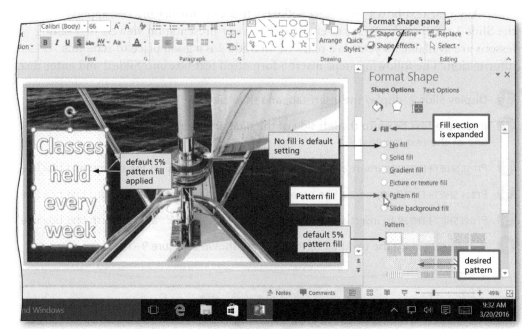

Figure 9–12

Q&A Can I experiment with previewing the patterns on the text box?
No, the live preview function is not available.

Can the default pattern gallery color vary?
Yes. You may find that your default color is black rather than the shade of blue shown in the figure.

3

- Click the 'Light upward diagonal' pattern (second pattern in third row) to apply this pattern to the Slide 2 text box.

Q&A How can I delete a pattern if I decide not to apply one to my slide?
If you already have applied the pattern, click the Undo button on the Quick Access Toolbar.

- If necessary, scroll down the Format Shape pane and then click the Foreground button to display the Color gallery (Figure 9–13).

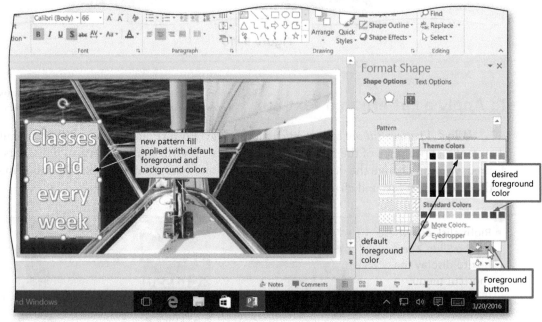

Figure 9–13

Q&A Can the default foreground color vary in the gallery?
Yes. You may find that your default color is black rather than the shade of blue shown in the figure.

- Click Dark Blue (ninth color in Standard Colors row) to apply this color to the text box pattern and to display the Pattern gallery with the new foreground color.

- Click the Background button to display the Color gallery (Figure 9–14).

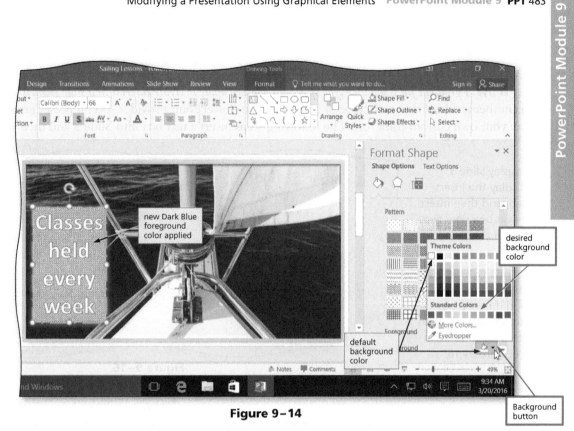

Figure 9–14

- Click Light Blue (seventh color in Standard Colors row) to apply this color to the text box background and to display the Pattern gallery with the new background color (Figure 9–15).

- Click the Close button to close the Format Shape pane.

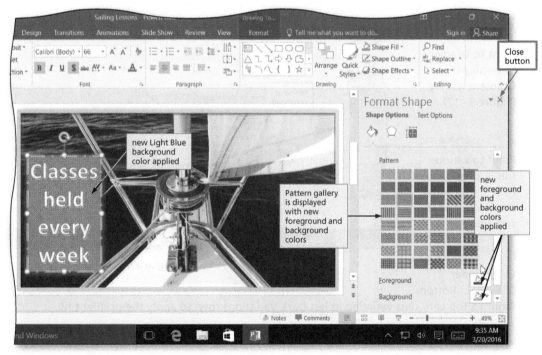

Figure 9–15

To Apply a Gradient Fill to a Text Box

Why? A gradient fill is another type of format you can apply to create interest in a slide element. It blends one color into another shade of the same color or another color. PowerPoint provides several preset gradients, or you can create your own custom color mix. The following steps insert a text box into Slide 3 and then apply a gradient fill.

- Display Slide 3, display the Insert tab, and then insert a text box near the top of the slide.

- Type **Class Highlights** as the text box text, and if necessary, drag the text box to the location shown in Figure 9–16.

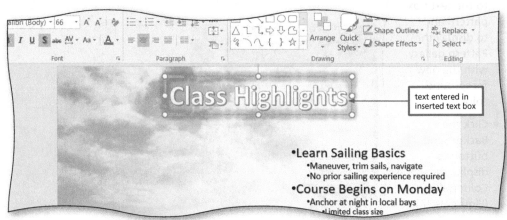

Figure 9–16

- Click the Drawing Tools Format tab and then click the Shape Fill arrow (Drawing Tools Format tab | Shape Styles group) to display the Shape Fill gallery.

- Point to Gradient to display the Gradient gallery (Figure 9–17).

Experiment

- Point to various fills in the Gradient gallery and watch the interior of the text box change.

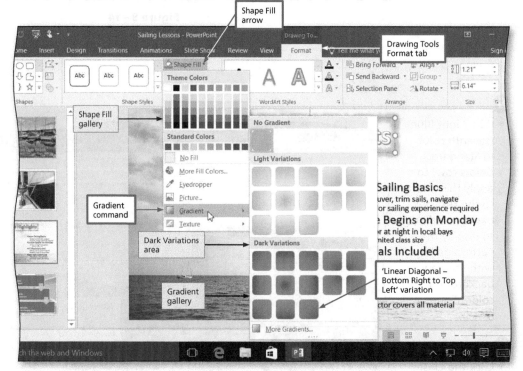

Figure 9–17

- Click 'Linear Diagonal - Bottom Right to Top Left' (last variation in last Dark Variations row) to apply the gradient fill.

To Align a Text Box

The text box on Slide 3 will serve as the title. You could attempt to position it horizontally on the slide and use the rulers to aid you in this process. You also can use PowerPoint's Align feature. *Why? Using the Align command is a more efficient method of positioning the text box in the slide.* You can align a slide element horizontally along the left or right sides or in the center of the slide, and you also can align an element vertically along the top, bottom, or middle of the slide. The following steps move the Slide 3 text box horizontally to the left edge of the slide.

- With the Slide 3 text box selected, click the Align button (Drawing Tools Format tab | Arrange group) to display the Align menu (Figure 9–18).

- Click Align Left to move the text box horizontally on the slide.

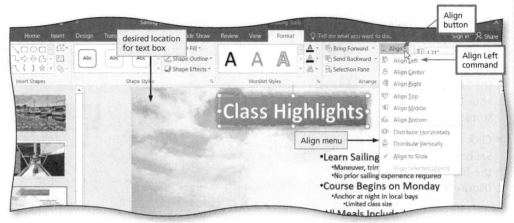

Figure 9–18

Q&A Can I position a text box in a precise location on a slide?

Yes. With the text box selected, right-click a border of the box to display the shortcut menu and then click Format Shape on the shortcut menu to display the Format Shape pane. Click the Size & Properties icon, click Position, and then enter Horizontal position and Vertical position measurements. Specify if these measurements should be from the Top Left Corner or the Center of the text box and then click the Close button (Format Shape pane).

To Change a Slide Picture

1 INSERT & CUSTOMIZE TEXT BOXES | 2 CONVERT WORDART TO SMARTART & FORMAT | 3 INSERT & FORMAT SHAPES
4 DRAW & FORMAT LINES | 5 CUSTOMIZE THE RIBBON | 6 EXPORT FILE & CREATE PICTURE PRESENTATION

PowerPoint allows you to change a picture on a slide easily. The following steps change the Slide 3 picture. **Why?** *The photograph on Slide 3 features one sailboat that is not prominently featured. A more dramatic photograph of many sailboats is located in the Data Files.*

- With Slide 3 displaying, click anywhere on the picture except the text box to select the picture and then click the Picture Tools Format tab (Figure 9–19).

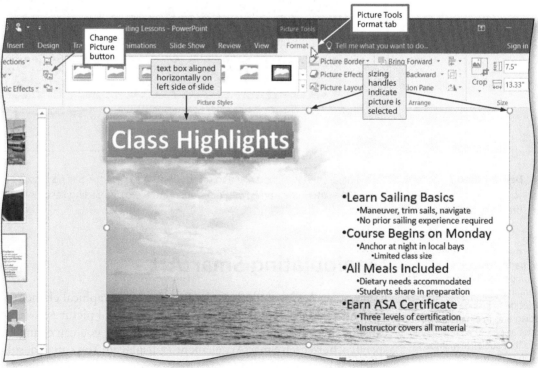

Figure 9–19

2

- Click the Change Picture button (Picture Tools Format tab | Adjust group) to display the Insert Pictures dialog box and then navigate to the location where your Data Files are stored.

- Click Reflected Sailboats to select the file name (Figure 9–20).

Q&A What if the picture is not in my Data Files folder?

Use the same process, but select the device containing the photograph. Another option is to locate this photograph or a similar one on Facebook, Flickr, and other websites.

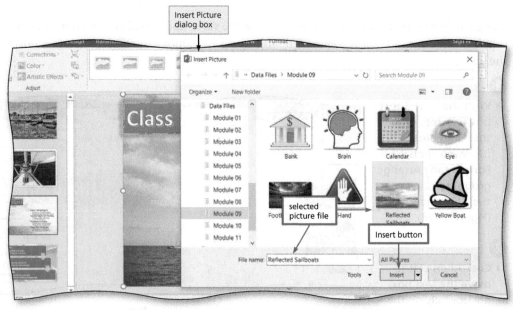

Figure 9–20

3

- Click the Insert button (Insert Picture dialog box) to change the Slide 3 picture. If necessary, drag the sizing handles to the borders of the slide (Figure 9–21).

Q&A What if I do not want to use this picture?

Click the Undo button on the Quick Access Toolbar.

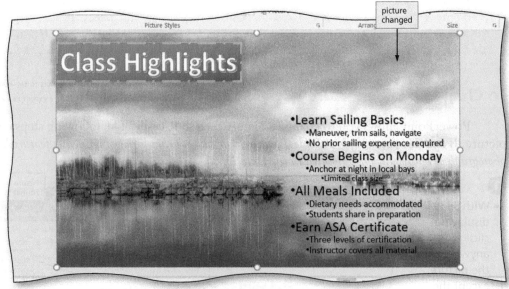

Figure 9–21

Break Point: If you wish to take a break, this is a good place to do so. Be sure to save the Sailing Lessons file again and then you can exit PowerPoint. To resume at a later time, run PowerPoint, open the file called Sailing Lessons, and continue following the steps from this location forward.

BTW

SmartArt in Handouts
SmartArt diagrams are composed of individual vector graphics. Some presenters decide to include these diagrams in a handout but not as part of a presentation so that audience members can study the relationships among the shapes after the presentation has concluded.

Manipulating SmartArt

Every SmartArt layout has a unique design and graphical elements. The shapes maximize vertical and horizontal space for text and pictures. When your presentation calls for special design needs or additional shapes, you can change the defaults that specify where each SmartArt element is displayed. You can add, subtract, and reorder shapes; promote and demote text; make a single shape smaller or larger; and change the SmartArt fill, outline, and colors.

In the following pages, you will perform these tasks on Slides 3 and 4:

1. Convert WordArt paragraphs to SmartArt.
2. Reorder two shapes in the SmartArt layout.
3. Reorder two bulleted paragraphs in a SmartArt shape.
4. Promote and demote SmartArt bulleted paragraphs.
5. Change the SmartArt layout, style, and color.
6. Remove a SmartArt shape.
7. Resize the entire SmartArt layout and shapes within the layout.
8. Apply a picture to the text box.
9. Convert the SmartArt graphic to text on Slide 4.

Use keywords in SmartArt graphics.

Most SmartArt shapes have very limited space for text. You must, therefore, carefully choose each word you are going to display in the graphic. The text you select can serve as **keywords**, or a speaking outline. If you glance at the SmartArt when you are presenting the slide show in front of an audience, each word should prompt you for the main point you are going to make. These keywords should jog your memory if you lose your train of thought or are interrupted.

To Convert WordArt to SmartArt

1 INSERT & CUSTOMIZE TEXT BOXES | 2 CONVERT WORDART TO SMARTART & FORMAT | 3 INSERT & FORMAT SHAPES
4 DRAW & FORMAT LINES | 5 CUSTOMIZE THE RIBBON | 6 EXPORT FILE & CREATE PICTURE PRESENTATION

The bulleted paragraphs on Slide 3 are formatted as WordArt. Although WordArt can add visual interest, using a graphical element such as SmartArt can be even more effective in helping the audience to grasp essential concepts. *Why? SmartArt diagrams are creative means to show processes, lists, cycles, and other relationships.* PowerPoint suggests layouts that might fit the concept you are trying to present and then easily converts WordArt to SmartArt. The following steps convert WordArt to SmartArt.

- With Slide 3 displaying, right-click anywhere in the WordArt bulleted list paragraphs to display the shortcut menu.

- Point to 'Convert to SmartArt' to display the SmartArt gallery (Figure 9–22).

Q&A Does it matter where I place the cursor?
No. As long as the cursor is placed in the WordArt text, you will be able to convert the paragraphs to SmartArt.

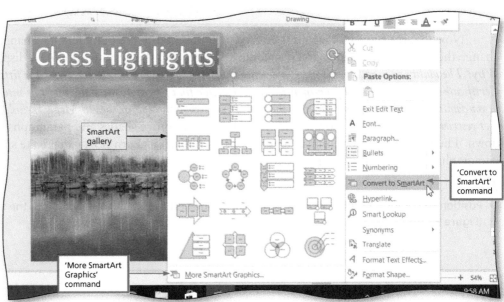

Figure 9–22

- Click 'More SmartArt Graphics' to display the Choose a SmartArt Graphic dialog box.

- Click Matrix in the list of graphic categories and then click Basic Matrix in the gallery to display a picture and a description of this SmartArt layout (Figure 9–23).

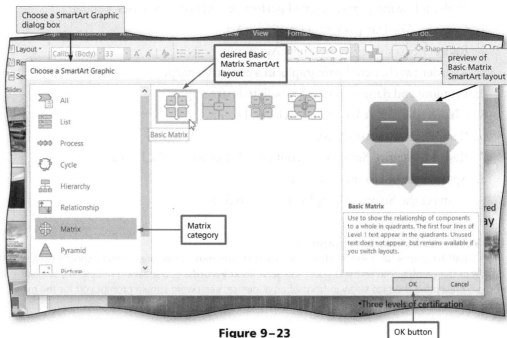

Figure 9–23

- Click the OK button (Choose a SmartArt Graphic dialog box) to convert the WordArt to that layout.

Q&A How is the text arranged in the Basic Matrix SmartArt layout?
The four first-level paragraphs are at the top of each shape in the graphic and have a larger font size than the eight bulleted second-level paragraphs.

To Reorder SmartArt Shapes

1 INSERT & CUSTOMIZE TEXT BOXES | **2 CONVERT WORDART TO SMARTART & FORMAT** | **3 INSERT & FORMAT SHAPES**
4 DRAW & FORMAT LINES | 5 CUSTOMIZE THE RIBBON | 6 EXPORT FILE & CREATE PICTURE PRESENTATION

Now that the SmartArt layout is created, you can modify the graphic. One change you can make is to change the order of the shapes. You decide that two items in the graphic should be displayed in a different order. *Why? The ability to earn a certificate is a desired component of the one-week schools, so it is fitting that the Earn ASA Certificate should be displayed prominently. You also decide that potential students might be interested in cooking onboard, so you want to move that information in the second bulleted paragraph in the All Meals Included shape above the fact that diet restrictions are addressed.* PowerPoint provides tools to move shapes and paragraphs in a vertical layout up or down. The following steps reorder the All Meals Included and Earn ASA Certificate shapes and the two bulleted paragraphs in the All Meals Included shape.

- Position the pointer in the Earn ASA Certificate shape and then click to select it and the two bulleted paragraphs (Figure 9–24).

Q&A

Is all the text selected in the Earn ASA Certificate shape?
Yes. The words, Earn ASA Certificate, are in a first-level paragraph, and the two bulleted second-level paragraphs are associated with it. When the shape is selected, all related paragraphs are selected with it.

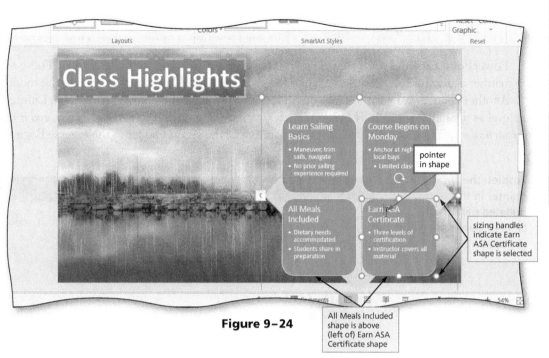

Figure 9–24

2

- With the SmartArt Tools Design tab displaying, click the Move Up button (SmartArt Tools Design tab | Create Graphic group) to reorder the Earn ASA Certificate shape to the left of the All Meals Included shape.

- Position the pointer in the bulleted paragraph, Dietary needs accommodated (Figure 9–25).

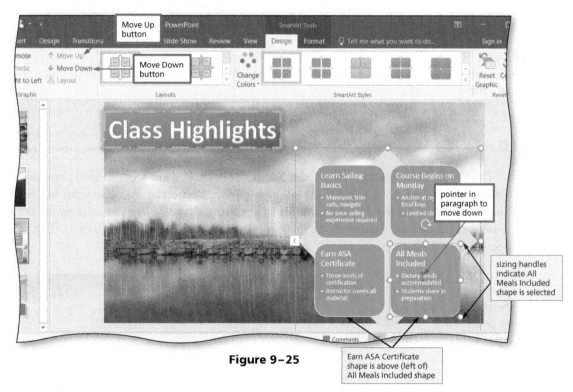

Figure 9–25

3

- Click the Move Down button (SmartArt Tools Design tab | Create Graphic group) to reorder the bulleted paragraph, Dietary needs accommodated, below the bulleted paragraph, Students share in preparation.

To Promote a SmartArt Bullet Level

PowerPoint provides tools that allow you to promote and demote bulleted text. These tools function in the same manner as the Increase List Level and Decrease List Level buttons that change the indents for bulleted text.

Another change you want to make on Slide 3 is to promote the bulleted paragraph, Limited class size, to the same level as the bullet above it. *Why? Because this fact may encourage people to register early, and it may be a selling feature of this particular sailing school.* The following steps promote the second bullet in the Course Begins on Monday shape.

- Position the pointer in the bulleted paragraph, Limited class size (Figure 9–26).

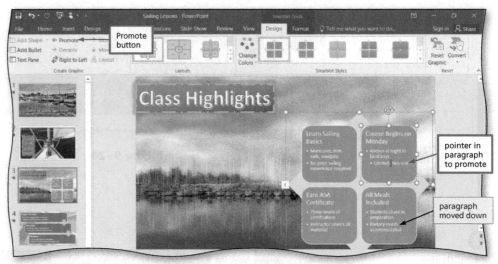

Figure 9–26

- Click the Promote button (SmartArt Tools Design tab | Create Graphic group) to decrease the indent of the bulleted paragraph.

To Demote a SmartArt Bullet Level

The two bulleted items in the Learn Sailing Basics shape are second-level paragraphs, but you decide to demote the second paragraph, No prior sailing experience required. You also want to demote the paragraph, Instructor covers all material in the Earn ASA Certificate shape. *Why? The information in these two paragraphs is not as important as the information in the first bulleted paragraphs in each of these shapes.* The following steps demote the second-level bulleted paragraphs.

- Position the pointer in the bulleted paragraph, No prior sailing experience required (Figure 9–27).

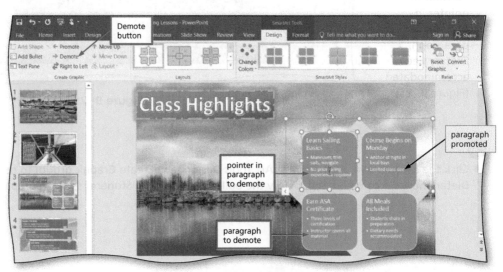

Figure 9–27

2

- Click the Demote button (SmartArt Tools Design tab | Create Graphic group) to increase the indent of the bulleted paragraph.

- Position the pointer in the bulleted paragraph, Instructor covers all material, and then click the Demote button to increase the indent of this paragraph (Figure 9–28).

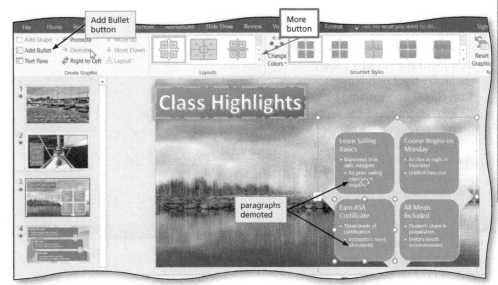

Figure 9–28

TO ADD A SMARTART BULLET

If you need to add information to a SmartArt shape, you can create a new bulleted paragraph. This text would display below the last bulleted paragraph in the shape. If you wanted to add a SmartArt bullet, you would perform the following steps.

1. Select the SmartArt graphic shape where you want to insert the bulleted paragraph.

2. Click the Add Bullet button (SmartArt Tools Design tab | Create Graphic group) to insert a new bulleted paragraph below any bulleted text.

To Change the SmartArt Layout

1 INSERT & CUSTOMIZE TEXT BOXES | 2 CONVERT WORDART TO SMARTART & FORMAT | 3 INSERT & FORMAT SHAPES
4 DRAW & FORMAT LINES | 5 CUSTOMIZE THE RIBBON | 6 EXPORT FILE & CREATE PICTURE PRESENTATION

Once you begin formatting a SmartArt shape, you may decide that another layout better conveys the message you are communicating to an audience. PowerPoint allows you to change the layout easily. Any graphical changes that were made to the original SmartArt, such as moving shapes or promoting and demoting paragraphs, are applied to the new SmartArt layout. The following steps change the SmartArt layout to Linear Venn. *Why? A Venn diagram has overlapping components. Similarly, the information in the individual Sailing Lessons SmartArt shapes overlaps the information in the other shapes. For example, the basic sailing techniques mentioned in the left shape are needed to earn an ASA certificate, which is the topic of the right shape.*

1

- With the SmartArt Tools Design tab displaying, click the More button (shown in Figure 9–28) in the Layouts group to expand the Layouts gallery (Figure 9–29).

Q&A
Can I select one of the layouts displaying in the Layouts group without expanding the layout gallery?
Yes. At times, however, you may want to display the gallery to view and preview the various layouts.

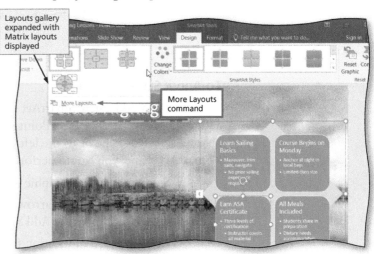

Figure 9–29

2

- Click More Layouts at the bottom of the Layouts gallery to display the Choose a SmartArt Graphic dialog box, click Relationship in the list of graphic categories, and then click the Linear Venn layout (first layout in last row) to display a picture and a description of this SmartArt layout (Figure 9–30).

3

- Click the OK button (Choose a SmartArt Graphic dialog box) to change the layout.

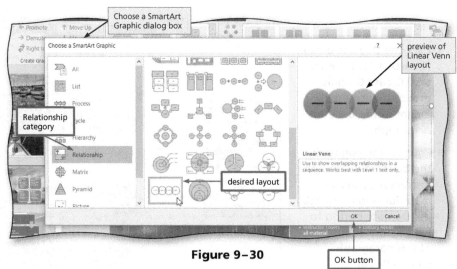

Figure 9–30

To Remove a SmartArt Shape

1 INSERT & CUSTOMIZE TEXT BOXES | 2 CONVERT WORDART TO SMARTART & FORMAT | 3 INSERT & FORMAT SHAPES
4 DRAW & FORMAT LINES | 5 CUSTOMIZE THE RIBBON | 6 EXPORT FILE & CREATE PICTURE PRESENTATION

Now that the new SmartArt layout is created, you can modify the graphic. One change you can make is to delete elements. You decide to delete the last shape on Slide 3. *Why? The slide contains information about what students will experience during the lessons, so the facts about meals are a different topic.* The following steps remove a SmartArt shape.

1

- Click a border of the right SmartArt shape, All Meals Included, to select the entire shape (Figure 9–31).

2

- Press the DELETE key to delete the right SmartArt shape.

Q&A | How do I delete the shape if I am using a touch screen? Press and hold the SmartArt shape and then tap Delete on the shortcut menu.

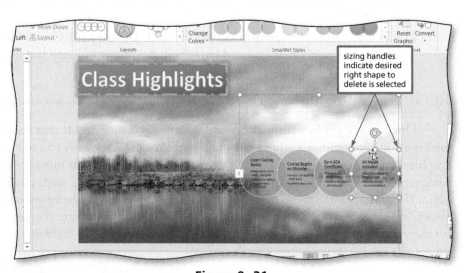

Figure 9–31

To Add a SmartArt Shape

You may add a new SmartArt shape to the layout if you need to display additional information. PowerPoint gives you the option of adding this shape above or below a selected shape or to the left or the right side of the shape. If you wanted to add a SmartArt shape, you would perform the following steps.

1. Select a SmartArt graphic shape near where you want to insert another shape.

2. Click the Add Shape arrow (SmartArt Tools Design tab | Create Graphic group) to display the Add Shape menu.

3. Click the desired location for the new shape, which would be after, before, above, or below the selected shape.

To Resize a SmartArt Graphic by Entering an Exact Measurement

Why? Adequate space exists on the slide to increase all the SmartArt shapes. You can resize a slide element by dragging the sizing handles or by specifying exact measurements for the height and width. The following steps resize the SmartArt graphic by entering an exact measurement.

- Select the entire SmartArt graphic by clicking an outer edge of the graphic (Figure 9–32).

Q&A How will I know the entire graphic is selected?
You will see the Text pane control and sizing handles around the outer edge of the SmartArt.

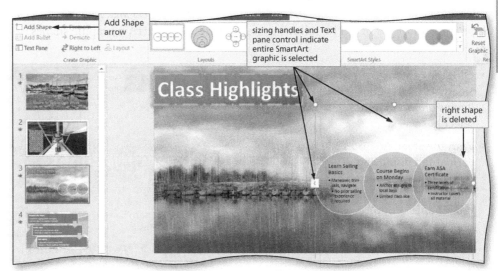

Figure 9–32

- Display the SmartArt Tools Format tab, if necessary click the Size button (SmartArt Tools Format tab | Size group) to display the Height and Width boxes, and then change the Height measurement to 9" and the Width measurement to 13" (Figure 9–33).

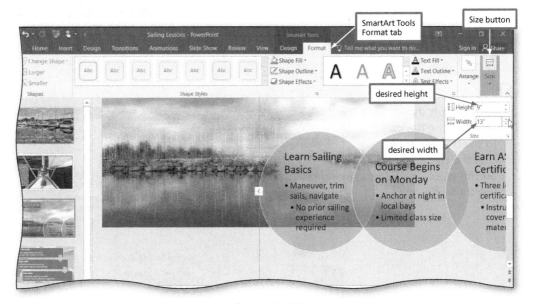

Figure 9–33

3

- Drag the SmartArt graphic upward so its upper edge is aligned with the top edge of the slide and then center the graphic between the left and right edges of the slide.

Other Ways

1. Right-click graphic, click 'Size and Position' on shortcut menu, if necessary click 'Size & Properties' icon (Format Shape pane), if necessary click Size, enter graphic height and width values in boxes, close Format Shape pane

To Resize a SmartArt Graphic Shape

The entire SmartArt shape and the text box now are the proper proportions to display together on the slide. In addition to changing the height and width of the SmartArt graphic, you also can change the height and width of one individual SmartArt shape in the graphic. *Why? Potential students desire to learn what their lessons will entail and would appreciate knowing they do not need to have sailed prior to enrolling. To emphasize this unique feature, you want to make the center SmartArt shape smaller than the others and, in contrast, emphasize the Learn Sailing Basics shape by increasing its size.* The following steps resize the SmartArt graphic shapes.

- Click the center SmartArt shape, Course Begins on Monday, to select it.

- With the SmartArt Tools Format tab displaying, click the Smaller button (SmartArt Tools Format tab | Shapes group) once to decrease the shape size (Figure 9–34).

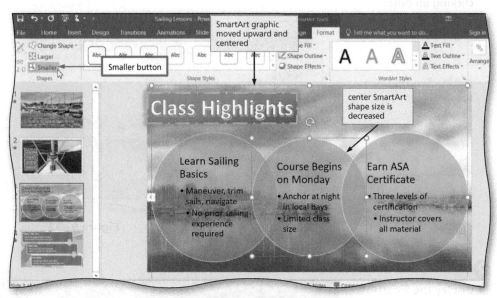

Figure 9–34

- Click the left shape, Learn Sailing Basics, to select it and then click the Larger button twice (Figure 9–35).

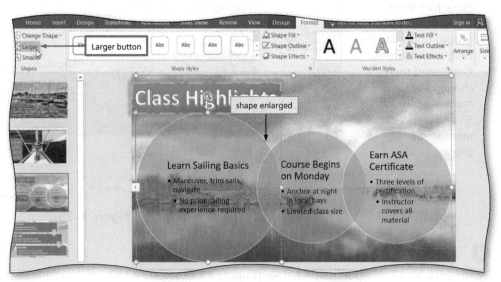

Figure 9–35

Other Ways

1. Right-click graphic, click 'Size and Position' on shortcut menu, if necessary click 'Size & Properties' icon (Format Shape pane), if necessary click Size, enter graphic height and width values in boxes, close Format Shape pane

To Add a SmartArt Style to the Graphic and Change the Color

To enhance the appearance of the circles in the Linear Venn layout, you can add a transparent three-dimensional style that hides some of the background details. You also can add more colors. The following steps add the Powder style and a Colorful range.

1 Select the entire SmartArt graphic, display the SmartArt Tools Design tab, and then click the More button in the SmartArt Styles group to expand the SmartArt Styles gallery.

2 Click Powder in the 3-D area (fourth graphic in first row) to apply this style to the graphic.

3 Click the Change Colors button (SmartArt Tools Design tab | SmartArt Styles group) to display the Change Colors gallery.

4 Click 'Colorful Range – Accent Colors 4 to 5' (fourth graphic in Colorful row) to apply this color variation to the graphic (Figure 9–36).

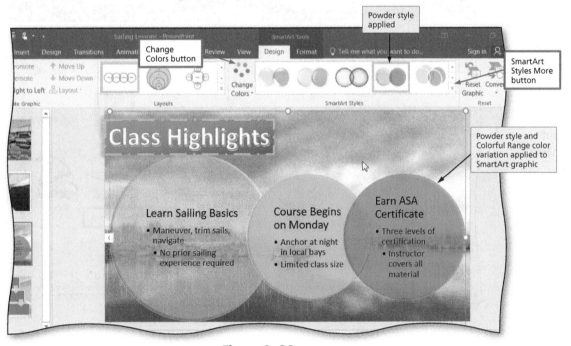

Figure 9–36

To Apply a Picture to a Text Box

1 INSERT & CUSTOMIZE TEXT BOXES | 2 CONVERT WORDART TO SMARTART & FORMAT | 3 INSERT & FORMAT SHAPES
4 DRAW & FORMAT LINES | 5 CUSTOMIZE THE RIBBON | 6 EXPORT FILE & CREATE PICTURE PRESENTATION

Sufficient space exists on both sides of the text box at the top of the slide to insert a picture. *Why? A picture helps to reinforce the written message and also calls attention to the sailing theme. A sailboat illustration provides contrast with the photograph background.* For consistency with the slide title, you can insert a text box that has the default formatting and then add a picture. The following steps add a text box and then apply a picture.

• Select the Slide 3 title text box, click the Align button (Drawing Tools Format tab | Arrange group), and then click Align Center to move the text box horizontally to the center of the slide.

• Display the Insert tab and then insert a text box to the left of the text box at the top of slide.

• Display the Drawing Tools Format tab and then click the Shape Fill arrow (Drawing Tools Format tab | Shape Styles group) to display the Shape Fill gallery (Figure 9–37).

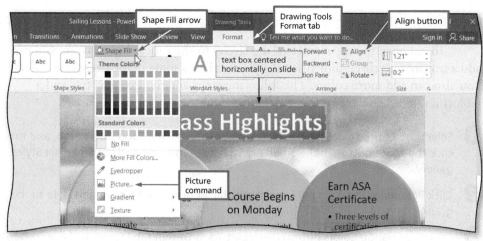

Figure 9–37

• Click Picture in the Shape Fill gallery to display the Insert Pictures dialog box and then navigate to the location where your Data Files are stored.

• Click Yellow Boat to select the file name (Figure 9–38).

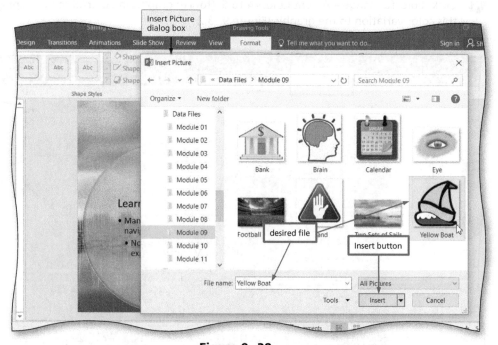

Figure 9–38

• Click the Insert button (Insert Picture dialog box) to insert the Yellow Boat picture into the text box.

• Increase the size of the text box to 1.5" x 1.5" and drag the box so that the right edge of the Yellow Boat text box overlaps the left edge of the title text box. Align the bottom edges of these text boxes (Figure 9–39).

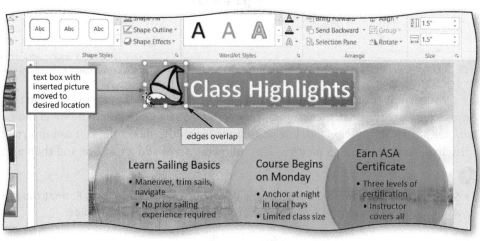

Figure 9–39

To Duplicate and Flip a Text Box Picture

1 INSERT & CUSTOMIZE TEXT BOXES | 2 CONVERT WORDART TO SMARTART & FORMAT | 3 INSERT & FORMAT SHAPES
4 DRAW & FORMAT LINES | 5 CUSTOMIZE THE RIBBON | 6 EXPORT FILE & CREATE PICTURE PRESENTATION

Once the text box and picture are inserted on the left side of the title text box, you can duplicate this slide element and then flip the picture so that the boat is pointed in the opposite direction. *Why? A picture on the right size of the title text box provides symmetry, and both sailboat illustrations will point toward the outer edges of the slide.* The following steps duplicate a text box and then flip the box horizontally.

- With the Yellow Boat text box selected, display the Home tab and then click the Copy arrow (Home tab | Clipboard group) to display the Copy menu (Figure 9–40).

Figure 9–40

- Click Duplicate in the list to create a second text box with the Yellow Boat picture. Drag this new text box to the right side of the title text box and then overlap the left edge of the Yellow Boat text box and right edge of the title text box. Align the bottom edges of the text boxes (Figure 9–41).

Figure 9–41

- Click the Arrange button (Home tab | Drawing group) to display the Arrange menu and then point to Rotate in the Position Objects group to display the Rotate list (Figure 9–42).

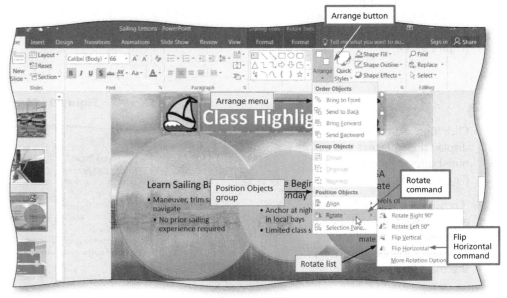

Figure 9–42

4

- Click Flip Horizontal in the Rotate menu to flip the Yellow Boat text box picture (Figure 9–43).

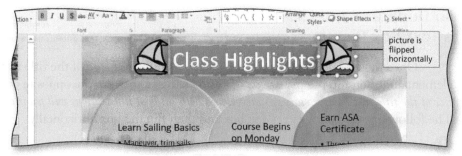

Figure 9–43

To Convert a SmartArt Graphic to Text

1 INSERT & CUSTOMIZE TEXT BOXES | 2 CONVERT WORDART TO SMARTART & FORMAT | 3 INSERT & FORMAT SHAPES
4 DRAW & FORMAT LINES | 5 CUSTOMIZE THE RIBBON | 6 EXPORT FILE & CREATE PICTURE PRESENTATION

Potential students would be curious about specific skills they will learn while sailing. The SmartArt graphic information on Slide 4 explains the basic objectives of the class. In a later portion of this module, you will supplement these details with a graphic pointing out the main components of a sailboat. At times, you may decide that SmartArt is not the optimal method of presenting information to an audience and instead want to depict the same concept using text. *Why? The SmartArt's visual elements may detract from the points being made, so the bulleted list might be useful for instructional purposes. In addition, SmartArt may take up so much room on the slide that other visual elements do not fit.* PowerPoint allows you to remove the shapes and change the text in the graphic to a bulleted list. The following steps convert the SmartArt graphic to text.

1

- Display Slide 4 and then select the entire SmartArt graphic.

Q&A
If one of the SmartArt shapes is selected, how do I select the entire graphic?
Be certain to click the edge of the graphic. You will see sizing handles and the Text pane control when the SmartArt graphic is selected.

- Display the SmartArt Tools Design tab and then click the Convert button (SmartArt Tools Design tab | Reset group) to display the Convert menu (Figure 9–44).

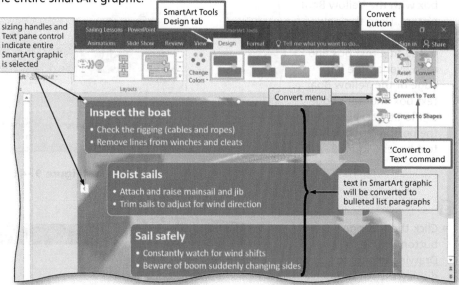

Figure 9–44

2

- Click 'Convert to Text' to display the SmartArt text as nine bulleted list paragraphs (Figure 9–45).

- If requested by your instructor, add the word, in, and the city or county in which you were born after the word, safely, in the third first-level paragraph.

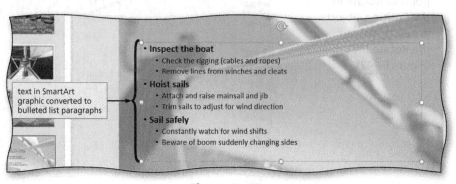

Figure 9–45

- Position the bulleted list placeholder in the upper-right corner of the slide. Drag the middle-right sizing handle to the right edge of the slide (Figure 9–46).

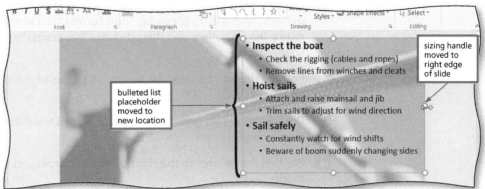

Figure 9–46

To Convert a SmartArt Graphic to Shapes

An alternative to changing a graphic to text is changing a graphic to shapes. In this manner, a shape can be moved, resized, or deleted independently of any other shape in the SmartArt. If you wanted to convert a SmartArt graphic to shapes, you would perform the following steps.

1. Select the entire SmartArt graphic.
2. Click the Convert button (SmartArt Tools Design tab | Reset group) to display the Convert menu.
3. Click 'Convert to Shapes'.

Break Point: If you wish to take a break, this is a good place to do so. Be sure to save the Sailing Lessons file again and then you can exit PowerPoint. To resume at a later time, run PowerPoint, open the file called Sailing Lessons, and continue following the steps from this location forward.

Inserting and Modifying Shapes

The items in the Shapes gallery provide a variety of useful shapes you can insert into slides. Diagrams with labels often help audiences identify the parts of an object. Text boxes with clear, large type and an arrow pointing to a precise area of the object work well in showing relationships between components. You also can use items in the Shapes gallery to create your own custom artwork.

A sailboat has several components: They include the hull, which might include a cabin for cooking, sleeping, and other activities. The front of the hull is called the bow and the rear is called the stern. Other components are the sails, called the jib and mainsail; and the mast, which attaches the sails. These parts can be depicted with a variety of items found in the Shapes gallery. You also want to add text boxes and arrows to identify the components. At times, you may be unable to find a shape in the gallery that fits your specific needs. In those instances, you might find a similar shape and then alter it to your specifications.

BTW
Inserting Shapes
The Shapes gallery is displayed on two tabs: the Drawing Tools Format tab (Insert Shapes group) and the Home tab (Drawing group). Shapes also are available if you display the Insert tab and then click the Shapes button (Illustrations group).

To Insert Shapes

You can draw parts of the sailboat with shapes located in the Shapes gallery: two trapezoids for the hull, which contains the cabin; circles for the portholes; right triangles for the sails, called the jib and the mainsail; and a can for the mast. In addition, the Notched Right Arrow shape can be inserted to serve as a leader line for labeling a sailboat part. The following steps insert five shapes into Slide 4.

1 Display the Drawing Tools Format tab. With Slide 4 displaying, click the More button in the Shapes gallery (Drawing Tools Format tab | Insert Shapes group) to display the entire Shapes gallery and then click the Trapezoid shape (sixth shape in first Basic Shapes row).

2 Position the pointer near the lower-left corner of the slide and then click to insert the Trapezoid shape.

3 Display the Shapes gallery and then click the Oval shape (second shape in first Basic Shapes row).

4 Position the pointer to the right of the Trapezoid and then click to insert the Oval shape.

5 Display the Shapes gallery, click the Right Triangle shape (fourth shape in first Basic Shapes row), and then insert this shape above the Trapezoid.

6 Display the Shapes gallery, click the Can shape (eleventh shape in second Basic Shapes row), and then insert this shape above the Right Triangle.

7 Display the Shapes gallery, click the Notched Right Arrow shape (sixth shape in the second Block Arrows row), and then insert this shape in the upper-left corner of the slide (Figure 9–47).

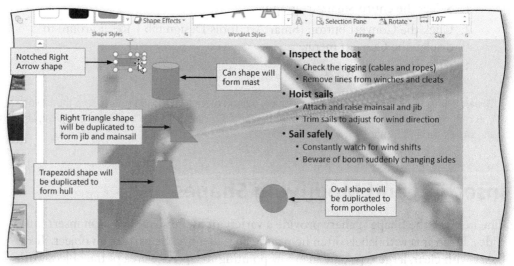

Figure 9–47

BTW

Vector Graphics
Geometric shapes, lines, arrows, and action buttons are vector graphics, which are drawn using mathematical formulas. The size, color, line width, starting and ending points, and other formatting attributes are stored as numeric values and are recalculated when you resize or reformat each shape. Most clip art and video games also use vector graphics.

To Resize and Move Shapes

The five shapes on Slide 4 are the default sizes, and they need to be proportioned to reflect accurate sailboat dimensions. If you are not using a touch screen, you can keep the resized shape proportions identical to the original shape by pressing the SHIFT key while tapping or clicking a sizing handle and then dragging the pointer inward or outward to decrease or increase the size. If you do not hold down the SHIFT key, you can elongate the height or the width to draw an object that is not identical to the shape shown in the Shapes gallery. If you want to alter the shape's proportions, drag one of the sizing handles inward or outward. The following steps resize the shapes and arrow.

1 Select the trapezoid and change the size to 0.2" x 2".

2 With the trapezoid still selected, display the Home tab, click the Copy arrow, and then click Duplicate in the menu. Move the duplicate trapezoid below the first trapezoid, position the pointer over the rotation handle and then turn the shape downward 180 degrees so that it turns upside down. Change the size to 1" x 5" and move the shape toward the bottom of the slide.

3 Drag the small trapezoid to the top of the large trapezoid and use the Smart Guide to center it along the top edge.

4 Select the oval and change the size to 0.5" x 0.5". Duplicate the oval. Drag one oval to the left side of the large trapezoid and the second oval to the right side. If necessary, you may need to bring one of the ovals to the front if it is hidden behind the trapezoid by clicking the Undo button so that this oval is visible and selected, clicking the Bring Forward arrow (Drawing Tools Format tab | Arrange group), clicking 'Bring to Front' in the menu, and then moving the oval back on the trapezoid. Use the Smart Guides to help align the ovals.

5 Select the can and change the size to 5" x 0.2". Drag the can to the smaller trapezoid's upper edge and use the Smart Guides to help you center this shape.

6 Select the right triangle and change the size to 4.2" x 2.4". Drag the shape to the right side of the can, leaving space between these two shapes and between the lower edge of the sail and the upper edge of the smaller trapezoid.

7 Duplicate the right triangle and change the size to 4.5" x 1.7". Flip the shape horizontally, and then drag this shape to left side of the can. The top of the triangle should be even with the top of the can. Leave space between these two shapes (Figure 9–48).

BTW

Displaying Smart Guides

If the Smart Guides are not displayed when you are attempting to align objects, you may need to specify that PowerPoint should show them. Display the View tab, click the Show Group launcher, and then click the 'Display Smart Guides when shapes are aligned' check box to select this option.

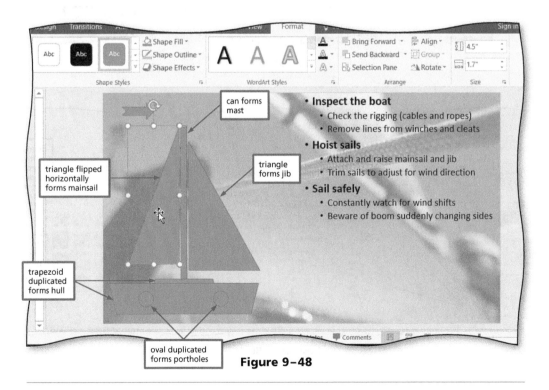

Figure 9–48

To Apply a Fill to a Shape

The shapes on Slide 4 have light blue fill. You can change the shape fill using the same types of fills you used for the text boxes in this presentation. For example, you can apply a gradient, pattern, texture, or picture. *Why? Using similar fills among the slides adds consistency and gives a uniform look to the presentation.* The method of applying these fill effects is similar to the steps you used to format text boxes. The following steps apply fills to the shapes.

1

- Select the two triangles. With the Drawing Tools Format tab displaying, click the Shape Fill arrow (Drawing Tools Format tab | Shape Styles group) to display the Shape Fill gallery and then point to Gradient to display the Gradient gallery (Figure 9–49).

Experiment

- Point to various gradients in the Gradient gallery and watch the interiors of the two shapes change.

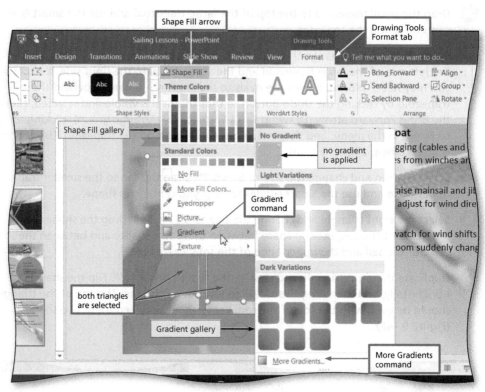

Figure 9–49

2

- Click More Gradients in the Gradient gallery to display the Format Shape pane.

- Click Gradient fill to expand the gradient options and then click the Preset gradients button to display the Preset gradients gallery (Figure 9–50).

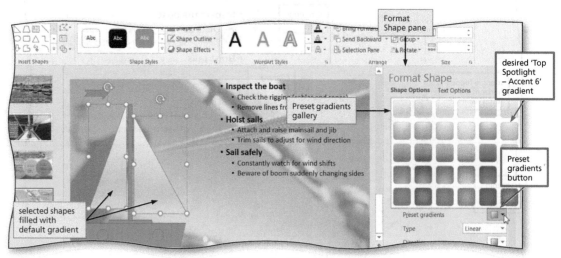

Figure 9–50

Q&A Can I experiment with previewing the gradient colors?
No, the live preview feature is not available.

3

- Click 'Top Spotlight - Accent 6' (last color in second row) to apply the gradient fill to the two triangles.

Q&A How can I delete a gradient fill if I decide not to apply one to the shape?
If you already have applied the pattern, you must click the Undo button on the Quick Access Toolbar.

4

- Select the two trapezoids, click Gradient fill, and then click the Preset gradients button (Figure 9–51).

Q&A Why did these two shapes fill with the green gradient fill when I tapped or clicked Gradient fill?
PowerPoint recalls the last gradient you selected.

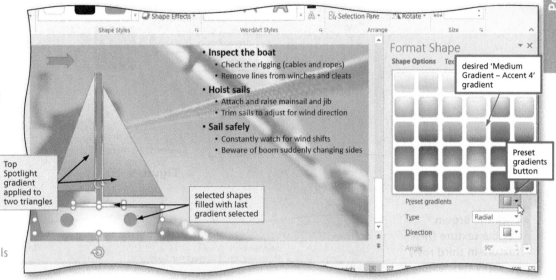

Figure 9–51

5

- Click 'Medium Gradient – Accent 4' (fourth color in third row) to apply this gradient to the shapes.

- Select the can and then click 'Picture or texture fill' to display the ' Picture or texture fill' section (Figure 9–52).

Q&A Why did the can fill with a texture?
Depending on previous settings for shape fills, PowerPoint may insert a fill or change the transparency when you click the 'Picture or texture fill' option button.

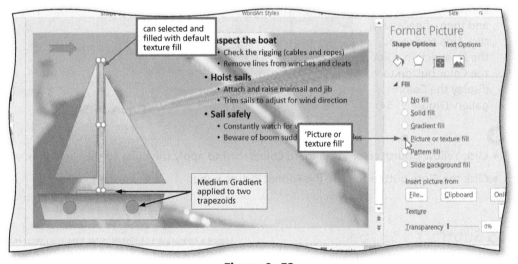

Figure 9–52

- Click the Texture button to display the Texture gallery (Figure 9–53).

Figure 9–53

- Click the Brown marble texture (first texture in third row) to apply this texture to the can.

- If necessary, set the Transparency slider to 0%.

- Scroll down the Format Picture pane and then, if necessary, click Line to expand the Line section. Click the Color button to display the Color gallery (Figure 9–54).

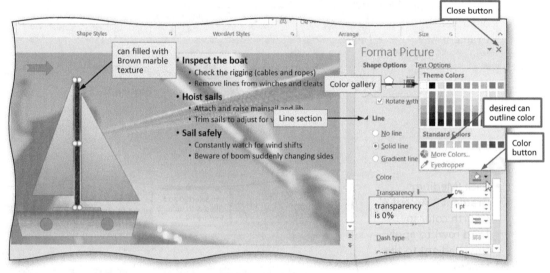

Figure 9–54

- Click Yellow (fourth color in Standard Colors row) to apply this color to the can edges.

- Click the Close button to close the Format Picture pane.

To Subtract a Shape

1 INSERT & CUSTOMIZE TEXT BOXES | 2 CONVERT WORDART TO SMARTART & FORMAT | 3 INSERT & FORMAT SHAPES
4 DRAW & FORMAT LINES | 5 CUSTOMIZE THE RIBBON | 6 EXPORT FILE & CREATE PICTURE PRESENTATION

The trapezoid hull you drew now has solid blue portholes, but you can easily give the effect of transparent portholes by subtracting the areas of the ovals that overlap the trapezoid. *Why? Your sailboat will look more accurate with this element.* The result is a blank area that displays the slide background. The following steps subtract the ovals.

- Click the larger trapezoid, press and hold down the CTRL key, click one oval to select it, and then click the second oval to select all three shapes.

Q&A | Can I perform this step using a touch screen?
No. You will need to use a keyboard to select multiple shapes.

- With the Drawing Tools Format tab displaying, click the Merge Shapes button (Drawing Tools Format tab | Insert Shapes group) to display the Merge Shapes list (Figure 9–55).

 Do I need to select the shapes in this order?
Yes. You first select the shape that you want to keep and then click the shape(s) that you want to delete.

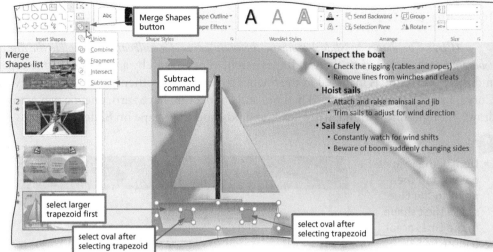

Figure 9–55

 **Experiment**

- Point to the commands in the Merge Shapes list and watch the results of the various merge commands.

2

- Click Subtract in the Merge Shapes list to delete the gold background behind the oval shapes.

To Merge Shapes

1 INSERT & CUSTOMIZE TEXT BOXES | 2 CONVERT WORDART TO SMARTART & FORMAT | 3 INSERT & FORMAT SHAPES
4 DRAW & FORMAT LINES | 5 CUSTOMIZE THE RIBBON | 6 EXPORT FILE & CREATE PICTURE PRESENTATION

The two trapezoids forming the hull and cabin have a common horizontal line where the two shapes intersect. You can eliminate this line if you merge the shapes. *Why? The two elements will appear seamless as part of the main structure of the sailboat.* The following steps merge the two trapezoids.

1

- Select the two trapezoids. With the Drawing Tools Format tab displaying, click the Merge Shapes button (Drawing Tools Format tab | Insert Shapes group) to display the Merge Shapes list (Figure 9–56).

2

- Click Union (Drawing Tools Format tab | Insert Shapes group) to combine the trapezoid shapes.

 When would I use the Union command instead of the Combine command?
The Union command joins the shapes using the formatting of the top shape. The Combine command also joins shapes, but it deletes the area where two shapes overlap.

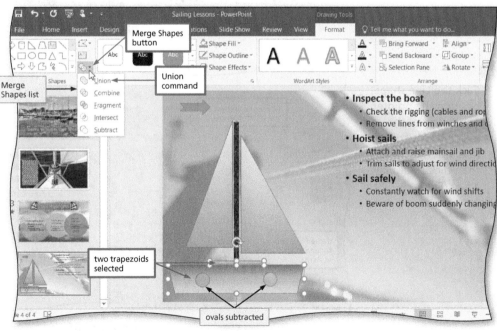

Figure 9–56

To Draw a Line

Why? *The shapes on Slide 4 comprise the main parts of a sailboat. To complete the drawing, you need to add the ropes that connect the sails to the hull.* Ropes can be represented by a line shape. One type of rope is a straight bar, and this type of line is included in the Shapes gallery. Some other lines in the gallery are the Elbow Connector, Curve, Freeform, and Scribble. The lines and connectors have zero, one, or two arrowheads. The following steps draw a straight line without arrowheads and position this shape on Slide 4.

1

• Display the Shapes gallery and then point to the Line shape (first shape in the Lines area) (Figure 9–57).

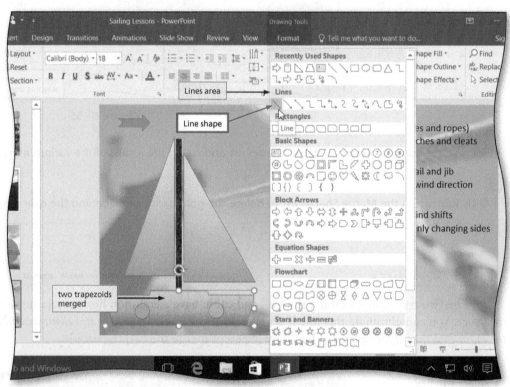

Figure 9–57

2

• Click the Line shape, position the pointer on the top of the left right triangle (the mainsail), and then click to display a line (Figure 9–58).

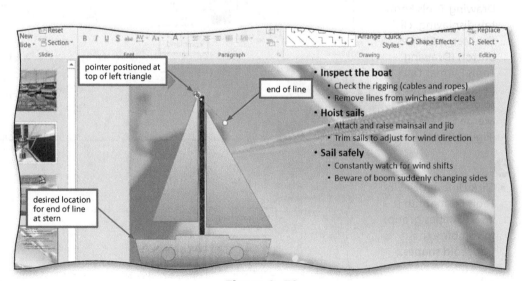

Figure 9–58

3

• Drag the lower sizing handle to the rear (stern) of the boat.

To Change a Line Weight and Color

In this project, you changed a text box and shape outline color and weight. In a similar fashion, you can change line outline formatting. *Why? The line you drew on Slide 4 is thin, and the color does not display well against the slide background.* You can increase the line thickness and change its color to enhance the shape. The following steps change the line thickness and color.

- With the line selected, click the Shape Outline arrow (Drawing Tools Format tab | Shape Styles group) and then point to Weight to display the Weight gallery.

- Point to 1½ pt to see a preview of that weight applied to the line (Figure 9–59).

 **Experiment**

- Point to various weights in the Weight gallery and watch the line thickness change.

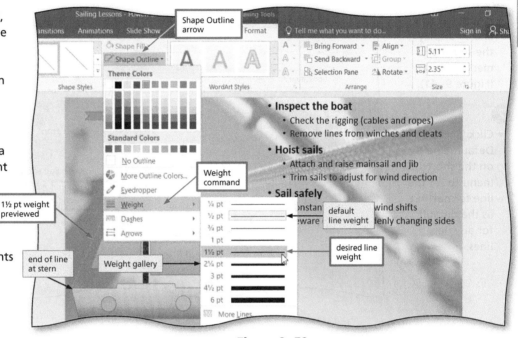

Figure 9–59

②

- Click 1½ pt in the Weight gallery to apply that weight to the line.

- Click the Shape Outline arrow again. Point to 'Gold, Accent 4, Darker 50%' (eighth color in last Theme Colors row) to see a preview of that color applied to the line (Figure 9–60).

 **Experiment**

- Point to various colors in the Theme Colors gallery and watch the line color change.

③

- Click 'Gold, Accent 4, Darker 50%' to apply that color to the line.

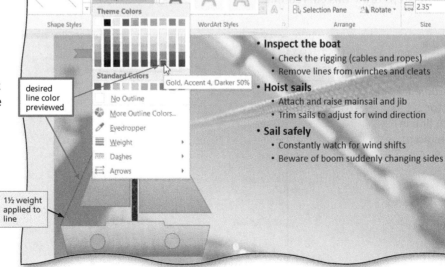

Figure 9–60

To Set Line Formatting as the Default

1 INSERT & CUSTOMIZE TEXT BOXES | 2 CONVERT WORDART TO SMARTART & FORMAT | 3 INSERT & FORMAT SHAPES
4 DRAW & FORMAT LINES | **5 CUSTOMIZE THE RIBBON** | **6 EXPORT FILE & CREATE PICTURE PRESENTATION**

The line you inserted and formatted is one of two ropes in the sailboat diagram. You can set these line attributes as the default for the other line you will draw in the presentation. *Why? Setting the default characteristics saves time when you add other lines because you do not need to repeat all the formatting steps. It also ensures consistency among the line shapes.* The following steps set the line shape on Slide 4 as the default.

- Right-click the line to display the shortcut menu (Figure 9–61).

- Click 'Set as Default Line' on the shortcut menu to set the line formatting as the default for any new lines.

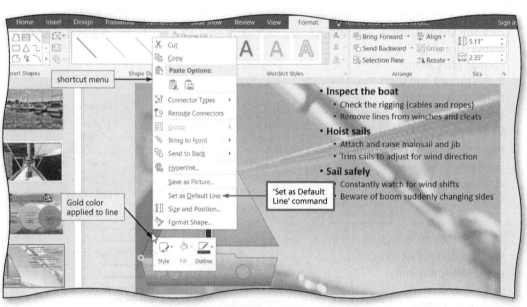

Figure 9–61

To Draw an Additional Line

1 INSERT & CUSTOMIZE TEXT BOXES | 2 CONVERT WORDART TO SMARTART & FORMAT | 3 INSERT & FORMAT SHAPES
4 DRAW & FORMAT LINES | **5 CUSTOMIZE THE RIBBON** | **6 EXPORT FILE & CREATE PICTURE PRESENTATION**

One more line is needed to connect the jib to the bow (front of the hull). A line with a curve is a good shape to use to connect these two shapes. *Why? This shape has two bends, which can be altered to create one curve.* The following steps draw this curved line.

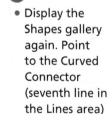

- Display the Shapes gallery again. Point to the Curved Connector (seventh line in the Lines area) (Figure 9–62).

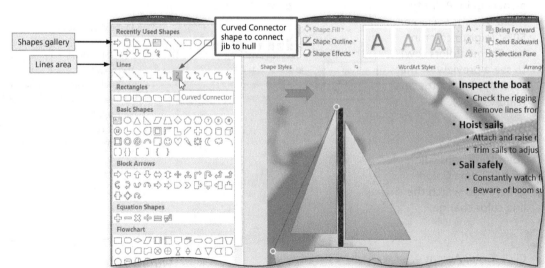

Figure 9–62

2

- Click the Curved Connector, position the pointer in the lower-right corner of the jib, and then click to insert one end of the line at this location (Figure 9–63).

Q&A What is the yellow dot in the middle of the line?
The dot is called a point. Every shape is formed by a series of points connected with lines that are straight or curved. If desired, you can drag a point to alter the shape's form.

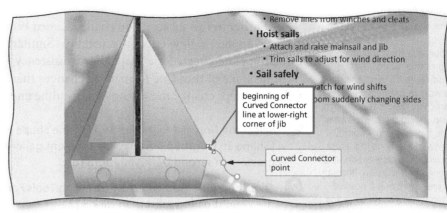

Figure 9–63

3

- Drag the sizing handle at the other end of the line near the front of the hull (Figure 9–64).

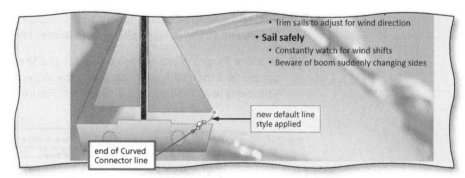

Figure 9–64

To Group and Size the Sailboat Objects

All the shapes comprising the sailboat are separate elements on the slide. You will need to move and enlarge the sailboat on the slide. You easily can complete these tasks if you group all the components so they no longer are individual pieces. The following steps group all these shapes and then enlarge the entire sailboat shape.

1 Select all the sailboat shapes and then display the Picture Tools Format tab.

2 Click the Group Objects button (Picture Tools Format tab | Arrange group) to display the Group list and then click Group in the list to combine all the shapes.

3 Size the sailboat object so that it is 6.5" x 5.5" and then move it to the location shown in Figure 9–65.

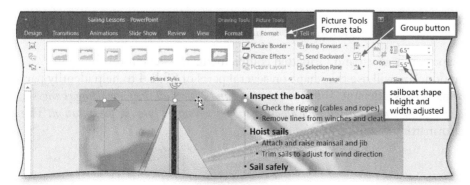

Figure 9–65

BTW
Revising Your Presentation
If you are going to present your slide show multiple times to a variety of audiences, consider the slides a work in progress. Each time you deliver your speech, you should be able to tweak the slides to clarify points, answer questions that arose during the presentation, and generate discussion. Revising a presentation is a positive step toward communicating your message clearly and powerfully.

To Change a Shape Fill and Outline and Apply Effects

Earlier in this project, you changed a text box outline color, weight, and style. You also applied a glow effect to a text box. Similarly, you can change the outline formatting and effects for a shape. For consistency, you can enhance the arrow shape by using some of the same formatting changes that you applied to the text box. The following steps change the arrow shape outline and apply an effect.

1 Select the Notched Right Arrow, click the Shape Fill arrow (Drawing Tools Format tab | Shape Styles group), display the Gradient gallery, and then click Linear Right (first gradient in second Dark Variations row).

2 Click the Shape Outline arrow (Drawing Tools Format tab | Shape Styles group), display the Weight gallery, and then click 3 pt.

3 Display the Shape Outline gallery again and then click Orange to change the shape border color.

4 Display the Shape Outline gallery again, display the Dashes gallery, and then click Square Dot (third style) to change the border style.

5 Click the Shape Effects button to display the Shape Effects gallery, display the Glow gallery, and then click 'Orange, 5 pt glow, Accent color 2' (second color in first Glow Variations row) to apply the glow effect (Figure 9–66).

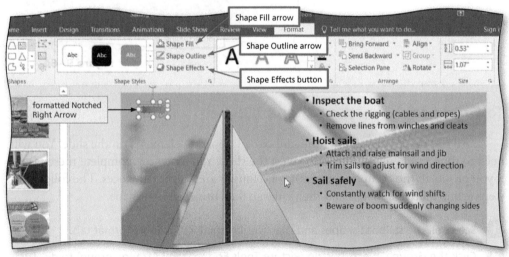

Figure 9–66

To Set Shape Formatting as the Default

1 INSERT & CUSTOMIZE TEXT BOXES | 2 CONVERT WORDART TO SMARTART & FORMAT | **3 INSERT & FORMAT SHAPES**
4 DRAW & FORMAT LINES | 5 CUSTOMIZE THE RIBBON | 6 EXPORT FILE & CREATE PICTURE PRESENTATION

The Notched Right Arrow shape you inserted and formatted complements the default text box you inserted on the slides in the presentation. You will use this shape on several parts of Slide 4 to help identify parts of the sailboat, so you can set its formatting as a default. *Why? To save time and ensure all the formatting changes are applied, you can set the formatting of one shape as the default for all other shapes you insert into the presentation.* The following steps set the arrow shape formatting on Slide 4 as the default.

1

- Right-click the Notched Right Arrow shape to display the shortcut menu (Figure 9–67).

2

- Click 'Set as Default Shape' on the shortcut menu to set the shape formatting as the default for any new shapes.

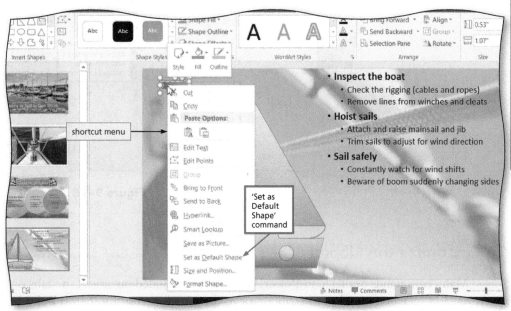

Figure 9–67

Use politically correct language.

Many companies have strict policies in order to prevent harassment in the workplace. These guidelines are developed to protect employees from adverse treatment based on race, religion, national origin, gender, or other personal traits. Keep these policies in mind as you label components on your slides. For example, some females may be offended if you refer to an adult woman as a "girl," or an older athlete may resent being labeled as an "aging" rather than as a "veteran" player.

To Label the Shapes

The final step in creating Slide 4 is to label the parts of the sailboat. The Notched Right Arrow shape and the text box are formatted as defaults, so the labeling process is easy to accomplish. The following steps insert text boxes and arrows into Slide 4 and then enter text in the text boxes.

1 With Slide 4 displaying, insert a text box into the left side of the slide near the upper hand in the background picture. Type `Mainsail` in the text box and then decrease the font size to 24 point.

2 Duplicate the Mainsail text box, type `Jib` in the box, and then move it under the bulleted list.

3 Drag the Notched Right arrow to the mainsail. Display the Drawing Tools Format tab, click the Bring Forward arrow (Drawing Tools Format tab | Arrange group), and then click 'Bring to Front' to display the arrow on top of the mainsail. Use the arrow keys to move the Mainsail text box to the left of the arrow.

4 Duplicate the Notched Right arrow, rotate it 180 degrees, drag it near the lower-right corner of the jib, and then use the arrow keys to move the Jib text box to the right of this arrow.

5 Select both the Jib text box and arrow, duplicate them, and then type `Hull` in the text box (Figure 9–68).

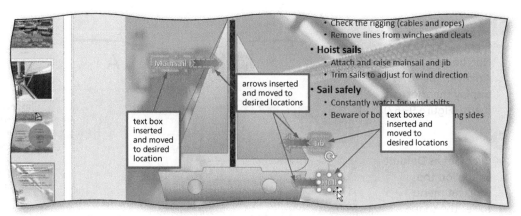

Figure 9–68

To Customize the Ribbon

Many commands available in PowerPoint are not included on any of the tabs on the ribbon. You can, however, add such commands to the ribbon or to the Quick Access Toolbar. *Why? Many of these commands perform tasks you commonly repeat, so it would be convenient to have the buttons accessible in a group on the ribbon.* The following steps customize the ribbon by adding the 'Print Preview and Print' and 'Create Handouts in Microsoft Word' commands to the ribbon and then arranging their order in the group.

1

• With the Home tab displaying, open the Backstage view and then click Options to display the PowerPoint Options dialog box.

• Click Customize Ribbon in the left pane to display the Customize the Ribbon pane (Figure 9–69).

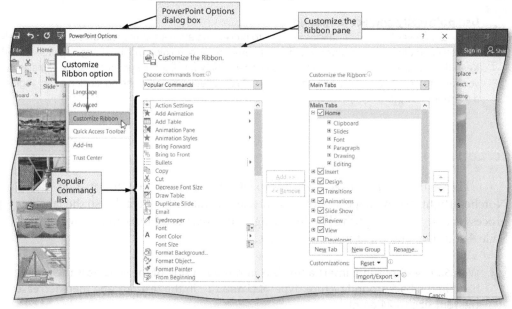

Figure 9–69

2

• Click the 'Choose commands from' arrow to display the 'Choose commands from' list (Figure 9–70).

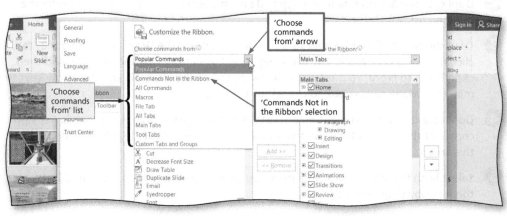

Figure 9–70

- Click 'Commands Not in the Ribbon' in the 'Choose commands from' list to display a list of commands that do not display in the ribbon (Figure 9–71).

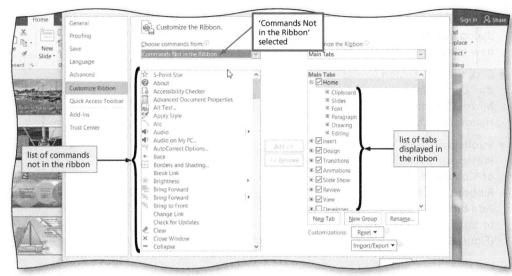

Figure 9–71

- Scroll down and then click 'Create Handouts in Microsoft Word' to select this button.

- Click Editing in the Main Tabs area under Home to specify that the 'Create Handouts in Microsoft Word' button will be added in a new group after the Editing group on the Home tab (Figure 9–72).

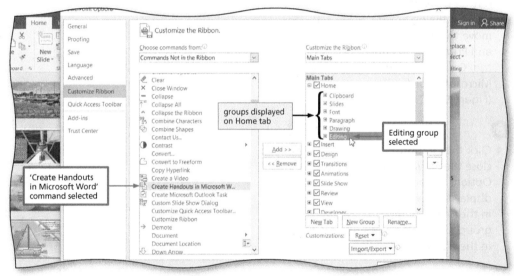

Figure 9–72

- Click the New Group button to create a new group.

- Click the Rename button and then type **Handouts** as the new group name in the Display name text box (Rename dialog box) (Figure 9–73).

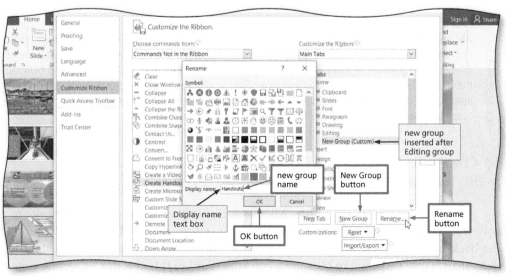

Figure 9–73

6

- Click the OK button (Rename dialog box) to rename the new group.
- Click the Add button to add the 'Create Handouts in Microsoft Word' button to the Handouts group.
- Scroll down, click 'Print Preview and Print' in the list of 'Commands Not in the Ribbon', and then click the Add button to add the button to the Handouts group (Figure 9–74).

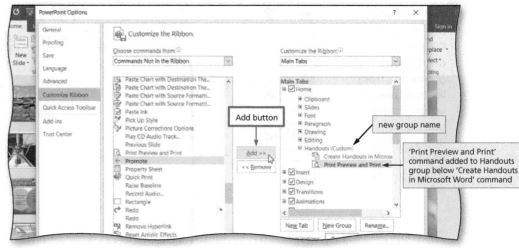

Figure 9–74

7

- Click the Move Up button (PowerPoint Options dialog box) to move the 'Print Preview and Print' button above the 'Create Handouts in Microsoft Word' button (Figure 9–75).

8

- Click the OK button to close the PowerPoint Options dialog box and display the two buttons in the new Handouts group on the Home tab in the ribbon.

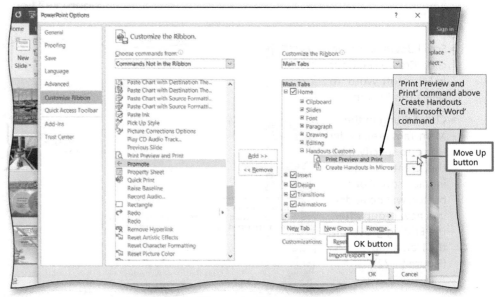

Figure 9–75

CONSIDER THIS

Work with a buddy.

Although you may believe you create your best work when you work alone, research shows that the work product generally improves when two or more people work together on a creative task. A classmate or team member at work can assist you in many ways. For example, this person can help you gather research for your graphics and bulleted text or provide feedback on the slides' clarity and readability. As you rehearse, a buddy can time your talk and identify the times when the presentation lacks interest. If a buddy attends your actual presentation, he or she can give objective feedback on the components that worked and those that can use revision for the next time you present the material.

To Create a Handout by Exporting a File to Microsoft Word

1 INSERT & CUSTOMIZE TEXT BOXES | 2 CONVERT WORDART TO SMARTART & FORMAT | 3 INSERT & FORMAT SHAPES
4 DRAW & FORMAT LINES | 5 CUSTOMIZE THE RIBBON | **6 EXPORT FILE & CREATE PICTURE PRESENTATION**

The handouts you create using Microsoft PowerPoint are useful to distribute to audiences. Each time you need to create these handouts, however, you need to open the file in PowerPoint and then print from the Backstage view. As an alternative, it might be convenient to save, or export, the file as a Microsoft Word document if you are going to be using Microsoft Word to type a script or lecture notes. *Why? The handout can have a variety of layouts; for example, the notes you type in the Notes pane can be displayed to the right of or beneath the slide thumbnails, blank lines can be displayed to the right of or beneath the slide thumbnails, or just an outline can be displayed.* The following steps use the 'Create Handouts in Microsoft Word' button you added to the new Handouts group on the Home tab to export the presentation to Microsoft Word and then create a handout.

1

- With the Home tab displaying, click the 'Create Handouts in Microsoft Word' button (Home tab | Handouts group) to display the Send to Microsoft Word dialog box (Figure 9–75).

2

- Click 'Blank lines next to slides' to add blank lines next to the slides when the handout is printed (Figure 9–76).

- Click the OK button to save the file with this layout.

3

- If the handout does not display in a new Microsoft Word window, click the Microsoft Word program button on the Windows taskbar to see a live preview of the handout. If you print the handouts, they will resemble the pages shown in Figure 9–77.

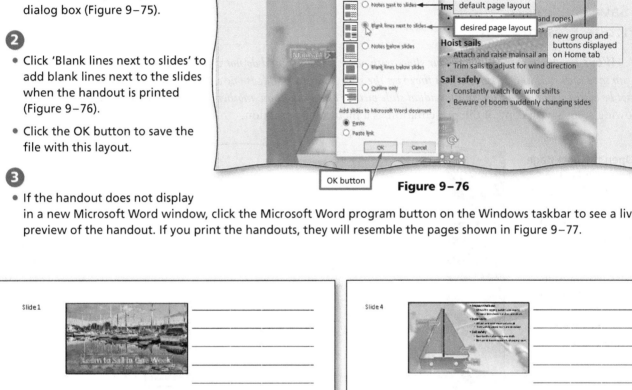

Figure 9–76

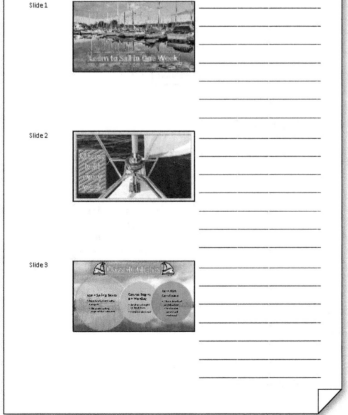

(a) Page 1

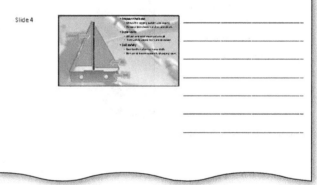

(b) Page 2

BTW

Conserving Ink and Toner
If you want to conserve ink or toner, you can instruct PowerPoint to print draft quality documents by clicking File on the ribbon to open the Backstage view, clicking the Options tab in the Backstage view to display the PowerPoint Options dialog box, clicking Advanced in the left pane (PowerPoint Options dialog box), scrolling to the Print area in the right pane, placing a check mark in the 'Use draft quality' check box, and then clicking the OK button. Then, use the Backstage view to print the document as usual.

Figure 9–77

- Save the Word file using the file name, Sailboat Word Handout.

- Close the Word file and, if necessary, exit Word.

Other Ways

1. Open Backstage view, display Export tab, click Create Handouts, click Create Handouts button

BTW
Distributing a Document
Instead of printing and distributing a hard copy of a document, you can distribute the document electronically. Options include sending the document via email; posting it on cloud storage (such as OneDrive) and sharing the file with others; posting it on social media, a blog, or other website; and sharing a link associated with an online location of the document. You also can create and share a PDF or XPS image of the document, so that users can view the file in Acrobat Reader or XPS Viewer instead of in PowerPoint.

To Save the Presentation as a Picture Presentation

1 INSERT & CUSTOMIZE TEXT BOXES | 2 CONVERT WORDART TO SMARTART & FORMAT | 3 INSERT & FORMAT SHAPES
4 DRAW & FORMAT LINES | 5 CUSTOMIZE THE RIBBON | **6 EXPORT FILE & CREATE PICTURE PRESENTATION**

Why? If you are going to share your slides with other presenters and do not want them to alter the slide content, you can save each slide as a picture. When they run the slide show, each slide is one complete picture, so the text and shapes cannot be edited. You also can use an individual slide picture as a graphic on another slide or in another presentation. The following steps save a copy of the presentation as a picture presentation.

- Open the Backstage view, display the Export tab, and then click 'Change File Type' to display the 'Change File Type' gallery.

- Click 'PowerPoint Picture Presentation' in the Presentation File Types area (Figure 9–78).

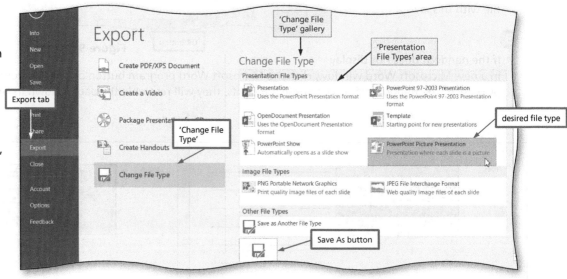

Figure 9–78

- Click the Save As button to display the Save As dialog box.

- Type **Sailing Lessons Picture Presentation** in the File name text box (Figure 9–79).

- Click the Save button (Save As dialog box) to save a copy of the presentation as a picture presentation.

- Click the OK button (Microsoft PowerPoint dialog box).

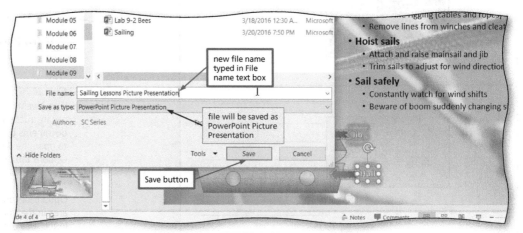

Figure 9–79

To Reset the Ribbon

Why? *Your work with the PowerPoint presentation is complete, so you can delete the group and buttons you added to the ribbon.* The following steps remove the Handouts group and the 'Print Preview and Print' and 'Create Handouts in Microsoft Word' commands from the Home tab.

- Open the Backstage view, click Options to display the PowerPoint Options dialog box, and then click Customize Ribbon in the left pane to display the Customize the Ribbon pane.

- Click the Reset button (PowerPoint Options dialog box) to display the Reset menu (Figure 9–80).

- Click 'Reset all customizations'.

- Click the Yes button (Microsoft Office dialog box) to delete all customizations.

- Click the OK button (PowerPoint Options dialog box) to close the dialog box.

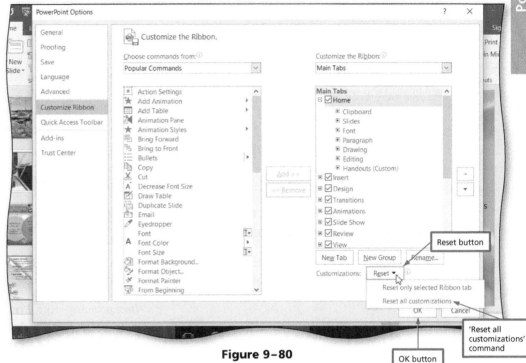

Figure 9–80

Q&A
Do I need to remove the group and commands from the ribbon?
No. For consistency, the ribbon is reset after the added group and commands no longer are needed. If you share a computer with others, you should reset the ribbon.

- Because the project now is complete, you can save the presentation again and then exit PowerPoint.

Summary

In this module you have learned how to modify a presentation using text boxes, SmartArt, and shapes. You customized a text box, set it as the default, and then inserted new text boxes and applied formatting, including a texture, gradient, and pattern. You also converted WordArt to SmartArt and then formatted the shapes and bulleted paragraphs. Then you created a diagram from shapes, which had gradients and patterns applied. Finally, you customized and reset the ribbon, created handouts in Microsoft Word, and saved the presentation as a picture presentation.

What decisions will you need to make when creating your next presentation?

Use these guidelines as you complete the assignments in this module and create your own slide show decks outside of this class.

1. **Choose colors wisely.** The appropriate use of color can add interest and help audience members retain information. Used inappropriately, however, mismatched colors will generate confusion and create an impression of unprofessionalism.

2. **Use keywords in SmartArt graphics.** The words you type into your SmartArt graphic can serve as a prompt of the key points you want to make in the presentation.

3. **Use politically correct language.** When you type words into text boxes, be mindful of the terms you are using to identify the images.

4. **Work with a buddy.** As you develop your slide content and then rehearse the presentation, ask a friend or work associate to assist you with various tasks.

Apply Your Knowledge

Reinforce the skills and apply the concepts you learned in this module.

Centering and Formatting Placeholders, Converting WordArt to SmartArt, and Formatting and Reordering Shapes

Note: To complete this assignment, you will be required to use the Data Files. Please contact your instructor for information about accessing the Data Files.

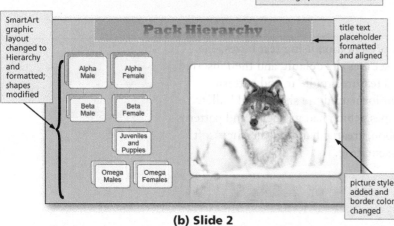

(a) Slide 1

(b) Slide 2

Figure 9–81

Instructions: Run PowerPoint. Open the presentation called Apply 9–1 Wolves, which is located in the Data Files. The two slides in this presentation are about the hierarchy of wolves in their packs. The document you open is a partially formatted presentation. You will center and format placeholders, convert WordArt to SmartArt, and then format and reorder the shapes. Your presentation should look like Figure 9–81.

Perform the following tasks:

1. On Slide 1 (Figure 9–81a), select the title text placeholder and align it in the center of the slide. With the title text placeholder still selected, apply the 40% pattern fill (last pattern in first row), change the outline color to Blue (eighth color in Standard Colors row), and then change the outline weight to 3 pt.

2. Convert the WordArt text at the bottom of the slide to the Continuous Block Process SmartArt graphic (first graphic in third Process row). Select the rightmost SmartArt shape (Two to twenty per pack) and delete it. Increase the size of the SmartArt graphic

to approximately 2.2" × 8". Apply the 'Gradient Range - Accent 5' color (third color in Accent 5 row) to the graphic and then apply the Inset style (second style in first 3-D row). Change the font to Arial, change the font size to 20 point, and then bold this text. Align the SmartArt graphic in the center of the slide to the location shown in Figure 9–81a.

3. On Slide 2 (Figure 9–81b), select the title text placeholder and align it in the center of the slide. With the title text placeholder still selected, apply the 'White, Background 1, Darker 35%' solid fill color (first color in fifth Theme Colors row) and then change the transparency to 50%. Change the shape outline to Square Dot dashed line (third line in Dashes gallery), change the outline weight to 2¼ pt, and then change the outline color to 'White, Background 1' (first color in first Theme Colors row).

4. Change the SmartArt graphic layout to Hierarchy (second style in second Hierarchy row). Select the shape labeled Alpha Male and add a shape after it. Type the text, **Alpha Female** in the added shape. Select the shape labeled Beta Female and demote it. Select the shape labeled Juveniles and Puppies and demote it. Select the shape labeled Omega Males and Females, demote it, and then delete the text, and Females. With this shape still selected, add a shape after it and type, **Omega Females** in the shape.

5. Increase the SmartArt graphic size to 5.5" × 4.7". Change the font in the SmartArt graphic to Arial and then change the font size to 20 point. Select the shapes labeled Alpha Male and Alpha Female and increase the size to approximately 1.3" × 1.6". Move the SmartArt graphic to the location shown in the figure.

6. Change the colors of the SmartArt graphic to 'Gradient Range - Accent 4' (third color in Accent 4 area) and then apply the Cartoon style (third effect in first 3-D row).

7. Apply the 'Reflected Bevel, White' picture style (fifth style in last row) to the wolf picture. Change the picture border color to 'Blue, Accent 5' (ninth color in first Theme Colors row) and then change the border weight to 3 pt.

8. If requested by your instructor, insert a text box in the lower-right corner of Slide 2 and then type your birth year, birth city, and birth state.

9. Apply the Flash transition (Subtle area) and change the duration to 4.00 for both slides.

10. Run the presentation and then save the file using the file name, Apply 9–1 Wolves Ranking Order.

11. Submit the revised document in the format specified by your instructor.

12. ❋ In this presentation, you converted the WordArt to a SmartArt graphic on Slide 1. Was the Continuous Block Process layout an appropriate choice? Would another layout be more suitable for the content? Does the hierarchy chart help your audience comprehend the wolf pack hierarchy? Why or why not?

Extend Your Knowledge

Extend the skills you learned in this module and experiment with new skills. You may need to use Help to complete the assignment.

Setting Default Line Formatting, Applying a Pattern and Outline Style to a Text Box, Modifying Shapes, and Editing SmartArt Shapes

Note: To complete this assignment, you will be required to use the Data Files. Please contact your instructor for information about accessing the Data Files.

Continued >

Extend Your Knowledge *continued*

Instructions: Run PowerPoint. Open the presentation, Extend 9–1 Driving, which is located in the Data Files. You will set line formatting as the default, apply a pattern to a text box, change a text box outline style, change a slide picture, apply a fill to a shape, apply a picture to a text box, and change text box outlines and fills to create the presentation shown in Figure 9–82.

Perform the following tasks:

1. On Slide 1 (Figure 9–82a), change the font for the first line in the title text placeholder to Gill Sans MT, increase the font size to 48 point, change the font color to Red, and then bold this text. Change the font for the second line to Gill Sans Ultra Bold and then increase the front size to 40 point. Apply the 'Wide downward diagonal' pattern fill (fifth pattern in third row) to this placeholder, change the Foreground color to 'Gray-25%, Background 2, Darker 50%' (third color in fourth Theme Colors row), and then change the Background color to 'Gold, Accent 4, Lighter 40%' (eighth color in fourth Theme Colors row).

2. Change the title text placeholder outline weight to 6 pt, change the outline color to 'Gold, Accent 4' (eighth color in Theme Colors row), and then change the outline style to Long Dash Dot (seventh style in Dashes gallery).

3. Select the body of the car that was drawn with the Freeform line and change the fill color to 'White, Background 1, Darker 50%' (first color in last Theme Colors row). Using Figure 9–82a as a guide, place the two window shapes on the car. Select both window shapes and then apply the 'Top Spotlight - Accent 3' gradient (third gradient in second Preset gradients row) to these two shapes.

4. To create the wheels for the car, insert an Oval shape, size the shape to 0.4" × 0.4", change the fill color to 'White, Background 1, Darker 50%' (first color in last Theme Colors row), change the outline color of this shape to 'Black, Text 1', and then change the outline weight (width) to 12 pt. Duplicate the shape and then move the shapes to the car's wheel wells, as shown in the figure.

5. To create the headlight, insert an Oval shape, size it to 0.2" × 0.15", change the shape fill color to Yellow, remove the outline, and then move the shape near the front of the car, as shown in the figure.

6. To create the door handle, insert another Oval shape, size it to 0.1" × 0.2", change the shape fill color to 'Black, Text 1', and then position this shape on the door, as shown in the figure. Select all the car shapes and then group them.

7. On Slide 1, create the goalpost base by inserting a vertical Line shape in the lower-left area of the slide, changing the weight (width) of the line to 12 pt, and then changing the outline color to Gold, Accent 4 (eighth color in first Theme Colors row). Set this line formatting as the default. Change the shape height to 1.5". To form the crossbar, insert a horizontal Line, change the length to 1.86", and then center this line perpendicular to the base. To form the posts, insert a vertical Line, change the height to 1.5", and then move this line to the left side of the crossbar. Duplicate this shape and then move the new line to the right side of the crossbar.

8. Select the four lines, group them, and then move the goalpost to the area shown in the figure.

9. Insert a text box at the bottom of Slide 1 and then type the text shown in Figure 9–82a. Change the font to Arial and then change the font size to 20 pt. Bold, italicize, and underline this text, align it right, and then align it in the middle of the text box. Adjust the size of the text box to approximately 1.35" × 13.33" and then move it to the bottom and side edges of the slide. Apply the 'Gold, Accent 4, Lighter 40%' shape fill color (eighth color in fourth Theme Colors row) to the text box.

10. On Slide 1, select the car, bring it to the front and then move it to the left side of the text box. Change the picture on Slide 1 to the picture called Football Stadium, which is located in the Data Files. Use the sizing handles to increase the size of the picture so that it fills the entire white area of the slide.

11. Change the Up Arrow shape to the Left-Right Arrow shape (fifth shape in Block Arrows group). [*Hint:* Select the shape, click the Edit Shape button (Drawing Tools Format tab | Insert Shapes group), point to Change Shape, and then select the new shape.] Use the rotation and sizing handles to adjust the shape and then move it to the position shown in the figure.

12. On Slide 2 (Figure 9–82b), move the Texting shape in the SmartArt graphic on the left side of the slide up to the top level. Promote the Reading shape one level. Change the SmartArt style from Powder to Inset (second style in first 3-D row).

13. Change the layout of the SmartArt graphic on the right to Trapezoid List (second layout in eighth row of List area). Change the colors to 'Colorful Range - Accent Colors 3 to 4' (third color in Colorful area) and then choose the Cartoon style (third style in first 3-D row). Adjust the size of the SmartArt graphic to approximately 5" × 7" and then move it to the area shown in the figure.

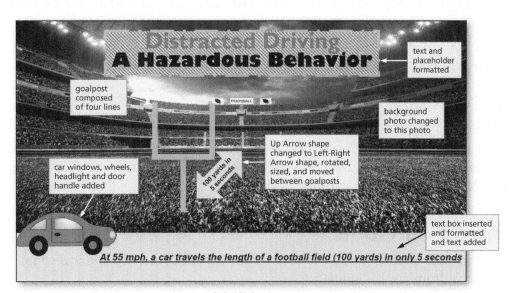

(a) Slide 1

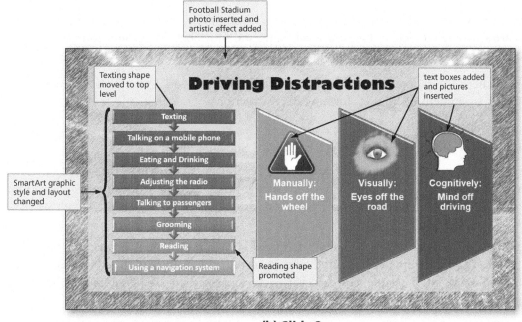

(b) Slide 2

Figure 9–82

Continued >

Extend Your Knowledge *continued*

14. Insert a text box above the text in the first shape of the SmartArt graphic on the right side of Slide 2. In the text box, insert the picture called Hand, which is located in the Data Files, and then adjust the size to 1.5" × 1.5". Insert a text box above the text in the middle shape of the SmartArt graphic, insert the picture called Eye, and then adjust the size to 1.5" × 1.5". Insert a text box above the text in the right shape, insert the picture called Brain, and then adjust the size of the text box to 1.3" × 1.3".

15. On Slide 2, insert a rectangle and then size it to 6.5" × 12". Apply the 'Green, Accent 6, Lighter 60%' shape fill (last color in third Theme Colors row), change the transparency to 20%, and then select no outline. Align the rectangle in the center and middle on the slide, and then send this shape to the back. Insert the Football Stadium picture and then apply the Line Drawing artistic effect to the picture (fifth effect in first row). Using the sizing handles, increase the size of the picture so that it fills the entire area of the slide, and then send this picture to the back.

16. If requested by your instructor, type your mother's maiden name in place of the text, Using a navigation system, in the text box on Slide 2 (Figure 9–82b).

17. Apply the Comb transition in the Exciting category to both slides and then change the duration to 4.00 seconds.

18. Run the presentation and then save the file using the file name, Extend 9–1 Distracted Driving.

19. Submit the revised document in the format specified by your instructor.

20. ✳ Was the pattern fill you applied to the title text placeholder on Slide 1 a good choice of designs? Why or why not? Does the slide content provide sufficient information to persuade people to avoid distracting activities while driving?

Expand Your World

Create a solution that uses cloud or web technologies by learning and investigating on your own from general guidance.

Reviewing Google Images SmartArt

Instructions: You want to add SmartArt to a presentation you have created to accompany a speech you are scheduled to deliver for your local skiing and snowboarding group. You need to add graphical interest to your slides, so you browse Google Images for SmartArt ideas.

Note: You will need Internet access to complete this assignment. If you do not have Internet access, read this assignment without performing the instructions.

Perform the following tasks:

1. Run PowerPoint and then open the file, Expand 9–1 Snowboarding.

2. Open your browser and navigate to Google.com. Click Images at the top of the screen to display the Google Images webpage. Click the Google Images search text box, type `smartart` as the search text, and then click the Search button (the magnifying glass) or press the ENTER key.

3. View several SmartArt images with designs that would be appropriate for the material on Slides 2 and 3. Select two different designs and then convert the bulleted lists in these slides to these designs in PowerPoint. If desired, you can change the SmartArt styles and colors and also arrange the slide elements.

4. If requested by your instructor, add a text box on Slide 1 with the name of your high school mascot.

5. Run the presentation and then save the file with the new file name, Expand 9–1 Snowboarding SmartArt.

6. Submit the revised presentation in the format specified by your instructor.

7. ✸ Which SmartArt images on the Google Images webpage did you use for your presentation? Why did you select these particular examples?

In the Labs

Design, create, modify, and/or use a presentation following the guidelines, concepts, and skills presented in this module. Labs 1 and 2, which increase in difficulty, require you to create solutions based on what you learned in the module; Lab 3 requires you to apply your creative thinking and problem-solving skills to design and implement a solution.

Lab 1: Converting WordArt and SmartArt, Formatting Text Boxes and Shapes, and Combining Shapes

Note: To complete this assignment, you will be required to use the Data Files. Please contact your instructor for information about accessing the Data Files.

Problem: The branch manager of your local bank has asked you to help prepare the slides to accompany her presentation regarding obtaining a car loan. She shows you two slides she has started to create and wants you to put the finishing touches on them. You create the presentation shown in Figure 9–83.

Perform the following tasks:

1. Run PowerPoint. Open the presentation, Lab 9–1 Car Loan, which is located in the Data Files.

2. On Slide 1 (Figure 9–83a), convert the WordArt to SmartArt using the 'Horizontal Bullet List' layout (second layout in third List row). Change the color of the SmartArt graphic to 'Colorful – Accent Colors' (first color in Colorful row) and then apply the Inset style (second style in first 3-D row). Size the SmartArt to approximately 5.8" × 13" and then move it to the location shown in the figure.

3. Insert the illustration, Bank, size it to approximately 1.8" × 2.19", and then move it to the lower area of the left shape. In the middle shape, demote the second bullet (Know your credit score). Insert the illustration, Calendar, size it to approximately 2" × 1.91", and then move it to the lower-right corner of the right shape.

4. Insert a text box in the blue sky area of Slide 1. Type, `Road to Car Loans` as the text box text. Change the text box outline weight to 3 pt, change the outline color to Dark Blue (ninth color in Standard Colors row), change the outline style to Long Dash (sixth style in Dashes gallery), apply the 'Offset Diagonal Top Right' shadow effect (first shadow in third Outer row), increase the font size to 60 point, apply the 'Pattern Fill - Olive Green, Accent 3, Narrow Horizontal, Inner Shadow' WordArt style, and then add the 'Olive Green, Accent 3, Lighter 80%' shape fill (seventh color in second Theme Colors row). Set this text box formatting as the default. Move the text box to the location shown in the figure.

5. On Slide 2 (Figure 9–83b), convert the SmartArt Graphic to text and then increase the font size of the three bulleted paragraphs to 32 point. Reduce the size of the bulleted list placeholder to include only the three bulleted paragraphs and then position the placeholder in the center of the slide.

Continued >

In the Labs *continued*

6. If requested by your instructor, add the name of your grade school or high school as a fourth bulleted paragraph.

7. Create the road shown in the figure by inserting the Curved Connector line and increasing its size to 6" × 6". Right-click the shape and then click Format Shape in the shortcut menu to display the Format Shape pane. Change the color to 'Black, Text 1' and then increase the width to 96 pt. Create the white dashed line by inserting another Curved Connector line and increasing its size to 6" × 6". Change the color to 'White, Background 1', increase the width to 6 pt, and then change the dash type to Dash (fourth dash in the Dash gallery). Close the Format Shape pane. Move the upper edges of the two Curved Connector shapes to the upper-left corner of the slide.

8. Create the car shown in Slide 2 by assembling the shapes on the slide. To begin, make a windshield by centering the yellow shape over the blue shape, selecting the blue shape, holding down the CTRL key and selecting the yellow shape, clicking the Merge Shapes button, and then clicking Subtract in the Merge Shapes list.

9. Make the front end of the car by moving the red headlights and license plate holder over the purple shape, selecting the purple shape, holding down the CTRL key and selecting the three red shapes, clicking the Merge Shapes button, and then clicking Subtract in the Merge Shapes list.

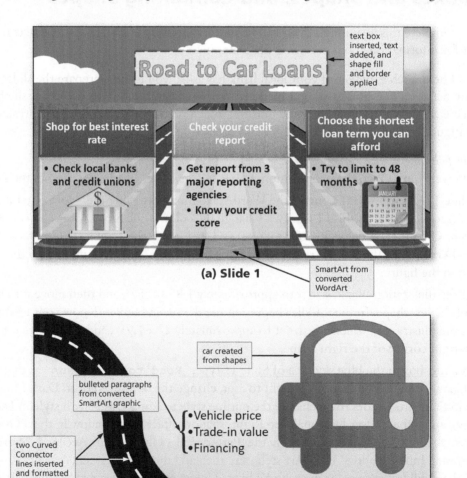

(a) Slide 1

(b) Slide 2

Figure 9–83

10. Move the two black tires up to the lower edge of the car's front end. Move the top of the car down to the upper edge of the car's front end. Select all the shapes, click the Merge Shapes button, and then click Union in the menu to merge all the shapes.

11. Apply a 'Blue, Accent 1' shape fill and the 'Linear Diagonal - Bottom Right to Top Left' gradient fill (last gradient in last Variations row). Size the car to approximately 5" × 5" and then move it to the upper-right corner of the slide.

12. Insert a text box in the lower-right corner. Type, **Negotiate the Loan** as the text box text and then move the text box next to the lower end of the road.

13. Apply the Doors transition in the Exciting category to both slides and then change the duration to 2.00 seconds.

14. Run the presentation and then save the file using the file name, Lab 9–1 Road to Car Loans.

15. Submit the document in the format specified by your instructor.

16. ✳ Is the Horizontal Bullet List a good choice for the SmartArt layout on Slide 1? Why or why not? Did changing the SmartArt graphic to text enhance Slide 2? Why? Did you encounter any difficulties using shapes to assemble the car?

Lab 2: Creating a Picture Background Using Shapes, Combining Shapes, Customizing and Resetting the Ribbon, and Creating a Handout by Exporting a File to Microsoft Word

Note: To complete this assignment, you will be required to use the Data Files. Please contact your instructor for information about accessing the Data Files.

Problem: The number of honey bees is declining. Some researchers think this trend is due to over-use of pesticides on crops and fungicides that contaminate the pollen bees collect for their hives. Tom Wilson is the owner of a local honey farm that has been in business since 1946. He wants community residents to help increase the honey bee population, so he is selling bees and all the equipment needed for a working hive. He recently created a flyer about his farm and asked you to develop a PowerPoint presentation to publicize his efforts. You create the slides shown in Figure 9–84.

Perform the following tasks:

1. Run PowerPoint and then open the presentation, Lab 9–2 Bees, which is located in the Data Files.

2. To begin creating the honeycomb background for Slide 1 (Figure 9–84a), insert a new blank slide. Insert a Hexagon shape (ninth shape in first Basics Shapes row) and resize the shape to 0.9" × 1.1". Change the shape fill color to Orange (third color in Standard Colors row) and then change the outline color to 'Black, Text 1' (second color in first Theme Colors row). Move the shape to the upper-left corner of the slide, as shown in Figure 9–84b.

3. With the hexagon shape still selected, press CTRL+D to duplicate this shape. Move the new shape below the original shape, leaving a small space between them. Press CTRL+D six more times so that you now have a column of eight shapes at the left edge of the slide.

4. Align the shapes horizontally in the column by selecting all eight shapes, clicking the Align arrow (Drawing Tools Format tab | Arrange group), and then clicking Distribute Horizontally in the menu. Align the shapes vertically in the column by clicking the Align arrow again and then clicking Distribute Vertically in the menu.

Continued >

5. With the eight hexagon shapes still selected, press CTRL+D to duplicate the column and then drag this new column upward and to the right, positioning it as shown in Figure 9–84b. Duplicate this second column of shapes and then it them downward and to the right so that the first shape is at the same height as the first shape in the first column. Repeat these steps until you have 14 columns of shapes. Use the arrow keys to adjust some of the shapes so they are not in perfect alignment.

6. Press CTRL+A to select all the shapes and then group them. Apply the 'Gradient Fill - Gold, Accent 4, No Outline' Shape Quick Style (fifth style in last Presets row) to the grouped shapes. Save the group as a picture with the file name, Honeycomb, using the PNG Portable Network Graphics Format file type. Delete this slide.

7. On Slide 1 (Figure 9–84a), create a background on the slide by inserting the Honeycomb picture you just created. Change the transparency to 50%.

8. To format the text box (Family owned and operated since 1946), select the box, click the Shape Fill arrow, display the Gradient gallery, and then click the Linear Down variation (second variation in first row).

9. To begin creating the beehive on Slide 2 (Figure 9–84c), insert an Oval shape (second shape in first Basic Shapes row), change the shape fill to 'Gold, Accent 4, Lighter 40%' (eighth color in fourth Theme Colors row), change the outline color to 'Gold, Accent 4, Darker 50%' (eighth color in last Theme Colors row), change the outline weight to 1½ pt. Type `We` in the shape and then change the font size to 20 point. Set this shape as the default shape.

10. Insert five Oval shapes under the shape you created. Adjust the size of the first shape to 0.55" × 1", the second shape to 0.8" × 2", the third shape to 0.86" × 2.7", the fourth shape to 1.16" × 3.7", the fifth shape to 1.5" × 4.5", and the sixth shape to 1.5" × 5.8". Type the text shown in the Figure 9–94c in each of the shapes. In the first two shapes, leave the font size at 20 point. In the rest of the shapes, decrease the font size to 16 point. Overlap the shapes and use the SmartGuides to center them under each other.

11. Insert an Oval shape, adjust the size to 0.5" × 0.5", change the shape fill color to 'Black Text 1, no outline', and then move the shape to the bottom-center of the last beehive shape to create the opening for the bees. Select the entire beehive, group the shapes, and then move it to the lower-left area of the slide. Move the bee illustration from the upper-left corner of the slide to the right of the hive opening. If necessary, bring the bee illustration to the front by clicking the Bring Forward button (Picture Tools Format tab | Arrange Group).

12. If requested by your instructor, substitute your mother's name for the word, bees, in the bottom beehive shape on Slide 2.

13. Apply the Honeycomb transition in the Exciting category to both slides and then change the duration to 5.00 seconds.

14. Customize the ribbon by adding the Create Handouts in Microsoft Word button to the Editing group on the Home tab. Click this new button to create a handout in Microsoft Word using the 'Blank lines below slides' page layout, as shown in Figure 9–84d, e. Save the document using the file name, Lab 9–2 Wilson's Honey Farm Word Handout. Close the Word file and then exit Word. Reset the ribbon.

15. Run the presentation and then save the file using the file name, Lab 9–2 Wilson's Honey Farm.

16. Save the presentation as a picture presentation using the file name, Lab 9–2 Wilson's Honey Farm Picture Presentation.

17. Submit the document in the format specified by your instructor.

18. ✸ Did creating a background using shapes on Slide 1 improve the look of the slide? Was saving the formatting as the default for shapes helpful? Why?

Honeycomb picture inserted as slide background

variation added to text box

(a) Slide 1

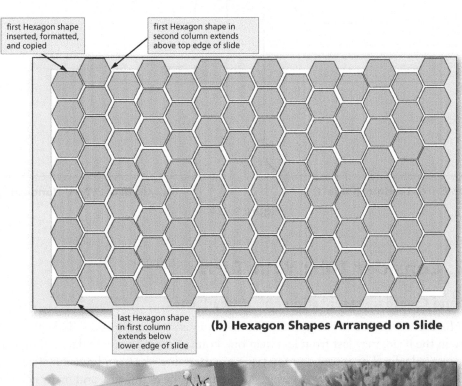

first Hexagon shape inserted, formatted, and copied

first Hexagon shape in second column extends above top edge of slide

last Hexagon shape in first column extends below lower edge of slide

(b) Hexagon Shapes Arranged on Slide

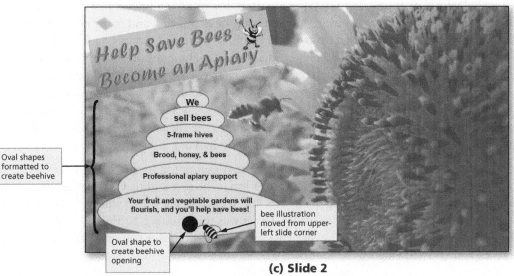

Oval shapes formatted to create beehive

bee illustration moved from upper-left slide corner

Oval shape to create beehive opening

(c) Slide 2

Figure 9–84 (Continued)

Continued >

In the Labs *continued*

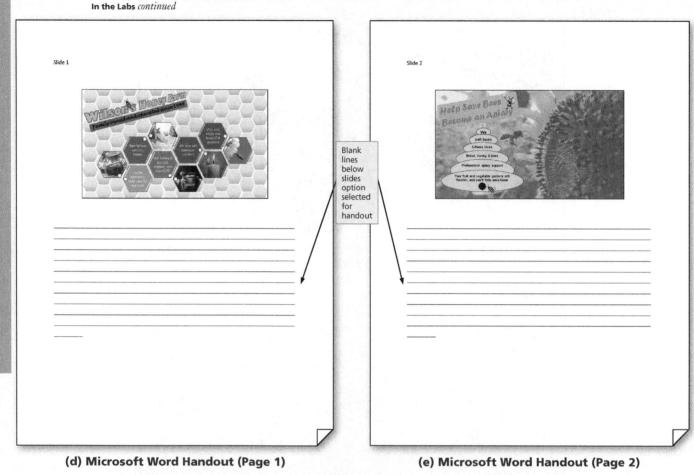

(d) Microsoft Word Handout (Page 1)   **(e) Microsoft Word Handout (Page 2)**

Figure 9–84

Lab 3: Consider This: Your Turn

Design and Create a Presentation about Headaches

Part 1:   Headaches are one of the more common nervous system disorders. This pain may occur anywhere in the head, may last from less than one hour to more than one day, and may develop suddenly or gradually. The most common types are migraine, sinus, and tension. They can result from lack of sleep, stress, allergies, exposure to chemicals, head injuries, and many other triggers. Headaches possibly could be prevented by avoiding some foods and beverages, such as caffeine, bananas, nuts, onions, and citrus fruits. Use the concepts and techniques presented in this module to create a presentation with this information and other facts you obtain from online sources. Use at least three objectives found at the beginning of this module to develop the slides, and include shapes, a formatted text box, and SmartArt. Print handouts and speaker notes for the presentation. Review and revise your presentation as needed and then save the file using the file name, Lab 9–3 Headaches. Submit your assignment in the format specified by your instructor.

Part 2:   ✳ You made several decisions while creating the presentation in this assignment: where to insert text boxes and shapes, what fills to use, how to format the text and text box backgrounds (such as font, font size, and colors), which image(s) to use, and which SmartArt graphic(s) to use to make the presentation look professional and consistent. What was the rationale behind each of these decisions? When you reviewed the document, what further revisions did you make and why? Where would you recommend showing this slide show?

10 | Developing a Presentation with Content from Outside Sources

Objectives

You will have mastered the material in this module when you can:

- Insert an object from a file
- Embed and edit a file
- Draw and format a table
- Resize, split, distribute, and arrange table columns and rows
- Insert and edit a linked Excel worksheet
- Switch chart rows and columns

- Change a chart type
- Apply a chart style
- Apply effects to chart elements
- Display chart elements
- Edit chart data
- Add a hyperlink to a table

Introduction

Adding visuals to a presentation could help audience members remember the important facts you want to share. Researchers have found that adding such graphics as tables, charts, graphs, and maps increases retention by more than 50 percent. Audiences also believe that speakers who include visuals in their presentations are more qualified and believable than speakers who do not have accompanying visuals. In addition, studies have shown that meeting times are reduced and decisions are reached more quickly when group members have seen visuals that help them reach a consensus.

PowerPoint has many features that allow you to insert visuals and then modify them directly on the slide. For example, you can embed a Microsoft Word document and then edit its text or replace its graphics. You can link an Excel worksheet with a PowerPoint slide so that when numbers are modified in the slide, the corresponding numbers on the worksheet also are updated. These tools help you work productively and generate slides with graphics that help your audience comprehend and remember your message.

Project — Presentation with Embedded and Linked Files and Formatted Table and Chart

The typical American family spends nearly $2,000 yearly on utility bills. Much of that expense can be reduced by making small changes in the household, such as buying energy efficient appliances, using CFL or LED light bulbs, and installing a programmable thermostat to keep the house a few degrees warmer in the summer and a few degrees cooler in the winter. These and many more energy-efficient improvements can help save natural resources and give long-term financial rewards.

The presentation you create in this module (Figure 10–1) would be useful to show during a workshop at your local home improvement store. You begin Slide 1 (Figure 10–1a) by inserting a flyer with graphics and text (Figure 10–1b). You then decide to emphasize that the workshop focuses on whole-house energy efficiency planning, so you edit the title text by adding the words, at Home, directly onto the slide.

The second slide (Figure 10–1c) includes a chart that you draw and enhance using PowerPoint's tools and graphical features. If you click a cell in the chart when running the presentation, a hyperlinked Adobe PDF file displays with easy, practical advice audience members can use throughout their home, especially pertaining to lighting, heating and cooling, and appliances (Figure 10–1d).

You insert the table on Slide 3 (Figure 10–1e) from a Microsoft Excel worksheet (Figure 10–1f) that contains computations of using incandescent, halogen, CFL, and LED bulbs for one or more hours a day. You will update this table by editing the number of bulbs and the number of hours each day they are turned on. These figures also will update the original Excel worksheet.

Several homeowners in your town took measures during the past winter to reduce their electric consumption, including installing programmable thermostats, adjusting the temperature, and cleaning their furnaces and air ducts. They provided you their electric bills from the summers prior to and after their improvements, and you used this data to average the kilowatts used and then develop the chart that is displayed on Slide 4 (Figure 10–1g) and created in Microsoft Excel (Figure 10–1h). You then obtain the electric bills from a few more community residents who made the heating and cooling enhancements, so you update the worksheet data that generated the chart, which, in turn, modifies the chart automatically.

BTW
Checking for Accessibility Issues
As you develop tables and other slide elements, you may want to check the presentation for content that people with disabilities may be unable to read. To identify possible accessibility problems, display the Info tab in the Backstage view and notice if the message, Content that people with disabilities are unable to read, is displayed next to the 'Check for Issues' button. If so, click the 'Check for Issues' button and then click Check Accessibility in the menu. The Accessibility Checker task pane will display issues that you can address.

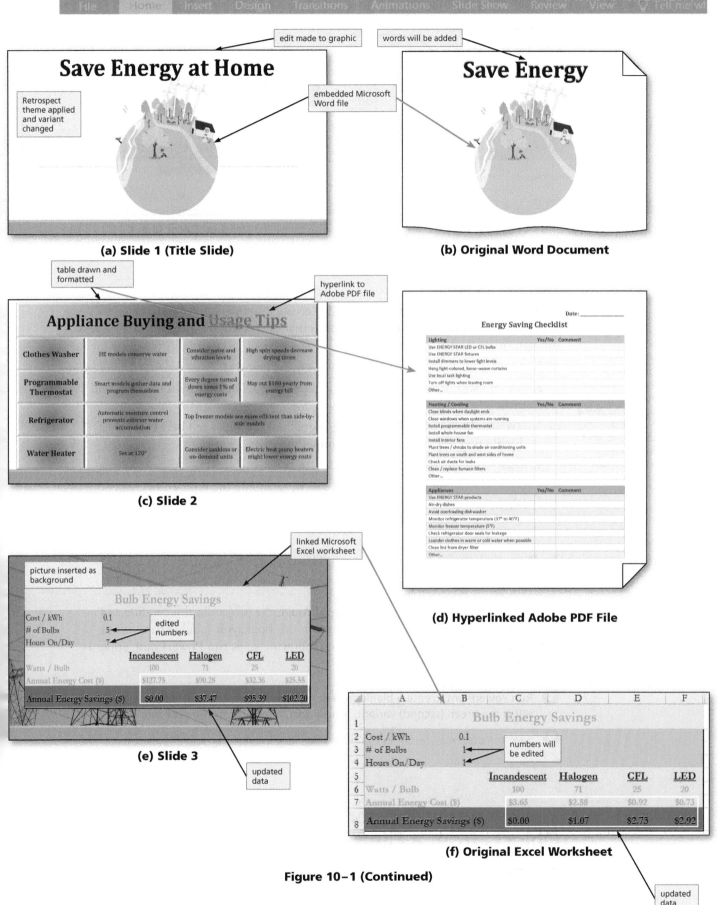

Microsoft PowerPoint 2016

(a) Slide 1 (Title Slide)

(b) Original Word Document

(c) Slide 2

(d) Hyperlinked Adobe PDF File

(e) Slide 3

(f) Original Excel Worksheet

Figure 10–1 (Continued)

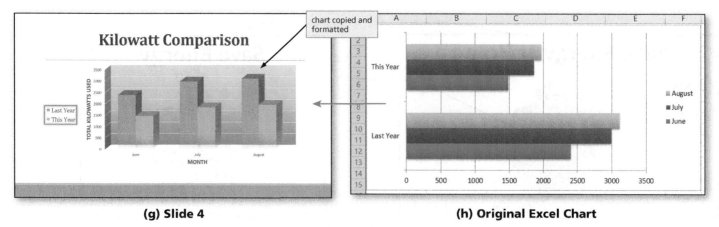

(g) Slide 4

(h) Original Excel Chart

Figure 10–1

In this module, you will learn how to create the slides shown in Figure 10–1. The following roadmap identifies general activities you will perform as you progress through this module:

1. INSERT AND EDIT a Microsoft WORD FILE by adding text.
2. CREATE TABLE ROWS AND COLUMNS and then erase lines and split columns and rows.
3. FORMAT a TABLE by adding shading, a gradient fill, and a cell bevel, and then distributing rows and resizing columns and rows.
4. INSERT AND EDIT a LINKED Excel WORKSHEET.
5. COPY, FORMAT and EDIT an Excel CHART by changing the type, colors, legend, labels, background, and data.

To Run PowerPoint, Choose a Theme and Variant, and Save a File

If you are using a computer to step through the project in this module and you want your screens to match the figures in this book, you should change your computer's resolution to 1366 × 768. The following steps run PowerPoint, apply a theme and variant, and then save a file.

1 Run PowerPoint, create a blank presentation, apply the Retrospect theme, and then select the green (second) variant. If necessary, maximize the PowerPoint window.

2 Save the presentation using the file name, Save Energy.

Inserting Graphics or Other Objects from a File

PowerPoint allows you to insert many types of objects into a presentation. You can insert clips, pictures, video and audio files, and symbols, and you also can copy and paste or drag and drop objects from one slide to another. At times you may want to insert content created with other Microsoft Office programs, such as a Word flyer, an Excel table or graph, a Paint graphic, or a document created with another Microsoft Windows-based application. The original document is called the **source**, and the new document that contains this object is called the **destination**. When you want to copy a source document object, such as a Word flyer, to a destination document, such as your PowerPoint slide, you can use one of three techniques.

- **Embedding** — An **embedded object** becomes part of the destination slide, but you edit and modify the contents using the source program's commands and features. In this project, for example, you will embed a Word document and then edit the text using Microsoft Word without leaving PowerPoint.

- **Linking** — Similar to an embedded object, a **linked object** also is created in another application and is stored in the **source file**, the original file in which the object was created. The linked object maintains a connection to its source and does not become part of the destination slide. Instead, a connection, or link, made between the source and destination objects gives the appearance that the objects are independent. In reality, the two objects work together so that when one is edited, the other is updated. If the original object is changed, the linked object on the slide also changes. In this project, for example, you will link a Microsoft Excel table and then edit the data using Excel. As the numbers in the table change, the numbers in the linked table on the PowerPoint slide also are updated to reflect those changes.

- **Copying and pasting** — An object that you copy from a source document and then paste in a destination document becomes part of the destination program. Any edits that you make are done using the destination software. When you paste the object, you have the options of embedding or linking the document. For example, if you copy a picture from a Word document, embed it into your slide, and then recolor or remove the background, those changes are made using PowerPoint's commands and do not affect the source object. In contrast, in this project you will copy an Excel chart and then paste it into a slide by linking the two documents. When you modify the object without leaving PowerPoint, any changes you make to the data in PowerPoint will be reflected in the original Excel source document.

The first two techniques described above are termed **object linking and embedding (OLE,** pronounced o-lay). This means of sharing material developed in various sources and then updating the files within a destination program is useful when you deliver presentations frequently that display current data that changes constantly. For example, your PowerPoint presentation may contain a chart reflecting current fitness center enrollment statistics, or you may include a table with the fitness center's membership totals for the previous year.

BTW

Importing Text Files
In this project you import a Microsoft Word file, but you also can import a text (.txt) file, which has alphanumeric characters with little or no visual formatting. To import a text file, perform the same steps you use to insert the Energy Flyer, but locate a file with the .txt file extension instead of the .docx file extension.

BTW

Touch Screen Differences
The Office and Windows interfaces may vary if you are using a touch screen. For this reason, you might notice that the function or appearance of your touch screen differs slightly from this module's presentation.

To Insert a File with Graphics and Text

1 INSERT & EDIT WORD FILE | **2 CREATE TABLE ROWS & COLUMNS** | **3 FORMAT TABLE**
4 INSERT & EDIT LINKED WORKSHEET | **5 COPY, FORMAT, & EDIT CHART**

The first object you will add to your presentation is a graphical flyer created in Microsoft Word. This flyer contains artwork and text developed as part of an advertising campaign for a previous energy-reduction workshop at the home improvement store. You desire to use this document in your slide show. *Why? The earth image and text fit well with the topic of your presentation.* The following steps insert a Microsoft Word file with a graphic and text.

1

- Delete both the title and subtitle placeholders.
- Display the Insert tab and then click the Object button (Insert tab | Text group) to display the Insert Object dialog box (Figure 10–2).

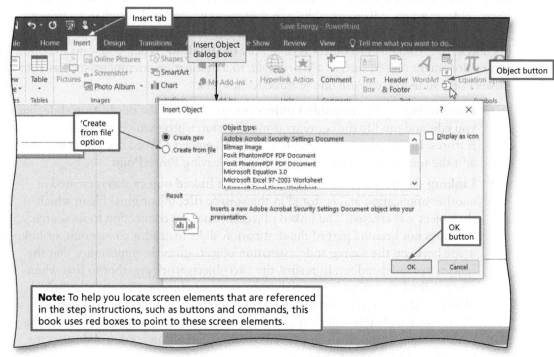

Figure 10–2

2

- Click 'Create from file' (Insert Object dialog box) to display the File box.
- Click the Browse button and then navigate to the location where your Data Files are stored.
- If necessary, scroll down, and then click Energy Flyer to select the Microsoft Word file (Figure 10–3).

Q&A What is the difference between the Create new and the 'Create from file' options?

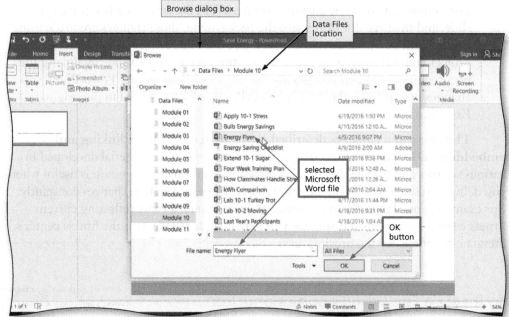

Figure 10–3

The Create new option opens an application and allows you to develop an original object. In contrast, the 'Create from file' option prompts you to locate a file that already is created and saved so you can modify the object using the program that was used to create it.

3

- Click the OK button (Browse dialog box) to insert the file name into the File box (Insert Object dialog box) (Figure 10–4).

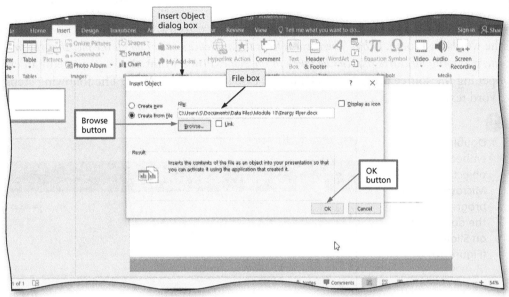

Figure 10–4

4

- Click the OK button (Insert Object dialog box) to display the Energy Flyer contents on Slide 1 (Figure 10–5).

Q&A Why did several seconds pass before this flyer was displayed on the slide?

PowerPoint takes more time to insert embedded and linked inserted objects than it takes to perform an ordinary cut-and-paste or copy-and-paste action. You must be patient while PowerPoint is inserting the object.

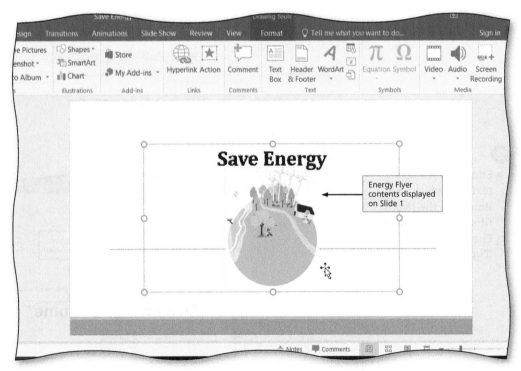

Figure 10–5

To Edit an Embedded File

The flyer provides an excellent graphic and text to use on Slide 1, but you want to edit the text by adding the words, at Home. *Why? These words focus the audience's attention on the fact that the presentation emphasizes energy-saving measures that can be taken in the home.* PowerPoint allows you to edit an embedded file easily by opening the source program, which in this case is Microsoft Word. The following steps edit the Microsoft Word text.

- Double-click the embedded earth object to run the Microsoft Word program and open the document on Slide 1 (Figure 10–6).

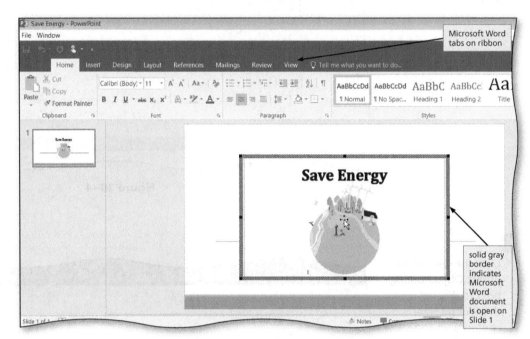

Figure 10–6

- Edit the document text by adding **at Home** to the flyer title to make it Save Energy at Home (Figure 10–7).

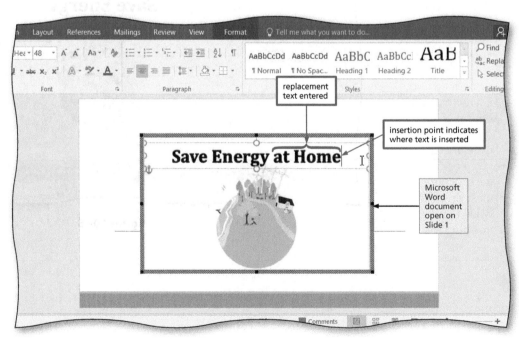

Figure 10–7

• Click outside the Word document to close Microsoft Word and display the edited flyer object on Slide 1.

• Display the Drawing Tools Format tab, size the object so that it is approximately 7" x 12", and then position the object as shown in Figure 10–8.

Q&A Does PowerPoint take more time to position embedded objects than copied objects?
Yes, you must be patient while PowerPoint responds to your touch, mouse, or arrow key movements.

How can I center the object precisely as shown in Figure 10–8?
Use the Align commands available when you click the Align Objects button (Drawing Tools Format tab | Arrange group). You then can use the ARROW keys to move the object in small increments.

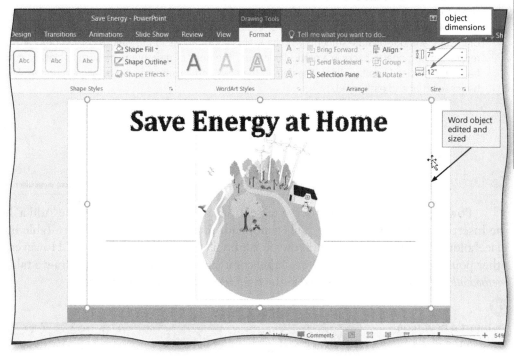

Figure 10–8

Other Ways

1. Right-click Word object, click Document Object on shortcut menu, click Edit

Drawing and Adjusting a Table

Tables are useful graphical elements to present data organized in descriptive rows and columns. Each cell created from the intersection of a row and column has a unique location name and contains numeric or textual data that you can edit.

In the following pages, you will perform these tasks on Slide 2:

1. Draw a table.
2. Create table rows.
3. Draw table columns.
4. Erase a table line and enter text in a table.
5. Split a table column and row.
6. Add shading to a table.
7. Add a gradient fill to a table.
8. Add a cell bevel.
9. Distribute table rows.
10. Resize table columns and rows and align data in cells.
11. Center the table and format table data.

BTW
Drawing a Table Using a Tablet
In this project, you will create a table using PowerPoint's pencil pointer. This tool allows you to use a mouse and draw rows and columns. On a touch screen, however, the pencil pointer is not available. You may, therefore, use a mouse, stylus, or other pointing device to draw a table. Or, you can create a table by tapping the 'Add a Table' button (Insert tab | Tables group) and then specifying the desired number of rows and columns.

Develop tables that are clear and meaningful.
Use a table to present complex material, but be certain the information makes useful comparisons. Tables generally are used to show relationships between sets of data. For example, they may show prices for grades of gasoline in three states, the number of in-state and out-of-state students who have applied for admission to various college programs, or the rushing and passing records among quarterbacks in a particular league. The units of measurement, such as dollars, specific majors, or yards, should be expressed clearly on the slides. The data in the rows and columns should be aligned uniformly. Also, the table labels should be meaningful and easily read.

To Draw a Table

1 INSERT & EDIT WORD FILE | **2 CREATE TABLE ROWS & COLUMNS** | **3 FORMAT TABLE**
4 INSERT & EDIT LINKED WORKSHEET | **5 COPY, FORMAT, & EDIT CHART**

PowerPoint allows you to insert a table in several ways. You can click the 'Add a Table' button on the Insert tab and click the Insert Table command. You also can click the Insert Table button in a content placeholder. Another method that allows flexibility is to draw the entire table. However, you must use a mouse or other pointing device to use the Draw Table command. The following steps draw a table on Slide 2. *Why? This method allows flexibility to draw the outer edges and then add the columns and rows.*

1

- Insert a new slide with the Blank layout. Display the View tab and then, if necessary, click the Ruler check box (View tab | Show group) to display the horizontal and vertical rulers.

- Display the Insert tab and then click the 'Add a Table' button (Insert tab | Tables group) to display the Insert Table gallery (Figure 10–9).

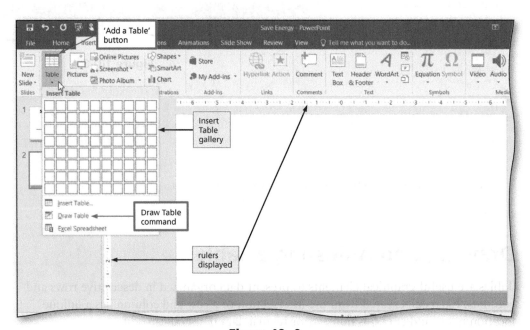

Figure 10–9

- Click Draw Table and then position the pointer, which has the shape of a pencil, in the upper-left area of the slide.

Q&A If I decide I do not want to draw a table, how can I change the pointer to the block arrow?
Press the ESC key.

- Drag the pencil pointer to the lower-right corner of the slide to draw the outer edges of the table (Figure 10–10).

- Release the mouse button to create the table frame.

Q&A Must my table be the same size or be positioned in the same location shown in the figure?
No. You will resize and reposition the table later in this project.

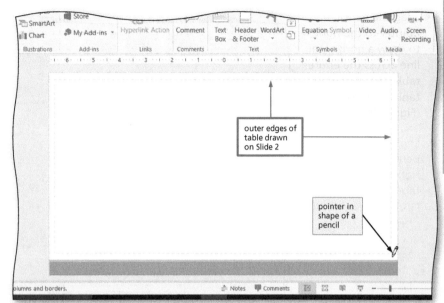

Figure 10–10

To Draw Table Rows

1 INSERT & EDIT WORD FILE | **2 CREATE TABLE ROWS & COLUMNS** | **3 FORMAT TABLE**
4 INSERT & EDIT LINKED WORKSHEET | **5 COPY, FORMAT, & EDIT CHART**

Once you draw the four sides of the table, you then can use the pointer as a pencil to draw lines for the columns and rows in the positions where you desire them to display. You could, therefore, draw columns having different widths and rows that are spaced in irregular heights. The following steps draw three lines to create four table rows. **Why?** *The first row will contain the table title, and the remaining rows will list specific appliances: clothes washer, refrigerator, and water heater.* You must use a mouse or other pointing device to draw table rows.

1

- With the Table Tools Design tab displaying, click the Draw Table button (Table Tools Design tab | Draw Borders group) to change the pointer to a pencil and then position the pencil pointer inside the table approximately 1" from the top table edge and 1" from the left table edge (Figure 10–11).

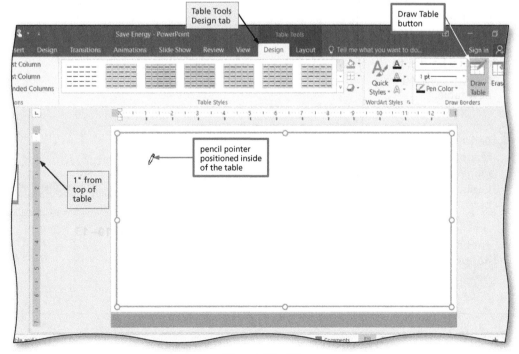

Figure 10–11

- Drag the pencil pointer to the right to draw a horizontal line across the entire table and divide the table into two cells (Figure 10–12).

Q&A

Should I drag the pencil pointer to the right edge of the table?

No. PowerPoint will draw a complete line when you begin to move the pencil pointer in one direction.

If I drew the line in an incorrect location, how can I erase it?

Press CTRL+Z, click the Undo button on the Quick Access Toolbar, or click the Table Eraser button (Table Tools Design tab | Draw Borders group) and then click the line.

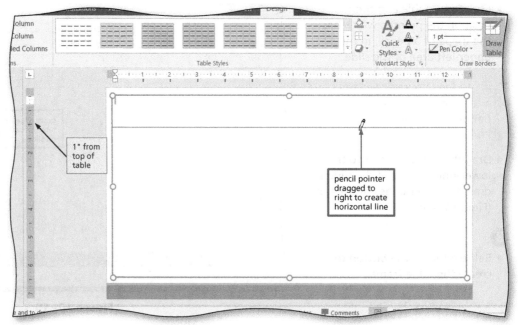

Figure 10–12

- Draw two additional horizontal lines, as shown in Figure 10–13. When you start drawing the lines, place your pencil pointer at a location away from the table border, not at a border, to prevent creating a new table.

Q&A

How can I get my pencil pointer to reappear if it no longer is displaying?

Click the Draw Table button again.

Do I need to align the lines in the precise positions shown?

No. You will create evenly spaced rows later in this project.

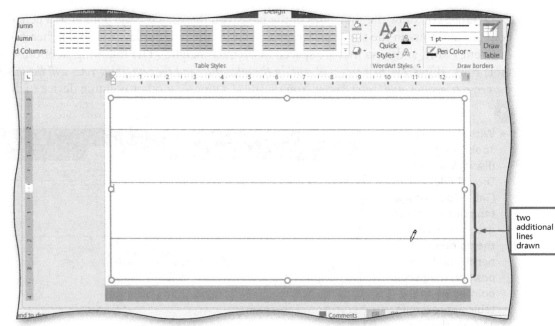

Figure 10–13

BTW

Displaying Gridlines

Gridlines can help you align charts, shapes, and other objects on slides. To show the gridlines, display the View tab and then select the Gridlines check box (View tab | Show group).

To Draw Table Columns

The pencil pointer is useful to draw table columns with varying widths. Each appliance row has either two or three usage tips. The clothes washer row will be subdivided. *Why? You have three important facts consumers should consider when they are purchasing a clothes washer, so you need to add a cell third in that row.* The following steps draw four vertical lines to create columns. You must use a mouse or other pointing device to draw table columns.

- Position the pencil pointer inside the table approximately 2.5" from the left table edge (Figure 10–14).

Q&A Can I change the line color?
Yes. Click the Pen Color button (Table Tools Design tab | Draw Borders group) and then select a different color.

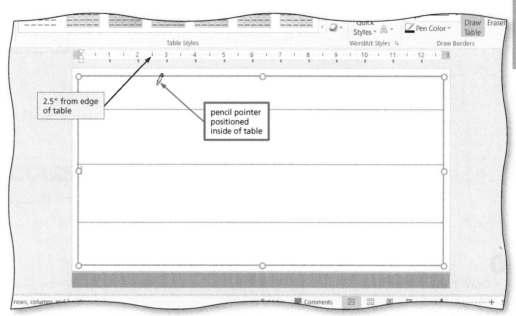

Figure 10–14

- Drag the pencil pointer down through all the horizontal lines to draw a vertical line that divides the table into eight cells.

- Position the pencil pointer inside the second cell in the second row approximately 6" from the left table edge (Figure 10–15).

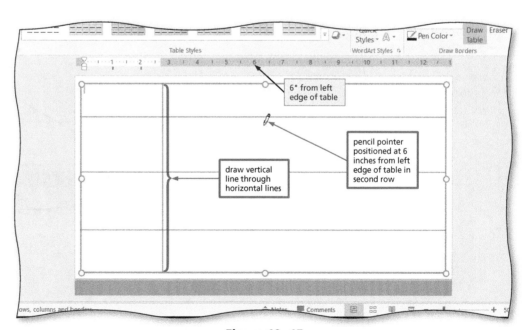

Figure 10–15

- Drag the pencil pointer down slightly to draw a vertical line in only that cell (Figure 10–16).

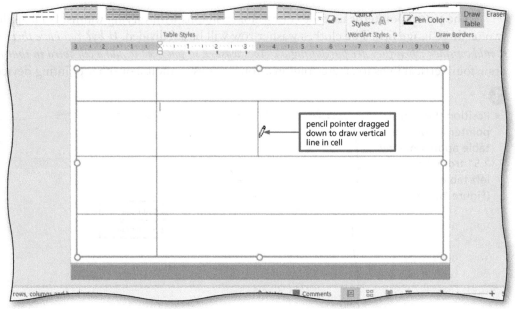

Figure 10–16

- Draw two additional vertical lines, as shown in Figure 10–17.

Q&A Are vertical and horizontal lines the only types of lines I can draw?
No. You also can draw a diagonal line from one corner of a cell to another corner.

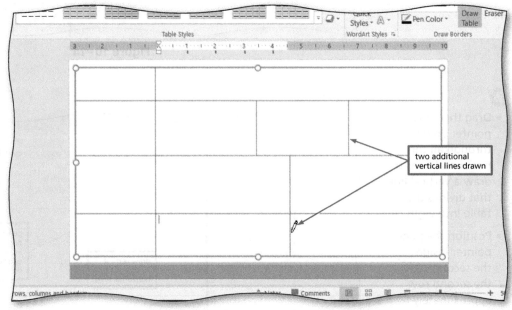

Figure 10–17

Developing a Presentation with Content from Outside Sources **PowerPoint Module 10** **PPT** 543

1 INSERT & EDIT WORD FILE | 2 CREATE TABLE ROWS & COLUMNS | 3 FORMAT TABLE
4 INSERT & EDIT LINKED WORKSHEET | 5 COPY, FORMAT, & EDIT CHART

PowerPoint Module 10

To Erase a Table Line

PowerPoint supplies an eraser tool that allows you to delete vertical and horizontal lines in a table. This eraser is useful to delete unnecessary column lines. You must use a mouse or other pointing device to use the eraser tool. The following steps use the eraser to delete one vertical line in a row. *Why? You decide to include only the title text in the first row.*

1
- Click the Table Eraser button (Table Tools Design tab | Draw Borders group).
- Position the pointer, which has the shape of an eraser, over the vertical line in the first row (Figure 10–18).

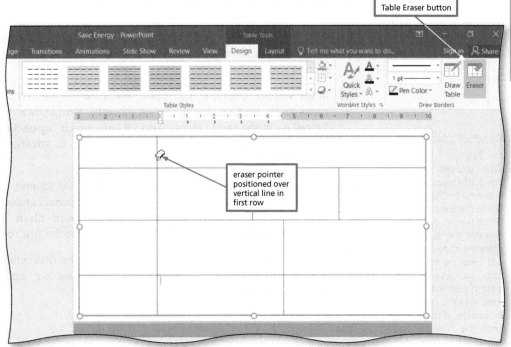

Figure 10–18

2
- Click the vertical line to erase it (Figure 10–19).
- Press the ESC key and then click inside the cell to change the pointer to the I-beam and display the insertion point.

3
- Display the View tab and then click the Ruler check box (View tab | Show group) to hide the horizontal and vertical rulers.

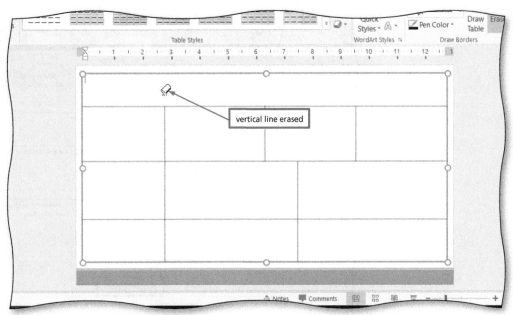

Figure 10–19

BTW
Navigating the Table
In this project, you advance the insertion point to the next cell by pressing the TAB key. To move to the previous cell, press the SHIFT+TAB keys. Press the DOWN ARROW key to move to the next row, and press the UP ARROW key to move up one row.

BTW
Symbol Character Codes
When you select a symbol to insert, its character code is displayed in Character code box in the lower-right corner of the Symbol dialog box. For example, the degree symbol's character code is 002F. If you know the character code, you can enter that code in your slide and then press ALT+X to convert it to a character. If you want to know the character code for a symbol you already inserted in your document, place the insertion point directly after the character and then press ALT+X.

To Enter Text in a Table

Four major appliances will be featured in your table: clothes washer, programmable thermostat, refrigerator, and water heater. The table you created will list these appliances on the left side of each row and give specific buying and usage tips on the right side. The first row will display the table title. To place data in a cell, you click the cell and then type text. The following steps enter text in the cells of the empty table.

1 With the pointer in the first row, type `Appliance Buying and Usage Tips` in the cell. Press the TAB key to advance the insertion point to the first cell in the second row.

2 In the second row, type `Clothes Washer` in the first column, `HE models conserve water` in the second column, `Consider noise and vibration levels` in the third column, and `High spin speeds decrease drying times` in the fourth column. Press the TAB key to advance the insertion point to the first column of the third row.

3 In the third row, type `Refrigerator` in the first column, `Automatic moisture control prevents exterior water accumulation` in the second column and `Top freezer models are more efficient than side-by-side models` in the third column. Advance the insertion point to the first column of the fourth row.

4 In the fourth row, type `Water Heater` in the first column, `Set at 120°` in the second column, and `Consider tankless or on-demand units` in the third column (Figure 10–20).

Q&A How do I insert the degree symbol after 120 in the second cell of the Water Heater row?
Position the insertion point after 120. Click the Symbol button (Insert tab | Symbols group) to display the Symbol dialog box. Scroll down, generally to the sixth or seventh row, to locate the symbol in the gallery and then click the Insert button (Symbol dialog box) to place the degree symbol to the left of the insertion point. Click the Close button to close the Symbol dialog box after inserting the symbol.

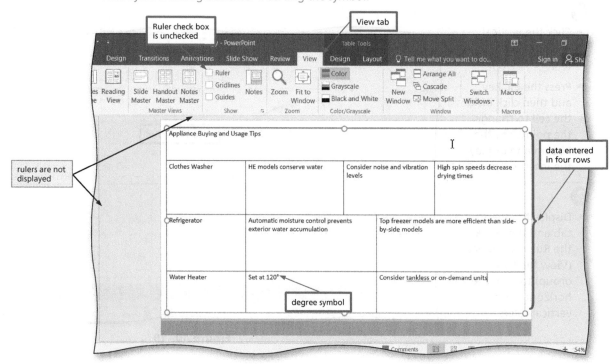

Figure 10–20

To Split a Table Column and Row

You easily can create additional table columns and rows by dividing current cells and rows. The following steps split a column and a row. *Why? You want to add information about electric heat pump heaters in the Water Heater row. In addition, the appliances shown in the first column are listed in alphabetical order, and you want to add another appliance, Programmable Thermostat.* To keep the alphabetical order, this new appliance should be inserted between the Clothes Washer and the Refrigerator rows.

1

- With the insertion point in the Consider tankless or on-demand units cell, click the Table Tools Layout tab to display the Table Tools Layout ribbon and then click the Split Cells button (Table Tools Layout tab | Merge group) to display the Split Cells dialog box (Figure 10–21).

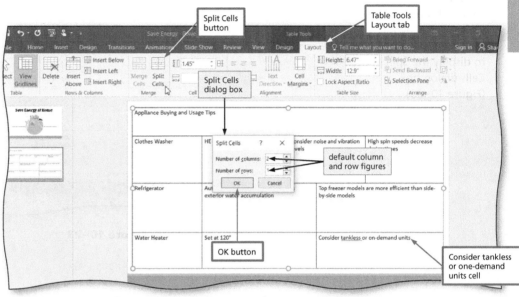

Figure 10–21

 Are the default numbers in the dialog box always 2 columns and 1 row?
Yes, but you can increase the numbers if you need to divide the cell into more than two halves or need to create two or more rows within one cell.

2

- Click the OK button (Split Cells dialog box) to create a fourth cell in the Water Heater row.

- Position the insertion point in the Clothes Washer cell.

- Click the Select Table button (Table Tools Layout tab | Table group) to display the Select Table menu (Figure 10–22).

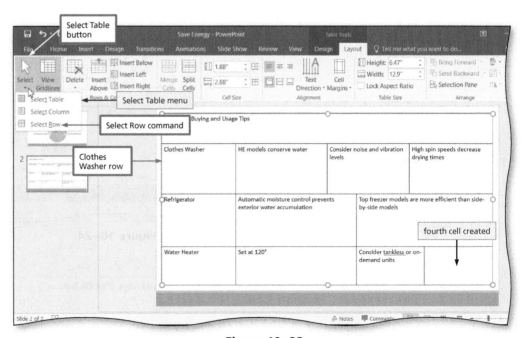

Figure 10–22

- Click Select Row in the Select Table menu to select the Clothes Washer row.
- With the Table Tools Layout tab displaying, click the Split Cells button (Table Tools Layout tab | Merge group) to display the Split Cells dialog box (Figure 10–23).

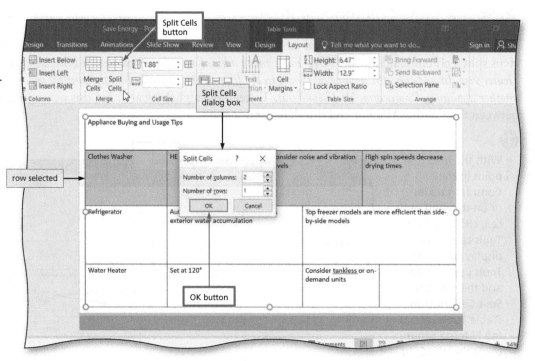

Figure 10–23

- Decrease the number of columns from 2 to 1.
- Increase the number of rows from 1 to 2 (Figure 10–24).

Q&A How many rows and columns can I create by splitting the cells? The maximum number varies depending upon the width and height of the selected cell.

- Click the OK button (Split Cells dialog box) to create a row below the Clothes Washer row.

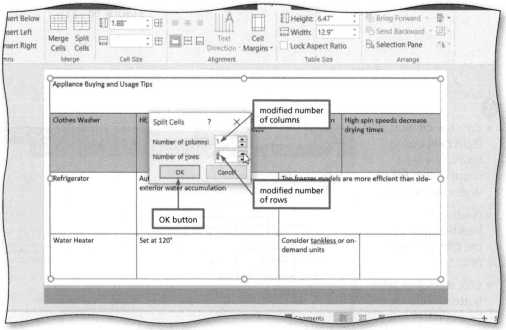

Figure 10–24

Other Ways

1. Right-click table, click Split Cells on shortcut menu, enter number of columns and rows, click OK button

To Enter Additional Text in a Table

With the additional row and column added to the table, you now can add the programmable thermostat information in the inserted row and also add electric heat pump heater information in the new cell in the Water Heater row. The following steps enter text in the new cells.

1 Position the pointer in the first cell of the new row and then type `Programmable Thermostat` in the cell. Advance the insertion point to the adjacent right column cell and then type `Smart models gather data and program themselves` in the second cell, `Every degree turned down saves 3% of energy costs` in the third cell, and `May cut $180 yearly from energy bill` in the last cell in this row.

2 Position the pointer in the new cell in the Water Heater row and then type `Electric heat pump heaters might lower energy costs` in the cell.

3 Drag the edges of the cells so the cell widths are similar to those in Figure 10–25. Use the Smart Guides to help align the cells vertically.

- If requested by your instructor, change the figure, 180, in the Programmable Thermostat row to the year your mother was born.

BTW
Customizing Table Formatting
PowerPoint applies a style to a table automatically based on the theme. To change this format, you can select a style in the Table Styles gallery, which presents several options to give a professional and colorful design and format. You, however, may desire to customize the layout by adding or modifying borders, the background color, or the font. To clear a style from a table, display the Table Tools Design tab, click the More button in the Table Styles group, and then click Clear Table.

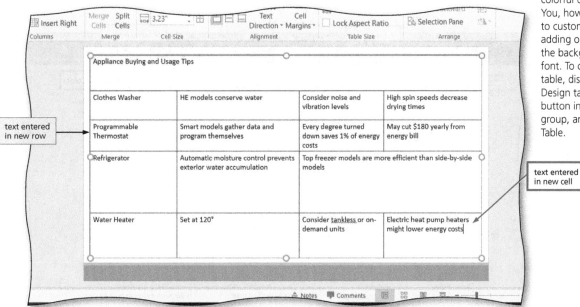

Figure 10–25

CONSIDER THIS

Use appropriate colors when formatting graphics you want people to remember.
Studies have shown that men and women differ slightly in their recall of graphics formatted with various colors. Men remembered objects colored with shades of violet, dark blue, olive green, and yellow. Women recalled objects they had seen with dark blue, olive green, yellow, and red hues.

To Add Shading to a Table

You can format the table in several ways, including adding shading to color the background. The following steps add shading to the table. *Why? Shading makes the table more visually appealing and helps distinguish each cell.*

- Click the Select Table button (Table Tools Layout tab | Table group) to display the Select Table menu (Figure 10–26).

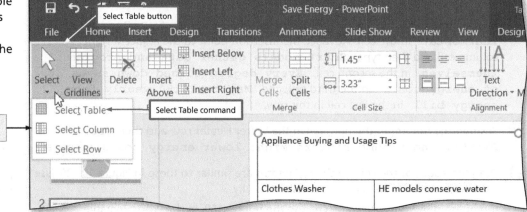

Figure 10–26

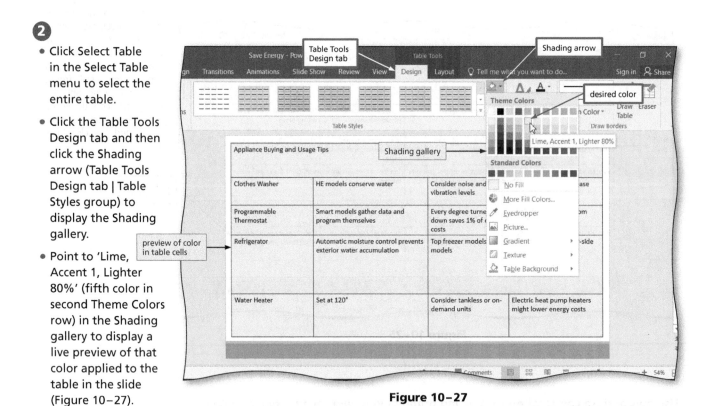

- Click Select Table in the Select Table menu to select the entire table.
- Click the Table Tools Design tab and then click the Shading arrow (Table Tools Design tab | Table Styles group) to display the Shading gallery.
- Point to 'Lime, Accent 1, Lighter 80%' (fifth color in second Theme Colors row) in the Shading gallery to display a live preview of that color applied to the table in the slide (Figure 10–27).

Figure 10–27

Experiment

- Point to various colors in the Shading gallery and watch the background of the table change.

- Click 'Lime, Accent 1, Lighter 80%' in the Shading gallery to apply the selected color to the table.

To Add a Gradient Fill to a Table

Another enhancement you can make to the table is to add a gradient fill so that one shade of the green color gradually progresses to another shade of the same color. The following steps add a gradient fill to the table. *Why? Using a gradient fill is another method of calling attention to each individual table cell.*

- With the table still selected, click the Shading arrow (Table Tools Design tab | Table Styles group) again to display the Shading gallery.

- Point to Gradient to display the Gradient gallery.

- Point to From Center (second gradient in second row of Variations area) to display a live preview of that gradient applied to the table in the slide (Figure 10–28).

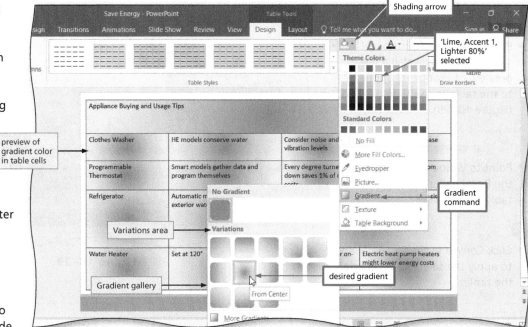

Figure 10–28

Q&A What if my Gradient gallery shows Light and Dark variations?
Select the last gradient in the Light Variations area.

Experiment
- Point to various gradients in the Gradient gallery and watch the background of the table change.

- Click From Center in the Shading gallery to apply the selected gradient to the table.

To Add a Cell Bevel

Why? Bevels modify the cell edges to give a 3-D effect, which makes each cell stand out. Some bevels give the appearance that the cell is protruding from the table, while others give the effect that the cell is depressed into the table. The steps on the next page add a bevel to the table cells.

- With the table still selected, click the Effects button (Table Tools Design tab | Table Styles group) to display the Effects menu.

- Point to Cell Bevel on the Effects menu to display the Cell Bevel gallery.

- Point to Convex (third bevel in second row) to display a live preview of that bevel applied to the table in the slide (Figure 10–29).

Experiment

- Point to various bevel effects in the Bevel gallery and watch the table cells change.

- Click Convex in the Bevel gallery to apply the selected bevel effect to the table.

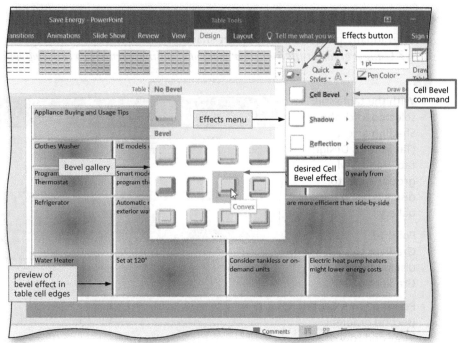

Figure 10–29

To Distribute Table Rows

1 INSERT & EDIT WORD FILE | 2 CREATE TABLE ROWS & COLUMNS | 3 FORMAT TABLE
4 INSERT & EDIT LINKED WORKSHEET | 5 COPY, FORMAT, & EDIT CHART

At times you may desire the row heights to vary. In the Slide 2 table, however, you desire the heights of the rows to be uniform. To make each selected row the same height, you distribute the desired rows. The following steps distribute table rows. **Why?** *The horizontal lines you drew are not spaced equidistant from each other, and distributing the rows is an efficient manner of creating rows with the same height.*

1

- With the table still selected, display the Table Tools Layout tab and then select the cells in the second, third, fourth, and fifth rows (Figure 10–30).

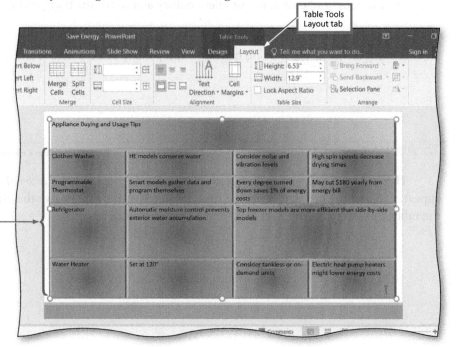

Figure 10–30

2

- Click the Distribute Rows button (Table Tools Layout tab | Cell Size group) to equally space these four rows vertically (Figure 10–31).

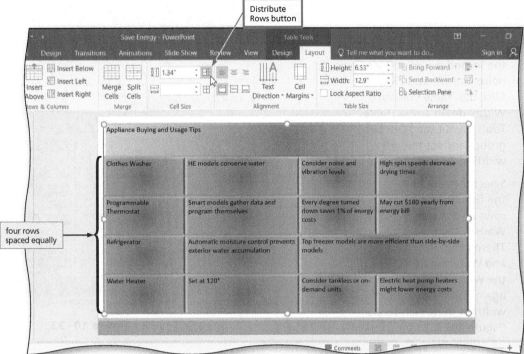

Figure 10–31

To Resize Table Columns and Rows

1 INSERT & EDIT WORD FILE | 2 CREATE TABLE ROWS & COLUMNS | 3 FORMAT TABLE
4 INSERT & EDIT LINKED WORKSHEET | 5 COPY, FORMAT, & EDIT CHART

The first table row should have a height taller than the rows beneath it. In addition, when a row has four cells, each cell should be somewhat narrower than the cells in rows with three cells. *Why? You will increase the heading text font size in a later part of this project, so you need to leave sufficient room for these letters.* The following steps resize the table columns and rows.

1

- With the Table Tools Layout tab displaying, position the insertion point in the first row.

- Click the 'Table Row Height' up arrow (Table Tools Layout tab | Cell Size group) and set the row height to 1.5" (Figure 10–32).

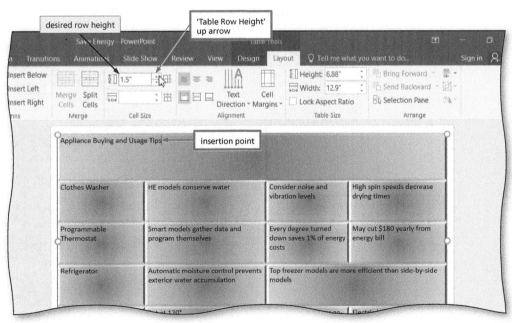

Figure 10–32

- Position the insertion point in the third cell in the second row (Consider noise and vibration levels). Click the 'Table Column Width' down arrow (Table Tools Layout tab | Cell Size group) and set the cell width to 2.5".

- Select the cells in the first column, rows 2 – 5 (Clothes Washer, Programmable Thermostat, Refrigerator, and Water Heater). Click the Width down arrow again and then set the width of these cells to 2.5" (Figure 10–33).

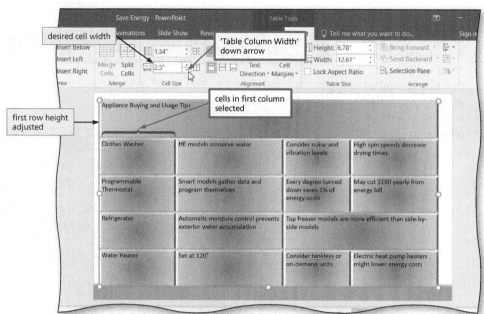

Figure 10–33

To Align Data in Cells

The next step is to change the alignment of the data in all the table cells. In addition to aligning text horizontally in a cell (left, center, or right), you can align it vertically within a cell (top, middle, or bottom). The following steps center data in the table both horizontally and vertically.

① Select all the table cells and then click the Center button (Table Tools Layout tab | Alignment group) to center the text horizontally in the cells.

② Click the Center Vertically button (Table Tools Layout tab | Alignment group) to center the contents of the cells vertically (Figure 10–34).

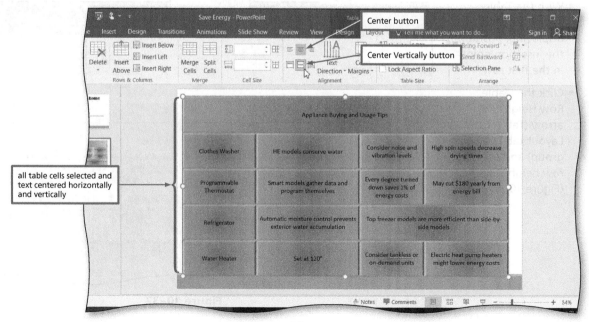

Figure 10–34

To Center a Table

Why? *The table should be positioned an equal distance between the left and right slide edges to balance this object in the slide.* To center the table, you align it in the middle of the slide. The following steps center the table horizontally.

- With the table selected, adjust the table vertically on the slide so that its lower edge is aligned with the top of the green bar at the bottom of the slide. If necessary, move the bottom sizing handle up to adjust the table size.

- Click the Align Objects button (Table Tools Layout tab | Arrange group) to display the Align Objects menu (Figure 10–35).

- Click Align Center on the Align Objects menu, so PowerPoint adjusts the position of the table evenly between the left and right sides of the slide.

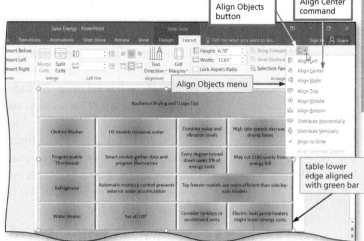

Figure 10–35

To Format Table Data

The final table enhancements are to format the text in the table cells. The following steps increase the font size and bold the text in the first row and column and then change the font for all the table data.

1 Select the text in the first row and then increase the font size to 48 point and bold this text.

2 Select the cells in the first column and then increase the font size to 24 and bold this text.

3 Select all the table cells and then change the font to Cambria. If necessary, change the width of the columns so the words display with adequate spacing on the left and right sides (Figure 10–36).

Figure 10–36

Break Point: If you wish to take a break, this is a good place to do so. Be sure to save the Save Energy file again and then you can exit PowerPoint. To resume at a later time, run PowerPoint, open the file called Save Energy, and continue following the steps from this location forward. Note: PowerPoint will prompt you to update any files that you modified.

Inserting a Linked Excel Worksheet

Linked files maintain a connection between the source file and the destination file. When you select the **Link check box** in the Insert Object dialog box, the object is inserted as a linked object instead of an embedded object. Your PowerPoint presentation stores a representation of the original file and information about its location. If you later move or delete the source file, the link is broken, and the object will not be available. Consequently, if you make a presentation on a computer other than the one on which the presentation was created, and the presentation contains linked objects, be certain to include a copy of the source files. The source files must be stored in the exact location as originally specified when you linked them to your presentation.

PowerPoint associates a linked file with a specific application, which PowerPoint bases on the file extension. For example, if you select a source file with the file extension **.docx**, PowerPoint recognizes the file as a Microsoft Word file. Additionally, if you select a source file with the file extension **.xlsx**, PowerPoint recognizes the file as a Microsoft Excel file.

In the following pages, you will insert a linked Excel worksheet, align it on the slide, and then edit three cells.

To Insert a Linked Excel Worksheet

1 INSERT & EDIT WORD FILE | 2 CREATE TABLE ROWS & COLUMNS | 3 FORMAT TABLE
4 INSERT & EDIT LINKED WORKSHEET | 5 COPY, FORMAT, & EDIT CHART

The Bulb Energy Savings Excel worksheet contains a table with data corresponding to computations that determine the cost of using of using incandescent, halogen, CFL, and LED bulbs for one or more hours a day. While the price of electricity can vary in each town and at different times of the year, this worksheet assumes a cost of 10 cents per kilowatt. The initial computations are for one light bulb and one hour of use. The results in the last three rows of the table show that a using an energy-efficient bulb could result in an 80 percent savings. You will update this table by editing the number of bulbs and the number of hours each day they are turned on. These figures also will update the original Excel worksheet. When you insert the Bulb Energy Savings chart, you can specify that it is linked from the PowerPoint slide to the Excel worksheet. *Why? Any edits made to specific cells are reflected in both the source and destination files.* The following steps insert and link the Microsoft Excel worksheet.

- Insert a new slide with the Blank layout.

- Click the Format Background button (Design tab | Customize group) to display the Format Background pane. Insert the Wires photo located in the Data Files as a background for the new slide (Figure 10–37).

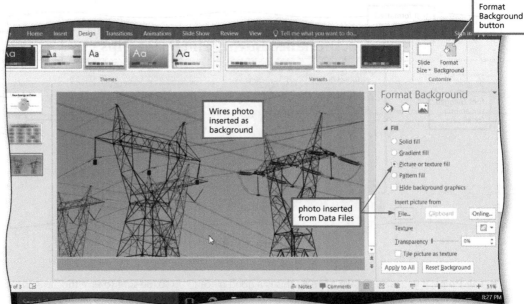

Figure 10–37

2

- Close the Format Background pane.

- Display the Insert tab and then click the Object button (Insert tab | Text group) to display the Insert Object dialog box.

- Click 'Create from file' (Insert Object dialog box) to display the File box (Figure 10–38).

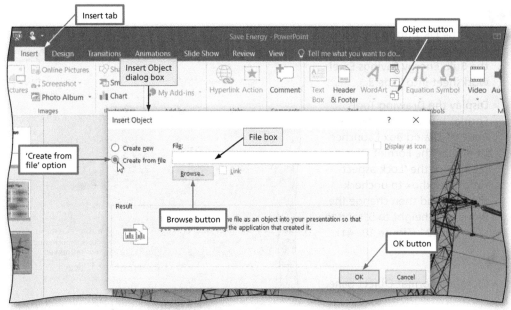

Figure 10–38

3

- Click the Browse button, navigate to the location of your Data Files, and then click Bulb Energy Savings to select the file name (Figure 10–39).

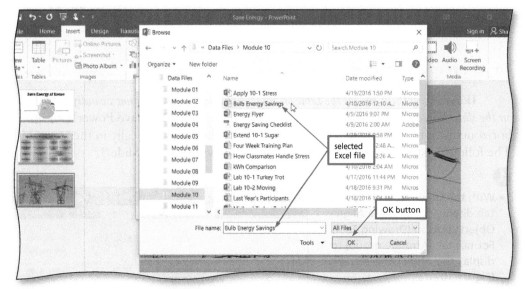

Figure 10–39

4

- Click the OK button (Browse dialog box) to insert the file name into the File box (Insert Object dialog box).

- Click the Link check box (Insert Object dialog box) to select the check box (Figure 10–40).

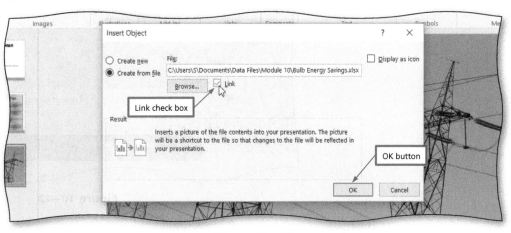

Figure 10–40

- Click the OK button (Insert Object dialog box) to insert the Bulb Energy Savings Excel worksheet into Slide 3.

- Display the Drawing Tools Format tab, click the 'Size and Position Dialog Box Launcher' to display the Format Object pane, click the 'Lock aspect ratio' checkbox to uncheck the box, and then change the worksheet height to 5" and the width to 12" (Figure 10–41).

- Close the Format Object pane.

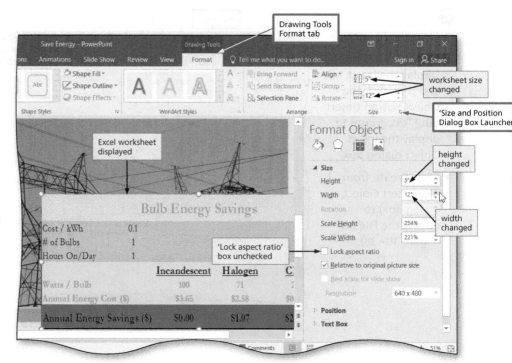

Figure 10–41

To Align a Worksheet

1 INSERT & EDIT WORD FILE | 2 CREATE TABLE ROWS & COLUMNS | 3 FORMAT TABLE
4 INSERT & EDIT LINKED WORKSHEET | 5 COPY, FORMAT, & EDIT CHART

Why? *PowerPoint inserts the table on Slide 3 in a location that is not visually appealing, so you want to center it on the slide.* You can drag the table to a location, but you also can have PowerPoint precisely align the object horizontally in the left, center, or right areas of the slide, and vertically in the top, middle, or bottom of the slide. The following steps align the table horizontally and vertically on Slide 3.

- With the Drawing Tools Format tab displaying, click the Align Objects button (Drawing Tools Format tab| Arrange group) to display the Align Objects menu (Figure 10–42).

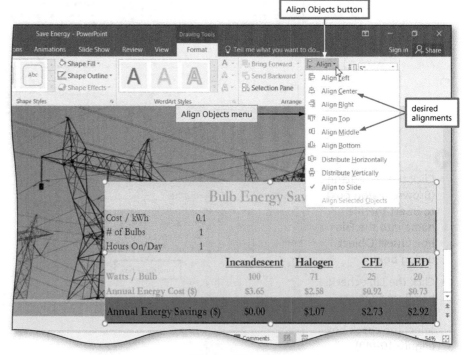

Figure 10–42

2

- Click Align Center on the Align Objects menu to position the worksheet evenly between the left and right edges of the slide.

- Click the Align Objects button again to display the Align Objects menu and then click Align Middle to position the worksheet in the center of the slide (Figure 10–43).

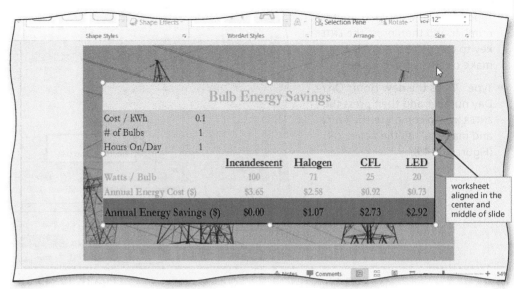

Figure 10–43

To Edit a Linked Worksheet

1 INSERT & EDIT WORD FILE | 2 CREATE TABLE ROWS & COLUMNS | 3 FORMAT TABLE
4 INSERT & EDIT LINKED WORKSHEET | 5 COPY, FORMAT, & EDIT CHART

Each table or worksheet cell is identified by a unique address, or **cell reference**, representing the intersection of a column and row. The column letter is first and is followed by the row number. For example, cell B3 is located at the intersection of the second column, B, and the third row. Three cells need updating. *Why? Most people use more than one bulb for more than one hour per day, so you want to show realistic figures and the corresponding energy savings.* The following steps edit cells in the linked table.

- Double-click the worksheet to open Microsoft Excel and display the worksheet.

- Click the number 1 to the right of the # of Bulbs cell to make cell B3 the active cell (Figure 10–44).

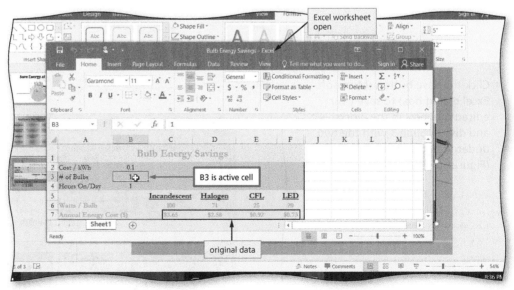

Figure 10–44

2

- Type **5** as the new # of Bulbs number and then press the ENTER key to complete the entry and make cell B4 the active cell.

- Type **7** as the new Hours On / Day number and then press the ENTER key to complete the entry and make cell B5 the active cell. (Figure 10–45).

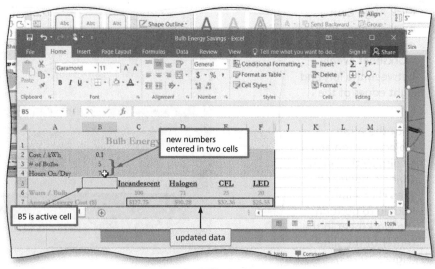

Figure 10–45

3

- Click the Close button in the upper-right corner of the Microsoft Excel window to exit Excel (Figure 10–46).

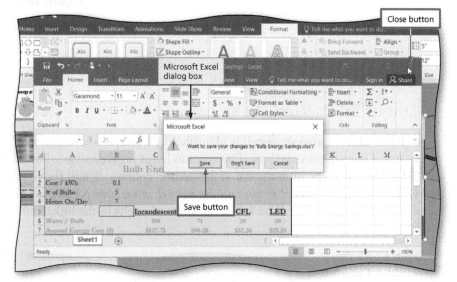

Figure 10–46

- Click the Save button (Microsoft Excel dialog box) to save your edited numbers in the worksheet and display Slide 3 with the two updated figures in the table (Figure 10–47).

Q&A | What would occur if I clicked the Don't Save button in the dialog box instead of the Save button? The new figures in cells B3 and B4 would not be updated in the Excel spreadsheet.

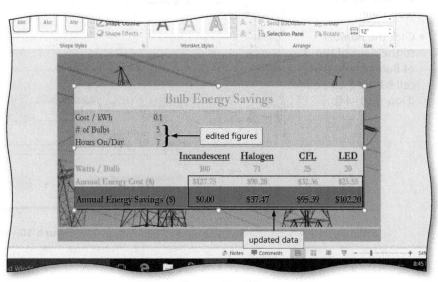

Figure 10–47

Break Point: If you wish to take a break, this is a good place to do so. Be sure to save the Save Energy file again and then you can exit PowerPoint. To resume at a later time, run PowerPoint, open the file called Save Energy, and continue following the steps from this location forward.

Copying and Modifying a Linked Excel Chart

The Microsoft Excel table you inserted into Slide 3 is a linked object. You added data to the table using the Microsoft Excel source program, and that change is reflected on the PowerPoint slide and in the original Excel document. Now you will insert and then modify a Microsoft Excel chart on Slide 4. This object will be linked, so any changes you make to the layout, legend, or background will be reflected in the destination object on the slide and in the original Excel worksheet.

Your local home improvement store held seminars this past winter to describe easy low-cost and no-cost methods consumers could take to save energy. Several homeowners attended these seminars and, in turn, made energy-efficient improvements. They gave you their electric bills from the summers prior to and after their improvements, and you averaged their kilowatt consumption and then used this data to develop a Microsoft Excel chart.

In the following pages, you will perform these tasks on Slide 4:

1. Copy a chart from a file.
2. Edit a linked worksheet.
3. Align the chart.
4. Switch rows and columns.
5. Change the chart type.
6. Apply a style.
7. Display and format axis titles.
8. Move and format a legend.
9. Format the background.
10. Edit data.

BTW
Positioning a Chart or Other Slide Object
At times you might desire to place a table, text box, shape, or other element in a precise location on the slide. To specify a position, right-click the object, click Format Shape on the shortcut menu to display the Format Shape pane, click 'Size & Properties' in the Shape Options tab, if necessary click Position, and then enter the precise measurements of the horizontal and vertical distances from either the top-left corner or the center of the slide.

BTW
File Sizes
Files with embedded objects typically have larger file sizes than those with linked objects because the source data is stored in the presentation. In order to keep file sizes manageable, Microsoft recommends inserting a linked object rather than an embedded object when the source file is large or complex.

To Copy an Excel Chart

1 INSERT & EDIT WORD FILE | 2 CREATE TABLE ROWS & COLUMNS | 3 FORMAT TABLE
4 INSERT & EDIT LINKED WORKSHEET | **5 COPY, FORMAT, & EDIT CHART**

The chart you want to insert into your slide show was created in Microsoft Excel. The file consists of two sheets: one for the chart and another for the numbers used to create the chart. The chart is on Sheet1. One method of placing this chart into a PowerPoint presentation is to copy this object from the Excel worksheet and then paste it into a slide. The following steps copy and link a chart from Sheet1 of the Microsoft Excel file using the destination formatting. *Why? Copying and linking allows you to modify the chart content easily. You want to use the destination formatting so the chart uses the Retrospect theme colors and styles.*

• Insert a new slide with the Title Only layout. Type **Kilowatt Comparison** as the title text, change the font to Cambria, and then bold this text. Center and align it in the middle of the placeholder (Figure 10–48).

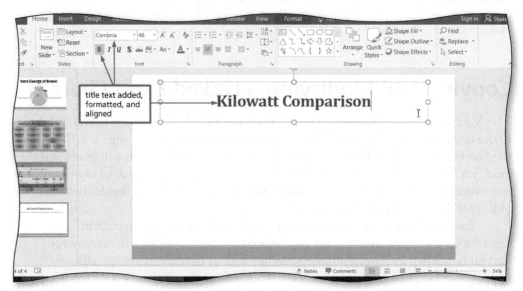

Figure 10–48

• Click the File Explorer app button on the taskbar to make the File Explorer window the active window. Navigate to the location where your Data Files are stored and then point to the kWh Comparison file in the Name list (Figure 10–49).

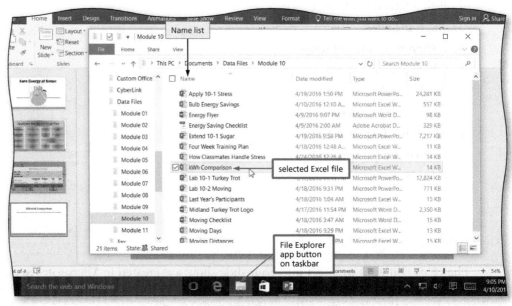

Figure 10–49

3

- Double-click the KWh Comparison file to run Microsoft Excel. If necessary, display the chart on Sheet1.

- Click a blank area above the chart legend in the Chart Area to select the entire chart.

- Click the Copy button (Home tab | Clipboard group) to copy the chart to the Office Clipboard (Figure 10–50).

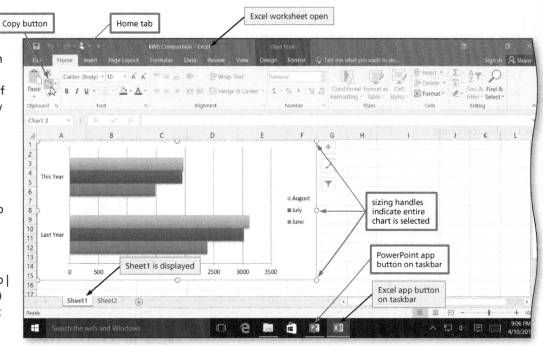

Figure 10–50

4

- Click the PowerPoint app button on the taskbar to make the PowerPoint window the active window. With Slide 4 and the Home tab displaying, click the Paste arrow (Home tab | Clipboard group) to display the Paste Options gallery.

- Point to the 'Use Destination Theme & Link Data' button to display a live preview of the chart in the slide (Figure 10–51).

 Why did I click the Paste arrow instead of the Paste button?
You want to use the colors and style of Retrospect theme (the destination theme), so you need to display the Paste Options gallery to make that choice and to link the chart to the original Excel worksheet. If you had clicked the Paste button, you would have embedded the chart using the Excel worksheet theme (the source theme).

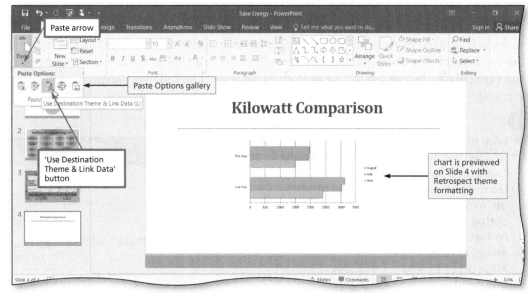

Figure 10–51

Experiment

- Point to the 'Use Destination Theme & Embed Workbook' button in the Paste Options gallery to display a live preview of the chart with the Retrospect theme applied.

5

- Click the 'Use Destination Theme & Link Data' button to paste the chart into Slide 4.

- Display the Chart Tools Format tab and then change the chart size to 4.5" x 11" (Figure 10–52).

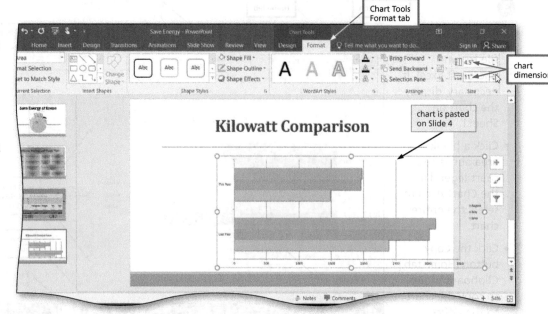

Figure 10–52

Other Ways

1. Right-click Excel chart, click Copy, exit Microsoft Excel, click Paste arrow (Home tab | Clipboard group), click 'Use Destination Theme & Link Data'

To Align a Chart

1 INSERT & EDIT WORD FILE | 2 CREATE TABLE ROWS & COLUMNS | 3 FORMAT TABLE
4 INSERT & EDIT LINKED WORKSHEET | **5 COPY, FORMAT, & EDIT CHART**

Why? *You aligned the table on Slide 3 horizontally and vertically. Likewise, you want to align the chart on Slide 4 so that it is displayed in an appropriate location on the slide.* Although you can drag the chart on the slide, you also can use PowerPoint commands to align the object horizontally in the left, center, or right areas of the slide, and vertically in the top, middle, or bottom of the slide. The following steps align the chart horizontally and vertically on Slide 4.

1

- With the chart selected and the Chart Tools Format tab displaying, click the Align Objects button (Chart Tools Format tab | Arrange group) to display the Align Objects menu (Figure 10–53).

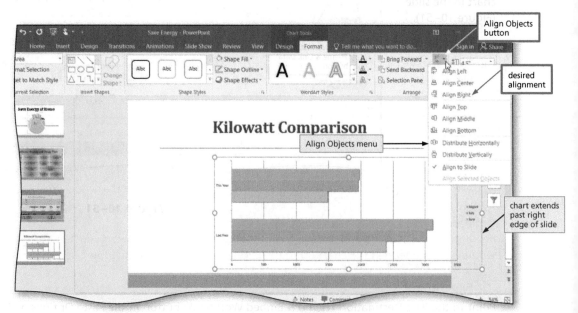

Figure 10–53

2

- Click Align Right on the Align Objects menu to position the chart along the right edge of the slide (Figure 10–54).

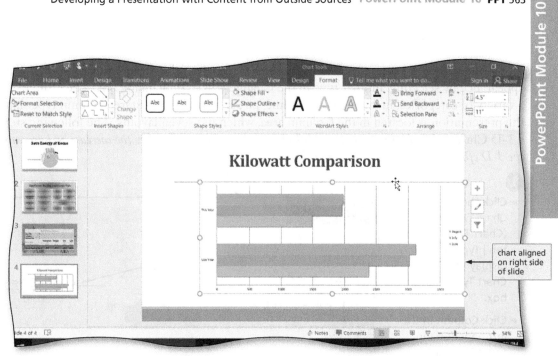

Figure 10–54

To Switch Rows and Columns in a Chart

1 INSERT & EDIT WORD FILE | 2 CREATE TABLE ROWS & COLUMNS | 3 FORMAT TABLE
4 INSERT & EDIT LINKED WORKSHEET | 5 COPY, FORMAT, & EDIT CHART

Excel created the chart on Slide 4 (Sheet1 in the Excel file) based on the values in the worksheet on Sheet2 of the Excel file. The scale is based on the values in the **y-axis**, which also is called the **vertical axis** or **value axis**. The titles along the **x-axis**, also referred to as the **horizontal axis** or **category axis**, are derived from the top row of the Sheet2 worksheet and are displayed along the left edge of the chart. Each bar in the chart has a specific color to represent one of the three months — June, July, and August — grouped by kilowatts used during the two previous summers. You can switch the data in the chart so that a kilowatts used bar is displayed for each of the three months. ***Why?*** *In your presentation to consumers, you want to emphasize the lower electricity consumption when energy-reduction measures have been taken.* The following step switches the rows and columns in the chart.

1

- Display the Chart Tools Design tab on the ribbon.

- Click the Switch Row/Column button (Chart Tools Design tab | Data group) to swap the data charted on the x-axis with the data on the y-axis (Figure 10–55).

Q&A
If the Switch Row/ Column button is dimmed, how can I switch the data?
Be certain the Excel worksheet is open. The button is active only when the worksheet is open.

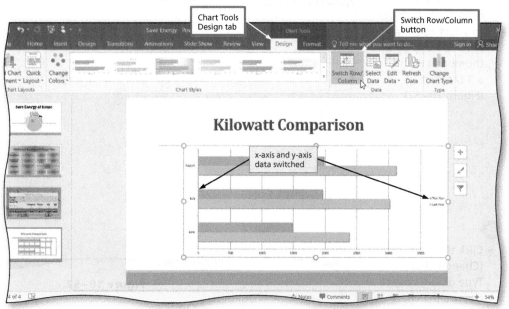

Figure 10–55

To Change the Chart Type

The bar chart represents data horizontally for each of the three summer months. You can change the chart appearance by selecting another type in the Change Chart Type dialog box. The sample charts are divided into a variety of categories, including column, line, pie, and bar. The clustered column type that you want to use in the presentation is located in the Column area, which has seven layouts. The following steps change the chart to a 3-D Clustered Column chart type. *Why? The vertical bars help show the increase and decrease of kilowatt usage, and the 3-D effect adds an interesting visual element.*

1

- Click the 'Change Chart Type' button (Chart Tools Design tab | Type group) to display the Change Chart Type dialog box.

- Click Column in the left pane (Change Chart Type dialog box) to display a Clustered Column thumbnail (Figure 10–56).

Figure 10–56

2

- Click the '3-D Clustered Column' chart (fourth chart) to select this chart type and display a thumbnail with a 3-D effect (Figure 10–57).

Q&A Can I see a larger preview of the chart?
Yes. You can point to the chart to enlarge the preview.

3

- Click the OK button (Change Chart Type dialog box) to change the chart type to 3-D Clustered Column.

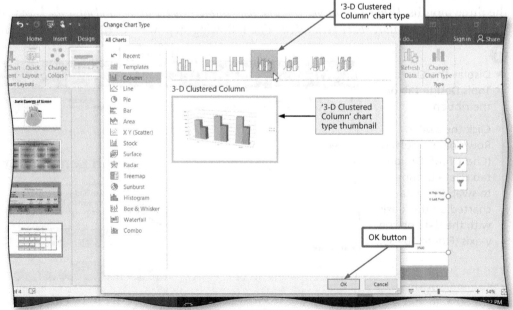

Figure 10–57

TO EXCLUDE DATA IN A CHART

If you have multiple categories (which display in the x-axis) or series (which display in the legend) of data and want to exclude one or more of them from displaying, you can instruct PowerPoint to exclude data elements. If you wanted to exclude a particular category or series, you would perform the following steps.

1. Click the Chart Filters button (funnel icon) on the right side of the chart to display a pane with each data element.

2. Clear the check boxes of the elements you want to exclude on the chart.

3. To display an excluded data element, select the check box.

To Apply a Style to a Chart

1 INSERT & EDIT WORD FILE | 2 CREATE TABLE ROWS & COLUMNS | 3 FORMAT TABLE
4 INSERT & EDIT LINKED WORKSHEET | 5 COPY, FORMAT, & EDIT CHART

Why? *You can modify the chart's appearance easily by selecting a predefined style.* The styles available in the Chart Styles gallery have a variety of colors and backgrounds and display in both 2-D and 3-D. The following steps apply a style to the chart.

- Click the Chart Style button (paintbrush icon) on the right side of the chart area to display the Chart Style gallery with the Style tab displayed.

- Scroll down until the eighth style (Style 8) in the Chart Style gallery is displayed and then point to this style to see a live preview on Slide 4 (Figure 10–58).

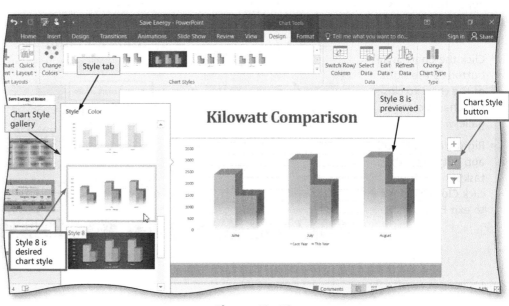

Figure 10–58

Ⓟ **Experiment**

- Point to various chart styles and watch the layouts change.

- Click Style 8 in the Chart Style gallery to apply the chart style to the chart.

To Change Chart Colors

You can modify a chart's colors easily by selecting one of the color groups available in the Chart Color gallery. These colors are grouped in two categories: Colorful and Monochromatic. For a unique look, PowerPoint also allows you create a custom color combination. The following steps change the chart colors. *Why? The two columns in the chart have very similar colors, so you want to distinguish the kilowatts used during the previous summer from those used this year by changing to a color scheme with more contrast.*

1

• With the Chart Style gallery still displaying, click the Color tab at the top of the pane to display the Chart Color gallery.

Experiment

• Point to various color groups and watch the chart colors change.

2

• Click Color 3 (the third row in the Colorful area) to apply these colors to the chart (Figure 10–59).

• Click the Chart Style button to the right of the chart to close the Chart Color gallery.

• Right-click the Excel app button on the taskbar and then click Close window to exit Excel.

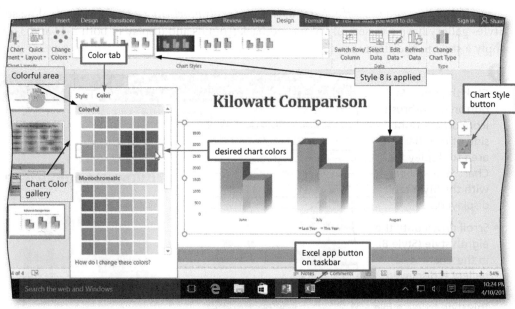

Figure 10–59

Other Ways

1. Click 'Chart Quick Colors' button (Chart Tools Design tab | Chart Styles group)

To Display and Format Axis Titles

The legend below the chart identifies the colors assigned to each of the bars. You can modify the default legend in a variety of ways, including moving its location, changing the fill and outline, adding an effect, and changing the font. The Chart Elements button on the right side of the chart area allows you to display or hide a chart element. When you click this button, the Chart Elements pane is displayed. A check mark appears in the check box for each chart element that is displayed. You can check and uncheck each chart element to display or hide axes, the chart title, labels, gridlines, and the legend. The following steps display the axis titles and then format the text. *Why? You want your audience to recognize that the y-axis represents the total number of kilowatts used and the x-axis represents the summer months.*

1

- Click the Chart Elements button (plus sign icon) on the right side of the chart area to display the CHART ELEMENTS pane.

- Click the Axis Titles check box to display the two default titles for the x and y axes (Figure 10–60).

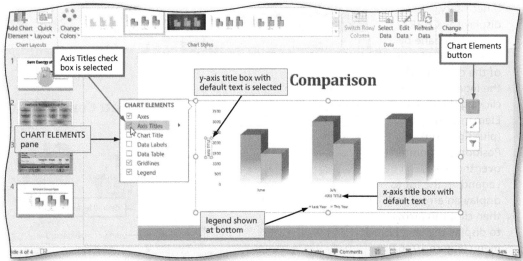

Figure 10–60

 2

- With the default y-axis title box selected, delete the default text and then type **Total Kilowatts Used** in the text box.

- Select the text and then increase the font size to 18 point and bold the text.

3

- Click the x-axis title to select it, delete the default text, and then type **Month** as the replacement text.

- Select the text and then increase the font size to 18 point and bold the text (Figure 10–61).

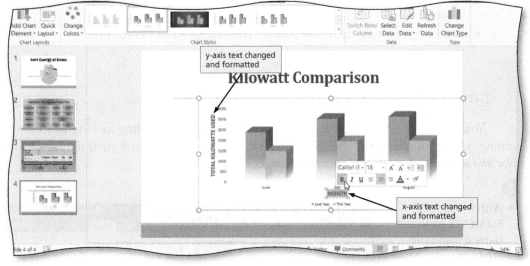

Figure 10–61

Other Ways

1. Click Add Chart Element button (Chart Tools Design tab | Chart Layouts group), click Axis Titles

---

To Move a Chart Legend

The legend below the chart identifies the colors assigned to each of the bars. You can modify the default legend in a variety of ways, including moving its location, changing the fill and outline, adding an effect, and changing the font. The following steps move the legend to the left side of the chart. *Why? A blank area is available on the left side of the chart, and you believe the legend will be more effective there.*

- If necessary, display the CHART ELEMENTS pane by clicking a blank area of the chart beside the legend and then clicking the Chart Elements button (plus sign icon). Position the pointer over the word, Legend, in the list to display an arrow and then click this arrow to display the Legend menu (Figure 10–62).

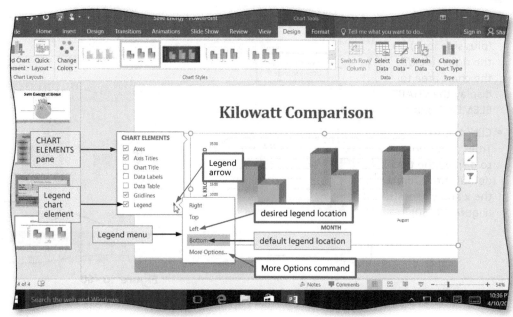

Figure 10–62

- Click Left to display the legend on the left side of the chart.

Other Ways

1. Click Add Chart Element button (Chart Tools Design tab | Chart Layouts group), click Legend arrow

---

To Format a Chart Legend

1 INSERT & EDIT WORD FILE | 2 CREATE TABLE ROWS & COLUMNS | 3 FORMAT TABLE
4 INSERT & EDIT LINKED WORKSHEET | **5 COPY, FORMAT, & EDIT CHART**

You can modify the default legend in a variety of ways, including moving its location, changing the fill and outline, adding an effect, and changing the font. The following steps format the legend. *Why? Changing the line color and adding a glow help call attention to the legend.*

- With the CHART ELEMENTS pane and Legend menu still displaying, click More Options to display the Format Legend pane. Click the 'Fill & Line' button and then, if necessary, click Border to display the Border area. Scroll down to display the Border area.

- Click Solid line and then, if necessary, scroll down and then click the Color button to display the Color gallery (Figure 10–63).

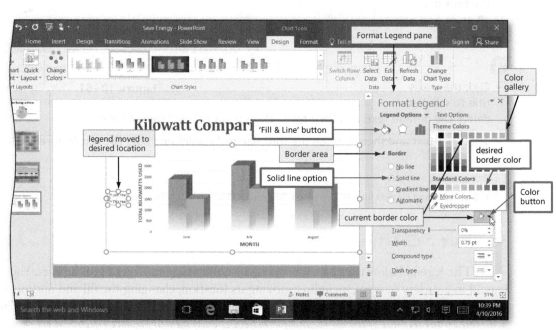

Figure 10–63

- Click Blue (eighth color in Standard Colors row) to change the legend border line color.

- Click the Width up arrow several times to increase the line width to 2 pt (Figure 10–64).

Q&A Is a live preview available?
No, this feature is not offered.

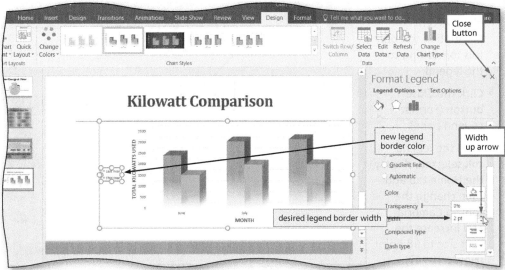

Figure 10–64

- Click the Effects button (Format Legend pane) and then, if necessary, display the Glow area (Figure 10–65).

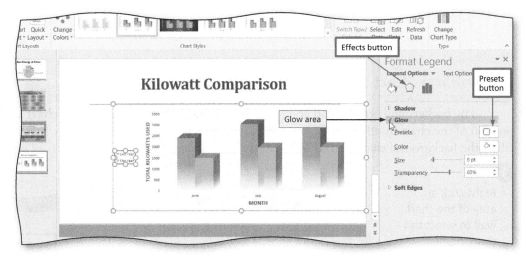

Figure 10–65

- Click the Presets button to display the Glow gallery.

- Point to 'Blue, 8 pt glow, Accent color 6' (last variation in second row) (Figure 10–66).

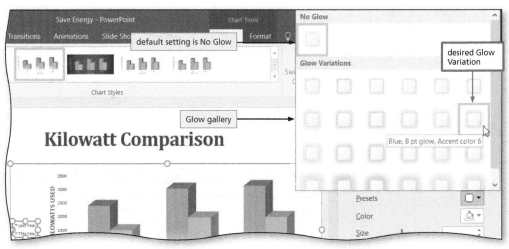

Figure 10–66

5

- Click the 'Blue, 8 pt glow, Accent color 6' variation to apply this formatting to the legend.

- Click the Close button (Format Legend pane).

- With the legend still selected, display the Home tab and then change the font to Cambria and increase the font size to 18 point (Figure 10–67).

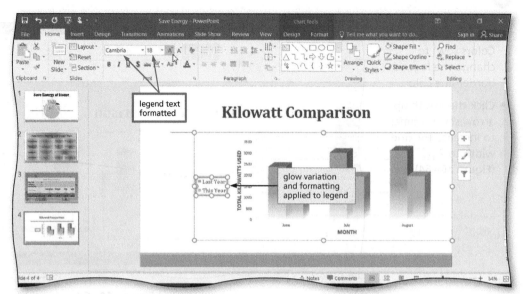

Figure 10–67

Other Ways

1. Right-click legend, click Format Legend on shortcut menu

To Format a Chart Background

1 INSERT & EDIT WORD FILE | 2 CREATE TABLE ROWS & COLUMNS | 3 FORMAT TABLE
4 INSERT & EDIT LINKED WORKSHEET | **5 COPY, FORMAT, & EDIT CHART**

The background area behind and to the left of the chart bars is called the **chart wall**. You can format this portion of the chart by adding a fill, an outline, and effects such as a shadow. The following steps add a gradient fill to the background chart wall. *Why? The gradient adds a visual element and helps call attention to the gridlines.*

1

- Right-click an area of the chart wall to select this chart element and to display a mini toolbar and shortcut menu. If necessary, click the Chart Elements arrow and then click Walls in the list (Figure 10–68).

Q&A

How will I know if this piece of the chart is selected? You will see six small blue circles, each one located at the upper or lower gridline corner.

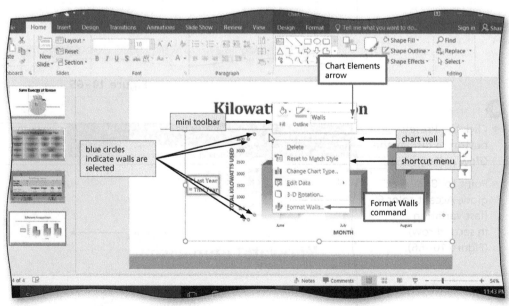

Figure 10–68

2

- If necessary, display the shortcut menu again and, if necessary, click Fill to expand the Fill section of the Format Walls pane (Figure 10–69).

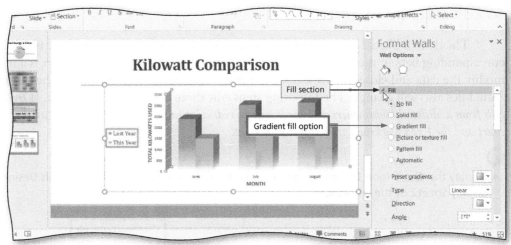

Figure 10–69

3

- Click Gradient fill to display options related to the gradient colors in the pane. Click the Preset gradients button to display a palette of built-in gradient fill colors (Figure 10–70).

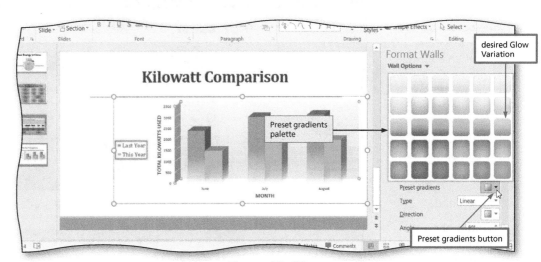

Figure 10–70

4

- Click 'Medium Gradient – Accent 6' (last gradient in third row) to apply this gradient to the chart walls (Figure 10–71).

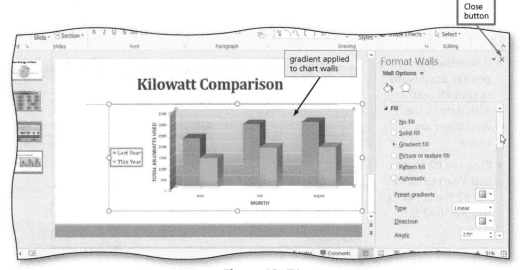

5

- Click the Close button (Format Walls pane).

Figure 10–71

Other Ways

1. Click the Chart Elements arrow (Chart Tools Format tab | Current Selection group), click Walls, click Format Selection (Chart Tools Format tab | Current Selection group), if necessary click Fill & Line button, if necessary click Fill, click Gradient fill (Format Walls pane)

To Edit Data in a Chart

The data in Sheet2 of the worksheet is used to create the chart on Slide 4. If you edit this data, the corresponding bars in the chart change height to reflect new numbers. The chart is a linked object, so when you modify the data and close the worksheet, the chart will reflect the changes and the original file stored in your Data Files also will change. The following steps edit three cells in the worksheet. *Why? You have obtained electric bills from additional homeowners who made energy-reduction improvements this past year, and you want to update your chart and the Excel worksheet with this information.*

1

• Display the Chart Tools Design tab and then click the Edit Data button (Chart Tools Design tab | Data group) to display Sheet2 of the worksheet.

Q&A Why might I want to click the Edit Data arrow instead of the Edit Data button? You would be given the option to run Microsoft Excel and then edit the worksheet using that app. More options would be available using Excel. If you simply need to edit data, you can perform that task easily using PowerPoint.

• Position the pointer in the lower-right corner of the worksheet (Figure 10–72).

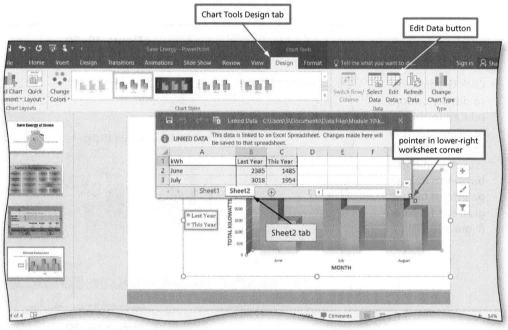

Figure 10–72

2

• If necessary, drag the pointer downward so that all cells with data in the worksheet are visible.

• Click cell B2 (June of Last Year) to make cell B2 the active cell (Figure 10–73).

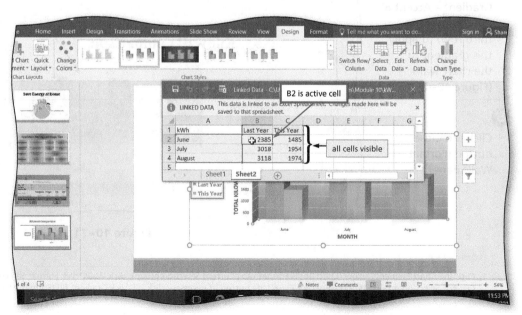

Figure 10–73

- Type **2401** as the replacement number and then press the DOWN ARROW key to make cell B3 (July of Last Year) the active cell.

- Type **2993** as the replacement number and then press the RIGHT ARROW key to make cell C3 (July of This Year) the active cell.

- Type **1861** as the replacement number and then press the ENTER key (Figure 10–74).

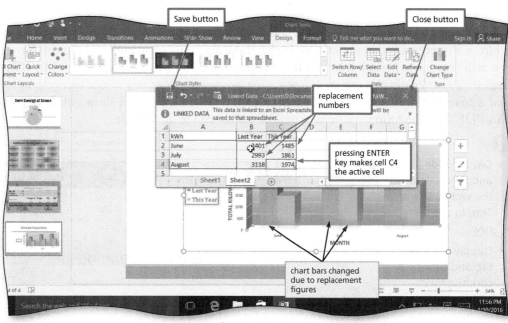

Figure 10–74

- Click the Save button on the spreadsheet toolbar to save the data to the Excel spreadsheet.

- Click the Close button on the spreadsheet to close the window.

- Display the Chart Tools Format tab, click the Align Objects button (Chart Tools Format tab | Arrange group), and then click Align Center to position the chart in the center of the slide (Figure 10–75).

Q&A

The Align Center command is dimmed. What should I do?
Click the chart area so that the chart walls are not selected and then click the Align Objects button again.

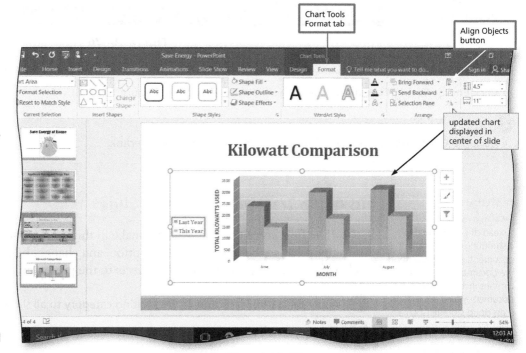

Figure 10–75

To Add a Hyperlink to a Table

A hyperlink connects one element on a slide to another slide, presentation, picture, file, webpage, or email address. Presenters use hyperlinks to display these elements to an audience. In this Save Energy presentation, you will create a hyperlink from a cell in the table on Slide 2 to an Adobe PDF file. *Why? You want to show your audience a simple form they can use to analyze the measures they can take to save energy in lighting, heating and cooling, and appliances.* When you click this particular table cell during a slide show, Adobe Acrobat starts and then opens this PDF file. The following steps hyperlink a table cell to a PDF file.

1

- Display Slide 2 and then select the words, Usage Tips, in the first row.

- Display the Insert tab and then click the 'Add a Hyperlink' button (Insert tab | Links group) to display the Insert Hyperlink dialog box.

- If necessary, click the 'Existing File or Web Page' button in the Link to area.

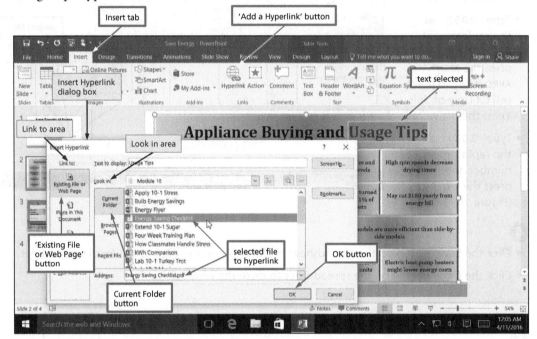

- If necessary, click the Current Folder button in the Look in area and then navigate to the location where your Data Files are stored.

- Click Energy Saving Checklist to select this file as the hyperlink (Figure 10–76).

Figure 10–76

2

- Click the OK button (Insert Hyperlink dialog box) to insert the hyperlink.

BTW

Distributing a Document

Instead of printing and distributing a hard copy of a document, you can distribute the document electronically. Options include sending the document via email; posting it on cloud storage (such as OneDrive) and sharing the file with others; posting it on social media, a blog, or other website; and sharing a link associated with an online location of the document. You also can create and share a PDF or XPS image of the document, so that users can view the file in Acrobat Reader or XPS Viewer instead of in PowerPoint.

To Add a Transition between Slides

The final enhancements you will make in this presentation are to apply a transition, change the transition effect option, and change the transition speed. The following steps apply these transition effects to the presentation.

1 Apply the Blinds transition in the Exciting category to all slides.

2 Change the effect option to Horizontal.

3 Change the transition speed from 1.40 to 3.00 seconds.

To Run, Print, Save, and Exit PowerPoint

The presentation now is complete. You should run the presentation, view the hyperlinked file, print the slides, save the presentation, and then exit PowerPoint.

① Run the Save Energy presentation. When Slide 2 is displayed, click Usage Tips in the first row of the table to display the Energy Saving Checklist document as the hyperlinked file. If the Microsoft PowerPoint Security Notice dialog box is displayed, click the Yes button, then click OK in the Microsoft Office dialog box, to open the PDF file.

② Review the contents of the Energy Saving Checklist. Point to the PowerPoint app button on the taskbar to see the PowerPoint window and a live preview of Slide 2.

③ Click the thumbnail of Slide 2 to display that slide and then display Slides 3 and 4.

④ End the slide show. Close the Energy Saving Checklist.

⑤ Print the Save Energy presentation as a handout with two slides per page.

⑥ Save the Save Energy presentation again with the same file name.

⑦ Because the project now is complete, you can exit PowerPoint, closing all open documents.

BTW
Conserving Ink and Toner
If you want to conserve ink or toner, you can instruct PowerPoint to print draft quality documents by clicking File on the ribbon to open the Backstage view, clicking the Options tab in the Backstage view to display the PowerPoint Options dialog box, clicking Advanced in the left pane (PowerPoint Options dialog box), scrolling to the Print area in the right pane, placing a check mark in the 'Use draft quality' check box, and then clicking the OK button. Then, use the Backstage view to print the document as usual.

Summary

In this module you have learned how to develop a presentation using information you inserted from a Microsoft Word flyer and Microsoft Excel worksheet and chart. These documents were either embedded or linked, and you edited each of them to update words or numbers. You also drew a table, enhanced and formatted it, and linked an Adobe PDF file to the table. You then altered a Microsoft Excel object by changing the chart type, background, gridlines, and legend.

CONSIDER THIS

What decisions will you need to make when creating your next presentation?
Use these guidelines as you complete the assignments in this module and create your own slide show decks outside of this class.

1. **Use powerful words to accompany the text on your slides.** The slides are meant to enhance your talk by clarifying main points and calling attention to key ideas. Your speech should use words that explain and substantiate your visuals.

2. **Develop tables that are clear and meaningful.** Tables are extremely useful vehicles for presenting complex relationships. Their design plays an important part in successfully conveying the information to the audience.

3. **Use appropriate colors when formatting graphics you want people to remember.** Numerous studies have shown that appropriate graphics help audiences comprehend and remember the information presented during a speech. Color has been shown to increase retention by as much as 80 percent. When choosing colors for your graphics, use hues that fit the tone and objective of your message.

Apply Your Knowledge

Reinforce the skills and apply the concepts you learned in this module.

Copying a Chart from an Excel file, Changing a Chart Type, and Drawing a Table

Note: To complete this assignment, you will be required to use the Data Files. Please contact your instructor for information about accessing the Data Files.

Instructions: Run PowerPoint. Open the presentation called Apply 10-1 Stress, which is located in the Data Files. You conducted a survey of your freshman class to find out how they handle stress and entered the results in an Excel worksheet. The document you open is a partially formatted presentation highlighting the results of your survey and information on reactions to stress. You will copy a chart from an Excel file, change the chart type, and draw a table. Your presentation should look like Figure 10–77.

Perform the following tasks:

1. Open the Microsoft Excel file called How Classmates Handle Stress, which is located in the Data Files, and then copy the doughnut pie chart located on Sheet1. Paste the chart onto Slide 1 (Figure 10–77a) with the ' Use Destination Theme & Link Data' option. Change the chart style to Style 7 and then change the chart type to Sunburst.

2. Increase the size of the chart to 4.5" × 6". Hide the legend. Change the font color of the data labels to 'Black, Background 1' and then bold this text. Change the chart colors to Color 4. Add a 6 pt black border. Move the chart to the lower-right corner of the slide.

3. On Slide 2 (Figure 10–77b), draw a table with four columns and three rows. Adjust the size of the table to 2.5" × 10.5". Set the height of the first row to 0.83" and the second and third rows to 0.75". Set the width of the first column to 3" and the width of the second, third, and fourth columns to 2.5". Merge the four cells in the first row. Enter the data shown in the figure. Center the data vertically in the cells.

4. If requested by your instructor, add your birth year after the word, Stress, in the table title.

5. Increase the font size of the table title to 32 point, change the font color to 'Green, Accent 6' (last color in first Theme Colors row), and then bold and center the text. Increase the font size of the text in the second and third rows to 20 point. Underline and bold the words, Emotional and Physical, in the first column and then center these words in the cells.

6. With the table still selected, click the Pen Weight arrow (Table Tools Design tab | Draw Borders group) and then click 3 pt in the Pen Weight gallery. Click the Pen Color button (Table Tools Design tab | Draw Borders group) and then change the pen color to 'Green, Accent 6'. Click the Borders arrow (Table Tools Design tab | Table Styles group) and then click All Borders in the Borders gallery to change all borders to this new weight and color. Add 'Dark Blue, Background 2, Darker 50%' (third color in last Theme Colors row) shading to the entire table. Move the table to the area shown in Figure 10–77b.

7. Apply the Fracture transition (Exciting category) and then change the duration to 3.25 seconds for both slides.

8. Run the presentation and then save the file using the file name, Apply 10-1 Stress Symptoms.

9. Submit the revised document in the format specified by your instructor.

10. ✺ Is the Sunburst chart type appropriate for the chart on Slide 1? Can you suggest other formatting changes to make for the Slide 2 table?

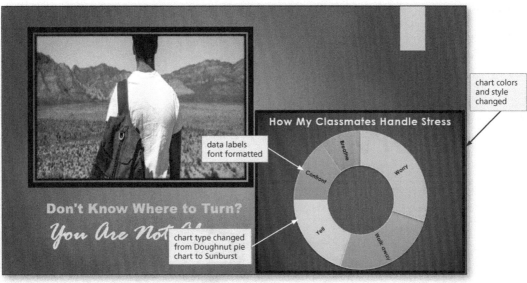

(a) Slide 1

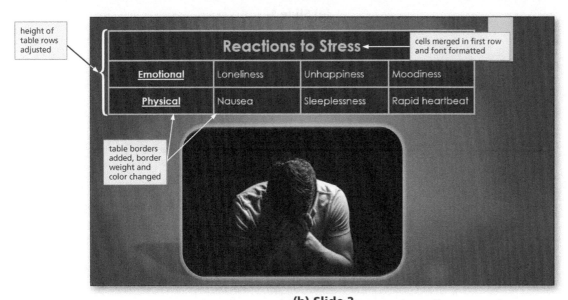

(b) Slide 2

Figure 10–77

Extend Your Knowledge

Extend the skills you learned in this module and experiment with new skills. You may need to use Help to complete the assignment.

Inserting a Linked Object and Drawing a Table

Note: To complete this assignment, you will be required to use the Data Files. Please contact your instructor for information about accessing the Data Files.

Instructions: Run PowerPoint. Open the presentation called Extend 10-1 Sugar, which is located in the Data Files. You will edit a table from a linked document and then draw and format a second table, as shown in Figure 10–78.

Continued >

Extend Your Knowledge *continued*

(a) Slide 1

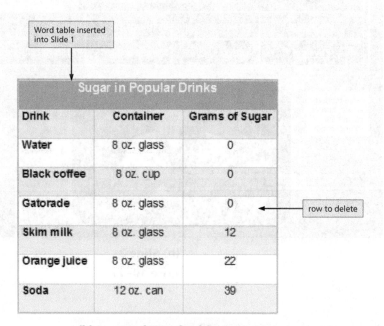

(b) Inserted Word Table

Figure 10–78 (Continued)

Perform the following tasks:

1. Display Slide 1 (Figure 10–78a). Insert the table object from the Microsoft Word file called Sugar in Popular Drinks (Figure 10–78b), which is located in the Data Files.

2. Delete the fourth row of the table, which contains the text, Gatorade, 8 oz. glass, and 0, by double-clicking the table to open Microsoft Word, double-clicking the table, placing the insertion point in the Gatorade row, displaying the Table Tools Layout tab (Microsoft Word), clicking the Delete Table button (Table Tools Layout tab | Rows & Columns group), and then clicking Delete Rows in the Delete Table menu. Exit Word by clicking the Close button in the upper-right corner of the screen. The edited table object is displayed on Slide 1.

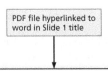

PDF file hyperlinked to word in Slide 1 title

Watermelon Breeze

Ingredients:

2 cups chopped seedless watermelon, chilled

½ cup pomegranate juice, no sugar added

Juice of ½ lemon

1 mint leaf

Directions:

Add all ingredients to the blender and blend until smooth. Pour over ice and garnish with additional mint if desired.

This recipe makes 2 servings and yields about 2 cups

(c) Hyperlinked Adobe PDF File

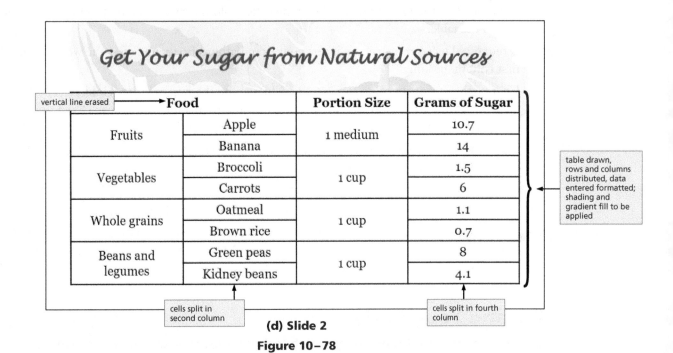

vertical line erased

cells split in second column

cells split in fourth column

table drawn, rows and columns distributed, data entered formatted; shading and gradient fill to be applied

Get Your Sugar from Natural Sources

Food		Portion Size	Grams of Sugar
Fruits	Apple	1 medium	10.7
	Banana		14
Vegetables	Broccoli	1 cup	1.5
	Carrots		6
Whole grains	Oatmeal	1 cup	1.1
	Brown rice		0.7
Beans and legumes	Green peas	1 cup	8
	Kidney beans		4.1

(d) Slide 2

Figure 10–78

Continued >

Extend Your Knowledge *continued*

3. Click outside the table object on Slide 1. If necessary, click the table object to select it. Display the Drawing Tools Format tab, click the Size and Position Dialog Box Launcher, and then unlock the aspect ratio. Change the table size to 5" × 5.5" and then move it to the lower-left corner of the slide.

4. Select the word, Drink, in the title text placeholder and then and hyperlink it to the PDF file called Watermelon Breeze (Figure 10–78c), which is located in the Data Files. (*Hint:* You might need to click the 'Existing File or Web Page' button in the Link to area.)

5. Display Slide 2 (Figure 10–78d) and then draw a table with five rows and four columns. Erase the vertical line between the first and second cells in the first row and then type, **Food**, in that cell as the column heading. Type **Portion Size** as the second column heading and **Grams of Sugar** as the third column heading.

6. Split each of the cells in the second and fourth columns so that they are displayed as one column and two rows. Distribute the rows and the columns. *Hint:* To distribute the columns, display the Table Tools Layout tab and then click the Distribute Columns button (Table Tools Layout tab | Cell Size group).

7. With the table selected, click the Pen Weight arrow (Table Tools Design tab | Draw Borders group) and then click 2 1/4 pt in the Pen Weight gallery. Click the Pen Color button (Table Tools Design tab | Draw Borders group) and then change the pen color to 'Gold, Accent 4, Darker 25%' (eighth color in fifth Theme Colors row). Click the Borders arrow (Table Tools Design tab | Table Styles group) and then click All Borders in the Borders gallery to apply the new border settings.

8. Enter the data in the table using Figure 10–78d as a guide. Select all text in the table and then change the font to Georgia and the font size to 24 point. Center the text vertically in each cell and then align the text in the middle of the cells. Bold the three column headings in the first row of the table.

9. If requested by your instructor, insert your grandfather's first name after the word, Food, in the first column heading.

10. Change the size of the table to 5" × 12". Change the shading color to 'Gold, Accent 4, Lighter 60%' (eighth color in third Theme Colors row) and then apply the Linear Down gradient (second gradient in first Variations row). Align the table in the center of the slide.

11. Apply the Flip transition in the Exciting category to both slides and then change the direction to Left. Change the duration to 3.00 seconds.

12. Run the presentation and then save the file using the file name, Extend 10-1 Sugar in Our Diet.

13. Submit the revised document in the format specified by your instructor.

14. ✸ In this presentation, you added borders to the table on Slide 2. Do these borders help separate the cells and make the data easier to read? Do the shading and gradient choices complement the slide background and overall presentation topic? Why or why not?

Expand Your World

Create a solution that uses cloud or web technologies by learning and investigating on your own from general guidance.

Creating a Slide with SmartArt Using PowerPoint Online

Instructions: You are at your local library waiting for your study partner to arrive. You notice that the computers in the library's Tech Link Lab can access the Internet, but they do not have Microsoft Office 2016 installed. To make the best use of your time, you decide to begin working on a project for your economics class about saving money when buying and using appliances. You use

PowerPoint Online and the data in Slide 2 of the Save Energy presentation in this module to create a SmartArt graphic (Figure 10–79). This graphic can be used as a replacement for Slide 2 if you decide to present the same information in an alternate manner. When you have access to Microsoft Office 2016, you open the file containing this slide and edit the slide contents using this software.

Perform the following tasks:

1. Run a browser and navigate to the Office Online website. You will need to sign in to your Microsoft account. Run PowerPoint Online.

2. Create a new presentation using the Ion Boardroom theme. Save the file using the file name, Expand 10-1 Appliance Energy Savings.

3. Change the layout to Title and Content layout and then change the Ion Boardroom variant to Variant 2.

4. Type **Appliance Buying and Usage Tips** as the title text. If requested by your instructor, type, **for** and your grandmother's or grandfather's first name or middle name. Change the font to Century Schoolbook, increase the font size to 40 point, and then center this text.

5. To begin creating the SmartArt graphic, click the SmartArt icon in the content placeholder, click the More Layouts arrow (SMARTART TOOLS DESIGN tab | Layouts group), and then select the Hierarchy List in the Layouts gallery (last design in third row).

6. Enter the data from Slide 2 of the Save Energy presentation, which is shown in Figure 10–1c. When you have typed all the data, click a blank area of the slide to display the graphic. If some of the data does not display properly in the individual graphic boxes, delete that text and continue performing the remaining steps in this assignment.

7. Select the SmartArt graphic and then right-click to display the mini toolbar. Click the Style button in the mini toolbar and then apply the Inset style (second style in second row). Click the Color button and then change the colors to Colorful – Accent Colors (first color in Colorful row). Change the font of all SmartArt text to Tahoma. Use the SmartArt corner sizing handles to increase the graphic's size, as shown in Figure 10–79.

8. Click the 'OPEN IN POWERPOINT' button and then click the Yes button (Microsoft Office dialog box) to open the document in the PowerPoint desktop app. If necessary, sign in to your Microsoft account when prompted. Note: You may need to respond to security warnings regarding viruses. If you are using a browser other than Microsoft Edge, you may need to respond to questions in that browser's dialog box.

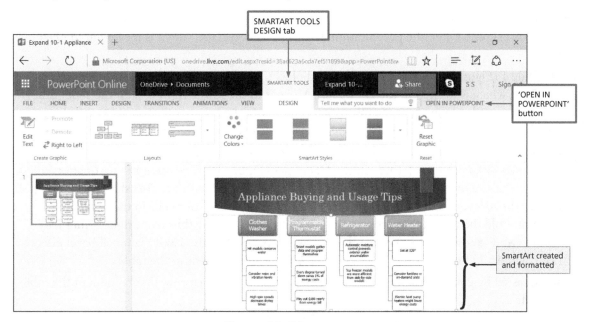

Figure 10–79

Continued >

Expand Your World *continued*

9. In the PowerPoint desktop app, apply the Metallic Scene SmartArt style to the graphic and bold the four column headings (Clothes Washer, Programmable Thermostat, Refrigerator, and Water Heater). Save the slide on your OneDrive account with the file name, Expand 10-1 Appliance Energy Savings Modified.

10. Submit the Expand 10-1 Appliance Energy Savings and the Expand 10-1 Appliance Energy Savings Modified documents in the format requested by your instructor. Sign out of your OneDrive account. Sign out of the Microsoft account in PowerPoint.

11. ✷ Which SmartArt features that are available in the PowerPoint desktop app are not available in PowerPoint Online? Is the information presented more clearly in the Save Energy chart or in the SmartArt graphic? Why?

In the Labs

Design, create, modify, and/or use a presentation following the guidelines, concepts, and skills presented in this module. Labs 1 and 2, which increase in difficulty, require you to create solutions based on what you learned in the module; Lab 3 requires you to apply your creative thinking and problem-solving skills to design and implement a solution.

Lab 1: Inserting Content from Word Documents and Excel Worksheets, Switching Rows and Columns in a Chart, and Entering Data in a Table

Note: To complete this assignment, you will be required to use the Data Files. Please contact your instructor for information about accessing the Data Files.

Problem: The town of Midland is hosting its ninth annual Thanksgiving Day Turkey Trot. More than 20,000 runners are expected to participate. In previous years, the runners have come from the five neighboring towns. The director of the Turkey Trot has asked for your help in publicizing the event. She gives you the Microsoft Word file with the logo she used for last year's event and wants you to update it for this race. You create the presentation shown in Figure 10–80.

Perform the following tasks:

1. Run PowerPoint. Open the presentation, Lab 10-1 Turkey Trot, which is located in the Data Files.

2. On Slide 1 (Figure 10–80a), insert the Word object, Midland Turkey Trot Logo (Figure 10–79b), which is located in the Data Files. Move it to the lower-right area of the slide. Edit the text in the flag by placing the insertion point before the number 8, typing `9,` and then deleting the number 8. Click outside the object to close the editing window.

3. On Slide 2, copy and paste the table from the Microsoft Word file called Reasons to Run (Figure 10–80c), which is located in the Data Files (Figure 10-80d) using the destination styles. Change the size of the table to 4" × 8" and then move the table to the area shown in the figure. Center the text vertically and then increase the font size of the four cells in the first column to 24 pt. Bold the text in the second column. Edit the text in the third row, right column, by typing `and scenic Downtown` after the word, parks. Add the Cool Slant cell bevel effect (fourth effect in first row) and then add the Linear Right gradient to the table.

4. If requested by your instructor, add your home address in the last row, first column of the table on Slide 2.

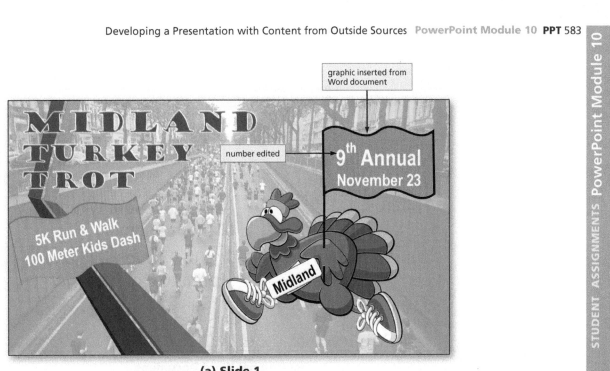

(a) Slide 1

(b) Original Word Graphic

Figure 10–80 (Continued)

Continued >

In the Labs *continued*

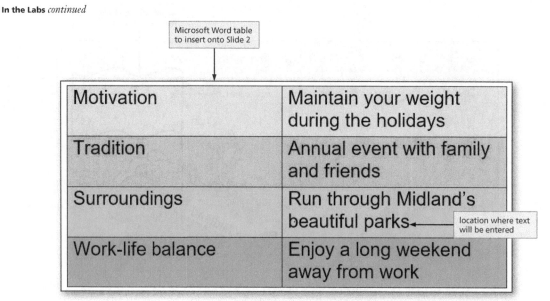

(c) Original Word Document

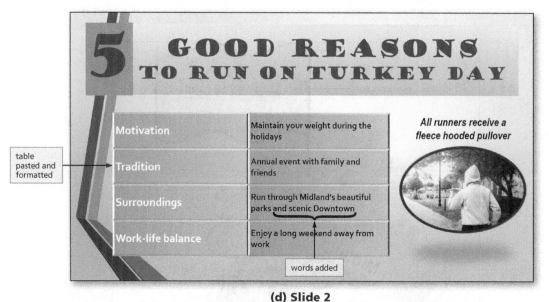

(d) Slide 2

Figure 10–80 (Continued)

5. On Slide 3 (Figure 10–80e), insert and link the Microsoft Excel table called Four Week Training Plan (Figure 10–80f), which is located in the Data Files. Unlock the aspect ratio, change the size to 4.5" × 11.5", and move it to the location shown in Figure 10–80e. For Week 4, change the running times in the Monday and Friday columns from 45 min to 50 min. Save the changes in the Excel worksheet.

6. Open the Microsoft Excel file called Last Year's Participants, which is located in the Data Files, and then copy the chart located on Sheet1 (Figure 10–80g). Paste the chart onto Slide 4 (Figure 10–80h) with the 'Use Destination Theme & Link Data' option and then resize it to 6" × 10". Switch the chart's rows and columns so the town names are listed at the bottom of the chart. Change the chart type to 3-D Column, the chart style to Style 11, the colors to Color 1.

table inserted onto Slide 3 and linked

data changed

data changed

(e) Slide 3

Microsoft Excel table to insert onto Slide 3

data to change

data to change

(f) Original Excel Table

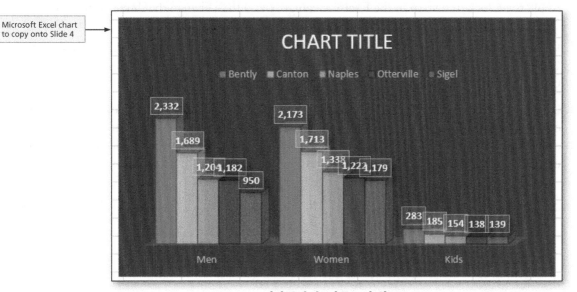

Microsoft Excel chart to copy onto Slide 4

(g) Original Excel Chart

Figure 10–80 (Continued)

Continued >

In the Labs *continued*

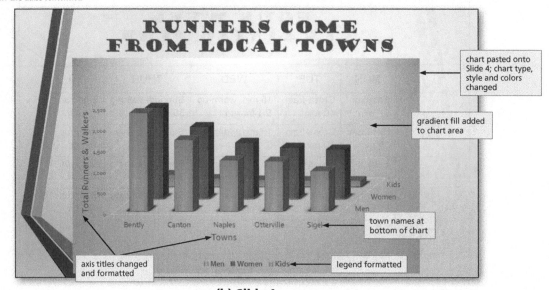

(h) Slide 4

Figure 10–80

7. Type **Total Runners & Walkers** as the vertical axis title and **Towns** as the horizontal axis title. Change the font size for both axis titles to 20 pt. Delete the chart title by displaying the CHART ELEMENTS pane and then clicking the Chart Title check box and the Data Labels check box to remove the check marks.

8. Format the chart area with the 'Top Spotlight - Accent 3' preset gradient fill (third gradient in second row). Click one of the depth axis labels (Men, Women, Kids) to select all three words, display the Home tab, and then increase the font size to 16 pt. Then, select a horizontal axis label and increase the font size to 16 point. Select all the legend items, increase the font size to 16 point, and then bold this text.

9. Align the chart in the center of the slide.

10. Apply the Clock transition in the Exciting category and then change the duration to 3.50 seconds for all slides.

11. Run the presentation and then save the file using the file name, Lab 10-1 Midland Turkey Trot. Close any open Microsoft Excel or Word files.

12. Submit the document in the format specified by your instructor.

13. ☀ Were the formatting changes you made to the Slide 2 table appropriate choices? What other changes could make the table more visually appealing? Would you choose a different chart type, chart style, or colors for the Slide 4 chart? Which Microsoft Word or Excel files would you find useful to insert in a PowerPoint presentation that you would create for your job or at school?

Lab 2: Copying and Pasting Graphics from PowerPoint and Excel Documents, Formatting a Table and a Chart, Adding a Hyperlink to a Table, and Editing Linked Files

Note: To complete this assignment, you will be required to use the Data Files. Please contact your instructor for information about accessing the Data Files.

Problem: You work for a moving and storage company, and your boss asked you to prepare a presentation to run on kiosks at both office locations. Some of the slides also will be added to the company's website. While developing content for your presentation, you learn that the most popular days to move are Friday and Saturday. You also find that approximately 40 percent of your customers moved to a new home that was located 100 miles or more from their current home. A smaller percentage of your customers — about 14 percent — moved 25 miles or less. You create the presentation shown in Figure 10–81.

Perform the following tasks:

1. Run PowerPoint. Open the presentation called Lab 10-2 Moving, which is located in the Data Files.

2. Display Slide 1 (Figure 10–81a). Open the PowerPoint presentation called, Why People Move, which is available in the Data Files, select the graphic on Slide 1, and then copy and paste it on Slide 1 of the Moving presentation. Use the SmartGuides to center the graphic below the title text.

3. On Slide 2 (Figure 10–81b), increase the table size to 5" × 11". Distribute all rows and columns. Select all text in the table and then change the font to Arial. Increase the font size of the column headings in the first row to 20 point. Increase the font size of the text in the five rows below the column headings to 18 point. Align the table in the center of the slide.

4. Change the table background shading to 'Red, Accent 2, Lighter 40%' (sixth color in fourth Theme Colors row) and then apply the Relaxed Inset cell bevel (second bevel in first Bevel row) to the table.

(a) Slide 1

Figure 10–81 (continued)

Continued >

In the Labs *continued*

(b) Slide 2

Moving Checklist

8 to 10 weeks before

- ☐ Set a moving date
- ☐ Get estimates from 3 professional movers
- ☐ Go through the house and make a list of what you are taking
- ☐ Decide what items you can donate or discard
- ☐ Get new-resident information from your new town

6 weeks before

- ☐ Get change-of-address forms from your post office
- ☐ If moving long distance, get medical, dental, and vet records
- ☐ If necessary, transfer school records

4 weeks before

- ☐ Get packing materials, including boxes, labels, markers, tape, and bubble wrap
- ☐ Start packing and labeling items you won't need (holiday decorations & off-season clothing, etc.)
- ☐ Decide what items you may want to store in a storage facility
- ☐ Arrange baby and dog sitters for moving day

3 weeks before

- ☐ Confirm delivery of new appliances and furnishings
- ☐ Contact electric, gas, and other utilities at both locations to set off/on dates
- ☐ Take packed items to storage facility

2 weeks before

- ☐ Contact local newspaper to set up new delivery address
- ☐ Give mail and/or email change-of-address forms to post office and creditors
- ☐ Contact bank and/or credit union with change of address

1 week before

- ☐ Sort and pack legal and valuable documents that you will move personally
- ☐ Notify family and friends of your new address
- ☐ Pack and label clearly other items except for clothing and kitchen items you may need

1 day before

- ☐ Label boxes "open first" with items such as tools, cleaning supplies, and lights
- ☐ Check and replenish cash needed for payments (movers, helpers, meals, etc.)
- ☐ Clean out refrigerator and donate perishable items

(c) Hyperlinked Word File

Figure 10–81 (Continued)

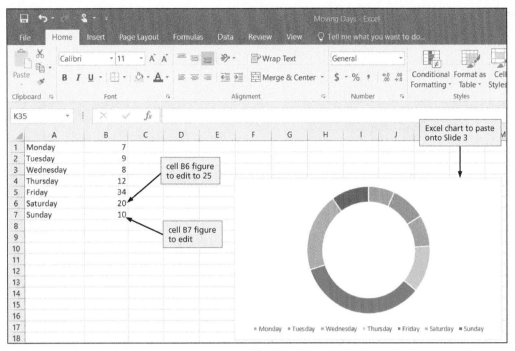

(d) Excel Worksheet

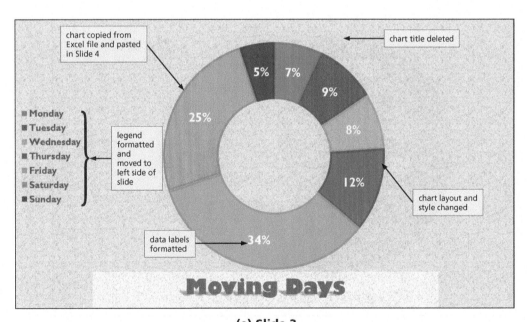

(e) Slide 3

Figure 10 – 81 (Continued)

5. On Slide 2, select the column heading, Personal, and then insert a hyperlink to the Microsoft Word file called Moving Checklist (Figure 10–81c), which is located in the Data Files.

6. If requested by your instructor, type the name of your current or previous pet after the word, Veterinarian, in the last row of the table.

7. Open the Microsoft Excel file called Moving Days, which is located in the Data Files, and then copy the chart (Figure 10–81d) located on Sheet1. Paste the chart onto Slide 3 (Figure 10–81e) with the 'Keep Source Formatting & Link Data' option and then resize

Continued >

In the Labs *continued*

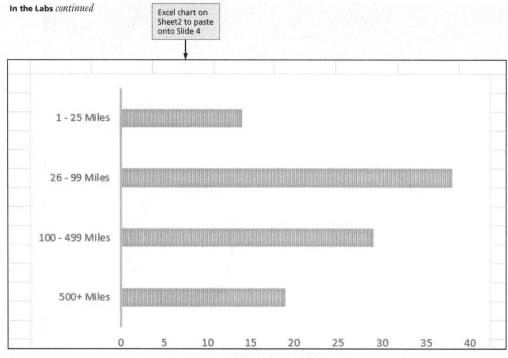

(f) Original Excel Chart

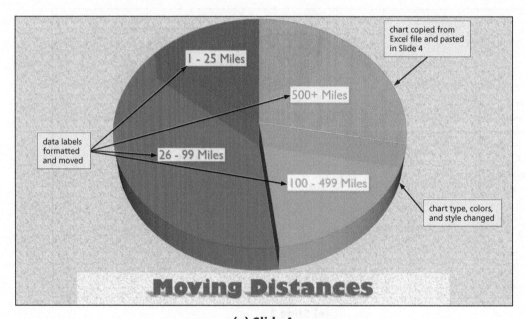

(g) Slide 4
Figure 10 – 81 (Continued)

it to 7.1" × 12". Click the Quick Layout button (Chart Tools Design tab | Chart Layouts group) and then change the layout to Layout 6. Change the chart style to Style 8.

8. Delete the chart title. Move the legend to the left side of the slide, change the font to Gill Sans MT, increase the font size to 18 point, and then bold this text. Select the data labels in the doughnut chart, change the font to Gill Sans MT, and then increase the font size to 24 point. Align the chart in the left and the top of the slide.

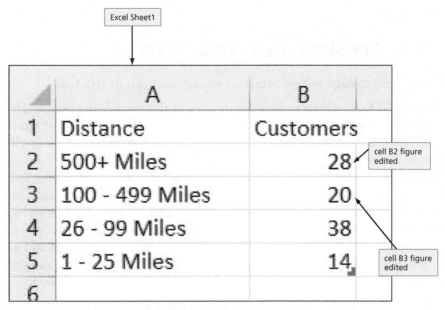

(h) Excel Worksheet

Figure 10–81

9. Edit the chart in Microsoft Excel by changing the figure in cell B6 (customers moving on Saturday) to 25 and the figure in cell B7 (customers moving on Sunday) to 5. Save the new values in the Moving Days worksheet.

10. Open the Microsoft Excel file called Moving Distances, which is located in the Data Files, and then copy the chart located on Sheet2 (Figure 10–81f). Paste the chart onto Slide 4 (Figure 10–81g) with the 'Keep Source Formatting & Link Data' option and then resize it to 7" × 11". Change the chart type to 3-D Pie, change the colors to Color 4 (last row in Colorful group), and then change the style to Style 2.

11. Edit the chart in Microsoft Excel by displaying Sheet1 and changing the figure in cell B2 (customers moving 500 or more miles) to 28 and the figure in cell B3 (customers moving 100 – 499 miles) to 20 (Figure 10–81h). Save the new values in the Moving Distances worksheet.

12. Change the font of the data labels to Gill Sans MT and then increase the font size to 24. Move the data labels to the locations shown in the figure. Align the chart in the center and the top of the slide.

13. Apply the Fade transition in the Subtle category and then change the duration to 2.50 seconds for all slides.

14. Run the presentation and then save the file using the file name, Lab 10-2 1st Class Moving and Storage. Close any open Microsoft Excel or Word files.

15. Submit the document in the format specified by your instructor.

16. ✳ On Slide 2, you distributed rows and columns in the table and added a shading and a bevel to the background. Did this improve the look of the table? Would a different chart type on Slide 3 better represent the moving days?

Continued >

In the Labs *continued*

Lab 3: **Consider This: Your Turn**

Design and Create a Presentation about Sodium in the Diet

Part 1: The Extend Your Knowledge exercise in this module discusses sugar levels in popular drinks and natural sources. Nutritionists recommend monitoring sugar intake because excessive sugar can negatively affect overall health. Eating foods with high sugar levels can lead to an impaired immune system, diabetes, and obesity. High sodium levels, likewise, may cause health issues, including high blood pressure and osteoporosis. Review the tables in Figure 10–78 and then use the concepts and techniques presented in this module to create a similar presentation on the topic of sodium in your diet. Obtain information about foods with high sodium contents. Also, explore healthier alternatives, and then present this information in a table. Use at least three objectives found at the beginning of this module to develop the slides, and include at least one table. Review and revise your presentation as needed and then save the file using the file name, Lab 10-3 Sodium. Submit your assignment in the format specified by your instructor.

Part 2: ✳ You made several decisions while creating the presentation in this assignment: where to research nutritional guidelines on sodium content, how to present this information in a table, how to format a table, and how to make the presentation look professional and consistent. What was the rationale behind each of these decisions? When you reviewed the document, what further revisions did you make and why? Where would you recommend showing this slide show?

11 | Organizing Slides and Creating a Photo Album

Objectives

You will have mastered the material in this module when you can:

- Create a section break
- Rename and reorder a section
- Create a custom slide show
- Create a photo album and add captions
- Reorder pictures in a photo album
- Adjust the quality of pictures in a photo album

- Look up information
- Change slide orientation
- Set up a custom size slide
- Copy and compress a video file
- Email a presentation
- Create a video from a presentation

Introduction

BTW

Using Photographs
A carefully selected image can convey an engaging message that your audience will remember long after the presentation has ended. One picture can evoke emotions and create a connection between the speaker and the listeners. The adage, "A picture is worth a thousand words," is relevant when audience members view PowerPoint slides.

Sharing photographs and videos has become a part of our everyday lives. We often use smartphones, digital cameras, and mobile devices, and we visit online social media websites to share our adventures, special occasions, and business activities. The presentations can be organized into sections so that particular slides are shown to specific audiences. For example, one large presentation created for freshmen orientation can be divided into one section for registration, another for financial aid, and a third for campus activities; each section could be shown to different audiences.

In addition, PowerPoint's ability to create a photo album allows you to organize and distribute your pictures by adding interesting layouts, vibrant backgrounds, and meaningful captions. These photo albums can be emailed, published to a website, or turned into a video to distribute to friends and business associates, who do not need PowerPoint installed on their computers to view your file.

Project — Presentation with Sections and a Photo Album

Iceland is a stunning country known as "The Land of Fire and Ice." Its diverse geographical regions feature forests, farmlands, volcanoes, lagoons, hot springs, and major towns. Whale watching excursions are plentiful, and visitors are apt to view a variety of marine mammals. The small Icelandic horse is a descendent of an ancient breed that lived more than one thousand years ago. Tourists also enjoy relaxing in geothermally heated water, the most famous being the Blue Lagoon. Many travel groups plan group vacations, and they welcome experts and vacationers who share insights and photos of travel destinations. Members of the Travel Club in your community have asked you to present highlights of that country during their monthly meeting at the library.

The presentation you create in this module (Figure 11–1) contains photos of Icelandic highlights. You divide the slide show into sections for Lagoons and Geysers (Figure 11–1a), Cities and Countrysides, Animals, and Glaciers. You then create a photo album, add pictures, make adjustments to brightness and contrast, and edit captions (Figures 11–1b and 11–1c). You also create a second photo album with black-and-white images (Figure 11–1d). In addition, you create two slides with a custom size to use as a marketing tool to promote your presentation at the library and insert a video file on one of the slides (Figure 11–1e). You then email the announcement file to a member and also convert another file to a video so that Travel Club members who do not have PowerPoint installed on their computers can view the Eyjafjallajokull volcano that erupted in 2010.

In this module, you will learn how to create the slides shown in Figure 11–1. The following roadmap identifies general activities you will perform as you progress through this module:

1. CREATE and ORGANIZE SECTIONS in a presentation.
2. Select specific slides to CREATE a CUSTOM SLIDE SHOW.
3. CREATE a PHOTO ALBUM and ENHANCE photo album ELEMENTS.
4. SPECIFY a CUSTOM SLIDE SIZE and ADD a VIDEO CLIP.
5. SHARE and DISTRIBUTE a PRESENTATION by emailing and creating a video.

To Run PowerPoint and Save a File

If you are using a computer to step through the project in this module and you want your screens to match the figures in this book, you should change your computer's resolution to 1366 × 768. The following steps run PowerPoint and then save a file.

1 Run PowerPoint. If necessary, maximize the PowerPoint window.

2 Open the presentation, Iceland, located in the Data Files.

3 Save the presentation using the file name, Discover Iceland.

text edited for Section Header layout

A Land of Lagoons and Geysers
DISCOVER ICELAND

(a) Discover Iceland Section Slide

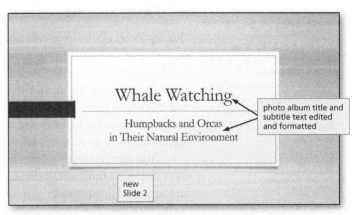

Whale Watching

Humpbacks and Orcas
in Their Natural Environment

photo album title and subtitle text edited and formatted

new Slide 2

(b) Photo Album Title Slide

Silica once was a major export of the whaling town, Husavik

caption edited

(c) Photo Album Slide

black and white picture in photo album

Visitors can view whales up close while enjoying the beautiful Icelandic scenery

caption edited

(d) Black-and-White Photo Album Slide

custom size slide has portrait orientation

Join us as we explore this vibrant country
• Learn about whaling adventures, sightseeing trips through the countryside, geysers, and much more

video copied and compressed

(e) Custom Size Slide

Figure 11–1

BTW
Touch Screen Differences
The Office and Windows interfaces may vary if you are using a touch screen. For this reason, you might notice that the function or appearance of your touch screen differs slightly from this module's presentation.

BTW
Hyperlinking Custom Shows
You can hyperlink to a custom show with slides relating to a specific topic in your presentation. Click the Hyperlink button (Insert tab | Links group), if necessary click the 'Place in This Document' button in the Link to area, and then select the custom show in the 'Select a place in this document' area.

Creating Sections and a Custom Slide Show

Quality PowerPoint presentations are tailored toward specific audiences, and experienced presenters adapt the slides to meet the listeners' needs and expectations. Speakers can develop one slide show and then modify the content each time they deliver the presentation. In the Discover Iceland slide show, for example, a speaker may decide to place the slides that showcase spectacular glaciers at the end of the presentation to build suspense. Or, these slides can appear at the beginning of the presentation to generate interest.

You can divide the slides into **sections** to help organize the slides. These sections serve the same function as dividers in a notebook or tabs in a manual: They help the user find required information and move material in a new sequence. In PowerPoint, you can create sections, give them unique names, and then move slides into each section. You then can move one entire section to another part of the slide show or delete the section if it no longer is needed. Each section can be displayed or printed individually.

A **custom show** is an independent set of slides to show to a specific audience. These slides can be in a different order than in the original presentation. For example, you may desire to show a title slide, the last nine slides, and then Slides 2, 5, and 8, in that order. One PowerPoint file can have several custom shows to adapt to specific audiences.

To Insert Slides with a Section Layout

1 CREATE & ORGANIZE SECTIONS | **2 CREATE CUSTOM SLIDE SHOW** | 3 CREATE PHOTO ALBUM & ENHANCE ELEMENTS
4 SPECIFY CUSTOM SLIDE SIZE & ADD VIDEO CLIP | 5 SHARE & DISTRIBUTE PRESENTATION

Your presentation will have four sections: Lagoons and Geysers, Cities and Countrysides, Animals, and Glaciers. One of PowerPoint's layouts is named Section Header, and it is similar to the Title Slide layout because it has a title and a subtitle placeholder. To ensure consistency and save time, you can create one slide with a Section Header layout and then duplicate and modify it for each section. *Why? You can help your audience understand the organization of your slide show if you have one slide announcing the content of each section.* The following steps insert the four section slides.

- With Slide 1 selected and the Home tab displaying, click the New Slide arrow (Home tab | Slides group) to display the Office Theme gallery (Figure 11–2).

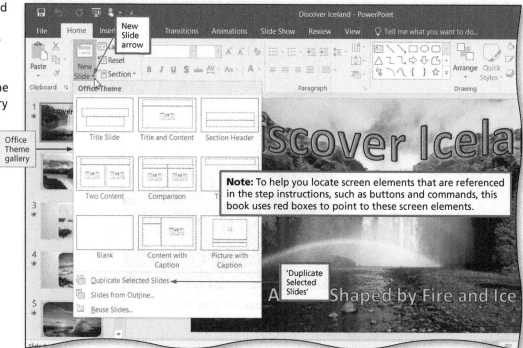

Figure 11–2

2

- Click 'Duplicate Selected Slides' in the Office Theme gallery to create a new Slide 2 that is a duplicate of Slide 1.

- Click the Slide Layout button (Home tab | Slides group) to display the Office Theme layout gallery (Figure 11–3).

Figure 11–3

3

- Click the Section Header layout to apply that layout to the new Slide 2 (Figure 11–4).

Figure 11–4

Other Ways

1. Right-click Slide 1, click Duplicate Slide on shortcut menu; then right-click Slide 2, click Layout on shortcut menu

To Edit the Subtitle

The slide with the Section Header layout should have characteristics similar to the title slide to give the presentation continuity. One method of slightly altering the title slide is to change the text to reflect the next set of slides in the presentation. The following steps edit the subtitle text.

1 With Slide 2 displaying, select the words, Shaped by Fire and Ice, in the subtitle text placeholder and then type **of Lagoons and Geysers** as the replacement text.

2 Select all the subtitle text, change the font size to 36 point, click the Character Spacing button (Home tab | Font group), and then change the character spacing to Loose.

3 Center this text in the placeholder and then change the subtitle text font color to 'Tan, Background 2' (third color in first Theme Colors row) (Figure 11–5).

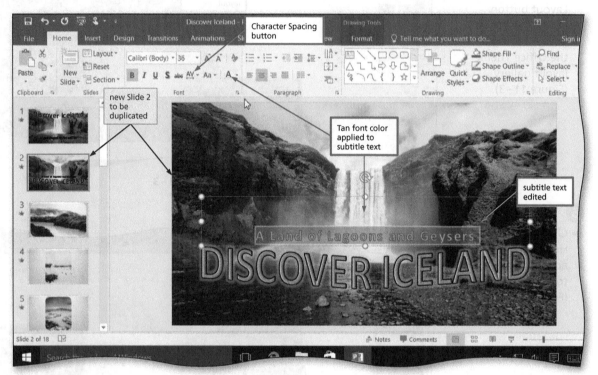

Figure 11–5

To Duplicate and Edit the Section Slides

Slide 2 is formatted appropriately to display at the beginning of the Lagoons and Geysers section of the slide show. A similar slide should display at the beginning of the Cities and Countrysides, Animals, and Glaciers sections. The following steps duplicate Slide 2 and edit the title text.

1 With Slide 2 selected and the Home tab displaying, click the New Slide arrow and then click 'Duplicate Selected Slides'.

2 Repeat Step 1 twice to insert two additional duplicate slides.

3 Display Slide 3, select the words, Lagoons and Geysers, and then type **Cities and Countrysides** in the subtitle text placeholder.

4 Display Slide 4, select the words, Lagoons and Geysers, and then type **Animals** in the subtitle text placeholder.

5 Display Slide 5, select the words, Lagoons and Geysers, and then type **Glaciers** in the subtitle text placeholder (Figure 11–6).

Figure 11–6

To Arrange Slides in Slide Sorter View

1 CREATE & ORGANIZE SECTIONS | **2 CREATE CUSTOM SLIDE SHOW** | **3 CREATE PHOTO ALBUM & ENHANCE ELEMENTS**
4 SPECIFY CUSTOM SLIDE SIZE & ADD VIDEO CLIP | **5 SHARE & DISTRIBUTE PRESENTATION**

The four slides with a Section Header layout currently are displayed after the title slide. They are followed by 16 slides grouped into four categories, each of which has a distinct photo style or effect and background. The Lagoons and Geysers slides have photos with a rounded border and a green background, the Cities and Countrysides slides have photos with a green border and a patterned background, the Animal photos have soft edges and a grass photo background, and Glaciers photos have a bevel effect and a water background. One of the four section slides you formatted should be positioned at the beginning of each category. When the presentation has only a few slides, you easily can drag and drop the slide thumbnails in the Slides pane. Your Discover Iceland presentation, however, has 21 slides. The following steps arrange the slides in Slide Sorter view. *Why? To easily arrange the slides, you can change to Slide Sorter view and drag and drop the thumbnails into their desired locations.*

1

- Click the Slide Sorter view button to display the slides in Slide Sorter view and then click the Slide 3 thumbnail (A Land of Cities and Countrysides) to select it.

- Drag the Zoom slider to the left to change the zoom percentage to 30% so that all the slides are displayed (Figure 11–7).

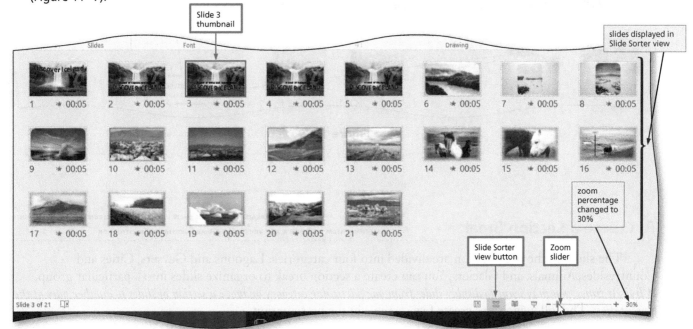

Figure 11–7

2

- Drag the Slide 3 thumbnail between the Slide 9 and Slide 10 thumbnails so that it is positioned in the desired location between these two slides (Figure 11–8).

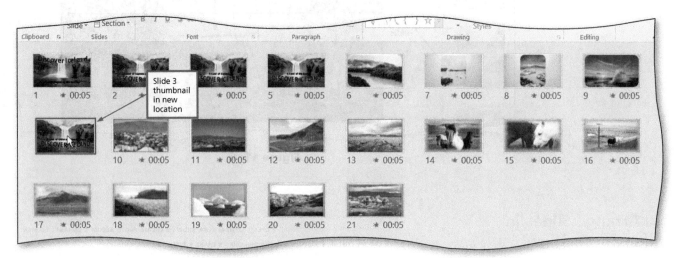

Figure 11–8

3

- Release the mouse button to display the Slide 3 thumbnail in a new location as Slide 9.
- Select the new Slide 3 (A Land of Animals) and drag it between Slide 13 and Slide 14.
- Select the new Slide 3 (A Land of Glaciers) and drag it between Slide 17 and Slide 18 (Figure 11–9).

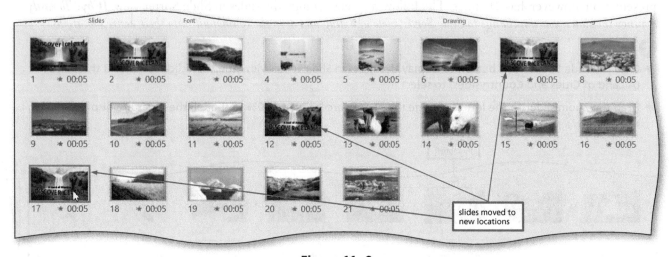

Figure 11–9

To Create a Section Break

1 CREATE & ORGANIZE SECTIONS | 2 CREATE CUSTOM SLIDE SHOW | 3 CREATE PHOTO ALBUM & ENHANCE ELEMENTS
4 SPECIFY CUSTOM SLIDE SIZE & ADD VIDEO CLIP | 5 SHARE & DISTRIBUTE PRESENTATION

The slides in the presentation are divided into four categories: Lagoons and Geysers, Cities and Countrysides, Animals, and Glaciers. You can create a section break to organize slides into a particular group. *Why? At times, you may want to display slides from one particular category or move a section of slides to another part of the presentation.* The following steps create five sections in the presentation.

- In Slide Sorter view, position the pointer between Slide 1 and Slide 2 and then click once to display the vertical bar (Figure 11–10).

Q&A I am using a touch screen. When I tap between the slides to display the vertical bar, a shortcut menu also displays with an Add Section button. Can I just tap that button instead of using the Home tab Section button?
Yes.

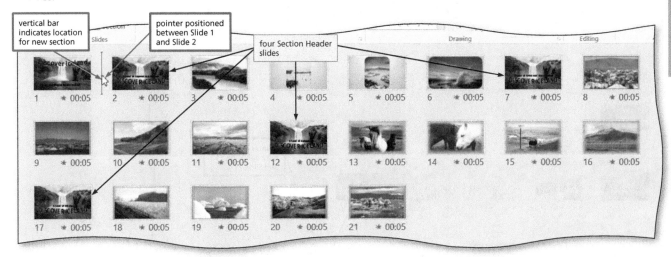

Figure 11–10

- With the Home tab displaying, click the Section button (Home tab | Slides group) to display the Section menu (Figure 11–11).

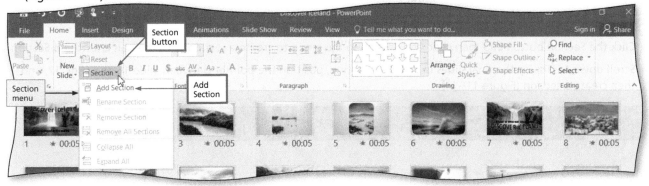

Figure 11–11

❸

- Click Add Section in the menu to create a section with the name, Untitled Section.

- Position the pointer between Slide 6 and Slide 7, which is the start of the slides with the Cities and Countrysides photos, and then click once to display the vertical bar (Figure 11–12).

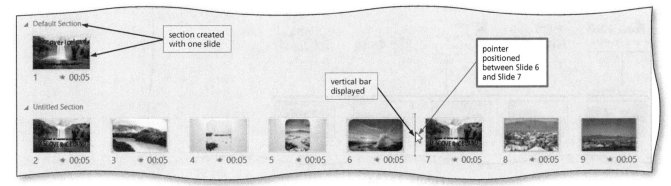

Figure 11–12

4

- Click the Section button (Home tab | Slides group) to display the Section menu and then click Add Section in the menu to create a section with the name, Untitled Section.

- Position the pointer between Slide 11 and Slide 12, which is the start of the slides with animal photos, and then click once (Figure 11–13).

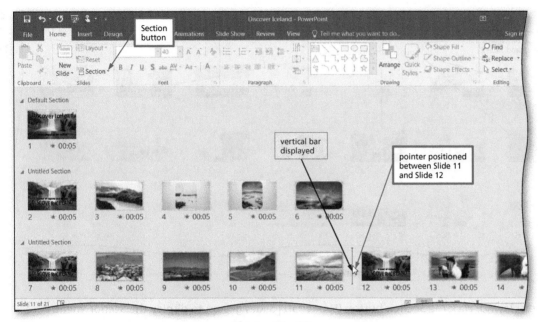

Figure 11–13

5

- Click the Section button and then click Add Section in the menu to create a section with the name, Untitled Section.

- Scroll down to display the final slides in the presentation, position the pointer between Slide 16 and Slide 17, and then create a section (Figure 11–14).

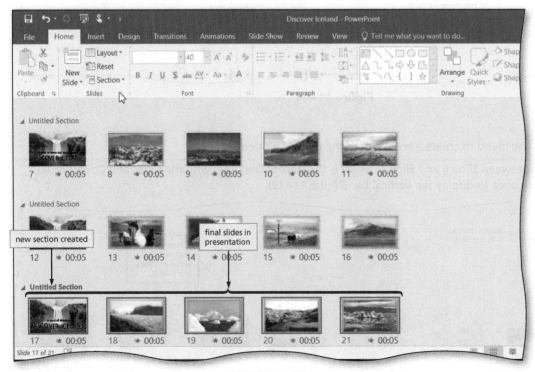

Figure 11–14

To Rename a Section

The default section names, Untitled and Default, do not identify the content of the slides in the group. The following steps rename each of the five sections in the presentation. *Why? Giving each section a unique name helps to categorize the slides easily.*

- With the last section featuring the glacier photos selected and the Home tab displaying, click the Section button (Home tab | Slides group) to display the Section menu (Figure 11–15).

Q&A
If the Glaciers section is not highlighted, how can I select it? Click the divider between the sections. You will know the section is selected when the thumbnails have a red border and the text and slide numbers have a red font color.

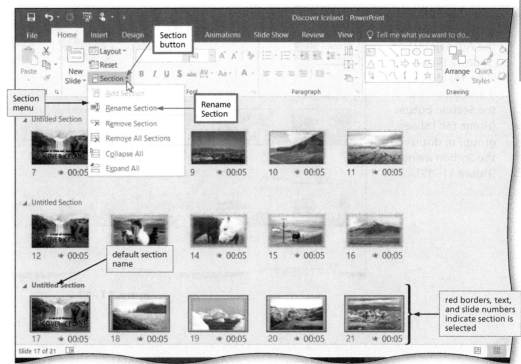

Figure 11–15

- Click Rename Section in the menu to display the Rename Section dialog box.

- Type **Glaciers** in the Section name box (Figure 11–16).

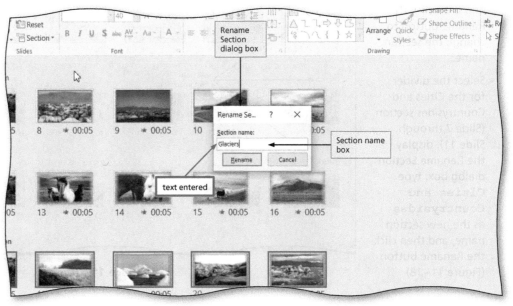

Figure 11–16

- Click the Rename button (Rename Section dialog box) to change the section name.

- Click the Untitled Section divider for the Animals section (Slide 12 through Slide 16) to select it and then click the Section button (Home tab | Slides group) to display the Section menu (Figure 11–17).

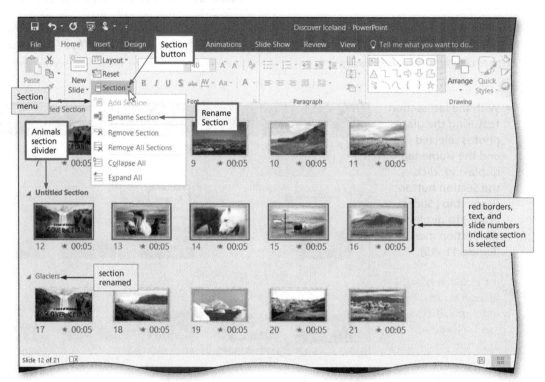

Figure 11–17

- Click Rename Section to display the Rename Section dialog box, type **Animals** in the Section name box, and then click the Rename button to change the section name.

- Select the divider for the Cities and Countrysides section (Slide 7 through Slide 11), display the Rename Section dialog box, type **Cities and Countrysides** as the new section name, and then click the Rename button (Figure 11–18).

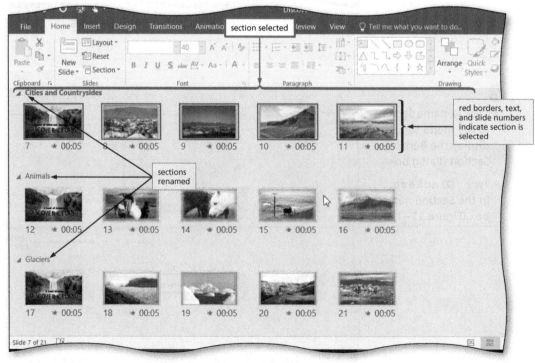

Figure 11–18

- Scroll up to display the first two sections, select the divider for the Lagoons and Geysers slides (Slide 2 through Slide 6), display the Rename Section dialog box, type **Lagoons and Geysers** as the new section name, and then click the Rename button.

- Select the Default Section divider for Slide 1, display the Rename Section dialog box, type **Discover Iceland Title** as the new section name, and then click the Rename button (Figure 11–19).

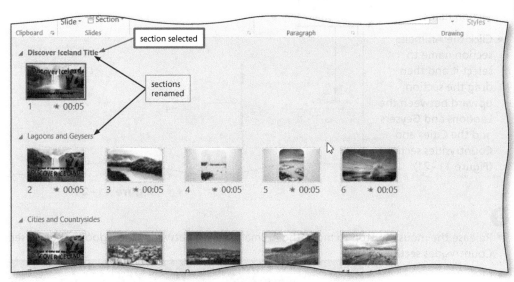

Figure 11–19

Other Ways

1. Right-click section divider, click Rename Section on shortcut menu

To Collapse and Reorder Sections

1 CREATE & ORGANIZE SECTIONS | 2 CREATE CUSTOM SLIDE SHOW | 3 CREATE PHOTO ALBUM & ENHANCE ELEMENTS
4 SPECIFY CUSTOM SLIDE SIZE & ADD VIDEO CLIP | 5 SHARE & DISTRIBUTE PRESENTATION

Why? *Travel Club members have expressed much more interest this year in animals than the cities and countryside landscape, so you want to change the order of these two sets of slides in your presentation.* When slides are organized into sections, it is easy to change the order in which the sections display. Because your presentation consists of multiple sections, you can collapse the sections so that only the section titles are displayed. You then can reorder the sections and expand the sections. The following steps collapse the sections, reorder the Animals and Cities and Countrysides sections, and expand the sections.

- With the first section, Discover Iceland Title, selected and the Home tab displaying, click the Section button (Home tab | Slides group) to display the Section menu (Figure 11–20).

Q&A

Can I remove a section?

Yes. To delete one section, select the section title and then click Remove Section in the Section menu. To remove all sections, display the Section menu and then click 'Remove All Sections'.

Figure 11–20

2

- Click Collapse All in the Section menu to display only the section names.

- Click the Animals section name to select it and then drag the section upward between the Lagoons and Geysers and the Cities and Countrysides sections (Figure 11–21).

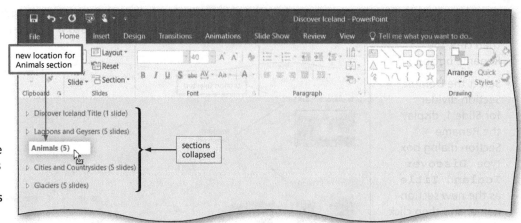

Figure 11–21

3

- Release the mouse button to move the Animals section between the Lagoons and Geysers and Cities and Countrysides sections.

- Click the Section button (Home tab | Slides group) to display the Section menu (Figure 11–22).

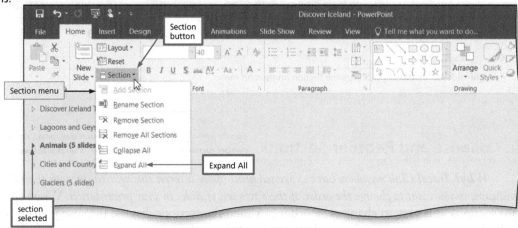

Figure 11–22

4

- Click Expand All in the Section menu to display all the slides in their corresponding sections (Figure 11–23).

5

- Run the presentation to display all the slides in the desired order.

Figure 11–23

Other Ways

1. Right-click section name, click Move Section Up, Move Section Down, Collapse All, or Expand All on shortcut menu

To Show a Presentation with Manual Timing

The Discover Iceland slides are set to display for specified times. If you desire to override the automatic timings and advance the slides manually, you would perform the following steps.

1. Display the Slide Show tab and then click the 'Set Up Slide Show' button (Slide Show tab | Set Up group) to display the Set Up Show dialog box.

2. Click Manually in the Advance slides area (Set Up Show dialog box) and then click the OK button.

Break Point: If you wish to take a break, this is a good place to do so. Be sure to save the Discover Iceland file again and then you can exit PowerPoint. To resume at a later time, run PowerPoint, open the file called Discover Iceland, and continue following the steps from this location forward.

To Create a Custom Slide Show

1 CREATE & ORGANIZE SECTIONS | 2 CREATE CUSTOM SLIDE SHOW | **3 CREATE PHOTO ALBUM & ENHANCE ELEMENTS**
4 SPECIFY CUSTOM SLIDE SIZE & ADD VIDEO CLIP | 5 SHARE & DISTRIBUTE PRESENTATION

Many presenters deliver their speeches in front of targeted audiences. For example, the director of human resources may present one set of slides for new employees, another set for potential retirees, and a third for managers concerned with new regulations and legislation. Slides for all these files may be contained in one file, and the presenter can elect to show particular slides to accompany specific speeches. PowerPoint allows you to create a **custom show** that displays only selected slides. The following steps create a custom show. *Why? You want to create a smaller file in case your speech time at the library is less than planned and you need to shorten your talk.*

①

- Click the Normal view button to display the slides in Normal view and then display the Slide Show tab.

- Click the 'Custom Slide Show' button (Slide Show tab | Start Slide Show group) to display the Custom Slide Show menu (Figure 11–24).

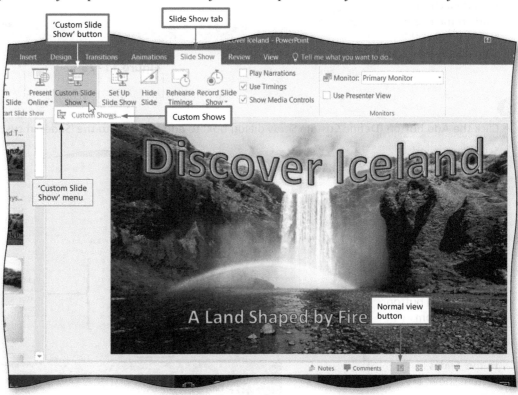

Figure 11–24

- Click Custom Shows to open the Custom Shows dialog box (Figure 11–25).

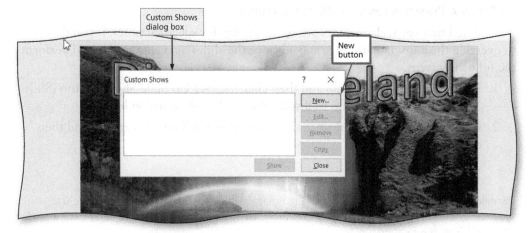

Figure 11–25

- Click the New button (Custom Shows dialog box) to display the Define Custom Show dialog box.

- Click '1. Discover Iceland' in the 'Slides in presentation' area to place a check mark in the check box and select this slide (Figure 11–26).

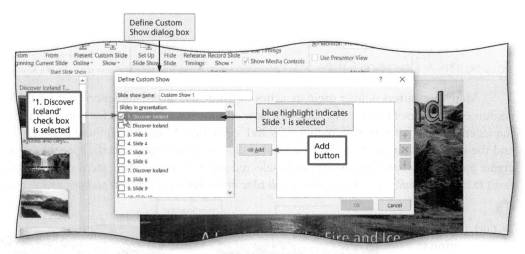

Figure 11–26

- Click the Add button (Define Custom Show dialog box) to add this slide to the 'Slides in custom show' area.

- Scroll down and then click the check boxes for Slide 3, Slide 6, Slide 9, Slide 11, Slide 13, Slide 14, Slide 19, and Slide 21 in the 'Slides in presentation' area.

- Click the Add button (Define Custom Show dialog box) to add these slides to the 'Slides in custom show' area (Figure 11–27).

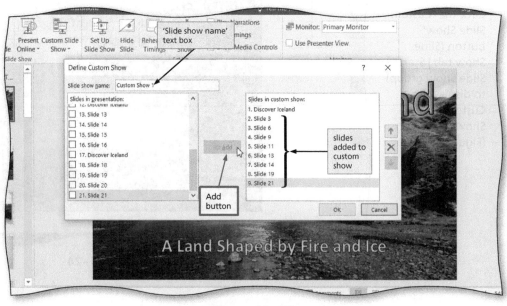

Figure 11–27

• Select the text in the 'Slide show name' text box (Define Custom Show dialog box) and then type **Popular Iceland Attractions** as the new name (Figure 11–28).

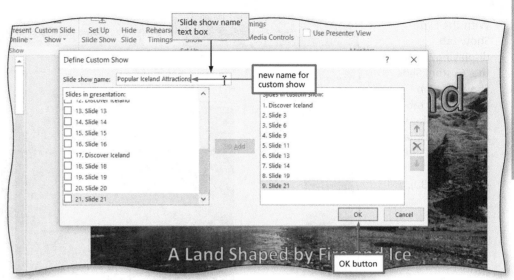

Figure 11–28

• Click the OK button (Define Custom Show dialog box) to create the new Popular Iceland Attractions custom show and display the Custom Shows dialog box (Figure 11–29).

• Click the Close button (Custom Shows dialog box) to close the dialog box.

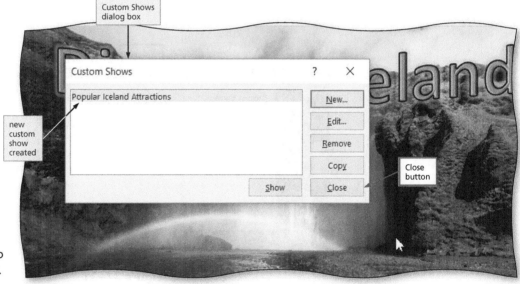

Figure 11–29

To Open and Edit a Custom Slide Show

1 CREATE & ORGANIZE SECTIONS | 2 CREATE CUSTOM SLIDE SHOW | 3 CREATE PHOTO ALBUM & ENHANCE ELEMENTS
4 SPECIFY CUSTOM SLIDE SIZE & ADD VIDEO CLIP | 5 SHARE & DISTRIBUTE PRESENTATION

A PowerPoint file can have several custom slide shows. You can elect to display one of them at any time depending upon the particular needs of your audience. If you need to reorder the slides, you can change the sequence easily. The following steps open a custom show and edit the slide sequence.

1

- With the Slide Show tab displaying, click the 'Custom Slide Show' button (Slide Show tab | Start Slide Show group) to display the Custom Slide Show menu (Figure 11–30).

Q&A

Why does 'Popular Iceland Attractions' display in the Custom Slide Show menu?
The names of any custom shows will be displayed in the menu. If desired, you could click this custom show name to run the slide show and display the selected slides.

Figure 11–30

2

- Click Custom Shows to display the Custom Shows dialog box (Figure 11–31).

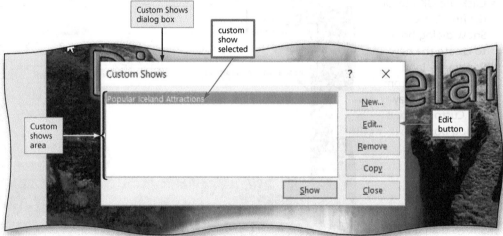

Figure 11–31

3

- With the Popular Iceland Attractions custom show selected in the Custom shows area, click the Edit button (Custom Shows dialog box) to display the Define Custom Show dialog box.

- Click '8. Slide 19' in the 'Slides in custom show' area to select it (Figure 11–32).

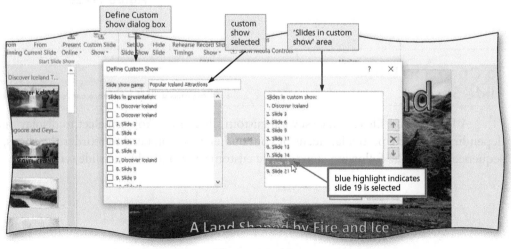

Figure 11–32

• Click the Up button six times to move Slide 19 below Slide 1 as the second slide in the custom show (Figure 11–33).

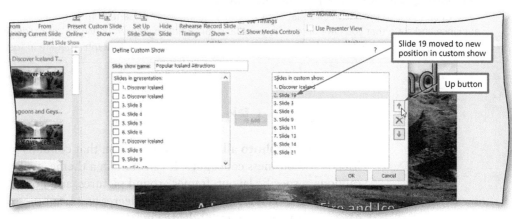

Figure 11–33

• Click '9. Slide 21' in the 'Slides in custom show' area to select it and then click the Up button six times to move Slide 21 below Slide 19 as the third slide in the custom show.

• Click '6. Slide 9' in the 'Slides in custom show' area to select it and then click the Down button once to move Slide 9 below Slide 11 as the seventh slide in the custom show (Figure 11–34).

Q&A Can I move the slides so they display later in the custom show? Yes. Select the slide you want to reorder and then click the Down button.

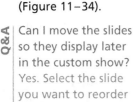

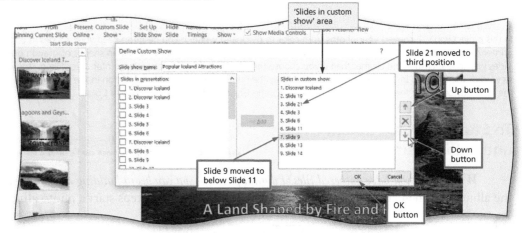

Figure 11–34

• Click the OK button (Define Custom Show dialog box) to create the revised Popular Iceland Attractions custom show and display the Custom Shows dialog box (Figure 11–35).

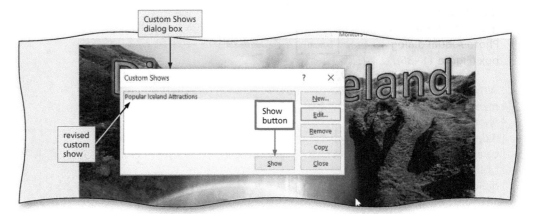

Figure 11–35

• Click the Show button (Custom Shows dialog box) to run the Popular Iceland Attractions custom show.

• When all the slides have displayed, exit the custom show.

• Save the Discover Iceland file. Do not close this file because you are going to use it later in this project.

Use photographs with sharp focus and contrast.
Clear, sharp pictures provide details that draw an audience into your presentation. High-quality photographs impress your audience and state that you have an eye for detail and take pride in your work. When your slides are projected on a large screen, any imperfection is magnified, so you must take care to select photographs that are in focus and have high contrast.

Creating a Photo Album

A PowerPoint **photo album** is a presentation that contains pictures to share with friends and business colleagues. It can contain a theme, a vibrant background, custom captions, a specific layout, frames around pictures, and boxes. You can enhance the quality of the pictures by increasing or decreasing brightness and contrast, and you can rotate the pictures in 90-degree increments. You also can change color pictures to display in black and white.

You can share your photo album in a variety of ways. You can, for example, email the file, publish it to the web, or print the pictures as handouts.

BTW
Printing in Grayscale
In this project you will convert your photos from color to black and white. If you desire to keep your images in color but you do not have a color printer or do not require a color printout, choosing Grayscale will print all the slide objects in shades of gray. In grayscale, some objects on the slides will appear crisper and cleaner than if you choose the Color option on a non-color printer. Click File on the ribbon to open the Backstage view, click the Print tab in the Backstage view to display the Print pane, click the Color button in the Settings area, click Grayscale, and then click the Print button. If you then want to print in color, click the Grayscale button and then click Color.

To Start a Photo Album and Add Pictures

Why? *Once you have gathered files of digital pictures, you can begin building a photo album.* You initially create the album and then later enhance its appearance. The following steps start a photo album and add pictures.

1
- Display the Insert tab and then click the 'New Photo Album' button (Insert tab | Images group) to display the Photo Album dialog box (Figure 11–36).

Q&A
Why am I viewing a menu with the 'New Photo Album' and 'Edit Photo Album' commands instead of the Photo Album dialog box?
You mistakenly clicked the 'New Photo Album' arrow instead of the 'New Photo Album' button.

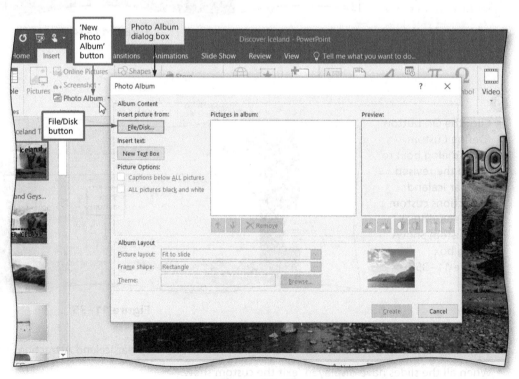

Figure 11–36

- Click the File/Disk button to display the Insert New Pictures dialog box.

- If necessary, navigate to the location where your Data Files are stored (Figure 11–37).

Figure 11–37

- If necessary, click the 'Change your view.' arrow, which has the ScreenTip, More options, on the toolbar (Insert New Pictures dialog box) to display the view settings (Figure 11–38).

BTW
Selecting Slides or Other Items
To select sequential or adjacent files or items, select the first item, press and hold down the SHIFT key, and then select the last item. All items between the first and last item will be highlighted. To select nonadjacent files or items, select the first item and then press and hold down the CTRL key. While holding down the CTRL key, select additional items.

Figure 11–38

- If necessary, click List in the view settings to change the view setting and display only the picture file names.

- Click on the left side of the Whale Head icon to select the file name and then select the file names Whale Mouth, Whale Pectoral, Whale Sunset, Whale Tail, Whale Town, and Whale Watching as additional files to insert (Figure 11–39).

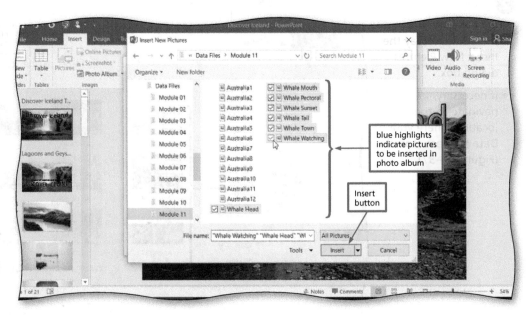

Figure 11–39

Q&A

If I mistakenly select a file name, how can I remove the selection?
Click the file name again to remove the check mark.

I'm using a touch screen and am having trouble selecting multiple files. What can I do?
You may need to use a mouse in combination with the onscreen keyboard CTRL key, or you can select and insert each file individually.

- Click the Insert button (Insert New Pictures dialog box) to add the pictures to the album.

To Reorder Pictures in a Photo Album

1 CREATE & ORGANIZE SECTIONS | 2 CREATE CUSTOM SLIDE SHOW | 3 CREATE PHOTO ALBUM & ENHANCE ELEMENTS
4 SPECIFY CUSTOM SLIDE SIZE & ADD VIDEO CLIP | 5 SHARE & DISTRIBUTE PRESENTATION

PowerPoint inserted the pictures in alphabetical order, which may not be the desired sequence for your album. You easily can change the order of the pictures in the same manner that you change the slide order in a custom show. The following steps reorder the photo album pictures. *Why? Showing the town of Husavik at the beginning of the presentation orientates your audience members to the area where many of the whaling excursions begin.*

- Click the check box for the sixth picture, Whale Town, to select it (Figure 11–40).

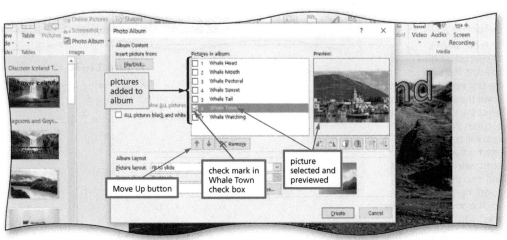

Figure 11–40

2

- Click the Move Up button five times to move the Whale Town photo upward so that it now is the first picture (picture 1) in the album.

Q&A I clicked the Move Up button, but the photo is not moving. What should I do?
Be patient. The photo eventually will move.

- Click the Whale Town check box to remove the check mark.

3

- Select the fifth picture, Whale Sunset, and then click the Move Down button two times to move this picture downward so that it now is the last picture (picture 7) in the album.

- Click the Whale Sunset check box to remove the check mark (Figure 11-41).

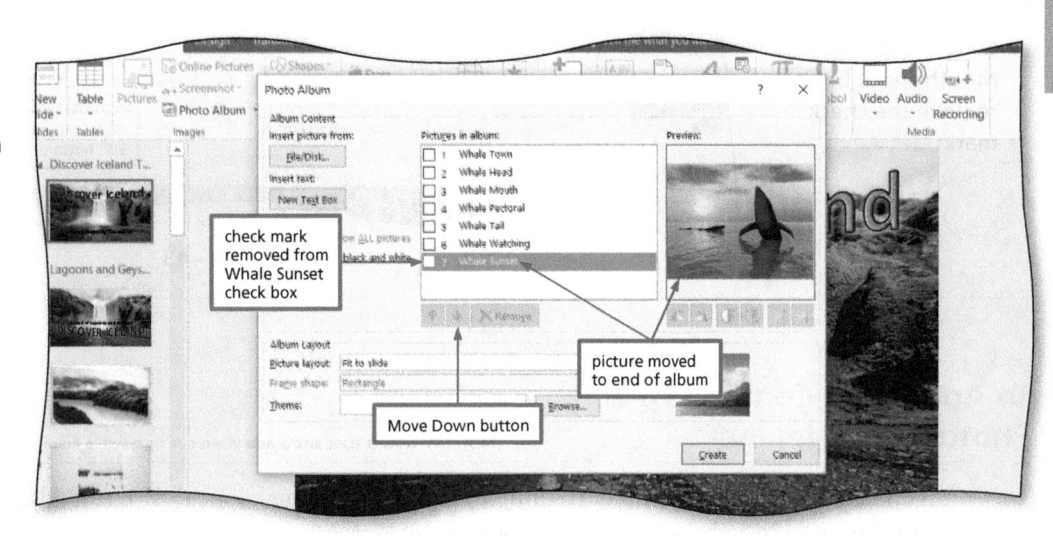

Figure 11–41

To Adjust the Rotation of a Photo Album Image

1 CREATE & ORGANIZE SECTIONS | 2 CREATE CUSTOM SLIDE SHOW | 3 CREATE PHOTO ALBUM & ENHANCE ELEMENTS
4 SPECIFY CUSTOM SLIDE SIZE & ADD VIDEO CLIP | 5 SHARE & DISTRIBUTE PRESENTATION

Digital images have either a portrait (vertical) or landscape (horizontal) orientation. If a picture is displayed in your album with the wrong orientation, you can rotate the image in 90-degree increments to the left or the right. The following steps rotate a photo album picture. *Why? The photo of the whale will be more dramatic if the mouth is facing the audience members.*

- Click the check box for the third picture, Whale Mouth, to select it and display a preview (Figure 11–42).

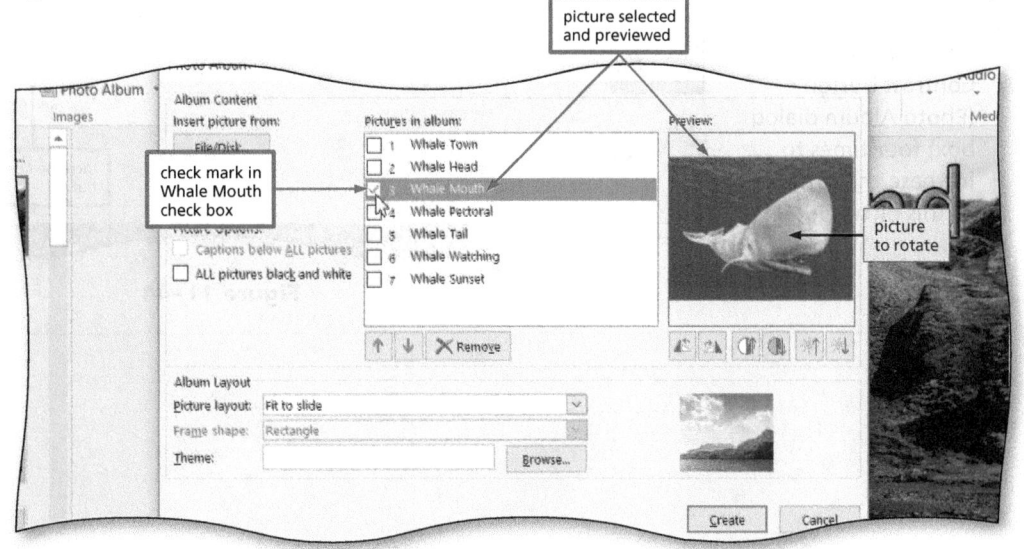

Figure 11–42

- Click the 'Rotate Right 90°' button (Photo Album dialog box) to turn the picture to the right (Figure 11–43).

- Click the Whale Mouth check box to remove the check mark.

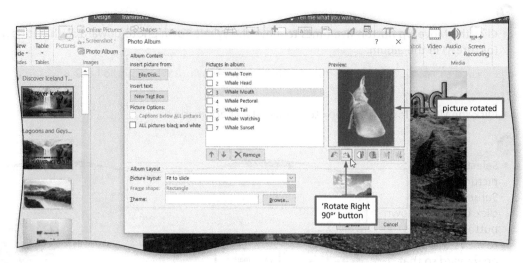

Figure 11–43

To Adjust the Contrast of a Photo Album Image

1 CREATE & ORGANIZE SECTIONS | 2 CREATE CUSTOM SLIDE SHOW | 3 CREATE PHOTO ALBUM & ENHANCE ELEMENTS
4 SPECIFY CUSTOM SLIDE SIZE & ADD VIDEO CLIP | 5 SHARE & DISTRIBUTE PRESENTATION

A picture you insert may need correcting to enhance its visual appeal. You can adjust the difference between the darkest and lightest areas of the picture by increasing or decreasing the contrast. The following steps adjust the contrast of a photo album picture. *Why? The Whale Head photo lacks contrast and has many light areas. It would be more dramatic if it had a wide variety of dark and light regions.*

- Click the check box for the second picture, Whale Head, to select it and display a preview (Figure 11–44).

- Click the Increase Contrast button (Photo Album dialog box) four times to increase the contrast of this picture.

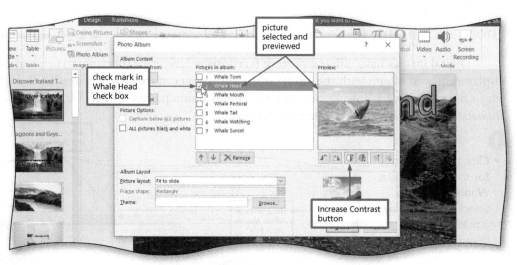

Figure 11–44

To Adjust the Brightness of a Photo Album Image

If a picture in the photo album is too light or too dark, you can adjust its brightness to enhance its appearance. The following step adjusts the brightness of a photo album picture. *Why? The Whale Head photo is somewhat light, so decreasing the brightness would help the colors stand out on the slide and give more depth to the image.*

1

- With the Whale Head picture selected, click the Decrease Brightness button (Photo Album dialog box) two times to intensify the colors in the picture (Figure 11–45).

- Click the Whale Head check box to remove the check mark.

Figure 11–45

To Change a Photo Album Layout

PowerPoint inserts each photo album picture so that it fills, or fits, one entire slide. You can modify this layout to display two or four pictures on a slide, display a title, or add white space between the image and the slide edges. You also can add a white or black frame around the perimeter of each picture. The following steps change an album layout. *Why? The photos are spectacular, so you want to display only one on each slide. Adding a frame provides contrast between the photos and the background.*

- With the Photo Album dialog box displayed, click the Picture layout arrow in the Album Layout area (Photo Album dialog box) to display the Picture layout list (Figure 11–46).

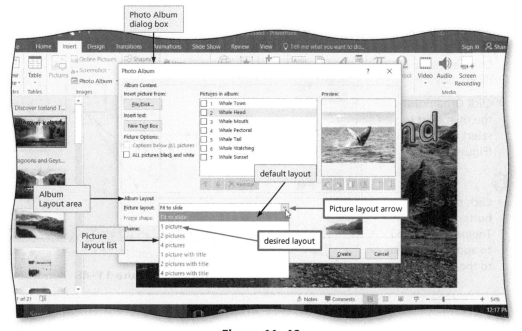

Figure 11–46

- Click 1 picture in the Picture layout list to change the layout so that one picture is displayed on each slide and a rectangular frame is displayed around each picture.

- Click the Frame shape arrow in the Album Layout area (Photo Album dialog box) to display the Frame shape list (Figure 11–47).

- Click 'Simple Frame, White' in the Frame shape list to add a white frame around the picture.

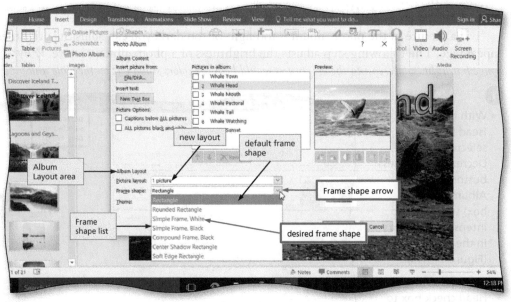

Figure 11–47

To Add a Photo Album Theme

1 CREATE & ORGANIZE SECTIONS | 2 CREATE CUSTOM SLIDE SHOW | **3 CREATE PHOTO ALBUM & ENHANCE ELEMENTS**
4 SPECIFY CUSTOM SLIDE SIZE & ADD VIDEO CLIP | 5 SHARE & DISTRIBUTE PRESENTATION

The themes that are used to design a presentation also are available to add to a photo album. These themes determine the colors and fonts that complement each other and increase the visual appeal of the slides. The following steps add a theme to the photo album. **Why?** *The photos feature outdoor scenes, so you want to select a theme that has natural colors and a simple layout and font that will complement the majestic photos.*

- Click the Browse button in the Album Layout area (Photo Album dialog box) to display the Choose Theme dialog box.

- Click Organic in the theme list to select this theme (Figure 11–48).

- Click the Select button (Choose Theme dialog box) to apply this theme to the presentation.

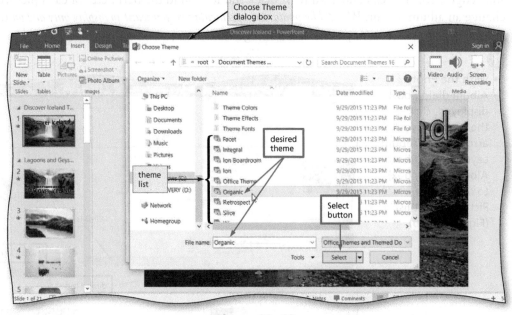

Figure 11–48

To Add Captions below
All Pictures

If you desire a caption below each picture, you can request PowerPoint add this feature to the slides. The file name is displayed as the caption text, but you can edit and add effects to this text. The following step selects the option to add a caption below all pictures in the photo album. *Why? The audience members will see the text on the slide and hear you describe the images. Because they are using these two senses, they should be able to recall the information you are presenting. In addition, absent Travel Club members could view the presentation during their free time and learn the names of the places and objects presented on the slides.*

1

- In the Picture Options area (Photo Album dialog box), click the 'Captions below ALL pictures' check box to select the check box (Figure 11–49).

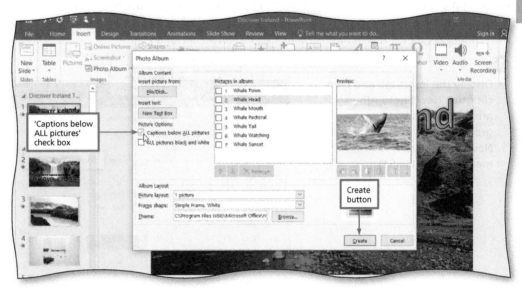

Figure 11–49

To Create a Photo Album

Once you have inserted the pictures, determined the picture sequence, layout, and frame shape, you are ready to make the photo album. *Why? You have specified all the information PowerPoint needs to create this album.* The following step creates the photo album.

- Click the Create button (Photo Album dialog box) to close the dialog box and create a photo album with a title slide and seven pictures (Figure 11–50).

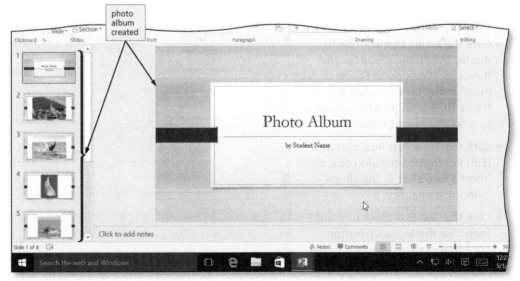

Figure 11–50

To Edit a Photo Album

1 CREATE & ORGANIZE SECTIONS | 2 CREATE CUSTOM SLIDE SHOW | 3 CREATE PHOTO ALBUM & ENHANCE ELEMENTS
4 SPECIFY CUSTOM SLIDE SIZE & ADD VIDEO CLIP | 5 SHARE & DISTRIBUTE PRESENTATION

Once you review the photo album PowerPoint creates, you can modify the contents by adding and
deleting pictures, changing the layout and frames, and adding transitions. The following steps edit the photo
album. *Why? You want to change the frame style and color, add a text box on a new slide, and add a transition to add
interest and to give additional information to your audience members.*

1

- Display the Insert tab and then
click the 'New Photo Album'
arrow (Insert tab | Images
group) to display the
New Photo Album
menu (Figure 11–51).

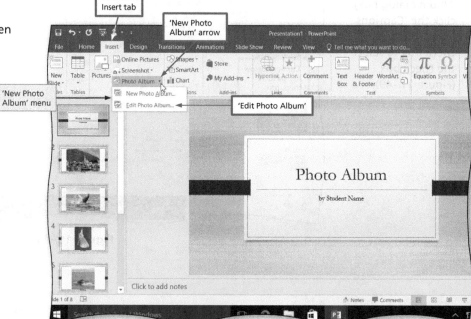

Figure 11–51

2

- Click 'Edit Photo Album' in the
menu to display the Edit Photo
Album dialog box.

- Click the Frame shape arrow to
display the Frame shape list and
then click 'Compound Frame,
Black' in the list to change the
frame from a single white border
to a double black border.

- Click the 'New Text Box' button
(Edit Photo Album dialog box) to
insert a new slide in the album
with the name, Text Box.

- Click the Text Box check box and
then click the Move Up button
once to move this picture upward
as the first slide in the 'Pictures
in album' list (Figure 11–52).

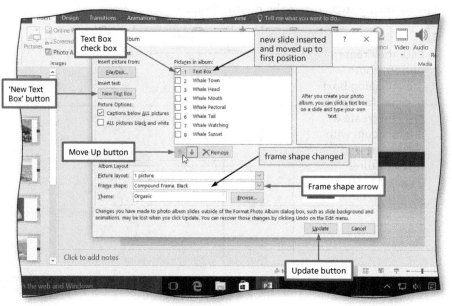

Figure 11–52

Q&A Can I insert a text box on a slide that already has a picture?
Yes. Click the Text Box button (Insert tab | Text group) and then click the slide where you want to insert the box. You then can arrange the box and picture on the slide.

- Click the Update button (Edit Photo Album dialog box) to make the changes to the photo album.

- Apply the Cube transition and then change the duration to 03.00 seconds for all slides.

To Insert and Format Text in a Photo Album

PowerPoint inserts text into the slides, such as the file name for captions and the user name associated with the Microsoft Office installation as the subtitle text on the title slide. You can revise and format this text by changing the font, font size, color, and any other font styles and effects. The following steps edit text in the photo album.

1 With Slide 1 displaying, select the title text, Photo Album, and then type **Whale Watching** as the replacement text.

2 Select the subtitle text, by [Student Name], type **Humpbacks and Orcas** as the first paragraph, press the SHIFT+ENTER keys, and then type **in Their Natural Environment** as the second paragraph replacement text.

3 Increase the font size of the subtitle text to 32 point.

4 Display Slide 2, select the words, Text Box, and then type **Husavik is Iceland's whale watching capital. Guests board traditional oak ships and sail into Skjalfandi Bay.** as the replacement text.

5 Press the ENTER key two times and then type **The best time to see the marine mammals in the cold Arctic waters is from April through September.** as the second paragraph.

6 Display Slide 3, select the caption text, and then type **Silica once was a major export of the whaling town, Husavik.** as the new caption.

7 Display Slide 8, select the caption text, and then type **Visitors can view whales up close while enjoying the beautiful Icelandic scenery.** as the new caption.

8 Display Slide 1 and then run the slide show.

9 Save the presentation with the file name, Whale Watching Photo Album (Figure 11–53).

BTW
Resetting Placeholders
You can reset all customization changes to the preset options. Click the Reset button (Home tab | Slides group) or right-click the slide or thumbnail and then click Reset Slide on the shortcut menu. To retain custom formatting changes and move the placeholders to their original locations, click the Layout button (Home tab | Slides group) or right-click the slide or thumbnail and then click Layout on the shortcut menu. Then, reapply the active layout from the Layout gallery.

BTW
Distributing a Document
Instead of printing and distributing a hard copy of a document, you can distribute the document electronically. Options include sending the document via email; posting it on cloud storage (such as OneDrive) and sharing the file with others; posting it on social media, a blog, or other website; and sharing a link associated with an online location of the document. You also can create and share a PDF or XPS image of the document, so that users can view the file in Acrobat Reader or XPS Viewer instead of in PowerPoint.

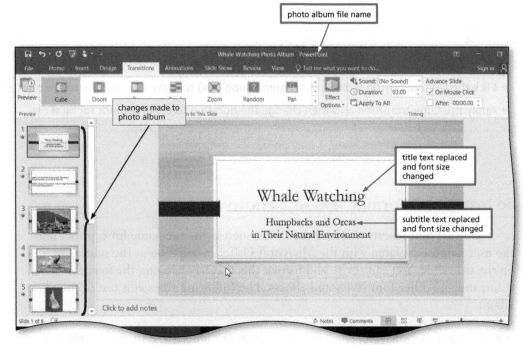

Figure 11–53

To Create Black-and-White Images in a Photo Album

1 CREATE & ORGANIZE SECTIONS | 2 CREATE CUSTOM SLIDE SHOW | **3 CREATE PHOTO ALBUM & ENHANCE ELEMENTS**
4 SPECIFY CUSTOM SLIDE SIZE & ADD VIDEO CLIP | 5 SHARE & DISTRIBUTE PRESENTATION

Why? Black-and-white pictures often generate interest and give a unique version of the color photographs. The series of shades ranging from black to white, or grayscale, provide a different perspective of our world. The following steps edit a photo album to use black-and-white images.

1
- Display the Insert tab, click the 'New Photo Album' arrow, and then click 'Edit Photo Album'.

- Click the 'ALL pictures black and white' check box to select the check box (Figure 11–54).

Q&A Can I change the view to see my slides in grayscale or black and white?
Yes. Display the View tab and then click the Grayscale or the 'Black and White' button (Color /Grayscale group). The Grayscale option shows a variety of shades ranging from white to black whereas the 'Black and White' option displays only black-and-white objects.

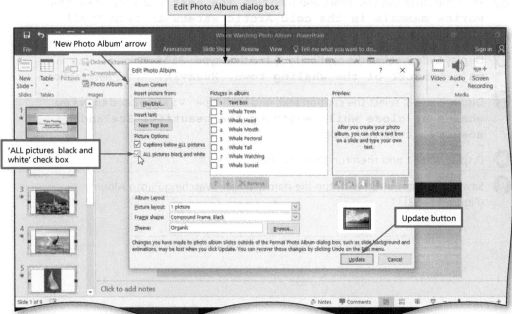

Figure 11–54

②

- Click the Update button (Edit Photo Album dialog box) to change the photographs from color to black-and-white images on the slides.

- Run the slide show.

- Save the presentation with the file name, Whale Watching Photo Album Black and White.

- Print the presentation as a handout with three slides per page (Figure 11–55).

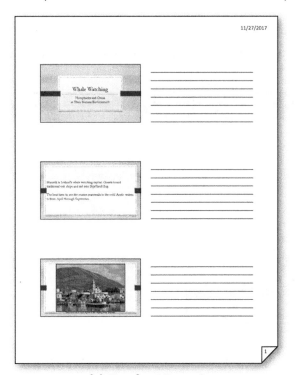

(a) Handout Page 1

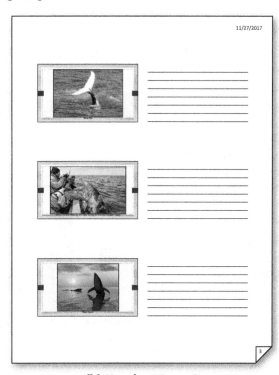

(b) Handout Page 2

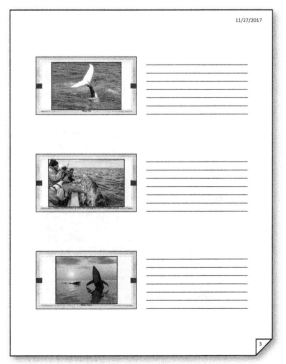

(c) Handout Page 3

Figure 11–55

BTW

Conserving Ink and Toner

If you want to conserve ink or toner, you can instruct PowerPoint to print draft quality documents by clicking File on the ribbon to open the Backstage view, clicking the Options tab in the Backstage view to display the PowerPoint Options dialog box, clicking Advanced in the left pane (PowerPoint Options dialog box), scrolling to the Print area in the right pane, placing a check mark in the 'Use draft quality' check box, and then clicking the OK button. Then, use the Backstage view to print the document as usual.

To Look Up Information

You can search for information regarding a wide variety of topics using PowerPoint's reference materials. If you are connected to the Internet, you can use the Insights task pane. The Explore tab provides reference information, including images and articles. The Define tab displays a definition and word origin. The following steps use the Insights task pane to locate material about a word. *Why? You want to know more about the word, silica, which you typed as part of the Slide 3 caption text.*

- Display Slide 3 and then select the word, Silica, in the caption.
- Display the Review tab and then click the Smart Lookup button (Review tab | Insights group) to display the Insights task pane.
- If necessary, click the Got it button in response to the "We value your privacy" message to allow Microsoft to send information to Bing regarding your search.
- If necessary, click the Explore tab (Figure 11–56).

Q&A Why does my Insights task pane look different?
Depending on your settings, your Insights task pane may appear different from the figure shown here.

What is Bing?
It is the name of Microsoft's search engine, which is a program that locates websites, webpages, images, videos, news, maps, and other information related to a specific topic.

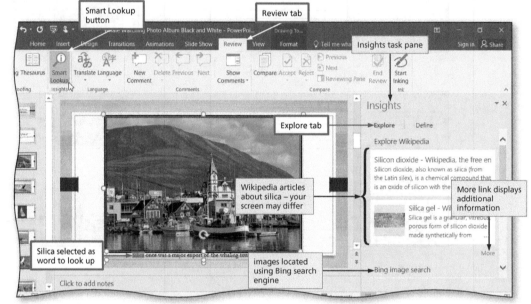

Figure 11–56

In the Insights task pane, read the Wikipedia opening paragraphs about silica, also called silicon dioxide, and then scroll down to see photos of this chemical compound and to view articles discussing this material (Figure 11–57).

Q&A Can I view additional articles and images?
Yes. Click the More link at the end of each research section to locate more information on the search topic.

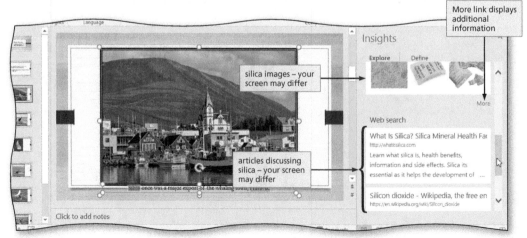

Figure 11–57

- Click the Define tab in the Insights task pane and then scroll up to display the definition and the origin of the word, silica.

- Click the speaker icon to hear the correct pronunciation of this word (Figure 11–58).

Q&A

Can I copy information from the Insights task pane into my slides?
Yes, you can use the Copy and Paste commands to insert the text. Be certain, however, that you do not plagiarize this material.

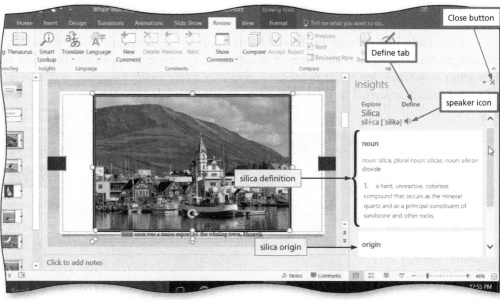

Figure 11–58

- Click the Close button in the Insights task pane.

To Close a Presentation

The second photo album with the black-and-white pictures is complete. The following step closes the Whale Watching Photo Album Black and White file.

Open the Backstage view and then click Close to close the open Whale Watching Photo Album Black and White file without exiting PowerPoint.

Break Point: If you wish to take a break, this is a good place to do so. You can exit PowerPoint now. To resume at a later time, run PowerPoint and continue following the steps from this location forward.

Sharing and Distributing a Presentation

Many people design PowerPoint presentations to accompany a speech given in front of an audience, and they also develop slide shows to share with family, work associates, and friends in a variety of ways. For example, they can print a slide on thick paper and send the document through the mail. They also can email the file or create a video to upload to a website or view on a computer. Video files can become quite large in file size, so PowerPoint allows you to reduce the size by compressing the file.

Use hyperlinks to show slides with landscape and portrait orientations.
When you are creating your presentation, you have the option to display all your slides in either the default landscape orientation or in portrait orientation. You may, however, desire to have slides with both orientations during a single presentation. Using hyperlinks is one solution to mixing the orientations. Apply a hyperlink to an object on the last slide in one orientation and then hyperlink to another presentation with slides in the other orientation. If you desire to hyperlink to one particular slide in a second presentation, click the Bookmark button in the Insert Hyperlink dialog box and then select the title of the slide you want to use as your link. Once you have displayed the desired slides in the second presentation, create another hyperlink from that presentation back to a slide in your original presentation.

To Change the Slide Orientation

By default, PowerPoint displays slides in landscape orientation, where the width dimension is greater than the height dimension. You can change this setting to specify that the slides display in portrait orientation. *Why?* *In portrait orientation, the height dimension is greater than the width dimension, so it is useful to display tall objects, people who are standing, or faces.* The following steps change the slide orientation.

- Open the presentation, Iceland Travel, located in the Data Files.

- Display the Design tab and then click the Slide Size button (Design tab | Customize group) to display the Slide Size gallery (Figure 11–59).

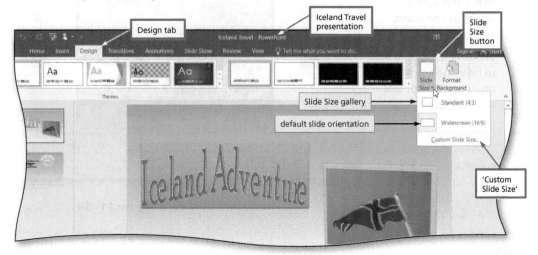

Figure 11–59

❷

- Click 'Custom Slide Size' to display the Slide Size dialog box and then click Portrait in the Slides area of the Orientation section to change the slide orientation from Landscape to Portrait (Figure 11–60).

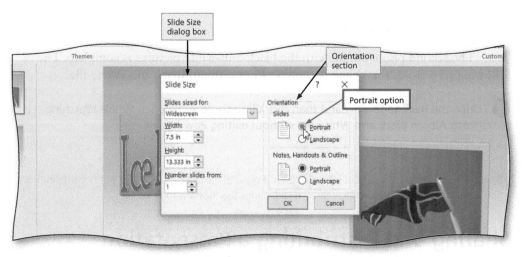

Figure 11–60

To Set Up a Custom Size

Why? *To announce your presentation at the library and encourage Travel Club members to attend, you want to mail postcards to their homes.* To simplify the process, you can create a PowerPoint slide that is the precise measurement of a postcard, print the card on heavy paper stock, and mail the card to Travel Club members. You can specify that your PowerPoint slides are a precise dimension. The following steps change the slide size to a custom size.

- With the Slide Size dialog box displaying, click the 'Slides sized for' arrow to display the size list (Figure 11–61).

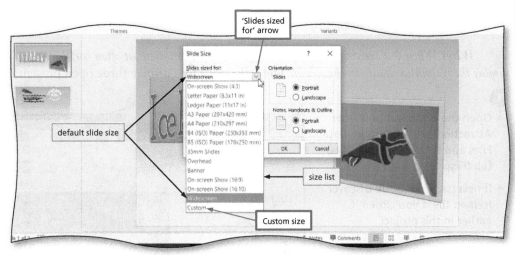

Figure 11–61

- Click Custom in the size list.
- Change the slide width to 5 inches in the Width box.
- Change the slide height to 7 inches in the Height box (Figure 11 – 62).

Q&A Can I type the width and height measurements in the boxes instead of clicking the down arrows repeatedly?
Yes. You also can click and hold down the mouse button instead of repeatedly clicking the arrows until the desired dimensions are displayed.

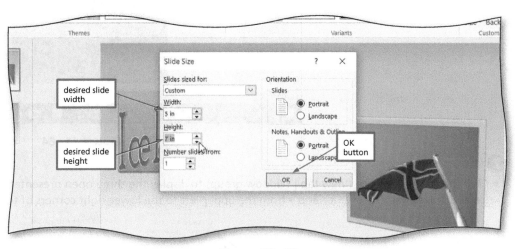

Figure 11–62

- Click the OK button (Slide Size dialog box) to display the Microsoft PowerPoint dialog box (Figure 11–63).

- Click the Ensure Fit button (Microsoft PowerPoint dialog box) to apply the custom sizes and close the dialog box.

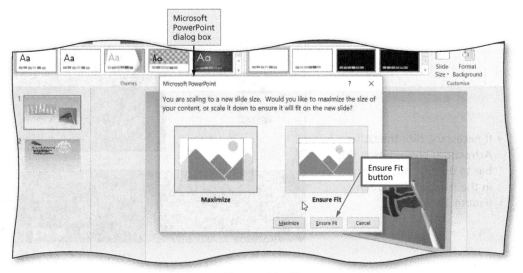

Figure 11–63

To Display Multiple Presentation Windows Simultaneously

Why? *When you are reviewing elements of several presentations, it often is efficient and convenient to open and display them simultaneously on the screen.* The following steps display three open presentations simultaneously.

1

- Open the presentation, Other Attractions, located in the Data Files and then display the View tab (Figure 11–64).

- If necessary, open the Discover Iceland file if you closed it earlier in this project.

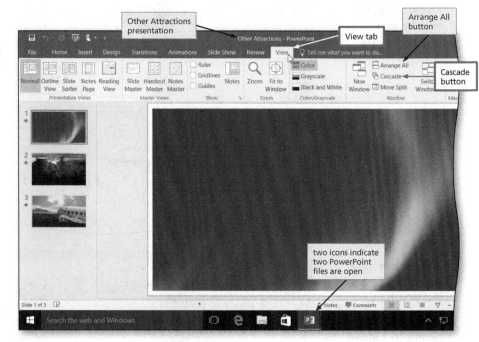

Figure 11–64

2

- Click the Cascade button (View tab | Window group) to display the three open presentations – Other Attractions, Iceland Travel, and Discover Iceland – from the upper-left to the lower-right corners of the screen.

Q&A What is the difference between the Cascade button and the Arrange All button?
When you click the Cascade button, the open windows display overlapped, or stacked, on each other. Tapping or clicking the Arrange All button tiles all the open windows side by side on the screen. Each window may display narrower than in Normal view so that all the open windows are visible simultaneously.

- If necessary, click the Other Attractions presentation title bar to display that presentation in the front of the screen (Figure 11–65).

Q&A The Other Attractions title bar is not visible on my screen. Can I move the presentation windows so that it is visible?
Yes. You can drag the presentation title bars to arrange the windows.

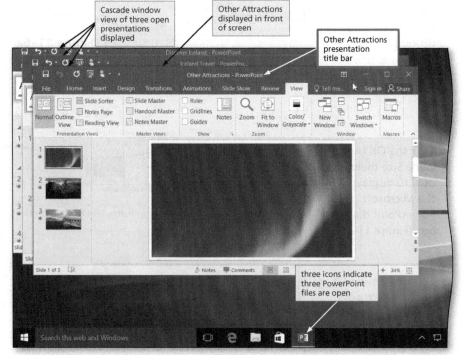

Figure 11–65

To Copy a Video File

Why? Slide 2 in the Other Attractions presentation contains a video clip of the Eyjafjallajokull volcano that you want to insert at the bottom of Slide 2 in the Iceland Travel file. With multiple presentations open simultaneously on your screen, you can view all the slides quickly and decide which elements of one presentation you desire to copy to another. The following steps copy the video file from Slide 2 of the Other Attractions presentation to Slide 2 of the Iceland Travel presentation.

1

- Click the Slide 2 thumbnail of the Other Attractions presentation to display that slide.

- Right-click the video image in the center of the slide to select it and to display the shortcut menu (Figure 11–66).

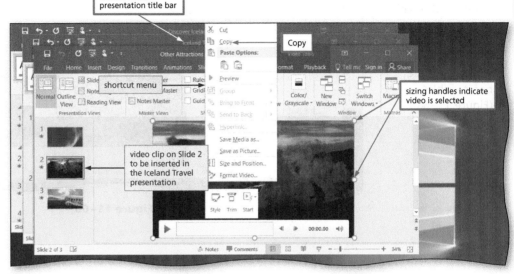

Figure 11–66

2

- Click Copy on the shortcut menu.

- Click the Iceland Travel presentation title bar to display that presentation in the front of the screen.

- Click the Slide 2 thumbnail of the Iceland Travel presentation to display that slide.

- Right-click the slide to display the shortcut menu and then point to the 'Use Destination Theme' button under Paste Options to display a preview of the video clip on that slide (Figure 11–67).

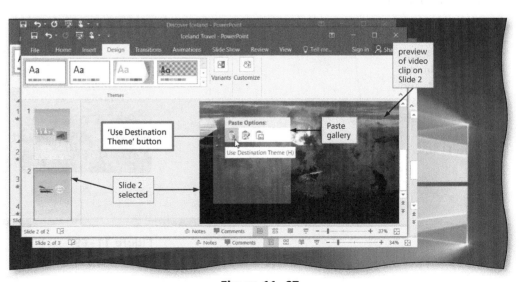

Figure 11–67

- Click the 'Use Destination Theme' button in the Paste gallery to insert the video into the slide.

- If necessary, drag the Iceland Travel presentation title bar downward so the Other Attractions title bar is visible (Figure 11–68).

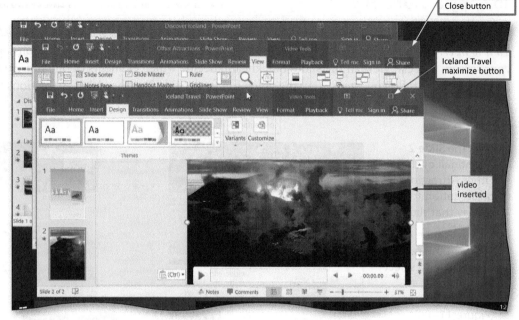

Figure 11–68

- Click the Other Attractions title bar and then click that presentation's Close button to close that presentation.

- Click the Maximize button in the Iceland Travel presentation to maximize the PowerPoint window.

- Select the video, display the Video Tools Format tab, size the video to 2.8" x 4.98", and then move the clip to the location shown in Figure 11–69.

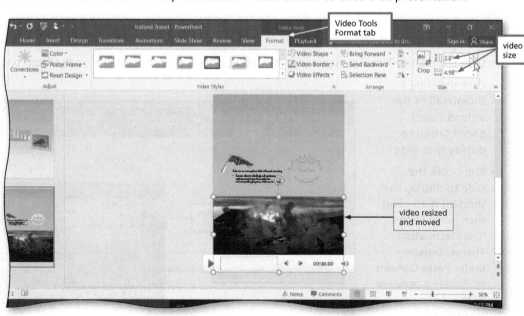

Figure 11–69

BTW

Screen Recording

You can include screen recordings in your PowerPoint presentations if you have a sound card, microphone, and speakers. Display the slide you would like to record at the beginning of the presentation, display the Insert tab, click the Screen Recording button (Insert tab | Media area), select an area of your screen to record, and then click the Record button. Capture the desired information, including voice narrations, slide timings, and ink and laser pointer gestures. Then, insert the recording directly into your presentation.

To Compress a Video File

Why? *The file size of videos can be quite large. This size can pose a problem if you desire to email a presentation or if the space on a storage device is small.* PowerPoint includes a feature that will compress your file to reduce its size. You can specify one of three compression qualities: Presentation, Internet, or Low. In this project, you are going to email the Iceland Travel file, so you desire to keep the file size as small as possible without sacrificing too much resolution quality. The following steps compress the video file.

1

- With the video clip selected on Slide 2, display the Backstage view and then click the Compress Media button (Info tab | Media Size and Performance section) to display the Compress Media menu (Figure 11–70).

Q&A

Why am I seeing an error message stating that the media could not be compressed? Graphics cards have acceleration capabilities that allow video, animation, transitions, and other graphics to display smoothly. Your PowerPoint file may have too many graphics that are consuming the resources of your graphics card. If so, you may need to disable hardware graphics acceleration. These settings are found in the Display section of the PowerPoint Options Advanced tab.

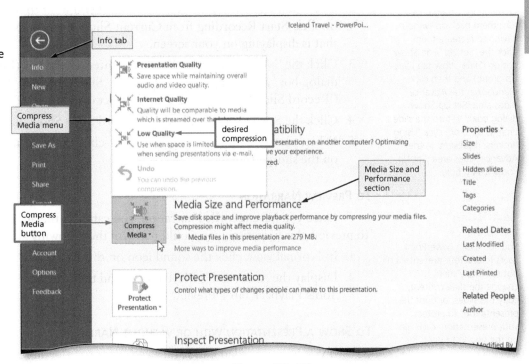

Figure 11–70

 2

- Click Low Quality to display the Compress Media dialog box and compress the file (Figure 11–71).

3

- When the video file has been compressed, click the Close button (Compress Media dialog box) to return to the Backstage view.

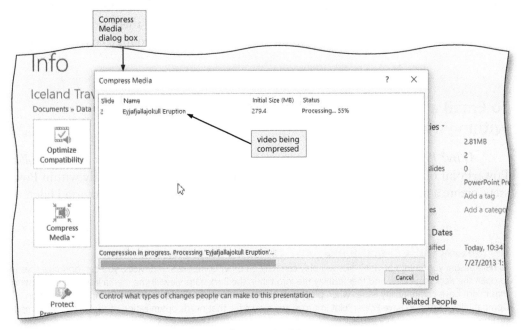

Figure 11–71

TO RECORD NARRATION

In some situations, you may want your viewers to hear recorded narration that accompanies slides. You can record narration separately and then add this file to the slide. You also can record narration while the slide show is running. To record this narration, you would perform the following steps.

1. Display the Slide Show tab and then click the 'Record Slide Show' arrow (Slide Show tab | Set Up group).
2. Click 'Start Recording from Beginning' if you want to begin with the first slide or click 'Start Recording from Current Slide' if you want to begin with the slide that is displaying on your screen.
3. Click the 'Narrations, ink, and laser pointer' check box (Record Slide Show dialog box) and, if appropriate, click the 'Slide and animation timings' check box ('Record Slide Show' dialog box) to select or remove the check mark.
4. Click the Start Recording button (Record Slide Show dialog box).
5. When you have finished speaking, right-click the slide and then click End Show on the shortcut menu.

TO PREVIEW NARRATION

Once you have recorded narration, you can play the audio to review the sound. To preview this narration, you would perform the following steps.

1. In Normal view, click the sound icon on the slide.
2. Display the Audio Tools Playback tab and then click the Play button (Audio Tools Playback tab | Preview group).

TO SHOW A PRESENTATION WITH OR WITHOUT NARRATION

If you have recorded narration to accompany your slides, you can choose whether to include this narration when you run your slide show. You would perform the following steps to run the slide show either with or without narration.

1. Display the Slide Show tab and then click the Play Narrations check box (Slide Show tab | Set Up group) to remove the check from the box.
2. If you have chosen to show the presentation without narration and then desire to allow audience members to hear this recording, click the Play Narrations check box (Slide Show tab | Set Up group) to check this option.

To Email a Slide Show from within PowerPoint

1 CREATE & ORGANIZE SECTIONS | 2 CREATE CUSTOM SLIDE SHOW | 3 CREATE PHOTO ALBUM & ENHANCE ELEMENTS
4 SPECIFY CUSTOM SLIDE SIZE & ADD VIDEO CLIP | **5 SHARE & DISTRIBUTE PRESENTATION**

Why? *Presenters often email their presentations to friends and colleagues to solicit feedback and share their work.* PowerPoint offers a convenient method of emailing a presentation directly within PowerPoint. The following steps create a message, attach a presentation, and send a slide show to Victoria Halen.

- With the Backstage view displaying, display the Share gallery.
- Click the Email button to display the Email options (Figure 11–72).

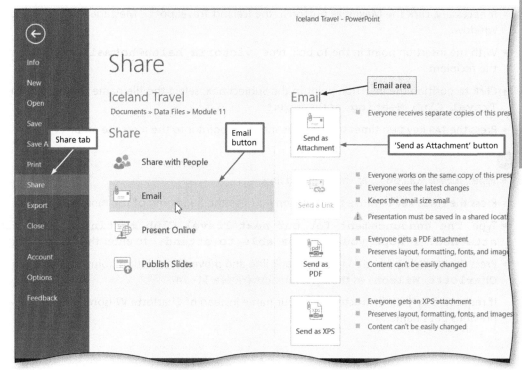

Figure 11–72

- Click the 'Send as Attachment' button in the Email area to open the Iceland Travel.pptx – Message (HTML) window in Microsoft Outlook (Figure 11–73). If necessary, enter your user name or password in the Windows Security dialog box.

Q&A Must I use Microsoft Outlook to send this email message?
No, you do not have to have Outlook installed; however, you need to have an email program installed in Windows to send the email. If you don't use Outlook, you could use Windows Mail or another email program.

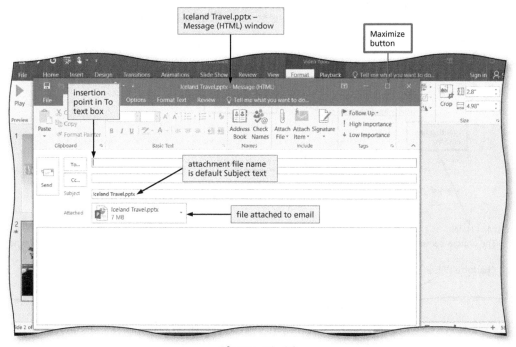

Figure 11–73

3

- If necessary, click the Maximize button in the Iceland Travel.pptx – Message (HTML) window to maximize the window.
- With the insertion point in the To box, type `victoria_halen@hotmail.com` to enter the email address of the recipient.
- Click to position the insertion point in the Subject box, select the file name that is displaying, and then type `Travel Club Meeting` as the subject.
- Press the TAB key two times to move the insertion point into the message area.

4

- Type `Miss Halen,` as the greeting line.
- Press the ENTER key to move the insertion point to the beginning of the next line.
- Type `The announcement for our next Travel Club meeting at the library is attached. I hope you will be able to attend.` to enter the message text.
- Press the ENTER key twice to insert a blank line and move the insertion point to the beginning of the next line. Type `Charlotte Wilson` as the signature line (Figure 11–74).

  If requested by your instructor, type your name instead of Charlotte Wilson's name followed by your current or previous pet's name.

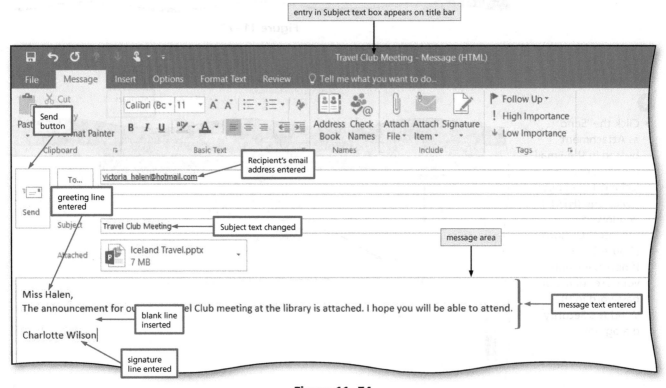

Figure 11–74

5

- Click the Send button in the message header to send the email message and to close the message window.

Rehearse, rehearse, rehearse.
Speakers should spend as much time practicing their presentations as they do preparing their PowerPoint slides. Frequently, however, they use the majority of their preparation time designing and tweaking the slides. Audience members expect to see a presenter who is prepared, confident, and enthusiastic. Practicing the presentation helps convey this image. As you rehearse, focus on a strong introduction that grasps the audience's attention and previews the main points of your talk. You have only one chance to make a good first impression, so begin the speech by establishing eye contact with audience members in various parts of the room. Resist the urge to stare at the slides projected on the screen. Your audience came to your presentation to hear you speak, and rehearsing will help you deliver a high-quality talk that exceeds their expectations.

To Run and Save the Presentation

When you run the Iceland Travel presentation, the video will play automatically because the file had that setting in the Other Attractions presentation. The following steps run the slide show and then save and close the document.

1 Display Slide 1 and then run the presentation.

2 Save the presentation with the file name, Iceland Travel Mail.

3 Display the Backstage view and then click Close to close the Iceland Travel Mail file without exiting PowerPoint.

TO PRESENT A SLIDE SHOW ONLINE

Microsoft's Office Presentation Service feature allows you to share your presentation remotely with anyone having an Internet connection. As you display your slides, they see a synchronized view of your slide show in their web browser, even if they do not have PowerPoint installed on their computers. To present your presentation online, you would perform the following steps.

1. Click the Present Online arrow (Slide Show tab | Start Slide Show group) to display the Present Online menu.

2. Click 'Office Presentation Service' to display the Present Online dialog box.

3. Click the CONNECT button to agree to the service terms, then, if necessary, sign in to your Microsoft account, and then click the Next button (Sign in dialog box).

4. After PowerPoint has connected to the service and completed preparing the presentation, share the presentation link with up to 50 remote viewers and then click the START PRESENTATION button (Present Online dialog box). People visiting the website can view your presentation with any annotations you make.

5. When you have displayed the last slide, click the 'End Online Presentation' button (Present Online tab | Present Online group) and then click the 'End Online Presentation' button (Microsoft PowerPoint dialog box).

BTW
Use Your Mouse as a Laser Pointer
When you are presenting, you can emphasize an important point in your slide by using your mouse as a laser pointer. In Slide Show view, click either the From Beginning or the 'From Current Slide' button (Slide Show tab | Start Slide Show group), press and hold the CTRL key, and then click and drag the left mouse button to point to specific slide contents. To change the laser pointer color, click the 'Set Up Slide Show' button (Slide Show tab | Set Up group) to display the Set Up Show dialog box. In the Show options area, click the 'Laser pointer color' button, select the desired color in the gallery, and then click the OK button.

BTW
Configuring Slide Show Resolution
You can change the resolution you want to use to display your presentation. This feature is valuable when your computer is connected to two different monitors, when you are delivering your presentation using a computer other than the one used to create the slides, or when the projector does not support the resolution you specified when you saved the presentation. To configure the resolution, click the 'Set Up Slide Show' button (Slide Show tab | Set Up group), click the Resolution arrow in the Multiple monitors area (Set Up Show dialog box), and then select the new resolution.

To Create a Video

Why? *Watching video files is a common activity with the advent of easy-to-use recording devices and websites that host these files.* You can convert your PowerPoint presentation to a video file and upload it to a video-sharing website or burn the file to a CD or DVD to distribute to people. You can include your narrations, timings, animations, transitions, and laser pointing gestures in the file, which can be saved in MPEG-4 or WMV format. The following steps create a video of the Discover Iceland presentation.

1

- Display the Discover Iceland file and, if necessary, click the Maximize button in the title bar to maximize the window.

- Display the Backstage view and then display the Export gallery.

- Click the 'Create a Video' button to display the Create a Video section.

- Click the Presentation Quality button in the Create a Video section to display a list of file sizes and screen resolutions (Figure 11–75).

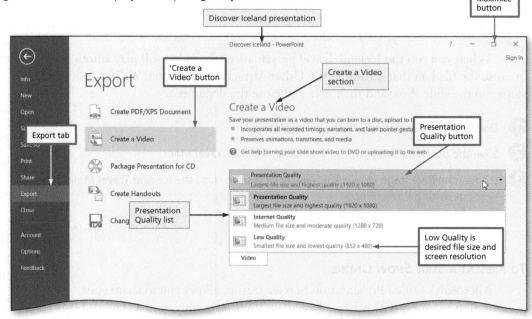

Figure 11–75

2

- If Low Quality is not the selected option, click Low Quality to select the smallest file size and 852 × 480 resolution.

- Change the 'Seconds spent on each slide' time to 10 seconds (Figure 11–76).

Q&A — Is 5 seconds always the default slide display time?
Yes. If you have not set transitions in your file, PowerPoint will display each slide for this amount of time in the video.

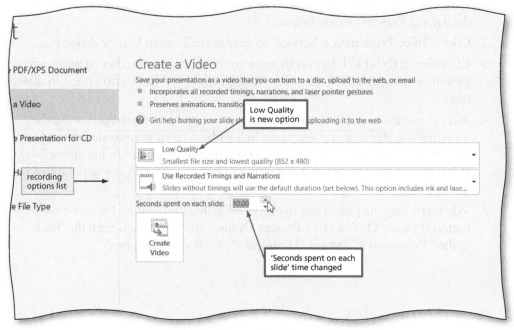

Figure 11–76

3
- Click the 'Use Recorded Timings and Narrations' button in the Create a Video section to display a list of recording options (Figure 11–77).

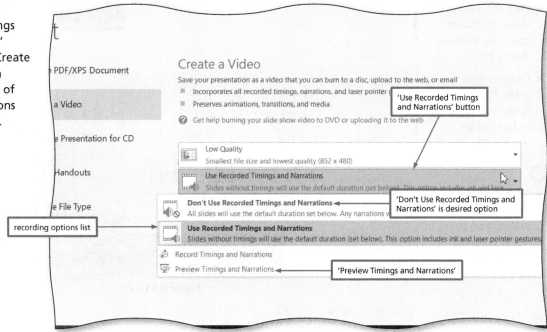

Figure 11–77

4
- Click 'Preview Timings and Narrations' to run the slide show.
- When all the slides in the presentation have displayed, end the slide show.
- Click the 'Use Recorded Timings and Narrations' button in the Create a Video section and then click the 'Don't Use Recorded Timings and Narrations' option (Figure 11-78).

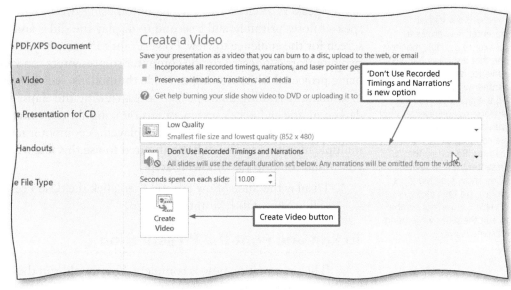

Figure 11–78

Q&A
When would I select the 'Use Recorded Timings and Narrations' option?
If you had recorded and timed narrations and also had turned you mouse into a laser pointer, then you would want to include these features in your video.

- Click the Create Video button to open the Save As dialog box.

- Change the video file name to Discover Iceland Video (Figure 11–79).

- Click the Save button (Save As dialog box) to begin creating the Discover Iceland Video file.

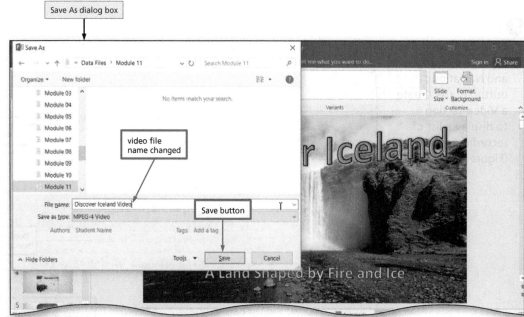

Save As dialog box

video file name changed

Save button

Figure 11–79

Q&A

Does PowerPoint take a long period of time to create the video?

Yes. It may take several minutes to export the presentation to a video. Do not attempt to open the video file while it is being created.

- When the video has been created, save the presentation again.

BTW
Practice Using Presenter View
Presenter view allows a speaker to use dual monitors: one that displays what the audience is seeing, and another with controls to aid the presenter. You can rehearse using Presenter view with one monitor so that you are comfortable using the features. Be certain that 'Use Presenter View' is selected (Slide Show tab | Monitors group) and then press ALT+F5. You will not be able to edit the slides while using Presenter view.

TO SET UP PRESENTER VIEW

Speakers often deliver a presentation using two monitors: one to display their speaker notes privately, and a second to display the slides and project them on a large screen for the audience to view. PowerPoint's **Presenter view** supports the use of two monitors connected to one computer so presenters can view the slide currently being projected while viewing the slide thumbnails, seeing a preview of the next slide or animation, reading their speaker notes, viewing the elapsed time, lightening or darkening the audience's screen, or customizing the presentation by skipping the next slide or reviewing a slide previously displayed. A computer must support the use of multiple monitors and must be configured to use this feature. To use Presenter view, you would perform the following step.

1. Display the Slide Show tab and then click the 'Use Presenter View' check box (Slide Show tab | Monitors group).

To Run and Print the Presentation

The presentation now is complete. You should run the slide show, print handouts, and then exit PowerPoint.

1 Run the slide show.

2 Print the presentation as a handout with six horizontal slides per page (Figure 11–80).

3 Because the project now is complete, you can exit PowerPoint, closing all open documents.

BTW
Printing Selections
When you are developing slides or creating handouts for a particular audience, you may not want to print every slide in your presentation. To print specific slides, select the desired slides in the Thumbnail pane. Then, click File on the ribbon to open the Backstage view, display the Print tab in the Backstage view, click the first button in the Settings area, click Print Selection in the list to specify you want to print the slides you have selected, and then click the Print button in the Print gallery to print these slides.

(a) Handout Page 1

(b) Handout Page 2

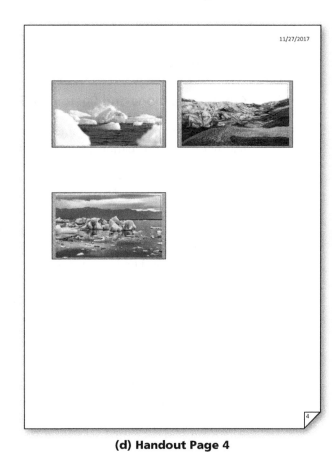

(c) Handout Page 3

(d) Handout Page 4

Figure 11–80

Summary

In this module you have learned how to organize a presentation into sections and then rename and move entire sections in the file. You then created a photo album, added and organized pictures, selected a theme and layout, adjusted a photo's contrast and brightness, and edited captions. You also changed the images to black and white in a separate photo album. Then, you specified a custom size and modified two slides by changing the slide orientation to portrait and inserting and compressing a video file. You then emailed the file and converted another file to video.

CONSIDER THIS: PLAN AHEAD

What decisions will you need to make when creating your next presentation?
Use these guidelines as you complete the assignments in this module and create your own slide show decks outside of this class.

1. **Use photographs with sharp focus and contrast.** The adage, "A picture is worth a thousand words," is relevant in a PowerPoint presentation. When your audience can see a visual representation of the concept you are describing during your talk, they are apt to understand and comprehend your message. Be certain your pictures are sharp and clear.

2. **Use hyperlinks to show slides with landscape and portrait orientations.** All slides in one presentation must be displayed in either landscape or portrait orientation. If you want to have variety in your slide show or have pictures or graphics that display best in one orientation, consider using hyperlinks to mix the two orientations during your presentation.

3. **Rehearse, rehearse, rehearse.** Outstanding slides lose their value when the presenter is unprepared to speak. Always keep in mind that the visual aspects are meant to supplement a speaker's verbal message. Practice your presentation before different types of audiences to solicit feedback, and use their comments to improve your speaking style.

Apply Your Knowledge

Reinforce the skills and apply the concepts you learned in this module.

Creating Sections and Custom Slide Shows

Note: To complete this assignment, you will be required to use the Data Files. Please contact your instructor for information about accessing the Data Files.

Instructions: Run PowerPoint. Open the presentation called Apply 11-1 Golf, which is located in the Data Files. The slides in this presentation provide information about golf lessons at the Harper Valley Golf Academy. Instructors at the golf academy teach all ages and skill levels, and they have developed programs for beginners, intermediate, and advanced skill levels. The manager mentioned that most students from last year are returning and probably will enroll in the intermediate or advanced classes. The beginners program may be eliminated, and classes may be changed to intermediate or advanced to accommodate the returning students. The document you open is a partially formatted presentation. You will insert slides, insert section breaks, rename and reorder sections, and create two custom slide shows. Your presentation should look like Figure 11–81.

Perform the following tasks:
1. Select Slide 1 (Figure 11–81a), and create a new Slide 2 that is a duplicate of Slide 1. Resize the golf ball illustration in the lower-right corner of Slide 2 to 2.5 × 2.46 and then move it by the sand trap, as shown in Figure 11-81b. Select the words, 'and skill levels', in the rectangle shape and then type **at beginner level** as the replacement text.

(a) Slide 1

(b) Slide 2

Figure 11–81 (Continued)

2. If requested by your instructor, add the city where you were born as the third line of the rectangle shape text.

3. Move the rectangle shape to the lower-right area of the slide, as shown in Figure 11-81b. Create a new Slide 3 that is a duplicate of Slide 2. Select the word, beginning, in the rectangle shape and then type `intermediate` as the new text. Duplicate Slide 3 and then replace the word, intermediate, with the word, `advanced`, in the new Slide 4.

4. In Slide Sorter view, add a section break after Slide 1 and the rename the new (Untitled) section, Beginners.

Continued >

Apply Your Knowledge *continued*

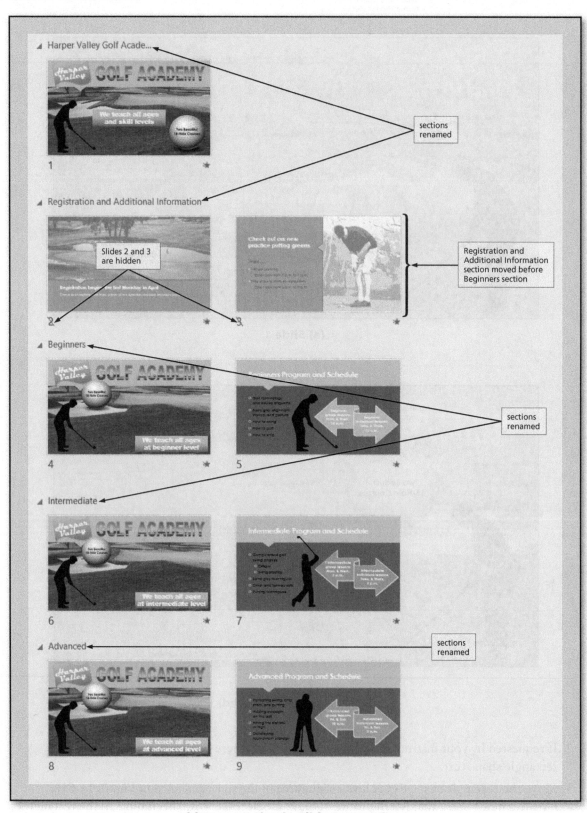

(c) Presentation in Slide Sorter View

Figure 11–81

5. Rename the Default Section divider (before Slide 1), Harper Valley Golf Academy.

6. Add a section break before Slide 3 and then rename it, Intermediate. Add a section break before Slide 4 and then rename it, Advanced.

7. Adjust the zoom so that all slides are visible. Move Slide 5 (Beginners Program and Schedule) to the Beginners section so that it becomes the second slide of that section and Slide 3 in the presentation. Move Slide 6 (Intermediate Program and Schedule) to the Intermediate section so that it becomes the second slide of that section and Slide 5 in the presentation. Slide 7 should remain as the second slide in the Advanced section.

8. Add a section break before Slide 8 and then rename it, Registration and Additional Information. Slide 9 should remain as the second slide in this section.

9. Collapse all sections and then move the Registration and Additional Information section before the Beginners section. Hide both slides in this section.

10. Apply the Wind transition (Exciting category) and change the duration to 03.50 for all slides.

11. Expand all the sections and then change the view to Normal. Create a custom slide show called Intermediate Golf Lessons. Include only Slides 1, 2, 3, 6, and 7 in this custom slide show. Show the custom presentation.

12. Create a second custom slide show called Advanced Golf Lessons. Include only Slides 1, 2, 3, 8, and 9 in this custom slide show. Show the custom presentation.

13. Run the Golf presentation and then save the file using the file name, Apply 11-1 Golf Lessons.

14. Submit the documents in the format specified by your instructor.

15. ✹ In this presentation, you duplicated the title slide and then created three new slides that served as the first slide of each section. How does this common element help guide audience members through the presentation? Is it more effective to display the Registration and Additional Information section at the beginning or the end of the presentation? Why? When might a presenter want to hide one or both slides in the Registration and Additional Information section?

Extend Your Knowledge

Extend the skills you learned in this module and experiment with new skills. You may need to use Help to complete the assignment.

Renaming Sections, Removing a Section, Using the Smart Lookup Tool to Find Information, and Setting Up a Custom Size

Note: To complete this assignment, you will be required to use the Data Files. Please contact your instructor for information about accessing the Data Files.

Instructions: Run PowerPoint. You volunteer at the local wildlife reserve where people can observe many kinds of birds. The lake on the reserve had been home to large colonies of flamingos and herons, but the heron colony no longer is present. You locate a presentation about these birds that was used at the visitors' center kiosk several years ago, and now you will revise it. You also will create a banner from the title slide that will be printed and posted near the path to the lake. Open the presentation called Extend 11-1 Flamingos and Herons, which is located in the Data Files. Create the presentation shown in Figure 11–82.

Continued >

Extend Your Knowledge *continued*

Perform the following tasks:

1. On Slide 1 (Figure 11–82a), delete the heron picture on the left side of the slide. Increase the size of the flamingo picture to 6.4" × 9.91" and then align it in the center and the middle of the slide. Delete the words, and Heron, from the text box and then change the text box shape fill color to Red (in Recent Colors row).

2. Use Smart Lookup to find the etymology (origin) of the word, flamingo. Copy and paste this information in the Notes pane on Slide 1.

3. Using Slide Sorter view (Figure 11–82b), remove the Heron Colony section and the three slides in this section. (*Hint:* You may need to use Help to learn how to remove a section and associated slides.)

4. Move the Flamingo Habitats section up so that is below the Flamingo - General Information section.

5. Remove the Flamingo Breeding section and slide.

6. Rename the first section, Flamingo Colony - Entry Sign.

7. Create a custom slide show called Flamingos. Include only Slides 2, 3, and 4 in this custom slide show. Move Slide 3 (Diet) up so that it becomes the second slide and displays after Slide 1 (FLAMINGO). Show the custom show.

8. If requested by your instructor, add the number of bones you have broken after the word, feathers, on Slide 2.

9. Change the transition from Fade to Uncover in the Subtle category, change the duration to 03.50 seconds, and then apply the transition to all slides.

10. Run the presentation and then save the file using file name, Extend 11-1 Flamingo Reserve.

(a) Slide 1

Figure 11–82 (Continued)

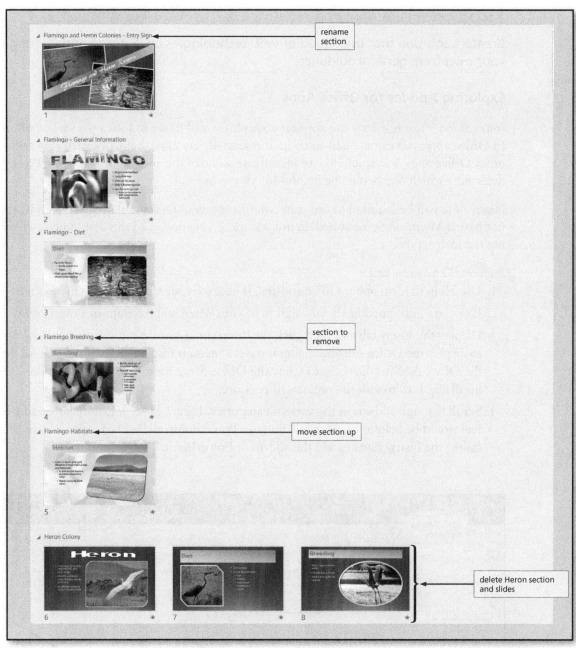

(b) Presentation in Slide Sorter View

Figure 11–82

11. Display Slide 1 and create a custom slide size for a banner. [*Hint:* Click the Slide Size button (Design tab | Customize group), click Custom Slide Size, click the 'Slides sized for' arrow (Slide Size dialog box), and then click Custom.] Change the banner width to 48" and the height to 32". Ensure the banner will fit on the new slide.

12. Delete Slides 2, 3, and 4 and the associated sections.

13. Save Slide 1 using the file name, Extend 11-1 Flamingo Reserve Banner.

14. Submit the revised documents in the format specified by your instructor.

15. ✹ In this presentation, you removed the section with the herons. Why? Which reference did you use to find the etymology for the word, flamingo? What other information about this bird is available in the Insights task pane's Explore tab?

Expand Your World

Create a solution that uses cloud or web technologies by learning and investigating on your own from general guidance.

Exploring Add-Ins for Office Apps

Instructions: You regularly use apps on your phone and tablet to look up a variety of information. In Office apps, you can use add-ins, which essentially are apps that work with PowerPoint and the other Office apps. You would like to investigate some of the add-ins available for PowerPoint to determine which ones would be helpful for you to use.

Note: You will be required to use your Microsoft account to complete this assignment. If you do not have a Microsoft account and do not want to create one, read this assignment without performing the instructions.

Perform the following tasks:

1. Use Help to learn about Office add-ins. If necessary, sign in to your Windows account.
2. If you are not signed in already, sign in to your Microsoft Account in PowerPoint.
3. Display the Insert tab and then click the 'Insert an Add-in' button (Insert tab | Add-Ins group) to display the Office Add-ins dialog box. (If a menu is displayed, click the See All link to display the Office Add-ins dialog box.) Click the Office Store button or the STORE tab (Office Add-ins dialog box) to visit the online Office Store.
4. Scroll through add-ins in the various categories (Figure 11–83). Locate a free add-in that you feel would be helpful to you while you use PowerPoint, click this desired add-in, and then follow the instructions to add the add-in to PowerPoint.

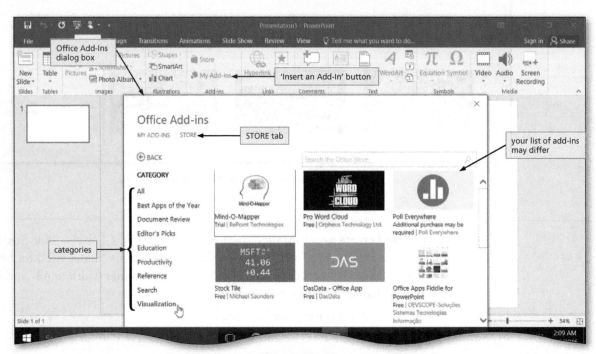

Figure 11–83

5. In PowerPoint, click the 'Insert an Add-in' button again to display the Office Add-ins dialog box. Click the add-in you added and then click the Insert button to use the add-in. Click the 'Insert an Add-in' arrow to see the added add-in in the list.

6. Practice using the add-in. Does the add-in work as you intended? Would you recommend the add-in to others?

7. ⊛ Which add-ins, if any, were already on your computer or mobile device? Which add-in did you download and why? Answer the questions in #6.

In the Labs

Design, create, modify, and/or use a presentation following the guidelines, concepts, and skills presented in this module. Labs 1 and 2, which increase in difficulty, require you to create solutions based on what you learned in the module; Lab 3 requires you to apply your creative thinking and problem-solving skills to design and implement a solution.

Lab 1: Working with Multiple Presentation Windows Simultaneously, Setting Manual Timings, and Creating a Video

Note: To complete this assignment, you will be required to use the Data Files. Please contact your instructor for information about accessing the Data Files.

Problem: You are preparing a presentation about jellyfish for your marine biology class and are working with two PowerPoint presentations simultaneously. One has basic facts about jellyfish and their life cycle. The second one contains information about different species of jellyfish and a video that you want to use in your presentation. You create a video of your final combined presentation, and email the presentation.

Perform the following tasks:

1. Run PowerPoint. Open the presentation, Lab 11-1 Jellyfish Facts, which is located in the Data Files. Remove all sections (but not the slides).

2. Open the presentation, Lab 11-1 Jellyfish with Video, which is located in the Data Files, and then cascade the two open document windows on the screen.

3. Copy the video on Slide 3 of the Jellyfish with Video presentation to Slide 4 of the Jellyfish Facts presentation using the destination theme. Change the video style to Reflected Bevel, White (fourth style in first Intense row). Increase the size of the video frame to 5.4" × 9.6 and then align it on the middle and the right side of the slide.

4. Display Slide 3 of the Jellyfish with Video presentation. Select the text box with the two bulleted paragraphs, copy it, and then paste it on Slide 4 of the Jellyfish Facts presentation using the 'Keep Source Formatting' option. Align the text box in the middle and the left side of the slide (Figure 11–84).

5. If requested by your instructor, add the name of your grade school or high school as a third paragraph in the bulleted text box on Slide 4.

6. Close the Jellyfish with Video presentation without saving changes.

7. Apply the Ripple transition in the Exciting category to Slide 4 and then change the duration to 03.50 seconds.

Continued >

In the Labs *continued*

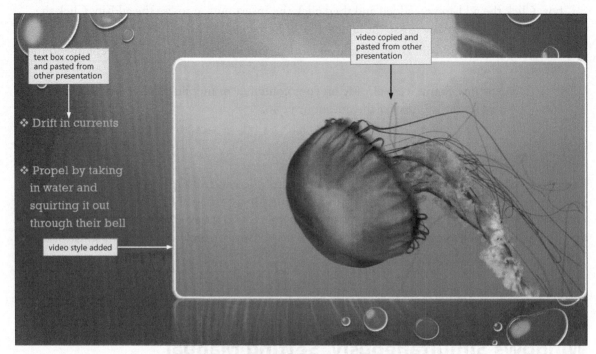

Figure 11–84 Remarkable Jellyfish Slide 4

8. Set up the slide show to advance slides manually. Run the presentation using Presenter View.

9. Save the presentation using the file name, Lab 11-1 Remarkable Jellyfish.

10. Create a video of the Lab 11-1 Remarkable Jellyfish presentation. Select Internet Quality, do not record timings and narrations, and then change seconds spent on each slide to 10.00. Save the video using the file name, Lab 11-1 Remarkable Jellyfish Video.

11. Email the presentation to your instructor.

12. ✳ You copied the video on Slide 4 from another presentation. Was the video style you added to it appropriate, or can you recommend another style that is more suitable? What other videos and photos would enhance this presentation?

Lab 2: Creating Photo Albums in Color and Black-and-White, Adjusting Brightness and Contrast of an Image, Copying and Compressing a Video File, and Recording a Narration

Note: To complete this assignment, you will be required to use the Data Files. Please contact your instructor for information about accessing the Data Files.

Problem: You recently vacationed in Australia and have decided to create a photo album to share your experiences. To add interest to the color photo album, you want to add a short video you took of a kangaroo with a beautiful sunset in the background. You will copy the video into your color photo album. Then, you will create a black-and-white photo album with narration. You create the slides shown in Figure 11–85.

Perform the following tasks:

Part 1:

1. Run PowerPoint. Apply the Blank Presentation theme. Insert a new photo album.

2. Insert the Australia1, Australia2, Australia3, Australia4, Australia5, Australia6, Australia7, and Australia8 pictures, which are located in the Data Files.

3. Move the Australia7 picture in the album above the Australia2 picture.

4. Move the Australia4 picture in the album to the end of the album after the Australia8 picture.

5. Change the album picture layout to 2 pictures, select the 'Simple Frame, White' frame shape, and then select the 'Captions below ALL pictures' option.

6. Create the photo album. Apply the Vapor Trail theme. Save the presentation using the file name, Lab 11-2 Australia Color Album.

7. On Slide 1, type, `Visit Australia` as the new title text and then, if necessary, type your name in the subtitle placeholder (Figure 11–85a).

8. If requested by your instructor, type the time of day you were born after the word, Australia.

9. On Slide 2, type, `Sydney Opera House` as the caption for the left picture and `Cathedral Range State Park` as the caption for the right picture (Figure 11–85b).

10. On Slide 3, type, `Melbourne` as the caption for the left picture and `Spectacular dive site` as the caption for the right picture. Edit the photo album and then rotate the right picture clockwise (Figure 11–85c).

11. On Slide 4, type `Mount Oberon` as the caption for the left picture and `Lake Eldon` as the caption for the right picture (Figure 11–85d).

12. On Slide 5, edit the photo album by removing the Australia8 picture. Increase the size of the beach picture to 6" × 8.25" and then align the picture in the center and the middle of the slide. Type the caption, `7-Mile Beach` (Figure 11–85e).

14. Insert a new slide after Slide 5 and select the Blank layout.

(a) Slide 1

Figure 11–85 (Continued)

Continued >

In the Labs *continued*

(b) Slide 2

(c) Slide 3

Figure 11–85 (Continued)

(d) Slide 4

(e) Slide 5

Figure 11–85 (Continued)

Continued >

In the Labs continued

(f) Slide 6

(g) Slide 1 (Narrated Presentation)

Figure 11–85 (Continued)

photo contrast increased

(h) Slide 2 (Narrated Presentation)

photo brightness
decreased

(i) Slide 3 (Narrated Presentation)

Figure 11–85

Continued >

In the Labs *continued*

15. Open the presentation, Lab 11-2 Australia Sunsets, which is located in the Data Files. Cascade the two open document windows on the screen. Copy the video from Slide 2 and paste it into Slide 6 of the Lab 11-2 Australia Color Album using the destination theme.

16. Close the Lab 11-2 Australia Sunsets presentation. Maximize the Lab 11-2 Australia Color Album presentation. Adjust the size of the video to 7" × 12.44" and then align it in the center and the middle of the slide. Change the start option to Automatically and then change the video style to 'Simple Frame, White' (sixth style in first Subtle row) (Figure 11–85f).

17. Apply the Comb transition (Exciting category), change the duration to 03.50 seconds, and then apply to all slides.

18. Set up the show to run in Presenter View.

19. Compress the media files in the presentation using the Low Quality setting. Save the presentation again using the same file name.

20. Run the presentation. Submit the revised document in the format specified by your instructor.

Part 2:

1. Insert a new photo album.

2. Insert the Australia9, Australia10, Australia11, and Australia12 pictures, which are located in the Data Files.

3. Change the album picture layout to 2 pictures, select the 'Compound Frame, Black' frame shape, select the 'ALL pictures blank and white' option, and then add the Ion theme.

4. Select the Australia10 picture and increase the contrast two times.

5. Select the Australia11 picture and decrease the brightness of the picture two times.

6. Create the photo album and then apply the Ion theme's blue variant.

7. Edit the album by removing the Australia9 picture. Insert the Australia4 picture and then move it to the beginning of the album. Update the slides.

8. On Slide 1, type, `Surfing in Australia` as the new title text and then, if necessary, type your name in the subtitle placeholder (Figure 11–85g).

9. If requested by your instructor, type the year you started college after the word, Australia.

10. Select Slide 2 (Figure 11–85h). Record the slide show from the current slide. Note: The following steps contain narration that you will read while progressing through the slides. Read the following narration: `"Australia has many great surfing spots to explore."` for this slide.

11. Advance to Slide 3 (Figure 11–85i) and then read the following narration: `"Whether you are a beginner or an experienced surfer, you can find your surfing spot somewhere in Australia."` for this slide.

12. Stop the presentation so that the recording session ends.

13. Display Slide 1 and then run the slide show to view the presentation and to hear the narration you just recorded.

14. Apply the Fall Over transition, change the duration to 03.00 seconds, and then apply to all slides.

15. Preview the presentation and then save the file using the file name, Lab 11-2 Surfing in Australia Narration.

16. Submit the revised document in the format specified by your instructor.

17. ✳ When you created the color and black-and-white photo albums of Australia pictures, you set up the albums with two photos per slide. Would another picture layout be more dramatic? Why or why not? Did changing the contrast and brightness of the photos enhance the quality? In the black-and-white photo album, you used the Ion design with the blue variant. Was this a good choice? Why?

Lab 3: Consider This: Your Turn

Design and Create a Presentation about Snakes

Part 1:   Naturalists at the nature center in your community work with teachers to bring environmental education into the classroom. One of the traveling exhibits features snakes. The outreach coordinator has asked you to develop a presentation to accompany her talk and then create a video from the presentation. She provides a video, called Garter Snake, and tells you that this reptile is non-venomous and grows to between 1 foot (0.3048 m) and 2 feet (0.6096 m) long. It eats bugs and small rodents, so it can help control mice or insects. While developing the slides, you use the Smart Lookup feature to gather more information about snakes, including their habitat, diet, and anatomy. Use the concepts and techniques presented in this module to create a presentation with sections and that includes the garter snake video. The Data Files contains the Garter Snake video and seven snake illustrations called Snake 1 - Cobra, Snake 2 - Copperhead, Snake 3 – Diamondback Water, Snake 4 – Eastern Coral, Snake 5 – Rattlesnake, Snake 6 – Timber Rattlesnake, and Snake 7 – Cartoon Snake. You also can add photos you found using Smart Lookup, as long as you cite the source of these photos in the caption or in the Notes pane. Create section breaks and format the background. Compress the video. Review and revise your presentation as needed and then save the file using the file name, Lab 11-3 Snakes. Then, create a video and save that file using the file name, Lab 11-3 Snakes Video. Submit your assignment in the format specified by your instructor.

Part 2:   ✳ You made several decisions while creating the presentation: how to organize the sections, how to order the photos and video, which photo enhancements to use, and which layout and theme to apply. What was the rationale behind each of these decisions? When you reviewed the document, what further revisions did you make and why?

8 | Working with Trendlines, PivotTables, PivotCharts, and Slicers

Objectives

You will have mastered the material in this module when you can:

- Analyze worksheet data using a trendline
- Create a PivotTable report
- Format a PivotTable report
- Apply filters to a PivotTable report
- Create a PivotChart report
- Format a PivotChart report
- Apply filters to a PivotChart report

- Analyze worksheet data using PivotTable and PivotChart reports
- Create calculated fields
- Create slicers to filter PivotTable and PivotChart reports
- Format slicers
- Analyze PivotTable and PivotChart reports using slicers

Introduction

In both academic and business environments, people are presented with large amounts of data that needs to be analyzed and interpreted. Data increasingly is available from a wide variety of sources and gathered with ease. Analysis of data and interpretation of the results are important skills to acquire. Learning how to ask questions that identify patterns in data is a skill that can provide businesses and individuals with information that can be used to make decisions about business situations.

Project — LinkMe Internet Service Provider

LinkMe ISP (Internet Service Provider) is a company that sells five different types of Internet connection service plans: Basic, Basic Plus, Hi-Speed, Deluxe 150, and T3. They keep records on sales regions, including city, suburban, and rural sales. They also keep track of online sales versus other venues such as retail outlets, trade shows, and telemarketing.

The owner of LinkMe ISP is interested in reviewing sales figures for the past six years. She also has requested that you compare the last two years of sales figures for the different service types, by region and by venue. In this module, you will learn how to use the trendline charting feature in Excel to examine data for trends. You also will analyze sales data for LinkMe ISP using PivotTable and PivotChart reports. The results of this analysis are shown in Figure 8–1.

A **trendline** (Figure 8–1a) is a visual way to show how two variables relate to each other. Trendlines often are used to represent changes in one set of data over time, but also can compare changes in one set of data with changes in another. Excel can overlay a trendline on certain types of charts.

In addition to trendlines, PivotTable reports and PivotChart reports provide methods to manipulate and visualize data. A PivotTable report (Figure 8–1b) is an interactive view of worksheet data that gives users the ability to summarize the data by selecting and grouping categories. When using a PivotTable report, you can change selected categories quickly, without needing to manipulate the worksheet itself. You can examine and analyze several complex organizations of the data and may spot relationships you might not otherwise see. For example, you can look at total sales for each region, broken down by service type, and then look at the quarterly sales for certain subgroupings, without having to do complex reorganization of the data.

A PivotChart report (Figure 8–1c) is an interactive chart that allows users to change the data groupings. For example, if LinkMe ISP wanted to view a pie chart showing percentages of total sales for each service type, a PivotChart could show that percentage categorized by city versus rural sales, without having to rebuild the chart from scratch for each view. PivotChart reports are visual representations of PivotTables. When you create a PivotChart report, Excel creates and associates a PivotTable with that PivotChart.

Slicers (Figure 8–1d) are graphic objects that you click to filter the data in PivotTables and PivotCharts. Each slicer button clearly identifies its purpose (the applied filter), making it easy to interpret the data displayed in the PivotTable report.

Using trendlines, PivotTables, PivotCharts, and slicers, a user with little knowledge of formulas, functions, and ranges can complete powerful what-if analyses on a set of data.

Figure 8–2 illustrates the requirements document for the LinkMe ISP Sales Analysis worksheet. It includes the needs, source of data, calculations, and other facts about the worksheet's development.

The following roadmap identifies general activities you will perform as you progress through this module:

1. CREATE the LINE CHART and TRENDLINE.
2. CREATE the PIVOTTABLE.
3. CHANGE the LAYOUT and VIEW of the PivotTable
4. FILTER the PIVOTTABLE.
5. FORMAT the PIVOTTABLE.
6. CREATE the PIVOTCHART.
7. CHANGE the PIVOTCHART VIEW and CONTENTS.
8. ADD SLICERS.

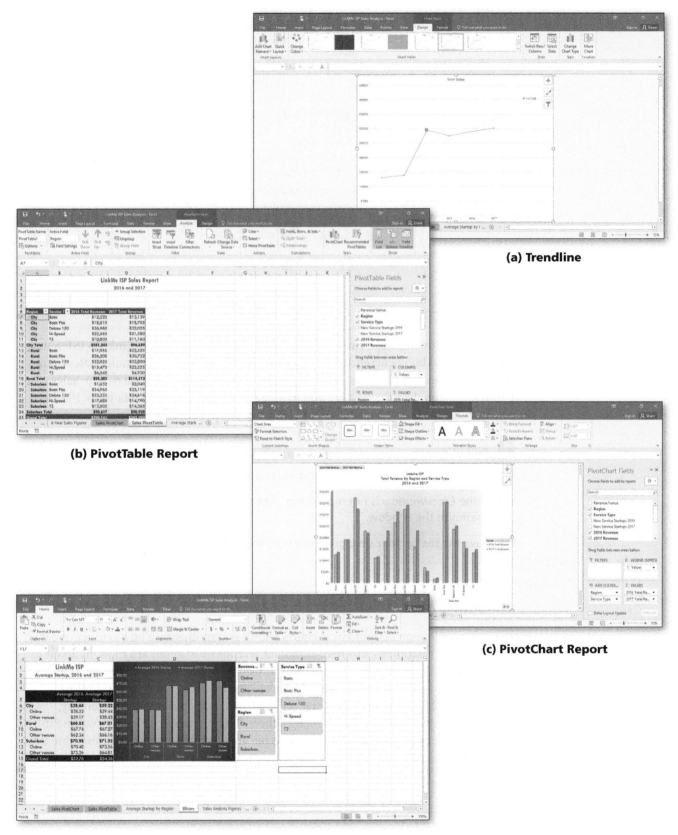

(a) Trendline

(b) PivotTable Report

(c) PivotChart Report

(d) Slicers

Figure 8–1

Worksheet Title	LinkMe ISP Sales Analysis
Needs	Evaluate different sets of sales data analysis: 1. Total Sales data for 2012–2017. Provide a visual representation of revenue over the past 6 years, and a forecast for the next 2 years based on the current trend. 2. Sales data for 2016 and 2017 for all venues, with details identifying region, service type, and number of start-ups sold. For this data, use PivotTables and PivotCharts to look for patterns and anomalies in the data, based on different breakouts. Some breakouts of interest include Total Sales and Average Sales for Region and Service type, by Revenue Venue. 3. Set up slicers to facilitate easy examination of various subgroupings for users with little or no Excel experience.
Source of Data	Data is available in the workbook LinkMe ISP Sales Data.xlsx.
Calculations	In addition to total sales for the various groupings, produce comparisons of average sales for those groupings. Finally, create calculations of the value of the average sales for various combinations.

Figure 8–2

To Run Excel and Open a Workbook

The following steps run Excel and open a workbook named LinkMe ISP Sales Data. The workbook currently has two worksheets, one showing detailed sales figures, named Sales Analysis Figures, and one summarizing the data, named 6-Year Sales Figures. To complete these steps, you will be required to use the Data Files. Please contact your instructor for information about accessing the Data Files.

1 Run Excel.

2 Open the file named LinkMe ISP Sales Data from the Data Files.

3 If the Excel window is not maximized, click the Maximize button on its title bar to maximize the window.

4 Save the file on your storage device with the name, LinkMe ISP Sales Analysis.

Adding a Trendline to a Chart

Using a trendline on certain Excel charts allows you to illustrate how one set of data is changing in relation to another set of data. Trends most often are thought about in terms of how a value changes over time, but trends also can describe the relationship between two variables, such as height and weight. In Excel, you add a trendline to most types of charts, such as unstacked 2-D area, bar, column, line, inventory, scatter (X, Y), and bubble charts, among others. Chart types that do not examine the relationship between two variables, such as pie and doughnut charts that examine the contribution of different parts to a whole, cannot include trendlines.

How do you determine which trends to analyze?

Before you add a trendline to a chart, you need to determine which data series to analyze. If the chart uses only one data series, Excel uses it automatically. If the chart involves more than one data series, you select the one you want to use as a trendline. You then can analyze current or future trends.

To analyze a current trend, make sure you have enough data available for the period you want to analyze. For example, two years of annual sales totals might not provide enough data to analyze sales performance. Five years of annual sales totals or two years of monthly sales totals are more likely to present a trend.

To analyze a future trend, you use a trendline to project data beyond the values or scope of the data set. This process is called forecasting. **Forecasting** helps predict data values that are outside of a data set. For example, if a data set is for a 10-year period and the data shows a trend in that 10-year period, Excel can predict values beyond that period or estimate what the values may have been before that period.

When you add a trendline to a chart, you can set the number of periods to forecast forward or backward in time. For example, if you have six years of sales data, you can forecast two periods forward to show the trend for eight years: six years of current data and two years of projected data. You also can display information about the trendline on the chart itself to help guide your analysis. For example, you can display the equation used to calculate the trend and show the **R-squared value**, which is a number from 0 to 1 that measures the strength of the trend. An R-squared value of 1 means the estimated values in the trendline correspond exactly to the actual data.

To Create a 2-D Line Chart

1 CREATE LINE CHART & TRENDLINE | **2 CREATE PIVOTTABLE** | **3 CHANGE LAYOUT & VIEW** | **4 FILTER PIVOTTABLE**
5 FORMAT PIVOTTABLE | **6 CREATE PIVOTCHART** | **7 CHANGE PIVOTCHART VIEW & CONTENTS** | **8 ADD SLICERS**

Why? *Line charts are suited to charting a variable, in this case sales, over a number of time periods.* The following steps create a 2-D line chart of the LinkMe ISP sales data. You will add a trendline to the chart later in the module.

- If necessary, click the '6-Year Sales Figures' sheet tab.
- Select cells A4:G5 to select the range to be charted (Figure 8–3).

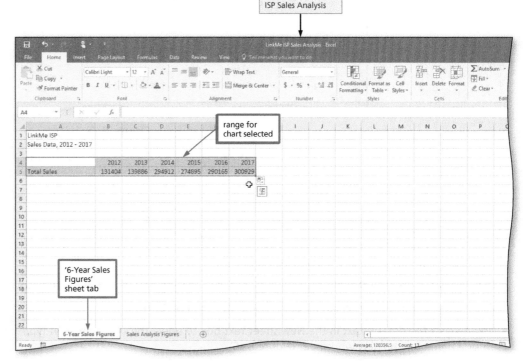

Figure 8–3

- Click Insert on the ribbon to display the Insert tab.
- Click the 'Insert Line or Area Chart' button (Insert tab | Charts group) to display the Insert Line and Area Chart gallery (Figure 8–4).

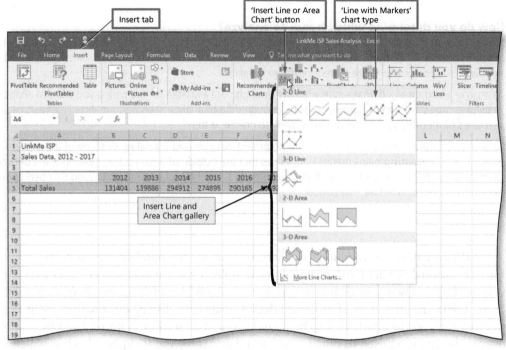

Figure 8–4

- Click 'Line with Markers' in the 2-D Line area to insert a 2-D line chart with data markers (Figure 8–5).

Q&A

What are data markers?

A data marker is the symbol in a chart that represents a single value from a worksheet cell. In this case, the data markers are circles that represent the six sales figures.

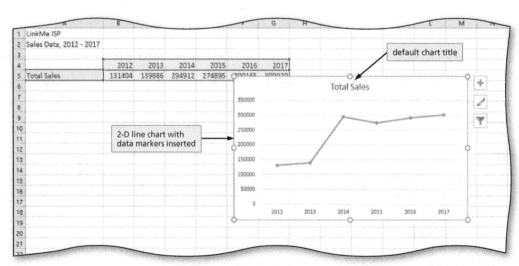

Figure 8–5

Why do the selected cells appear with colored fill?

Excel uses colors to identify chart elements when preparing to create a chart. In this case, the red cell is the chart title, the purple cells are the x-axis or category values (in this case, years), and the blue cells are the data or values.

- If necessary, display the Chart Tools Design tab.
- Click the Move Chart button (Chart Tools Design tab | Location group) to display the Move Chart dialog box.
- Click New sheet (Move Chart dialog box) to select the option button.
- Double-click the default text in the New sheet text box to select the text, and then type **Trendline Chart** to enter a name for the new worksheet (Figure 8–6).

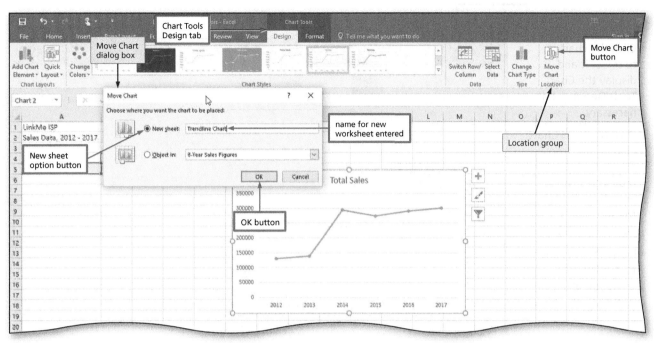

Figure 8–6

- Click the OK button (Move Chart dialog box) to move the chart to a new worksheet.

- Click the chart title and select the text.

- Type **LinkMe ISP Sales 2012 – 2017** to enter the new chart title.

- Click outside of the chart area to deselect the chart (Figure 8–7).

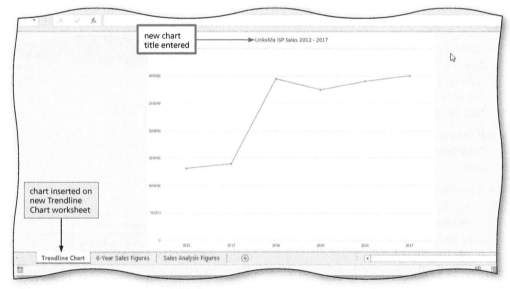

Figure 8–7

Other Ways

1. Click Quick Analysis button, click Charts tab, click Line button

To Add a Trendline to a Chart

1 CREATE LINE CHART & TRENDLINE | 2 CREATE PIVOTTABLE | 3 CHANGE LAYOUT & VIEW | 4 FILTER PIVOTTABLE
5 FORMAT PIVOTTABLE | 6 CREATE PIVOTCHART | 7 CHANGE PIVOTCHART VIEW & CONTENTS | 8 ADD SLICERS

The following steps add a trendline to the LinkMe ISP Total Sales 2012 – 2017 chart. *Why? You add a trendline to a chart to analyze current and/or future trends. A trendline must be added to an existing chart.* The chart will predict the total sales two years beyond the data set in the six-year sales figures worksheet.

- Click the chart to select it and display the Chart Tools Design tab if necessary.

- Click the 'Add Chart Element' button (Chart Tools Design tab | Chart Layouts group) to display the Add Chart Element menu.

- Point to Trendline to display the Trendline gallery (Figure 8–8).

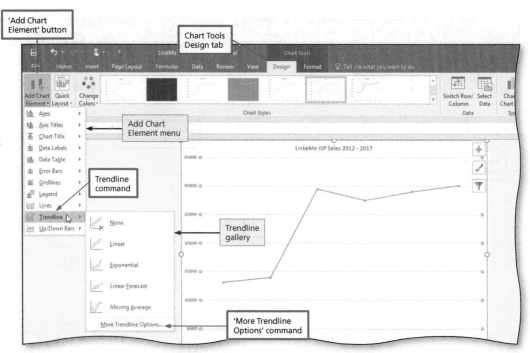

Figure 8–8

- Click 'More Trendline Options' (Trendline gallery) to display the Format Trendline task pane.

- If necessary, click the Trendline Options tab.

- If necessary, click Linear in the Trendline Options area to select a linear trendline type (Figure 8–9).

Q&A Why should I select the Linear option button in this case?
The 2-D line chart you created is a basic line chart, so it is appropriate to apply a linear trendline, which shows values that are increasing or decreasing at a steady rate.

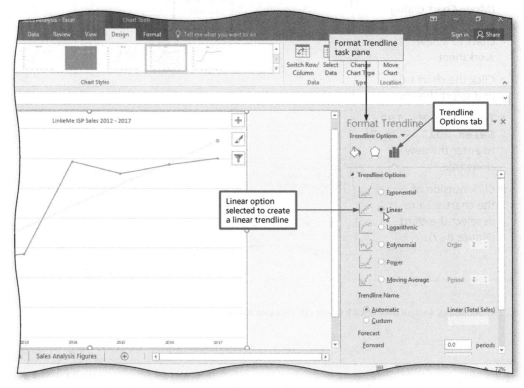

Figure 8–9

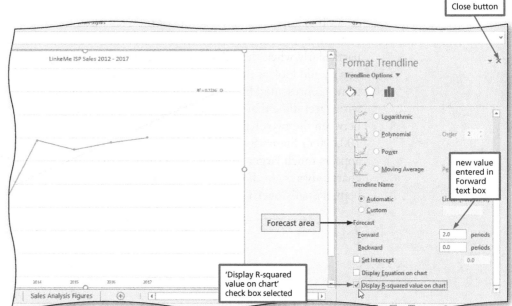

Figure 8–10

- If necessary, scroll down in the Format Trendline task pane until the Forecast area is visible.

- Select the Forward text box and type **2.0** to add a trendline to the chart with a two-period forward forecast.

Q&A | What does it mean to enter a two-period forward forecast?

A two-period forward forecast estimates the values for the two time periods that follow the data you used to create the line chart. In this case, it will estimate total sales for the next two years.

- Click the 'Display R-squared value on chart' check box to display the R-squared value on the chart (Figure 8–10).

Q&A | What is the R-squared value?

The R-squared value is a measure of how well the trendline describes the relationship between total sales and time. The closer the value is to 1, the more accurate the trendline.

- Click the Close button (Format Trendline task pane) to add the trendline with the selected options.

- Display the Page Layout tab.

- Use the Themes button (Page Layout tab | Themes group) to apply the Integral theme to the workbook (Figure 8–11).

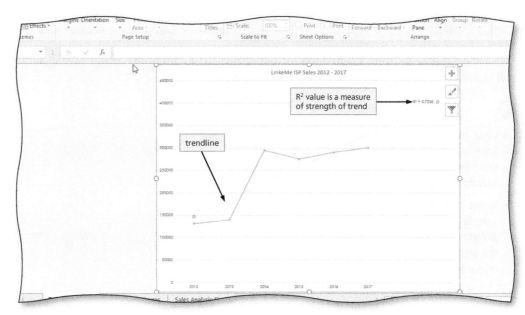

Figure 8–11

Other Ways

1. Right-click graphed line, click Add Trendline on shortcut menu

More about Trendlines

It is important to take note of the axes when looking at trendlines. Charts with trendlines often are reformatted to start the vertical axis at a number other than zero, particularly when the values on the vertical axis are high. When interpreting a trendline, you should look at the vertical axis to see if it starts at zero. If it does not, be aware that trends represented by the trendline may appear exaggerated. Figure 8–12 shows a chart with a trendline that uses the same data as the chart in Figure 8–11. The difference between the two charts is in the vertical axis, which starts at zero in Figure 8–11 and at 100,000 in Figure 8–12. The difference between the projected values for 2018 and 2019 appears much larger in Figure 8–12 where the axis starts at 100,000. When looking at charts, always check the axes to be sure that the differences shown in the chart are not being visually overstated.

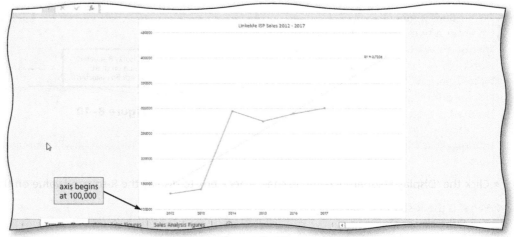

Figure 8–12

To Change the Format of a Data Point

1 CREATE LINE CHART & TRENDLINE | 2 CREATE PIVOTTABLE | 3 CHANGE LAYOUT & VIEW | 4 FILTER PIVOTTABLE
5 FORMAT PIVOTTABLE | 6 CREATE PIVOTCHART | 7 CHANGE PIVOTCHART VIEW & CONTENTS | 8 ADD SLICERS

The following steps change the format of the 2014 data point. *Why? When graphing data, you may want to call visual attention to a particular data point or points.*

- Click the 2014 data point twice to select the single point. Do not double-click.

- Right-click the selected data point to display the shortcut menu (Figure 8–13).

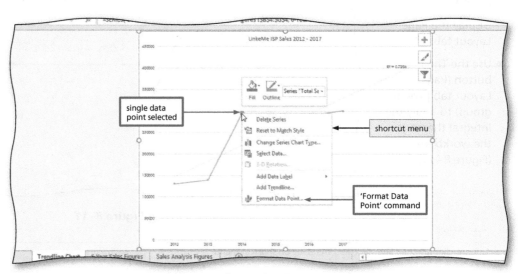

Figure 8–13

- Click 'Format Data
  Point' on the
  shortcut menu to
  display the Format
  Data Point task
  pane.
- Click the 'Fill & Line'
  tab (Format Data
  Point task pane) to
  display the Fill &
  Line options.
- Click Marker, and
  then if necessary,
  click Marker Options
  to expand the
  section.
- Select the contents
  of the Size box, and
  then type **12** as
  the new size.

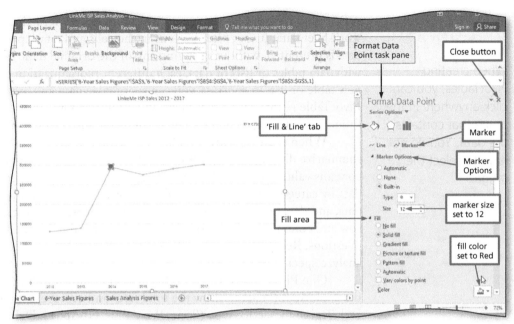

Figure 8–14

- If necessary, click Fill to expand the Fill section.
- Click the Color button and then click Red in the Standard Colors area to change the color of the data point to red
  (Figure 8–14).

- Click the Close
  button (Format Data
  Point task pane)
  and then click away
  from the data point
  to view the change
  (Figure 8–15).

- Click the Save
  button (Quick Access
  Toolbar) to save the
  workbook with the
  same name in the
  same location.

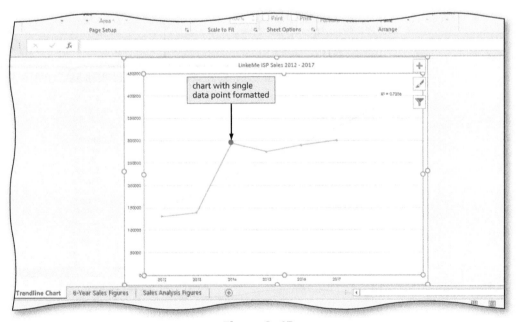

Figure 8–15

Break Point: If you wish to take a break, this is a good place to do so. Exit Excel. To resume at a later time, run
Excel and open the file named LinkMe ISP Sales Analysis, and then continue following the steps from this location
forward.

Creating and Formatting PivotTable Reports

BTW

Selecting PivotTable Ranges

When creating PivotTables, you can click anywhere in the range that contains the data. You do not have to select the range.

A PivotTable report, also called a PivotTable, is an interactive tool that summarizes worksheet data. It uses filter buttons in the cells and a task pane to change the way the data is presented, without changing any of the original data. Normally, when working with data tables or lists of data, each different reorganization of the data requires a new table or list. In contrast, you can reorganize data and examine summaries in a PivotTable report with a few clicks. PivotTable reports allow you to view different summaries of the data quickly and easily, using just a single table.

When creating a PivotTable report, you can use categories in the data to summarize different groups or totals. PivotTables use two types of fields: data, which contains values that the PivotTable will summarize, and category, which describes the data by categorizing it. Category fields typically correspond to columns in the original data, and data fields correspond to summary values across categories. You can change row and column groupings quickly to summarize the data in different ways to ask new questions. Reorganizing the table reveals different levels of detail and allows you to analyze specific subgroups.

One PivotTable created in this project is shown in Figure 8–16. It summarizes the LinkMe ISP data to show the total sales and average sales in 2016 and 2017 for each region by service type (Basic, Basic Plus, Hi-Speed, Deluxe 150, and T3). The filter button in cell A6 filters the results by region, and the filter button in cell B6 filters the results by service type. Columns C and D show the values for the total sales in 2016 and 2017, and columns E and F show the values for the average sales in 2016 and 2017.

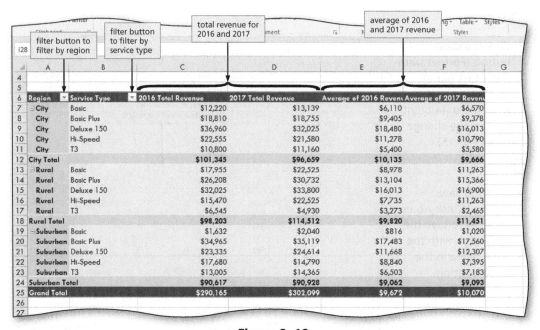

Figure 8–16

How do you determine which fields to use in a PivotTable?

CONSIDER THIS

You can create PivotTable and PivotChart reports in almost any configuration of your existing data. To use this powerful tool effectively, you need to create these reports with various questions in mind. Look at the categories you can use to describe your data and think about how the various categories can interact. Common questions relate to how the data changes over time, and how the data varies in geographical locations, such as states or regions, different functional groups within an organization, different product groupings, and demographic groupings, such as age and gender.

You can create PivotTable reports either on the same worksheet as the data to be analyzed or on a new worksheet in the same workbook.

To Create a Blank PivotTable

1 CREATE LINE CHART & TRENDLINE | 2 CREATE PIVOTTABLE | 3 CHANGE LAYOUT & VIEW | 4 FILTER PIVOTTABLE
5 FORMAT PIVOTTABLE | 6 CREATE PIVOTCHART | 7 CHANGE PIVOTCHART VIEW & CONTENTS | 8 ADD SLICERS

The following steps create a blank PivotTable report using the ribbon. *Why? Creating a blank PivotTable allows the user to create a framework within which to use the available data.* When you create a PivotTable, each column heading from your original data will represent a field of data accessible via the PivotTable Fields task pane.

- Click the 'Sales Analysis Figures' sheet tab to make the worksheet active.
- Click cell B3 to select a cell containing data for the PivotTable.
- Display the Insert tab.

Experiment
- Click the Recommended PivotTables button to view the various ways the data might be represented in tabular form. Click the Cancel button (Recommend PivotTables dialog box) to continue.

- Click the PivotTable button (Insert tab | Tables group) to display the Create PivotTable dialog box (Figure 8–17).

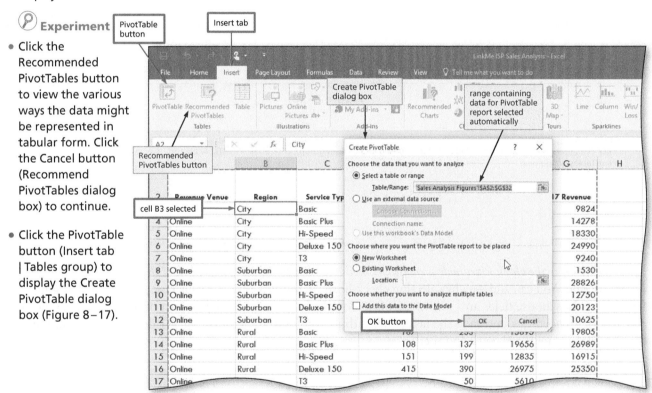

Figure 8–17

- Click the OK button (Create PivotTable dialog box) to create a blank PivotTable report on a new worksheet and display the PivotTable Fields task pane (Figure 8–18).

Q&A | Why is the PivotTable blank?
When you create a PivotTable, you first insert the structure. The resulting PivotTable is blank until you add content to it, which you do in the next set of steps.

My PivotTable Fields task pane just disappeared. What happened?
If you click outside of the PivotTable, the task pane no longer will be displayed. To redisplay the pane, click in the PivotTable.

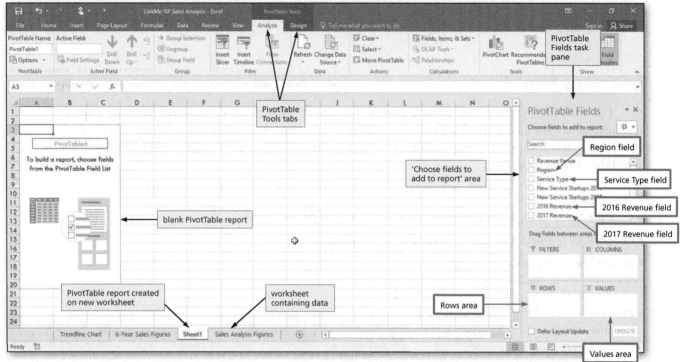

Figure 8–18

Other Ways

1. Click cell in range, click Recommended PivotTables (Insert tab | Tables group), click Blank PivotTable button (Recommended PivotTables dialog box)

To Add Data to the PivotTable

1 CREATE LINE CHART & TRENDLINE | **2 CREATE PIVOTTABLE** | 3 CHANGE LAYOUT & VIEW | 4 FILTER PIVOTTABLE
5 FORMAT PIVOTTABLE | 6 CREATE PIVOTCHART | 7 CHANGE PIVOTCHART VIEW & CONTENTS | 8 ADD SLICERS

Why? Once the blank PivotTable is created, it needs to be populated using any or all of the fields in the PivotTable Fields task pane. You can add data by selecting check boxes in the PivotTable Fields task pane or by dragging fields from the Choose fields area to the one of the four boxed areas in the lower part of the task pane. Once you add a field, it becomes a button in the task pane, with its own button menu. Table 8–1 describes the four areas in the PivotTable Fields task pane and their common usage.

Table 8–1 Field Areas in the PivotTable Fields Task Pane	
Areas	**Use**
FILTERS	Fields added to the Filters area create a report filter and filter button in the PivotTable, representing a subset that meets a selection criterion.
COLUMNS	Normally, Excel creates a field in the Columns area when multiple fields are dragged to the Values area. Fields directly added to the Columns fields should contain summary numeric data
ROWS	Fields added to the Rows area become rows in the PivotTable. Subsequent fields added to the Rows area become subsets of the first field.
VALUES	Fields added to the Values area must contain numeric data from the source data

The following step adds data to the PivotTable. The rows will show the Service Type and within that the region. As you add the 2016 Total Revenue and 2017 Total Revenue fields to the Values area, Excel will create columns.

- Drag the Service Type field from the 'Choose fields to add to report' area to the Rows area to add the field to a row in the PivotTable.

- Click the Region check box in the 'Choose fields to add to report' area to add the Region field to the Rows area below the Service Type field.

Q&A How did the Region field end up in the Rows area?
Excel places a checked field in the group it determines is correct for that field. You can drag the field to a different group if you choose.

Figure 8–19

- Drag the 2016 Revenue field to the Values area to add the field to column B of the PivotTable.

- Drag the 2017 Revenue field to the Values area to add the field to column C of the PivotTable (Figure 8–19).

Q&A What is shown in the PivotTable?
Excel displays the Service Type and Region fields as rows in the PivotTable. The 2016 Sales and 2017 Sales display as columns.

Other Ways

1. Click check box for each field name (PivotTable Fields task pane)

To Change the Layout of a PivotTable

1 CREATE LINE CHART & TRENDLINE | 2 CREATE PIVOTTABLE | 3 CHANGE LAYOUT & VIEW | 4 FILTER PIVOTTABLE
5 FORMAT PIVOTTABLE | 6 CREATE PIVOTCHART | 7 CHANGE PIVOTCHART VIEW & CONTENTS | 8 ADD SLICERS

You can display a PivotTable in one of three layouts. By default, PivotTable reports are presented in a compact layout. **_Why change the layout?_** _When using multiple row labels, a different layout can make identifying the groups and subgroups easier for the reader._ The following steps change the layout of the PivotTable report to the tabular layout and then add item labels to all rows.

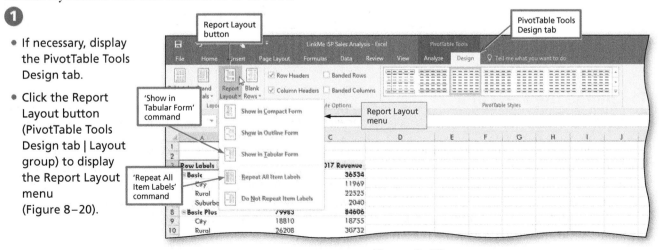

- If necessary, display the PivotTable Tools Design tab.

- Click the Report Layout button (PivotTable Tools Design tab | Layout group) to display the Report Layout menu (Figure 8–20).

Figure 8–20

2

• Click 'Show in Tabular Form' to display the PivotTable report in a tabular format (Figure 8–21).

🔍 **Experiment**

• Click all the layout options to review the differences in the layout. When done, click 'Show in Tabular Form' once again.

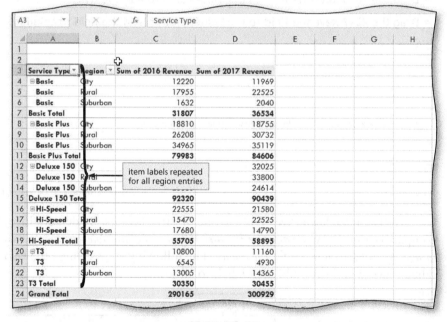

Figure 8–21

3

• Click the Report Layout button (PivotTable Tools Design tab | Layout group) again, and then click 'Repeat All Item Labels' to display Service Type labels for all Region entries (Figure 8–22).

Figure 8–22

To Change the View of a PivotTable Report

1 CREATE LINE CHART & TRENDLINE | 2 CREATE PIVOTTABLE | 3 CHANGE LAYOUT & VIEW | 4 FILTER PIVOTTABLE
5 FORMAT PIVOTTABLE | 6 CREATE PIVOTCHART | 7 CHANGE PIVOTCHART VIEW & CONTENTS | 8 ADD SLICERS

If you use the sort and summary features in Excel, comparing the revenue for each service type and region would require many steps. With PivotTable reports, this comparison is accomplished quickly. The PivotTable report in the LinkMe ISP Sales Analysis workbook currently shows the sum of the sales revenue for each year by service type and then region (Figure 8–22). ***Why change the view of a PivotTable report?*** *You can change the view of this data depending on what you want to analyze.* The following step changes the view of the PivotTable to show the total revenue by region for each service type.

1

- In the Rows area (PivotTable task pane), drag the Service Type button below the Region button to group total sales by Region (rather than by Service Type) (Figure 8–23).

🔍 **Experiment**

- Drag other fields to the Rows area and rearrange it to see how the data in the PivotTable changes. When you are finished, remove all fields in the Rows area but Region and Service Type as shown in Figure 8–23.

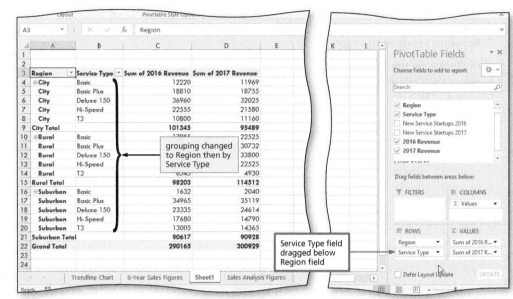

Figure 8–23

Other Ways
1. Click Service Type arrow, click Move Down on menu

To Filter a PivotTable Report Using a Report Filter

1 CREATE LINE CHART & TRENDLINE | 2 CREATE PIVOTTABLE | 3 CHANGE LAYOUT & VIEW | **4 FILTER PIVOTTABLE**
5 FORMAT PIVOTTABLE | 6 CREATE PIVOTCHART | 7 CHANGE PIVOTCHART VIEW & CONTENTS | 8 ADD SLICERS

Why? *In a PivotTable report, you can add detail by further categorizing the data to focus on a particular subgroup or subgroups.* You can use the Revenue Venue field to view sales in a particular venue by service type and region. Viewing a PivotTable report for a subset of data that meets a selection criterion is known as filtering. The following steps add a report filter to change the view of the PivotTable and then filter the PivotTable by Revenue Venue.

- Drag the Revenue Venue field from the 'Choose field to add to report' area (PivotTable Fields task pane) to the Filters area to create a report filter in the PivotTable (Figure 8–24).

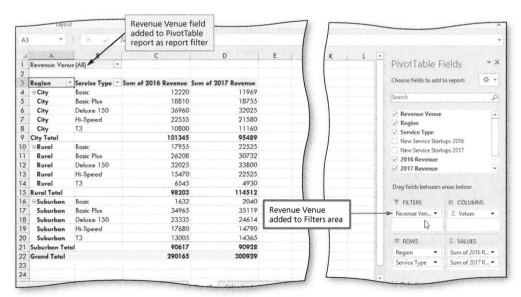

Figure 8–24

• Click the filter button in cell B1 to display the filter menu for column B, Revenue Venue in this case.

• Click Online on the filter menu to select the Online criterion (Figure 8–25).

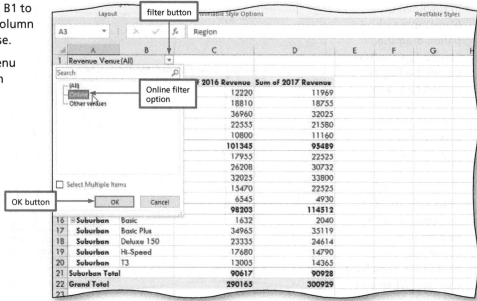

Figure 8–25

• Click the OK button to display totals for online sales only (Figure 8–26).

Q&A What is shown now in the PivotTable report?
Now the PivotTable shows total sales for each region and service type for online sales only.

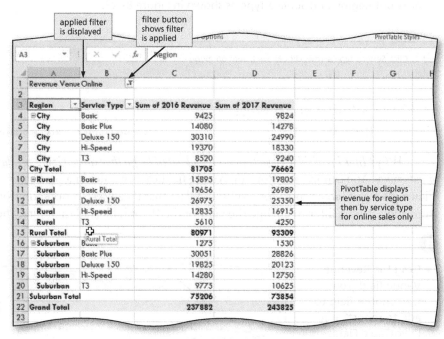

Figure 8–26

To Filter a PivotTable Report Using Multiple Selection Criteria

1 CREATE LINE CHART & TRENDLINE | 2 CREATE PIVOTTABLE | 3 CHANGE LAYOUT & VIEW | **4 FILTER PIVOTTABLE** | **5 FORMAT PIVOTTABLE** | **6 CREATE PIVOTCHART** | **7 CHANGE PIVOTCHART VIEW & CONTENTS** | **8 ADD SLICERS**

Why? *You may need to identify a subset that is defined by more than one filter criterion.* The following steps change the filter field and select multiple criteria on which to filter.

1

- Drag the Service Type button from the Rows area to the Filters area.

- Drag the Revenue Venue button from the Filters area to the Rows area below Region (Figure 8–27).

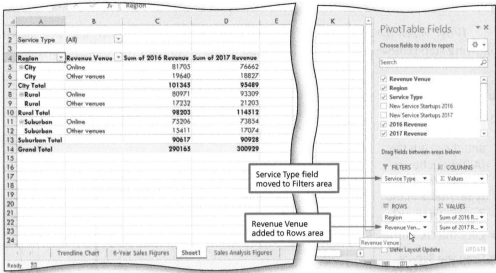

Figure 8–27

2

- Click the filter button in cell B2 to display the filter menu for the Service Type field.

- Click the 'Select Multiple Items' check box to prepare to select multiple criteria.

- Click to remove the check mark in each of the Basic, Hi-Speed, and T3 check boxes to deselect these criteria (Figure 8–28).

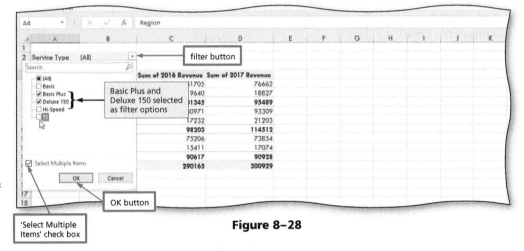

Figure 8–28

3

- Click the OK button to display sales totals for Basic Plus and Deluxe 150 service types (Figure 8–29).

Q&A How do I know which criteria have been selected? With a filter, you need to click the filter button to see which criteria have been selected.

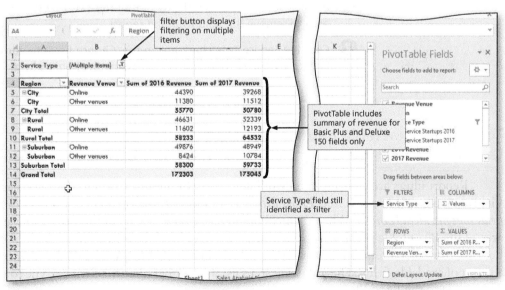

Figure 8–29

To Remove a Report Filter from a PivotTable Report

Why? *When you no longer need to display filtered data in a PivotTable, you can remove the filter easily.* The following step removes the Service Type report filter from the PivotTable report.

- Click the filter button in cell B2 and then click the (All) check box to include all service type criteria in the PivotTable report.
- Click the OK button.
- Drag the Service Type button out of the Filters area (PivotTable Fields task pane) to remove the field from the PivotTable report (Figure 8–30).

Q&A Should I drag it to a specific location?
No. You can drag it out of the box to any blank area on the worksheet.

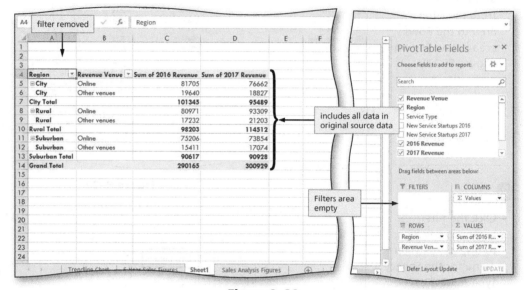

Figure 8–30

To Remove and Add Data to the PivotTable Report

The following steps remove the Revenue Venue field from the Rows area and add the Service Type field.

1 In the PivotTable Fields task pane, drag the Revenue Venue button out of the Rows area to remove the field from the report.

2 Click the Service Type check box in the 'Choose fields to add to report' area to add the Service Type field to the Rows area below the Region field.

To Filter a PivotTable Report Using the Row Label Filter

Report filters are added to the PivotTable report by adding a field to the Filters area of the PivotTable Fields task pane. *Why use a Row Label filter?* *In a PivotTable report, you may want to look at a subset of data based on fields that are already in use.* When the field of interest is already part of the PivotTable and included in the Rows area of the PivotTable Fields task pane, you can use row label filters to view a subset of the data. Like other filter buttons, row label filters display within the column heading. When you click the filter button, Excel displays a menu of available fields. The following steps use a row label filter for Service Type to restrict data in the PivotTable to the Basic Plus and Deluxe 150 service types.

● Click the filter
button in cell B4
to display the filter
menu for the Service
Type field
(Figure 8–31).

Q&A

I do not have a filter
button in cell B4.
How do I access the
filter?
The filter buttons
may be hidden. Click
the Field Headers
button (PivotTable
Tools Analyze tab |
Show group) to turn
on the field headers
and make the filter
buttons visible.

Why does cell B4
not appear selected
when I use the filter button?
Filtering happens independently of cell selection. You do not need to select the cell in which the filter button is
located in order to use the filter. In Figure 8–31, for example, the filter button for Service Type has been clicked
while cell A4 is the active or selected cell.

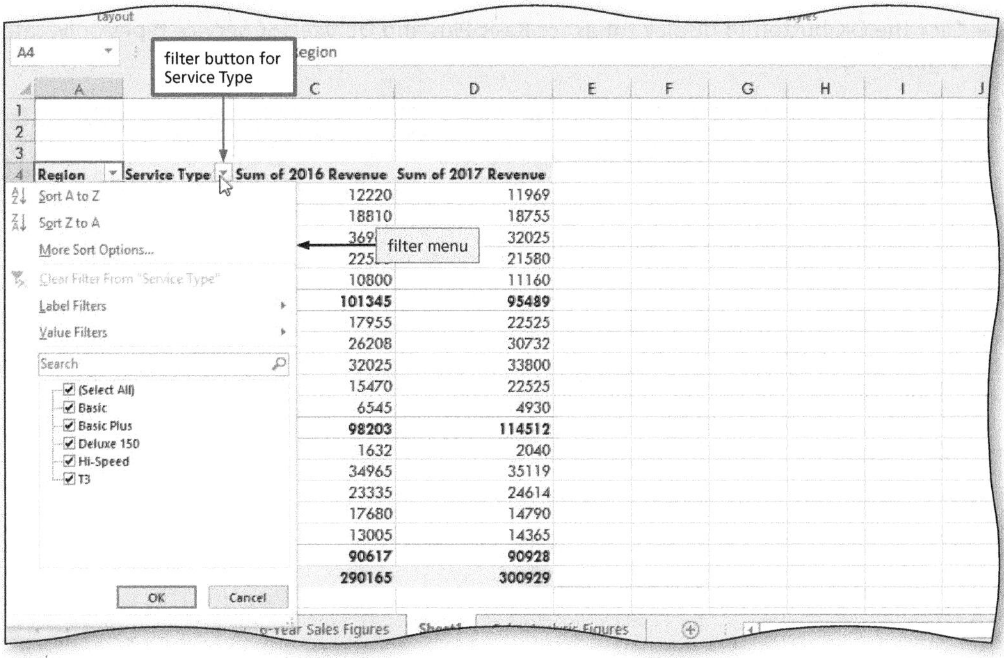

Figure 8–31

●❷

● Click the Basic,
Hi-Speed, and T3
check boxes on the
filter menu to leave
only the Basic Plus
and Deluxe 150
service plans selected
(Figure 8–32).

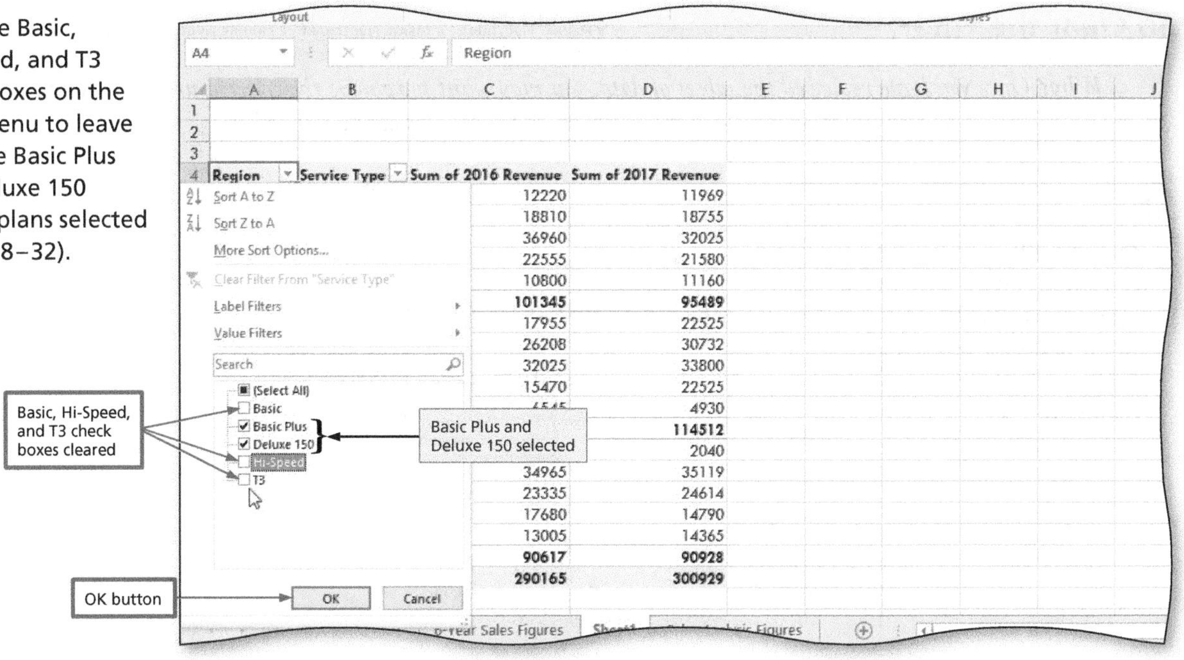

Figure 8–32

- Click the OK button to display totals for Basic Plus and Deluxe 150 service types only, categorized by region (Figure 8–33).

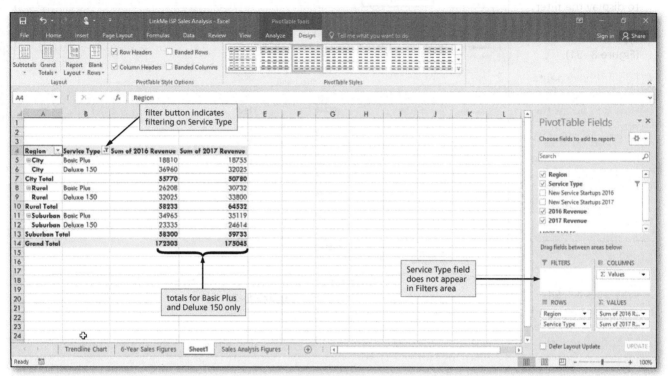

Figure 8–33

To Clear the Filter

1 CREATE LINE CHART & TRENDLINE | 2 CREATE PIVOTTABLE | 3 CHANGE LAYOUT & VIEW | **4 FILTER PIVOTTABLE**
5 FORMAT PIVOTTABLE | 6 CREATE PIVOTCHART | 7 CHANGE PIVOTCHART VIEW & CONTENTS | 8 ADD SLICERS

Why? *Once you have reviewed the subset of data, you may want to remove the criteria using the Row Label filter to display all records.* The following steps clear the filter in order to display all records.

- Click the filter button in cell B4 again to display the filter menu for the Service Type field (Figure 8–34).

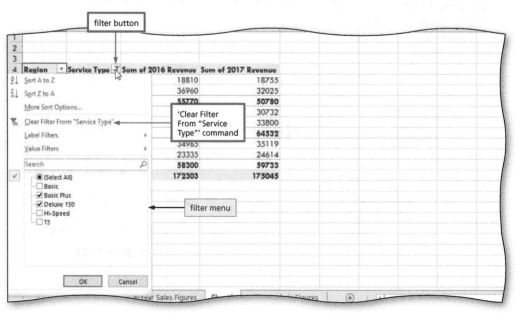

Figure 8–34

②

- Click 'Clear Filter From "Service Type"' on the filter menu to display totals for all service types in all regions (Figure 8–35).

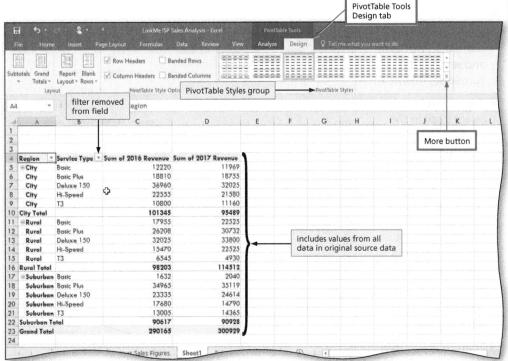

Figure 8–35

Other Ways

1. Click filter button, click (Select All) check box on filter menu, click OK button

---

Formatting PivotTable Reports

You can use several formatting options to enhance the appearance of PivotTable reports and make the content easier to read. Excel includes a number of preset PivotTable report styles to simplify this task. These styles function in a similar fashion to Excel's table styles. Care should be taken when formatting PivotTable reports, however, because formatting techniques that work for regular tables of data do not behave in the same fashion in PivotTable reports. PivotTable report formatting requires the use of PivotTable styles and field settings.

How do you choose a particular PivotTable style?

When you plan PivotTables and PivotCharts, consider what information you want to display in each report. As you are developing a report, review the galleries of PivotTable and PivotChart styles to find the best one to display your data. For example, some PivotTable styles include banded rows and columns, which can make it easier to scan and interpret the report.

CONSIDER THIS

To Format a PivotTable Report

1 CREATE LINE CHART & TRENDLINE | 2 CREATE PIVOTTABLE | 3 CHANGE LAYOUT & VIEW | 4 FILTER PIVOTTABLE
5 FORMAT PIVOTTABLE | 6 CREATE PIVOTCHART | 7 CHANGE PIVOTCHART VIEW & CONTENTS | 8 ADD SLICERS

Why? *PivotTable reports benefit from formatting to enhance their readability.* The following steps format a PivotTable report by applying a PivotTable style and specifying number formats for the fields.

- Name the Sheet1 tab, Sales PivotTable and set the color to Turquoise, Accent 1.

- Click cell A7 to select a cell in the PivotTable.

- Click the More button in the PivotTable Styles gallery (PivotTable Tools Design tab | PivotTable Styles group) to expand the gallery.

- Scroll down until the Dark section of the gallery is visible.

- Point to 'Pivot Style Dark 9' (PivotTable Styles gallery) to display a preview of the style in the PivotTable (Figure 8–36).

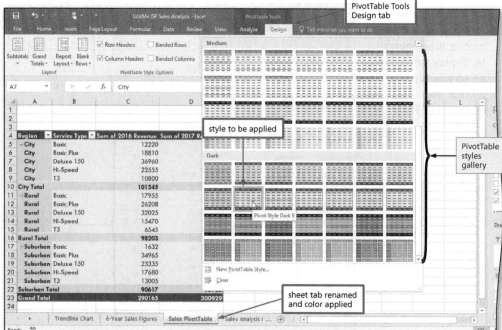

Figure 8–36

- Click 'Pivot Style Dark 9' in the PivotTable Styles gallery to apply the style to the PivotTable report.

- Right-click cell C6 and then click Number Format on the shortcut menu to display the Format Cells dialog box.

- Click Currency in the Category list (Format Cells dialog box) to select the Currency number format.

- Type 0 in the Decimal places box to specify no decimal places (Figure 8–37).

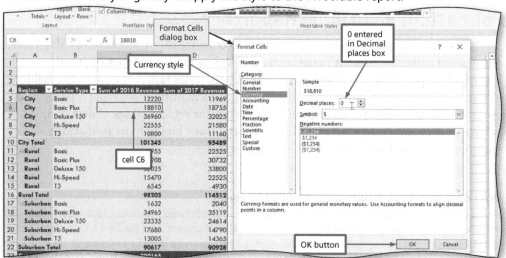

Figure 8–37

- Click the OK button to apply the Currency style to all 2016 revenue values in the PivotTable report.

Q&A

Why does the number format change apply to all Revenue values?
In a PivotTable, when you format a single cell using Number Format, that formatting is applied to the entire set of values to which that single cell belongs.

Can I use the formatting options on the Home tab?
Yes, but you would have to highlight all of the cells first and then apply the formatting. The Number Format command is easier.

- Select cell D6 and then repeat Step 3 to apply the Currency style to all 2017 revenue values.

- Click cell E24 to deselect the PivotTable report.

- Click the Save button on the Quick Access Toolbar to save the workbook (Figure 8–38).

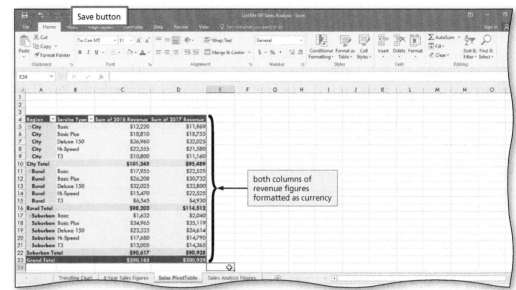

Figure 8–38

Break Point: If you wish to take a break, this is a good place to do so. Exit Excel. To resume at a later time, run Excel and open the file named LinkMe ISP Sales Analysis, and then continue following the steps from this location forward.

Summary Functions

In PivotTable reports, you easily can change the function used to summarize data in the original table. For example, in Figure 8–38, the data is totalled for 2016 and 2017 using a SUM function. You can change that to other summary functions. Summary functions can be inserted in one of three ways: by using the shortcut menu of a cell in the PivotTable, by using the field button menu in the Values area (PivotTable Fields task pane), or by using the Field Settings button (PivotTable Tools Analyze tab | Active Field group).

Table 8–2 lists the summary functions Excel provides for analysis of data in PivotTable reports. These functions also apply to PivotChart Reports.

Table 8–2 Summary Functions for PivotTable Report and PivotChart Report Data Analysis

Summary Function	Description
Sum	Sum of the values (default function for numeric source data)
Count	Number of data values
Average	Average of the values
Max	Largest value
Min	Smallest value
Product	Product of the values
Count Numbers	Number of data values that contain numeric data
StdDev.s	Estimate of the standard deviation of all of the data to be summarized, used when data is a sample of a larger population of interest
StdDev.p	Standard deviation of all of the data to be summarized, used when data is the entire population of interest
Var.s	Estimate of the variance of all of the data to be summarized, used when data is a sample of a larger population of interest
Var.p	Variance of the data to be summarized, used when data is the entire population of interest

To Switch Summary Functions

Why? *The default summary function in a PivotTable is the SUM function.* For some comparisons, using a different summary function will yield more useful measures. In addition to analyzing the total revenue by region and service type, you are interested in looking at average sales. Currently, the PivotTable report for LinkMe ISP displays the total sales for each region by service type. Average sales by service type and by region might be a better measure for comparing the revenue. The following steps switch summary functions in a PivotTable using the shortcut menu.

- Right-click cell C5 to display the shortcut menu and then point to 'Summarize Values By' to display the Summarize Values By submenu (Figure 8–39).

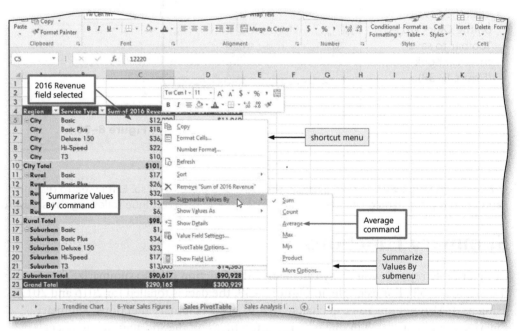

Figure 8–39

2

- Click Average on the Summarize Values By submenu to change the summary function from Sum to Average (Figure 8–40).

Q&A

Why did the column title in cell C4 change?

When you change a summary function, the column heading automatically updates to reflect the new summary function chosen.

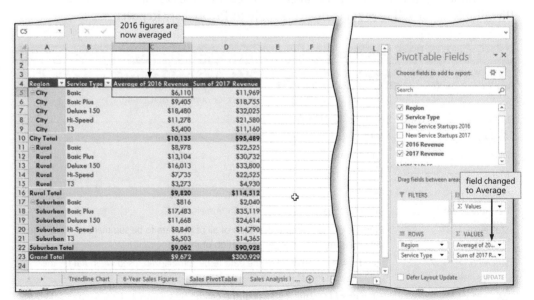

Figure 8–40

- Repeat Steps 1 and 2 to change the summary function used in column D from Sum to Average (Figure 8–41).

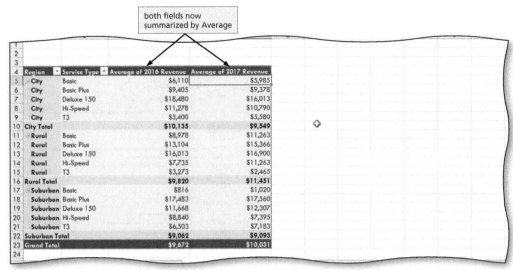

Figure 8–41

To Insert a New Summary Function

1 CREATE LINE CHART & TRENDLINE | 2 CREATE PIVOTTABLE | 3 CHANGE LAYOUT & VIEW | 4 FILTER PIVOTTABLE
5 FORMAT PIVOTTABLE | 6 CREATE PIVOTCHART | 7 CHANGE PIVOTCHART VIEW & CONTENTS | 8 ADD SLICERS

Why? In addition to changing summary functions, you may need to add new fields to analyze additional or more complex questions. You have been asked to review and compare both total and average sales for 2016 and 2017. You will need to add value fields and change the summary function to meet this request. The following steps add a second value calculation for each of the two years and use these fields to add a summary function in the PivotTable report. This time, you will use the menu displayed when you click the value field button to access the Value Field Settings dialog box.

- In the PivotTable Fields task pane, drag the 2016 Revenue field to the Values area above the 'Average of 2016 Sales' button to add the field to the PivotTable.

- In the Values area, click the 'Sum of 2016 Revenue' button to display the Sum of 2016 Sales menu (Figure 8–42).

Q&A Why did I place the new field above the other items in the Values area?
Dragging the new field to a location above the other fields will place the data in a new column before the others in the PivotTable report, in this case in column C.

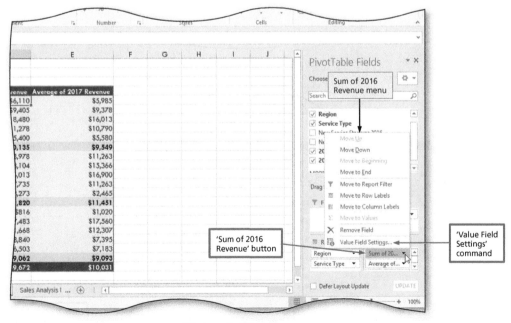

Figure 8–42

- Click 'Value Field Settings' to display the Value Field Settings dialog box.

- In the Custom Name text box (Value Field Settings dialog box), type **2016 Total Revenue** to change the field name (Figure 8–43).

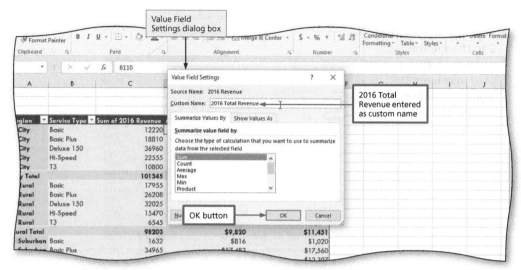

Figure 8–43

- Click the OK button (Value Field Settings dialog box) to apply the custom name.

- In the PivotTable Fields task pane, drag the 2017 Revenue field to the Values area, and place it between the '2016 Total Revenue' button and the 'Average of 2016 Revenue' button.

- In the Values area, click the 'Sum of 2017 Revenue' button to display its menu, and then click 'Value Field Settings' to display the Value Field Settings dialog box.

- In the Custom Name text box, type **2017 Total Revenue** and then click the OK button (Value Field Settings dialog box) to rename the field.

- Using the buttons in the Values area, rename the other two fields to customize the column headings in cells E4 and F4 as shown in Figure 8–44.

- Format the values in columns C and then D to the Currency category, 0 decimal places, and the $ symbol (Figure 8–44).

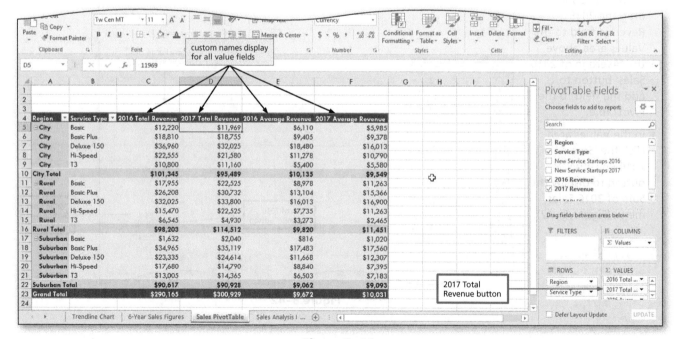

Figure 8–44

To Customize the Field Headers and Field List

The following steps hide the PivotTable Fields task pane, hide the field headers, and then turn off column autofitting. *Why? Customizing the display of the field headers and field list can provide a less-cluttered worksheet.*

- Display the PivotTable Tools Analyze tab.
- Click the Field List button (PivotTable Tools Analyze tab | Show group) to hide the PivotTable Fields task pane.
- Click the Field Headers button (PivotTable Tools Analyze tab | Show group) to hide the field headers (Figure 8–45).

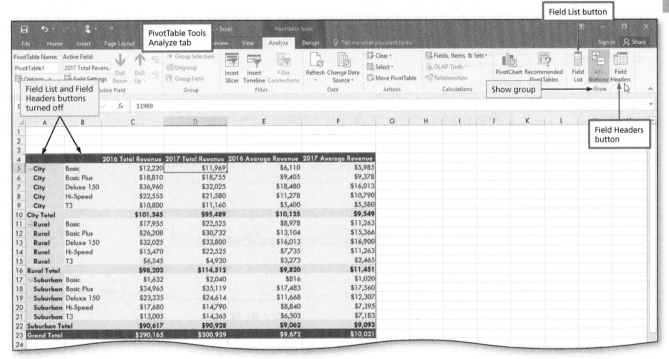

Figure 8–45

Q&A How can I display the PivotTable Fields task pane and field headers after hiding them?

The Field List and Field Headers buttons (PivotTable Tools Analyze tab | Show group) are toggle buttons—clicking them again turns the display back on.

- Click the PivotTable Options button (PivotTable Tools Analyze tab | PivotTable group) to display the PivotTable Options dialog box.
- Click the 'Autofit column widths on update' check box to remove the check mark (Figure 8–46).

- Click the OK button (PivotTable Options dialog box) to turn off the autofitting of column widths.

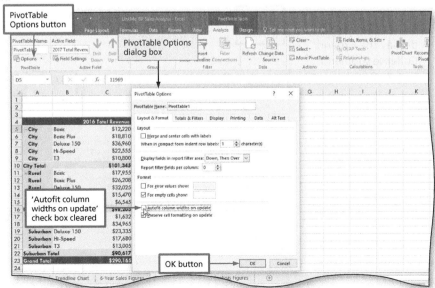

Figure 8–46

To Expand and Collapse Categories

The Expand and Collapse buttons expand and collapse across categories, reducing the amount of detail visible in the report without removing the field from the report. *Why customize the display of these buttons? In some instances, the report may be more visually appealing without the Expand or Collapse buttons in the report.* The following steps expand and collapse categories using the buttons and shortcut menus, and then suppress the display of the Expand and Collapse buttons in the report.

- Click the Collapse button in cell A5 to collapse the City information (Figure 8–47).

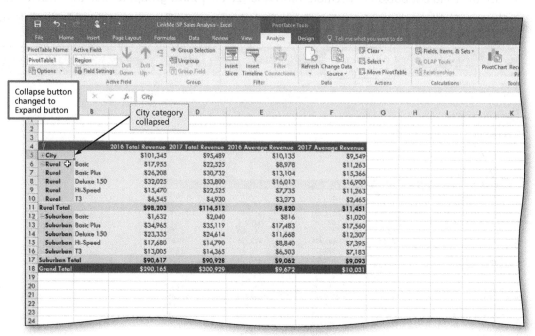

Figure 8–47

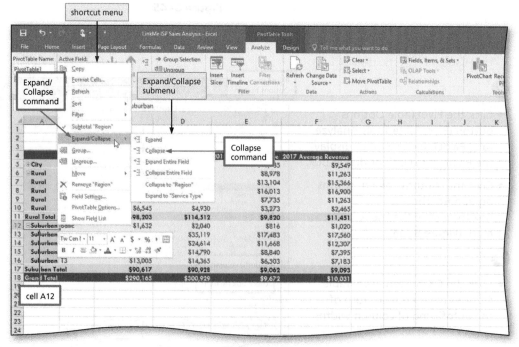

- Right-click cell A12 to display the shortcut menu and then point to Expand/Collapse to display the Expand/Collapse submenu (Figure 8–48).

Q&A

Which method should I use to expand and collapse?
Either way is fine. Sometimes the Collapse button is not visible, in which case you would have to use the shortcut menu.

Figure 8–48

- Click Collapse on the Expand/Collapse submenu to collapse the Suburban data.
- Click the '+/– Buttons' button (PivotTable Tools Analyze tab | Show group) to hide the Expand and Collapse buttons in the PivotTable (Figure 8–49).

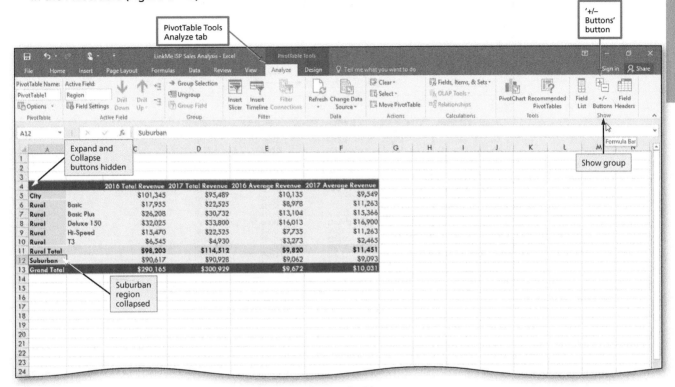

Figure 8–49

- Right-click cell A5 and then point to Expand/Collapse on the shortcut menu to display the Expand/Collapse submenu.
- Click 'Expand Entire Field' on the Expand/Collapse submenu to redisplay all data (shown in Figure 8–50).

To Create a Title

The following steps insert two blank rows and create a title for the PivotTable. You must insert new rows because Excel requires the two rows above the PivotTable to be reserved for extra filters.

1. Insert two blank rows above row 1 for the title and subtitle.

2. In cell A1, enter the title **LinkMe ISP Sales Report** and then enter the subtitle **2016 and 2017** in cell A2.

3. Merge and center the text in cell A1 across A1:F1.

4. Merge and center the text in cell A2 across A2:F2.

⑤ Apply the Title style to cell A1 and bold the cell.

⑥ Apply the Heading 2 style to cell A2 (Figure 8–50).

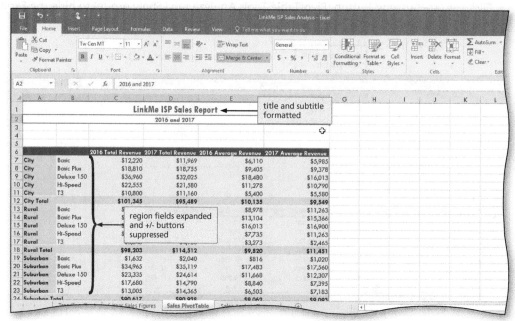

Figure 8–50

To Update a PivotTable

1 CREATE LINE CHART & TRENDLINE | 2 CREATE PIVOTTABLE | 3 CHANGE LAYOUT & VIEW | 4 FILTER PIVOTTABLE
5 FORMAT PIVOTTABLE | 6 CREATE PIVOTCHART | 7 CHANGE PIVOTCHART VIEW & CONTENTS | 8 ADD SLICERS

When you update cell contents in Excel, you also update related tables, formula calculations, and charts. *Why does this not work for PivotTables? PivotTables do not update automatically when you change the underlying data for the PivotTable report. You must update the PivotTable manually to recalculate summary data in the PivotTable report.* Two figures in the original data worksheet are incorrect: the New Service Startups 2017 and the 2017 Revenue for Basic City service sold in Other Venues. The following steps correct the typographical errors in the underlying worksheet, and then update the PivotTable report.

- Click the 'Sales Analysis Figures' sheet tab to make it the active worksheet.

- Click cell E18 and then type   51 as the new value.

- Click cell G18, type   3315,   and then press the ENTER key to change the contents of the cell (Figure 8–51).

Q&A

What data will this change in the PivotTable?

The changed value is for sales of Basic City Service sold in Other Venues. This change will be reflected in cells D7 and F7 in the Sales PivotTable worksheet when the update is performed.

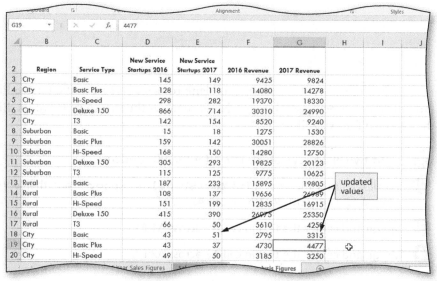

Figure 8–51

2

- Click the Sales PivotTable sheet tab to make it the active worksheet.

- If necessary, click inside the PivotTable report to make it active.

- Display the PivotTable Tools Analyze tab on the ribbon.

- Click the Refresh button (PivotTable Tools Analyze tab | Data group) to update the PivotTable report to reflect the change to the underlying data.

- Click the Save button on the Quick Access Toolbar to save the workbook (Figure 8–52).

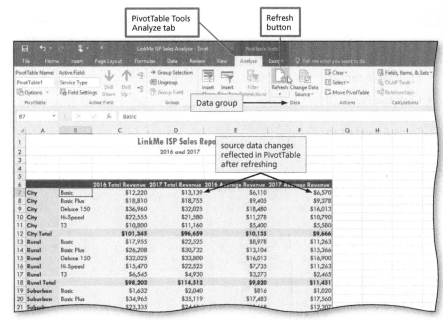

Figure 8–52

Q&A Do I always have to refresh the data?

Yes. The contents of a PivotTable are not refreshed when the data from which they are created changes. This means you must refresh the PivotTable manually when underlying data changes.

If I add rows or columns to the data, will refreshing update the PivotTable?

If your data is in a data table, yes. Otherwise, you will have to create a new PivotTable.

Break Point: If you wish to take a break, this is a good place to do so. Exit Excel. To resume at a later time, run Excel and open the file named LinkMe ISP Sales Analysis, and then continue following the steps from this location forward.

Creating and Formatting PivotChart Reports

A PivotChart report, also called a PivotChart, is an interactive chart that allows users to change, with just a few clicks, the groupings that graphically present the data in chart form. As a visual representations of PivotTables, each PivotChart Report must be associated or connected with a PivotTable report. Most users create a PivotChart from an existing PivotTable; however, you can create a new PivotTable and PivotChart at the same time. If you create the PivotChart first, Excel will create the PivotTable automatically.

To Create a PivotChart Report from an Existing PivotTable Report

1 CREATE LINE CHART & TRENDLINE | 2 CREATE PIVOTTABLE | 3 CHANGE LAYOUT & VIEW | 4 FILTER PIVOTTABLE

5 FORMAT PIVOTTABLE | 6 CREATE PIVOTCHART | **7 CHANGE PIVOTCHART VIEW & CONTENTS** | 8 ADD SLICERS

If you already have created a PivotTable report, you can create a PivotChart report for that PivotTable using the PivotChart button (PivotTable Tools Analyze tab | Tools group). The following steps create a 3-D clustered column PivotChart report from the existing PivotTable report. *Why? The PivotChart will show the two-year data for revenue side by side.*

- If necessary, click cell A7 to select it in the PivotTable report.
- Click the Field List button (PivotTable Tools Analyze tab | Show group) to display the PivotTable Fields task pane.
- Click the PivotChart button (PivotTable Tools Analyze tab | Tools group) to display the Insert Chart dialog box.
- Click '3-D Clustered Column' in the Column Chart gallery to select the chart type (Figure 8–53).

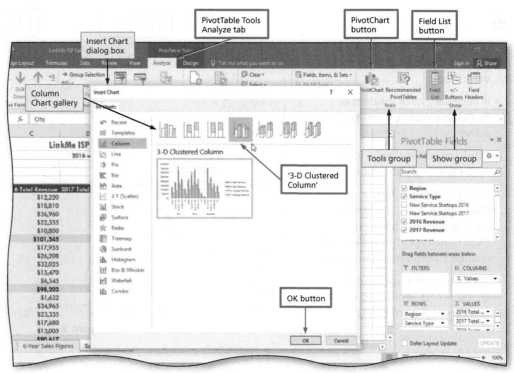

Figure 8–53

- Click the OK button (Insert Chart dialog box) to add the chart to the Sales PivotTable worksheet (Figure 8–54).

Q&A My chart does not display field buttons across the top. Did I do something wrong?
No. It may be that they are just turned off. Click the Field Buttons button (PivotChart Tools Analyze tab | Show/ Hide Group) to turn them on.

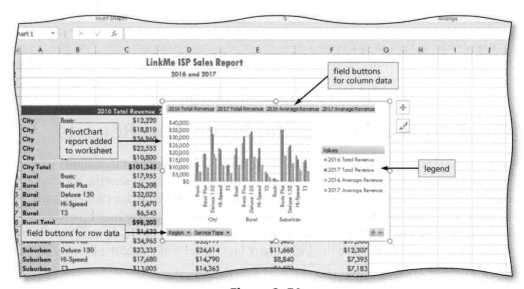

Figure 8–54

Other Ways

1. Click Insert PivotChart button (Insert tab | Charts group), select chart type (Insert Chart dialog box), click OK button

To Move the PivotChart Report

By default, a PivotChart report will be created on the same page as the associated PivotTable report. The following steps move the PivotChart report to a separate worksheet and then change the tab color to match that of the PivotTable report tab.

1 Display the PivotChart Tools Design tab.

2 With the 3-D Clustered Column chart selected, use the Move Chart button (PivotChart Tools Design tab | Location group) to move the chart to a new worksheet named Sales PivotChart.

3 Set the tab color to Turquoise, Accent 1 (shown in Figure 8–55).

To Remove Fields

The following step deletes the average Sales Data from the PivotTable and PivotChart Reports. Because the PivotTable and PivotChart are connected, removing the fields from one worksheet automatically removes the fields from the other.

1 In the PivotChart Fields task pane, drag 2016 Average Revenue and 2017 Average Revenue out of the Values area to remove the average sales data from the PivotChart report and PivotTable report (Figure 8–55).

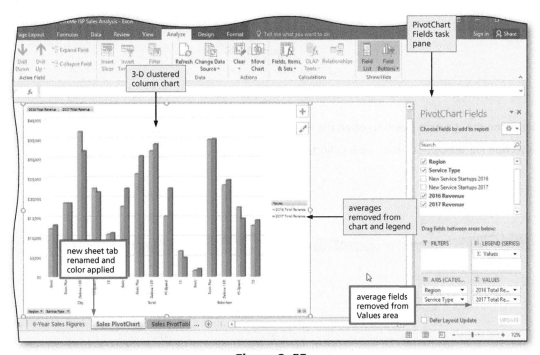

Figure 8–55

To Change the PivotChart Type and Format the Chart

1 CREATE LINE CHART & TRENDLINE | 2 CREATE PIVOTTABLE | 3 CHANGE LAYOUT & VIEW | 4 FILTER PIVOTTABLE
5 FORMAT PIVOTTABLE | 6 CREATE PIVOTCHART | **7 CHANGE PIVOTCHART VIEW & CONTENTS** | 8 ADD SLICERS

Why? *Selecting a chart type instead of using the default type provides variety for the reader.* The default chart type for a PivotChart is a clustered column chart, however PivotCharts can support most chart types, except scatter (X, Y), stock, and bubble. The following steps change the PivotChart type to 3-D cylinder, add a title to the PivotChart report, and apply formatting options to the chart.

1

• Click one of the lighter blue '2016 Total Revenue' columns to select the data series.

• Right-click to display the shortcut menu (Figure 8–56).

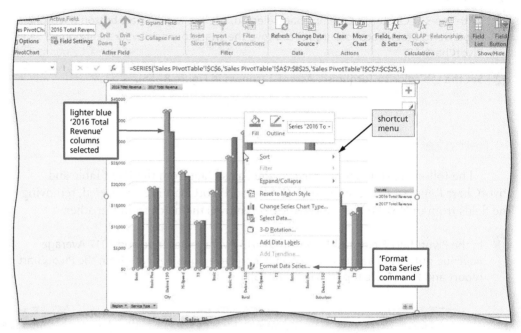

Figure 8–56

2

• Click 'Format Data Series' on the shortcut menu to open the Format Data Series task pane.

• In the Column shape section (Series Options tab), click Cylinder (Figure 8–57).

◁ | I cannot see a difference. What changed?
Q&A | The lighter blue data columns now display a rounded top. It will be more obvious later in the module and when printed.

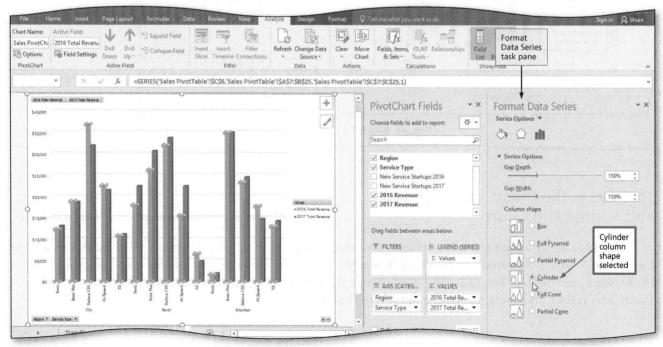

Figure 8–57

3

- Repeat the process to change the 2017 Total Revenue column to a cylinder and then close the Format Data Series task pane.

- Click the Chart Elements button to display the menu and then click to place a check mark in the Chart Title check box.

- Select the chart title and then type **LinkMe ISP** as the first line in the chart title. Press the ENTER key to move to a new line.

- Type **Total Revenue by Region and Service Type** as the second line in the chart title and then press the ENTER key to move to a new line.

- Type **2016 and 2017** as the third line in the chart title.

- Select all of the text in the title and change the font color to black (Figure 8–58).

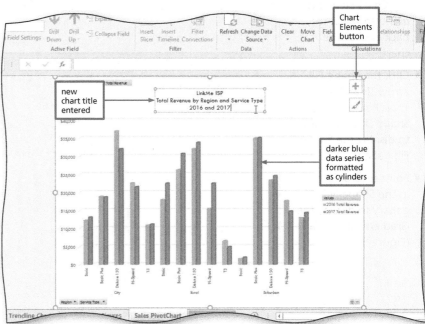

Figure 8–58

4

- Display the PivotChart Tools Format tab.

- Click the Chart Elements arrow (PivotChart Tools Format tab | Current Selection group) to display the Chart Elements menu (Figure 8–59).

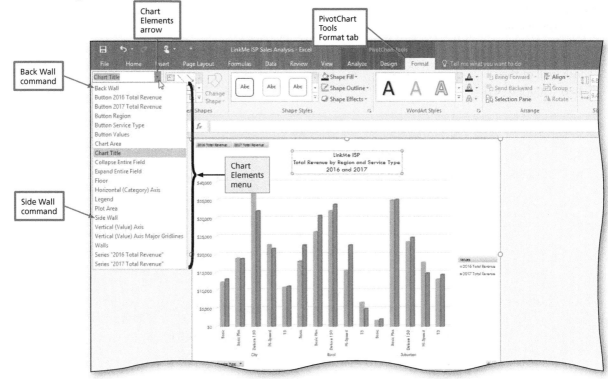

Figure 8–59

- Click Back Wall on the Chart Elements menu to select the back wall of the chart.
- Click the Shape Fill arrow (PivotChart Tools Format tab | Shape Styles group) to display the Shape Fill gallery.
- Point to Gradient in the Shape Fill gallery to display the Gradient submenu (Figure 8–60).

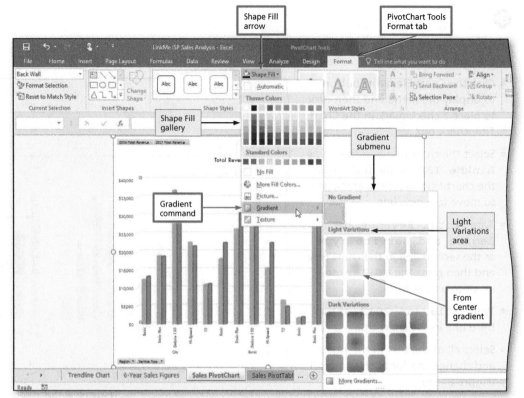

Figure 8–60

- Click From Center in the Light Variations area to apply a gradient fill to the back wall of the chart (Figure 8–61).

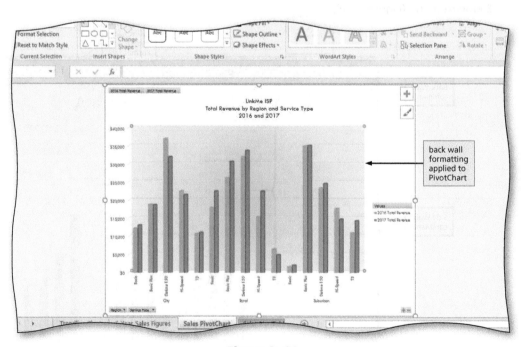

Figure 8–61

- Repeat Steps 5 and 6 after selecting Side Wall on the Chart Elements menu (Figure 8–62).

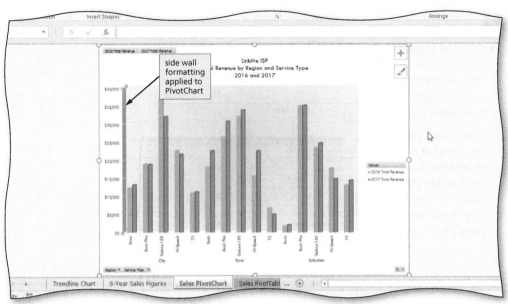

Figure 8–62

To Change the View of a PivotChart Report

1 CREATE LINE CHART & TRENDLINE | 2 CREATE PIVOTTABLE | 3 CHANGE LAYOUT & VIEW | 4 FILTER PIVOTTABLE
5 FORMAT PIVOTTABLE | 6 CREATE PIVOTCHART | **7 CHANGE PIVOTCHART VIEW & CONTENTS** | **8 ADD SLICERS**

Why change the view of a PivotChart? Changing the view of the PivotChart lets you analyze different relationships graphically. As with regular charts, when the source data is changed, any charts built upon that data update to reflect those changes. Unique to PivotCharts, however, is that the reverse is also true. Changes made to the view of the PivotChart are reflected automatically in the view of the PivotTable. The following steps change the view of the PivotChart report that causes a corresponding change in the view of its associated PivotTable report.

- Display the PivotChart Tools Analyze tab.

- If necessary, click the Field List button (PivotChart Tools Analyze tab | Show /Hide group) to display the PivotChart Fields task pane.

- Click the Region check box in the 'Choose fields to add to report' area to deselect the Region field.

- Place a check mark in the Revenue Venue check box to select the field and add it to the Axis area (Figure 8–63).

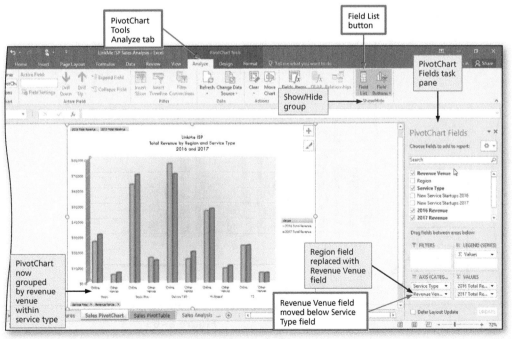

Figure 8–63

2

- Click the Sales PivotTable sheet tab to view the changes in the corresponding PivotTable report.

- If necessary, click the Field List button (PivotTable Tools Analyze tab | Show group) to display the Pivot Table Fields task pane (Figure 8–64).

Q&A
What usually happens when the view of the PivotChart report changes?
Changes to the PivotChart are reflected automatically in the PivotTable. Changes to category (x-axis) fields, such as Revenue Venue, are made to row fields in the PivotTable. Changes to series (y-axis) fields appear as changes to column fields in the PivotTable.

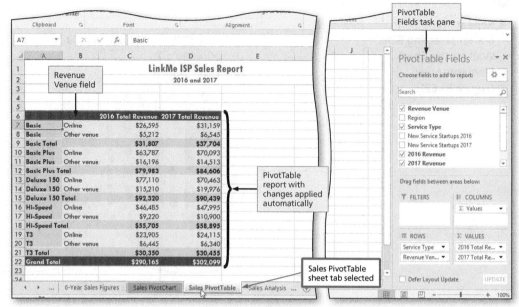

Figure 8–64

3

- In the PivotTable task pane remove the Revenue Venue field from the Rows area and replace it with the Region field.

- If necessary, change the order of the row labels to display the data first by Region and then by Service type.

- Click the Sales PivotChart sheet tab to make it the active tab (Figure 8–65).

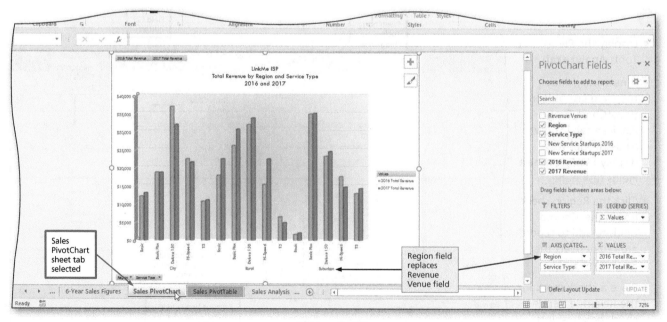

Figure 8–65

4

- Click the Save button on the Quick Access Toolbar to save the workbook.

To Create a PivotChart and PivotTable Directly from Data

The requirements document included a request to create a second PivotChart and PivotTable that examine the average sale amount, controlling for different variables. *Why? Creating a second PivotChart and PivotTable offers a platform for pursuing multiple inquiries of the data simultaneously.* The following steps create a PivotChart report and an associated PivotTable report directly from the available data.

1

- Click the 'Sales Analysis Figures' sheet tab to display the worksheet.

- Click cell A3 to select a cell displaying revenue data and then display the Insert tab.

- Click the PivotChart arrow (Insert tab | Charts group) to display the PivotChart menu (Figure 8–66).

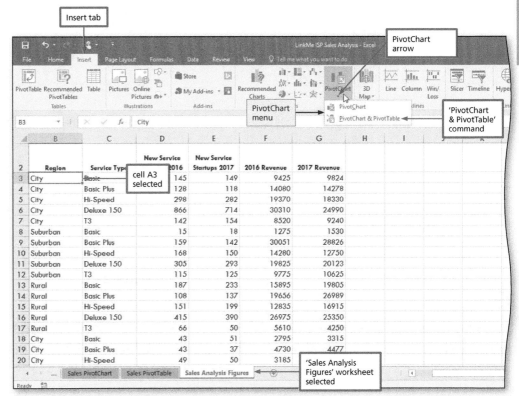

Figure 8–66

2

- Click 'PivotChart & PivotTable' on the PivotChart menu to display the Create PivotTable dialog box.

- If necessary, click New Worksheet (Create PivotTable dialog box) (Figure 8–67).

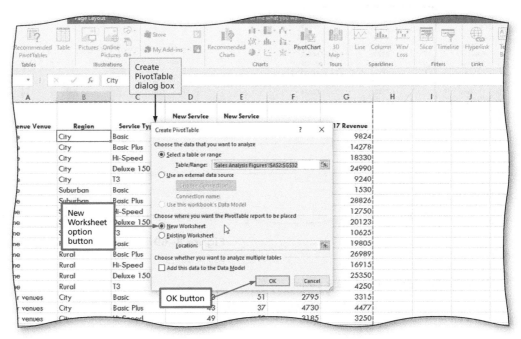

Figure 8–67

3

- Click the OK button to add a new worksheet containing a blank PivotTable and blank PivotChart (Figure 8–68).

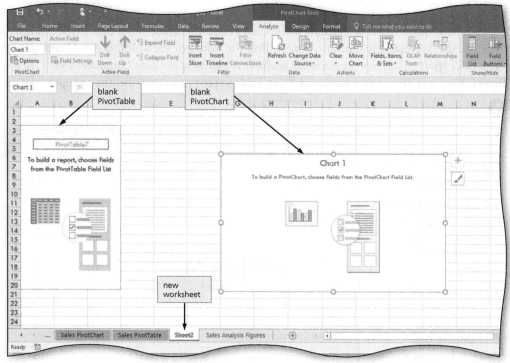

Figure 8–68

4

- Use the PivotChart Fields task pane to add the Region and Revenue Venue fields to the Axis area.

- Add the 2016 Revenue and 2017 Revenue fields to the Values area in the PivotChart Fields task pane (Figure 8–69).

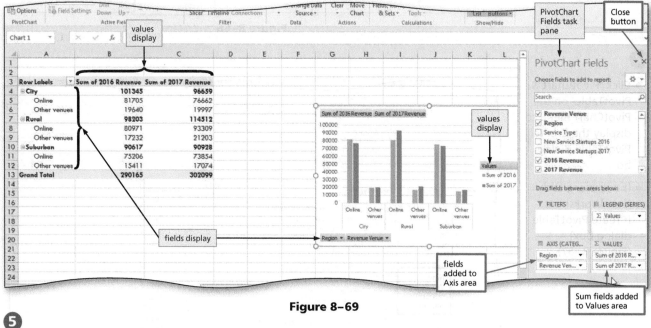

Figure 8–69

5

- Close the PivotChart Fields task pane.

- Rename the new worksheet as Average Startup by Region.

To Create a Calculated Field to a PivotTable Report

The following steps create calculated fields to use in the PivotTable and PivotChart reports. *Why? You would like to review the average start-up sales by region and venue for 2016 and 2017, but this information currently is not part of the data set with which you are working.* You will need to calculate the values you need through the use of a calculated field. A **calculated field** is a field with values not entered as data but determined by computation involving data in other fields. In this case, Average 2016 Startup and Average 2017 Startup will be new calculated fields, based on dividing the existing values of the 2016 Revenue and 2017 Revenue by the New Service Startups 2016 and 2017 respectively.

1

- If necessary, click the PivotTable to make it active and display the PivotTable Tools Analyze tab.

- Click the 'Fields, Items, & Sets' button (PivotTable Tools Analyze tab | Calculations group) to display the Fields, Items, & Sets menu (Figure 8–70).

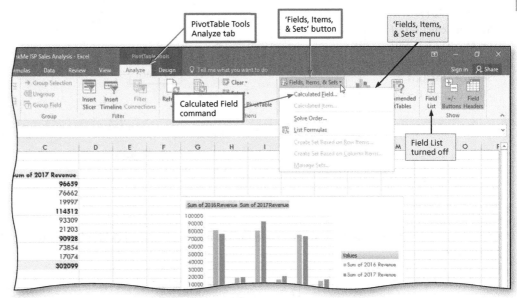

Figure 8–70

2

- Click Calculated Field to display the Insert Calculated Field dialog box.

- In the Name box, type **Average 2016 Startup**.

- In the Formula text box, delete the value to the right of the equal sign, in this case, 0.

- In the Fields list, double-click the 2016 Revenue field to insert it in the Formula text box.

- Type / (slash), and then double-click the 'New Service Startups 2016' field to complete the formula, which should read = '2016 Revenue' / 'New Service Startups 2016' (Figure 8–71).

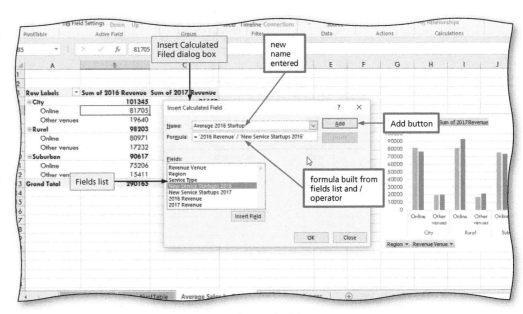

Figure 8–71

- Click the Add button (Insert Calculated Field dialog box) to add the calculated field to the Fields list.

- Repeat Step 2 to create a calculated field named Average 2017 Startup, calculated using 2017 Revenue divided by New Service Startups 2017 (Figure 8–72).

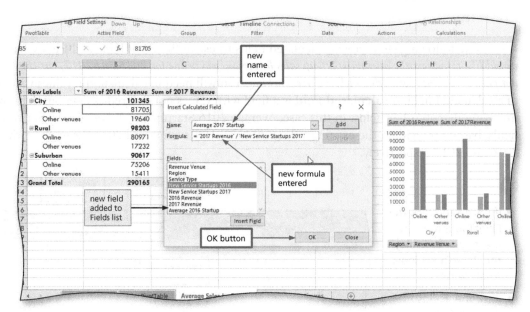

Figure 8–72

- Click the Add button (Insert Calculated Field dialog box) and then click the OK button to close the dialog box (Figure 8–73).

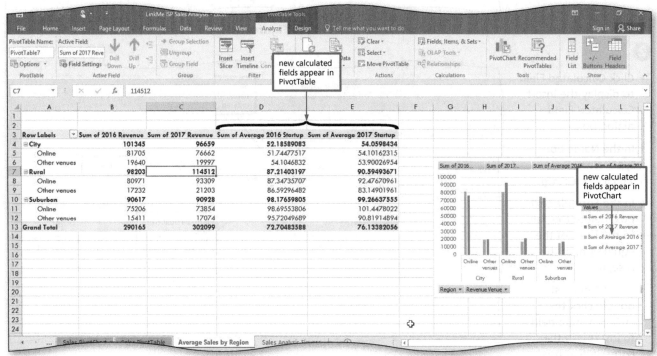

Figure 8–73

To Format the PivotTable

Now that you have added a calculated field, you can format the PivotTable and PivotChart so they look professional and are easy to interpret. The following steps format the PivotTable report.

1 If necessary, click the Field List button (PivotTable Tools Analyze tab | Show group) to display the PivotTable Fields task pane and then click to remove the check mark in the 2016 Revenue check box and the 2017 Revenue check box to remove these fields.

2 If necessary, click cell A3 to select it. Display the PivotTable Tools Design tab and then apply 'Pivot Style Medium 12' to the PivotTable.

3 Insert two blank rows above the PivotTable. In cell A1, enter the title **LinkMe ISP**. In cell A2, enter the subtitle **Average Startup, 2016 and 2017**.

4 Merge and center the text across A1:C1 and A2:C2. Apply the Title style to cell A1 and bold the text. Apply the Heading 2 style to cell A2.

5 Change the field name in cell B5 to Average 2016 Startup. Change the field name in cell C5 to Average 2017 Startup. If Excel displays a message about the field name already existing, place a space in front of the field name.

6 Apply the currency number format with 2 decimal places and the $ symbol to the Average 2016 Startup and Average 2017 Startup fields.

7 Change the column widths for columns B and C to 12.00, and change the width for column D to 50.

8 Wrap and center the field names in cells B5 and C5.

9 Use the Field List button, the '+/– Buttons' button, and the Field Headers button (PivotTable Tools Analyze tab | Show group) to hide the field list, the Expand/Collapse buttons, and the field headers (Figure 8–74).

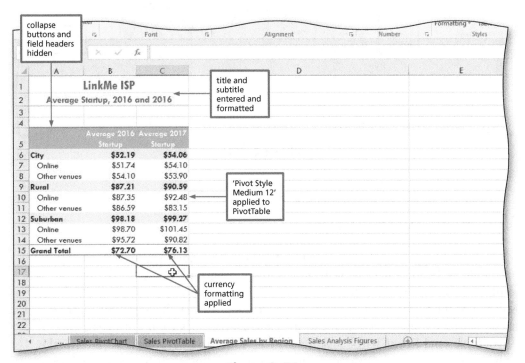

Figure 8–74

To Format the PivotChart

The following steps format the PivotChart report.

1 If necessary, click in the PivotChart report to select it. Move and resize the PivotChart report so that it fills the range D1:D15.

2 Apply Style 12 in the Chart Styles gallery (PivotChart Tools Design tab | Chart Styles group).

3 Use the 'Chart Quick Colors' button (PivotChart Tools Design tab | Chart Styles group) to change the colors to Color 3 in the Colorful area.

4 Use the 'Add Chart Element' button (PivotChart Tools Design tab | Chart Layouts group) to position the legend at the top of the PivotChart report.

5 Click the Field Buttons button (PivotChart Tools Analyze tab | Show/Hide group) to hide the field buttons.

6 Save the workbook (Figure 8–75).

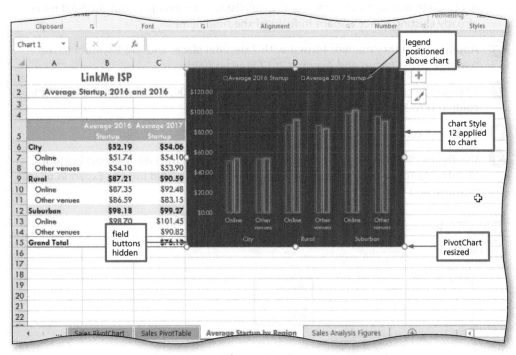

Figure 8–75

Working with Slicers

One of the strengths of PivotTables is that you can ask questions of the data by using filters. Being able to identify and examine subgroups is a useful analytical tool; however, when using filters and autofilters, the user cannot always tell which subgroups the filters and autofilters have selected, without clicking filter buttons to see the subgroups selected. Slicers are buttons you click to filter the data in PivotTables and PivotCharts, making the data easier to interpret. With Slicers, the subgroups are immediately identifiable and can be changed with a click of a button or buttons.

Why would you use slicers rather than row, column, or report filters?

One effective way to analyze PivotTable data is to use slicers to filter the data in more than one field. Slicers let you refine the display of data in a PivotTable. They offer the following advantages over filtering directly in a PivotTable:

• In a PivotTable, you use the filter button to specify how to filter the data, which involves a few steps. After you create a slicer, you can perform this same filtering task in one step.

• You can filter only one PivotTable at a time, whereas you can connect slicers to more than one PivotTable to filter data.

• Excel treats slicers as graphic objects, which means you can move, resize, and format them as you can any other graphic object. As graphic objects, they invite interaction.

The owner of LinkMe ISP has asked you to set up a PivotChart and PivotTable with a user-friendly way for anyone to explore the average start-up sales data. You can use slicers to complete this task efficiently.

To Copy a PivotTable and PivotChart

To create a canvas for exploratory analysis of revenue data, you first need to create a new PivotTable and a PivotChart. The following steps copy an existing PivotTable and PivotChart to a new worksheet, format the PivotTable, and rename the worksheet.

1 Create a copy of the Average Startup by Region worksheet and then move the copy so that it precedes the Sales Analysis Figures worksheet.

2 Rename the new worksheet, Slicers.

3 Apply chart Style 8 to the PivotChart to format the PivotChart.

4 Apply the Pivot Style Medium 20 style to the PivotTable.

5 Set the column widths of columns E to 17.00 and column F to 19.00.

6 If necessary, turn off the display of field headers and +/− buttons (Figure 8–76).

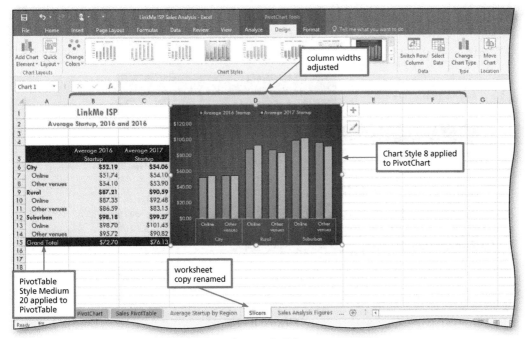

Figure 8–76

To Add Slicers to the Worksheet

The following steps add a slicer that provides an easier way to filter the new PivotTable and PivotChart. *Why? To analyze sales data for specific subgroups, you can use slicers instead of PivotTable filters.*

- If necessary, click to make the PivotChart active and display the PivotChart Tools Analyze tab.

- Click the Insert Slicer button (PivotChart Tools Analyze tab | Filter group) to display the Insert Slicers dialog box.

- Click to place check marks in the Revenue Venue, Region, and Service Type check boxes (Figure 8–77).

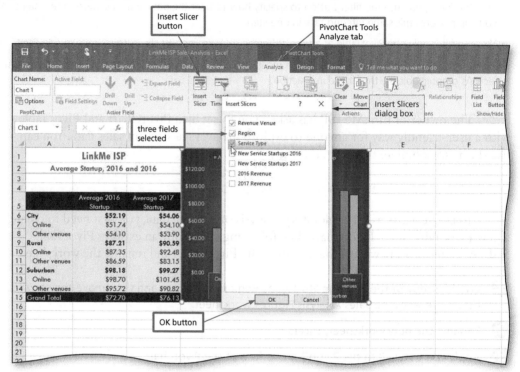

Figure 8–77

- Click the OK button (Insert Slicers dialog box) to display the selected slicers on the worksheet (Figure 8–78).

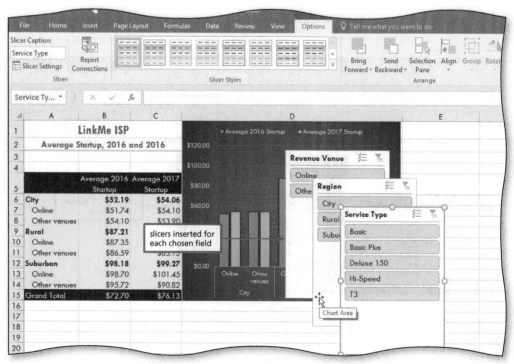

Figure 8–78

To Format Slicers

The following steps move the slicers to the right of the PivotChart and then format them. *Why? The slicers need to be moved and formatted so that they do not obscure the PivotTable or PivotChart and are easy to read and use.*

1

- Click the title bar of the Revenue Venue slicer and then drag the slicer to column E. Use the sizing handles to adjust the length of the slicer so that it ends at the bottom of row 6, and fits the width of the slicer so that it ends at the right edge of column E.

- Click and drag the Service Type slicer to column F. Use the sizing handles to adjust the length of the slicer so that it ends at the bottom of row 15 and the width so that it fits in column F.

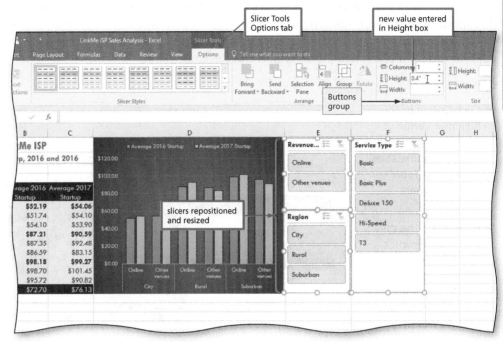

Figure 8–79

- Click and then drag the Region slicer to column E, just below the Revenue Venue slicer. Use the sizing handles to change the length of the slicer so that it ends at the bottom of row 15 and the width so that it fits in column E.

- Hold down the CTRL key and then, one at a time, click each of the slicer title bars to select all three.

- Select the text in the Height box (Slicer Tools Options tab | Buttons group), type **.4**, and then press the ENTER key to set the button height (Figure 8–79).

2

- Click the 'Slicer Style Light 5' Slicer style (Slicer Tools Options tab | Slicer Styles group) to apply it to the slicers (Figure 8–80).

3

- Click any cell to deselect the slicers.

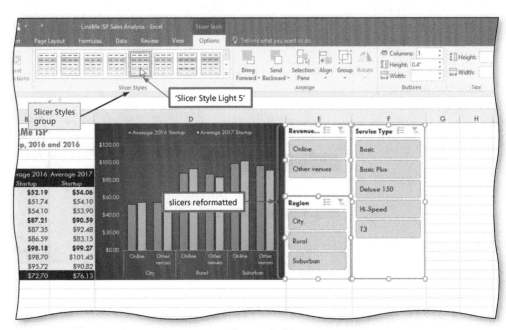

Figure 8–80

To Use the Slicers

Why use slicers? Slicers provide you with a visual means of filtering data. You do not need knowledge of Excel to use slicers. Instead, you click the subgroups of interest. Slicers based on row label fields provide the same results as filters in a PivotTable. They narrow the table down to a visible subgroup or subgroups. Clicking a slicer displays only that slicer's data. You can select multiple fields by using the Multi-Select button in the slicer title bar or by using CTRL+click to add a button (in the same slicer) to the display. The following steps use slicers to review average sales for different combinations of Region and Revenue Venue.

1

- Click Online in the Revenue Venue slicer to display the data for online sales in the PivotTable and PivotChart calculations.

- Hold down the CTRL key and then click City in the Region slicer to remove the City data and show the rural and suburban areas only (Figure 8–81).

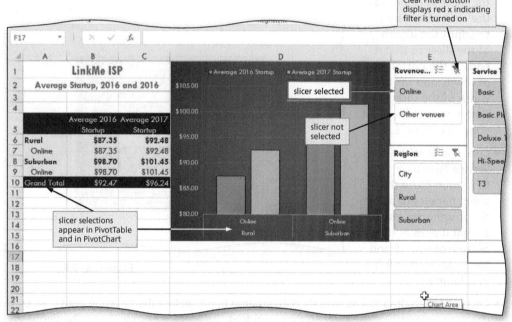

Figure 8–81

2

- Click Other venues in the Revenue Venue slicer to see the data for other venues from the rural and suburban areas only (Figure 8–82).

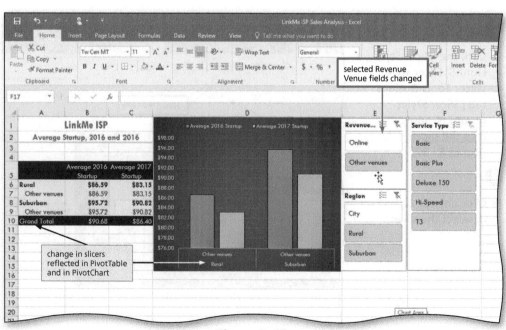

Figure 8–82

To Use the Slicers to Review Data Not in the PivotTable

You can look for possible explanations of patterns by using slicers to analyze data other than that which displays in the PivotTable. *Why? Slicers based on fields not included in the PivotTable provide the same results as report filters.* Slicers regroup and narrow the PivotTable content to groups not visible in the PivotTable. The following steps use slicers to review data not currently visible in the PivotTable.

- Click the Clear Filter button on the Revenue slicer and on the Region slicer to remove the filters and return the PivotTable and PivotChart to their unfiltered states.

- Click the Deluxe 150 button in the Service Type slicer to see the aggregate data for the average start-up prices for customers who chose the Deluxe 150 service, broken down by Revenue Venue and Region (Figure 8–83).

ⓟ Experiment

- Click different service types and combinations of service types to see how the aggregate data changes.

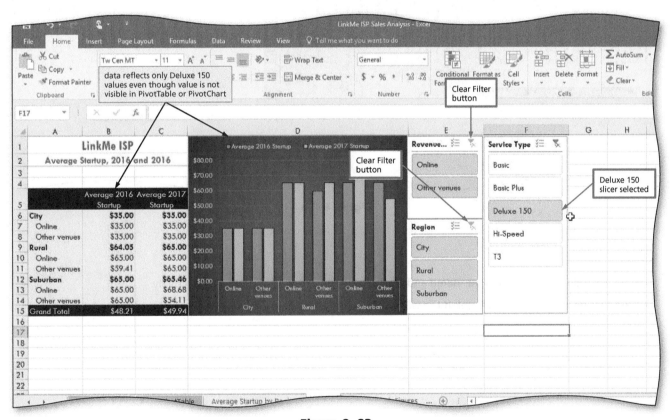

Figure 8–83

- If necessary, click the Deluxe 150 button in the Service Type slicer to select it, click the Multi-Select button in the slicer header, and then click the T3 button in the Service type slicer to view the aggregate data, broken down by Revenue Venue and Region (Figure 8–84).

Q&A

How can I save a particular PivotTable setup?

PivotTables are dynamic by nature. To save a particular configuration, make a copy of the worksheet, and use the Protect Sheet command (Review tab | Changes group) to keep changes from being made to the worksheet copy. You can continue to use the PivotTable on the original worksheet to analyze the data.

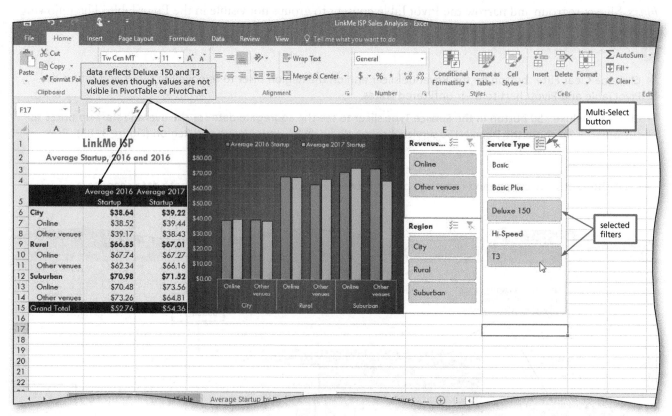

Figure 8–84

3

> If instructed to do so, enter your name and course number in cell F17 and F18 respectively.

- Save the workbook and exit Excel. If the Microsoft Office Excel dialog box is displayed, click the Don't Save button.

Summary

In this module, you learned how to create a 2-D line chart and add a trendline to extend the trend to two more time periods. You added an R-squared (R^2) value to the trendline to measure the strength of the trend and formatted a data point. You created and formatted a PivotTable report based on raw data. Using the PivotTable Fields task pane, you added row fields and columns to the PivotTable. You created calculated fields in the PivotTable using summary functions. To see the power of the PivotTable, you inserted, deleted, and organized fields to view the data in different ways. You created and formatted a PivotChart Report from a PivotTable, filtering and analyzing data. You then created both a PivotTable and PivotChart from scratch and added a calculated field. Finally, you created slicers to make manipulating PivotTables and PivotCharts easier.

What decisions will you need to make when creating your next worksheet to analyze data using trendlines, PivotCharts, and PivotTables?
Use these guidelines as you complete the assignments in this module and create your own worksheets for evaluating and analyzing data outside of this class.

1. Identify trend(s) to analyze with a trendline.

    a) Determine data to use.

    b) Determine time period to use.

    c) Determine type and format of trendline.

2. Identify questions to ask of your data.

    a) Determine which variables to combine in a PivotTable or PivotChart.

3. Create and format PivotTables and PivotCharts.

    a) Add all fields to the field list.

    b) Use formatting features for PivotTables and PivotCharts.

4. Manipulate PivotTables and PivotCharts to analyze data.

    a) Select fields to include in PivotTables and PivotCharts.

    b) Use filters to review subsets of data.

    c) Use calculated fields and summary statistics to look at different measures of data.

    d) Create and use slicers to look at subsets of data.

CONSIDER THIS: PLAN AHEAD

Apply Your Knowledge

Reinforce the skills and apply the concepts you learned in this module.

Creating a PivotTable

Note: To complete these steps, you will be required to use the Data Files. Please contact your instructor for information about accessing the Data Files.

Instructions: Run Excel. Open the document Apply 8-1 Totes & Bags from the Data Files and then save the workbook as Apply 8-1 Totes & Bags Complete. The owner of Totes & Bags wants you to create a PivotTable from the current inventory and then manipulate it to display different totals. Figure 8–85 shows the completed Inventory PivotTable worksheet.

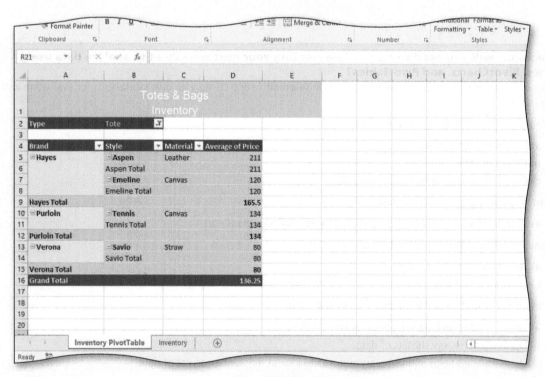

Figure 8–85

Perform the following tasks:
1. Select cell A3 and then click the PivotTable button (Insert tab | Tables group) to display the Create PivotTable dialog box. Make sure New Worksheet is selected and then click the OK button.
2. Drag the Brand field from the 'Choose fields to add to report' area to the Rows area to add the Brand field to the PivotTable. Repeat this step for the Style, Material, and Type fields.
3. Drag the Price field from the 'Choose fields to add to report' area to the Values area to add the sum of the Price field to the PivotTable.
4. Change the summary calculation for Price from Sum to Average by clicking the 'Sum of Price' button in the Values area of the PivotTable Fields task pane, click Value Field Settings, and then choose Average in the Value Field Settings dialog box.

5. Click the Report Layout button (PivotTable Tools Design tab | Layout group) to display the Report Layout menu. Change the PivotTable report layout to tabular. Widen the columns as necessary to read the column headings.

6. If instructed to do so, enter the brand names in column G and the averages in column H, or write them down.

7. Click the filter button in cell A3 to display the filter menu. Select only Kipling Leathers and Donna and then click the OK button. If instructed to do so, enter the averages for those two brands and the overall average in a blank area of the worksheet, or write them down.

8. Remove the Brand filter so that all data is displayed.

9. If necessary, click the Field List button (PivotTable Tools Analyze tab | Show group) to display the PivotTable Fields task pane. Drag the Type button in the Rows area to the Filters area in the PivotTable Fields task pane to create a new filter.

10. In the filter area above the PivotTable, click the filter button for the Type field, click Tote, and then click the OK button. If instructed to do so, enter the averages for the brands and the overall total in a blank area of the worksheet, or write them down.

11. Click cell A4, click the PivotTable Styles More button (PivotTable Tools Design tab | PivotTable Styles group), and then click 'Pivot Style Dark 2' to apply the style to the PivotTable.

12. Add a blank line at the top of the worksheet. Copy the heading from the Inventory worksheet and change the height of the row as necessary.

13. If requested by your instructor, in cell A20, type **List compiled by**, followed by your name.

14. Name the worksheet Inventory PivotTable. Save the workbook with the PivotTable, and then close the workbook.

15. Submit the revised document in the format specified by your instructor.

16. ✳ List two changes you would make to the PivotTable report to make it more easily interpreted by the user, and explain why you would make these changes. These changes could be to formatting, layout, or both.

Extend Your Knowledge

Extend the skills you learned in this module and experiment with new skills. You may need to use Help to complete the assignment.

Grouping Content in PivotTables

Note: To complete these steps, you will be required to use the Data Files. Please contact your instructor for information about accessing the Data Files.

Instructions: Run Excel. Open the workbook Extend 8-1 Mervin's Barbecue from the Data Files and then save the workbook using the file name, Extend 8-1 Mervin's Barbecue Complete. Create a PivotTable and PivotChart for Mervin's Barbecue that analyzes a year's worth of sales data. Figure 8–86 shows the completed Income Review worksheet.

Extend Your Knowledge *continued*

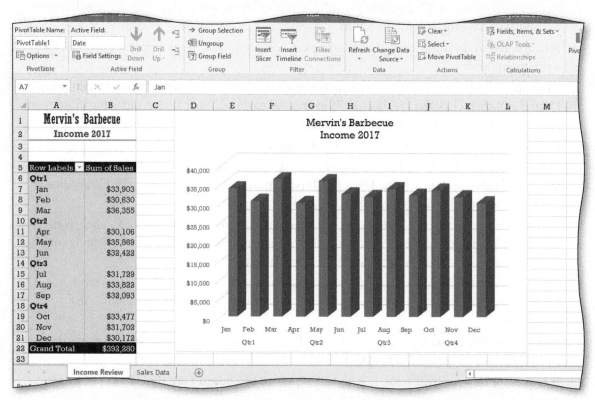

Figure 8–86

Perform the following tasks:

1. Use Help to learn about using dates in a PivotTable and PivotChart and using the Grouping dialog box.

2. Create a PivotTable based on the data in the Sales Data worksheet. Use Date as the Rows field and use Sales as the Values field. Note that Excel breaks the date fields down into months and days. Name the new worksheet containing the PivotTable, Income Review. Change the PivotTable style to 'Pivot Style Medium 17'. Add a title and subtitle to the PivotTable, as shown in Figure 8–86. Merge and center the titles across columns A and B. Format cell A1 using the Title cell style and A2 using the Heading 2 cell style. Change the font color in both cells to black, if necessary. Insert two blank rows for future filters.

3. Format the Sales data using the Number Format command to format the values to be currency with no decimal places.

4. Use the Group Field command (PivotTable Tools Analyze tab | Group group) to group the daily sales figures by months and quarters. Display the Expand and Collapse buttons.

5. Create a PivotChart, and locate it on the same worksheet as the PivotTable. Use the 3-D Clustered Column chart type, and set up the chart to have no legend. Hide the Expand and Collapse buttons in the PivotChart. Right-click in the chart area, choose '3-D Rotation' on the shortcut menu, and set X rotation to 100° and Y rotation to 50°. Change chart colors to Color 17. Edit the chart title to match the PivotTable title and resize the PivotChart as shown in Figure 8–86.

6. If requested by your instructor, add a worksheet header with your name and course number.

7. Preview and then print the PivotTable worksheet in landscape orientation.

8. Save the workbook with the new page setup characteristics.

9. Submit the revised document in the format specified by your instructor.

10. ✺ What other chart type would you use to present this data for the user? Why would you choose that particular chart type?

Expand Your World

Create a solution that uses cloud and web technologies by learning and investigating on your own from general guidance.

Creating Charts for a School District

Note: To complete these steps, you will be required to use the Data Files. Please contact your instructor for information about accessing the Data Files.

Problem: You volunteer with the Northville school district. The district would like to make available for parents some summary results from the latest round of statewide testing of the students in 4th, 7th, 10th, and 12th grade. Data has been compiled for the three testing areas, Math, Science, and English, for each of the eight schools in the district. The data includes both the average score for each grade and school combination and the test goal the various grades were charged with meeting. Assume for computation purposes that the class sizes for the schools across grades are within one or two students of each other, allowing calculation of goal averages without weighting. You have been tasked with creating a PivotTable for the school district for use on the publicly available portion of their OneDrive. The school district would like a PivotTable that would allow parents to visit OneDrive and, using slicers, examine the data for any school/grade combinations that are of interest to them. In addition to the PivotTable, you need to create brief instructions for visitors on how to use slicers to view combinations of grade and school.

Instructions:
1. Open the workbook Expand 8-1 Northville School District from the Data Files and then save the workbook using the file name, Expand 8-1 Northville School District Complete.

2. Create a PivotTable for the data provided. Set up the PivotTable to allow users to compare average scores and goals by school and/or grade.

3. Format the PivotTable and slicers to provide the user with a visually pleasing, easy-to-use product. You will need to decide which PivotTable elements to display, and how to display them. You also will need to make decisions about how to format various elements, taking into account color, size, default text, etc. (*Hint:* If the filter button menu does not produce the desired results, you may need to use the shortcut menu to move the grades up or down.) As you create the slicers, select multiple fields by using the Multi-Select button in the slicer title bar.

4. Write a brief instruction guide for users. You can place this guide in a group of merged cells, or you can insert a text box on the worksheet (visit Help to learn about text boxes and how to use them). You will need to make formatting decisions to ensure that the instructions are

Expand Your World *continued*

readable and fit on the worksheet with the PivotTable and slicers. Remember when setting up this worksheet that if you have content on your worksheet that you need available to set up the table, but the user does not need to see to use the PivotTable, you can hide specific rows/columns/worksheets without affecting the performance of the workbook contents. This can free up space on the worksheet for the content that needs to be visible.

5. If requested by your instructor, add a line at the bottom of your guide identifying you as the author of the guide.

6. Save the workbook on OneDrive, and test its performance. Make any changes necessary. Submit the revised document in the format specified by your instructor.

7. ✸ Evaluate the strengths and weaknesses of this method of making information available to parents. List three concerns, and suggest how you might begin to address them.

In the Labs

Design, create, modify, and/or use a workbook following the guidelines, concepts, and skills presented in this module. Labs 1 and 2, which increase in difficulty, require you to create solutions based on what you learned in the module; Lab 3 requires you to apply your creative thinking and problem-solving skills to design and implement a solution.

Lab 1: Creating a PivotTable, PivotChart, and Trendline

Note: To complete these steps, you will be required to use the Data Files. Please contact your instructor for information about accessing the Data Files.

Problem: You work for Altar Holdings and help the financial director prepare and analyze revenue and expense reports. He has asked you to create two PivotTables and corresponding PivotCharts based on sales data. One PivotTable and PivotChart summarize the sales by Supplier (Figure 8–87a). The other PivotTable and PivotChart summarize the Digital Products sales by month for the top supplier (Figure 8–87b).

Perform the following tasks:
1. Open the workbook Lab 8-1 Altar Holdings from the Data Files and then save the workbook using the file name, Lab 8-1 Altar Holdings Complete.

2. Using the data in the Sales Results worksheet, create the PivotTable and associated PivotChart shown in Figure 8–87a in a separate worksheet in the workbook. Name the worksheet Sales by Supplier.

3. Change the contents of cell A4 to Supplier and cell B3 to Store. Apply the 'Pivot Style Dark 21' style to the PivotTable. Format the values as currency values with a dollar sign and no decimal places. Apply the chart Style 14 to the PivotChart. Resize the PivotChart to cover the range A18:G35 and then hide the field buttons.

4. Create a second PivotTable and associated PivotChart, as shown in Figure 8–87b, in a separate worksheet in the workbook. Name the worksheet Digital Product Sales by Month.

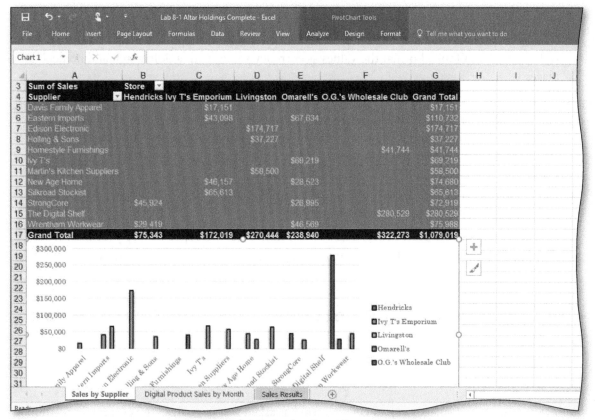

(a) Sales by Supplier

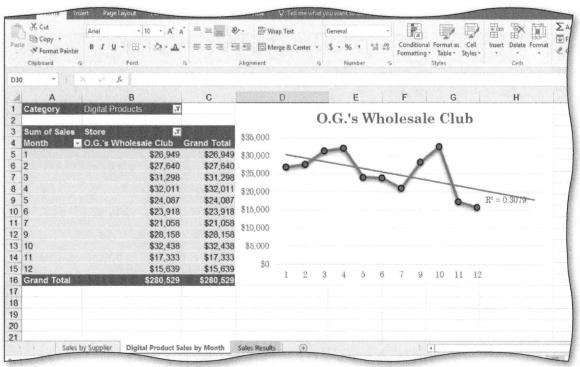

(b) Digital Products Sales by Month

Figure 8–87

In the Labs *continued*

5. Change the contents of cell A4 to Month and cell B3 to Store. Apply the 'Pivot Style Dark 4' style to the PivotTable. Format the values as currency values with a dollar sign and no decimal places.

6. Filter the category by Digital Products. Filter the store to O.G.'s Wholesale Club.

7. Change the chart type to Line and then add a linear trendline that forecasts the trend for three more months. Add the R-squared value to the trendline. Apply the chart Style 15 to the PivotChart and then hide the field buttons. Delete the legend. Resize the chart to the range D1:H16.

8. If requested by your instructor, add the text, Contact number, followed by your phone number to cell B66 of the Sales Results worksheet.

9. Save the workbook. Submit the revised document in the format specified by your instructor.

10. ✸ How helpful is the monthly breakdown when analyzing sales of various products?

Lab 2: **Manipulating PivotTables and PivotCharts with Slicers**

Note: To complete these steps, you will be required to use the Data Files. Please contact your instructor for information about accessing the Data Files.

Problem: The office manager at Evans Law Firm has asked you to analyze the current week's billing worksheet using PivotTables and PivotCharts. She wants you to create them for three scenarios: (a) the payment amount totals for hours billed, (b) the averages of the hours per region, and (c) the cost of the miscellaneous hours if they had been billable. The PivotTables and PivotCharts should appear as shown in Figure 8–88.

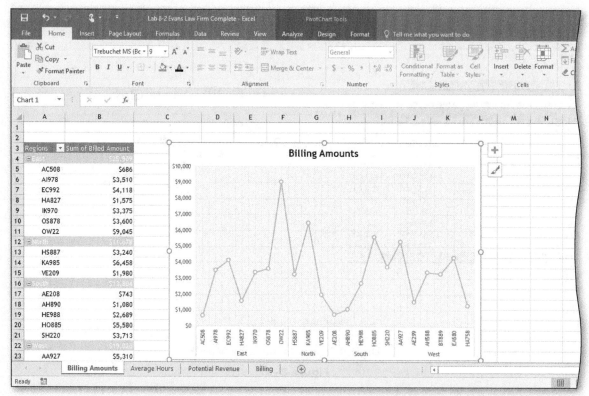

(a) Total Billed Amounts and Hours by Region

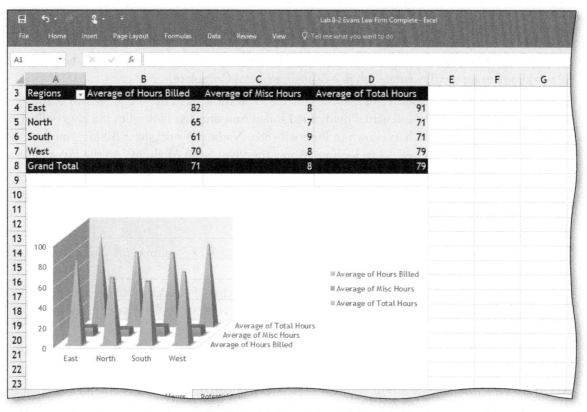

(b) **Average Hours by Region**

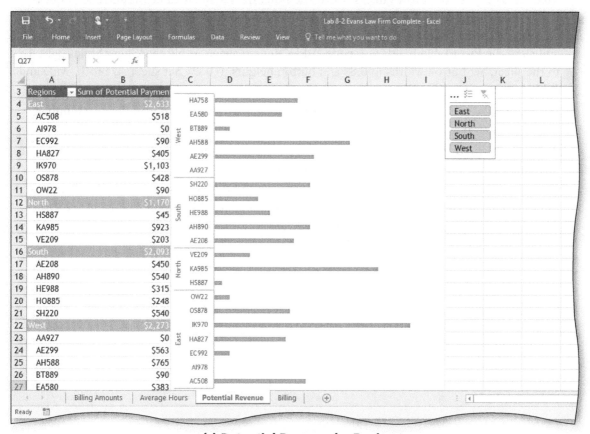

(c) **Potential Revenue by Region**

Figure 8–88

In the Labs *continued*

Perform the following tasks:

1. Run Excel. Open the workbook Lab 8-2 Evans Law Firm from the Data Files and then save the workbook using the file name, Lab 8-2 Evans Law Firm Complete.

2. Create the PivotTable shown in Figure 8–88a based on the data in the range A4:F26 in the Billing worksheet. Add a calculated field called Billed Amount that multiplies the hours billed by 45. Create the PivotChart shown in Figure 8–88a. Name the worksheet Billing Amounts. Change the contents of cell A3 to Regions. Apply the Pivot Style Medium 2 to the PivotTable. Format the Billed Amount values as currency values with a dollar sign and no decimal places. Apply the chart Style 6 to the PivotChart.

3. On a new worksheet create the PivotTable and Partial Pyramids PivotChart shown on the Average Hours worksheet in Figure 8–88b.

   a. To create the Partial Pyramids PivotChart, begin with a 3-D column chart. Format each data series with the Partial Pyramid option.

   b. Change the calculations to averages. Change the contents of cell A3 to Regions. Apply the 'Pivot Style Medium 17' style to the PivotTable. Format all value fields as number with no decimal places.

   c. Apply the chart Style 11 to the PivotChart. Change the fill of the back wall and wide wall to the Gradient style, 'Linear Diagonal – Top Left to Bottom Right'.

4. Create the PivotTable shown in Figure 8–88c. Add a calculated field called Potential Payment that multiplies the miscellaneous hours by 45. Create the PivotChart shown in Figure 8–88c. Name the worksheet Potential Revenue. Change cell A3 to Regions. Apply the 'Pivot Style Medium 5' style to the PivotTable. Format the Potential Payment values as currency values with a dollar sign and no decimal places. Apply the chart Style 2 to the PivotChart and change colors to Monochromatic Color 8. Remove the legend and chart title. Hide all field buttons, and close the PivotTable Fields task pane. Add a Region slicer. Apply the 'Slicer Style Light 4' to the slicer. Set button widths to 0.8" and button heights to 0.2". Set slicer size to 1" wide and 1.37" high. Position the slicer as shown in Figure 8–88c.

5. If requested by your instructor, add a worksheet header with your name and course number.

6. Select all three PivotTable sheets. With the three sheets selected, preview and then print the sheets. Save the workbook with the new page setup characteristics. Submit the revised document in the format specified by your instructor.

7. ✳ In this exercise, you have to scroll to see all parts of the PivotTable. Did you find this a hindrance when working on the PivotTables and PivotCharts? How could you address this when setting up your PivotTables and PivotCharts?

Lab 3: **Consider This: Your Turn**

Apply your creative thinking and problem-solving skills to design and implement a solution.

Budget Analysis

Note: To complete these steps, you will be required to use the Data Files. Please contact your instructor for information about accessing the Data Files.

Part 1:   You have created a table that shows your household income and expenses. You would now like to create charts to help you analyze your budget. Part of this includes identifying a trend in your spending habits. Open the workbook Lab 8-3 Budget Analysis from the Data Files and then save the workbook using the file name, Lab 8-3 Household Budget Analysis Complete.

Create a chart using the expenses from the budget. Create a second chart using the cash flow data from the budget. Add a trendline to the chart that shows trends for the next four months. Submit your assignment in the format specified by your instructor.

Part 2:   In Part 1, you made choices about which type(s) of chart(s) to use to present budget data. What was the rationale behind those selections? How did the data in the Household Expenses pose a special challenge? How might you address that challenge?

9 Formula Auditing, Data Validation, and Complex Problem Solving

Objectives

You will have mastered the material in this module when you can:

- Use formula auditing techniques to analyze a worksheet
- Trace precedents and dependents
- Use error checking to identify and correct errors
- Add data validation rules to cells
- Enable the Solver add-in
- Use trial and error to solve a problem on a worksheet

- Use goal seeking to solve a problem
- Circle invalid data on a worksheet
- Use Solver to solve a complex problem
- Use the Scenario Manager to record and save sets of what-if assumptions
- Create a Scenario Summary report
- Create a Scenario PivotTable report

Introduction

Excel offers many tools that can be used to solve complex problems. In previous modules, simple what-if analyses have shown the effect of changing one value on another value of interest. This module introduces you to auditing the formulas in a worksheet, validating data, and solving complex problems. **Formula auditing** allows you to examine formulas to determine which cells are referenced by those formulas and examine cells to determine which formulas are built upon those cells. Auditing the formulas in a worksheet can give insight into how a worksheet is structured and how cells are related to each other. Formula auditing is especially helpful when presented with a workbook created by someone else.

    Data validation allows you to set cells so that the values they accept are restricted in terms of type and range of data. This feature can be set up to display prompts and error messages when users select a cell or enter invalid data. You also can use data validation to circle cells containing data that does not meet the criteria you specified.

When trying to solve some problems, you can make an educated guess if you are familiar with the data and the structure of the workbook. This process is called **trial and error**. For simpler problems, you may find a solution using this process. For more complex problems, you might need to use software, such as Excel, to find a satisfactory solution.

One of the tools that Excel provides to solve complex problems is Solver, which allows you to specify up to 200 cells that can be adjusted to find a solution to a problem. Solver also lets you place limits or constraints on allowable values for some or all of those cells. A **constraint** is a limitation on the possible values that a cell can contain. Solver will try many possible solutions to find one that solves the problem subject to the constraints placed on the data.

Project — Life Coach Services Scheduling Analysis

In this module, you will learn how to use the Life Coach Services Analysis workbook shown in Figure 9–1. Life Coach Services provides three types of coaching services to their clients: business coaching, individual coaching, and mentoring. The company employs three coaches who can provide all or some of the specific coaching services offered. The three coaches have different schedule capacities for a 40-hour work week. Paula schedules in 30-minute intervals and is able to see two clients per hour. Frank and Kristen schedule in 60-minute intervals and are able to see one client per hour. Additionally, Paula cannot take on mentoring clients and Frank cannot serve business clients. Service types that cannot be scheduled for a specific coach are shaded in gray.

The Scheduling Plan worksheet, shown in Figure 9–1a, was created to determine the most cost-effective way of scheduling coaching time to meet the needs of existing clients. The worksheet includes the details of the scheduling requirements for the three coaches, taking into account their schedule capacities as well as labor and material costs per client. A second worksheet, on the Costs tab, details the material costs and prices for the three different types of service.

The details of the first solution determined by Solver are shown in Figure 9–1b. Solver was given the goal of minimizing the total costs (cell E14) while also accommodating the following constraints: the number of clients assigned to each coach (range B7:D9) cannot be negative or fractional, the total number of clients of each type (range E7:E9) must equal the totals shown in the scheduling constraints area, and the total hours for any individual coach (range B11:D11) must not exceed the value shown in cell B18. Applying these constraints, Solver calculated the optimal distribution of coaching services among the coaches, shown in the range B7:D9, necessary to achieve the goal of minimizing the total costs (and maximizing total profit). Solver modified the values for each service type (rows 7 through 9) that resulted in changes in the total hours and costs per coach (rows 11 through 14) and minimized the total cost to Life Coach Services. However, if you applied a different set of scheduling constraints, Solver would determine a new solution. When Solver finishes solving a problem, you can create an Answer Report. An Answer Report (Figure 9–1c) summarizes the answer found by Solver, by identifying which constraints were in place and which values in the worksheet were manipulated in order to solve the problem within the constraints.

Excel's Scenario Manager is a what-if analysis tool that allows you to record and save different sets, or scenarios, of what-if assumptions for the same worksheet. In this case, you will use Scenario Manager to manage the two sets of Solver data for the Scheduling Plan worksheet. The Scenario Manager also allows you to create reports that summarize the scenarios on your worksheet. Both the Scenario Summary report (Figure 9–1d) and the Scenario PivotTable (Figure 9–1e) concisely present the differences among different scheduling scenarios. Like any PivotTable, the Scenario PivotTable allows you to interact with the data easily.

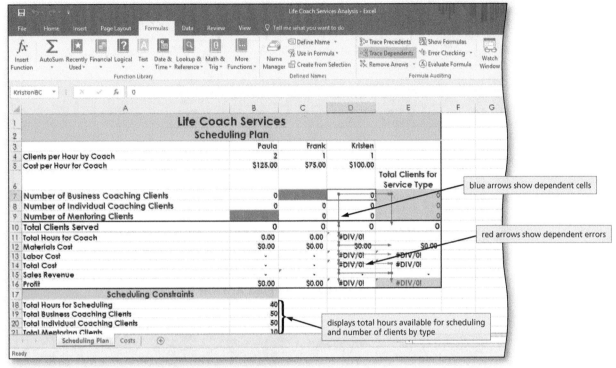

(a) Scheduling Plan Worksheet

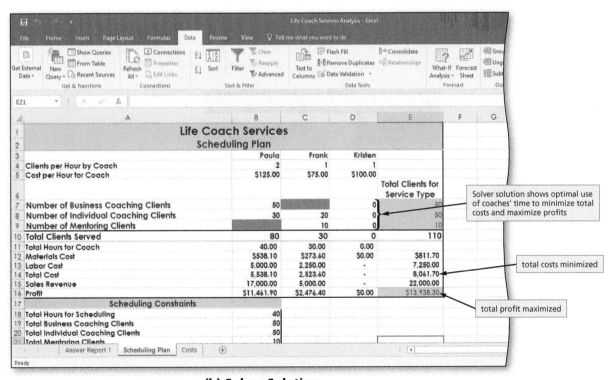

(b) Solver Solution

Figure 9–1 (Continued)

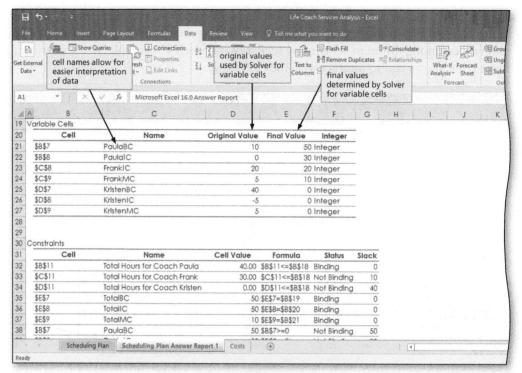

(c) Scheduling Plan Answer Report

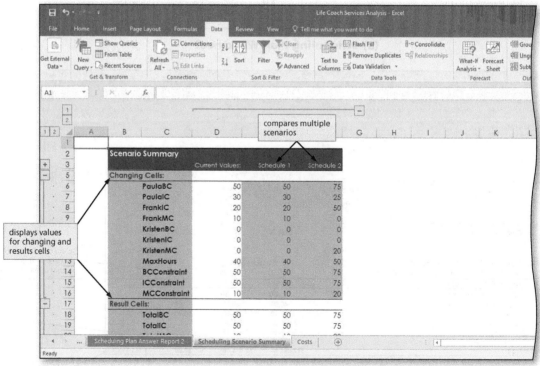

(d) Scheduling Scenario Summary Table

Figure 9–1 (Continued)

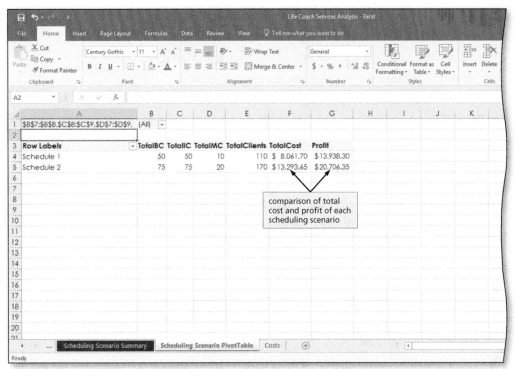

(e) Scheduling Scenario PivotTable

Figure 9–1

Figure 9–2 illustrates the requirements document for the Life Coach Services Analysis workbook. It includes the needs, source of data, and other facts about its development.

Worksheet Title	Life Coach Services Analysis
Needs	Evaluate two different sets of scheduling data to determine the optimal scheduling distribution to minimize total cost. Data include: • Three coaches, two of whom can coach only two types of clients • Three types of clients: business, individual, and mentoring • Labor and materials costs per coach Constraints include: • The numbers of coaching clients must be nonnegative integer values • The total number of clients for each type of service must equal the totals shown within the scheduling constraints area • Do not exceed the total hours for any individual coach
Source of Data	Cost and price information is available in the Life Coach Services workbook on the Costs worksheet.
Calculations	All formulas are set up in the workbook. The worksheets in the workbook should be reviewed to familiarize yourself with the calculations.
Other Requirements	None

Figure 9–2

With a good understanding of the requirements document and an understanding of the necessary decisions, the next step is to use Excel to create the workbook. In this module, you will learn how to create the Life Coach Services Analysis workbook shown in Figure 9–1.

The following roadmap identifies general activities you will perform as you progress through this module:

1. ANALYZE the WORKBOOK FORMULAS in the existing workbook.

2. SET DATA VALIDATION RULES to restrict cell contents.

3. CUSTOMIZE Excel ADD-INS to enable the Solver tool.

4. SOLVE COMPLEX PROBLEMS using what-if analysis tools.

5. CREATE AND EVALUATE SCENARIOS using Scenario Manager.

6. PRODUCE summary REPORTS from Scenario Manager.

To Run Excel and Open a Workbook

The following steps run Excel and open a workbook named Life Coach Services. The workbook currently contains two worksheets. The Scheduling Plan tab shows the overall scheduling plan and scheduling constraints for the coaches and services, while the Costs tab summarizes the related costs for each of the coaching services. To complete these steps, you will be required to use the Data Files. Please contact your instructor for information about accessing the Data Files.

1 Run Excel.

2 Open the file named Life Coach Services from the Data Files.

3 If the Excel window is not maximized, click the Maximize button on its title bar to maximize the window.

4 Save the workbook on your hard drive, OneDrive, or other storage location using Life Coach Services Analysis as the file name (Figure 9–3).

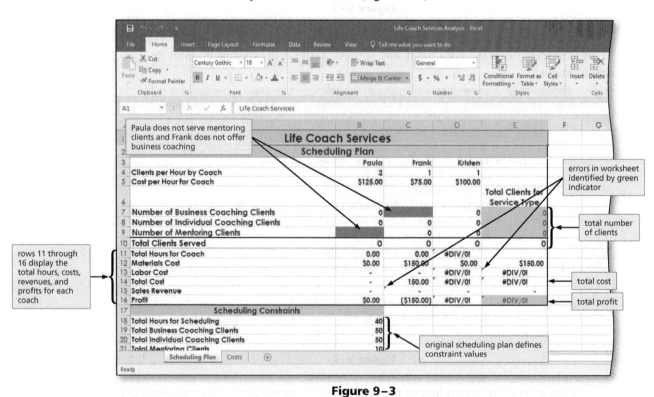

Figure 9–3

About the Scheduling Plan Worksheet

The Scheduling Plan worksheet shown in Figure 9–3 provides information about three coaches and three types of services. Rows 4 and 5 contain the hourly capacity and cost for each of the three coaches. The range B7:D9 will show the optimal combination of clients served by each coach that minimizes the total cost to Life Coach Services, which is the problem that needs to be solved in this module.

The gray cells indicate that a particular coach cannot provide a certain type of service. The total hours, costs, revenues, and profits for each coach (rows 11 to 16) are based on the numbers of clients shown in the range B7:D9. As the numbers of clients change, the values in the range B10:D16 are updated. Your goal is to determine the best distribution of clients, without exceeding the maximum number of hours per coach (cell B18), while minimizing total cost to the company (cell E14).

The current worksheet displays the scheduling constraints for the first scenario in the range B18:B21. As outlined in the requirements document in Figure 9–2, a second set of constraints also must be analyzed. Thus the information in the range B18:B21 will be modified to reflect the constraints associated with the different scenario.

Formula Auditing

Errors can be introduced into a worksheet when using formulas. Formula auditing is the process of reviewing formulas for errors. Errors may be obvious, with results that indicate that a formula is incorrect. For example, in Figure 9–3, cells D11, D13, E13, D14, E14, D16, and E16 display error codes. These errors are flagged by both the error code #DIV/0! and the error indicator, a green triangle, in the upper-left corner of those cells. Errors also may be less obvious, introduced through formulas that, while technically correct, result in unintended results in the worksheet. Error indicators with no accompanying error code, such as that found in cell C15, should be examined for these less-obvious errors. A complex worksheet should be reviewed to correct obvious errors *and* to correct formulas that do not produce error indicators but still do not produce the intended results.

Excel provides formula auditing tools, found in the Formula Auditing group on the Formulas tab, that can be used to review the formulas in a worksheet. Some tools, such as the Error Checking command, deal with identified errors. Other auditing tools provide visual cues to identify how cells in a worksheet are related to each other. Tracer arrows are drawn from one cell to another, identifying cells that are related to other cells through their use in a formula. A tracer arrow can be drawn from a cell that appears in a formula in another cell or from a cell that contains a formula with cell references. Red tracer arrows indicate that one of the referenced cells contains an error.

A cell containing a formula that references other cells is said to have precedents. Each cell referenced in the formula is a **precedent** of the cell containing the formula. For example, in the formula C24 = C23/$B$1, cells C23 and B1 are precedents of cell C24. Cells C23 and B1 also can have precedents, and these cells also would be precedents of cell C24. Tracing precedents can highlight where a formula may be incorrect.

BTW
Tracing Precedents and Dependents
When all levels of precedents or dependents have been identified, Excel will sound a beep if you try to trace another level.

To Trace Precedents

1 ANALYZE WORKBOOK FORMULAS | 2 SET DATA VALIDATION RULES | 3 CUSTOMIZE ADD-INS
4 SOLVE COMPLEX PROBLEMS | 5 CREATE & EVALUATE SCENARIOS | 6 PRODUCE REPORTS

Why? *Tracing precedents in Excel allows you to identify upon which cells a particular cell is based, not only directly by the formula in the cell but indirectly via precedents for the precedent cells.* The following steps trace the precedent cells for cell E12, which displays the Total Materials Cost for accommodating the scheduling needs.

- If necessary, make Scheduling Plan the active sheet.
- Display the Formulas tab and then select cell E12.
- Click the Trace Precedents button (Formulas tab | Formula Auditing group) to draw a tracer arrow across precedents of the selected cell (Figure 9–4).

Q&A How do I interpret the precedent arrows?

The arrow in Figure 9–4 terminates with an arrowhead on the traced cell, in this case cell E12. The heavy blue line that runs through the range of cells B12:D12 indicates that all cells in the range are precedents of the traced cell, E12.

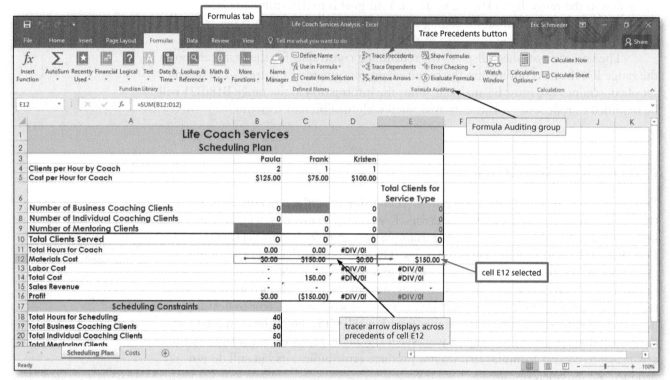

Figure 9–4

2

• Click the Trace Precedents button (Formulas tab | Formula Auditing group) again to draw arrows indicating precedents of cells B12:D12 (Figure 9–5).

Q&A How do I interpret the new precedent arrows?

The new arrows in Figure 9–5 have arrowheads on traced cells and dots on cells that are direct precedents of the cells with arrowheads. For instance, cell B12 has a tracer arrow to it with a blue line

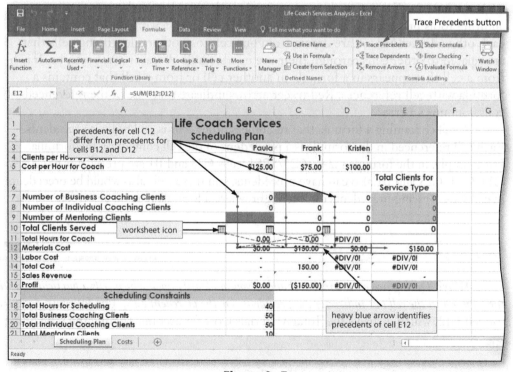

Figure 9–5

appearing in the range B7:B11 and dots in cell B7 and B8. This indicates that the cells containing dots, cells B7 and B8, are precedents of cell B12, while the other cells, without dots, are not. In addition, there is a black dashed line connecting cell B12 to a worksheet icon that indicates that precedent cells exist on another worksheet.

To Review Precedents on a Different Worksheet

Why? *Precedents also can be located on different worksheets in the same workbook or in different workbooks.* In Figure 9–5, the dashed precedent arrows and worksheet icons identify precedents on another worksheet. Cell C12, which has precedents on a different worksheet, displays a value of $150.00 in material costs, although no clients have been assigned to Frank. This is inconsistent with the surrounding cell values that accurately display no initial material costs for Paula and Kristen. The following steps review the precedents for cell C12.

- Click cell C12 to display the formula in the formula bar (Figure 9–6).

Q&A
I am having difficulty selecting cell C12. Is this cell locked?
When precedent or dependent arrows are drawn through a cell, the area that you can click in the cell to select it is reduced. Click near the boundaries of the cell in order to select it.

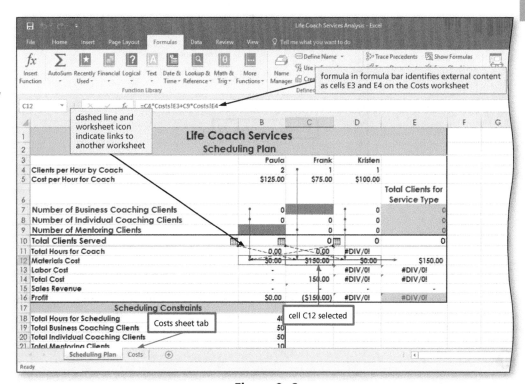

Figure 9–6

- Review the formula in the formula bar to identify the location of the precedent cell or cells, in this case cells E3 and E4 on the Costs worksheet.

- Display the Costs worksheet.

- Review the precedent cells to determine if the reference to them in the formula is correct as written (Figure 9–7).

Q&A
Are the cells referenced in the formula in cell C12 in the Scheduling Plan worksheet correct?
The formula in cell C12 should calculate the material costs for Frank. However, the formula contains multiple errors. In the Costs worksheet, the formula incorrectly references the Price per Session values (cells E3 and E4) instead of the Material Cost per Session values (cells C3 and C4). In the Scheduling Plan worksheet, the formula incorrectly references the Clients per Hour by Coach that Frank can serve (cell C4) instead than the Number of Individual Coaching Clients served by Frank (cell C8).

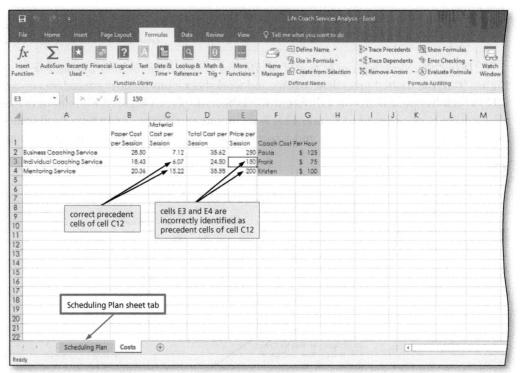

Figure 9–7

To Remove the Precedent Arrows

Why? Reducing visual clutter makes the worksheet easier to edit. After reviewing the precedents of cell E12, you determine that the formula in cell C12 needs to be changed to calculate the total material cost correctly for Frank. The following steps remove the precedent arrows level by level and then correct the formula in cell C12.

- Display the Scheduling Plan worksheet and then select cell E12.

- Click the 'Remove All Arrows' arrow (Formulas tab | Formula Auditing group) to display the 'Remove All Arrows' menu (Figure 9–8).

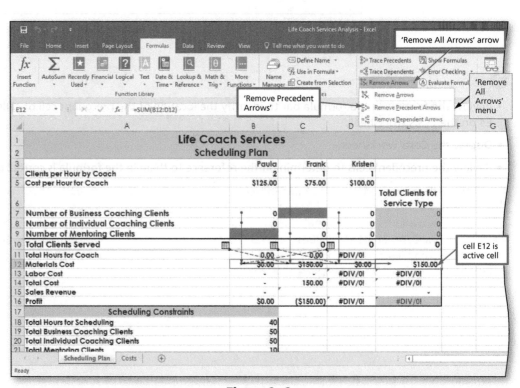

Figure 9–8

- Click 'Remove Precedent Arrows' on the 'Remove All Arrows' menu to remove precedent arrows linking to the Costs sheet.

- Click the 'Remove All Arrows' button (Formulas tab | Formula Auditing group) to remove the remaining tracer arrows.

- Edit the formula in cell C12 to read `=C8*Costs!C3+C9*Costs!C4` to correct the error.

- Click the Enter button to accept the change (Figure 9–9).

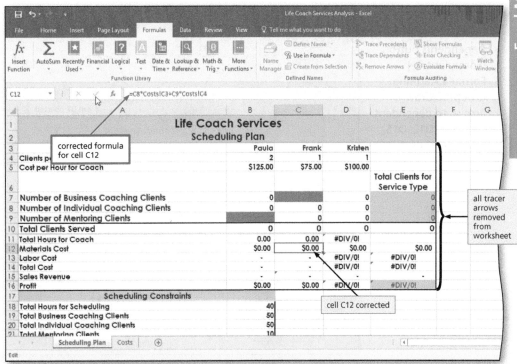

Figure 9–9

TO REVIEW PRECEDENTS ON A DIFFERENT WORKSHEET USING THE GO TO COMMAND

You can use precedent arrows to navigate directly to precedents on a different worksheet or different workbook. If you choose to use this feature, you would use the following steps:

1. Double-click on the dashed precedent arrow to display the Go To dialog box.

2. Select the cell reference to navigate to from the Go to list (Go To dialog box).

3. Click the OK button (Go To dialog box) to navigate to the selected cell reference.

To Trace Dependents

1 ANALYZE WORKBOOK FORMULAS | 2 SET DATA VALIDATION RULES | 3 CUSTOMIZE ADD-INS
4 SOLVE COMPLEX PROBLEMS | 5 CREATE & EVALUATE SCENARIOS | 6 PRODUCE REPORTS

Why? *Identifying dependents highlights where changes will occur in the worksheet as a result of changing the value in the cell you are identifying as a referenced cell.* A cell that references another cell is said to be a **dependent** of that referenced cell. If cell A3 contained the formula =B2/B4, cell A3 would be a dependent of cells B2 and B4. Changing the value in cell B2 or cell B4 also changes the result in the dependent cell A3. The following steps trace the dependents of cell D7, which will display the optimal number of business coaching clients for Kristen.

1

- Select cell D7.

- Click the Trace Dependents button (Formulas tab | Formula Auditing group) to draw arrows to dependent cells D10, D12, D15, and E7 (Figure 9–10).

Q&A What is the meaning of the dependent arrows?

As shown in Figure 9–10, the arrowheads indicate which cells directly depend on the selected cell. In this case, cell D7 is explicitly referenced in formulas in cells D10, D12, D15, and E7.

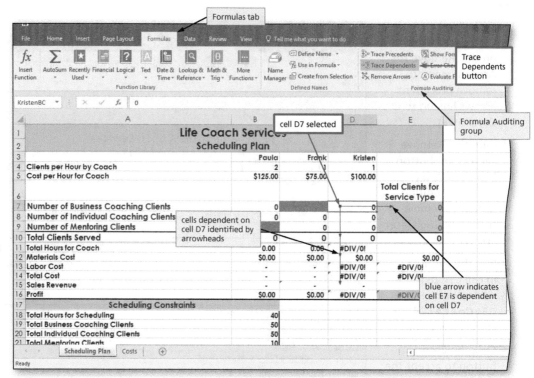

Figure 9–10

2

- Click the Trace Dependents button three more times to draw arrows indicating the indirectly dependent cells — those cells which depend on cells that directly or indirectly depend on the selected cell — of cell D7 (Figure 9–11).

Q&A How do I know when I have identified all remaining dependents?

If no additional dependents are present when you click the Trace Dependents button, Excel does not draw additional arrows but plays an error tone.

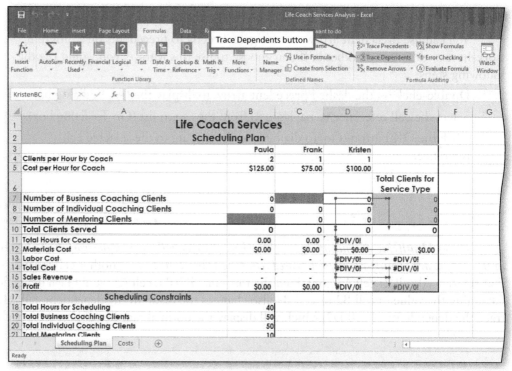

Figure 9–11

To Remove the Dependent Arrows

Why? *Tracing dependents identified the cells that depend on cell D7, which will help to correct the #DIV/0! errors in the worksheet. Once dependent cells are identified, you may want to remove the arrows to clear the worksheet of extraneous content.* The following step clears the dependent arrows from the worksheet.

1

- Click the 'Remove All Arrows' button (Formulas tab | Formula Auditing group) to remove all of the dependent arrows (Figure 9–12).

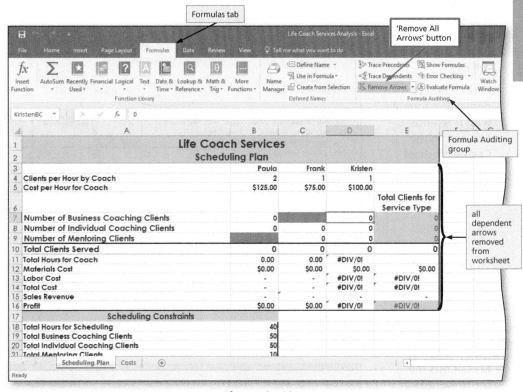

Figure 9–12

To Use Error Checking to Correct Errors

Why use error checking? *Excel can provide assistance in determining the source of errors in the worksheet.* Cells D11, D13:E14, and D16:E16 all contain error codes. Their contents indicate that these cells are in error because the formulas they contain attempt to divide a number by zero. For example, cell E16 contains references to cells E14 and E15. Cell E14 refers to the range B14:D14. The cells in the range B14:D14 also contain references to other cells. The source of the error in cell E16 could be in any of the directly or indirectly referenced cells. To identify the source, it is important to review all precedents to the cell containing the error. The following steps use error checking features to find the source of these errors and correct them.

1

• Select cell E16.

• Click the Trace Precedents button (Formulas tab | Formula Auditing group) six times to identify all precedents of cell E16.

• Click cell D5 to display the formula with reference to a cell on the Costs worksheet (Figure 9–13).

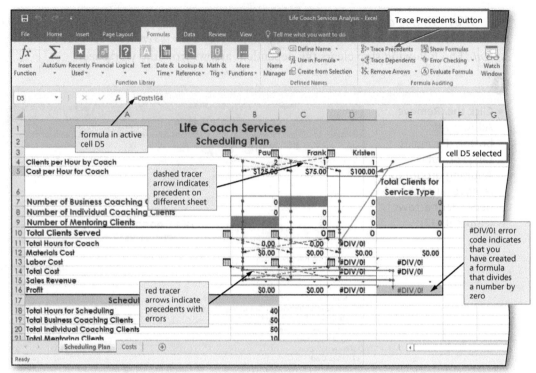

Figure 9–13

2

• Make Costs the active worksheet.

• Review cell G4 (Costs worksheet) to determine if the reference to it in the formula in cell D5 of the Scheduling Plan worksheet is correct (Figure 9–14).

Q&A Is cell G4 (Costs worksheet) the correct reference for the formula in cell D5 (Scheduling worksheet)?
Cell G4 is the Coach Cost Per Hour for Kristen and contains the value 100. Cell D5 on the Scheduling Plan worksheet represents the cost per hour for Kristen. Thus cell G4 is the correct reference for cell D5.

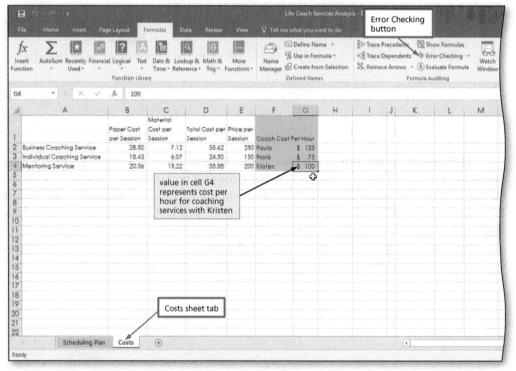

Figure 9–14

- Make Scheduling Plan the active worksheet and then select cell E16.
- Click the Error Checking button (Formulas tab | Formula Auditing group) to display the Error Checking dialog box (Figure 9–15).

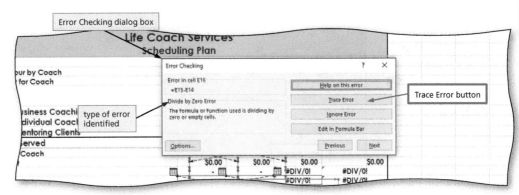

Figure 9–15

- Click the Trace Error button (Error Checking dialog box) to highlight the precedents of the active cell, which also contain error codes (Figure 9–16).

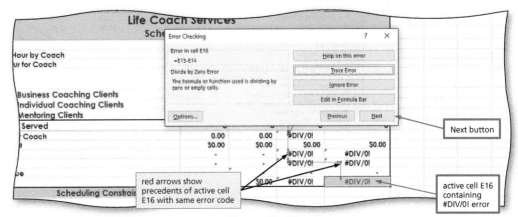

Figure 9–16

- Click the Next button (Error Checking dialog box) to move to the next error in the workbook, found in cell D11 in this case (Figure 9–17).

Experiment

- Drag the Error Checking dialog box to view empty cell E4, referenced in the formula in cell D11.

Q&A What happens when I click the Next button?
Excel will move to the next cell in which it finds an error code or an error indicator.

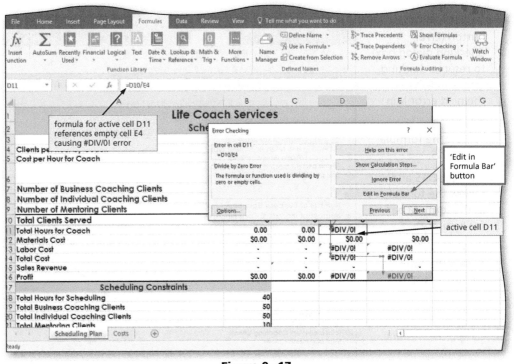

Figure 9–17

Excel moves forward or backward through the workbook, row by row, when you click the Next or Previous button. Clicking the Next button does not move to a precedent or dependent cell. In this case, clicking the Next button displayed the first error in the workbook, because the workbook contains no errors after cell E16.

6

- Click the 'Edit in Formula Bar' button (Error Checking dialog box) and edit cell D11 to read =**D10/D4**.

- Click the Enter button in the formula bar to complete the edit of the cell and to correct the remaining #DIV/0! errors (Figure 9–18).

Q&A Why did correcting one error in cell D11 correct all the #DIV/0! errors in the worksheet?
The other cells containing #DIV/0! errors were directly or indirectly dependent on the value in cell D11, thus correcting the error in cell D11 provided a valid value for use in the other formulas.

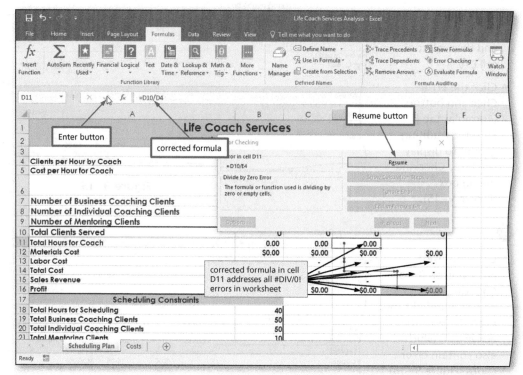

Figure 9–18

7

- Click the Resume button (Error Checking dialog box) to resume checking errors, in this case the next error is in cell C15.

- Review the formula in cell C15.

- Click cell D15 and review the formula in the formula bar for accuracy.

- Click cell B15 and review the formula (Figure 9–19).

Q&A Why did Excel jump to cell C15 when I clicked the Resume button?
Clicking the Resume button selects the next cell containing an error if the error in the previously selected cell is corrected. If the error was not corrected, the selected cell would not change.

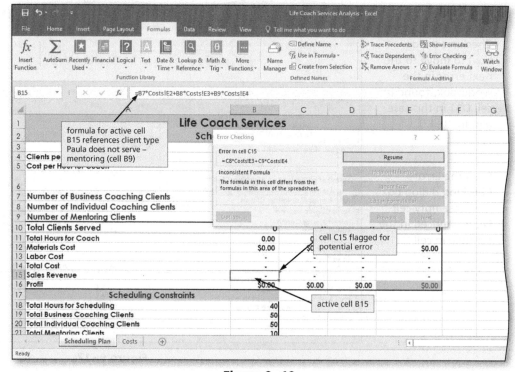

Figure 9–19

Are the formulas in cells B15, C15, and D15 accurate?

Although all three formulas produce accurate results, the formula in cell C15 is flagged as a potential error because it is inconsistent with the other two. The formula in cell C15 references only the types of clients Frank serves. For greater accuracy, the formula in cell B15 should reference only the types of clients that Paula serves.

- Edit the formula in cell B15 to read `=B7*Costs!E2+B8*Costs!E3` (Figure 9–20).

- Click the Resume button (Error Checking dialog box) to complete the edit.

Q&A Why did the error flag in cell C15 disappear after editing the formula in cell B15?

The formula in cell C15 was originally flagged as a potential error because the formula was inconsistent with the cells on either side of it. Once the formula in cell B15 was edited, Excel no longer expects consistency because none of the cells in the range B15:D15 contain formulas that are consistent with each other, so the error flag is removed.

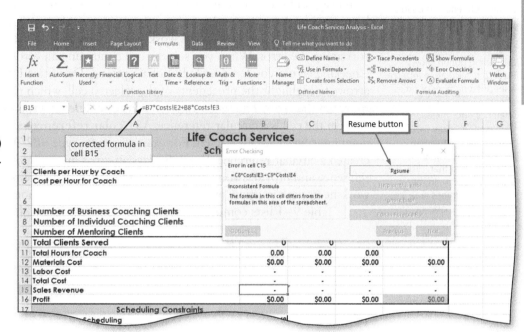

Figure 9–20

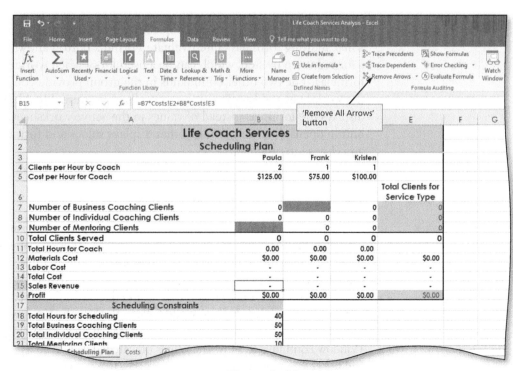

- Click the OK button in the Microsoft Excel dialog box to close the open dialog boxes.

- If necessary, click the 'Remove All Arrows' button (Formulas tab | Formula Auditing group) to remove all of the dependent arrows (Figure 9–21).

Figure 9–21

BTW
**Setting Iterative
Calculation Options**
In certain situations, you will
want Excel to recalculate
a formula that contains a
circular reference, to enable
Excel to converge upon
an acceptable solution.
Changing the iterative
calculation option allows
Excel to recalculate a formula
a specified number of times
after the initial circular
reference error message is
dismissed. To allow Excel
to recalculate a formula,
display the Excel Options
dialog box and then click
the Formulas tab. In the
Calculation options area, click
to select the 'Enable iterative
calculation' check box. You
can specify the maximum
number of iterations and
maximum amount of
change between iterations.
Be aware that turning on
this option will slow down
the worksheet due to the
additional computations.

More about the Formula Auditing Group

In the previous steps, you used some of the buttons in the Formula Auditing group on the Formulas tab to identify and correct errors in your worksheet. You already have used the Trace Precedents, Trace Dependents, and 'Remove All Arrows' buttons to gain insight into the structure of the worksheet. You also have used the Error Checking button to check for errors throughout the worksheet. When Error Checking is clicked, Excel highlights each error in the worksheet in sequence and displays options for correcting the error. When you select a cell containing an error and then click the Error Checking arrow, you have two additional options. The Trace Error command uses red arrows to highlight the precedents of the selected cell, which may help you identify the source of the error. The second option, Circular References, is available only when the error in the cell is a circular reference. A **circular reference** occurs when one of the defining values in a cell is itself. For example, if you type =B2/A2 in cell B2, you have created a circular reference. Excel displays an error message when you create a circular reference and provides you with access to the appropriate Help topic. In complex worksheets with multiple precedent levels, these errors are not uncommon.

Table 9–1 lists common error codes identified in Excel.

Table 9–1 Common Excel Error Codes	
Error Code	**Description**
#DIV/0!	Indicates that a formula divides a number by zero
#N/A!	Indicates that a formula cannot locate a referenced value
#NAME?	Indicates use of an invalid function name
#NULL!	Indicates that a formula incorrectly contains a space between two or more cell references
#NUM!	Indicates that a formula contains invalid numeric values
#REF!	Indicates that a cell reference in a formula is not valid; it may be pointing to an empty cell, for instance
#VALUE!	Indicates that a calculation includes nonnumeric data

The Formula Auditing group contains three other commands you can use when auditing formulas. The Evaluate Formula button allows you to move through a formula step by step, which can be a useful tool when working with long, complex formulas. The two other commands in the group provide you with options for viewing the worksheet and keeping an eye on cells of interest. The Show Formulas button displays the formulas instead of values in the active worksheet. The Watch Window button opens a separate window that displays values and formulas for specific cells that you choose to monitor.

Using the Watch Window

The Watch Window (Figure 9–22a) allows you to keep an eye on cells that you have identified as being related; this allows you to observe changes to the cells even when viewing a different worksheet or workbook. For example, if you were watching cell E12, which displays total material costs, and you changed the value in cell C3 on the Costs worksheet, the Watch Window would display the updated value of cell E12 on the Scheduling Plan worksheet. You add cells to the Watch Window using the Add Watch button in the Watch Window and the Add Watch dialog box (Figure 9–22b). The Watch Window continues to show the values of watched cells even as you navigate the worksheet and the cells no longer are in view. Similarly, if you change the view to another worksheet or workbook, the Watch Window allows you to continue to monitor the cell values.

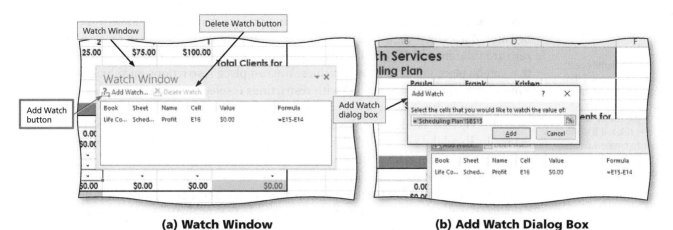

| **(a) Watch Window** | **(b) Add Watch Dialog Box** |

Figure 9–22

To Open the Watch Window

If you wanted to open the Watch Window, you would perform the following steps:

1. If necessary, display the Formulas tab.
2. Click the Watch Window button (Formulas tab | Formula Auditing group) to open the Watch Window (Figure 9–22a).
3. If necessary, move the Watch Window to a location where it does not obscure cells you want to observe to make it easier to select the cells you want to add.

To Add Cells to the Watch Window

If you wanted to add cells to the Watch Window, you would perform the following steps:

1. Click the Add Watch button on the Watch Window toolbar to display the Add Watch dialog box (Figure 9–22b).
2. Select the cell or cells to be watched.
3. Click the Add button (Add Watch dialog box) to add the selected cells to the Watch Window.

To Delete Cells from the Watch Window

If you wanted to delete cells from the Watch Window, you would perform the following steps:

1. In the Watch Window dialog box, select the cell you want to stop watching.
2. Click the Delete Watch button in the Watch Window to delete the selected cell from the Watch Window.

Data Validation

When calculating formulas, some values used in calculations might not have any useful meaning for the problem at hand. For example, cells B7 and D7 in the Scheduling Plan worksheet display the number of business coaching clients served. Because you cannot

BTW

Errors and Data Validation
Excel cannot identify cells that contain formulas that are mathematically correct, but logically incorrect, without the use of data validation rules. It is up to the user to create validation rules that restrict solutions to logical values.

serve a negative number of clients, only values greater than or equal to zero should be entered in cells B7 and D7. In other words, only values greater than or equal to zero are valid in cells B7 and D7. Excel provides you with tools to restrict the values that can be placed in cells to valid values. You can place restrictions on values, provide a message to the user when a cell with restrictions is selected, and create an error message that is displayed when an invalid value is entered.

Excel's data validation rules apply only when you enter data into the cell manually. Excel does not check the validation rules if a cell is calculated by a formula or set in a way other than by direct input by the user.

The types of data validation criteria you can use include specific values, whole numbers, a value in a list (such as a text value), dates, and custom values. When using the custom validation type, you can use a formula that evaluates to either true or false. If the value is false, users may not enter data in the cell. Suppose, for example, you have a cell that contains an employee's salary. If the salary is zero, which indicates the employee no longer is with the company, you may want to prohibit a user from entering a percentage in another cell that contains the employee's raise for the year.

To Add Data Validation to Cells

1 ANALYZE WORKBOOK FORMULAS | 2 SET DATA VALIDATION RULES | 3 CUSTOMIZE ADD-INS
4 SOLVE COMPLEX PROBLEMS | 5 CREATE & EVALUATE SCENARIOS | 6 PRODUCE REPORTS

Why add data validation? In the *Scheduling Plan worksheet, the numbers of each type of client served by each coach must be nonnegative whole numbers.* The cells that need to be restricted are cells B7:B8, C8:C9, and D7:D9 because they display the number of each type of client. You can use data validation to apply these conditions and restrictions to the cells. The following steps add data validation to cells in the ranges B7:B8, C8:C9, and D7:D9.

- Display the Data tab and then select cells B7 and D7.

- Click the Data Validation button (Data tab | Data Tools group) to display the Data Validation dialog box.

- Click the Allow arrow (Data Validation dialog box) and then click Whole number in the Allow list to select it as the validation criteria type.

- Click the Data arrow and then click 'greater than or equal to' in the Data list to select it.

- Type 0 in the Minimum box to specify that the values in the selected cells must be whole numbers greater than or equal to zero (Figure 9–23).

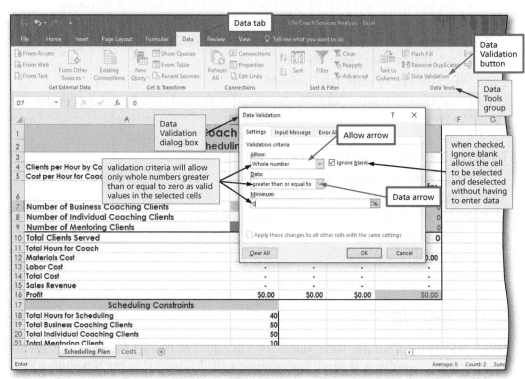

Figure 9–23

How else can I validate data?

Excel allows several types of validation to be set in the Settings sheet (Data Validation dialog box) shown in Figure 9–23. Each selection in this sheet changes the type of value that Excel allows a user to enter in the cell. In the Allow list, the Any value selection allows you to enter any value but still allows you to specify an input message for the cell. The Whole number, Decimal, Date, and Time selections permit only values of those types to be entered in the cell. The List selection allows you to specify a range that contains a list of valid values for the cell. The Text length selection allows only a certain length of text string to be entered in the cell. The Custom selection allows you to specify a formula that validates the data entered by the user.

- Click the Input Message tab (Data Validation dialog box) to display the Input Message sheet.

- Type **Number of Business Clients** in the Title text box to enter a title for the message displayed when cell B7 or D7 is selected.

- Type **Enter the number of business coaching clients to be served by this coach. The number**

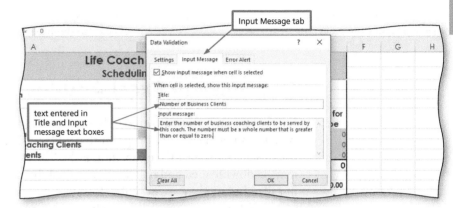

Figure 9–24

must be a whole number that is greater than or equal to zero. in the Input message text box to enter the text for the message (Figure 9–24).

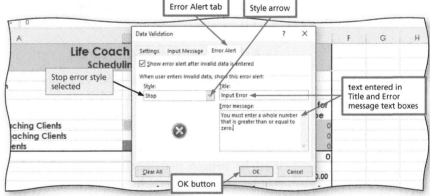

Figure 9–25

- Click the Error Alert tab (Data Validation dialog box) to display the Error Alert sheet.

- If necessary, Click the Style arrow and then click Stop to select the Stop error style.

- Type **Input Error** in the Title text box to enter a title for the error message displayed if invalid data is entered in cell B7 or D7.

- Type **You must enter a whole number that is greater than or equal to zero.** in the Error message text box to enter the text for the error message (Figure 9–25).

What is a Stop error style?

You can select one of three types of error styles. Stop prevents users from entering invalid data in a cell. Warning displays a message that the data is invalid and lets users accept the invalid entry, edit it, or remove it. Information displays a message that the data is invalid but still allows users to enter it.

- Click the OK button (Data Validation dialog box) to accept the data validation settings for cells B7 and D7.

- Repeat Steps 1 through 4 two more times, once for individual clients in cells B8:D8 and once for mentoring clients in cells C9:D9. Use the same settings in the Settings sheet for the values that can be entered in the cells. When creating the title for the input message for cells B8:D8, use **Number of Individual Clients**. Similarly, use the title **Number of Mentoring Clients** for cells C9:D9. Make the appropriate changes for the text in the input messages and error alerts.

- Click cell E21 to make it the active cell.

- Save the workbook again on the same storage location with the same file name.

Q&A What is the result of these validation rules?

When a user selects one of the cells in the ranges B7:B8, C8:C9, or D7:D9, Excel displays the input message defined in Figure 9–24. When the user enters a value that either is less than zero or is not a whole number in cells in the ranges B7:B8, C8:C9, and D7:D9, Excel displays the error message defined in Figure 9–25 and forces the user to change the value to a valid number before deselecting the cell. The validation rules will be tested later in the module.

Break Point: If you wish to take a break, this is a good place to do so. You can exit Excel now. To resume at a later time, run Excel, open the file called Life Coach Services Analysis, and continue following the steps from this location forward.

Customizing Excel Add-Ins

Excel provides optional commands and features through the inclusion of add-ins. An add-in is an accessory program that adds functionality to Excel. Although some add-ins are built into Excel, including the Solver add-in used in this module, others may be downloaded and installed as needed. In any case, add-ins for Excel must be installed before they are available for use.

Add-ins are managed through the Add-ins tab accessible through the Excel Options dialog box. Once activated, the add-in and related commands are accessible through the ribbon, often in custom tabs or groups. The Solver and Analysis ToolPak add-ins are represented by buttons in the Analyze group on the Data tab. Euro Currency Tools, another built-in add-in for Excel, appears as commands in the Solutions group on the Formulas tab.

The Solver Add-In

The Solver add-in is a tool you use to generate the best possible solution for complex problems from a wide range of possibilities. Solver works to optimize a specific cell, called an objective cell, by maximizing, minimizing, or setting it to a specific value. For example, you may want to minimize total cost (cell E14) or maximize profit (cell E16). Because of the number of precedents to these cell values, it can be difficult to determine which values should change. When you decrease the number of business coaching clients for one coach, you have to increase the number assigned to another coach to ensure that all clients are being served. This change not only has an impact on costs and resulting profit but also impacts the number of hours required of the individual coaches. Solver takes into account all of the various constraints when determining the best solution. In the scheduling plan problem, constraints include the number of hours an individual coach can work in a week (cell B18) and the number of clients in each category of coaching service (B19:B21). The countless options make it difficult to identify the best solution to the problem using other methods of what-if analysis such as trial and error or Goal Seek.

To Enable the Solver Add-In

1 ANALYZE WORKBOOK FORMULAS | 2 SET DATA VALIDATION RULES | 3 CUSTOMIZE ADD-INS
4 SOLVE COMPLEX PROBLEMS | 5 CREATE & EVALUATE SCENARIOS | 6 PRODUCE REPORTS

Many of the advanced features of Excel, such as the Solver add-in, are hidden until the user adds the feature to the user interface. *Why? Excel is a powerful application with many features that the average user does not need to access on a regular basis. These features are hidden to keep the interface from becoming too overwhelming.* The following steps will add the Solver add-in to Excel and verify the additional features on the Data tab of the ribbon.

1

- Display the Backstage view.
- Click the Options tab to display the Excel Options dialog box (Figure 9–26).

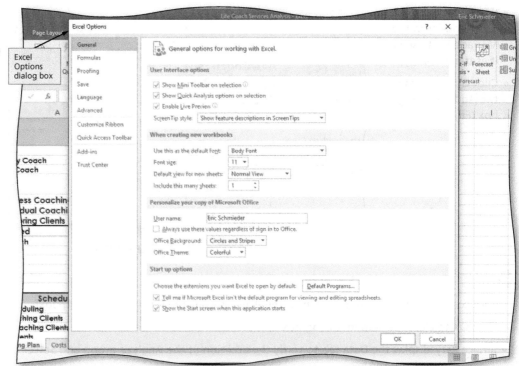

Figure 9–26

2

- Click the Add-ins tab to display the View and manage Microsoft Office Add-ins (Figure 9–27).

 Why is my list of add-ins different? Depending on the applications installed and enabled for use in Excel, the list of active, inactive, and available add-ins may be different.

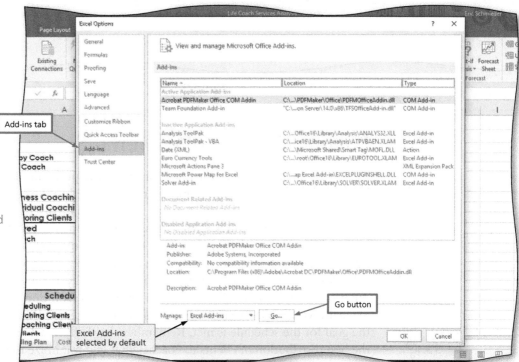

Figure 9–27

- If necessary, click Excel Add-ins in the Manage list to select it as the add-in type.
- Click Go to display the Add-ins dialog box (Figure 9–28).

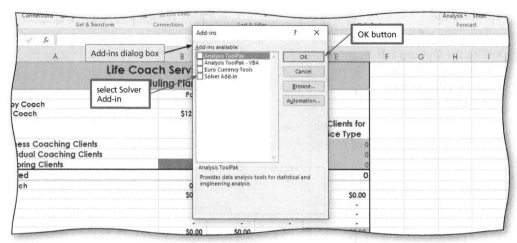

Figure 9–28

- Click to select the Solver Add-in item in the Add-ins available list (Add-ins dialog box).
- Click OK to close the Add-ins dialog box.
- If necessary, display the Data tab to verify the addition of the Analyze group and Solver button (Figure 9–29).

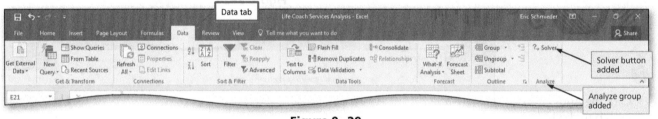

Figure 9–29

Solving Complex Problems

In the Life Coach Services Analysis workbook, the problem of determining how to schedule client services to minimize total cost within the constraints provided is not straightforward, due to the number of variables involved. Remember from the requirements document that these constraints include the number of hours each individual coach can work in a week (cell B18), the number of clients that need to be served in each category (cells B19:B21), and the types of clients each coach serves.

You can attempt to solve the problem manually, through trial and error, or you can use an Excel tool to automate some or all of the solution. To solve the problem manually, you could try adjusting values in the ranges B7:B8, C8:C9, and D7:D9 until the goal for the schedule is met. Remember that Life Coach Services wants to identify the best distribution of clients to coaches that will minimize their total costs. Because so many possible combinations could meet the criteria, you could hold one or more of the cells affected by constraints constant and make adjustments to the other cells to attempt to meet the rest of the criteria. For example, you could assign all ten of the mentoring clients to Kristen (cell D9) and reassign a corresponding number of individual coaching clients to Frank (cell C8) to see how that one change affects the total costs.

How should you approach solving a complex problem?

When considering an approach to a complex problem in Excel, start with the least complex method of attempting to solve the problem. In general, the following methods can be useful in the order shown:

1. **Use trial and error** to modify the values in the worksheet. Use a commonsense approach, and keep in mind the range of acceptable answers to your problem. For example, the number of coaching clients should not be a negative number.

2. **Use Excel's Goal Seek feature** to have Excel automatically modify a cell's value in a worksheet in an attempt to reach a certain goal in a dependent cell.

3. **Use Excel's Solver feature** to provide Excel with all of the known rules, or constraints, of your problem as well as the goal you are seeking. Allow Solver to attempt as many different solutions to your problem as possible.

To Use Trial and Error to Attempt to Solve a Complex Problem

1 ANALYZE WORKBOOK FORMULAS | 2 SET DATA VALIDATION RULES | 3 CUSTOMIZE ADD-INS
4 SOLVE COMPLEX PROBLEMS | **5 CREATE & EVALUATE SCENARIOS** | **6 PRODUCE REPORTS**

Trial and error is not making blind guesses. Trial and error is a process of making incremental changes in order to observe the impact on the desired result. *Why use trial and error? With an understanding of how the worksheet is set up and how the various values interact, you can make informed and incremental changes, or trials, based on how each decision affects the worksheet.* In the first trial for the Life Coach Services workbook, you will set up the schedule so that all the services are delivered by Kristen, the one coach that can deliver all three types of services, and then make some adjustments based on the results. The following steps illustrate the process of using trial and error to attempt to solve a complex problem.

- Click cell D7 to make it the active cell and display the Number of Business Clients input message.

- Type **47.5** and then press the ENTER key to enter the number of business coaching clients for Kristen and display the Input Error dialog box (Figure 9–30).

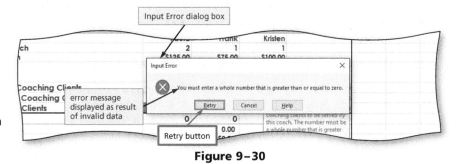

Figure 9–30

Q&A Why does the Input Error dialog box appear after entering 47.5 in cell D7?
You set a data validation rule in cell D7 that accepts only whole numbers greater than or equal to zero. Because 47.5 is not a whole number, Excel displays the Input Error dialog box with the title and error message you specified when you set the data validation rule.

- Click the Retry button (Input Error dialog box) to return to cell D7.

- Enter **50** in cell D7 as the number of business clients to schedule with Kristen and then press the ENTER key.

- Enter **50** in cell D8 as the number of individual clients to schedule with Kristen and then press the ENTER key.

- Enter **10** in cell D9 as the number of mentoring clients to schedule with Kristen and then press the ENTER key (Figure 9–31).

Q&A Do the values entered in Step 2 solve the scheduling problem for Kristen?
No. Each coach must be scheduled for 40 hours or less, as indicated by cell B18. The values entered in Step 2 mean that Kristen will spend 110 hours to deliver the scheduled services, as shown in cell D11.

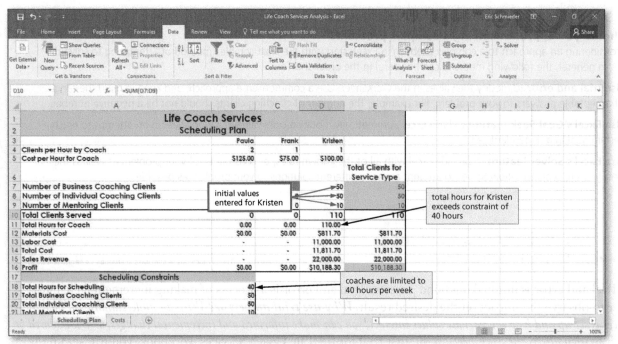

Figure 9–31

- Click cell D7 to make it the active cell.

- Type **40** and then press the ENTER key to reduce the number of business coaching clients for Kristen.

- Click cell B7 to make it the active cell. Type **10** and then press the ENTER key to enter the number of business coaching clients to be served by Paula.

- Click an empty cell, in this case cell A6, to view the results (Figure 9–32).

Q&A | Do the values entered in Step 3 solve the scheduling problem for Kristen?

No. The values entered in Step 3 mean that Kristen still needs to allocate 100 hours for coaching clients in her schedule, which is greater than the 40-hour constraint (B18).

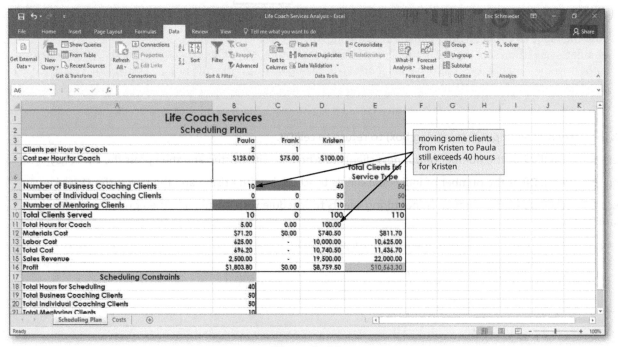

Figure 9–32

4

- Click cell C8 to make it the active cell.

- Enter `20` as the number of individual coaching clients for Frank.

- Enter `30` in cell D8 to reduce the number of individual coaching clients for Kristen.

- Enter `5` in cell C9 as the number of mentoring clients for Frank.

- Enter `5` in cell D9 and then press the ENTER key to reduce the number of mentoring clients for Kristen (Figure 9–33).

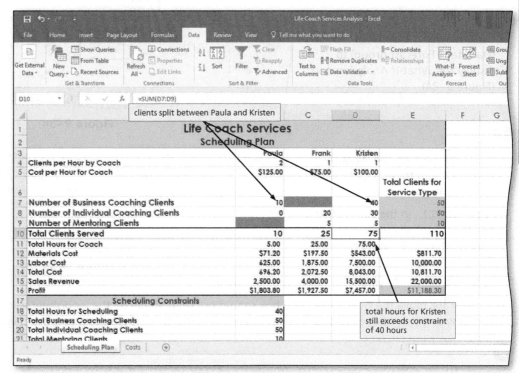

Figure 9–33

Q&A

Do the values entered in Step 4 solve the scheduling problem for all the coaches?
No. The scheduled time for Kristen still exceeds the 40-hour scheduling constraint.

What are some problems with using trial and error?
While trial and error can be used on simple problems, it has many limitations when used to solve complex problems. The Scheduling Plan worksheet has seven cells (B7, B8, C8, C9, D7, D8, and D9) that can be adjusted to solve the problem. Endless combinations of values could be entered in those seven cells to try to come up with a solution. Using trial and error, it is difficult to determine if a solution you reach satisfies the goal of minimizing the total cost.

To Use Goal Seek to Attempt to Solve a Complex Problem

1 ANALYZE WORKBOOK FORMULAS | 2 SET DATA VALIDATION RULES | 3 CUSTOMIZE ADD-INS
4 SOLVE COMPLEX PROBLEMS | 5 CREATE & EVALUATE SCENARIOS | 6 PRODUCE REPORTS

The previous set of steps illustrates a situation where Goal Seek may help you to solve a complex problem. The total hours for Kristen, as shown in cell D11, needs to be less than or equal to 40 hours. The formula in cell D11 is =D10/ D4, where D10 is the sum of cells D7:D9. Therefore, D11 depends on cells D7:D9 and cell D4. With Goal Seek, you can manipulate one of these precedent cells to find a solution for cell D11 that meets the 40-hour constraint. Goal seeking will change the value of one cell until the specified goal is met in another cell. You decide to have Goal Seek manipulate cell D8, because Paula is not currently scheduled for individual coaching. Any reduction in Kristen's individual clients would produce an equal increase in Paula's individual clients. In using Goal Seek, you hope that the problem of scheduling the other client types has already been solved.

The following steps use Goal Seek to change the number of individual clients for Kristen to keep the total hours for Kristen at less than or equal to 40.

- If necessary, display the Data tab.
- Click the 'What-If Analysis' button (Data tab | Forecast group) to display the What-If Analysis menu (Figure 9–34).

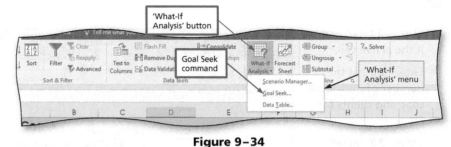

Figure 9–34

❷

- Click Goal Seek on the What-If Analysis menu to display the Goal Seek dialog box.
- Type **$D$11** in the Set cell text box (Goal Seek dialog box) to specify which cell should contain the goal value.
- Type **40** in the To value text box as the goal value.

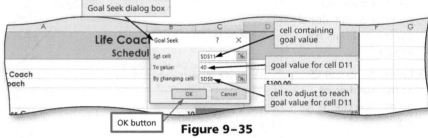

Figure 9–35

- If necessary, move the Goal Seek dialog box so that cell D8 is visible on the worksheet, click the 'By changing cell' text box, and then click cell D8 to enter its reference in the 'By changing cell' text box (Figure 9–35).

❸

- Click the OK button (Goal Seek dialog box) to seek the goal of 40 hours in cell D11 and display the Goal Seek Status dialog box, which indicates that goal seeking found a solution (Figure 9–36).

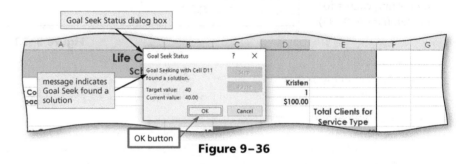

Figure 9–36

❹

- Click the OK button (Goal Seek Status dialog box) to close the dialog box and display the updated worksheet.
- Click cell E21 to deselect any other cell (Figure 9–37).

Q&A How can the number of individual coaching clients (cell D8) contain a negative number when data validation rules allow only numbers greater than or equal to zero? Data validation rules are applied only to data that is entered into a cell. Entries that are the result of calculations will not produce a data validation error.

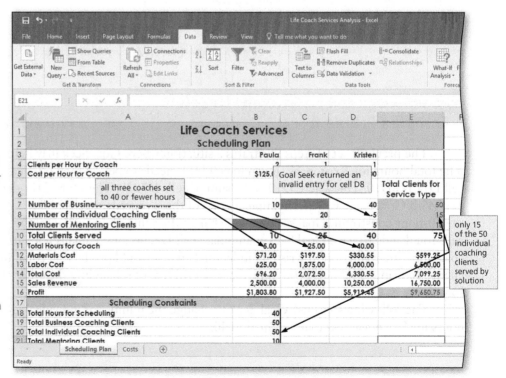

Figure 9–37

To Circle Invalid Data

Why? *The 'Circle Invalid Data' command checks for invalid data entered as the result of a formula or automated tool, such as Goal Seek.* The previous set of steps illustrates how the data validation rules apply only to data directly entered into a cell, not to the results of actions such as Goal Seek. In this case, Goal Seek found a solution that satisfied the criteria specified for the goal, but that solution violated the conditions specified for data validation. It is good practice to check your worksheet for invalid data periodically through use of the 'Circle Invalid Data' command. The following steps check for and circle any invalid data on the Scheduling Plan worksheet.

- Click the Data Validation arrow (Data tab | Data Tools group) to display the Data Validation menu (Figure 9–38).

Figure 9–38

- Click 'Circle Invalid Data' on the Data Validation menu to place a red validation circle around any invalid data, in this case cell D8 (Figure 9–39).

Q&A

Now that I have identified invalid data, what do I do with that information?
Once you identify invalid data in a worksheet, you should determine how to correct the data.

What are some limitations of using goal seeking?
Goal seeking allows you to manipulate

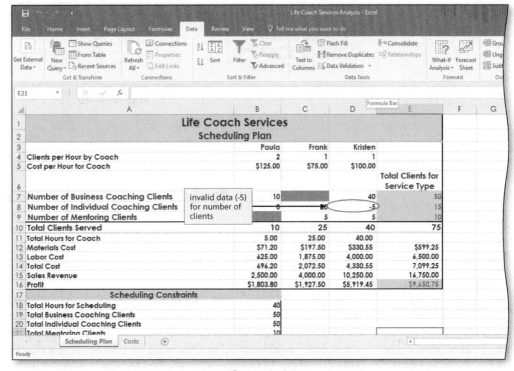

Figure 9–39

only one cell in order to reach a goal. In this example, to change the total number of hours scheduled for Kristen to 40, the number of individual coaching clients is changed to –5. Goal Seek can produce a result that is acceptable mathematically, but not logically, as is the case here.

To Clear Validation Circles

Why? Once the invalid data has been identified, it is easier to work when the worksheet is clear of extraneous marks. The following step clears the validation circles.

- Click the Data Validation arrow (Data tab | Data Tools group) to display the Data Validation menu.

- Click 'Clear Validation Circles' on the Data Validation menu to remove the red validation circle.

- Select cell E21 to deselect any other cell and then save the workbook (Figure 9–40).

Q&A

Has the scheduling problem been solved?
No. Although each coach's schedule is meeting the 40-hour constraint, not enough individual clients are being served. (And there is the issue of the invalid data.) But even if all the scheduling constraints were met, you still would have no way of knowing whether the goal to minimize cost (cell E14) has been achieved.

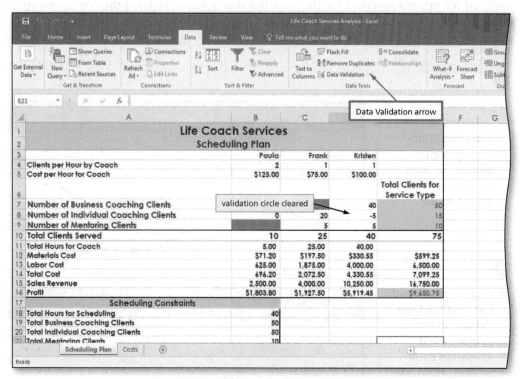

Figure 9–40

Using Solver to Solve Complex Problems

BTW
Solver Requirements
Regardless of the technique Solver uses to solve a problem, it requires three different types of input from the user: the objective, or the result you need for the target cell; variable cells, the values that can change; and constraints, the conditions that the solution has to meet.

Solver allows you to solve complex problems where a number of variables can be changed in a worksheet in order to meet a goal in a particular cell. Unlike Goal Seek, Solver is not restricted to changing one cell at a time and can efficiently evaluate many combinations for a solution.

The technique Solver uses to solve a problem depends on the model that the user selects as best representing the data. For the current scheduling problem, you will use LP Simplex, a technique in Solver associated with linear programming. **Linear programming** is a complex mathematical process used to solve problems that include multiple variables and the minimizing or maximizing of result values. Solver essentially tries as many possible combinations of solutions as it can. On each attempt to solve the problem, Solver checks to see if it has found a solution. The other two techniques are beyond the scope of this book.

In order for Solver to solve the scheduling problem, Solver must modify data until an optimum value is reached for the selected cell. The cells modified by Solver are called **decision variable cells**, also known as changing cells or adjustable cells. In this case, these are cells in the ranges B7:B8, C8:C9, and D7:D9. The cell that Solver is working to optimize, either by finding its maximum or its minimum value, is known as the **objective cell**, or target cell. In this case, Solver is trying to minimize the total cost of providing coaching services, which makes cell E14 the objective or target cell.

Solver will attempt to minimize the value of cell E14 by varying the values in the decision variable, or changing, cells, within the constraints set by Life Coach Services. Figure 9–41a displays the result of using Solver on the Scheduling Plan worksheet.

Constraints are the requirements that have been placed on certain values in the problem and are listed in the requirements document. For example, one constraint is that no coach should be scheduled for more than 40 hours. Other constraints include the types of clients that each coach is certified to work with and the number of each type of client served by Life Coach Services.

When Solver reaches a solution to a problem, it generates an Answer Report. An Answer Report is a worksheet summarizing a Solver calculation. It shows the answer for the target cell, the values used in the changing cells to arrive at that answer, and the constraints that were applied to the calculation. Figure 9–41b shows a Solver Answer Report. By creating an Answer Report, you satisfy the requirement to document the results of the scheduling calculation.

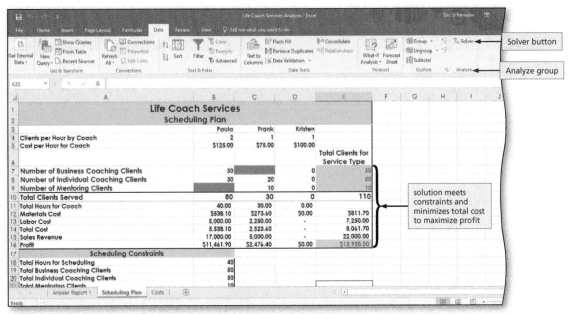

(a) Scheduling Plan Solver Results

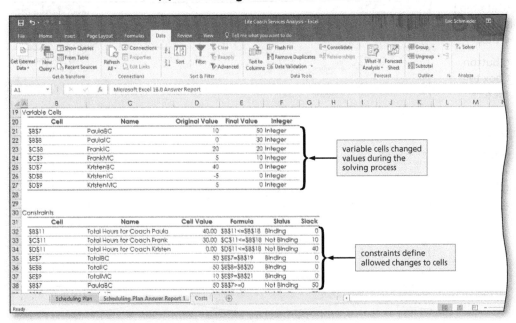

(b) Scheduling Plan Answer Report

Figure 9–41

Note: If the Solver button does not appear on the Data tab, then you must complete the steps earlier in this module to enable the Solver add-in.

To Use Solver to Find the Optimal Solution to a Complex Problem

To solve the scheduling problem for Life Coach Services, you set Solver the goal of minimizing the total cost of the coaching services, shown in cell E14, within the constraints set in the Requirements Document. To accomplish this goal, Solver can modify the number of clients of each type served by each coach (represented by the ranges B7:B8, C8:C9, and D7:D9). **Why use Solver?** *Solver allows Excel to evaluate multiple combinations of values for changing variables to find an optimal solution to a complex problem.* The constraints are summarized in Table 9–2. The following steps use Solver to find the optimal solution to the scheduling problem in the Scheduling Plan worksheet within the given constraints.

Table 9–2 Constraints for Solver		
Cell or Range	**Operator**	**Constraint**
$B$7:$B$8	>=	0
$B$7:$B$8	int	integer
$C$8:$C$9	>=	0
$C$8:$C$9	int	integer
$D$7:$D$9	>=	0
$D$7:$D$9	int	integer
$E$7	=	$B$19
$E$8	=	$B$20
$E$9	=	$B$21
$B$11	<=	$B$18
$C$11	<=	$B$18
$D$11	<=	$B$18

1

- Click the Solver button (Data tab | Analyze group) to display the Solver Parameters dialog box.

- Click the Collapse Dialog button in the Set Objective text box to collapse the Solver Parameters dialog box.

- Click cell E14 to set the target cell.

- Click the Expand Dialog button on the right side of the collapsed Solver Parameters dialog box to expand the dialog box (Figure 9–42).

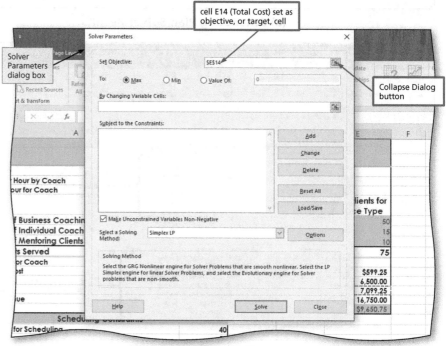

Figure 9–42

2

- Click Min in the To area to specify that the value of the target cell should be as small as possible.

- Click the Collapse Dialog button in the 'By Changing Variable Cells' box to collapse the Solver Parameters dialog box.

- Select the range B7:B8, hold down the CTRL key, and then select the ranges C8:C9 and D7:D9.

- Click the Expand Dialog button on the right side of the collapsed Solver Parameters dialog box to expand the dialog box (Figure 9–43).

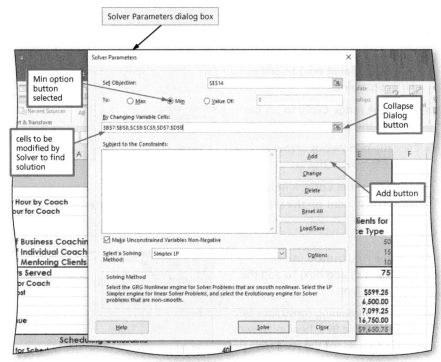

Figure 9–43

3

- Click the Add button to display the Add Constraint dialog box.

- If necessary, move the Add Constraint dialog box so that the range B7:B8 is visible.

- Select the range B7:B8 to set the value of the Cell Reference text box.

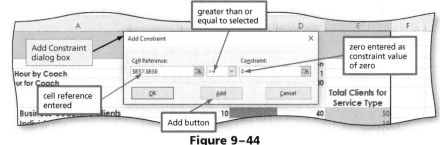

Figure 9–44

- Click the middle arrow and then select >= in the list.

- Type   0   in the Constraint text box to set the constraint on the cells in the range B7:B8 to be greater than or equal to zero (Figure 9–44).

Q&A

How do I use the Constraint text box?
When adding constraints, as shown in Figure 9–44, you first enter a cell reference followed by an operator. If the operator is <=, >=, or =, then you enter the constraint value in the Constraint text box. The constraint can be a value or a cell reference. Other valid operators are int, for an integer value; bin, for cells that contain only one of two values, such as yes/no or true/false; or dif, for an "all different" constraint where no two values are the same.

What do the entries in the Add Constraint dialog box in Figure 9–44 mean?
The entries limit the number of clients served by Paula (cells B7:B8) to a number greater than or equal to zero.

4

- Click the Add button (Add Constraint dialog box) to add a second constraint.

- Select the range B7:B8 to set the value of the Cell Reference box.

- Click the middle box arrow and then select int in the list to set a constraint on the cells in the range B7:B8 to be assigned only integer values (Figure 9–45).

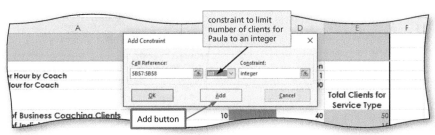

Figure 9–45

5

- Click the Add button (Add Constraint dialog box) to add a third constraint.

- Select the range C8:C9 to set the value of the Cell Reference box.

- Click the middle box arrow and then select >= in the list.

- Type 0 in the Constraint box to set the constraint on the cells in the range C8:C9 to be greater than or equal to zero (Figure 9–46).

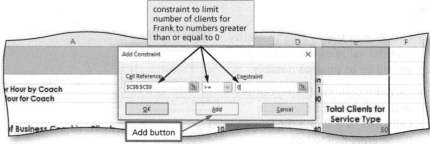

Figure 9–46

6

- Click the Add button (Add Constraint dialog box) to add the next constraint.

- Enter the remaining constraints as shown in Table 9–2, beginning with the constraints for the range C8:C9.

- After entering the last constraint, click the OK button (Add Constraint dialog box) to close the dialog box and display the Solver Parameters dialog box (Figure 9–47).

Q&A What should I do if a constraint does not match the ones shown in Figure 9–47?
Select the constraint, click the Change button (Solver Parameters dialog box), and then enter the constraints as shown in the table.

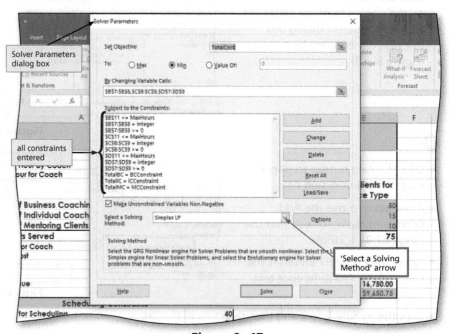

Figure 9–47

7

- If necessary, click Simplex LP in the 'Select a Solving Method' list to select the linear progression method (Figure 9–48).

Q&A What does Simplex LP mean?
LP stands for linear progression, and Simplex refers to the basic problem-solving method used to solve linear problems. Linear problems are ones in which a "straight-line" approach of cause and effect can seek to determine a goal value by modifying values that impact the goal. For example, a decrease in costs results in an increase in profits.

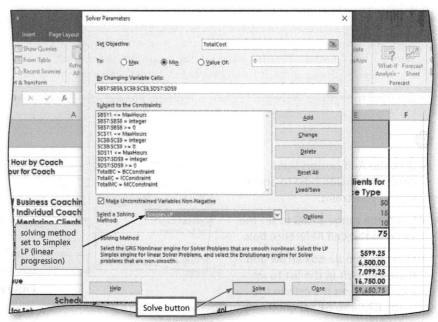

Figure 9–48

- Click the Solve button (Solver Parameters dialog box) to display the Solver Results dialog box, indicating that Solver found a solution to the problem.

- Click Answer in the Reports list to select the type of report to generate (Figure 9–49).

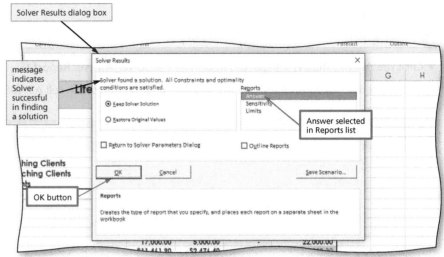

Figure 9–49

- Click the OK button (Solver Results dialog box) to display the values found by Solver and the newly recalculated totals (Figure 9–50).

Q&A
What is the result of using Solver?
Solver found a solution to the scheduling problem, shown in Figure 9–50, that meets the constraints and minimizes the total cost of the coaching services. This solution has Paula being assigned 80 clients, Frank being assigned 30 clients, and Kristen not being scheduled with any clients. Paula was assigned so many clients because she can see two clients per hour, so her labor cost is the lowest of all three coaches at $62.50 per client. The other two coaches only see one client per hour and therefore have a higher per client cost.

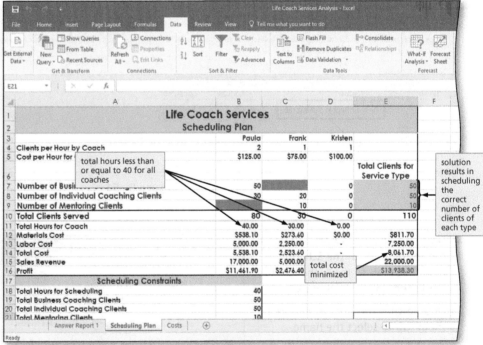

Figure 9–50

To View the Solver Answer Report

1 ANALYZE WORKBOOK FORMULAS | 2 SET DATA VALIDATION RULES | 3 CUSTOMIZE ADD-INS
4 SOLVE COMPLEX PROBLEMS | 5 CREATE & EVALUATE SCENARIOS | 6 PRODUCE REPORTS

Solver generates the requested Answer Report on a separate worksheet after it finds a solution. The Answer Report summarizes the problem that you have presented to Solver. It shows the original and final values of the target, or objective, cell along with the original and final values of the changing cells (decision variable cells) that Solver modified to find the answer. Additionally, it lists all of the constraints that you entered.

Why view the Answer Report generated by Solver? The Answer Report documents that a particular problem has been solved correctly. Because it lists all of the relevant information in a concise format, you can use the Answer Report to make certain that you have entered all of the constraints and allowed Solver to modify all the necessary values to solve the problem. You also can use the report to reconstruct the Solver model in the future.

The following steps view the Solver Answer Report.

1

● Click the Answer Report 1 sheet tab to display the Solver Answer Report (Figure 9–51).

If requested by your instructor, add the name of your hometown in cell A3, following the content already in that cell.

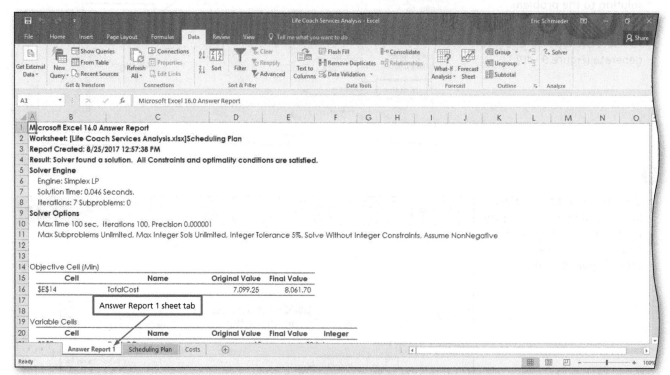

Figure 9–51

2

● Drag the Answer Report 1 sheet tab to the right of the Scheduling Plan sheet tab to move the worksheet in the workbook.

● Double-click the Answer Report 1 sheet tab to select the name.

● Type **Scheduling Plan Answer Report 1** and then press the ENTER key to rename the worksheet.

● Change the color of the sheet tab to 'Red, Accent 5' (column 9, row 1).

● Scroll down to view the remaining cells of the Answer Report (Figure 9–52).

● Save the workbook again on the same storage location with the same file name.

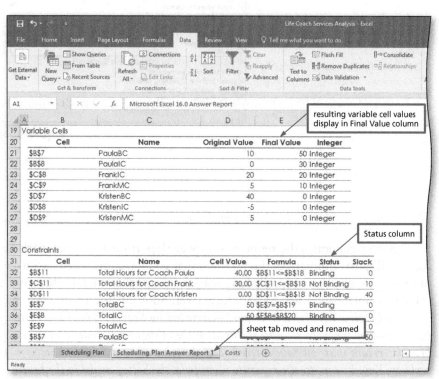

Figure 9–52

What is shown in the Answer Report?

The Answer Report shows additional information about the constraints and how they were used to solve the problem. The Status column, column F, indicates whether a constraint was binding. A constraint that is **binding** is one that limited the final solution in some way. For example, the total number of hours in cell B11 in the Scheduling Plan worksheet is binding because the solution generated the maximum number allowed by the constraints, 40 hours. No more time could be allocated to scheduling for that coach given that constraint. A constraint that is not binding is one that was not a limiting factor in the solution that Solver provided.

Working with Solver Options

When you selected the Simplex LP method of solving the production problem in the Solver Parameters dialog box, you selected a linear programming method that assumes the problem follows a cause and effect relationship, by which changes to one value have a direct impact on another value. After choosing the Solver method, you can select various options to further configure the inner workings of Solver. Note that Excel saves the most recently used Solver parameters and options. Discussion of many of these parameters is beyond the scope of this book. Table 9–3 presents some of the more commonly used Solver options.

BTW
Viewing Other Solutions
If you want to view solutions other than the one Solver identifies as optimal, select the Show Iteration Results check box in the Solver Parameters dialog box. After each iteration, the Show Trial Solution dialog box will be displayed and you will have the option of saving that scenario and then stopping Solver or continuing on to the next solution.

Table 9–3 Commonly Used Solver Parameters	
Parameter	**Meaning**
Max Time	The total time that Solver should spend trying different solutions, expressed in seconds
Iterations	The number of possible answer combinations that Solver should try
Constraint Precision	Instructs Solver in how close it must come to the target value in order to consider the problem to be solved. For example, if the target value is 100 and and you set tolerance to 5%, then generating a solution with a target value of 95 is acceptable
Use Automatic Scaling	Selected by default, automatic scaling specifies that Solver should internally rescale values of variables, restraints, and the objective to reduce the effect of outlying values.

When using Solver, three issues must be kept in mind. First, some problems do not have solutions. The constraints may be constructed in such a way that Solver cannot find an answer that satisfies all of the constraints. Second, sometimes multiple answers solve the same problem. Solver does not indicate when this is the case, and you will have to use your own judgment to determine if you should seek another solution. As long as you are confident that you have given Solver all of the constraints for a problem, however, all answers should be equally valid. Finally, if Solver fails to find a solution, more time or more iterations may be required to solve the problem.

Break Point: If you wish to take a break, this is a good place to do so. You can now exit Excel. To resume at a later time, run Excel, open the file called Life Coach Services Analysis, and continue following the steps from this location forward.

Using Scenarios and Scenario Manager to Analyze Data

Scenarios are named combinations of values, or what-if assumptions, that are assigned to variables in a model. In this project, you will create different scheduling plans—scenarios—based on different assumptions. For example, you have created a scheduling plan that required distributing 50 business coaching clients, 50 individual coaching clients, and 10 mentoring clients among three coaches while not exceeding 40 hours for any coach. Changing the number of clients in any or all of the categories

BTW
Naming Cell Ranges
Naming ranges for use with input variables is helpful when dealing with multiple input variables. Assign names to all the input variables before creating your first scenario. Named ranges will make scenario reports easier to understand and interpret.

would create a new scenario. Each set of values in these examples represents a what-if assumption. You use the Scenario Manager to keep track of various scenarios, and produce a report detailing the what-if assumptions and results for each scenario.

The primary uses of the Scenario Manager are to:

1. Create different scenarios with multiple sets of changing cells;
2. Build summary worksheets that contain the different scenarios; and
3. View the results of each scenario on your worksheet.

You will use the Scenario Manager for each of these three applications. After you create the scenarios, you will instruct Excel to build the summary worksheets, including a Scenario Summary worksheet and a Scenario PivotTable worksheet.

To Save the Current Data as a Scenario

1 ANALYZE WORKBOOK FORMULAS | 2 SET DATA VALIDATION RULES | 3 CUSTOMIZE ADD-INS
4 SOLVE COMPLEX PROBLEMS | **5 CREATE & EVALUATE SCENARIOS** | **6 PRODUCE REPORTS**

Why? *The current data on the Scheduling Plan worksheet consists of constraints and the values that correctly solve the scheduling problem.* These values can be saved as a scenario named Schedule 1 that can be accessed later or compared with other scenarios. The following steps save the current data for the Schedule 1 scenario using the Scenario Manager dialog box.

- Make Scheduling Plan the active sheet.
- Click the 'What-If Analysis' button (Data tab | Forecast group) to display the What-If Analysis menu (Figure 9–53).

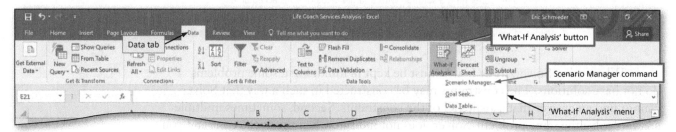

Figure 9–53

- Click Scenario Manager on the What-If Analysis menu to display the Scenario Manager dialog box, which indicates that no scenarios are defined (Figure 9–54).

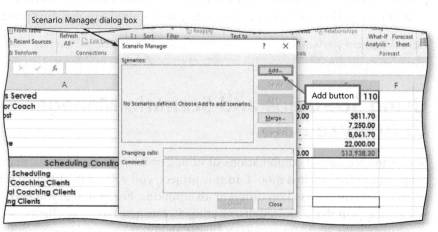

Figure 9–54

- Click the Add button (Scenario Manager dialog box) to open the Add Scenario dialog box.

- Type **Schedule 1** in the Scenario name text box (Add Scenario dialog box) to provide a name for the scenario (Figure 9–55).

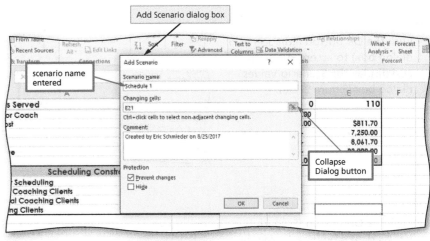

Figure 9–55

- Click the Collapse Dialog button (Add Scenario dialog box) to collapse the dialog box.

- Select the range B7:B8, type , (comma), select the ranges C8:C9, type , (comma), select D7:D9, type , (comma), and then select B18:B21 to enter the ranges in the Changing cells box (Figure 9–56).

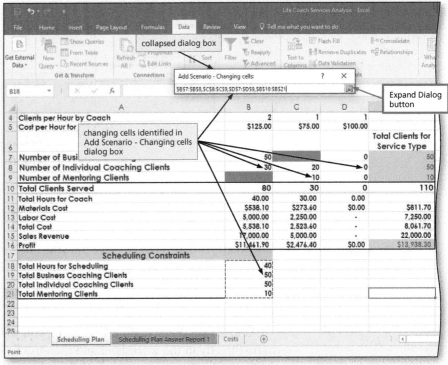

Figure 9–56

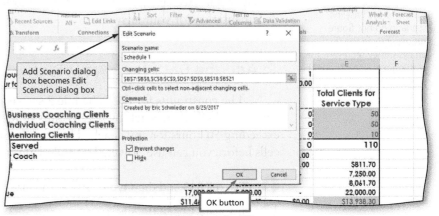

- Click the Expand Dialog button (Add Scenario dialog box) to display the Edit Scenario dialog box (Figure 9–57).

Figure 9–57

- Click the OK button (Edit Scenario dialog box) to accept the settings and display the Scenario Values dialog box (Figure 9–58).

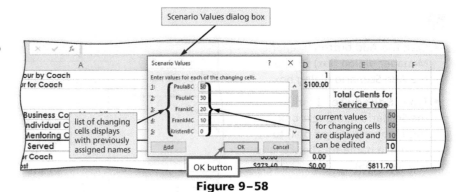

Figure 9–58

- Click the OK button (Scenario Values dialog box) to display the Scenario Manager dialog box with the Schedule 1 scenario selected in the Scenarios list (Figure 9–59).

Q&A

What can I do with the scenario? After the scenario has been saved, you can recall it at any time using the Scenario Manager. In Figure 9–58, the values of the changing cells in the Scenario Values dialog box default to the current values in the worksheet. By changing the text boxes next to the cell names, you can save the scenario using values different from the current values.

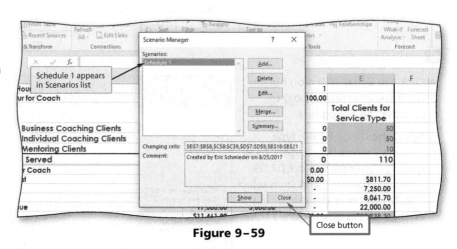

Figure 9–59

- Click the Close button (Scenario Manager dialog box) to save the Schedule 1 scenario in the workbook.

Adding Data for a New Scenario

BTW

Baseline Scenarios
For each model, it is helpful to define a baseline scenario that represents the starting assumptions. Even if the results of the baseline scenario do not figure prominently in the final analysis, they represent the starting point and should be saved.

After saving the Schedule 1 scenario, you will enter the data for the Schedule 2 scenario directly in the worksheet and then use Solver to solve the Schedule 2 scenario in the same way that you solved the Schedule 1 scenario. Because both scenarios are based on the same model, you do not need to reenter the constraints into the Scenario Manager. The Answer Report meets the requirement that you create supporting documentation for your answer.

To Add the Data for a New Scenario

The constraints for the Schedule 2 scenario require that 75 business coaching clients, 75 individual coaching clients, and 20 mentoring clients be served without exceeding 50 hours for any coach. These values must be entered into the appropriate cells before you can use Solver. The following steps add the data for a new scenario.

1. Click cell B18 and then type 50 as the maximum hours for scheduling.

2. Click cell B19 and then type 75 as the number of business coaching clients.

3. Click cell B20 and then type 75 as the number of individual coaching clients.

④ Click cell B21, type   20   as the number of mentoring clients, and then click cell E21 to deselect cell B21 (Figure 9–60).

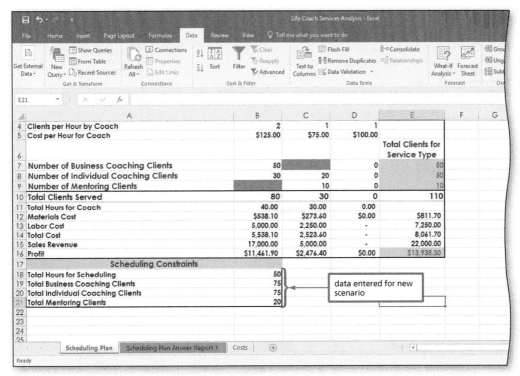

Figure 9–60

To Use Solver to Find a New Solution

Why? *After entering the new values, the total number of clients shown in the range E7:E9 no longer satisfies the scheduling constraints for the Schedule 2 scenario.* You now must use Solver to determine if a solution exists for the constraints of Schedule 2. The following steps use Solver to seek a solution.

①

- Click the Solver button (Data tab | Analyze group) to display the Solver Parameters dialog box with the objective cell, changing cells, and constraints used with the previous scenario (Figure 9–61).

 Why am I not updating the constraints?

When you set up the constraints in Solver for Schedule 1, you used cell references rather than actual values for the number of each type of client. Entering the new values in cells B18:B21 automatically updated the constraints.

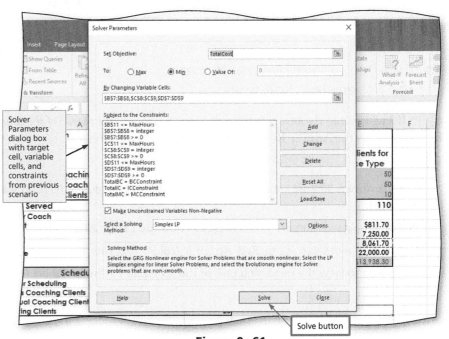

Figure 9–61

2

- Click the Solve button (Solver Parameters dialog box) to solve the problem using Solver and display the Solver Results dialog box.

- Click Answer in the Reports list to select a report type (Figure 9–62).

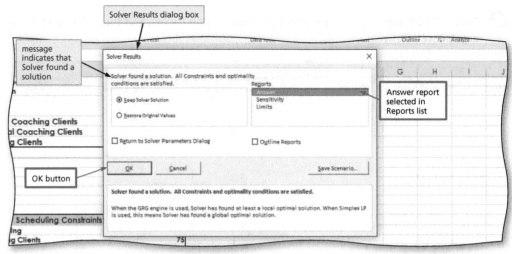

Figure 9–62

3

- Click the OK button (Solver Results dialog box) to display the solution found by Solver (Figure 9–63).

Q&A What did Solver accomplish?

As shown in Figure 9–63, Solver found a solution that satisfies all of the constraints and minimizes the total cost. In this new scenario, total cost will be $13,293.65.

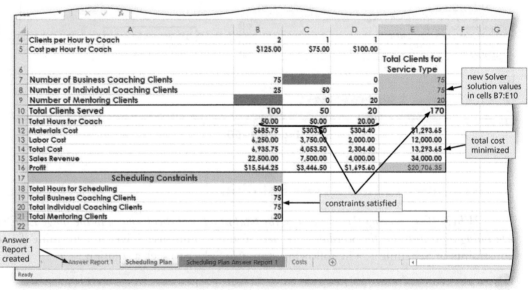

Figure 9–63

To View the Solver Answer Report for the Schedule 2 Solution

1 ANALYZE WORKBOOK FORMULAS | 2 SET DATA VALIDATION RULES | 3 CUSTOMIZE ADD-INS
4 SOLVE COMPLEX PROBLEMS | 5 CREATE & EVALUATE SCENARIOS | 6 PRODUCE REPORTS

Why? *Viewing the answer report allows you to compare the results of the Schedule 1 and Schedule 2 solutions.* The next step views the Answer Report for the Schedule 2 solution.

1

- Drag the Answer Report 1 sheet tab to the right of the Scheduling Plan Answer Report 1 sheet tab to move the worksheet.

- Rename the Answer Report 1 worksheet as **Scheduling Plan Answer Report 2**.

- Change the sheet tab color to 'Red, Accent 6' (column 10, row 1).

- Scroll down to view the remaining cells of the Schedule 2 Answer Report (Figure 9–64).

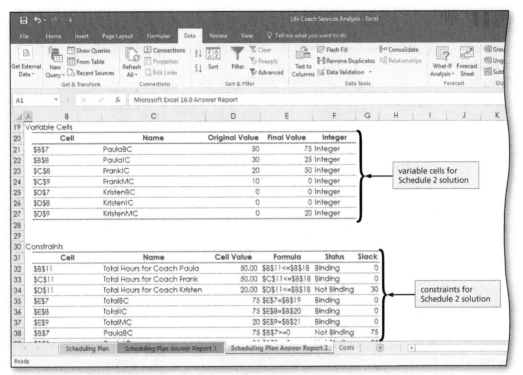

Figure 9–64

To Save the Second Solver Solution as a Scenario

1 ANALYZE WORKBOOK FORMULAS | 2 SET DATA VALIDATION RULES | 3 CUSTOMIZE ADD-INS
4 SOLVE COMPLEX PROBLEMS | 5 CREATE & EVALUATE SCENARIOS | 6 PRODUCE REPORTS

Why? *With a second scenario created, you can begin to take advantage of the Scenario Manager.* The Scenario Manager allows you to compare multiple scenarios side by side. In order to use the Scenario Manager for this, you first must save the second Solver solution as a scenario. The following steps save the second Solver solution as a scenario.

- Make Scheduling Plan the active worksheet.

- Click the 'What-If Analysis' button (Data tab | Forecast group) to display the What-If Analysis menu (Figure 9–65).

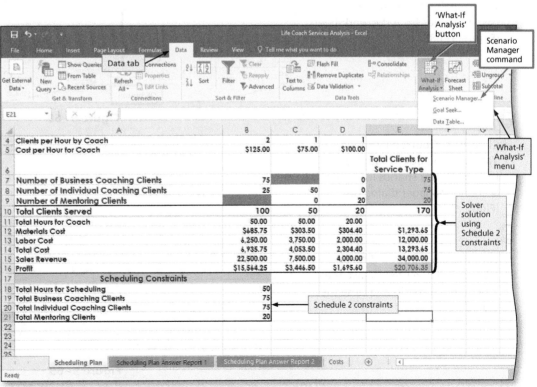

Figure 9–65

- Click Scenario Manager on the What-If Analysis menu to display the Scenario Manager dialog box (Figure 9–66).

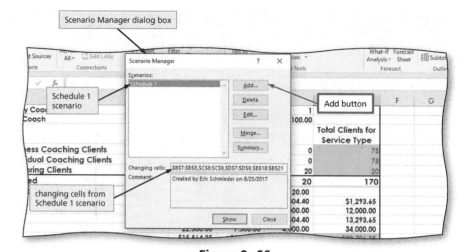

Figure 9–66

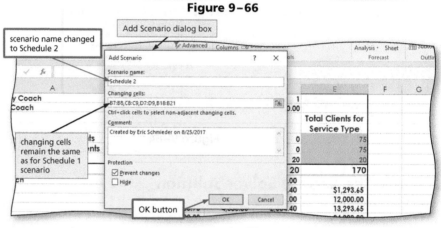

- Click the Add button (Scenario Manager dialog box) to display the Add Scenario dialog box.

- Type **Schedule 2** in the Scenario name text box to name the new scenario (Figure 9–67).

Figure 9–67

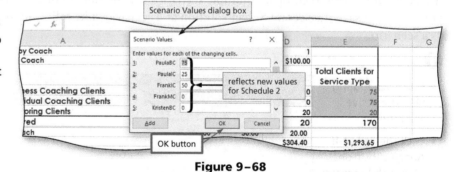

- Click the OK button (Add Scenario dialog box) to display the Scenario Values dialog box with the current values from the worksheet (Figure 9–68).

Figure 9–68

- Click the OK button (Scenario Values dialog box) to display the updated Scenarios list in the Scenario Manager dialog box (Figure 9–69).

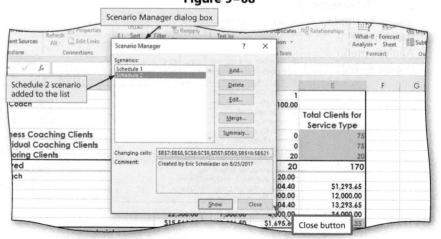

- Click the Close button (Scenario Manager dialog box) to save the Schedule 2 scenario and close the dialog box.

Figure 9–69

To Show a Saved Scenario

Why? *You can display and review any scenario in the workbook by using the Show button in the Scenario Manager dialog box.* The following steps display the Schedule 1 scenario created earlier.

- Click the 'What-If Analysis' button (Data tab | Forecast group) to display the What-If Analysis menu.

- Click Scenario Manager on the What-If Analysis menu to display the Scenario Manager dialog box.

- Click the scenario of interest, Schedule 1 in this case, to select it (Figure 9–70).

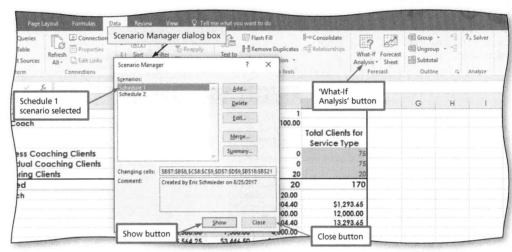

Figure 9–70

- Click the Show button (Scenario Manager dialog box) to display the data for the selected scenario in the worksheet.

- Click the Close button (Scenario Manager dialog box) to close the dialog box (Figure 9–71).

Q&A Do I have to use the Scenario Manager to switch between scenarios?
Once you have viewed two or more scenarios consecutively, you can use the Undo and Redo commands to switch between them as an alternative to using the Scenario Manager.

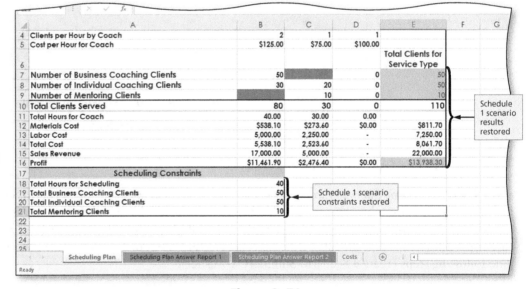

Figure 9–71

Summarizing Scenarios

You can create a Scenario Summary worksheet or a Scenario PivotTable worksheet to review and analyze various what-if scenarios when making decisions. A Scenario Summary worksheet, generated by the Scenario Manager, is a worksheet in outline format (Figure 9–72a) that you can print and manipulate just like any other worksheet. Module 6 presented skills that you can use to manipulate outline features for information presentation.

BTW
Scenario Summary Details
Clicking the show detail button on the Scenario Summary worksheet will display any information entered in the Comments box of the Scenario Manager dialog box, along with creation and modification information.

The Scenario PivotTable worksheet (Figure 9–72b) generated by the Scenario Manager also is a worksheet that you can print and manipulate like other worksheets. PivotTables summarize large amounts of data, and can be rearranged and regrouped to show the data in various forms. Module 8 presented skills that can be used to analyze summary data using PivotTables. The Scenario PivotTable worksheet allows you to compare the results of multiple scenarios.

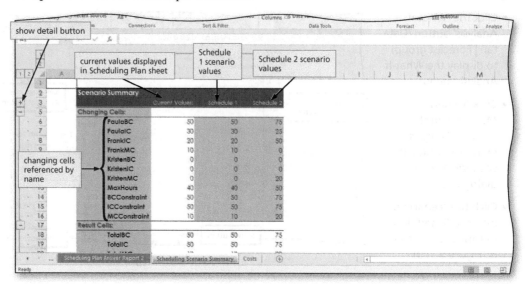

(a) Scheduling Scenario Summary

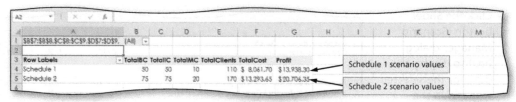

(b) Scheduling Scenario PivotTable

Figure 9–72

To Create a Scenario Summary Worksheet

1 ANALYZE WORKBOOK FORMULAS | 2 SET DATA VALIDATION RULES | 3 CUSTOMIZE ADD-INS
4 SOLVE COMPLEX PROBLEMS | 5 CREATE & EVALUATE SCENARIOS | 6 PRODUCE REPORTS

Why? *A Scenario Summary worksheet is a useful decision-making tool.* The Scenario Summary worksheet in Figure 9–72a shows the number of each type of coaching service scheduled and total cost of the scheduled services for the current worksheet values and the Schedule 1 and Schedule 2 scenarios. The optimal number of each type of service to be scheduled for each coach, as calculated by Solver, is shown for both scheduling plans. The following steps create a Scenario Summary worksheet.

- Click the 'What-If Analysis' button (Data tab | Forecast group) to display the What-If Analysis menu.

- Click Scenario Manager on the What-If Analysis menu to display the Scenario Manager dialog box (Figure 9–73).

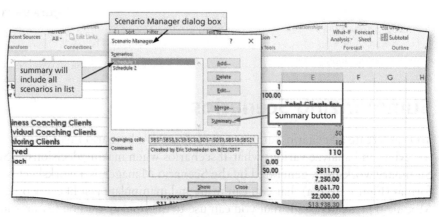

Figure 9–73

2

- Click the Summary button (Scenario Manager dialog box) to display the Scenario Summary dialog box.

- Click the Collapse Dialog button (Scenario Summary dialog box) and then select the cells E7:E10, E14, and E16. (You can use CTRL+click to select multiple cells or add commas in between selecting each range or cell.)

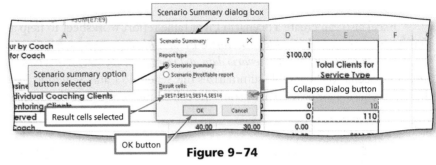

Figure 9–74

- Click the Expand Dialog button to return to the Scenario Summary dialog box (Figure 9–74).

3

- Click the OK button (Scenario Summary dialog box) to generate a Scenario Summary report.

- Rename the Scenario Summary worksheet as **Scheduling Scenario Summary** to provide a descriptive name for the sheet.

- Change the sheet tab color to 'Gray-80%, Text 2' (column 4, row 1).

- Drag the Scheduling Scenario Summary sheet tab to the right of the Scheduling Plan Answer Report 2 sheet tab to reposition the worksheet in the workbook (Figure 9–75).

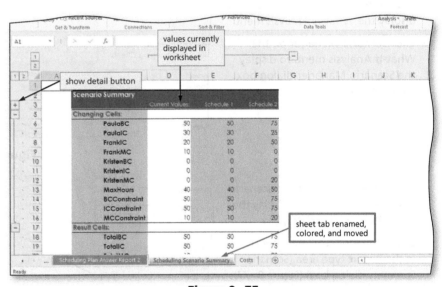

Figure 9–75

Q&A

What is shown in the Scheduling Scenario Summary worksheet?

The Scheduling Scenario Summary worksheet shows the current values in the Scheduling Plan worksheet next to the results of any scenarios you have created. In Figure 9–75, current values are shown in column D, and scenarios Schedule 1 and Schedule 2 are shown side by side (in columns E and F) allowing you to compare results and determine the best available option.

Working with an Outlined Worksheet

Excel automatically outlines the Scheduling Scenario Summary worksheet. The symbols for expanding and collapsing the rows appear above and to the left of the worksheet. You can hide or display levels of detail by using the hide detail and show detail symbols. You can also use the row- and column-level show detail buttons to collapse or expand rows and columns.

The outline feature is especially useful when working with very large worksheets. With smaller worksheets, the feature may not provide any real benefits. You can remove an outline by clicking the Ungroup arrow (Data tab | Outline group) and then clicking Clear Outline on the Ungroup menu.

To Create a Scenario PivotTable Worksheet

Excel also can create a Scenario PivotTable report worksheet to help analyze and compare the results of multiple scenarios. ***Why create a Scenario PivotTable report worksheet?*** *A Scenario PivotTable report worksheet gives you the ability to summarize the scenario data and reorganize the rows and columns to obtain different views of the summarized data.* The Scenario PivotTable summarizes the Schedule 1 and Schedule 2 scenarios and displays the result cells for the two scenarios for easy comparison. The following steps create the Scenario PivotTable worksheet.

- Click the Scheduling Plan sheet tab to make Scheduling Plan the active worksheet. You may have to scroll through the sheet tabs to locate the worksheet.

- Click the 'What-If Analysis' button (Data tab | Forecast group) to display the What-If Analysis menu.

- Click Scenario Manager on the What-If Analysis menu to display the Scenario Manager dialog box (Figure 9–76).

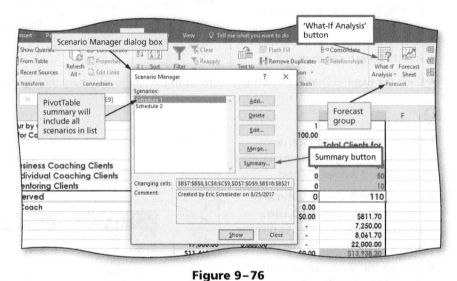

Figure 9–76

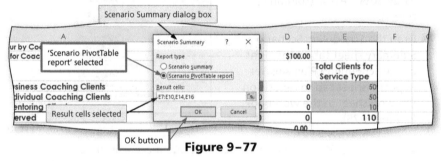

- Click the Summary button (Scenario Manager dialog box) to display the Scenario Summary dialog box.

- Click 'Scenario PivotTable report' in the Report type area (Scenario Summary dialog box) (Figure 9–77).

Figure 9–77

- Click the OK button to create the Scenario PivotTable (Figure 9–78).

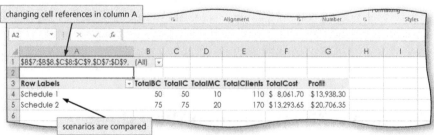

Figure 9–78

- Rename the Scenario PivotTable worksheet as **Scheduling Scenario PivotTable** to provide a descriptive name for the worksheet.

- Change the sheet tab color for the Scheduling Scenario PivotTable worksheet to 'Dark Teal, Accent 1' (column 5, row 1).

- Drag the Scheduling Scenario PivotTable sheet tab to the right of the Scheduling Scenario Summary sheet tab to reposition the worksheet in the workbook.

- Format cells F4:G5 using the Accounting number format.

- Click cell A2 to deselect any other cell.

- If necessary, close the PivotTable Fields task pane (Figure 9–79).

Q&A How can I use the PivotTable? After creating the PivotTable, you can treat it like any other worksheet. Thus, you can print or chart a PivotTable. If you update the data in one of the scenarios, click the Refresh All button (Data tab | Connections group) to update the PivotTable. Note that if you merely change values on a scenario worksheet, it is not the same as changing the scenario. If you want to change the data in a scenario, you must enter the new data using the Scenario Manager.

⑤

- Save the workbook and exit Excel.

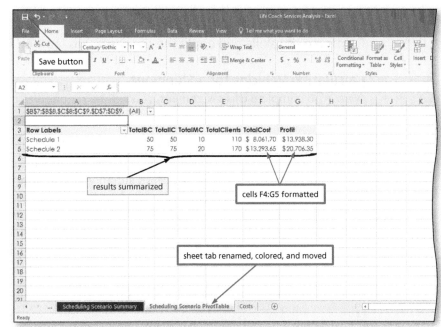

Figure 9–79

Summary

In this module, you learned how to analyze a worksheet using formula auditing techniques and tracer arrows. You established data validation rules, and informed users about the validation rules. You solved a complex problem with Excel, including using trial and error, goal seeking, and Solver. You used the Scenario Manager to manage different problems on the same worksheet, and then summarized the results of the scenarios with a Scenario Summary worksheet and a Scenario PivotTable worksheet.

What decisions will you need to make when creating your next worksheet to solve a complex problem?
Use these guidelines as you complete the assignments in this module and create your own worksheets for evaluating and analyzing data outside of this class.

1. Review and analyze workbook structure and organization.
    a) Review all formulas.
    b) Use precedent and dependent tracing to determine dependencies.
    c) Use formula auditing tools to correct formula errors.
2. Establish data validation rules.
    a) Identify changing cells.
    b) Determine data restrictions to address using data validation.
3. Configure useful add-ins.
    a) Identify missing add-ins.
    b) Use Excel Options to enable necessary add-ins.
    c) Verify inclusion on the ribbon.
4. Determine strategies for problem solving.
    a) Use trial and error to modify input or changing values.
    b) Use Goal Seek.
    c) Use Solver to address multiple constraints and changing cells.
5. Create and store scenarios.
    a) Use the Scenario Manager to keep track of multiple scenarios.
    b) Use a Scenario Summary worksheet to present and compare multiple scenarios.
    c) Use a Scenario PivotTable report to manipulate and interpret scenario results.

CONSIDER THIS: PLAN AHEAD

Apply Your Knowledge

Reinforce the skills and apply the concepts you learned in this module.

Calculating Vehicles for a Shipment

Note: To complete this assignment, you will be required to use the Data Files. Please contact your instructor for information about accessing the Data Files.

Instructions: Run Excel. Open the workbook Apply 9-1 American Auto Imports LLC from the Data Files and then save the workbook as Apply 9-1 American Auto Imports LLC Complete.

American Auto Imports LLC ships automobiles from various European nations for resale in North America. Vehicles are shipped to the North American distribution hub in standard shipping containers with a maximum capacity of 800 cubic feet. Use Solver to find the optimal mix of vehicles so that each shipment includes at least one of each type of vehicle and no more than four of Vehicle 2. Maximize total profit for the shipment. Figure 9–80 shows the completed Costs and Shipping worksheet.

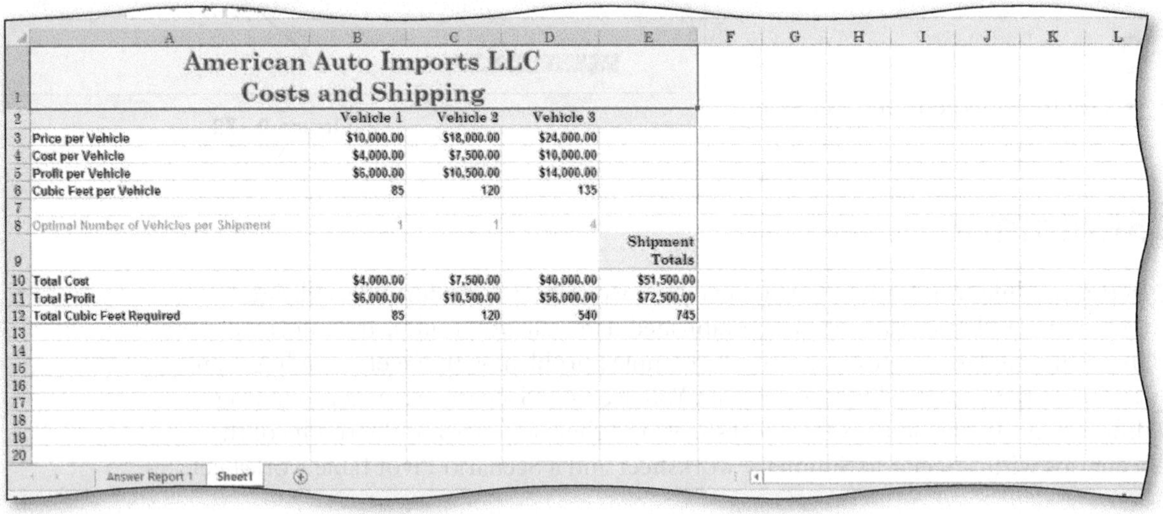

Figure 9–80

Perform the following tasks:

1. Use Solver to find a solution to the problem so that the Total Profit on the shipment (cell E11) is maximized. Allow Solver to change cells B8, C8, and D8. The results in cells B8, C8, and D8 should be integer values. Add constraints to Solver to limit the number of vehicles to no more than four of Vehicle 2 and to include at least one of each vehicle type. The Total Cubic Feet Required (cell E12) should be limited to no more than 800 to accommodate the maximum volume constraint. Use the Simplex LP option in Solver. Solver should find the answer as shown in Figure 9–80.

2. Instruct Solver to create the Answer Report for your solution.

3. Trace precedents for cell E12 by clicking the Trace Precedents button (Formulas tab | Formula Auditing group) two times. Remove the precedent arrows. Trace dependents for cell C8 by clicking the Trace Dependents button (Formulas tab | Formula Auditing group) two times. Remove the dependent arrows.

4. Use the Watch Window to monitor cells E10:E12. Change values in the range B8:D8 and view changes in the Watch Window. Close the Watch Window.

5. If requested by your instructor, add the month and year of your birth to the end of the first line in cell A1.

6. Save the workbook. Submit the revised workbook in the format specified by your instructor.

7. ⊛ How would you adjust the constraints to further investigate maximizing total profit? Which constraints would you change and why?

Extend Your Knowledge

Extend the skills you learned in this module and experiment with new skills. You may need to use Help to complete the assignment.

Working with Data Validation Rules

Note: To complete this assignment, you will be required to use the Data Files. Please contact your instructor for information about accessing the Data Files.

Instructions: Run Excel. Open the workbook Extend 9-1 Travel League Registration and then save the workbook as Extend 9-1 Travel League Registration Complete.

You have been asked to create data validation rules in an Excel worksheet that calculates registration fees for a travel league program that runs three leagues: baseball/softball, football, and soccer. These leagues are popular and space is limited, so players are restricted to one league per year. Registration fees vary according to the league. The league provides some add-on services such as equipment and private coaching. They also offer a discount for registrations paid in full when registering. Figure 9–81 shows the completed League Registration worksheet.

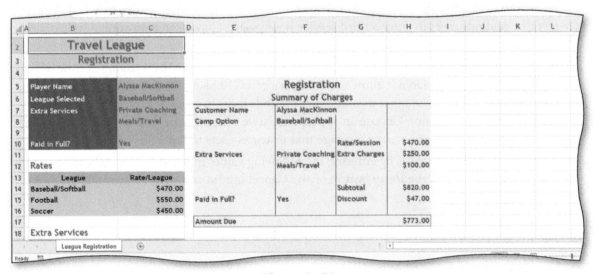

Figure 9–81

Perform the following tasks:

1. In cell C5 on the League Registration worksheet, enter a data validation rule that allows users to enter any value. Use the following:

   Input message title: Player Name

   Input message: Please enter the player's full name.

   Error alert title: Input Error

   Error message: Enter player name.

   Error alert style: Stop

2. In cell C6, enter a data validation rule that requires users to select a league from a list. Allow users to select the data from a list of leagues, which is contained in the range B14:B16. Do not allow users to leave cell C6 blank. Use the following for data validation:

   Input message title: Which League?

   Input message: Click the arrow to select the desired league.

   Error alert title: Invalid League

   Error message: Select Baseball/Softball, Football, or Soccer from the list.

   Error alert style: Stop

Continued >

Extend Your Knowledge *continued*

3. In cell C7, enter another data validation rule that allows users to select a valid entry from a list of extra services, which are included in cells B20:B22. These are optional services, so you can allow users to leave cell C7 blank. For the input message, use an appropriate title and display text that reminds users to enter the first extra service the customer needs. Choose a style of error alert considering that if users enter a service, they must select one of the three services in the list. Enter an appropriate error alert title and an error message that instructs users to select a service from the list.

4. In cell C8, enter a data validation rule that uses the custom formula =AND(C8<>C7,C8<>C9) as its validation criteria to verify that the value entered in cell C8 is not the same as the value in cell C7 or C9. For the input message, use an appropriate title and display text that reminds users to enter a second service if desired. Choose a style of error alert considering that if users enter a second service, they must enter one of the three services not already entered. Enter an appropriate error alert title and an error message.

5. In cell C9, enter a data validation rule that uses a custom formula similar to the one you entered for cell C8. This formula, however, should verify that the value entered in cell C9 is not the same as the value in cell C7 or C8. For the input message, use an appropriate title and display text that reminds users to enter a third service if necessary. Choose an appropriate style of error, error alert title, and error message.

6. In cell C10, enter a data validation rule that instructs users to enter Yes if paying at time of registration, No if not. Do not allow users to leave cell C10 blank. Use Payment as the input message title and enter an input message that reminds users to enter Yes if paying at time of registration, and No if not. Choose an appropriate style of error alert. Use Invalid Entry as the error alert title and enter an error message that instructs users to enter Yes or No.

7. Test the data validation rules by entering the following values in the specified cells. If an error message appears, Click the Retry button or the Cancel button and then enter valid data.

   C5: Alyssa MacKinnon

   C6: Baseball/Softball

   C7: Private Coaching

   C8: Meals/Travel

   C9:

   C10: Yes

8. If requested by your instructor, enter the following text in cell E20: **Registered by <yourname>**, substituting your initials for <yourname>.

9. Save the workbook. Submit the revised workbook in the format specified by your instructor.

10. ✳ The range C7:C9 used two different approaches to prompting users for information, selecting from a list or typing information based on a screen prompt. Which do you think is more effective, and why? List a weakness of the approach you feel is more effective.

Expand Your World

Create a solution that uses cloud and web technologies by learning and investigating on your own from general guidance.

Add-ins for Excel Online

Problem: You use Excel Online through your OneDrive account and understand that there are limitations to the online versions of the Office apps compared to the desktop applications, but are interested in what add-ins may improve your overall productivity with Excel Online.

Instructions:
1. Sign into OneDrive and create a new workbook using Excel Online.
2. Explore the Office Add-ins collection available from the Insert tab of the ribbon in the new workbook.
3. Browse options in the Education and Productivity categories of the Store as well as those in another category of your choice.
4. Create a document that summarizes the features of an add-in from each of the three categories.
5. Save the document. Submit the document as specified by your instructor.
6. ✳ Compare the add-ins available in Excel 2016 to those available for Excel Online. What are the strengths and weaknesses of each? Which would you recommend, and why?

In the Labs

Design, create, modify, and/or use a workbook following the guidelines, concepts, and skills presented in this module. Labs 1 and 2, which increase in difficulty, require you to create solutions based on what you learned in the module; Lab 3 requires you to apply your creative thinking and problem-solving skills to design and implement a solution.

Lab 1: **Reaching Monthly Budget Goals**

Note: To complete this assignment, you will be required to use the Data Files. Please contact your instructor for information about accessing the Data Files.

Problem: You want to select the best payback options for a car loan you will be getting. You have created a data table to examine the effects of interest rates from 3.5% to 6.5% for a loan. You want to use Goal Seek to determine how many months it will take to pay off a loan of $22,000.00 with an interest rate of 5.9% using different monthly payment goals.

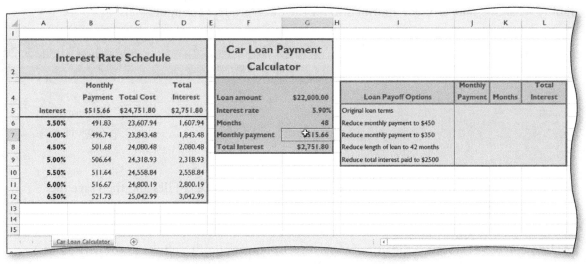

Figure 9–82

Perform the following tasks:
1. Open the workbook Lab 9-1 Car Loan from the Data Files and then save the workbook as Lab 9-1 Car Loan Complete (Figure 9–82).
2. Enter a loan amount of 22,000 (cell G4), interest rate of 5.9% (cell G5), and months of 48 (cell G6) in the payment calculator portion of the workbook.

Continued >

In the Labs *continued*

3. Enter the Monthly Payment, Months, and Total Interest Paid values from the Car Loan Payment Calculator in the Original loan terms row of the Loan Payoff Options table found in the range I4:L9.

4. Select cell G7. Use Goal Seek (Data tab | Forecast group) to determine how many months you will need to pay off the loan if you pay $450.00 per month by setting cell G7 to the value 450 and changing cell G6. Update the Loan Payoff Options table with the results of this Goal Seek.

5. Use Goal Seek to determine how many months you would need to pay off the loan if you pay $350.00 per month. Update the Loan Payoff Options table with the results of this Goal Seek.

6. Reduce the loan term to 42 months and record the monthly payment and total interest paid in the Loan Payoff Options table.

7. If requested by your instructor, enter your name in cell I2.

8. Save the workbook. Submit the revised workbook as specified by your instructor.

9. ☀ Use Goal Seek to determine the Monthly Payment and Months for the final option in the Loan Payoff Options table, reducing the total interest paid to $2500. Which variable did you choose to change? What other variable could you change to reach a total interest of $2,500?

Lab 2: **Finding the Optimal Product Mix**

Note: To complete this assignment, you will be required to use the Data Files. Please contact your instructor for information about accessing the Data Files.

Problem: Michaels Chocolates sells chocolates in single bars, 6-packs, and 12-packs to convenience and grocery stores. They are expanding to a national chain big box store where they have purchased 45 square feet of shelf space. They want to optimize the use of that shelf space to ensure that they showcase all three configurations of their product while maximizing profit as best they can. Table 9–4 shows the pertinent information for the three product configurations.

Table 9–4 Michaels Chocolates Information			
Item	**Profit per Item**	**Square Feet per Item**	**Display Constraints**
Single bars	0.08	0.0625	50 maximum
6-packs	0.45	0.4	30 minimum
12-packs	0.88	0.75	30 minimum

Perform the following tasks:

1. Open the workbook Lab 9-2 Michaels Chocolates from the Data Files and then save the workbook with the file name, Lab 9-2 Michaels Chocolates Complete.

2. Enter the data in Table 9–4 into the worksheet.

3. Use Solver to determine the mix of items that maximizes profit, subject to the constraints shown in Table 9–4. Use the Simplex LP option in Solver. Instruct Solver to create an Answer Report if it can find a solution to the problem. Save the scenario as Maximize Profit 1. (Hint: use the Save Scenario button in the Solver Results dialog box.) Rename the Answer Report containing the scenario as Maximize Profit 1. Figure 9–83 shows the values Solver should find.

	Singles	6-Packs	12-Packs	
Michaels Chocolates				
Stock Plan, Big Box Store				
5 Profit per Item	$0.08	$0.45	$0.88	
6 Space Taken in Square Feet	0.0625	0.4	0.75	
8 Optimal Number of Each Item	50	30	40	
9				Totals
10 Total Profit per Item	$4.00	$13.50	$35.05	$52.55
11 Total Space per Item in Square Feet	3	12	30	45

Figure 9–83

4. If the company decides to set the maximum number of 12-packs at 30, how would this affect the mix of items? Use Solver to determine the new mix. Instruct Solver to create an Answer Report if it can find a solution to the problem. Save the scenario as Maximize Profit 2, and rename the Answer Report containing the scenario as Maximize Profit 2.

5. Create a Scenario Summary showing the two scenarios you saved in the Scenario Manager.

6. If requested by your instructor, change the name of the store in cell A2 from Big Box Store to <streetname> Store, where <streetname> is the name of the street you lived on in high school.

7. Save the workbook. Submit the workbook as specified by your instructor.

8. ✳ What changes would you suggest to the company to maximize profit, other than raising prices? How could you use scenarios to make your point?

Lab 3: **Consider This: Your Turn**

Apply your creative thinking and problem-solving skills to design and implement a solution.

Using Solver to Plan Professional Development Programs

Part 1:   You have started a new position at a progressive technology company that uses a professional development skill point model in its annual review process. You have been asked to create a worksheet that managers could use with their employees to determine an optimal training plan for professional development. The managers are interested in being able to review combinations of courses for an employee and to vary the length of training. The managers will provide you with a list of courses, and the number of skill points per 15 minutes of coursework, for each entry on the list, for technicians and developers.

   You have explained that this is a complex problem-solving exercise, and that the best approach is to build a simple workbook to test first. Your goal is to create a test workbook that reflects the structure needed to solve this problem. For test data, use four professional development

Continued >

In the Labs *continued*

activities and fictitious skills points per 15-minute block, or unit. You will want to solve for how many units of different types, or the same type, of coursework would give the individual the most benefit, subject to constraints. You can constrain which courses the individual can elect to register and how many units of each course he or she does. As indicated, you need to take an individual's position into account. You will have different skill points for technicians and developers for each unit of each course.

Part 2: In addition to type and length of course, what other information would you consider building into a more complex model? What are the challenges associated with introducing the information you are suggesting?

10 | Data Analysis with Power Tools and Creating Macros

Objectives

You will have mastered the material in this module when you can:

- Explain Excel's power tools
- Customize the ribbon and enable data analysis
- Use the Get & Transform data commands
- Create a query using Query Editor
- Build a PivotTable using Power Pivot
- Explain data modelling
- Create a measure
- View cube functions

- Use Power View
- Create tiles in a Power View report
- Use 3D Maps
- Save a tour as an animation
- Explain Power BI
- Create hyperlinks
- Use the macro recorder to create a macro
- Execute a macro

Introduction

Excel has a wide range of interlinked power tools — Get & Transform, Power Pivot, Power View, 3D Maps, and Power BI (Business Intelligence) — to analyze business data, whether you need to export data for business intelligence, pivot or manipulate data to find trends, create data models, or show data more visually.

Table 10–1 describes the five power tools available with Excel 2016. In this module, you only will touch on each of the power tools. The topic is vast and would require a lot of time and data modelling experience to explore all of the features associated with each tool. Power Pivot and Power View are not available in all versions of Excel. While you may have limited access to these tools, you will be able to work through the majority of the steps in this module.

Table 10–1 Power Tools	
Tool	**Purpose**
Get & Transform (formerly called Power Query)	The Get & Transform commands enable you to extract, connect, refine, and transform large amounts of data into an accessible Excel file. You can use Get & Transform to exert greater control over columns, formulas, and filtering tools, and also to modify data types and extract PivotTables.
Power Pivot	Power Pivot enables you to import and compare large amounts of data from multiple sources to build analytical relationships. You can use Power Pivot to create and model data tables, feed data to other Power Tools, and use data analysis expressions. Power Pivot is not available with all versions of Excel.
Power View	Power View is an interactive visualization tool used to provide a drag-and-drop interface for rapid model building. You can use Power View to connect to different data models within the same workbook, create new relationships among current data, and introduce key performance indicators (KPIs) based on those relationships. Power View can group (or smart group) data automatically to create advanced pie charts, maps, data cards, and other data visualizations.
3D Maps (formerly called Power Map)	3D Maps let you plot and visualize geographic or temporal data on a three-dimensional map. With filtering, you can compare how different factors affect your data. You can use a 3D Map to build custom regions, capture screenshots, and build cinematic time tours or animations through your data.
Power BI	Power BI, or Power Business Intelligence, is an Excel-based cloud tool that combines the other Power Tools with some additional features to enable you to find and visualize data, share, and collaborate. Power BI includes a wide range of forecasting tools, a drag-and-drop canvas, dashboards, report generation, and data modelling. Currently Power BI is available only to businesses, Office 365 subscribers, or as a download.

In addition to using Excel's power tools, you will create hyperlinks to move quickly to other parts of the workbook, animations, and external websites. You also will record a macro to automate a task.

Project — Business Decisions Demographics

The project in this module follows proper design guidelines and uses Excel to create the workbook shown in Figures 10 – 1 and 10 – 2. Business Decisions is a data analytics firm that specializes in examining raw data, looking for patterns, correlations, and other associations to help companies and organizations make better business decisions. Business Decisions has a new client who wants to open a business offering high-end replacement windows in South Carolina, but who first needs to understand the demographics of various communities who could support her business. Making use of data from the U.S. Census Bureau, Business Decisions plans to present several forms of visual data to its client using Excel's power tools.

Figure 10–1a shows the opening worksheet that includes a picture and hyperlinks to the other pages. Figure 10–1b queries the external data to display the top 15 most populous counties. Figure 10–1c lists the cities, along with the number of housing units and total area from a different data table.

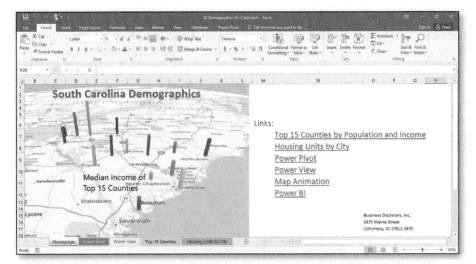

(a) Homepage with Hyperlinks

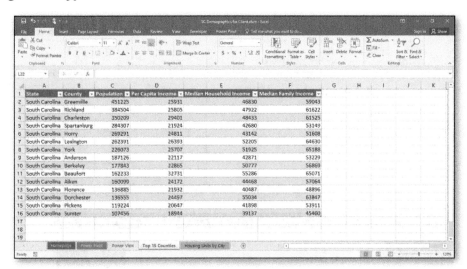

(b) Top 15 Most Populous Counties

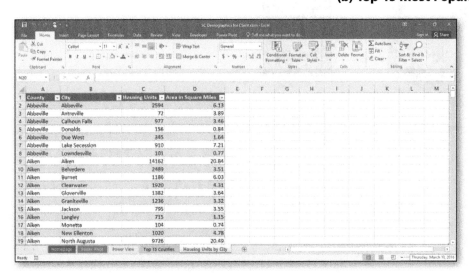

(c) Housing Units by City

Figure 10–1

Figure 10–2a displays a PivotTable that merges the two data sources to display the number of housing units per county. Figure 10–2b displays a Power View report. Figure 10–2c displays the data represented in Power BI. Power BI (pronounced bee-eye) or Business Intelligence is a powerful web-based tool to visualize and share data. Finally, the data then will be transformed into an interactive map. The 3D Maps window is shown in Figure 10–2d.

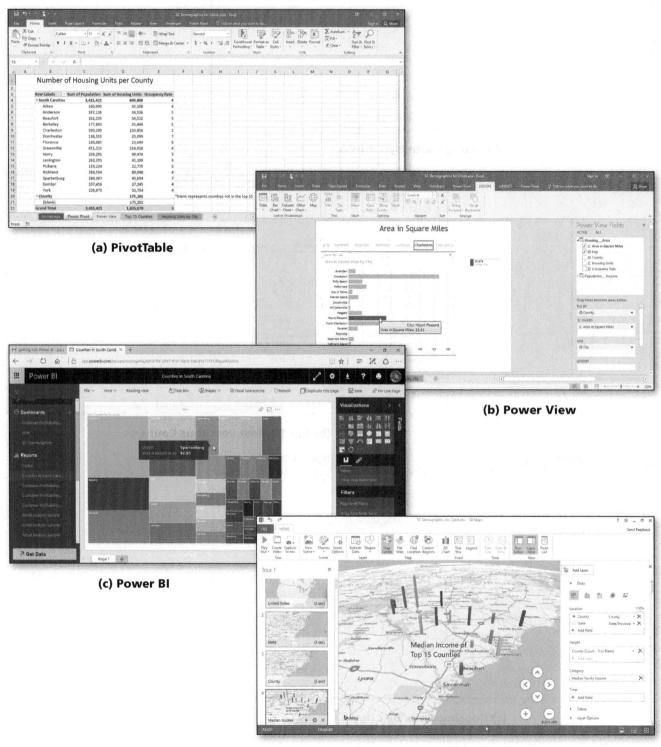

(a) PivotTable

(b) Power View

(c) Power BI

(d) 3D Map

Figure 10–2

Figure 10–3 illustrates the requirements document for the Business Decisions Demographics workbook. It includes the needs, source of data, and other facts about its development.

Worksheet Title	Demographic Analysis for Proposed Car Dealership
Needs	Business Decisions would like to present a variety of data visualizations to the client, including: 1. Top 15 most populous counties in order from most to least. 2. A list of all of the incorporated cities in the state, along with the number of housing units in each, and the total area represented in square miles. 3. A Power Pivot report combining the data sources to show the relationship between city, population, and housing units. 4. A Power View report showing the square miles and housing units for individual cities. 5. An animated map showing the counties with the highest median household income. 6. An attractive opening worksheet with hyperlinks to each of the above items, 1 through 5, and a hyperlink to the Power BI website.
Source of Data	Data is available in two external sources, downloaded from the U.S. Census Bureau: SC Housing Units by City and SC Population & Income by County.
Calculations	Average occupancy rate for each county that is calculated by taking the population of the county divided by the number of housing units. This calculation will appear in the Power Pivot report.

Figure 10–3

Workflow

Recall that in previous modules you imported data from a variety of sources including an Access database, Word table, a comma-delimited text file, and a table from the web. The workflow to create connections for use with the power tools is similar:

- Connect to the data — make connections to data in the cloud, in a service, or from local sources. You can work with the connected data by creating a permanent connection from your workbook to that data source, ensuring that the data you work with is always up-to-date.

- Transform the data — shape the data locally to meet your needs; the original source remains unchanged.

- Combine data from various sources— create a data model from multiple data sources and get a unique view into the data.

- Share the data —save, share, or use transformed data for reports and presentations.

The following roadmap identifies general activities you will perform as you progress through this module:

1. ENABLE DATA ANALYSIS and customize the ribbon.
2. GET and TRANSFORM data.
3. USE POWER PIVOT.
4. USE POWER VIEW.
5. USE 3D MAP.
6. CREATE a home page with HYPERLINKS.
7. RECORD, save, and execute MACROS.

To Create a Workbook in a New Folder

The following steps run Excel and open a blank workbook. Then, after changing the color scheme, you will use the Save As dialog box to create a new folder and save the workbook on your storage device.

1 Run Excel.

2 Click the Blank workbook from the template gallery.

3 If necessary, maximize the Excel window.

4 Set the color scheme to Orange Red.

5 Display the Backstage view, click the Save As tab, and then click Browse to open the Save As dialog box.

6 Browse to your storage device and then click the New folder button. Name the new folder Module 10.

7 Double-click the new folder, Module 10, to open it.

8 In the File name box, type `SC Demographics for Client` as the file name.

9 Click the Save button (Save As dialog box) to save the file in the new folder.

To Copy Data Files

Sometimes data sources move to different locations. You probably have noticed while surfing the web that some webpages no longer exist or have been redirected. On your computer, you may have links that no longer work after moving a file to a different folder. Anytime your workbook is connected to data, there is a chance that the data file might be moved. Therefore, if you are using local data — that is the data stored on your computer — it is a good idea to store the workbook and any connected data sources in the same folder location.

The following steps copy two files from the Data Files to your storage location (the new folder you just created). See the Office 2016 and Windows 10 Module for more information about this process. If you already have downloaded the Data Files to the same storage location that you are using to create and save files in this module, you can skip these steps.

To complete these steps, you will be required to use the Data Files. Please contact your instructor for information about accessing the Data Files.

1 Click the File Explorer button on the Windows taskbar to open a File Explorer window.

2 Navigate to the location of the Data Files for this module.

3 Select both the 'SC Housing Units by City' file and the 'SC Population & Income by County' file, and then copy and paste the files in to the new folder you just created.

4 Close the File Explorer window.

To Enable Data Analysis

1 ENABLE DATA ANALYSIS | 2 GET & TRANSFORM | 3 USE POWER PIVOT | 4 USE POWER VIEW
5 USE 3D MAPS | 6 CREATE HYPERLINKS | 7 RECORD MACROS

The following steps verify that Data Analysis has been enabled in the version of Excel that you are running. *Why? Data analysis commands are required in order to use the power tools.*

1

- Display the Backstage view and then click the Options tab to open the Excel Options dialog box.

- In the left pane of the dialog box, click Advanced to display the Advanced Options.

- Scroll to the Data area.

- If necessary, click to display a check mark in the 'Enable Data Analysis add-ins: Power Pivot, Power View, and Power Map' check box (Figure 10–4).

Q&A I do not see the Enable option. What should I do?

You may have a version of Excel that does not support data analysis and the power tools. Continue with the steps and contact your instructor.

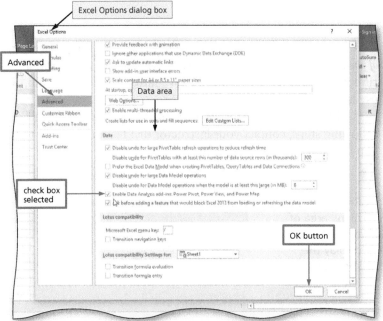

Figure 10–4

2

- Click the OK button (Excel Options dialog box) to close the dialog box and enable the data analysis tools.

Q&A Should I see a change in Excel?

No. Changing the setting assures that you will not see an error message when you try to use the power tools later in the module.

To Add in Power Map

If you could not enable data analysis in the previous steps, you may need to add Power Map to your version of Excel in order to run 3D Maps. Recall from a previous module that you used the Add-ins option to add Solver to Excel. The following steps add in Power Map.

1. Display the Backstage view and then click the Options tab to open the Excel Options dialog box.

2. In the left pane of the dialog box, click Add-ins to display the Add-ins Options.

3. Near the bottom of the dialog box, click the Manage arrow and then click COM Add-ins.

4. Click the Go button to open the COM Add-ins dialog box.

5. Click to display a check mark in the Microsoft Power Map for Excel check box. If you have check boxes for Power View or Power Pivot, select those as well.

6. Click the OK button (COM Add-ins dialog box).

CONSIDER THIS

What should I keep in mind when customizing the ribbon?

- Customize the ribbon when you need to access new features of Excel, or when you regularly need to access commands that are not part of the ribbon already.

- If the new command will be used at various times, with different tabs, consider adding the command or button to the Quick Access Toolbar.

- If you need to add a single command to the ribbon, choose a tab with plenty of room to hold the new command and its new group.

- If you need to add several commands, consider creating a new tab on the ribbon.

- If you are using a computer in a lab situation, reset the ribbon when you are done.

To Customize the Ribbon

The following steps customize the ribbon. *Why? Due to space constraints on the ribbon and the advanced nature of the power tools, some of the commands do not display automatically.* You will enable the Power Pivot tab on the ribbon, add the 'Insert a Power View' button to the Insert tab, and then enable the Developer tab that you will use later in the module.

The Power Pivot tool is not available in all versions of Excel. If you do not see the Power Pivot tab in the following steps, contact your instructor or IT administrator to see if your version of Excel can run Power Pivot; you may have to use an Add-in process.

①

- Right-click a blank area of the ribbon to display the shortcut menu (Figure 10–5).

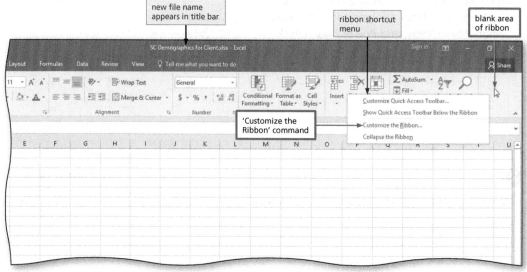

Figure 10–5

②

- Click 'Customize the Ribbon' on the shortcut menu to display the Excel Options dialog box.

- In the Main Tabs area, scroll as necessary, and then click to display a check mark in both the Developer and the Power Pivot check boxes, if necessary (Figure 10–6).

Q&A I do not see Power Pivot. What should I do?
Contact your instructor to see if your version of Excel can run Power Pivot. If not, you can still continue with these steps and use the Developer ribbon.

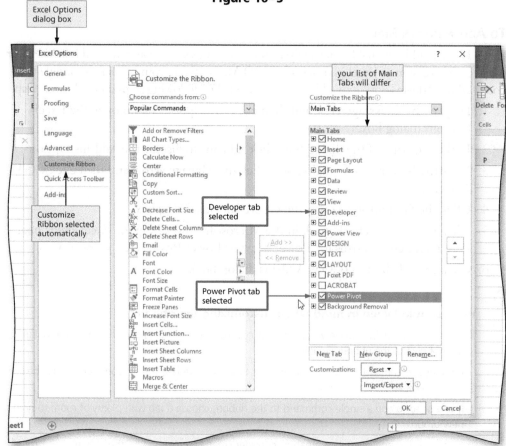

Figure 10–6

- In the Main Tabs area, click Insert (not the check box) to select the Insert tab.

- Click the New Group button to insert a new group on the selected tab (in this case, the Insert tab) (Figure 10–7).

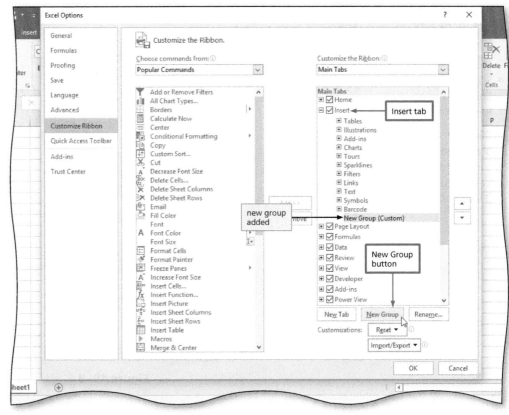

Figure 10–7

- Click the 'Choose commands from' button to display the menu (Figure 10–8).

Q&A Can I add a command directly to a tab?
No. You only can add commands to new groups.

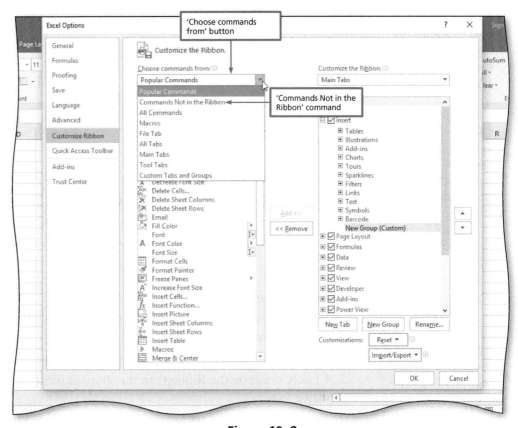

Figure 10–8

- Click 'Commands Not in the Ribbon' to display only those commands.
- Scroll down and click 'Insert a Power View Report' to select it.
- Click the Add button to add the command to the new group (Figure 10–9).

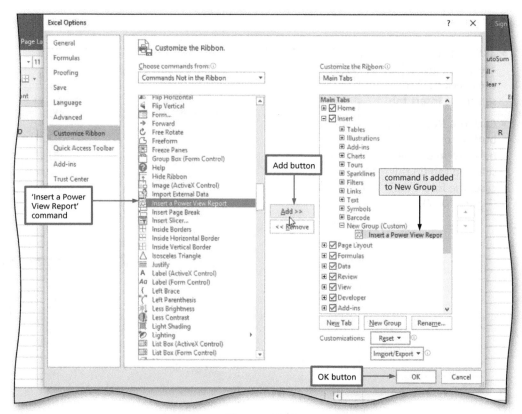

Figure 10–9

- Click the OK button (Excel Options dialog box) to display the customization on the ribbon (Figure 10–10).

Experiment

- Click the Insert tab and look at the new group and new button. Click the Home tab.

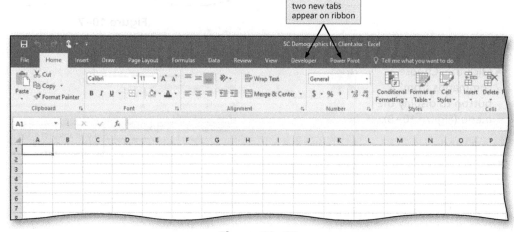

Figure 10–10

Other Ways

1. Display Backstage view, click Options, click Customize Ribbon (Excel Options dialog box), click appropriate check box in Main Tabs list, add necessary commands, click OK button

TO RENAME A NEW GROUP

If you wanted to rename a new group to customize the ribbon further, you would perform the following steps.

1. Right-click a blank area of the ribbon to display the shortcut menu.
2. Click 'Customize the Ribbon' on the shortcut menu to display the Excel Options dialog box.
3. In the Main Tabs area, navigate to and then click 'New Group (Custom)' to select it.
4. Click the Rename button to display the Rename dialog box.

5. Choose an appropriate symbol and enter a display name.

6. Click the OK button (Rename dialog box).

7. Click the OK button (Excel Options dialog box).

Get & Transform

Formerly called Power Query, the Get & Transform commands located on the Data tab allow you to extract, connect, clean, and transform large amounts of data into an accessible Excel table. Importing data in this fashion is different from the way you imported data in previous modules. The Get & Transform commands allow you to edit, as well as query or transform, imported data without making a permanent change to the data. Excel uses a dedicated window named Query Editor to facilitate and display data transformations. Recall that you queried tables in a previous module by searching for and limiting the display of certain data. When you use the Query Editor, you are provided with many more tools to group rows, replace values, remove duplicates, and edit columns, among others. The resulting query table then becomes a displayed subset of the actual data.

BTW

Getting Data from Access Databases
When you click the New Query button (Data Tab | Get & Transform group) and choose an Access database, the Navigator window appears so you can select which table (or tables) you want to use in your query. When you select a table, a preview of its data is shown in the right pane of the Navigator window.

To Get Data

1 ENABLE DATA ANALYSIS | 2 GET & TRANSFORM | 3 USE POWER PIVOT | 4 USE POWER VIEW
5 USE 3D MAPS | 6 CREATE HYPERLINKS | 7 RECORD MACROS

The following steps connect to a table with data provided by the U.S. Census Bureau from the 2010 Census from the state of South Carolina. The table is located in the Data Files. *Why? Connecting with the U.S. Census Bureau website is somewhat cumbersome and requires many steps.* You will use the New Query button (Data tab | Get & Transform group) to connect to the data. When you bring the data into Excel, you are working with a local copy; you will not change the original data source in any way. Should the data source be updated externally however, you easily can refresh your local copy. The local data becomes a table, also called a query.

To complete these steps, you will be required to use the Data Files. Please contact your instructor for information about accessing the Data Files.

- Display the Data tab.

- Click the New Query button (Data tab | Get & Transform group) to display the New Query menu.

- Point to the From File command to display the From File submenu (Figure 10–11).

 Experiment

- Point to the other commands on the New Query menu and look at the various sources from which you can get data. When you are done, point to From File again.

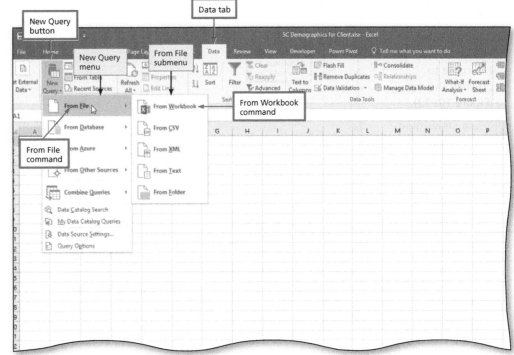

Figure 10–11

2

- Click From Workbook on the From File submenu to display the Import Data dialog box.

- If necessary, navigate to the Module 10 folder to display the files (Figure 10–12).

Q&A Could I have clicked From Web and navigated to the Census data?
Yes; however, you would have had to perform many additional steps to drill down to the desired data for this project.

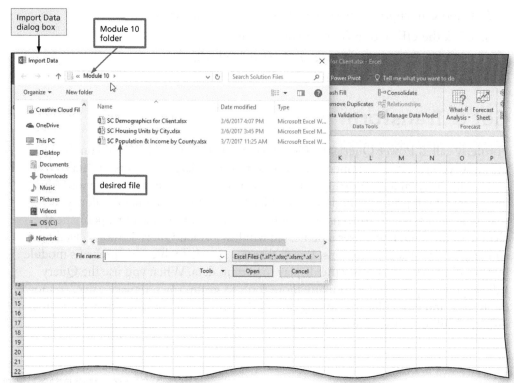

Figure 10–12

3

- Double-click the file named 'SC Population & Income by County' to display the Navigator dialog box.

- Click the table named Population & Income to preview the data (Figure 10–13).

Q&A Could I have used the Get External Data button on the Data tab, as I did in a previous module?
No. Using that command imports the data without the ability to query and transform the data using the power tools.

What does the Edit button do?
If you know that you want to edit the data before creating the query, you can click the Edit button to display the Query Editor window.

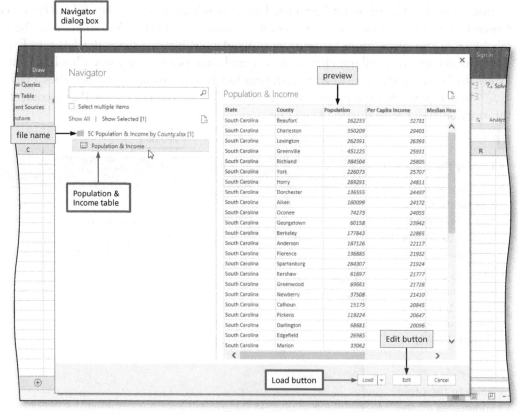

Figure 10–13

4

- Click the Load button (Navigator dialog box) to import the data (Figure 10–14).

Q&A How is the data displayed?
Excel shows 46 rows of data for the counties in South Carolina in a table format.

State	County	Population	Per Capita Income	Median Household Income	Median Family Income
South Carolina	Beaufort	162233	32731	55286	65071
South Carolina	Charleston	350209	29401	48433	61525
South Carolina	Lexington	262391	26393	52205	64630
South Carolina	Greenville	451225	25931	46830	59043
South Carolina	Richland	384504	25805	47922	61622
South Carolina	York	226073	25707	51925	65188
South Carolina	Horry	269291	24811	43142	51608
South Carolina	Dorchester	136555	24497	55034	63847
South Carolina	Aiken	160099	24172	44468	57064
South Carolina	Oconee	74273	24055	42266	52332
South Carolina	Georgetown	60158	23942	42666	54115
South Carolina	Berkeley	177843	22865	50777	56869
South Carolina	Anderson	187126	22117	42871	53229
South Carolina	Florence	136885	21932	40487	48896
South Carolina	Spartanburg	284307	21924	42680	53149
South Carolina	Kershaw	61697	21777	44064	53053
South Carolina	Greenwood	69661	21728	38797	49785
South Carolina	Newberry	37508	21410	41815	49560
South Carolina	Calhoun	15175	20845	36790	51975
South Carolina	Pickens	119224	20647	41898	53911
South Carolina	Darlington	68681	20096	38379	46894
South Carolina	Edgefield	26985	19901	42834	57114

loaded data appears in table format on new sheet

Figure 10–14

To Transform the Data

1 ENABLE DATA ANALYSIS | 2 GET & TRANSFORM | 3 USE POWER PIVOT | 4 USE POWER VIEW
5 USE 3D MAPS | 6 CREATE HYPERLINKS | 7 RECORD MACROS

When you get data using a Get & Transform command, Excel provides advanced editing and querying techniques to use with that data. The Worksheet Queries task pane shows all of the files connected to your workbook. In the following steps you will use the Query Editor to sort the data and only display the top 15 most populous counties. *Why? The client wants you to narrow down the counties to the places with the most people.*

1

- If necessary, display the Data tab.

- If necessary, click the Show Queries button (Data tab | Get & Transform group) to display the Worksheet Queries task pane (Figure 10–15).

Experiment

- Point to the Population & Income query in the Worksheet Queries task pane to display information about the file.

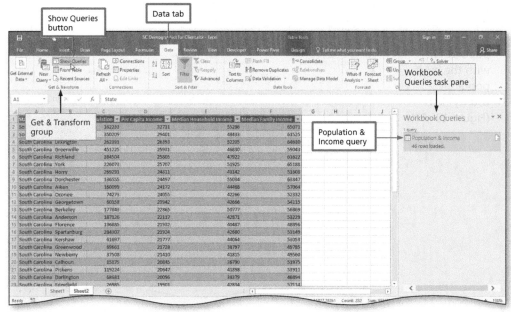

Figure 10–15

2

- Double-click the Population & Income query in the Worksheet Queries task pane to display the Query Editor window.

- In the third column, click the Population column filter button to display the filter menu (Figure 10–16).

Q&A
Is the Query Editor a separate app?
Query Editor is like an app within an app. The Query Editor window has its own ribbon, tabs, and groups and is navigated independently from Excel. The Query Settings task pane allows you to make changes to the data and keeps track of each change, in order.

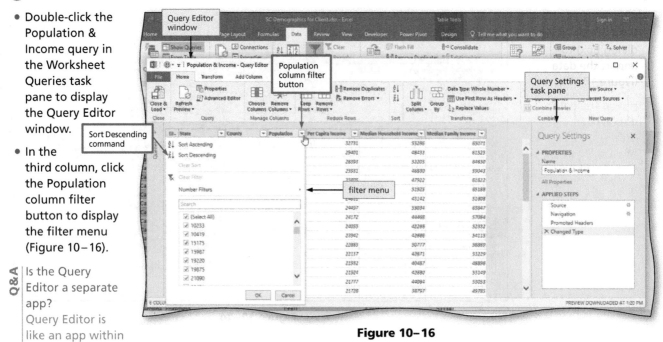

Figure 10–16

3

- On the filter menu, click Sort Descending to sort the data in order by population with the most populous county first (Figure 10–17).

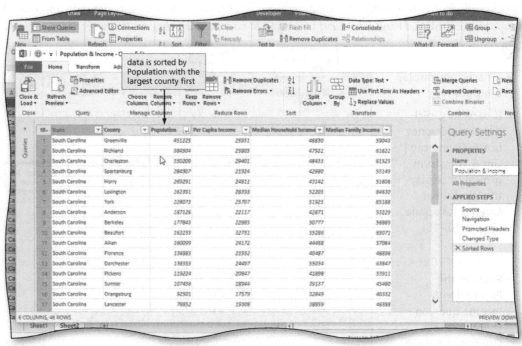

Figure 10–17

4

- Click the Keep
Rows button
(Home tab |
Reduce Rows
group) to
display
the menu
(Figure 10–18).

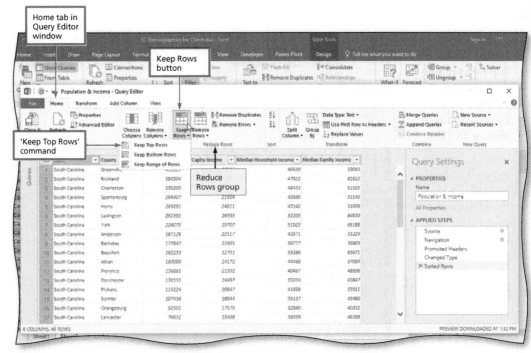

Figure 10–18

5

- Click the 'Keep Top
Rows' command to
display the Keep
Top Rows dialog
box.

- Type **15** in the
Number of
rows text box
(Figure 10–19).

Could I have just
deleted the rows
in the main Excel
window?
You could have;
however, that
would permanently
delete the local
copy of the data.
Using the Query
Editor, you can
restore the data if
you need it later.

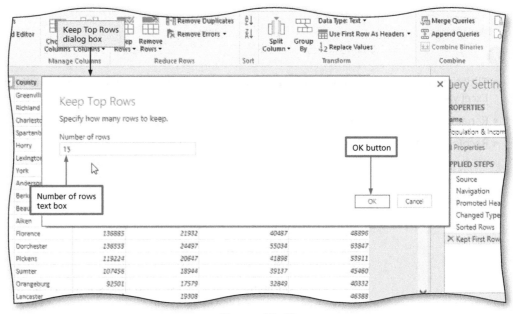

Figure 10–19

- Click the OK button (Keep Top Rows dialog box) to return to the Query Editor window (Figure 10–20).

Q&A What happens if my source data moves?

If you suspect that your source data has moved, display the Query Editor window and then click the Refresh Preview button (Query Editor window | Home tab | Query group). If an error message appears, click the 'Go To Error' button, click the Edit Details button, and then navigate to the new location of the file.

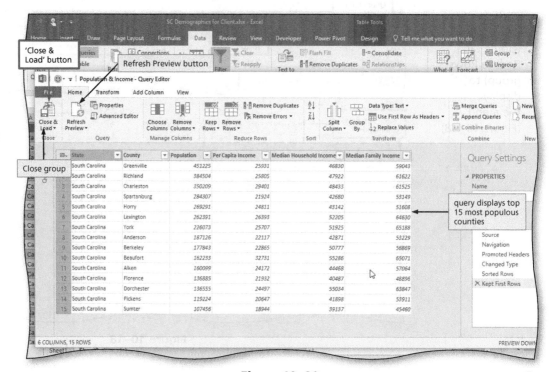

Figure 10–20

- Click the Close & Load button (Home tab | Close group) to load the transformed data into the worksheet in the Excel window.

- Rename the sheet tab with the name Top 15 Counties.

- Recolor the sheet tab with the color Light Green.

Q&A What is the new tab on the ribbon?

It is the Query Tools Query tab (shown in Figure 10–22), which allows you to make additional queries easily.

To Get Another Data Source

The following steps add a second data source to the workbook.

1 In the Excel window, click the New Query button (Data tab | Get & Transform group), point to From File to display the From File submenu, and then click From Workbook to display the Import Data dialog box.

2 If necessary, navigate to the Module 10 folder to display the files.

3 Click the file named 'SC Housing Units by City' to select it and then click the Open button to display the Navigator dialog box.

4 Click the 'Housing & Area' table to preview the data.

5 Click the Load button (Navigator dialog box) to import the data (Figure 10–21).

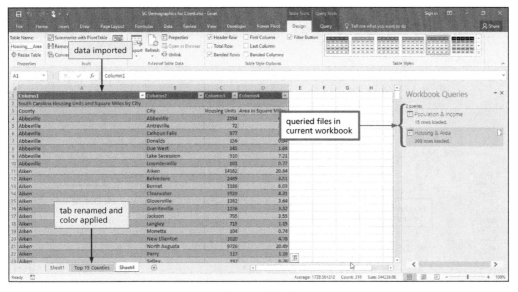

Figure 10–21

To Edit Using the Query Tab

The following steps edit the query to remove a heading from the imported data and to convert the second row into column headings. This time you will use the Query Tools Query tab to access the Query Editor window. *Why? Depending on where you in the process of getting and transforming your data, the Query Tool Query tab may be more convenient than using the Worksheet Queries task pane.* You also will save the file again.

- Display the Query Tools Query tab.

- Click the Edit button (Query Tools Query tab | Edit group) to display the Query Editor window.

- In the Query Editor window, click the Remove Rows button (Home tab | Reduce Rows group) to display the Remove Rows menu (Figure 10-22).

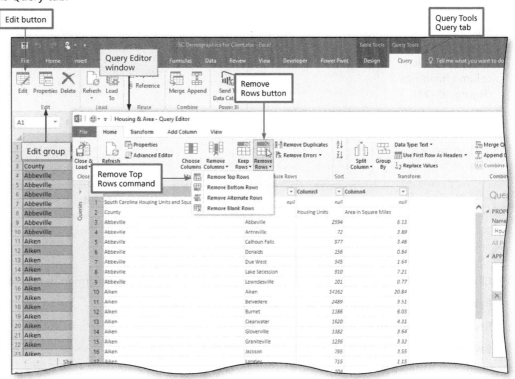

Figure 10–22

2

- Click Remove Top Rows to display the Remove Top Rows dialog box.

- Type 1 in the Number of rows text box (Figure 10–23).

Q&A Why am I removing the first row?
The first row is the title of the imported worksheet; it is not part of the data itself.

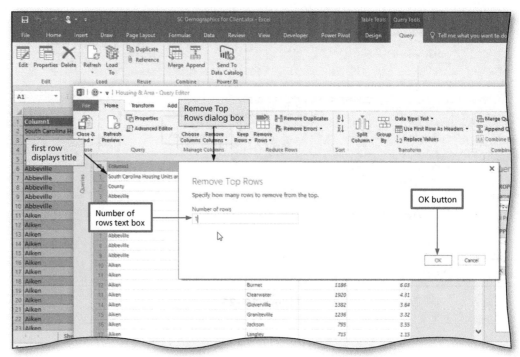

Figure 10–23

3

- Click the OK button (Remove Top Rows dialog box) to remove the first row.

- Click the 'Use First Row As Headers' button (Home tab | Transform group) to use the imported table's column headings (Figure 10–24).

Q&A What is the Applied Steps area in the Query Settings task pane?
The Applied Steps area displays each manipulation that you performed on the data, in order. You can click a step to return to that view of the data or delete the step.

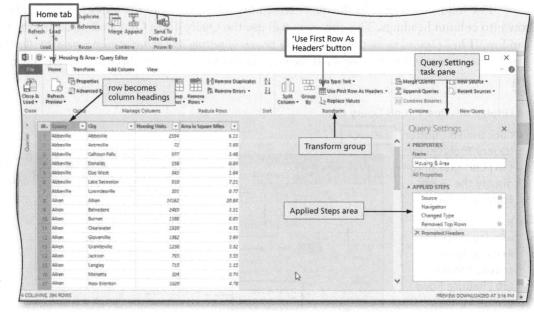

Figure 10–24

4

- Click the Close & Load button (Home tab | Close group) to load the transformed data into the worksheet.

- Rename the sheet tab with the name Housing Units by City.

- Recolor the sheet tab with the color Light Blue.

- Save the file.

Break Point: If you wish to take a break, this is a good place to do so. Exit Excel. To resume at a later time, run Excel, open the file named SC Demographics for Client, and then continue following the steps from this location forward.

Power Pivot

Power Pivot is a tool that extends the analytical functionality of PivotTables in Excel. It includes the capability to include data from multiple data sources into one PivotTable. Valued as a Business Intelligence (BI) tool by the business community, Power Pivot especially is helpful when analyzing large, complex sets of related tables. Using Power Pivot, you can import some or all of the tables from a relational database into Excel in order to analyze the data using PivotTables and the enhanced features.

Data Models

Power Pivot, along with the other power tools, provides a data modelling tool to help you explore, analyze, and manage your data. **Data modelling** is the process of creating a model, simulation, or small-scale representation of data and the relationships among pieces of data. Data modelling often includes multiple ways to view the same data and ensure that all data and processes are identified. A **data model** documents the processes and events to capture and translate complex data into easy-to-understand information. It is an approach for integrating data from multiple tables, effectively building a relational database inside Excel. A **relational database** is any collection of data that can be accessed or reassembled without having to reorganize the tables.

Are data models unique to Power Pivot?

No. You used the concept of a data model when you created PivotTable and PivotChart reports; a field list is a visual representation of a data model. The difference between Power Pivot and a PivotTable is that you can create a more sophisticated data model using Power Pivot. When importing relational data, the creation of a data model occurs automatically when you select multiple tables. However, if the tables are from different sources, they may have to be added to the data model manually.

CONSIDER THIS

1 ENABLE DATA ANALYSIS | 2 GET & TRANSFORM | 3 USE POWER PIVOT | **4 USE POWER VIEW**
5 USE 3D MAPS | 6 CREATE HYPERLINKS | 7 RECORD MACROS

To Add a Query to a Data Model

The following steps add a query to the data model. *Why? You cannot create the Power Pivot PivotTable unless both queries are added to the data model.* You will use the Add to Data Model command. If you do not have Power Pivot, simply read these steps.

1

- If necessary, display the Housing Units by City worksheet and then click in the table to make it active.

- Click Power Pivot on the ribbon to display the Power Pivot tab (Figure 10–25).

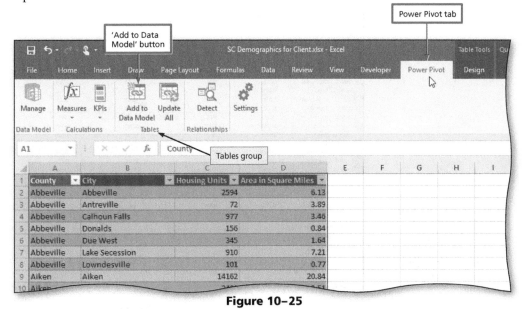

Figure 10–25

● Click the 'Add
to Data Model'
button (Power
Pivot tab | Tables
group) to add the
data on the current
worksheet to the
data model
(Figure 10–26).

Q&A
What window is
displayed?
Excel displays
the maximized
Power Pivot for
Excel window that
contains tabs and
groups used when working with multiple tables from multiple sources.

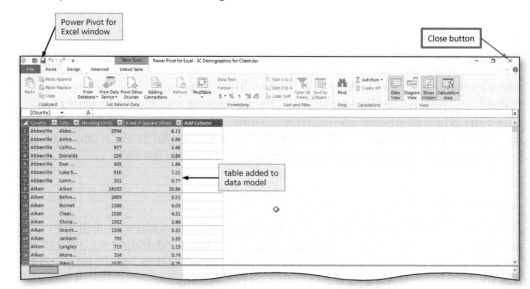

Figure 10–26

● Close the Power Pivot for Excel window to return to the regular Excel window.

To Add Another Query to the Data Model

The following steps add another query to the data model. If you do not have
Power Pivot, skip these steps.

① Click the Top 15 Counties tab to display the worksheet.

② Click any cell in the data.

③ Click the 'Add to Data Model' button (Power Pivot tab | Tables group) to add a second
query to the data model (Figure 10–27).

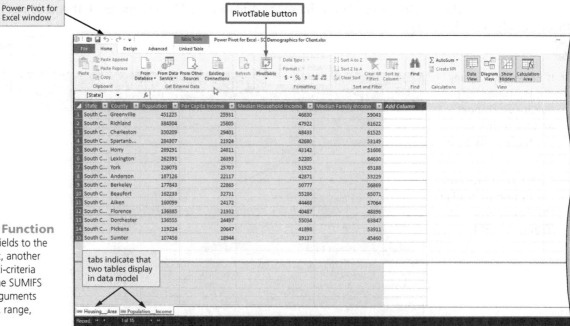

BTW
The SUMIFS Function
Besides adding fields to the
PivotTable report, another
way to find multi-criteria
sums is to use the SUMIFS
function with arguments
of range, critera, range,
criteria, etc.

Figure 10–27

To Build a PivotTable Using Power Pivot

The following steps create a PivotTable using Power Pivot, based on the two queries. *Why? Using Power Pivot provides you with the most flexibility and functionality when building a PivotTable.* If you do not have access to Power Pivot, you can create a regular PivotTable report.

 1

- With the Power Pivot for Excel window still open, click the PivotTable button to display the Create PivotTable dialog box.

- If necessary, click the New Worksheet option button to select it (Figure 10–28).

Q&A Can I make a PivotTable without Power Pivot?

Yes. Click the PivotTable button (Insert tab | Tables group). In the Create PivotTable dialog box, click to display a check mark in the 'Add this data to the Data Model' check box.

Figure 10–28

2

- Click the OK button to create a PivotTable on a new sheet and to display the PivotTable Fields task pane (Figure 10–29).

Q&A Why do I not see both of my tables?

In the PivotTable Fields task pane, click the All tab. If you see a More Tables link, click the Yes button (Create a New Table dialog box).

You later can delete any unused worksheets that might be created by this process.

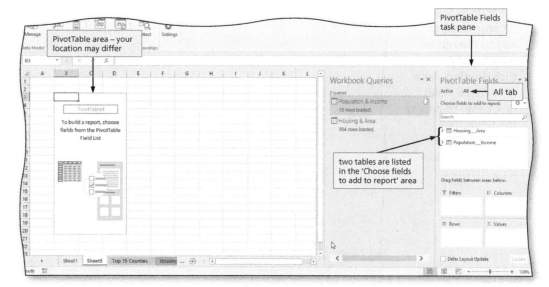

Figure 10–29

3

- In the Choose fields to add to the report area, click Population_Income (PivotTable Fields task pane) to display the fields from the query table.

- Click the check boxes beside the State field and the County field to add the fields to the Rows area.

- Click the Population check box to add the field to the Values area (Figure 10–30).

Why do the query tables use an underscore in their name?

Database structures rarely allow spaces in the names of files or fields. Excel wants to make sure the data can be used in many kinds of databases.

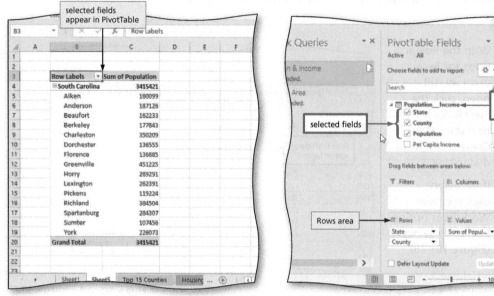

Figure 10–30

4

- Scroll up in the 'Choose fields to add to the report' area and then click Housing_Area (PivotTable Fields task pane) to display the fields from the query table (Figure 10–31).

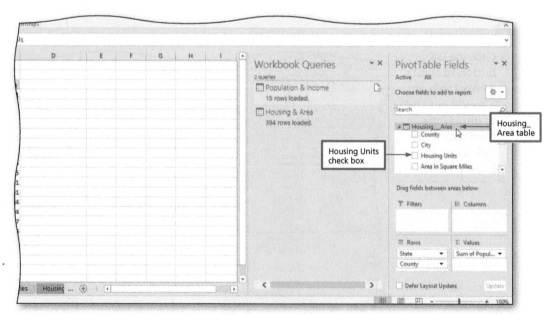

Figure 10–31

- Click the Housing Units check box to add the field to the Values area (Figure 10–32).

Q&A

Why do all of the counties have the same number of housing units?
The PivotTable does not associate the housing units with the counties automatically. You will create that relationship in the next series of steps.

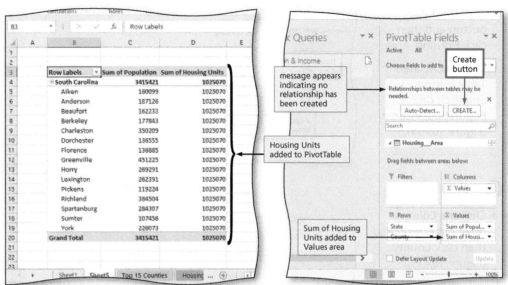

Figure 10–32

To Create a Relationship

1 ENABLE DATA ANALYSIS | 2 GET & TRANSFORM | 3 USE POWER PIVOT | 4 USE POWER VIEW
5 USE 3D MAPS | 6 CREATE HYPERLINKS | 7 RECORD MACROS

A **relationship** is a field or column that two data sources have in common. For example, a payroll file and a human resource file might each have a field named employee_number. Sometimes that field is named identically in the two files and has the same number of rows; other times the name is different. One file might use the field name last_name and another file might call it LastName. Those two fields would have to be manually associated.

When the number of rows are different, the relationship is said to be **one-to-many**. For example, both a client file and an employee file might have a field named salesperson. In the employee file, there is only one record for each salesperson; however, in the client file, several clients might be assigned to the same salesperson.

The following steps create a relationship using the County field. **Why?** Both query tables have a column named County, although it is a one-to-many relationship. The Population_Income query has one line of data for each county. The Housing_Units query table has many cities listed for each county.

- Click the Create button in the PivotTable Fields task pane to display the Create Relationship dialog box (Figure 10–33).

Q&A

I do not have a Create button or it did not work. What should I do?
Click the Relationships button (Data tab | Data Tools) to display the Manage Relationships dialog box. Click the New button.

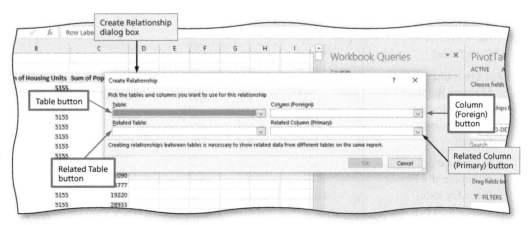

Figure 10–33

• Click the Table button and then click Housing_Area.

• Click the Related Table button and then click Population_Income (Figure 10–34).

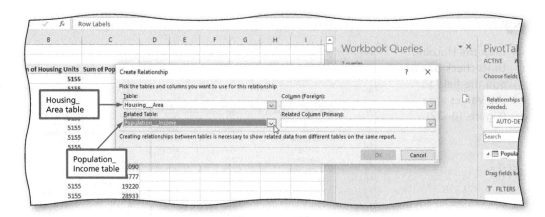

Figure 10–34

• Click the Column (Foreign) button and then click County (Figure 10–35).

Q&A Why is it called a foreign column? Foreign, or foreign key, refers to a *field* in one *table* that uniquely identifies a row in a different table. Even though the names may be the same, the field is foreign to the second table. For most Excel purposes, it does not matter which table you use for the foreign versus primary key.

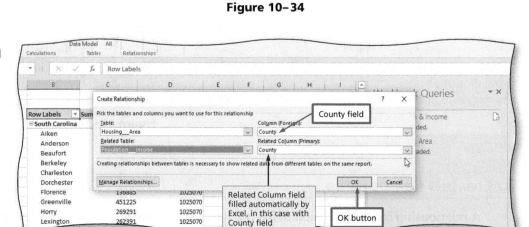

Figure 10–35

• Click the OK button (Create Relationship dialog box) to create the relationship between the tables and adjust the numbers in the PivotTable.

• If Excel displays the Manage Relationships dialog box, click the Close button.

• If necessary, minimize the Power Pivot for Excel window to return to the regular Excel window (Figure 10–36).

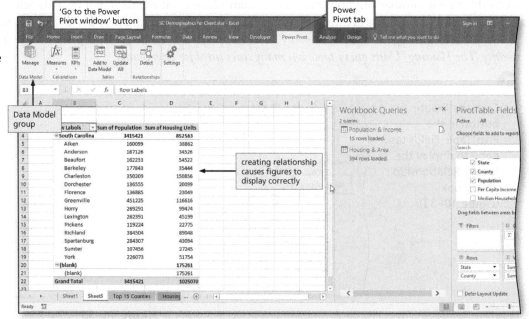

Figure 10–36

Other Ways

1. Click Detect Relationships button (Power Pivot tab | Relationship group), select relationships

To View Relationships

The following steps graphically display the relationship that you created in the previous steps using the Power Pivot window. *Why? Sometimes looking at a picture makes the concept clearer.* If you do not have Power Pivot, simply read these steps.

- Click the 'Go to the Power Pivot window' button (Power Pivot tab | Data Model group) to make the Power Pivot for Excel window active.

- Click the Diagram View button (Home tab | View group) to see a visual display.

- Resize each of the table views to display all of the data, and then drag the tables slightly to see the relationship of one-to-many (Figure 10–37).

- Click the Data View button (Home tab | View group) to return to the Data View.

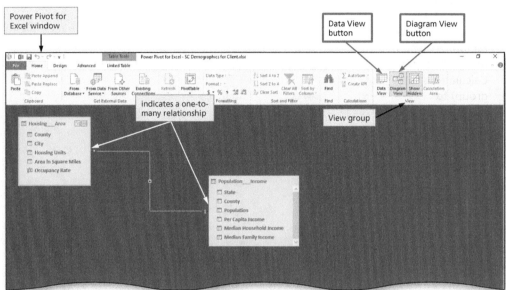

Figure 10–37

TO MANAGE RELATIONSHIPS

You can set up multiple relationships using Power Pivot. You may need to add, edit, or delete relationships at some point. To do this, you would use the Manage Relationships command in the Power Pivot window, as shown in the following steps.

1. Click the 'Go to the Power Pivot window' button (Power Pivot tab | Data Model group) to make the Power Pivot for Excel window active.

2. Display the Design tab and then click the Manage Relationships button in the Power Pivot for Excel window (Design tab | Relationships group) to display the Manage Relationships dialog box.

3. Use the Create, Edit, or Delete button to make changes to the selected relationship and then click the Close button (Manage Relationships dialog box) to close the dialog box.

4. Minimize the Power Pivot for Excel window.

To Create a Measure

A **measure** is a calculated named field in Power Pivot. Measures use a special set of functions and commands called data analysis expressions or DAX. Measures have several advantages over simple formulas and other calculated fields. *Why? With measures, you can create aggregate formulas that use one or multiple rows from multiple sources, which will adjust as you rearrange the pivot. You can format measures as you create them for global formatting benefits. Measures become fields in pivot field lists and can be used in multiple reports and across multiple worksheets. In regular PivotTables, you cannot create calculated fields using multiple data sources.*

The following steps create a measure to calculate the average number of people in each household. If you do not have Power Pivot, simply read these steps.

1

- If necessary, minimize the Power Pivot for Excel window.

- Click any cell in the PivotTable and then click the Measures button (Power Pivot tab | Calculations group) to display the menu (Figure 10–38).

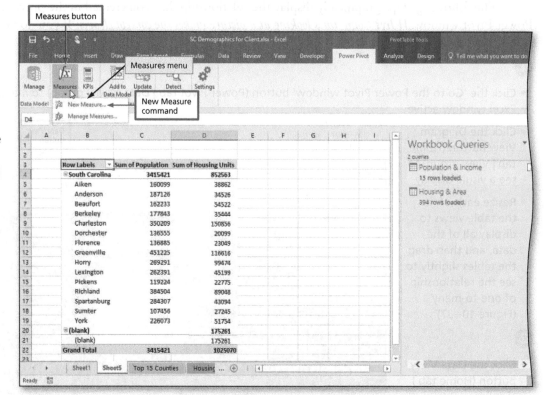

Figure 10–38

2

- Click New Measure in the Measures menu to display the Measure dialog box.

- In the Measure name text box, select any default text and then type `Occupancy Rate` to name the column.

- In the Description text box, select any default text and then type `number of people per housing unit` to create a description.

- In the Formula box following the equal sign, type `[` (left bracket) to prompt Excel to display the available fields that exist in the PivotTable (Figure 10–39).

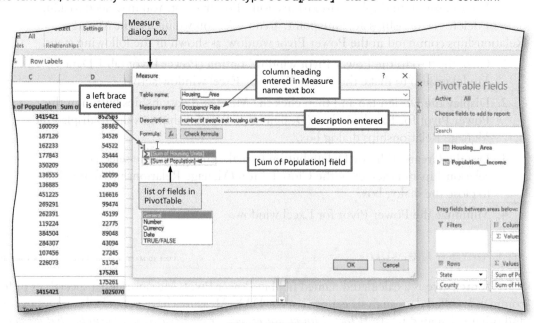

Figure 10–39

- Double-click the [Sum of Population] field to insert it into the formula.

- Type /[to enter the division symbol and to display again the available fields.

- Double-click the [Sum of Housing Units] field to insert it into the formula.

- In the Category box, click Number.

- Click the Format button and then click Whole Number to choose the format (Figure 10–40).

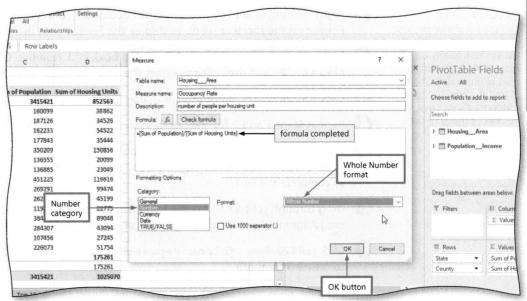

Figure 10–40

- Click the OK button (Measure dialog box) to create the measure and display the new column (Figure 10–41).

Q&A Could I obtain the same result by creating a calculated field in the PivotTable?
No. The Calculated Field option is unavailable to PivotTable data with multiple data sources.

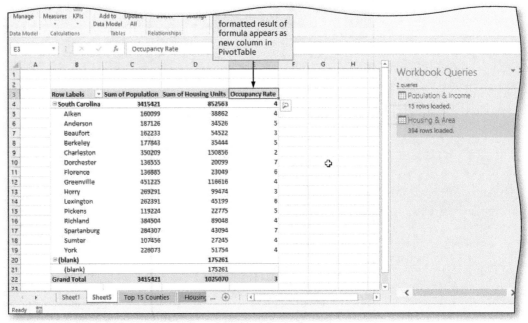

Figure 10–41

To Finish Formatting the PivotTable

The following steps format the other columns of numbers, insert a heading for the page, add a footnote, and save the file.

① Right-click any number in the 'Sum of Population' column and then click Number Format on the shortcut menu to display the Format Cells dialog box.

② In the Category area (Format Cells dialog box), click Number. Change the decimal places to 0 and then click to select the 'Use 1000 Separator' check box.

③ Click the OK button (Format Cells dialog box) to return to the PivotTable.

④ Repeat Steps 1 and 2 for the numbers in the Sum of Housing Units column.

⑤ Click cell A1. If necessary, change the font color to black. Change the font size to 20. Type **Number of Housing Units per County** and then press the ENTER key to complete the text.

⑥ Drag through cells A1 through E1 and then click the Merge & Center button (Home tab | Alignment group) to merge and center the title.

⑦ Click cell F20. Type ***blank represents counties not in the top 15** to create a footnote.

⑧ Rename the worksheet tab with the name, Power Pivot.

⑨ Recolor the worksheet tab with the color, Blue.

⑩ Save the file again (Figure 10–42).

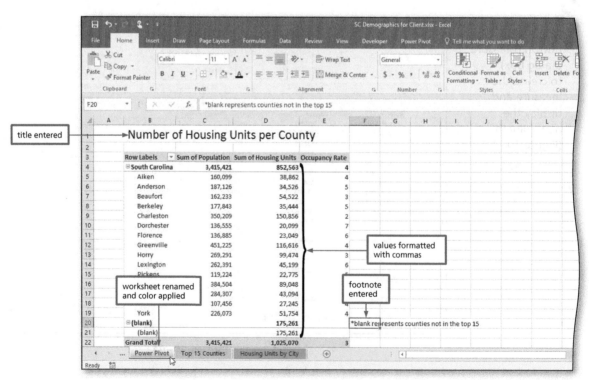

Figure 10–42

Cube Functions

Normally if you want to reference a piece of data, you use a cell reference such as B4. If the data in that cell changes, your reference will reflect that change as well. And when you want to replicate a formula containing a reference that should not change, you use an absolute reference, such as $B$4. In PivotTables, however, neither of those cell references work. The data is prone to change dramatically, from numeric to text, from field to field, or even to blank. Formula or other references to that data immediately become invalid or display errors when the data is pivoted.

The solution to that problem is to use cube functions. **Cube functions** are a set of advanced analytic functions that you can use with multidimensional data, also called **data cubes**. A Power Pivot report is considered a data cube because of its 3-D cube-like structure. With a cube function, you can reference any piece of data in the PivotTable to use in formulas or in other functions, or merely to display the data in other places in the workbook. The cube function will adjust automatically if you change the way your data pivots.

Table 10–2 lists the cube functions.

BTW

The AVERAGEIFS Function

Like its single-criteria counterpart AVERAGEIF, the AVERAGEIFS function averages all arguments that meet multiple criteria.

Table 10–2 Cube Functions

Function	Return Value	Purpose
CUBEKPIMEMBER	Returns the name of a key performance indicator (KPI)	Produces a quantifiable measure such as net income
CUBEMEMBER	Returns a member or tuple from the cube	Validates that the member or tuple exists in the cube
CUBEMEMBERPROPERTY	Returns the value of a member property from the cube	Validates that a member name exists within the cube and to return the specified property for this member
CUBERANKEDMEMBER	Returns the nth, or ranked, member in a set	Returns one or more elements in a set, such as the top salesperson or the top 10 athletes
CUBESET	Defines a set of members by sending an expression to the cube	Identifies sets for use in other cube functions
CUBESETCOUNT	Returns the number of items in a set	Finds how many entries are in a set
CUBEVALUE	Returns an aggregated value from the cube	Displays values from the cube

The cube functions use a variety of arguments in their construction. Recall than an argument refers to any piece of information that the function needs in order to do its job. Arguments are placed in parentheses following the function name. Arguments are separated by commas. Table 10–3 lists some of the arguments used in the construction of cube functions.

For example, the following CUBEMEMBER function includes a reference to the connection or data model, and then the name of the table followed by the name of the value. The function would return the calculated sum from the PivotTable.

```
=CUBEMEMBER("ThisWorkbookDataModel"," [Measures].[Sum
            of Housing Units]"
```

The reference to "ThisWorkbookDataModel" and the reference to Measures are standard references called constants; they should be entered exactly as written above. The reference to Sum of Housing Units is a variable and would be changed to match the field name in the PivotTable.

BTW

The GETPIVOTDATA Function

Another way to extract data stored in a PivotTable is to use the GETPIVOTDATA function. The function takes at least two arguments: the name of the data field and a reference to any cell in the PivotTable report. It returns the sum of that field. An optional third argument allows you to enter a search term. The GETPIVOTDATA function also can search calculated fields.

Table 10–3 Cube Function Arguments	
Argument	**Definition**
Caption or property	An alternate text to display in the cell that is perhaps more user-friendly than the database, field or row name
Connection	Names the table, query, or data model
Key performance indicator (KPI)	A quantifiable measurement, such as net profit, used to monitor performance
Measures	A pivot calculation such as sum, average, minimum, or maximum
Member expression	Uses database field-like references to the data rather than cell references
Rank	An integer to represent which piece of data to return in an ordered list
Set	A string to represent a set of values that has been defined or returned by another cube function
Sort by	A field name to sort by when a function returns a set of values
Sort order	An integer to represent how the data should be ordered when a function returns a set of values
Tuple	A row of values in a relational database

To View Cube Functions

1 ENABLE DATA ANALYSIS | 2 GET & TRANSFORM | 3 USE POWER PIVOT | 4 USE POWER VIEW
5 USE 3D MAPS | 6 CREATE HYPERLINKS | 7 RECORD MACROS

The following steps use the Convert to Formulas command. *Why? The command converts the cells in a Power Pivot report or a PivotTable report to cube references, allowing you to see the functions behind the scenes.*

- Click cell E3 in the PivotTable.

- Display the PivotTable Tools Analyze tab.

- Click the OLAP Tools button (PivotTable Tools Analyze tab | Calculations group) to display the menu (Figure 10–43).

Q&A

What does OLAP stand for?
OLAP stands for Online Analytical Processing that is an advanced analytic tool to assist users in data warehousing and data mining, especially with multidimensional data such as a PivotTable with two outside sources.

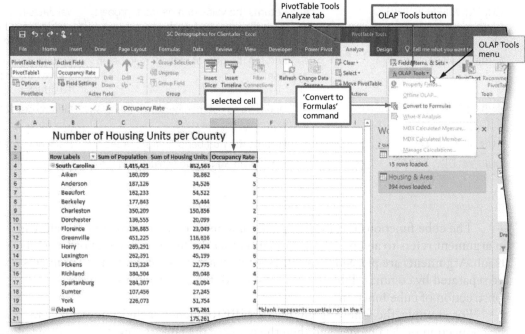

Figure 10–43

- Click Convert to Formulas on the OLAP Tools menu to view the cube function in the formula bar (Figure 10–44).

Experiment

- Click various cells in the table, including the row and column headings, while watching the formula bar. Note the various cube functions that make up the PivotTable.

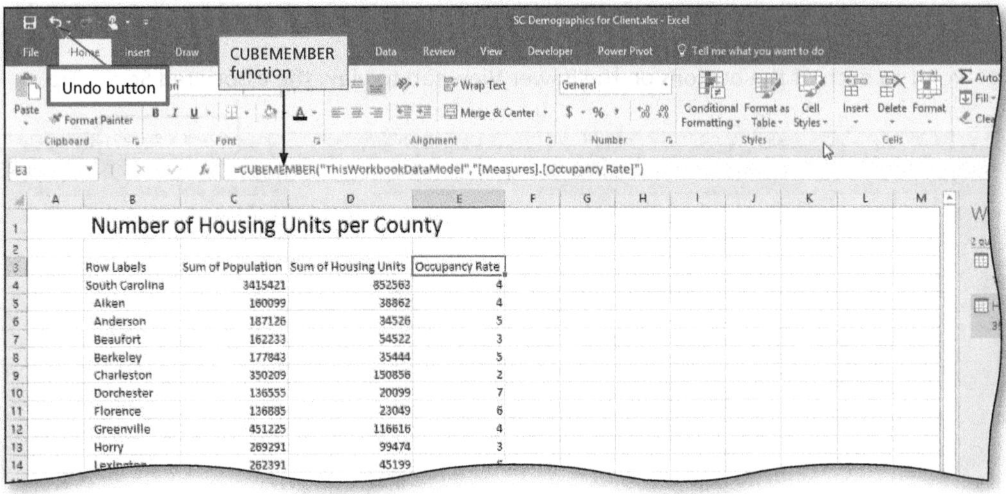

Figure 10–44

- Click the Undo button on the Quick Access Toolbar, to hide the cube functions and display the PivotTable.

- If necessary, close the Power Pivot window and return to the Excel window.

Power View

Power View is another of the interactive visualization power tools. Power View uses a drag-and-drop interface to create a variety of charts, maps, data cards, and other data visualizations. A unique feature of a Power View report is the use of tiles and filters. A **tile** is a button on a Power View navigation strip that is used to group data. A Power View filter is a way to focus on a particular piece of data by clicking on it, similar to a PivotTable slicer. Power View supports multiple views of the data, tiles, and filters in the same view or report.

To Start Power View

1 ENABLE DATA ANALYSIS | 2 GET & TRANSFORM | 3 USE POWER PIVOT | **4 USE POWER VIEW**
5 USE 3D MAPS | 6 CREATE HYPERLINKS | 7 RECORD MACROS

Earlier in this module, you added the Insert a Power View Report button to the Insert tab. The following steps use the new button to start Power View. Power View will display two new tabs on the ribbon. *Why? Power View uses many tools and needs its own ribbons to display the buttons and menus.* The Power View tab helps you add objects to the view. Once you add data to the view, the Design tab appears with access to charts many formatting tools. If you could not enable the data analysis features earlier in this module, you may not have access to Power View.

- Display the tab containing the New Group you added earlier in the module (in this case, the Insert tab).

- Click the 'Insert a Power View Report' button (Insert tab | New Group group) to open Power View and to display the Power View tab.

- Close the Workbook Queries task pane, if necessary (Figure 10–45).

Q&A   My Power View button did not work. What should I do?
See your instructor regarding access to Power View. If you do not have access, read through these steps and study the figures.

Does the order of the worksheet tabs matter?
No. Your order may vary depending on how you minimized or closed other windows.

⌕ **Experiment**

● Point to each of the buttons on the Power View tab to view the associated ScreenTip.

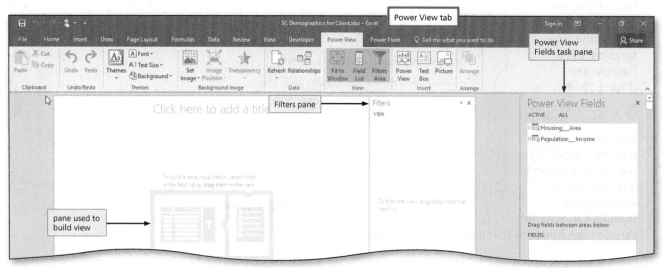

Figure 10–45

To Create a Power View Report with Tiles

1 ENABLE DATA ANALYSIS | 2 GET & TRANSFORM | 3 USE POWER PIVOT | **4 USE POWER VIEW**
5 USE 3D MAPS | 6 CREATE HYPERLINKS | 7 RECORD MACROS

The following steps add data to the Power View data visualization area to create a Power View report that shows city and square miles data by county. You will create a tile for each county. *Why? Using a tile for each county will help you navigate the large amount of data and reduce the need to scroll. When you click a tile, only data related to that field value is displayed.* If you do not have Power View, simply read these steps.

● In the Power View Fields task pane, click the triangle beside the Housing_Area table to display the fields.

● Click the check boxes for County, City, and 'Area in Square Miles' to display them in the report (Figure 10–46).

⌕ **Experiment**

● Scroll in the report to see more of the data.

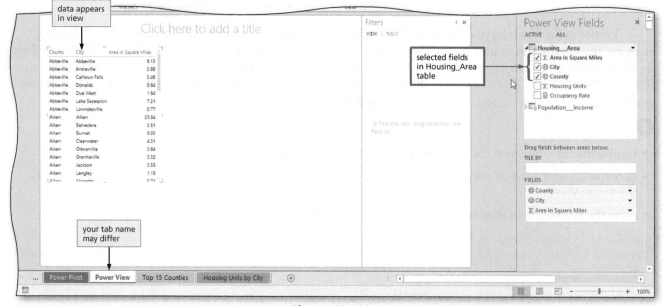

Figure 10–46

2

- If necessary, display the Design tab.

- Click the Tiles button (Design tab | Tiles group) to tile the data.

- Near the light blue line at the bottom of the table itself, rather than the tiles, drag the lower-right corner of the table to fill approximately two-thirds of the pane.

- In the Power View Fields task pane, click to remove the check mark in the County check box, as you no longer need the field in the report table (Figure 10–47).

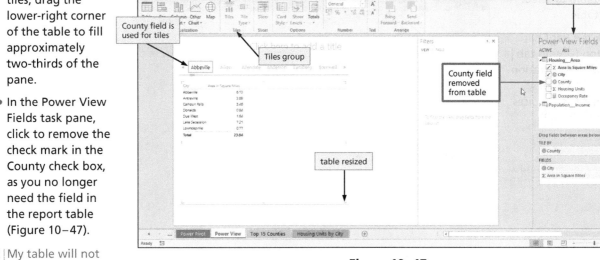

Figure 10–47

Q&A My table will not resize. What did I do wrong?

Try resizing the tiles area or resize using the upper-right sizing handle.

3

- In the Power View Fields task pane, drag the Housing Units field to the report pane to create a second table to the right of the first one (Figure 10–48).

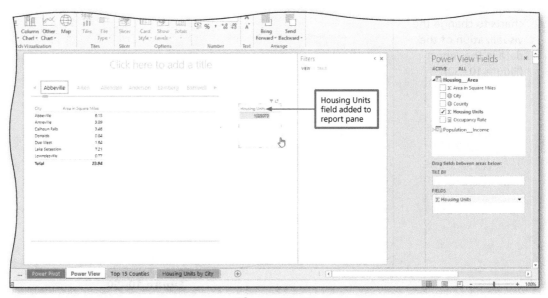

Figure 10–48

To Switch Visualizations

The following steps convert the left table to a bar chart visualization and convert the right table to a card visualization. *Why? Different kinds of visualizations add variety and aid in reading the data.* If you do not have Power View, simply read these steps.

- Click any item in the left table to select the table.
- Click the Bar Chart button (Design tab | Switch Visualization group) to display the bar chart choices (Figure 10–49).

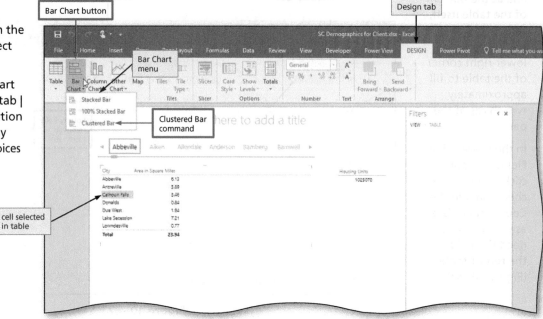

Figure 10–49

- Click Clustered Bar in the list of bar charts to change the visualization of the data in the report (Figure 10–50).

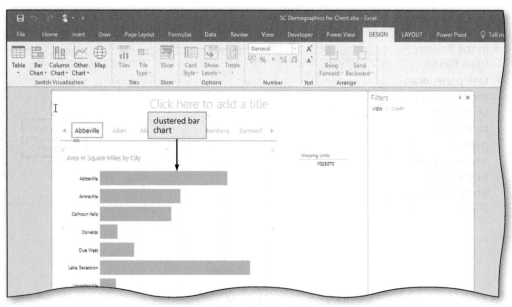

Figure 10–50

- Click the Housing Units data in the table to select the table.
- Click the Table button (Design tab | Switch Visualization group) and then click Card in the list to display the data in the Card format.

To Format the Power View Report

The following steps format the Power View report. *Why? Adding a theme and title enhance the report and improves comprehension.* You also will format the numbers. If you do not have Power View, simply read these steps.

1

- Display the Power View tab.

- Click the Themes button (Power View tab | Themes group) to display the Power View themes.

- Scroll to display more themes (Figure 10–51).

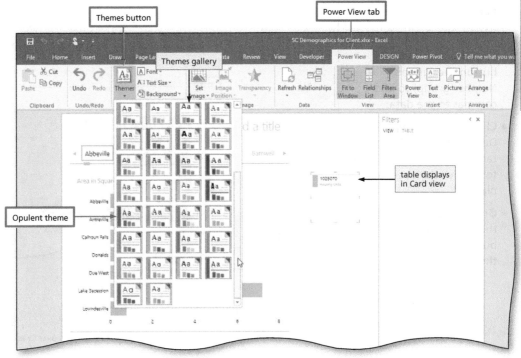

Figure 10–51

2

- Click the Opulent theme to change the colors in the Power Pivot report.

- In the report pane, click the title area. Type **Area in Square Miles** to enter the title text (Figure 10–52).

Q&A Could I add a background to the report?
Yes. You can use the Background button (Power View tab | Themes group) to add a colored background; or you can insert a picture in the background using the Set Image button (Power View tab | Background Image group).

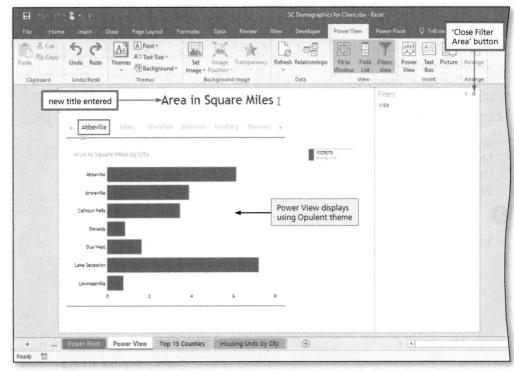

Figure 10–52

- Click the data in the Housing Units table card on the right side of the pane.

- Display the Design tab.

- Click the Comma Style button (Design tab | Number group) to add commas to the data.

- Click the Decrease Decimal button (Design tab | Number group) twice to remove the decimal places.

- On the Filters pane, click the 'Close Filter Area' button to remove it from the display (Figure 10–53).

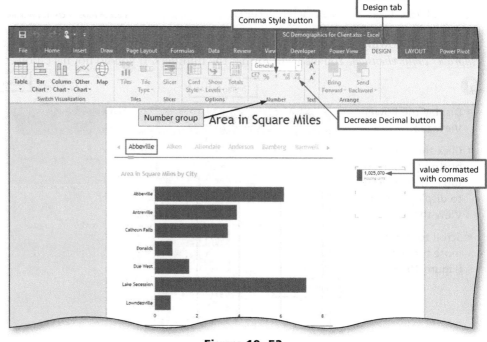

Figure 10–53

To Highlight Data in the Visualization

1 ENABLE DATA ANALYSIS | 2 GET & TRANSFORM | 3 USE POWER PIVOT | 4 USE POWER VIEW
5 USE 3D MAPS | 6 CREATE HYPERLINKS | 7 RECORD MACROS

The following steps use the tiles and filters to highlight specific data items. *Why? Sometimes when presenting data, you may want to focus in on a piece of data (in this case, one city in one county).* You also will save the file. If you do not have Power View, simply read these steps.

- Above the bar chart, click the right-arrow in the tile navigation strip until Charleston county is displayed.

- Click the Charleston tile.

- In the bar chart, click Mount Pleasant to display the data for that specific city (Figure 10–54).

- Save the file again.

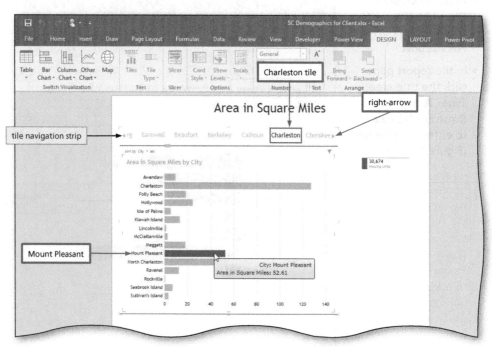

Figure 10–54

Break Point: If you wish to take a break, this is a good place to do so. Exit Excel. To resume at a later time, run Excel, open the file named SC Demographics for Client, and then continue following the steps from this location forward.

3D Maps

The 3D Maps power tool, formerly called Power Map, helps show your data in relation to a geographical area on a map. You can create a single map, or several maps, that become an animation focusing in on your data. The animation is called a tour, and each map is called a scene. If you are going to create a tour, you should plan out each scene and decide what data you want to display in each one.

The 3D Maps command opens a new window that uses a lot of your computer's resources. It is a good idea to close any apps other than Excel while working with 3D Maps.

To Open the 3D Maps Window

1 ENABLE DATA ANALYSIS | 2 GET & TRANSFORM | 3 USE POWER PIVOT | 4 USE POWER VIEW
5 USE 3D MAPS | **6 CREATE HYPERLINKS** | **7 RECORD MACROS**

The following steps open the 3D Maps window. *Why? The 3D Maps windows has the tools to create a map or tour.*

- Click the Housing Units by City sheet tab and click anywhere within the data.
- Display the Insert tab (Figure 10–55).

Q&A Do I have to be in a specific worksheet to access 3D Maps?
No. 3D Maps can be accessed from any worksheet or window. Excel will add a note to the current worksheet explaining that a map is associated with it, however.

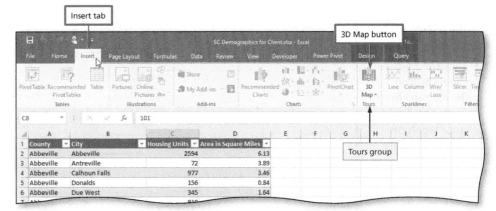

Figure 10–55

- Click the 3D Map button (Insert tab | Tours group) to open the 3D Maps window (Figure 10–56).

Q&A I do not see two tables in my field list. What should I do?
It is possible that the second table was not added to the data model. Minimize the 3D Map window and return to the main Excel window. Click the sheet tab of the missing data and click any cell in the table. Click the 3D Map arrow (Insert tab | Tours group) and then click 'Add the Selected Data to 3D Maps' on the menu.

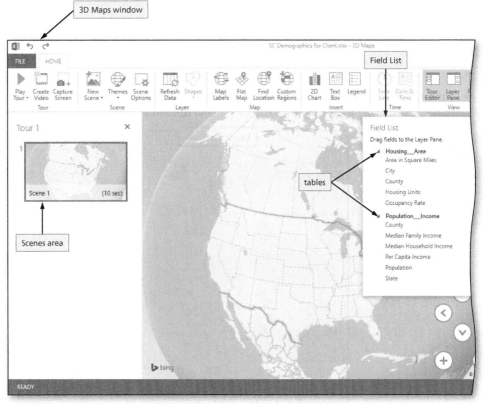

Figure 10–56

To Create Scenes

If you want to create more than just a single static map, you must add scenes to the tour. The following steps add three scenes to the tour. *Why? The first scene will focus in on the state, the second one will focus on the counties with map labels, and the third will display the population for each of the 15 most populous counties.*

- In the 3D Maps window, click the New Scene button (Home tab | Scene group) to add a new scene to the tour.

- In the Field List, drag the State field from the Population_Income table to the Location area in the Layer pane to focus in on the state.

- If the map does not zoom to South Carolina, click the Select One button and then click State/Province in the list.

- Click the Map Labels button (Home tab | Map group) to display state labels on the map (Figure 10–57).

Q&A Does the map have its own worksheet tab?
No. You can save the tour as an animation, but the only way to revisit your map is to use the 3D Map button (Insert tab | Tours group).

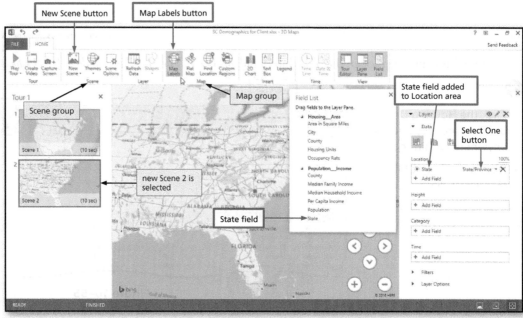

Figure 10–57

②

- Click the New Scene button (Home tab | Scene group) to add a Scene 3 to the tour.

- In the Field List, drag the County field from the Population_Income table to the Location area in the Layer pane to change the map. If necessary, click the Select One button and then click County in the list.

- Click the Zoom in button several times to zoom in on the state of South Carolina.

- If necessary, drag in the map to better position the state and adjust the Field List (Figure 10–58).

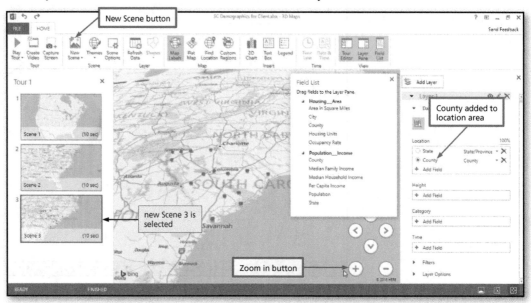

Figure 10–58

3

- Click the New Scene button (Home tab | Scene group) to add a Scene 4 to the tour.

- In the Field List, drag the Median Family Income field to the Category area in the Layer pane to change the map.

- In the Field List, drag the County field from the Housing_Area table, to the Height area in the Layer pane (Figure 10–59).

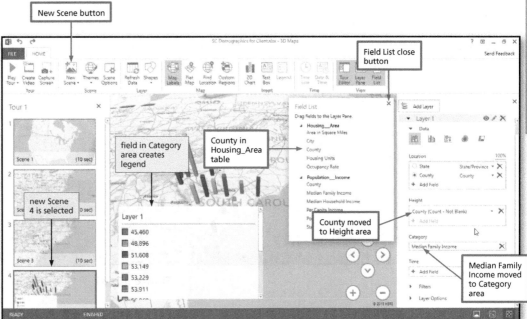

Figure 10–59

4

- Close the Field List.

- Right-click the Layer 1 legend and then click Remove.

- In the map, click the Tilt down button three times and click the Zoom in button several times.

- Drag in the map to better position the state.

- Point to any of the data bars to display the data card (Figure 10–60).

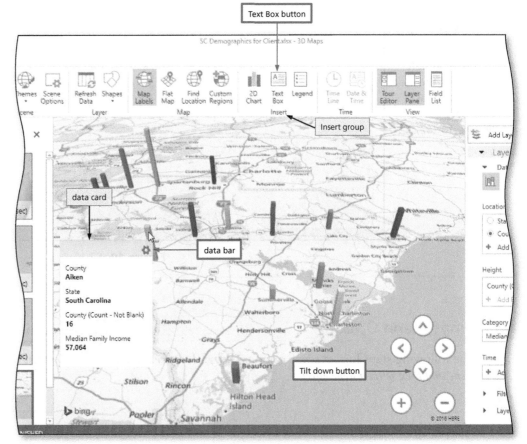

Figure 10–60

- Click the Text Box button (Home tab | Insert group) to display the Add Text Box dialog box.

- Change the font size to 24.

- In the Title text box, type Median Income of Top 15 Counties to enter the title (Figure 10–61).

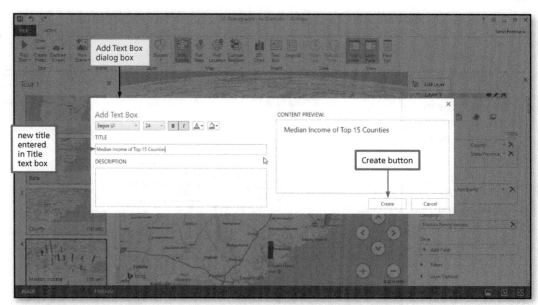

Figure 10–61

- Click the Create button (Add Text Box dialog box) to create a text box title for the map.

- Drag the text box to the lower left portion of the map and resize it as necessary (Figure 10–62).

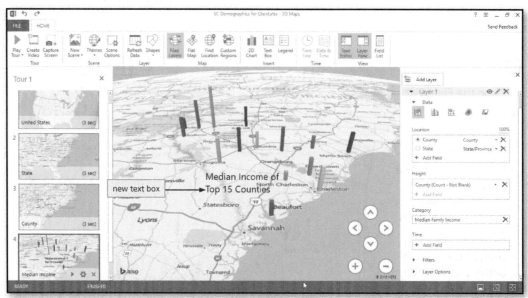

Figure 10–62

To Format Scene Options

1 ENABLE DATA ANALYSIS | 2 GET & TRANSFORM | 3 USE POWER PIVOT | 4 USE POWER VIEW
5 USE 3D MAPS | 6 CREATE HYPERLINKS | 7 RECORD MACROS

The following steps format scene options. *Why? To make the animation smoother, you will change the duration of each scene and then select a scene effect.*

- Click Scene 1 in the Tour pane.

- Click the Scene Options button (Home tab | Scene group) to display the Scene Options dialog box.

- Select the text in the Scene duration box and then type **3** to change the scene to a length of three seconds.

- In the Scene Name text box type **United States** to change the name.

- Click the Effect button to display the list of effects (Figure 10–63).

- Click Push In to select the effect.

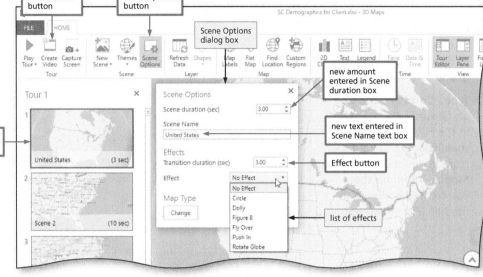

Figure 10–63

- Repeat Steps 1 and 2 for scene 2. Use the name State.

- Repeat Steps 1 and 2 for scene 3. Use the name County.

- Repeat Steps 1 and 2 for scene 4. Use the name Median Income.

To Finish the Animation Steps

1 ENABLE DATA ANALYSIS | 2 GET & TRANSFORM | 3 USE POWER PIVOT | 4 USE POWER VIEW
5 USE 3D MAPS | **6 CREATE HYPERLINKS** | **7 RECORD MACROS**

The following steps play the tour, save a copy of the tour, and take a screen shot of the final map. *Why? You will paste the screen shot to Sheet1 in preparation for creating a home page for the workbook.* You also will save the file.

- Click the Play Tour button (Home tab | Tour group) to play the animation. When the animation is finished, click the "Go back to Edit view." button in the lower left corner of the animation window to return to the 3D Maps window.

- Adjust any of the maps as necessary.

- Click the Create Video button (Home tab | Tour group) to display the Create Video dialog box.

- Click the 'Computers & Tablets' option button (Figure 10–64).

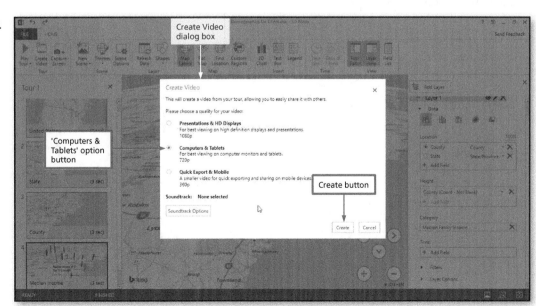

Figure 10–64

- Click the Create button (Create Video dialog box) to display the Save Movie dialog box.

- Type **County Income in South Carolina** in the File name box and then navigate to your storage device and the Module 10 folder that you created earlier in the module (Figure 10–65).

- Click the Save button to save the video. When Excel has finished saving the video, click the Close button, if necessary.

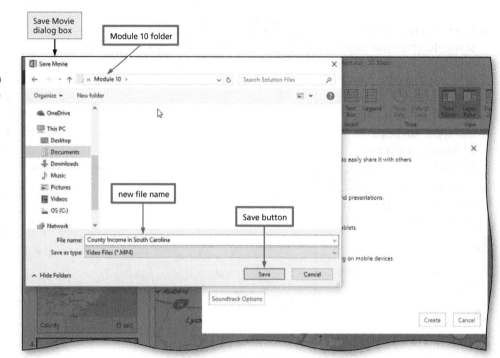

Figure 10–65

Q&A Can I play the video?
Yes, if you wish to view the video, navigate to the storage location, right-click the file, and then click Open or Play on the shortcut menu. When the video is finished, click the Close button in the video window.

To Capture a Screen

1 ENABLE DATA ANALYSIS | 2 GET & TRANSFORM | 3 USE POWER PIVOT | 4 USE POWER VIEW
5 USE 3D MAPS | 6 CREATE HYPERLINKS | 7 RECORD MACROS

The following steps capture a screen. *Why? A screen capture is a picture that can be used in other places in the workbook and in other applications because it is stored on the clipboard.*

- If necessary, click the Close button of any open dialog boxes.

- If necessary, select Scene 4 and then click the Capture Screen button (Home tab | Tour group) to place a copy of the map on the clipboard (Figure 10–66).

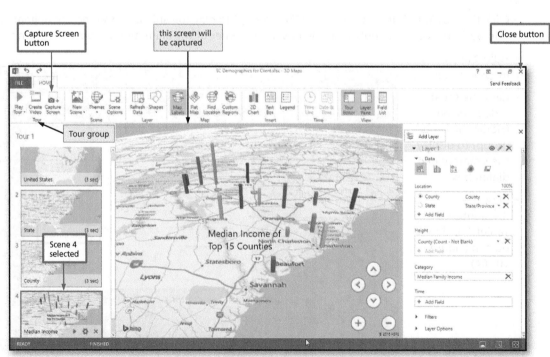

Figure 10–66

- Close the 3D Maps window and navigate to Sheet1 in the workbook.

- Click the Paste button (Home tab | Clipboard group) to paste the map to Sheet1 (Figure 10–67).

❸

- Save the file.

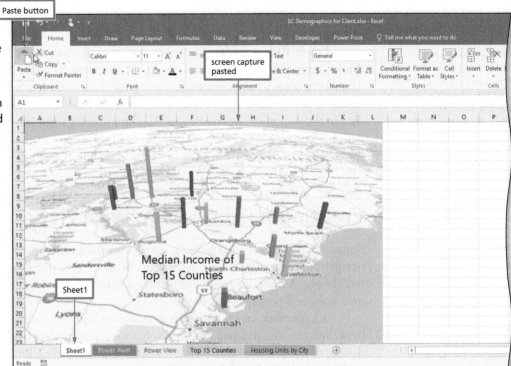

Figure 10–67

Power BI

Microsoft's Power BI is a business intelligence tool to visualize and share data. It is a web-based tool designed to help business users gain insights from their data. Power BI can generate reports with a wide variety of tools including the Excel power tools. Currently, Power BI is free for businesses; otherwise, you are required to have an Office 365 subscription to publish to Power BI.

In Power BI, a dashboard is the file management system where you can upload many different types of files. You can create multiple dashboards. Files in the dashboard are then used to create reports. Figure 10–68 displays a treemap chart using

BTW
Power BI Website
Microsoft's Power BI website has many samples, blogs, and a guided learning tutorial about how to use Power BI. Visit powerbi.microsoft.com for more information.

Figure 10–68

BTW

Accessing 3D Maps
You cannot create a direct hyperlink to the 3D Maps window. You must click the 3D Map arrow (Insert tab | Tours group) and then click the 'Open 3D Maps' command on the menu. You can create a macro that opens the 3D Maps window or create a hyperlink to a saved tour.

the South Carolina demographic information. Notice the tools in the Visualizations task pane are similar to those in the various Power Tool task panes. The Navigation pane is on the left.

Power BI is integrated into Excel in several ways. For example, on the Query Tools Query tab, which appears on the ribbon after you have used the Get & Transform tools to perform a query on your data, there is a Send to Data Catalog button (for version of Excel with data analysis enabled) that automatically loads the data in the query and opens Power BI. Data Catalogs can be shared with everyone within a business. After saving your file to OneDrive, you can publish the entire spreadsheet to Power BI by clicking Publish in the Backstage view.

Creating a Home Page with Hyperlinks

BTW

Email Hyperlinks
You can create a hyperlink that will open the user's default email handler such as Outlook or Gmail. Click the Email Address button in the Insert Hyperlink dialog box (shown in Figure 10–72).

Some Excel users create a home page or introductory worksheet to help with navigation, especially when novice users of Excel may need to interact with complex workbooks. A home page should display a title, links to other worksheets or pertinent materials, and perhaps a graphic.

A **hyperlink**, or hypertext, is a computer link or reference to another location. A hyperlink can link to a page on the web, to an email address, to a location on a storage device, or another location within a workbook. Users click links to navigate or browse to the location. In Excel, hyperlinks can be created using cell data or linked to a graphic.

To Create a Home Page

1 ENABLE DATA ANALYSIS | 2 GET & TRANSFORM | 3 USE POWER PIVOT | 4 USE POWER VIEW
5 USE 3D MAPS | 6 CREATE HYPERLINKS | **7 RECORD MACROS**

Earlier you copied a screen shot of the 3D map and pasted it to Sheet1. The following steps insert a title for the home page using a text box. *Why? A text box can be placed in front of a graphic; if you try to type in a cell, the text will appear behind the graphic.*

- Display the Insert tab.

- Click the Text Box button (Insert tab | Text group) and then draw a text box across the top of the graphic. Do not cover up any of the data bars on the map.

- Change the font size to 28 and the font color to purple. Set the text to bold. Click the Center button (Home tab | Alignment group).

- Type South Carolina Demographics to enter the text (Figure 10–69).

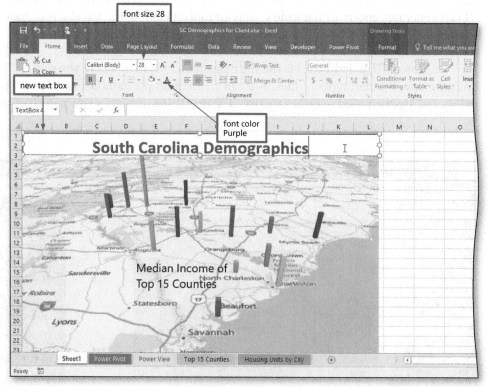

Figure 10–69

- Display the Drawing Tools Format tab.
- Click the Shape Fill arrow (Drawing Tools Format tab | Shape Styles group) and then click No Fill in the Shape Fill gallery.
- Click the Shape Outline arrow (Drawing Tools Format tab | Shape Styles group) and then click No Outline in the Shape Outline gallery.
- Click outside the textbox to display the results (Figure 10–70).

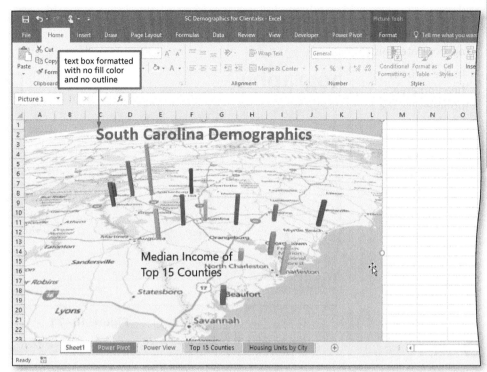

Figure 10–70

To Insert a Hyperlink

1 ENABLE DATA ANALYSIS | 2 GET & TRANSFORM | 3 USE POWER PIVOT | 4 USE POWER VIEW
5 USE 3D MAPS | 6 CREATE HYPERLINKS | 7 RECORD MACROS

To create a hyperlink in Excel, you select the cell or graphic and then decide from among four type of hyperlinks: links to places in the workbook, links to files or webpages, a link to create a new file, or links to email addresses. Table 10–4 displays the text and hyperlinks that you will enter on the home page of the SC Demographics for Client workbook.

Table 10–4 Homepage Text and Hyperlinks			
Cell	**Text**	**Hyperlink location**	**Hyperlink**
M6	Links:	<none>	<none>
N7	Top 15 Counties by Population and Income	Place in current document	Top 15 Counties
N8	Housing Units by City	Place in current document	Housing Units by City
N9	Power Pivot	Place in current document	Power Pivot
N10	Power View	Place in current document	Power View
N11	Map Animation	Existing file	County Income in South Carolina.mp4
N12	Power BI	Eternal webpage	http://powerbi.microsoft.com

The following steps create hyperlinks on the home page. *Why? Creating links to other tabs, files, and websites will help users navigate through the workbook.*

1

- Enter the text from Table 10–4 into the appropriate cells.

- In the column heading area, double-click the border between columns N and O to widen column N.

- Zoom to 150% (Figure 10–71).

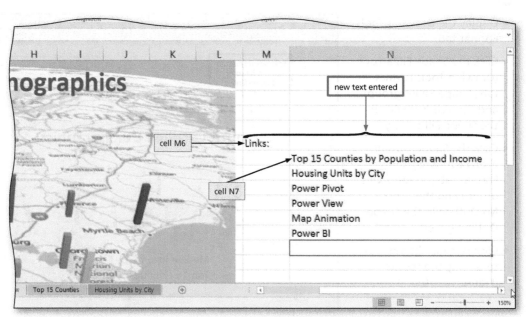

Figure 10–71

2

- Display the Insert tab.

- Select the cell you wish to make a hyperlink (in this case, cell N7) and then click the 'Add a Hyperlink' button (Insert tab | Links group) to display the Insert Hyperlink dialog box.

- In the Link to area, click the 'Place in This Document' button to identify the type of hyperlink.

- In the 'Or select a place in this document' area, click 'Top 15 Counties' (Figure 10–72).

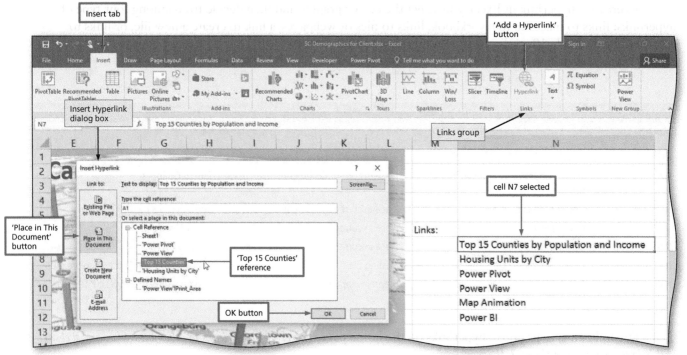

Figure 10–72

③

- Click the OK button (Insert Hyperlink dialog box) to assign the hyperlink.

- Repeat the process for cells N8, N9, and N10, referring to Table 10–4 as necessary.

- Click cell N11 to select it (Figure 10–73).

Q&A

How can I tell if a cell is hyperlinked?
Excel will underline a hyperlink and, when a user hovers over a hyperlink, the pointer will appear as a hand.

How do I edit a hyperlink if I make a mistake?
Right-click the hyperlink to display the shortcut menu and then click Edit Hyperlink to display the Edit Hyperlink dialog box.

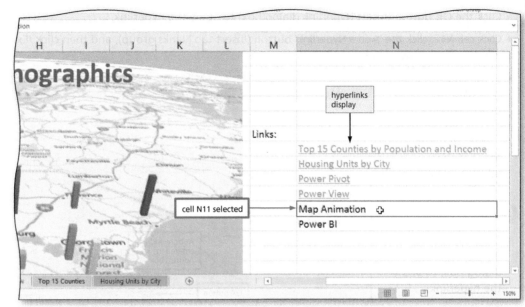

Figure 10–73

④

- Click the 'Add a Hyperlink' button (Insert tab | Links group) again and then click the 'Existing File or Web Page' button to identify the type of hyperlink.

- If necessary, click Current Folder in the Look in area.

- Click 'County Income in South Carolina. mp4' to select the file (Figure 10–74).

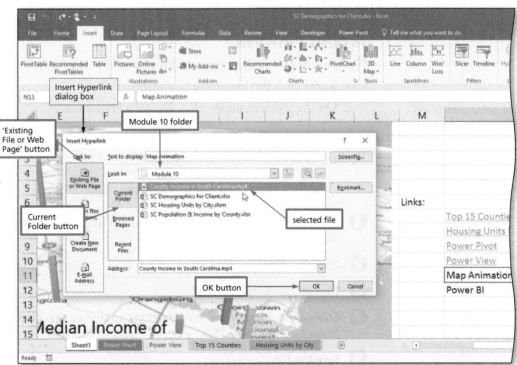

Figure 10–74

• Click the OK button (Insert Hyperlink dialog box) to apply the hyperlink.

• Click cell N12, click the 'Add a Hyperlink' button (Insert tab | Links group), and then click 'Existing File or Web Page' to identify the last hyperlink.

• In the Address box, type `http:// powerbi .microsoft .com` to enter the webpage address (Figure 10–75).

6

• Click the OK button (Insert Hyperlink dialog box) to apply the hyperlink.

• One at a time, click each of the hyperlinks to verify its functionality.

• Save the file.

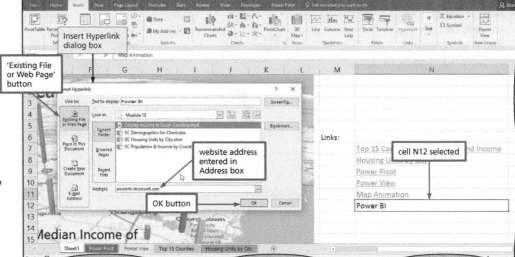

Figure 10–75

Other Ways

1. Right-click cell, click Hyperlink, enter settings and hyperlink address (Insert Hyperlink dialog box), click OK button

2. Press CTRL+K, enter settings and hyperlink address (Insert Hyperlink dialog box), click OK button

TO DELETE A HYPERLINK

BTW
Distributing a Workbook
Instead of printing and distributing a hard copy of a workbook, you can distribute the workbook electronically. Options include sending the workbook via email; posting it on cloud storage (such as OneDrive) and sharing the file with others; posting it on a social networking site, blog, or other website; and sharing a link associated with an online location of the workbook. You also can create and share a PDF or XPS image of the workbook, so that users can view the file in Acrobat Reader or XPS Viewer instead of in Excel.

If you wanted to delete a hyperlink you would perform the following steps.

1. Right-click the hyperlink you wish to delete.
2. On the shortcut menu, click Remove Hyperlink.

To Format the Home Page

The following steps format the home page.

1 On Sheet1, drag to select cells M6 through N12. Change the font color to purple and change the font size to 20.

2 Zoom to 100%.

3 Turn off gridlines.

4 Change the name of the worksheet tab to Homepage. Change the color to purple (shown in Figure 10–75).

5 Save the file.

Break Point: If you wish to take a break, this is a good place to do so. Exit Excel. To resume at a later time, run Excel, open the file named SC Demographics for Client, and then continue following the steps from this location forward.

Macros

A **macro** is a set of commands and instructions grouped together to allow a user to accomplish a task automatically. Because Excel does not have a command or button for every possible worksheet task, you can create a macro to group together commonly used combinations of tasks, which then can be reused later. People also use macros to record commonly used text, to ensure consistency in calculations and formatting, as well as to manipulate nonnumeric data. In this module, you will learn how to create a macro using the macro recorder. After recording a macro, you can play it back, or execute it, as often as you want to repeat the steps you recorded with the macro recorder.

Three steps must be taken in preparation for working with macros in Excel. First, you must display the Developer tab (which you did earlier in the module). Second, a security setting in Excel must be modified to enable macros whenever you use Excel. Finally, Excel requires that a workbook which includes macros be saved as an Excel Macro-Enabled Workbook file type; the file extension is xlsm.

> **BTW**
> **Naming Macros**
> If you use an uppercase letter when naming a macro, the user will have to use the SHIFT key when executing the macro.

> **BTW**
> **Enabling Macros**
> Excel remembers your decision about enabling macros. If you have enabled macros in a worksheet, Excel will not ask you about enabling them the next time you open the worksheet, but will open the worksheet with macros enabled.

Should you customize applications with macros?
Casual Microsoft Office users do not know that customization is available. Creating special macros, events, or buttons on the ribbon can really help a user to be more productive. Creating a macro for repeating tasks also saves time and reduces errors. If you understand how to do so, customization is an excellent productivity tool.

CONSIDER THIS

To Enable Macros

1 ENABLE DATA ANALYSIS | 2 GET & TRANSFORM | 3 USE POWER PIVOT | 4 USE POWER VIEW
5 USE 3D MAPS | 6 CREATE HYPERLINKS | **7 RECORD MACROS**

The following steps enable macros in the workbook. *Why? Enabling macros allows the workbook to open with executable macros.*

1
- Click the Developer tab to make it the active tab.
- Click the Macro Security button (Developer tab | Code group) to display the Trust Center dialog box.
- Click 'Enable all macros' to select the option button (Figure 10–76).

2
- Click the OK button (Trust Center dialog box) to close the dialog box and enable macros.

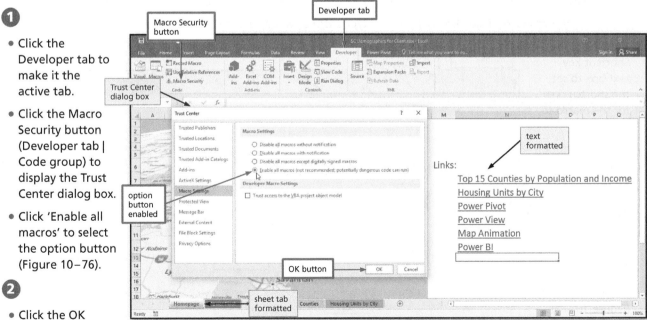

Figure 10–76

BTW

Storing Macros
In the Record Macro dialog box, you can select the location to store the macro in the 'Store macro in' box. If you want a macro to be available to use in any workbook whenever you use Excel, select Personal Macro Workbook in the Store macro in list. This selection causes the macro to be stored in the Personal Macro Workbook, which is part of Excel. If you click New Workbook in the Store macro in list, then Excel stores the macro in a new workbook. Most macros created with the macro recorder are workbook-specific and thus are stored in the active workbook.

BTW

Shortcut Keys
Macro shortcut keys take precedence over Excel's existing shortcut keys. If you assign an existing shortcut key to a macro, it no longer will work for its original purpose. For instance, assigning CTRL+C to a macro means that you no longer will be able to use that shortcut key to copy content.

Recording Macros

A macro is created by recording a set of steps as they are performed. The steps and their order should be determined and rehearsed before creating the macro. When you create a macro, you assign a name to it. A macro name can be up to 255 characters long; it can contain numbers, letters, and underscores, but it cannot contain spaces or other punctuation. The name is used later to identify the macro when you want to execute it. Executing a macro causes Excel to perform each of the recorded steps in order.

Entering a cell reference always directs the macro to that specific cell. Navigating to a cell using keyboard navigation, however, requires the use of relative cell addressing. If you will be using keyboard navigation, you must ensure that the Use Relative References button (Developer tab | Code group) is selected so that the macro works properly. For example, suppose you record a macro in cell C1 that moves to cell C4 and enters text. If the Use Relative References button is not selected, the macro will always move to C4 and enter text; C4 would be considered an absolute reference. If the Use Relative References button is selected while recording, the macro will move three cells to the right of the current position and enter text (which will not always be cell C4).

You can copy macros to other workbooks by copying the macro code. You will learn more about coding in the next module.

To Record a Macro

1 ENABLE DATA ANALYSIS | 2 GET & TRANSFORM | 3 USE POWER PIVOT | 4 USE POWER VIEW
5 USE 3D MAPS | 6 CREATE HYPERLINKS | 7 RECORD MACROS

The following steps record a macro named Address_Block, with the shortcut key CTRL+M to execute the macro. *Why? The company wants to be able to use the shortcut to display company information.*

- Select cell O15.

- Click the 'Use Relative References' button (Developer tab | Code group) to indicate relative references.

- Click the Record Macro button (Developer tab | Code group) to display the Record Macro dialog box.

- When the Record Macro dialog box is displayed, type **Address_Block** in the Macro name text box.

- Type **m** in the Shortcut key text box to set the shortcut key for the macro to CTRL+M.

- In the Description text box, type **This macro prints the name of the company and the address in a block of three cells.** to enter the text (Figure 10–77).

Q&A

Where are macros stored?

In this module, the macro will be stored in the current workbook. If you want a macro to be available in any workbook, you would click the 'Store macro in' button and then select Personal Macro Workbook.

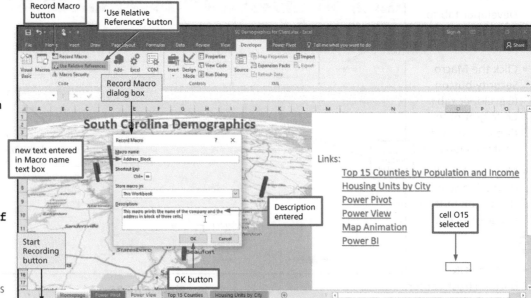

Figure 10–77

2

- Click the OK button (Record Macro dialog box) to begin recording the macro and to change the Record Macro button to the Stop Recording button (Figure 10–78).

Q&A What will be included in the macro?
Any task you perform in Excel will be part of the macro. When you are finished recording the macro, clicking the Stop Recording button on the ribbon or on the status bar ends the recording.

What is the purpose of the Record Macro button on the status bar?
You can use the Record Macro button on the status bar to start or stop recording a macro. When you are not recording a macro, this button is displayed as the Record Macro button. If you click it to begin recording a macro, the button changes to become the Stop Recording button.

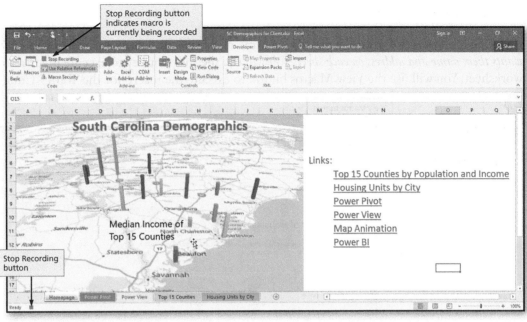

Figure 10–78

3

- Type **Business Decisions, Inc.** and press the DOWN ARROW key.

- Type **1475 Maine Street** and press the DOWN ARROW key.

- Type **Columbia, SC 27811-1475** and press the DOWN ARROW key to complete the text (Figure 10–79).

4

- Click the Stop Recording button (Developer tab | Code group) to stop recording the worksheet activities.

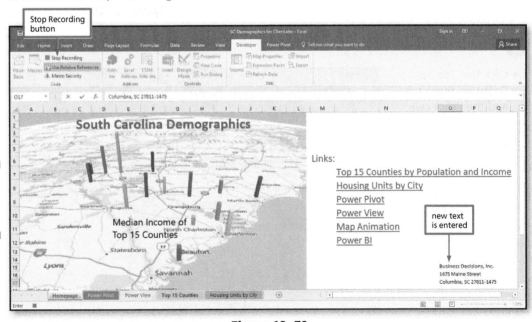

Figure 10–79

Q&A What if I make a mistake while recording the macro?
If you make a mistake while recording a macro, delete the macro and record it again. You delete a macro by clicking the View Macros button (Developer tab | Code group), clicking the name of the macro in the Macro dialog box, and then clicking the Delete button. You then can record the macro again with the same macro name.

Other Ways

1. Click Record Macro button on status bar, enter macro information (Record Macro dialog box), click OK button, enter steps, click Stop Recording button on status bar

To Execute a Macro

The following steps execute or playback the macro on the other worksheet pages. *Why? The company wants their name and address on each sheet.* You will use the shortcut key to execute the macro on the Power Pivot worksheet. You will use the View Macros button to execute the macro for the Top 15 Counties worksheet.

1

- Click the Power Pivot sheet tab and then click cell L19.

- Press **CTRL+M** to execute the macro with the shortcut key (Figure 10–80).

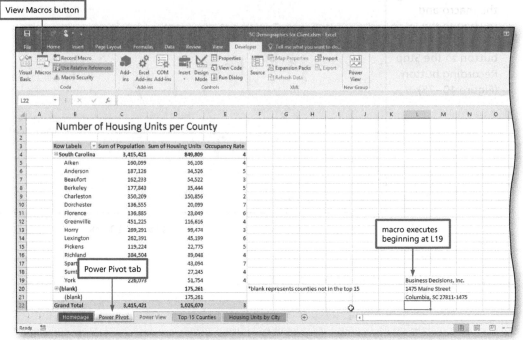

Figure 10–80

2

- Click the 'Top 15 Counties' sheet tab and then click cell L19.

- Click the View Macros button (Developer tab | Code group) to display the Macro dialog box (Figure 10–81).

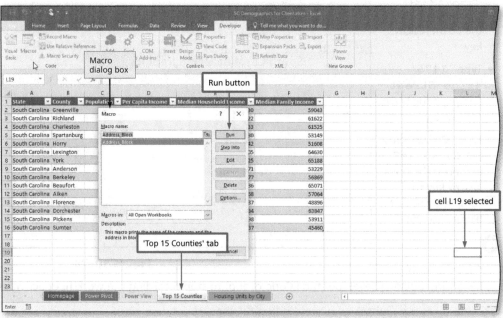

Figure 10–81

- Click the Run button (Macros dialog box) to execute the macro (Figure 10–82).

- Repeat the process for the Housing Units by City tab. Because the Power View worksheet is a chart, it has no specific cells. Do not apply the macro on that worksheet.

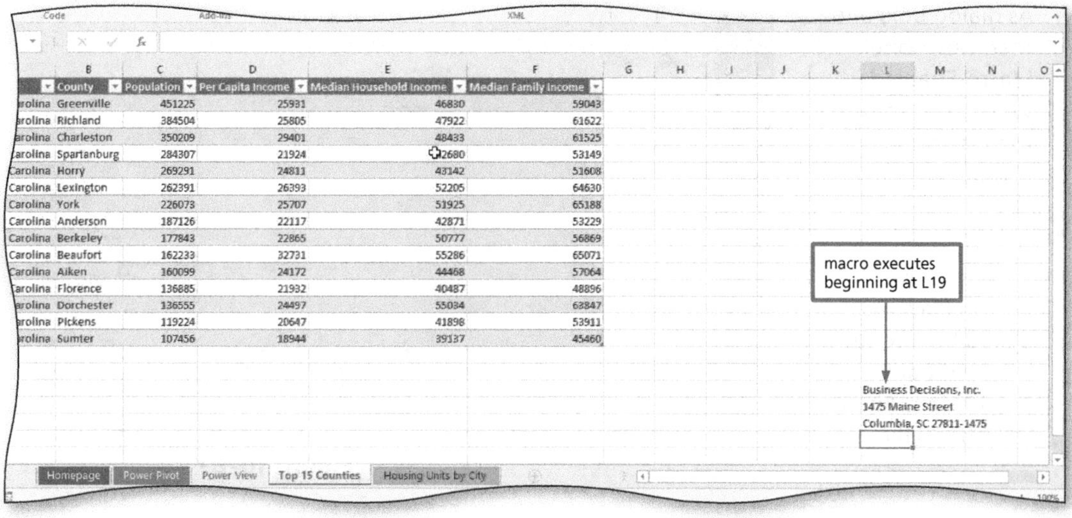

Figure 10–82

Other Ways

1. Press ALT+F8, select macro, click Run button (Macro dialog box)

TO CREATE A MACRO BUTTON ON THE QUICK ACCESS TOOLBAR

If you wanted to create a button on the Quick Access Toolbar to run the macro, you would perform the following steps.

1. Right-click anywhere on the Quick Access Toolbar to display the shortcut menu.

2. Click 'Customize Quick Access Toolbar' on the shortcut menu to display the Customize the Quick Access Toolbar options in the Excel Options dialog box.

3. Click the 'Choose commands from' arrow in the right pane to display a list of commands to add to the Quick Access Toolbar.

4. Click Macros in the Choose commands from list to display a list of macros.

5. Click the name of the macro in the Macros list to select it.

6. Click the Add button (Excel Options dialog box) to add the macro to the Customize Quick Access Toolbar list.

7. Click the OK button (Excel Options dialog box) to close the dialog box.

BTW

Starting Macros
Before recording a macro, you should select your starting cell. If you select it after you begin recording the macro, the macro always will start in that particular cell, which may limit the macro's usefulness.

To Save a Workbook as a Macro-Enabled Workbook

1 ENABLE DATA ANALYSIS | 2 GET & TRANSFORM | 3 USE POWER PIVOT | 4 USE POWER VIEW
5 USE 3D MAPS | 6 CREATE HYPERLINKS | **7 RECORD MACROS**

The following steps save the workbook as a macro-enabled workbook. *Why? Workbooks with macro must be saved as macro-enabled.*

- Display the Backstage view, click the Save As tab, click the Browse button, and then navigate to your storage location.

- Click the 'Save as type' button (Save As dialog box) and then click 'Excel Macro-Enabled Workbook' to select the file format (Figure 10–83).

- Click the Save button (Save As dialog box) to save the workbook as an Excel Macro-Enabled Workbook file.

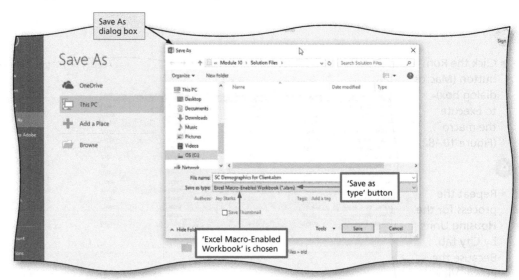

Figure 10–83

To Reset the Ribbon

1 ENABLE DATA ANALYSIS | 2 GET & TRANSFORM | 3 USE POWER PIVOT | 4 USE POWER VIEW | 5 USE 3D MAPS | 6 CREATE HYPERLINKS | 7 RECORD MACROS

It is a good idea to reset the ribbon when you are finished using the customized tools. *Why? Other Excel users may not expect to see new tabs and new button groups, especially in lab situations.* The following steps reset the ribbon, removing all customization, and then exit Excel.

- Right-click a blank area of the ribbon and then click 'Customize the Ribbon' on the shortcut menu to display the Excel Options dialog box.

- Click the Reset button to display its menu (Figure 10–84).

- Click 'Reset all customizations' in the Reset menu.

- When Excel displays a Microsoft Office dialog box asking if you want to delete all customizations, click the Yes button.

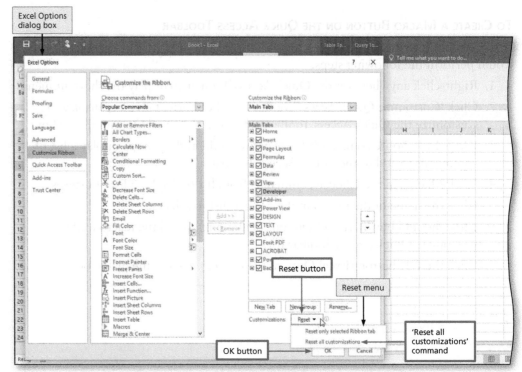

Figure 10–84

- Click the OK button to close the Excel Options dialog box.

- Exit Excel. If the Microsoft Office Excel dialog box is displayed, click the Don't Save button.

Summary

In this module, you learned how to use Excel's power tools. You learned how to enable data analysis in workbooks and customize the ribbon to display different tabs and all groups. You imported data by using the Get & Transform commands to create query tables. You used the Query Editor window to make changes to the data before using it as a table. Using Power Pivot, you added tables to the data model, created a PivotTable with relationships, and used a measure to create a calculated column. You also viewed the cube functions in Power Pivot.

You used Power View to create a report with tiles. You learned how to switch visualizations and highlight data in the Power View report. After opening the 3D Maps window, you create scenes with different map views, map labels, and displayed data related to geography. You created a tour animation and saved it.

You learned that Power BI is a tool that is used to create visualizations of your data to share in the cloud.

Finally, you created a home page with a captured screen shot and hyperlinks to the other tabs and webpages. You recorded a reusable macro with the company information.

What decisions will you need to make when using Power Tools, creating hyperlinks and recording macros?

Use these guidelines as you complete the assignments in this module and create your own worksheets for evaluating and analyzing data outside of this class.

1. Select your data carefully. Make sure it is in a tabular format. If the original data could possibly move, copy the data in a new folder and create your spreadsheet in that folder.

2. Choose the kind of visualization you wish to create.

3. If you want to create a PivotTable from multiple sources of data, use Power Pivot.

4. If you want to create a chart with multiple data sources, or to use interactive tiles or data card visualizations, use Power View.

5. If you have data that is geographic in nature, use 3D Maps.

6. Design a user interface to access your data more conveniently. Include hyperlinks, macro instructions, screen captures, and graphics.

7. Determine any actions you want to automate and create a macro. The steps and their order should be determined and rehearsed before creating the macro.

8. Test the user interface. The final step in creating a user interface is to verify that the interface behaves as designed and as a user expects.

CONSIDER THIS: PLAN AHEAD

Apply Your Knowledge

Reinforce the skills and apply the concepts you learned in this module.

Creating a Power View Report

Note: To complete this assignment, you will be required to use the Data Files. Please contact your instructor for information about accessing the Data Files. This assignment also requires access to Power View.

Instructions: Run Excel. Open a blank workbook and then save the workbook as Apply 10–1 Peppers Complete. The owner of a local restaurant wants you to create a Power View report that they eventually will upload to their website. The report should describe the peppers they use in various dishes on the menu as shown in Figure 10–85. They have provided you with a database file that has two tables in it.

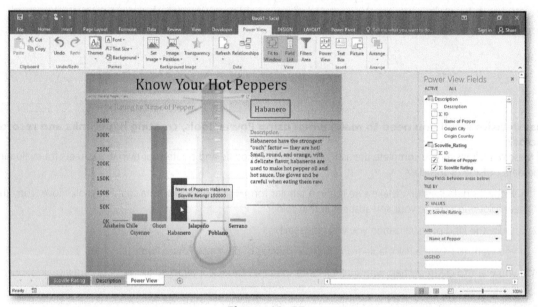

Figure 10–85

Perform the following tasks:

1. Open a File Explorer window. Copy and paste the Apply 10–1 Peppers.accdb data file from the Data Files for Module 10 to the location where you stored the Apply 10–1 Peppers Complete Excel file.

2. If necessary, customize the ribbon as described in the module to include a new group with the Insert a Power View Report command.

3. In the Excel window, set the color scheme to Aspect.

4. Click the New Query button (Data tab | Get & Transform group), point to From Database, and then click From Microsoft Access Database. Navigate to your storage location and double-click the Apply 10–1 Peppers file.

5. When the Navigator dialog box is displayed, load the Description table. Change the table style to Table Style Medium 5 (Table Tools Design tab | Table Styles group). Rename the sheet tab, Description, and color the tab Green.

6. Change the column width of column C, Description, to 35. Wrap the text. Change the row height of rows 2 through 8 to 115. You may need to zoom out while changing the row height.

7. Repeat Steps 4 and 5 to load the Scoville Rating table. Use Table Style Medium 3. Rename the sheet tab, Scoville Rating, and color the tab Red.

8. Click the 'Insert a Power View Report' button that you added to the ribbon, which will open a new worksheet, labelled Power View or Power View1.

9. If necessary, in the Power View Fields task pane, click the triangle next to the Scoville_Rating table to view the fields. If necessary, click the Name of Pepper and Scoville Rating check boxes to add them to the table. Remove the check mark in the ID check box, if necessary.

10. Click the Column Chart button (Design tab | Switch Visualization group) and then click Clustered Column. Resize the chart to cover approximately 2/3 of the report area.

11. In the Power View Fields task pane, click the All tab if necessary, and then click the triangle next to the Description table. Drag the Description field to an area beside the table, creating a second visualization. Drag the Name of Pepper field to the Tile By area.

12. To create the relationship between the two tables, click the Relationships button (Power View tab | Data group). When Excel displays the Manage Relationships dialog box, click the New button and link the two tables by the common field Name of Pepper. Resize the tables as shown in Figure 10–85. *Hint:* you may need to resize the inner table in the second visualization to wrap the text correctly.

13. Display the Power View tab. Use the Themes group to change the theme to NewsPrint, the font to Cambria, the Text Size to 150%, and the Background to Light1 Center Gradient. Edit the title as shown in Figure 10–85.

14. Use the Background Image group to set the image to the Apply 10–1 Thermometer.png file in the Data Files. Change the Transparency to 80%.

15. Click one of the bars in the column chart to verify that the tables are synchronized.

16. If instructed to do so, insert a text box with your name and course number in the lower-right corner of the Power View report.

17. Delete Sheet1 in the workbook. Save the file again.

18. Display the Backstage view and then click Print. Change the print settings to landscape and fit the Power View report to the paper size. Print the report.

19. Submit the revised workbook and the report printout in the format specified by your instructor.

20. Reset the ribbon customization and close Excel.

21. ✷ How might you use the other fields in the Description table? Would they be appropriate for the Power View? Why or why not?

Extend Your Knowledge

Extend the skills you learned in this module and experiment with new skills. You may need to use Help to complete the assignment.

Creating a Macro, Editing a Macro, and Assigning It to a Button

Note: To complete this assignment, you will be required to use the Data Files. Please contact your instructor for information about accessing the Data Files.

Instructions: Run Excel. Open the workbook Extend 10–1 Avia Salon from the Data Files for Students and then save the workbook as an Excel Macro-Enabled Workbook file type using the file name, Extend 10–1 Avia Salon Complete.

Continued >

Extend Your Knowledge *continued*

In the following steps, you will create a macro to add a column to a worksheet, assign the macro to a button on the Quick Access Toolbar, and then execute the macro. Figure 10–86 shows the completed worksheet.

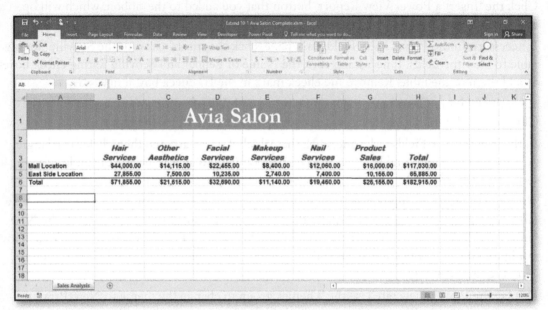

Figure 10–86

Perform the following tasks:

1. If the Developer tab is not displayed on the ribbon, display the Backstage view, click Options in the left pane to display the Excel Options dialog box, click Customize Ribbon, click the Developer check box in the Customize the Ribbon area, and then click the OK button.

2. Create a macro that adds a column before the Product Sales column by doing the following:

    a. Click the Record Macro button (Developer tab | Code group).

    b. When the Record Macro dialog box appears, name the macro, AddColumn, assign the keyboard shortcut CTRL+N. Store the macro in this workbook, enter your name in the Description box, and then click the OK button (Record Macro dialog box) to start the macro recording process.

    c. Select cell C3, click the Insert Cells arrow (Home tab | Cells group), and then click the 'Insert Sheet Columns' command from the Insert Cells menu.

    d. Select cell C6, sum the cell range C4:C5, set the column width to 15, and then click the Stop Recording button (Developer tab | Code group).

3. In the newly added column, enter **Nail Services** in cell C3, **12060** in cell C4, and **7400** in cell C5.

4. Click the View Macros button (Developer tab | Code group) to display the Macro dialog box. Run the AddColumn macro to add a column. Enter the following data: **Makeup Services**, **8400**, and **2740**.

5. Right-click anywhere on the Quick Access Toolbar and then click 'Customize Quick Access Toolbar' on the shortcut menu. When the Excel Options dialog box is displayed, click the 'Choose commands from' arrow and click Macros. Click AddColumn, click the Add button, and then click the OK button to add a Macro button to the Quick Access Toolbar.

6. While still in column C, run the macro as follows:

   a. Click the AddColumn button on the Quick Access Toolbar and then enter `Facial Services`, `22455`, and `10235` for the column values.

   b. Press CTRL+SHIFT+N and then enter `Other Aesthetics`, `14115`, and `7500` for the column values.

7. If requested by your instructor, add the following text to the end of the text in cell A1: `(EST. <year of birth>)`, replacing <year of birth> with your year of birth.

8. Right-click the AddColumn button on the Quick Access Toolbar and then click 'Remove from Quick Access Toolbar' on the shortcut menu.

9. Use Help to learn how to access the VBA window. In the VBA window, click File on the menu bar and then click print to print the AddColumn macro.

10. Save the workbook. Submit the revised workbook and the macro printout in the format specified by your instructor.

11. ✳ How would using the 'Use Relative References' button when recording your macro change how you insert columns using the AddColumn macro?

Expand Your World

Create a solution that uses cloud and web technologies by learning and investigating on your own from general guidance.

Creating a Power BI Treemap

Note: To complete these steps, you will be required to use the file you created in this module, named SC Demographics for Client. If you did not create this file, see your instructor for ways to complete this assignment. You must be connected to the Internet to perform these steps. If you are working in a lab situation, your IT administrator must have turned on access to Power BI. If you are working from home, you will need access to your Office 365 account.

Problem: You decide to create a Power Bi visualization to share with others via the web (Figure 10–87).

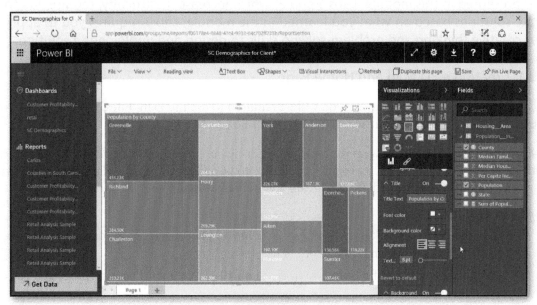

Figure 10–87

Continued >

Expand Your World *continued*

Instructions:

1. Open a browser and navigate to https://powerbi.microsoft.com. If you have an Office 365 account, Sign in. If not, see your instructor for login assistance.

2. In the upper-left corner, click the 'Show the navigation pane' button, if necessary. (If the 'Show the navigation pane' button is unavailable, click the Get button (local files) to display the Get Data > Files window.)

3. Click the plus sign next to Dashboards in the My Workspace pane on left side of the screen. Type `SC Demographics` to name a new dashboard and then press the ENTER key.

4. Click the Get Data button at the bottom of the navigation pane. Follow the instructions to import a local file. Navigate to your storage location and double-click the SC Demographics for Client.xlsx that you created in this module.

5. Double-click the file to open a blank report.

6. If necessary, click Edit report on the toolbar to open the Visualizations task pane and the Fields task pane.

7. In the Visualizations task pane, click the Treemap icon.

8. In the Fields task pane, open the Population_Income table and click the County and Populations check boxes. Resize the treemap chart as necessary.

9. In the Visualizations task pane, click the Format tab. Turn on Data labels. Set the background color to gray and the title font color to white.

10. If instructed to do so, enter your name in the Title Text box (Visualizations task pane).

11. Delete the Power View tab.

12. Save the file. Send a link to your instructor. Close Power BI.

13. ✳ How was creating a treemap visualization in Power BI different than creating it in Excel. In Power BI, what advantages do you have with regard to sharing the report?

In the Labs

Design, create, modify, and/or use a workbook following the guidelines, concepts, and skills presented in this module. Labs 1 and 2, which increase in difficulty, require you to create solutions based on what you learned in the module; Lab 3 requires you to apply your creative thinking and problem-solving skills to design and implement a solution.

Lab 1: Creating a 3D Map and Home Page

Note: To complete this assignment, you will be required to use the Data Files. Please contact your instructor for information about accessing the Data Files.

Problem: The State of Alaska wants a visual report displaying the number of visitors to its top 10 National Parks in a recent year. They also would like to be able to access the National Park Service website within the report. You decide to create a workbook with a home page and 3D Map.

Perform the following tasks:

1. Run Excel and open a blank workbook. Save the file on your storage location with the name, Lab 10–1 National Parks in Alaska Complete.

2. Using File Explorer, copy the Data File named Lab 10–1 National Parks in Alaska and paste it to your storage location.

3. Click the New Query button (Data tab | Get & Transform group) and choose to import from a workbook. Using the Import Data dialog box, navigate to your storage location and import the Lab 10–1 National Parks in Alaska file.

4. When Excel displays the Navigator dialog box, click the Top 10 Parks table and then click the Edit button.

5. Using the Query Editor window, remove the first row, which is a title. Make the next row the header row. Close and load the query.

6. Widen columns as necessary to view all of the data. Add commas to the visitor figures.

7. Click the 3D Map button (Insert tab | Tours group) to open the 3D Maps window.

8. For Scene 1:

   a. Remove any locations in the Layer Pane.

   b. Zoom out and reposition the map to show the entire United States.

9. Create Scene 2.

   a. In the Location area (Layer Pane), click the Add Field button and then click State in the field list.

   b. Create a text box with the word, Alaska.

10. Create Scene 3.

   a. Remove the text box and turn on Map Labels.

   b. In the Location area (Layer Pane), click the Add Field button (Layer Pane) and then click National Park in the field list. Click the Select One button and then click Other in the list.

   c. In the Height area (Layer Pane), click the Add Field button and then click Visitors in 2015.

   d. In the Category area (Layer Pane), click the Add Field button and then click National Park. Right-click the Legend and then click Remove.

   e. Zoom in as close as possible, while keeping all of the data bars on the map.

   f. For each data bar, right-click the data bar and then click Add Annotation. In the Add Annotation dialog box, click the National Park option button, click the Custom option button, and then edit the title field to display only the name of the park. Choose a position for the annotation (left or right), and how high on the bar you want the annotation to display. As you add annotations, try not to overlap.

11. For Scenes 1 and 2, change the scene options to a duration of 3 seconds and use the Fly Over Effect. For Scene 3, change the scene option to a duration of 3 seconds and use the Push In effect.

12. Play the tour (Figure 10–88) and then make any adjustments necessary. Capture a screenshot of scene 3. Create a video of the tour with the name Alaska State Parks.

13. Close the 3D Maps window and return to the Excel window. Save the file.

14. Navigate to Sheet1 in the workbook. Rename the worksheet Homepage. Paste the screen capture.

15. In cell M3, type `Links:` to enter a heading.

16. Navigate to the Top 15 Parks worksheet and copy the range, B2:B11. Paste the range to cell M5 on the home page.

17. Open a browser and navigate to http://www.nps.gov/state/ak/index.htm. Scroll down to Bering Land Bridge National Preserve. Right-click the heading and then click Copy link on the shortcut menu.

Continued >

In the Labs continued

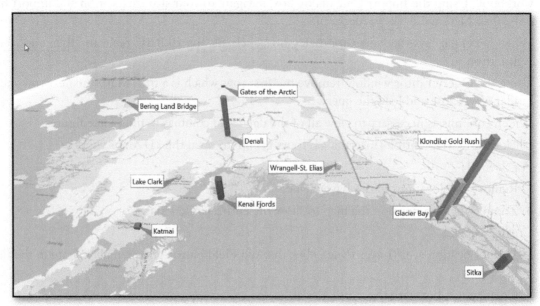

Figure 10–88

18. Return to the workbook. Right-click cell M5 and then click Hyperlink on the shortcut menu. Paste the web address in the Address box. Click the OK button.

19. Repeat Steps 17 and 18 for each of the other nine parks.

20. In cell M15, type **Map Animation**. Hyperlink the cell to the stored video you created.

21. If instructed to do so, enter your name and course number on the home page.

22. Save the file. See your instructor for ways to submit this file.

23. ✳ Would you use Excel for a presentation? What are the advantages and disadvantages of using visualizations in Excel versus apps like PowerPoint or Prezi?

Lab 2: Using Power Pivot

Note: To complete this assignment, you will be required to use the Data Files. Please contact your instructor for information about accessing the Data Files. You also will need access to Power Pivot.

Problem: The Resident Life office at your school has a list of approved dormitories, resident halls, and apartments, both on- and off-campus. They have asked you to merge two data files related to locations and occupancy. You create the PivotTable shown in Figure 10–89.

Perform the following tasks:

1. Run Excel and open a blank workbook. If necessary, customize the ribbon as described in the module to include the Power Pivot tab. Save the file on your storage location with the file name Lab 10–2 Residences Complete.

2. Using File Explorer, copy the Data Files named Lab 10–2 Residence Halls and Lab 10–2 Locations, and paste them to your storage location.

3. Use the commands in the Get & Transform group on the Data tab to import two query tables: Lab 10–2 Residence Halls and Lab 10–2 Locations. Use the Query Editor window as necessary to format the data.

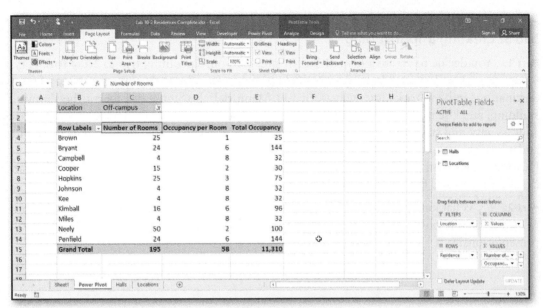

Figure 10–89

4. In the Excel workbook, format the two tables and rename the sheet tabs. Name the tabs, Halls and Locations.

5. If you have access to Power Pivot, use the Power Pivot tab to add each worksheet to the data model. Use the Power Pivot for Excel window to create a PivotTable on a new worksheet. If you do not have access to Power Pivot, create a PivotTable using the Insert tab.

6. In the Excel window, access the PivotTable Fields task pane. Place check marks in the Residence, # of Rooms, and Max Occupancy check boxes from the Halls table and a check mark in the Location check box from the Locations table. Create a relationship as necessary.

7. Double click the column headings and rename them Number of Rooms and Occupancy per Room.

8. In the PivotTable Fields task pane, drag the Location field to the Filters area.

9. If you have access to Power Pivot, click the Measures button and then click New Measure on the menu. Name the new measure, Total Occupancy, and use the LEFT BRACKET key ([ ) to help you multiply the Number of Rooms times the Occupancy per Room.

10. Format the PivotTable as necessary. Name the sheet tab, Power Pivot. Delete the Sheet1 tab.

11. Click the filter button in cell C1, click the All tab if necessary, and then click Off-campus to display only the off campus housing choices as shown in Figure 10–89.

12. If instructed to do so, create a home page with a picture of your school, and your name and course number.

13. Save the workbook. Remove the ribbon customization. Submit the revised document in the format specified by your instructor.

14. ✳ What other measure might you create with this data? How would the Residence Life office use this data to manage room assignments?

Continued >

In the Labs *continued*

Lab 3: Creating a Tourist Map

Part 1: You decide to create a map of tourist sites for your upcoming trip to New York City. Create a workbook named Lab 10–3 NYC Highlights. In column A, enter the name of five tourist destinations in New York City, such as the 911 Memorial, the Statue of Liberty, the Empire State Building, etc. Use the web to find the address for those locations. For each location, enter the street address, city, and state into your spreadsheet. Convert the data to a table. Edit the column headings and adjust the column widths, as necessary. Access 3D Maps and add the appropriate fields to the location area. Zoom in. Create a flat map with map labels and data cards that display the name of the destination and the address. Post a screen capture to your social media.

Part 2: ✳ What kind of industries might use the 3D Maps tool on a regular basis? Why might 3D Maps be the tool of choice over map-specific apps? How could you use the 3D Maps tool in presentations?

11

User Interfaces, Visual Basic for Applications (VBA), and Collaboration Features in Excel

Objectives

You will have mastered the material in this module when you can:

- Add and configure worksheet form controls such as command buttons, option buttons, and check boxes

- Record user input to another location on the worksheet

- Understand Visual Basic for Applications (VBA) code and explain event-driven programs

- Explain sharing and collaboration techniques

- Use passwords to assign protected and unprotected status to a worksheet

- Compare and merge workbooks

- Review a digital signature on a workbook

- Insert, edit, delete, and review comments in a workbook

- Manage tracked changes in a shared workbook

- Format a worksheet background

- Enhance charts and sparklines

- Save a custom view of a worksheet

Introduction

This module introduces you to user interface design using form controls and ActiveX controls in a worksheet, the Visual Basic for Applications (VBA) programming environment, sharing and collaboration features of worksheets and workbooks, the use of comments in Excel, and the process of tracking changes in shared workbooks.

With Excel, you can design a user-friendly interface that permits users to easily enter information into the workbook, regardless of their experience with the app.

Form controls include interface elements such as option buttons, check boxes, and group boxes. ActiveX controls, including the text box and command button controls used in this module, provide the same core functionality as the form controls, but allow you, as the designer, greater power to customize the appearance of the control. The VBA programming environment is used to program the functionality of the ActiveX controls.

When working on a team, the sharing features of Excel make it easy to provide team members access to worksheet data, protect information as necessary, and track changes made throughout the workbook. Distributing a workbook through OneDrive, Office 365, or SharePoint maintains ownership of the file while providing all members of the team access to the most current version of the data at all times. Commenting features of Excel encourage feedback on specific content within the worksheet.

Additional collaboration tools permit users to view multiple versions of the same workbook side by side for comparison or to compare and merge copies of the same workbook after editing by individual team members.

Project — Global Pharmaceutical Company Sales Analysis

The project in this module follows proper design guidelines and uses Excel to create the workbooks shown in Figure 11–1. Global Pharmaceutical Company (GPC) develops and markets generic drugs to hospitals and health clinics worldwide. Because GPC's reach is global, there are members of the sales team located in offices throughout the world. The head of sales wants to use advanced features of Excel to share information about GPC's prospective clients and projected revenue among the sales team. The GPC Sales Analysis workbook consists of three worksheets — Prospect Recorder, Sales Data Analysis, and a hidden Prospect List. The GPC Events workbook consists of two worksheets — Event Expenses and Prior Years. Multiple copies of both workbooks exist with changes made by multiple users.

The Prospect Recorder worksheet (Figure 11–1a) in the GPC Sales Analysis workbook provides a framework for recording information about sales prospects. You will add form controls and ActiveX controls to finish the interface development. You will then create VBA code to add functionality to the command button controls added to the worksheet. The functionality added through the VBA programming environment will present a series of dialog boxes instructing the salesperson to enter the prospect's contact information, and then will copy the prospect's information into the hidden Prospect List worksheet.

The Sales Data Analysis worksheet (Figure 11–1b) in the GPC Sales Analysis workbook provides production details for 2017 and 2018 related to the three production lines (production facilities are located in Brazil, India, and Mexico) and four product types (generic versions of antihistamine, antihypertensive, anti-inflammatory, and antithyroid drugs). You will add comments and track changes made by other users of the shared workbook.

The Event Expenses worksheet (Figure 11–1c) in the GPC Events workbook contains estimated costs for three sales events throughout the year 2018. Colleagues Noah and Serenity have made changes to their individual shared copies of the workbook that you will merge into a single workbook file. You will add a watermark to this worksheet.

The Prior Years worksheet (Figure 11–1d) in the GPC Events workbook contains attendance figures for prior events (2011 through 2017) and a chart representing the data. You will add a background to this worksheet. You will add finishing touches to the existing chart and add sparklines for each event. You will also create a custom view for the worksheet and prepare the workbook for distribution to users of older versions of Excel.

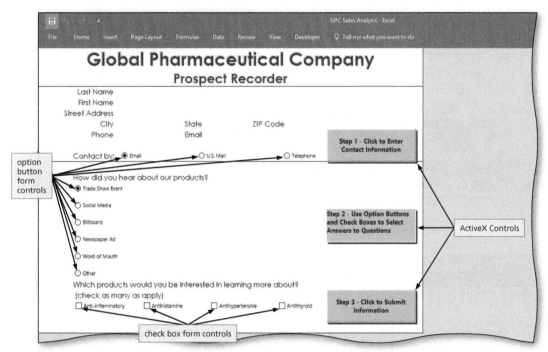

(a) Prospect Recorder Form

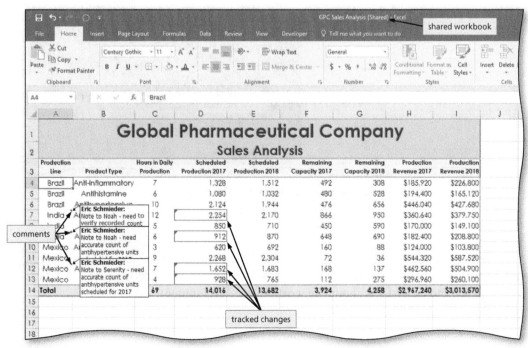

(b) GPC Sales Analysis

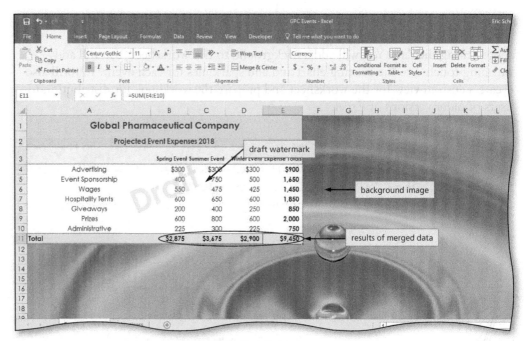

(c) Event Expenses

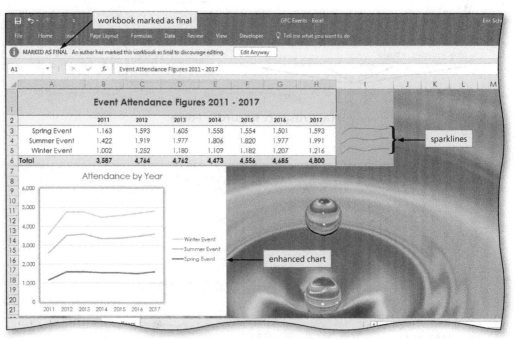

(d) Prior Years Event Attendance

Figure 11–1

The requirements document for Global Pharmaceutical Company Sales Analysis and Events workbooks is shown in Figure 11–2. It includes the needs, source of data, calculations, and other facts about the worksheets' development.

Worksheet Titles	Prospect Recorder, Sales Data Analysis, Event Expenses, and Prior Years
Needs	Global Pharmaceutical Company (GPC) develops and markets four types of generic drugs (antihistamine, antihypertensive, anti-inflammatory, and antithyroid) to hospitals and health clinics worldwide through three production facilities in Brazil, India, and Mexico.
	The company would like a workbook to record information about sales prospects and maintain current information regarding scheduled production and sales. Additionally, a second workbook is needed to maintain current data on the upcoming 2018 sales events and consolidate historic attendance information on events held from 2011 through 2017.
	Several copies of each workbook exist. The information required of the prospects has been structured in a hidden Prospect List worksheet, but the sales manager wants a form created to make data entry easier. Changes have been made to sales analysis data in a shared copy of the workbook and those changes need to be reviewed and accepted or rejected. Finally, three copies of the shared events workbook exist with different cost values for the events. These values need to be merged into a single workbook and visual enhancements to the worksheets are desired for presentation purposes.
Source of Data	Updated values for 2018 event costs are included in the GPC Events Noah and GPC Events Serenity workbooks. Changes have been made and tracked in the GPC Sales Analysis Changed workbook.
Calculations	All formulas are set up in the workbook. The worksheets in the workbook should be reviewed to familiarize yourself with the calculations.
Other Requirements	None.

Figure 11–2 Requirements Document

The following roadmap identifies general activities you will perform as you progress through this module:

1. DESIGN the USER INTERFACE.
2. RECORD USER INPUT to another location using the user interface.
3. WRITE the Visual Basic for Applications (VBA) CODE.
4. TEST the USER INTERFACE.
5. SHARE AND COLLABORATE on a workbook.
6. USE COMMENTS for review discussion.
7. TRACK CHANGES made to the workbook.
8. FINALIZE the WORKBOOK.

To Run Excel and Open a Workbook

The following steps run Excel and open a workbook named GPC Sales Analysis. To complete these steps, you will be required to use the Data Files. Please contact your instructor for information about accessing the Data Files.

1 Run Excel.

2 Open the file named GPC Sales from the Data Files.

3 If the Excel window is not maximized, click the Maximize button on its title bar to maximize the window.

4 Save the workbook on your hard drive, OneDrive, or other storage location as a macro-enabled workbook (.xlsm format) using GPC Sales Analysis as the file name (Figure 11–3).

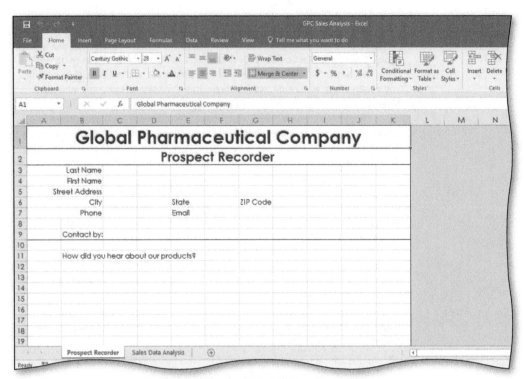

Figure 11–3

Designing the User Interface

The GPC sales team is using Excel to maintain information on prospects and their product interests. The head of sales has requested a simple user interface that can be used by salespeople to record details about prospects in the workbook. You will create a method of entering data for people with little or no knowledge of Excel, who might not know which cells to select or how to navigate the worksheet. Figure 11–4 shows the approach that will be used to create the user interface and how the Prospect Recorder worksheet will look when complete.

When a user clicks the 'Click to Enter Contact Information' command button, it will trigger Excel to display a series of input dialog boxes to capture contact information. The remaining data (the prospect's preferred method of communication, how they heard about GPC's products, and their specific product interest) will be entered using check boxes and option buttons to help reduce input errors that can be caused by mistyped data. Multiple check boxes can be selected for product interests. Unlike check boxes, option buttons restrict users to one selection per group, in this case to one preferred method of contact and one source of information. Because all of the data entry will use controls and input dialog boxes, you can protect the workbook to restrict the user's interaction with the worksheet to those controls and dialog boxes.

Planning Controls into the Worksheet Design

Two types of controls are used to create the user interface: form controls and ActiveX controls. Form controls and ActiveX controls look identical in the controls gallery. They do have functional differences, however, that can help determine which one is the best choice for an object.

Step 1 — Create the User Interface

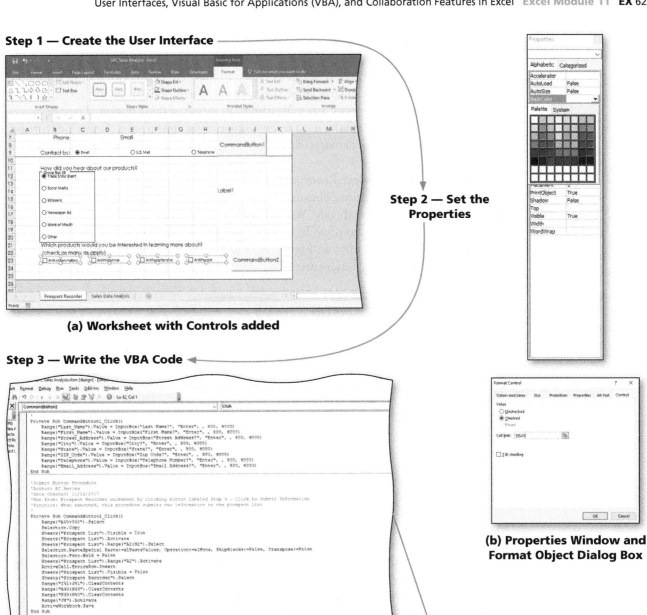

(a) Worksheet with Controls added

Step 2 — Set the Properties

Step 3 — Write the VBA Code

(c) VBA Code Associated with Controls

(b) Properties Window and Format Object Dialog Box

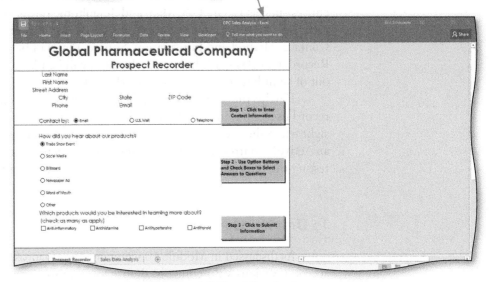

(d) Final Product

Figure 11–4

Form controls require no knowledge of VBA to use. You can assign an Excel macro directly to a form control, allowing the macro to be run with a click. Form controls also allow you to reference cells easily and use Excel functions and expressions to manipulate data. You can customize their appearance at a rudimentary level.

ActiveX controls provide great flexibility in terms of their design. They have extensive properties that can be used to customize their appearance. ActiveX controls cannot be assigned an Excel macro directly. The macro code must be part of the VBA code for the control.

To create the Prospect Recorder interface, you will use form controls for the check box and option buttons, because of their ease of use and ability to use Excel functions with no additional code. You will use ActiveX controls for the command button and label controls to provide a more visually appealing interface than would be possible just using form controls. Figure 11-5 displays the gallery of controls available to use when constructing a user interface.

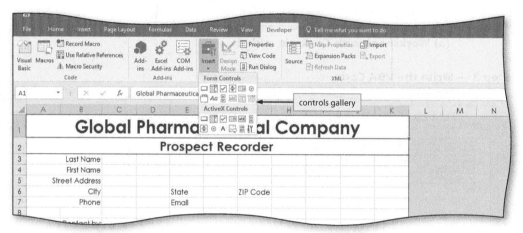

Figure 11–5

The option button controls will be used with the INDEX function to record the single selections for two entries: the prospect's preferred method of contact and how prospects heard about the products. When selected, the control will return a number indicating which option button was selected. The INDEX function matches that selection to a list and returns the entry in the list. This allows the workbook to contain entries such as Email, U.S. Mail, and Telephone, rather than values that the control returns such as 1, 2, and 3. The INDEX function will make use of the named ranges, Contact_Method and Information_Source, that will be created in the Prospect Recorder worksheet. These named ranges will be placed in column W to keep them out of sight but still on the same worksheet as the user interface.

Finally, the user interface will record input in two places. It will temporarily record user input in row 40 of the Prospect Recorder worksheet, which is out of sight when the user interface is visible. Once the user input is recorded in row 40, an ActiveX control will copy the input to a hidden worksheet, Prospect List. When testing the interface, you will verify the data recorded in the hidden worksheet.

To Display the Developer Tab

As discussed in Module 10 when creating macros, the Developer tab provides access to various VBA controls. Before you can work with VBA, you need to prepare the workbook by providing access to the necessary tools. The following steps display the Developer tab on the ribbon.

1 Display the Backstage view.

2 Click Options in the left pane to display the Excel Options dialog box.

3 Click Customize Ribbon in the left pane (Excel Options dialog box) to display the Customize the Ribbon tools.

4 Click the Developer check box in the Main Tabs list to select the Developer tab for display on the ribbon.

5 Click the OK button (Excel Options dialog box) to close the dialog box.

To Add Form Controls to a Worksheet

1 DESIGN USER INTERFACE | 2 RECORD USER INPUT | 3 WRITE VBA CODE | 4 TEST USER INTERFACE
5 SHARE & COLLABORATE | 6 USE COMMENTS | 7 TRACK CHANGES | 8 FINALIZE WORKBOOK

Why? *You will use form controls not only to ensure consistent data entry but also to make the final interface one that someone unfamiliar with Excel will be able to use easily.* The following steps create the form controls. Do not be concerned about the exact placement of controls on the form. The option buttons and check boxes will be aligned later in the module.

1

- If necessary, display the Prospect Recorder worksheet.

- Display the Developer tab and then click the Insert Controls button (Developer tab | Controls group) to display the Controls gallery (Figure 11–6).

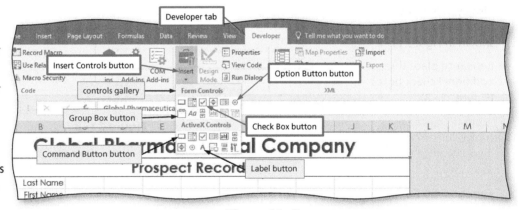

Figure 11–6

2

- Click the Option Button button in the Form Controls area (column 6, row 1) in the Controls gallery.

- Drag the pointer to place the option button control in cell C9 (approximately), as shown in Figure 11–7.

- Repeat to place eight additional option buttons (Figure 11–7).

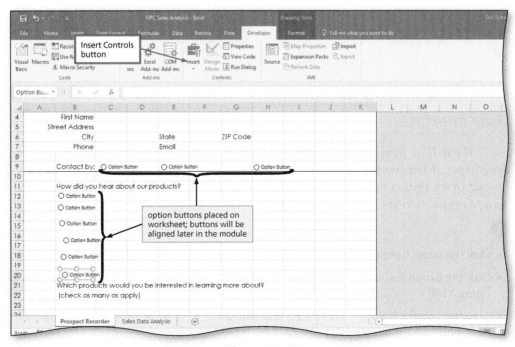

Figure 11–7

Q&A Why does my option button have more label text showing than in the figure?

The amount of text visible is determined by the size of the control. Dragging through a larger space on the worksheet will result in more label text being displayed. You can adjust the amount of visible label text by resizing the control.

3

- Click the Insert Controls button (Developer tab | Controls group) to display the Controls gallery, as shown in Figure 11–6.

- Click the Check Box button in the Form Controls area (column 3, row 1) in the Controls gallery.

- Drag so that the check box control is displayed in cell B24 (approximately), as shown in Figure 11–8.

- Repeat to place three additional check boxes (Figure 11–8).

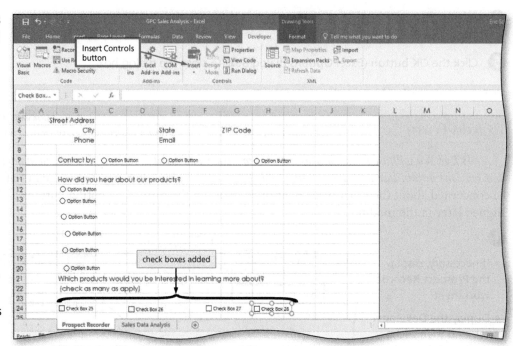

Figure 11–8

Q&A What if I placed a control incorrectly?

If you want to reposition a control, right-click the control to select it and then drag it to its new location. You can delete a control by right-clicking the control and selecting Cut on the shortcut menu.

The check box is not the size I need it to be. What can I do?

Check boxes are resized easily. The check boxes here will be resized after the captions are changed later in this module.

Other Ways

1. Select control, click Copy button (Home tab | Clipboard group), click Paste button (Home tab | Clipboard group)

2. Right-click control, click Copy on shortcut menu, right-click worksheet, click Paste on shortcut menu

3. Select control, press CTRL+C to copy, press CTRL+V to paste

To Group Option Buttons in the User Interface

1 DESIGN USER INTERFACE | 2 RECORD USER INPUT | 3 WRITE VBA CODE | 4 TEST USER INTERFACE
5 SHARE & COLLABORATE | 6 USE COMMENTS | 7 TRACK CHANGES | 8 FINALIZE WORKBOOK

Why? *With form controls, only one of the option buttons on the entire form can be selected unless the option buttons are grouped. When grouped, only one option button per group can be selected.* Use the group box form control to group one set of the option buttons together. The following step first creates the group box form control, and then groups option buttons inside it.

- Click the Insert Controls button (Developer tab | Controls group) to display the Controls gallery.

- Click the Group Box button in the Form Controls area (column 1, row 2) in the Controls gallery, as shown in Figure 11–6.

- Drag the pointer from cell B12 to C20, approximately, so that the group box control encloses the six 'How did you hear' option buttons (Figure 11–9).

Q&A How accurately do I have to draw the group box?
The option button controls need to be completely enclosed in the group box control in order for it to work correctly.

Why did I not add a group box control around the Contact by option buttons?
Group boxes are used to logically collect option buttons in order to limit the selection of options to only one choice from the group. Any option buttons not contained within a group box are treated as a group contained by the form, so the Contact by option buttons are grouped by default. Without the addition of one group box on the form, the user would only be able to select one option button out of the nine option buttons.

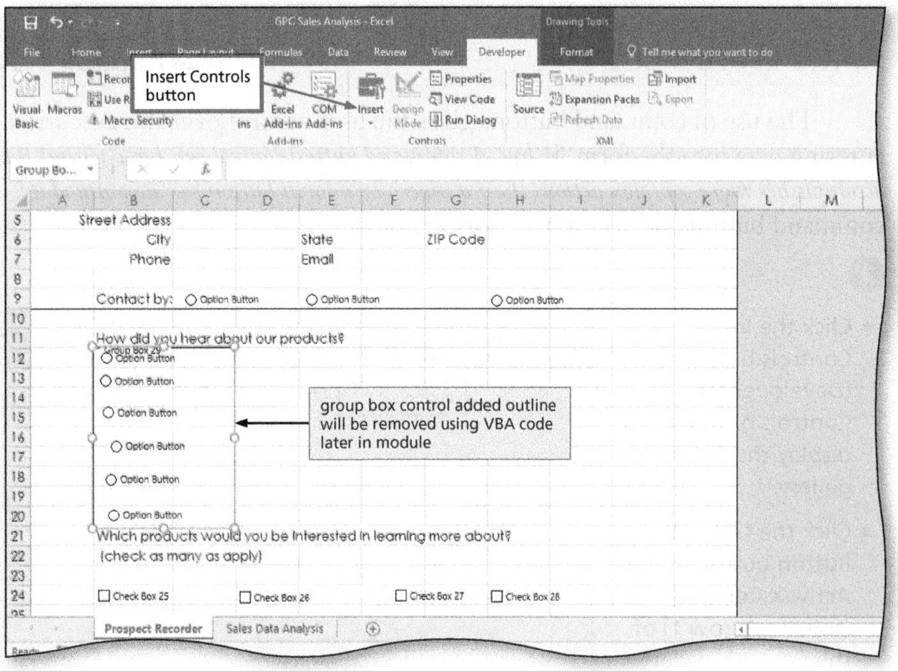

Figure 11–9

To Add a Label Control to the Worksheet

1 DESIGN USER INTERFACE | 2 RECORD USER INPUT | 3 WRITE VBA CODE | 4 TEST USER INTERFACE
5 SHARE & COLLABORATE | 6 USE COMMENTS | 7 TRACK CHANGES | 8 FINALIZE WORKBOOK

A total of 13 option buttons and check box controls have been added to the form so far. Adding a label can guide the user on the use of these controls within the process of entering the prospect information. ***Why?*** *A label control can be used to impart information in a user interface.* The following step adds a label control to the worksheet.

1

- Click cell I14.
- Click the Insert Controls button (Developer tab | Controls group) to display the Controls gallery.
- Click the Label button in the ActiveX Controls area (column 3, row 2) of the Controls gallery as shown in Figure 11–6.
- Using the selected cell I14 as a guide, drag the pointer (a crosshair) from the upper-left corner of cell I14 to the lower-right corner of cell J15 to insert the label control (Figure 11–10).

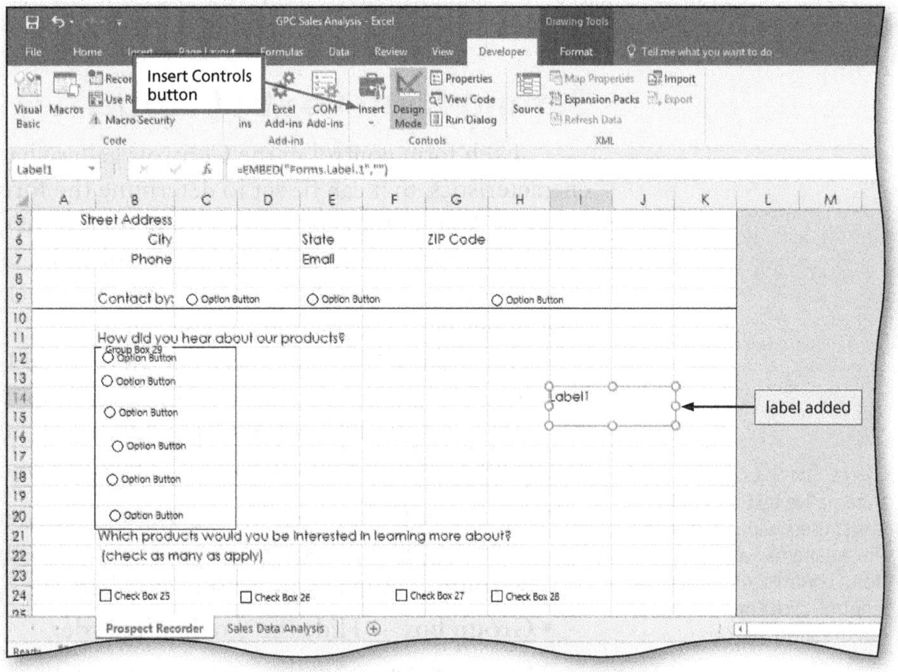

Figure 11–10

To Add a Command Button Control to the Worksheet

The use of command buttons gives the user control over the execution of each step of the process when entering data into the form. *Why? A command button control can have Visual Basic code associated with it that accomplishes more complex actions than a macro or a form button can accommodate.* The following steps add two command button controls to the worksheet.

 1

- Click the Insert Controls button (Developer tab | Controls group) to display the Controls gallery.
- Click the Command Button button in the ActiveX Controls area (column 1, row 1) of the Controls gallery.
- Drag the pointer (a crosshair) from the upper-left corner of cell I7 to the lower-right corner of cell J9, as shown in Figure 11–11.

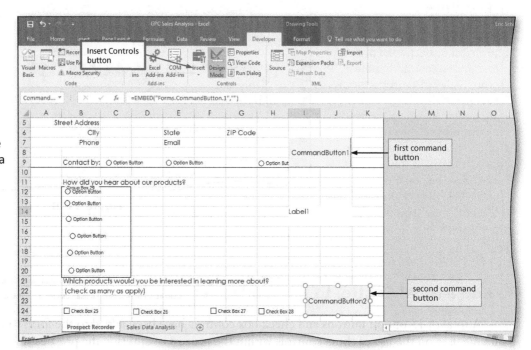

Figure 11–11

2

- Repeat Step 1 to add a second command button in the location shown in Figure 11–11.
- Save the workbook again on the same storage location with the same file name (Figure 11–11).

Setting Form Control Properties

Each form control in the Controls gallery has many properties, or characteristics, that can be set to determine the form control's appearance and behavior. You set these properties using the Format Control dialog box, which can be accessed by right-clicking the form control and selecting Format Control from the shortcut menu, or by selecting the control and clicking the Control Properties button (Developer tab | Controls group) on the ribbon.

The next step is to set the properties for the 13 form controls in the user interface. The group box, while technically a form control, will not be formatted here. This will be formatted using VBA later in the module. The three ActiveX controls also will be formatted later in the module. The form control properties will be set as follows:

BTW
Adding Alternative Text for Accessibility
Alternative text is used to assist users with disabilities. To set alternative text on form controls, right-click the control, click Format Control on the shortcut menu, and then enter the desired alternative text on the Alt Text tab of the Format Control dialog box.

- **Option buttons** — Set the captions to match those in Figure 11–4d. Resize the controls so that the entire caption shows. Align and horizontally distribute the Contact by controls. Align and vertically distribute the option buttons inside the group box.
- **Group box** — Hide the group box border.
- **Check boxes** — Set the captions to match those in Figure 11–4d. Resize the controls so that the entire caption shows. Align and horizontally distribute the check box controls.

To Format the Form Controls

Why? The option button controls must be formatted to identify their purpose for the user. Other formatting options can be used to make the controls and the worksheet upon which they are found easier and more pleasant to use. The following steps change the text associated with the option button controls, resize the controls, and align and distribute the controls.

- Right-click the first option button control in the Contact by area to display the shortcut menu (Figure 11–12).

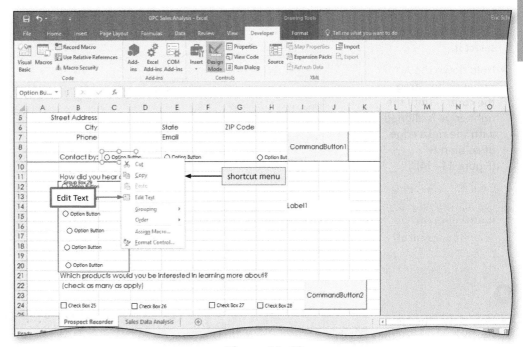

Figure 11–12

- Click Edit Text on the shortcut menu to edit the control text.
- Delete the text in the control and type **Email** to replace the text.
- Resize the control so that it just encloses the new text (Figure 11–13).

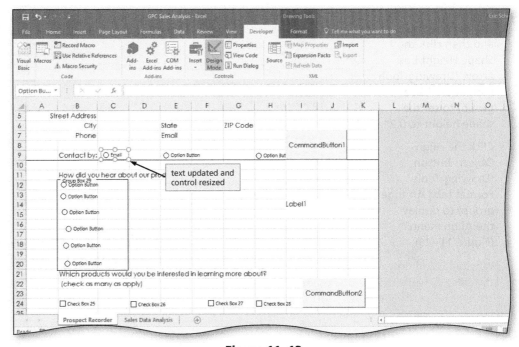

Figure 11–13

- Repeat Steps 1 and 2 to resize and rename the other two contact controls, naming them as shown in Figure 11–14.

- If necessary, click the Telephone control to select it.

- Hold down the ALT key and then drag the control until the right edge is aligned with the right edge of column H (Figure 11–14).

Q&A Why did I hold down the ALT key while positioning the Telephone control?
Using the ALT key aligns the controls to the grid making it easier to place items on the form.

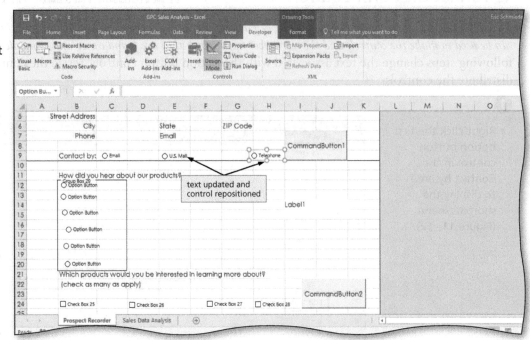

Figure 11–14

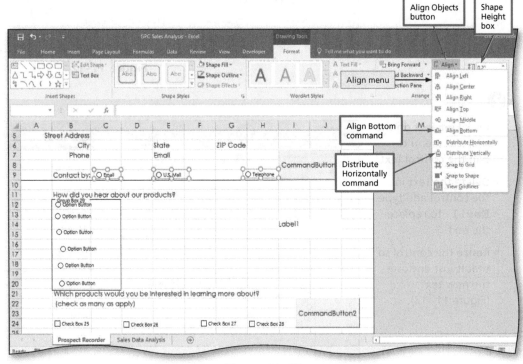

Figure 11–15

- Hold down the CTRL key and then click the other two controls to select all three option button controls.

- Display the Drawing Tools Format tab and then click the Shape Height box arrow (Drawing Tools Format tab | Size group) to set the shape height to 0.2".

- Click the Align Objects button (Drawing Tools Format tab | Arrange group) to display the Align menu (Figure 11–15).

Q&A Why did I hold down the CTRL key while clicking the other two controls?
The CTRL key adds additional controls to the selection so that formatting and alignment options can be adjusted on the set of controls rather than individually.

5

- Click Align Bottom on the Arrange menu to align the three controls along their bottom borders.

- Click the Align Objects button again (Drawing Tools Format tab | Arrange group) to display the alignment options.

- Click Distribute Horizontally on the Arrange menu to space the three controls evenly between columns C and H.

- Make C8 the active cell to deselect the option buttons and then click to select the Email option button (Figure 11–16).

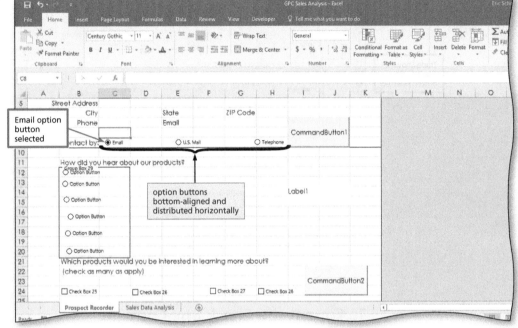

Figure 11–16

Q&A

How can I make the controls more visible?
You can format the controls with borders and fill colors to make them stand out from the background. From the shortcut menu, you can select Format Control and then use the Color and Lines tab in the Format Control dialog box to apply colors and patterns.

Can I make the controls a specific size?
The size of controls can also be set using the Format Control command on the shortcut menu.

To Format the Controls in the Group Box

The following steps format the option buttons in the group box control.

1 Right-click each of the six option buttons in the group box in turn and edit the text to match the text in Figure 11–17.

2 Move the top option button so that its upper-left corner aligns with the upper-left corner of cell B12, and then move the bottom option button so that its lower-left corner aligns with the lower-left corner of cell B20.

3 Select all six controls, and using the Shape Height and Shape Width boxes (Drawing Tools Format tab | Size group), set the control height to 0.2" and the shape width to 1.1".

4 With the six controls still selected, using the Align Objects button (Drawing Tools Format tab | Arrange group), apply the Align Left and Distribute Vertically formats to the group.

5 Make A10 the active cell to deselect the option buttons, and then click to select the Trade Show Event option button (Figure 11–17).

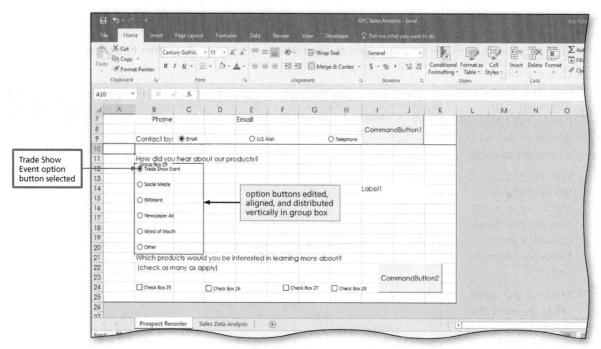

Figure 11–17

To Format the Check Box Controls

The check box controls are formatted in the same fashion as the option button controls. The following steps format and align the check box controls.

1 Select each of the four check box buttons , and in turn, type the following: **Anti-inflammatory, Antihistamine, Antihypertensive,** and **Antithyroid.**

2 Move the leftmost check box button so that its upper-left corner aligns with the upper-left corner of cell B23, and move the rightmost check box button so that its upper-right corner aligns with the upper-right corner of cell H23.

3 Select all four controls and then using the Shape Height and Shape Width boxes (Drawing Tools Format tab | Size group), set the control height to 0.2″ and the shape width to 1.2″.

4 If necessary select all four controls and then using the Align Objects button (Drawing Tools Format tab | Arrange group), apply the Align Top and Distribute Horizontally formats to the group (Figure 11–18).

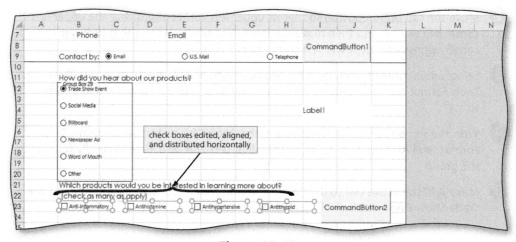

Figure 11–18

Setting ActiveX Control Properties

Like with form controls, each ActiveX control in the Controls gallery has many properties that determine the control's appearance and behavior. You set these properties in Design mode, which is entered by using the Design Mode button in the Controls group on the Developer tab on the ribbon. This will open the Properties dialog box where the control properties can be set or edited.

The user interface contains three ActiveX controls: two command buttons and a text box. The color, font, and effects for these controls will be modified by applying property values.

To Format the ActiveX Controls

1 DESIGN USER INTERFACE | 2 RECORD USER INPUT | 3 WRITE VBA CODE | 4 TEST USER INTERFACE
5 SHARE & COLLABORATE | 6 USE COMMENTS | 7 TRACK CHANGES | 8 FINALIZE WORKBOOK

Why? *Format the command button and label controls to provide instructions to the user and to make them visually prominent. Adding color, font formatting, shadow properties, and detailed captions to the ActiveX controls draw a user's attention.* The following steps set the properties using the Properties window.

- Select the two command button controls and the label control.

- Display the Developer tab and then click the Control Properties button (Developer tab | Controls group) to open the Properties window.

- Click the BackColor property to display the BackColor arrow.

- Click the BackColor arrow to display the BackColor options.

- Click the Palette tab to display the color options (Figure 11–19).

Q&A Why does the Properties window look different from other dialog boxes in Excel?
The Properties window is part of the VBA interface and is used to manage ActiveX controls in Excel.

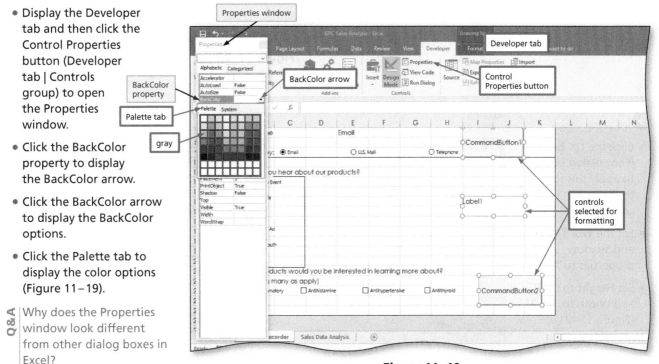

Figure 11–19

2

- Click gray (column 1, row 3) to add a gray background to the command buttons.
- Click the Font property to display the ellipsis button.
- Click the ellipsis button to display the Font dialog box.
- Select Segoe UI in the Font list, Bold in the Font style list, and 10 in the Size list to change the font on the command buttons and in the label (Figure 11–20).

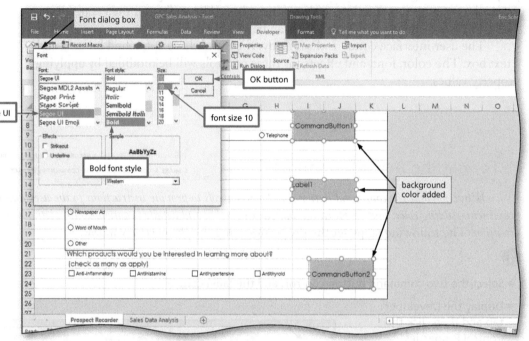

Figure 11–20

3

- Click the OK button (Font dialog box) to apply this font to the text in the controls.
- Set the WordWrap and Shadow properties to True.
- Set Height to 50.25 and Width to 140.25 (Figure 11–21).

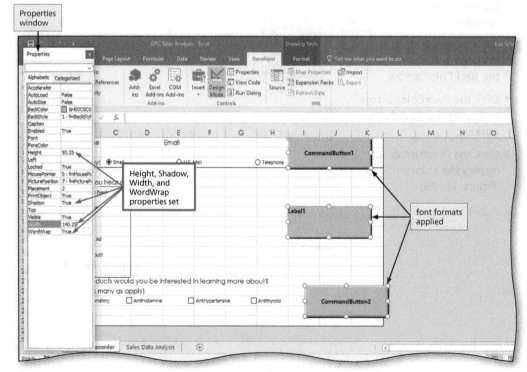

Figure 11–21

- Select the command button controls individually and then enter the text shown in Figure 11–22 into the Caption property for each command button.

- Select the label control and then enter the text shown in the figure into the Caption property (Figure 11–22).

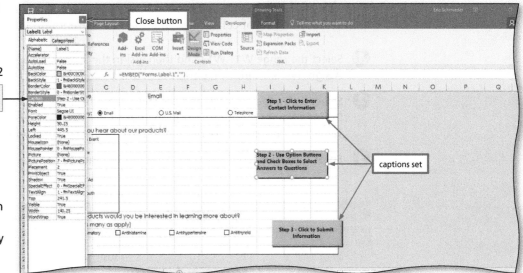

Figure 11–22

- Close the Properties window.

- Select the command buttons and the label and use the Align Objects button (Drawing Tools Format tab | Arrange group) to apply the Align Right and Distribute Vertically formats to the group.

- With the three controls still selected, use the arrow keys to move the controls as a group to the locations shown in Figure 11–23.

- Save the workbook again on the same storage location with the same file name (Figure 11–23).

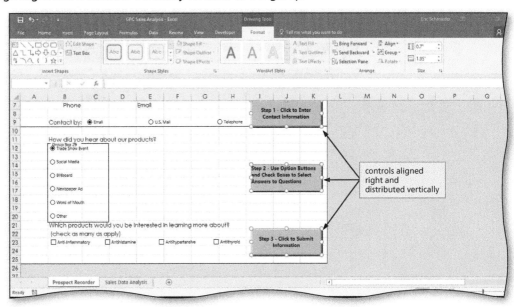

Figure 11–23

Recording User Input

Once you have added the controls to the worksheet, consider where the information will be stored within the workbook, so that it will be accessible to Excel and experienced users, but not distracting to users entering data in the form. For this project, you will temporarily store input in row 40 of the worksheet before copying that information into the Prospects List worksheet for long-term retention. To prepare for the user input you will name the cells for each of fields directly entered by the user and use INDEX functions to look up values selected with the option button controls.

To Assign Names to Ranges and Cells

The following steps assign names to ranges and cells and enter necessary references. The lists of cell names and references are found in Tables 11–1 and 11–2.

1 Select the range W11:W13 and then assign the name Contact_Method to the range. Assign the name Information_Source to the range W3:W8.

2 Select the range A39:H40 and use the 'Create from Selection' button (Formulas tab | Defined Names group) to assign the names in cells A39:H39 to the cells A40:H40. Using Table 11–1 as a guide, verify that the names have been assigned to the correct cells.

3 Enter the cell references listed in Table 11–2 into the appropriate cells.

Table 11–1 Cell Names	
Cell	**Name**
A40	Last_Name
B40	First_Name
C40	Street_Address
D40	City
E40	State
F40	Zip_Code
G40	Telephone
H40	Email_Address

Table 11–2 Cell References	
Cell	**Reference**
C3	=A40
C4	=B40
C5	=C40
C6	=D40
F6	=E40
H6	=F40
C7	=G40
F7	=H40

To Record User Input for Controls

1 DESIGN USER INTERFACE | 2 RECORD USER INPUT | 3 WRITE VBA CODE | 4 TEST USER INTERFACE

5 SHARE & COLLABORATE | 6 USE COMMENTS | 7 TRACK CHANGES | 8 FINALIZE WORKBOOK

The option button controls you added to the form will be used with the INDEX function to record the user's selections for two data points: the prospect's preferred method of contact and how the prospect heard about GPC's products. When a user selects one of the Contact by options, Excel interprets that input as a number (1, 2, or 3, reflecting which option button was selected) and then records that number in cell I41. You will enter an INDEX function in cell I40 that matches that number to a list, found in the named range in column W. By using the INDEX function, Excel will record the user's selections as Email, U.S. Mail, and Telephone, rather than the numerical values (1, 2, or 3) returned by the control. *Why? User input has to be changed from a numerical value to*

User Interfaces, Visual Basic for Applications (VBA), and Collaboration Features in Excel **Excel Module 11** **EX** 637

Excel Module 11

one that salespeople can understand. The following steps record the user's Contact by option to another place on the worksheet.

1

- Right-click the Email option button control to display the shortcut menu.

- Click Format Control to display the Format Control dialog box.

- If necessary, click the Control tab (Format Control dialog box) to display the Control sheet.

- Type **$I$41** in the Cell link box (Format Control dialog box) to link the option button output to cell I41 (Figure 11–24).

Q&A Why did I link only one of the option buttons to cell I41?
Option buttons work collectively as a group with a single identity assigned to the set of options. The specific value of the selected option button will be assigned to the output cell I41.

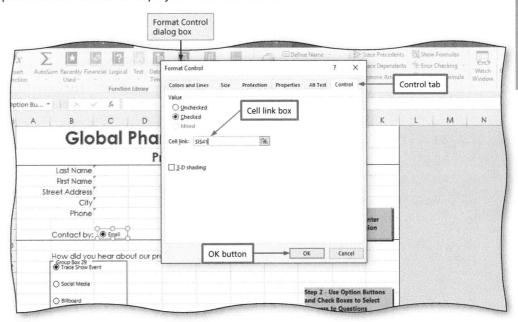

Figure 11–24

2

- Click the OK button (Format Control dialog box) to close the dialog box.

- Scroll down and then click cell I40 to make it the active cell.

- Type **=INDEX (Contact_ Method,$I$41)** to record text from named range Contact_Method rather than numbers in cell I40 (Figure 11–25).

- Click the Enter button.

Q&A How does the INDEX function work here?
In this instance, the INDEX function looks at the value in cell I41, which identifies which option button was selected, and returns the entry associated with that value from the named range, Contact_Method. The named range contact is found in column W in this worksheet.

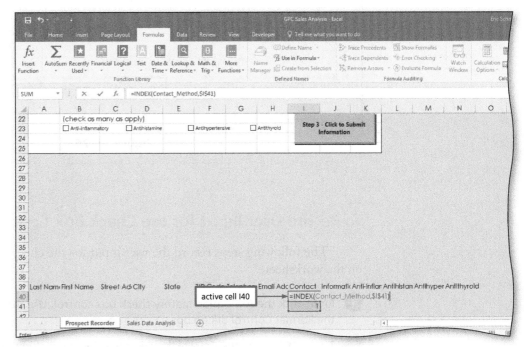

Figure 11–25

To Record User Input for the Group Box Controls

The following steps record the user response to the 'How did you hear about our products?' question in another place on the worksheet.

1 Right-click the Trade Show Event option button control and then click Format Control on the shortcut menu. If necessary, click the Control tab.

2 Type **$J$41** in the Cell link box (Format Control dialog box).

3 Click the OK button (Format Control dialog box).

4 Make cell J40 the active cell. Enter **=INDEX(Information_Source,$J$41)** to return text from the named range Information_Source rather than numbers in row 40 (Figure 11–26).

5 Click the Enter button.

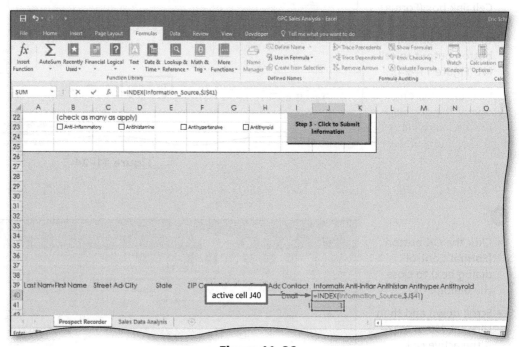

Figure 11–26

To Record User Input for the Check Box Controls

The following steps record the user input for the check boxes at another place on the worksheet.

1 Right-click the Anti-inflammatory check box control. Use the shortcut menu to display the Format Control dialog box.

2 Type **$K$40** in the Cell link box (Format Control dialog box, Control tab).

3 Click the OK button (Format Control dialog box).

4 Repeat Steps 1 through 3 for each of the remaining three check box controls, using cells $L$40, $M$40, and $N$40 for the cell links.

5 Save the workbook again on the same storage location with the same file name.

Q&A
Why do I have to link each check box control to a specific cell?
Unlike option buttons that work in groups, check box controls can each be either checked or unchecked representing TRUE or FALSE values.

Writing Code for a Command Button

Using the Controls gallery to insert a command button control into a worksheet places the object only. To have the button take action when a user clicks it, you must write VBA code that tells Excel what to do after the command button is clicked.

The next step is to write the procedure that will execute when the user clicks the 'Step 1 - Click to Enter Contact Information' button. A **procedure** is the code executed in response to an event. In VBA, procedures are blocks of code that begin with the words Private Sub and end with the line End Sub. You will enter code in the Visual Basic Editor, which is accessed from the Developer tab on the ribbon. The Visual Basic Editor is like an app within an app. The Visual Basic Editor window has its own ribbon, tabs, and groups and is navigated independently from Excel.

The Visual Basic Editor is a full-screen editor, which allows you to enter a procedure by typing the lines of VBA code as if you were using word processing software. At the end of each line, you press the ENTER key or use the DOWN ARROW key to move to the next line. If you make a mistake in a line of code, also called a statement, you can use the arrow keys and the DELETE or BACKSPACE key to correct it. You also can move the insertion point to previous lines to make corrections. As an app inside an app, the code entered in the Visual Basic Editor is saved with the macro-enabled Excel workbook. Saving from either the Visual Basic Editor or Excel will save the macro-enabled workbook and related VBA code.

When you trigger the event that executes a procedure, such as clicking a button, Excel steps through the Visual Basic statements one at a time, beginning at the top of the procedure. The statements should reflect the steps you want Excel to take, in the exact order in which they should occur. An **event-driven program** includes procedures that are executed when specific actions are taken by the user or other events occur.

After you determine what you want the procedure to do, write the VBA code on paper, creating a table similar to Table 11–3. Test the code before you enter it in the Visual Basic Editor, by stepping through the instructions one at a time yourself. As you do so, think about how the procedure affects the worksheet.

BTW
Printing VBA Code
Some people find it easier to review and edit code by working with a printout. To print out VBA code while using the Visual Basic Editor, click File on the menu bar and then click Print on the file menu.

BTW
Copying Macros Between Workbooks
Macros consist of VBA code that can be edited or copied between workbooks using the Visual Basic Editor. To copy macros between workbooks, open the workbook containing the existing macro and the destination workbook. Open the Visual Basic Editor. In the Project pane, drag the module that you want to copy to the destination workbook.

Should you document your code? Yes. Use comments to document each procedure. This will help you remember the purpose of the code or help somebody else understand the code. In Table 11–3, the first six lines are comments. Comments begin with the word Rem (short for Remark) or an apostrophe ('). Comments have no effect on the execution of a procedure; they simply provide information about the procedure, such as name, creation date, and function. Comments can be placed at the beginning before the Private Sub statement, in between lines of code, or at the end of a line of code, as long as each comment begins with an apostrophe ('). It is good practice to place comments containing overall documentation and information at the beginning, before the Sub statement.

CONSIDER THIS

To Enter the Command Button Procedures
Using the Visual Basic Editor

Why? To enter a procedure, you use the Visual Basic Editor. Each command button has a separate function. The first button displays a series of dialog boxes that collect information about the prospect and enter it into appropriate locations on the worksheet. The second button copies the information to the hidden Prospect List worksheet. To activate the Visual Basic Editor, Excel must be in Design mode. The following steps activate the Visual Basic Editor and create the procedure for the two command buttons.

- If necessary, display the Developer tab and then click the Design Mode button (Developer tab | Controls group) to make Design Mode active.

- Click the Step 1 button on the worksheet to select the button.

- Click the View Code button (Developer tab | Controls group) to display the Microsoft Visual Basic for Applications editor and then, if necessary, maximize the window.

- Click the Object arrow at the top of the window and then select CommandButton1 from the list.

- Enter the VBA code shown in Table 11–3 (Figure 11–27).

Table 11–3 Enter Prospect Contact Information Button Procedure
'Enter Prospect Contact Information Button Procedure
'Author: SC Series
'Date Created: 11/12/2017
'Run from: Prospect Recorder worksheet by clicking button labeled Step 1 - Click to Enter Contact Information
'Function: When executed, this procedure enters contact information for the prospect
'
Private Sub CommandButton1_Click()
Range("Last_Name").Value = InputBox("Last Name?", "Enter", , 800, 6000)
Range("First_Name").Value = InputBox("First Name?", "Enter", , 800, 6000)
Range("Street_Address").Value = InputBox("Street Address?", "Enter", , 800, 6000)
Range("City").Value = InputBox("City?", "Enter", , 800, 6000)
Range("State").Value = InputBox("State?", "Enter", , 800, 6000)
Range("ZIP_Code").Value = InputBox("Zip Code?", "Enter", , 800, 6000)
Range("Telephone").Value = InputBox("Telephone Number?", "Enter", , 800, 6000)
Range("Email_Address").Value = InputBox("Email Address?", "Enter", , 800, 6000)
End Sub

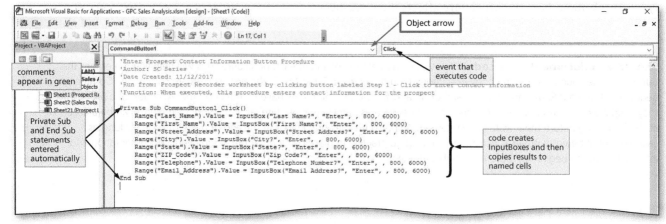

Figure 11–27

- Click the Object arrow and then click CommandButton2 in the list.
- Enter the VBA code shown in Table 11–4 (Figure 11–28).
- If requested by your instructor, enter your place of birth following the Author entry.

Table 11–4 Submit Button Procedure

'Submit Button Procedure

'Author: SC Series

'Date Created: 11/12/2017

'Run from: Prospect Recorder worksheet by clicking button labeled Step 3 - Click to Submit Information

'Function: When executed, this procedure submits new information to the prospect list

'

Private Sub CommandButton2_Click()

   Range("A40:O40").Select

   Selection.Copy

   Sheets("Prospect List").Visible = True

   Sheets("Prospect List").Activate

   Sheets("Prospect List").Range("A2:N2").Select

   Selection.PasteSpecial Paste:=xlPasteValues, Operation:=xlNone, SkipBlanks:=False, Transpose:=False

   Selection.Font.Bold = False

   Sheets("Prospect List").Range("A2").Activate

   ActiveCell.EntireRow.Insert

   Sheets("Prospect List").Visible = False

   Sheets("Prospect Recorder").Select

   Range("I41:J41").ClearContents

   Range("A40:H40").ClearContents

   Range("K40:N40").ClearContents

   Range("J8").Activate

   ActiveWorkbook.Save

End Sub

Figure 11–28

- Verify your code by comparing it with the content of Tables 11–3 and 11–4.

To Remove the Outline from the Group Control

1 DESIGN USER INTERFACE | 2 RECORD USER INPUT | **3 WRITE VBA CODE** | **4 TEST USER INTERFACE**
5 SHARE & COLLABORATE | **6 USE COMMENTS** | **7 TRACK CHANGES** | **8 FINALIZE WORKBOOK**

Why? Removing the outline from the group control will result in a more visually pleasing user interface. Removing the outline requires a line of VBA code. You will enter this in the Immediate window in the Visual Basic Editor. The Immediate window often is used for debugging and executing statements during design. As its name suggests, code entered in this window is executed immediately upon exiting the Visual Basic Editor. The following step removes the outline from the group control.

- Press CTRL+G to open the Immediate window.

- Type `activesheet.
groupboxes.visible =
false` and then press the ENTER key to remove the box from around the group control (Figure 11–29).

- Close the Visual Basic Editor window.

- Save the workbook again on the same storage location with the same file name.

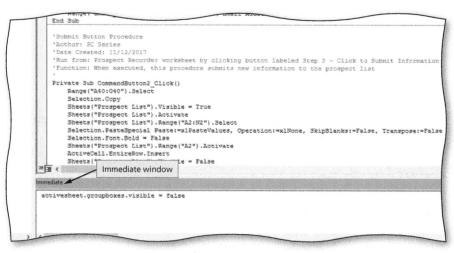

Figure 11–29

Break Point: If you wish to take a break, this is a good place to do so. You can now exit Excel. To resume at a later time, run Excel, open the file called GPC Sales Analysis, and continue following the steps from this location forward.

Sharing and Collaboration

If others need to edit a workbook or suggest changes, Excel provides three ways to collaborate. In addition, Excel offers several methods to protect your privacy or hide data that you may not want to share with others. Before distributing your workbook to others, you should consider what type of hidden information might be in your document. In previous modules, you have learned to hide rows and columns, protect cells, protect worksheets, and protect workbooks. Other types of information may be hidden in a workbook. Excel provides a tool called the Document Inspector to inspect and report such information. You then easily can remove the hidden information or choose to leave the information in the document.

When distributing a workbook, you also should consider whether the intended recipients have the most recent version of Excel. If this is not the case, Excel allows you to save a workbook for use in previous versions of Excel, such as Excel 97-2003. When you save a workbook in the Excel 97-2003 Workbook file format, Excel will invoke the Compatibility Checker, which notifies you if any of the content of your workbook cannot be saved in that format. Additionally, the Compatibility Checker will inform you if any content will not appear the same in the new format, such as cell or chart formatting.

To Prepare and Protect the Worksheet

Why? *You are removing the ribbon from view and protecting the worksheet to restrict what the user can do in this worksheet.* The following steps prepare and protect the worksheet, and then save the workbook.

- If necessary, click the Design Mode button (Developer tab | Controls group) to exit Design mode.

- Display the Backstage view.

- Click Options to display the Excel Options dialog box.

- Click the Advanced tab (Excel Options dialog box) to display the advanced options.

- Scroll to the 'Display options for this worksheet' area in the right pane and then, if necessary, click the 'Show page breaks' and 'Show a zero in cells that have zero value' check boxes to remove the check marks (Figure 11–30).

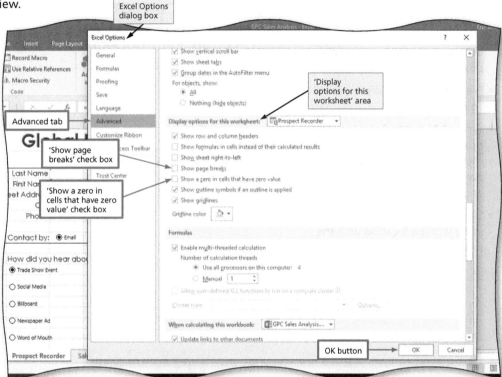

Figure 11–30

- Click the OK button to close the dialog box.

- Display the View tab.

- Click the View Gridlines, Formula Bar, and View Headings check boxes (View tab | Show group) to remove the check marks (Figure 11–31).

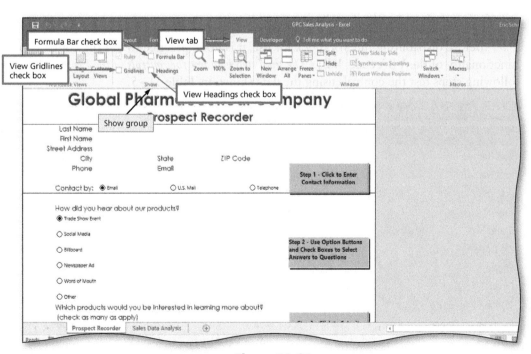

Figure 11–31

- Click the 'Collapse the Ribbon' button on the ribbon to collapse the ribbon.
- Display the Review tab and then click the Protect Sheet button (Review tab | Changes group) to display the Protect Sheet dialog box.
- Type **Prospect17** in the 'Password to unprotect sheet' text box and then click the OK button (Protect Sheet dialog box) to display the Confirm Password dialog box.
- Type **Prospect17** in the 'Reenter password to proceed' text box and then click the OK button (Confirm Password dialog box) to close the dialog boxes.
- Press the F5 key to display the Go To dialog box.
- Type **J8** in the Reference text box (Go To dialog box) and then click the OK button (Go To dialog box) to make cell J8 the active cell and close the dialog box.
- Save the workbook again on the same storage location with the same file name (Figure 11–32).

Q&A
Do any rules apply to passwords?
Yes. Passwords in Excel can contain, in any combination, letters, numbers, spaces, and symbols, and can be up to 15 characters long. Passwords are case sensitive. If you decide to password-protect a worksheet, make sure you save the password in a secure place. If you lose the password, you will not be able to open or gain access to the password-protected worksheet.

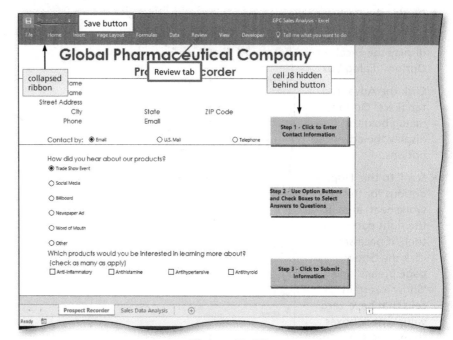

Figure 11–32

To Test the Controls in the Worksheet

1 DESIGN USER INTERFACE | 2 RECORD USER INPUT | 3 WRITE VBA CODE | 4 TEST USER INTERFACE
5 SHARE & COLLABORATE | 6 USE COMMENTS | 7 TRACK CHANGES | 8 FINALIZE WORKBOOK

Before distributing the workbook for use, it is good practice to test the controls and verify the proper functionality of the VBA code. *Why? The final step is to test the controls in the Prospect Recorder worksheet.* The following steps test the controls using the data shown in Table 11–5.

Table 11–5 Prospect Records		
Field	**Record 1**	**Record 2**
Last Name	Derringer	Shum
First Name	Kevin	Laurie
Address	572 Birch Street	31 Windsor Road
City	Clayton	Parkville
State	NC	MD
Zip Code	27520	21234
Phone	555-555-1212	555-555-1313
Email	kderringer@scseries.com	lshum@scseries.com
Contact Preference	Telephone	Email
Information Source	Social Media	Trade Show Event
Interest(s)	Antihypertensive	Anti-inflammatory & Antithyroid

1

- For each of the records in Table 11–5, use the command buttons to enter the data, follow the prompts, and then submit the data.

- Unhide the Prospect List worksheet (right-click the Prospect Recorder worksheet tab, click Unhide, and then click OK), and confirm that the records were copied correctly (Figure 11–33).

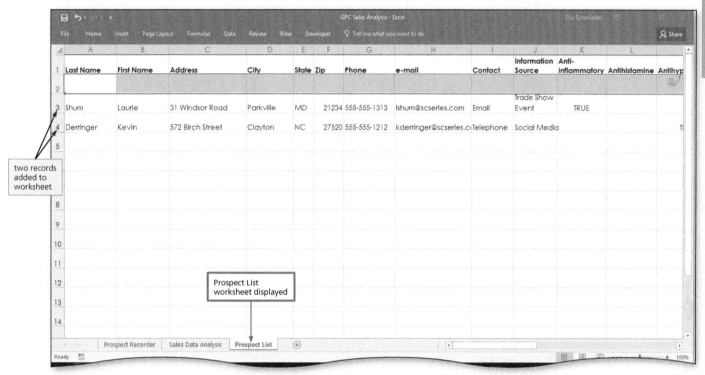

Figure 11–33

2

- Hide the Prospect List worksheet.

Collaborating with Others

Collaborating means working together on a document in cooperation with other Excel users. Excel provides three ways to collaborate.

The first option is to distribute the workbook to others, physically on storage media, through email using the Share gallery in the Backstage view, or via OneDrive. In the Share gallery, the document can be embedded as part of the email message, which allows users to view the spreadsheet upon opening the email message, or the file can be sent as an email attachment, which allows recipients of the email message to open the file if Excel is installed on their computer or mobile device.

A second option is to collaborate by sharing the workbook using the Sharing feature in Excel. Sharing involves more than simply giving another user a copy of a file; it allows multiple people to work independently on the same workbook at the same time if they are in a networked environment. Sharing a workbook puts restrictions on the types of edits a user can make, which provides a degree of control over the editing process that distributing the workbook does not. If users are not in a networked environment, workbook sharing allows them to work on the workbook in turn, while keeping track of who was responsible for each edit.

BTW

Passwords and Workbook Sharing
Excel keeps a change history of 30 days by default for a shared workbook. You can use passwords with a shared workbook to protect the change history. Use the Protect Shared Workbook button (Review tab | Changes group). The workbook cannot be shared at the time the password is added.

A third option is to collaborate interactively with other people through discussion threads or online meetings. SharePoint Services with Microsoft Office 2016 allows people at different sites to share and exchange files.

Sharing can be turned on for a workbook using the Share Workbook button on the Review tab. When workbook sharing is enabled, a number of Excel features — merging cells, deleting worksheets, changing or removing passwords, using scenarios, creating data tables, modifying macros, using data validation, and creating PivotTables — are disabled for the workbook. For this reason, limit the number of occasions when a workbook is shared; further, sharing should be used only for the purpose of reviewing and modifying the contents of worksheet data.

To Distribute a Workbook via OneDrive

1 DESIGN USER INTERFACE | 2 RECORD USER INPUT | 3 WRITE VBA CODE | 4 TEST USER INTERFACE
5 SHARE & COLLABORATE | 6 USE COMMENTS | 7 TRACK CHANGES | 8 FINALIZE WORKBOOK

You can use OneDrive to distribute workbooks instead of sending them as attachments to email messages. Just as with sharing via email, colleagues can make changes, and then save the workbook on OneDrive for review. Saving workbooks for distribution on OneDrive does not differ from using OneDrive to save your own files, although you do need to make the workbook available to others by saving it in an accessible location. *Why? You may need to have a workbook reviewed by someone who does not share network access with you.* You can send a shared workbook using OneDrive. When the recipient sends the edited workbook back to you for review, his or her changes will be tagged just as they would be if the recipient opened the workbook on the network. The following steps save the workbook and send it by OneDrive.

- Display the Backstage view.
- Click the Share tab to display the Share gallery.
- If necessary, click the 'Share with People' button to display the 'Share with People' options in the right pane (Figure 11–34).

Q&A
Why do I have a 'Save to Cloud' button instead of the 'Share with People' button?
Your file is saved on the local computer or USB file storage location and must be saved to a OneDrive location for sharing. Click the 'Save to Cloud' button and navigate to a storage location on your OneDrive before proceeding to Step 2.

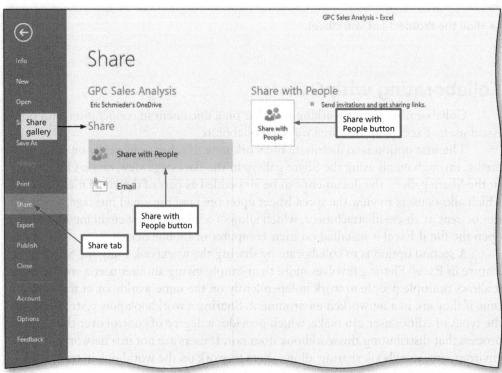

Figure 11–34

- Click the 'Share with People' button in the right pane to display the Share task pane for sending invitations and getting sharing links.

- Enter a recipient's email address in the Invite people text box (Figure 11–35).

- Verify that Can edit is selected.

- Add a brief message to the recipient and then click the Share button to send the message with a link to the shared workbook.

- Close the Share task pane.

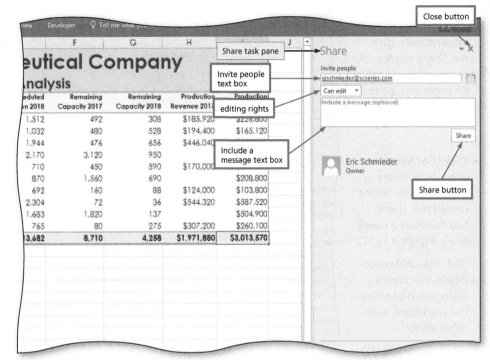

Figure 11–35

Q&A A Sharing Information dialog box was displayed after I clicked the Share button. Why?

To prevent automated programs from sharing spam documents, OneDrive may request completion of an additional authentication step.

To Share and Collaborate on a Workbook

1 DESIGN USER INTERFACE | 2 RECORD USER INPUT | 3 WRITE VBA CODE | 4 TEST USER INTERFACE
5 SHARE & COLLABORATE | 6 USE COMMENTS | 7 TRACK CHANGES | 8 FINALIZE WORKBOOK

Working together in the same workbook at the same time can improve efficiency in networked team environments. **Why?** *Sharing a workbook can provide you with a timely, interactive editing process with colleagues.* The following steps turn on sharing for the GPC Sales Analysis workbook and then allow collaboration with another user in a networked environment to make changes to the workbook.

- If necessary, display the Sales Data Analysis worksheet.

- Display the View tab and then click the 'Pin the ribbon' button on the ribbon to keep the ribbon open.

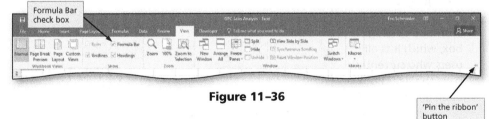

Figure 11–36

- Click the Formula Bar check box (View tab | Show group) to redisplay the formula bar (Figure 11–36).

- Display the Review tab and then click the Share Workbook button (Review tab | Changes group) to display the Share Workbook dialog box.

- Click the 'Allow changes by more than one user at the same time' check box to insert a check mark (Figure 11–37).

- Click the OK button (Share Workbook dialog box) to share the workbook with other users.

- When Excel displays the Microsoft Excel dialog box, click the OK button to save and then share the workbook.

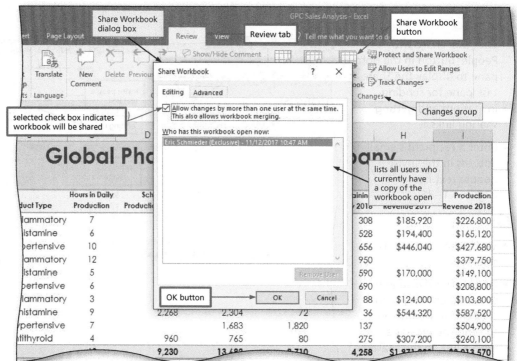

Figure 11–37

- If possible, have a classmate open a second copy of the workbook.

- With a second copy of the workbook open, click the Share Workbook button (Review tab | Changes group) to display the Share Workbook dialog box, which lists all users who currently have the workbook open (Figure 11–38).

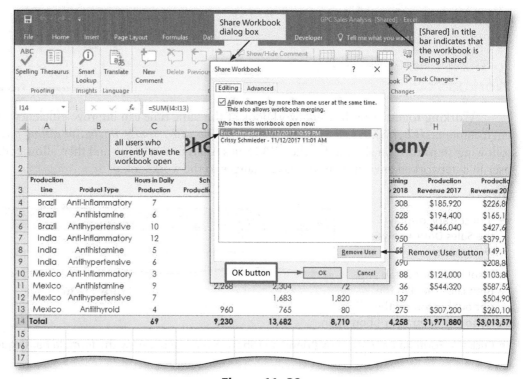

Figure 11–38

- Click the OK button (Share Workbook dialog box) to close the dialog box.

- Ask the second workbook user to click cell D7, enter **2254** as the new value, and then save the workbook.

• In your copy of the workbook, click the Save button on the Quick Access Toolbar to display the Microsoft Excel dialog box indicating that the workbook has been updated with changes saved by another user (Figure 11–39).

Q&A
Must I save the workbook before I am notified of another user's changes?
Yes. Until the workbook is saved, Excel provides no indication that another user has changed the shared workbook. To prohibit another user from saving additional updates to the workbook, click the user name in the Share Workbook dialog box and then click the Remove User button.

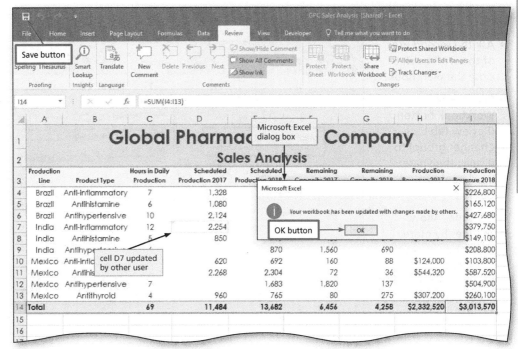

Figure 11–39

⑤

• Click the OK button (Microsoft Excel dialog box) to close the dialog box.

• Point to the triangle in cell D7 to display the comment that identifies the other user's changes (Figure 11–40).

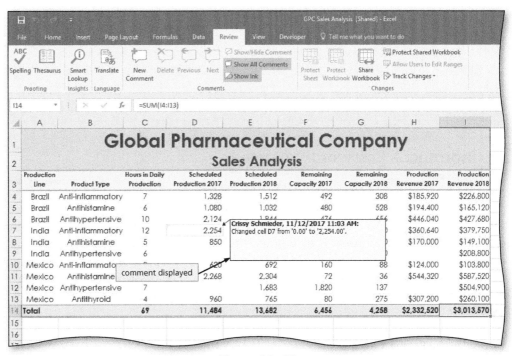

Figure 11–40

- Ask the second user of the workbook to close the workbook.

- Click the Share Workbook button (Review tab | Changes group) to display the Share Workbook dialog box.

- Click the 'Allow changes by more than one user at the same time' check box to remove the check mark (Figure 11–41).

- Click the OK button (Share Workbook dialog box) to stop sharing the workbook.

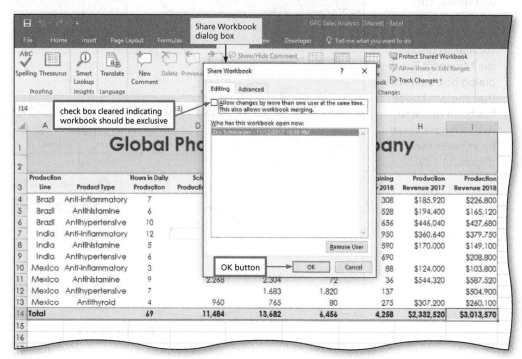

Figure 11–41

- If Excel displays the Microsoft Excel dialog box asking whether the workbook should be removed from shared use, click the Yes button.

- If desired, save the workbook in the same storage location where you save your files.

Q&A How long are changes kept?
The changes made to a workbook are called the change history. When a workbook is shared, Excel keeps the changes made for 30 days unless you set the change history to store changes for a different number of days. To alter the length of time the change history will be kept, select the Advanced tab in the Share Workbook dialog box, and set 'Keep change history for' to the desired interval.

To Unprotect a Password-Protected Worksheet

1 DESIGN USER INTERFACE | 2 RECORD USER INPUT | 3 WRITE VBA CODE | 4 TEST USER INTERFACE
5 SHARE & COLLABORATE | 6 USE COMMENTS | 7 TRACK CHANGES | 8 FINALIZE WORKBOOK

The Prospect Recorder worksheet in the GPC Sales Analysis workbook is protected, which restricts the changes you can make to the worksheet to unlocked cells only. You cannot make changes to locked cells or modify the worksheet itself. *Why unprotect the worksheet? You will unprotect the worksheet to allow changes to locked cells and the worksheet itself.* Recall from Module 4 that a password ensures that users cannot unprotect the worksheet simply by clicking the Unprotect button. The password for the worksheet is Prospect17. The following steps unprotect the password-protected Prospect Recorder worksheet.

- Display the Prospect Recorder worksheet.

- If necessary, display the Review tab, and then click the Unprotect Sheet button (Review tab | Changes group) to display the Unprotect Sheet dialog box.

- When the Unprotect Sheet dialog box appears, type **Prospect17** in the Password text box (Figure 11–42).

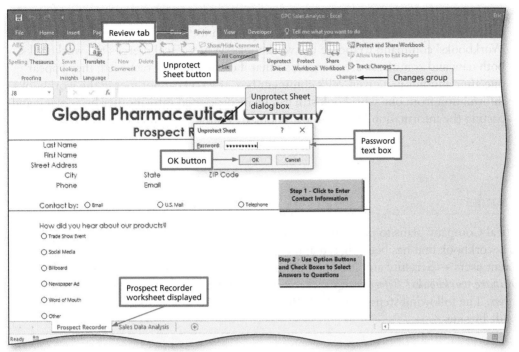

Figure 11–42

- Click the OK button (Unprotect Sheet dialog box) to unprotect the Prospect Recorder worksheet.

- Save and close the GPC Sales Analysis workbook.

Q&A Can I work with the entire worksheet now?
Yes. With the worksheet unprotected, you can modify the contents of cells, regardless of whether they are locked or unlocked. Cells must both be locked and the worksheet protected to restrict what users can do to cell contents.

Comparing and Merging Workbooks

Excel provides you with two methods to use when working with multiple versions of a workbook. You can open multiple copies of the same workbook and move through the workbooks in a synchronized manner so that the same area of each workbook is always in view. For example, as a user scrolls down a worksheet, Excel automatically updates the view of the second worksheet to show the same rows as the first worksheet. This functionality allows for a side-by-side visual comparison of two workbooks.

In the case of multiple copies of a workbook, Excel provides the capability to merge multiple copies into a single workbook. This feature requires you to do some preparation. To merge the changes from one or more workbooks into another, all workbooks must satisfy the following requirements:

- The original workbook must be shared before making copies, and each workbook must be a copy of the same workbook.

- When copies of the workbook are made, track changes or sharing must be enabled, so that the change history of the workbook is kept.

- Clicking the Share Workbook button on the Review tab displays a dialog box with a tab for recording the number of days to record the change history. Shared workbooks must be merged within that time period.

- If the workbooks have been assigned passwords, all workbooks involved in the merge must have the same password.

- Each copy of the workbook must have a different file name.

BTW

Merging and the Change History
If there are any concerns about how long it will take to get all copies of a workbook back, err on the side of caution and set a high number of days for recording the change history.

When all of the copies of the workbook are available on your hard disk, USB drive, OneDrive, or other storage medium, you can use the 'Compare and Merge Workbooks' command to merge the workbooks. When Excel merges the workbooks, both data and comments are merged, so that if comments are recorded, they appear one after another in a given cell's comment box. If Excel cannot merge the workbooks, information from one workbook still can be incorporated into another by copying and pasting the information from one workbook to another.

To Compare Workbooks

1 DESIGN USER INTERFACE | 2 RECORD USER INPUT | 3 WRITE VBA CODE | 4 TEST USER INTERFACE
5 SHARE & COLLABORATE | 6 USE COMMENTS | 7 TRACK CHANGES | 8 FINALIZE WORKBOOK

Global Pharmaceutical Company plans to participate in three sales events in 2018. Proposed event expenditures are saved in a workbook that has been shared and copied to two other members of the staff for review. Because two different users — Serenity and Noah — modified the separate workbooks, the workbooks must be merged. ***Why compare workbooks?*** *Before merging the workbooks, they can be compared visually to note the changes made by different users.* The following steps open the GPC Events and GPC Events Noah workbooks and compare the workbooks side by side.

- Open the file GPC Events from the Data Files.
- If the file opens in a maximized state, click the workbook's Restore Down button to resize the window.
- Open the file GPC Events Noah from the Data Files.
- If the file opens in a maximized state, click the workbook's Restore Down button to resize the window.
- Display the View tab and then click the 'View Side by Side' button (View tab | Window group) to display the workbooks side by side (Figure 11–43).
- Use the scroll bar in the active window to scroll the GPC Events worksheet.

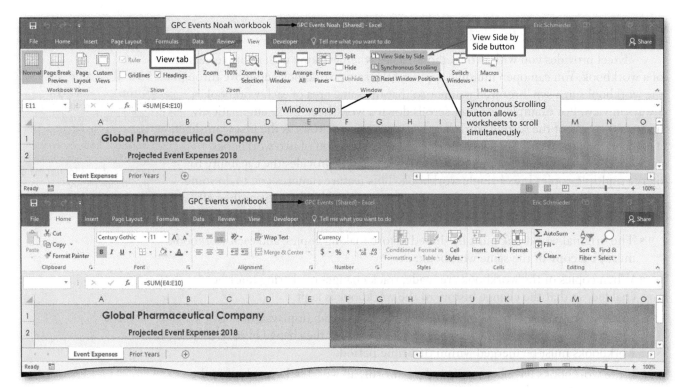

Figure 11–43

User Interfaces, Visual Basic for Applications (VBA), and Collaboration Features in Excel **Excel Module 11** **EX** 653

Excel Module 11

How should the workbooks be arranged after clicking the 'View Side by Side' button?

Depending on how previous Excel windows were arranged on your computer, the workbooks may appear next to each other left-to-right, or with one window above the other. To change how the windows are positioned, drag one workbook window to the desired screen edge to dock it. Dock the second workbook window on the opposite edge.

What happens when I scroll the worksheet?

Because the Synchronous Scrolling button is selected, both worksheets scroll at the same time so that you can make a visual comparison of the workbooks.

- Click the 'View Side by Side' button (View tab | Window group) again to display the windows separately and turn off synchronous scrolling.

- Close the GPC Events Noah workbook.

- If Excel displays a Microsoft Excel dialog box, click the Don't Save button.

- Click the Maximize button in the GPC Events window to maximize the window.

To Merge Workbooks

Why? *When multiple users have made changes to copies of a workbook, merging can be more efficient and accurate than copying changes over to a single workbook.* After the initial review, the next step is to merge the two workbooks changed by Serenity and Noah into the original GPC Events workbook. All three of the workbooks are shared. The following steps merge the workbooks containing changes from Serenity and Noah with the original workbook, GPC Events.

- Save the GPC Events workbook as GPC Events Merged in the same storage location where you save your files.

- Click the 'Customize Quick Access Toolbar' arrow next to the Quick Access Toolbar and then click More Commands on the Customize Quick Access Toolbar menu to display the Excel Options dialog box.

- Select All Commands in the 'Choose commands from' list.

- Scroll to and click the 'Compare and Merge Workbooks' command in the All Commands list.

- Click the Add button (Excel Options dialog box) to add the 'Compare and Merge Workbooks' command to the Customize Quick Access Toolbar list on the right of the dialog box (Figure 11–44).

How do I undo changes from a merge?

Merged changes cannot be undone. Make sure you make a copy of your files before you perform the merge.

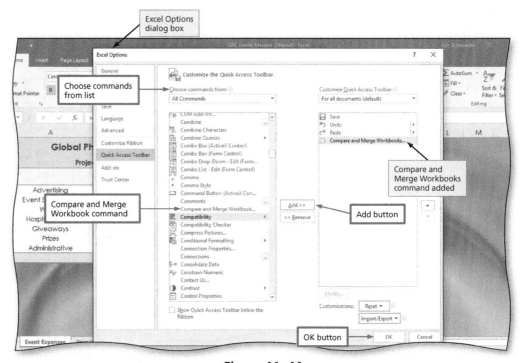

Figure 11–44

2

- Click the OK button to add the 'Compare and Merge Workbooks' button to the Quick Access Toolbar.

- Click the 'Compare and Merge Workbooks' button on the Quick Access Toolbar to display the Select Files to Merge Into Current Workbook dialog box.

- If necessary, navigate to the location of your data files.

- Click 'GPC Events Noah', hold down the SHIFT key, and then click 'GPC Events Serenity' to select both files (Figure 11–45).

Q&A Why is my 'Compare and Merge Workbooks' button gray?
The workbook must be shared before you can use the 'Compare and Merge Workbooks' button. Check to make sure your workbook is shared.

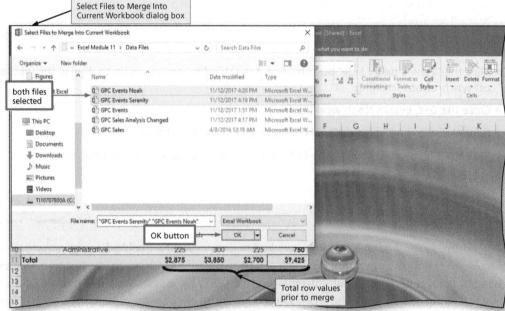

Figure 11–45

3

- Click the OK button (Select Files to Merge Into Current Workbook dialog box) to merge the workbooks (Figure 11–46).

Q&A What is the result of the merge?
The workbooks have been merged, and the GPC Events worksheet reflects the changes from Serenity and Noah. If Serenity and Noah had changed a common cell with different values, Excel would have displayed a prompt, asking which change to keep in the merged workbook.

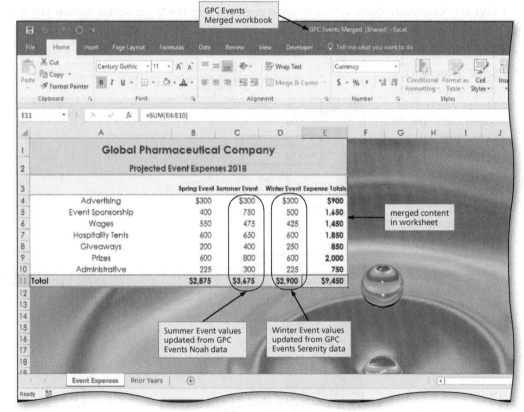

Figure 11–46

To Turn Off Workbook Sharing

Now that the three copies of the shared workbook have been merged into a single file, workbook sharing is no longer necessary. ***Why?*** *Turn off workbook sharing once the workbooks have been merged to have access to all of Excel's features.* The following steps turn off workbook sharing so that the data can be manipulated.

- Display the Review tab and then click the Share Workbook button (Review tab | Changes group) to display the Share Workbook dialog box.
- Click the 'Allow changes by more than one user at the same time' check box to remove the check mark (Figure 11–47).

- Click the OK button (Share Workbook dialog box) to turn off workbook sharing.
- If Excel displays the Microsoft Excel dialog box, Click the Yes button.
- Save and close the GPC Events Merged workbook.

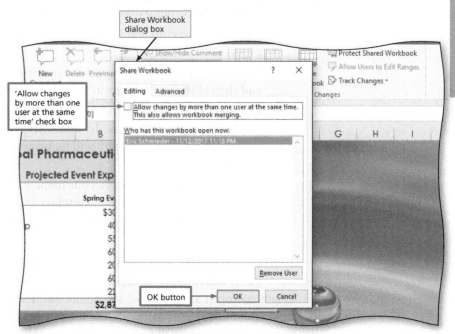

Figure 11–47

Digital Signatures

Some users prefer to attach a digital signature to verify the authenticity of a document. A **digital signature** is an electronic, encrypted, and secure stamp of authentication on a document. This signature confirms that the file originated from the signer (file developer) and that it has not been altered.

A digital signature may be visible or invisible. In either case, the digital signature references a digital certificate. A **digital certificate** is an attachment to a file or email message that vouches for its authenticity, provides secure encryption, or supplies a verifiable signature. Many users who receive files containing macros enable the macros based on whether they are digitally signed by a developer on the user's list of trusted sources.

You can obtain a digital certificate from a commercial **certificate authority** (CA), from your network administrator, or you can create a digital signature yourself. A digital certificate you create yourself is not issued by a formal certification authority. Thus, signed macros using such a certificate are referred to as **self-signed projects**. Certificates you create yourself are considered unauthenticated and still will generate a warning when opened if the security level is set to very high, high, or medium. Many users, however, consider self-signed projects safer to open than those with no certificates at all.

To Add a Signature Box and Digital Signature to a Workbook

After adding a digital signature, Excel will display the digital signature whenever the document is opened. If you wanted to add a digital signature to an Excel workbook, you would perform the following steps.

1. Open the GPC Sales Analysis workbook and, if necessary, unprotect the Prospect Recorder worksheet using the password, Prospect17.
2. Click the Insert tab and then click the 'Add a Signature Line' button in the Text group.
3. Enter your name in the Suggested signer text box (Signature Setup dialog box) and then click the OK button to add the signature box to the workbook.
4. Right-click the signature box and then click Sign on the shortcut menu to display the Sign dialog box. To sign a Microsoft Office document you need a digital ID. If necessary, you will be prompted to get one from a Microsoft Partner.
5. In the Sign dialog box, enter your name in the signature box or click the Select Image link to select a file that contains an image of your signature.
6. Click the Sign button (Sign dialog box) to digitally sign the document.

To Review a Digital Signature on a Workbook

Excel will display the digital signature whenever the document is opened. When you open a digitally signed document, Excel displays a message announcing the signature on the status bar while the file opens. After the file is opened, Excel displays a certification icon on the status bar. You can click the icon to find out who digitally signed the document. The word, Signed, also appears on the title bar in parentheses, indicating the document is signed digitally. If you wanted to review a digital signature on an Excel workbook, you would perform the following steps.

1. Display the Backstage view. If necessary, click the Info tab and then click View Signatures to open the Signatures task pane.
2. Select a name from the Valid signature list (Signature task pane), click the arrow to display the shortcut menu, and then click Signature Details to display the certificate.
3. When you are finished reviewing the certificate, click the Close button (Signature Details dialog box) and then close the workbook.

Gathering Feedback Using Comments

Comments are the electronic version of sticky notes or annotations in the margin. They can request additional information or clarification of existing information. Comments can provide direction to the reader about how to interpret content or describe what type of content to add. You can add a comment to any cell in a worksheet. Once added, you can edit, format, move, copy, or resize comments. You can choose to show comments in a worksheet, to display only a comment indicator, or to hide comments. Comments work well when multiple people are collaborating on a worksheet. Comments added by each user are identified by a name in the comment, set by the user.

Depending on the nature of the comments, you may decide to delete some or all comments after reading them and making edits to the worksheet, if appropriate.

BTW

Copying Comments
You can copy comments from one cell to other cells using the Paste Special command. Select the cell that contains the comment you need to copy, click the Copy button (Home tab | Clipboard group), select the cell or cells to which you want to apply the comment, click the Paste arrow, and then click Paste Special. In the Paste Special dialog box, in the Paste list, select Comments, and then click the OK button.

To Add Comments to a Worksheet

Why? *Comments in Excel can be used to remind the user of material that needs to be added or updated.* The Sales Analysis worksheet in the GPC Sales Analysis workbook has some missing data. The following steps add comments to the worksheet in cells A7, A9, and A12.

- If necessary, open the GPC Sales Analysis workbook and then click the Enable Content button in the yellow Security Warning bar below the ribbon.

- If necessary, display the Sales Data Analysis worksheet.

- Display the Review tab and, if necessary, click the 'Show All Comments' button (Review tab | Comments group) to toggle the option off and hide all comments in the workbook.

- Right-click cell A7 to display the shortcut menu (Figure 11–48).

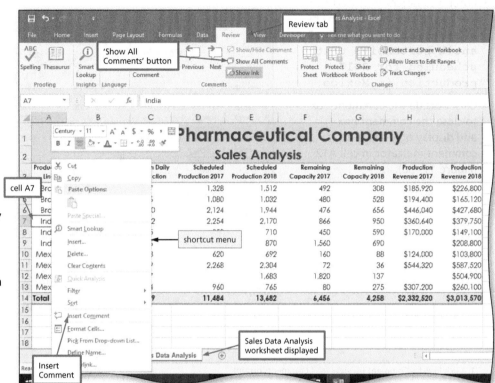

Figure 11–48

2

- Click Insert Comment on the shortcut menu to open a comment box next to the selected cell and display a comment indicator in the cell.

- Enter the text **Note to Noah - need count of anti-inflammatory units scheduled for 2017 production in India.** in the comment box (Figure 11–49).

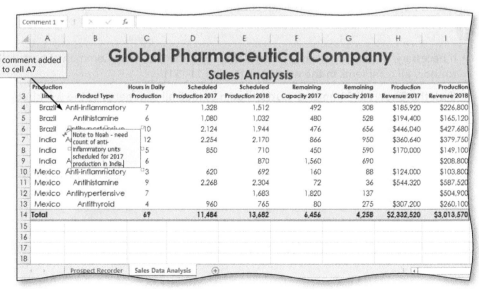

Figure 11–49

- Click outside the comment box to close the comment box and display only the red comment indicator in cell A7.

- Enter a comment in cell A9 with the text `Note to Noah - need accurate count of antihypertensive units scheduled for 2017 production in India.`

- Click outside the comment box to close the comment box and display only the red comment indicator in cell A9.

- Enter a comment in cell A12 with the text `Note to Serenity - need accurate count of antihypertensive units scheduled for 2017 production in Mexico.`

- Click outside the comment box to close the comment box and display only the red comment indicator in cell A12 (Figure 11–50).

Q&A

My comment boxes do not close when I click outside the comment box. Why?

The Show All Comments option must be active. To turn it off and display only the red comment indicators, click the Show All Comments button (Review tab | Comments group).

Global Pharmaceutical Company
Sales Analysis

Production Line	Product Type	Hours in Daily Production	Scheduled Production 2017	Scheduled Production 2018	Remaining Capacity 2017	Remaining Capacity 2018	Production Revenue 2017	Re
Brazil	Anti-Inflammatory	7	1,328	1,512	492	308	$185,920	
Brazil	Antihistamine	6	1,080	1,032	480	528	$194,400	
Brazil	Antihypertensive	10	2,124	1,944	476	656	$446,040	
India	Anti-Inflammatory		2,254	2,170	866	950	$360,640	
India	Antihistamine		850	710	450	590	$170,000	
India	Antihypertensive			870	1,560	690		
Mexico	Anti-Inflammatory		620	692	160	88	$124,000	
Mexico	Antihistamine	9	2,268	2,304	72	36	$544,320	
Mexico	Antihypertensive	7		1,683	1,820	137		
Mexico	Antithyroid	4	960	765	80	275	$307,200	
Total		69	11,484	13,682	6,456	4,258	$2,332,520	

comment indicators in cells A7, A9, and A12

Figure 11–50

Other Ways

1. Click Insert a Comment (Review tab | Comments group)
2. SHIFT+F2

To Display All Comments on a Worksheet

1 DESIGN USER INTERFACE | 2 RECORD USER INPUT | 3 WRITE VBA CODE | 4 TEST USER INTERFACE
5 SHARE & COLLABORATE | 6 USE COMMENTS | 7 TRACK CHANGES | 8 FINALIZE WORKBOOK

Why? *While editing the worksheet, you may find it helpful to have comments visible.* The comments currently are hidden. The following step makes all comments visible.

- If necessary, display the Review tab and then click the 'Show All Comments' button (Review tab | Comments group) to show all comments in the workbook (Figure 11–51).

- Click the 'Show All Comments' button again to hide all comments in the workbook.

Q&A

Can I quickly read a hidden comment in a worksheet?

Point to a comment indicator to display the related comment.

Can I print comments?

Yes. You can print comments where they appear on the worksheet by displaying all comments and then printing the sheet. You can print a list of comments separately using the Sheet tab in the Page Setup dialog box. To do so, click the Page Setup Dialog Box Launcher (Page Layout tab | Page Setup group), click the Sheet tab (Page Setup dialog box), click the Comments arrow, and then click 'At end of sheet' in the Comments list.

What is the Show Ink button and should it be selected?

Comments can be added to worksheets using ink annotations from tablet or touch screen users. If the Show Ink button is turned off, these annotations will not be visible. No ink annotations are recorded in this worksheet, so the button has no impact on which comments are displayed.

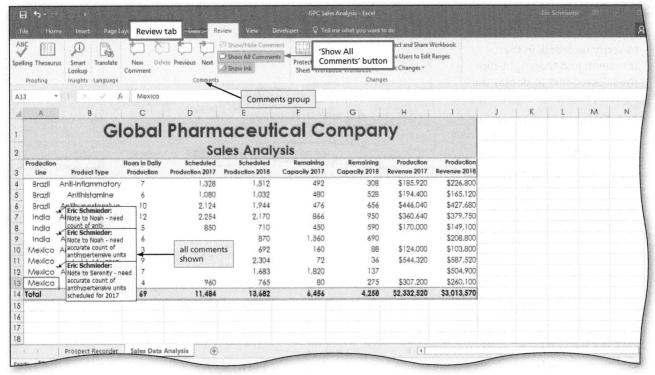

Figure 11–51

To Edit Comments on a Worksheet

1 DESIGN USER INTERFACE | 2 RECORD USER INPUT | 3 WRITE VBA CODE | 4 TEST USER INTERFACE
5 SHARE & COLLABORATE | 6 USE COMMENTS | 7 TRACK CHANGES | 8 FINALIZE WORKBOOK

You want to alert Noah to the need for verification of a recorded value related to the initial comment in cell A7. *Why? After adding comments to a worksheet, you may need to edit them to add or change information or you may want to change the appearance of a particular comment to make it stand out from other comments.* The following steps edit and format the comment in cell A7.

- Click cell A7 to make active the cell containing the comment to format.

- Click the Edit Comment button (Review tab | Comments group) to open the comment for editing.

- Change the comment by typing the words, `to verify recorded`, between the words, need and count, so that the text reads as follows: Note to Noah - need to verify recorded count of anti-inflammatory units scheduled for 2017 production in India (Figure 11–52).

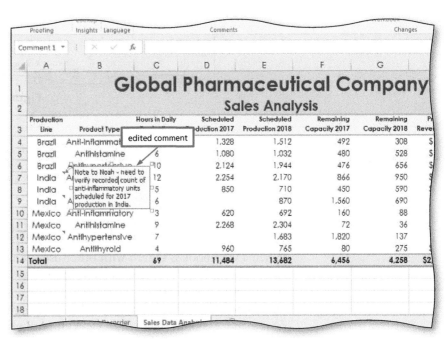

Figure 11–52

2

- Select the words you just added, to verify recorded, in the comment, and then right-click the selected text to display the shortcut menu.

- Click Format Comment on the shortcut menu to display the Format Comment dialog box.

- Change the Color to Red (column 1, row 3) and change the Font style to Bold for the selected text (Figure 11–53).

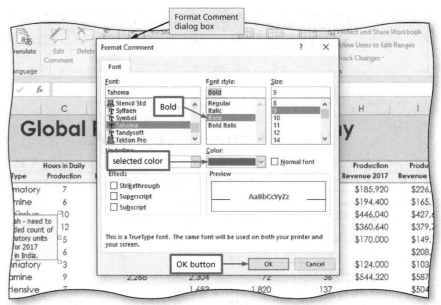

Figure 11–53

3

- Click the OK button (Format Comment dialog box) to apply the selected formatting to the comment text. Use the sizing handles to resize the comment box as necessary so that all the text is visible (Figure 11–54).

- Click cell A4 to deselect and hide the comment.

- Save the workbook again on the same storage location with the same file name.

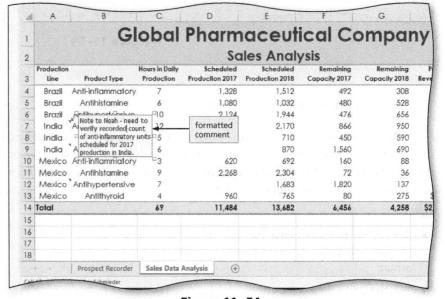

Figure 11–54

Break Point: If you wish to take a break, this is a good place to do so. You can now exit Excel. To resume at a later time, run Excel, open the file called GPC Sales Analysis, and continue following the steps from this location forward.

Tracking Changes on a Workbook

When a workbook is shared with other users, changes made and saved by the other users are visible only when you attempt to save changes. When Excel recognizes that another user has modified a shared workbook, Excel displays a dialog box indicating that the workbook has been updated with changes saved by other users; you then can review and accept or reject their work. If both you and another user change the same cell, Excel displays a Resolve Conflicts dialog box when the workbook is saved. The

User Interfaces, Visual Basic for Applications (VBA), and Collaboration Features in Excel **Excel Module 11** **EX** 661

Excel Module 11

dialog box lists the conflicting changes and provides options to choose which change to accept in the workbook.

Tracking changes means that Excel, through the Track Changes command, will display the edited cells with a comment indicating who made the change, when the change was made, and what the original value was of the cell that was changed. If either tracking or sharing is enabled, Excel enables the other by default.

To Turn On Track Changes

1 DESIGN USER INTERFACE | 2 RECORD USER INPUT | 3 WRITE VBA CODE | 4 TEST USER INTERFACE
5 SHARE & COLLABORATE | 6 USE COMMENTS | 7 TRACK CHANGES | 8 FINALIZE WORKBOOK

Multiple users may make changes to the workbook and you want to ensure that a history of changes is recorded for review. *Why? Tracking changes when working collaboratively keeps a record of the changes that others make to a workbook.* The following steps turn on track changes.

- If necessary, display the Review tab and then click the Track Changes button (Review tab | Changes group) to display the Track Changes menu (Figure 11–55).

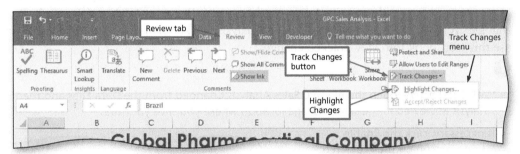

Figure 11–55

- Click Highlight Changes on the Track Changes menu to display the Highlight Changes dialog box.
- Click the 'Track changes while editing. This also shares your workbook.' check box to insert a check mark.
- If necessary, click all of the check boxes in the Highlight which changes area to clear them (Figure 11–56).

Q&A

What is the purpose of clearing the check marks?

Clicking the 'Track changes while editing. This also shares your workbook.' check box enables track changes and shares the workbook. The When, Who, and Where check boxes play no role when you first enable track changes.

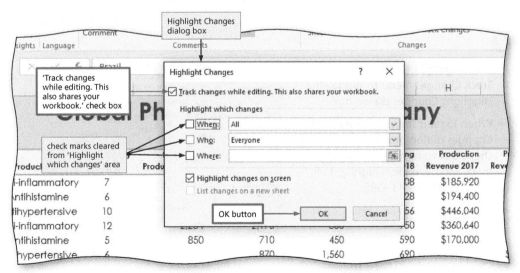

Figure 11–56

- Click the OK button (Highlight Changes dialog box) to close the dialog box.
- If a Microsoft Excel dialog box appears, click the OK button (Microsoft Excel dialog box) to save, share, and track changes in the workbook.

Reviewing Tracked Changes

Instead of writing suggestions and changes on a printed copy and sending it to the person in charge of a workbook, Excel's track changes feature allows users to enter suggested changes directly in the workbook. The owner of the workbook then looks through each change and makes a decision about whether to accept it.

To Open a Workbook and Review Tracked Changes

1 DESIGN USER INTERFACE | 2 RECORD USER INPUT | 3 WRITE VBA CODE | 4 TEST USER INTERFACE
5 SHARE & COLLABORATE | 6 USE COMMENTS | 7 TRACK CHANGES | 8 FINALIZE WORKBOOK

After others have reviewed a workbook, it usually is returned to the owner. When track changes is enabled for a workbook, the file, when returned to the owner, will contain other users' changes, corrections, and comments. *Why review tracked changes? The owner of the workbook then can review those changes and make decisions about whether to accept the changes.* A workbook named GPC Sales Analysis Changed, which includes tracked changes from other users to the GPC Sales Analysis workbook, is saved in the Data Files. The following steps use this workbook to review tracked changes.

- With Excel active, open the file GPC Sales Analysis Changed from the Data Files and then save it as GPC Sales Analysis Reviewed in the same storage location where you save your files.

- If necessary, click the Enable Editing button on the Protected View bar to open the workbook for editing and display the Sales Data Analysis worksheet.

- Display the Review tab and then click the Track Changes button (Review tab | Changes group) to display the Track Changes menu (Figure 11–57).

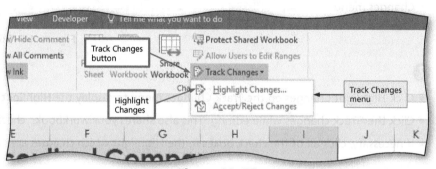

Figure 11–57

- Click Highlight Changes on the Track Changes menu to display the Highlight Changes dialog box.

- When Excel displays the Highlight Changes dialog box, click the When check box to remove the check mark and have Excel highlight all changes (Figure 11–58).

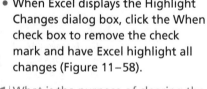

Q&A What is the purpose of clearing the When check mark?

Clearing the check mark from the When check box indicates to Excel

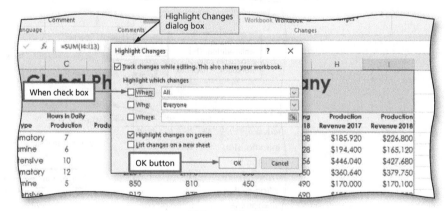

Figure 11–58

that all changes in the change history should be available for review. Excel can track three categories of changes in the change history. The When check box allows you to specify the time period from which you want to review changes. The Who check box allows you to specify which individual users changes you want to review. The Where check box allows you to specify a range of cells to check for changes.

Why would I select the When, Who, and Where check boxes?
You would select these check boxes when you want to highlight only some changes, such as those made since you last saved or those made by everyone except you.

3

- Click the OK button (Highlight Changes dialog box) to close the dialog box.
- Point to cell D9 to display a comment box with information about the change made to the cell D9 (Figure 11–59).

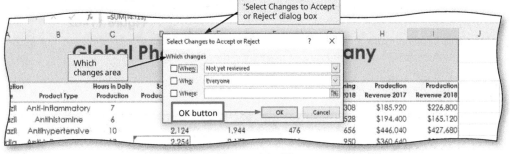

Figure 11–59

4

- Click the Track Changes button (Review tab | Changes group) to display the Track Changes menu.
- Click 'Accept/Reject Changes' on the Track Changes menu to display the 'Select Changes to Accept or Reject' dialog box.
- If necessary, clear all the check boxes in the Which changes area, indicating that all changes in the change history file should be reviewed (Figure 11–60).

Figure 11–60

5

- Click the OK button ('Select Changes to Accept or Reject' dialog box) to display the first tracked change (Figure 11–61).

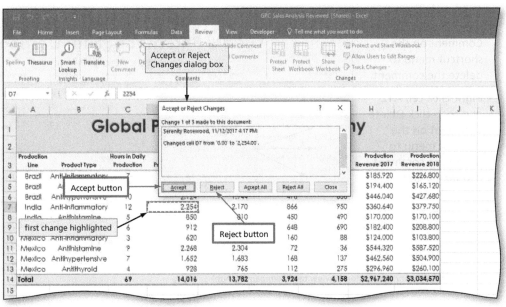

Figure 11–61

6

- Click the Accept button (Accept or Reject Changes dialog box) to accept the change to cell D7 and display the second tracked change.

- Click the Reject button (Accept or Reject Changes dialog box) to reject the change to cell E8 and display the next tracked change.

- As Excel displays each change in the Accept or Reject Changes dialog box, read the details of the change, and then click the Accept button until the dialog box closes.

- Click the 'Show All Comments' button (Review tab | Comments group) to display all comments in the worksheet (Figure 11–62).

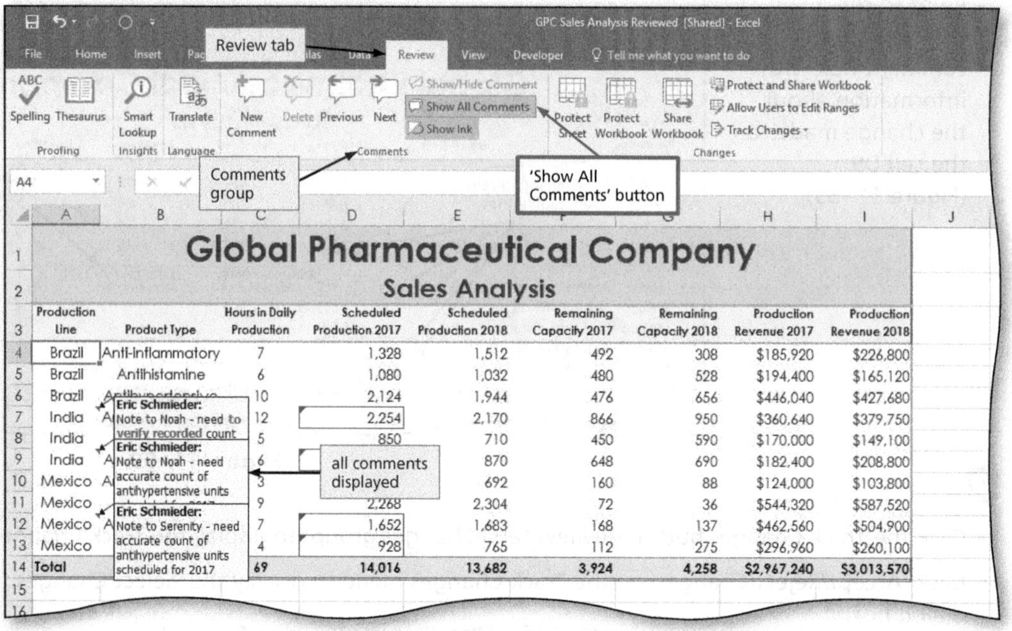

Q&A Could I click the Accept All button to accept all remaining changes?
Yes, though when you click the Accept All button, you cannot review the details of each change.

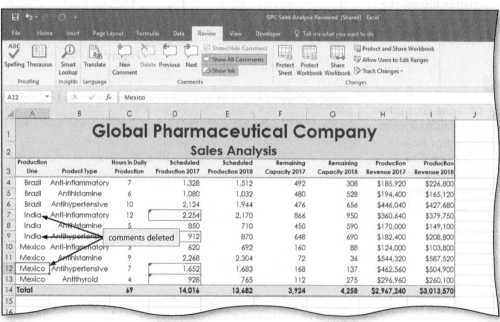

Figure 11–62

7

- Right-click cell A7 and then click Delete Comment on the shortcut menu to delete the comment.

- Right-click cell A9 and then click Delete Comment on the shortcut menu to delete the comment.

- Right-click cell A12 and then click Delete Comment on the shortcut menu to delete the comment (Figure 11–63).

Figure 11–63

Other Ways

1. Click Delete Comment button (Review tab | Comments group)

To Turn Off Track Changes

Why? *When workbook sharing is enabled, Excel denies access to a number of features. Turning off track changes, which also turns off sharing and saves the workbook, provides access to those features again.* The workbook is saved as an **exclusive workbook**, one that is not shared and can be opened only by a single user. The following steps turn off track changes and make the workbook exclusive.

- Click the Track Changes button (Review tab | Changes group) to display the Track Changes menu.

- Click Highlight Changes on the Track Changes menu to display the Highlight Changes dialog box.

- Click the 'Track changes while editing' check box to remove the check mark (Figure 11–64).

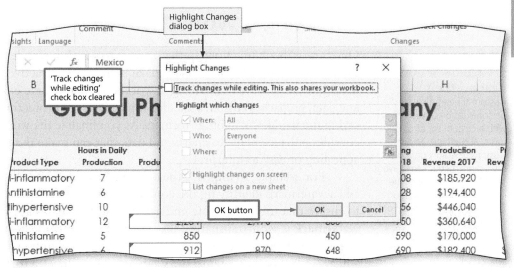

Figure 11–64

- Click the OK button (Highlight Changes dialog box) to turn off track changes, close the dialog box, and display the Microsoft Excel dialog box asking if the workbook should be made exclusive (Figure 11–65).

Q&A

What is the change history, and how can it be protected?

Excel keeps a change history with each shared workbook. In the case of a shared workbook in which changes should be tracked, Excel provides a way for users to make data entry changes but does not allow them to modify the change history. To protect the change history associated with a shared workbook, click the Protect and Share Workbook button (Review tab | Changes group). When Excel displays the Protect Shared Workbook dialog box, click 'Sharing with track changes' to select it and then click the OK button. After a shared workbook is protected, no one can unprotect or change it except the owner.

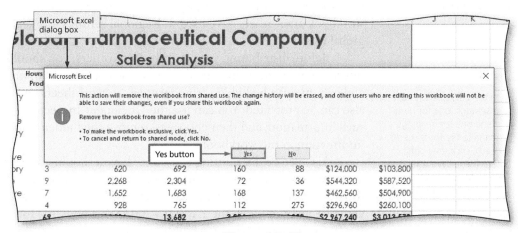

Figure 11–65

- Click the Yes button to make the workbook exclusive.

- Save changes and close the GPC Sales Analysis Reviewed workbook.

What happens when track changes is disabled?
When track changes is disabled, sharing is disabled as well. At the same time, Excel erases the change history. The workbook is saved automatically, as an exclusive workbook, which is not shared and can be opened only by a single user.

How do I know that the workbook is an exclusive workbook?
The text, Shared, is no longer displayed on the title bar.

Finalizing a Workbook

BTW
Create and Modify Custom Themes
Custom themes allow for personalization of workbooks with a custom set of colors, fonts, and effects. Use the Customize Colors option on the Colors menu (Page Layout tab | Themes group) or the Customize Fonts option on the Fonts menu (Page Layout tab | Themes group) to create custom options and select the desired effect setting from the Effects gallery. After selecting your desired options, click the Themes button and then click Save Current Theme to save your custom theme.

Once a workbook functions in the manner to which it was designed, final touches can be added to the worksheets to make them more attractive and easy to use. Excel provides several ways of finalizing a workbook that include enhancing existing objects and data, preparing custom views for multiple users, protecting your privacy, and saving the workbook in other formats. As you finalize the workbook, you should consider enhancements to charts and data that can make the information more visually appealing or easy to interpret.

For example, to improve the appearance of the Prior Years worksheet, you will add a watermark identifying the content on the Event Expenses worksheet as draft, to ensure that the salespeople understand that the details are subject to change. A **watermark** is semi-transparent text overlaid on the worksheet that is used to convey something about the state of the worksheet, such as Draft or Confidential status. You will also add a background to the Prior Years worksheet. Worksheet backgrounds place an image behind the data in cells of a worksheet.

When preparing the workbook for distribution, consider establishing a custom view so that the content will display in your preferred way when you access the workbook after others have used it. Regional settings in Excel allow for support of global users.

BTW
Managing Theme Fonts
Each theme includes two font settings: one for body text and one for headings. To manage the fonts used for each, click the Fonts button (Page Layout tab | Themes group) and then click Customize Fonts to display the Create New Theme Fonts dialog box. Select the desired heading and body font options, enter a name for the theme, and then click Save to update and apply the font selections.

Before distributing your workbook to others, you should consider what hidden information might be in your workbook. As you learned in previous modules, rows and columns can be hidden from view, as can worksheets and workbooks. Cells also can be protected. You can use the Document Inspector to inspect and report such information, and then choose to remove the hidden information or leave the information in the workbook.

Also before distributing a workbook, you should consider whether the intended recipients have the most recent version of Excel. If this is not the case, Excel allows you to save a workbook for use in previous versions of Excel, such as Excel 97-2003. When you save a workbook in the Excel 97-2003 Workbook file format, Excel will invoke the Compatibility Checker, which notifies you if any of the content of the workbook cannot be saved in that format. Additionally, the Compatibility Checker will inform you if any content will appear differently in the Excel 97-2003 Workbook format, such as cell or chart formatting.

To Add a Watermark to a Worksheet

1 DESIGN USER INTERFACE | 2 RECORD USER INPUT | 3 WRITE VBA CODE | 4 TEST USER INTERFACE
5 SHARE & COLLABORATE | 6 USE COMMENTS | 7 TRACK CHANGES | **8 FINALIZE WORKBOOK**

Why? A watermark can be used to provide a reminder to the user. In this case, it will remind the users that the worksheet contains draft content. Excel does not have a watermark function, but you can use WordArt to mimic one. The following steps add a watermark to the Event Expenses worksheet.

1

- Reopen the GPC Events Merged workbook from the storage location where your files are saved and then make Event Expenses the active worksheet. If necessary, turn off workbook sharing.

- Display the Insert tab and then click the Insert WordArt button (Insert tab | Text group) to display the Insert WordArt gallery (Figure 11–66).

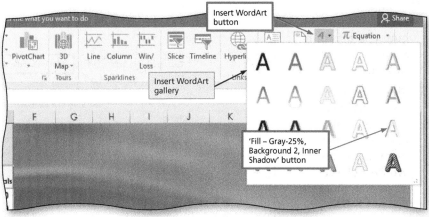

Figure 11–66

2

- Click 'Fill - Gray-25%, Background 2, Inner Shadow' (column 5, row 3 of the Insert WordArt gallery) to insert a new WordArt object.

- If necessary, select the text in the WordArt object and then type **Draft** as the watermark text.

- Point to the border of the WordArt object, and when the pointer changes to a four-headed arrow, drag the WordArt object to the center of the worksheet content, as shown in Figure 11–67.

- With the WordArt text selected, right-click the WordArt object to display a shortcut menu (Figure 11–67).

Figure 11–67

3

- Click 'Format Text Effects' on the shortcut menu to open the Format Shape task pane.

- If necessary, click the Text Options tab (Format Shape task pane) to display the sheet.

- Click the 'Text Fill & Outline' tab (Format Shape task pane) and then expand the Text Fill section.

- Set the Transparency slider to 80% to change the transparency of the Word Art (Figure 11–68).

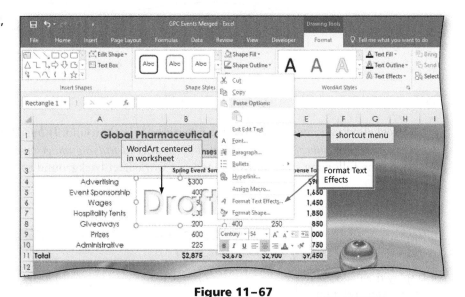

Figure 11–68

- Click the Close button in the Format Shape task pane to close it.
- With the WordArt object still selected, drag the rotation handle until the orientation of the WordArt object appears as shown in Figure 11–69.

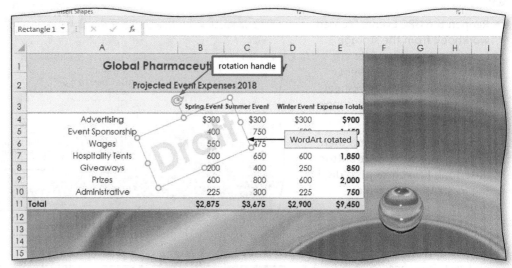

Figure 11–69

To Format a Worksheet Background

1 DESIGN USER INTERFACE | 2 RECORD USER INPUT | 3 WRITE VBA CODE | 4 TEST USER INTERFACE
5 SHARE & COLLABORATE | 6 USE COMMENTS | 7 TRACK CHANGES | **8 FINALIZE WORKBOOK**

Excel allows an image to be used as a worksheet background. *Why? Worksheet backgrounds can provide visual appeal to a worksheet, allowing for a corporate logo or other identifying image to serve as the background for an entire worksheet.* The following steps add an image as a worksheet background to the Prior Years worksheet.

- Display the Prior Years worksheet.
- Display the Page Layout tab and then click the Background button (Page Layout tab | Page Setup group) to display the Insert Pictures dialog box (Figure 11–70).

Q&A Why do I have additional locations listed in my Insert Pictures dialog box? If you are logged in to your Microsoft account, you will have additional, cloud-based locations listed.

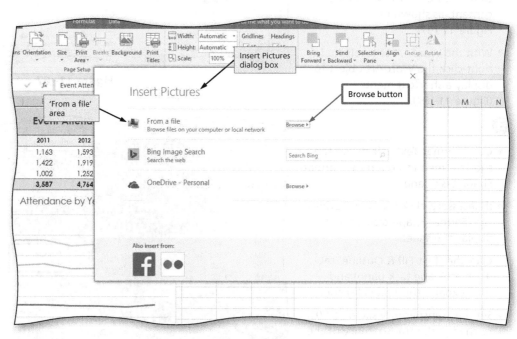

Figure 11–70

User Interfaces, Visual Basic for Applications (VBA), and Collaboration Features in Excel **Excel Module 11** **EX** 669

Excel Module 11

- Click the Browse button in the From a file area to display the Sheet Background dialog box.
- Navigate to the location of the Data Files, and then select the waterdroplet image file (Figure 11–71).

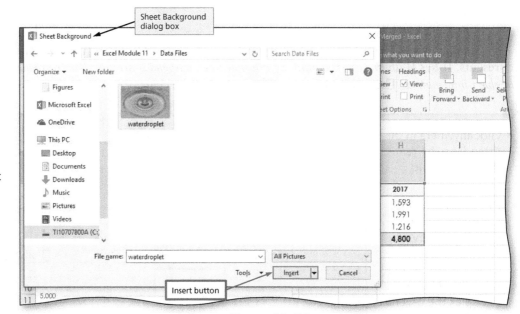

Figure 11–71

- Click the Insert button (Sheet Background dialog box) to display the image as the worksheet background.
- If gridlines are displayed, click the View Gridlines check box (Page Layout tab | Sheet Options group) to remove the check mark and turn off gridlines (Figure 11–72).

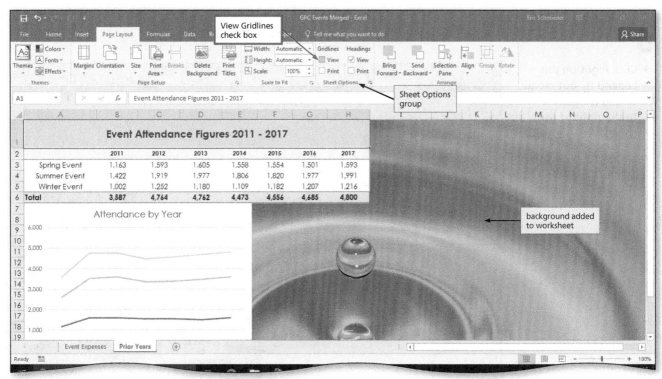

Figure 11–72

To Add a Legend to a Chart

Adding a legend to the chart will improve the readability of the chart by identifying which event each line represents. *Why? With line charts containing multiple lines, a legend is necessary for the reader to be able to understand the chart information.* The following steps add a legend to the chart.

1

- Click anywhere in the Attendance by Year chart to select it.

- Click the Chart Elements button to display the Chart Elements gallery. Point to Legend to display an arrow and then click the arrow to display the Legend fly-out menu (Figure 11–73).

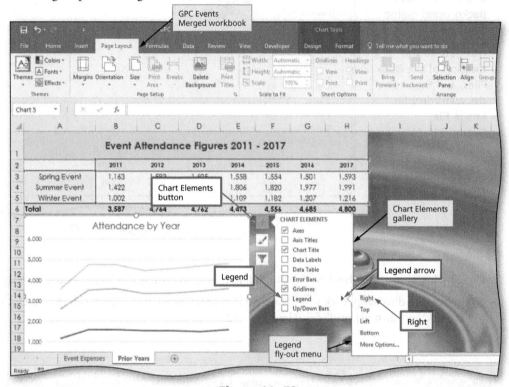

Figure 11–73

2

- Click Right on the Legend fly-out menu to add a legend to the right of the chart.

- Click the Chart Elements button to close the gallery (Figure 11–74).

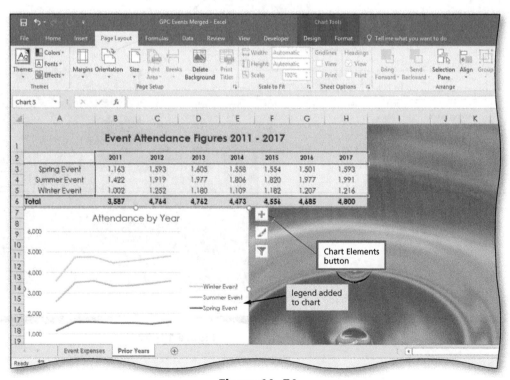

Figure 11–74

To Add a Shadow to a Chart Element

Adding a shadow to the plot area separates it from the other chart elements and improves the visual appeal of the chart. *Why? Shadows and other design features can add depth and a more professional look to your charts.* The following steps add a shadow to the plot area of the chart.

- Click anywhere in the plot area to select it.
- Right-click the plot area to display a shortcut menu (Figure 11–75).

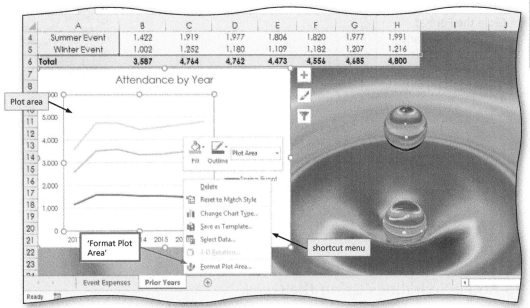

Figure 11–75

- Click 'Format Plot Area' on the shortcut menu to open the Format Plot Area task pane.
- If necessary, click the Effects tab (Format Plot Area task pane) and then expand the Shadow settings.
- Click the Presets/ Shadow button to display the Shadow gallery (Figure 11–76).

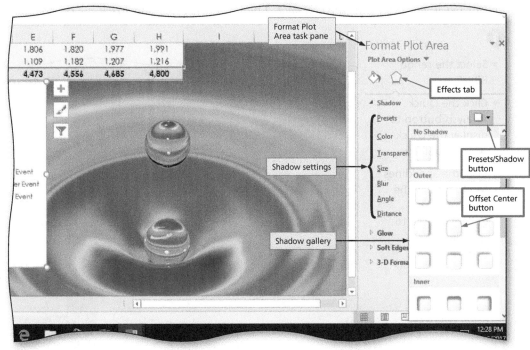

Figure 11–76

- Click the Offset Center button (Outer area) to apply a shadow effect to the plot area of the chart.

- Close the Format Plot Area task pane and then deselect the plot area (Figure 11–77).

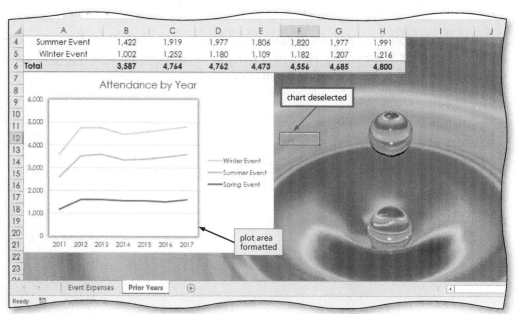

Figure 11–77

To Add a Sparklines Using the Quick Analysis Gallery

1 DESIGN USER INTERFACE | 2 RECORD USER INPUT | 3 WRITE VBA CODE | 4 TEST USER INTERFACE
5 SHARE & COLLABORATE | 6 USE COMMENTS | 7 TRACK CHANGES | 8 FINALIZE WORKBOOK

Why? Sparklines are charts that are inserted immediately beside the data that creates them, allowing for easy comparison of numerical and graphical data. The following steps add sparkline charts for attendance figures.

- Select the range B3:H5.

- Click the Quick Analysis button to display the Quick Analysis gallery.

- Click the Sparklines tab to display the Quick Analysis gallery related to sparklines (Figure 11–78).

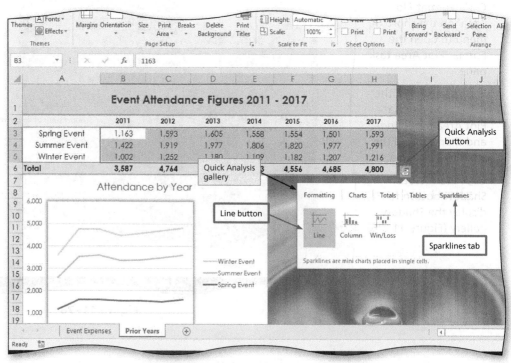

Figure 11–78

2

- Click the Line button (Quick Analysis gallery) to insert sparklines in cells I3:I5.

- Apply the Tan, Accent 2 (column 6, row 1) fill color (Home tab | Font group) to the range I1:I6.

- Make cell A1 the active cell to deselect the range (Figure 11–79).

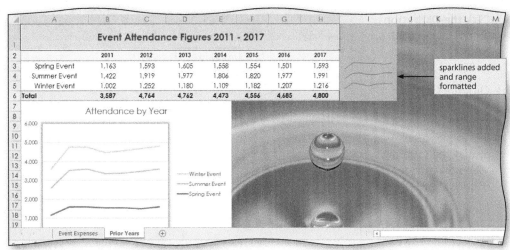

Figure 11–79

Saving Custom Views

Custom views allow certain layout and printing characteristics of a workbook to be saved and then used later. When a custom view of a workbook is saved, Excel stores information about the workbook's current window size and print settings. Before saving a custom view, make sure the workbook reflects the desired layout and print settings.

The Custom Views button on the View tab is used to save, delete, and display custom views. When a user saves a custom view, Excel also stores the name of the current worksheet. When a user displays a custom view by clicking the Show button in the Custom Views dialog box, Excel switches to the worksheet that was active in the workbook when the custom view was saved.

BTW
Save a Chart as a Template
Chart objects can be saved as templates for reuse. To save a chart as a template, right-click the chart, click Save as Template on the shortcut menu, enter a file name for the template in the Save Chart Template dialog box, and then click Save.

To Save a Custom View of a Workbook

1 DESIGN USER INTERFACE | 2 RECORD USER INPUT | 3 WRITE VBA CODE | 4 TEST USER INTERFACE
5 SHARE & COLLABORATE | 6 USE COMMENTS | 7 TRACK CHANGES | **8 FINALIZE WORKBOOK**

Why? *If a workbook requires that you customize certain layout and printing settings to use it effectively, using a custom view allows you to save those settings with the workbook. Whenever the workbook is opened, it will be opened with those settings active.* The following steps create and save a custom view of the GPC Events workbook.

1

- Click View on the ribbon to display the View tab.

- Click the Zoom button (View tab | Zoom group) to display the Zoom dialog box.

- Click the 75% option button (Zoom dialog box) to select 75% magnification (Figure 11–80).

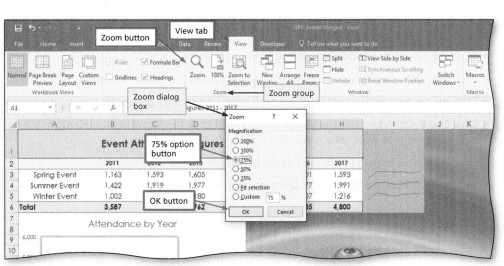

Figure 11–80

2

- Click the OK button (Zoom dialog box) to set the zoom to 75%.

- Click the Custom Views button (View tab | Workbook Views group) to display the Custom Views dialog box (Figure 11–81).

Q&A

Why does my Custom Views dialog box contain a list of views?

The views listed will reflect the authors of any open documents as well as any users signed in to Windows.

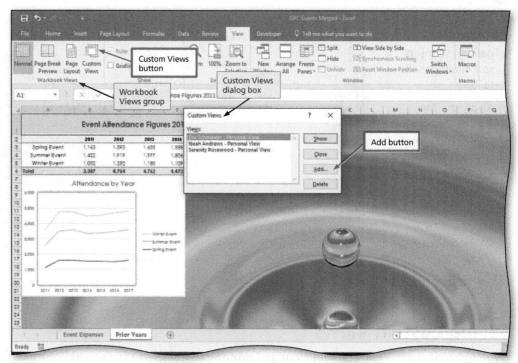

Figure 11–81

3

- Click the Add button (Custom Views dialog box) to display the Add View dialog box.

- Type **Event Attendance** in the Name text box to provide a name for the custom view (Figure 11–82).

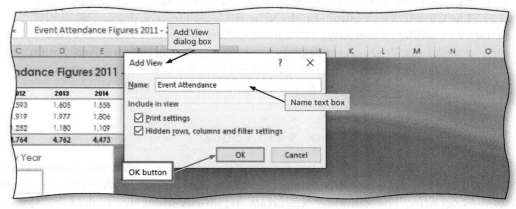

Figure 11–82

4

- Click the OK button (Add View dialog box) to close the dialog box.

- Click the 100% button (View tab | Zoom group) to set the zoom to 100%.

- Click the Custom Views button (View tab | Workbook Views group) to display the Custom Views dialog box.

- Click Event Attendance in the Views list and then click the Show button (Custom Views dialog box) to display the Event Attendance view, which includes a zoom to 75%.

- Click the 100% button (View tab | Zoom group) to set the zoom to 100%.

- Save the workbook again on the same storage location with the same file name.

Q&A

Can I delete a custom view?

Yes. To delete custom views, use the Delete button in the Custom Views dialog box shown in Figure 11–81.

Internationalization Features

Excel provides internationalization features you can use when creating workbooks. Use of these features should be determined based on the intended audience of the workbook. For instance, if you are creating a workbook that will be used in European countries where decimal notation differs from that used in North America, consider setting up the workbook to use the European notation by creating custom number formats or changing the symbol used with the Currency or Accounting number formats.

By default, workbooks use formatting consistent with the country or region selected when installing Windows. Situations exist where a workbook will need to contain text or number formatting consistent with a different country or region. Several options are available for applying international formats to content.

Displaying International Symbols

You can format a cell or range of cells with international currency symbols using the Format Cells dialog box. Both the Accounting and Currency number categories provide a selection of symbols for use when formatting monetary cell entries. You also can select from the more commonly used currency symbols when applying the accounting number format by clicking the 'Accounting Number Format' arrow (Home tab | Number group) and selecting the desired currency from the list.

You can use the Symbol button (Insert tab | Symbols group) to enter international characters and monetary symbols as cell entries. To insert a character, click the Symbol button to display the Symbol dialog box, select the font you are using from the Font list, and then scroll until you see the symbol of interest. Select the symbol and then click the Insert button (Symbol dialog box) to insert the symbol at the location of the insertion point in your worksheet.

Displaying Data in Multiple International Formats

Data formatting varies from country to country and region to region globally, including the use of different characters to separate decimal places and differing date formats. If preparing a workbook for use in another region, consider changing the location setting in Windows to the region of your audience. Use the Windows search box to search for Region to access the settings and format options for a specific region.

Collaborating with Users Who Do Not Use Excel 2016

It is not unusual to collaborate with others who are using different software versions, or different software entirely, to do their work. You even can find different versions of software being used within the same company. When collaborating with others, you should make decisions about how to save and distribute files after considering how your colleagues will be using the workbooks you create. In instances where people are working with earlier versions of software or different software, you need to provide workbooks in formats that they can use.

Before sharing a workbook with others, you can mark the workbook as being final. When another user of your workbook opens the workbook, he or she will be notified that you have marked the workbook as final. The workbook can still be edited, but only if the user clicks a button to indicate that he or she wants to edit the workbook.

To Save a Workbook in an Earlier Version of Excel and Mark as Final

Why? You occasionally need to save a workbook for use in previous versions of Excel. Each version of Excel includes varying features, so you can use the Compatibility Checker to determine if the features used in your workbook are compatible with earlier versions of Excel. The following steps check the compatibility of the workbook while saving the workbook in the Excel 97-2003 Workbook file format.

1

- Display the Backstage view, click the Save As tab, and then navigate to the location where you store your files.

- Click the 'Save as type' arrow (Save As dialog box) and then click 'Excel 97-2003 Workbook' to select the file format (Figure 11–83).

Q&A Would saving the file using the same name overwrite the original version of the workbook?
No. It is not necessary to save the workbook with a new file name. The 'Excel 97-2003' version of the workbook will have a file extension of .xls, while the original has a file extension of .xlsx.

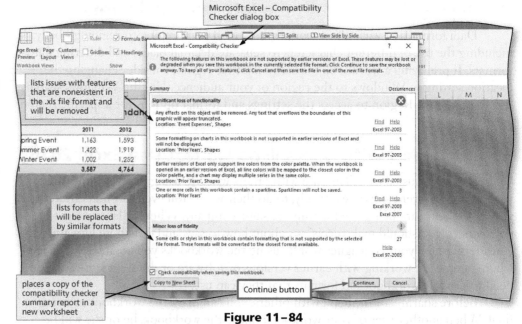

Figure 11–83

2

- Click the Save button (Save As dialog box) to display the Microsoft Excel - Compatibility Checker dialog box.

- Resize the dialog box so that it displays all the issues (Figure 11–84).

Q&A What is shown in the Microsoft Excel - Compatibility Checker dialog box?
The Summary states that some of the chart elements and the sparklines used on the Prior Years worksheet are not compatible with previous versions of Excel. While the workbook still will be saved in the Excel 97-2003 file format, the sparklines will not be saved. In addition, some cell formatting is unique to Excel 2016. These formats will be converted to the nearest approximation in the earlier version of Excel.

Figure 11–84

Excel Module 11

- Click the Continue button (Microsoft Excel - Compatibility Checker dialog box) to save the workbook in the Excel 97-2003 Workbook file format.
- Display the Backstage view.
- Click the Protect Workbook button in the Info gallery to display the Protect Workbook menu (Figure 11–85).

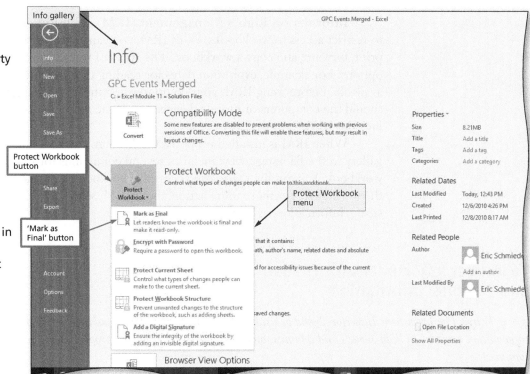

Figure 11–85

- Click 'Mark as Final' on the Protect Workbook menu to display the Microsoft Excel dialog box.
- Click the OK button (Microsoft Excel dialog box) to indicate you want to mark the workbook as final.
- If necessary, click the Continue button on the Microsoft Excel - Compatibility Checker dialog box.
- Click the OK button to close the Microsoft Excel dialog box and mark the workbook as final (Figure 11–86).
- Close the workbook.

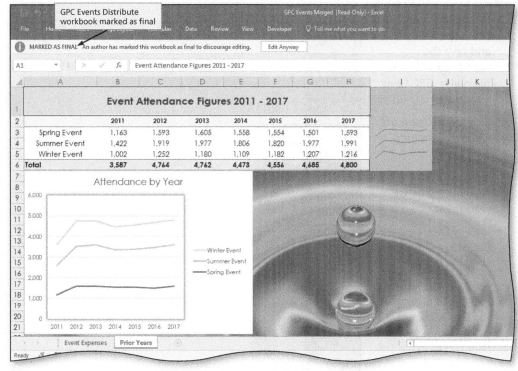

Figure 11–86

Q&A

I have saved the workbook in .xls format, but the sparklines are still showing. Why?

Although the .xls format does not support newer features such as sparklines, Excel 2016 does. If you close the file and reopen the workbook saved in the older format, the sparklines will be missing.

Information Rights Management

Information Rights Management (IRM) is a feature of Excel that allows you to restrict access to workbooks. With IRM, you can restrict who can view, modify, print, forward, and copy a workbook. The types of restrictions include a variety of options. For example, expiration dates for reading or modifying a workbook are available. Before using IRM, your computer first must be configured with IRM, as should the computers or mobile devices of anyone attempting to use a document that includes IRM features.

When IRM is installed properly, the Protect Workbook menu in the Info gallery in the Backstage view includes several commands for limiting access to the workbook. You can limit who can access the workbook and who can make changes to the workbook. For more information about IRM, search Excel Help using the search string, information rights management.

To Inspect a Document for Hidden and Personal Information

1 DESIGN USER INTERFACE | 2 RECORD USER INPUT | 3 WRITE VBA CODE | 4 TEST USER INTERFACE
5 SHARE & COLLABORATE | 6 USE COMMENTS | 7 TRACK CHANGES | **8 FINALIZE WORKBOOK**

Why? *The Document Inspector should be used before sharing a workbook publicly or when you suspect extraneous information remains in hidden rows and columns, hidden worksheets, document properties, headers and footers, or worksheet comments.*

The following steps make a copy of the GPC Sales Analysis workbook and then inspect the copy for hidden and personal information.

- If necessary, reopen GPC Sales Analysis and save the workbook with the file name, GPC Sales Distribute.

- If necessary, turn off workbook sharing.

- If necessary, make Sales Data Analysis the active worksheet.

- Display the Backstage view.

- Click the 'Check for Issues' button (Info gallery) to display the Check for Issues menu (Figure 11–87).

Q&A Why did I save this workbook with a different file name?

When preparing a workbook for distribution, you may decide to use the Document Inspector to make changes to the document. Saving the workbook with a different file name ensures that you will have a copy of the workbook with all of the original information intact for your records.

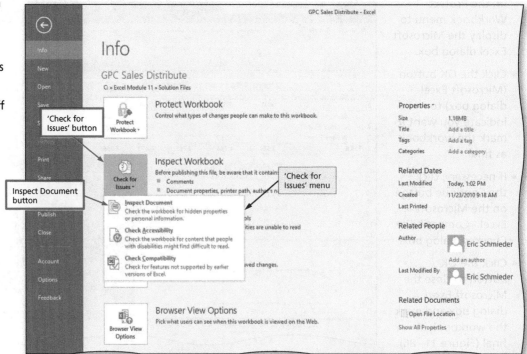

Figure 11–87

- Click Inspect
  Document (Check
  for Issues menu)
  to display the
  Document Inspector
  dialog box
  (Figure 11–88).

Q&A What is shown in the
  Document Inspector
  dialog box?
  The Document
  Inspector dialog box
  allows you to choose
  which types of
  content to inspect.
  Typically you would
  leave all of the items
  selected, unless you
  are comfortable
  with some types of
  content not being
  inspected.

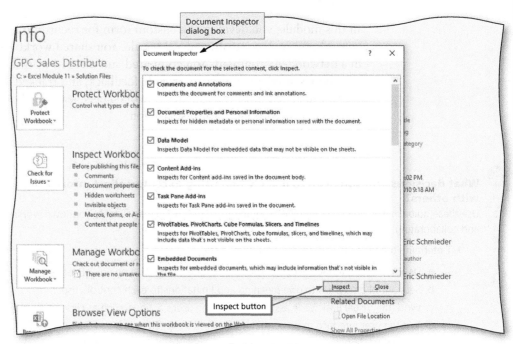

Figure 11–88

- Click the Inspect
  button (Document
  Inspector dialog box)
  to run the Document
  Inspector and
  display its results
  (Figure 11–89).

Q&A What did the
  Document Inspector
  find?
  The Document
  Inspector found the
  hidden Prospect
  List worksheet,
  comments, and
  personal information
  (Figure 11–89),
  including document
  properties, author
  information, related
  dates, absolute path

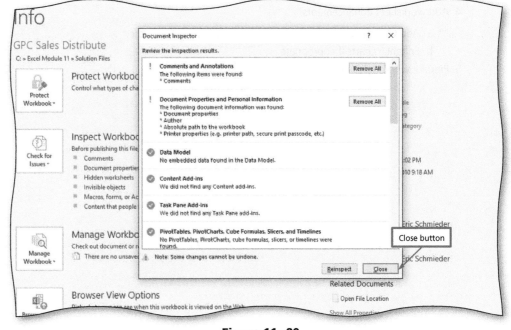

Figure 11–89

to the workbook, and printer properties. The Remove All button in the dialog box allows you quickly to remove
the items found if needed. In many instances, you may want to take notes of the results and then investigate and
remedy each one separately. In this workbook, all of these items found by the Document Inspector are expected
and do not need to be remedied.

- Click the Close button (Document Inspector dialog box) to close the dialog box.

- Save the workbook and exit Excel.

Summary

In this module, you developed a custom form for recording information, using form controls, ActiveX controls, and VBA code. You shared workbooks on OneDrive and in a network environment. You compared and merged worksheet data from shared workbooks, used comments to provide feedback, and tracked changes made by other users. You added finishing touches to worksheets, learned about internationalization, and prepared workbooks for distribution.

CONSIDER THIS

What decisions will you need to make when using Excel to collect information or collaborate with others?

Use these guidelines as you complete the assignments in this module and create your own worksheets for creating Excel forms and collaborating with others outside of this class.

1. Determine the purpose and needs of the form data.

    a. Design a user interface with controls appropriate to the data being entered.

    b. Set control properties to give meaning and limitations to each control's use.

    c. Write the Visual Basic code associated with the user's actions, such as clicking a button.

    d. Test the user interface to prove that it behaves as expected.

2. Determine the audience, purpose, and options available for the collaboration.

3. Evaluate changes made by colleagues.

    a. With a single distributed workbook, use Track Changes and Accept/Reject changes.

    b. With multiple workbooks, use Compare and Merge and then Accept/Reject changes.

4. Add worksheet enhancements.

    a. Add watermarks and worksheet backgrounds as appropriate.

    b. Enhance charts if appropriate.

5. Prepare workbook(s) for distribution.

Apply Your Knowledge

Reinforce the skills and apply the concepts you learned in this module.

Working with Comments and Tracked Changes

Note: To complete this assignment, you will be required to use the Data Files. Please contact your instructor for information about accessing the Data Files.

Instructions: Run Excel. Open the workbook Apply 11–1 Travel Expenses from the Data Files and then save the workbook using the file name, Apply 11–1 Travel Expenses Complete.

Figure 11–90 shows the initial workbook. You need to make changes based on comments, create a worksheet showing the history of tracked changes, and accept or reject tracked changes.

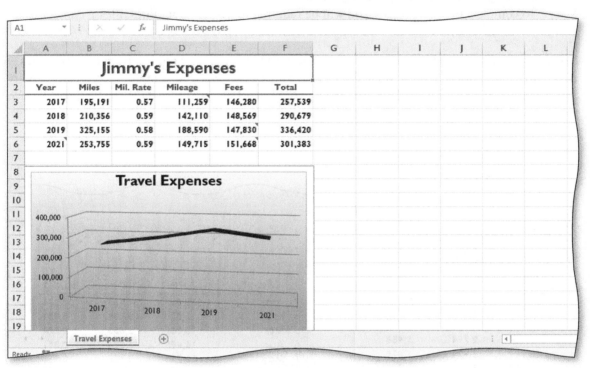

Figure 11–90

Perform the following tasks:

1. If necessary, share the workbook. Click the Track Changes button (Review tab | Changes group) and then click Highlight Changes. Clear the three check boxes in the 'Highlight which changes' area. Click the 'List changes on a new sheet' check box, and then click the OK button.

2. Make the Travel Expenses worksheet active, click the Track Changes button (Review tab | Changes group) and then click 'Accept/Reject Changes'. Clear the When check box and then click the OK button. Accept the change to cell B6. Reject the other change.

3. Click the 'Show All Comments' button (Review tab | Comments group). Make the changes as indicated in the comments. Delete the comments.

4. If requested by your instructor, add a comment to cell A2 noting your date of birth.

Continued >

Apply Your Knowledge *continued*

5. Save your changes to the workbook and then submit the revised workbook as specified by your instructor.

6. ⚙ You can review changes made to the worksheet either by generating the History worksheet or by reviewing the comments added to the worksheet by the Highlight Changes command. Which method of reviewing changes do you prefer, and why?

Extend Your Knowledge

Extend the skills you learned in this module and experiment with new skills. You may need to use Help to complete the assignment.

Consolidating Worksheets by Category

Note: To complete this assignment, you will be required to use the Data Files. Please contact your instructor for information about accessing the Data Files.

Instructions: Run Excel. Open the workbook Extend 11–1 N&S Art Supplies from the Data Files and then save the workbook using the file name, Extend 11– 1 N&S Art Supplies Complete. Modify the workbook so that it consolidates data from existing worksheets. The data in the worksheets have the same column and row labels (Figure 11–91).

Month	In-Store	Online	Catalog
Jan	$13,274	$3,657	$1,791
Feb	13,935	2,488	1,803
Mar	14,764	2,642	1,791
Apr	15,154	2,794	1,488
May	15,799	2,974	1,879
Jun	16,567	3,216	1,861
Jul	16,369	2,988	1,518
Aug	16,387	3,331	1,780
Sep	16,433	3,569	1,756
Oct	17,805	3,497	1,865
Nov	19,338	3,815	1,932
Dec	19,887	3,572	2,715

(a) N & S Art Supplies NC worksheet

Month	In-Store	Online	Catalog
Jan	$15,957	$4,466	$2,274
Feb	17,220	3,159	2,982
Mar	15,307	3,553	2,274
Apr	16,685	3,776	2,341
May	16,723	3,677	2,386
Jun	18,982	4,083	2,634
Jul	17,320	3,679	2,304
Aug	18,578	4,922	2,260
Sep	16,222	4,645	2,230
Oct	15,310	4,440	2,393
Nov	17,467	4,845	2,453
Dec	19,664	6,288	3,196

(b) N & S Art Supplies SC worksheet

Figure 11–91

Perform the following tasks:

1. Select the N&S Art Supplies NC worksheet. Select the range A2:D14, and then name the range NC.

2. Select the N&S Art Supplies SC worksheet. Select the range A2:D14, and then name the range SC.

3. Insert a blank worksheet. Name the worksheet Consolidated and color the tab blue. Copy the range A1:D1 from the N&S Art Supplies NC worksheet and then paste it to the range A1:D1 on the Consolidated worksheet. Change the background color of the range to Light Blue from the Standard Colors area in the background color palette. Edit the text in cell A1 to N&S Art Supplies Consolidated Monthly Sales.

4. Select cell A2. Click the Consolidate button (Data tab | Data Tools group). In the Consolidate dialog box, type NC in the Reference text box and then click the Add button (Consolidate dialog box). Type SC in the Reference text box, and then click the Add button. Click the Top row and Left column check boxes to insert check marks. Click the OK button (Consolidate dialog box) to consolidate the worksheets. If necessary, type Month in cell A2. Use Paste Special to copy the formatting and column widths for the ranges A2:D14 from either state worksheet to the consolidated worksheet.

5. If requested by your instructor, change NC to the abbreviation for the state in which you were born.

6. Save the workbook. Submit the revised workbook in the format specified by your instructor.

7. ✳ How does consolidation differ from copying and pasting content from one worksheet to another? How does it differ from using Compare and Merge?

Expand Your World

Create a solution that uses cloud and web technologies by learning and investigating on your own from general guidance.

Preparing Surveys

Problem: You have been asked to create a survey related to either education or employment to illustrate how to use form controls and ActiveX controls in Excel to create a survey and record responses.

Instructions:

1. Run a browser and navigate to http://zoho.com/survey. Search the website for a survey template in either education or employment that you can create in Excel with form controls. Select a template that contains at least 10 questions. Record the web address of the survey template and print a copy.

2. Run Excel and open a blank workbook. Using the skills you learned in this module, create a survey that includes the questions from the survey you found on zoho.com. You should use more than one type of control in creating your survey.

3. Write a VBA procedure to collect the entered data each time the survey is completed and store it on a separate, hidden worksheet.

Continued >

Expand Your World *continued*

4. Use worksheet protection and formatting to set up your survey so that a user can answer questions but not gain access to the hidden worksheet or areas on the current worksheet outside of the survey.

5. Save the file as Expand 11–1 Survey Complete and submit it in the format specified by your instructor.

6. ✳ Did you use ActiveX controls, form controls, or a combination of both in your survey? Explain why you chose one type of control over the other and give one benefit of using the other type of control.

In the Labs

Design, create, modify, and/or use a workbook following the guidelines, concepts, and skills presented in this module. Labs 1 and 2, which increase in difficulty, require you to create solutions based on what you learned in the module; Lab 3 requires you to apply your creative thinking and problem-solving skills to design and implement a solution.

Lab 1: **Merging Workbooks**

Note: To complete this assignment, you will be required to use the Data Files. Please contact your instructor for information about accessing the Data Files.

Problem: As the college-wide tutoring coordinator, you have created a workbook using the time sheets from the tutors and have shared the workbook with the tutoring center managers who made their own copies. They have sent their copies back with their changes to the timesheet data for the various tutors from the Fine Arts, Sciences, and Technology departments of Eastbrook Cole University. Damon, Addyson, and Carlee are the tutoring center managers for the three departments. You now need to merge their changes into one workbook. The result of the merge is shown in Figure 11–92.

Perform the following tasks:

1. Open the workbook Lab 11–1 ECU Tutoring from the Data Files, and then save the workbook as Lab 11–1 ECU Tutoring Complete.

2. If necessary, add the 'Compare and Merge Workbooks' button to the Quick Access Toolbar. Use the 'Compare and Merge Workbooks' button to merge the workbooks Lab 11–1 ECU Tutoring Addyson, Lab 11–1 ECU Tutoring Carlee, and Lab 11–1 ECU Tutoring Damon into Lab 11–1 ECU Tutoring Complete.

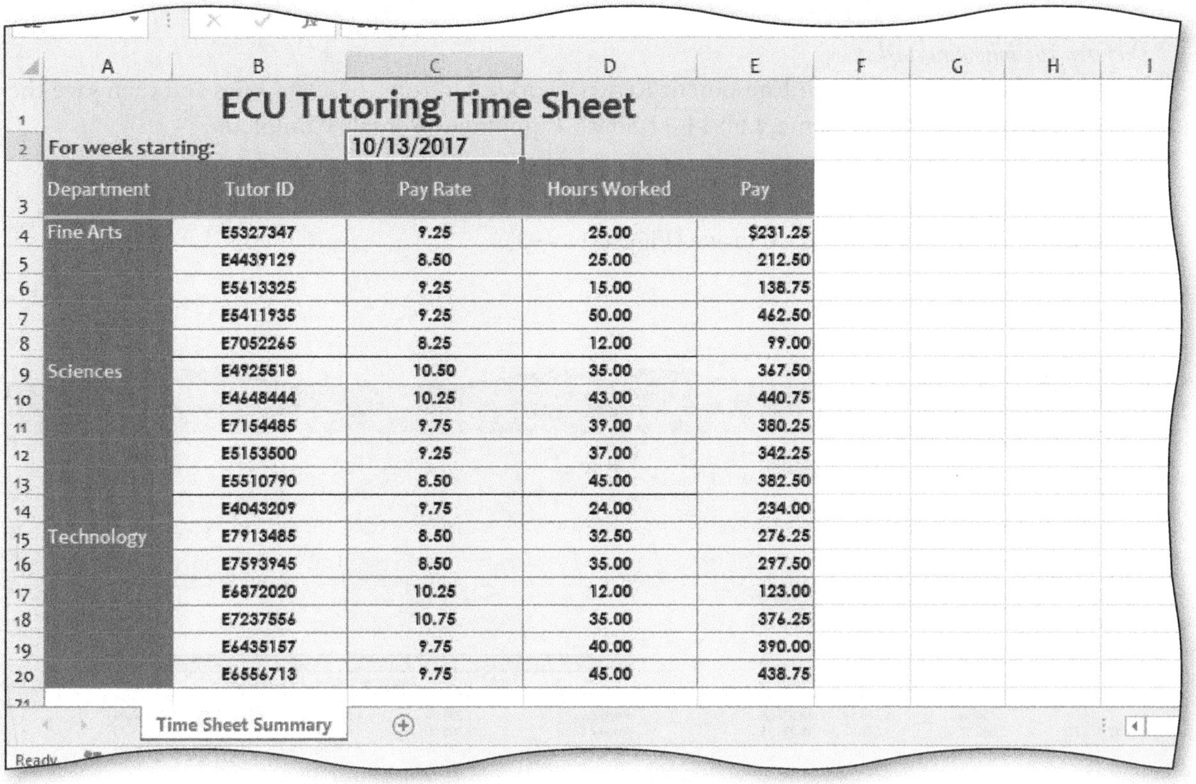

	A	B	C	D	E	F	G	H	I
1		**ECU Tutoring Time Sheet**							
2	For week starting:		10/13/2017						
3	Department	Tutor ID	Pay Rate	Hours Worked	Pay				
4	Fine Arts	E5327347	9.25	25.00	$231.25				
5		E4439129	8.50	25.00	212.50				
6		E5613325	9.25	15.00	138.75				
7		E5411935	9.25	50.00	462.50				
8		E7052265	8.25	12.00	99.00				
9	Sciences	E4925518	10.50	35.00	367.50				
10		E4648444	10.25	43.00	440.75				
11		E7154485	9.75	39.00	380.25				
12		E5153500	9.25	37.00	342.25				
13		E5510790	8.50	45.00	382.50				
14		E4043209	9.75	24.00	234.00				
15	Technology	E7913485	8.50	32.50	276.25				
16		E7593945	8.50	35.00	297.50				
17		E6872020	10.25	12.00	123.00				
18		E7237556	10.75	35.00	376.25				
19		E6435157	9.75	40.00	390.00				
20		E6556713	9.75	45.00	438.75				

Time Sheet Summary

Figure 11–92

3. In the Lab 11–1 ECU Tutoring Complete workbook, use 'Accept/Reject Changes' on the Track Changes menu to accept all changes except for those in cells D7 and D10, which should be rejected. (*Hint:* Clear the When check box.)

4. Turn off sharing so that the workbook is exclusive.

5. If requested by your instructor, add a comment to cell A3 with your date of birth.

6. Save the workbook and submit the assignment in the format requested by your instructor.

7. ✷ What do you see as the disadvantages of merging and accepting/rejecting changes as compared with using comments exclusively for updating content?

Lab 2: Merging Sales Data and Working with Charts and Backgrounds

Note: To complete this assignment, you will be required to use the Data Files. Please contact your instructor for information about accessing the Data Files.

Problem: You work for Smith Equipment Rentals. You have been asked to merge revenue data from the three sectors where the equipment is rented. After you have merged the data, you will save a version in a previous version of Excel for sharing with your supervisor, who has Excel 2003.

Continued >

In the Labs *continued*

Perform the following tasks:

1. Open the Lab 11–2 Smith Equipment Rentals workbook from the Data Files and then save the workbook with the file name, Lab 11–2 Smith Equipment Rentals Complete.

2. Merge the workbooks Lab 11–2 Smith Equipment Rentals Sector 2 and Lab 11–2 Smith Equipment Rentals Sector 3 into Lab 11–2 Smith Equipment Rentals Complete. Turn off sharing so the workbook is exclusive (Figure 11–93).

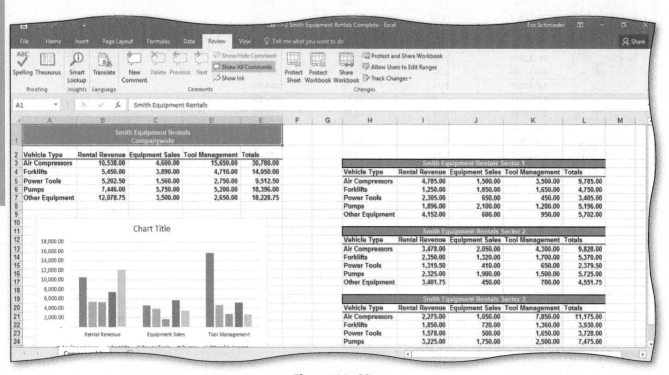

Figure 11–93

3. Enhance the chart by adding an appropriate chart title and a shadow to the plot area.

4. Add sparklines to the range F3:F7 representing the data in B3:E7.

5. Add a worksheet background that reflects the company's products and services. [*Hint:* Click the Background button (Page Layout tab | Page Setup group) and then use the search term, equipment, in the Bing Image Search text box in the Insert Pictures dialog box. Remember that although the Bing Image Search finds images licensed under Creative Commons, the resulting images may or may not be royalty and copyright free. You must read the specific license for any image you plan to use, even for educational purposes.]

6. Make any additional formatting changes to the page that you think are necessary now that the worksheet contains a background image.

7. If requested by your instructor, add a comment to cell A27 containing the name of your hometown.

8. Save the workbook.

9. Save a copy of the workbook using the file name, Lab 11–2 Smith Equipment Rentals Complete 2003, and the file type of Excel 97-2003 Workbook. After reviewing the Compatibility Checker results, click the Continue button (Compatibility Checker dialog box) to save the workbook.

10. Submit the assignment as specified by your instructor.

11. ✳ What formatting changes did you make to the worksheet to accommodate the image you used as a background?

Lab 3: **Consider This: Your Turn**

Apply your creative thinking and problem solving skills to design and implement a solution.

Using Commenting and Track Changes to Evaluate Report Differences

Part 1: Open the workbook Lab 11–3 On Time Delivery on the Data Files and then save the workbook with the file name, Lab 11–3 On Time Delivery Complete. You have two reports for 2 years of On Time Delivery staffing that contain discrepancies in actual recorded hours by position. You have been charged with identifying discrepancies and then gathering information to better understand these discrepancies. Use the collaborative features of Excel to design a strategy for gathering information and presenting it. Use position titles rather than names for any comments or requests that are to be directed to a particular person. You should prepare a workbook or workbooks containing the collaborative content needed to gather information. In the workbook (or workbooks), insert a new sheet named Instructions. Insert a text box on this sheet and use it to describe how you would use your workbook(s) to gather and present the information requested. Save the workbook(s). Submit the assignment as requested by your instructor.

Part 2: ✳ Identify an alternative approach in Excel to this task, and explain why you chose the method you did over this alternative.

Microsoft Access 2016

File   Home   Create   External Data   Database Tools   Tell me what you want to do...

PrattLast Associates : Database- C:\Users\Owner\Documents\CIS

8 | Macros, Navigation Forms, and Control Layouts

Objectives

You will have mastered the material in this module when you can:

- Create and modify macros and submacros
- Create a menu form with command buttons
- Create a menu form with an option group
- Create a macro for the option group
- Use an IF statement in a macro
- Create datasheet forms

- Create user interface (UI) macros
- Create navigation forms
- Add tabs to a navigation form
- Create data macros
- Create and remove control layouts
- Use the Arrange tab to modify control layouts on forms and reports

Introduction

In this module, you will learn how to create and test macros that open forms and that preview reports and export reports. You will create a menu form with command buttons as well as a menu form with an **option group**, which is an object that enables you to make a selection by choosing the option button corresponding to your choice. You will also create and use user interface (UI) macros in forms. PrattLast Associates requires a navigation form that will allow users to open forms and reports simply by clicking appropriate tabs and buttons. You will learn about the use of data macros for ensuring that updates to the database are valid. Finally, you will learn how to use control layouts on forms and reports.

Project—Macros, Navigation Forms, and Control Layouts

PrattLast Associates would like its users to be able to access forms and reports by simply clicking tabs and buttons, rather than by using the Navigation Pane. A **navigation form** like the one shown in Figure 8–1a is a form that includes tabs to display forms and reports. This navigation form contains several useful features. With the Account tab selected, you can click the account number on any row to see the data for the selected account displayed in the Account View and Update Form (Figure 8–1b). The form does not appear in a tabbed sheet, the way tables, queries, forms, and reports normally do. Rather, it appears as a **pop-up form**, a form that stays on top of other open objects, even when another object is active.

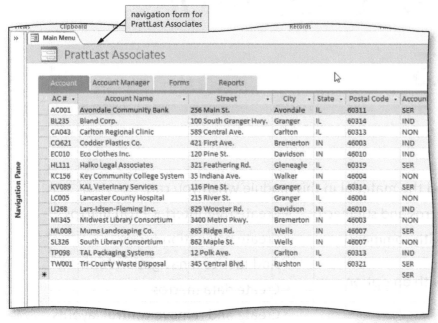

Figure 8–1(a) Navigation Form

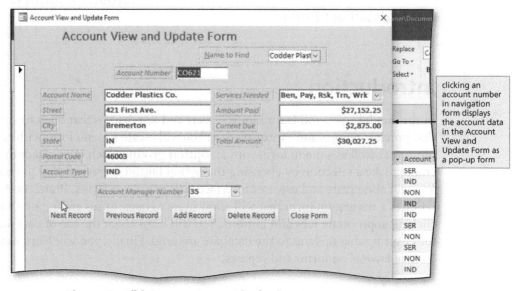

Figure 8–1(b) Pop-up Form Displaying Account Data

Clicking the Account Manager tab of the navigation form displays account manager data. As with accounts, clicking the account manager number on any record displays data for that account manager in a pop-up form.

Clicking the Forms tab in the PrattLast Associates navigation form displays buttons for each of the available forms (Figure 8–1c). You can open the desired form by clicking the appropriate button.

Clicking the Reports tab displays an option group for displaying reports (Figure 8–1d). You can preview or export any of the reports one at a time by clicking the corresponding option button. PrattLast plans to use the navigation form because they believe it will improve the user-friendliness of the database, thereby improving employee satisfaction and efficiency.

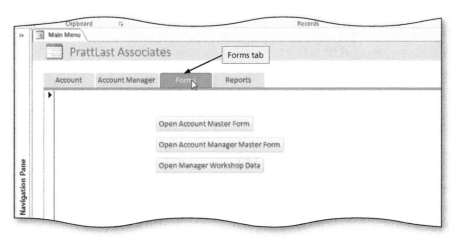

Figure 8–1(c) Forms Tab

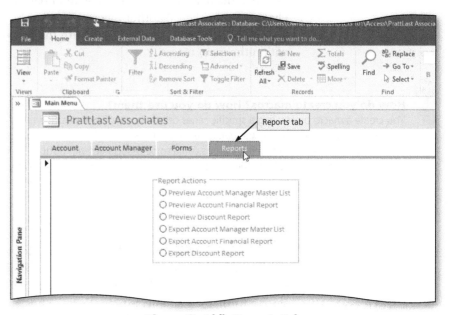

Figure 8–1(d) Reports Tab

Before creating the navigation form, PrattLast will create **macros**, which are collections of actions designed to carry out specific tasks. To perform the actions in a macro, you run the macro. When you run a macro, Access will execute the various steps, called **actions**, in the order indicated by the macro. You run the navigation form macros by clicking certain buttons in the form.

BTW
The Ribbon and
Screen Resolution
Access may change how the
groups and buttons within
the groups appear on the
ribbon, depending on the
computer's screen resolution.
Thus, your ribbon may look
different from the ones in
this book if you are using a
screen resolution other than
1366 x 768.

PrattLast will also create another type of macro, a data macro. A **data macro** is a special type of macro that enables you to add logic to table events such as adding, changing, or deleting data. You typically use data macros to ensure data validity.

In this module, you will learn how to create and use the navigation form shown in Figure 8–1. The following roadmap identifies general activities you will perform as you progress through this module:

1. Create and modify a MACRO WITH SUBMACROS
2. Create a menu FORM with COMMAND BUTTONS
3. Create a menu FORM with an OPTION GROUP
4. Create a MACRO for the OPTION GROUP
5. Create DATASHEET FORMS
6. Create USER INTERFACE (UI) MACROS
7. Create a NAVIGATION FORM
8. Create a DATA MACRO

Creating and Using Macros

BTW
Touch Screen
Differences
The Office and Windows
interfaces may vary if you are
using a touch screen. For this
reason, you might notice that
the function or appearance
of your touch screen differs
slightly from this module's
presentation.

Similar to other Office apps, Access allows you to create and use macros. A macro consists of a series of actions that Access performs when the macro is run. When you create a macro, you specify these actions. Once you have created a macro, you can simply run the macro, and Access will perform the various actions you specified. For example, the macro might open a form in read-only mode, a mode that prohibits changes to the data. Another macro might export a report as a PDF file. You can group related macros into a single macro, with the individual macros existing as submacros within the main macro.

CONSIDER THIS

How do you create macros? How do you use them?
You create a macro by entering a specific series of actions in a window called the Macro Builder window. Once a macro is created, it exists as an object in the database, and you can run it from the Navigation Pane by right-clicking the macro and then clicking Run on the shortcut menu. Macros can also be associated with buttons on forms. When you click the corresponding button on the form, Access will run the macro and complete the corresponding action. Whether a macro is run from the Navigation Pane or from a form, the effect is the same: Access will execute the actions in the order in which they occur in the macro.

BTW
Enabling the Content
For each of the databases
you use in this module,
you will need to enable the
content.

In this module, you will create macros for a variety of purposes. Access provides a collection of standard actions in the Macro Builder; as you enter actions, you will select them from a list. The names of the actions are self-explanatory. The action to open a form, for example, is OpenForm. Thus, it is not necessary to memorize the specific actions that are available.

To Begin Creating a Macro

1 MACRO WITH SUBMACROS | 2 FORM COMMAND BUTTONS | 3 FORM OPTION GROUP | 4 MACRO FOR OPTION GROUP
5 DATASHEET FORMS | 6 USER INTERFACE MACROS | 7 NAVIGATION FORM | 8 DATA MACRO

The following steps begin creating a macro. *Why? Once you have created the macro, you will be able to add the appropriate actions.*

- Run Access and open the database named PrattLast Associates from your hard disk, OneDrive, or other storage location.
- If necessary, close the Navigation Pane.
- Display the Create tab (Figure 8–2).

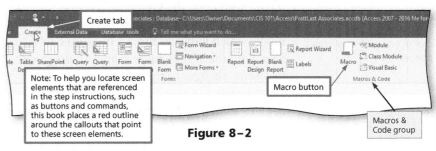

Figure 8–2

- Click the Macro button (Create tab | Macros & Code group) to create a new macro.
- Click the Action Catalog button (Macro Tools Design tab | Show/Hide group) if necessary to display the action catalog (Figure 8–3).

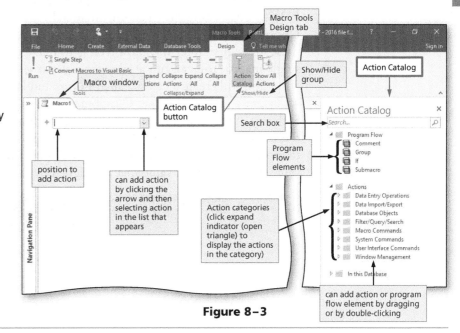

Figure 8–3

The Macro Builder Window

You create a macro by adding actions in the macro window, shown in Figure 8–3. You can add actions by clicking the 'Add New Action' arrow and selecting the desired action from the list of possible actions. You can also use the Action Catalog, which is a list of macro actions organized by type. If the Action Catalog does not appear, click the Action Catalog button (Macro Tools Design tab | Show/Hide group) to display it. You can add an action by double-clicking the action in the Action Catalog or by dragging it.

Access arranges the available actions in categories. To see the actions in a category, click the **expand indicator** (the open triangle) in front of the category. The actions will appear and the expand indicator will change to a solid triangle. To hide the actions in a category, click the solid triangle.

How can you find an action if you are not sure which category contains the action?
You can search the list by typing in the Search box. Access will then reduce the list of actions displayed to only those actions whose names or descriptions contain the text you have typed.

Many actions require additional information, called the **arguments** of the action. For example, if the action is OpenForm, Access needs to know which form is to be opened. You indicate the form to be opened by setting the value of the Form Name argument to the desired form. If the value for the Form Name argument for the OpenForm action is Manager Workshop Data, then Access will open the Manager Workshop Data form when it executes this action.

BTW
Macros
A macro is a series of commands used to automate repeated tasks. You can create macros in other Office apps, such as Word and Excel.

CONSIDER THIS

BTW
Touch and Pointers
Remember that if you are
using your finger on a touch
screen, you will not see the
pointer.

Actions can have more than one argument. For example, in addition to the Form Name argument, the OpenForm action also has a Data Mode argument. If the value of the Data Mode argument is Read Only, then the form will be opened in read-only mode, which indicates users will be able to view but not change data. When you select an action, the arguments will appear along with the action, and you can make any necessary changes to them.

In the forms you will create later in this module, you need macros for opening the Manager Workshop Data form as read-only (to prevent updates), opening the Account Manager Master Form, opening the Account Master Form, previewing the Account Manager Master List, previewing the Account Financial Report, previewing the Discount Report, exporting the Account Manager Master List as a PDF file, exporting the Account Financial Report as a PDF file, and exporting the Discount Report as a PDF file. You could create nine separate macros to accomplish these tasks. A simpler way, however, is to make each of these a submacro within a single macro. You can run a submacro just as you can run a macro.

You will create a macro called Forms and Reports that contains these nine submacros. Table 8–1 shows the submacros. Submacros can contain many actions, but each one in this table includes only a single action. For each submacro, the table gives the action, those arguments that need to be changed, and the values you need to assign to those arguments. If an argument is not listed, then you do not need to change the value from the default value that is assigned by Access.

Table 8–1 Forms and Reports Macro

Submacro	Action	Arguments to be Changed
Open Manager Workshop Data		
	OpenForm	Form Name: Manager Workshop Data Data Mode: Read Only
Open Account Manager Master Form		
	OpenForm	Form Name: Account Manager Master Form
Open Account Master Form		
	OpenForm	Form Name: Account Master Form
Preview Account Manager Master List		
	OpenReport	Report Name: Account Manager Master List View: Print Preview
Preview Account Financial Report		
	OpenReport	Report Name: Account Financial Report View: Print Preview
Preview Discount Report		
	OpenReport	Report Name: Discount Report View: Print Preview
Export Account Manager Master List		
	ExportWithFormatting	Object Type: Report Object Name: Account Manager Master List Output Format: PDF Format (*.pdf)
Export Account Financial Report		
	ExportWithFormatting	Object Type: Report Object Name: Account Financial Report Output Format: PDF Format (*.pdf)
Export Discount Report		
	ExportWithFormatting	Object Type: Report Object Name: Discount Report Output Format: PDF Format (*.pdf)

To Add an Action to a Macro

To continue creating the Forms and Reports macro, enter the actions in the Macro Builder. In these steps, you will enter actions by double-clicking the action in the Action Catalog. *Why? The actions in the Action Catalog are organized by function, making it easier to locate the action you want.* Access will add the action to the Add New Action box. If there is more than one Add New Action box, you need to ensure that the one where you want to add the action is selected before you double-click.

The following steps add the first action. They also make the necessary changes to any arguments. Finally, the steps save the macro.

1

- Double-click the Submacro element from the Program Flow section of the Action Catalog to add a submacro and then type **Open Manager Workshop Data** as the name of the submacro (Figure 8–4).

Q&A How can I tell the purpose of the various actions?

If necessary, expand the category containing the action so that the action appears. Point to the action. An expanded ScreenTip will appear, giving you a description of the action.

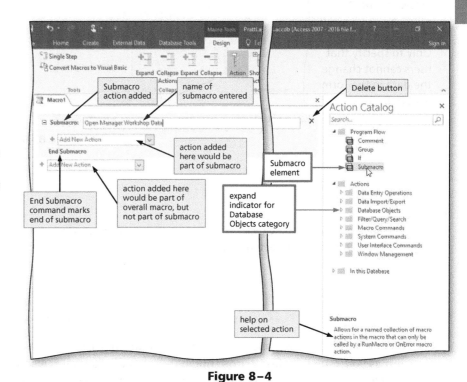

Figure 8–4

2

- Click the expand indicator for the Database Objects category of actions to display the actions within the category.

- Double-click the OpenForm action to add it to the submacro (Figure 8–5).

Q&A What should I do if I add an action in the wrong position? What should I do if I add the wrong action?

If you add an action in the wrong position, use the Move up or Move down buttons to move it to the correct position. If you added the wrong action, click the DELETE button to delete the action, and then fix the error by adding the correct action.

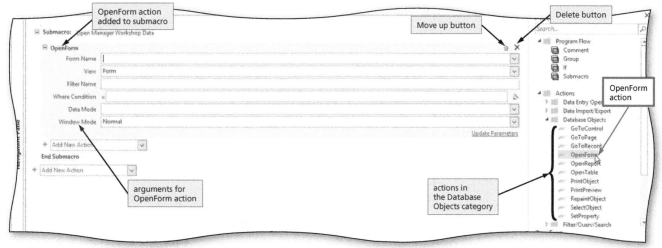

Figure 8–5

- Click the drop-down arrow for the Form Name argument and then select Manager Workshop Data as the name of the form to be opened.

- Click the drop-down arrow for the Data Mode argument and then select Read Only to specify that users cannot change the data in the form (Figure 8–6).

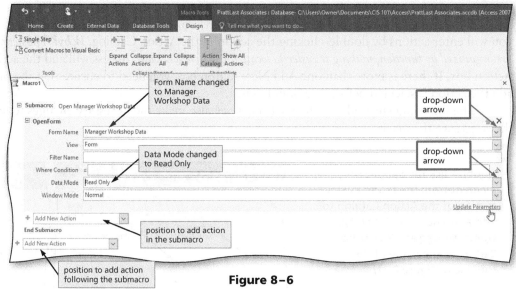

Figure 8–6

Q&A What is the effect of the other Data Mode options?

Add allows viewing records and adding new records, but not updating records. Edit allows viewing records, adding new records, and updating existing records.

- Click the Save button on the Quick Access Toolbar, type **Forms and Reports** as the name of the macro, and then click the OK button to save the macro.

To Add More Actions to a Macro

1 MACRO WITH SUBMACROS | 2 FORM COMMAND BUTTONS | 3 FORM OPTION GROUP | 4 MACRO FOR OPTION GROUP
5 DATASHEET FORMS | 6 USER INTERFACE MACROS | 7 NAVIGATION FORM | 8 DATA MACRO

To complete the macro, you need to add the additional actions shown in Table 8–1. You add the additional actions just as you added the first action. Initially, Access displays all the actions you have added with their arguments clearly visible. After you have added several actions, you might want to collapse some or all of the actions. **Why?** *Collapsing actions makes it easier to get an overall view of your macro.* You can always expand any action later to see details concerning the arguments. The following steps add additional actions to a macro, collapsing existing actions when necessary to provide a better view of the overall macro structure.

- Click the minus sign (–) in front of the OpenForm action to collapse the action (Figure 8–7).

Q&A Could I also use the buttons on the ribbon?

Yes, you can use the buttons in the Collapse/Expand group on the Macro Tools Design tab. Click the Expand Actions button to expand the selected action, or click the Collapse Actions button to collapse the selected action. You can expand all actions at once by clicking the Expand All button, or you can collapse all actions at once by clicking the Collapse All button.

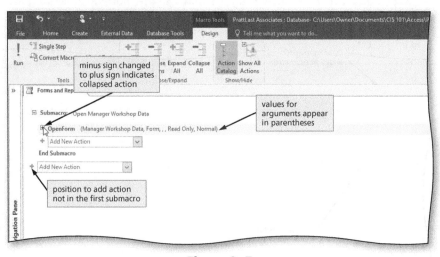

Figure 8–7

2

- Double-click the Submacro element from the Program Flow section of the Action Catalog to add a submacro and then type **Open Account Manager Master Form** as the name of the submacro.

- Double-click the OpenForm action to add it to the submacro.

- Click the drop-down arrow for the Form Name argument and then select 'Account Manager Master Form.'

- In a similar fashion, add the 'Open Account Master Form' submacro.

- Add the OpenForm action to the submacro.

- Select Account Master Form as the value for the Form Name argument (Figure 8–8).

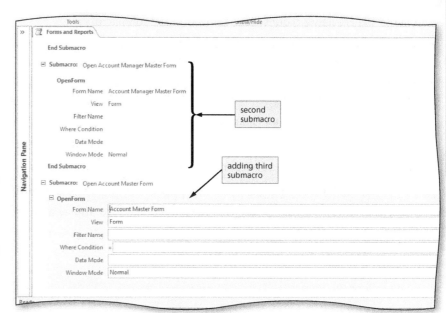

Figure 8–8

Q&A | Do I have to change the values of any of the other arguments?
No. The default values that Access sets are appropriate.

3

- For each of the submacros, click the minus sign in front of the submacro to collapse the submacro.

- Add a submacro named Preview Account Manager Master List.

- Add the OpenReport action to the macro.

- Select Account Manager Master List as the report name.

- Select Print Preview as the view (Figure 8–9).

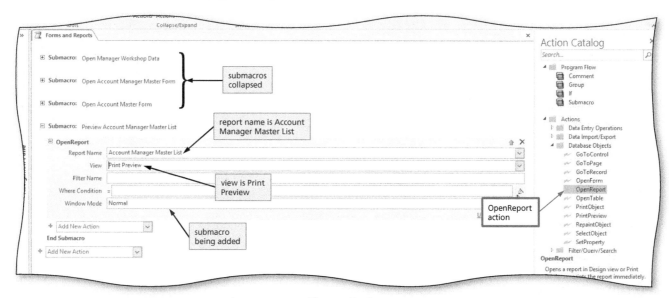

Figure 8–9

- Collapse the Preview Account Manager Master List submacro.
- Add the Preview Account Financial Report submacro. Include the action described in Table 8–1. The report name is Account Financial Report and the view is Print Preview.
- Add the Preview Discount Report submacro. Include the action described in Table 8–1. The report name is Discount Report and the view is Print Preview.
- Collapse the Preview Account Financial Report and Preview Discount Report submacros.
- Collapse the Database Objects category and then expand the Data Import/Export category.
- Add a submacro called Export Account Manager Master List.
- Add the ExportWithFormatting action, which will export and maintain any special formatting in the process.
- Click the drop-down arrow for the Object Type argument to display a list of possible object types (Figure 8–10).

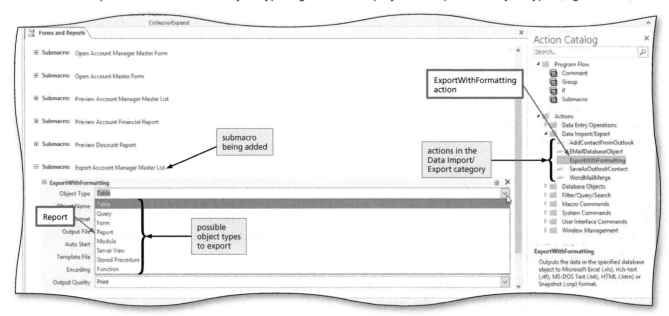

Figure 8–10

- Click Report in the list to indicate that Access is to export a report.

- Click the drop-down arrow for the Object Name argument and select Account Manager Master List as the object name.

- Click the drop-down arrow for the Output Format argument and then select PDF Format (*.pdf) as the Output Format to export the report in PDF format (Figure 8–11).

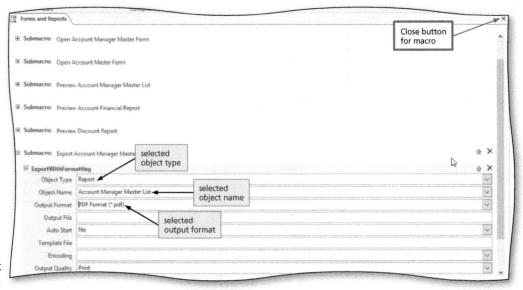

Figure 8–11

- Add the Export Account Financial Report submacro and the action from Table 8–1.

- Select Report as the Object Type and select Account Financial Report as the report name.

- Select PDF Format (*.pdf) as the Output Format to export the report in PDF format.

- Add the Export Discount Report submacro and the action from Table 8–1.

- Select Report as the Object Type and Discount Report as the report name.

- Select PDF Format (*.pdf) as the Output Format to export the report in PDF format.

- Save the macro.

- Close the macro by clicking its Close button, shown in Figure 8–11.

Opening Databases Containing Macros

It is possible that a macro stored in a database can contain a computer virus. By default, Access disables macros when it opens a database and displays a Security Warning. If the database comes from a trusted source and you are sure that it does not contain any macro viruses, click the Enable Content button. You can make adjustments to Access security settings by clicking File on the ribbon to open the Backstage view, and then clicking Options to display the Access Options dialog box, clicking Trust Center, clicking Trust Center Settings, and then clicking Macro Settings.

Errors in Macros

Macros can contain errors. The macro may abort. It might open the wrong table or produce a wrong message. If you have problems with a macro, you can **single-step the macro**, that is, proceed through a macro a step at a time in Design view.

Figure 8–12 shows a macro open in Design view. This macro first has an action to open the Account table in Datasheet view in Read Only mode. It then changes the view to Print Preview. Next, it opens the Account table in Datasheet view, this time in Edit mode. Finally, it opens the Manager-Account Query in Datasheet view in Edit mode. The macro in the figure is a common type of macro that opens several objects at once. To open all these objects, the user only has to run the macro. Unfortunately, this macro contains an error. The name of the Account table is written as "Accounts" in the second OpenTable action.

BTW
Converting a Macro to VBA Code
If you want to use many of the resources provided by Windows or communicate with another Windows app, you will need to convert any macros to VBA (Visual Basic for Applications) code. To convert a macro to VBA code, open the macro in Design view and click the 'Convert Macros to Visual Basic' button (Macro Tools Design tab | Tools group). When the Convert Macro dialog box appears, select the appropriate options, and then click Convert.

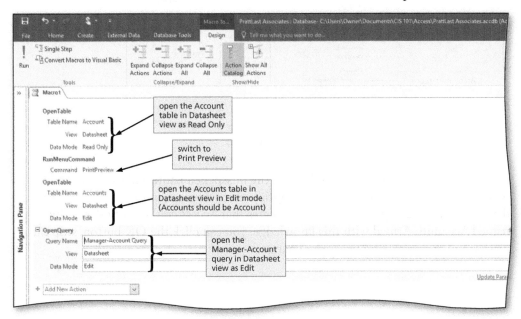

Figure 8–12

BTW
Saving a Macro as a VBA Module
You can save a macro as a VBA module using the 'Save Object As' command in Backstage view. Open the macro in Design view, click File on the ribbon to open Backstage view, and then click Save As. When the Save As gallery appears, click 'Save Object As' in the File Types area, and then click the Save As button. When the Save As dialog box appears, click Module in the As text box and then click the OK button.

To run this macro in single-step mode, you would first click the Single Step button (Macro Tools Design tab | Tools group). You would next click the Run button (Macro Tools Design tab | Tools group) to run the macro. Because you clicked the Single Step button, Access would display the Macro Single Step dialog box (Figure 8–13). The dialog box shows the action to be executed and the values of the various arguments. You can click the Step button to proceed to the next step.

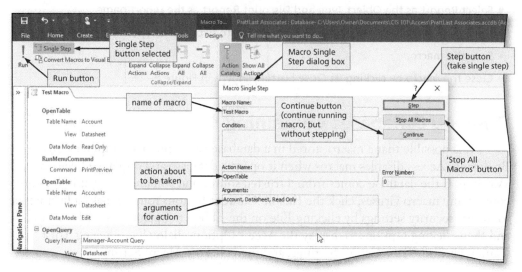

Figure 8–13

BTW
Program Flow Actions
Actions in the Program Flow category can change the order macro actions are executed or help structure a macro.

With this macro, after you clicked the Step button twice, you would arrive at the screen shown in Figure 8–14. Access is about to execute the OpenTable command. The arguments are Accounts, Datasheet, and Edit. At this point, you might spot the fact that "Accounts" is misspelled. It should be "Account." If so, you could click the 'Stop All Macros' button and then correct the object name.

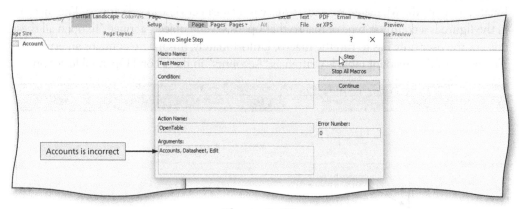

Figure 8–14

If you instead click the Step button, the misspelled name will cause the macro to abort. Access would display the appropriate error message in the Microsoft Access dialog box (Figure 8–15). This error indicates that Access could not find the object named Accounts. Armed with this knowledge, you can click the OK button, stop the macro, and then make the necessary change.

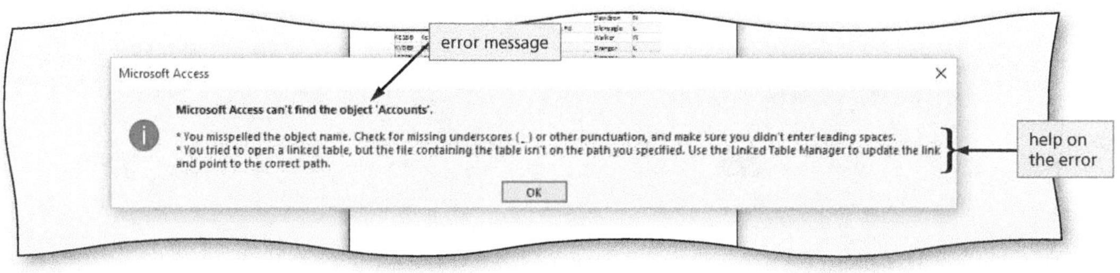

Figure 8–15

You do not need to step through a macro to discover the error. You can simply run the macro, either by clicking the Run button (Macro Tools Design tab | Tools group) with the macro open or by right-clicking the macro in the Navigation Pane and clicking Run. In either case, Access will run the macro until it encounters the error. When it does, it will display the same message shown in Figure 8–15. Just as with stepping through the macro, you would click the OK button, stop the macro, and then make the necessary change.

Break Point: If you wish to stop working through the module at this point, you can resume the project later by running Access, opening the database called PrattLast Associates, and continuing to follow the steps from this location forward.

Creating and Using a Navigation Form

Figure 8–1a showed a navigation form for PrattLast Associates. A navigation form is a form that contains a **navigation control**, a control that can display a variety of forms and reports. Like the form in Figure 8–1, navigation controls contain tabs. Clicking the tab displays the corresponding form or report. The tabs can be arranged across the top and/or down the sides.

You can only include forms and reports on the tabs; you cannot include either tables or queries. The navigation form in Figure 8–1, however, appears to have a tab corresponding to the Account table. If you would find it desirable to display tables or queries on a navigation control tab, you can make it appear as though the navigation form contains these objects by creating a datasheet form based on the table or query. Figure 8–1 actually shows a datasheet form based on the Account table and does not show the Account table itself.

Before creating the navigation form, you have some other forms to create. For example, you might want the users to be able to click a tab in the navigation form and then choose from a list of forms or reports. Figure 8–16 shows a list of forms presented as buttons; the user would click the button for the desired form. Clicking the 'Open Account Master Form' button, for example, would display the Account View and Update Form as shown in Figure 8–17.

BTW
Navigation Forms
A navigation form often is used as a switchboard or main page for a database to reduce clutter and target the most commonly used database objects. A navigation form contains a navigation control and a subform control. After you create a navigation form, you can use the Navigation Where Clause property associated with a navigation control to automatically apply a filter.

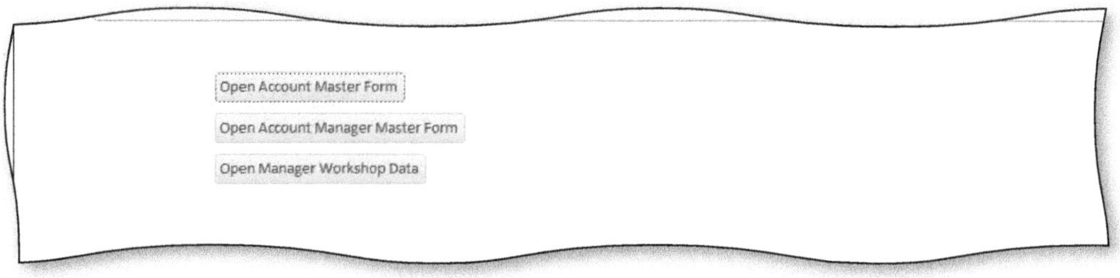

Figure 8–16

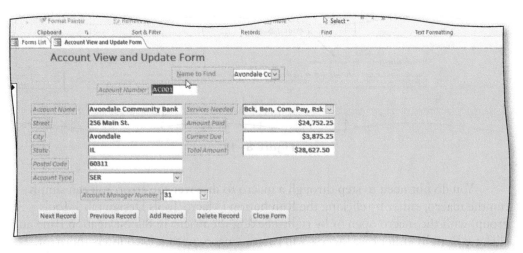

Figure 8–17

To implement options like these, you create blank forms and add either the command buttons or the option group. You then include the form you have created in the navigation form. When users click the corresponding tab, Access displays the form and users can then click the appropriate button.

To Create a Menu Form Containing Command Buttons

1 MACRO WITH SUBMACROS | 2 FORM COMMAND BUTTONS | 3 FORM OPTION GROUP | 4 MACRO FOR OPTION GROUP
5 DATASHEET FORMS | 6 USER INTERFACE MACROS | 7 NAVIGATION FORM | 8 DATA MACRO

Why? *A menu form in which you make a selection by clicking the appropriate command button provides a convenient way to select a desired option.* You can create a menu form by adding command buttons to the form. The following steps use this technique to create a menu form with three buttons: 'Open Account Master Form,' 'Open Account Manager Master Form,' and 'Open Manager Workshop Data.' The actions assigned to each button will run a macro that causes the desired action to occur. For example, the action for the Open Account Master Form button will run the Open Account Master Form submacro, which in turn will open the Account Master Form.

The following steps create a form in Design view and then add the necessary buttons.

- Display the Create tab.

- Click the Form Design button (Create tab | Forms group) to create a blank form in Design view.

- If a field list appears, click the 'Add Existing Fields' button (Form Design Tools Design tab | Tools group) to remove the field list.

- If a property sheet appears, click the Property Sheet button (Form Design Tools Design tab | Tools group) to remove the property sheet (Figure 8–18).

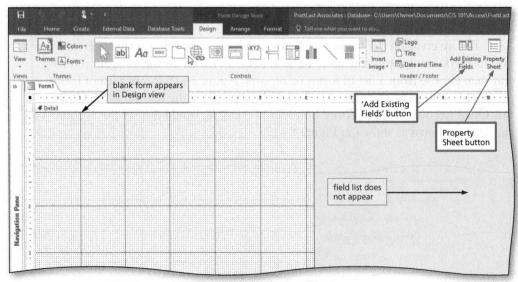

Figure 8–18

- Make sure the 'Use Control Wizards' button is selected.
- Click the Button tool (Form Design Tools Design tab | Controls group) and move the pointer to the approximate position shown in Figure 8–19.

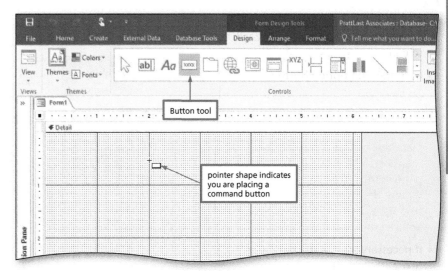

Figure 8–19

- Click the position shown in Figure 8–19 to display the Command Button Wizard dialog box.
- Click Miscellaneous in the Categories box, and then click Run Macro in the Actions box (Figure 8–20).

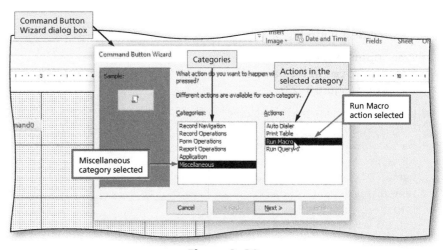

Figure 8–20

- Click the Next button to display the next screen in the wizard.
- Click Forms and Reports.Open Account Master Form to select the macro to be run (Figure 8–21).

Q&A What does this notation mean? The portion before the period is the macro and the portion after the period is the submacro. Thus, this notation means the Open Account Master Form submacro within the Forms and Reports macro.

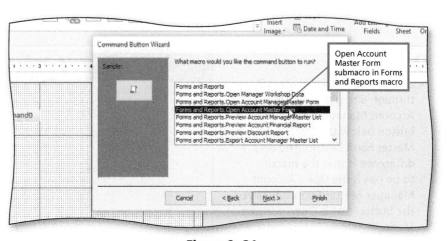

Figure 8–21

- Click the Next button to display the next Command Button Wizard screen.
- Click the Text option button.

Q&A What is the purpose of these option buttons?
Choose the first option button to place text on the button. You can then specify the text to be included or accept the default choice. Choose the second option button to place a picture on the button. You can then select a picture.

- If necessary, delete the default text and then type **Open Account Master Form** as the text (Figure 8–22).

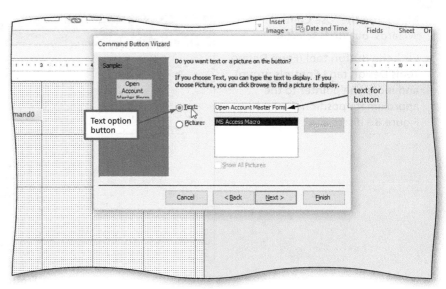

Figure 8–22

- Click the Next button.
- Type **Open_Account_ Master_Form** as the name of the button (Figure 8–23).

Q&A Why do you include the underscores in the name of the button?
If you are working with macros or VBA, you cannot have spaces in names. One way to avoid spaces and still make readable names is to include underscores where you would normally use spaces. Thus, Open Account Master Form becomes Open_Account_Master_ Form.

- Click the Finish button to finish specifying the button.

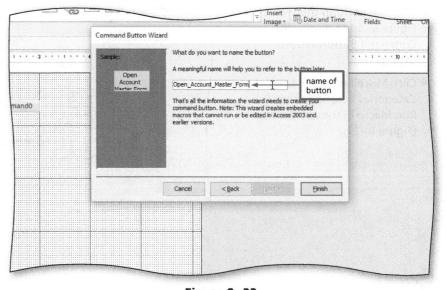

Figure 8–23

- Use the techniques in Steps 2 through 6 to place the Open Account Manager Master Form button below the Open Account Master Form button. The only difference is that the macro to be run is the Open Account Manager Master Form submacro, the button text is Open Account Manager Master Form, and the name of the button is Open_ Account_Manager_Master_Form.

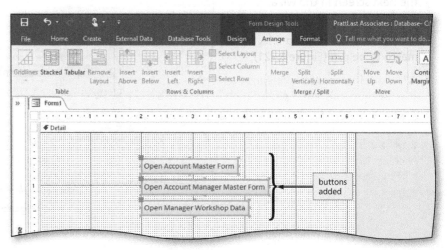

Figure 8–24

- Use the techniques in Steps 2 through 6 to place the Open Manager Workshop Data button below the Open Account Manager Master Form button. The only difference is that the macro to be run is the Open Manager Workshop Data submacro, the text is Open Manager Workshop Data, and the name of the button is Open_Manager_Workshop_Data.

- Adjust the size and spacing of the buttons to approximately match those in Figure 8–24, using the Arrange tab, if necessary.

- Save the form using the name, Forms List.

Q&A How can I test the buttons to make sure the macros work?
Right-click the Forms List form in the Navigation Pane and click Open. Click each of the buttons on the form. If there are errors in any of the macros, open the macro in the Macro Builder window and correct the errors.

 Experiment

- Test each of the buttons on the form. Ensure that the correct form opens. If there are errors, correct the corresponding macro.

8

- Close the form.

Option Groups

You might find it useful to allow users to make a selection from some predefined options by including an option group. An **option group** is a rectangle containing a collection of option buttons. To perform an action, you simply click the corresponding option button. Figure 8–25 shows a list of reports presented in an option group where the user would click the desired option button. Notice that the user could click an option button to preview a report. The user could click a different option button to export the report as a PDF file. Clicking the 'Preview Account Manager Master List' option button, for example, would display a preview of the Account Manager Master List (Figure 8–26). Clicking the Close Print Preview button would return you to the option group.

BTW
Viewing VBA Code
You can view VBA code that is attached to a form or report. To do so, open the form or report in Design view and click the View Code button (Report Design Tools Design tab | Tools group) for reports or (Form Design Tools Design tab | Tools group) for forms.

Figure 8–25

Figure 8–26

To Create a Menu Form Containing an Option Group

The form you are creating will contain an option group. *Why? The option group allows users to select an option button to indicate either a report to preview or a report to export.*

The following steps use the Option Group tool to create the option group named Form Options.

1

- Display the Create tab.

- Click the Form Design button (Create tab | Forms group) to create a blank form in Design view.

- If a field list appears, click the 'Add Existing Fields' button (Form Design Tools Design tab | Tools group) to remove the field list (Figure 8–27).

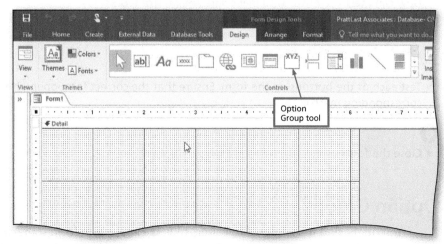

Figure 8–27

2

- With the 'Use Control Wizards' button selected, click the Option Group tool (Form Design Tools Design tab | Controls group) and then move the pointer to the approximate position shown in Figure 8–28.

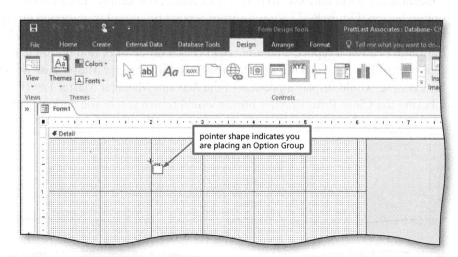

Figure 8–28

3

- Click the position shown in Figure 8–28 to place an option group and start the Option Group Wizard (Figure 8–29).

Q&A The Option Group Wizard did not start for me. What should I do? You must not have had the 'Use Control Wizards' button selected. With the option group selected, press the DELETE key to delete the option group. Select the 'Use Control Wizards' button, and then add the option group a second time.

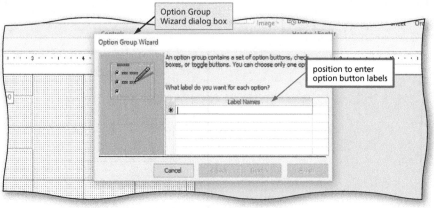

Figure 8–29

- Type **Preview Account Manager Master List** in the first row of label names and press the DOWN ARROW key to specify the label for the first button in the group.

- Type **Preview Account Financial Report** in the second row of label names and press the DOWN ARROW key.

- Type **Preview Discount Report** in the third row of label names and press the DOWN ARROW key.

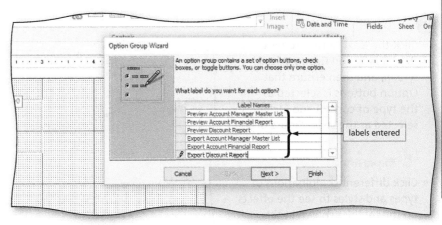

Figure 8–30

- Type **Export Account Manager Master List** in the fourth row of label names and press the DOWN ARROW key.

- Type **Export Account Financial Report** in the fifth row of label names and press the DOWN ARROW key.

- Type **Export Discount Report** in the sixth row of label names (Figure 8–30).

- Click the Next button to move to the next Option Group Wizard screen.

- Click the 'No, I don't want a default.' option button to select it (Figure 8–31).

Q&A | What is the effect of specifying one of the options as the default choice?
The default choice will initially be selected when you open the form. If there is no default choice, no option will be selected.

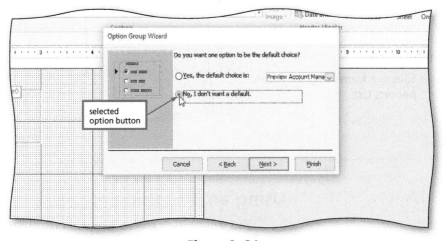

Figure 8–31

- Click the Next button to move to the next Option Group Wizard screen and then verify that the values assigned to the labels match those shown in Figure 8–32.

Q&A | What is the purpose of the values that appear for each option?
You can use the values in macros or VBA. You will use them in a macro later in this module.

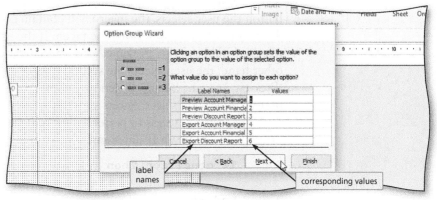

Figure 8–32

- Click the Next button to move to the next Option Group Wizard screen, and then ensure that Option buttons is selected as the type of control and Etched is selected as the style (Figure 8–33).

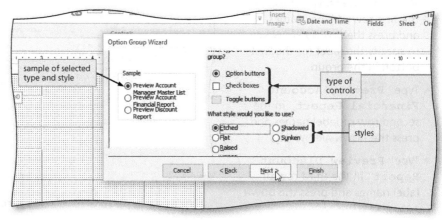

Experiment

- Click different combinations of types and styles to see the effects on the samples shown in the dialog box. When finished, select Option buttons as the type and Etched as the style.

Figure 8–33

- Click the Next button to move to the next Option Group Wizard screen and then type **Report Actions** as the caption.

- Click the Finish button to complete the addition of the option group (Figure 8–34).

- Save the form using the name, Reports List.

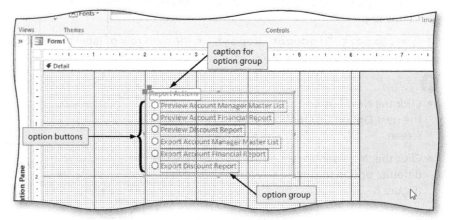

Figure 8–34

Using an If Statement

You will create a macro that will take appropriate action when the user updates the option group, that is, when the user clicks an option button in the group. The macro will run the appropriate submacro, depending on which option the user has selected.

Because the specific actions that the macro will perform depend on the option button the user selects, the macro will contain conditions. The conditions will determine which action should be taken. If the user selects the first option button, Access should run the 'Preview Account Manager Master List' submacro. If, on the other hand, the user selects the second option button, Access should instead run the 'Preview Account Financial Report' submacro. For each of the six possible option buttons a user can select, Access should run a different submacro.

To instruct Access to perform different actions based on certain conditions, the macro will contain an If statement. The simplest form of an If statement is:

```
If condition Then
        action
End If
```

If the condition is true, Access will take the indicated action. If the condition is false, no action will be taken. For example, the condition could be that the user selects the first option button, and the action could be to run the Account Manager Master List submacro. No action would be taken if the user selects any other button.

Another form of the If statement contains an Else clause. This form is:

```
If condition Then
      first action
Else
      second action
End If
```

If the condition is true, the first action is taken; if the condition is false, the second action is taken. For example, the condition could be that the user selects option button 1; the first action could be to run the 'Preview Account Manager Master List' submacro, and the second action could be to run the 'Preview Account Financial Report' submacro. If the user selects option button 1, Access would run the 'Preview Account Manager Master' list submacro. If the user selects any other option button, Access would run the 'Preview Account Financial Report' submacro. Because there are six option buttons, the macro needs to use an If statement with multiple Else Ifs to account for all of the options. This type of If statement has the form:

```
If first condition Then
      first action
Else If second condition Then
      second action
Else If third condition Then
      third action
...
End If
```

The first condition could be that the user selects the first option button; the second condition could be that the user selects the second option button; the third condition could be that the user selects the third option button, and so on. The first action could be that Access runs the first submacro; the second action could be that it runs the second submacro; and the third could be that it runs the third submacro. In this case, there are six option buttons and six submacros. For six conditions, as required in this macro, the If statement will contain five Else Ifs. The If statement along with the five Else Ifs will collectively contain six conditions: one to test if the user selected option 1, one for option 2, one for option 3, one for option 4, one for option 5, and one for option 6.

To Create a Macro with a Variable for the Option Group

1 MACRO WITH SUBMACROS | 2 FORM COMMAND BUTTONS | 3 FORM OPTION GROUP | 4 MACRO FOR OPTION GROUP
5 DATASHEET FORMS | 6 USER INTERFACE MACROS | 7 NAVIGATION FORM | 8 DATA MACRO

The following steps begin creating the macro and add an action to set a variable to the desired value. *Why? The expression that contains the option number is [Forms]![Account Master Form]![Form_Options]. Because this expression is fairly lengthy, the macro will begin by setting a temporary variable to this expression. A **variable** is a named* location in computer memory. You can use a variable to store a value that you can use later in the macro. You will assign the name Optno (short for option number) as the variable name for the expression. This location can contain a value, in this case, the option number on the form. In each of the conditions, you can then use Optno rather than the full expression.

1

- With the option group selected, display a property sheet.

- If necessary, click the All tab.

- Change the name of the option group to Form_Options (Figure 8–35).

Q&A Why this name?
The name Form_Options reflects the fact that these are options that control the action that will be taken on this form. The underscore keeps the name from containing a space.

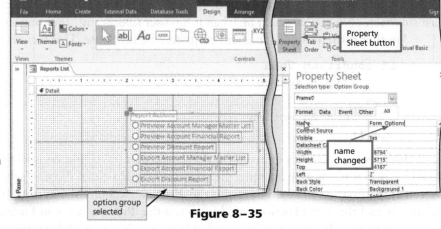

Figure 8–35

2

- Click the After Update property.

- Click the Build button to display the Choose Builder dialog box (Figure 8–36).

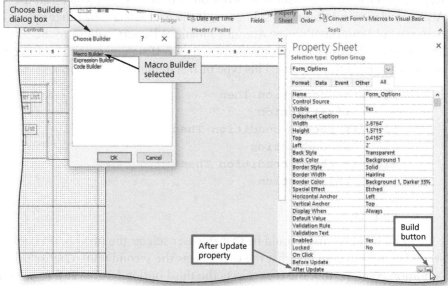

Figure 8–36

3

- With Macro Builder selected in the Choose Builder dialog box, click the OK button to create a macro.

- If necessary, click the Action Catalog button (Macro Tools Design tab | Show/Hide group) to display the Action Catalog.

- If necessary, collapse any category that is expanded.

- Expand the Macro Commands action category.

- Double-click the SetTempVar action in the Action Catalog to add the SetTempVar action to the macro.

- Type **Optno** as the value for the Name argument.

- Type **[Form_Options]** as the value for the Expression argument (Figure 8–37).

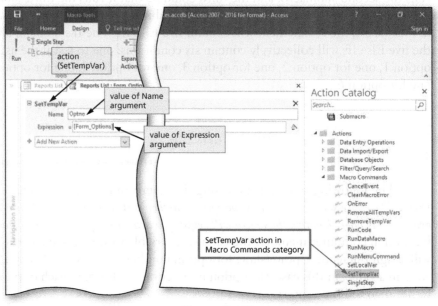

Figure 8–37

How does Access make it easier to enter values for arguments?

Access helps you in three ways. First, if you point to the argument, Access displays a description of the argument. Second, many arguments feature a drop-down list, where you can display the list and then select the desired value. Finally, if you begin typing an expression, a feature called IntelliSense will suggest possible values that start with the letters you have already typed and that are appropriate in the context of what you are typing. If you see the value you want in the list, you can simply click it to select the value.

Macro for Option Group

As mentioned previously, the macro contains six conditions. The first is [TempVars]! [Optno]=1, which simply means the value in the temporary variable Optno is equal to 1. In other words, the user selected the first option button. The action associated with this condition is RunMacro. The argument is the name of the macro. Because the macro to be run is a submacro, the name of the macro includes both the name of the macro containing the submacro, a period, and then the name of the submacro. Because the submacro to be run is Preview Account Manager Master List and is contained in the Forms and Reports macro, the value of the Macro Name argument is Forms and Reports.Preview Account Manager Master List.

The conditions and actions for options 2 through 6 are similar to the first submacro. The only difference is which submacro is associated with each option button. The conditions, actions, and arguments that you will change for the Form_ Options macro are shown in Table 8–2. If the option number is 1, for example, the action is RunMacro. For the RunMacro action, you will change the Macro Name argument. You will set the Macro Name argument to the Preview Account Manager Master List submacro in the Forms and Reports macro. On the other hand, if the option number is 2, for example, the action is again RunMacro. If the option number is 2, however, you will set the Macro Name argument to the Preview Account Financial Report submacro in the Forms and Reports macro. Similar actions take place for the other possible values for the Optno variable, that is, for option buttons 3-6. Because the temporary variable, Optno, is no longer needed at the end of the macro, the macro concludes with the RemoveTempVar command to remove this variable.

Table 8–2 Macro for After Update Property of the Option Group		
Condition	**Action**	**Arguments to be Changed**
	SetTempVar	Name: Optno Expression: [Form_Options]
If [TempVars]![Optno]=1		
	RunMacro	Macro Name: Forms and Reports.Preview Account Manager Master List
Else If [TempVars]![Optno]=2		
	RunMacro	Macro Name: Forms and Reports.Preview Account Financial Report
Else If [TempVars]![Optno]=3		
	RunMacro	Macro Name: Forms and Reports.Preview Discount Report
Else If [TempVars]![Optno]=4		
	RunMacro	Macro Name: Forms and Reports.Export Account Manager Master List
Else If [TempVars]![Optno]=5		
	RunMacro	Macro Name: Forms and Reports.Export Account Financial Report
Else If [TempVars]![Optno]=6		
	RunMacro	Macro Name: Forms and Reports.Export Discount Report
End If		
	RemoveTempVar	Name: Optno

To Add Actions to the Form Options Macro

The following steps add the conditions and actions to the Form_Options macro. *Why? The macro is not yet complete. Adding the conditions and actions will complete the macro.*

- Double-click the If element from the Program Flow section of the Action Catalog to add an If statement to the submacro and then type   `[TempVars] ! [Optno] =1`   as the condition in the If statement.

- With the Macro Commands category expanded, double-click RunMacro to add the RunMacro action.

- Click the drop-down arrow for the Macro Name argument and select the 'Preview Account Manager Master List' submacro within the Forms and Reports macro as the value for the argument (Figure 8–38).

Q&A What should I do if I add an action in the wrong position? What should I do if I add the wrong action?

If you add an action in the wrong position, use the Move up or Move down buttons to move it to the correct position. If you added the wrong action, click the DELETE button to delete the action, and then fix the error by adding the correct action.

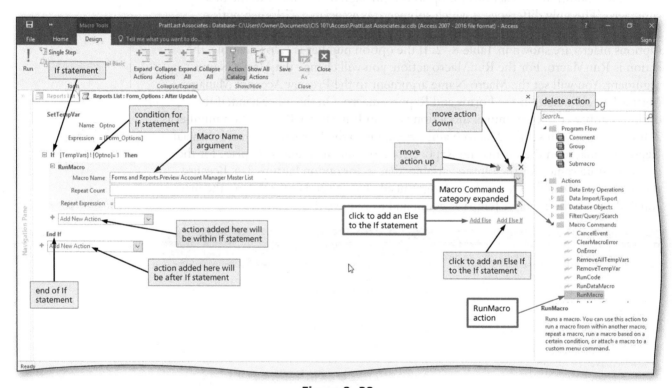

Figure 8–38

- Click 'Add Else If' to add an Else If clause to the If statement.

- Add the conditions and actions associated with options 2, 3, 4, 5, and 6 as described in Table 8–2, and specify the arguments for the actions. Click 'Add Else If' after adding each action except for the last one.

Q&A Do I have to enter all these actions? They seem to be very similar to the ones associated with option 1.

You can copy and paste the action for option 1. Right-click the action to select it and display a shortcut menu. Click Copy on the shortcut menu. Right-click the action just above where you want to insert the selected action and then click Paste. If the new action is not inserted in the correct position, select the new action and then click either the Move up or Move down buttons to move it to the correct location. Once the action is in the correct location, you can make any necessary changes to the arguments.

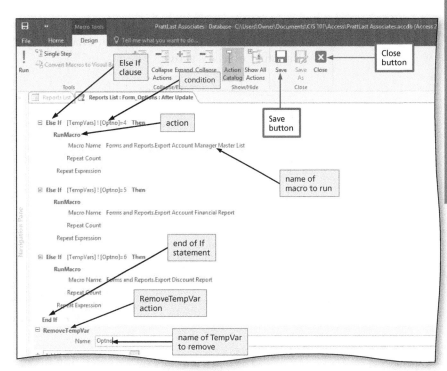

Figure 8–39

• Add the RemoveTempVar action and argument after the end of the If statement, as shown in Figure 8–39.

• Type **Optno** as the name of the TempVar to remove.

Q&A Do I need to remove the temporary variable?

Technically, no. In fact, if you plan to use this temporary variable in another macro and want it to retain the value you assigned in this macro, you would definitely not remove it. If you do not plan to use it elsewhere, it is a good idea to remove it, however.

• Click the Save button (Macro Tools Design tab | Close group) to save the macro.

• Click the Close button (Macro Tools Design tab | Close group) to close the macro and return to the form.

• Close the property sheet, save the form, and close the form.

 **Experiment**

• Test each of the buttons in the option group. If you do not preview or export the correct report, correct the error in the corresponding macro. If you get an error indicating that the section width is greater than the page width, you have an error in the corresponding report. Correct the error using the instructions in the Errors in Macros section of this module.

Break Point: If you wish to stop working through the module at this point, you can resume the project at a later time by running Access, opening the database called PrattLast Associates, and continuing to follow the steps from this location forward.

User Interface (UI) Macros

A **user interface (UI) macro** is a macro that is attached to a user interface object, such as a command button, an option group, or a control on a form. The macro you just created for the option group is thus a UI macro, as were the macros you attached to command buttons. A common use for UI macros is to associate actions with the clicking of a control on a form. In the Account form shown in Figure 8–40, for example, if you click the account number on the row in the datasheet where the account number is CO621, Access displays the data for that account in a pop-up form (Figure 8–41), that is, a form that stays on top of other open objects, even when another object is active.

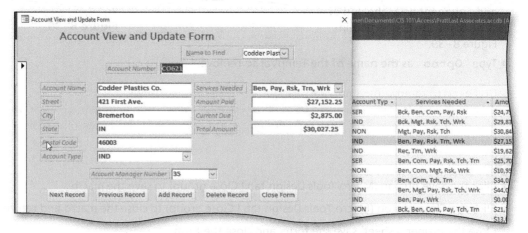

Figure 8–40

Figure 8–41

Similarly, in the Account Manager form shown in Figure 8–42, for example, if you click the account manager number on the row in the datasheet where the account manager number is 58, Access displays the data for that account manager in a pop-up form (Figure 8–43).

Figure 8–42

Figure 8–43

Recall that you can only use forms and reports for the tabs in a navigation form, yet the Account tab appears to display the Account table in Datasheet view. You can make it appear as though you are displaying the Account table in Datasheet view by creating a datasheet form that you will call Account. You will create a UI macro in this Account datasheet form. The UI macro that will be associated with the clicking of the account number on some record in the Account form will display the selected account in the Account Master Form.

To display the Account Master Form, the UI macro will use the OpenForm action. You must set the Form Name argument of the OpenForm action to the actual name of the form to be opened, Account Master Form. (Account View and Update Form is just the form caption.) PrattLast wants to prevent the user from updating data using this form, so the Data Mode argument is set to Read Only. The form should appear as a pop-up, which you accomplish by setting the value of the Window Mode argument to Dialog.

The form should display only the record that the user selected. If the user clicks account number CO621 in the Account form, for example, the form should display only the data for account CO621. To restrict the record that appears in the form, you include the Where Condition argument in the UI macro. The condition needs to indicate that the Account Number in the form to be opened, Account Master Form, needs to be equal to the Account Number the user selected in the Account form.

In the Where Condition, you can simply refer to a control in the form to be opened by using its name. If the name has spaces, you must enclose it in square brackets. Thus, the name for the Account Number in the Account Master Form is simply [Account Number]. To reference a control that is part of any other form, the expression must include both the name of the form and the name of the control, separated by an exclamation point. Thus, the Account Number in the Account form would be [Account]![Account Number]. This declaration works correctly when you are programming a macro that simply opens the Account form. However, when you associate the Account form with a tab in the navigation form, the Account form becomes a subform, which requires modification to the expression. This means that a form that works correctly when you open the form may not work correctly when the form is assigned to a tab in a navigation form. A safer approach avoids these issues by using a temporary variable.

Table 8–3 shows the UI macro for the Account form. It is associated with the On Click event for the Account Number control. When a user clicks an account number, the UI macro will display the data for the selected account in the Account Master Form. The main function of the macro is to open the appropriate form using the OpenForm action.

BTW
Distributing a Document
Instead of printing and distributing a hard copy of a document, you can distribute the document electronically. Options include sending the document via email; posting it on cloud storage (such as OneDrive) and sharing the file with others; posting it on a social networking site, blog, or other website; and sharing a link associated with an online location of the document. You also can create and share a PDF or XPS image of the document, so that users can view the file in Acrobat Reader or XPS Viewer instead of in Access.

Table 8–3 UI Macro Associated with On Click Event in the Account Form		
Condition	**Action**	**Arguments to Be Changed**
	SetTempVar	Name: AN Expression: [Account Number]
	OpenForm	Form Name: Account Master Form Where Condition: [Account Number]=[TempVars]![AN] Data Mode: Read Only Window Mode: Dialog
	RemoveTempVar	Name: AN

In the macro shown in Table 8–3, the first action, SetTempVar, assigns the temporary variable AN to the Account Number. The two arguments are Name, which is set to AN, and Expression, which is set to [Account Number]. The AN temporary variable refers to the Account Number in the Account form; recall that the completed macro will open the Account Master Form. You then can use that temporary variable in the Where Condition argument. The expression is thus [Account Number]=[TempVars]![AN]. The [Account Number] portion refers to the Account Number in the Account Master Form. The [TempVars]![AN] portion is the temporary variable that has been set equal to the Account Number in the Account form. The macro ends by removing the temporary variable.

Table 8–4 shows the macro for the Account Manager form, which is very similar to the macro for the Account form.

Table 8–4 UI Macro Associated with On Click Event in the Account Manager Form		
Condition	**Action**	**Arguments to Be Changed**
	SetTempVar	Name: MN Expression: [Account Manager Number]
	OpenForm	Form Name: Account Manager Master Form Where Condition: [Account Manager Number]=[TempVars]![MN] Data Mode: Read Only Window Mode: Dialog
	RemoveTempVar	Name: MN

To Create Datasheet Forms

1 MACRO WITH SUBMACROS | 2 FORM COMMAND BUTTONS | 3 FORM OPTION GROUP | 4 MACRO FOR OPTION GROUP
5 DATASHEET FORMS | 6 USER INTERFACE MACROS | 7 NAVIGATION FORM | 8 DATA MACRO

The following steps create two datasheet forms, one for the Account table and one for the Account Manager table. *Why? The datasheet forms enable the Account and Account Manager tables to appear as if displayed in Datasheet view, despite the Access restriction that prevents tables from being used on tabs in a navigation form.*

- Open the Navigation Pane and select the Account table.
- Display the Create tab and then click the More Forms button (Create tab | Forms group) to display the More Forms gallery (Figure 8–44).

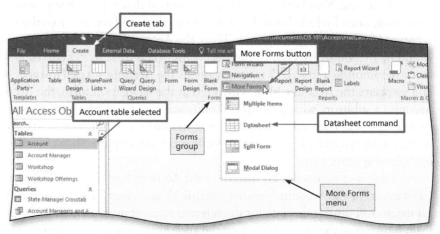

Figure 8–44

2

- Click Datasheet to create a datasheet form.
- Save the form using the name, Account.

Q&A Is it acceptable to use the same name for the form as for the table?
Yes. In this case, you want it to appear to the user that the Account table is open in Datasheet view. One way to emphasize this fact is to use the same name as the table.

What is the difference between this form, Account, and the form named Account Form?
The Account Form is a simple form that displays only one record at a time. The form you just created displays all of the account data in a datasheet.

- Use the same technique to create a datasheet form named Account Manager for the Account Manager table.
- Close both forms.

To Create UI Macros for the Datasheet Forms

1 MACRO WITH SUBMACROS | 2 FORM COMMAND BUTTONS | 3 FORM OPTION GROUP | 4 MACRO FOR OPTION GROUP
5 DATASHEET FORMS | 6 USER INTERFACE MACROS | 7 NAVIGATION FORM | 8 DATA MACRO

The following steps create the UI macro for the Account datasheet form shown in Table 8–3 and the UI macro for the Account Manager datasheet form shown in Table 8–4. ***Why?*** *The UI macros will cause the appropriate pop-up forms to appear as a result of clicking the appropriate position on the forms.*

1

- Open the Account datasheet form and then close the Navigation Pane.
- Click the Account Number (AC #) heading to select the Account Number column in the datasheet.
- If necessary, click the Property Sheet button (Form Tools Datasheet tab | Tools group) to display a property sheet.
- Click the Event tab to display only event properties.

Q&A Why click the Event tab? Why not just use the All tab as we have before?
You can always use the All tab; however, if you know the category that contains the property in which you are interested, you can greatly reduce the number of properties that Access will display by clicking the tab for that category. That gives you fewer properties to search through to find the property you want. Whether you use the All tab or one of the other tabs is strictly a matter of personal preference.

- Click the On Click event and then click the Build button (the three dots) to display the Choose Builder dialog box (Figure 8–45).

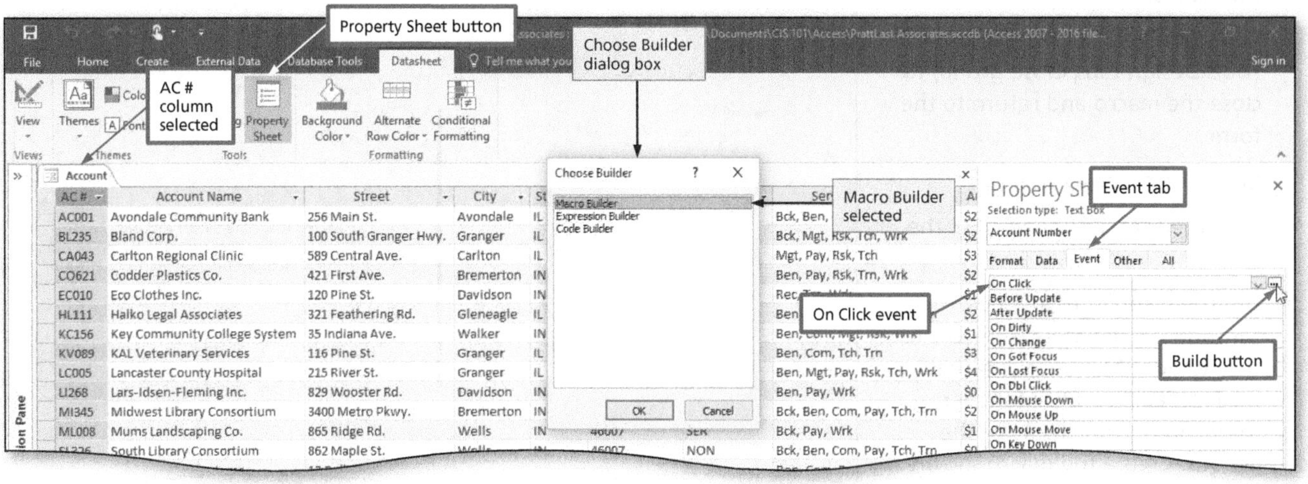

Figure 8–45

2

- Click the OK button (Choose Builder dialog box) to display the Macro Builder window.

- Add the SetTempVar action to the macro, enter **AN** as the value for the Name argument, and enter **[Account Number]** as the value for the Expression argument.

- Add the OpenForm action to the macro, select Account Master Form as the value for the Form Name argument, leave the value of the View argument set to Form, enter **[Account Number]=[TempVars]![AN]** as the value for the Where Condition argument, select Read Only as the value for the Data Mode argument, and select Dialog as the value for the Window Mode argument.

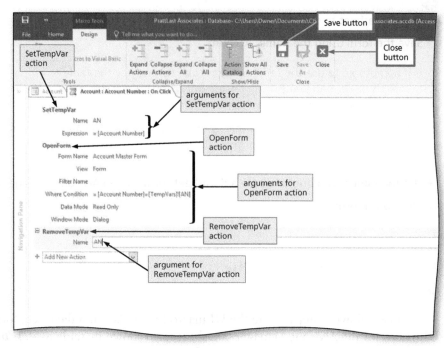

Figure 8–46

Q&A | What does this expression mean?

The portion before the equal sign, [Account Number], refers to the Account Number in the form just opened, that is, in the Account Master Form. The portion to the right of the equal sign, [TempVars]![AN], is the temporary variable that was set equal to the Account Number on the selected record in the Account form. This Where Condition guarantees that the record displayed in the Account Master Form will be the record with the same Account Number as the one selected in the Account form.

- Add the RemoveTempVar action to the macro and enter **AN** as the value for the Name argument (Figure 8–46).

Q&A | Why do you need to remove the temporary variable?

Technically, you do not. It has fulfilled its function, however, so it makes sense to remove it at this point.

3

- Click the Save button (Macro Tools Design tab | Close group) to save the macro.

- Click the Close button (Macro Tools Design tab | Close group) to close the macro and return to the form.

- Close the property sheet.

- Save the form and then close the form.

- Use the techniques in Steps 1 through 3 to create a UI macro for the Account Manager datasheet form called Account Manager, referring to Table 8–4 for the actions. Create the macro shown in Figure 8–47 associated with clicking the Account Manager Number (AM #) column.

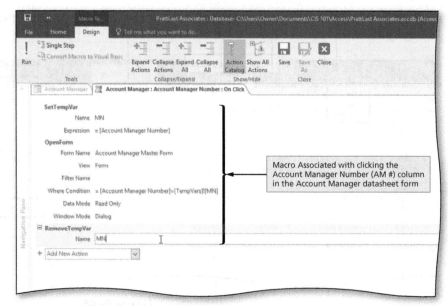

Figure 8–47

- Click the Save button (Macro Tools Design tab | Close group) to save the macro.
- Click the Close button (Macro Tools Design tab | Close group) to close the macro and return to the datasheet form.
- Close the property sheet.
- Save the form and then close the form.

To Create a Navigation Form

1 MACRO WITH SUBMACROS | 2 FORM COMMAND BUTTONS | 3 FORM OPTION GROUP | 4 MACRO FOR OPTION GROUP
5 DATASHEET FORMS | 6 USER INTERFACE MACROS | **7 NAVIGATION FORM** | **8 DATA MACRO**

You now have all the forms you need to include in the navigation form. The following steps create the navigation form using horizontal tabs. *Why? Horizontal tabs are common on navigation forms and are easy to use.* The steps then save the form and change the title.

- If necessary, open the Navigation Pane.
- Click the Create tab and then click the Navigation button (Create tab | Forms group) to display the gallery of available navigation forms (Figure 8–48).

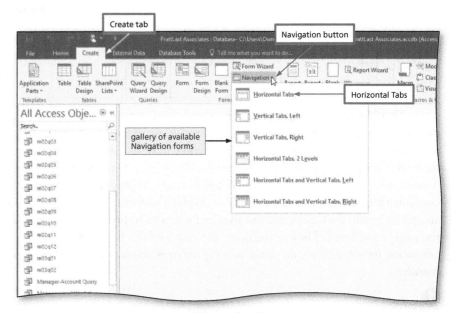

Figure 8–48

- Click Horizontal Tabs in the gallery to create a form with a navigation control in which the tabs are arranged horizontally in a single row.
- If a field list appears, click the 'Add Existing Fields' button (Form Layout Tools Design tab | Tools group) to remove the field list (Figure 8–49).

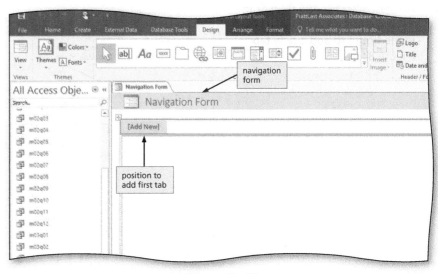

Figure 8–49

- Save the form using the name, Main Menu.

- Click the form title twice: once to select it and the second time to produce an insertion point.

- Erase the current title and then type **PrattLast Associates** as the new title (Figure 8–50).

- Save the form.

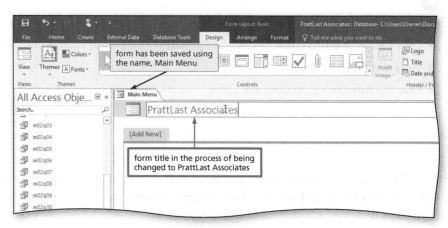

Figure 8–50

To Add Tabs to a Navigation Form

1 MACRO WITH SUBMACROS | 2 FORM COMMAND BUTTONS | 3 FORM OPTION GROUP | 4 MACRO FOR OPTION GROUP
5 DATASHEET FORMS | 6 USER INTERFACE MACROS | **7 NAVIGATION FORM** | **8 DATA MACRO**

To add a form or report to a tab in a navigation form, be sure the Navigation Pane is open and then drag the form or report to the desired tab. As a result, users can display that form or report by clicking the tab. For the PrattLast Associates navigation form, you will drag four forms to the tabs. The Account form is a datasheet form that appears to display the Account table open in Datasheet view. Similarly, the Account Manager form is a datasheet form that appears to display the Account Manager table open in Datasheet view. The Forms List form contains three buttons users can click to display the form of their choice. Finally, the Reports List form contains an option group that users can use to select a report to preview or export. The following steps add the tabs to the navigation form. They also change the name of the Forms List and Reports List tabs. *Why? The names of the tabs do not have to be the same as the name of the corresponding forms. By changing them, you can often make tabs more readable.*

- Scroll down in the Navigation Pane so that the form named Account appears, and then drag the form to the position shown in the figure to add a new tab (Figure 8–51).

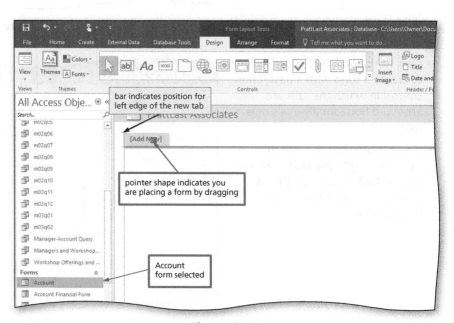

Figure 8–51

2

- Release the left mouse button to add the Account form as the first tab.
- Drag the Account Manager form to the position shown in the figure to add a new tab (Figure 8–52).

What should I do if I made a mistake and added a form or report to the wrong location? You can rearrange the tabs by dragging them. Often, the simplest way to correct a mistake is to click the Undo button to reverse your most recent action, however. You can also choose to simply close the form without saving it and then start over.

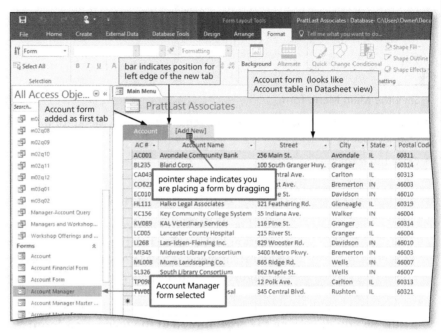

Figure 8–52

3

- Release the left mouse button to add the Account Manager form as the second tab.
- Using the techniques illustrated in Steps 1 and 2, add the Forms List form as the third tab and the Reports List form as the fourth tab (Figure 8–53).

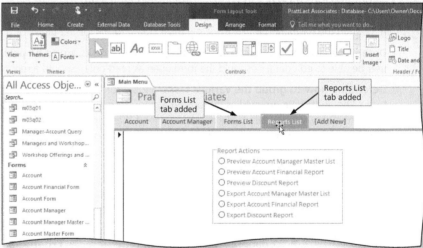

Figure 8–53

4

- Click the Forms List tab twice: once to select it and the second time to produce an insertion point.
- Change the name from Forms List to Forms.
- In a similar fashion, change the name of the Reports List tab from Reports List to Reports (Figure 8–54).

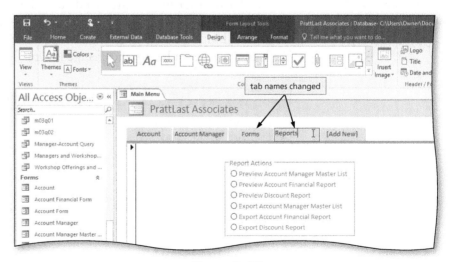

Figure 8–54

Q&A I created these two forms using the names Forms List and Reports List. Now I have changed the names to Forms and Reports. Why not call them Forms and Reports in the first place, so I would not have to rename the tabs?
Because the words, forms and reports, have specific meaning in Access, you cannot use these names when creating the forms. Thus, you needed to use some other names, like Forms List and Reports List. Because tabs within forms are not database objects, you can rename them to be any name you want.

5

- Save the Main Menu form.
- If requested to do so by your instructor, rename the Main Menu form as LastName Main Menu where LastName is your last name.
- Close the form.

Using a Navigation Form

The Main Menu navigation form is complete and ready for use. To use the navigation form, right-click the form in the Navigation Pane, and then click Open on the shortcut menu. The Main Menu form then will appear with the first tabbed object (see Figure 8–1). To display the other forms, simply click the appropriate tab.

CONSIDER THIS

How do you determine the organization of the navigation form?
Once you decide you want a navigation form, you need to decide how to organize the form.

- **Determine which tasks should be accomplished by having the user click tabs or buttons in the navigation form.** Which forms should be opened? Which reports should be opened? Are there any tables or queries that you need to be able to open in the navigation form? If so, you must create forms for the tables or queries.
- **Determine any special requirements for the way the tasks are to be performed.** When a form is opened, should a user be able to edit data, or should the form open as read-only? Should a report be exported or simply viewed on the screen?
- **Determine how to group the various tasks.** Should forms or reports simply be assigned to the tabs in the navigation form? Should they be grouped as buttons on a menu form? Should they be placed as options within an option group? (For consistency, you would usually decide on one of these approaches and use it throughout. In this module, one menu form uses command buttons, and the other uses an option group simply to illustrate both approaches.) As far as the navigation form is concerned, is a single set of horizontal tabs sufficient, or would you also like vertical tabs? Would you like two rows of horizontal tabs?

BTW
Data Macros
Data macros are similar to SQL triggers. You attach logic to record or table events and any forms and code that update those events inherit the logic. Data macros are stored with the table.

Data Macros

A data macro is a special type of macro that is associated with specific table-related events, such as updating a record in a table. The possible events are Before Change, Before Delete, After Insert, After Update, and After Delete. Data macros allow you to add logic to these events. For example, the data macro shown in Table 8–5 is associated with the Before Change event, an event that occurs after the user has changed the data but before the change is actually made in the database.

Table 8–5 Data Macro for Before Change Event		
Condition	**Action**	**Arguments to Be Changed**
If [Hours Spent]>[Total Hours]		
	SetField	Name: [Hours Spent] Value: [Total Hours]
Else If [Hours Spent]<0		
	SetField	Name: [Hours Spent] Value: 0
End If		

This macro will examine the value in the Hours Spent field in the Workshop Offerings table. If the user's update would cause the value in the Hours Spent field to be greater than the value in the Total Hours field, the macro will change the value in the Hours Spent field so that it is equal to the value in the Total Hours field. Likewise, if the update would cause the value in the Hours Spent field to be less than zero, the macro will set the value in the Hours Spent field to 0. These changes take place after the user has made the change on the screen but before Access commits the change to the database, that is, before the data in the database is actually changed.

There are other events to which you can assign data macros. The actions in a data macro associated with the Before Delete event will take place after a user has indicated that he or she wants to delete a record, but before the record is actually removed from the database. The actions in a macro associated with the After Insert event will take place immediately after a record physically is added to the database. The actions in a macro associated with the After Update event will take place immediately after a record is physically changed in the database. The actions in a macro associated with the After Delete event will take place immediately after a record is physically removed from the database.

To Create a Data Macro

1 MACRO WITH SUBMACROS | 2 FORM COMMAND BUTTONS | 3 FORM OPTION GROUP | 4 MACRO FOR OPTION GROUP
5 DATASHEET FORMS | 6 USER INTERFACE MACROS | 7 NAVIGATION FORM | **8 DATA MACRO**

The following steps create the data macro in Table 8–5, a macro that will be run after a user makes a change to a record in the Workshop Offerings table, but before the record is updated in the database. *Why? PrattLast Associates management wants a way to prevent users from entering invalid data into the database.*

1

- Open the Workshop Offerings table in Datasheet view and close the Navigation Pane.
- Display the Table Tools Table tab (Figure 8–55).

Q&A What is the meaning of the events in the Before Events and After Events groups?
Actions in macros associated with the Before Events group will occur after the user has taken action to change or delete a record, but before the change or deletion is made permanent in the database. Actions in macros associated with the After Events group will occur after the corresponding update has been made permanent in the database.

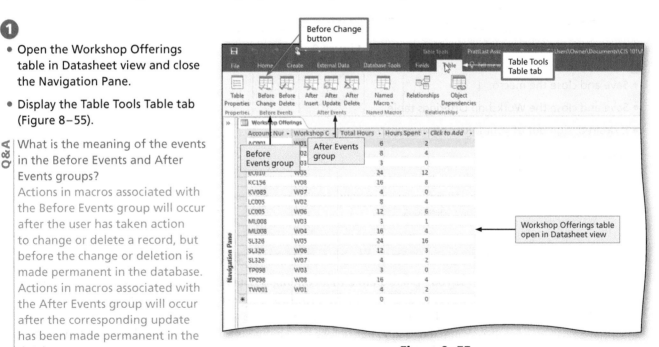

Figure 8–55

- Click the Before Change button (Table Tools Table tab | Before Events group).
- Create the macro shown in Figure 8–56.

Q&A What happened to all the actions that were in the list? In the previous macros we created, there seemed to be many more actions available.

There are only certain actions that make sense in data macros. Only those actions appear. Therefore, the list of actions that appears is much smaller in a data macro than in other macros.

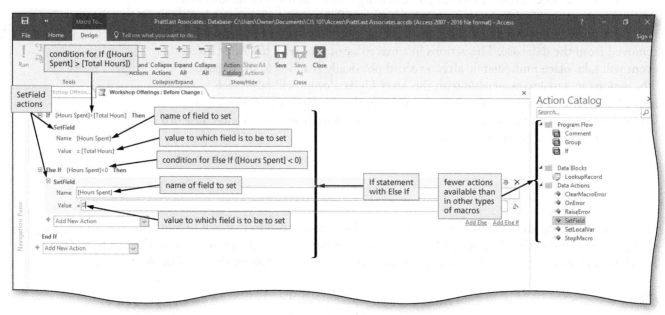

Figure 8–56

- Save and close the macro.
- Save and close the Workshop Offerings table.
- If desired, sign out of your Microsoft account.
- Exit Access.

Note: Unless your instructor indicates otherwise, you are encouraged to simply read the material in this module from this point on for understanding without carrying out any operations.

Using a Table That Contains a Data Macro

If you update a table that contains a data macro, the actions in the data macro will be executed whenever the corresponding event takes place. If the data macro corresponds to the Before Change event, the actions will be executed after the user has changed the data, but before the change is saved in the database. With the data macro you just created, for example, if a user attempts to change the data in such a way that the Hours Spent is greater than the Total Hours (Figure 8–57a), as soon as the user takes an action that would require saving the record, Access makes Hours Spent equal to Total Hours (Figure 8–57b). Likewise, if a user attempts to set Hours Spent to a negative number (Figure 8–58a), as soon as the user takes an action that would require saving the record, Access will set Hours Spent to 0 (Figure 8–58b). This change will take place automatically, regardless of whether the user changes the values in Datasheet view, with a form, in an update query, or in any other fashion.

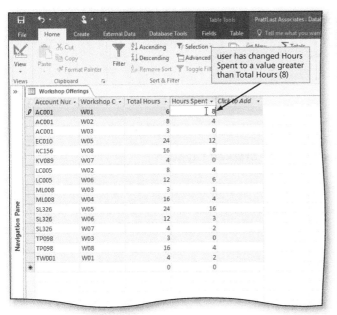

Figure 8–57(a)

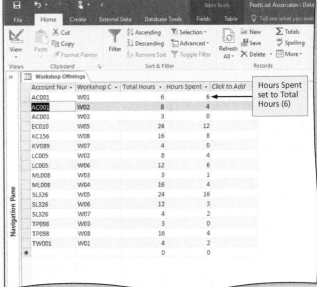

Figure 8–57(b)

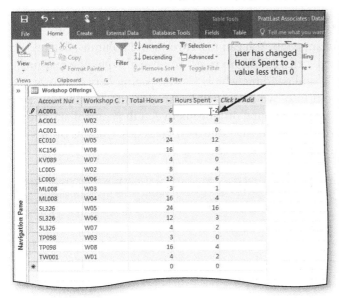

Figure 8–58(a)

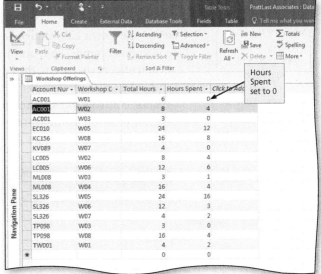

Figure 8–58(b)

Using Control Layouts on Forms and Reports

In earlier modules, you worked with control layouts in forms and reports. In a control layout, the data is aligned either horizontally or vertically. The two types of layouts are stacked layouts, which are most commonly used in forms, and tabular layouts, which are most commonly used in reports (Figure 8–59). Using a control layout gives you more options for moving rows or columns than you would have without the layout.

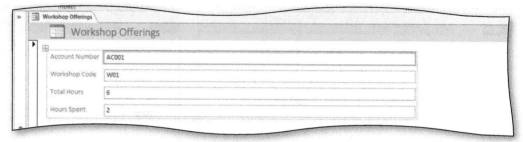

Figure 8–59(a) Stacked Layout

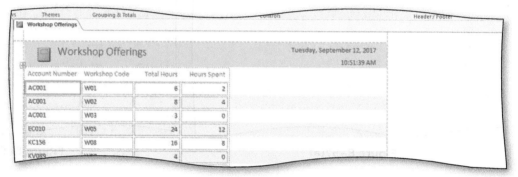

Figure 8–59(b) Tabular Layout

BTW
Quick Styles for Controls
To make a navigation form more visually appealing, you can change the style of a command button and/or tabs. Quick styles change how the different colors, fonts, and effects are combined. To change the style of a command button or tab, open the navigation form in Layout view. Select the control(s) for which you want to change the style, and click Quick Styles. When the Quick Styles gallery appears, select the desired style. You also can change the style of a control in Design view.

In working with control layouts, there are many functions you can perform using the Form Layout Tools Arrange tab. You can insert rows and columns, delete rows and columns, split and merge cells, and move rows. You can also change margins, which affects spacing within cells, and padding, which affects spacing between rows and columns. You can split a layout into two layouts and move layouts. Finally, you can anchor controls so that they maintain the same distance between the control and the anchor position as the form or report is resized. Table 8–6 gives descriptions of the functions available on the Form Layout Tools Arrange tab.

Table 8–6 Arrange Tab	
Button	**Enhanced ScreenTip**
Gridlines	Gridlines
Stacked	Create a layout similar to a paper form, with labels to the left of each field.
Tabular	Create a layout similar to a spreadsheet, with labels across the top and data in columns below the labels.
Insert Above	Insert Above
Insert Below	Insert Below
Insert Left	Insert Left
Insert Right	Insert Right
Select Layout	Select Layout
Select Column	Select Column
Select Row	Select Row
Merge	Merge Cells
Split Vertically	Split the selected layout into two rows.
Split Horizontally	Split the selected layout into two columns.
Move Up	Move Up
Move Down	Move Down
Control Margins	Control Margins
Control Padding	Control Padding
Anchoring	Tie a control to a section or another control so that it moves or resizes in conjunction with movement or resizing of the parent.

TO CREATE A LAYOUT FOR A FORM OR REPORT

If you create a form using the Form button (Create tab | Forms group), Access automatically creates a stacked layout. If you create a report using the Report button (Create tab | Reports group), Access automatically creates a tabular layout. In other cases, you can create a layout using the Form Layout Tools Arrange tab for forms or the Report Layout Tools Arrange tab for reports. If you no longer want controls to be in a control layout, you can remove the layout.

To create a layout in either a form or report, you would use the following steps.

1. Select all the controls that you want to place in a layout.
2. Click the Stacked button (Form Layout Tools Arrange tab | Table group) to create a stacked layout or the Tabular button (Form Layout Tools Arrange tab | Table group) to create a tabular layout.

TO REMOVE A LAYOUT FOR A FORM OR REPORT

To remove a layout from either a form or report, you would use the following steps.

1. Right-click any control in the layout you want to remove to produce a shortcut menu.
2. Point to Layout on the shortcut menu and then click Remove Layout on the submenu to remove the layout.

Using Undo

When making changes with the Form Layout Tools Arrange tab buttons, it is not uncommon to make a change that you did not intend. Sometimes taking appropriate action to reverse the change can prove difficult. If so, remember that you can undo the change by clicking the Undo button on the Quick Access Toolbar. It is also a good idea to save your work frequently. That way, you can always close the form or report without saving. When you reopen the form or report, it will not have any of your most recent changes.

TO INSERT A ROW

You can insert a blank row either above or below a selected row (Figure 8–60). You can then fill in the row by either typing a value or dragging a field from a field

BTW

Change the Shape of a Control
Command buttons and tabs have a default shape. For example, both command buttons and tabs have a rounded rectangle shape as the default shape. You can change the shape of a button or tab control on a navigation form. To do so, open the navigation form in Layout view. Select the control(s) for which you want to change the shape and click Change Shape. When the Change Shape gallery appears, select the desired shape. You also can change the shape of a command button or tab in Design view.

Figure 8–60(a) Selecting a Row

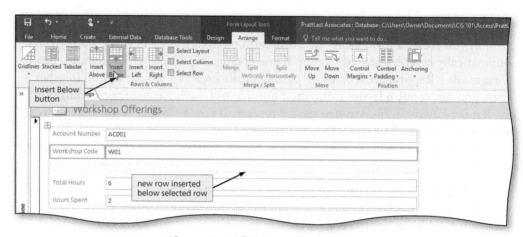

Figure 8–60(b) Inserting a Row

BTW

PivotTables and PivotCharts
PivotTable view and PivotChart view are no longer available in Access. To create a PivotChart or PivotTable, create a new workbook in the Microsoft Excel app, click the From Access button (Data tab | Get External Data group) and follow the directions in the Select Data Source dialog box to import an Access table. You then can use the PivotTable and PivotChart features of Excel.

list. In a similar fashion, you can insert a blank column either to the left or right of a selected column.

You would use the following steps to insert a blank row.

1. Select any control in the row above or below where you want to insert a new row.

2. Click the Select Row button (Form Layout Tools Arrange tab | Rows & Columns group) to select the row.

3. Click the Insert Above button (Form Layout Tools Arrange tab | Rows & Columns group) to insert a blank row above the selected row or the Insert Below button (Form Layout Tools Arrange tab | Rows & Columns group) to insert a blank row below the selected row.

As you have seen earlier in the text, you also can insert a row containing a field by simply dragging the field from the field list to the desired location.

TO INSERT A COLUMN

You would use the following steps to insert a new column.

1. Select any control in the column to the right or left of where you want to insert a new column.

2. Click the Select Column button (Form Layout Tools Arrange tab | Rows & Columns group) to select the column.

3. Click the Insert Left button (Form Layout Tools Arrange tab | Rows & Columns group) to insert a blank column to the left of the selected column or the Insert Right button (Form Layout Tools Arrange tab | Rows & Columns group) to insert a blank column to the right of the selected column.

TO DELETE A ROW

You can delete any unwanted row or column from a control layout. You would use the following steps to delete a row.

1. Click any control in the row you want to delete.

2. Click Select Row (Form Layout Tools Arrange tab | Rows & Columns group).

3. Press the DELETE key to delete the row.

TO DELETE A COLUMN

You would use the following steps to delete a column.

1. Click any control in the column you want to delete.
2. Click Select Column (Form Layout Tools Arrange tab | Rows & Columns group).
3. Press the DELETE key to delete the column.

Splitting and Merging Cells

You can split a cell into two cells either horizontally, as shown in Figure 8–61, or vertically. You can then enter contents into the new cell. For example, in Figure 8–61, you could type text into the new cell that gives information about account numbers. You can also merge two cells into one.

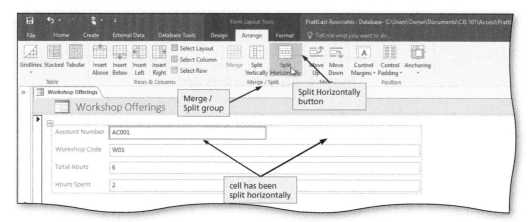

Figure 8–61

TO SPLIT A CELL

To split a cell, you would use the following steps.

1. Click the cell to be split.
2. Click the Split Vertically button (Form Layout Tools Arrange tab | Merge / Split group) to split the selected cell vertically or the Split Horizontally button (Form Layout Tools Arrange tab | Merge / Split group) to split the selected cell horizontally.

TO MERGE CELLS

You would use the following steps to merge cells.

1. Select the first cell to be merged.
2. While holding down the CTRL key, click all the other cells to be merged.
3. Click the Merge button (Form Layout Tools Arrange tab | Merge / Split group) to merge the cells.

Moving Cells

You can move a cell in a layout by dragging it to its new position. Most often, however, you will not want to move individual cells, but rather whole rows (Figure 8–62). You can move a row by selecting the row and then dragging it to the new position or you can use the Move buttons on the Form Layout Tools Arrange tab.

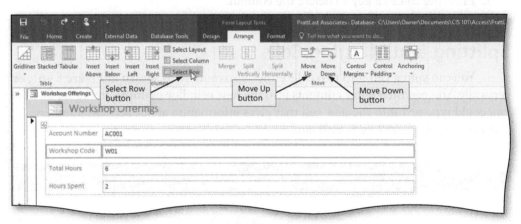

Figure 8–62(a) Row Selected

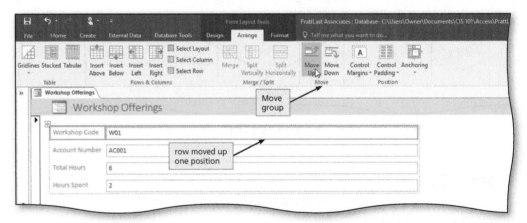

Figure 8–62(b) Row Moved

BTW
Control Padding
The term, padding, refers to the amount of space between a control's border and its contents. Effectively, you can increase or decrease the amount of white space in a control.

TO MOVE ROWS USING THE MOVE BUTTONS

You would use the following steps to move a row.

1. Select any cell in the row to be moved.
2. Click the Select Row button (Form Layout Tools Arrange tab | Rows & Columns group) to select the entire row.
3. Click the Move Up button (Form Layout Tools Arrange tab | Move group) to move the selected row up one row or the Move Down button (Form Layout Tools Arrange tab | Move group) to move the selected row down one row.

Margins and Padding

You can change the spacing within a layout by changing the control margins and the control padding. The control margins, which you change with the Control Margins button, affect the spacing around the text inside a control. Figure 8–63 shows the various options as well as samples of two of the options.

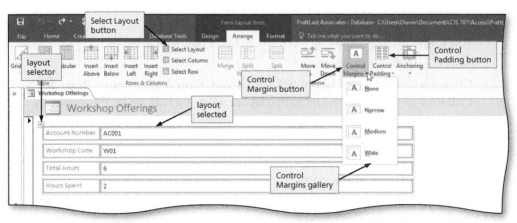

Figure 8–63(a) Changing Control Margins

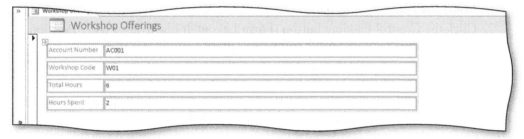

Figure 8–63(b) Control Margins Set to None

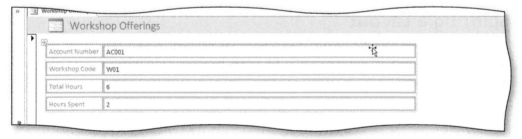

Figure 8–63(c) Control Margins Set to Medium

The control padding, which you change with the Control Padding button, affects the spacing around the outside of a control. The options are the same as those for control margins. Figure 8–64 shows samples of two of the options.

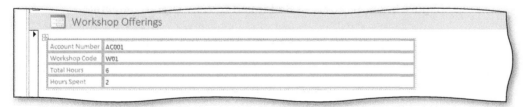

Figure 8–64(a) Control Padding Set to None

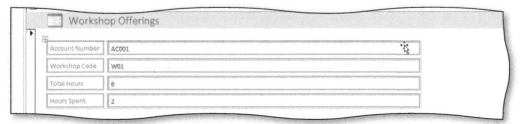

Figure 8–64(b) Control Padding Set to Medium

TO CHANGE CONTROL MARGINS

You would use the following steps to change a control's margins.

1. Select any cell in the layout.
2. Click the Select Layout button (Form Layout Tools Arrange tab | Rows & Columns group) to select the entire layout. (You also can select the layout by clicking the layout selector.)
3. Click the Control Margins button (Form Layout Tools Arrange tab | Position group) to display the available margin settings.
4. Click the desired margin setting.

TO CHANGE CONTROL PADDING

You would use the following steps to change control padding.

1. Select the layout.
2. Click the Control Padding button (Form Layout Tools Arrange tab | Position group) to display the available padding settings.
3. Click the desired padding setting.

Although you can make the margin and padding changes for individual controls, it is much more common to do so for the entire layout. Doing so gives a uniform appearance to the layout.

Splitting a Layout

You can split a single control layout into two separate layouts (Figure 8–65) and then modify each layout separately. They can be moved to different locations and formatted differently.

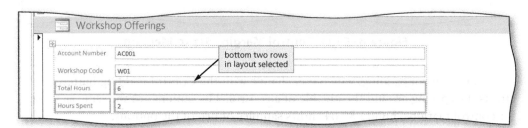

Figure 8–65(a) Rows to Be Moved to New Layout Selected

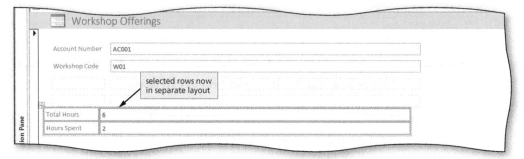

Figure 8–65(b) Rows Moved to New Layout

TO SPLIT A LAYOUT

To split a layout, you would use the following steps.

1. Select all the cells that you want to move to a new layout.
2. Click the Stacked button (Form Layout Tools Arrange tab | Table group) to place the cells in a stacked layout or the Tabular button (Form Layout Tools Arrange tab | Table group) to place the cells in a tabular layout.

Moving a Layout

You can move a control layout to a different location on the form (Figure 8–66).

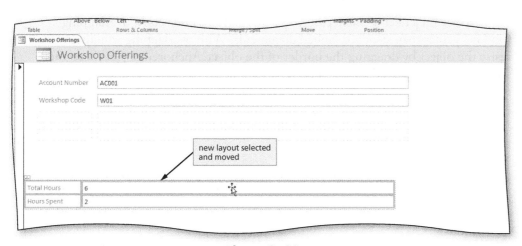

Figure 8–66

TO MOVE A LAYOUT

You would use the following steps to move a layout.

1. Click any cell in the layout to be moved and then click the Select Layout button (Form Layout Tools Arrange tab | Rows & Columns group) to select the layout.
2. Drag the layout to the new location.

Anchoring Controls

The Anchoring button allows you to tie (anchor) controls to a section or to other controls so that they maintain the same distance between the control and the anchor position as the form is resized. To anchor the controls you have selected, you use the Anchoring gallery (Figure 8–67).

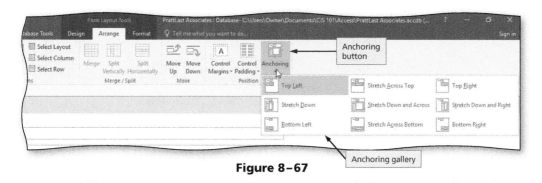

Figure 8–67

The Top Left, Top Right, Bottom Left, and Bottom Right options anchor the control in the indicated position on the form. The other five operations also stretch the controls in the indicated direction.

TO ANCHOR CONTROLS

You would use the following steps to anchor controls.

1. Select the control or controls to be anchored.
2. Click the Anchoring button (Form Layout Tools Arrange tab | Position group) to produce the Anchoring gallery.
3. Select the desired Anchoring option from the Anchoring gallery.

To see the effect of anchoring you need to display objects in overlapping windows rather than standard tabbed documents. With overlapping windows, you can resize the object by dragging the border of the object. Anchored objects keep their same relative position (Figure 8–68).

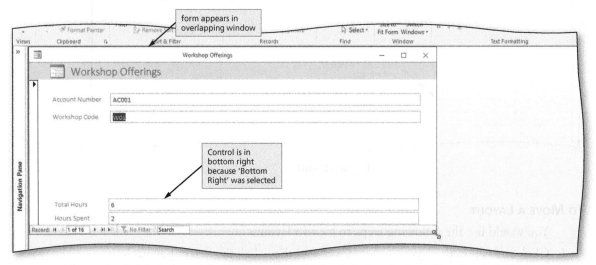

Figure 8–68(a) Form with Anchored Controls Appears in Overlapping Window

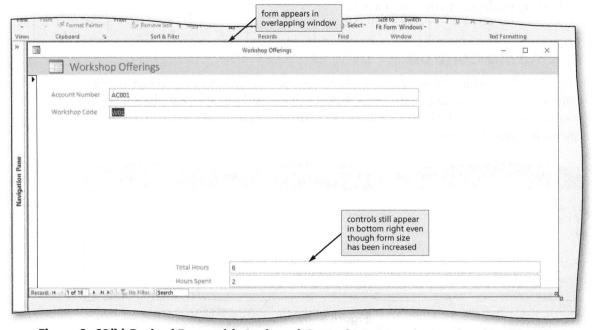

Figure 8–68(b) Resized Form with Anchored Controls Appears in Overlapping Window

If you want to display objects in overlapping windows, you have to modify the appropriate Access option.

To Display Objects in Overlapping Windows

You would use the following steps to overlap windows.

1. Click File on the ribbon to open the Backstage view.
2. Click Options to display the Access Options dialog box.
3. Click Current Database to display the Current Database options.
4. In the Application Options area, click the Overlapping Windows option button.
5. Click the OK button to close the Access Options dialog box.
6. For the changes to take effect, you will need to close and then reopen the database.

You use a similar process to return to displaying objects in tabbed documents.

To Display Objects in Tabbed Documents

You would use the following steps to display tabbed documents.

1. Click File on the ribbon to open the Backstage view.
2. Click Options to display the Access Options dialog box.
3. Click Current Database to display the Current Database options.
4. In the Application Options area, click the Tabbed Documents option button.
5. Click the OK button to close the Access Options dialog box.
6. For the changes to take effect, you will need to close and then reopen the database.

BTW
Overlapping Windows
When you display objects in overlapping windows, each database object appears in its own window. When multiple objects are open, these windows overlap each other. By default, Access 2016 displays database objects in a single pane separated by tabs.

Summary

In this module you have learned to create and use macros; create a menu form that uses command buttons for the choices; create a menu form that uses an option group for the choices; create a macro that implements the choices in the option group; create datasheet forms that utilize user interface macros; create a navigation form; add tabs to a navigation form; and create data macros. You also learned to modify control layouts.

What decisions will you need to make when creating your own macros and navigation forms?
Use these guidelines as you complete the assignments in this module and create your own macros and navigation forms outside of this class.

1. Determine when it would be beneficial to automate tasks in a macro.
    a. Are there tasks involving multiple steps that would be more conveniently accomplished by running a macro than by carrying out all the individual steps? For example, opening a form in read-only mode could be accomplished conveniently through a macro.
    b. Are there tasks that are to be performed when the user clicks buttons on a menu form?
    c. Are there tasks to be performed when a user clicks a control on a form?
    d. Are there tasks to be performed when a user updates a table? These tasks can be placed in a macro that can be run when the button is clicked.
2. Determine whether it is appropriate to create a navigation form.
    a. If you want to make it easy and convenient for users to perform a variety of tasks just by clicking tabs and buttons, consider creating a navigation form.
    b. You can associate the performance of the various tasks with the tabs and buttons in the navigation form.
3. Determine the organization of the navigation form.
    a. Determine the various tasks that need to be performed by clicking tabs and buttons.
    b. Decide the logical grouping of the tabs and buttons.

CONSIDER THIS

How should you submit solutions to questions in the assignments identified with a symbol?
Every assignment in this book contains one or more questions identified with a symbol. These questions require you to think beyond the assigned database. Present your solutions to the questions in the format required by your instructor. Possible formats may include one or more of these options: write the answer; create a document that contains the answer; present your answer to the class; discuss your answer in a group; record the answer as audio or video using a webcam, smartphone, or portable media player; or post answers on a blog, wiki, or website.

Apply Your Knowledge

Reinforce the skills and apply the concepts you learned in this module.

Creating UI Macros and a Navigation Form

Note: To complete this assignment, you will be required to use the Data Files. Please contact your instructor for information about accessing the Data Files.

Instructions: Run Access. Open the Apply AllAround Services database and enable the content. AllAround Services is a company that provides all types of cleaning and maintenance services for businesses and organizations.

Perform the following tasks:

1. Create a datasheet form for the Client table and name the form Client. Create a UI macro for the Client form. Use CN as the temporary variable name. When a user clicks a client number on a row in the datasheet form, the Client Financial Form should appear in a pop-up form in read-only mode.

2. Create a datasheet form for the Supervisor table and name the form Supervisor. Create a UI macro for the Supervisor form. Use SN as the temporary variable name. When a user clicks a supervisor number on a row in the datasheet form, the Supervisor Master Form should appear in a pop-up form in read-only mode.

3. Create the navigation form shown in Figure 8–69. The purpose of the form is to display the two datasheet forms in the database as horizontal tabs. Name the form Datasheet Forms Menu and change the title to AllAround Services Navigation Form.

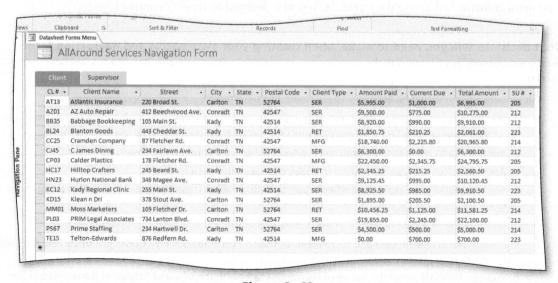

Figure 8–69

4. If requested to do so by your instructor, open the Supervisor datasheet form and change the first and last names of supervisor 212 to your first and last name.

5. Submit the revised database in the format specified by your instructor.

6. ✸ How could you add the Supervisor Services Data form to the navigation form?

Extend Your Knowledge

Extend the skills you learned in this module and experiment with new skills. You may need to use Help to complete the assignment.

Modifying Navigation Forms

Note: To complete this assignment, you will be required to use the Data Files. Please contact your instructor for information about accessing the Data Files.

Instructions: Run Access. Open the Extend Craft Cooperative database and enable the content. Craft Cooperative is run by the local school district to showcase the various crafts made by students.

Perform the following tasks:
1. Open the Main Menu form in Design view and change the theme for this object only to Facet. Expand the size of the form header and add the current date to the form header. Add a command button to the form header that closes the form. Save the changes and switch to Form view. Resize the Price field in the Item datasheet form to best fit, save the changes, and close the form.

2. Open the Reports List form in Design view. Select the Report Options label, and change the font weight to semi-bold and the special effect to Raised. Enlarge the label so that the complete label displays. Select all the option buttons and use the Size/Space menu to adjust the labels to be the same width as the widest label. Select the option group and change the special effect to Shadowed. Change the theme colors to Green for this object only. Use the Background Color button to change the background color of the form to White, Background 1, Darker 5%. Save the changes to the form.

3. Open the Forms List form in Design view and make the same changes that you made to the Reports List form. Save the changes to the form.

4. Convert the Forms and Reports macro to Visual Basic code.

5. Open the Main Menu navigation form in Layout view. Change the shape of the Forms tab to Rounded Rectangle and the shape of the Reports tab to Snip Single Corner Rectangle.

6. If requested to do so by your instructor, add a label to the form header for the Main Menu form with your first and last name.

7. Submit the revised database in the format specified by your instructor.

8. ✸ Why would you convert a macro to Visual Basic code?

Expand Your World

Create a solution which uses cloud and web technologies, by learning and investigating on your own from general guidance.

Problem: The local electric company is actively engaged in educating the community on ways to conserve energy. They regularly provide energy-saving tips and sell devices designed to conserve energy resources. The company has created macros and a navigation form but would like to link a workbook containing fuel usage statistics and add two hyperlinks to a form.

Continued >

Expand Your World *continued*

Note: To complete this assignment, you will be required to use the Data Files. Please contact your instructor for information about accessing the Data Files.

Perform the following tasks:

1. Open your browser and navigate to the U. S. Energy Information Administration website, www.eia.gov/consumption/residential/data/2009/. Select the Housing characteristics tab, and then select Fuels used & end uses. Download the workbook of your choice from the list provided, for example, by type of housing or by region.

2. Open the Expand Electric Company database from the Data Files and link the workbook you downloaded to the database.

3. Access any website containing royalty-free images and search for an energy-related image suitable for a navigation form.

4. Open the Main Menu navigation form in Design view and add the image to the form header. Add a hyperlink to the home page for the U.S. Energy Information Administration website to the form header. Add another link to your local electric utility company.

5. Save your changes.

6. Submit the revised database in the format specified by your instructor.

7. ✸ Which workbook did you download and link? What image did you choose for the navigation form? Why did you make those choices?

In the Labs

Design, create, modify, and/or use a database following the guidelines, concepts, and skills presented in this module. Labs are listed in order of increasing difficulty. Labs 1 and 2, which increase in difficulty, require you to create solutions based on what you learned in the module; Lab 3 requires you to apply your creative thinking and problem solving skills to design and implement a solution.

Lab 1: Creating Macros and a Navigation Form for the Gardening Supply Database

Note: To complete this assignment, you will be required to use the Data Files. Please contact your instructor for information about accessing the Data Files.

Problem: Gardening Supply is a wholesale distributor that supplies businesses such as florists, green houses, and nurseries with plants, pottery, mulch, and other gardening essentials. The company would like an easy way to access the various tables, forms, and reports included in the database. This would make the database easier to maintain and update.

Instructions: Perform the following tasks:

1. Open the Lab 1 Gardening Supply database, enable the content, and create a macro named Forms and Reports that will include submacros to perform the following tasks:

   a. Open the Sales Rep Order Data form in read-only mode.
   b. Open the Sales Rep Master Form. Do not specify a Data Mode.
   c. Open the Customer Master Form. Do not specify a Data Mode.

d. Preview the Sales Rep Master List.
e. Preview the Customer Financial Report.
f. Preview the Customer Discount Report.
g. Export the Sales Rep Master List in PDF format.
h. Export the Customer Financial Report in PDF format.
i. Export the Customer Discount Report in PDF format.

2. Create the menu form shown in Figure 8–70. The command buttons should use the macros you created in Step 1 to open the three forms.

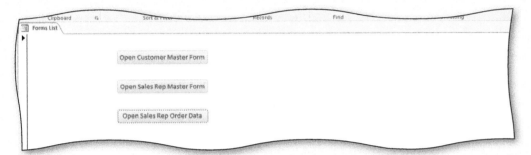

Figure 8–70

3. Create the menu form shown in Figure 8–71. The option group should use the macros you created in Step 1 to preview and export the three reports.

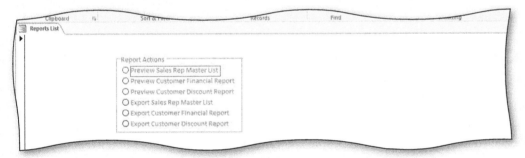

Figure 8–71

4. Create a datasheet form for the Customer table and name the form Customer. Create a UI macro for the Customer form. When a user clicks a customer number on a row in the datasheet, the Customer Master Form should appear in a pop-up, read-only form.

5. Create a datasheet form for the Sales Rep table and name the form Sales Rep. Create a UI macro for the Sales Rep form. When a user clicks a sales rep number on a row in the datasheet, the Sales Rep Master Form should appear in a pop-up, read-only form.

6. Create the navigation form shown in Figure 8–72 for the Gardening Supply database. Use the same design for your navigation form as the one illustrated in this module. For example, the Customer tab should display the Customer form you created in Step 4, and the Sales Rep tab should display the Sales Rep form you created in Step 5. The Forms tab should display the Forms List form you created in Step 2, and the Reports tab should display the Reports List form you created in Step 3.

Continued >

In the Labs *continued*

CU #	Customer Name	Street	City	State	Postal Code	Products Needed	Amount Paid	Balance Due	Total Amount	SR #
AA30	All About Landscapes	84 Berton St.	Greer	PA	19158	FERTL, MULCH, SEEDS	$1,510.00	$625.00	$2,135.00	24
CD02	Christmas Decors	483 Cantor Rd.	Pleasantburg	NJ	07025	FERTL, SEEDS, SOIL	$2,375.75	$740.25	$3,116.00	27
GG01	Garden Gnome	10 Main St.	Gossett	PA	19157	FERTL, MULCH, PLNTS, POTS	$1,300.00	$297.50	$1,597.50	27
GT34	Green Thumb Florists	26 Jefferson Hwy.	Pleasantburg	NJ	07025	FERTL, MULCH, SEEDS	$3,325.45	$865.50	$4,190.95	30
LH15	Lawn & Home Stores	33 Maple St.	Chambers	NJ	07037	FERTL, MULCH, PLNTS, POTS	$1,395.00	$0.00	$1,395.00	24
ML25	Mum's Landscaping	196 Lincoln Ave.	Quaker	DE	19719	FERTL, SEEDS, SOIL	$0.00	$1,995.00	$1,995.00	27
OA45	Outside Architects	234 Magnolia Rd.	Gaston	DE	19723	PLNTS, POTS	$4,205.50	$945.00	$5,150.50	30
PL10	Pat's Landscaping	22 Main St.	Chesnee	NJ	07053	FERTL, MULCH, PLNTS	$1,425.00	$380.75	$1,805.75	24
PN18	Pyke Nurseries	10 Grant Blvd.	Adelphia	PA	19159	FERTL, MULCH, SEEDS, SOIL	$2,465.00	$530.00	$2,995.00	30
SL25	Summit Stores	345 Oaktree Rd.	Chesnee	NJ	07053	MULCH, PLNTS, POTS, SEEDS	$3,125.45	$375.50	$3,500.95	24
TW34	TAL Floral Design	234 Cantor Rd.	Pleasantburg	NJ	07025	FERTL, MULCH, SEEDS, SOIL	$4,125.00	$350.00	$4,475.00	24
TY03	TLC Yard Care	24 Berton St.	Greer	PA	19158	PLNTS, POTS, Watr	$1,845.00	$689.45	$2,534.45	27
YS04	Yard Shoppe	124 Elm St.	Quaker	DE	19719	PLNTS, POTS, SEEDS	$445.00	$575.00	$1,020.00	30
YW01	Young's Garden Center	5239 Lancaster Hwy.	Adelphia	PA	19156	FERTL, MULCH, SEEDS, SOIL	$1,785.50	$145.60	$1,931.10	30
*				PA						

Figure 8–72

7. If requested to do so by your instructor, add your name to the title for the Main Menu navigation form.

8. Submit the revised database in the format specified by your instructor.

9. ✸ In this exercise, you have created both command buttons and option groups to run macros. Which do you prefer? Why?

Lab 2: Creating Macros and a Navigation Form for the Discover Science Database

Problem: Discover Science is an outreach of the local university. Science faculty at the university promote science education through programs at schools, libraries, and special events. As a way to promote science education among young people and raise funds for activities, the university has an online store of science-related items. The store manager would like an easy way to access the various tables, forms, and reports included in the database. This would make the database easier to maintain and update.

Note: To complete this assignment, you will be required to use the Data Files. Please contact your instructor for information about accessing the Data Files.

Instructions: Perform the following tasks:
1. Open the Lab 2 Discover Science database, enable the content, and create a macro named Forms and Reports that will include submacros to perform the following tasks:
   a. Open the Vendor Orders Data form in read-only mode.
   b. Open the Vendor Master Form. Do not specify a Data Mode.
   c. Open the Item Master Form. Do not specify a Data Mode.
   d. Preview the Vendor Master List.
   e. Preview the Item Status Report.
   f. Preview the Item Discount Report.
   g. Export the Vendor Master List in XPS format.

h. Export the Item Status Report in XPS format.

i. Export the Item Discount Report in XPS format.

2. Create the menu form shown in Figure 8–73. The command buttons should use the macros you created in Step 1 to open the three forms. Be sure to include the title on the form.

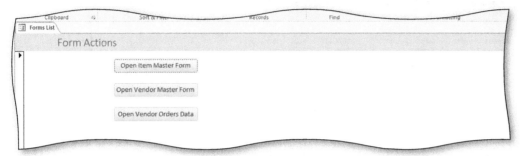

Figure 8–73

3. Create the menu form shown in Figure 8–74. The command buttons should use the macros you created in Step 1 to preview and export the three reports. Be sure to include the title on the form.

Figure 8–74

4. Create a datasheet form for the Item table and name the form Item. Create a UI macro for the Item form. When a user clicks an item number on a row in the datasheet, the Item Master Form should appear in a pop-up form.

5. Create a datasheet form for the Vendor table and name the form Vendor. Create a UI macro for the Vendor form. When a user clicks a vendor code on a row in the datasheet, the Vendor Master Form should appear in a pop-up form.

6. Create the navigation form shown in Figure 8–75 for the Discover Science database. Use the same design for your navigation form as the one illustrated in this module. For example, the Item tab should display the Item form you created in Step 4, and the Vendor tab should display the Vendor form you created in Step 5. The Forms tab should display the Forms List form you created in Step 2, and the Reports tab should display the Reports List form you created in Step 3.

Continued >

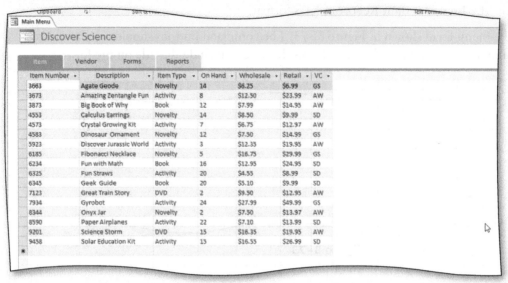

In the Labs *continued*

Figure 8–75

7. If requested to do so by your instructor, add your name to the title for the Forms List form.

8. Submit the revised database in the format specified by your instructor.

9. ✲ In this exercise, you exported reports in XPS format. How would you create a macro to export the Item table in Excel format?

Lab 3: **Consider This: Your Turn**

Creating Macros and a Navigation Form for the Marketing Analytics Database

Note: To complete this assignment, you will be required to use the Data Files. Please contact your instructor for information about accessing the Data Files.

Part 1: Marketing Analytics is a marketing research firm that focuses on the needs of small business owners. You are doing an internship with Marketing Analytics and the owners have asked you to create macros and a navigation form to make the database easier to use.

Open the Lab 3 Marketing Analytics database from the Data Files. Then, use the concepts and techniques presented in this module to perform the following tasks:

 a. Create a macro that includes submacros to open the Client Master Form, the Marketing Analyst Master Form, and the Analyst Seminar Data form. The Analyst Seminar Data form should open as read-only. The macro should also include submacros to preview and export in PDF format the Client Financial Report, the Marketing Analyst Master Report, and the Clients by Marketing Analyst report.

 b. Create a menu form for the forms and a menu form for the reports. Use an option group for each form and include a descriptive title on each form.

 c. Create a datasheet form for the Client table and name the form Client. Create a UI macro for the Client form. When a user clicks a client number on a row in the datasheet form, the Client Master Form should appear in a pop-up form.

 d. Create a datasheet form for the Marketing Analyst table and name the form Marketing Analyst. Create a UI macro for the Marketing Analyst form. When a user clicks a marketing analyst number on a row in the datasheet form, the Marketing Analyst Master Form should appear in a pop-up form.

  e. Create a data macro for the Seminar Offerings table. The macro will examine the value in the Hours Spent field. If the user's update would cause the value to be greater than the Total Hours, the macro will change the value to Total Hours. If the user's update would cause the value to be less than 0, the macro will change the value to 0.

  f. Create a navigation form for the Marketing Analytics database. Use the same design for your navigation form as that shown in Figure 8–1a. Include the Client form, the Marketing Analyst form, and the menu forms you created in Step b.

Submit your assignment in the format specified by your instructor.

Part 2:   You made several decisions while completing this assignment, including creating a macro to open a pop-up form. What was the rationale behind your decisions? The window mode to open a form as a pop-up form is Dialog. What would be the effect if the form opened in Normal mode?

9 | Administering a Database System

Objectives

You will have mastered the material in this module when you can:

- Convert a database to and from earlier versions of Access
- Use the Table Analyzer, Performance Analyzer, and Documenter
- Create custom categories and groups in the Navigation Pane
- Use table, database, and field properties
- Create indexes
- Enable and use automatic error checking

- Create custom data type parts
- Create a database for a template
- Create a custom template
- Encrypt a database and set a password
- Lock a database and split a database
- Create a custom web app
- Create custom views for a web app

Introduction

Administering a database system is an important activity that has many facets. Administration activities are an important aspect of database management because they improve the usability, accessibility, security, and efficiency of the database.

Project — Administering a Database System

PrattLast Associates realizes the importance of database administration, that is, the importance of administering its database system properly. Making a database available on the web using a web app (Figure 9–1) is part of this activity. The Customers and Reps database shown in Figure 9–1 is a database that contains information about a software company, a PrattLast subsidiary, that specializes in applications for the health sciences. Figure 9–1a shows the Rep table selected in List view. Not only does the data about the rep appear on the screen, but data concerning the customers of the selected rep does as well. Figure 9–1b shows the Customer table selected in By City view, which has grouped the customers by City. Customers in the selected city, Berridge in this case, appear on the screen. Clicking an individual customer causes all the data for the customer to appear, as shown in Figure 9–1c.

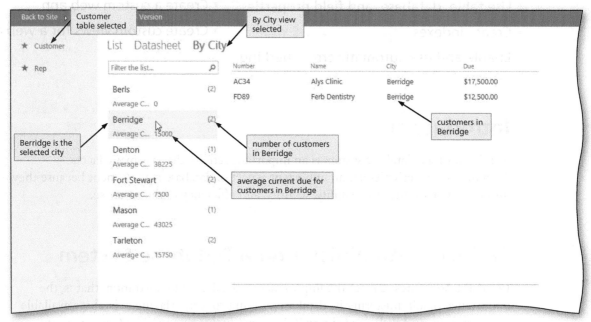

Figure 9–1(a) Rep Table Shown in Web App

Figure 9–1(b) Customer Table Shown in Web App

Another important activity in administering databases is the creation of custom templates, application parts, and data type parts. **Application parts** and **data type parts** are templates included in Access that you can add to your database to extend its functionality. Clicking an application part adds to your database a predetermined collection of objects such as tables, queries, forms, reports, and/or macros. Clicking a data type part adds a predetermined collection of fields to a table.

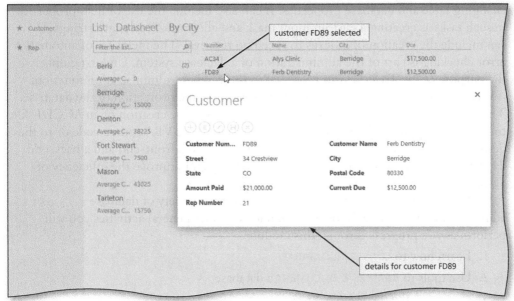

Figure 9–1(c) Customer Details Shown in Web App

Figure 9–2 illustrates the range of activities involved in database administration, including the conversion of an Access database to an earlier version of Access. Database administration usually includes such activities as analyzing tables for potential problems, analyzing performance to see if changes could make the system perform more efficiently, and documenting the various objects in the database. It

BTW
Enabling the Content
For each of the databases you use in this module, you will need to enable the content.

Figure 9–2

can include creating custom categories and groups in the Navigation Pane as well as changing table and database properties. It can also include the use of field properties in such tasks as creating a custom input mask and allowing zero-length strings. It can include the creation of indexes to speed up retrieval. The inclusion of automatic error checking is part of the administration of a database system. Understanding the purpose of the Trust Center is critical to the database administration function. Another important area of database administration is the protection of the database. This protection includes locking the database through the creation of an ACCDE file to prevent unauthorized changes from being made to the VBA source code or to the design of forms and reports. Splitting the database into a front-end and a back-end database is another way to protect the functionality and improve the efficiency of a database.

In this module, you will learn how to perform a variety of database administration tasks. The following roadmap identifies general activities you will perform as you progress through this module:

1. Learn how to CONVERT a DATABASE
2. Use tools to ANALYZE & DOCUMENT a database
3. CUSTOMIZE the NAVIGATION PANE
4. Use custom PROPERTIES & create INDEXES
5. CREATE a custom DATA PART
6. Create a custom TEMPLATE
7. ENCRYPT, LOCK, & SPLIT a database
8. Learn how to create a custom WEB APP
9. Learn how to create CUSTOM VIEW in a web app

Converting Databases

Access 2007, Access 2010, Access 2013, and Access 2016 all use the same file format, the .accdb format. The format is usually referred to as the Access 2007 file format. Thus, in Access 2016, you can use any database created in Access 2007. You should be aware of the following changes in Access 2013 and Access 2016 from the earlier versions.

1. Unlike previous versions, these versions do not support PivotTables or PivotCharts.
2. The Text data type is now Short Text and the Memo data type is now Long Text.
3. Smart Tags are no longer supported.
4. Replication is no longer available.

To convert an Access 2007 database to an earlier version, the database cannot contain any features that are specific to Access 2007, 2010, 2013, or 2016. These include attachments, multivalued fields, offline data, or links to external files not supported in earlier versions of Access. They also include objects published to the web, data macros, and calculated columns. Provided the database does not contain such features, you can convert the database by clicking the Save As tab in the Backstage view (Figure 9–3). You can then choose the appropriate format.

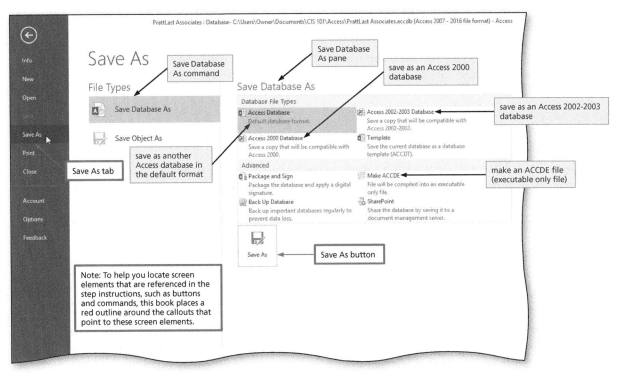

Figure 9–3

TO CONVERT AN ACCESS 2007–2016 DATABASE TO AN EARLIER VERSION

Specifically, to convert an Access 2007–2016 database to an earlier version, you would use the following steps.

1. With the database to be converted open, click File on the ribbon to open the Backstage view.
2. Click the Save As tab.
3. With the 'Save Database As' command selected, click the desired format, and then click the Save As button.
4. Type the name you want for the converted database, select a location in which to save the converted database, and click the Save button.

TO CONVERT AN ACCESS 2000 OR 2002–2003 DATABASE TO AN ACCESS 2016 DATABASE

To convert an Access 2000 or Access 2002–2003 database to the default database format for Access 2016, you open the database in Access 2016. Initially, the database is open in compatibility mode, where features that are new to Access 2016 and that cannot easily be displayed or converted are disabled. In this mode, the database remains in its original format. If you want to convert it so that you can use it in Access 2016, you use the Access Database command on the Backstage view. Once the database is converted, the disabled features will be enabled. You will no longer be able to share the database with users of Access 2000 or Access 2002–2003, however.

Specifically, to convert an Access 2000 or 2002–2003 database to the default database format for Access 2016, you would use the following steps.

1. With the database to be converted open, click File on the ribbon to open the Backstage view.
2. Click the Save As tab.

BTW
Saving Databases to External Locations
You also can save a database to an external location such as OneDrive, and to any portable storage device, such as a USB flash drive. To do so, select the desired external location or portable storage device when you browse to specify a location for your database.

BTW
Exporting XML Data
Database administration also may include responsibility for exchanging data between dissimilar systems or apps. Extensible Markup Language (XML) is a data interchange standard for describing and delivering data on the web. With XML, you can describe both the data and the structure (schema) of the data. You can export tables queries, forms, or reports. To export a database object, select the object and click the XML File button (External Data tab | Export group). Select the appropriate options in the Export XML dialog box.

3. With the Save Database As command selected, click Access Database and then click the Save As button.

4. Type the name you want for the converted database, select a location, and click the Save button.

Microsoft Access Analysis Tools

Microsoft Access has a variety of tools that are useful in analyzing databases. Analyzing a database gives information about how the database functions and identifies opportunities for improving functionality. You can use the Access analysis tools to analyze tables and database performance, and to create detailed documentation.

To Use the Table Analyzer

1 CONVERT DATABASE | **2 ANALYZE & DOCUMENT** | 3 NAVIGATION PANE | 4 PROPERTIES & INDEXES
5 DATA PART | 6 TEMPLATE | 7 ENCRYPT LOCK & SPLIT | 8 WEB APP | 9 CUSTOM VIEW

Access contains a Table Analyzer tool that performs three separate functions. This tool can analyze tables while looking for potential redundancy (duplicated data). The Table Analyzer can also analyze performance and check for ways to make queries, reports, or forms more efficient. Then the tool will make suggestions for possible changes. The final function of the analyzer is to produce detailed documentation describing the structure and content of the various tables, queries, forms, reports, and other objects in the database.

The following steps use the Table Analyzer to examine the Account table for **redundancy**, or duplicated data. *Why? Redundancy is one of the biggest potential sources of problems in a database.* If redundancy is found, the Table Analyzer will suggest ways to split the table in order to eliminate the redundancy.

1
- Run Access and open the database named PrattLast Associates from your hard disk, OneDrive, or other storage location.
- If necessary, close the Navigation Pane.
- Display the Database Tools tab (Figure 9–4).

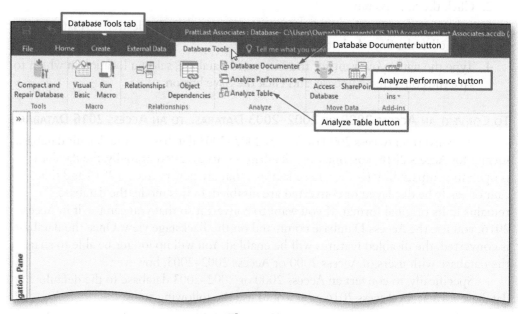

Figure 9–4

2

- Click the Analyze Table button (Database Tools tab | Analyze group) to display the Table Analyzer Wizard dialog box (Figure 9–5).

Where did the data in the figure come from? It does not look like my data. The data is fictitious. It is just intended to give you an idea of what the data might look like.

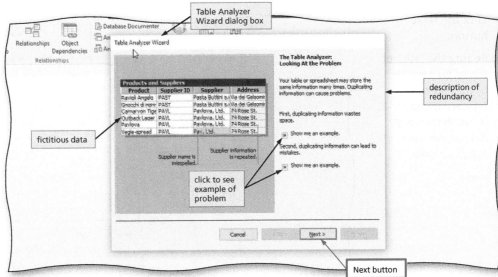

Figure 9–5

3

- Click the Next button to display the next Table Analyzer Wizard screen (Figure 9–6).

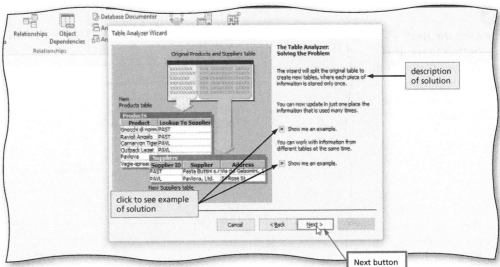

Figure 9–6

4

- Click the Next button to display the next Table Analyzer Wizard screen.

- If necessary, select the Account table (Figure 9–7).

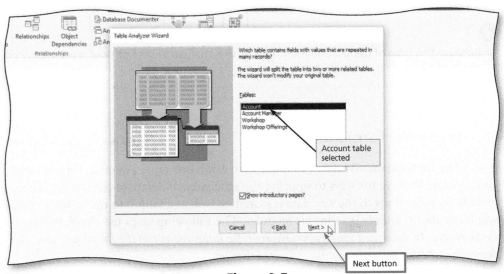

Figure 9–7

- Click the Next button.

- Be sure the 'Yes, let the wizard decide.' option button is selected (Figure 9–8) to let the wizard determine what action to take.

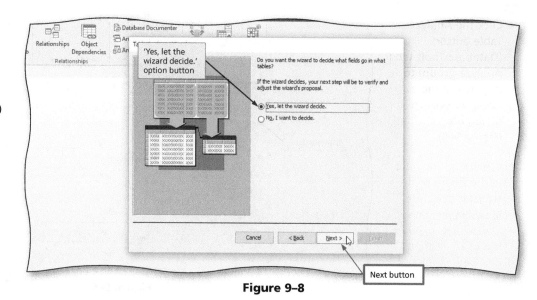

Figure 9–8

- Click the Next button to run the analysis (Figure 9–9), which indicates redundancy in the database.

Q&A | I do not really want to put the city and postal code in a different table, even though I realize that this data does appear to be duplicated. Do I have to follow this advice?

Certainly not. This is only a suggestion.

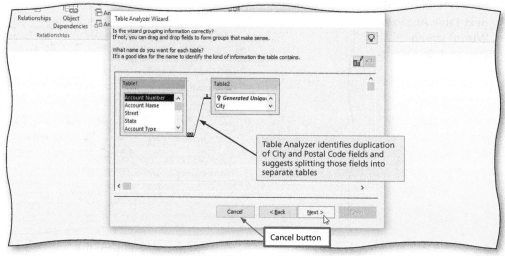

Figure 9–9

- Because the type of duplication identified by the analyzer does not pose a problem, click the Cancel button to close the analyzer.

To Use the Performance Analyzer

1 CONVERT DATABASE | 2 ANALYZE & DOCUMENT | 3 NAVIGATION PANE | 4 PROPERTIES & INDEXES 5 DATA PART | 6 TEMPLATE | 7 ENCRYPT LOCK & SPLIT | 8 WEB APP | 9 CUSTOM VIEW

The Performance Analyzer examines the database's tables, queries, reports, forms, and other objects in your system, looking for ways to improve the efficiency of database operations. These improvements could include modifications to the way data is stored, as well as changes to the indexes created for the system. (You will learn about indexes later in this module.) The following steps use the Performance Analyzer. **Why?** *The Performance Analyzer will identify possible areas for improvement in the PrattLast Associates database. Users then can determine whether to implement the suggested changes.*

1

- Click the Analyze Performance button, shown in Figure 9–4 (Database Tools tab | Analyze group), to display the Performance Analyzer dialog box.

- If necessary, click the Tables tab (Figure 9–10).

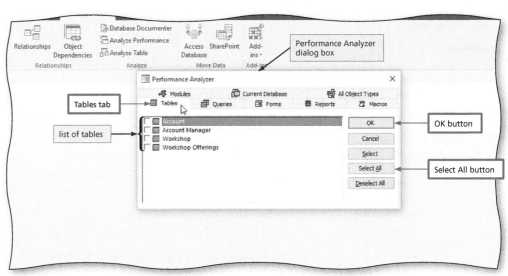

Figure 9–10

2

- Click the Select All button to select all tables.

- Click the OK button to display the results (Figure 9–11).

Q&A What do the results mean?
Because both fields contain only numbers, Access is suggesting that you might improve the efficiency of the table by changing the data types of the fields to Long Integer. As the icon

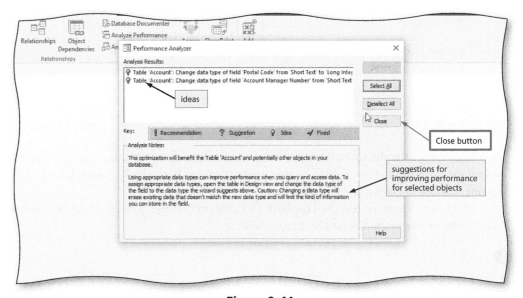

Figure 9–11

in front of the suggestions indicates, this is simply an idea — something to consider. Short Text is a better type for these particular fields, however, so you should ignore this suggestion.

3

- Click the Close button to finish working with the Performance Analyzer.

To Use the Database Documenter

1 CONVERT DATABASE | 2 ANALYZE & DOCUMENT | 3 NAVIGATION PANE | 4 PROPERTIES & INDEXES
5 DATA PART | 6 TEMPLATE | 7 ENCRYPT LOCK & SPLIT | 8 WEB APP | 9 CUSTOM VIEW

The Database Documenter allows you to produce detailed documentation of the various tables, queries, forms, reports, and other objects in your database. Documentation is required by many organizations. It is used for backup, disaster recovery, and planning for database enhancements. Figure 9–12 shows a portion of the documentation for the Account table. The complete documentation is much lengthier than the one shown in the figure.

C:\Users\Owner\Documents\CIS 101\Access\PrattLast Associates.accdb

Tuesday, September 12, 2017

Table: Account Page: 1

Columns

Name	Type	Size
Account Number	Short Text	5
Account Name	Short Text	30
Street	Short Text	25
City	Short Text	20
State	Short Text	2
Postal Code	Short Text	5
Account Type	Short Text	255

    RowSource: "SER";"NON";"IND"
    RowSourceType: Value List
    ValidationRule: ="SER" Or ="NON" Or ="IND"
    ValidationText: Must be SER, NON, or IND

Services Needed		4

    RowSource: "Bck";"Ben";"Com";"Mgt";"Pay";"Rec";"Rsk";"Tch";"Trn";"Wrk"
    RowSourceType: Value List

Amount Paid	Currency	8
Current Due	Currency	8

    ValidationRule: >=0 And <=10000
    ValidationText: Must be at least $0.00 and at most $10,000.00

Total Amount	Currency (Calculated)	8

    Expression: [Amount Paid]+[Current Due]

Account Manager Number	Short Text	2

Figure 9–12

Notice that the documentation of the Account Type field contains the row source associated with the Lookup information for the field. The documentation for both the Account Type and the Current Due fields contains validation rules and validation text.

The following steps use the Database Documenter. **Why?** *The Database Documenter is the easiest way to produce detailed documentation for the Account table.*

- Click the Database Documenter button, shown in Figure 9–4 (Database Tools tab | Analyze group), to display the Documenter dialog box.

- If necessary, click the Tables tab and then click the Account check box to specify documentation for the Account table (Figure 9–13).

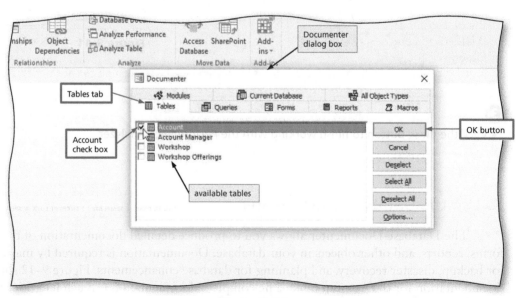

Figure 9–13

2

- Click the OK button to produce a preview of the documentation (Figure 9–14).

Q&A What can I do with this documentation? You could print it by clicking the Print button (Print Preview tab | Print group). You could create a PDF or XPS file containing the documentation by clicking the PDF or XPS button (Print Preview tab | Data group) and following the directions. You could create a Word (RTF) file by clicking the More button (Print

Preview tab | Data group), and then clicking Word and following the directions. Whatever option you choose, you may need to use this documentation later if you make changes to the database design.

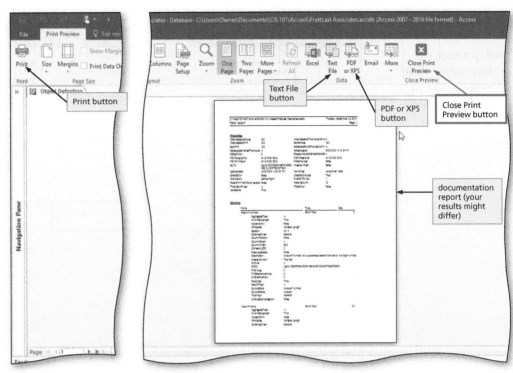

Figure 9–14

- Click the 'Close Print Preview' button (Print Preview tab | Close Preview group) to close the preview of the documentation.

ⓟ Experiment

- Try other options within the Database Documenter to see the effect of your choice on the documentation produced. Each time, close the preview of the documentation.

BTW
Touch Screen Differences
The Office and Windows interfaces may vary if you are using a touch screen. For this reason, you might notice that the function or appearance of your touch screen differs slightly from this module's presentation.

Navigation Pane Customization

You have already learned how to customize the Navigation Pane by selecting the category and the filter as well as how to use the Search Bar to restrict the items that appear in the Navigation Pane. You can also create custom categories and groups that you can use to categorize the items in the database in ways that are most useful to you.

To Create Custom Categories and Groups

1 CONVERT DATABASE | 2 ANALYZE & DOCUMENT | 3 NAVIGATION PANE | 4 PROPERTIES & INDEXES
5 DATA PART | 6 TEMPLATE | 7 ENCRYPT LOCK & SPLIT | 8 WEB APP | 9 CUSTOM VIEW

You can create custom categories in the Navigation Pane. You can further refine the objects you place in a category by adding custom groups to the categories. *Why? Custom categories and groups allow you to tailor the Navigation Pane for your own specific needs.* The following steps create a custom category called Financial Items. They then add two custom groups, Detailed and Summary, to the Financial Items category.

- Display the Navigation Pane.
- Right-click the Navigation Pane title bar to display a shortcut menu (Figure 9–15).

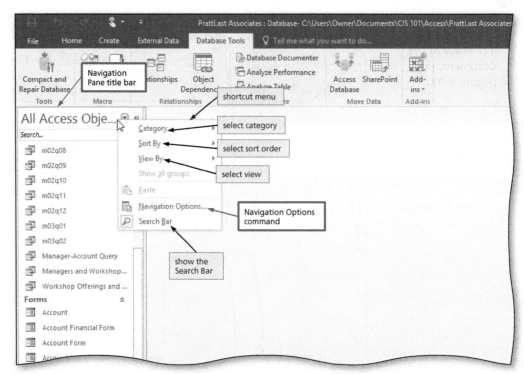

Figure 9–15

- Click the Navigation Options command on the shortcut menu to display the Navigation Options dialog box (Figure 9–16).

Q&A What else could I do with the shortcut menu?
You could select a category, select a sort order, or select how to view the items within the Navigation Pane.

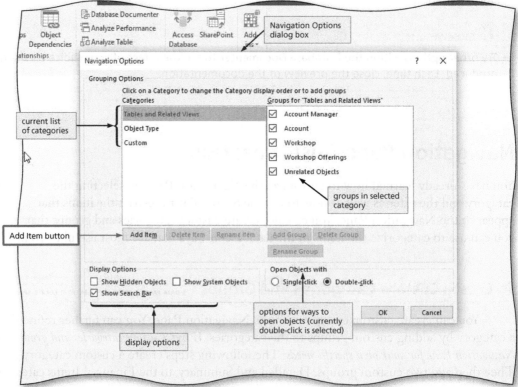

Figure 9–16

3

- Click the Add Item button to add a new category (Figure 9–17).

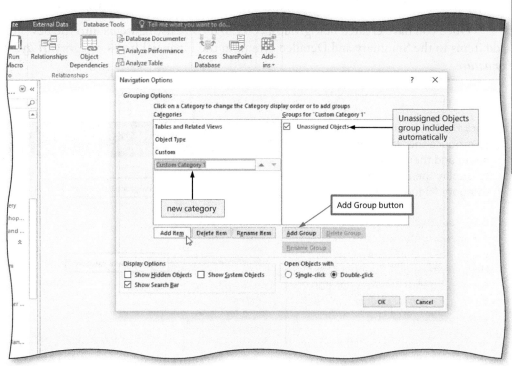

Figure 9–17

4

- Type **Financial Items** as the name of the category.

- Click the Add Group button to add a group and then type **Detailed** as the name of the group.

- Click the Add Group button to add a group and then type **Summary** as the name of the group (Figure 9–18).

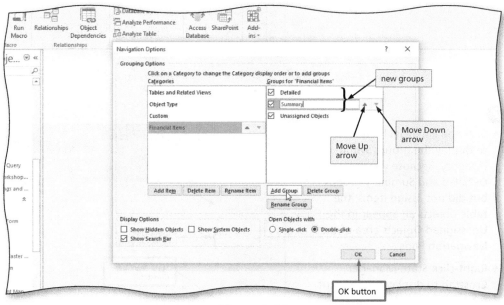

Figure 9–18

Q&A I added the groups in the wrong order. How can I change the order?
Select the group that is in the wrong position. Click the Move Up or Move Down arrow to move the group to the correct location.

If I made a mistake in creating a new category, how can I fix it?
Select the category that is incorrect. If the name is wrong, click the Rename Item button and change the name appropriately. If you do not want the category, click the Delete Item button to delete the category and then click the OK button.

5

- Click the OK button to create the new category and groups.

To Add Items to Groups

1 CONVERT DATABASE | 2 ANALYZE & DOCUMENT | **3 NAVIGATION PANE** | **4 PROPERTIES & INDEXES**
5 DATA PART | 6 TEMPLATE | 7 ENCRYPT LOCK & SPLIT | 8 WEB APP | 9 CUSTOM VIEW

Once you have created new groups, you can move existing items into the new groups. The following steps add items to the Summary and Detailed groups in the Financial Items category. *Why? These items are all financial in nature.*

1

- Click the Navigation Pane arrow to produce the Navigation Pane menu and then scroll as necessary to display the Financial Items category (Figure 9–19).

Q&A
Do I have to click the arrow?
No. If you prefer, you can click anywhere in the title bar for the Navigation Pane. Clicking arrows is a good habit, however, because there are many situations where you must click the arrow.

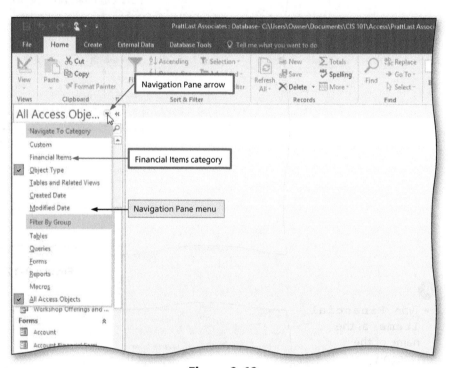

Figure 9–19

2

- Click the Financial Items category to display the groups within the category. Because you created the Detailed and Summary groups but did not assign items, the table objects all appear in the Unassigned Objects area of the Navigation Pane.

- Right-click State-Manager Crosstab to display the shortcut menu.

- Point to the 'Add to group' command on the shortcut menu to display the list of available groups (Figure 9–20).

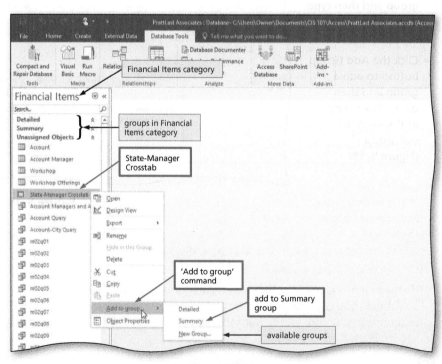

Figure 9–20

Q&A I did not create an Unassigned Objects group. Where did it come from?
Access creates the Unassigned Objects group automatically. Until you add an object to one of the groups you created, it will be in the Unassigned Objects group.

What is the purpose of the New Group on the submenu?
You can create a new group using this submenu. This is an alternative to using the Navigation Options dialog box. Use whichever approach you find most convenient.

3

- Click Summary to add the State-Manager Crosstab to the Summary group.

- Using the same technique, add the items shown in Figure 9–21 to the Detailed and Summary groups.

Q&A What is the symbol that appears in front of the items in the Detailed and Summary groups?
It is the link symbol. You do not actually add an object to your group. Rather, you create a link to the object. In practice, you do not have to worry about this. The process for opening an object in one of your custom groups remains the same.

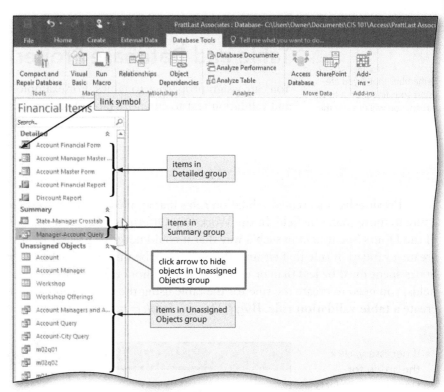

Figure 9–21

4

- Click the arrow in the Unassigned Objects bar to hide the unassigned objects (Figure 9–22).

Q&A Do I have to click the arrow?
No. Just as with the Navigation Pane, you can click anywhere in the Unassigned Objects bar.

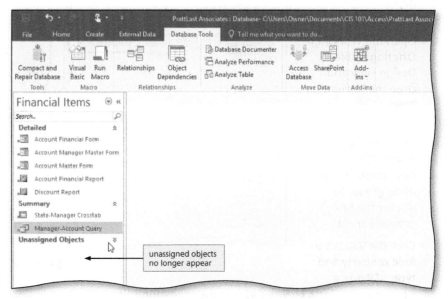

Figure 9–22

Break Point: If you wish to stop working through the module at this point, you can close Access now. You can resume the project at a later time by running Access, opening the PrattLast Associates database, and continuing to follow the steps from this location forward.

CONSIDER THIS

What issues do you consider in determining the customization of the Navigation Pane?

The types of issues to consider are the following:

• Would a new category be useful?

• If so, are there new groups that would be useful to include in the new category?

• If you have created a new category and new groups, which items should be included in the new groups, and which should be left uncategorized?

BTW
Touch and Pointers
Remember that if you are using your finger on a touch screen, you will not see the pointer.

Table and Database Properties

You can assign properties to tables. For example, you could assign a validation rule and validation text to an entire table. You can also assign properties to the database, typically for documentation purposes.

To Create a Validation Rule for a Table

1 CONVERT DATABASE | 2 ANALYZE & DOCUMENT | 3 NAVIGATION PANE | **4 PROPERTIES & INDEXES**
5 DATA PART | 6 TEMPLATE | 7 ENCRYPT LOCK & SPLIT | 8 WEB APP | 9 CUSTOM VIEW

Previously, you created validation rules that applied to individual fields within a table. Some, however, apply to more than one field. In the Workshop Offerings table, you created a macro that would change the value of the Hours Spent field in such a way that it could never be greater than the Total Hours field. You can also create a validation rule that ensures this will never be the case; that is, the validation rule would require that the hours spent must be less than or equal to the total hours. To create a validation rule that involves two or more fields, you need to create the rule for the table using the table's Validation Rule property. The following steps create a **table validation rule**. *Why? This rule involves two fields, Hours Spent and Total Hours.*

1

• If necessary, click the arrow for Unassigned Objects to display those objects in the Navigation Pane.

• Open the Workshop Offerings table in Design view and close the Navigation Pane.

• If necessary, click the Property Sheet button (Table Tools Design tab | Show /Hide group) to display the table's property sheet.

• Click the Validation Rule property and type `[Hours Spent]<=[Total Hours]` as the validation rule.

• Click the Validation Text property and type `Hours spent cannot exceed total hours` as the validation text (Figure 9–23).

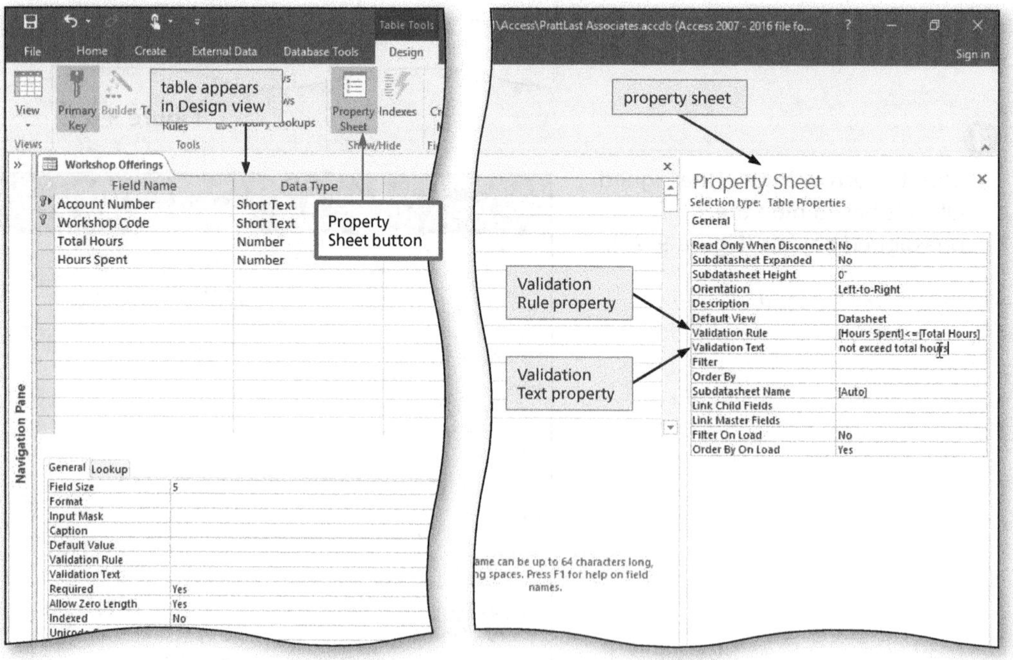

Figure 9–23

Q&A

Could I use the Expression Builder to create the validation rule?
Yes. Use whichever method you find the most convenient.

- Close the property sheet.
- Click the Save button on the Quick Access Toolbar to save the validation rule and the validation text.
- When asked if you want to test existing data, click the No button.
- Close the Workshop Offerings table.

To Create Custom Properties

1 CONVERT DATABASE | 2 ANALYZE & DOCUMENT | 3 NAVIGATION PANE | **4 PROPERTIES & INDEXES**
5 DATA PART | **6 TEMPLATE** | **7 ENCRYPT LOCK & SPLIT** | **8 WEB APP** | **9 CUSTOM VIEW**

In addition to the general database property categories, you can also use custom properties. *Why? You can use custom properties to further document your database in a variety of ways. If you have needs that go beyond the custom properties, you can create your own original or unique properties.* The following steps **populate** the Status custom property; that is, they set a value for the property. In this case, they set the Status property to Live Version, indicating this is the live version of the database. If the database were still in a test environment, the property would be set to Test Version. The steps also create and populate a new property, Production, which represents the date the database was placed into production.

1

- Click File on the ribbon to open the Backstage view.
- Ensure the Info tab is selected (Figure 9–24).

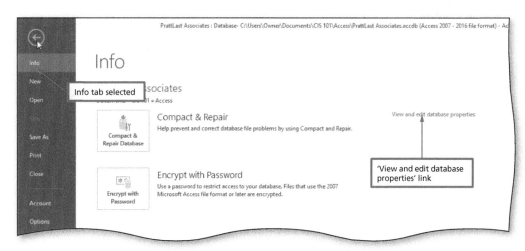

Figure 9–24

2

- Click the 'View and edit database properties' link to display the PrattLast Associates.accdb Properties dialog box.
- Click the Custom tab.
- Scroll down in the Name list so that Status appears, and then click Status.
- If necessary, click the Type arrow to set the data type to Text.
- Click the Value box and type **Live Version** as the value to create the custom property (Figure 9–25).

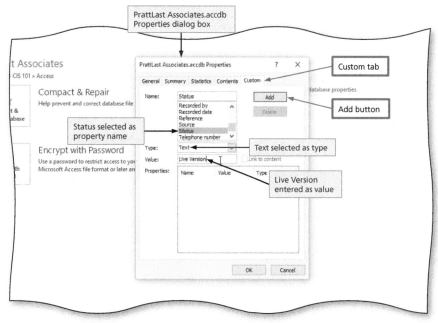

Figure 9–25

- Click the Add button to add the property.
- Type **Production** in the Name box.
- If requested to do so by your instructor, type your first and last name in the Name box.
- Select Date as the Type.
- Type **03/03/2018** as the value (Figure 9–26) to indicate that the database went into production on March 3, 2018.

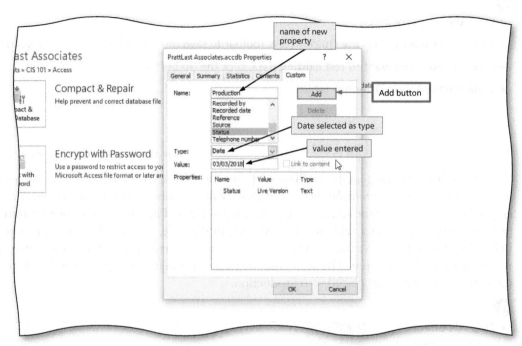

Figure 9–26

- Click the Add button to add the property (Figure 9–27).

Q&A What if I add a property that I decide I do not want?
You can delete it. To do so, click the property you no longer want and then click the Delete button.

- Click the OK button to close the PrattLast Associates.accdb Properties dialog box.

Q&A How do I view these properties in the future?
The same way you created them. Click File on the ribbon, click the Info tab, and then click the 'View and edit database properties' link. Click the desired tab to see the properties you want.

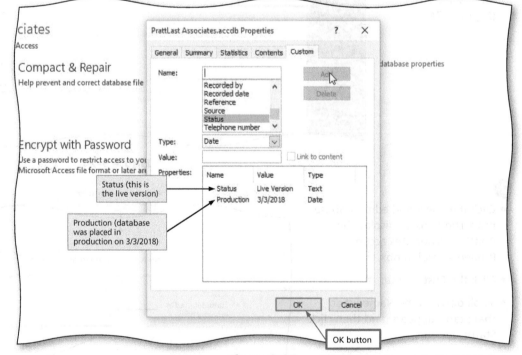

Figure 9–27

Special Field Properties

Each field in a table has a variety of field properties available. Recall that field properties are characteristics of a field. Two special field properties, the Custom Input Mask property and the Allow Zero Length property, are described in this section.

Custom Input Masks

One way to help users enter data using a certain format is to use an input mask. You have already used the Input Mask Wizard to create an input mask. Using the wizard, you can select the input mask that meets your needs. This is often the best way to create the input mask.

If the input mask you need to create is not similar to any in the list provided by the wizard, you can create a custom input mask by entering the appropriate characters as the value for the Input Mask property. In doing so, you use the symbols from Table 9–1.

Table 9–1	Input Mask Symbols	
Symbol	**Type of Data Accepted**	**Data Entry**
0	Digits 0 through 9 without plus (+) or minus (–) sign are accepted. Positions left blank appear as zeros.	Required
9	Digits 0 through 9 without plus (+) or minus (–) sign are accepted. Positions left blank appear as spaces.	Optional
#	Digits 0 through 9 with plus (+) or minus (–) sign are accepted. Positions left blank appear as spaces.	Optional
L	Letters A through Z are accepted.	Required
?	Letters A through Z are accepted.	Optional
A	Letters A through Z or digits 0 through 9 are accepted.	Required
a	Letters A through Z or digits 0 through 9 are accepted.	Optional
&	Any character or a space is accepted.	Required
C	Any character or a space is accepted.	Optional
<	Symbol converts any letter entered to lowercase.	Does not apply
>	Symbol converts any letter entered to uppercase.	Does not apply
!	Characters typed in the input mask fill it from left to right.	Does not apply
\	Character following the slash is treated as a literal in the input mask.	Does not apply

For example, to indicate that account numbers must consist of two letters followed by three numbers, you would enter LL999. The Ls in the first two positions indicate that the first two positions must be letters. Using L instead of a question mark indicates that the users are required to enter these letters. If you had used the question mark instead of the L, they could leave these positions blank. The 9s in the last three positions indicate that the users can enter only digits 0 through 9. Using 9 instead of 0 indicates that they could leave these positions blank; that is, they are optional. Finally, to ensure that any letters entered are displayed as uppercase, you would use the > symbol at the beginning of the input mask. The complete mask would be >LL999.

BTW
Changing Data Formats
To create custom data formats, enter various characters in the Format property of a table field. The characters can be placeholders (such as 0 and #), separators (such as periods and commas), literal characters, and colors. You can create custom formats for short text, date, number, and currency fields. Date, number, and currency fields also include a number of standard data formats.

BTW
Table Descriptions
To add a description for a table, right-click the table in the Navigation Pane and then click Table Properties on the shortcut menu. When the Properties dialog box for the table appears, enter the description in the Description property and then click the OK button. To enter a description for a table in Design view, click the Property Sheet button, and then enter a description in the Description property on the property sheet (see Figure 9–23).

To Create a Custom Input Mask

The following step creates a custom input mask for the Account Number field. *Why? None of the input masks in the list meet the specific needs for the Account Number field.*

- Open the Navigation Pane, open the Account table in Design view, and then close the Navigation Pane.

- With the Account Number field selected, click the Input Mask property, and then type **>LL999** as the value (Figure 9–28).

Q&A

What is the difference between the Format property and the Input Mask property?

The Format property ensures that data is displayed consistently, for example, always in uppercase. The Input Mask property controls how data is entered by the user.

What is the effect of this input mask?

From this point on, anyone entering an account number will be restricted to letters in the first two positions and numeric digits in the last three. Further, any letters entered in the first two positions will be displayed as uppercase.

In Figure 9–28, the Account Number field has both a custom input mask and a format. Is this a problem?

Technically, you do not need both. When the same field has both an input mask and a format, the format takes precedence. However, because the format specified for the Account Number field is the same as the input mask (uppercase), it will not affect the data.

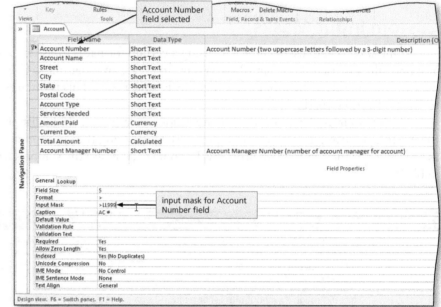

Figure 9–28

To Not Allow Zero Length

You can use zero-length strings to distinguish data that does not exist from data that is unknown. *Why? A zero-length string is different from a field that is blank.* For example, in the Account Manager table, you may want to set the Required property for the Special Skills field to Yes, so that users do not forget to enter an account manager's special skills. If the user forgets to enter a special skill, Access will display an error message and not add the record until the user enters a special skill. If, on the other hand, there are certain account managers for whom no special skill is appropriate, users can enter a **zero-length string** — a string that contains no characters — and Access will accept the record without generating an error message. To enter a zero-length string, you type two quotation marks with no space in between (""). If you enter a zero-length string into a Short Text or Long Text field whose Required property is set to Yes, Access will not report an error.

If you want to ensure that data is entered in the field and a zero-length string is not appropriate, you can set the Required property to Yes and the Allow Zero Length property to No. The following steps set the Allow Zero Length property for the Account Name field to No. (The Required property has already been set to Yes.)

1
- Click the row selector for the Account Name field to select the field.
- Click the 'Allow Zero Length' property and then click the arrow that appears to display a menu.
- Click No in the menu to change the value of the 'Allow Zero Length' property from Yes to No (Figure 9–29).

Q&A
Could I just type the word, No?
Yes. In fact, you could type the letter, N, and Access would complete the word, No. Use whichever technique you prefer.

2
- Save your changes and click the No button when asked if you want to test existing data.
- Close the table.

Q&A
What is the effect of this change?
If the value for the Allow Zero Length property is set to No, an attempt to enter a zero-length string (" ") will result in an error message.

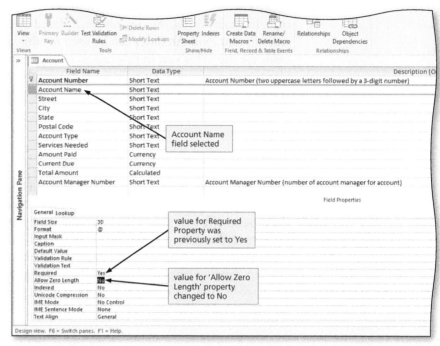

Figure 9–29

Creating and Using Indexes

You are already familiar with the concept of an index. The index in the back of a book contains important words or phrases along with a list of pages on which the given words or phrases can be found. An **index** for a table is similar. An index is a database object that is created based on a field or combination of fields. An index on the Account Name field, for example, would enable Access to rapidly locate a record that contains a particular account name. In this case, the items of interest are account names instead of keywords or phrases, as is the case for the index in the back of this book. The field or fields on which the index is built is called the **index key**. Thus, in the index on account names, the Account Name field is the index key.

Each name occurs in the index along with the number of the record on which the corresponding account is located. Further, the names appear in the index in alphabetical order, so Access can use this index to rapidly produce a list of accounts alphabetized by account name.

Another benefit of indexes is that they provide an efficient way to order records. That is, if the records are to appear in a certain order in a database object, Access can use an index instead of physically having to rearrange the records in the database. Physically rearranging the records in a different order can be a very time-consuming process.

To gain the benefits of an index, you must first create one. Access automatically creates an index on some special fields. If, for example, a table contains a field called Postal Code, Access would create an index for this field automatically. You must create any other indexes you determine would improve database performance, indicating the field or fields on which the index is to be built.

BTW
Changing Default Sort Order
To display the records in a table in an order other than the primary key (the default sort order), use the Order By property on the table's property sheet (see Figure 9–23).

BTW
Indexes
The most common structure for high-performance indexes is called a B-tree. It is a highly efficient structure that supports very rapid access to records in the database as well as a rapid alternative to sorting records. Virtually all systems use some version of the B-tree structure.

Although the index key will usually be a single field, it can be a combination of fields. For example, you might want to sort records by amount paid within account type. In other words, the records are ordered by a combination of fields: Account Type and Amount Paid. An index can be used for this purpose by using a combination of fields for the index key. In this case, you must assign a name to the index. It is a good idea to assign a name that represents the combination of fields. For example, an index whose key is the combination of the Account Type and Amount Paid fields might be called TypePaid.

How Access Uses Indexes

Access uses indexes automatically. If you request that data be sorted in a particular order and Access determines that an index is available that it can use to make the process efficient, it will do so automatically. If no index is available, it will still sort the data in the order you requested; it will just take longer than with the index.

Similarly, if you request that Access locate a particular record that has a certain value in a particular field, Access will use an index if an appropriate one exists. If not, it will have to examine each record until it finds the one you want.

To Create a Single-Field Index

1 CONVERT DATABASE | 2 ANALYZE & DOCUMENT | 3 NAVIGATION PANE | **4 PROPERTIES & INDEXES**
5 DATA PART | 6 TEMPLATE | 7 ENCRYPT LOCK & SPLIT | 8 WEB APP | 9 CUSTOM VIEW

The following steps create a single-field index on the Account Name field. *Why? This index will make finding accounts based on their name more efficient than it would be without the index. It will also improve the efficiency of sorting by account name.*

- Open the Navigation Pane, open the Account table in Design view, and then close the Navigation Pane.

- Select the Account Name field.

- Click the Indexed property box in the Field Properties pane to select the property.

- Click the arrow that appears to display the Indexed list (Figure 9–30).

- Click Yes (Duplicates OK) in the list to specify that duplicates are to be allowed.

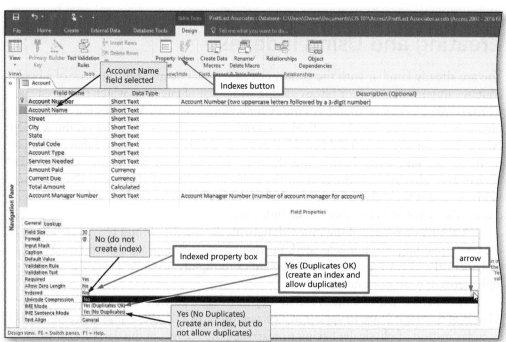

Figure 9–30

To Create a Multiple-Field Index

Creating **multiple-field indexes** — that is, indexes whose key is a combination of fields — involves a different process than creating single-field indexes. To create multiple-field indexes, you will use the Indexes button, enter a name for the index, and then enter the combination of fields that make up the index key. The following steps create a multiple-field index on the combination of Account Type and Amount Paid. *Why? PrattLast needs to sort records on the combination of Account Type and Amount Paid and wants to improve the efficiency of this sort.* The steps assign this index the name TypePaid.

1

• Click the Indexes button, shown in Figure 9–30 (Table Tools Design tab | Show/Hide group), to display the Indexes: Account window (Figure 9–31).

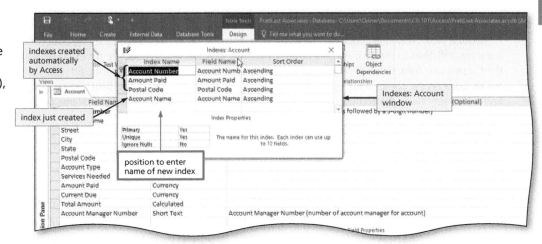

Figure 9–31

2

• Click the blank row (the row below Account Name) in the Index Name column in the Indexes: Account window to select the position to enter the name of the new index.

• Type `TypePaid` as the index name, and then press the TAB key.

• Click the arrow in the Field Name column to produce a list of fields in the Account table, and then select Account Type to enter the first of the two fields for the index.

• Press the TAB key three times to move to the Field Name column on the following row.

• Select the Amount Paid field in the same manner as the Account Type field (Figure 9–32).

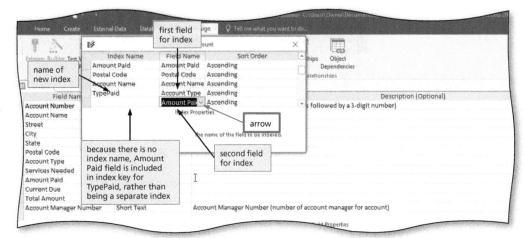

Figure 9–32

3

• Close the Indexes: Account window by clicking its Close button.

• Save your changes and close the table.

CONSIDER THIS

How do you determine when to use an index?

An index improves efficiency for sorting and finding records. On the other hand, indexes occupy space on your storage device. They also require Access to do extra work. Access must keep current all the indexes that have been created. The following guidelines help determine how and when to use indexes to their fullest advantage.

Create an index on a field (or combination of fields) if one or more of the following conditions are present:

1. The field is the primary key of the table. (Access creates this index automatically.)

2. The field is the foreign key in a relationship you have created.

3. You will frequently need your data to be sorted on the field.

4. You will frequently need to locate a record based on a value in this field.

Because Access handles condition 1 automatically, you only need to concern yourself about conditions 2, 3, and 4. If you think you will need to see account data arranged in order of current due amounts, for example, you should create an index on the Current Due field. If you think you will need to see the data arranged by amount paid within account type, you should create an index on the combination of the Account Type field and the Amount Paid field. Similarly, if you think you will need to find an account given the account's name, you should create an index on the Account Name field.

Automatic Error Checking

Access can automatically check for several types of errors in forms and reports. When Access detects an error, it warns you about the existence of the error and provides you with options for correcting it. The types of errors that Access can detect and correct are shown in Table 9–2.

Table 9–2 Types of Errors	
Error Type	**Description**
Unassociated label and control	A label and control are selected and are not associated with each other.
New unassociated labels	A newly added label is not associated with any other control.
Keyboard shortcut errors	A shortcut key is invalid. This can happen because an unassociated label has a shortcut key, there are duplicate shortcut keys assigned, or a blank space is assigned as a shortcut key.
Invalid control properties	A control property is invalid. For example, the property contains invalid characters.
Common report errors	The report has invalid sorting or grouping specifications, or the report is wider than the page size.

To Enable Error Checking

1 CONVERT DATABASE | 2 ANALYZE & DOCUMENT | 3 NAVIGATION PANE | **4 PROPERTIES & INDEXES**
5 DATA PART | **6 TEMPLATE** | **7 ENCRYPT LOCK & SPLIT** | **8 WEB APP** | **9 CUSTOM VIEW**

Why? *For automatic error checking to take place, it must be enabled.* The following steps ensure that error checking is enabled and that errors are found and reported.

1

- Click File on the ribbon and then click the Options tab to display the Access Options dialog box.

- Click Object Designers to display the options for creating and modifying objects.

- Scroll down so that the Error checking area appears.

- Ensure the 'Enable error checking' check box is checked (Figure 9–33).

Q&A

What is the purpose of the other check boxes in the section?
All the other check boxes are checked, indicating that Access will perform all the various types of automatic error checking that are possible. If there were a particular type of error checking that you would prefer to skip, you would remove its check mark before clicking the OK button.

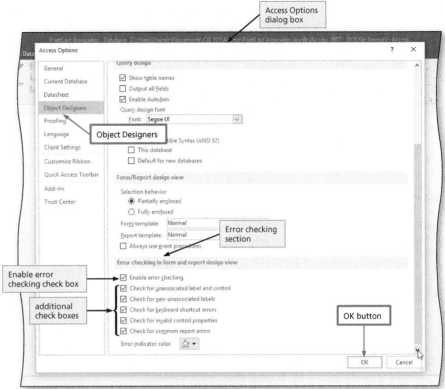

Figure 9–33

2

- Click the OK button to close the Access Options dialog box.

Error Indication

With error checking enabled, if an error occurs, a small triangle called an **error indicator** appears in the appropriate field or control. For example, you could change the label for Account Manager Number in the Account Master Form to include an ampersand (&) before the letter, N, making it a keyboard shortcut for this control. This would be a problem because N is already a shortcut for Name to Find. If this happens, an error indicator appears in both controls in which N is the keyboard shortcut, as shown in Figure 9–34.

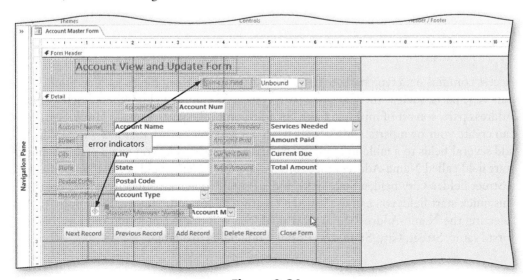

Figure 9–34

BTW
Freezing Fields
The Freeze Fields command allows you to place a column or columns in a table on the left side of the table. As you scroll to the right, the column or columns remain visible. To freeze a column or columns, select the column(s) in Datasheet view, right-click and click Freeze Fields on the shortcut menu. To unfreeze fields, click the 'Unfreeze All Fields' command on the shortcut menu. When you freeze a column, Access considers it a change to the layout of the table. When you close the table, Access will ask you if you want to save the changes.

Selecting a control containing an error indicator displays an 'Error Checking Options' button. Clicking the 'Error Checking Options' button produces the 'Error Checking Options' menu, as shown in Figure 9–35. The first line in the menu is simply a statement of the type of error that occurred, and the second is a description of the specific error. The Change Caption command gives a submenu of the captions that can be changed. The 'Edit Caption Property' command allows you to change the caption directly and is the simplest way to correct this error. The 'Help on This Error' command gives help on the specific error that occurred. You can choose to ignore the error by using the Ignore Error command. The final command, 'Error Checking Options', allows you to change the same error checking options shown in Figure 9–33.

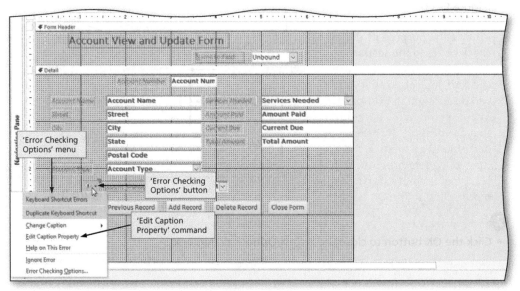

Figure 9–35

The simplest way to fix the duplicate keyboard shortcut error is to edit the caption property. Clicking the 'Edit Caption Property' command produces a property sheet with the Caption property highlighted. You could then change the Caption property of one of the controls, making another letter the shortcut key. For example, you could make the letter, A, the shortcut key by typing `&Account Manager Number` as the entry.

Data Type Parts

Access contains data type parts that are available on the More Fields gallery. Some data type parts, such as the Category part, consist of a single field. Others, such as the Address part, consist of multiple fields. In addition to the parts provided by Access, you can create your own parts. Quick Start fields act as a framework that lets you rapidly add several fields to a table in a single operation. For example, you could create a quick start field called Name-Address that consists of a Last Name field, a First Name field, a Street field, a City field, a State field, and a Postal Code field. Once you have created this quick start field, you can use it when creating tables in the future. By simply selecting the Name-Address quick start field, you will immediately add the Last Name, First Name, Street, City, State, and Postal Code fields to a table.

To Create Custom Data Parts

1 CONVERT DATABASE | 2 ANALYZE & DOCUMENT | 3 NAVIGATION PANE | 4 PROPERTIES & INDEXES

5 DATA PART | **6 TEMPLATE** | **7 ENCRYPT LOCK & SPLIT** | **8 WEB APP** | **9 CUSTOM VIEW**

PrattLast has decided that combining several address-related fields into a single data part would make future database updates easier. To create data parts in the Quick Start category from existing fields, you select the desired field or fields and then select the Save Selection as New Data Type command in the More Fields gallery. If you select multiple fields, the fields must be adjacent.

The following steps create a Quick Start field consisting of the Last Name, First Name, Street, City, State, and Postal Code fields in the Account Manager table. *Why? Once you have created this Quick Start field, users can add this collection of fields to a table by simply clicking the Quick Start field.*

1

- Open the Navigation Pane, open the Account Manager table in Datasheet view, and then close the Navigation Pane.

- Click the column heading for the Last Name field to select the field.

- Hold the SHIFT key down and click the column heading for the Postal Code field to select all the fields from the Last Name field to the Postal Code field.

- Display the Table Tools Fields tab.

- Click the More Fields button (Table Tools Fields tab | Add & Delete group) to display the More Fields gallery (Figure 9–36).

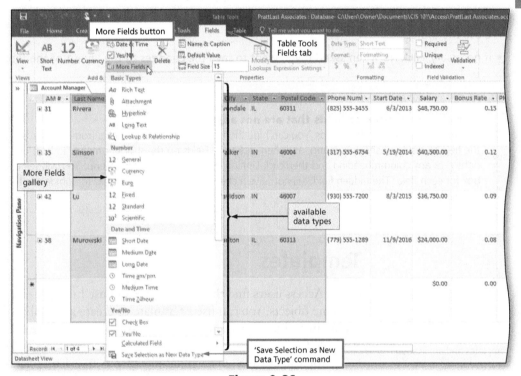

Figure 9–36

2

- Click 'Save Selection as New Data Type' to display the Create New Data Type from Fields dialog box.

- Enter **Name-Address** as the name.

- Enter **Last Name, First Name, Street, City, State, and Postal Code** as the description.

Q&A

What is the purpose of the description?

When a user points to the Quick Start field you created, a ScreenTip will appear containing the description you entered.

Figure 9–37

- Click the Category arrow to display a list of available categories (Figure 9–37).

- Click Quick Start to indicate the new data type will be added to the Quick Start category.

Q&A
What is the difference between the Quick Start and User Defined Types category?
If you select the Quick Start category, the data type you create will be listed among the Quick Start data types that are part of Access. If you select the User Defined Types category, the data type you create will be in a separate category containing only those data types you create. In either case, however, clicking the data type will produce the same result.

- Click the OK button (Create New Data Type from Fields dialog box) to save the data type.
- When Access indicates that your template (that is, your Quick Start field) has been saved, click the OK button (Microsoft Access dialog box).
- Close the table.
- If necessary, click No when asked if you want to save the changes to the layout of the table.

CONSIDER THIS

How do you rearrange fields that are not adjacent?
When adding new data type fields, you can hide the fields that keep your fields from being adjacent. To hide a field, right-click the field to display a shortcut menu, and then click Hide Fields on the shortcut menu. To later unhide a field you have hidden, right-click any column heading and then click Unhide Fields on the shortcut menu. You will see a list of fields with a check box for each field. The hidden field will not have a check mark in the check box. To unhide the field, click the check box for the field.

Templates

BTW
Templates and Application Parts
By default, user-created templates and application parts are stored in the C:\ Users\user name\AppData\ Roaming\Microsoft\ Templates\Access folder.

Often, Access users find that they create and use multiple databases containing the same objects. You can use a template to create a complete database application containing tables, forms, queries, and other objects. There are many templates available for Access.

You can create your own template from an existing database. To do so, you must first ensure that you have created a database with all the characteristics you want in your template. In this module, the database you create will have two tables, a query, two single-item forms, two datasheet forms that use macros, and a navigation form that will serve as the main menu. In addition, the navigation form will be set to appear automatically whenever you open the database. Once you have incorporated all these features, you will save the database as a template. From that point on, anyone can use your template to create a new database. The database that is created will incorporate all the same features as your original database.

Later in this module, you will create a web app, which is a database that anyone can use through a browser. The easiest way to create the tables for the web app is to import them from an existing database. You will use your template to create such a database. While the queries and forms that are part of the template will not be included in the web app, the tables will.

Access enforces some restrictions to tables used in web apps, so the tables in your template should adhere to these restrictions, as follows:

- While you can change the name of the default autonumber primary key, you cannot change its data type. If you have a text field that you want to be the primary key, the best you can do is to specify that the field must be both required and unique.

- You cannot create relationships as you can do with a typical desktop database. Rather, any relationships must be specified through lookup fields.

To Create a Desktop Database

The following steps create the Customers and Reps **desktop database**, that is, a database designed to run on a personal computer. *Why? This database will become the basis for a template.*

- Click File on the ribbon to open the Backstage view.
- Click the New tab.
- Click the 'Blank desktop database' button.
- Type **Customers and Reps** as the name of the database file.
- Click the 'Browse for a location to put your database' button to display the File New Database dialog box, navigate to the desired

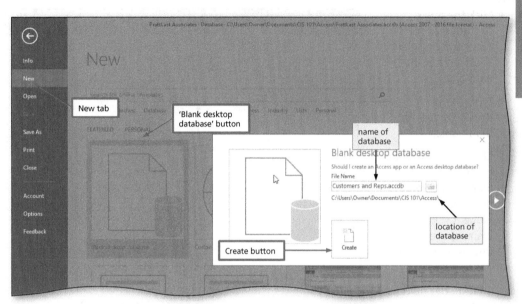

Figure 9–38

save location (for example, the Access folder in the CIS 101 folder), and then click the OK button to return to the Backstage view (Figure 9–38).

- Click the Create button to create the database (Figure 9–39).

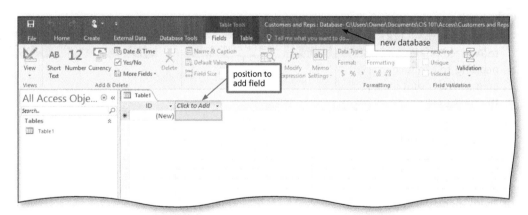

Figure 9–39

To Add Fields to the Table

The tables will have an autonumber ID field as the primary key. *Why? You will later import the tables in this database to a web app, and tables in a web app must have an autonumber field as a primary key.* In addition, the field that would normally be the primary key will be designated both required and unique, two characteristics of the primary key.

The following steps add the Rep Number, Last Name, First Name, Street, City, State, Postal Code, Rate, and Commission to a table. The Rate field is a Number field and the Commission field is a Currency field.

The steps designate the Rep Number field as both required and unique. They add the Last Name, First Name, Street, City, State, and Postal Code as a single operation by using the Quick Start field created earlier. After adding the fields, they save the table using the name, Rep. They also change the field size for the Rate field (a Number data type field) to Single so that the field can contain decimal places.

1

• Click the 'Click to Add' column heading and select Short Text as the data type.

• Type **Rep Number** as the field name.

• Click the white space below the field name to complete the change of the name. Click the white space a second time to select the field.

• Change the field size to 2.

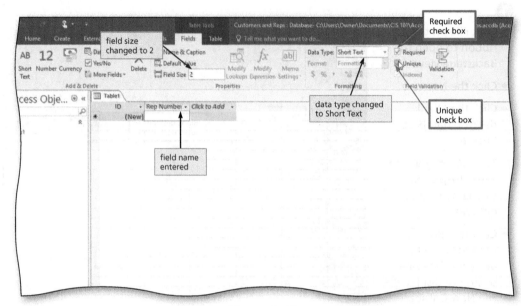

Figure 9–40

• Click the Required check box (Table Tools Fields tab | Field Validation group) to make the field a required field.

• Click the Unique check box (Table Tools Fields tab | Field Validation group) so that Access will ensure that values in the field are unique (Figure 9–40).

2

• Click under the 'Click to Add' column heading to produce an insertion point in the next field.

• Click the More Fields button (Table Tools Fields tab | Add & Delete group) to display the More Fields menu (Figure 9–41).

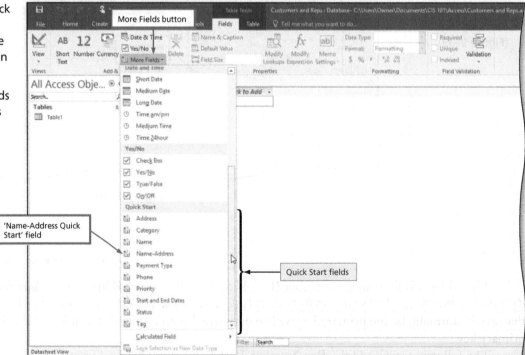

Figure 9–41

- Scroll as necessary to display the Name-Address Quick Start field you created earlier and then click the Name-Address Quick Start field to add the Last Name, First Name, Street, City, State, and Postal Code fields (Figure 9–42).

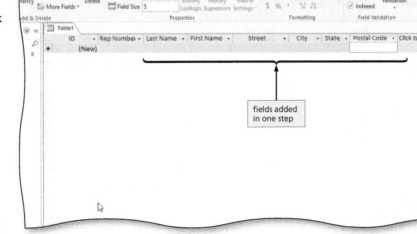

fields added in one step

Figure 9–42

- Add the Rate and Commission fields as the last two fields. The Rate field has the Number data type and the Commission field has the Currency data type.

- Save the table, assigning **Rep** as the table name.

- Switch to Design view, select the Rate field, and change the field size to Single so that the Rate field can include decimal places.

- Save and close the table.

To Create a Second Table

1 CONVERT DATABASE | 2 ANALYZE & DOCUMENT | 3 NAVIGATION PANE | 4 PROPERTIES & INDEXES
5 DATA PART | 6 TEMPLATE | **7 ENCRYPT LOCK & SPLIT** | 8 WEB APP | 9 CUSTOM VIEW

The following steps create the Customer table. The steps add a lookup field for Rep Number to relate the two tables. **Why?** *Because the tables will be used in a web app, the relationship between the tables needs to be implemented using a lookup field.*

- Display the Create tab (Figure 9–43).

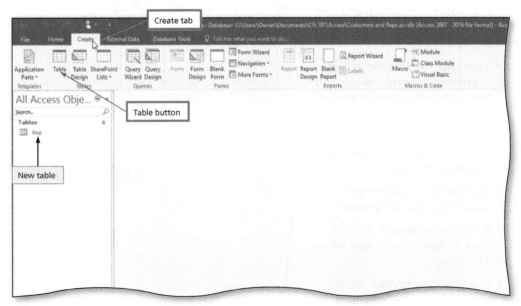

Figure 9–43

- Click the Table button (Create tab | Tables group) to create a new table.

- Click the 'Click to Add' column heading and select Short Text as the data type.

- Type **Customer Number** as the field name.

- Click the white space below the field name to complete the change of the name. Click the white space a second time to select the field.

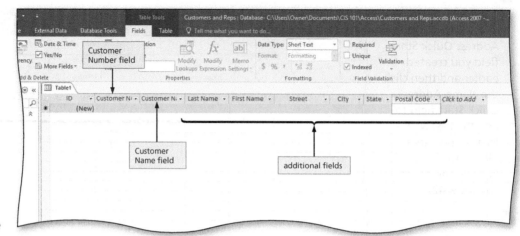

Figure 9–44

- Change the field size to 5.

- Click the Required check box (Table Tools Fields tab | Field Validation group) to make the field a required field.

- Click the Unique check box (Table Tools Fields tab | Field Validation group) so that Access will ensure that values in the field are unique.

- In a similar fashion, add the Customer Name field and change the field size to 30. Do not check the Required or Unique check boxes.

- Click under the 'Click to Add' column heading to produce an insertion point in the next field.

- Click the More Fields button (Table Tools Fields tab | Add & Delete group) to display the More Fields menu (see Figure 9–41).

- Click the Name-Address Quick Start field that you added earlier to add the Last Name, First Name, Street, City, State, and Postal Code fields (Figure 9–44).

- Right-click the Last Name field to produce a shortcut menu, and then click Delete Field to delete the field.

- Right-click the First Name field to produce a shortcut menu, and then click Delete Field to delete the field.

- Add the Amount Paid and Current Due fields. Both fields have the Currency data type.

- Save the table, assigning Customer as the table name.

- Scroll, if necessary, so that the 'Click to Add' column appears on your screen.

- Click the 'Click to Add' column heading to display a menu of available data types (Figure 9–45).

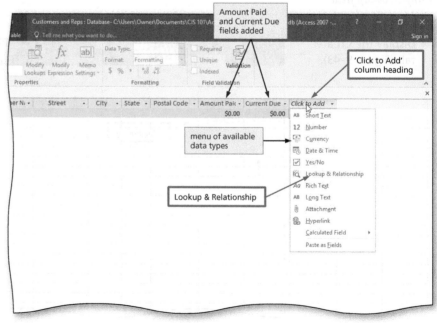

Figure 9–45

4
- Click Lookup &
  Relationship to
  display the Lookup
  Wizard dialog box
  (Figure 9–46).

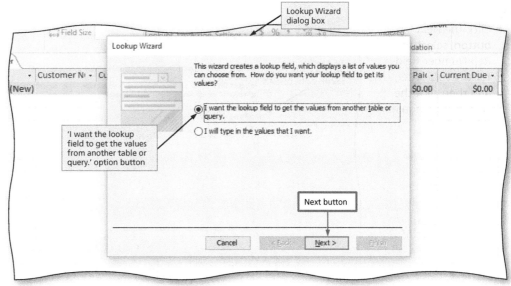

Figure 9–46

5
- Click the Next
  button to display
  the next Lookup
  Wizard screen, and
  then click the Rep
  table to select it so
  that you can add
  a lookup field for
  the Rep Number to
  the Customer table
  (Figure 9–47).

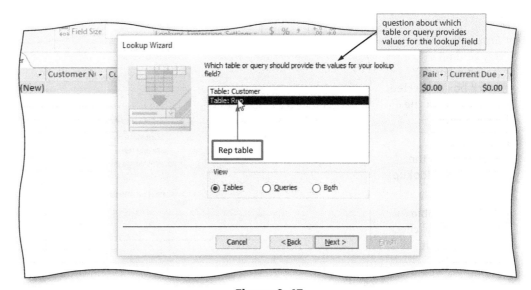

Figure 9–47

6
- Click the Next
  button, and then
  select the Rep
  Number, First Name,
  and Last Name fields
  for the columns in
  the lookup field
  (Figure 9–48).

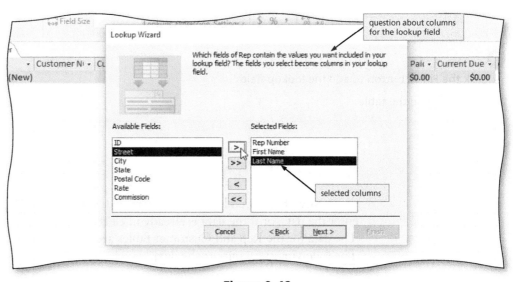

Figure 9–48

- Click the Next button, select the Rep Number field for the sort order, and then click the Next button again. (Figure 9–49).

I see the ID field listed when I am selecting the Rep Number field for the sort order. Did I do something wrong?
No. Access automatically included the ID field.

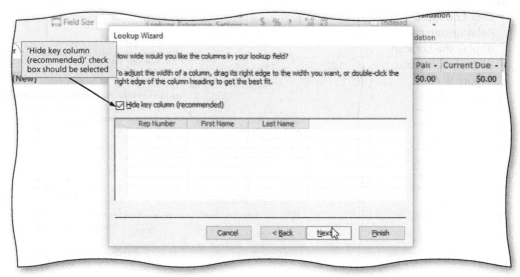

Figure 9–49

- Ensure the 'Hide key column (recommended)' check box is selected, and then click the Next button.

- Type **Rep Number** as the label for the lookup field.

- Click the 'Enable Data Integrity' check box to select it (Figure 9–50).

What is the effect of selecting Enable Data Integrity?
Access will enforce referential integrity for the Rep Number. That is, Access will not allow a rep number in a customer record that does not match the number of a rep in the Rep table.

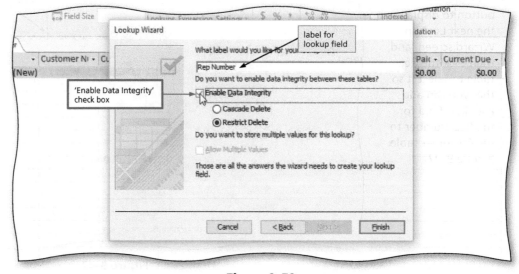

Figure 9–50

- Click the Finish button to add the lookup field.

- Save and close the table.

To Import the Data

Now that the tables have been created, you need to add data to them. You could enter the data, or if the data is already in electronic form, you could import the data. The data for the Rep and Customer tables are included in the Data Files as text files. The following steps import the data.

1. With the Customers and Reps database open, display the External Data tab, and then click the Text File button (External Data tab | Import & Link group) to display the Get External Data - Text File dialog box.

2. Click the Browse button (Get External Data - Text File dialog box) and select the location of the files to be imported (for example, the Access folder in the CIS 101 folder).

3. Select the Rep text file and then click the Open button.

4. Select the 'Append a copy of records to the table' option button, select the Rep table, and then click the OK button.

5. Be sure the Delimited option button is selected, and then click the Next button.

6. Be sure the Comma option button is selected, click the Next button, and then click the Finish button.

7. Click the Close button to close the Get External Data - Text File dialog box without saving the import steps.

8. Use the technique shown in Steps 1 through 7 to import the Customer text file into the Customer table.

To Create a Query Relating the Tables

The following steps create a query that relates the Customer and Rep tables.

1. Display the Create tab and then click the Query Design button (Create tab | Queries group) to create a new query.

2. Click the Customer table, click the Add button, click the Rep table, click the Add button, and then click the Close button to close the Show Table dialog box.

3. Double-click the Customer Number, Customer Name, and Rep Number fields from the Customer table. Double-click the First Name and Last Name fields from the Rep table to add the fields to the design grid.

4. Click the Save button on the Quick Access Toolbar to save the query, type `Customer-Rep Query` as the name of the query, and then click the OK button.

5. Close the query.

Creating Forms

There are several types of forms that need to be created for this database. The Customer and Rep detail forms show a single record at a time. The Customer, Rep, and Customer-Rep Query forms are intended to look like the corresponding table or query in Datasheet view. Finally, the main menu is a navigation form.

To Create Single-Item Forms

The following steps create two single-item forms, that is, forms that display a single record at a time. The first form, called Customer Details, is for the Customer table. The second form is for the Rep table and is called Rep Details.

1 Select the Customer table in the Navigation Pane and then display the Create tab.

2 Click the Form button (Create tab | Forms group) to create a single-item form for the Customer table.

3 Click the Save button on the Quick Access Toolbar and then type `Customer Details` as the name of the form, click the OK button (Save As dialog box) to save the form, and then close the form.

4 Select the Rep table, display the Create tab, and then click the Form button (Create tab | Forms group) to create a single-item form for the Rep table.

5 Save the form, using `Rep Details` as the form name.

6 Close the form.

To Create Datasheet Forms

1 CONVERT DATABASE | 2 ANALYZE & DOCUMENT | 3 NAVIGATION PANE | 4 PROPERTIES & INDEXES
5 DATA PART | 6 TEMPLATE | **7 ENCRYPT LOCK & SPLIT** | 8 WEB APP | 9 CUSTOM VIEW

The following steps create two datasheet forms, that is, forms that display the data in the form of a datasheet. *Why? These forms enable you to make it appear that you are displaying datasheets in a navigation form; recall that navigation forms can display only forms.* The first form is for the Customer table and is also called Customer. The second is for the Rep table and is also called Rep. The steps also create macros that will display the data for a selected record in a single-item form, as you did in Module 8.

- Select the Customer table and then display the Create tab.

- Click the More Forms button (Create tab | Forms group) to display the More Forms menu (Figure 9–51).

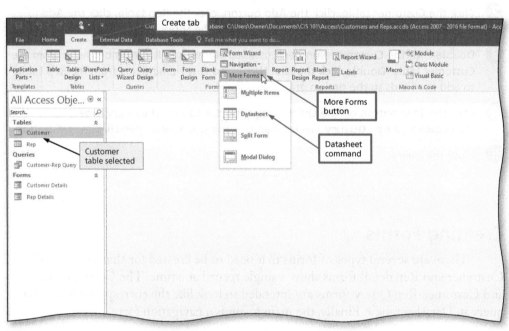

Figure 9–51

2

- Click Datasheet to create a datasheet form for the Customer table.

- Click the Save button on the Quick Access Toolbar and then accept Customer as the default name of the form.

- Click the column heading for the ID field to select the field.

- Display the property sheet and click the Event tab to display only the event properties (Figure 9–52).

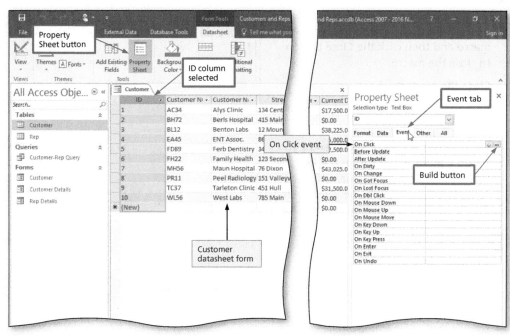

Figure 9–52

3

- Click the Build button (the three dots) for the On Click event, click the OK button (Choose Builder dialog box), and then use the techniques in the User Interface (UI) Macros section of Module 8 to enter the macro shown in Figure 9–53.

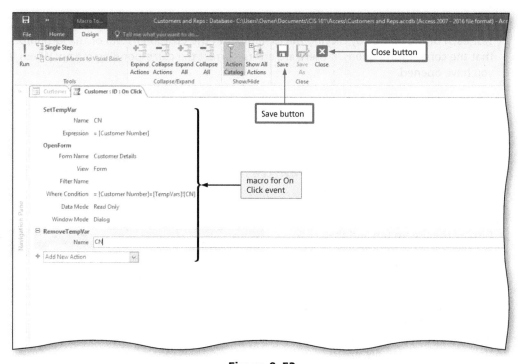

Figure 9–53

- Click the Save button (Macro Tools Design tab | Close group) to save the macro and then click the Close button to close the macro.

- Close the property sheet.

- Save the Customer datasheet form and then close the form.

- Use the techniques in Steps 1 and 2 to create a datasheet form for the Rep table. Use **Rep** as the name for the form. The macro for the On Click event for the ID field is shown in Figure 9–54.

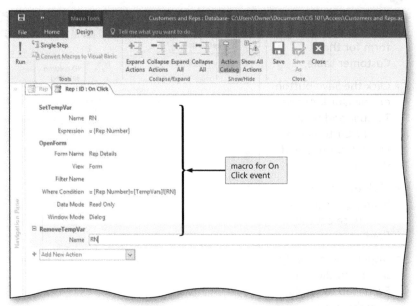

- Save and close the macro.

- Close the property sheet.

- Save and close the form.

- Select the Customer-Rep Query.

- Create a datasheet form for the Customer-Rep Query. Save the form, using **Customer-Rep Query** as the form name.

- Close the Customer-Rep Query form.

Figure 9–54

 Experiment

- Test each of the macros by clicking the ID number in the Customer form or the ID number in the Rep form. Ensure that the correct form opens. If there are errors, correct the corresponding macro. When finished, close any form you have opened.

To Create a Navigation Form

1 CONVERT DATABASE | 2 ANALYZE & DOCUMENT | 3 NAVIGATION PANE | 4 PROPERTIES & INDEXES
5 DATA PART | 6 TEMPLATE | 7 ENCRYPT LOCK & SPLIT | 8 WEB APP | 9 CUSTOM VIEW

The following steps create a navigation form containing a single row of horizontal tabs. The steps save the form using the name, Main Menu. **Why?** *This form is intended to function as a menu.* The steps change the form title and add the appropriate tabs.

1

- Display the Create tab and then click the Navigation button (Create tab | Forms group) to show the menu of available navigation forms.

- Click Horizontal Tabs in the menu to create a form with a navigation control in which the tabs are arranged in a single row, horizontally.

- If a field list appears, click the 'Add Existing Fields' button (Form Layout Tools Design tab | Tools group) to remove the field list.

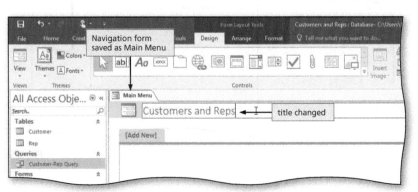

Figure 9–55

- Save the navigation form, using Main Menu as the form name.

- Click the form title twice, once to select it and the second time to produce an insertion point.

- Erase the current title and then type **Customers and Reps** as the new title (Figure 9–55).

- One at a time, drag the Customer form, the Rep form, the Customer-Rep Query form, the Customer Details form, and the Rep Details form to the positions shown in Figure 9–56.

- Save and close the form.

Q&A

What should I do if I made a mistake and added a form to the wrong location? You can rearrange the tabs by dragging. However, the simplest way to correct a mistake is to click the Undo button to reverse your most recent action. You can also choose to simply close the form without saving it and then start over.

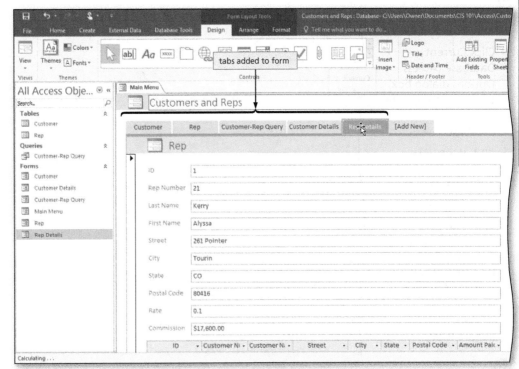

Figure 9–56

To Select a Startup Form

1 CONVERT DATABASE | 2 ANALYZE & DOCUMENT | 3 NAVIGATION PANE | 4 PROPERTIES & INDEXES
5 DATA PART | 6 TEMPLATE | **7 ENCRYPT LOCK & SPLIT** | 8 WEB APP | 9 CUSTOM VIEW

If the database includes a navigation form, it is common to select the navigation form as a **startup form,** which launches when the user opens the database. *Why? Designating the navigation form as a startup form ensures that the form will appear automatically when a user opens the database.* The following steps designate the navigation form as a startup form.

- Click File on the ribbon to display the Backstage view (Figure 9–57).

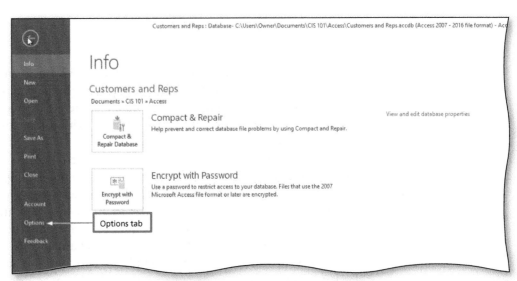

Figure 9–57

2

- Click the Options tab.

- Click Current Database (Access Options dialog box) to select the options for the current database.

- Click the Display Form arrow to display the list of available forms.

- Click Main Menu to select it as the form that will be automatically displayed whenever the database is opened (Figure 9–58).

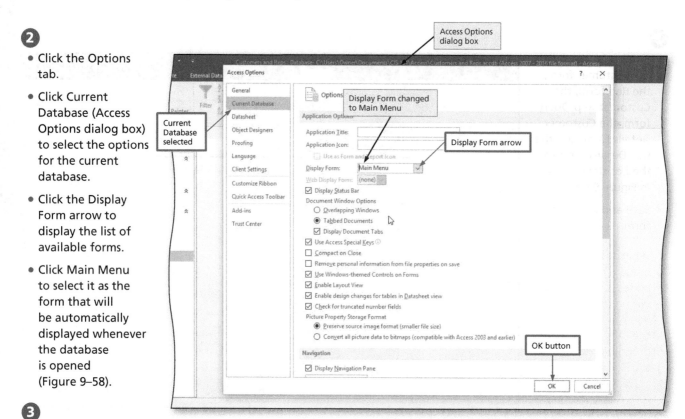

Figure 9–58

3

- Click the OK button (Access Options dialog box) to save your changes.

- Click the OK button (Microsoft Access dialog box) when Access displays a message indicating that you must close and reopen the database for the change to take effect.

- Close the database.

Break Point: If you wish to stop working through the module at this point, you can close Access now. You can resume the project at a later time by running Access, and continuing to follow the steps from this location forward.

Templates

An Access **template** is a file that contains the elements needed to produce a specific type of complete database. You can select a template when you create a database. The resulting database will contain all the tables, queries, forms, reports, and/or macros included in the template. In addition, with some templates, the resulting database might also contain data.

Some templates are also available as **application parts**. Application parts are very similar to templates in that selecting a single application part can create tables, queries, forms, reports, and macros. The difference is you select a template when you first create a database, whereas you select an application part after you have already created a database. The objects (tables, queries, forms, reports, and macros) in the application part will be added to any objects you have already created.

Access provides a number of templates representing a variety of types of databases. You can also create your own template from an existing database. When you create a template, you can choose to create an application part as well. When creating templates and application parts, you can also include data if desired.

To Create a Template and Application Part

The following steps create a template from the Customers and Reps database. *Why? The Customers and Reps database now contains all the tables, queries, and forms you want in the template. You will then be able to use the template when you want to create similar databases.* The steps also create an application part from the database so that you can reuse the parts in other databases.

1
- Open the Customers and Reps database and enable the content (Figure 9–59).

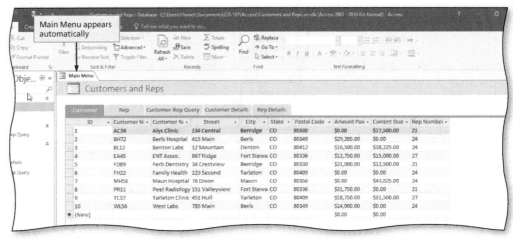

Figure 9–59

2
- Close the Main Menu form.
- Open the Backstage view.
- Click the Save As tab.
- Click the Template button in the Save Database As area to indicate you are creating a template (Figure 9–60).

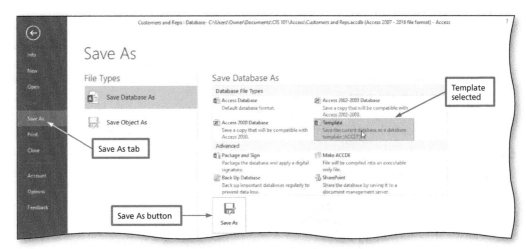

Figure 9–60

3
- Click the Save As button to display the Create New Template from This Database dialog box.
- Type **Customers and Reps** as the name for the new template.
- Type **Database of customers and reps with navigation form menu.** as the description.
- Click the Application Part check box to indicate that you also want to create an application part.

- Click the 'Include All Data in Package' check box to indicate you want to include the data in the database as part of the template (Figure 9–61).

Why include data?

Anytime a user creates a database using the template, the database will automatically include data. This enables the users to see what any reports, forms, or queries look like with data in them. Once the users have the reports, forms, and queries the way they want them, they can delete all this data. At that point, they can begin adding their own data to the database.

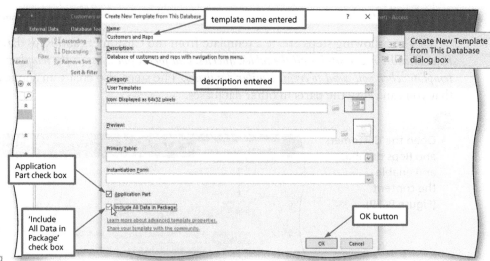

Figure 9–61

4

- Click the OK button (Create New Template from This Database dialog box) to create the template.
- When Access indicates that the template has been successfully saved, click the OK button (Microsoft Access dialog box).

To Use the Template

1 CONVERT DATABASE | 2 ANALYZE & DOCUMENT | 3 NAVIGATION PANE | 4 PROPERTIES & INDEXES
5 DATA PART | 6 TEMPLATE | **7 ENCRYPT LOCK & SPLIT** | 8 WEB APP | 9 CUSTOM VIEW

You can use the Customers and Reps template just as you would use any other template, such as the Blank database template you previously used. The only difference is that, after clicking the New tab in the Backstage view, you need to click the PERSONAL link. **Why?** *The PERSONAL link displays any templates you created and lets you select the template you want.*

The following steps use the template created earlier to create the PJP Customers database. Later in the module, you will learn how to use this database to import tables to a web app.

1

- Click File on the ribbon to open the Backstage view, if necessary.
- Click the New tab (Figure 9–62).

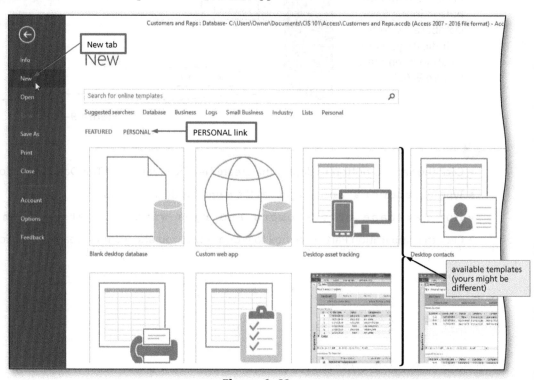

Figure 9–62

- Click the PERSONAL link to display the templates you have created (Figure 9–63).

Figure 9–63

- Click the 'Customers and Reps' template that you created earlier.

- Type **PJP Customers** as the name of the database and then navigate to the location where you will store the new database (for example, the Access folder in the CIS 101 folder).

- Click the Create button to create the database from the template.

- Close the database.

- If desired, sign out of your Microsoft account.

- Exit Access.

Note: Unless your instructor indicates otherwise, you are strongly encouraged to simply read the material in this module from this point on without carrying out any operations. If you decide to try it for yourself, it is important to make a backup copy of your database and store it in a secure location before performing the operation. That way, if something damages your database or you can no longer access your database, you still can use the backup copy. In addition, for the material on web apps, you must have access to a SharePoint site.

Using an Application Part

To use the application part you created, you first need to create a database. After doing so, you click the Application Parts button (Create tab | Templates group) to display the Application Parts menu (Figure 9–64).

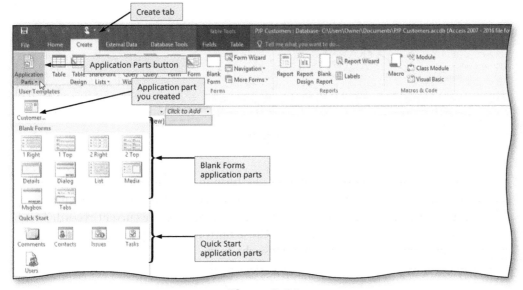

Figure 9–64

You can then click the application part you created, which will be located in the User Templates section of the Application Parts menu. If you have any open objects, Access will indicate that "all open objects must be closed before instantiating this application part" and ask if you want Access to close all open objects. After you click the Yes button, Access will add all the objects in the Application part to the database. If you had already created other objects in the database, they would still be included.

TO USE THE APPLICATION PART

Specifically, to use the application part created earlier, you would use the following steps.

1. Create or open the database in which you want to use the application part.
2. Display the Create tab and then click the Application Parts button (Create tab | Templates group).
3. Click the application part to be added.
4. If Access indicates that open objects must be closed, click the Yes button.

Blank Forms Application Parts

Blank Forms application parts (see Figure 9–64) represent a way to create certain types of forms. To do so, you click the Application Parts button to display the gallery of application part styles, and then click the desired type of form, for example, 1 Right. Access then creates a form with the desired characteristics and assigns it a name. It does not open the form, but you can see the form in the Navigation Pane (Figure 9–65).

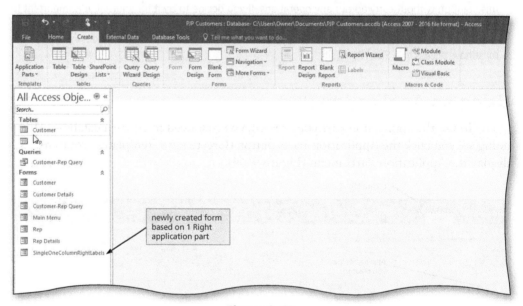

Figure 9–65

You can modify the form by opening the form in Layout or Design view (Figure 9–66). This particular form automatically creates a Save button. Clicking this button when you are using the form will save changes to the current record. The form also automatically includes a Save & Close button. Clicking this button will save changes to the current record and then close the form.

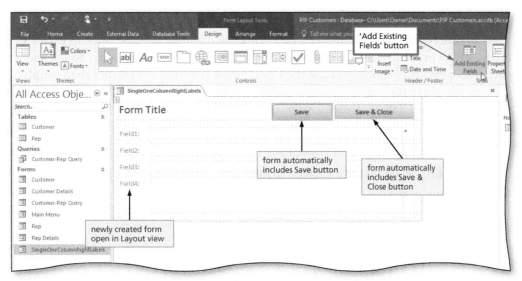

Figure 9–66

To add the specific fields you want to the form, display a field list. You can then drag a field onto the form while holding down the CTRL key (Figure 9–67). Once you have added the field, you can change the corresponding label by clicking the label to select it, clicking the label a second time to produce an insertion point, and then making the desired change.

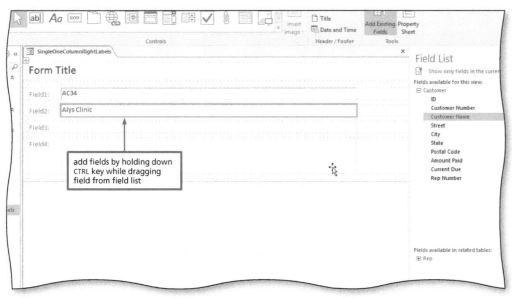

Figure 9–67

Encrypting a Database

Encrypting refers to the storing of data in the database in an encoded, or encrypted, format. Anytime a user stores or modifies data in the encrypted database, the database management system (DBMS) will encode the data before actually updating the database. Before a legitimate user retrieves the data using the DBMS, the data will be decoded. The whole encrypting process is transparent to a legitimate user; that is, he or she is not even aware it is happening. If an unauthorized user attempts to bypass all the controls of the DBMS and get to the database through a utility program or a word processor, however, he or she will only be able to see the encoded, and unreadable, version of the data. In Access, you encrypt a database and set a password as part of the same operation.

BTW

Encryption and Passwords
Encryption helps prevent unauthorized use of an Access database. Consider using encryption when the database contains sensitive data, such as medical records or employee records. Passwords should be eight or more characters in length. The longer the length of the password and the more random the characters, the more difficult it is for someone to determine. Use a combination of uppercase and lowercase letters as well as numbers and special symbols when you create a password. Make sure that you remember your password. If you forget it, there is no method for retrieving it. You will be unable to open the encrypted database.

To Open a Database in Exclusive Mode

To encrypt a database and set a password, the database must be open in exclusive mode, which prevents other users from accessing the database in any way. To open a database in exclusive mode, you use the Open arrow (Figure 9–68) rather than simply clicking the Open button.

To open a database in exclusive mode, you would use the following steps.

1. If necessary, close any open databases.
2. Click Open or click 'Open Other Files' in Backstage view to display the Open screen.
3. Click Browse on the Open screen to display the Open dialog box.
4. Navigate to the location of the database to be opened.
5. Click the name of the database to be opened.
6. Click the Open arrow to display the Open button menu.
7. Click Open Exclusive to open the database in exclusive mode.

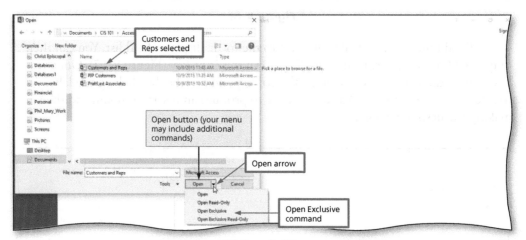

Figure 9–68

CONSIDER THIS

What is the purpose of the other modes?
The Open option opens the database in a mode so that it can be shared by other users. Open Read-Only allows you to read the data in the database, but not update the database.

Encrypting a Database with a Password

If you wanted to encrypt the database with a password, you would open the Backstage view (Figure 9–69).

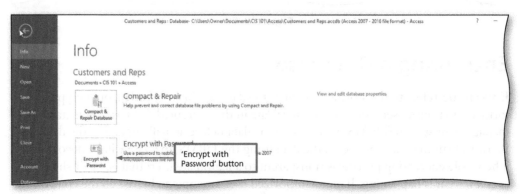

Figure 9–69

You would then select 'Encrypt with Password' and enter the password you have chosen in both the Password text box and Verify text box (Figure 9–70).

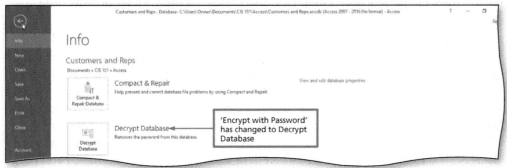

Figure 9–70

TO ENCRYPT A DATABASE WITH A PASSWORD

With the database open in exclusive mode, you would use the following steps to encrypt the database with a password.

1. Click File on the ribbon to open the Backstage view and ensure the Info tab is selected.
2. Click the 'Encrypt with Password' button to display the Set Database Password dialog box.
3. Type the desired password in the Password text box in the Set Database Password dialog box.
4. Press the TAB key and then type the password again in the Verify text box.
5. Click the OK button to encrypt the database and set the password.
6. If you get a message indicating that row level locking will be ignored, click the OK button.
7. Close the database.

Is the password case sensitive?
Yes, you must enter the password using the same case you used when you created it.

Opening a Database with a Password

When you open a database that has a password, you will be prompted to enter your password in the Password Required dialog box. Once you have done so, click the OK button. Assuming you have entered your password correctly, Access will then open the database.

Decrypting a Database and Removing a Password

If the encryption and the password are no longer necessary, you can decrypt the database. The database will no longer have a password. If you later found you needed the database to be encrypted, you could repeat the steps to encrypt the database and add a password. The button to encrypt a database with a password has changed to Decrypt Database (Figure 9–71).

Figure 9–71

TO DECRYPT THE DATABASE AND REMOVE THE PASSWORD

To decrypt a database that you have previously encrypted and remove the password, you would use the following steps.

1. Open the database to be decrypted in exclusive mode, entering your password when requested.
2. Open the Backstage view and ensure the Info tab is selected.
3. Click the Decrypt Database button to display the Unset Database Password dialog box.
4. Type the password in the Password dialog box.
5. Click the OK button to remove the password and decrypt the database.
6. Close the database.

The Trust Center

BTW
Security
Security is the prevention of unauthorized access to a database. Within an organization, the database administrator determines the types of access individual users can have to the database. Various government rules and regulations, such as the Sarbannes-Oxley Act (SOX) and the Health Insurance Portability and Accountability Act (HIPPA), require database administrators to have strict security procedures in place to protect data from unauthorized users.

The Trust Center is a feature within Access where you can set security options and also find the latest information on technology related to privacy, safety, and security. To use the Trust Center, you click File on the ribbon and then click the Options tab to display the Access Options dialog box. You then click Trust Center to display the Trust Center content (Figure 9–72). You would then click the 'Trust Center Settings' button to display the Trust Center dialog box in which you can make changes in the following categories.

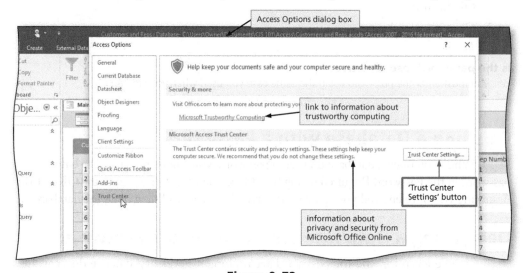

Figure 9–72

Trusted Publishers. Clicking Trusted Publishers in the Trust Center dialog box shows the list of trusted software publishers. To view details about a trusted publisher, click the publisher and then click the View button. To remove a trusted publisher from the list, click the publisher and then click the Remove button. Users may also add trusted publishers.

Trusted Locations. Clicking Trusted Locations shows the list of trusted locations on the Internet or within a user's network. To add a new location, click the 'Add new location' button. To remove or modify an existing location, click the location and then click the Remove or Modify button.

Trusted Documents. You can designate certain documents, including database, Word, Excel, and other files, as trusted. When opening a trusted document, you will not be prompted to enable the content, even if the content of the document has changed. You should be very careful when designating a document as trusted and only do so when you are absolutely sure the document is from a trusted source.

Add-ins. Add-ins are additional programs that you can install and use within Access. Some come with Access and are typically installed using the Access Setup program. Others can be purchased from other vendors. Clicking Add-ins gives you the opportunity to specify restrictions concerning Add-ins.

ActiveX Settings. When you use ActiveX controls within an Office app, Office prompts you to accept the controls. The ActiveX settings allow you to determine the level of prompting from Office.

Macro Settings. Macros written by other users have the potential to harm your computer; for example, a macro could spread a virus. The Trust Center uses special criteria, including valid digital signatures, reputable certificates, and trusted publishers, to determine whether a macro is safe. If the Trust Center discovers a macro that is potentially unsafe, it will take appropriate action. The action the Trust Center takes depends on the Macro Setting you have selected. Clicking Macro Settings enables you to select or change this setting.

Message Bar. Clicking Message Bar lets you choose whether the message bar should appear when content has been blocked.

Privacy Options. Clicking Privacy Options lets you set security settings to protect your personal privacy.

Trusted Add-in Catalogs. Use this option to specify trusted catalogs of web add-ins. You can also indicate whether Access will allow web add-ins to start.

BTW
Active X controls
Active X controls are small programs that can run within an Office app. The calendar control is an example of an Active X control.

Locking a Database

By **locking** a database, you can prevent users from viewing or modifying VBA code in your database or from making changes to the design of forms or reports while still allowing them to update records. When you lock the database, Access changes the file name extension from .accdb to .accde. To do so, you would use the Make ACCDE command shown in Figure 9–3.

BTW
Locked Databases
When you create a locked database, the original database remains unchanged and is still available for use.

TO CREATE A LOCKED DATABASE (ACCDE FILE)

To lock a database, you would use the following steps.

1. With the database open, click File on the ribbon to open the Backstage view.
2. Click the Save As tab.
3. Click Make ACCDE in the Advanced area.
4. Click the Save As button.
5. In the Save As dialog box, indicate a location and name for the ACCDE file.
6. Click the Save button in the Save As dialog box to create the file.

Using the Locked Database

You would use an ACCDE file just as you use the databases with which you are now familiar, with two exceptions. First, you must select ACCDE files in the 'Files of type' box when opening the file. Second, you will not be able to modify any source code or change the design of any forms or reports. If you right-clicked the Customer form, for example, you would find that the Design View command on the shortcut menu is dimmed, as are many other commands (Figure 9–73).

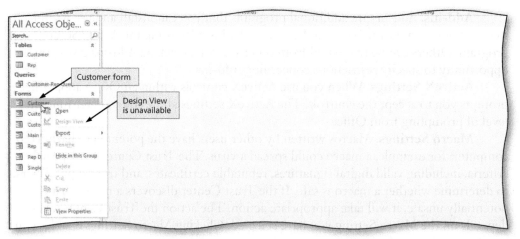

Figure 9–73

It is very important that you save your original database in case you ever need to make changes to VBA code or to the design of a form or report. You cannot use the ACCDE file to make such changes, nor can you convert the ACCDE file back to the ACCDB file format.

Record Locking

You can indicate how records are to be locked when multiple users are using a database at the same time. To do so, click File on the ribbon, click the Options tab, and then click Client Settings. Scroll down so that the Advanced area appears on the screen (Figure 9–74).

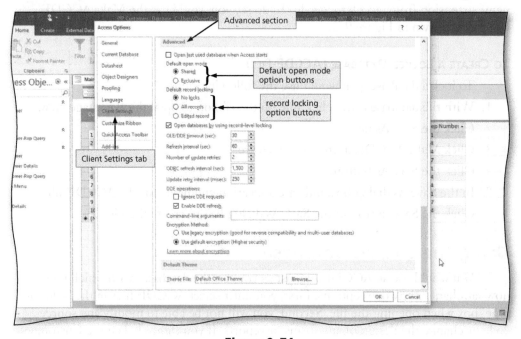

Figure 9–74

If you wanted the default open mode to be exclusive (only one user can use the database at a time) rather than shared (multiple users can simultaneously use the database), you could click the Exclusive option button. You can also select the approach you want for record locking by clicking the appropriate record locking option button. The possible approaches to record locking are shown in Table 9–3.

Table 9–3 Record Locking Approaches	
Locking Type	**Description**
No locks	When you edit a record, Access will not lock the record. Thus, other users also could edit the same record at the same time. When you have finished your changes and attempt to save the record, Access will give you the option of overwriting the other user's changes (not recommended), copying your changes to the clipboard, or canceling your changes.
All records	All records will be locked as long as you have the database open. No other user can edit or lock the records during this time.
Edited record	When you edit a record, Access will lock the record. When other users attempt to edit the same record, they will not be able to do so. Instead, they will see the locked record indicator.

Database Splitting

You can **split** a database into two databases, one called the **back-end database** containing only the table data, and another database called the **front-end database** containing the other objects. Only a single copy of the back-end database can exist, but each user could have his or her own copy of the front-end database. Each user would create the desired custom reports, forms, and other objects in his or her own front-end database, thereby not interfering with any other user.

When splitting a database, the database to be split must be open. In the process, you will identify a name and location for the back-end database that will be created by the Access splitter. In the process, you would display the Database Splitter dialog box (Figure 9–75).

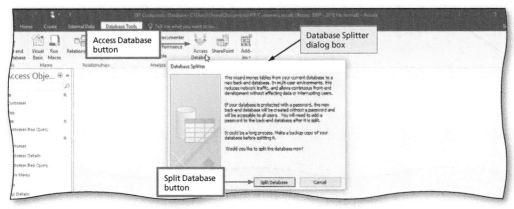

Figure 9–75

You would also have to select a location for the back-end database (Figure 9–76). Access assigns a name to the back-end database that ends with an underscore and the letters, be. You can override this name if you prefer.

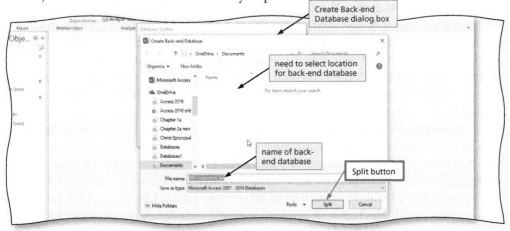

Figure 9–76

TO SPLIT THE DATABASE

To split a database, you would use the following steps.

1. Open the database to be split.
2. Display the Database Tools tab.
3. Click the Access Database button (Database Tools tab | Move Data group) to display the Database Splitter dialog box.
4. Click the Split Database button to display the Create Back-end Database dialog box.
5. Either accept the file name Access suggests or change it to the one you want.
6. Select a location for the back-end database.
7. Click the Split button to split the database.
8. Click the OK button to close the dialog box reporting that the split was successful.

The Front-End and Back-End Databases

The database has now been split into separate front-end and back-end databases. The front-end database is the one that you will use; it contains all the queries, reports, forms, and other components from the original database. The front-end database only contains links to the tables, however, instead of the tables themselves (Figure 9–77). The back-end database contains the actual tables but does not contain any other objects.

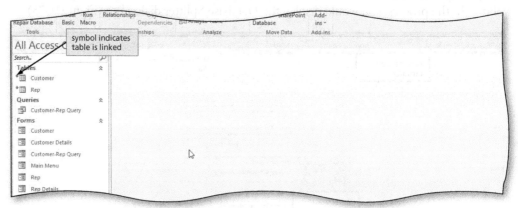

Figure 9–77

Web Apps

A **web app** is a database that you use in a web browser. You do not need to have Access installed to use the web app. You design and modify the web app using Access 2016, but users do not need Access 2016 to use the web app. To create or use a web app, you need a SharePoint server to host the web app. There are three typical ways of getting access to a SharePoint server. If your company has a SharePoint server using the full version of SharePoint, you could use that. You could also purchase an Office 365 subscription plan that includes SharePoint. Finally, you could get SharePoint 2016 hosting from some other company.

Access provides a specific interface for creating web apps. When you create web apps, Access restricts some of the available database features. Tables in web apps must have AutoNumber fields as the primary key. Relationships between tables must be accomplished through lookup fields. Web apps viewed in a browser consist solely of a collection of related tables and various views of those tables. List view, which is similar to Form view, and Datasheet view are automatically included. You can define additional summary views that group data on selected fields.

Creating Web Apps

You can create custom web apps, in which you will indicate the specific tables and fields you want to include. Alternatively, you can select one of the web app templates. In either case, you must enter a name for your app as well as a web location for the app (Figure 9–78).

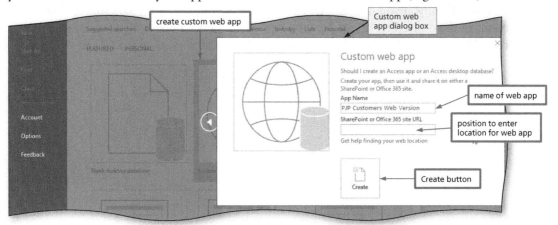

Figure 9–78

TO CREATE A WEB APP

To create a web app, you would use the following steps.

1. In Backstage view, on the New tab, click either 'Custom web app' to create a web app of your own design or one of the web app templates to create a web app matching the template.

2. Enter a descriptive name for the web app.

3. If you see a list of available locations for the web app, you can select one of the locations. If not, or if none of the available locations is appropriate, enter the URL that points to your SharePoint site.

4. Click the Create button to create the web app.

5. If requested, enter the User ID and password for your SharePoint site and click the Sign In button to finish creating the web app on your SharePoint site.

Figure 9–79 shows the result of creating a custom web app called PJP Customers Web Version.

BTW
SharePoint 2016
SharePoint offers users the ability to store data on the web so that access to that data can be shared across a network. It is essentially a storage location that can be accessed collaboratively. No special software is required on the customer side. SharePoint 2016 allows users to share calendars, blogs, wikis, surveys, document libraries, and task lists.

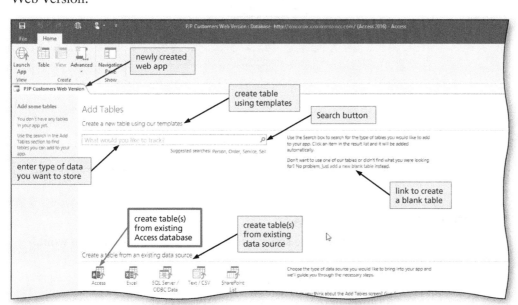

Figure 9–79

Creating Tables for the Web App

BTW

Distributing a Document

Instead of printing and distributing a hard copy of a document, you can distribute the document electronically. Options include sending the document via email; posting it on cloud storage (such as OneDrive) and sharing the file with others; posting it on a social networking site, blog, or other website; and sharing a link associated with an online location of the document. You also can create and share a PDF or XPS image of the document, so that users can view the file in Acrobat Reader or XPS Viewer instead of in Access.

There are three ways of creating the tables for the web app. First, you can use a template, in which case Access will determine the fields to be included in the table. Alternatively, you can create a blank table and then enter the fields and data types yourself. Finally, if you have an Access database or other existing data source that contains the desired tables, such as the PJP Customers database, you can import the data. In importing the data, you would need to identify the name and location of the file that contains the desired data (Figure 9–80).

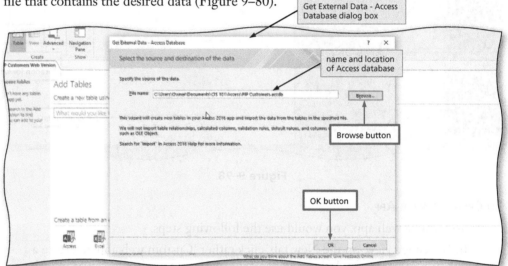

Figure 9–80

After identifying the file containing the tables, you would be presented with a list of tables in that file (Figure 9–81). You could select individual tables in the list or select all the tables by clicking the Select All button. Once you have made your selection, you would click the OK button to import the data.

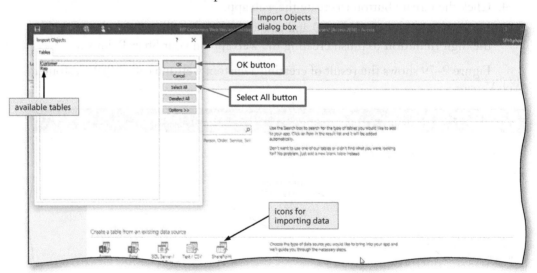

Figure 9–81

To Create Tables by Importing Data

To import data from an existing source such as an Access database, you would use the following steps.

1. Click the icon for the type of data to import.
2. Browse to the location of the data to import and select the file to import.
3. Click the OK button.

4. Select the tables to import. If you want to import all the tables in the data source, click the Select All button.

5. Click the OK button to import the data.

TO CREATE TABLES FROM TEMPLATES

Access provides templates to assist in the creation of tables. To create a table for a web app from a template, you would use the following steps.

1. Enter the type of object for which you will be storing data and click the Search button.

2. When Access presents a list of options, click the option that best fits your needs.

TO CREATE BLANK TABLES

You can create a blank table for the web app and then enter the names, data types, and other characteristics of the fields in Design view just as you have created other tables. To create a blank table, you would use the following step.

1. Click the 'add a new blank table' link to create the table and display the table in Design view.

CONSIDER THIS

The Rate field has a special field size, Single, which is necessary to display decimal places. If you create the Rep table as a blank table in a web app, do you still have the option to change the field size to Single?
Not exactly. The possible field sizes for Number fields are slightly different when you create a web app than when you create a desktop database. The possibilities are Whole Number (no decimal places), Fixed-point number (6 decimal places), and Floating-point number (variable decimal places). If you import a table from a desktop database in which you have set the field size to Single, Access will automatically assign the field the Floating-point number field size, which is appropriate.

Using Views

Figure 9–82 shows the web app with the two tables created during the import process. The Customer table is currently selected. The web app offers two views, List view and Datasheet view. List view, in which the data appears as a form, is currently selected. Figure 9–82 shows the appearance of the view, not the actual data. You will see the data when you run the app.

To make changes to the way the table appears in List view, you would click the floating Edit button, which appears in the middle of the list.

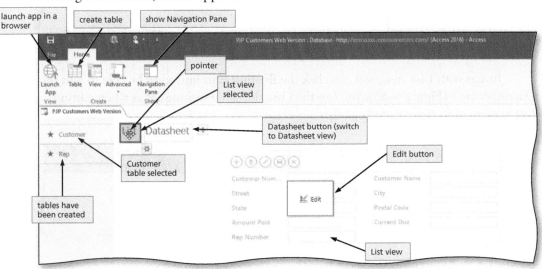

Figure 9–82

If you click the Edit button, you will be able to edit the view (Figure 9–83). Editing the view allows you to change the appearance of the view, not the underlying data. The process is similar to modifying the layout of a form in either Layout or Design view. You can display a field list as shown in the figure by clicking the 'Add Existing Fields' button. You can add a field by dragging it from the field list into the desired location in the view. You can delete an existing field from the view by clicking the field, and then pressing the DELETE key. You can move fields within the list by dragging them to the desired location. You can also click a field and then click the Formatting button to display the FORMATTING menu. Using that menu, you can display a tooltip for the field, choose whether the field is visible, or choose whether the field is enabled.

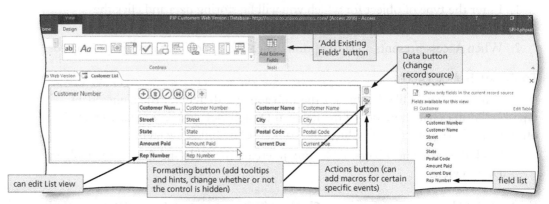

Figure 9–83

Clicking the Datasheet view button for the same table displays the Datasheet view, which is similar to the normal Datasheet view you see when working with a desktop database (Figure 9–84).

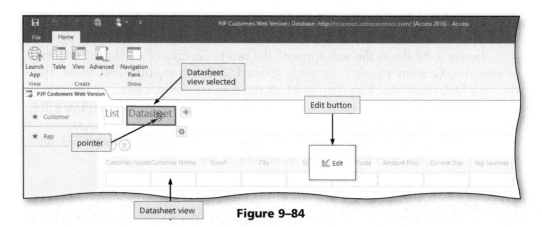

Figure 9–84

Just as with List view, you can click the floating Edit button to be able to edit the Datasheet view (Figure 9–85). You can then use the same techniques as when editing List view to make any desired changes.

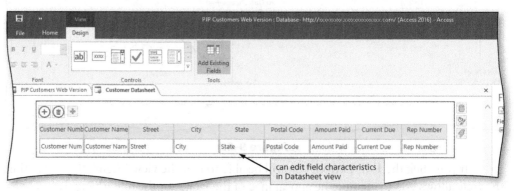

Figure 9–85

To Edit Views

To edit a view, you would use the following steps.

1. Click the table whose view you want to edit.

2. Click the view to edit.

3. Click the Edit button.

4. When finished editing, click the Close button for the view you are editing.

5. Click the Yes button to save your changes. Click the No button if you do not want to save your changes.

Viewing Data

When you later run the web app, you will see the actual data in the database. You can view the data in either List or Datasheet view or you can make changes to the data, which are immediately available to other users.

You can also view the data in a typical Access format. To do so, select the table you want to view and click the Settings/Action button, or right-click the table, to display the Settings/Action menu (Figure 9–86).

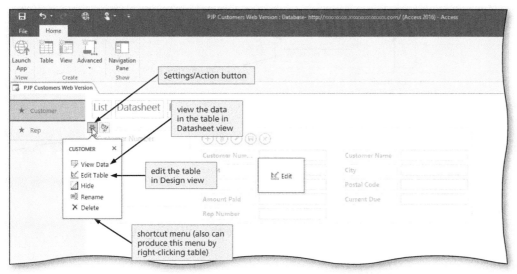

Figure 9–86

If you click View Data on the Settings/Action menu, you will see the data in Datasheet view. You can both view and change the data.

You can also modify the design of a table using the Settings/Action button. To do so, you would click Edit Table rather than View Data. You would then see the table displayed in Design view. You can make changes to the table design similar to how you have updated other tables in Design view.

What is the purpose of the other commands on the Settings/Action menu?

If you select Hide, the selected table will not appear when you run the app. If you hide a table, you can later select Unhide, in which case it will once again appear. You can rename a table by selecting Rename and delete the table by selecting Delete.

Creating an Additional View

You can create additional views that are then included in the app. To do so, click the 'Add New View' button (Figure 9–87) to display the ADD NEW VIEW dialog box. You also can click the View button (Home tab | Create group) to display the dialog box. Figure 9–87 also shows the list of available view types. The available types are List Details (List view), Datasheet, Summary, and Blank. You have already seen List and Datasheet views. You will see how to create a Summary view later in this module. A Blank view allows you to create a view from scratch, similar to using a blank form.

In the ADD NEW VIEW dialog box, you enter a name for the view, select the View Type, and then select the record source. The record source can be either a table or a query.

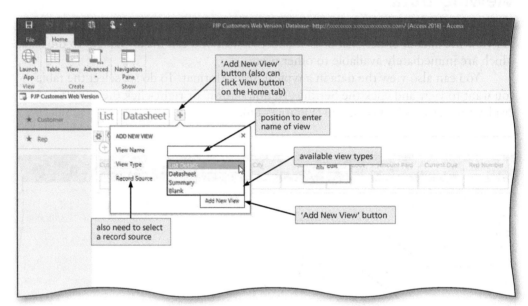

Figure 9–87

TO CREATE AN ADDITIONAL VIEW

To create an additional view, you would use the following steps.

1. Click the 'Add New View' button.
2. Enter a name for the view.
3. Click the View Type arrow to display the menu of available view types.
4. Click the desired view type.
5. Click the Record Source arrow to display a list of the available tables and queries.
6. Click the desired table or query.
7. Click the 'Add New View' button to create the new view.

CONSIDER THIS

How can you delete a view you do not want?

Click the view to select the view. Click the Settings/Action button that will appear near the view to display a shortcut menu. Click Delete on the shortcut menu. Click the OK button to confirm the deletion.

Creating Additional Objects

You can create tables by clicking the Table button (Home tab | Create group). You will then see the same Add Tables screen you saw earlier in Figure 9–79. You then have the same three options for creating tables: You can create the table using a template, create a blank table, or import a table from an existing data source.

You can create other objects, such as queries, by clicking the Advanced button (Home tab | Create group) to produce the Advanced menu (Figure 9–88). The Advanced menu gives you options for creating queries, blank views, blank List views, blank Datasheet views, and various types of macros.

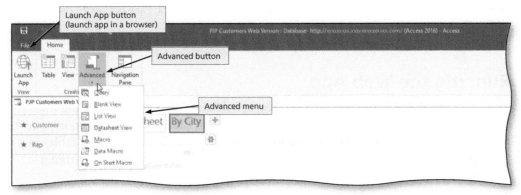

Figure 9–88

To use any of the blank views, you can place fields in the view by dragging the field from a field list, just as you have done in previous modules with forms and reports. Creating macros uses the same process you have seen earlier. However, creating macros in the web app does limit some of the available options for macros. Creating a query in the web app is also similar to the process you used to create queries earlier; the design grid used in the web app is similar to that used in Access (Figure 9–89). As with macros, creating queries in the web app limits some of the options, but the options that are present function in the manner you would expect. Once you have created a query, you can then use it as the record source for a view.

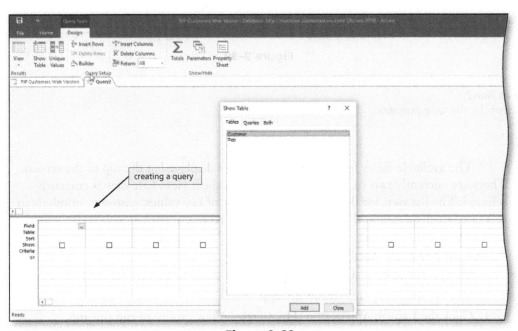

Figure 9–89

TO CREATE ADDITIONAL OBJECTS

To create an additional object, you would use the following steps.

1. To create a table, click the Table button (Home tab | Create group), and then indicate whether you will create the table using a template, create a blank table, or import a table from an existing data source.

2. To create another type of object, click the Advanced button (Home tab | Create group) to display the Advanced menu, and then select the type of object to create.

How can you see the additional objects you have created?
You can only see them in the Navigation Pane. To display the Navigation Pane, click the Navigation Pane button (Home tab | Show group).

Running the Web App

You run the web app in a browser. You can do so from Access by clicking the Launch App button (Home tab | View group). You will then see the web app in your browser (Figure 9–90). On the left side of the screen, you will see the list of tables in the app. At any time, one of the tables will be selected. In the figure, the Customer table is currently selected.

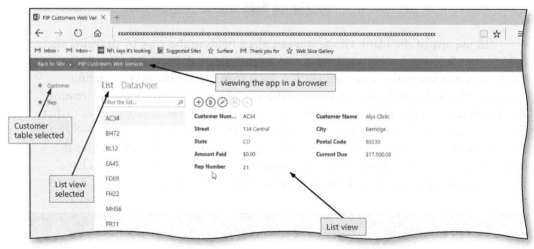

Figure 9–90

Is Launch the same as Run?
Yes. They are different words for the same operation.

The available views for the selected table are displayed at the top of the screen. There are currently two views, List view and Datasheet view. List view is currently selected. The list view for the table as well as a list of key values, customer numbers in this case, are displayed in the center area of the screen.

TO RUN AN APP FROM ACCESS

To run an app from Access, the app must be open in Access. Assuming it is, you would use the following step to run the app.

1. Click the Launch App button (Home tab | View group) to run the app.

To display a table in Datasheet view, first be sure the desired table is selected. Next, click the Datasheet link. The table will appear in Datasheet view (Figure 9–91).

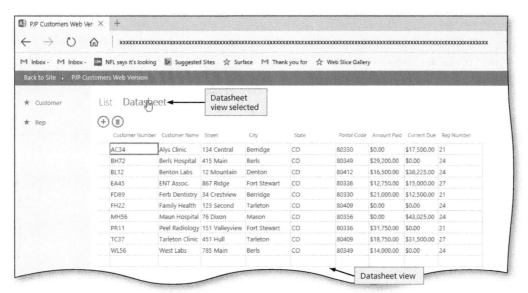

Figure 9–91

If you click the List link, the table will again appear in List view (Figure 9–92). Click one of the customer numbers on the left to display the data for that customer. You can update the data for the customer currently on the screen, add a new customer, or delete a customer. To do so, click the button for the desired action. If you click the Add button, the form will be blank and you can type the data for the new customer. If you click the Delete button, you will be asked to confirm the deletion. If you do, the customer currently on the screen will be deleted.

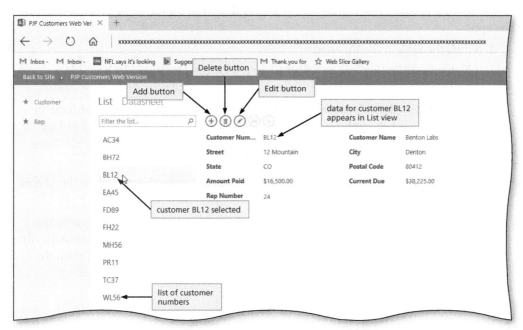

Figure 9–92

If you click the Edit button, the buttons change slightly (Figure 9–93). The Add, Delete, and Edit buttons are dimmed, whereas the Save and Cancel buttons are not. After making a change, such as the change of the state as shown in the figure, you can click the Save button to save the change or the Cancel button to cancel the change.

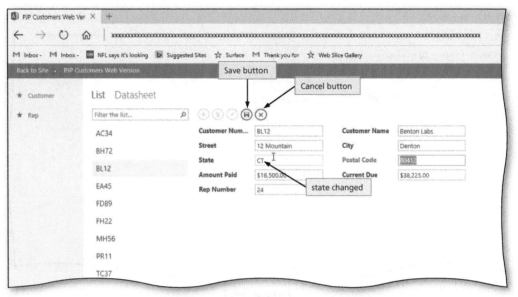

Figure 9–93

You can also update data in Datasheet view. To add a record, click the Add button and type the contents of the new record. To delete a record, click anywhere in the record, click the Delete button, and then confirm the deletion. To edit a record, click in the field to be changed and make the desired change.

TO UPDATE DATA USING A WEB APP

To update data using a web app, you would use the following steps after running the app.

1. Click the table to be updated.
2. Click either the List link to select List view or the Datasheet link to select Datasheet view.
3. To add a record in Datasheet view, click the Add button, enter the contents of the record, and press the TAB key after entering the final field. To add in List view, click the Add button, enter the contents of the record, and click the Save button.
4. To delete a record in either view, select the record to be deleted, click the Delete button, and then confirm the deletion.
5. To edit a record in Datasheet view, click the field to be changed and make the necessary change. As soon as you leave the record, the change will automatically be saved. To edit a record in List view, select the record to be edited, click the Edit button, make the change, and then click the Save button.

Showing a Relationship in List View

If you view the "one" table in a one-to-many relationship in List view, you will see the corresponding records in the "many" table appear in a datasheet. Figure 9–94 shows the Rep table appearing in List view. The data for the selected rep appears in List view. The customers of the selected rep appear in a datasheet just below the data for the rep. Note that this is the only way to see the relationship. Viewing the "one" table in Datasheet view will not show the relationship, nor will viewing the "many" table in either view.

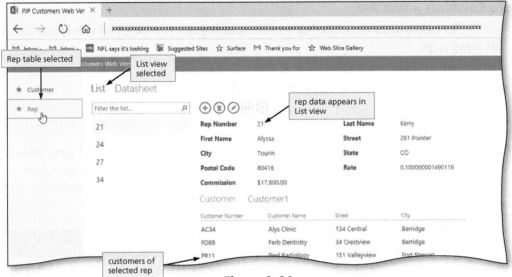

Figure 9–94

Running a Web App from a Browser

To run a web app, you navigate to your SharePoint site and simply run the app. You do not have to run Access, open the app, and then run the app. It is not even necessary to have Access on your computer. You can run the app directly from your browser.

TO RUN A WEB APP FROM A BROWSER

To run a web app from a browser, you would use the following steps.

1. Type the URL for your SharePoint site and press the ENTER key.
2. When requested, type your user name and password.
3. Click the OK button to display the contents of your SharePoint site.
4. Click the desired web app to run the app.

Customizing a Web App

You can customize a web app from within Access. If you are running the app in a browser, you launch Access by clicking the Settings button and then clicking the 'Customize in Access' command (Figure 9–95).

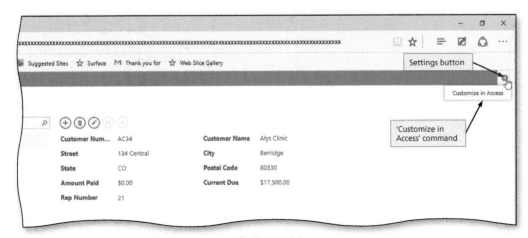

Figure 9–95

To Customize a Web App

To customize a web app that you are running in a browser, you would use the following steps.

1. Click the Settings button.
2. Click the 'Customize in Access' command.

Adding a Summary View

One of the ways you can customize a web app is to add an additional view, such as a Summary view. After selecting the table for which you want to add the view, you would use the 'Add New View' button to select Summary as the view type and then select the record source table (Figure 9–96).

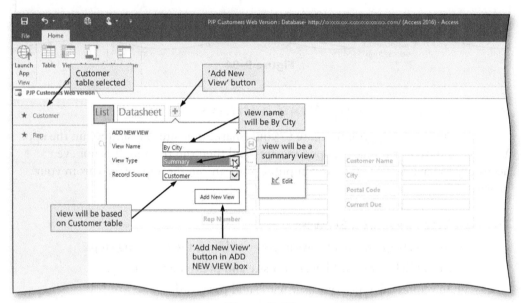

Figure 9–96

Clicking the 'Add New View' button in the ADD NEW VIEW dialog box creates the view. You can edit the view using the EDIT button. Then, you can use the Data button to display the DATA box, where you indicate a Group By field, Sort Order, Calculation Field, and Calculation Type (Figure 9–97).

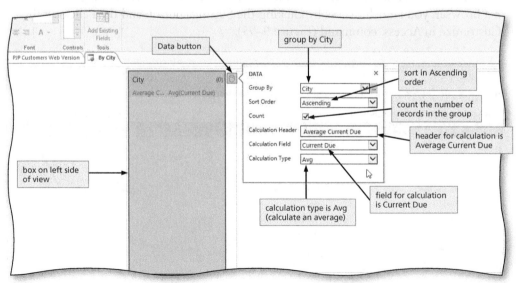

Figure 9–97

By clicking the box on the right and then clicking the Data button, you can enter up to four fields to be displayed and optionally display captions for the fields. Specifying the popup view determines the view that will appear as a popup when the user clicks a specific record and will give additional information about that record. The final step is to enter the sort order (Figure 9–98).

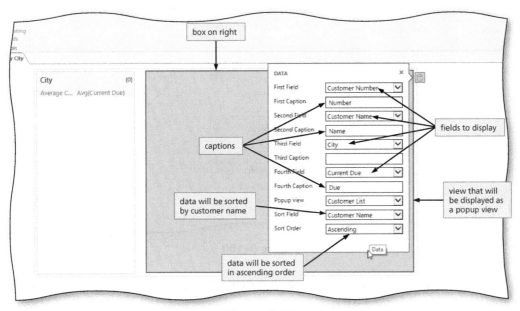

Figure 9–98

After closing the view and saving the changes, you can run the app by clicking the Launch App button, being sure the appropriate table is selected. You click the new view to test the view, and then close the view (Figure 9–99).

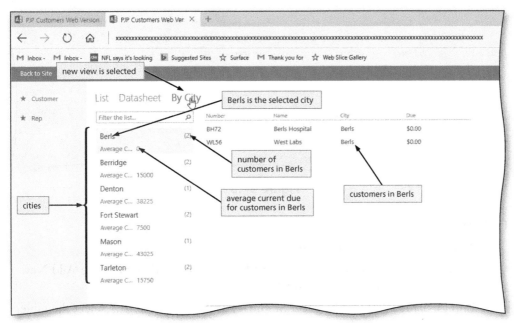

Figure 9–99

If you select another value in the left-hand column, all the corresponding records will now appear in the right-hand column (Figure 9–100).

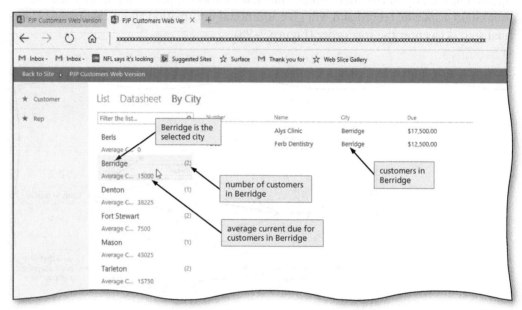

Figure 9–100

Select one of the records in the group to display details concerning that record in a popup view (Figure 9–101).

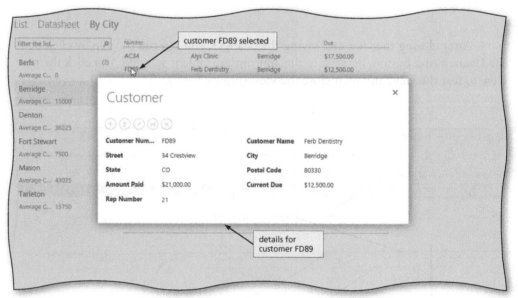

Figure 9–101

To Create a Summary View

To create a Summary view, you would use the following steps.

1. Click the table for which you want to add the view and then click the 'Add New View' button to display the ADD NEW VIEW box.
2. Enter a name for the view, select Summary as the view type, and select the table that will be the record source.

3. Click the 'Add New View' button (ADD NEW VIEW dialog box) to create the view.

4. Click the Edit button to edit the view.

5. Click the box on the left side of the view and then click the Data button to display the DATA box.

6. Enter the Group By field, sort order, whether you want a count displayed, the header for the calculation, the field for the calculation, and the calculation type (average or sum).

7. Close the DATA box, click the box on the right, and then click its Data button.

8. Enter up to four fields to be displayed. You can optionally enter captions for any of the fields.

9. Enter the popup view.

10. Enter the sort order.

11. Close the view and click the Yes button when asked if you want to save your changes.

Summary

In this module you have learned to convert Access databases to and from earlier versions; use Microsoft Access tools to analyze and document an Access database; add custom categories and groups to the Navigation Pane; use table and database properties; use field properties to create a custom input mask; allow zero-length strings; create indexes; use automatic error checking; create custom data parts; create and use templates and application parts; encrypt a database and set a password; understand the Trust Center; lock a database; split a database; create and run a web app; and customize a web app.

CONSIDER THIS: PLAN AHEAD

What decisions will you need to make when administering your own databases?

Use these guidelines as you complete the assignments in this module and administer your own databases outside of this class.

1. Determine whether a database needs to be shared over the web.

   a. Do you have users who would profit from being able to access a database over the web? If so, you will need to create a web app, which requires you to have access to a SharePoint server.

   b. Determine the tables that should be in the web app.

   c. Determine the views of the tables that should be included in the web app.

2. Determine whether you should create any templates, application parts, or data type parts.

   a. Is there a particular combination of tables, queries, forms, reports, and/or macros that you would like to enable users to easily include in their databases? If so, you could create a template and an application part containing the specific objects you want them to be able to include.

   b. Is there a particular collection of fields that you would like to enable users to include in a table with a single click? If so, you could create a data type part containing those fields.

3. Determine whether a database needs to be converted to or from an earlier version.

   a. Do users of a previous version of Access need to be able to use the database? If so, you will need to be sure the database does not contain any features that would prevent it from being converted.

   b. Do you use a database that was created in an earlier version of Access that you would like to use in Access 2016? If so, you can convert the database for use in Access 2016.

4. Determine when to analyze and/or document the database.

   a. Once you create a database, you should use the table and performance analyzers to determine if any changes to the structure are warranted.

   b. You should also document the database.

5. Determine the most useful way to customize the Navigation Pane.

    a. Would it be helpful to have custom categories and groups?

    b. What objects should be in the groups?

    c. Would it be helpful to restrict the objects that appear to only those whose names contain certain characters?

6. Determine any table-wide validation rules.

    a. Are there any validation rules that involve more than a single field?

7. Determine any custom database properties.

    a. Are there properties that would be helpful in documenting the database that are not included in the list of database properties you can use?

8. Determine indexes.

    a. Examine retrieval and sorting requirements to determine possible indexes. Indexes can make both retrieval and sorting more efficient.

9. Determine whether the database should be encrypted.

    a. If you need to protect the security of the database's contents, you should strongly consider encryption.

    b. As part of the process, you will also set a password.

10. Determine whether the database should be locked.

    a. Should users be able to change the design of forms, reports, and/or macros?

11. Determine whether the database should be split.

    a. It is often more efficient to split the database into a back-end database, which contains only the table data, and a front-end database, which contains other objects, such as queries, forms, and reports.

CONSIDER THIS

How should you submit solutions to questions in the assignments identified with a symbol?

Every assignment in this book contains one or more questions identified with a symbol. These questions require you to think beyond the assigned database. Present your solutions to the questions in the format required by your instructor. Possible formats may include one or more of these options: write the answer; create a document that contains the answer; present your answer to the class; discuss your answer in a group; record the answer as audio or video using a webcam, smartphone, or portable media player; or post answers on a blog, wiki, or website.

Apply Your Knowledge

Reinforce the skills and apply the concepts you learned in this module.

Administering the AllAround Services Database

Instructions: Run Access. Open the Apply AllAround Services database that you modified in Module 8. (If you did not complete the exercise, see your instructor for a copy of the modified database.)

Perform the following tasks:

1. Open the Client table in Design view and create an index that allows duplicates on the Client Name field. Zero-length strings should not be allowed in the Client Name field.

2. Create a custom input mask for the Client Number field. The first two characters of the client number must be uppercase letters and the last two characters must be numerical digits.

3. Create an index on the combination of Client Type and Amount Paid. Name the index TypePaid.

4. Save the changes to the Client table.

5. Use the Database Documenter to produce detailed documentation for the Services table. Export the documentation to a Word RTF file. Change the name of the file to LastName _Documentation.rtf where LastName is your last name.

6. Use the Table Analyzer to analyze the table structure of the Client table. Open the Word RTF file that you created in Step 5 and make a note of the results of the analysis at the end of the file.

7. Use the Performance Analyzer to analyze all the tables in the database. Describe the results of your analysis in your RTF file.

8. Populate the Status property for the database with the value Apply AllAround Services.

9. If requested to do so by your instructor, populate the Status property with your first and last name.

10. Create a custom property with the name, Due Date. Use Date as the type and enter the current date as the value.

11. Submit the revised Apply AllAround Services database and the RTF file in the format specified by your instructor.

12. ✸ Can you convert the Apply AllAround Services database to an Access 2002–2003 database? Why or why not?

Extend Your Knowledge

Extend the skills you learned in this module and experiment with new skills. You may need to use Help to complete the assignment.

Note: To complete this assignment, you will be required to use the Data Files. Please contact your instructor for information about accessing the Data Files.

Instructions: Run Access. Open the Extend Paws for a Cause database. The Extend Paws for a Cause database contains information about a thrift store that raises money for a local animal shelter.

Perform the following tasks:
1. Change the Current Database options to ensure that the Main Menu opens automatically.

2. Currently, when you open the Items table in Datasheet view, the table is ordered by Item Number. Change the property for the table so the table is in order by Description.

3. Customize the Navigation Pane by adding a custom category called Thrift Store. Then add two custom groups, Regular and Reduced, to the Thrift Store category.

4. Add the Item Master Form and Available Items Report to the Regular group. Add the Item Sale Report, the Reduced Price Report, and the Seller and Items Query to the Reduced group.

5. Add the Address Quick Start field to the Seller table. Move the Phone Number field so that it follows the Country Region field. Save the changes to the table.

6. If requested to do so by your instructor, add a table description to the Seller table that includes your first and last name.

7. Submit the revised database in the format specified by your instructor.

8. ✸ What advantages are there to listing items by Description rather than by Item Number?

Expand Your World

Create a solution which uses cloud and web technologies by learning and investigating on your own from general guidance.

Problem: There are many ways to share an Access database. Some ways require each user to have Microsoft Access installed on their computer, while others do not. The method you select depends on factors such as need and available resources.

Instructions: Perform the following tasks:
1. Create a blog, a Google document, or a Word document on OneDrive on which to store your findings.
2. Use the web to research different ways to share an Access database such as PrattLast Associates with others. Be sure to note any specific resources needed, such as an Access database or a SharePoint server, any costs involved, and provide examples of different reasons for sharing a database such as PrattLast Associates. Record your findings in your blog, Google document, or Word document, being sure to appropriately reference your sources.
3. Submit the assignment in the format specified by your instructor.
4. ✺ Based on your research, what method would you choose to share your Access databases?

In the Labs

Design, create, modify, and/or use a database following the guidelines, concepts, and skills presented in this module. Labs are listed in order of increasing difficulty. Labs 1 and 2, which increase in difficulty, require you to create solutions based on what you learned in the module; Lab 3 requires you to apply your creative thinking and problem solving skills to design and implement a solution.

Lab 1: **Administering the Gardening Supply Database**

Problem: Gardening Supply has determined a number of database administration tasks that need to be done. These include creating indexes and custom input masks, adding table and database properties, creating a template, and splitting a database.

Instructions: Perform the following tasks:
1. Run Access and open the Lab 1 Gardening Supply database that you modified in Module 8. (If you did not complete the exercise, see your instructor for a copy of the modified database.)
2. Open the Open Orders table in Datasheet view and add the Quick Start Priority field to the end of the table. In Datasheet view, use a filter to assign the value Normal to all records where the Amount is less than $400.00. Assign the value High to all other orders.
3. Open the Customer table in Design view and create custom input masks for the following fields: Customer Number, State, Postal Code, and Sales Rep Number. The Customer Number field should consist of two uppercase letters followed by two numbers. The State field should contain two uppercase letters. Both the Postal Code and Sales Rep Number fields can only contain numbers.
4. Create an index on the Customer Name field that allows duplicates.
5. Change the options to ensure that the Main Menu form is displayed automatically when a user opens the database.

6. Save the Lab 1 Gardening Supply database as a template with data but not as an application part. Name the template Lab 1 Gardening Supply Template. You do not need a description. Create a new database from the Lab 1 Gardening Supply template. Name the database Lab 1 Gardening Supply New. Split the Lab 1 Gardening Supply New database.

7. If requested to do so by your instructor, open the front-end database, open the Forms List in Layout view, and add a title with your first and last name.

8. Submit the revised databases in the format specified by your instructor.

9. ✺ In this exercise, you split a database into a front-end and a back-end. Why would you split a database?

Lab 2: **Administering the Discover Science Database**

Problem: Discover Science has determined a number of database administration tasks that need to be done. These include creating indexes and custom input masks, adding table and database properties, and creating a locked database.

Instructions: Perform the following tasks:

1. Run Access and open the Lab 2 Discover Science database that you modified in Module 8. (If you did not complete the exercise, see your instructor for a copy of the modified database.)

2. Open the Item table in Design view and add a validation rule that ensures that the wholesale cost is always less than the retail price of an item. Include validation text.

3. Create an index on the combination of item type and description. Name the index TypeDesc.

4. Do not allow zero-length strings for the Description field.

5. Create custom input masks for the Item Number and the Vendor Code fields.

6. Save the changes to the table design.

7. In Datasheet view, add the Address Quick Start field to the Vendor table following the Vendor Name field. Delete the Attachments field.

8. If requested to do so by your instructor, change the Vendor Name for Vendor Code GS to your last name and change the phone to your phone number.

9. Rename the Main Menu form to Discover Science Menu.

10. Change the Current Database options to ensure that the Discover Science Menu opens automatically.

11. Create a locked database for the Lab 2 Discover Science database.

12. Submit the revised database and the locked database in the format specified by your instructor.

13. ✺ Why would you lock a database?

Lab 3: **Consider This: Your Turn**

Administering the Marketing Analytics Database

Part 1:   The management of the Marketing Analytics company has asked you to perform a number of administration tasks. Open the Lab 3 Marketing Analytics database that you modified in Module 8. (If you did not complete the exercise, see your instructor for a copy of the modified database.) Use the concepts and techniques presented in this module to perform each of the following tasks.

Continued >

In the Labs *continued*

a. Change the Current Database options to ensure that the Main Menu form opens automatically when the user opens the database.

b. Open the Client table in Design view and add custom input masks for the Client Number and Postal Code fields. Create an index for the Client Name field that allows duplicates. Do not allow zero-length strings for the Client Name field.

c. Open the Marketing Analyst table in Design view and create an index named LastFirst on the last name and the first name.

d. Open the Seminar Offerings table in Design view and create a validation rule to ensure that Hours Spent are less than or equal to Total Hours. Include validation text.

e. Open the Seminar Offerings table in Datasheet view and add the Quick Start Status field to the table. In Datasheet view, use a filter to assign the value, Not Started, to all offerings where the Hours Spent is 0. Assign the value, In Progress, to all other offerings.

f. Populate the Editor custom database property with your first and last name.

g. Use the 1 Right Blank Forms application part to create a form for the Seminar Offerings table. Include all fields except Status on the form. Change the title and the name of the form to Seminar Offerings.

Submit your assignment in the format specified by your instructor.

Part 2: You made several decisions while completing this project, including using an application part to create a form. What was the rationale behind your decisions? Would you use an application part to create another form? Why or why not?

Microsoft Access 2016

File   Home   Create   External Data   Database Tools   Tell me what you want to do...

PrattLast Associates : Database- C:\Users\Owner\Documents\CIS

10 | Using SQL

Objectives

You will have mastered the material in this module when you can:

- Understand the SQL language and how to use it
- Change the font or font size for queries
- Create SQL queries
- Include fields in SQL queries
- Include simple and compound criteria in SQL queries
- Use computed fields and built-in functions in SQL queries
- Sort the results in SQL queries
- Use aggregate functions in SQL queries
- Group the results in SQL queries
- Join tables in SQL queries
- Use subqueries
- Compare SQL queries with Access-generated SQL
- Use INSERT, UPDATE, and DELETE queries to update a database

Introduction

The language called **SQL (Structured Query Language)** is a very important language for querying and updating databases. It is the closest thing to a universal database language, because the vast majority of database management systems, including Access, use it in some fashion. Although some users will be able to do all their queries through the query features of Access without ever using SQL, those in charge of administering and maintaining the database system should be familiar with this important language. You can also use Access as an interface to other database management systems, such as SQL Server. Using or interfacing with SQL Server requires knowledge of SQL. Virtually every DBMS supports SQL.

Project — Using SQL

PrattLast Associates wants to be able to use the extended data management capabilities available through SQL. As part of becoming familiar with SQL, PrattLast would like to create a wide variety of SQL queries.

Similar to creating queries in Design view, SQL provides a way of querying relational databases. In SQL, however, instead of making entries in the design grid, you type commands into SQL view to obtain the desired results, as shown in Figure 10–1a. You can then click the View button to view the results just as when you are creating queries in Design view. The results for the query in Figure 10–1a are shown in Figure 10–1b.

Figure 10–1 (a) Query in SQL

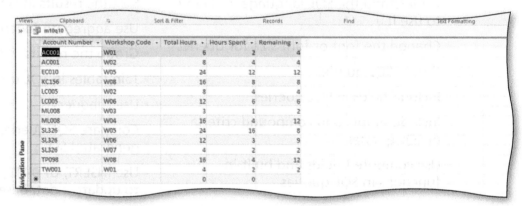

Figure 10–1 (b) Results

In this module, you will learn how to create and use SQL queries like the one shown in Figure 10–1. The following roadmap identifies general activities you will perform as you progress through this module:

1. Create a query in SQL VIEW
2. Use SIMPLE CRITERIA in a query
3. Use COMPOUND CRITERIA in a query
4. SORT RESULTS of a query
5. GROUP RESULTS of a query
6. JOIN TABLES in a query
7. USE a SUBQUERY in a query
8. UPDATE DATA with a query

SQL Background

In this module, you query and update a database using the language called **SQL (Structured Query Language)**. Similar to using the design grid in the Access Query window, SQL provides users with the capability of querying a relational database.

Microsoft Access 2016

File   Home   Create   External Data   Database Tools   Tell me what you want to do...

Prattl ast Associates : Database- C:\Users\Owner\Documents\CIS

Because SQL is a language, however, you must enter **commands** to obtain the desired results, rather than completing entries in the design grid. SQL uses commands to update tables and to retrieve data from tables. The commands that are used to retrieve data are usually called **queries**.

SQL was developed under the name SEQUEL at the IBM San Jose research facilities as the data manipulation language for IBM's prototype relational model DBMS, System R, in the mid-1970s. In 1980, it was renamed SQL to avoid confusion with an unrelated hardware product called SEQUEL. Most relational DBMSs, including Microsoft Access and Microsoft SQL Server, use a version of SQL as a data manipulation language.

Some people pronounce SQL by pronouncing the three letters, that is, "ess-que-ell." It is very common, however, to pronounce it as the name under which it was developed originally, that is, "sequel."

BTW
Enabling the Content
For each of the databases you use in this module, you will need to enable the content.

To Change the Font Size

1 SQL VIEW | 2 SIMPLE CRITERIA | 3 COMPOUND CRITERIA | 4 SORT RESULTS
5 GROUP RESULTS | 6 JOIN TABLES | 7 USE SUBQUERY | 8 UPDATE DATA

You can change the font and/or the font size for queries using the Options button in the Backstage view and then Object Designers in the list of options in the Access Options dialog box. There is not usually a compelling reason to change the font, unless there is a strong preference for some other font. It often is worthwhile to change the font size, however. *Why? With the default size of 8, the queries can be hard to read. Increasing the font size to 10 can make a big difference.* The following steps change the font size for queries to 10.

- Run Access and open the database named PrattLast Associates from your hard disk, OneDrive, or other storage location.

- Click File on the ribbon to open the Backstage view.

- Click Options to display the Access Options dialog box.

- Click Object Designers to display the Object Designer options.

- In the Query design area, click the Size box arrow, and then click 10 in the list to change the size to 10 (Figure 10–2).

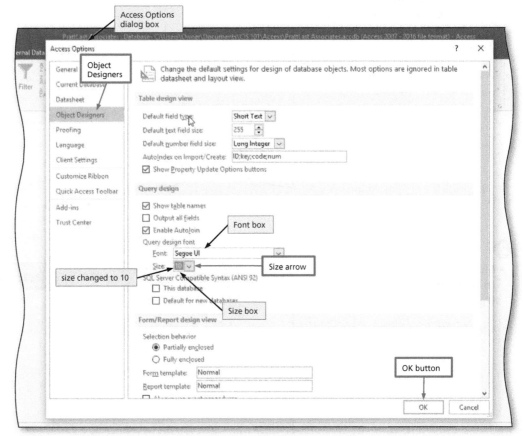

- Click the OK button to close the Access Options dialog box.

Figure 10–2

SQL Queries

When you query a database using SQL, you type commands in a blank window rather than filling in the design grid. When the command is complete, you can view your results just as you do with queries you create using the design grid.

To Create a New SQL Query

1 SQL VIEW | 2 SIMPLE CRITERIA | 3 COMPOUND CRITERIA | 4 SORT RESULTS
5 GROUP RESULTS | 6 JOIN TABLES | 7 USE SUBQUERY | 8 UPDATE DATA

You begin the creation of a new **SQL query**, which is a query expressed using the SQL language, just as you begin the creation of any other query in Access. The only difference is that you will use SQL view instead of Design view. *Why? SQL view enables you to type SQL commands rather than making entries in the design grid.* The following steps create a new SQL query.

- Close the Navigation Pane.
- Display the Create tab.
- Click the Query Design button (Create tab | Queries group) to create a query.
- Close the Show Table dialog box without adding any tables.
- Click the View button arrow (Query Tools Design tab | Results group) to display the View menu (Figure 10–3).

Q&A
Why did the icon on the View button change to SQL, and why are there only two items on the menu instead of the usual five?
Without any tables selected, you cannot view any results. You can only use the normal Design view or SQL view. The change in the icon indicates that you could simply click the button to transfer to SQL view.

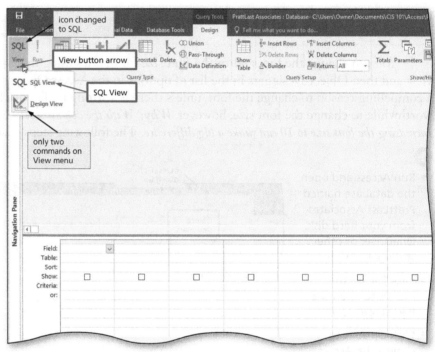

Figure 10–3

- Click SQL View on the View menu to view the query in SQL view (Figure 10–4).

Q&A
What happened to the design grid?
In SQL view, you specify the queries by typing SQL commands rather than making entries in the design grid.

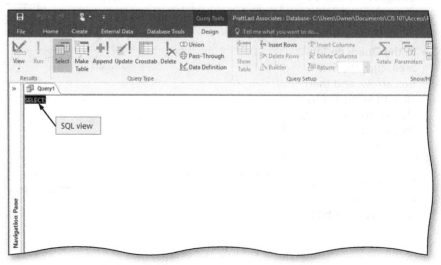

Figure 10–4

SQL Commands

The basic form of SQL expressions is quite simple: SELECT-FROM-WHERE. The command begins with a **SELECT clause**, which consists of the word, SELECT, followed by a list of those fields you want to include. The fields will appear in the results in the order in which they are listed in the expression. Next, the command contains a **FROM clause**, which consists of the word FROM followed by a list of the table or tables involved in the query. Finally, there is an optional **WHERE clause**, which consists of the word WHERE followed by any criteria that the data you want to retrieve must satisfy. The command ends with a semicolon (;), which in this text will appear on a separate line.

SQL has no special format rules for placement of terms, capitalization, and so on. One common style is to place the word FROM on a new line, and then place the word WHERE, when it is used, on the next line. This style makes the commands easier to read. It is also common to show words that are part of the SQL language in uppercase and others in a combination of uppercase and lowercase. This text formats SQL terms in uppercase letters. Because it is a common convention, and necessary in some versions of SQL, you will place a semicolon (;) at the end of each command.

Microsoft Access has its own version of SQL that, unlike some other versions of SQL, allows spaces within field names and table names. There is a restriction, however, to the way such names are used in SQL queries. When a name containing a space appears in SQL, it must be enclosed in square brackets. For example, Account Number must appear as [Account Number] because the name includes a space. On the other hand, City does not need to be enclosed in square brackets because its name does not include a space. For consistency, all names in this text are enclosed in square brackets. Thus, the City field would appear as [City] even though the brackets are not technically required by SQL.

BTW
Touch Screen Differences
The Office and Windows interfaces may vary if you are using a touch screen. For this reason, you might notice that the function or appearance of your touch screen differs slightly from this module's presentation.

BTW
Touch and Pointers
Remember that if you are using your finger on a touch screen, you will not see the pointer.

To Include Only Certain Fields

1 SQL VIEW | **2 SIMPLE CRITERIA** | **3 COMPOUND CRITERIA** | **4 SORT RESULTS**
5 GROUP RESULTS | **6 JOIN TABLES** | **7 USE SUBQUERY** | **8 UPDATE DATA**

To include only certain fields in a query, list them after the word, SELECT. If you want to list all rows in the table, you do not include the word, WHERE. **Why?** *If there is no WHERE clause, there is no criterion restricting which rows appear in the results. In that case, all rows will appear.* The following steps create a query for PrattLast Associates that will list the number, name, amount paid, and current due amount of all accounts.

1

- Type `SELECT [Account Number],[Account Name],[Amount Paid],[Current Due]` as the first line of the command, and then press the ENTER key.

Q&A What is the purpose of the SELECT clause?
The SELECT clause indicates the fields that are to be included in the query results. This SELECT clause, for example, indicates that the Account Number, Account Name, Amount Paid, and Current Due fields are to be included.

- Type `FROM [Account]` as the second line to specify the source table, press the ENTER key, and then type a semicolon (`;`) on the third line.

Q&A What is the purpose of the FROM clause?
The FROM clause indicates the table or tables that contain the fields used in the query. This FROM clause indicates that all the fields in this query come from the Account table.

- Click the View button (Query Tools Design tab | Results group) to view the results (Figure 10–5).

Q&A My screen displays a dialog box that asks me to enter a parameter value. What did I do wrong?
You typed a field name incorrectly. Click Cancel to close the dialog box and then correct your SQL statement.

Q&A Why does AC # appear as the column heading for the Account Number field?
This is the caption for the field. If the field has a special caption defined, Access will use the caption rather than the field name. You will learn how to change this later in this module.

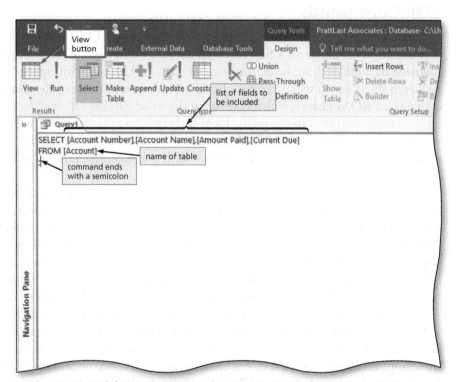

Figure 10–5 (a) Query to List the Account Number, Account Name, Amount Paid, and Current Due for All Accounts

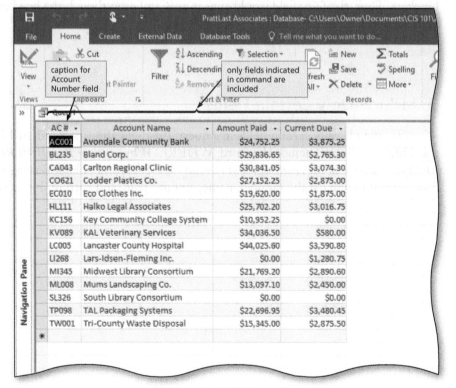

Figure 10–5 (b) Results

2

- Click the Save button on the Quick Access Toolbar, type `m10q01` as the name in the Save As dialog box, and click the OK button to save the query as m10q01.

To Prepare to Enter a New SQL Query

1 SQL VIEW | 2 SIMPLE CRITERIA | 3 COMPOUND CRITERIA | 4 SORT RESULTS
5 GROUP RESULTS | 6 JOIN TABLES | 7 USE SUBQUERY | 8 UPDATE DATA

To enter a new SQL query, you could close the window, click the No button when asked if you want to save your changes, and then begin the process from scratch. A quicker alternative is to use the View menu and then select SQL View. *Why? You will be returned to SQL view with the current command appearing. At that point, you could erase the current command and then enter a new one. If the next command is similar to the previous one, however, it often is simpler to modify the current command instead of erasing it and starting over.* The following step shows how to prepare to enter a new SQL query.

1

- Click the View button arrow (Home tab | Views group) to display the View menu (Figure 10–6).

- Click SQL View to return to SQL view.

Q&A

Could I just click the View button, or do I have to click the arrow?
Because the icon on the button is not the icon for SQL view, you must click the arrow.

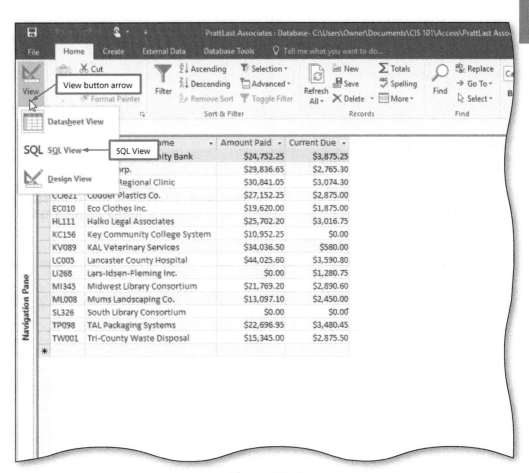

Figure 10–6

To Include All Fields

1 SQL VIEW | 2 SIMPLE CRITERIA | 3 COMPOUND CRITERIA | 4 SORT RESULTS
5 GROUP RESULTS | 6 JOIN TABLES | 7 USE SUBQUERY | 8 UPDATE DATA

To include all fields, you could use the same approach as in the previous steps, that is, list each field in the Account table after the word SELECT. There is a shortcut, however. Instead of listing all the field names after SELECT, you can use the asterisk (*) symbol. *Why? Just as when working in the design grid, the asterisk symbol represents all fields.* This indicates that you want all fields listed in the order in which you described them to the system during data definition. The following steps list all fields and all records in the Account table.

● Delete the current command, type
SELECT * as the first line of
the command, and then press the
ENTER key.

● Type **FROM [Account]** as the
second line, press the ENTER key,
and type a semicolon (**;**) on
the third line.

● View the results (Figure 10–7).

Q&A Can I use copy and paste
commands when I enter SQL
commands?
Yes, you can use copy and paste as
well as other editing techniques,
such as replacing text.

● Click File on the ribbon to open
the Backstage view, click the Save
As tab to display the Save As
gallery, click 'Save Object As' in
the File Types area, click the Save
As button to display the Save As
dialog box, type **m10q02** as the
name for the saved query, then
click the OK button to save the
query as m10q02 and return to
the query.

Q&A Can I just click the Save button on
the Quick Access Toolbar as I did
when I saved the previous query?
If you did, you would replace the
previous query with the version
you just created. Because you
want to save both the previous
query and the new one, you need
to save the new version with a
different name. To do so, you
must use 'Save Object As', which
is available through the Backstage
view.

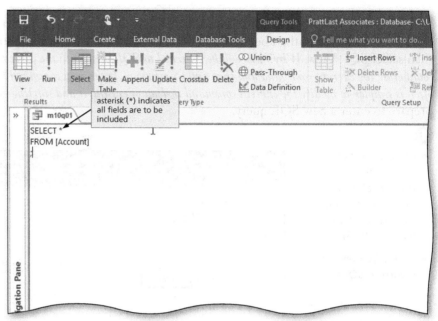

**Figure 10–7 (a) Query to List All Fields and All Records
in the Account Table**

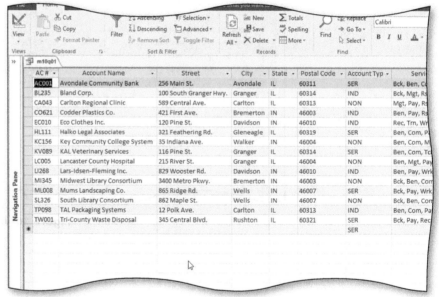

Figure 10–7 (b) Results

To Use a Criterion Involving a Numeric Field

To restrict the records to be displayed, include the word WHERE followed by a criterion as part of the command. If the field involved is a numeric field, you simply type the value. In typing the number, you do not type commas or dollar signs. *Why? If you enter a dollar sign, Access assumes you are entering text. If you enter a comma, Access considers the criterion invalid.* The following steps create a query to list the account number and name of all accounts whose current due amount is $0.00.

1

- Return to SQL view and delete the current command.

- Type **SELECT [Account Number],[Account Name]** as the first line of the command.

- Type **FROM [Account]** as the second line.

- Type **WHERE [Current Due]=0** as the third line, and then type a semicolon (**;**) on the fourth line.

Q&A What is the purpose of the WHERE clause?
The WHERE clause restricts the rows to be included in the results to only those that satisfy the criteria included in the clause. With this WHERE clause, for example, only those rows on which Current Due is equal to 0 will be included.

- View the results (Figure 10–8).

Q&A On my screen, the accounts are listed in a different order. Did I do something wrong?
No. The order in which records appear in a query result is random unless you specifically order the records. You will see how to order records later in this module.

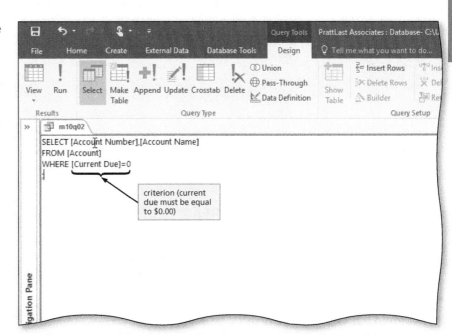

Figure 10–8 (a) Query to List the Account Number and Account Name for Those Accounts Where Current Due Is Equal to 0

2

- Save the query as m10q03.

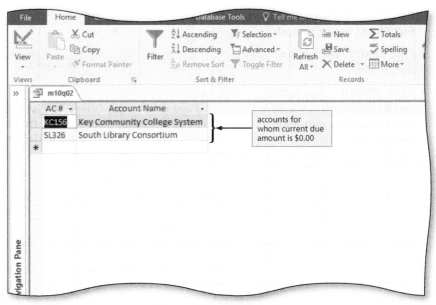

Figure 10–8 (b) Results

Simple Criteria

The criterion following the word WHERE in the preceding query is called a simple criterion. A **simple criterion** has the form: field name, comparison operator, then either another field name or a value. The possible comparison operators are shown in Table 10–1.

Table 10–1 Comparison Operators

Comparison Operator	Meaning
=	equal to
<	less than
>	greater than
<=	less than or equal to
>=	greater than or equal to
<>	not equal to

To Use a Comparison Operator

1 SQL VIEW | 2 SIMPLE CRITERIA | 3 COMPOUND CRITERIA | 4 SORT RESULTS
5 GROUP RESULTS | 6 JOIN TABLES | 7 USE SUBQUERY | 8 UPDATE DATA

In the following steps, PrattLast Associates uses a comparison operator to list the account number, account name, amount paid, and current due for all accounts whose amount paid is greater than $20,000. *Why? A comparison operator allows you to compare the value in a field with a specific value or with the value in another field.*

- Return to SQL view and delete the current command.

- Type **SELECT [Account Number],[Account Name],[Amount Paid],[Current Due]** as the first line of the command.

- Type **FROM [Account]** as the second line.

- Type **WHERE [Amount Paid] >20000** as the third line, and then type a semicolon (;) on the fourth line.

- View the results (Figure 10–9).

- Save the query as m10q04.

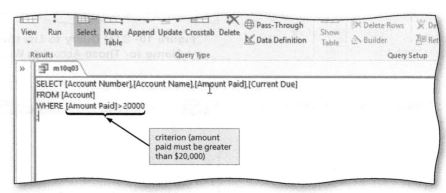

Figure 10–9 (a) Query to List the Account Number, Account Name, Amount Paid, and Current Due for Those Accounts Where Amount Paid Is Greater Than $20,000

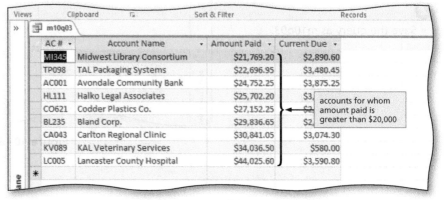

Figure 10–9 (b) Results

To Use a Criterion Involving a Text Field

If the criterion involves a text field, the value must be enclosed in quotation marks. *Why? Unlike when you work in the design grid, Access will not insert the quotation marks around text data for you in SQL view. You need to include them.* The following example lists the account number and name of all of PrattLast Associates' accounts located in Granger, that is, all accounts for whom the value in the City field is Granger.

- Return to SQL view, delete the current command, and type **SELECT [Account Number],[Account Name]** as the first line of the command.

- Type **FROM [Account]** as the second line.

- Type **WHERE [City]='Granger'** as the third line and type a semicolon (**;**) on the fourth line.

- View the results (Figure 10–10).

Q&A Could I enclose the text field value in double quotation marks instead of single quotation marks?
Yes. It is usually easier, however, to use single quotes when entering SQL commands.

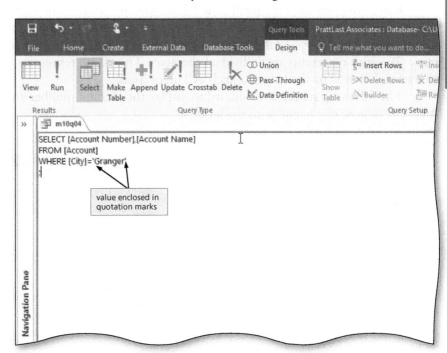

Figure 10–10 (a) Query to List the Account Number and Account Name for Those Accounts Whose City Is Granger

- Save the query as m10q05.

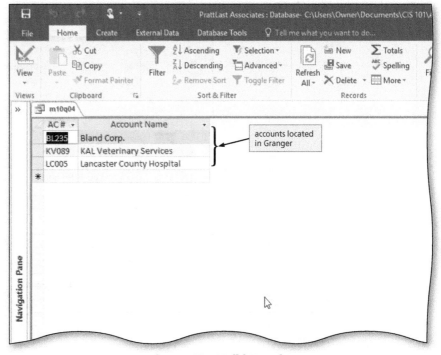

Figure 10–10 (b) Results

To Use a Wildcard

In most cases, the conditions in WHERE clauses involve exact matches, such as retrieving rows for each account located in the city of Granger. In some cases, however, exact matches do not work. *Why? You might only know that the desired value contains a certain collection of characters.* In such cases, you use the LIKE operator with a wildcard symbol.

Rather than testing for equality, the LIKE operator uses one or more wildcard characters to test for a pattern match. One common wildcard in Access, the **asterisk** (*), represents any collection of characters. Thus, G* represents the letter, G, followed by any string of characters. Another wildcard symbol is the question mark (?), which represents any individual character. Thus, T?m represents the letter T, followed by any single character, followed by the letter, m, such as Tim or Tom.

The following steps use a wildcard to display the account number and name for every account of PrattLast Associates whose city begins with the letter, G.

- Return to SQL view, delete the previous query, and type **SELECT [Account Number], [Account Name], [City]** as the first line of the command.

- Type **FROM [Account]** as the second line.

- Type **WHERE [City] LIKE 'G*'** as the third line and type a semicolon (;) on the fourth line.

- View the results (Figure 10–11).

2

- Save the query as m10q06.

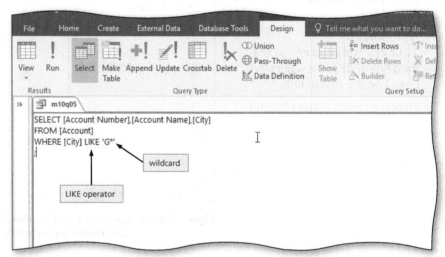

Figure 10–11 (a) Query to List the Account Number, Account Name, and City for Those Accounts Whose City Begins with the Letter G

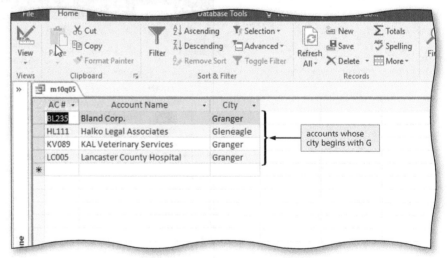

Figure 10–11 (b) Results

Break Point: If you wish to stop working through the module at this point, you can close Access now. You can resume the project later by running Access, opening the database called PrattLast Associates, creating a new query in SQL view, and continuing to follow the steps from this location forward.

Compound Criteria

You are not limited to simple criteria in SQL. You can also use compound criteria. **Compound criteria** are formed by connecting two or more simple criteria using AND, OR, and NOT. When simple criteria are connected by the word AND, all the simple criteria must be true in order for the compound criterion to be true. When simple criteria are connected by the word OR, the compound criterion will be true whenever any of the simple criteria are true. Preceding a criterion by the word NOT reverses the truth or falsity of the original criterion. That is, if the original criterion is true, the new criterion will be false; if the original criterion is false, the new one will be true.

BTW

Entering Field Names
Be sure to enclose field names in square brackets. If you accidentally use parentheses or curly braces, Access will display a syntax error (missing operator) message.

To Use a Compound Criterion Involving AND

1 SQL VIEW | 2 SIMPLE CRITERIA | 3 COMPOUND CRITERIA | **4 SORT RESULTS**
5 GROUP RESULTS | 6 JOIN TABLES | 7 USE SUBQUERY | 8 UPDATE DATA

The following steps use a compound criterion. *Why? A compound criterion allows you to impose multiple conditions.* In particular, the steps enable PrattLast to display the number and name of those accounts that are located in Wells and who have a current due amount of $0.00.

- Return to SQL view, delete the previous query, and type **SELECT [Account Number],[Account Name]** as the first line of the command.

- Type **FROM [Account]** as the second line.

- Type **WHERE [City]= 'Wells'** as the third line.

- Type **AND [Current Due]=0** as the fourth line and type a semicolon (;) on the fifth line.

Q&A

What is the purpose of the AND clause?
The AND clause indicates that there are multiple criteria, all of which must be true. With this AND clause, only rows on which BOTH City is Wells AND Current Due is 0 will be included.

- View the results (Figure 10–12).

- Save the query as m10q07.

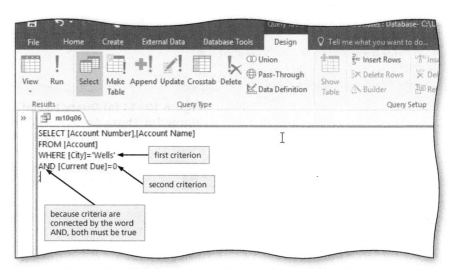

Figure 10–12 (a) Query to List the Account Number and Account Name for Those Accounts Whose City Is Wells and Whose Current Due Amount Is Equal to $0

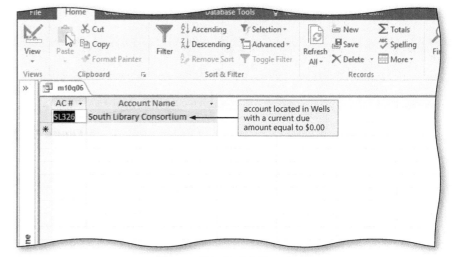

Figure 10–12 (b) Results

To Use a Compound Criterion Involving OR

The following steps use a compound criterion involving OR to enable PrattLast Associates to display the account number and name of those accounts located in Wells or for whom the current due amount is $0.00. *Why? In an OR criterion only one of the individual criteria needs to be true in order for the record to be included in the results.*

- Return to SQL view, delete the previous query, and type **SELECT [Account Number],[Account Name]** as the first line of the command.

- Type **FROM [Account]** as the second line.

- Type **WHERE [City]='Wells'** as the third line.

- Type **OR [Current Due]=0** as the fourth line and type a semicolon (**;**) on the fifth line.

Q&A

What is the purpose of the OR clause?

The OR clause indicates that there are multiple criteria, only one of which needs to be true. With this OR clause, those rows on which EITHER City is Wells OR Current Due is 0 (or both) will be included.

- View the results (Figure 10–13).

- Save the query as m10q08.

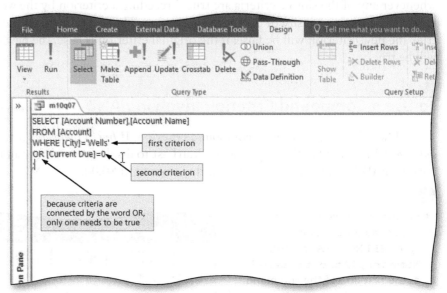

Figure 10–13 (a) Query to List the Account Number and Account Name for Those Accounts Whose City Is Wells or Whose Current Due Amount Is Equal to $0

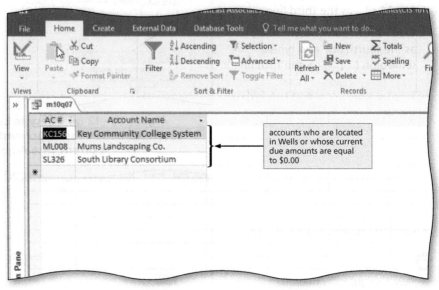

Figure 10–13 (b) Results

To Use NOT in a Criterion

Why? *You can negate any criterion by preceding the criterion with the word NOT.* The following steps use NOT in a criterion to list the numbers and names of the accounts of PrattLast Associates not located in Wells.

- Return to SQL view and delete the previous query.

- Type `SELECT [Account Number],[Account Name],[City]` as the first line of the command.

- Type `FROM [Account]` as the second line.

- Type `WHERE NOT [City]= 'Wells'` as the third line and type a semicolon (`;`) on the fourth line.

- View the results (Figure 10–14).

- Save the query as m10q09.

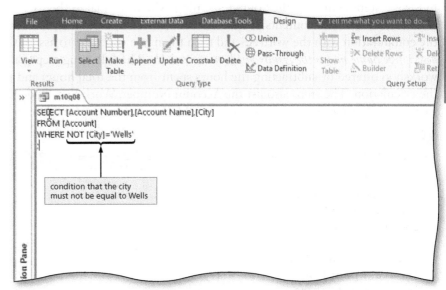

Figure 10–14 (a) Query to List the Account Number, Account Name, and City for Those Accounts Whose City Is Not Wells

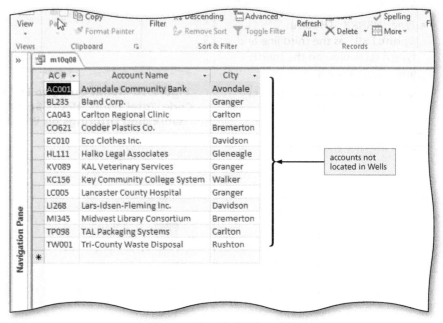

Figure 10–14 (b) Results

To Use a Computed Field

   Just as with queries created in Design view, you can include fields in queries that are not in the database, but that can be computed from fields that are. Such a field is called a **computed** or **calculated field**. Computations can involve addition (+), subtraction (-), multiplication (*), or division (/). The query in the following steps computes the hours remaining, which is equal to the total hours minus the hours spent.

   To indicate the contents of the new field (the computed field), you can name the field by following the computation with the word AS and then the name you want to assign the field. *Why? Assigning the field a descriptive name makes the results much more readable.* The following steps calculate the hours remaining for each workshop offered by subtracting the hours spent from the total hours and then assigning the name Remaining to the calculation. The steps also list the Account Number, Workshop Code, Total Hours, and Hours Spent for all workshop offerings for which the number of hours spent is greater than 0.

- Return to SQL view and delete the previous query.

- Type `SELECT [Account Number],[Workshop Code],[Total Hours],[Hours Spent],[Total Hours]-[Hours Spent] AS [Remaining]` as the first line of the command.

- Type `FROM [Workshop Offerings]` as the second line.

- Type `WHERE [Hours Spent]>0` as the third line and type a semicolon on the fourth line.

- View the results (Figure 10–15).

- Save the query as m10q10.

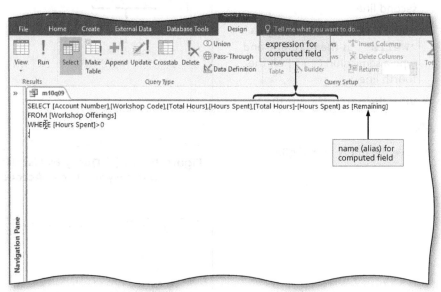

Figure 10–15 (a) Query to List the Account Number, Workshop Code, Total Hours, Hours Spent, and Hours Remaining for Those Workshop Offerings on Which Hours Spent Is Greater Than 0

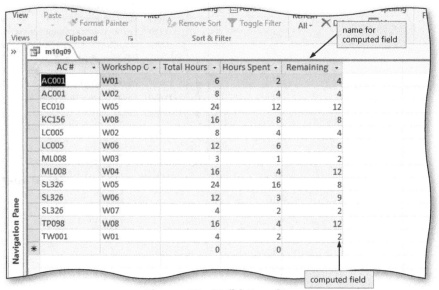

Figure 10–15 (b) Results

Sorting

Sorting in SQL follows the same principles as when using Design view to specify sorted query results, employing a sort key as the field on which data is to be sorted. SQL uses major and minor sort keys when sorting on multiple fields. By following a sort key with the word DESC with no comma in between, you can specify descending sort order. If you do not specify DESC, the data will be sorted in ascending order.

To sort the output, you include an **ORDER BY clause**, which consists of the words ORDER BY followed by the sort key. If there are two sort keys, the major sort key is listed first. Queries that you construct in Design view require that the major sort key is to the left of the minor sort key in the list of fields to be included. In SQL, there is no such restriction. The fields to be included in the query are in the SELECT clause, and the fields to be used for sorting are in the ORDER BY clause. The two clauses are totally independent.

To Sort the Results on a Single Field

1 SQL VIEW | 2 SIMPLE CRITERIA | 3 COMPOUND CRITERIA | **4 SORT RESULTS**
5 GROUP RESULTS | **6 JOIN TABLES** | **7 USE SUBQUERY** | **8 UPDATE DATA**

The following steps list the account number, name, amount paid, and current due for all accounts sorted by account name. ***Why?** PrattLast Associates wants this data to appear in alphabetical order by account name.*

- Return to SQL view and delete the previous query.

- Type `SELECT [Account Number],[Account Name],[Amount Paid],[Current Due]` as the first line of the command.

- Type `FROM [Account]` as the second line.

- Type `ORDER BY [Account Name]` as the third line and type a semicolon on the fourth line.

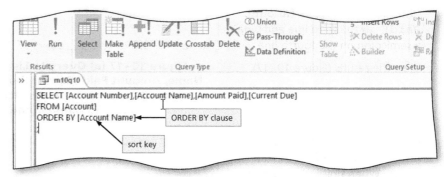

Figure 10–16 (a) Query to List the Account Number, Account Name, Amount Paid, and Current Due for All Accounts with the Results Sorted by Account Name

Q&A | What is the purpose of the ORDER BY clause?
The ORDER BY clause indicates that the results of the query are to be sorted by the indicated field or fields. This ORDER BY clause, for example, would cause the results to be sorted by Account Name.

- View the results (Figure 10–16).

- Save the query as m10q11.

AC #	Account Name	Amount Paid	Current Due
AC001	Avondale Community Bank	$24,752.25	$3,875.25
BL235	Bland Corp.	$29,836.65	$2,765.30
CA043	Carlton Regional Clinic	$30,841.05	$3,074.30
CO621	Codder Plastics Co.	$27,152.25	$2,875.00
EC010	Eco Clothes Inc.	$19,620.00	$1,875.00
HL111	Halko Legal Associates	$25,702.20	$3,016.75
KV089	KAL Veterinary Services	$34,036.50	$580.00
KC156	Key Community College System	$10,952.25	$0.00
LC005	Lancaster County Hospital	$44,025.60	$3,590.80
LI268	Lars-Idsen-Fleming Inc.	$0.00	$1,280.75
MI345	Midwest Library Consortium	$21,769.20	$2,890.60
ML008	Mums Landscaping Co.	$13,097.10	$2,450.00
SL326	South Library Consortium	$0.00	$0.00
TP098	TAL Packaging Systems	$22,696.95	$3,480.45
TW001	Tri-County Waste Disposal	$15,345.00	$2,875.50

rows sorted by account name

Figure 10–16 (b) Results

To Sort the Results on Multiple Fields

The following steps list the account number, name, amount paid, current due, and account manager number for all accounts. The data is to be sorted on multiple fields. *Why? PrattLast wants the data to be sorted by amount paid within account manager number. That is, the data is to be sorted by account manager number. In addition, within the group of accounts that have the same manager number, the data is to be sorted further by amount paid.* To accomplish this sort, the Account Manager Number field is the major (primary) sort key and the Amount Paid field is the minor (secondary) sort key. Remember that the major sort key must be listed first.

1

- Return to SQL view and delete the previous query.

- Type `SELECT [Account Number],[Account Name],[Amount Paid],[Current Due],[Account Manager Number]` as the first line of the command.

- Type `FROM [Account]` as the second line.

- Type `ORDER BY [Account Manager Number],[Amount Paid]` as the third line and type a semicolon on the fourth line.

- View the results (Figure 10–17).

 Experiment

- Try reversing the order of the sort keys to see the effect. View the results to see the effect of your choice. When finished, return to the original sorting order for both fields.

2

- Save the query as m10q12.

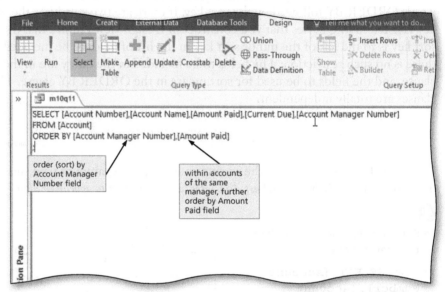

Figure 10–17 (a) Query to List the Account Number, Account Name, Amount Paid, Current Due, and Account Manager Number for All Accounts with Results Sorted by Account Manager Number and Amount Paid

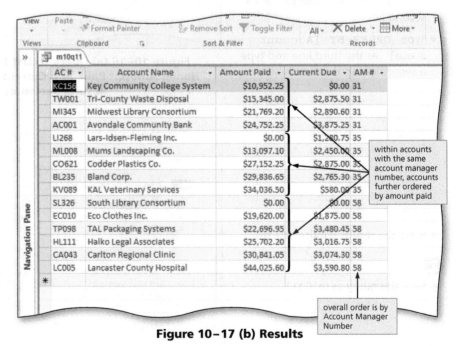

Figure 10–17 (b) Results

To Sort the Results in Descending Order

Why? *To show the results in high-to-low rather than low-to-high order, you sort in descending order.* To sort in descending order, you follow the name of the sort key with the DESC operator. The following steps list the account number, name, amount paid, current due, and account manager number for all accounts. PrattLast wants the data to be sorted by descending current due within account manager number. That is, within the accounts having the same manager number, the data is to be sorted further by current due in descending order.

- Return to SQL view and delete the previous query.

- Type **SELECT [Account Number],[Account Name],[Amount Paid],[Current Due],[Account Manager Number]** as the first line of the command.

- Type **FROM [Account]** as the second line.

- Type **ORDER BY [Account Manager Number],[Current Due] DESC** as the third line and type a semicolon on the fourth line.

Q&A
Do I need a comma between [Current Due] and DESC?
No. In fact, you must not use a comma. If you did, SQL would assume that you want a field called DESC. Without the comma, SQL knows that the DESC operator indicates that the sort on the Current Due field is to be in descending order.

- View the results (Figure 10–18).

2

- Save the query as m10q13.

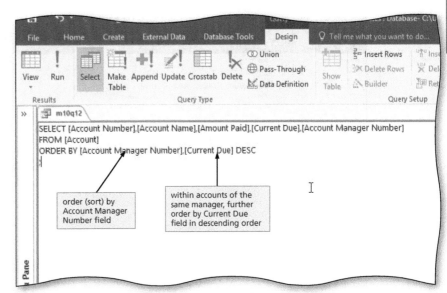

Figure 10–18 (a) Query to List the Account Number, Account Name, Amount Paid, Current Due, and Account Manager Number for All Accounts with Results Sorted by Account Manager Number and Descending Current Due

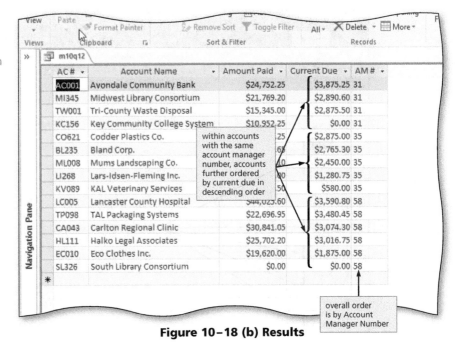

Figure 10–18 (b) Results

To Omit Duplicates When Sorting

When you sort data, duplicates are normally included. For example, the query in Figure 10–19 sorts the account numbers in the Workshop Offerings table. Because any account can be offered many workshops at a time, account numbers can be included more than once. PrattLast does not find this useful and would like to eliminate these duplicate account numbers. To do so, use the DISTINCT operator in the query. *Why? The DISTINCT operator eliminates duplicate values in the results of a query.* To use the operator, you follow the word DISTINCT with the field name in parentheses.

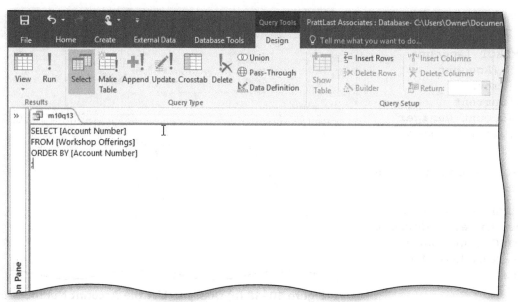

Figure 10–19 (a) Query to List the Account Numbers in the Workshop Offerings Table Sorted by Account Number

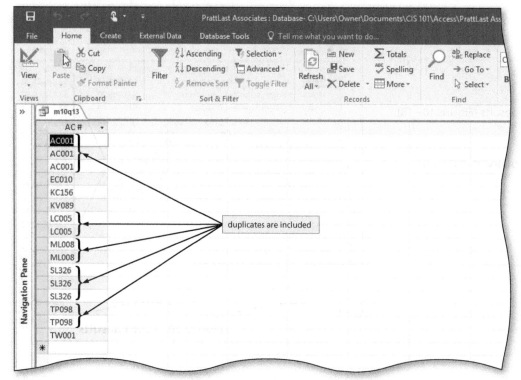

Figure 10–19 (b) Results

The following steps display the account numbers in the Workshop Offerings table in account number order, but with any duplicates removed.

- Return to SQL view and delete the previous query.
- Type **SELECT DISTINCT([Account Number])** as the first line of the command.
- Type **FROM [Workshop Offerings]** as the second line.
- Type **ORDER BY [Account Number]** as the third line and type a semicolon on the fourth line.
- View the results (Figure 10–20).

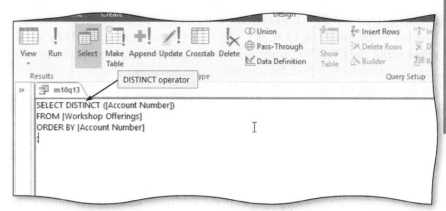

Figure 10–20 (a) Query to List the Account Numbers in the Workshop Offerings Table Sorted by Account Number, Ensuring That No Account Number Is Listed More Than Once

- Save the query as m10q14. Return to the query.

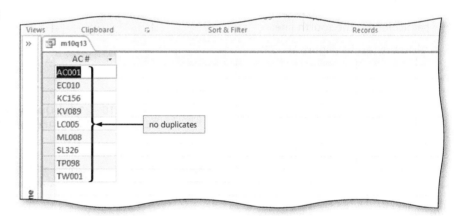

Figure 10–20 (b) Results

How do you determine sorting when creating a query?

Examine the query or request to see if it contains words such as *order* or *sort* that would imply that the order of the query results is important. If so, you need to sort the query.

- **Determine whether data is to be sorted.** Examine the requirements for the query looking for words like *sorted by*, *ordered by*, *arranged by*, and so on.

- **Determine sort keys.** Look for the fields that follow sorted by, ordered by, or any other words that signify sorting. If the requirements for the query include the phrase, ordered by account name, then Account Name is a sort key.

- **If there is more than one sort key, determine which one will be the major sort key and which will be the minor sort key.** Look for words that indicate which field is more important. For example, if the requirements indicate that the results are to be ordered by amount paid within account manager number, Account Manager Number is the more important sort key.

Break Point: If you wish to stop working through the module at this point, you can close Access now. You can resume the project later by running Access, opening the database called PrattLast Associates, creating a new query in SQL view, and continuing to follow the steps from this location forward.

To Use a Built-In Function

SQL has built-in functions, also called aggregate functions, to perform various calculations. Similar to the functions you learned about in an earlier module, these functions in SQL are COUNT, SUM, AVG, MAX, and MIN, respectively. PrattLast uses the following steps to determine the number of accounts assigned to manager number 35 by using the COUNT function with an asterisk (*). ***Why use an asterisk rather than a field name when using the COUNT function?*** *You could select a field name, but that would be cumbersome and imply that you were just counting that field. You are really counting records. It does not matter whether you are counting names or street addresses or anything else.*

1

- Return to SQL view and delete the previous query.

- Type `SELECT COUNT (*)` as the first line of the command.

- Type `FROM [Account]` as the second line.

- Type `WHERE [Account Manager Number]='35'` as the third line and type a semicolon on the fourth line.

- View the results (Figure 10–21).

Q&A Why does Expr1000 appear in the column heading of the results? Because the field is a computed field, it does not have a name. Access assigns a generic expression name. You can add a name for the field by including the AS clause in the query, and it is good practice to do so.

2

- Save the query as m10q15.

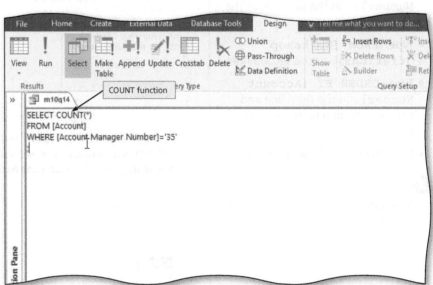

Figure 10–21 (a) Query to Count the Number of Accounts Whose Account Manager Number Is 35

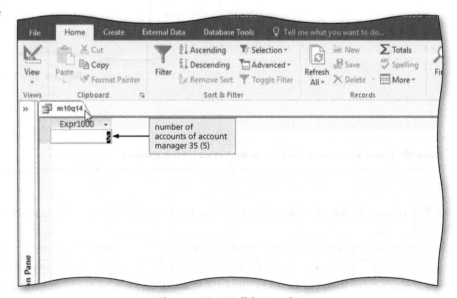

Figure 10–21 (b) Results

To Assign a Name to the Results of a Function

PrattLast Associates would prefer to have a more meaningful name than Expr1000 for the results of counting account numbers. *Why? The default name of Expr1000 does not describe the meaning of the calculation.* Fortunately, just as you can assign a name to a calculation that includes two fields, you can assign a name to the results of a function. To do so, follow the expression for the function with the word AS and then the name to be assigned to the result. The following steps assign the name, Account Count, to the expression in the previous query.

- Return to SQL view and delete the previous query.

- Type **SELECT COUNT(*) AS [Account Count]** as the first line of the command.

- Type **FROM [Account]** as the second line.

- Type **WHERE [Account Manager Number]='35'** as the third line and type a semicolon on the fourth line.

- View the results (Figure 10–22).

- Save the query as m10q16.

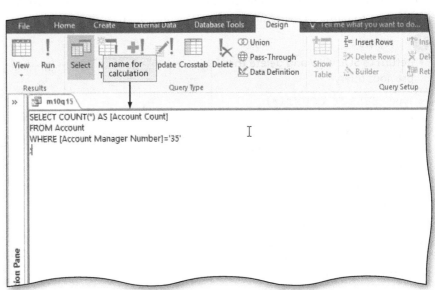

Figure 10–22 (a) Query to Count the Number of Accounts Whose Account Manager Number Is 35 with Results Called Account Count

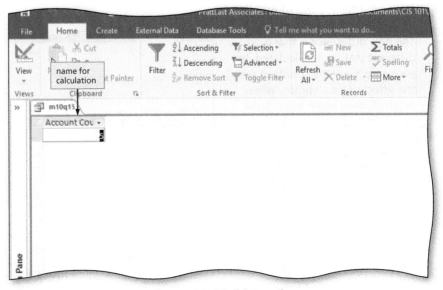

Figure 10–22 (b) Results

To Use Multiple Functions in the Same Command

There are two differences between COUNT and SUM, other than the obvious fact that they are computing different statistics. First, in the case of SUM, you must specify the field for which you want a total, instead of an asterisk (*); second, the field must be numeric. *Why? If the field is not numeric, it does not make sense to calculate a sum. You could not calculate a sum of names or addresses, for example.* The following steps use both the COUNT and SUM functions to count the number of accounts whose account manager number is 35 and calculate the sum (total) of their amounts paid. The steps use the word AS to name COUNT(*) as Account Count and to name SUM([Amount Paid]) as Sum Paid.

- Return to SQL view and delete the previous query.

- Type `SELECT COUNT(*) AS [Account Count], SUM([Amount Paid]) AS [Sum Paid]` as the first line of the command.

- Type `FROM [Account]` as the second line.

- Type `WHERE [Account Manager Number]='35'` as the third line and type a semicolon on the fourth line.

- View the results (Figure 10–23).

 Experiment

- Try using the other functions in place of SUM. The use of AVG, MAX, and MIN is similar to SUM. The only difference is that a different statistic is calculated. In each case, view the results to see the effect of your choice. When finished, once again select SUM.

- Save the query as m10q17.

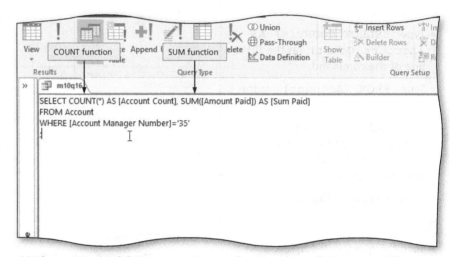

Figure 10–23 (a) Query to Count the Number of Accounts Whose Account Manager Number Is 35 with Results Called Account Count and Calculate the Sum of Amount Paid with Results Called Sum Paid

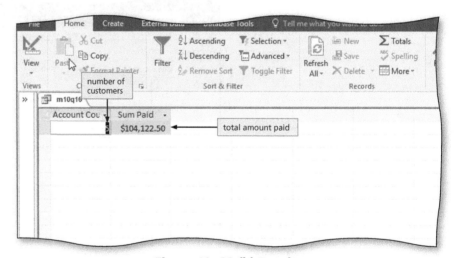

Figure 10–23 (b) Results

Grouping

Recall that grouping means creating groups of records that share some common characteristic. When you group rows, any calculations indicated in the SELECT command are performed for the entire group.

To Use Grouping

1 SQL VIEW | 2 SIMPLE CRITERIA | 3 COMPOUND CRITERIA | 4 SORT RESULTS
5 GROUP RESULTS | 6 JOIN TABLES | 7 USE SUBQUERY | 8 UPDATE DATA

PrattLast Associates wants to calculate the totals of the Amount Paid field, called Sum Paid, and the Current Due field, called Sum Due, for the accounts of each manager. To calculate the totals, the command will include the calculations, SUM([Amount Paid]) and SUM([Current Due]). To get totals for the accounts of each manager, the command will also include a **GROUP BY clause**, which consists of the words, GROUP BY, followed by the field used for grouping, in this case, Account Manager Number. *Why? Including GROUP BY Account Manager Number will cause the accounts for each manager to be grouped together; that is, all accounts with the same account manager number will form a group. Any statistics, such as totals, appearing after the word SELECT will be calculated for each of these groups.* Using GROUP BY does not mean that the information will be sorted.

The following steps use the GROUP BY clause to produce the results PrattLast wants. The steps also rename the total amount paid as Sum Paid and the total current due as Sum Due by including appropriate AS clauses; finally, the steps sort the records by account manager number.

- Return to SQL view and delete the previous query.

- Type `SELECT [Account Manager Number], SUM([Amount Paid]) AS [Sum Paid], SUM([Current Due]) AS [Sum Due]` as the first line of the command.

- Type `FROM [Account]` as the second line.

- Type `GROUP BY [Account Manager Number]` as the third line.

Q&A

What is the purpose of the GROUP BY clause?

The GROUP BY clause causes the rows to be grouped by the indicated field. With this GROUP BY clause, the rows will be grouped by Account Manager Number.

- Type `ORDER BY [Account Manager Number]` as the fourth line and type a semicolon on the fifth line.

- View the results (Figure 10–24).

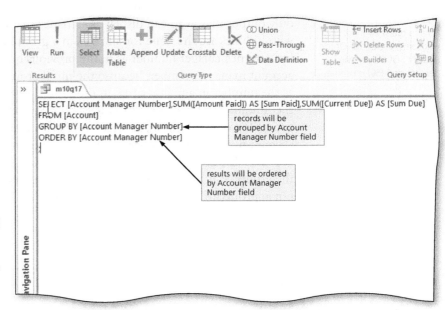

Figure 10–24 (a) Query to Group Records by Account Manager Number and List the Account Manager Number, the Sum of Amount Paid, and the Sum of Current Due

2

• Save the query as m10q18.

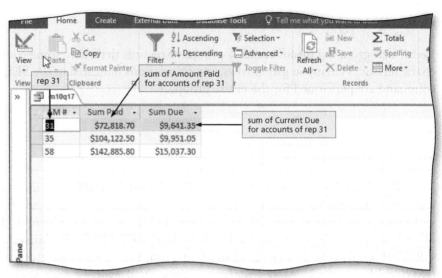

Figure 10–24 (b) Results

BTW
Wildcards
Other implementations of
SQL do not use the asterisk
(*) and question mark (?)
wildcards. In SQL for Oracle
and for SQL Server, the
percent sign (%) is used as
a wildcard to represent any
collection of characters.
In Oracle and SQL Server,
the WHERE clause shown
in Figure 10-11a would be
WHERE [City] LIKE 'G%'.

Grouping Requirements

When rows are grouped, one line of output is produced for each group. The only output that SQL can display is statistics that are calculated for the group or fields whose values are the same for all rows in a group. For example, when grouping rows by account manager number as in the previous query, it is appropriate to display the account manager number, because the number in one row in a group must be the same as the number in any other row in the group. It is appropriate to display the sum of the Amount Paid and Current Due fields because they are statistics calculated for the group. It would not be appropriate to display an account number, however, because the account number varies on the rows in a group; the manager is associated with many accounts. SQL would not be able to determine which account number to display for the group. SQL will display an error message if you attempt to display a field that is not appropriate, such as the account number.

To Restrict the Groups That Appear

1 SQL VIEW | 2 SIMPLE CRITERIA | 3 COMPOUND CRITERIA | 4 SORT RESULTS
5 GROUP RESULTS | 6 JOIN TABLES | 7 USE SUBQUERY | 8 UPDATE DATA

In some cases, PrattLast Associates may want to display only certain groups. For example, management may want to display only those account managers for whom the sum of the current due amounts are less than $10,000.00. This restriction does not apply to individual rows, but instead to groups. You cannot use a WHERE clause to accomplish this restriction. *Why? WHERE applies only to rows, not groups.*

Fortunately, SQL provides the **HAVING clause**, which functions with groups similarly to the way WHERE functions with rows. The HAVING clause consists of the word HAVING followed by a criterion. It is used in the following steps, which restrict the groups to be included to those for which the sum of the current due is less than $10,000.00.

1

- Return to SQL view.

- Click the beginning of the fourth line (ORDER BY [Account Manager Number]) and press the ENTER key to insert a new blank line.

- Click the beginning of the new blank line, and then type **HAVING SUM([Current Due])<10000** as the new fourth line.

What is the purpose of the HAVING clause?

The HAVING clause restricts the groups that will be included to only those satisfying the indicated criteria. With this clause, only groups for which the sum of the current due amount is less than $10,000 will be included.

- View the results (Figure 10–25).

2

- Save the query as m10q19.

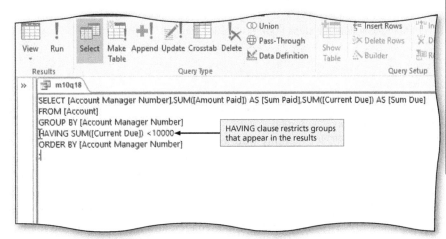

Figure 10–25 (a) Query to Restrict the Results of the Previous Query to Only Those Groups for Which the Sum of Current Due Is Less Than $10,000

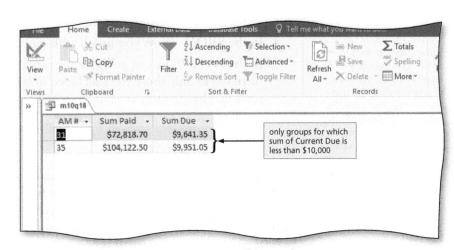

Figure 10–25 (b) Results

How do you determine grouping when creating a query?

Examine the query or request to determine whether records should be organized by some common characteristic.

- **Determine whether data is to be grouped in some fashion.** Examine the requirements for the query to see if they contain individual rows or information about groups of rows.

- **Determine the field or fields on which grouping is to take place.** By which field is the data to be grouped? Look to see if the requirements indicate a field along with several group calculations.

- **Determine which fields or calculations are appropriate to display.** When rows are grouped, one line of output is produced for each group. The only output that can appear are statistics that are calculated for the group or fields whose values are the same for all rows in a group. For example, it would make sense to display the manager number, because all the accounts in the group have the same manager number. It would not make sense to display the account number, because the account number will vary from one row in a group to another. SQL could not determine which account number to display for the group.

CONSIDER THIS

Break Point: If you wish to stop working through the module at this point, you can close Access now. You can resume the project later by running Access, opening the database called PrattLast Associates, creating a new query in SQL view, and continuing to follow the steps from this location forward.

BTW
Inner Joins
A join that compares the tables in the FROM clause and lists only those rows that satisfy the condition in the WHERE clause is called an inner join. SQL has an INNER JOIN clause. You could replace the query shown in Figure 10–26a with FROM [Account] INNER JOIN [Account Manager] ON [Account].[Account Manager Number]=[Account Manager]. [Account Manager Number] to get the same results as shown in Figure 10–26b.

BTW
Outer Joins
Sometimes you need to list all the rows from one of the tables in a join, regardless of whether they match any rows in the other table. For example, you can perform a join on the Account and Workshop Offerings table but display all accounts — even the ones without workshop offerings. This type of join is called an outer join. In a left outer join, all rows from the table on the left (the table listed first in the query) will be included regardless of whether they match rows from the table on the right (the table listed second in the query). Rows from the right will be included only if they match. In a right outer join, all rows from the table on the right will be included regardless of whether they match rows from the table on the left. The SQL clause for a left outer join is LEFT JOIN and the SQL clause for a right outer join is RIGHT JOIN.

Joining Tables

Many queries require data from more than one table. Just as with creating queries in Design view, SQL should provide a way to **join** tables, that is, to find rows in two tables that have identical values in matching fields. In SQL, this is accomplished through appropriate criteria following the word WHERE.

If you want to list the account number, name, account manager number, first name of the manager, and last name of the manager for all accounts, you need data from both the Account and Account Manager tables. The Account Manager Number field is in both tables, the Account Number field is only in the Account table, and the First Name and Last Name fields are only in the Account Manager Table. You need to access both tables in your SQL query, as follows:

1. In the SELECT clause, you indicate all fields you want to appear.

2. In the FROM clause, you list all tables involved in the query.

3. In the WHERE clause, you give the criterion that will restrict the data to be retrieved to only those rows included in both of the two tables, that is, to the rows that have common values in matching fields.

Qualifying Fields

There is a problem in indicating the matching fields. The matching fields are both called Account Manager Number. There is a field in the Account table called Account Manager Number, as well as a field in the Account Manager Table called Account Manager Number. In this case, if you only enter Account Manager Number, it will not be clear which table you mean. It is necessary to **qualify** Account Manager Number, that is, to specify to which field in which table you are referring. You do this by preceding the name of the field with the name of the table, followed by a period. The Account Manager Number field in the Account table, for example, is [Account].[Account Manager Number].

Whenever a query is potentially ambiguous, you must qualify the fields involved. It is permissible to qualify other fields as well, even if there is no confusion. For example, instead of [Account Name], you could have typed [Account].[Account Name] to indicate the Account Name field in the Account table. Some people prefer to qualify all fields, and this is not a bad approach. In this text, you will only qualify fields when it is necessary to do so. Each field is qualified individually.

To Join Tables

1 SQL VIEW | 2 SIMPLE CRITERIA | 3 COMPOUND CRITERIA | 4 SORT RESULTS
5 GROUP RESULTS | 6 JOIN TABLES | 7 USE SUBQUERY | 8 UPDATE DATA

PrattLast Associates wants to list the account number, account name, account manager number, first name of the manager, and last name of the manager for all accounts. The following steps create a query to join the tables. *Why? The data comes from two tables.* The steps also order the results by account number.

- Return to SQL view and delete the previous query.

- Type **SELECT [Account Number],[Account Name],[Account].[Account Manager Number],[First Name],[Last Name]** as the first line of the command.

- Type **FROM [Account], [Account Manager]** as the second line.

Q&A
Why does the FROM clause contain more than one table?
The query involves fields from both tables.

- Type **WHERE [Account].[Account Manager Number]=[Account Manager].[Account Manager Number]** as the third line.

Q&A
What is the purpose of this WHERE clause?
The WHERE clause specifies that only rows for which the manager numbers match are to be included. In this case, the manager number in the Account table ([Account].[Account Manager Number]) must be equal to the manager number in the Account Manager table ([Account Manager].[Account Manager Number]).

- Type **ORDER BY [Account Number]** as the fourth line and type a semicolon on the fifth line.

- View the results (Figure 10–26).

2

- Save the query as m10q20.

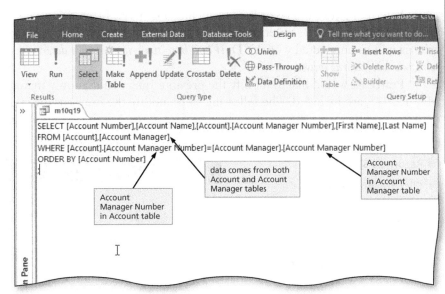

Figure 10–26 (a) Query to List the Account Number, Account Name, Account Manager Number, First Name, and Last Name for All Accounts

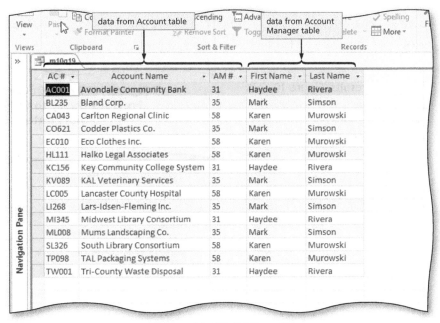

Figure 10–26 (b) Results

To Restrict the Records in a Join

You can restrict the records to be included in a join by creating a compound criterion. The compound criterion will include the criterion necessary to join the tables along with a criterion to restrict the records. The criteria will be connected with AND. *Why? Both the criterion that determines the records to be joined and the criterion to restrict the records must be true.*

PrattLast would like to modify the previous query so that only managers whose start date is prior to May 1, 2015, are included. The following steps modify the previous query appropriately. The date is enclosed between number signs (#), which is the date format used in the Access version of SQL.

- Return to SQL view.

- Click the end of line 1.

- Type **, [Start Date]** to add the Start Date field to the SELECT clause.

- Click immediately prior to the ORDER BY clause.

- Type **AND [Start Date]<#5/1/2015#** and press the ENTER key.

Q&A Could I use other formats for the date in the criterion?
Yes. You could type #May 1, 2015# or #1-May-2015#.

- View the results (Figure 10–27).

2

- Save the query as m10q21.

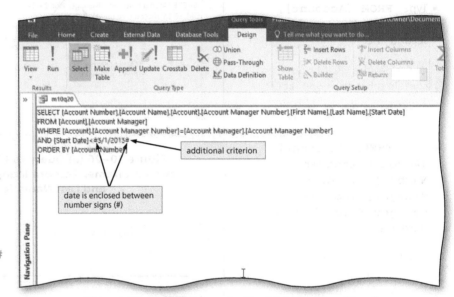

Figure 10–27 (a) Query to Restrict the Results of Previous Query to Only Those Accounts Whose Start Date Is Before 5/1/2015

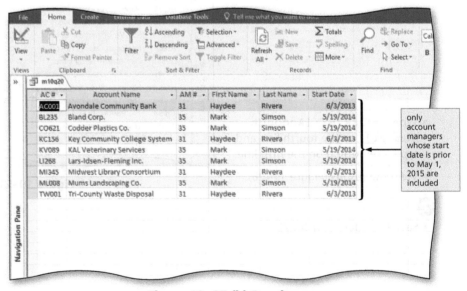

Figure 10–27 (b) Results

Aliases

When tables appear in the FROM clause, you can give each table an **alias**, or an alternative name, that you can use in the rest of the statement. You create an alias by typing the name of the table, pressing the spacebar, and then typing the name of the alias. No commas or periods are necessary to separate the two names.

You can use an alias for two basic reasons: for simplicity or to join a table to itself. Figure 10–28 shows the same query as in Figure 10–27, but with the Account table assigned the letter, A, as an alias and the Account Manager table assigned the letter, M. The query in Figure 10–28 is less complex. Whenever you need to qualify a field name, you can use the alias. Thus, you only need to type M.[Account Manager Number] rather than [Account Manager].[Account Manager Number].

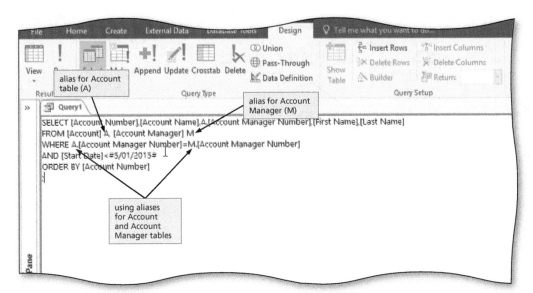

BTW

Qualifying Fields
There is no space on either side of the period that is used to separate the table name from the field name. Adding a space will result in an error message.

Figure 10–28

To Join a Table to Itself

1 SQL VIEW | 2 SIMPLE CRITERIA | 3 COMPOUND CRITERIA | 4 SORT RESULTS
5 GROUP RESULTS | 6 JOIN TABLES | 7 USE SUBQUERY | 8 UPDATE DATA

The other use of aliases is in joining a table to itself. An example of this type of join would enable PrattLast to find account numbers and names for every two accounts located in the same city. One such pair, for example, would be account BL235 (Bland Corp.) and account KV089 (KAL Veterinary Services) because both accounts are located in the same city (Granger). Another example would be account BL235 (Bland Corp.) and account LC005 (Lancaster County Hospital) because both accounts are also located in the same city (Granger). Finally, because both KV089 and LC005 are located in the same city (Granger), there would be a third pair: KV089 (KAL Veterinary Services) and LC005 (Lancaster County Hospital).

If there were two Account tables in the database, PrattLast could obtain the results they want by simply joining the two Account tables and looking for rows where the cities were the same. Even though there is only one Account table, you can actually treat the Account table as two tables in the query by creating two aliases. You would change the FROM clause to:

```
FROM [Account] F, [Account] S
```

SQL treats this clause as a query of two tables. The clause assigns the first Account table the letter, F, as an alias. It also assigns the letter, S, as an alias for the Account table. The fact that both tables are really the single Account table is not a problem. The following steps assign two aliases (F and S) to the Account table and list the account number and account name of both accounts as well as the city in which both are located. The steps also include a criterion to ensure F.[Account Number] < S.[Account Number]. **Why?** *If you did not include this criterion, the query would contain four times as many results. On the first row in the results, for example, the first account number is BL235 and the second is KV089. Without this criterion, there would be a row on which both the first and second account numbers are BL235, a row on which both are KV089, and a row on which the first is KV089 and the second is BL235. This criterion only selects the one row on which the first account number (BL235) is less than the second account number (KV089).*

- Return to SQL view and delete the previous query.

- Type `SELECT F.[Account Number],F.[Account Name],S.[Account Number],S.[Account Name],F.[City]` as the first line of the command to select the fields to display in the query result.

- Type `FROM [Account] F,[Account] S` as the second line to create the aliases for the first and second Account tables.

- Type `WHERE F.[City]=S.[City]` as the third line to indicate that the cities in each table must match.

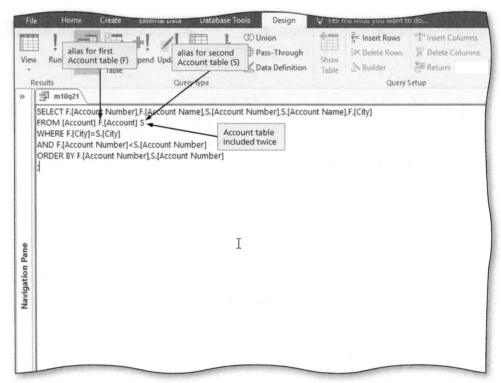

Figure 10–29 (a) Query to List the Account Name and Account Number for Pairs of Accounts Located in the Same City

- Type `AND F.[Account Number]<S.[Account Number]` as the fourth line to indicate that the account number from the first table must be less than the account number from the second table.

- Type `ORDER BY F.[Account Number], S.[Account Number]` as the fifth line to ensure that the results are sorted by the account number from the first table and further sorted by the account number from the second table.

- Type a semicolon on the sixth line.

- View the results (Figure 10–29).

- Save the query as m10q22.

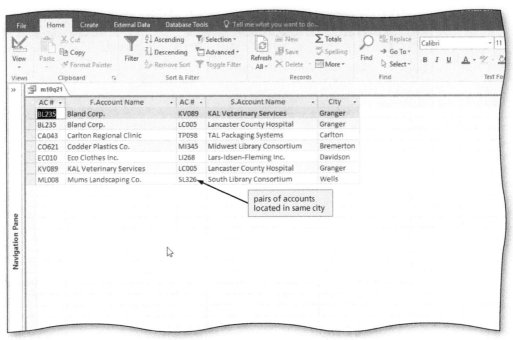

Figure 10–29 (b) Results

How do you determine criteria when creating a query?

Examine the query or request to determine any restrictions or conditions that records must satisfy to be included in the results.

- **Determine the fields involved in the criteria.** For any criterion, determine the fields that are included. Determine the data types for these fields. If the criterion uses a value that corresponds to a Text field, enclose the value in single quotation marks. If the criterion uses a date, enclose the value between number signs (for example, #4/15/2015#).

- **Determine comparison operators.** When fields are being compared to other fields or to specific values, determine the appropriate comparison operator (equals, less than, greater than, and so on). If a wildcard is involved, then the query will use the LIKE operator.

- **Determine join criteria.** If tables are being joined, determine the fields that must match.

- **Determine compound criteria.** If more than one criterion is involved, determine whether all individual criteria are to be true, in which case you will use the AND operator, or whether only one individual criterion needs to be true, in which case you will use the OR operator.

CONSIDER THIS

Subqueries

It is possible to place one query inside another. You will place the query shown in Figure 10–30 inside another query. When you have done so, it will be called a **subquery**, which is an inner query, contained within parentheses, that is evaluated first. Then the outer query can use the results of the subquery to find its results. In some cases, using a subquery can be the simplest way to produce the desired results, as illustrated in the next set of steps.

BTW
SELECT clause
When you enter field names in a SELECT clause, you do not need to enter a space after the comma. Access inserts a space after the comma when you save the query and close it. When you re-open the query in SQL view, a space will appear after each comma that separates fields in the SELECT clause.

BTW
SQL Standards
The International Standards
Organization (ISO) and the
American National Standards
Institute (ANSI) recognize SQL
as a standardized language.
Different relational database
management systems may
support the entire set of
standardized SQL commands
or only a subset.

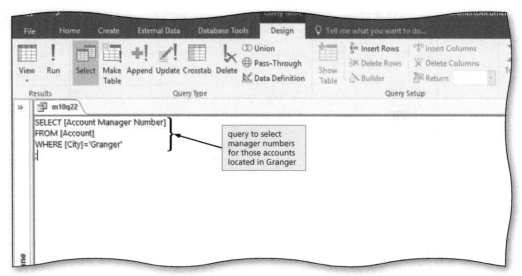

**Figure 10–30 (a) Query to List the Account Manager Number for All Records
in the Account Table on Which the City Is Granger**

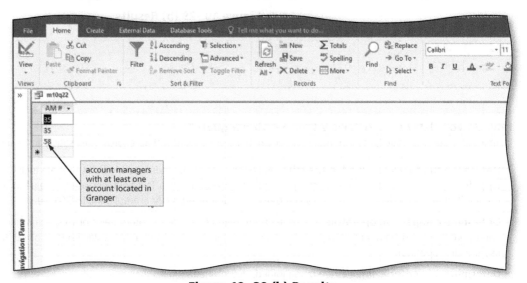

Figure 10–30 (b) Results

Why does account manager 35 appear twice?

The PrattLast Associates database includes two accounts whose city is Granger and whose account manager number is 35. This is not a problem because in the next query it is only important what numbers are included, not how many times they appear. If you wanted the numbers to only appear once, you would order the results by Account Manager Number and use the DISTINCT operator.

CONSIDER THIS

To Use a Subquery

The following steps use the query shown in Figure 10–30 as a subquery. *Why? PrattLast Associates can use this query to select manager numbers for those managers who have at least one account located in Granger.* After the subquery is evaluated, the outer query will select the manager number, first name, and last name for those managers whose manager number is in the list produced by the subquery.

- Return to SQL view and delete the previous query.
- Type **SELECT [Account Manager Number], [First Name], [Last Name]** as the first line of the command.
- Type **FROM [Account Manager]** as the second line.
- Type **WHERE [Account Manager Number] IN** as the third line.
- Type **(SELECT [Account Manager Number]** as the fourth line.
- Type **FROM [Account]** as the fifth line.
- Type **WHERE [City]='Granger')** as the sixth line and type a semicolon on the seventh line.
- View the results (Figure 10–31).

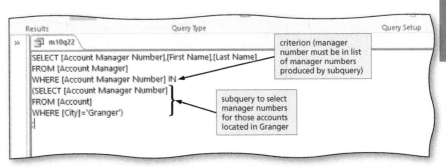

Figure 10–31 (a) Query to List Account Manager Number, First Name, and Last Name for All Account Managers Who Represent at Least One Account Located in Granger

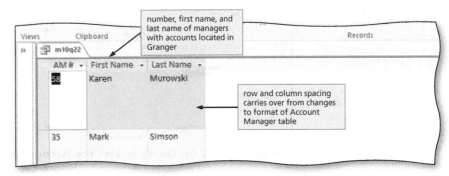

Figure 10–31 (b) Results

- Save the query as m10q23.

Using an IN Clause

The query in Figure 10–31 uses an IN clause with a subquery. You can also use an IN clause with a list as an alternative to an OR criterion when the OR criterion involves a single field. For example, to find accounts whose city is Granger, Rushton, or Wells, the criterion using IN would be City IN ('Granger', 'Rushton', 'Wells'). The corresponding OR criterion would be City='Granger' OR City= 'Rushton' OR City= 'Wells'. The choice of which one to use is a matter of personal preference.

You can also use this type of IN clause when creating queries in Design view. To use the criterion in the previous paragraph, for example, include the City field in the design grid and enter the criterion in the Criteria row.

BTW
BETWEEN Operator
The BETWEEN operator allows you to search for a range of values in one field. For example, to find all accounts whose amount paid is between $10,000.00 and $20,000.00, the WHERE clause would be WHERE [Amount Paid] BETWEEN 10000 AND 20000.

Comparison with Access-Generated SQL

When you create a query in Design view, Access automatically creates a corresponding SQL query that is similar to the queries you have created in this module. The Access query shown in Figure 10–32, for example, was created in Design view and includes the Account Number and Account Name fields. The City field has a criterion (Granger).

BTW

Union, Pass-Through, and Data Definition Queries
There are three queries that cannot be created in Design view. When you click the button on the ribbon for any of these three queries in Design view, the SQL view window opens. The Union query combines fields from more than one table into one query result set. The Pass-Through query enables you to send SQL commands directly to ODBC (Open Database Connectivity) databases using the ODBC database's SQL syntax. The Data Definition query allows you to create or alter database tables or create indexes in Access directly.

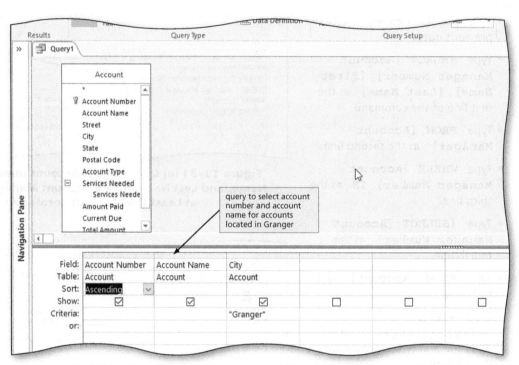

Figure 10–32 (a) Query to List the Account Number and Account Name for All Accounts Whose City Is Granger

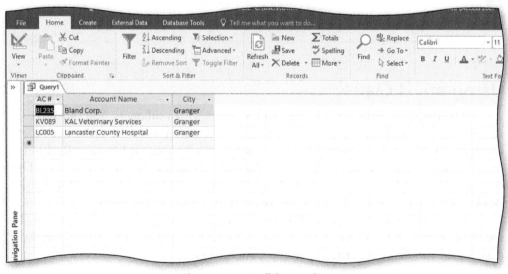

Figure 10–32 (b) Results

The SQL query that Access generates in correspondence to the Design view query is shown in Figure 10–33. The query is very similar to the queries you have entered, but there are three slight differences. First, the Account.[Account Number] and Account.[Account Name] fields are qualified, even though they do not need to be; only one table is involved in the query, so no qualification is necessary. Second, the City field is not enclosed in square brackets. The field is legitimately not enclosed in square brackets because there are no spaces or other special characters in the field name. Finally, there are extra parentheses in the criteria.

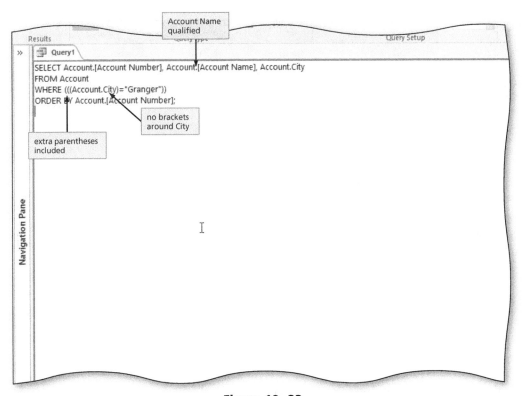

Figure 10–33

Both the style used by Access and the style you have been using are legitimate. The choice of style is a personal preference.

Updating Data Using SQL

Although SQL is often regarded as a language for querying databases, it also contains commands to update databases. You can add new records, update existing records, and delete records. To make the change indicated in the command, you will click the Run button.

BTW
Action Queries
When you use the INSERT, UPDATE, or DELETE commands in SQL, you are creating action queries. The query is making a change to the database. To effect this change, you must click the Run button in the Results group.

To Use an INSERT Command

You can add records to a table using the SQL INSERT command. The command consists of the words INSERT INTO followed by the name of the table into which the record is to be inserted. Next is the word VALUE, followed by the values for the fields in the record. Values for text fields must be enclosed within quotation marks. *Why? Just as you needed to type the quotation marks when you used text data in a criterion, you need to do the same when you use text values in an INSERT INTO command.* The following steps add a record that PrattLast Associates wants to add to the Workshop Offerings table. The record is for account EC010 and Workshop W04, and indicates that the workshop will be offered for a total of 16 hours, of which 0 hours have already been spent.

- If necessary, return to SQL view and delete the existing query.

- Type **INSERT INTO [Workshop Offerings]** as the first line of the command.

Q&A What is the purpose of the INSERT INTO clause?
The clause indicates the table into which data is to be inserted.

- Type **VALUES** as the second line.

- Type **('EC010','W04' ,16,0)** as the third line and type a semicolon on the fourth line (Figure 10–34).

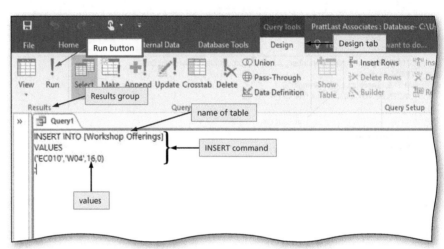

Figure 10–34

Q&A What is the purpose of the VALUES clause?
The VALUES clause, which typically extends over two lines, indicates the values that are to be inserted into a new record in the table. For readability, it is common to place the word VALUES on one line and the actual values on a separate line.

- Run the query by clicking the Run button (Query Tools Design tab | Results group).

- When Access displays a message indicating the number of records to be inserted (appended), click the Yes button to insert the records.

Q&A I clicked the View button and did not get the message. Do I need to click the Run button?
Yes. You are making a change to the database, so you must click the Run button, or the change will not be made.

How can I see if the record was actually inserted?
Use a SELECT query to view the records in the Workshop Offerings table.

3

- Save the query as m10q24.

To Use an UPDATE Command

You can update records in SQL by using the UPDATE command. The command consists of UPDATE, followed by the name of the table in which records are to be updated. Next, the command contains one or more SET clauses, which consist of the word SET, followed by a field to be updated, an equal sign, and the new value. The SET clause indicates the change to be made. Finally, the query includes a WHERE clause. *Why? When you execute the command, all records in the indicated table that satisfy the criterion will be updated.* The following steps use the SQL UPDATE command to perform an update requested by PrattLast Associates. Specifically, they change the Hours Spent to 4 on all records in the Workshop Offerings table on which the account number is EC010 and the workshop code is W04. Because the combination of the Account Number and Workshop Code fields is the primary key, only one record will be updated.

- Delete the existing query.
- Type **UPDATE [Workshop Offerings]** as the first line of the command.

Q&A What is the purpose of the UPDATE clause?
The UPDATE clause indicates the table to be updated. This clause indicates that the update is to the Workshop Offerings table.

- Type **SET [Hours Spent]=4** as the second line.

Q&A What is the purpose of the SET clause?
The SET clause indicates the field to be changed as well as the new value. This SET clause indicates that the hours spent is to be set to 4.

- Type **WHERE [Account Number]='EC010'** as the third line.
- Type **AND [Workshop Code]='W04'** as the fourth line and type a semicolon on the fifth line (Figure 10–35).

Q&A Do I need to change a field to a specific value such as 4?
No. You could use an expression. For example, to add $100 to the Current Due amount, the SET clause would be SET [Current Due]=[Current Due]+100.

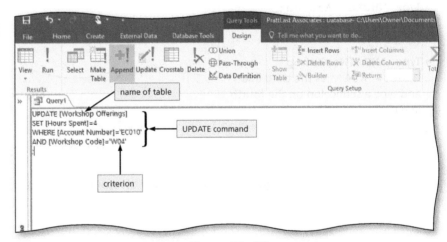

Figure 10–35

- Run the query.
- When Access displays a message indicating the number of records to be updated, click the Yes button to update the records.

Q&A How can I see if the update actually occurred?
Use a SELECT query to view the records in the Workshop Offerings table.

- Save the query as m10q25.

To Use a DELETE Command

You can delete records in SQL using the DELETE command. The command consists of DELETE FROM, followed by the name of the table from which records are to be deleted. Finally, you include a WHERE clause to specify the criteria. *Why? When you execute the command, all records in the indicated table that satisfy the criterion will be deleted.* The following steps use the SQL DELETE command to delete all records in the Workshop Offerings table on which the account number is EC010 and the workshop code is W04, as PrattLast Associates has requested. Because the combination of the Account Number and Workshop Code fields is the primary key, only one record will be deleted.

1

- Delete the existing query.
- Type **DELETE FROM [Workshop Offerings]** as the first line of the command.

Q&A

What is the purpose of the DELETE clause?

The DELETE clause indicates the table from which records will be deleted. This DELETE clause indicates that records will be deleted from the Workshop Offerings table.

- Type **WHERE [Account Number]='EC010'** as the second line.

- Type **AND [Workshop Code]='W04'** as the third line and type a semicolon on the fourth line (Figure 10–36).

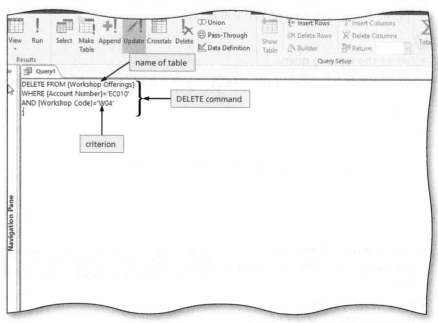

Figure 10–36

2

- Run the query.

- When Access displays a message indicating the number of records to be deleted, click the Yes button to delete the records.

Q&A

How can I see if the deletion actually occurred?

Use a SELECT query to view the records in the Workshop Offerings table.

3

- Save the query as m10q26.

- Close the query.

How do you determine any update operations to be performed?

Examine the database to determine if records must be added, updated, and/or deleted.

- **Determine INSERT operations.** Determine whether new records need to be added. Determine to which table they should be added.

- **Determine UPDATE operations.** Determine changes that need to be made to existing records. Which fields need to be changed? Which tables contain these fields? What criteria identify the rows that need to be changed?

- **Determine DELETE operations.** Determine which tables contain records that are to be deleted. What criteria identify the rows that need to be deleted?

To Restore the Font Size

Earlier you changed the font size from its default setting of 8 to 10 so the SQL queries would be easier to read. Unless you prefer to retain this new setting, you should change the setting back to the default. The following steps restore the font size to its default setting.

1 Click File on the ribbon to open the Backstage view.

2 Click Options to display the Access Options dialog box.

3 If necessary, click Object Designers to display the Object Designer options.

4 In the Query design area, click the Size box arrow, and then click 8 in the list that appears to change the size back to 8.

5 Click the OK button to close the Access Options dialog box.

6 If desired, sign out of your Microsoft account.

7 Exit Access.

BTW

Datasheet Font Size
You also can use the Access Options dialog box to change the default font and font size for datasheets. To do so, click Datasheet in the Access Options dialog box and make the desired changes in the Default font area.

Summary

In this module you have learned to create SQL queries; include fields in a query; use criteria involving both numeric and text fields as well as use compound criteria; use computed fields and rename the computation; sort the results of a query; use the built-in functions; group records in a query and also restrict the groups that appear in the results; join tables and restrict the records in a join; and use subqueries. You looked at a SQL query that was generated automatically by Access. Finally, you used the INSERT, UPDATE, and DELETE commands to update data.

CONSIDER THIS: PLAN AHEAD

What decisions will you need to make when creating your own SQL queries?
Use these guidelines as you complete the assignments in this module and create your own queries outside of this class.

1. Select the fields for the query.
 a. Examine the requirements for the query you are constructing to determine which fields are to be included.

2. Determine which table or tables contain these fields.
 a. For each field, determine the table in which it is located.

3. Determine criteria.
 a. Determine any criteria that data must satisfy to be included in the results.
 b. If there are more than two tables in the query, determine the criteria to be used to ensure the data matches correctly.

4. Determine sort order.
 a. Is the data to be sorted in some way?
 b. If so, by what field or fields is it to be sorted?

5. Determine grouping.
 a. Is the data to be grouped in some way?
 b. If so, by what field is it to be grouped?
 c. Identify any calculations to be made for the group.

6. Determine any update operations to be performed.
 a. Determine whether rows need to be inserted, changed, or deleted.
 b. Determine the tables involved.

CONSIDER THIS

How should you submit solutions to questions in the assignments identified with a symbol?
Every assignment in this book contains one or more questions identified with a symbol. These questions require you to think beyond the assigned database. Present your solutions to the questions in the format required by your instructor. Possible formats may include one or more of these options: write the answer; create a document that contains the answer; present your answer to the class; discuss your answer in a group; record the answer as audio or video using a webcam, smartphone, or portable media player; or post answers on a blog, wiki, or website.

Apply Your Knowledge
Reinforce the skills and apply the concepts you learned in this module.

Using Criteria, Joining Tables, and Sorting in SQL Queries

Instructions: Run Access. Open the Apply AllAround Services database that you modified in Module 9. (If you did not complete the exercise, see your instructor for a copy of the modified database.) Use SQL to query the Apply AllAround Services database.

Perform the following tasks:
 1. Find all clients whose client type is RET. Display all fields in the query result. Save the query as AYK Step 1 Query.
 2. Find all clients whose amount paid or current due is $0.00. Display the Client Number, Client Name, Amount Paid, and Current Due fields in the query result. Save the query as AYK Step 2 Query.

3. Find all clients in the Client table who are not located in Carlton. Display the Client Number, Client Name, and City in the query results. Save the query as AYK Step 3 Query.

4. Display the Client Number, Client Name, Supervisor Number, First Name, and Last Name for all clients. Sort the records in ascending order by supervisor number and client number. Save the query as AYK Step 4 Query.

5. Display the Supervisor Number, First Name, Last Name, and Hourly Rate for all supervisors whose Hourly Rate is greater than $13.50. Save the query as AYK Step 5 Query.

6. If requested to do so by your instructor, rename the AYK Step 5 Query as Last Name Query where Last Name is your last name.

7. Submit the revised database in the format specified by your instructor.

8. ✷ What WHERE clause would you use if you wanted to find all clients located in cities beginning with the letter K?

Extend Your Knowledge

Extend the skills you learned in this module and experiment with new skills. You may need to use Help to complete the assignment.

Note: To complete this assignment, you will be required to use the Data Files. Please contact your instructor for information about accessing the Data Files.

Instructions: Run Access. Open the Extend Helping Hands database. The Extend Helping Hands database contains information about a local business that provides nonmedical services to adults who need assistance with daily living.

Perform the following tasks:

1. Find all clients where the client's first name is either Tim or Jim. Display the Client Number, First Name, Last Name, and Address fields in the query result. Save the query as EYK Step 1 Query.

2. Find all clients who live in Upper Darby or Drexel Hill. Use the IN operator. Display the Client Number, First Name, Last Name, and City fields in the query result. Save the query as EYK Step 2 Query.

3. Find all clients whose amount paid is greater than or equal to $500.00 and less than or equal to $600.00. Use the BETWEEN operator. Display the Client Number, First Name, Last Name, and Amount Paid fields in the query result. Save the query as EYK Step 3 Query.

4. Use a subquery to find all helpers whose clients are located in Springfield. Display the Helper Number, First Name, and Last Name fields in the query result. Save the query as EYK Step 4 Query.

5. If requested to do so by your instructor, rename the EYK Step 4 Query as First Name City Query where First Name is your first name and City is the city where you currently reside.

6. Submit the revised database in the format specified by your instructor.

7. ✷ What WHERE clause would you use to find the answer to Step 2 without using the IN operator?

Continued >

Expand Your World

Create a solution, which uses cloud and web technologies, by learning and investigating on your own from general guidance.

Problem: Many SQL tutorials are available on the web. One site, www.w3schools.com/sql, has an online SQL editor that allows you to edit SQL commands and then run commands. You will use this editor to create and run queries.

Note: For each SQL statement that you create and run, use the asterisk (*) to select all fields in the table. Copy the SQL statement and the number of results retrieved to your blog, Google document, or Word document.

Perform the following tasks:
1. Create a blog, Google document, or Word document on OneDrive on which to store your SQL statements and the number of results obtained from the query. Include your name and the current date at the beginning of the blog or document.
2. Access the www.w3schools.com/sql website and spend some time becoming familiar with the tutorial and how it works.
3. Using the website, create a query to find all records in the OrderDetails table where the ProductID is 4 and the Quantity is greater than 20.
4. Create a query to find all records in the Customers table where the ContactName begins with the letter P. (*Hint:* Use the percent symbol (%), not the asterisk in this query.)
5. Create a query to find all records in the Employees table where the birth date of the employee is after January 1, 1960. (*Hint:* View all the records in the table first to determine how dates are stored. Enclose the date with single quotes.)
6. Submit the document containing your statements and results in the format specified by your instructor.
7. ✴ What differences did you notice between the online SQL editor and Access SQL? Which one would you prefer to use? Why?

In the Labs

Design, create, modify, and/or use a database following the guidelines, concepts, and skills presented in this module. Labs are listed in order of increasing difficulty. Labs 1 and 2, which increase in difficulty, require you to create solutions based on what you learned in the module; Lab 3 requires you to apply your creative thinking and problem solving skills to design and implement a solution.

Lab 1: Querying the Gardening Supply Database Using SQL

Problem: Gardening Supply wants to learn more about SQL and has determined a number of questions it wants SQL to answer. You must obtain answers to the questions using SQL.

Instructions: Perform the following tasks:

1. Run Access and open the Lab 1 Gardening Supply database that you modified in Module 9. (If you did not complete the exercise, see your instructor for a copy of the modified database.) Create a new query in SQL view.

2. Find all customers who are located in the city of Quaker. Include the Customer Number, Customer Name, and City in the query results. Save the query as ITL 1 Step 2 Query.

3. Find all customers located in New Jersey (NJ) with an amount paid greater than $3,000.00. Include the Customer Number, Customer Name, and Amount Paid fields in the query results. Save the query as ITL 1 Step 3 Query.

4. Find all customers whose names begin with the letter P. Include the Customer Number, Customer Name, and City fields in the query results. Save the query as ITL 1 Step 4 Query.

5. List all states in descending alphabetical order. Each state should appear only once. Save the query as ITL 1 Step 5 Query.

6. Display the customer number, customer name, sales rep number, sales rep first name, and sales rep last name for all customers. Sorts the results in ascending order by sales rep number and customer number. Save the query as ITL 1 Step 6 Query.

7. List the average balance due grouped by sales rep number. Include the sales rep number in the result and name the average balance as Average Balance. Save the query as ITL 1 Step 7 Query.

8. Find the customer numbers, names, and sales rep numbers for all customers that have open orders. Use the alias O for the Open Orders table and C for the Customer table. Each customer should appear only once in the results. Save the query as ITL 1 Step 8 Query.

9. Find the customer number, name, and city for every two customers who are located in the same city. Save the query as ITL 1 Step 9 Query.

10. Find the average amount paid for sales rep 30. Name the average amount paid as Average Paid. Save the query as ITL 1 Step 10 Query.

11. If requested to do so by your instructor, open the Sales Rep table and change the first and last name for sales rep 30 to your first and last name.

12. Submit the revised database in the format specified by your instructor.

13. ✸ What WHERE clause would you use to find all records where one of the Products Needed was MULCH?

Continued >

In the Labs *continued*

Lab 2: Querying the Discover Science Database Using SQL

Problem: Discover Science wants to learn more about SQL and has determined a number of questions it wants SQL to answer. You must obtain answers to the questions using SQL.

Instructions: Perform the following tasks:
1. Run Access and open the Lab 2 Discover Science database that you modified in Module 9. (If you did not complete the exercise, see your instructor for a copy of the modified database.) Create a new query in SQL view.

2. Find all records in the Item table where the difference between the retail price and the wholesale cost of an item is less than $5.00. Display the item number, description, wholesale cost, and retail price in the query results. Save the query as ITL 2 Step 2 Query.

3. Display the item number, description, and inventory value for all items. Inventory value is the result of multiplying wholesale cost by the number of items on hand. Name the computed field Inventory Value. Save the query as ITL 2 Step 3 Query.

4. Find all items where the description begins with the letter G. Include the item number and description in the query results. Save the query as ITL 2 Step 4 Query.

5. Display the vendor name, item number, description, retail price, and quantity on hand for all items where the number on hand is greater than 15. Sort the results in ascending order by vendor name and descending order by on hand. Save the query as ITL 2 Step 5 Query.

6. Find the average wholesale cost by vendor. Name the computed field Avg Wholesale. Include the vendor code in the result. Save the query as ITL 2 Step 6 Query.

7. Find the total number of reordered items in the Reorder table. Name the computed field Total Ordered. Save the query as ITL 2 Step 7 Query.

8. Add the following record to the Reorder table. (*Hint:* Use # symbols at the beginning and the end of the date ordered value.)

Item Number	Date Ordered	Number Ordered
9201	9/7/2017	5

Save the query to add the record as ITL 2 Step 8 Query.

9. If requested to do so by your instructor, rename the ITL 2 Step 8 Query as LastName Reorder Query where LastName is your last name.

10. Update the Number Ordered field to 7 for those records where the Item Number is 9201. Save the query to update the records as ITL 2 Step 10 Query.

11. Delete all records from the Reorder table where the Item Number is 9201. Save the query to delete the records as ITL 2 Step 11 Query.

12. Submit the revised database in the format specified by your instructor.

13. ✹ How would you write an SQL query to increment the number ordered by 2 for all items where the Item Number was 8344?

Lab 3: **Consider This: Your Turn**

Querying the Marketing Analytics Database Using SQL

Instructions: Open the Lab 3 Marketing Analytics database that you modified in Module 9. (If you did not complete the exercise, see your instructor for a copy of the modified database.)

Part 1:   Use the concepts and techniques presented in this module to create queries using SQL for the following. Save each query using the format ITL 3 Step x Query where x is the step letter.

a. Find the names of all clients who have the letters, ion, in their client name.

b. Find the totals of the amount paid and current due amounts for all clients. Assign the names Total Paid and Total Due.

c. Find all marketing analysts who started before 1/1/2016. Display the marketing analyst first name, last name, and start date. (*Hint:* Use # symbols at the beginning and the end of the start date value.)

d. Find the marketing analyst for each client. List the marketing analyst number, first name, last name, client number, and client name. Assign the alias C to the Client table and M to the Marketing Analyst table. Sort the results in ascending order by marketing analyst number and client number.

e. Restrict the records retrieved in Step d above to only those records where the current due amount is greater than $3,000.00.

f. Find the average current due amount grouped by marketing analyst number. Include the marketing analyst number in the results and assign the name Average Due to the average current due amount.

g. Restrict the records retrieved in Step f above to only those groups where the average current due amount is greater than $2,000.00.

h. List the client number, client name, seminar code, seminar description, and hours spent for all seminar offerings. Sort the results by client number and seminar code.

Submit your assignment in the format specified by your instructor.

Part 2:   You made several decisions while completing this assignment. What was the rationale behind your decisions? How could you modify the query in Step h to find only those clients where hours spent is equal to zero?

11 | Database Design

Objectives

You will have mastered the material in this module when you can:

- Understand the terms entity, attribute, and relationship
- Understand the terms relation and relational database
- Understand functional dependence and identify when one column is functionally dependent on another
- Understand the term primary key and identify primary keys in tables
- Design a database to satisfy a set of requirements
- Convert an unnormalized relation to first normal form
- Convert tables from first normal form to second normal form
- Convert tables from second normal form to third normal form
- Understand how to represent the design of a database using diagrams

Introduction

This module presents a method for determining the tables and fields necessary to satisfy a set of requirements. **Database design** is the process of determining the particular tables and fields that will comprise a database. In designing a database, you must identify the tables in the database, the fields in the tables, the primary keys of the tables, and the relationships between the tables.

The module begins by examining some important concepts concerning relational databases and then presents the design method. To illustrate the process, the module presents the requirements for the PrattLast Associates database. It then applies the design method to those requirements to produce the database design. The module applies the design method to a second set of requirements, which are requirements for a company called TDK Distributors. It next examines normalization, which is a process

Microsoft Access 2016

PrattLast Associates : Database C:\Users\Owner\Documents\CIS

File   Home   Create   External Data   Database Tools   ♀ Tell me what you want to do...

that you can use to identify and fix potential problems in database designs. The module concludes by explaining how to use a company's policies and objectives — which are typically addressed in existing documentation — to plan and design a database. Finally, you will learn how to represent a database design with a diagram.

Project — Design a Database

BTW
Systems Analysis
The determination of database requirements is part of a process known as systems analysis. A systems analyst interviews users, examines existing and proposed documents, investigates current procedures, and reviews organizational policies to determine exactly the type of data needs the database must support.

This module expands on the database design guidelines presented earlier. Without a good understanding of database design, you cannot use a database management system such as Access effectively. In this module, you will learn how to design two databases by using the database design process shown in Figure 11–1.

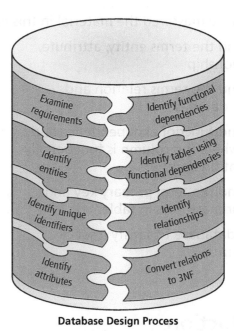

Database Design Process

Figure 11–1

You will design a database for PrattLast Associates that is similar to the database you have used in the previous modules. You will also design a database for TDK Distributors, a distributor of energy-saving and water-conservation devices.

Entities, Attributes, and Relationships

Working in the database environment requires that you be familiar with some specific terms and concepts. The terms *entity*, *attribute*, and *relationship* are fundamental when discussing databases. An **entity** is like a noun: it is a person, place, thing, or event. The entities of interest to PrattLast Associates, for example, are such things as account managers, accounts, and workshops. The entities that are of interest to a college include students, faculty, and classes; a real estate agency is interested in buyers, sellers, properties, and agents; and a used car dealer is interested in vehicles, accounts, salespeople, and manufacturers. When creating a database, an entity is represented as a table.

An **attribute** is a property of an entity. The term is used here exactly as it is used in everyday English. For the entity *person*, for example, the list of attributes might include such things as eye color and height. For PrattLast Associates, the attributes of interest for the entity *account* are such things as name, address, city, and so on. For the entity *faculty* at a school, the attributes would be such things as faculty number, name, office number, phone, and so on. For the entity *vehicle* at a car dealership, the attributes are such things as the vehicle identification number, model, price, year, and so on. In databases, attributes are represented as the fields in a table or tables.

A **relationship** is an association between entities. There is an association between account managers and accounts, for example, at PrattLast Associates. An account manager is associated with all of his or her accounts, and an account is associated with the one account manager to whom the account is assigned. Technically, you say that an account manager is *related* to all of his or her accounts, and an account is *related* to his or her account manager.

The relationship between account managers and accounts is an example of a one-to-many relationship because one account manager is associated with many accounts, but each account is associated with only one account manager. In this type of relationship, the word *many* is used in a way that is different from everyday English; it might not always mean a large number. In this context, for example, the term *many* means that an account manager might be associated with *any* number of accounts. That is, one account manager can be associated with zero, one, or more accounts.

There is also a relationship between accounts and workshops. Each account can be offered many workshops, and each workshop can be offered to many accounts. This is an example of a many-to-many relationship.

How does a relational database handle entities, attributes of entities, and relationships between entities? Entities and attributes are fairly simple. Each entity has its own table; in the PrattLast Associates database, there is one table for account managers, one table for accounts, and so on. The attributes of an entity become the columns in the table. In the table for accounts, for example, there is a column for the account number, a column for the account name, and so on.

What about relationships? Relationships are implemented through matching fields. One-to-many relationships, for example, are implemented by including matching fields in the related tables. Account managers and accounts are related, for example, by including the Account Manager Number field in both the Account Manager table and the Account table.

Many-to-many relationships are implemented through an additional table that contains matching fields for both of the related tables. Accounts and workshops are related, for example, through the Workshop Offerings table. Both the Account table and the Workshop Offerings table contain Account Number fields. In addition, both the Workshop and the Workshop Offerings table contain Workshop Code fields.

BTW
Entities
PrattLast Associates could include many other entities in a database, such as entities for employees, and for inventories of software and hardware. The decisions on which entities to include are part of the process of determining database requirements based on user needs.

BTW
Relationships
One-to-one relationships also can occur but they are not common. To implement a one-to-one relationship, treat it as a one-to-many relationship. You must determine which table will be the one table and which table will be the many table. To do so, consider what may happen in the future. In the case of one project that has one employee assigned to it, more employees could be added. Therefore, the project table would be the one table and the employee table would be the many table.

Relational Databases

A relational database is a collection of tables similar to the tables for PrattLast Associates that appear in Figure 11–2. In the PrattLast Associates database, the Account table contains information about the accounts to which PrattLast Associates provides human resource services (Figure 11–2a). Note that, for simplification purposes, the tables in the figure do not include all the fields of the final PrattLast database in Module 10.

Account

Account Number	Account Name	Street	City	State	Postal Code	Amount Paid	Current Due	Account Manager Number
AC001	Avondale Community Bank	256 Main St.	Avondale	IL	60311	$24,752.25	$3,875.25	31
BL235	Bland Corp.	100 South Granger Hwy.	Granger	IL	60314	$29,836.65	$2,765.30	35
CA043	Carlton Regional Clinic	589 Central Ave.	Carlton	IL	60313	$30,841.05	$3,074.30	58
CO621	Codder Plastics Co.	421 First Ave.	Bremerton	IN	46003	$27,152.25	$2,875.00	35
EC010	Eco Clothes Inc.	120 Pine St.	Davidson	IN	46010	$19,620.00	$1,875.00	58
HL111	Halko Legal Associates	321 Feathering Rd.	Gleneagle	IL	60319	$25,702.20	$3,016.75	58
KC156	Key Community College System	35 Indiana Ave.	Walker	IN	46004	$10,952.25	$0.00	31
KV089	KAL Veterinary Services	116 Pine St.	Granger	IL	60314	$34,036.50	$580.00	35
LC005	Lancaster County Hospital	215 River St.	Granger	IL	46004	$44,025.60	$3,590.80	58
LI268	Lars-Idsen-Fleming Inc.	829 Wooster Rd.	Davidson	IN	46010	$ 0.00	$1,280.75	35
MI345	Midwest Library Consortium	3400 Metro Pkwy.	Bremerton	IN	46003	$21,769.20	$2,890.60	31
ML008	Mums Landscaping Co.	865 Ridge Rd.	Wells	IN	46007	$13,097.10	$2,450.00	35
SL126	South Library Consortium	862 Maple St.	Wells	IN	46007	$ 0.00	$0.00	58
TP098	TDK Packaging Systems	12 Polk Ave.	Carlton	IL	60313	$22,696.95	$3,480.45	58
TW001	Tri-County Waste Disposal	345 Central Blvd.	Rushton	IL	60321	$15,345.00	$2,875.50	31

Figure 11–2 (a) Account Table

PrattLast assigns each account to a specific account manager. The Account Manager table contains information about the managers to whom these accounts are assigned (Figure 11–2b).

Account Manager

Account Manager Number	Last Name	First Name	Street	City	State	Postal Code	Salary	Bonus Rate
31	Rivera	Haydee	325 Twiddy St.	Avondale	IL	60311	$36,750.00	0.15
35	Simson	Mark	1467 Hartwell St.	Walker	IN	46004	$24,000.00	0.12
42	Lu	Peter	5624 Murray Ave.	Davidson	IN	46007	$48,750.00	0.09
58	Murowski	Karen	168 Truesdale Dr.	Carlton	IL	60313	$40,500.00	0.08

Figure 11–2 (b) Account Manager Table

The Workshop table lists the specific workshops that the account managers at PrattLast Associates offer to their accounts (Figure 11–2c). Each workshop has a code and a description. The table also includes the number of hours for which the workshop is usually offered and the workshop's increments, that is, the standard time blocks in which the workshop is usually offered. The first row, for example, indicates that workshop W01 is Dealing with Unacceptable Employee Behavior. The workshop is typically offered in 2-hour increments for a total of 4 hours.

Workshop			
Workshop Code	Workshop Description	Hours	Increments
W01	Dealing with Unacceptable Employee Behavior	4	2
W02	Writing Effective Policies and Procedures	8	4
W03	Payroll Law	3	1
W04	Workplace Safety	16	4
W05	The Recruitment Process	24	4
W06	Diversity in the Workplace	12	3
W07	Americans with Disabilities Act (ADA)	4	2
W08	Workers' Compensation	16	4

Figure 11–2 (c) Workshop Table

The Workshop Offerings table contains an account number, a workshop code, the total number of hours for which the workshop is scheduled, and the number of hours the account has already spent in the workshop (Figure 11–2d). The first record shows that account number AC001 has currently scheduled workshop W01. The workshop is scheduled for 6 hours, of which 2 hours have currently been spent. The total hours are usually the same as the number of hours indicated for the workshop in the Workshop table, but it can differ.

Workshop Offerings			
Account Number	Workshop Code	Total Hours	Hours Spent
AC001	W01	6	2
AC001	W02	8	4
AC001	W03	3	0
EC010	W05	24	12
KC156	W08	16	8
KV089	W07	4	0
LC005	W02	8	4
LC005	W06	12	6
ML008	W03	3	1
ML008	W04	16	4
SL126	W05	24	16
SL126	W06	12	3
SL126	W07	4	2
TP098	W03	3	0
TP098	W08	16	4
TW001	W01	4	2

Figure 11–2 (d) Workshop Offerings Table

The formal term for a table is relation. If you study the tables shown in Figure 11–2, you might see that there are certain restrictions you should place on relations. Each column in a table should have a unique name, and entries in each column should match this column name. For example, in the Postal Code column, all entries should in fact *be* postal codes. In addition, each row should be unique. After all, if two rows in a table contain identical data, the second row does not provide any information that you do not already have. In addition, for maximum flexibility, the order in which columns and rows appear in a table should be immaterial. Finally, a table's design is less complex if you restrict each position in the table to a single entry, that is, you do not permit multiple entries, often called **repeating groups,** in the table. These restrictions lead to the following definition:

A **relation** is a two-dimensional table in which:

1. The entries in the table are single-valued; that is, each location in the table contains a single entry.
2. Each column has a distinct name, technically called the *attribute name*.
3. All values in a column are values of the same attribute; that is, all entries must correspond to the column name.
4. Each row is distinct; that is, no two rows are identical.

Figure 11–3a shows a table with repeating groups, which violates Rule 1. Figure 11–3b shows a table in which two columns have the same name, which violates Rule 2. Figure 11–3c shows a table in which one of the entries in the Workshop Description column is not a workshop description, which violates Rule 3. Figure 11–3d shows a table with two identical rows, which violates Rule 4.

Figure 11–3 (a) Workshop Offerings Table Violation of Rule 1 — Table Contains Repeating Groups

Figure 11–3 (b) Workshop Table Violation of Rule 2 — Each Column Should Have a Distinct Name

Workshop			
Workshop Code	**Workshop Description**	**Hours**	**Increments**
W01	Dealing with Unacceptable Employee Behavior	4	2
W02	Writing Effective Policies and Procedures	8	4
W03	?@!	3	1
W04	Workplace Safety	16	4
W05	The Recruitment Process	24	4
W06	Diversity in the Workplace	12	3
W07	Americans with Disabilities Act (ADA)	4	2
W08	Workers' Compensation	16	4

value does not correspond to column name; that is, it is not a workshop description

Figure 11–3 (c) Workshop Table Violation of Rule 3 — All Entries in a Column Must Correspond to the Column Name

Workshop			
Workshop Code	**Workshop Description**	**Hours**	**Increments**
W01	Dealing with Unacceptable Employee Behavior	4	2
W02	Writing Effective Policies and Procedures	8	4
W03	Payroll Law	3	1
W03	Payroll Law	3	1
W04	Workplace Safety	16	4
W05	The Recruitment Process	24	4
W06	Diversity in the Workplace	12	3
W07	Americans with Disabilities Act (ADA)	4	2
W08	Workers' Compensation	16	4

identical rows

Figure 11–3 (d) Workshop Table Violation of Rule 4 — Each Row Should Be Distinct

In addition, in a relation, the order of columns is immaterial. The order of rows is also immaterial. You can view the columns or rows in any order you want.

A **relational database** is a collection of relations. Rows in a table (relation) are often called **records** or **tuples**. Columns in a table (relation) are often called **fields** or **attributes**. Typically, the terms *record* and *field* are used in Access.

To depict the structure of a relational database, you can use a commonly accepted shorthand representation: you write the name of the table and then within parentheses list all of the fields in the table. Each table should begin on a new line. If the entries in the table occupy more than one line, the entries that appear on the next line should be indented so it is clear that they do not constitute another table. Using this method, you would represent the PrattLast Associates database as shown in Figure 11–4.

Account (Account Number, Account Name, Street, City, State, Postal Code, Amount Paid, Current Due, Account Manager Number)

Account Manager (Account Manager Number, Last Name, First Name, Street, City, State, Postal Code, Salary, Bonus Rate)

Workshop (Workshop Code, Workshop Description, Hours, Increments)

Workshop Offerings (Account Number, Workshop Code, Total Hours, Hours Spent)

Figure 11–4

The PrattLast Associates database contains some duplicate field names. For example, the Account Manager Number field appears in *both* the Account Manager table *and* the Account table. This duplication of names can lead to possible confusion. If you write Account Manager Number, it is not clear to which Account Manager Number field you are referring.

When duplicate field names exist in a database, you need to indicate the field to which you are referring. You do so by writing both the table name and the field name, separated by a period. You would write the Account Manager Number field in the Account table as Account.Account Manager Number and the Account Manager Number field in the Account Manager table as Account Manager.Account Manager Number. As you learned previously, when you combine a field name with a table name, you say that you **qualify** the field names. It is *always* acceptable to qualify field names, even if there is no possibility of confusion. If confusion may arise, however, it is *essential* to qualify field names.

Functional Dependence

BTW
Functional
Dependence
To help identify functional dependencies, ask yourself the following question. If you know a unique value for an attribute, do you know the unique values for another attribute? For example, when you have three attributes — Account Manager Number, Last Name, and First Name — and you know a unique value for Account Manager Number, do you also know a unique value for Last Name and First Name? If so, then Last Name and First Name are functionally dependent on Account Manager Number.

In the PrattLast Associates database (Figure 11–2), a given account number in the database will correspond to a single account because account numbers are unique. Thus, if you are given an account number in the database, you could find a single name that corresponds to it. No ambiguity exists. The database terminology for this relationship between account numbers and names is that Account Number determines Account Name, or, equivalently, that Account Name is functionally dependent on Account Number. Specifically, if you know that whenever you are given a value for one field, you will be able to determine a single value for a second field, the first field is said to **determine** the second field. In addition, the second field is said to be **functionally dependent** on the first.

There is a shorthand notation that represents functional dependencies using an arrow. To indicate that Account Number determines Account Name, or, equivalently, that Account Name is functionally dependent on Account Number, you would write Account Number → Account Name. The field that precedes the arrow determines the field that follows the arrow.

If you were given a city and asked to find a single account's name, you could not do it. Given Granger as the city, for example, you would find two account names, Bland Corp. and KAL Veterinary Services (Figure 11–5). Formally, you would say the City does *not* determine Account Name, or that Account Name is *not* functionally dependent on City.

CONSIDER THIS

In the Account Manager table, is Last Name functionally dependent on Account Manager Number?
Yes. If you are given a value for Account Manager Number, for example 42, you will always find a *single* last name, in this case Lu, associated with it.

In the Account table, is Account Name functionally dependent on Account Manager Number?
No. A given Account Manager Number occurs on multiple rows. Account Manager Number 35, for example, occurs on a row in which the Account Name is Bland Corp. It also occurs on a row in which the Account Name is KAL Veterinary Services. Thus, rep number 35 is associated with more than one account name.

Account								
Account Number	Account Name	Street	City	State	Postal Code	Amount Paid	Current Due	Account Manager Number
AC001	Avondale Community Bank	256 Main St.	Avondale	IL	60311	$24,752.25	$3,875.25	31
BL235	Bland Corp.	100 South Granger Hwy.	Granger	IL	60314	$29,836.65	$2,765.30	35
CA043	Carlton Regional Clinic	589 Central Ave.	Carlton	IL	60313	$30,841.05	$3,074.30	58
CO621	Codder Plastics Co.	421 First Ave.	Bremerton	IN	46003	$27,152.25	$2,875.00	35
EC010	Eco Clothes Inc.	120 Pine St.	Davidson	IN	46010	$19,620.00	$1,875.00	58
HL111	Halko Legal Associates	321 Feathering Rd.	Gleneagle	IL	60319	$25,702.20	$3,016.75	58
KC156	Key Community College System	35 Indiana Ave.	Walker	IN	46004	$10,952.25	$0.00	31
KV089	KAL Veterinary Services	116 Pine St.	Granger	IL	60314	$34,036.50	$580.00	35
LC005	Lancaster County Hospital	215 River St.	Granger	IL	46004	$44,025.60	$3,590.80	58
LI268	Lars-Idsen-Fleming Inc.	829 Wooster Rd.	Davidson	IN	46010	$0.00	$1,280.75	35
MI345	Midwest Library Consortium	3400 Metro Pkwy.	Bremerton	IN	46003	$21,769.20	$2,890.60	31
ML008	Mums Landscaping Co.		Wells	IN	46007	$13,097.10	$2,450.00	35
SL126	South Library Consortium	862 Maple St.	Wells	IN	46007	$0.00	$0.00	58
TP098	TDK Packaging Systems	12 Polk Ave.	Carlton	IL	60313	$22,696.95	$3,480.45	58
TW001	Tri-County Waste Disposal	345 Central Blvd.	Rushton	IL	60321	$15,345.00	$2,875.50	31

Annotation (top): city is Granger; name is Bland Corp.

Annotation (middle): city is also Granger, but name is KAL Veterinary Services (same city, but different account name)

Figure 11–5

In the Workshop Offerings table, is Hours Spent functionally dependent on Account Number?
No. There is a row, for example, in which the Account Number is AC001 and the Hours Spent is 2. There is another row in which the Account Number is AC001 but the Hours Spent is 4, a different number.

In the Workshop Offerings table, is Hours Spent functionally dependent on Workshop Code?
No. There is a row, for example, in which the Workshop Code is WO3 and the Hours Spent is 0. There is another row in which the Workshop Code is W03 but the Hours Spent is 1, a different number.

On which fields is Hours Spent functionally dependent?
To determine a value for Hours Spent, you need both an Account Number and a Workshop Code. In other words, Hours Spent is functionally dependent on the combination, formally called the **concatenation**, of Account Number and Workshop Code. That is, given an Account Number *and* a Workshop Code, you can find a single value for Hours Spent.

On which fields is Total Hours functionally dependent?
Because the Total Hours field for a given workshop can vary from one account to another, Total Hours is also functionally dependent on the combination of Account Number and Workshop Code.

On which fields would Total Hours be functionally dependent if every time a workshop was scheduled, Total Hours had to be the same as the number of hours given in the Workshop table?
In that case, to determine Total Hours, you would only need to know the Workshop Code. Thus, Total Hours would be functionally dependent on Workshop Code.

Primary Key

The **primary key** of a table is the field or minimum collection of fields — the fewest number of fields possible — that uniquely identifies a given row in that table. In the Account Manager table, the account manager's number uniquely identifies a given row. Any account manager number appears on only one row of the table. Thus, Account Manager Number is the primary key. Similarly, Account Number is the primary key of the Account table, and Workshop Code is the primary key of the Workshop table.

Is the Account Number field the primary key for the Workshop Offerings table?
No, because it does not functionally determine either Total Hours or Hours Spent.

Is the Workshop Code field the primary key for the Workshop Offerings table?
No, because, like Account Number, it does not functionally determine either Total Hours or Hours Spent.

What is the primary key of the Workshop Offerings table?
The primary key is the combination of the Account Number and Workshop Code fields. You can determine all other fields from this combination. Further, neither the Account Number nor the Workshop Code alone has this property.

Is the combination of the Workshop Code and Workshop Description fields the primary key for the Workshop table?
No. Although it is true that you can determine all fields in the Workshop table by this combination, Workshop Code alone also has this property. The Workshop Code field is the primary key.

BTW
Candidate Keys
According to the definition of a candidate key, a Social Security number is a legitimate primary key. Many databases use a person's Social Security number as a primary key. However, many institutions and organizations are moving away from using Social Security numbers because of privacy issues. Instead, many institutions and organizations use unique student numbers or employee numbers as primary keys.

The primary key provides an important way of distinguishing one row in a table from another. In the shorthand representation, you underline the field or collection of fields that comprise the primary key for each table in the database. Thus, the complete shorthand representation for the PrattLast Associates database is shown in Figure 11–6.

Account (<u>Account Number</u>, Account Name, Street, City, State, Postal Code, Amount Paid, Current Due, Account Manager Number)

Account Manager (<u>Account Manager Number</u>, Last Name, First Name, Street, City, State, Postal Code, Salary, Bonus Rate)

Workshop (<u>Workshop Code</u>, Workshop Description, Hours, Increments)

Workshop Offerings (<u>Account Number</u>, <u>Workshop Code</u>, Total Hours, Hours Spent)

Figure 11–6

Occasionally, but not often, there might be more than one possibility for the primary key. For example, if the PrattLast Associates database included the account manager's Social Security number in the Account Manager table, either the account manager number or the Social Security number could serve as the primary key. In this case, both fields are referred to as candidate keys. Similar to a primary key, a **candidate key** is a field or combination of fields on which all fields in the table are functionally dependent. Thus, the definition for primary key really defines candidate key as well. There can be many candidate keys, although having more than one is very rare. By contrast, there is only one primary key. The remaining candidate keys are called **alternate keys.**

Database Design

This section presents a specific database design method, based on a set of requirements that the database must support. The section then presents a sample of such requirements and illustrates the design method by designing a database to satisfy these requirements.

Design Process

The following is a method for designing a database for a set of requirements.

1. Examine the requirements and identify the entities, or objects, involved. Assign names to the entities. The entities will become tables. If, for example, the design involves the entities departments and employees, you could assign the names, Department and Employee. If the design involves the entities accounts, orders, and parts, you could assign the names, Account, Orders, and Part.

NOTE: The word, Order, has special meaning in SQL. If you use it for the name of a table, you will not be able to use SQL to query that table. A common approach to avoid this problem is to make the name plural. That is the reason for choosing Orders rather than Order as the name of the table.

2. Assign a unique identifier to each entity. For example, if one of the entities is "item," you would determine what it takes to uniquely identify each individual item. In other words, what enables the organization to distinguish one item from another? For an item entity, it may be Item Number. For an account entity, it may be Account Number. If there is no such unique identifier, it is a good idea to add one. Perhaps the previous system was a manual one where accounts were not assigned numbers, in which case this would be a good time to add Account Numbers to the system. If there is no natural candidate for a primary key, you can add an AutoNumber field, which is similar to the ID field that Access adds automatically when you create a new table.

3. Identify the attributes for all the entities. These attributes will become the fields in the tables. It is possible that more than one entity has the same attribute. At PrattLast Associates, for example, accounts and account managers both have the attributes of street address, city, state, and postal code. To address this duplication, you can follow the name of the attribute with the corresponding entity in parentheses. Thus, Street (Account) would be the street address of an account, whereas Street (Account Manager) would be the street address of an account manager.

4. Identify the functional dependencies that exist among the attributes.

5. Use the functional dependencies to identify the tables. You do this by placing each attribute with the attribute or minimum combination of attributes on which it is functionally dependent. The attribute or attributes on which all other attributes in the table are dependent will be the primary key of the table. The remaining attributes will be the other fields in the table. Once you have determined all the fields in the table, you can assign an appropriate name to the table.

6. Determine and implement relationships among the entities. The basic relationships are one-to-many and many-to-many.

One-to-many. You implement a one-to-many relationship by including the primary key of the "one" table as a foreign key in the "many" table. A **foreign key** is a field in one table whose values are required to match the *primary key* of another table. In the one-to-many relationship between account managers and accounts, for example, you include the primary key of the Account Manager Table, which is Account Manager Number, as a foreign key in the Account table. You may have already included this field in the earlier steps. If so, you would simply designate it as a foreign key. If you had not already added it, you would need to add it at this point, designating it as a foreign key.

Many-to-many. A many-to-many relationship is implemented by creating a new table whose primary key is the combination of the keys of the original tables. To implement the many-to-many relationship between accounts and workshops, for example, you would create a table whose primary key is the combination of Account Number and Workshop Code, which are the primary keys of the original tables. Both of the fields that make up the primary key of the new table will also be foreign keys. The Account Number field, for example, will be a foreign key required to match the primary key of the Account table. Similarly, the Workshop Code field will be a foreign key required to match the primary key of the Workshop table.

You may have already identified such a table in the earlier steps, in which case, all you need to do is to be sure you have designated each portion of the primary key as a foreign key that is required to match the primary key of the appropriate table. If you have not, you would add the table at this point. The primary key will consist of the primary keys from each of the tables to be related. If there are any attributes that depend on the combination of fields that make up the primary key, you need to include them in this table. (*Note:* There may not be any other fields that are dependent on this combination. In that case, there will be no fields besides the fields that make up the primary key.)

The following sections illustrate the design process by designing the database for PrattLast Associates. The next section gives the requirements that this database must support, and the last section creates a database design based on those requirements.

Requirements for the PrattLast Associates Database

Systems analysts have examined the needs and organizational policies at PrattLast Associates and have determined that the PrattLast Associates database must support the following requirements:

1. For an account, PrattLast needs to maintain the account number, name, street address, city, state, postal code, amount paid, and the amount that is currently due. They also need the total amount, which is the sum of the amount already paid and the current amount due.

2. For an account manager, store the account manager number, last name, first name, street address, city, state, postal code, salary paid, and bonus rate.

3. For a workshop, store the workshop code, workshop description, hours, and increments. In addition, for each offering of the workshop, store the number of the account for whom the workshop is offered, the total number of hours planned for the offering of the workshop, and the number of hours already spent in the workshop. The total hours spent may be the same as the normal total number of hours for the workshop, but it need not be. This gives PrattLast the flexibility of tailoring the offering of the workshop to the specific needs of the account.

4. Each account has a single account manager to which the account is assigned. Each account manager may be assigned many accounts.

5. An account may be offered many workshops and a workshop may be offered to many accounts.

Design of the PrattLast Associates Database

The following represents the application of the design method for the PrattLast Associates requirements.

1. There appear to be three entities: accounts, account managers, and workshops. Reasonable names for the corresponding tables are Account, Account Manager, and Workshop, respectively.

2. The unique identifier for accounts is the account number. The unique identifier for account managers is the account manager number. The unique identifier for workshops is the workshop code. Reasonable names for the unique identifiers are Account Number, Account Manager Number, and Workshop Code, respectively.

3. The attributes are:

>**Account Number**
>
>**Account Name**
>
>**Street (Account)**
>
>**City (Account)**
>
>**State (Account)**
>
>**Postal Code (Account)**
>
>**Amount Paid**
>
>**Current Due**
>
>**Account Manager Number**
>
>**Last Name**
>
>**First Name**
>
>**Street (Account Manager)**
>
>**City (Account Manager)**
>
>**State (Account Manager)**
>
>**Postal Code (Account Manager)**
>
>**Salary**
>
>**Bonus Rate**
>
>**Workshop Code**

> **Workshop Description**
>
> **Hours**
>
> **Increments**
>
> **Total Hours**
>
> **Hours Spent**

Remember that parentheses after an attribute indicate the entity to which the attribute corresponds. Thus, Street (Account) represents the street address of an account in a way that distinguishes it from Street (Account Manager), which represents the street address of an account manager.

CONSIDER THIS

Why is Total Amount not included?

Total Amount, which is Amount Paid plus Current Due, can be calculated from other fields. You can perform this calculation in queries, forms, and reports. Thus, there is no need to include it as a field in the Account table. Further, by including it, you introduce the possibility of errors in the database. For example, if Amount Paid is $5,000, Current Due is $2,000, yet you set Total Amount equal to $8,000, you have an error. You would also need to be sure to change Total Amount appropriately whenever you change either Amount Paid or Current Due. If it is not stored, but rather calculated when needed, you avoid all these problems.

If including the Total Amount field is not appropriate, why did we include the Total Amount field in the Account table in earlier modules?

Access allows calculated fields. Rather than storing a value, you simply indicate the calculation. Access will calculate the value when needed. This approach avoids the above problems, so you actually could include the field. Often, however, you will still decide to not include a calculated field. If you plan to use another database management system, for example, an earlier version of Access, you should not include it. In addition, if you are using Access but plan to use the database with SQL Server, you should not include it.

4. The functional dependencies among the attributes are:

> **Account Number → Account Name, Street (Account), City (Account), State (Account), Postal Code (Account), Amount Paid, Current Due, Account Manager Number**
>
> **Account Manager Number → Last Name, First Name, Street (Account Manager), City (Account Manager), State (Account Manager), Postal Code (Account Manager), Salary, Bonus Rate**
>
> **Workshop Code → Workshop Description, Hours, Increments**
>
> **Account Number, Workshop Code → Total Hours, Hours Spent**

CONSIDER THIS

Why is Total Hours listed with Account Number and Workshop Code rather than just with Workshop Code?

If the total hours were required to be the same as the number of hours for the workshop, then it would indeed be listed with Workshop Code because it would not vary from one account to another. Because PrattLast wants the flexibility of tailoring the number of hours for which a particular workshop is offered to the specific needs of the account, Total Hours is also dependent on Account Number.

The account's name, street address, city, state, postal code, amount paid, and current due are dependent only on account number. Because an account has a single account manager, the account manager number is dependent on account number as well. The account manager's last name, first name, street address, city, state, postal code, salary, and bonus rate are dependent only on account manager number. A workshop description, the number of hours for the workshop, and the increments in which the workshop is offered are dependent only on workshop code. The total hours for a particular workshop offering as well as the hours already spent are dependent on the combination of account number and workshop code.

5. The shorthand representation for the tables is shown in Figure 11–7.

Account (<u>Account Number</u>, Account Name, Street, City, State, Postal Code, Amount Paid, Current Due, Account Manager Number)

Account Manager (<u>Account Manager Number</u>, Last Name, First Name, Street, City, State, Postal Code, Salary, Bonus Rate)

Workshop (<u>Workshop Code</u>, Workshop Description, Hours, Increments)

Workshop Offerings (<u>Account Number</u>, <u>Workshop Code</u>, Total Hours, Hours Spent)

Figure 11–7

6. The following are the relationships between the tables:

a. The Account and Account Manager tables are related using the Account Manager Number fields, which is the primary key of the Account Manager table. The Account Manager Number field in the Account table is a foreign key.

b. The Account and Workshop Offerings tables are related using the Account Number field, which is the primary key of the Account table. The Account Number field in the Workshop Offerings table is a foreign key.

c. The Workshop and Workshop Offerings tables are related using the Workshop Code field, which is the primary key of the Workshop table. The Workshop Code field in the Workshop Offerings table is a foreign key.

Does a many-to-many relationship exist between accounts and workshops?
Yes. The Workshop Offerings table will implement a many-to-many relationship between accounts and workshops. You identified this table as part of the database design process. If you had not, you would need to add it at this point.

In the Workshop Offerings table, the primary key consists of two fields, Account Number and Workshop Code. There are two additional fields, Total Hours and Hours Spent. What if the design requirements did not require these additional fields? Would we still need the Workshop Offerings table?
Yes, because this table implements the many-to-many relationship between accounts and workshops. It is perfectly legitimate for the table that implements a many-to-many relationship to contain no columns except the two columns that constitute the primary key.

In the Workshop Offerings table, the primary key consists of two fields, Account Number and Workshop Code. Does the Account Number field have to come first?
No. The Workshop Code could have come first just as well.

CONSIDER THIS

NOTE: In the shorthand representation for a table containing a foreign key, you would represent the foreign key by using the letters FK, followed by an arrow, followed by the name of the table in which that field is the primary key. For example, to indicate that the Account Manager Number in the Account table is a foreign key that must match the primary key of the Account Manager table, you would write FK Account Manager Number → Account Manager.

The shorthand representation for the tables and foreign keys is shown in Figure 11–8. It is common to list a table containing a foreign key after the table that contains the corresponding primary key, when possible. Thus, in the figure, the Account Manager table has been moved so that it comes before the Account table.

Account Manager (<u>Account Manager Number</u>, Last Name, First Name, Street, City, State, Postal Code, Salary, Bonus Rate)

Account (<u>Account Number</u>, Account Name, Street, City, State, Postal Code, Amount Paid, Current Due, Account Manager Number)
FK Account Manager Number → Account Manager

Workshop (<u>Workshop Code</u>, Workshop Description, Hours, Increments)

Workshop Offerings (<u>Account Number</u>, <u>Workshop Code</u>, Total Hours, Hours Spent)
FK Account Number → Account
FK Workshop Code → Workshop

Figure 11–8

TDK Distributors

The management of TDK Distributors, a distributor of energy-saving and water-conservation items, has determined that the company's rapid growth requires a database to maintain customer, order, and inventory data. With the data stored in a database, management will be able to ensure that the data is current and more accurate. In addition, managers will be able to obtain answers to their questions concerning the data in the database quickly and easily, with the option of producing a variety of reports.

Requirements for the TDK Distributors Database

A system analyst has interviewed users and examined documents at TDK Distributors, and has determined that the company needs a database that will support the following requirements:

1. For a sales rep, store the rep's number, last name, first name, street address, city, state, postal code, total commission, and commission rate.

2. For a customer, store the customer's number, name, street address, city, state, postal code, balance owed, and credit limit. These customers are businesses, so it is appropriate to store a single name, rather than first name and last name as you would if the customers were individuals. Additional fields you need to store are the number, last name, and first name of the sales rep representing this customer. The analyst has also determined that a sales rep can represent many customers, but a customer must have exactly one sales rep. In other words, one sales rep must represent each customer; a customer cannot be represented by zero or more than one sales rep.

3. For an item, store the item's number, description, units on hand, the category the item is in, and the price.

4. For an order, store the order number, order date, the number and name of the customer placing the order, and the number of the sales rep representing that customer. For each line item within an order, store the item's number and description, the number ordered, and the quoted price. The analyst also obtained the following information concerning orders:

a. There is only one customer per order.

b. On a given order, each item is listed as a single line. For example, item DR93 cannot appear on multiple lines within the same order.

c. The quoted price might differ from the actual price in cases in which the sales rep offers a discount for a certain item on a specific order.

Design of the TDK Distributors Database

The following steps apply the design process to the requirements for TDK Distributors to produce the appropriate database design:

1. Assign entity names. There appear to be four entities: reps, customers, items, and orders. The names assigned to these entities are Rep, Customer, Item, and Orders, respectively.

2. Determine unique identifiers. From the collection of entities, review the data and determine the unique identifier for each entity. For the Rep, Customer, Item, and Orders entities, the unique identifiers are the rep number, the customer number, the item number, and the order number, respectively. These unique identifiers are named Rep Number, Customer Number, Item Number, and Order Number, respectively.

3. Assign attribute names. The attributes mentioned in the first requirement all refer to sales reps. The specific attributes mentioned in the requirement are the sales rep's number, last name, first name, street address, city, state, postal code, total commission, and commission rate. Assigning appropriate names to these attributes produces the following list:

> **Rep Number**
> **Last Name**
> **First Name**
> **Street**
> **City**
> **State**
> **Postal Code**
> **Commission**
> **Rate**

The attributes mentioned in the second requirement refer to customers. The specific attributes are the customer's number, name, street address, city, state, postal code, balance, and credit limit. The requirement also mentions the number, first name, and last name of the sales rep representing this customer. Assigning appropriate names to these attributes produces the following list:

> **Customer Number**
> **Customer Name**
> **Street**
> **City**
> **State**

BTW
Line Items
A line item is a unit of information that appears on its own line. For example, when you purchase groceries, each grocery item appears on its own line. Line items also can be referred to as order line items or item detail lines.

Postal Code

Balance

Credit Limit

Rep Number

Last Name

First Name

CONSIDER THIS

Do you need to include the last name and first name of a sales rep in the list of attributes for the second requirement?
There is no need to include them in this list, because they can both be determined from the sales rep number and are already included in the list of attributes determined by Rep Number. They will be removed in a later step.

There are attributes named Street, City, State, and Postal Code for sales reps as well as attributes named Street, City, State, and Postal Code for customers. To distinguish these attributes in the final collection, the name of the attribute is followed by the name of the corresponding entity. For example, the street for a sales rep is Street (Rep) and the street for a customer is Street (Customer).

The attributes mentioned in the third requirement refer to items. The specific attributes are the item's number, description, units on hand, category, and price. Assigning appropriate names to these attributes produces the following list:

Item Number

Description

On Hand

Category

Price

The attributes mentioned in the fourth requirement refer to orders. The specific attributes include the order number, order date, the number and name of the customer placing the order, and the number of the sales rep representing the customer. Assigning appropriate names to these attributes produces the following list:

Order Number

Order Date

Customer Number

Customer Name

Rep Number

The statement concerning orders indicates that there are specific attributes to be stored for each line item within the order. These attributes are the item number, description, the number ordered, and the quoted price. If the quoted price must be the same as the price in the Item table, you could simply call it Price. According to requirement 4c, however, the quoted price might differ from the item price. Thus, you must add the quoted price to the list. Assigning appropriate names to these attributes produces the following list:

Item Number

Description

Number Ordered

Quoted Price

The complete list grouped by entity is as follows:

Rep

  Rep Number
  Last Name
  First Name
  Street (Rep)
  City (Rep)
  State (Rep)
  Postal Code (Rep)
  Commission
  Rate

Customer

  Customer Number
  Customer Name
  Street (Customer)
  City (Customer)
  State (Customer)
  Postal Code (Customer)
  Balance
  Credit Limit
  Rep Number
  Last Name
  First Name

Item

  Item Number
  Description
  On Hand
  Category
  Price

Orders

  Order Number
  Order Date
  Customer Number
  Customer Name
  Rep Number

For line items within an order:

  Order Number
  Item Number
  Description
  Number Ordered
  Quoted Price

4. Identify functional dependencies. The fact that the unique identifier for sales reps is the Rep Number gives the following functional dependencies:

Rep Number → Last Name, First Name, Street (Rep), City (Rep), State (Rep), Postal Code (Rep), Commission, Rate

The fact that the unique identifier for customers is the Customer Number gives the following preliminary list of functional dependencies:

Customer Number → Customer Name, Street (Customer), City (Customer), State (Customer), Postal Code (Customer), Balance, Credit Limit, Rep Number, Last Name, First Name

The fact that the unique identifier for items is the Item Number gives the following functional dependencies:

Item Number → Description, On Hand, Category, Price

The fact that the unique identifier for orders is the Order Number gives the following functional dependencies:

Order Number → Order Date, Customer Number, Customer Name, Rep Number

CONSIDER THIS

Do you need to include the name of a customer and the number of the customer's rep in the list of attributes determined by the order number?
There is no need to include the customer name and the rep number in this list because you can determine them from the customer number, and they are already included in the list of attributes determined by customer number. They will be removed in the next step.

The final attributes to be examined are those associated with the line items within the order: Item Number, Description, Number Ordered, and Quoted Price.

CONSIDER THIS

Why are Number Ordered and Quoted Price not included in the list of attributes determined by the Order Number?
To uniquely identify a particular value for Number Ordered or Quoted Price, Order Number alone is not sufficient. It requires the combination of Order Number and Item Number.

The following shorthand representation indicates that the combination of Order Number and Item Number functionally determines Number Ordered and Quoted Price:

Order Number, Item Number → Number Ordered, Quoted Price

CONSIDER THIS

Does Description need to be included in this list?
No, because Description can be determined by the Item Number alone, and it already appears in the list of attributes dependent on the Item Number.

The complete list of functional dependencies with appropriate revisions is as follows:

Rep Number → Last Name, First Name, Street (Rep), City (Rep), State (Rep), Postal Code (Rep), Commission, Rate

Customer Number → Customer Name, Street (Customer), City (Customer),
   State (Customer), Postal Code (Customer), Balance, Credit Limit,
   Rep Number

Item Number → Description, On Hand, Category, Price

Order Number → Order Date, Customer Number

Order Number, Item Number → Number Ordered, Quoted Price

5. Create the tables. Using the functional dependencies, you can create tables with the attribute(s) to the left of the arrow being the primary key and the items to the right of the arrow being the other fields. For tables corresponding to those entities identified in Step 1, you can simply use the name you already determined. Because you did not identify any entity that had a unique identifier that was the combination of Order Number and Item Number, you need to assign a name to the table whose primary key consists of these two fields. Because this table represents the individual line items within an order, the name Line Item is a good choice. The final collection of tables for TDK Distributors is shown in Figure 11–9.

Rep (Rep Number, Last Name, First Name, Street,
   City, State, Postal Code, Commission, Rate)

Customer (Customer Number, Customer Name, Street,
   City, State, Postal Code, Balance, Credit Limit,
   Rep Number)

Item (Item Number, Description, On Hand, Category, Price)

Orders (Order Number, Order Date, Customer Number)

Line Item (Order Number, Item Number, Number Ordered,
   Quoted Price)

Figure 11–9

6. Identify relationships.

   a. The Customer and Rep tables are related using the Rep Number fields. The Rep Number field in the Rep table is the primary key. The Rep Number field in the Customer table is a foreign key.

   b. The Orders and Customer tables are related using the Customer Number fields. The Customer Number field in the Customer table is the primary key. The Customer Number field in the Orders table is a foreign key.

   c. The Line Item and Orders tables are related using the Order Number fields. The Order Number field in the Orders table is the primary key. The Order Number field in the Line Item table is a foreign key.

   d. The Line Item and Item tables are related using the Item Number fields. The Item Number field in the Item table is the primary key. The Item Number field in the Line Item table is a foreign key.

Does a many-to-many relationship exist between orders and items?
Yes. The Line Item table will implement a many-to-many relationship between orders and items. You identified this table as Line Item in the database design process. If you had not, you would need to add it at this point.

CONSIDER THIS

In the Line Item table, the primary key consists of two fields, Order Number and Item Number. There are two additional fields, Number Ordered and Quoted Price. What if the design requirements did not require these additional fields? Would we still need the Line Item table?
Yes, because this table implements the many-to-many relationship between orders and items. It is perfectly legitimate for the table that implements a many-to-many relationship to contain only the two columns that constitute the primary key.

The shorthand representation for the tables and foreign keys is shown in Figure 11–10.

Rep (<u>Rep Number</u>, Last Name, First Name, Street,
   City, State, Postal Code, Commission, Rate)

Customer (<u>Customer Number</u>, Customer Name, Street,
   City, State, Postal Code, Balance, Credit Limit,
   Rep Number)
   FK Rep Number → Rep

Item (<u>Item Number</u>, Description, On Hand, Category, Price)

Orders (<u>Order Number</u>, Order Date, Customer Number)
   FK Customer Number → Customer

Line Item (<u>Order Number</u>, <u>Item Number</u>, Number Ordered,
   Quoted Price)
   FK Order Number → Orders
   FK Item Number → Item

Figure 11–10

Sample data for the TDK Distributors database is shown in Figure 11–11.

Rep

Rep Number	Last Name	First Name	Street	City	State	Postal Code	Commission	Rate
20	Kaiser	Valerie	624 Randall	Georgetown	NC	28794	$2,542.50	0.05
35	Hull	Richard	532 Jackson	Kyle	SC	28797	$3,216.00	0.07
65	Perez	Juan	1626 Taylor	Byron	SC	28795	$2,487.00	0.05

Customer

Customer Number	Customer Name	Street	City	State	Postal Code	Balance	Credit Limit	Rep Number
148	Al's Hardware Store	2837 Greenway	Oxford	TN	37021	$2,550.00	$7,500.00	20
282	Brookings Direct	3827 Devon	Ashton	VA	20123	$431.50	$2,500.00	35
356	Ferguson's	382 Wildwood	Georgetown	NC	28794	$2,785.00	$7,500.00	65
408	The Energy Shop	1828 Raven	Granger	NC	27036	$1,285.25	$5,000.00	35
462	Walburg Energy Alternatives	12 Polk	Walburg	NC	28819	$1,412.00	$2,500.00	65
524	Kline's	838 Ridgeland	Oxford	TN	37021	$3,762.00	$7,500.00	20
608	Conservation Foundation	372 Oxford	Ashton	VA	20123	$106.00	$5,000.00	65
687	CleanPlanet	282 Evergreen	Lowton	TN	37084	$2,851.00	$5,000.00	35
725	Patricia Jean's Home Center	282 Columbia	Walburg	NC	28819	$248.00	$7,500.00	35
842	The Efficient Home	28 Lakeview	Pineville	VA	22503	$4,221.00	$7,500.00	20

Figure 11–11 (Continued)

Orders

Order Number	Order Date	Customer Number
12608	4/5/2018	148
12610	4/5/2018	356
12613	4/6/2018	408
12614	4/6/2018	282
12617	4/8/2018	608
12619	4/8/2018	148
12623	4/8/2018	608

Item

Item Number	Description	On Hand	Category	Price
AT94	Air Deflector	50	General	$5.45
BV06	Energy Saving Kit	45	Energy	$42.75
CD52	Fluorescent Light Bulb	65	Energy	$4.75
DL71	Low Flow Shower Head	21	Water	$8.75
DR93	Smoke Detector	38	General	$6.10
DW11	Retractable Clothesline	12	General	$13.25
FD21	Water Conservation Kit	22	Water	$13.45
KL62	Toilet Tank Water Saver	32	Water	$3.35
KT03	Programmable Thermostat	8	Energy	$34.25
KV29	Windows Insulator Kit	19	Energy	$4.95

Line Item

Order Number	Item Number	Number Ordered	Quoted Price
12608	AT94	11	$5.45
12610	DR93	5	$6.10
12610	DW11	3	$12.50
12613	KL62	10	$3.35
12614	KT03	6	$33.00
12617	BV06	2	$40.25
12617	CD52	20	$4.25
12619	DR93	12	$6.00
12623	KV29	8	$4.95

Figure 11–11

Normalization

After you create your database design, you should analyze it using a process called
normalization to make sure the design is free of potential update, redundancy,
and consistency problems. This process also supplies methods for correcting these
problems.

The normalization process involves converting tables into various types of
normal forms. A table in a particular normal form possesses a certain desirable set
of properties. Several normal forms exist, the most common being first normal form
(1NF), second normal form (2NF), and third normal form (3NF). The forms create a
progression in which a table that is in 1NF is better than a table that is not in 1NF;

a table that is in 2NF is better than one that is in 1NF; and so on. The goal of normalization is to take a table or collection of tables and produce a new collection of tables that represents the same information but is free of problems.

First Normal Form

A table that contains a **repeating group**, or multiple entries for a single row, is called an **unnormalized table**. Recall from the definition of relation that an unnormalized table actually violates the definition of relation.

Removal of repeating groups is the starting point in the goal of having tables that are as free of problems as possible. In fact, in most database management systems, tables cannot contain repeating groups. A table (relation) is in **first normal form (1NF)** if it does not contain repeating groups.

In designing a database, you may have created a table with a repeating group. For example, you might have created a Workshop Offerings table in which the primary key is the Account Number and there is a repeating group consisting of Workshop Code, Total Hours, and Hours Spent. In the example, each account appears on a single row and Workshop Code, Total Hours, and Hours Spent are repeated as many times as necessary for each account (Figure 11–12).

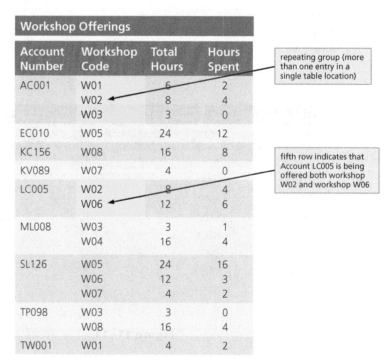

Figure 11–12

In the shorthand representation, you represent a repeating group by enclosing the repeating group within parentheses. The shorthand representation for the Workshop Offerings table from Figure 11–12 is shown in Figure 11–13.

Workshop Offerings (<u>Account Number</u>, (Workshop Code, Total Hours, Hours Spent))

Figure 11–13

Conversion to First Normal Form

Figure 11–14 shows the normalized version of the table. Note that the fifth row of the unnormalized table (Figure 11–12) indicates that account LC005 is currently being offered both workshop W02 and workshop W06. In the normalized table, this information is represented by *two* rows, the seventh and the eighth. The primary key for the unnormalized Workshop Offerings table was the Account Number only. The primary key for the normalized table is now the combination of Account Number and Workshop Code.

Workshop Offerings			
Account Number	Workshop Code	Total Hours	Hours Spent
AC001	W01	6	2
AC001	W02	8	4
AC001	W03	3	0
EC010	W05	24	12
KC156	W08	16	8
KV089	W07	4	0
LC005	W02	8	4
LC005	W06	12	6
ML008	W03	3	1
ML008	W04	16	4
SL126	W05	24	16
SL126	W06	12	3
SL126	W07	4	2
TP098	W03	3	0
TP098	W08	16	4
TW001	W01	4	2

seventh row indicates that Account LC005 is being offered workshop W02

eighth row indicates that Account LC005 is being offered workshop W06

Figure 11–14

In general, when converting a non-1NF table to 1NF, the primary key will typically include the original primary key concatenated with the key of the repeating group, that is, the field that distinguishes one occurrence of the repeating group from another within a given row in the table. In this case, Workshop Code is the key to the repeating group and thus becomes part of the primary key of the 1NF table.

To convert the table to 1NF, remove the parentheses enclosing the repeating group and expand the primary key to include the key to the repeating group. The shorthand representation for the resulting table is shown in Figure 11–15. Notice that the primary key is now the combination of the Account Number field and the Workshop Code field.

Workshop Offerings (Account Number, Workshop Code, Total Hours, Hours Spent)

Figure 11–15

Second Normal Form

Even though the following table is in 1NF, problems may exist that will cause you to want to restructure the table. In the database design process, for example, you might have created the Workshop Offerings table shown in Figure 11–16.

Workshop Offerings (Account Number, Account Name, Workshop Code, Workshop Description, Total Hours, Hours Spent)

Figure 11–16

This table contains the following functional dependencies:

Account Number → Account Name

Workshop Code → Workshop Description

Account Number, Workshop Code → Total Hours, Hours Spent

This notation indicates that Account Number alone determines Account Name, and Workshop Code alone determines Workshop Description, but it requires *both* an Account Number *and* a Workshop Code to determine either Total Hours or Hours Spent. Figure 11–17 shows a sample of this table.

description of workshop W06 occurs more than once

Account					
Account Number	**Account Name**	**Workshop Code**	**Workshop Description**	**Total Hours**	**Hours Spent**
AC001	Avondale Community Bank	W01	Dealing with Unacceptable Employee Behavior	6	2
AC001	Avondale Community Bank	W02	Writing Effective Policies and Procedures	8	4
AC001	Avondale Community Bank	W03	Payroll Law	3	0
EC010	Eco Clothes Inc.	W05	The Recruitment Process	24	12
KC156	Key Community College System	W08	Workers' Compensation	16	8
KV089	KAL Veterinary Services	W07	Americans with Disabilities Act (ADA)	4	0
LC005	Lancaster County Hospital	W02	Writing Effective Policies and Procedures	8	4
LC005	Lancaster County Hospital	W06	Diversity in the Workplace	12	6
ML008	Mums Landscaping Co.	W03	Payroll Law	3	1
ML008	Mums Landscaping Co.	W04	Workplace Safety	16	4
SL126	South Library Consortium	W05	The Recruitment Process	24	16
SL126	South Library Consortium	W06	Diversity in the Workplace	12	3
SL126	South Library Consortium	W07	Americans with Disabilities Act (ADA)	4	2
TP098	TDK Packaging Systems	W03	Payroll Law	3	0
TP098	TDK Packaging Systems	W08	Workers' Compensation	16	4
TW001	Tri-County Waste Disposal	W01	Dealing with Unacceptable Employee Behavior	4	2

name of Account LC005 occurs more than once

Figure 11–17

The name of a specific account, LC005 for example, occurs multiple times in the table, as does the description of a workshop. This redundancy causes several problems. It is certainly wasteful of space, but that is not nearly as serious as some of the other problems. These other problems are called **update anomalies**, and they fall into four categories:

1. **Update.** A change to the name of account LC005 requires not one change to the table, but several: you must change each row in which LC005 appears. This certainly makes the update process much more cumbersome; it is logically more complicated and takes longer to update.

2. **Inconsistent data.** There is nothing about the design that would prohibit account LC005 from having two or more different names in the database. The first row, for example, might have Lancaster County Hospital as the name, whereas the second row might have Lancaster Community Hospital.

3. **Additions.** There is a real problem when you try to add a new workshop and its description to the database. Because the primary key for the table consists of both Account Number and Workshop Code, you need values for both of these to add a new row. If you have an account to add but there are so far no workshops scheduled for it, what do you use for a Workshop Code? The only solution would be to make up a placeholder Workshop Code and then replace it with a real Workshop Code once the account requests a workshop. This is certainly not an acceptable solution.

4. **Deletions.** In Figure 11–17, if you delete workshop W01 from the database, you would need to delete all rows on which the Workshop Code is W01. In the process, you will delete the only row on which account TW001 appears, so you would also *lose* all the information about account TW001. You would no longer know that the name of account TW001 is Tri-County Waste Disposal.

These problems occur because there is a field, Account Name, that is dependent only on an Account Number, which is just a portion of the primary key. There is a similar problem with Workshop Description, which depends only on the Workshop Code, not the complete primary key. This leads to the definition of second normal form. Second normal form represents an improvement over first normal form because it eliminates update anomalies in these situations. In order to understand second normal form, you need to understand the term, nonkey field.

A field is a **nonkey field**, also called a **nonkey attribute**, if it is not a part of the primary key. A table (relation) is in **second normal form (2NF)** if it is in first normal form and no nonkey field is dependent on only a portion of the primary key.

Note that if the primary key of a table contains only a single field, the table is automatically in second normal form. In that case, there could not be any field dependent on only a portion of the primary key.

Conversion to Second Normal Form

To correct the problems, convert the table to a collection of tables in second normal form. Then name the new tables. The following is a method for performing this conversion.

1. Take each subset of the set of fields that make up the primary key and begin a new table with this subset as its primary key. The result of applying this step to the Workshop Offerings table is shown in Figure 11–18.

(Account Number,

(Workshop Code,

(Account Number, Workshop Code,

Figure 11–18

2. Place each of the other fields with the appropriate primary key; that is, place each one with the minimal collection of fields on which it depends. The result of applying this step to the Workshop Offerings table is shown in Figure 11–19.

(<u>Account Number</u>, Account Name)
(<u>Workshop Code</u>, Workshop Description)
(<u>Account Number</u>, <u>Workshop Code</u>, Total Hours, Hours Spent)

Figure 11–19

3. Give each of these new tables a name that is descriptive of the meaning of the table, such as Account, Workshop, and Workshop Offerings.

Figure 11–20 shows samples of the tables.

Account	
AC #	**Account Name**
AC001	Avondale Community Bank
BL235	Bland Corp.
CA043	Carlton Regional Clinic
CO621	Codder Plastics Co.
EC010	Eco Clothes Inc.
HL111	Halko Legal Associates
KC156	Key Community College System
KV089	KAL Veterinary Services
LC005	Lancaster County Hospital
LI268	Lars-Idsen-Fleming Inc.
MI345	Midwest Library Consortium
ML008	Mums Landscaping Co.
SL126	South Library Consortium
TP098	TDK Packaging Systems
TW001	Tri-County Waste Disposal

name of Account LC005 occurs only once

Workshop	
Workshop Code	**Workshop Description**
W01	Dealing with Unacceptable Employee Behavior
W02	Writing Effective Policies and Procedures
W03	Payroll Law
W04	Workplace Safety
W05	The Recruitment Process
W06	Diversity in the Workplace
W07	Americans with Disabilities Act (ADA)
W08	Workers' Compensation

description of workshop W06 occurs only once

Figure 11–20 (Continued)

Access Module 11

Workshop Offerings			
Account Number	Workshop Code	Total Hours	Hours Spent
AC001	W01	6	2
AC001	W02	8	4
AC001	W03	3	0
EC010	W05	24	12
KC156	W08	16	8
KV089	W07	4	0
LC005	W02	8	4
LC005	W06	12	6
ML008	W03	3	1
ML008	W04	16	4
SL126	W05	24	16
SL126	W06	12	3
SL126	W07	4	2
TP098	W03	3	0
TP098	W08	16	4
TW001	W01	4	2

Figure 11–20

The new design eliminates the update anomalies. An account name occurs only once for each account, so you do not have the redundancy that you did in the earlier design. Changing the name of an account is now a simple process involving a single change. Because the name of an account occurs in a single place, it is not possible to have multiple names for the same account in the database at the same time.

To add a new account, you create a new row in the Account table, and thus there is no need to have a workshop offering already scheduled for that account. In addition, deleting workshop W01 has nothing to do with the Account table and, consequently, does not cause account TW001 to be deleted. Thus, you still have its name, Tri-County Waste Disposal, in the database. Finally, you have not lost any information in the process.

CONSIDER THIS

Can I reconstruct the data in the original design from the data in the new design?
Yes, and SQL is the best way to accomplish this. The following SQL query would produce the data in the form shown in Figure 11–17:

```
SELECT [Account].[Account Number], [Account Name],
  [Workshop].[Workshop Code], [Workshop Description],
  [Total Hours], [Hours Spent]
FROM [Account],[Workshop],[Workshop Offerings]
WHERE [Account].[Account Number]=
  [Workshop Offerings].[Account Number]
AND [Workshop].[Workshop Code]=
  [Workshop Offerings].[Workshop Code];
```

BTW

3NF
The definition given for third normal form is not the original definition. This more recent definition, which is preferable to the original, is often referred to as Boyce-Codd normal form (BCNF) when it is important to make a distinction between this definition and the original definition. This text does not make such a distinction but will take this to be the definition of third normal form.

Third Normal Form

Problems can still exist with tables that are in 2NF, as illustrated in the Account table whose shorthand representation is shown in Figure 11–21.

Account (<u>Account Number</u>, Account Name, Street, City, State, Postal Code, Amount Paid, Current Due, Account Manager Number, Last Name, First Name)

Figure 11–21

The functional dependencies in this table are:

Account Number → Account Name, Street, City, State, Postal Code, Amount Paid, Current Due, Account Manager Number, Last Name, First Name

Account Manager Number → Last Name, First Name

As these dependencies indicate, Account Number determines all the other fields. In addition, Account Manager Number determines Last Name and First Name.

Because the primary key of the table is a single field, the table is automatically in second normal form. As the sample of the table shown in Figure 11–22 demonstrates, however, this table has problems similar to those encountered earlier, even though it is in 2NF. In this case, it is the last name and first name of a manager that can occur many times in the table; see manager 31, Haydee Rivera, for example. (Note that the three dots represent fields that do not appear due to space limitations.)

Account

Account Number	Account Name	...	Amount Paid	Current Due	Account Manager Number	Last Name	First Name
AC001	Avondale Community Bank	...	$24,752.25	$3,875.25	31	Rivera	Haydee
BL235	Bland Corp.	...	$29,836.65	$2,765.30	35	Simson	Mark
CA043	Carlton Regional Clinic	...	$30,841.05	$3,074.30	58	Murowski	Karen
CO621	Codder Plastics Co.	...	$27,152.25	$2,875.00	35	Simson	Mark
EC010	Eco Clothes Inc.	...	$19,620.00	$1,875.00	58	Murowski	Karen
HL111	Halko Legal Associates	...	$25,702.20	$3,016.75	58	Murowski	Karen
KC156	Key Community College System	...	$10,952.25	$0.00	31	Rivera	Haydee
KV089	KAL Veterinary Services	...	$34,036.50	$580.00	35	Simson	Mark
LC005	Lancaster County Hospital	...	$44,025.60	$3,590.80	58	Murowski	Karen
LI268	Lars-Idsen-Fleming Inc.	...	$0.00	$1,280.75	35	Simson	Mark
MI345	Midwest Library Consortium	...	$21,769.20	$2,890.60	31	Rivera	Haydee
ML008	Mums Landscaping Co.	...	$13,097.10	$2,450.00	35	Simson	Mark
SL126	South Library Consortium	...	$0.00	$0.00	58	Murowski	Karen
TP098	TDK Packaging Systems	...	$22,696.95	$3,480.45	58	Murowski	Karen
TW001	Tri-County Waste Disposal	...	$15,345.00	$2,875.50	31	Rivera	Haydee

Figure 11–22

name of manager 31 occurs more than once

This redundancy results in the same set of problems described previously with the Workshop Offerings table. In addition to the problem of wasted space, you have similar update anomalies, as follows:

1. **Updates.** A change to the name of a manager requires not one change to the table, but several changes. Again, the update process becomes very cumbersome.

2. **Inconsistent data.** There is nothing about the design that would prohibit a manager from having two different names in the database. On the first row, for example, the name for manager 31 might read Haydee Rivera, whereas on the third row (another row on which the manager number is 31), the name might be Haydee Muniz.

3. **Additions.** In order to add rep 71, whose name is Marilyn Webb, to the database, she must have at least one account. If she has not yet been assigned any accounts, either you cannot record the fact that her name is Marilyn Webb, or you have to create a fictitious account for her to represent. Again, this is not a desirable solution to the problem.

4. **Deletions.** If you were to delete all the accounts of manager 31 from the database, then you would also lose all information concerning manager 31.

These update anomalies are due to the fact that Account Manager Number determines Last Name and First Name, but Account Manager Number is not the primary key. As a result, the same Account Manager Number and consequently the same Last Name and First Name can appear on many different rows.

You have seen that 2NF is an improvement over 1NF, but to eliminate 2NF problems, you need an even better strategy for creating tables in the database. Third normal form provides that strategy.

Before looking at third normal form, you need to become familiar with the special name that is given to any field that determines another field, like Account Manager Number in the Account table. Any field or collection of fields that determines another field is called a **determinant**. Certainly the primary key in a table is a determinant. Any candidate key is a determinant as well. (Remember that a candidate key is a field or collection of fields that could function as the primary key.) In this case, Account Manager Number is a determinant, but because several rows in the Account table could have the same Account Manager Number, that field is not a candidate key for the Account table shown in Figure 11–22, and that is the problem.

A table is in **third normal form** (3NF) if it is in second normal form and if the only determinants it contains are candidate keys.

Conversion to Third Normal Form

You have now identified the problem with the Account table: it is not in 3NF. You need a way to correct the deficiency in the Account table and in all tables having similar deficiencies. Such a method follows.

First, for each determinant that is not a candidate key, remove from the table the fields that depend on this determinant, but do not remove the determinant. Next, create a new table containing all the fields from the original table that depend on this determinant. Finally, make the determinant the primary key of this new table.

In the Account table, for example, Last Name and First Name are removed because they depend on the determinant Account Manager Number, which is not a candidate key. A new table is formed, consisting of Account Manager Number as the primary key, Last Name, and First Name. Specifically, you would replace the Account table in Figure 11–22 with the two tables shown in Figure 11–23.

Account (<u>Account Number</u>, Account Name, Street, City, State, Postal Code, Amount Paid, Current Due, Account Manager Number)

Account Manager (<u>Account Manager Number</u>, Last Name, First Name)

Figure 11–23

Figure 11–24 shows samples of the tables.

Account

Account Number	Account Name	...	Amount Paid	Current Due	Account Manager Number
AC001	Avondale Community Bank	...	$24,752.25	$3,875.25	31
BL235	Bland Corp.	...	$29,836.65	$2,765.30	35
CA043	Carlton Regional Clinic	...	$30,841.05	$3,074.30	58
CO621	Codder Plastics Co.	...	$27,152.25	$2,875.00	35
EC010	Eco Clothes Inc.	...	$19,620.00	$1,875.00	58
HL111	Halko Legal Associates	...	$25,702.20	$3,016.75	58
KC156	Key Community College System	...	$10,952.25	$0.00	31
KV089	KAL Veterinary Services	...	$34,036.50	$580.00	35
LC005	Lancaster County Hospital	...	$44,025.60	$3,590.80	58
LI268	Lars-Idsen-Fleming Inc.	...	$0.00	$1,280.75	35
MI345	Midwest Library Consortium	...	$21,769.20	$2,890.60	31
ML008	Mums Landscaping Co.	...	$13,097.10	$2,450.00	35
SL126	South Library Consortium	...	$0.00	$0.00	58
TP098	TDK Packaging Systems	...	$22,696.95	$3,480.45	58
TW001	Tri-County Waste Disposal	...	$15,345.00	$2,875.50	31

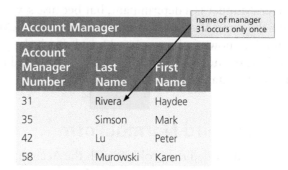

Account Manager

name of manager 31 occurs only once

Account Manager Number	Last Name	First Name
31	Rivera	Haydee
35	Simson	Mark
42	Lu	Peter
58	Murowski	Karen

Figure 11–24

This design corrects the previously identified problems. A manager's name appears only once, thus avoiding redundancy and making the process of changing a manager's name a very simple one. With this design, it is not possible for a manager to have two different names in the database. To add a new account manager to the database, you add a row in the Account Manager table; it is not necessary to have a pre-existing account for the manager. Finally, deleting all the accounts of a given manager will not remove the manager's record from the Account Manager table, so you retain the manager's name; all the data in the original table can be reconstructed from the data in the new collection of tables. All previously mentioned problems have indeed been solved.

Can I reconstruct the data in the original design from the data in the new design?
Yes. The following SQL query would produce the data in the form shown in Figure 11–22:

```
SELECT [Account Number], [Account Name], [Street],
   [City], [State], [Postal Code], [Amount Paid],
   [Current Due], [Account].[Account Manager Number],
   [Last Name], [First Name]
FROM [Account],[Account Manager]
WHERE [Account].[Account Manager Number]=
   [Account Manager].[Account Manager Number];
```

Special Topics

In addition to knowing how to design a database and how to normalize tables, there are two other topics with which you should be familiar. First, you may be given a requirement for a database in the form of a document that the database must be capable of producing; for example, an invoice. In addition, you should know how to represent your design with a diagram.

Obtaining Information from Existing Documents

Existing documents can often furnish helpful information concerning the database design. You need to know how to obtain information from the document that you will then use in the design process. An existing document, like the invoice for the company named TDK Distributors shown in Figure 11–25, will often provide the details that determine the tables and fields required to produce the document.

The first step in obtaining information from an existing document is to identify and list all fields and give them appropriate names. You also need to understand the business policies of the organization. For example, in the order shown in Figure 11–25, the information on TDK Distributors is preprinted on the form, and it is not necessary to describe the company. The following is a list of the fields you can determine from the invoice shown in Figure 11–25.

> **Order Number**
> **Order Date**
> **Customer Number**
> **Customer Name**
> **Street (Customer)**
> **City (Customer)**
> **State (Customer)**
> **Postal Code (Customer)**
> **Rep Number**
> **Last Name (Rep)**
> **First Name (Rep)**
> **Item Number**
> **Description**
> **Number Ordered**
> **Price**
> **Total**
> **Order Total**

TDK Distributors

INVOICE

543 Main Street
Kyle, SC 28797
Phone (803)-555-0190 Fax (803)-555-0191

ORDER: 12617
DATE: APRIL 8, 2018

TO:
Customer: 462
Walburg Energy Alternatives
12 Polk
Walburg, NC 28819

SALES REP: 65
Juan Perez

ITEM NUMBER	DESCRIPTION	NUMBER ORDERED	PRICE	TOTAL
BV06	Energy Saving Kit	2	40.25	80.50
CD52	Fluorescent Light Bulb	20	4.25	85.00
			TOTAL	165.50

Make all checks payable to TDK Distributors
Total due in 15 days. Overdue accounts subject to a service charge of 1% per month.

Thank you for your business!

Figure 11–25

Next, you need to identify functional dependencies. If the document you are examining is unfamiliar to you, you may have difficulty determining the dependencies and may need to get all the information directly from the user. On the other hand, you can often make intelligent guesses based on your general knowledge of the type of document you are studying. You may make mistakes, of course, and these should be corrected when you interact with the user. After initially determining the functional dependencies, you may discover additional information. The following are possible initial functional dependencies:

> **Customer Number → Customer Name, Street (Customer), City (Customer),
>   State (Customer), Postal Code (Customer), Rep Number,
>   Last Name (Rep), First Name (Rep)**
>
> **Item Number → Description, Price**
>
> **Order Number → Order Date, Customer Number, Order Total**
>
> **Order Number, Item Number → Number Ordered, Price, Total**

You may find, for example, that the price for a particular item on an order need not be the same as the standard price for the item. If that is the case, Price and Total are functionally dependent on the combination of Order Number and Item Number, not just Item Number alone. You may also decide to change the field name to Quoted Price to indicate the fact that it can vary from one order to another.

For the same reasons that you did not include Total Amount in the PrattLast Associates database, you would probably not want to include either Total or Order Total. Both can be computed from other data. The other correction that you should make to the functional dependencies is to realize that the last name and first name of a rep depend on the data in the Rep Number field.

Given these corrections, a revised list of functional dependencies might look like the following:

> **Rep Number → Last Name, First Name**
>
> **Customer Number → Customer Name, Street (Customer), City (Customer),
>   State (Customer), Postal Code (Customer), Rep Number**
>
> **Item Number → Description, Price**
>
> **Order Number → Order Date, Customer Number**
>
> **Order Number, Item Number → Number Ordered, Quoted Price**

After you have determined the preliminary functional dependencies, you can begin determining the tables and assigning fields. You could create tables with the determinant – the field or fields to the left of the arrow – as the primary key and with the fields to the right of the arrow as the remaining fields. This would lead to the following initial collection of tables shown in Figure 11–26.

Rep (<u>Rep Number</u>, Last Name, First Name)

Customer (<u>Customer Number</u>, Customer Name, Street, City, State, Postal Code,
    Rep Number)

Item (<u>Item Number</u>, Description, Price)

Orders (<u>Order Number</u>, Order Date, Customer Number)

OrderLine (<u>Order Number</u>, <u>Item Number</u>, Number Ordered, Quoted Price)

Figure 11–26

Adding the foreign key information produces the shorthand representation shown in Figure 11–27.

Rep (<u>Rep Number</u>, Last Name, First Name)

Customer (<u>Customer Number</u>, Customer Name, Street, City, State, Postal Code, Rep Number)
   FK Rep Number → Rep

Item (<u>Item Number</u>, Description, Price)

Orders (<u>Order Number</u>, Order Date, Customer Number)
   FK Account Number → Customer

OrderLine (<u>Order Number</u>, <u>Item Number</u>, Number Ordered, Quoted Price)
   FK Order Number → Orders
   FK Item Number → Item

Figure 11–27

BTW
Merging Entities
When you merge entities, do not assume that the merged entities will be in 3NF. Apply normalization techniques to convert all entities to 3NF.

At this point, you would need to verify that all the tables are in third normal form. If any are not in 3NF, you need to convert them. If you had not determined the functional dependency of Last Name and First Name on Rep Number earlier, for example, you would have had Last Name and First Name as fields in the Account table. These fields are dependent on Rep Number, making Rep Number a determinant that is not a primary key, which would violate third normal form. Once you converted that table to 3NF, you would have the tables shown in Figure 11–27.

You may have already created some tables in your database design. For example, you may have obtained financial data on customers from the Accounting department. If so, you would need to merge the tables in Figure 11–27 with those tables you already created. To merge tables, you combine tables that have the same primary key. The new table contains all the fields in either individual table and does not repeat fields that are present in both tables. Figure 11–28, for example, illustrates the merging of two tables that both have the Customer Number field as the primary key. In addition to the primary key, the result contains the Customer Name and Rep Number fields, which are included in both of the original tables; the Street, City, State, and Postal Code fields, which are only in the first table; and the Balance and Credit Limit fields, which are only in the second table. The order in which you decide to list the fields is immaterial.

Merging

Customer (<u>Customer Number</u>, Account Name, Street, City, State, Postal Code, Rep Number)

and

Customer (<u>Customer Number</u>, Customer Name, Balance, Credit Limit, Rep Number)

gives

Customer (<u>Customer Number</u>, Customer Name, Street, City, State, Postal Code, Balance, Credit Limit, Rep Number)

Figure 11–28

Diagrams for Database Design

You have now seen how to represent a database design as a list of tables, fields, primary keys, and foreign keys. It is often helpful to also be able to represent a database design with a diagram. If you have already created the database and relationships in Access, the Relationships window and Relationships report provide a helpful diagram of the design. Figure 11–29 shows the Access Relationship diagram and report for the PrattLast Associates database. In these diagrams, rectangles represent tables. The fields in the table are listed in the corresponding rectangle with a key symbol appearing in front of the primary key. Relationships are represented by lines with the "one" end of the relationship represented by the number, 1, and the "many" end represented by the infinity symbol (∞).

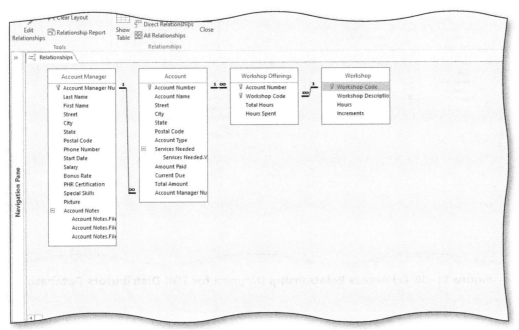

Figure 11–29 (a) Access Relationship Diagram for PrattLast Associates Database

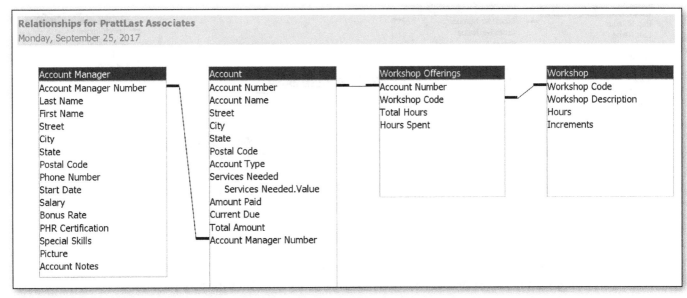

Figure 11–29 (b) Access Relationship Report for PrattLast Associates Database

Figure 11–30 shows the Access Relationship diagram and report for the TDK Distributors database.

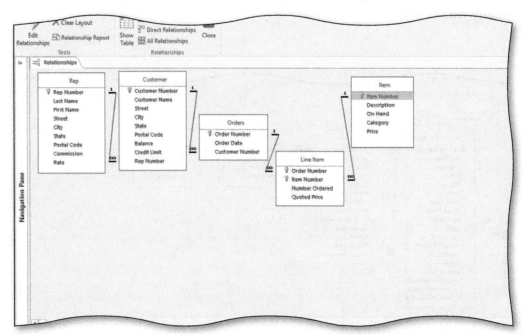

Figure 11–30 (a) Access Relationship Diagram for TDK Distributors Database

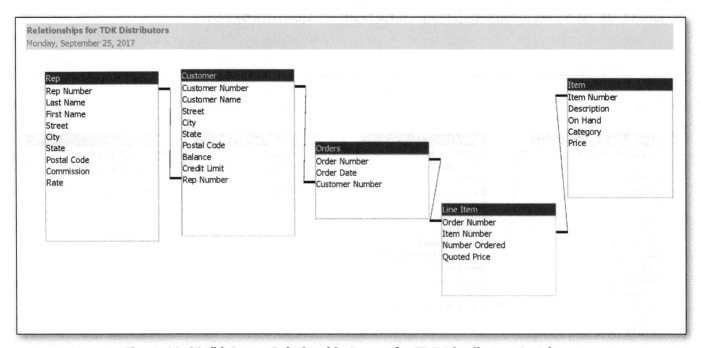

Figure 11–30 (b) Access Relationship Report for TDK Distributors Database

Another popular option for diagramming a database design is the **entity-relationship diagram (ERD)**. Figure 11–31 shows a sample ERD for the PrattLast Associates database. In this type of diagram, rectangles represent the tables. The primary key is listed within the table above a line. Below the line are the other fields in the table. The arrow goes from the rectangle that represents the many part of the relationship to the one part of the relationship.

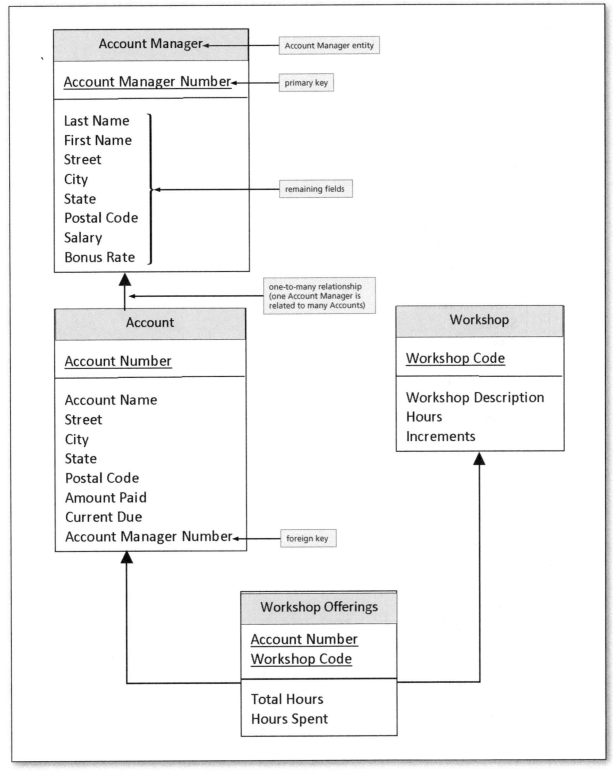

Figure 11–31

Figure 11–32 shows a similar diagram for the TDK Distributors database.

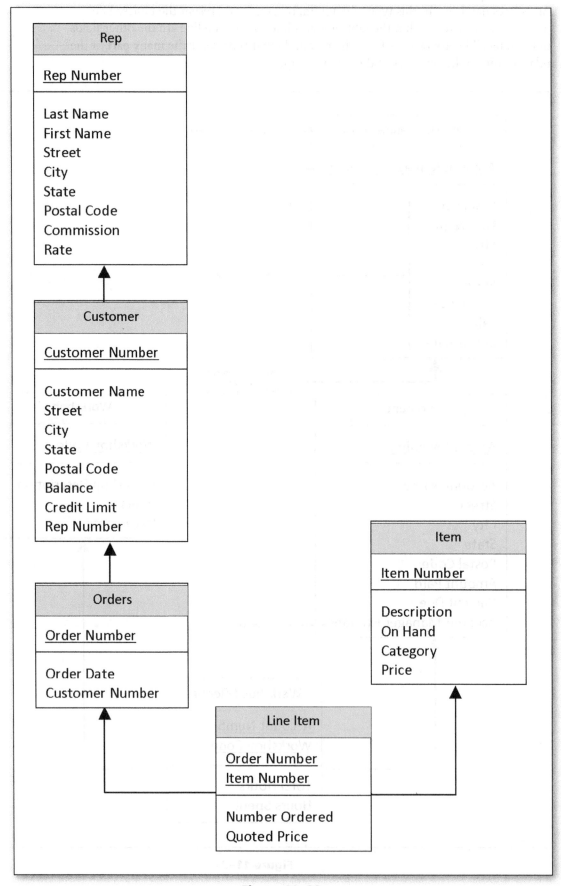

Figure 11–32

There are many options for such diagrams. Some options include more detail than shown in the figure. You can include, for example, such details as data types and indexes. Other options have less detail, showing only the name of the table in the rectangle, for example. There are also other options for the appearance of the lines representing relationships.

Summary

In this module, you have learned the following concepts.

1. An entity is a person, place, thing, or event. An attribute is a property of an entity. A relationship is an association between entities.

2. A relation is a two-dimensional table in which the entries in the table are single-valued, each column has a distinct name, all values in a column are values of the same attribute (that is, all entries must correspond to the column name), and each row is distinct.

3. In a relation, the order of columns is immaterial. You can view the columns in any order you want. The order of rows is also immaterial. You can view the rows in any order you want.

4. A relational database is a collection of relations.

5. Rows in a table (relation) are often called records or tuples. Columns in a table (relation) are often called fields or attributes. Typically, the terms *record* and *field* are used in Access.

6. If you know that whenever you are given a value for one field, you will be able to determine a single value for a second field, then the first field is said to determine the second field. In addition, the second field is said to be functionally dependent on the first.

7. The primary key of a table is the field or minimum collection of fields that uniquely identifies a given row in that table.

8. The following is a method for designing a database for a set of requirements.

   a. Examine the requirements and identify the entities (objects) involved. Assign names to the entities.
   b. Identify a unique identifier for each entity.
   c. Identify the attributes for all the entities. These attributes will become the fields in the tables.
   d. Identify the functional dependencies that exist among the attributes.
   e. Use the functional dependencies to identify the tables.
   f. Identify any relationships between tables by looking for matching fields where one of the fields is a primary key. The other field will then be a foreign key. In the shorthand representation for the table containing the primary key, represent the foreign key by using the letters FK, followed by an arrow, followed by the name of the table containing the primary key.

9. A table (relation) is in first normal form (1NF) if it does not contain repeating groups.

10. To convert a table to 1NF, remove the parentheses enclosing the repeating group and expand the primary key to include the key to the repeating group.

11. A field is a nonkey field (also called a nonkey attribute) if it is not a part of the primary key. A table (relation) is in second normal form (2NF) if it is in first normal form and no nonkey field is dependent on only a portion of the primary key.

12. To convert a table to 2NF, take each subset of the set of fields that make up the primary key and begin a new table with this subset as its primary key. Place each of the other fields with the appropriate primary key; that is, place each one with the minimal collection of fields on which it depends. Give each of these new tables a name that is descriptive of the meaning of the table.

13. Any field (or collection of fields) that determines another field is called a determinant. A table is in third normal form (3NF) if it is in second normal form and if the only determinants it contains are candidate keys.

14. To convert a table to 3NF, for each determinant that is not a candidate key, remove from the table the fields that depend on this determinant, but do not remove the determinant. Create a new table containing all the fields from the original table that depend on this determinant and make the determinant the primary key of this new table.

15. An entity-relationship diagram (ERD) is a diagram used to represent database designs. In ERDs, rectangles represent tables and lines between rectangles represent one-to-many relationships between the corresponding tables. You can also diagram a database design by using the Access relationship window.

CONSIDER THIS

How should you submit solutions to questions in the assignments identified with a ✸ symbol?

Every assignment in this book contains one or more questions identified with a ✸ symbol. These questions require you to think beyond the assigned database. Present your solutions to the questions in the format required by your instructor. Possible formats may include one or more of these options: write the answer; create a document that contains the answer; present your answer to the class; discuss your answer in a group; record the answer as audio or video using a webcam, smartphone, or portable media player; or post answers on a blog, wiki, or website.

Apply Your Knowledge

Reinforce the skills and apply the concepts you learned in this module.

Understanding Keys and Normalization

Instructions: Answer the following questions in the format specified by your instructor.

1. Figure 11–33 contains sample data for a Student table. Use this figure to answer the following:
    a. Is the table in first normal form (1NF)? Why or why not?
    b. Is the table in second normal form (2NF)? Why or why not?
    c. Is the table in third normal form (3NF)? Why or why not?
    d. Identify candidate keys for the table.

Student

SSN	Student_ID	Name	Major Department Code	Major Department Name
1111	123-6788	Theresa	CS	Computer Science
2222	346-8809	Juan	IT	Information Technology
3333	433-7676	Lee	CS	Computer Science
4444	654-4312	Barbara	ACC	Accounting

Figure 11–33

2. Figure 11–34 contains sample data for items and vendors who supply these items. In discussing the data with users, you find that item numbers – but not descriptions – uniquely identify items, and that vendor names uniquely identify vendors. Multiple vendors can supply the same item. For example, agate bookends can be purchased from either Atherton Group or Gift Specialties.
   a. Convert the data in Figure 11–34 into a relation in first normal form (1NF) using the shorthand representation used in this module.
   b. Identify all functional dependencies using the notation demonstrated in the module.

Item

Item Number	Description	Vendor Name	City	Wholesale Cost
3663	Agate Bookends	Atherton Group	Rock Hill	16.25
		Gift Specialties	Indian Land	16.20
4573	Crystal Growing Kit	Atherton Group	Rock Hill	6.75
		Gift Specialties	Indian Land	6.80
		Smith Distributors	Ballantyne	6.70

Figure 11–34

3. ✸ Using only the data in Figure 11–33, how could you identify the entities and attributes that would be the starting point for a database design?

Extend Your Knowledge

Extend the skills you learned in this module and experiment with new skills. You may need to use Help to complete the assignment.

Modifying a Database Design and Understanding Diagrams
Instructions: Answer the following questions in the format specified by your instructor.
1. Using the shorthand representation illustrated in this module, indicate the changes you would need to make to the PrattLast Associates database design shown in Figure 11–8 in order to support the following requirements:
   a. An account may not necessarily work with one account manager; it can work with several account managers.
   b. Hours and Total Hours do not vary based on account.

Continued >

Extend Your Knowledge *continued*

2. Using the shorthand representation illustrated in this module, indicate the changes you would need to make to the TDK Distributors data design shown in Figure 11–10 to support the following requirements:

    a. The price for an item does not change; it is the same for all customers.

    b. TDK also needs to keep track of the wholesale cost of an item.

3. Use the Access Relationships Report for the Marketing Analytics database shown in Figure 11–35 to answer the following:

    a. Identify the foreign keys in the Seminar Offerings table.

    b. What is the purpose of the Seminar Offerings table?

    c. What is the primary key of the Seminar Offerings table?

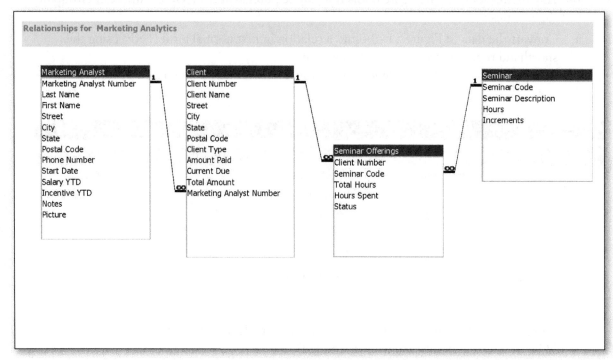

Figure 11–35

4. ❉ TDK Distributors has decided to add its suppliers to the database. One supplier can supply many items but an item has only one supplier. What changes would you need to make to the database design for TDK Distributors?

Expand Your World

Create a solution which uses cloud and web technologies, by learning and investigating on your own from general guidance.

Instructions: There are several websites that provide examples of database models, such as www.databaseanswers.org/data_models/index.htm. These models provide a good starting point for creating your own database design.

1. Create a blog, a Google document, or a Word document on OneDrive on which to store your assignment. Include your name and the current date at the beginning of the blog or document.

2. Access the www.databaseanswers.org/data_models/index.htm website or another website of your choice that provides data models.

3. Browse the different database models and select one in which you have an interest.

4. In your own words, create a scenario for which the database model would work. Study the model to see if you need to modify it to make it applicable to your scenario. If changes are necessary, document the required modifications.

5. ✸ Why did you select the model that you did? How easy was it to understand the entities, attributes, and relationships? Were the relations in 3NF?

In the Labs

Design, create, modify, and/or use a database following the guidelines, concepts, and skills presented in this module. Labs are listed in order of increasing difficulty. Labs 1 and 2, which increase in difficulty, require you to create solutions based on what you learned in the module; Lab 3 requires you to apply your creative thinking and problem solving skills to design and implement a solution.

Lab 1: Designing a Database for Sports Leagues

Instructions: Answer the following questions in the format specified by your instructor.

1. A database for a local community center that offers multiple sports leagues for adults must support the following requirements:

   a.   For a league, store its number and name, for example, 072, Basketball. Each league has a participant cost associated with it, a start date for the league, and a maximum number of participants.

   b.   For a participant, store his or her number, first name, last name, home telephone number, and mobile telephone number.

   One participant can enroll in many sports leagues, and one league can include many participants.

2. Based on these requirements:

   a.   Identify and list the entities and attributes of those entities.

   b.   Identify and list the functional dependencies.

   c.   Create a set of third normal form (3NF) relations using the shorthand notation given in the module. Be sure to identify all primary keys and foreign keys appropriately.

   Submit your database design in the format specified by your instructor.

Continued >

3. ✸ Because each league plays at a different location, the community center director would like to add locations to the database. He would also like to include the participant's birth date. In which table(s) would you place these attributes?

Lab 2: **Normalizing a Client Relation**

Instructions: Answer the following questions in the format specified by your instructor.

Consider the following relation:

> Client (Client#, ClientName, Balance Due, TherapistID, TherapistName, ServiceCode, ServiceDesc, ServiceFee, ServiceDate)

This is a relation concerning data about clients of physical therapy practice and the services the therapists perform for their clients. The following dependencies exist in Client:

> Client# → ClientName, BalanceDue
>
> TherapistID → TherapistName
>
> ServiceCode → ServiceDesc, ServiceFee
>
> Client#, TherapistID, ServiceCode → ServiceDate

1. Convert Client to 1NF based on the functional dependencies given.
2. Convert to a set of relations in 3NF.
3. ✸ The database design needs to include an attribute for the date of the client's last visit. In what table would you place this attribute?

Lab 3: **Consider This: Your Turn**

Designing a Database for Outdoor Adventure

Instructions: Outdoor Adventures is a small business that organizes day-long guided trips of New England. You have been asked to create a database to keep track of the trips and the guides who lead these trips as well as customers who reserve these trips. Use the concepts and techniques presented in this module to design a database to meet the following requirements:

Part 1:   The Outdoor Adventure database must support the following requirements:

a. For each guide, store his or her guide number, last name, first name, street address, city, state, postal code, telephone number, and date hired.

b. For each trip, store the trip ID number, the trip name, the location from which the trip starts, the state in which the trip originates, the trip distance, the maximum group size, the type of trip (hiking, biking, or paddling), and the guide number, first name, and last name of each guide. A guide may lead many trips and a trip may be led by many different guides.

c. For each customer, store the customer number, last name, first name, street address, city, state, postal code, and telephone number.

d. For each reservation, store the reservation number, the trip ID number, the trip date, the number of persons included in the reservation, and the customer number, first name, and last name of the customer who made the reservation.

Based on these requirements:

  a. Identify and list the entities and attributes of those entities.
  b. Identify and list the functional dependencies.
  c. Create a set of third normal form (3NF) relations using the shorthand notation given in this module. Be sure to identify all primary keys and foreign keys appropriately.

Submit your database design in the format specified by your instructor.

Part 2: ✷ You made several decisions while designing this database. What was the rationale behind these decisions? Are there other requirements that would have been helpful to you in the design process?

4 | Creating and Managing Tasks with Outlook

Objectives

You will have mastered the material in this module when you can:

- Create a new task
- Create a task with a status
- Create a task with a priority
- Create a task with a reminder
- Create a recurring task
- Categorize a task
- Configure Quick Clicks
- Categorize email messages

- Update a task
- Attach a file to a task
- Assign a task
- Forward a task
- Send a status report
- Print tasks
- Create a note
- Change the view of notes

Creating and Managing Tasks with Outlook

This introductory module covers features and functions common to creating and managing tasks in Outlook 2016.

Roadmap

In this module, you will learn how to create and manage tasks. The following roadmap identifies general activities you will perform as you progress through this module:

1. CREATE a NEW TASK
2. CATEGORIZE a TASK
3. CATEGORIZE an EMAIL MESSAGE
4. ASSIGN a TASK
5. PRINT a TASK
6. CREATE AND USE NOTES

At the beginning of step instructions throughout the module, you will see an abbreviated form of this roadmap. The abbreviated roadmap uses colors to indicate module progress: gray means the module is beyond that activity, blue means the task being shown is covered in that activity, and black means that activity is yet to be covered. For example, the following abbreviated roadmap indicates the section would be about categorizing an email message.

1 CREATE NEW TASK | 2 CATEGORIZE TASK | **3 CATEGORIZE EMAIL MESSAGE**
4 ASSIGN TASK | 5 PRINT TASK | 6 CREATE AND USE NOTES

Use the abbreviated roadmap as a progress guide while you read or step through the instructions in this module.

Introduction to Outlook Tasks

Whether you are keeping track of your school assignments that are due next week or the action items that your boss needs completed as soon as possible, you can use Outlook tasks to manage your to-do list by generating a checklist and tracking activities. Instead of keeping a paper list of the things you need to do, you can use Outlook to combine your various tasks into one list that has reminders and tracking. A **task** is an item that you create in Outlook to track until its completion. A **to-do item** is any Outlook item such as a task, an email message, or a contact that has been flagged for follow-up later.

Creating and managing tasks in Outlook allows you to keep track of projects, which might include school assignments, work responsibilities, or personal activities. Using a task, you can record information about a project such as start date, due date, status, priority, and percent complete. Outlook can also remind you about the task so that you do not forget to complete it. If you are managing a project, for example, you can assign tasks to people so that everyone can complete their portion of the project.

Project — Managing Tasks

People and businesses create tasks to keep track of projects that are important to them or their organizations. Tasks can be categorized and monitored to ensure that all projects are completed in a timely fashion. You can track one-time tasks as well as tasks that recur over a period of time. You can also prioritize tasks so that you can decide which ones must be completed first.

The project in this module follows general guidelines and uses Outlook to create the task list shown in Figure 4–1. The task list in the Sophia Module 4 mailbox includes tasks that are organized using class, personal, and project team categories.

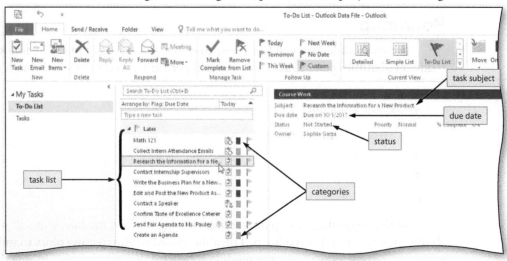

Figure 4–1

Inbox - Outlook Data File - Outlook

Microsoft Outlook 2016

File   Home   Send / Receive   Folder   View   ? Tell me what you want to do...

Creating a Task

The first step in creating a task for your to-do list is to open the Tasks category in Outlook. After you create a list of tasks, you can sync your tasks across multiple devices such as your smartphone and laptop, staying up to date and improving your productivity.

What advantages does an Outlook task list provide beyond a basic to-do list?
Many business employees use an Outlook task list to detail their hours, business expenses, and mileage. Instead of jotting down how many hours you worked on Tuesday to report later, remembering the tolls paid on a business trip, or how many miles you must list on your expense report, you can store this information in a task. When it is time to turn in your work hours or expense report, you can easily retrieve the details from your task list.

BTW
The Ribbon and Screen Resolution
Outlook may change how the groups and buttons within the groups appear on the ribbon, depending on the computer or mobile device's screen resolution. Thus, your ribbon may look different from the ones in this book if you are using a screen resolution other than 1366 × 768.

CONSIDER THIS

To-Do List Window

The To-Do List - Outlook Data File - Outlook window shown in Figure 4–2 includes features to help you manage your tasks. The main elements of the To-Do List window are the Navigation Pane, the To-Do list pane, and the Preview pane. The My Tasks folder in the Navigation Pane displays the To-Do list link and Tasks folder. Clicking the To-Do list link displays the tasks in the To-Do list view, and clicking Tasks displays the tasks in the task folder in Simple List view.

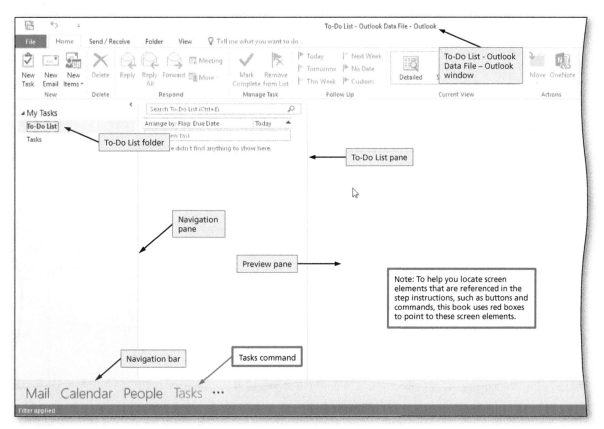

Figure 4–2

Creating a To-Do List

The first step in creating a To-Do list is to select a folder for storing your tasks. By default, Outlook stores tasks in the Tasks folder, but you can also create a personal folder in which to store your tasks, using the technique presented in Module 2. In this module, you will create tasks in the Tasks folder.

To Create a New Task

1 CREATE NEW TASK | 2 CATEGORIZE TASK | 3 CATEGORIZE EMAIL MESSAGE
4 ASSIGN TASK | 5 PRINT TASK | 6 CREATE AND USE NOTES

Sophia Garza, a student work study employee in the Pathways Internship Office, wants to create a task list to keep track of the internships and her own classes. The first task is to invite the internship supervisors to the rescheduled Pathways Internship Fair at least a month before the meeting now scheduled on November 3 so that she does not forget to complete the task. The following steps create a new task. *Why? To stay organized, you should create Outlook tasks to make sure you complete all the items on your to-do list.*

- Run Outlook 2016.
- Open the Sophia Module 4.pst Outlook Data File from the Data Files for Module 4.
- Click Tasks (shown in Figure 4–2) on the Navigation bar to display the Outlook Tasks.
- Click the New Task button (Home tab | New group) to display the Untitled – Task window (Figure 4–3).

Q&A Why is my screen different? My Untitled – Task window does not have the two buttons named Assign Task and Send Status Report in the Manage Task group as shown in Figure 4–3.

If you do not have an email account connected to Outlook (covered in Module 1), you will not have these two buttons.

The New Task button does not appear on the Home tab. What should I do?

Click the New Items button (Home tab | New group), and then click Task. Now the New Task button should appear on the Home tab.

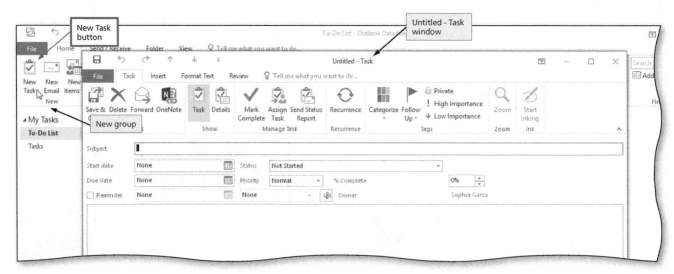

Figure 4–3

2

- Type `Contact Internship Supervisors` in the Subject text box to enter a subject for the task.

- Type `Pathways Internship Fair rescheduled for November 3` in the task body area to enter a description for the task (Figure 4–4).

Q&A Why did the title of the Task window change after I entered the subject?
As soon as you enter the subject, Outlook updates the Task window title to reflect the information you entered. The task is not saved, however; only the window title is updated.

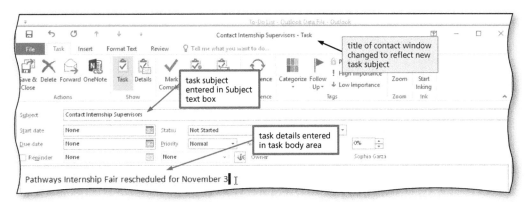

Figure 4–4

3

- Click the Start date Calendar button to display a calendar for the current month (Figure 4–5).

Q&A Why does my calendar display a different month?
Depending on the actual calendar month, your current month may be different.

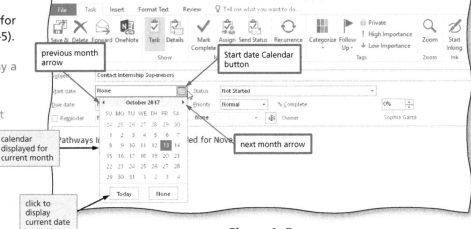

Figure 4–5

4

- If necessary, click the next month arrow or previous month arrow an appropriate number of times to advance to October 2017.

- Click 3 to select Tues 10/3/2017 as the start date (Figure 4–6).

Q&A Why did the due date change?
If you enter a start date, the due date automatically changes to match the start date. You can change the due date if needed.

Can I just type the date?
Yes, you can type the date. Using the calendar allows you to avoid potential errors due to typing mistakes.

What if October 2017 is in the past?
If October 2017 is in the past, click the previous month arrow an appropriate number of times until you reach October 2017.

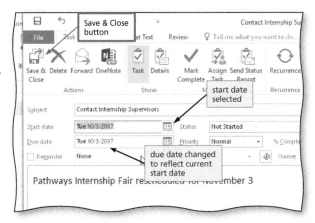

Figure 4–6

5

• Click the Save & Close button (Task tab | Actions group) (shown in Figure 4–6) to save the task and close the Task window (Figure 4–7).

Q&A My tasks are displayed in an arrangement different from the one in Figure 4–7. What should I do?
Click the Change View button or the More button (Home tab | Current View group), and then click To-Do List.

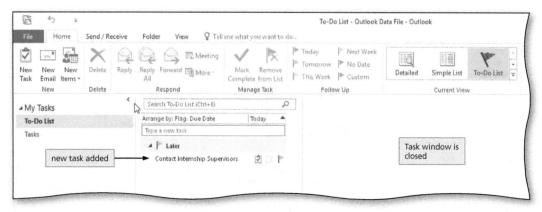

Figure 4–7

Other Ways

1. Press CTRL+N

To Create a Task with a Due Date

1 CREATE NEW TASK | 2 CATEGORIZE TASK | 3 CATEGORIZE EMAIL MESSAGE
4 ASSIGN TASK | 5 PRINT TASK | 6 CREATE AND USE NOTES

When you create the first task, the due date is set automatically after you enter the start date. If you have a specific due date, you can enter it when you create a task. Sophia needs to create a meeting agenda before the meeting on November 3. The following steps create a task with a due date. *Why? You can quickly add a specific due date to set a deadline for a task. You also can sort by the due date, placing the most urgent tasks at the top of your list.*

1

• Click the New Task button (Home tab | New group) to display the Untitled – Task window.

• Type **Create an Agenda** in the Subject text box to enter a subject for the task (Figure 4–8).

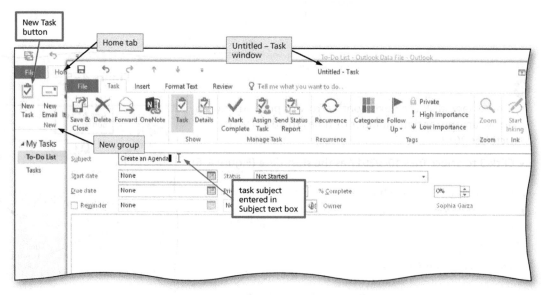

Figure 4–8

- Click the Due date Calendar button to display a calendar for the current month.

- Click the next or previous month arrow an appropriate number of times to display November 2017.

- Click 3 to select Fri 11/3/2017 as the due date (Figure 4–9).

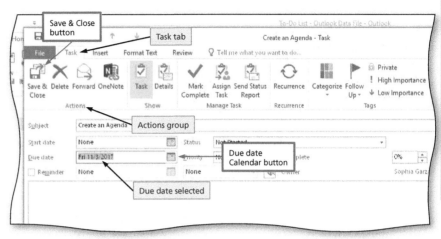

Figure 4–9

- Click the Save & Close button (Task tab | Actions group) to save the task and close the Task window (Figure 4–10).

Figure 4–10

To Create a Task with a Status

1 CREATE NEW TASK | 2 CATEGORIZE TASK | 3 CATEGORIZE EMAIL MESSAGE
4 ASSIGN TASK | 5 PRINT TASK | 6 CREATE AND USE NOTES

You can assign a status to a task using any of five status indicators: Not Started, In Progress, Completed, Waiting on someone else, and Deferred. Sophia is planning to provide a speaker for the Land Your Perfect Internship event on 10/27/2017 and wants to create a task to remind herself to contact a speaker. She has already started working on a few speaker ideas, so the task status should be set to In Progress. The following steps create a task with a status. *Why? You can reflect your current progress by changing the status of a task.*

- Click the New Task button (Home tab | New group) to display the Untitled – Task window.

- Type **Contact a Speaker** in the Subject text box to enter a subject for the task.

- Type **Speaker needed for the Land Your Perfect Internship event** in the task body area to enter a description for the task.

- Click the Due date Calendar button to display a calendar for the current month.

- Click the appropriate month arrow button to go to October 2017.

- Click 27 to select Fri 10/27/2017 as the due date (Figure 4–11).

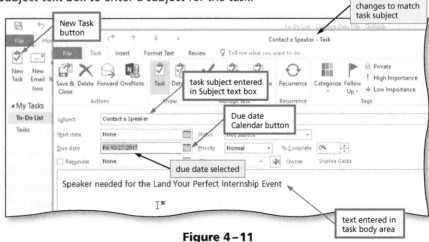

Figure 4–11

• Click the Status box
arrow to display
the status options
(Figure 4–12).

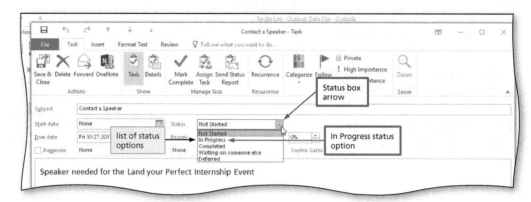

Figure 4–12

• Click In Progress to
change the status
of the task (Figure
4–13).

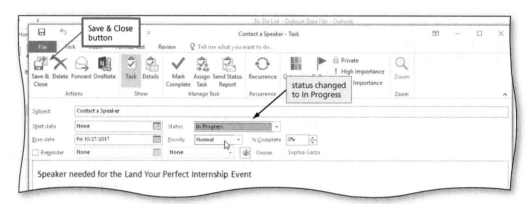

Figure 4–13

• Click the Save &
Close button (Task
tab | Actions group)
to save the task
and close the Task
window (Figure
4–14).

Figure 4–14

To Create a Task with a Priority

1 CREATE NEW TASK | 2 CATEGORIZE TASK | 3 CATEGORIZE EMAIL MESSAGE
4 ASSIGN TASK | 5 PRINT TASK | 6 CREATE AND USE NOTES

Outlook can organize each task by setting priorities to reflect its importance. Outlook allows for three priority levels: Low, Normal, and High. The Pathways Internship Fair on November 3 will be catered by Taste of Excellence, and Sophia needs to confirm the catering details at least four days in advance. As you enter the task in Outlook, assign a high priority. The following steps set the priority of a task. *Why? After setting priorities, you can sort by the importance of the task to determine how best to focus your time.*

1

- Click the New Task button (Home tab | New group) to display the Untitled – Task window.

- Type `Confirm Taste of Excellence Caterer` in the Subject text box to enter a subject for the task.

- Click the Due date Calendar button to display a calendar for the current month.

- Click the next or previous month arrow an appropriate number of times to display October 2017.

- Click 30 to select Mon 10/30/2017 as the due date (Figure 4–15).

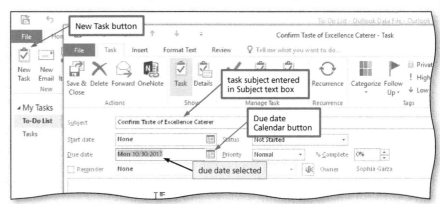

Figure 4–15

2

- Click the Priority box arrow to display the priority options (Figure 4–16).

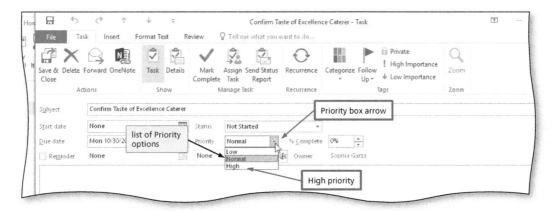

Figure 4–16

3

- Click High to set the priority (Figure 4–17).

4

- Click the Save & Close button (Task tab | Actions group) to save the task and close the Task window.

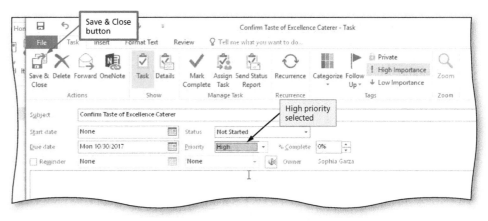

Figure 4–17

Can a project manager in a business team assign tasks in Outlook to keep track of what work the team has completed?

Outlook provides an easy way for project managers to assign tasks. For example, a manager might want to receive status reports and updates on the progress of a task. If the person who is assigned a task rejects it, the manager can reassign the task to someone else and set a high priority for the task.

To Create a Task with a Reminder

1 CREATE NEW TASK | 2 CATEGORIZE TASK | 3 CATEGORIZE EMAIL MESSAGE
4 ASSIGN TASK | 5 PRINT TASK | 6 CREATE AND USE NOTES

To make sure you remember to complete a task, set a reminder before the task is due so you have enough time to complete the task. Ms. Pauley, the faculty advisor, asked Sophia to send her the Pathways Internship Fair agenda by the end of October. Sophia can create a task with a reminder to respond to Ms. Pauley's request. *Why? By adding a reminder to a task, Outlook can remind you about the task automatically.* The following steps add a task and set the reminder option for a week before the task is due.

• Click the New Task button (Home tab | New group) to display the Untitled – Task window.

• Type **Send Fair Agenda to Ms. Pauley** in the Subject text box to enter a subject for the task.

• Type **Pathways Internship Fair detailed agenda** in the task body area to enter a description for the task.

• Click the Due date Calendar button to display a calendar for the current month.

• Click the next month arrow an appropriate number of times to advance to October 2017.

• Click 31 to select Tue 10/31/2017 as the due date (Figure 4–18).

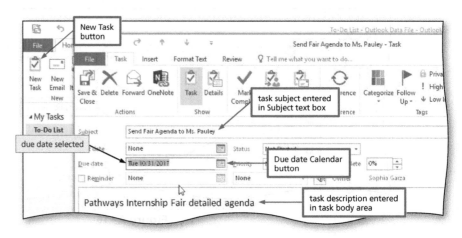

Figure 4–18

• Click the Reminder check box to insert a check mark, enable the Reminder boxes, and configure Outlook to display a reminder (Figure 4–19).

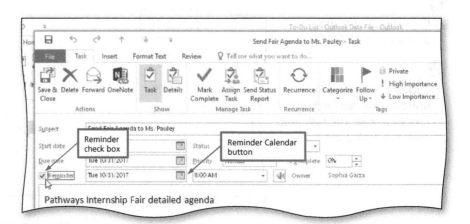

Figure 4–19

③

- Click the Reminder Calendar button to display a calendar for October.

- Click 24 to select Tue 10/24/2017 as the Reminder date (Figure 4–20).

Q&A Can I change the time that Outlook displays the reminder?
Yes. When you set a reminder, Outlook automatically sets the time for the reminder to 8:00 AM. You can change the time by clicking the Reminder box arrow and then selecting a time. You can also use the Outlook Options dialog box to change the default time.

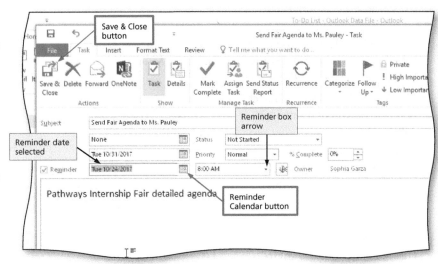

Figure 4–20

④

- Click the Save & Close button (Task tab | Actions group) to save the task and close the Task window (Figure 4–21).

Q&A How does Outlook remind me of a task?
Outlook displays the Task window for the task at the specified time. If you used the Sound icon to set an alarm for the reminder, Outlook also plays the sound when it displays the Task window.

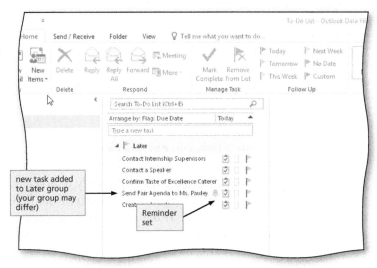

Figure 4–21

To Create More Tasks

1 CREATE NEW TASK | 2 CATEGORIZE TASK | 3 CATEGORIZE EMAIL MESSAGE
4 ASSIGN TASK | 5 PRINT TASK | 6 CREATE AND USE NOTES

Sophia has three tasks to add regarding a project in her economics course to develop a new product plan. The first task is to research the information for a new product. Another task is to write the business plan for the new product. She also needs a task for editing and posting the new product assignment. Table 4–1 displays the business plan tasks with their due dates.

Table 4–1 Additional Tasks	
Subject	**Due Date**
Research the Information for a New Product	10/2/2017
Write the Business Plan for a New Product	10/9/2017
Edit and Post the New Product Assignment	10/16/2017

The following step creates the remaining tasks in the Task window. *Why? By adding academic tasks to your list, an item that requires attention will not be overlooked.*

- Click the New Task button (Home tab | New group) to display the Untitled – Task window.

- Enter the subject in the Subject text box for the first task in Table 4–1.

- Click the Due date Calendar button to display a calendar for the current month, and then select the due date for the task as shown in Table 4–1.

- Click the Save & Close button (Task tab | Actions group) to save the task and close the Task window.

- Repeat the actions in bullets 1 through 4 for the two remaining tasks in Table 4–1 (Figure 4–22).

Figure 4–22

To Create a Recurring Task

1 CREATE NEW TASK | 2 CATEGORIZE TASK | 3 CATEGORIZE EMAIL MESSAGE
4 ASSIGN TASK | 5 PRINT TASK | 6 CREATE AND USE NOTES

When you create a task, you can specify it is a recurring task by selecting whether the task recurs daily, weekly, monthly, or yearly. For each of those options, you can provide specifics, such as the day of the month the task occurs. You can have the task recur indefinitely or you can specify the exact end date. Sophia has a weekly assignment due in her Math 121 course on Mondays from September 11 until December 11. The following steps add a recurring weekly task. *Why? When you have a task that occurs at regular intervals, you should set a recurring task to keep you informed.*

- Click the New Task button (Home tab | New group) to display the Untitled – Task window.

- Type `Math 121` in the Subject text box to enter a subject for the task.

- Type `Submit assignment online` in the task body area to enter a description for the task.

- Click the Start date Calendar button to display a calendar for the current month.

- Click the next or previous month arrow an appropriate number of times to display September 2017.

- Click 11 to select Mon 9/11/2017 as the start date (Figure 4–23).

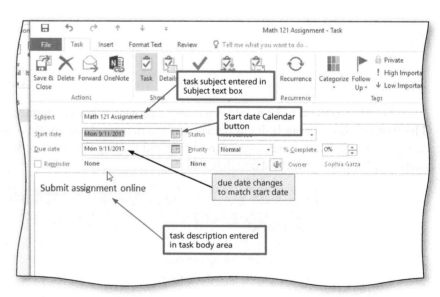

Figure 4–23

2

- Click the Recurrence button (Task tab | Recurrence group) to display the Task Recurrence dialog box (Figure 4–24).

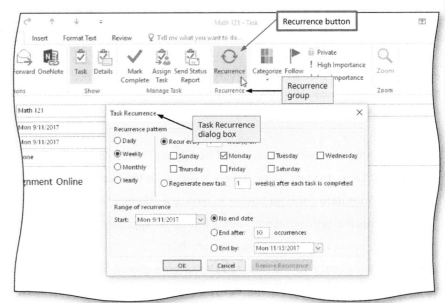

Figure 4–24

3

- Click the End by option button to select it.

- Click the End by box arrow to display a calendar.

- If necessary, click the next or previous month arrow an appropriate number of times to display December 2017.

- Click 11 to select Mon 12/11/2017 as the End by date (Figure 4–25).

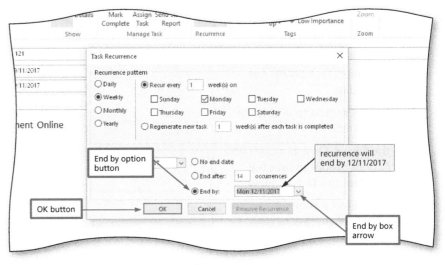

Figure 4–25

4

- Click the OK button (Task Recurrence dialog box) to accept the recurrence settings (Figure 4–26).

5

- Click the Save & Close button (Task tab | Actions group) to save the task and close the Task window.

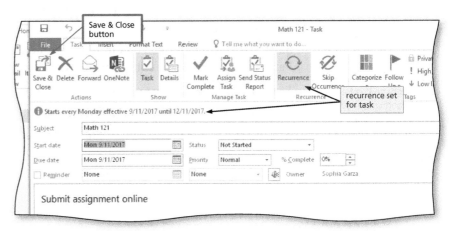

Figure 4–26

To Create Another Recurring Task

Sophia also needs a recurring task for collecting the intern attendance emails. The intern supervisors email each intern's attendance to Sophia every Friday from September 15 until December 8. The following step adds another recurring task. *Why? When you have a task that occurs at regular intervals, you should add it as a recurring task to keep you informed.*

1

- Click the New Task button (Home tab | New group) to display the Untitled – Task window.

- Type `Collect Intern Attendance Emails` in the Subject text box to enter a subject for the task.

- Click the Start date Calendar button to display a calendar for the current month.

- Click the next or previous month arrow button an appropriate number of times to display September 2017.

- Click 15 to select Fri 09/15/2017 as the start date.

- Click the Recurrence button (Task tab | Recurrence group) to display the Task Recurrence dialog box.

- Click the End by option button to select it.

- Click the End by box arrow to display a calendar.

- Click the next or previous month arrow button an appropriate number of times to return to December 2017.

- Click 8 to select Fri 12/8/2017 as the End by date.

- Click the OK button to accept the recurrence settings.

- Click the Save & Close button (Task tab | Actions group) to save the task and close the Task window.

- Click the Collect Intern Attendance Emails task to view the task details (Figure 4–27).

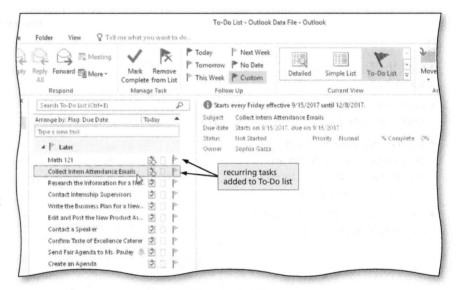

Figure 4–27

BTW

Task Options
You can modify options for tasks, such as changing the default reminder time for tasks with due dates, changing default colors for overdue and completed tasks, and setting the Quick Click flag. To access task options, open the Backstage view, click Options, and then click Tasks.

TO ADD A TASK USING THE TO-DO LIST PANE

If you need to add a task quickly, you can use the To-Do List Pane to create a quick task due the day you add it. If you wanted to add a task using the To-Do List Pane, you would use the following steps.

1. Click the 'Type a new task' box to select the text box.

2. Type a description to enter a description of the task.

3. Press the ENTER key to finish adding the task and display it in the To-Do list with the current date.

Categorizing Tasks

Outlook allows you to categorize email messages, contacts, tasks, and calendar items so that you can identify which ones are related to each other and quickly identify the items by their color. Module 2 used color categories to organize calendar items. In the same way, you can use color categories to organize tasks.

Six color categories are available by default, but you can also create your own categories and select one of 25 colors to associate with them. After you create a category, you can set it as a **Quick Click** category, which is applied by default when you click an item's category column in the To-Do list pane. For example, the default Quick Click category is the red category. If you click a task's category column in the To-Do list pane, the red category automatically is assigned to it.

To Create a New Category

1 CREATE NEW TASK | 2 CATEGORIZE TASK | 3 CATEGORIZE EMAIL MESSAGE
4 ASSIGN TASK | 5 PRINT TASK | 6 CREATE AND USE NOTES

Why? Custom categories can organize tasks listed in Outlook. The first category you want to create is the Pathways Internship Office category, which you can use for all tasks related to the internship program at Langford College. When you select a task and then create the category, Outlook applies the category to the selected task. After you create a category, apply it to other tasks as necessary. The following steps create a category and apply it to a task.

- Click the `Contact Internship Supervisors` task to select it.
- Click the Categorize button (Home tab | Tags group) to display the Categorize menu (Figure 4–28).

Q&A Why do I have to select the Contact Internship Supervisors task?
To activate the Categorize button, you first need to select a task or group of tasks.

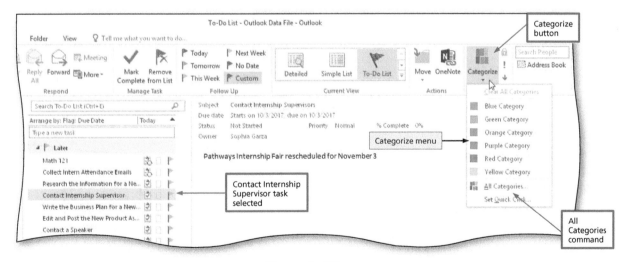

Figure 4–28

- Click All Categories to display the Color Categories dialog box (Figure 4–29).

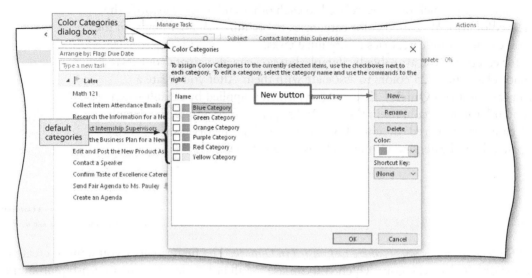

Figure 4–29

- Click the New button (Color Categories dialog box) to display the Add New Category dialog box (Figure 4–30).

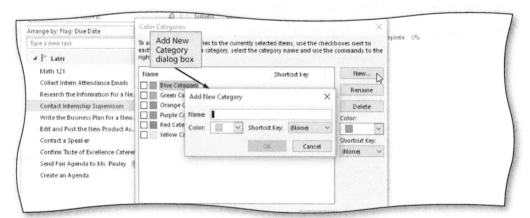

Figure 4–30

- Type **Pathways Internship** in the Name text box to enter a name for the category.

- Click the Color box arrow to display a list of colors (Figure 4–31).

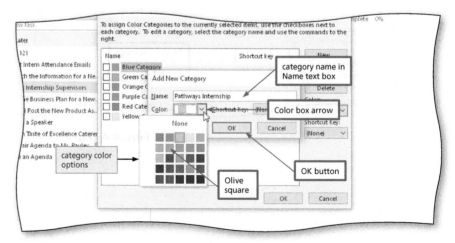

Figure 4–31

5

- Click the Olive square (column 2, row 2) to select a category color.
- Click the OK button (Add New Category dialog box) to create the new category and display it in the Color Categories dialog box (Figure 4–32).

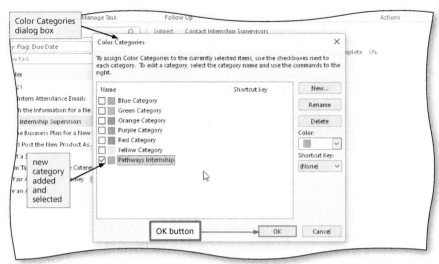

Figure 4–32

6

- Click the OK button (Color Categories dialog box) to assign the Contact Internship Supervisors task to the Pathways Internship category (Figure 4–33).

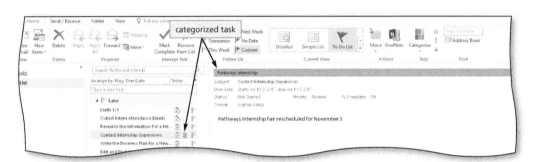

Figure 4–33

To Categorize a Task

1 CREATE NEW TASK | 2 CATEGORIZE TASK | 3 CATEGORIZE EMAIL MESSAGE
4 ASSIGN TASK | 5 PRINT TASK | 6 CREATE AND USE NOTES

After creating a category, you can apply other tasks that are related to that category. *Why? You can easily identify all the tasks for a specific category by using color categories.* The following steps assign a task to an existing color category.

1

- Click the Create an Agenda task to select it.
- Click the Categorize button (Home tab | Tags group) to display the Categorize menu (Figure 4–34).

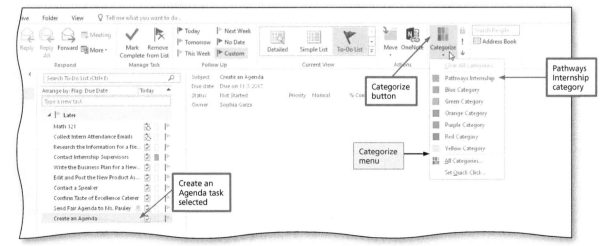

Figure 4–34

• Click Pathways Internship to assign the Create an Agenda task to that category (Figure 4–35).

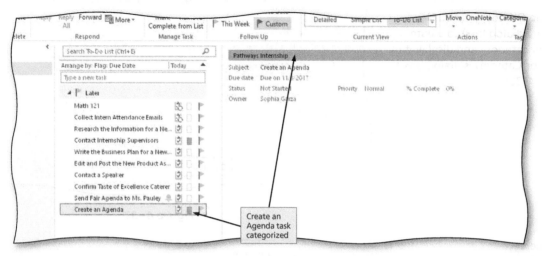

Figure 4–35

To Categorize Multiple Tasks

1 CREATE NEW TASK | 2 CATEGORIZE TASK | 3 CATEGORIZE EMAIL MESSAGE
4 ASSIGN TASK | 5 PRINT TASK | 6 CREATE AND USE NOTES

Outlook allows you to categorize multiple tasks at the same time. All of the course-related tasks can be assigned to a new category called Course Work, including the three new product assignments in the Economics class and the Math course task. The following steps create the Course Work category and apply it to the course-related tasks. *Why? As a student, you can view a single category to locate all of your assignments.*

• Select the Math 121, Research the Information for a New Product, Write the Business Plan for a New Product, and Edit and Post the New Product Assignment tasks.

• Click the Categorize button (Home tab | Tags group) to display the Categorize menu (Figure 4–36).

Q&A | How do I select more than one task?
Click the first task, press and hold the CTRL key, and then click the other tasks to select them.

Figure 4–36

2

- Click All Categories to display the Color Categories dialog box.

- Click the New button (Color Categories dialog box) to display the Add New Category dialog box (Figure 4–37).

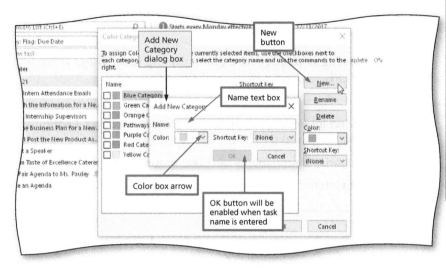

Figure 4–37

3

- Type `Course Work` in the Name text box to enter a name for the category.

- Click the Color box arrow to display a list of colors.

- Click the Dark Red square (column 1, row 4) to select the category color.

- Click the OK button (Add New Category dialog box) to create the Course Work category (Figure 4–38).

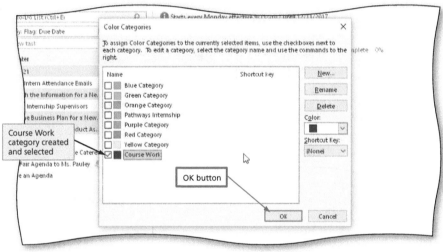

Figure 4–38

4

- Click the OK button (Color Categories dialog box) to assign the selected tasks to a category (Figure 4–39).

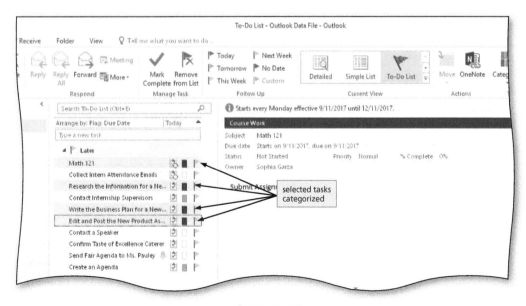

Figure 4–39

To Categorize Remaining Tasks

1 CREATE NEW TASK | 2 CATEGORIZE TASK | 3 CATEGORIZE EMAIL MESSAGE
4 ASSIGN TASK | 5 PRINT TASK | 6 CREATE AND USE NOTES

The following steps categorize the remaining tasks. *Why? When you sort by category, you will be able to view at a glance what tasks need completion in each facet of your life.*

- Select the Collect Intern Attendance Emails, Contact a Speaker, Confirm Taste of Excellence Caterer, and Send Fair Agenda to Ms. Pauley tasks.
- Click the Categorize button (Home tab | Tags group) to display the Categorize menu.
- Click Pathways Internship to categorize the selected tasks (Figure 4–40).

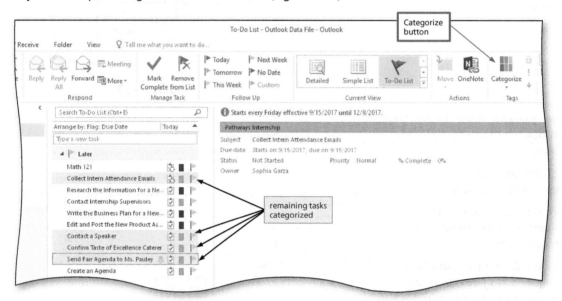

Figure 4–40

To Rename a Category

1 CREATE NEW TASK | 2 CATEGORIZE TASK | 3 CATEGORIZE EMAIL MESSAGE
4 ASSIGN TASK | 5 PRINT TASK | 6 CREATE AND USE NOTES

Sophia decides to change the name of the Pathways Internship category to the Pathways Internship Program category. The following steps rename a color category. *Why? By renaming the color categories, you can assign names that are meaningful to you.*

- Click the Categorize button (Home tab | Tags group) to display the Categorize menu.
- Click All Categories to display the Color Categories dialog box (Figure 4–41).

Q&A
Do the category tasks have to be selected before renaming the category?
No, any task can be selected. When you change the name, Outlook will update every task in that category.

Figure 4–41

- Click the Pathways Internship category to select it.

- Click the Rename button (Color Categories dialog box) to select the category name for editing.

- Type `Pathways Internship Program` and then press the ENTER key to change the category name (Figure 4–42).

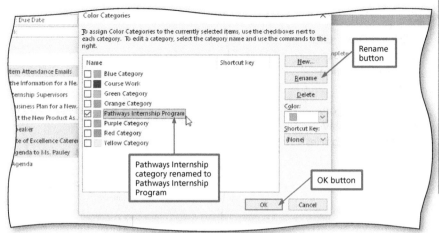

Figure 4–42

- Click the OK button (Color Categories dialog box) to apply the changes (Figure 4–43).

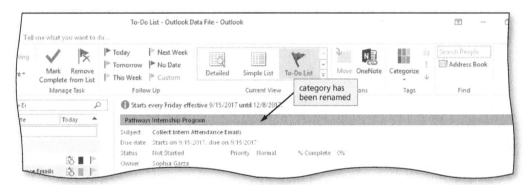

Figure 4–43

To Set a Quick Click

1 CREATE NEW TASK | 2 CATEGORIZE TASK | 3 CATEGORIZE EMAIL MESSAGE
4 ASSIGN TASK | 5 PRINT TASK | 6 CREATE AND USE NOTES

Instead of categorizing tasks using the Categorize menu options, you can assign a task to a category by clicking the category box for a task in the To-Do list pane. If you click the category box, the default category is applied. You can change the default category by setting one as a Quick Click. *Why? You can assign a frequently used color category (Quick Click category) by selecting it as your default color category.* Sophia realizes that most of her tasks are related to the Pathways Internship Program, so she decides to set the default category as the Pathways Internship Program category. The following steps assign the default category using a Quick Click.

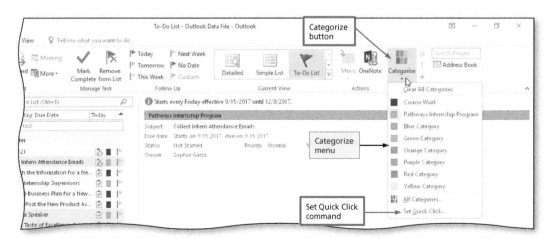

- Click the Categorize button (Home tab | Tags group) to display the Categorize menu (Figure 4–44).

Figure 4–44

- Click Set Quick Click to display the Set Quick Click dialog box.

- Click the category button to display the list of categories (Figure 4–45).

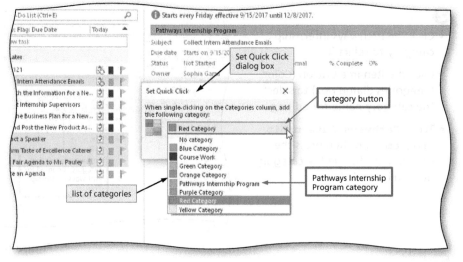

Figure 4–45

- Click Pathways Internship Program to set it as the Quick Click category (Figure 4–46).

- Click the OK button (Set Quick Click dialog box) to apply the changes.

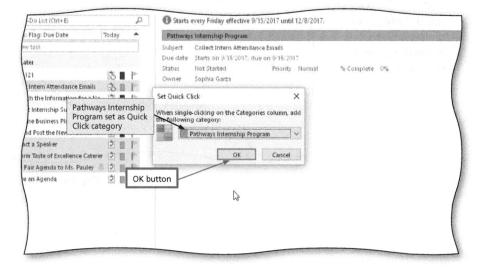

Figure 4–46

Break Point: If you wish to take a break, this is a good place to do so. To resume at a later time, continue to follow the steps from this location forward.

BTW
Copying and Moving Tasks
To move or copy a task to another folder, select the task, and then click the Move button (Home tab | Actions group). Click the Other Folder command to move the task; click the Copy to Folder command to copy the task. Select the folder to which you want to move or copy the task, and then click the OK button.

Categorizing Email Messages

Recall that you can use categories with email messages, contacts, tasks, and calendar items. Any category you create for a task can be used for your email messages. Categorizing your email messages allows you to create a link between them and other related items in Outlook. By looking at the category, you quickly can tell which Outlook items go together.

To Categorize an Email Message

Sophia received a couple of email messages from interns in the internship program. These email messages can be assigned to the Pathways Internship Program category. The following steps categorize email messages. *Why? Color categories can be assigned to email messages, enabling you to quickly identify them and associate them with related tasks.*

1

- Click the Mail button on the Navigation bar and open the Inbox folder to switch to your Inbox.

- Select the Zion Gibson and Yumi Mori email messages.

- Click the Categorize button (Home tab | Tags group) to display the Categorize menu (Figure 4–47).

Q&A What should I do if my Inbox email messages are not displayed?
Expand the Inbox folder in the Navigation Pane to view the messages.

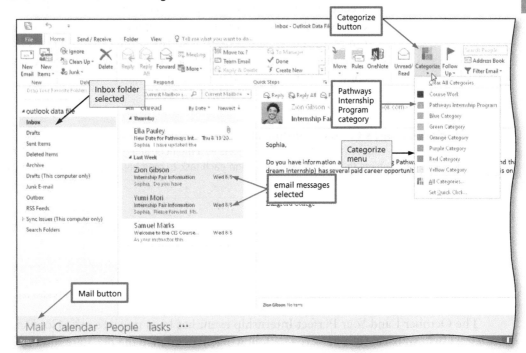

Figure 4–47

2

- Click Pathways Internship Program to assign the selected email messages to the Pathways Internship Program category (Figure 4–48).

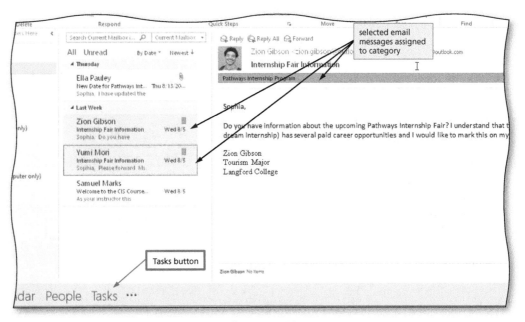

Figure 4–48

Managing Tasks

After creating one or more tasks in your To-Do list, you can manage them by marking tasks complete when you finish them, updating them, assigning some tasks to other people, adding attachments, and removing them. For example, when you email the agenda for the meeting to Ms. Pauley, mark the task as complete. That way, you will not have to remember later whether you completed the assignment.

When you are working on a project with others, you sometimes may want to assign tasks to them. Outlook allows you to assign tasks to other people and still monitor the tasks. When a task has been assigned to another person, that person can accept or reject the task. If the task is rejected, it comes back to you. If it is accepted, the task belongs to that person to complete. When you assign a nonrecurring task, you can retain a copy and request a **status report** that indicates how much progress has been made in completing the task. If the task is a recurring task, you cannot retain a copy, but you can still request a status report.

CONSIDER THIS

Can you assign tasks to others within a business or club setting?

In the professional world, you typically work on projects as a member of a group or team. As you organize the large and small tasks required to complete the project, you can assign each task to members of your team and track the progress of the entire project.

To Update a Task

1 CREATE NEW TASK | 2 CATEGORIZE TASK | 3 CATEGORIZE EMAIL MESSAGE
4 ASSIGN TASK | 5 PRINT TASK | 6 CREATE AND USE NOTES

The October Land Your Perfect Internship event has been moved so the Contact a Speaker task is due on October 24 instead of on October 27. The following steps change the due date for a task. *Why? As tasks change, be sure to update the due dates of your tasks.*

- Click the Tasks button on the Navigation bar (shown in Figure 4–48) to display the To-Do list.

- Double-click the Contact a Speaker task to display the Contact a Speaker – Task window (Figure 4–49).

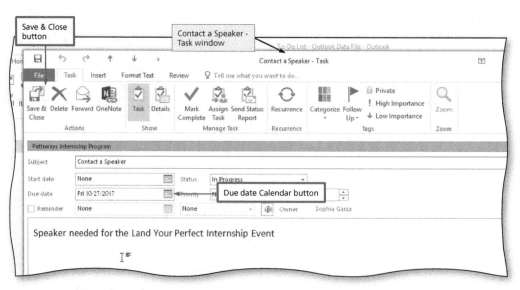

Figure 4–49

2

- Click the Due date Calendar button to display a calendar for October.
- Click 24 to select Tue 10/24/2017 as the due date.
- Click the Save & Close button (Task tab | Actions group) to save the changes (Figure 4–50).

Q&A How do I change the task name only?

Click the task name in the task list to select it, and then click it again to edit the name.

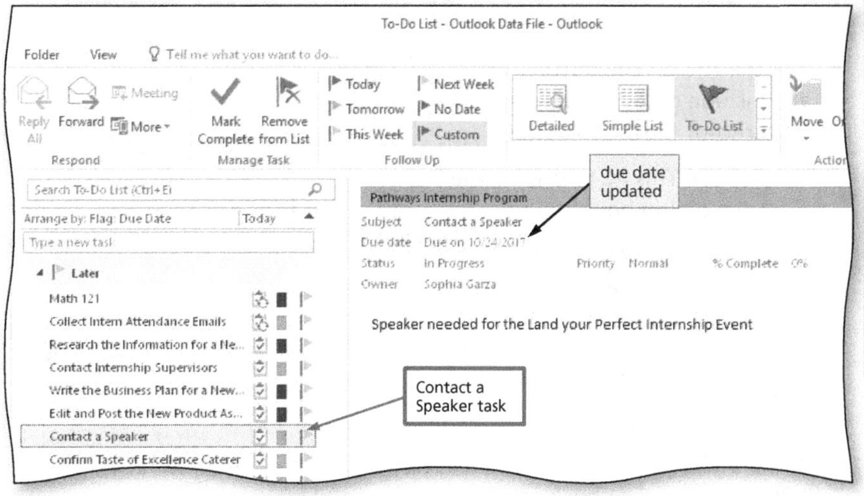

Figure 4–50

To Attach a File to a Task

1 CREATE NEW TASK | 2 CATEGORIZE TASK | 3 CATEGORIZE EMAIL MESSAGE
4 ASSIGN TASK | **5 PRINT TASK** | **6 CREATE AND USE NOTES**

***Why?** Attaching a file to a task is helpful if you want quick access to information when you are looking at a task.* Ella Pauley has emailed you an updated Pathways Internship Fair flyer, which you already have saved to your computer. You decide that you should attach it to the Confirm Taste of Excellence Caterer task so that you can share the flyer with the catering staff for room and timing information. The following steps attach a document to a task.

1

- Double-click the Confirm Taste of Excellence Caterer task (shown in Figure 4–50) to display the Confirm Taste of Excellence Caterer - Task window.
- Click Insert on the ribbon to display the Insert tab (Figure 4–51).

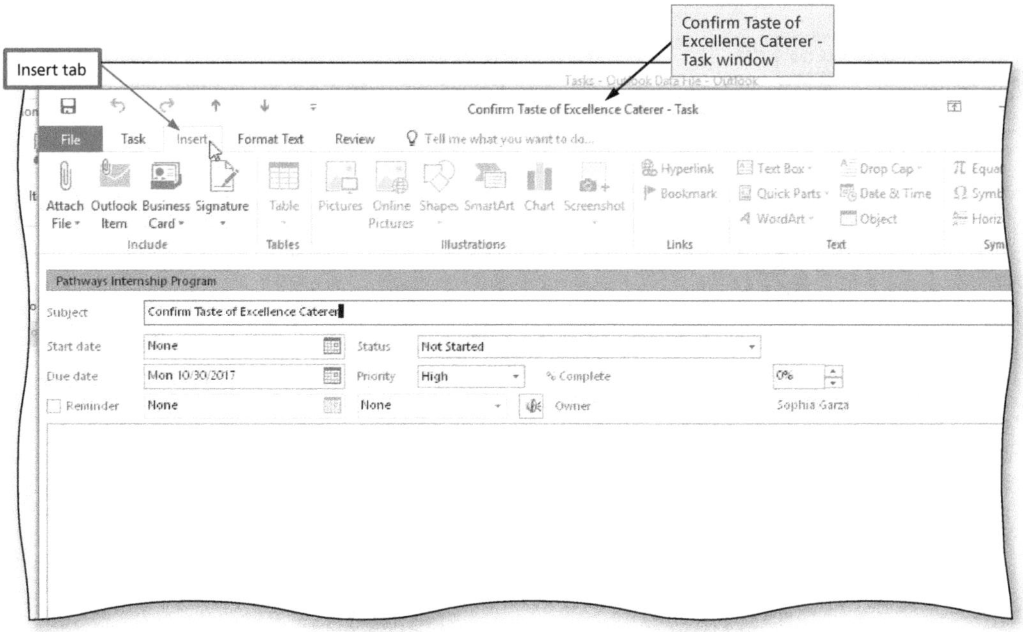

Figure 4–51

2

- Click the Attach File button (Insert tab | Include group) to display a list of recent files.

- Click Browse This PC to display the Insert File dialog box.

- If necessary, navigate to the folder containing the data files for this module (in this case, the Module 04 folder in the Outlook folder in the Data Files for Students folder).

- Click Fair (Word document) to select the file to attach (Figure 4–52).

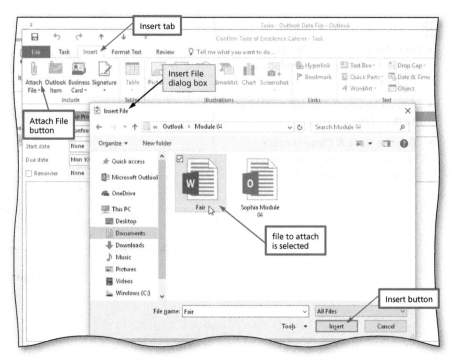

Figure 4–52

3

- Click the Insert button (Insert File dialog box) to attach the file (Figure 4–53).

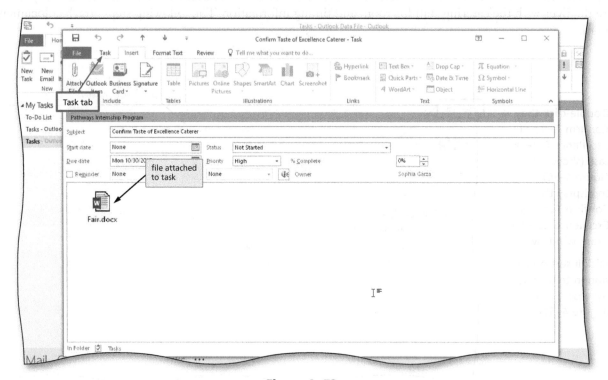

Figure 4–53

- Click Task on the ribbon to display the Task tab.

- Click the Save & Close button (Task tab | Actions group) to save the changes (Figure 4–54).

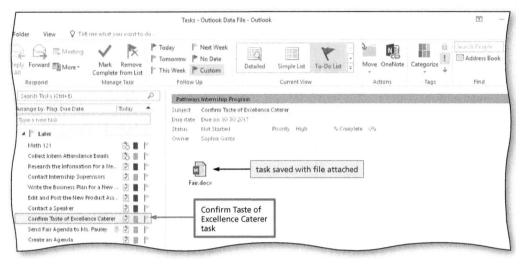

Figure 4–54

To Assign a Task

1 CREATE NEW TASK | 2 CATEGORIZE TASK | 3 CATEGORIZE EMAIL MESSAGE
4 ASSIGN TASK | 5 PRINT TASK | 6 CREATE AND USE NOTES

In addition to creating your own tasks, you can create tasks to assign to others. Yumi Mori, the Alumni Outreach coordinator, has volunteered to find a speaker for the Land Your Perfect Internship event. To assign a task, you first create the task, and then send it as a task request to someone. *Why? You can assign a task to someone else while ensuring that you retain a copy of the task and receive a status report once the task is completed.* The following steps assign a task.

1

- Double-click the Contact a Speaker task (shown in Figure 4–54) to reopen the Contact a Speaker - Task window (Figure 4–55).

Figure 4–55

2

• Click the Assign Task button (Task tab | Manage Task group) to add the To text box to the task to add an email address (Figure 4–56).

Q&A Why did the Assign Task button disappear after it was clicked? If you do not want to assign the task to an individual, click the Cancel Assignment button that replaced the Assign Task button.

Figure 4–56

3

• Type `yumi.mori@outlook.com` in the To text box to enter a recipient (Figure 4–57).

Figure 4–57

4

- Click the Send button (shown in Figure 4–57) to send the task to Yumi Mori (Figure 4–58).

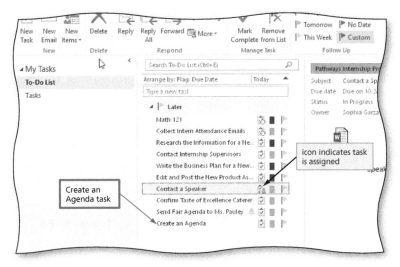

Figure 4–58

To Forward a Task

Why? *When you forward a task, you send a copy of the task to the person who can add it to their To-Do list for tracking.* Zion Gibson has agreed to assist you in creating the agenda for the Pathways Internship Fair. By forwarding the task to Zion, the task appears on his to-do list so he can track it on his own. The following steps forward a task.

1

- Double-click the Create an Agenda task (shown in Figure 4–58) to display the Create an Agenda – Task window (Figure 4–59).

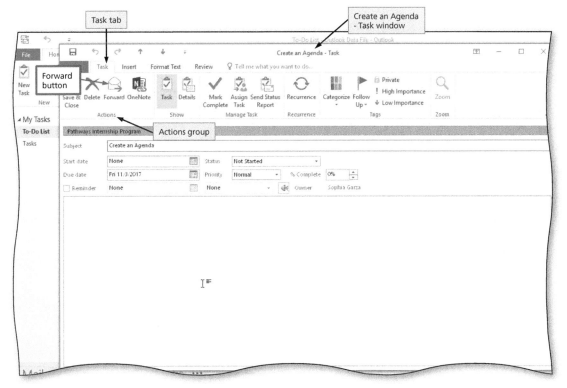

Figure 4–59

2

- Click the Forward button (Task tab | Actions group) to display the FW: Create an Agenda – Message (HTML) window (Figure 4–60).

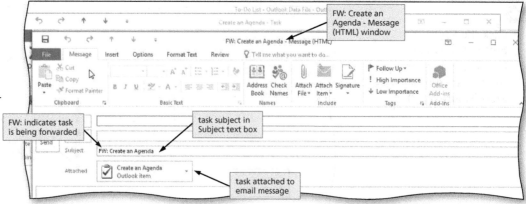

Figure 4–60

3

- Type `zion.gibson@outlook.com` in the To text box to enter a recipient.

- Type `Attached is the agenda task for you to add to your to-do list.` in the message body area to enter a message.

- Press the ENTER key two times and then type `Sophia` to complete the message (Figure 4–61).

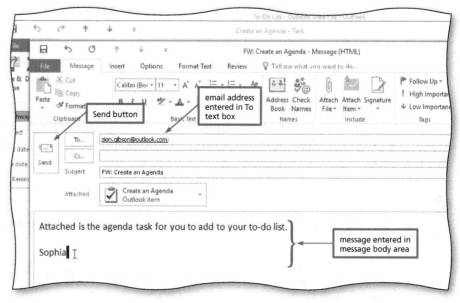

Figure 4–61

4

- Click the Send button to forward the task to Zion Gibson.

- Click the Save & Close button (Task tab | Actions group) to save the changes (Figure 4–62).

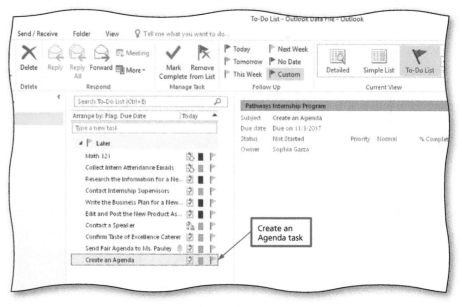

Figure 4–62

To Send a Status Report

While a task is in progress, you can send status reports to other people indicating the status and completion percentage of the task. Ms. Ella Pauley wants to be informed about the agenda for the November internship fair. Sophia has completed 25 percent of the work and wants to inform her that the task is in progress. The following steps create and send a status report. *Why? If you have been assigned a task, you can submit a status report before you complete the task to explain why the task has not been completed or why the task needs to be amended.*

- Double-click the Create an Agenda task to display the Create an Agenda - Task window.

- Click the Status box arrow to display a status list.

- Click In Progress to change the status of the task (Figure 4–63).

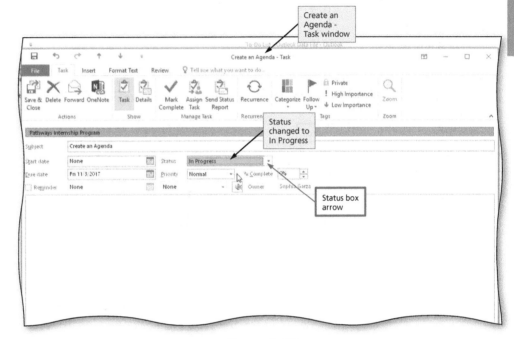

Figure 4–63

- Click the Up arrow to change the % Complete to 25% (Figure 4–64).

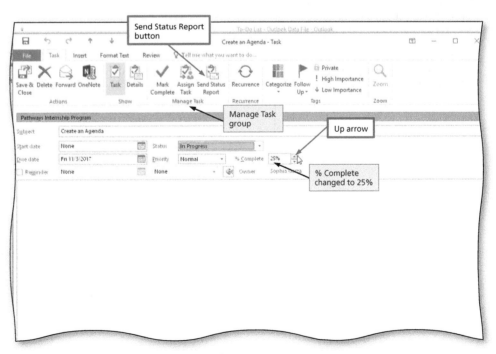

Figure 4–64

- Click the Send Status Report button (Task tab | Manage Task group) to display the Task Status Report: Create an Agenda - Message (Rich Text) window.

- Type `ella.pauley@outlook.com` in the To text box to enter a recipient.

- Type `Ms. Pauley,` and then press the ENTER key two times in the message body area to enter the greeting line of the message.

- Type `Here is my first update on this task.` in the message.

- Press the ENTER key two times, and then type `Sophia` to complete the message (Figure 4–65).

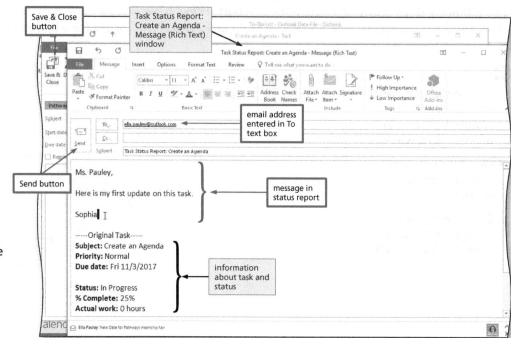

Figure 4–65

- Click the Send button to send the status report to Ella Pauley.

- Click the Save & Close button (Task tab | Actions group) to save the changes to the task (Figure 4–66).

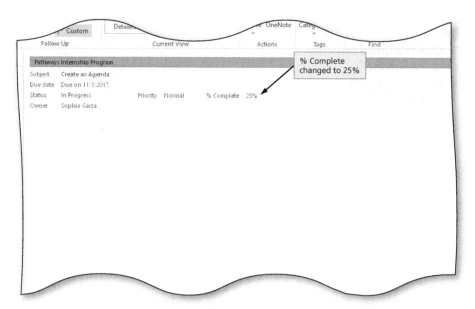

Figure 4–66

To Mark a Task Complete

You have just completed the research for the new product assignment for your economics class, so you can mark it as complete. *Why? Mark a task as complete so that you know it is finished.* The following steps mark a task as complete.

- Click the Research the Information for a New Product task to select it (Figure 4–67).

Figure 4–67

- Click the Mark Complete button (Home tab | Manage Task group) to mark the Research the Information for a New Product task as completed (Figure 4–68).

Q&A

Why was the Research the Information for a New Product task removed from the To-Do list?
Once you mark a task as complete, Outlook removes it from the To-Do list and places it in the Completed list. You can see the Completed list by changing your view to Completed using the Change View button (Home tab | Current View group).

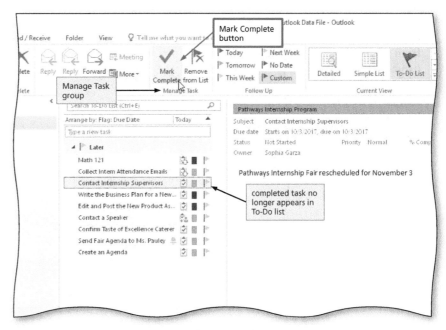

Figure 4–68

To Remove a Task

You sometimes may need to remove a task. **Why?** *When you remove a task, it is no longer displayed in your To-Do List.* The Pathways Internship Office has decided to remove the Contact Speaker for the Land Your Perfect Internship event task until the internship office has time to promote the event. The following steps remove a task.

1

- Click the Contact a Speaker task to select it (Figure 4–69).

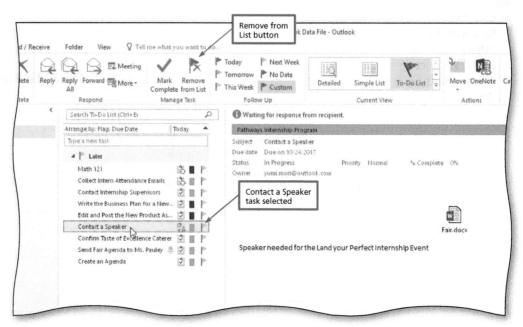

Figure 4–69

2

- Click the Remove from List button (Home tab | Manage Task group) to remove the task (Figure 4–70).

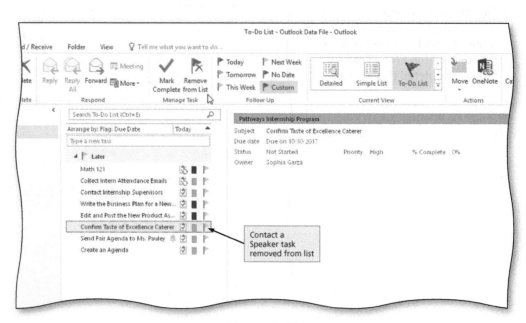

Figure 4–70

To DELETE A CATEGORY

When you no longer need a category, you can delete it. Deleting a category removes it from the category list but not from the tasks that already have been assigned to it. If you wanted to delete a category, you would use the following steps.

1. Click a task within the category that you would like to delete.
2. Click the Categorize button (Home tab | Tags group) to display the Categorize menu.
3. Click All Categories to display the Color Categories dialog box.
4. Click the category that you want to delete to select it.
5. Click the Delete button (Color Categories dialog box) to delete the color category.
6. Click the Yes button (Microsoft Outlook dialog box) to confirm the deletion.
7. Click the OK button (Color Categories dialog box) to close the dialog box.

BTW

Touch Screen Differences
The Office and Windows interfaces may vary if you are using a touch screen. For this reason, you might notice that the function or appearance of your touch screen differs slightly from this module's presentation.

Choosing Display and Print Views

When working with tasks, you can change the view to view your tasks as a detailed list, simple list, priority list, or a complete list. Change the view of your tasks to fit your current needs. For example, if you want to see tasks listed according to their priority (High, Normal, or Low), you can display the tasks in the Prioritized view. You can also print tasks in a summarized list or include the details for each task.

To Change the Task View

Tasks can be displayed in different customized view layouts. By displaying tasks in Detailed view, you can view all tasks, including completed tasks. The following steps change the view to Detailed view. *Why? To see the total picture of what you have to accomplish, the Detailed view provides all the task details, including task subject, status, due date, and categories.*

- Click View on the ribbon to display the View tab.

- Click the Change View button (View tab | Current View group) to display the Change View gallery (Figure 4–71).

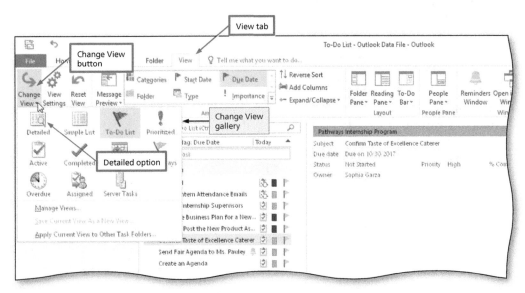

Figure 4–71

2

● Click Detailed to change the view (Figure 4–72).

Experiment

● Click the other views in the Current View gallery to view the tasks in other arrangements. When you are finished, click Detailed to return to Detailed view.

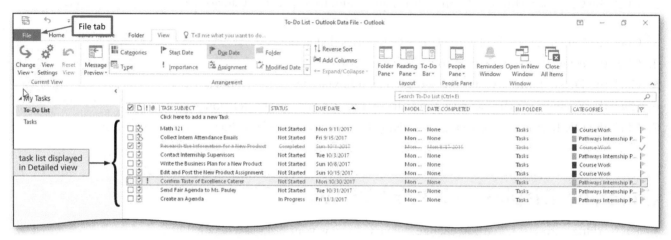

Figure 4–72

To Print Tasks

1 CREATE NEW TASK | 2 CATEGORIZE TASK | 3 CATEGORIZE EMAIL MESSAGE
4 ASSIGN TASK | 5 PRINT TASK | 6 CREATE AND USE NOTES

Outlook provides printing options based on the view and tasks you have selected. For example, in the To-Do List view, you can select a single task and print in Table Style or Menu Style. In Detailed view, which is the current view, you can print only in Table Style. The following steps print the tasks using Table Style. *Why?* *You might need a printed To-Do list to view when you are not working at your computer.*

1

● Click File on the ribbon to open the Backstage view.

● Click the Print tab in the Backstage view to display the Print gallery.

● If necessary, click Table Style in the Settings section to select a print format (Figure 4–73).

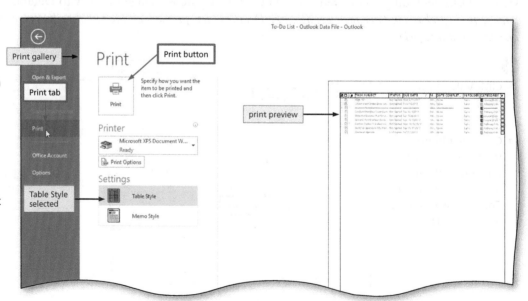

Figure 4–73

2

- Click the Print button to print the tasks in Table Style (Figure 4–74).

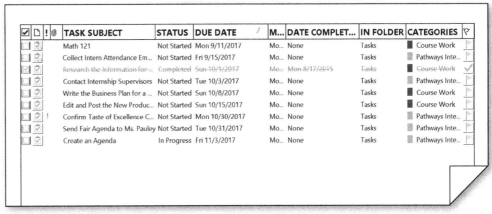

Figure 4–74

Using Notes

Outlook allows you to create the equivalent of paper notes using the Notes feature. Use notes to record ideas, spur-of-the-moment questions, and even words that you would like to recall or use at a later time. You can leave notes open on the screen while you continue using Outlook, or you can close them and view them in the Notes window. The Notes window contains the Navigation Pane and Notes Pane.

Can I use the Outlook Notes as sticky notes?

Notes are the electronic equivalent of yellow paper sticky notes. You can jot down notes for the directions that you find online to your interview, for example, or write questions that you want to remember to ask.

To Create a Note

1 CREATE NEW TASK | 2 CATEGORIZE TASK | 3 CATEGORIZE EMAIL MESSAGE
4 ASSIGN TASK | 5 PRINT TASK | 6 CREATE AND USE NOTES

Why? A note can be a reminder from a phone conversation, information you find online for future reference, or even a grocery list. When you enter text into a note, Outlook saves with the last modified date shown at the bottom of the note; you do not have to click a Save button. As Sophia was surfing the web, she found information that she wants to share with the interns. The following steps create a note reminder.

1

- Click the Navigation Options button (three dots) on the Navigation bar to display the Navigation Options menu (Figure 4–75).

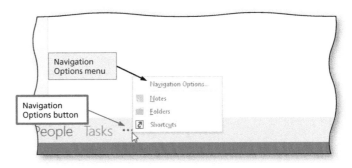

Figure 4–75

2

- Click Notes to open the Notes – Outlook Data File – Outlook window.
- Click the New Note button (Home tab | New group) to display a new blank note.
- Type `85% of companies use internships to recruit for their full-time workforce` as the note text to enter a note (Figure 4–76).

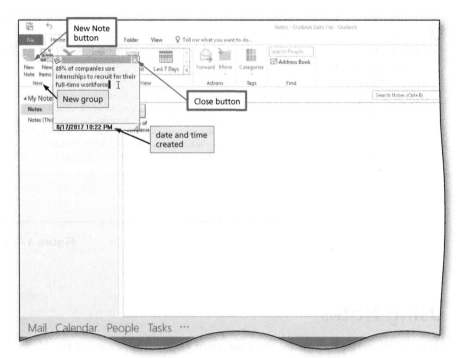

Figure 4–76

3

- Click the Close button to save and close the note (Figure 4–77).

Q&A Why is my Notes view different from Figure 4–77?
There are three basic Notes views: Icon, Notes List, and Last 7 Days. Figure 4–77 displays the note in Icon view. To switch to Icon view, click the Icon button (Home tab | Current View group).

Can I print notes?
Yes. First, select the note(s) you want to print. To select multiple notes, hold the CTRL key while clicking the notes to print. Next, click the File tab to open the Backstage view, click the Print tab, and then click the Print button.

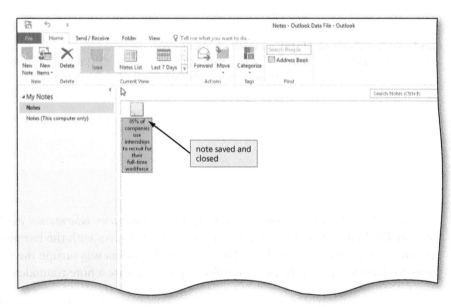

Figure 4–77

Other Ways

1. Press CTRL+SHIFT+N

To Change the Notes View

Why? *You would like to display your notes as a list instead of in the sticky note layout.* You decide to change your notes view to Notes List. The following step changes the view to Notes List view.

- Click the Notes List button (Home tab | Current View group) to change the view to Notes List (Figure 4–78).

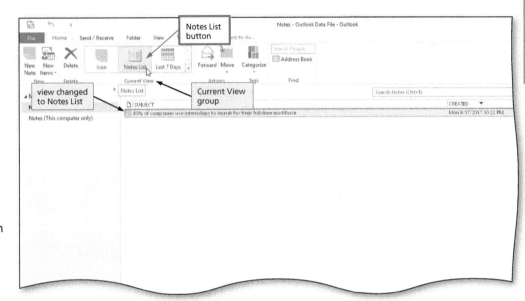

Experiment

- Click the other views in the Current View group to view the notes in other arrangements. When you are finished, click Notes List to return to Notes List view.

Figure 4–78

To Delete a Note

Why? *When you no longer need a note, you should delete it.* After sharing the note about recruiting interns for full-time positions, you decide to delete the note because you no longer need it. The following steps delete a note and close Outlook.

- If necessary, click the note about companies use of internships to select it.
- Click the Delete button (Home tab | Delete group) to delete the note (Figure 4–79).

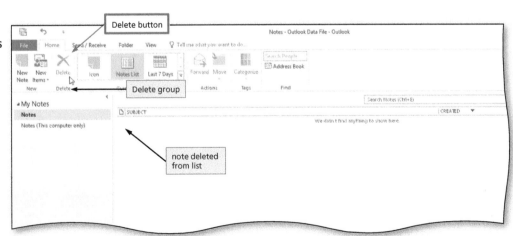

2

- Close Outlook.

Figure 4–79

Summary

In this module, you have learned how to use Outlook to create tasks, categorize tasks, categorize email messages, manage tasks, print tasks, create notes, and print notes.

CONSIDER THIS

Consider This: Plan Ahead

What decisions will you need to make when creating tasks, categorizing email messages, choosing views, and using notes in the future?

1. Create tasks.

   a. Determine what projects you want to track. People use tasks to keep track of the projects that are most important to them.

   b. Determine the information you want to store for a task. For any task, you can store basic information, add attachments, and add detailed instructions.

2. Categorize tasks and email messages.

   a. Plan categories for tasks. To identify and group tasks and other Outlook items easily, assign the items to categories.

   b. Assign emails to the same categories as tasks.

3. Manage tasks.

   a. Determine which tasks may need to be assigned to others.

4. Choose display and print views.

   a. Determine the preferred way to view the tasks to find the information you are seeking.

   b. Determine how you want to view your tasks.

5. Use notes.

   a. Determine what reminder notes would assist you.

CONSIDER THIS

How should you submit solutions to questions in the assignments identified with a **symbol?**

Every assignment in this book contains one or more questions with a symbol. These questions require you to think beyond the assigned file. Present your solutions to the question in the format required by your instructor. Possible formats may include one or more of these options: write the answer; create a document that contains the answer; present your answer to the class; discuss your answer in a group; record the answer as audio or video using a webcam, smartphone, or portable media player; or post answers on a blog, wiki, or website.

Apply Your Knowledge

Reinforce the skills and apply the concepts you learned in this module.

Note: To complete this assignment, you will be required to use the Data Files. Please contact your instructor for information about accessing the Data Files.

Editing a Task List

Instructions: Run Outlook. Import the Apply Your Knowledge 4-1 Youth in Politics Tasks file from the Data Files folder into Outlook. This file contains tasks for Shea Padilla, a student leader of the Youth in Politics Club on campus. Many of the tasks have changed and some are incomplete. You need to revise the tasks and then create categories for her. Then, you will print the resulting task list (Figure 4–80).

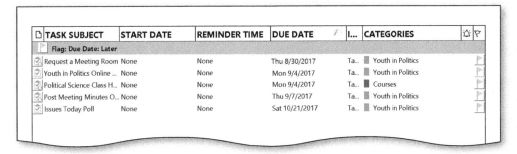

Figure 4–80

Perform the following tasks:

1. Display the Apply Your Knowledge 4-1 Youth in Politics Tasks folder in the Outlook Tasks window as a To-Do List.

2. Change the due date of the Youth in Politics Online Newsletter task to September 4, 2017. Change the % Complete to 75%.

3. Change the task name of Post Minutes Online to Post Meeting Minutes Online. Configure the task as a recurring task that occurs every Thursday from September 7, 2017, until December 7, 2017.

4. Make Request a Meeting Room a recurring task that occurs every Wednesday from August 30, 2017, until December 6, 2017. Change the status to Waiting on Someone Else.

5. Change the due date of the Issues Today Poll task to October 21, 2017. In the Task body, type **Create an online poll with 10 questions gauging which issues are important to our student population.**

6. Make Political Science Class Homework a recurring task that occurs every Monday, Wednesday, and Saturday from September 4, 2017, until December 15, 2017.

7. Create two color categories. Name the first one Youth in Politics and the second one Courses. Use the colors of your choice. Categorize each task accordingly.

8. Print the final task list in Table Style, as shown in Figure 4–80, and then submit it in the format specified by your instructor.

Continued >

Apply Your Knowledge *continued*

9. Export the Apply Your Knowledge 4-1 Tasks folder to a USB flash drive and then delete the folder from the hard disk. Submit the .pst file in the format specified by your instructor.

10. ✸ What task categories would you create to categorize the tasks in your personal life? Name at least five categories.

Extend Your Knowledge

Extend the skills you learned in this module and experiment with new skills. You may need to use Help to complete the assignment.

Creating Notes

Instructions: Run Outlook. Import the Extend Your Knowledge 4-1 Notes file from the Data Files folder into Outlook. This file has no notes, so you will create notes, categorize them, and then print the notes.

Perform the following tasks:

1. Use Help to learn about customizing notes.

2. Display the Extend Your Knowledge 4-1 Notes folder in the Outlook Notes window.

3. Create the following notes for a landscaper:
   - Send an email message to Lila Lucas about the mulch delivery time.
   - Pick up seasonal flowers for Layton job.
   - Order irrigation system for Poplar Forest Golf Course.
   - Create a snow removal contract for Liberty Public School System.
   - Create a formal bid for a landscape design for Tracey Thompson.
   - Advertise our snow removal services on website.

4. Select the Irrigation system task, and then create a color category named ASAP. Use a color of your choosing.

5. Categorize the notes about snow removal with a new "Snow Removal" category. Use a color of your choosing.

6. Categorize the remaining notes using a new "Complete This Week" category. Use a color of your choosing.

7. Replace "Tracey Thompson" in the "Create a formal bid for a landscape design for Tracey Thompson." note with the name of your favorite teacher.

8. Change the view to Notes List. Print the notes in Table Style, as shown in Figure 4–81, and then submit them in the format specified by your instructor.

9. Export the Extend Your Knowledge 4-1 Notes folder to a USB flash drive and then submit the file in the format specified by your instructor.

10. ✸ When is it appropriate to create a note instead of creating a task?

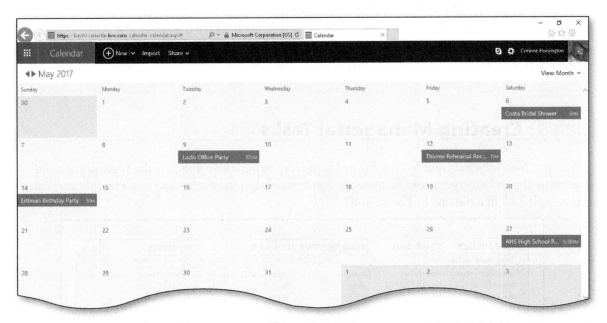

SUBJECT	CREATED	CATEGORIES
Advertise our snow removal services on website.	Fri 8/21/2018 10:24 AM	Snow Removal
Create a formal bid for a landscape design for Tracey Thompson.	Fri 8/21/2018 10:24 AM	Complete This Week
Create a snow removal contract for Liberty Public School System.	Fri 8/21/2018 10:23 AM	Snow Removal
Order irrigation system for Poplar Forest Golf Course.	Fri 8/21/2018 10:23 AM	ASAP
Pick up seasonal flowers for Layton job.	Fri 8/21/2018 10:20 AM	Complete This Week
Send an email message to Lila Lucas about the mulch delivery time.	Fri 8/21/2018 10:20 AM	Complete This Week

Figure 4–81

Expand Your World: Cloud and Web Technologies

Creating an Outlook.com Web-Based Task List Online

Create a solution that uses cloud or web technologies by learning and investigating on your own from general guidance.

Instructions: Outlook.com allows you to enter and maintain a task list from any computer with a web browser and an Internet connection. You are to use Outlook.com to create a task list for Bravo Tapas Café using the information in Table 4–2. You have five events coming up in the next month and want to create the tasks along with the reminders for them.

Figure 4–82

Continued >

Expand Your World: Cloud and Web Technologies *continued*

Perform the following tasks:

1. Start your web browser and navigate to outlook.com.

2. Sign in to outlook.com. If necessary, sign up for a Microsoft account.

3. View the calendar.

4. Create the tasks shown in Table 4–2.

Table 4–2 Bravo Tapas Cafe Tasks				
Event	**Due Date**	**Time**	**Reminder Time**	**How Long**
Costa Bridal Shower	May 6, 2017	6:00 PM	2 days before	2 hours
Lazlo Office Party	May 9, 2017	12:00 PM	2 weeks before	1.5 hours
Thieme Rehearsal Dinner	May 12, 2017	7:00 PM	1 week before	3 hours
Littman Birthday Party	May 14, 2017	3:00 PM	1 hour before	2 hours
AHS High School Reunion	May 27, 2017	6:30 PM	1 week before	4.5 hours

5. When you finish adding the tasks, share the calendar with your instructor. Your instructor should be able to view the details on your calendar but should not be able to edit anything. If you have additional items on your calendar that you do not want to share with your instructor, contact your instructor and determine an alternate way to submit this assignment.

6. ❋ When would you want to add your tasks to Outlook.com instead of using Microsoft Outlook? Is there a way to automatically get your tasks in Microsoft Outlook to appear in your Outlook.com account?

In the Labs

Design, create, modify, and/or use files following the guidelines, concepts, and skills presented in this module. Labs 1 and 2, which increase in difficulty, require you to create solutions based on what you learned in the module; Lab 3 requires you to apply your creative thinking and problem-solving skills to design and implement a solution.

Lab 1: **Creating Managerial Tasks**

Problem: You are a manager for the Fresh Air grocery store. Table 4–3 lists the regular tasks and the recurring tasks for your role as manager. Enter the tasks into the To-Do list. The task list you create will look like the one in Figure 4–83.

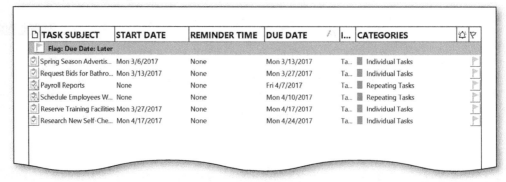

	TASK SUBJECT	START DATE	REMINDER TIME	DUE DATE	I...	CATEGORIES	
	Flag: Due Date: Later						
	Spring Season Advertis...	Mon 3/6/2017	None	Mon 3/13/2017	Ta...	Individual Tasks	
	Request Bids for Bathro...	Mon 3/13/2017	None	Mon 3/27/2017	Ta...	Individual Tasks	
	Payroll Reports	None	None	Fri 4/7/2017	Ta...	Repeating Tasks	
	Schedule Employees W...	None	None	Mon 4/10/2017	Ta...	Repeating Tasks	
	Reserve Training Facilities	Mon 3/27/2017	None	Mon 4/17/2017	Ta...	Individual Tasks	
	Research New Self-Che...	Mon 4/17/2017	None	Mon 4/24/2017	Ta...	Individual Tasks	

Figure 4–83

Perform the following tasks:

1. Create an Outlook Data File named Lab 4-1 Fresh Air Grocery Store.

2. Create a Tasks folder named Lab 4-1 Tasks.

3. Create the regular tasks in the Lab 4-1 Tasks folder using the information listed in Table 4–3.

Table 4–3 Fresh Air Grocery Story Managerial Tasks				
Task	**Start Date**	**Due Date**	**Status**	**Priority**
Spring Season Advertisements	3/6/2017	3/13/2017	In Progress	Normal
Request Bids for Bathroom Update	3/13/2017	3/27/2017		Normal
Reserve Training Facilities	3/27/2017	4/17/2017		High
Research New Self-Checkout System	4/17/2017	4/24/2017		High

4. Create the recurring tasks in the Lab 4-1 Tasks folder using the information listed in Table 4–4.

Table 4–4 Fresh Air Grocery Store Managerial Recurring Tasks			
Task	**Start Date**	**Due Date**	**Recurrence**
Schedule Employees Work Hours	4/10/2017	end of year	Monthly, second Monday
Payroll Reports	4/7/2017	20 occurrences	Weekly, Fridays

5. Open the Schedule Employees Work Hours task and add the detail in the task body that **Noah Cunningham cannot work on Monday or Wednesday due to college classes.**

6. Create a color category called Individual Tasks, using a color of your choice. Categorize the tasks in Table 4–3.

7. Create a color category called Repeating Tasks, using a color of your choice. Categorize all tasks with this category in Table 4–4.

8. Print the Lab 4-1 Tasks list in Table Style, and then submit it in a format specified by your instructor (Figure 4–83).

9. Export the Lab 4-1 Tasks folder to your USB flash drive and then delete the folder from the hard disk.

10. ✳ Why is it a good idea to include as much detail as possible in each task?

Lab 2: **Creating a Car Maintenance Task List**

Problem: You are the owner of a Toyota Prius and decide to enter the recommended car maintenance checklist into Outlook. You need to create a list of all the tasks and categorize them appropriately (Figure 4–84).

Continued >

In the Labs *continued*

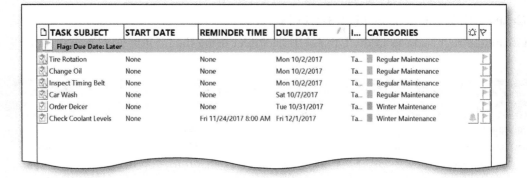

Figure 4–84

Perform the following tasks:

1. Create an Outlook Data File named Lab 4-2 Car Maintenance Tasks.

2. Create the tasks using the information listed in Table 4–5.

Table 4–5	Car Maintenance Tasks					
Task	**Task Body**	**Due Date**	**Status**	**Priority**	**Reminder**
Check Coolant Levels	Complete before first freeze	12/1/2017		High	11/24/2017
Order Deicer	Sale on Amazon	10/31/2017	In Progress	Low	

3. Create the recurring tasks using the information listed in Table 4–6.

Table 4–6	Car Maintenance Recurring Tasks		
Task	**Due Date**	**Task Body**	**Recurrence**
Tire Rotation	10/2/2017	Request wheel alignment	Yearly, No End Date
Change Oil	10/2/2017	Replace oil filter	First Monday of Each Month, Every 2 Months, No End Date
Inspect Timing Belt	10/2/2017	Replace as needed	Yearly, No End Date
Car Wash	10/7/2017	Exterior and interior	Weekly, Saturday, No End Date

4. Categorize the Winter tasks as Winter Maintenance by creating a new color category.

5. Categorize the remaining tasks as Regular Maintenance by creating a new color category.

6. Add a note `A Toyota Prius battery replacement costs approximately $2500`.

7. Print the tasks in Table Style, and then submit the task list in the format specified by your instructor.

8. Export the Lab 4-2 Car Maintenance Tasks to a USB flash drive and then submit the file in the format specified by your instructor.

9. ☀ Why is it a good idea to update the status of a task as it changes?

Lab 3: **Creating and Assigning Tasks**

Research and Collaboration

Part 1:   Your Western Civilization History instructor has assigned a term paper to be completed by a team of three people. Each person in the team is responsible for researching one aspect of the topic "Class Struggles in European History." The three subtopics are Feudalism, Immigration, and Industrial Revolution. After you perform adequate research and write your part of the paper, send it to another team member for a peer review. After all team members have performed a peer review, finalize the content, compile into one document, and prepare it for submission. Using Outlook, each team member should create tasks for the work they have to perform on the term paper (for example, research, writing the first draft, sending for peer review, performing a peer review, finalizing content, compiling into one master document, preparing for submission, and submitting the paper). Add as much information to the tasks as possible, such as the start date, due date, priority, status, and percent complete. Categorize the tasks appropriately. Assign the peer review task to the team member who will review your content. Finally, send a status report to all team members showing how much of each task you currently have completed. Submit the task list in a format specified by your instructor.

Part 2:   ❂ You have made several decisions while creating the task list in this assignment, such as which tasks to create, what details to add to each task, and how to categorize each task. What was the rationale behind each of these decisions?

5 | Customizing Outlook

Objectives

You will have mastered the material in this module when you can:

- Add another email account
- Insert Quick Parts in email messages
- Insert hyperlinks in email messages
- Insert images in email messages
- Create a search folder
- Set the default message format
- Create an email signature
- Format a signature

- Assign signatures
- Customize personal stationery
- Configure junk email options
- Create rules
- Configure AutoArchive settings
- Adjust calendar settings
- Subscribe to a news feed

This module covers features and functions common to customizing Outlook 2016.

Roadmap

In this module, you will learn how to perform basic customizing tasks. The following roadmap identifies general activities you will perform as you progress through this module:

1. CUSTOMIZE EMAIL MESSAGES
2. CUSTOMIZE SIGNATURES and STATIONERY
3. MANAGE JUNK EMAIL FILTERS
4. CONFIGURE RULES
5. CHANGE CALENDAR OPTIONS
6. ADD a NEWS FEED

At the beginning of step instructions throughout the module, you will see an abbreviated form of this roadmap. The abbreviated roadmap uses colors to indicate module progress: gray means the module is beyond that activity, blue means the task being shown is covered in that activity, and black means that activity is yet to be covered. For example, the following abbreviated roadmap indicates the section would be about managing junk email filters.

1 CUSTOMIZE EMAIL MESSAGES | 2 CUSTOMIZE SIGNATURES & STATIONERY | **3 MANAGE JUNK EMAIL FILTERS**
4 CONFIGURE RULES | 5 CHANGE CALENDAR OPTIONS | 6 ADD NEWS FEED

Use the abbreviated roadmap as a progress guide while you read or step through the instructions in this module.

Introduction to Customizing Outlook

Outlook provides many options for customizing your experience when working with email messages, calendars, and other items. From creating custom email signatures to adjusting how the workweek is displayed in your calendar, you can make Outlook fit your requirements so that you can use it more efficiently. For example, a rule is a command that tells Outlook how to process an email message. Using rules, you quickly can categorize or flag your email messages as they arrive so that you can identify at a glance which ones you first want to address. You can change the fonts and colors that are used by default as well. Outlook's customization options can help you become more productive.

Project — Adding a New Email Account and Customizing Options

People often have more than one email account. In fact, some people have more than they can remember. Outlook allows you to manage multiple email accounts. That way, you can read your email messages from all accounts without needing to use several email programs such as one for a Microsoft email account, another for a Gmail account, and a third for a school or work email account.

The project in this module follows general guidelines and uses Outlook to add a new email account and customize Outlook options, as shown in Figure 5–1.

(a) New Email Account

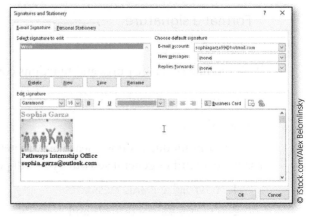

(b) Signature

© iStock.com/Alex Belomlinsky

(c) Customized Calendar

(d) Email Rules

Figure 5–1

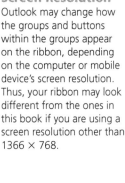

Adding New Email Accounts

As you learned in Module 1, when setting up an email account, you need to know basic information such as the email address and password. For example, in Figure 5–2, the first mailbox is displayed as Outlook Data File (Sophia Module 5.pst). The second mailbox displayed in Figure 5–2 is an additional Internet-based email account named sophiagarza99@hotmail.com.

BTW
The Ribbon and Screen Resolution
Outlook may change how the groups and buttons within the groups appear on the ribbon, depending on the computer or mobile device's screen resolution. Thus, your ribbon may look different from the ones in this book if you are using a screen resolution other than 1366 × 768.

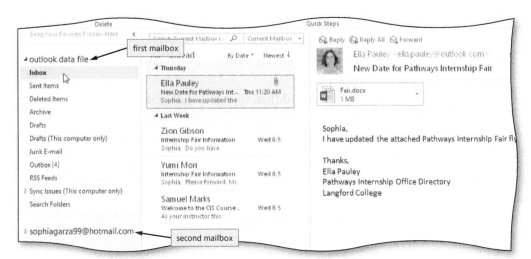

Figure 5–2

After you install Outlook, the Auto Account Setup feature runs and helps you to set up the first email account that Outlook manages. You can add another account and then use Outlook to manage two or more mailboxes.

Depending on your instructor's preferences and your email services, you can perform the steps in this module by opening an Outlook data file provided with the book and by adding a new email account to Outlook. Before you can add a new email account in Outlook, you must have an account set up with an email service provider that is different from any other account already set up in Outlook. For example, you might have a Microsoft account that provides email service. If you have not configured this account in Outlook, you can complete the steps in this module to do so.

To add a new account, you use the Add Account option in the Backstage view, which lets you add an account using the Add Account dialog box. If you want to add an account and change advanced settings, you should use the Account Settings dialog box instead.

My work email address requires additional information to set up my account. Where do I place this server information?

For the work email account you plan to add, make sure you know the account properties and settings before you start to add the account. Gather the following information: type of account, such as email, text messaging, or fax mail; your name, email address, and password; and the server information, including account type and the addresses of incoming and outgoing mail servers. You typically receive the server information from the IT staff at your place of employment. If additional server information is needed, click Manual setup or additional server types when you create an account to add this information.

CONSIDER THIS

To Add an Email Account

Sophia has a second email address that she dedicates to mailing lists. Sophia uses a second email account (sophiagarza99@hotmail.com) within Outlook so that she can manage both her primary and secondary email accounts. To follow all the steps within this module, an additional email account is necessary.

If you choose to add an email account to Outlook, you would use the following steps. If you are performing these steps on your computer, enter the name, email address, and password for an email account you own but have not yet added to Outlook.

BTW

Multiple Email Accounts

If you have multiple email accounts configured in Outlook, you can decide which email account to use each time you compose and send a new email message. To select the account from which to send the email message, click the From button in the Untitled - Message window, and then click the desired email account.

1. Run Outlook.
2. Click the File tab and then click Add Account.
3. Click the Your Name text box and then type your first and last name to associate your name with the account.
4. Click the E-mail Address text box and then type your full email address to associate your email address with the account.
5. Click the Password text box and then type your password to verify the password to your email account.
6. Click the Retype Password text box and then type your password again to confirm your password.
7. Click the Next button to configure your account settings and sign in to your mail server.
8. Click the Finish button to add the secondary email account.
9. Click the new email account to select it.

BTW

Touch Screen Differences

The Office and Windows interfaces may vary if you are using a touch screen. For this reason, you might notice that the function or appearance of your touch screen differs slightly from this module's presentation.

Customizing Email Messages

No matter what type of message you are composing in Outlook, whether business or personal, you always can find a way to add your unique style. With a variety of features such as background colors, graphics, designs, hyperlinks, and custom signatures, your email message starts as a blank, generic canvas and becomes an attractive, memorable communication.

To Add a Hyperlink to an Email Message

1 CUSTOMIZE EMAIL MESSAGES | 2 CUSTOMIZE SIGNATURES & STATIONERY | 3 MANAGE JUNK EMAIL FILTERS
4 CONFIGURE RULES | 5 CHANGE CALENDAR OPTIONS | 6 ADD NEWS FEED

Zion Gibson asked Sophia to send him the web address of the Kennedy Center internship site. Zion is hoping to land an internship at the Kennedy Center and wants to check the webpage for more information. Sophia can send him the web address as a hyperlink in an email message. *Why? Outlook automatically formats hyperlinks so that recipients can use them to access a website directly.* To follow the link, the recipient can hold down the CTRL key and click the hyperlink, which is formatted as blue, underlined text by default. The following steps add a hyperlink within an email message.

- If the Sophia Module 5.pst Outlook Data File is not open in Outlook, click outlook data file in the Navigation Pane to display its contents.
- Click the Inbox folder to display the mailbox.
- Click the New Email button (Home tab | New group) to open the Untitled - Message (HTML) window.
- Type `zion.gibson@outlook.com` in the To text box to enter the email address of the recipient.

- Click the Subject text box, and then type **Kennedy Center Internship** to enter the subject line.

- Press the TAB key to move the insertion point into the message area (Figure 5–3).

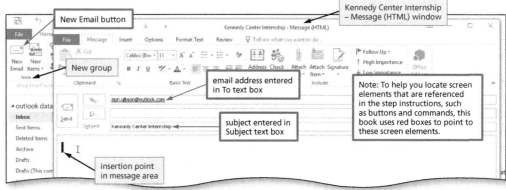

Figure 5–3

2

- Type **Zion,** as the greeting line and then press the ENTER key to insert a new line.

- Type **Per your request, the Kennedy Center internship site can be found at** and then press the SPACEBAR to enter the message text.

- Click Insert on the ribbon to display the Insert tab (Figure 5–4).

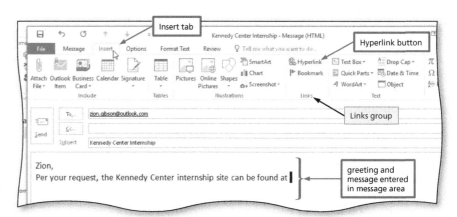

Figure 5–4

- Click the Hyperlink button (Insert tab | Links group) to display the Insert Hyperlink dialog box.

- In the Address box, type **kennedy-center.org/education/internships** to enter a hyperlink to a web address (Figure 5–5).

Q&A
Why do I not have to type the http:// part of the web address?
When you insert a hyperlink, Outlook does not require the hypertext transfer protocol (http) portion of the address.

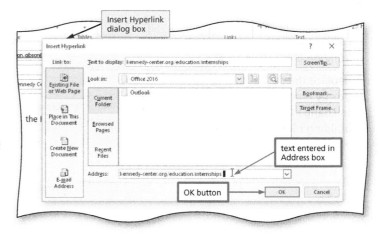

Figure 5–5

- Click the OK button to insert the hyperlink in the message body (Figure 5–6).

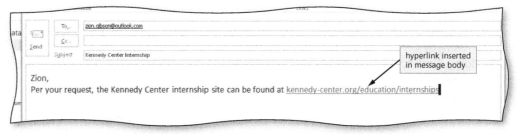

Figure 5–6

Other Ways

1. Press CTRL+K

To Create and Insert Quick Parts

How often do you include the same snippet or phrase in your correspondence, such as directions to your home, answers to frequently answered questions, or even the full name of a school or business? To assist you in these situations, Outlook includes **Quick Parts**, common building blocks that can be recycled and used again within your email messages. The first step in creating a Quick Part is to select the content that you want to reuse. After naming the contents and saving them to the Quick Parts gallery, you can use the Quick Part whenever you need to repeat that phrase. *Why? Quick Parts allow you to save pieces of content to reuse them easily within your email messages.* Several students have requested that Sophia send them the link to the Kennedy Center internship opportunity in the past month. The following steps save a phrase to the Quick Parts gallery.

- Select the phrase 'Per your request, the Kennedy Internship site can be found at kennedy-center. org/education/ internships'.

- Click the Quick Parts button (Insert tab | Text group) to display the Quick Parts list of options (Figure 5–7).

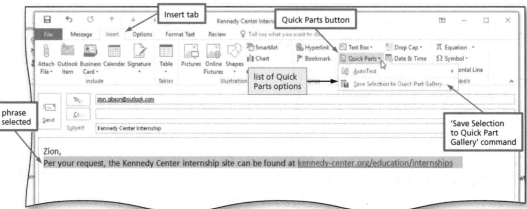

Figure 5–7

- Click 'Save Selection to Quick Part Gallery' to display the Create New Building Block dialog box.

- Replace the text in the Name text box by typing **Kennedy Center** to change the name of the new building block (Figure 5–8).

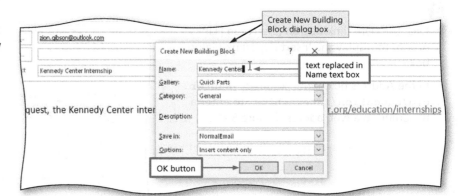

Figure 5–8

- Click the OK button (Create New Building Block dialog box) to add the Kennedy Center Building Block to the Quick Parts gallery (Figure 5–9).

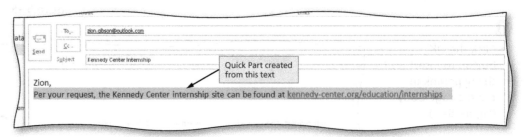

Figure 5–9

Experiment

- Click the Quick Parts button (Insert tab | Text group) to display a list of Quick Parts options. Click Kennedy Center to insert the building block into the email message. When you are finished, click the Undo button on the Quick Access Toolbar to remove the Kennedy Center internship text.

To Insert an Image into an Email Message

As you learned in Module 1, you can attach files to an email message, including image files. Outlook also provides the ability to insert an image directly within the message body of an email message. *Why? The recipient can quickly view the image without downloading an attachment or saving the picture on their computer.* Sophia would like to add a recent picture taken by one of their interns of the Kennedy Center. The picture is available with the Data Files for Module 05. The following steps insert an image into an email message.

- Click after the kennedy-center.org/ education/internships web address, and then press the ENTER key twice to move the insertion point to a new line.

- Click the Pictures button (Insert tab | Illustrations group) to display the Insert Picture dialog box.

- Navigate to the file location, in this case, the Module 05 folder in the Outlook folder provided with the Data Files.

- Click Kennedy to select the photo of the Kennedy Center (Figure 5–10).

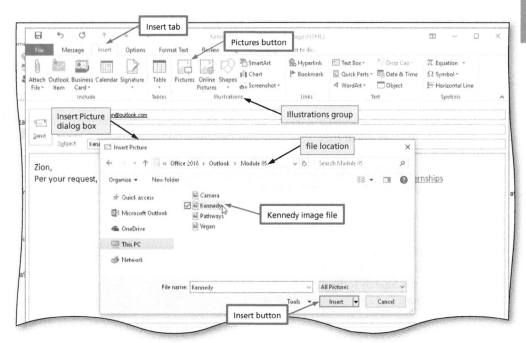

Figure 5–10

- Click the Insert button (shown in Figure 5–10) to add an image to the message body (Figure 5–11).

- Click the Save button on the Quick Access Toolbar to save the email message in the Drafts folder.

- Close the Kennedy Center Internship - Message (HTML) window.

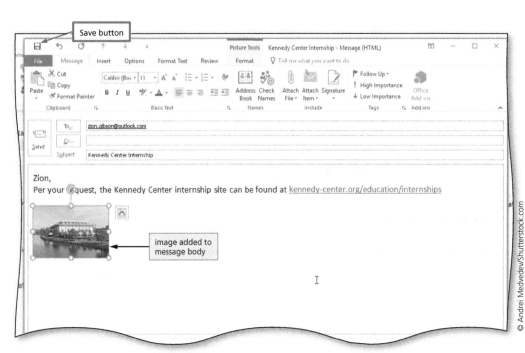

Figure 5–11

Can I use Outlook to allow a message recipient to vote, such as when I want to poll club members for their preferred speaker for our next event?

When composing a message, you can configure voting options by using the Properties dialog box. For example, you can choose to use voting buttons as well as request delivery and read receipts. To configure voting options:

1. While composing a message, click Options on the ribbon to display the Options tab.

2. Click the Use Voting Buttons button (Options tab | Tracking group) to display a list of options.

3. Click Custom to display the Properties dialog box.

4. Select voting options in the Voting and Tracking options area.

5. Click the Close button to close the Properties dialog box.

To Search Using Advanced Find

1 CUSTOMIZE EMAIL MESSAGES | 2 CUSTOMIZE SIGNATURES & STATIONERY | 3 MANAGE JUNK EMAIL FILTERS
4 CONFIGURE RULES | 5 CHANGE CALENDAR OPTIONS | 6 ADD NEWS FEED

At the top of the message pane is the **Instant Search** text box, which displays search results based on any matching words in your email messages. You can use the options on the Search Tools Search tab to broaden or narrow the scope of your search using the Advanced Find features. For example, Sophia would like to search for messages that have attachments. The following steps use instant search with Advanced Find features to locate email messages with attachments. *Why? Using Advanced Find features, you can quickly search for an email with an attachment.*

- If necessary, select your Inbox, and then click the Instant Search text box to display the Search Tools Search tab (Figure 5–12).

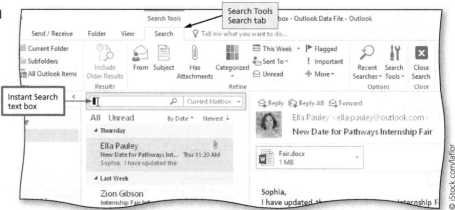

Figure 5–12

- Click the Has Attachments button (Search Tools Search tab | Refine group) to display email messages with attachments (Figure 5–13).

- Click the Close Search button (shown in Figure 5–13) to display the Inbox messages without the search criteria.

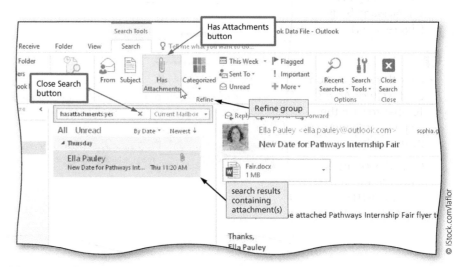

Figure 5–13

To Create a New Search Folder

Use search folders to gather email messages and other items into a folder based on search criteria. For example, Sophia wants to place messages with attachments into a separate search folder. You might want to create other search folders to view all messages that you have not read yet or to combine messages from a specific person. The following steps create a new search folder for email messages with attachments. *Why? By using search folders, you can better manage large amounts of email.*

1

- Click Folder on the ribbon to display the Folder tab.

- Click the New Search Folder button (Folder tab | New group) to display the New Search Folder dialog box (Figure 5–14).

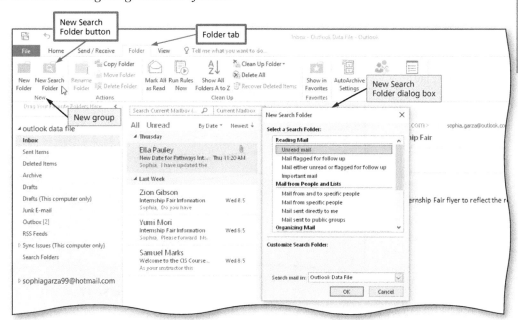

Figure 5–14

2

- Scroll down to view the Organizing Mail category.

- Click 'Mail with attachments' (New Search Folder dialog box) to select the type of email to store in a search folder (Figure 5–15).

Figure 5–15

3

- Click the OK button (New Search Folder dialog box) to create a new search folder that searches for and collects email messages with attachments (Figure 5–16).

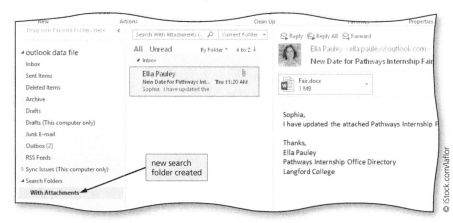

Figure 5–16

© iStock.com/laflor

To Display Outlook Options

Why? *To customize your Outlook email with default settings such as the message format, you use the Outlook Options dialog box.* The following step displays the Outlook Options dialog box.

1

- Click File on the ribbon to open the Backstage view.

- Click the Options tab in the Backstage view to display the Outlook Options dialog box (Figure 5–17).

Q&A
What options can I set in the General category?
The General category allows you to customize the user interface by enabling the Mini Toolbar and Live Preview, and by changing the

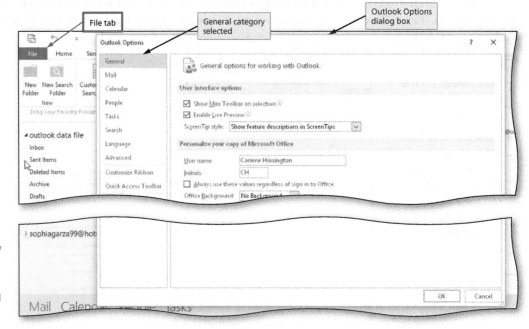

ScreenTip style and Theme. You can also personalize Microsoft Outlook by specifying your user name and initials. The Start up options allow you to specify whether Outlook should be the default program for email, contacts, and calendar.

Figure 5–17

To Set the Message Format

Email messages can be formatted as HTML, Plain Text, or Rich Text. As you learned in Module 1, you can format an individual email message using one of these message formats. To make sure that all your email messages use the HTML format by default, set the message format in the Outlook Options dialog box. The HTML message format allows the most flexibility when composing email messages. The following steps set the default message format to HTML. *Why?* *Instead of changing each email message to a different format, you can set a default in the Outlook options. All new messages are displayed in the default format.*

1

- Click Mail in the Category list to display the Mail options (Figure 5–18).

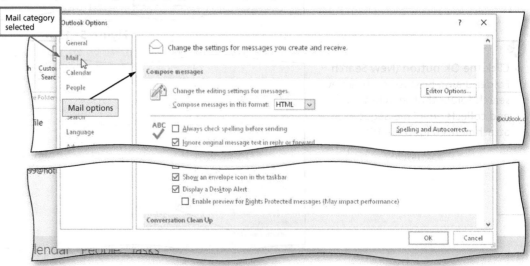

Figure 5–18

2

- Click the 'Compose messages in this format' box arrow to display a list of formatting options (Figure 5–19).

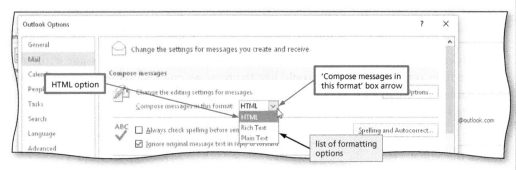

Figure 5–19

3

- If necessary, click HTML to set the default message format to HTML (Figure 5–20).

Q&A

What if HTML already is selected as the default message format?
Depending on who set up Outlook, the default message format already might be HTML. In that case, you can skip Step 3.

What if I want to choose a different format?
When you display the available message formats, choose the type you want to use. For example, if you want all new email messages to be in the Plain Text format, click the Plain Text option.

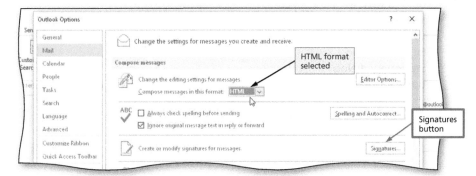

Figure 5–20

CONSIDER THIS

Can I sort my email messages by conversation instead of by date, which is the default setting?

Yes, you can sort by conversation if you prefer to sort your email messages by their subject field grouped by conversation. To sort by conversation:

1. Click View on the ribbon to display the View tab.

2. Click the Show as Conversations check box (View tab | Messages group) to select Show as Conversations.

Your Inbox is re-sorted, linking email messages in the same conversation together. Individual messages that do not belong to a conversation will look the same as before, while those involved in conversations will have a white triangle on the upper-left part of the message header.

Creating Signatures and Stationery

You can configure Outlook to add signatures to your email messages automatically. A **signature** is similar to a closing set of lines in a formal letter. It can include your full name, job title, email address, phone number, company information, and logo. You even can include business cards in your signature.

If you have more than one email account, you need to select the account for which you want to create the signature. You can create the signature while you are creating an email message or you can use the Outlook Options dialog box at any other time. If you create the signature while writing an email message, you have to apply the signature to the email message, because Outlook will not insert it automatically. If you create a signature using the Outlook Options dialog box, it is added automatically to all subsequent messages.

Besides adding signatures to your email messages, you can customize the **stationery**, which determines the appearance of your email messages, including background, fonts, and colors. You can pick fonts to use in the email message text, or you can select a theme or stationery design and apply that to your email messages.

To Create an Email Signature

An email signature provides a consistent closing to every email message without requiring you to retype signature lines repeatedly. Sophia would like to create an email signature named Work that includes her name, office name, and email address. The following steps create an email signature. *Why? An email signature provides your contact information in a condensed format, typically two to four lines.*

- Click the Signatures button (Outlook Options dialog box) (shown in Figure 5–20) to display the Signatures and Stationery dialog box (Figure 5–21).

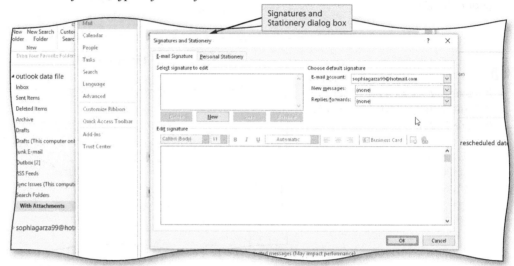

Figure 5–21

- Click the New button (Signatures and Stationery dialog box) to display the New Signature dialog box (Figure 5–22).

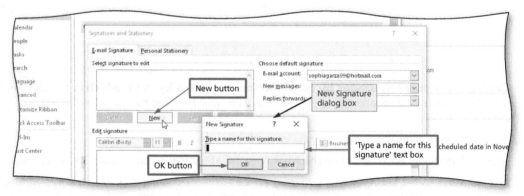

Figure 5–22

❸

- Type `Work` in the 'Type a name for this signature' text box to enter a name for the signature.

- Click the OK button (shown in Figure 5–22) to name the signature (Figure 5–23).

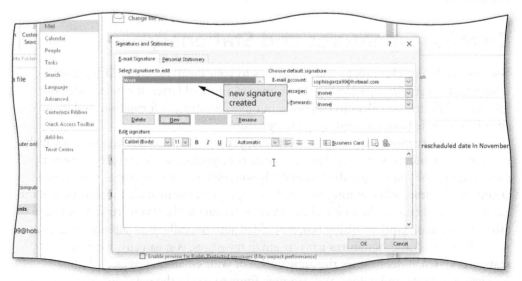

Figure 5–23

To Format an Email Signature

The email message signature will include Sophia's name, office name, and email address. In addition, she wants to use a format that suits her style. The format of the signature should be attractive, but maintain a professional, clean appearance. The following steps format and add the text for the signature. *Why? An email signature should convey the impression you are trying to make. A company might require employees to use a certain email signature when communicating with customers to create a consistent look.*

- Click the Font box arrow (Signatures and Stationery dialog box) to display a list of fonts (Figure 5–24).

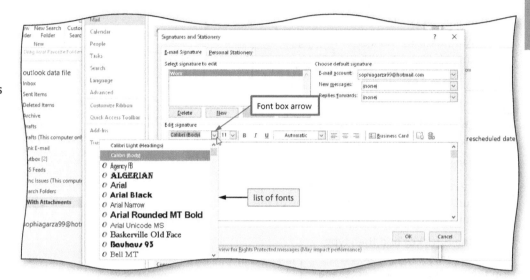

Figure 5–24

②

- Scroll down until Garamond is visible, and then click Garamond to select the font.

- Click the Font Size box arrow to display a list of font sizes (Figure 5–25).

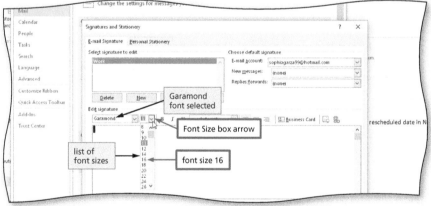

Figure 5–25

③

- Click 16 to change the font size.
- Click the Bold button to change the font to bold.
- Click the Font Color box arrow to display a list of colors (Figure 5–26).

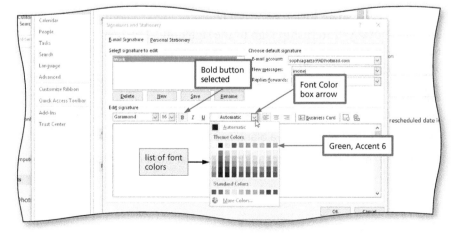

Figure 5–26

- Click Green, Accent 6 (first row, last column) to change the font color.
- Type `Sophia Garza` in the signature body to enter the first line of the signature.
- Click the Font Color box arrow to display a list of colors.
- Click Automatic to change the font color to automatic, which is black (Figure 5–27).

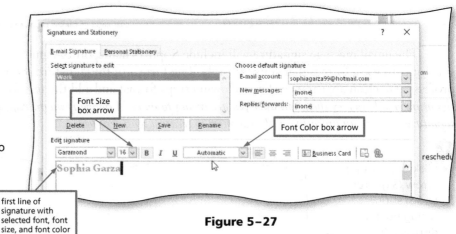

Figure 5–27

- Press the ENTER key and then click the Font Size box arrow to display a list of font sizes.
- Click 12 to change the font size.
- Type `Pathways Internship Office` in the signature body to enter the second line of the signature.
- Press the ENTER key and then type `sophia.garza@outlook.com` in the signature body to enter the third line of the signature (Figure 5–28).

Q&A Outlook capitalized the S in Sophia after I entered the email address. What should I do?
If you want the signature to match the figures in this module, change the S to lowercase.

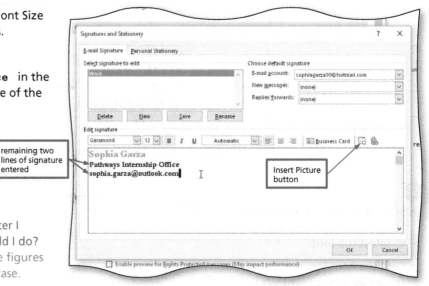

Figure 5–28

To Add an Image to an Email Signature

1 CUSTOMIZE EMAIL MESSAGES | 2 CUSTOMIZE SIGNATURES & STATIONERY | **3 MANAGE JUNK EMAIL FILTERS**
4 CONFIGURE RULES | 5 CHANGE CALENDAR OPTIONS | 6 ADD NEWS FEED

You can add an image such as a photo or logo to your signature to create visual appeal. Sophia wants to add the Pathways Internship logo in the signature. The picture is available in the Data Files for Module 05. The following steps add a logo image to a signature and save the changes. *Why? Adding a logo can promote brand or organization identity.*

- Move the insertion point to the end of the first line of the signature text.
- Press the ENTER key to place a blank line between the signature name and office name.
- Click the Insert Picture button (Signatures and Stationery dialog box) to display the Insert Picture dialog box.

- Navigate to the file location, in this case, the Module 05 folder in the Outlook folder provided with the Data Files.

- Click Pathways to select the Pathways Internship logo (Figure 5–29).

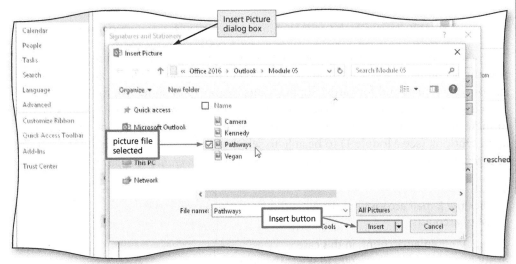

Figure 5–29

2

- Click the Insert button (Insert Picture dialog box) (shown in Figure 5–29) to insert the image into the signature (Figure 5–30).

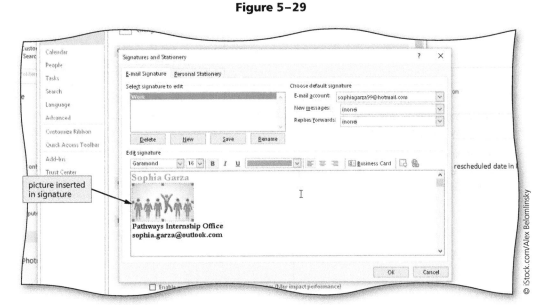

© iStock.com/Alex Belomlinsky

Figure 5–30

3

- Click the Save button (Signatures and Stationery dialog box) to save the changes to the signature (Figure 5–31).

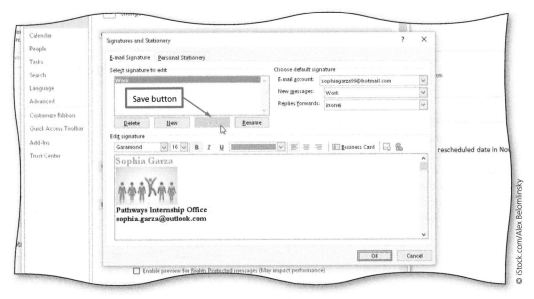

© iStock.com/Alex Belomlinsky

Figure 5–31

To Configure Signature Options

After creating a signature, you need to assign it to an email account. You can associate the signature with as many accounts as you want. You can set two default signatures for a single account: one for new messages and one for replies and forwards. Sophia wants to apply her signature for new messages to her email account named sophiagarza99@hotmail.com (select your own account). The following steps set the default signature for new messages. If you are completing these steps on a personal computer, your email account must be set up in Outlook (see Module 1) to be able to select an email account to apply the signature. *Why? By associating a signature with a particular email account, your signature automatically appears at the bottom of new messages.*

1

- Click the E-mail account box arrow to display a list of accounts.

- Click your email account, in this case sophiagarza99@hotmail.com, to select the email account (Figure 5–32).

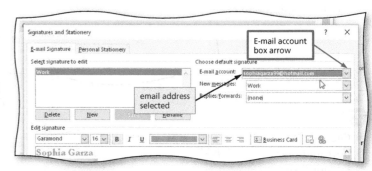

Figure 5–32

2

- Click the New messages box arrow to display a list of signatures.

- Click Work to make it the default signature for new messages (Figure 5–33).

Q&A

How do I place a signature in all messages including replies and forwards?

Click the Replies/forwards box arrow and then click a signature to make it the default signature for all message replies and forwards.

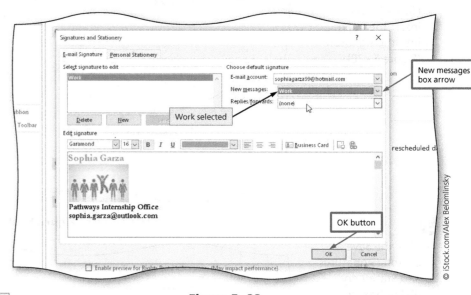

Figure 5–33

3

- Click the OK button (Signatures and Stationery dialog box) to save the changes to the signature settings, close the Signatures and Stationery dialog box, and return to the Outlook Options dialog box (Figure 5–34).

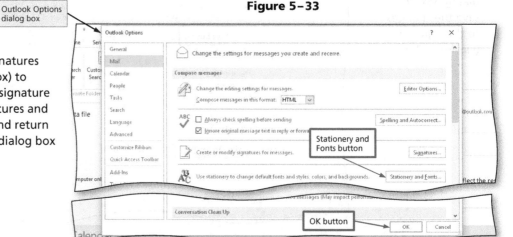

Figure 5–34

To Customize Stationery

Outlook provides backgrounds and patterns for email message stationery and offers themes, which are sets of unified design elements, such as fonts, bullets, colors, and effects that you can apply to messages. Sophia decides to use a stationery named Edge, which provides a professional, stylish design. The following steps customize the email message stationery. *Why? Stationery provides a distinctive look for your email messages.*

1

- Click the Stationery and Fonts button (Outlook Options dialog box) to display the Signatures and Stationery dialog box (Figure 5–35).

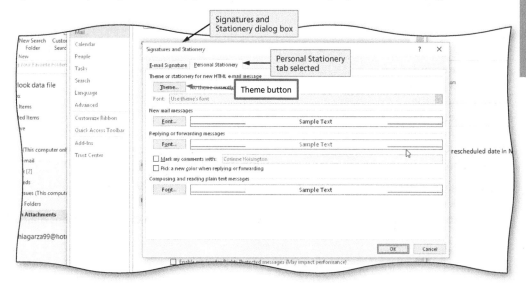

Figure 5–35

2

- Click the Theme button (Signatures and Stationery dialog box) to display the Theme or Stationery dialog box (Figure 5–36).

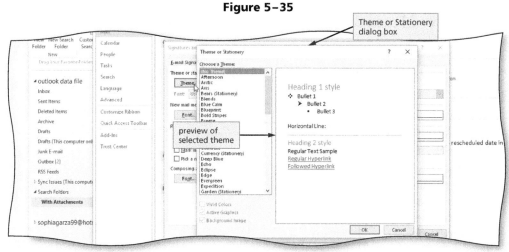

Figure 5–36

3

- Click Edge to select it and display a preview of its formats (Figure 5–37).

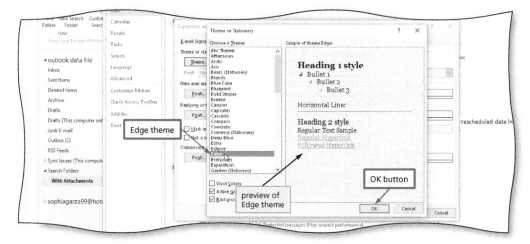

Figure 5–37

- Click the OK button (Theme or Stationery dialog box) to apply the theme to the stationery (Figure 5–38).

- Click the OK button (Signatures and Stationery dialog box) to save the theme settings and return to the Outlook Options dialog box.

- Click the OK button (Outlook Options dialog box) (shown in Figure 5–34 on page OUT 224) to close the Outlook Options dialog box.

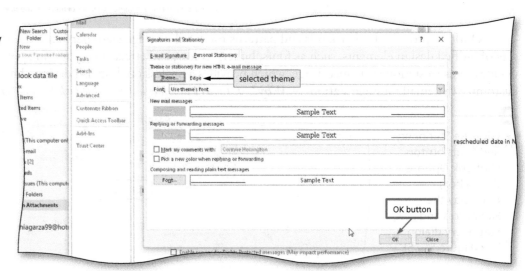

Figure 5–38

1 CUSTOMIZE EMAIL MESSAGES | 2 CUSTOMIZE SIGNATURES & STATIONERY | 3 MANAGE JUNK EMAIL FILTERS
4 CONFIGURE RULES | 5 CHANGE CALENDAR OPTIONS | 6 ADD NEWS FEED

To Preview Message Changes

Why? *You want to preview the changes you made to your email signature and stationery and see how they look in an email message.* The following steps display a new email message without sending it.

- Click Home on the ribbon to display the Home tab.

- Click the New Email button (Home tab | New group) to create a new email message (Figure 5–39).

2

- Close the email message without sending it.

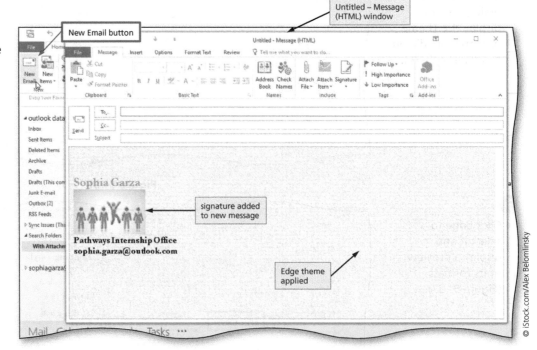

Figure 5–39

© iStock.com/Alex Belomlinsky

To Assign Signatures to a Single Email Message

If you use multiple email accounts, you can set a signature for each account or you can apply a signature to an individual email message. Sophia still needs to send the email about the Kennedy Center internship link to Zion and wants to apply the Work signature to that message, which is now stored in the Drafts folder. *Why? Instead of assigning your email address to one signature, you may want to create different signatures and apply a signature to individual email messages before you send them.* The following steps assign a signature to a single email message.

- Click the Drafts folder in the Navigation Pane to display the message header for the Kennedy Center Internship email message in the message list.

- Double-click the Kennedy Center Internship message header in the messages pane to open the Kennedy Center Internship - Message (HTML) window (Figure 5–40).

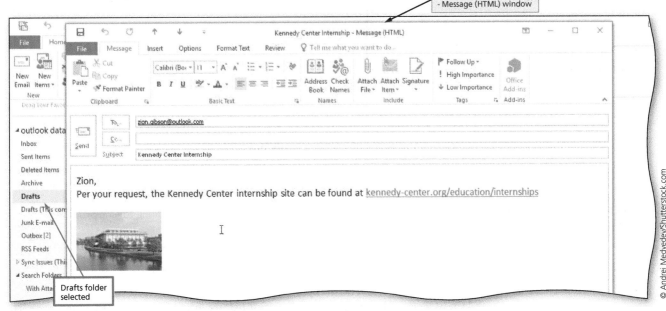

Figure 5–40

- Place the insertion point to the right of the Kennedy Center image and then press the ENTER key to move to the next line.

- Click Insert on the ribbon to display the Insert tab.

- Click the Signature button (Insert tab | Include group) to display a list of signatures (Figure 5–41).

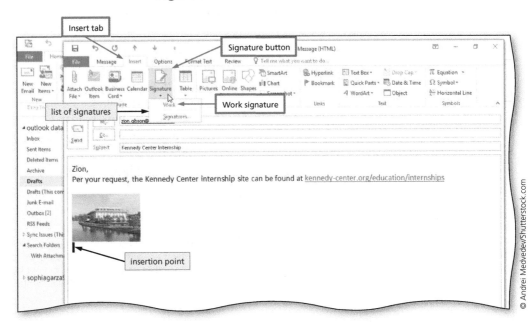

Figure 5–41

3

- Click Work to add the Work signature to the email message body.
- Scroll down to view the full signature (Figure 5–42).

4

- Click the Save button on the Quick Access Toolbar to save the email message in the Drafts folder.
- Click the Close button to close the email message.

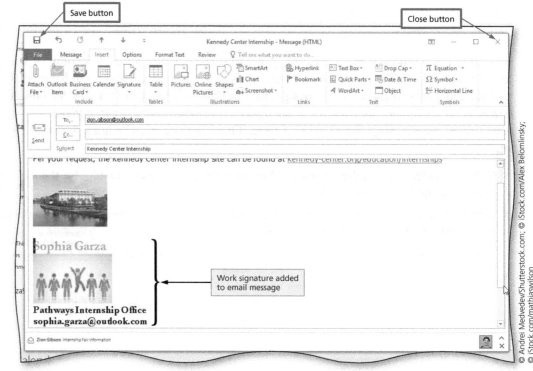

Figure 5–42

Break Point: If you wish to take a break, this is a good place to do so. To resume at a later time, continue to follow the steps from this location forward.

Managing Junk Email Options

As you learned in Module 1, junk email is bulk email, spam, or other unwanted email messages. Outlook uses a filter to control the amount of junk email you receive. The junk email filter evaluates incoming messages and sends to the Junk E-mail folder those messages that meet the criteria for junk email. You can use the Junk button in the Delete group on the Home tab to override the default criteria when viewing email messages by deciding to block the sender, never block the sender, never block the sender's domain, or never block a group or mailing list.

Using the Junk E-mail Options dialog box, you can change even more settings (Figure 5–43). Table 5–1 describes the options you can adjust using the Junk E-mail Options dialog box.

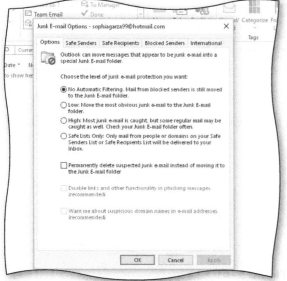

Figure 5–43

BTW

Junk Email
It usually is a good idea to check your Junk E-mail folder regularly to make sure no items are labeled as junk inadvertently. If, after clicking the Junk E-mail folder, you find an email message that is not junk, select the email message, click the Junk button (Home tab | Delete group), click Not Junk, and then click the OK button.

Table 5–1	Junk E-mail Options
Tab	**Description**
Options	Allows you to choose the level of protection (No Automatic Filtering, Low, High, Safe Lists Only), as well as set whether junk email is deleted, links are disabled in phishing messages, and warnings are provided for suspicious domain names.
Safe Senders	Permits the specification of safe email addresses and domains. Email messages from the listed email addresses and domains will not be treated as junk email.
Safe Recipients	Specifies that email messages sent to email addresses or domains in the safe recipient list will not be treated as junk email.
Blocked Senders	Allows you to manage your list of blocked email addresses and domains.
International	Manages which domains and encodings you would like to block based on languages used.

To Add a Domain to the Safe Senders List

1 CUSTOMIZE EMAIL MESSAGES | 2 CUSTOMIZE SIGNATURES & STATIONERY | 3 MANAGE JUNK EMAIL FILTERS
4 CONFIGURE RULES | 5 CHANGE CALENDAR OPTIONS | 6 ADD NEWS FEED

The junk email filter in Outlook is turned on by default, providing a protection level that is set to Low. This level is designed to catch only the most obvious junk email messages. Sophia feels that too many incoming messages from Microsoft are being sent to her Junk E-mail folder. Microsoft.com can be added to the Safe Senders list, which adjusts the filter sensitivity of Outlook, so the Microsoft messages are sent to the Inbox instead of the Junk E-mail folder. If you are completing these steps on a personal computer, your email account must be set up in Outlook (see Module 1) to be able to select an email account to configure the junk email options. The following steps configure the junk email options for an email account. *Why? The Junk E-mail folder helps to sort out relevant email messages from junk mail.*

1
- Click your personal email account (in this case, sophiagarza99@hotmail.com) in the Navigation Pane to select the mailbox (Figure 5–44).

Q&A Why did I have to select the email account?
To change junk email options for an account, the account first should be selected. If you selected a different mailbox, you would have changed junk email settings for that account.

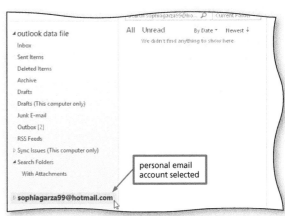

Figure 5–44

2
- Click the Junk button (Home tab | Delete group) to display the Junk options (Figure 5–45).

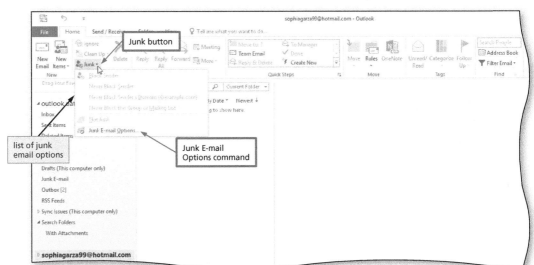

Figure 5–45

3

- Click Junk E-mail Options to display the Junk E-mail Options dialog box (Figure 5–46).

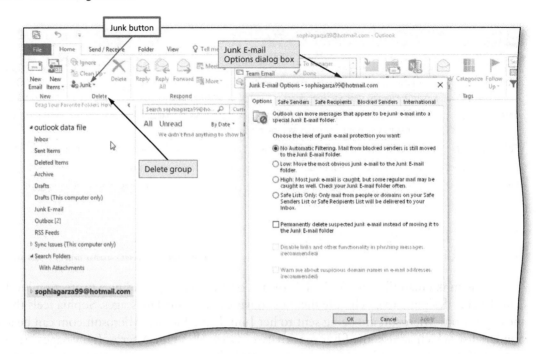

Figure 5–46

4

- Click the Safe Senders tab (Junk E-mail Options dialog box) to display the Safe Senders options (Figure 5–47).

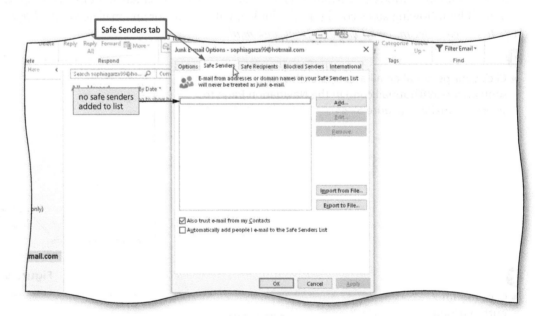

Figure 5–47

5

- Click the Add button (Junk E-mail Options dialog box) to display the Add address or domain dialog box (Figure 5–48).

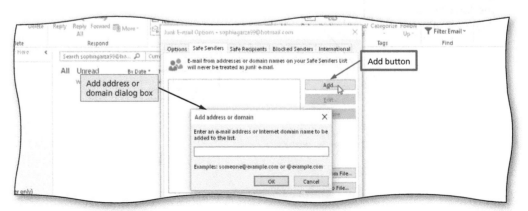

Figure 5–48

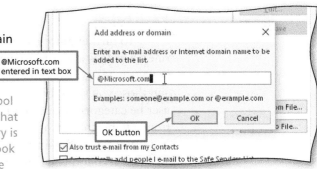

6

- Type **@Microsoft.com** in the text box to enter a domain name to add to the Safe Senders list (Figure 5–49).

Do I have to type the @ symbol?

Although Outlook recommends that you type the @ symbol to indicate a domain name, you can omit the symbol. In that case, you leave it up to Outlook to determine if your entry is a domain name or email address. Most of the time, Outlook interprets the entry correctly; however, to be certain, type the @ symbol.

Figure 5–49

7

- Click the OK button (Add address or domain dialog box) to add the domain to the Safe Senders List (Figure 5–50).

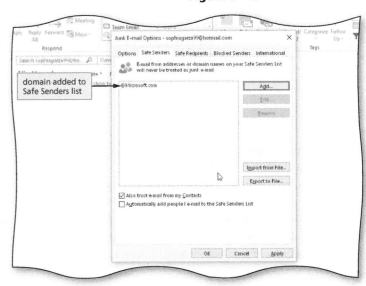

BTW

Using the Clutter Feature

If you have an Office 365 subscription, a feature called **Clutter** assists in filtering low-priority email, saving you time to focus on important emails. If you turn on Clutter, the Office 365 Exchange server automatically keeps track of the email messages you read and the email messages that you ignore. Office 365 moves the ignored messages to a folder in your Inbox called the Clutter items folder.

Figure 5–50

To Block a Specific Email Address

Why? *You may want to block a specific email address or domain to prevent people or companies from sending you messages you do not want to receive.* Sophia has received multiple unwanted emails from the following email address: getrich2@live.com. She considers these messages as junk email. The following steps block a specific email address using the junk filters.

1

- Click the Blocked Senders tab (Junk E-mail Options dialog box) to display the Blocked Senders options.

- Click the Add button (Junk E-mail Options dialog box) to display the Add address or domain dialog box.

- Type **getrich2@live.com** in the text box to enter the domain name to add to the Blocked Senders list (Figure 5–51).

2

- Click the OK button (Add address or domain dialog box) to add the domain to the Blocked Senders List.

- Click the OK button (Junk E-mail Options dialog box) to close the Junk E-mail Options dialog box.

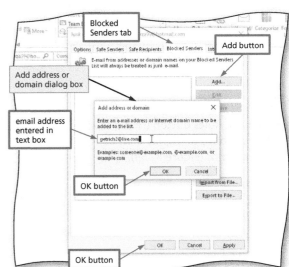

Figure 5–51

Working with Rules

To further automate the processing of email messages in Outlook, you can create rules. A **rule** is a set of instructions that tells Outlook how to handle email messages in your mailbox. You can create rules that apply to email messages you have received and those you send. For example, you can specify that email messages from a particular user be categorized automatically or placed in a specified folder. You can create rules from a template or from scratch based on conditions you specify. Rules apply to an email account, not a single folder or file. If you are working with a data file instead of an email account, you cannot create rules.

To simplify the process of creating rules, Outlook provides a Rules Wizard, which presents a list of conditions for selecting an email message and then lists actions to take with messages that meet the conditions. If necessary, you can also specify exceptions to the rule. For example, you can move certain messages to a specified folder unless they are sent with high importance.

To Create a New Rule

1 CUSTOMIZE EMAIL MESSAGES | 2 CUSTOMIZE SIGNATURES & STATIONERY | 3 MANAGE JUNK EMAIL FILTERS
4 CONFIGURE RULES | 5 CHANGE CALENDAR OPTIONS | 6 ADD NEWS FEED

Sophia would like to create a rule to flag all email messages from the director of the Pathways Internship Office, Ella Pauley, for follow-up. This way, she easily can remember to follow up with Ms. Pauley on important tasks. If you are completing these steps on a personal computer, your email account must be set up in Outlook so that you can select an email account to create a rule. The following steps create a rule that automatically flags email messages. **Why?** *Rules help you file and follow up on email messages. For example, your instructor can create a rule for messages from a specific course section, such as CIS 101. You can set CIS 101 in the Subject line to be flagged for follow-up and moved to a folder named Literacy.*

- Click the outlook data file Inbox to display the Inbox messages.

- If necessary, click the Ella Pauley email message to select it (Figure 5–52).

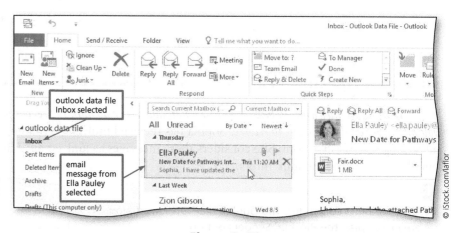

Figure 5–52

- Click the Rules button (Home tab | Move group) to display a list of rule options (Figure 5–53).

Q&A Why is my Rules button missing? An active email address must be set up in Outlook to view the Rules button.

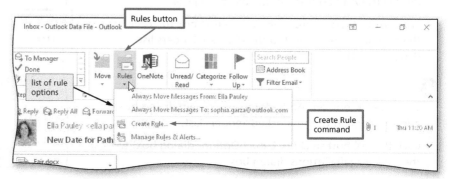

Figure 5–53

• Click the Create
  Rule command to
  display the Create
  Rule dialog box
  (Figure 5–54).

Figure 5–54

• Click the 'From
  Ella Pauley' check
  box to select it
  (Figure 5–55).

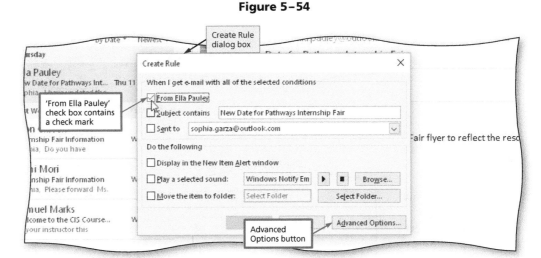

Figure 5–55

• Click the Advanced
  Options button
  (Create Rule dialog
  box) to display the
  Rules Wizard dialog
  box (Figure 5–56).

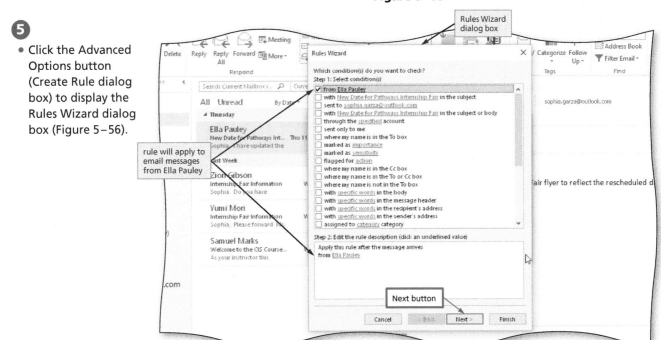

Figure 5–56

6

- Click the Next button (Rules Wizard dialog box) to continue to the next step, where you specify one or more actions to take with a selected message (Figure 5–57).

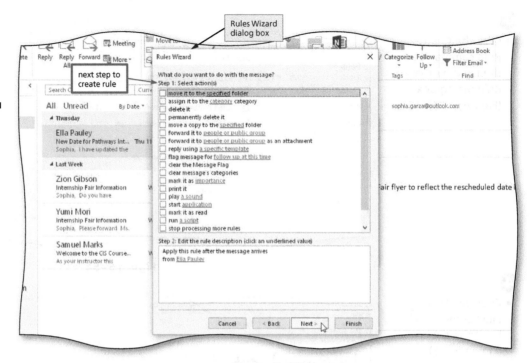

Figure 5–57

7

- Click the 'flag message for follow up at this time' check box to select it.

- If necessary, click the Yes button if a dialog box opens informing you that the rule you are creating can never be edited in previous versions of Outlook (Figure 5–58).

Q&A What is the effect of selecting the 'flag message for follow up at this time' check box?
Messages that meet the conditions you specify, in this case, messages from Ella Pauley, appear in the message list with a flag icon to indicate they need to be followed up.

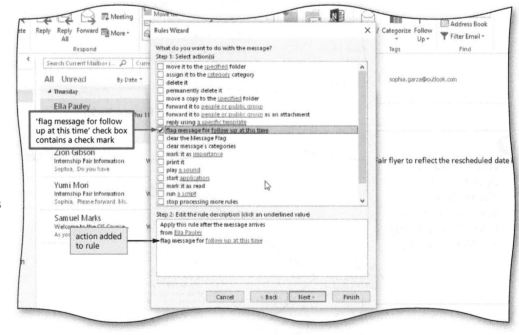

Figure 5–58

8

- Click the 'follow up at this time' link in the Step 2 area to display the Flag Message dialog box (Figure 5–59).

Q&A

For what purposes can I use the Flag Message dialog box? You can flag a message for follow up (the default) or for other options, including For Your Information, No Response Necessary, and Reply. You can also specify when to follow up: Today (the default), Tomorrow, This Week, Next Week, No Date, or Complete.

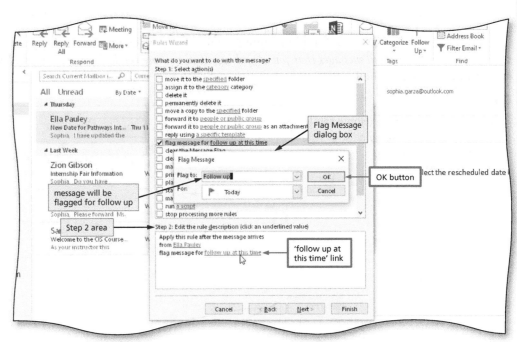

Figure 5–59

9

- Click the OK button (Flag Message dialog box) to accept the default settings and return to the Rules Wizard dialog box (Figure 5–60).

10

- Click the Finish button (Rules Wizard dialog box) to save the rule.

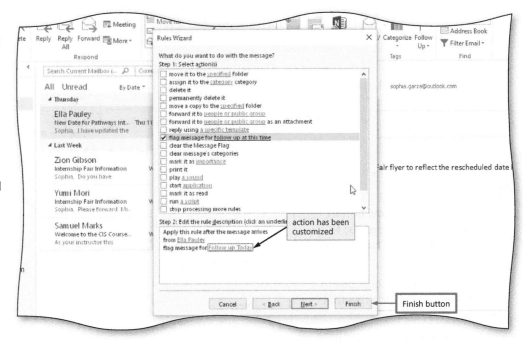

Figure 5–60

To Run Rules

Rules that you create run for all incoming email messages received after you create the rule. *Why? If you want to apply rules to email messages that you already received, you use the Rules and Alerts dialog box.* The following steps run the newly created rule.

- Click the Rules button (Home tab | Move group) to display a list of rule options (Figure 5–61).

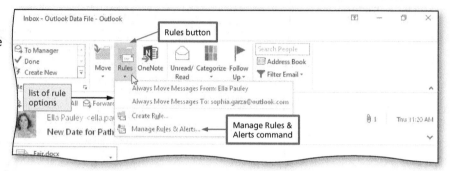

Figure 5–61

- Click the Manage Rules & Alerts command to display the Rules and Alerts dialog box (Figure 5–62).

Q&A

After I create a rule, can I modify it?
Yes. To modify an existing rule, select the rule you want to modify, click the Change Rule button, and then click the Edit Rule Settings command. Next, make the desired changes in the Rules Wizard. Click the Finish button after making all necessary changes.

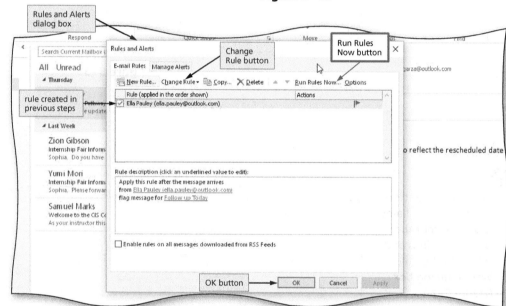

Figure 5–62

- Click the Run Rules Now button (Rules and Alerts dialog box) to display the Run Rules Now dialog box.

- Click the Ella Pauley check box to select it and specify the rule that will run.

- Click the Run Now button (Run Rules Now dialog box) to run the rule (Figure 5–63).

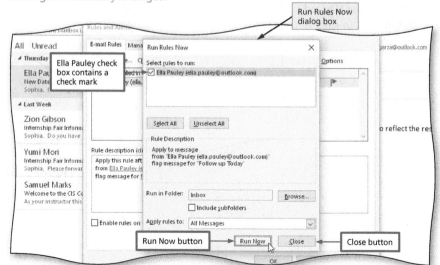

Figure 5–63

4

- Click the Close button (Run Rules Now dialog box) to close the Run Rules Now dialog box.

- Click the OK button (Rules and Alerts dialog box) (shown in Figure 5–62) to close the Rules and Alerts dialog box (Figure 5–64).

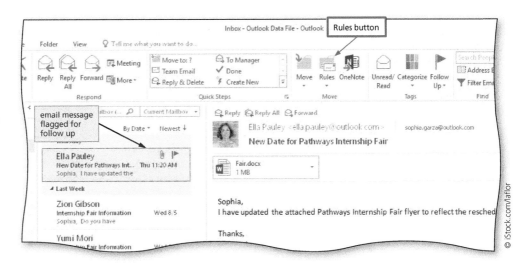

Figure 5–64

To Delete a Rule

1 CUSTOMIZE EMAIL MESSAGES | 2 CUSTOMIZE SIGNATURES & STATIONERY | 3 MANAGE JUNK EMAIL FILTERS
4 CONFIGURE RULES | **5 CHANGE CALENDAR OPTIONS | 6 ADD NEWS FEED**

Why? *When you no longer need a rule, you should delete it.* After further consideration, you decide that you do not need to flag all email messages from your faculty advisor; therefore, you decide to delete the rule. The following steps delete a rule.

1

- Click the Rules button (Home tab | Move group) (shown in Figure 5–64) to display a list of rule options.

- Click the Manage Rules & Alerts command to display the Rules and Alerts dialog box (Figure 5–65).

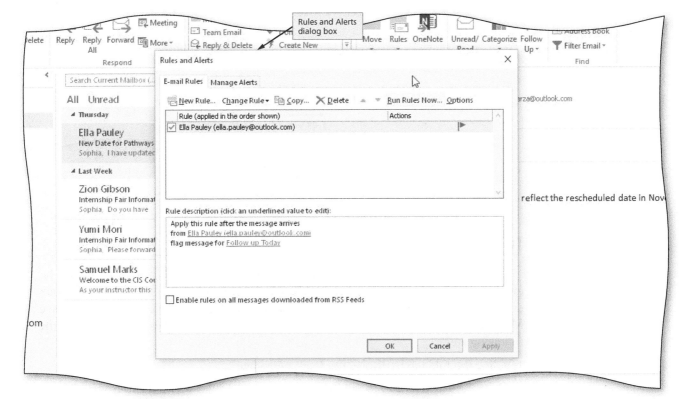

Figure 5–65

- Click the Delete button (Rules and Alerts dialog box) to display the Microsoft Outlook dialog box (Figure 5–66).

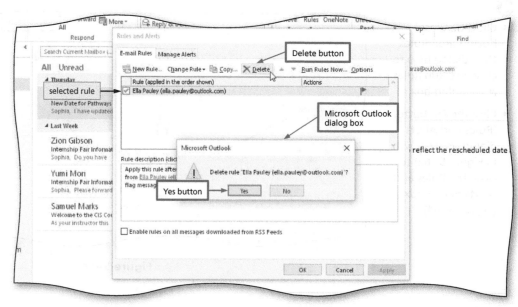

Figure 5–66

- Click the Yes button (Microsoft Outlook dialog box) to delete the Ella Pauley rule (Figure 5–67).

- Click the OK button (Rules and Alerts dialog box) to close the Rules and Alerts dialog box.

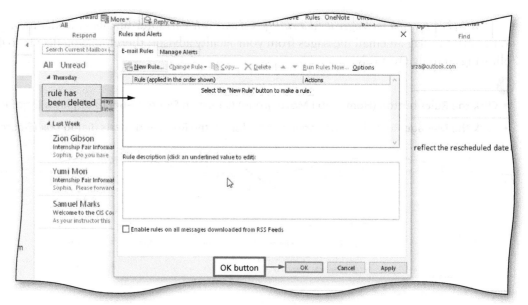

Figure 5–67

TO SET UP AUTOMATIC REPLIES

Outlook provides a quick way to set up automatic replies for when you may be away from your email account, such as when you are out of the office; however, your email account must support automatic replies using Microsoft Exchange. If you have a Microsoft Exchange account and want to set up automatic replies, you would use the following steps.

1. Click the File tab to display the Backstage view.

2. If necessary, click Info in the Backstage view to display account information.

3. Click Automatic Replies to display the Automatic Replies dialog box.

4. Click 'Send automatic replies' to turn on automatic replies.

5. Change the Start time to select the day and time for the automatic replies to start.

6. Change the End time to select the day and time for the automatic replies to stop.

7. Select Inside My Organization and enter an email message for email messages to be sent inside your organization.

8. Select Outside My Organization and enter an email message for email messages to be sent outside your organization.

9. Click OK to save the rule for automatic replies.

BTW
Cleanup Tools
In addition to archiving email messages, Outlook provides cleanup tools to help control the size of your mailbox. To access the various cleanup tools, display the Backstage view, click the Info tab, if necessary, click the Cleanup Tools button, and then click the desired cleanup tool you want to access.

To Set AutoArchive Settings

1 CUSTOMIZE EMAIL MESSAGES | 2 CUSTOMIZE SIGNATURES & STATIONERY | 3 MANAGE JUNK EMAIL FILTERS
4 CONFIGURE RULES | **5 CHANGE CALENDAR OPTIONS** | 6 ADD NEWS FEED

Why? *You can have Outlook transfer old items to a storage file. Items are only considered old after a certain number of days that you specify.* Sophia decides that she should back up the email messages in her email account. By default, when AutoArchive is turned on, Outlook archives messages every 14 days. The following steps turn on AutoArchive.

• Click the File tab to display the Backstage view.

• Click Options in the Backstage view to display the Outlook Options dialog box.

• Click Advanced in the Category list to display the Advanced options (Figure 5–68).

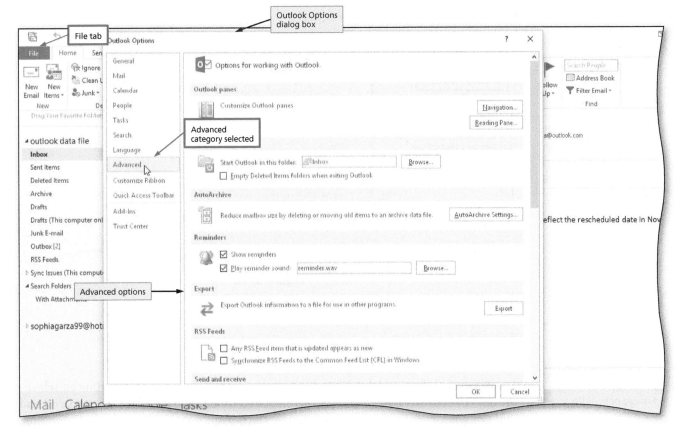

Figure 5–68

- Click the AutoArchive Settings button (Outlook Options dialog box) to display the AutoArchive dialog box (Figure 5–69).

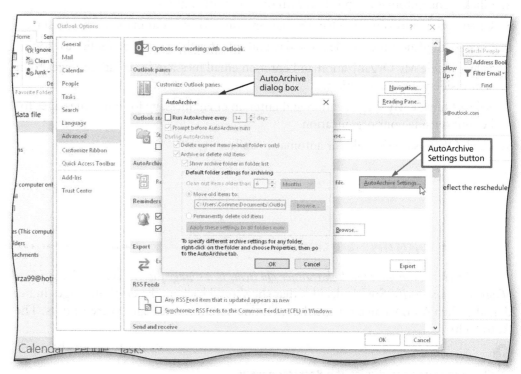

Figure 5–69

- Click the 'Run AutoArchive every' check box to select it and enable AutoArchive (Figure 5–70).

- Click the OK button (AutoArchive dialog box) to close the AutoArchive dialog box.

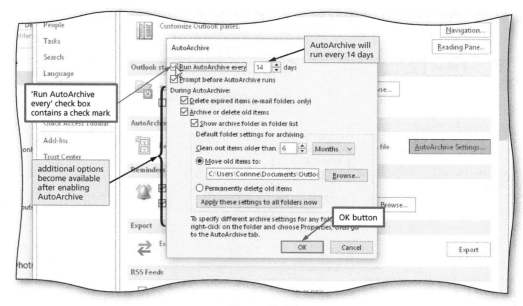

Figure 5–70

BTW
Advanced Options
In addition to the various Outlook options presented in this module, Outlook allows users to view and change advanced options. To access the advanced options, open the Outlook Options dialog box and then click Advanced in the Category list.

Customizing the Calendar

You can customize the Calendar to better suit your needs. For example, you can select the days of your work week and set the displayed time range to reflect the start and end times of your workday. You can also change the default reminder time from 15 minutes to any other interval, such as five minutes or a half-hour. Other Calendar options you can customize include the calendar font and current time zone.

To Change the Work Time on the Calendar

Sophia would like to customize the work time on the Calendar so that it reflects her work schedule. She normally works from 9:00 AM to 4:30 PM on Mondays, Wednesdays, Fridays, and Saturdays. The following steps change the Calendar settings to match the work schedule and make Monday the first day of the week. *Why? By default, the Calendar Work Week is set for Monday through Friday, but you can select which days comprise your work week.*

- Click Calendar in the Category list in the Outlook Options dialog box to display the Calendar options (Figure 5–71).

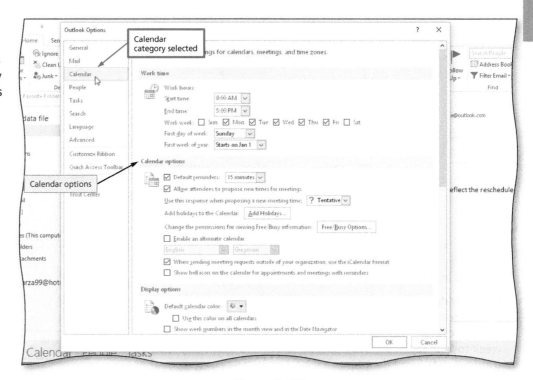

Figure 5–71

- Click the Start time box arrow to display a list of start times.

- Select 9:00 AM to change the start time.

- Click the End time box arrow to display a list of end times.

- Select 4:30 PM to change the end time (Figure 5–72).

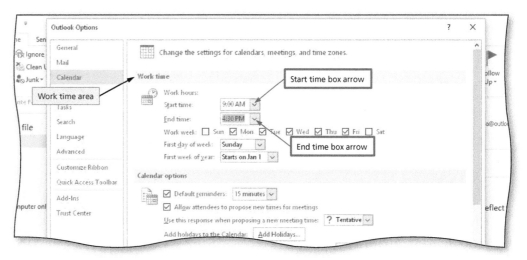

Figure 5–72

- Click the Tue check box to deselect it.
- Click the Thu check box to deselect it.
- Click the Sat check box to select it (Figure 5–73).

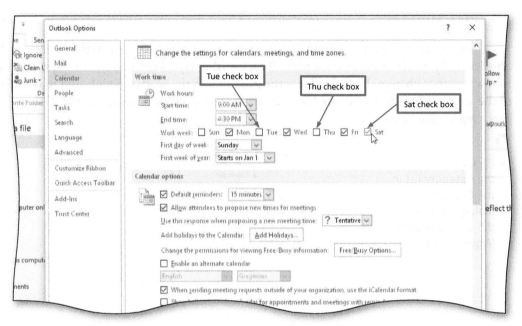

Figure 5–73

- Click the 'First day of week' box arrow to display a list of days.
- Click Monday to change the first day of the week to Monday (Figure 5–74).

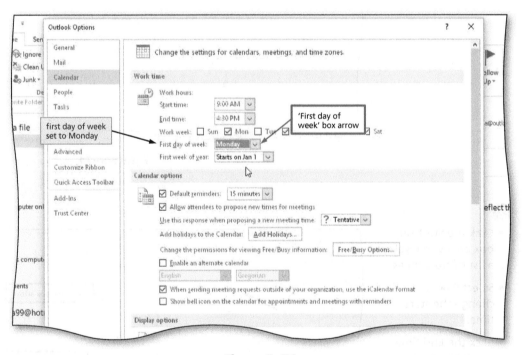

Figure 5–74

To Change the Time for Calendar Reminders

1 CUSTOMIZE EMAIL MESSAGES | 2 CUSTOMIZE SIGNATURES & STATIONERY | 3 MANAGE JUNK EMAIL FILTERS
4 CONFIGURE RULES | **5 CHANGE CALENDAR OPTIONS** | 6 ADD NEWS FEED

To further customize the Outlook calendar, Sophia would like to increase the time for reminders to 30 minutes. The following step changes the time for reminders. *Why?* *By default, the Calendar reminders are set for 15 minutes prior to an appointment or meeting.*

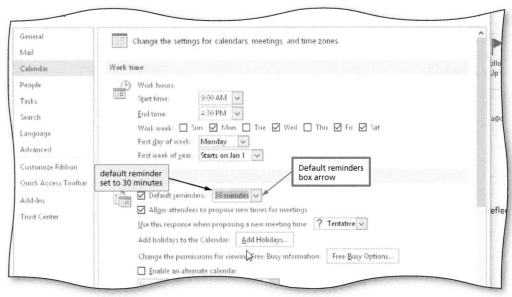

1

- Click the Default reminders box arrow to display a list of times.

- Click 30 minutes to select it as the default time for reminders (Figure 5–75).

Figure 5–75

To Change the Time Zone Setting

1 CUSTOMIZE EMAIL MESSAGES | 2 CUSTOMIZE SIGNATURES & STATIONERY | 3 MANAGE JUNK EMAIL FILTERS
4 CONFIGURE RULES | 5 CHANGE CALENDAR OPTIONS | 6 ADD NEWS FEED

Why? When you travel, your time zone may change and your calendar should be updated. If you change the time zone setting in Calendar, Outlook updates your appointments to display the new time zone when you arrive. Sophia is participating in an internship summit this summer with the director, Ms. Pauley in Honolulu, Hawaii, and needs to change the time zones accordingly. The following steps change the time zone.

- Scroll down until the Time zones settings are visible in the Outlook Options dialog box (Figure 5–76).

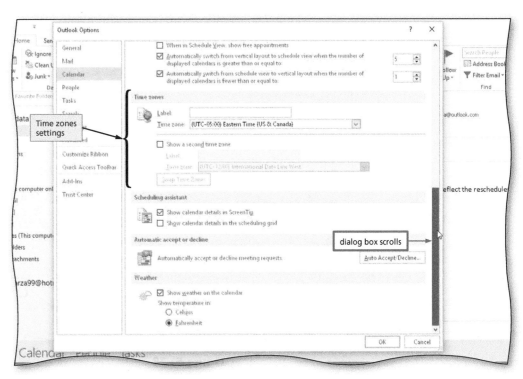

Figure 5–76

● Click the Time zone box arrow to display a list of time zones (Figure 5–77).

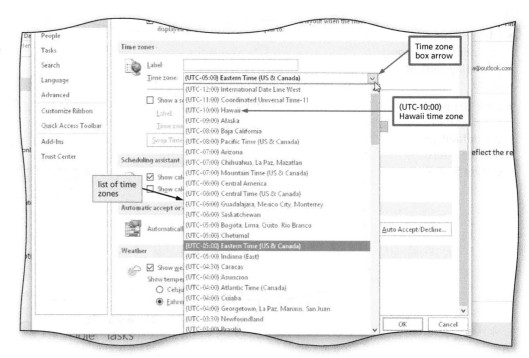

Figure 5–77

● Scroll and then click (UTC-10:00) Hawaii to select the time zone (Figure 5–78).

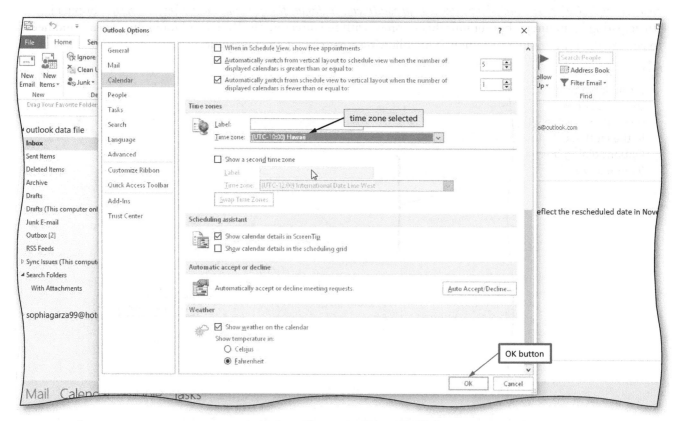

Figure 5–78

4

- Click the OK button (Outlook Options dialog box) to close the Outlook Options dialog box.

- Click the Calendar button in the Navigation Bar to display the Calendar to view the changes (Figure 5–79).

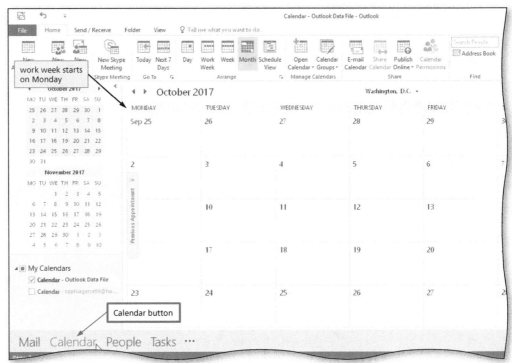

Figure 5–79

Working with RSS Feeds

Really Simple Syndication (RSS) is a way for content publishers to make news, blogs, and other content available to subscribers. RSS feeds typically are found on news websites, political discussion boards, educational blogs, and other sites that frequently update their content. For example, the PBS website contains an RSS feed on the Frontline webpage that allow people to view recent news stories in one convenient location. If you frequently visit websites that offer RSS feeds, you quickly can review the feed content of all the websites in a simple list in your browser by subscribing to their RSS feeds, without having to first navigate to each individual site.

If you want to use Outlook to read the feed, you can add the RSS feed to your account using the Account Settings dialog box. Outlook creates an easy way to manage and work with your RSS feed. Some accounts let you access the feeds from your web browser if they are using a common feeds folder; however, not all accounts allow for this.

To Subscribe to an RSS Feed

1 CUSTOMIZE EMAIL MESSAGES | 2 CUSTOMIZE SIGNATURES & STATIONERY | 3 MANAGE JUNK EMAIL FILTERS
4 CONFIGURE RULES | 5 CHANGE CALENDAR OPTIONS | 6 ADD NEWS FEED

Sophia subscribes to several RSS feeds in her web browser. To view the feed using Outlook, she needs to set up an RSS feed from http://www.nirmaltv.com/feed/. The following steps subscribe to an RSS feed and display the messages. *Why? The benefit of displaying an RSS feed in Outlook is the ability to combine feeds from multiple web sources in one place. You no longer have to visit different websites for news, weather, blogs, and other information.*

1

- Click the Mail button in the Navigation Bar to display the mailboxes in the Navigation Pane.

- Right-click the RSS Feeds folder in the Navigation Pane to display a shortcut menu (Figure 5–80).

Q&A

What should I do if an RSS Feeds folder does not appear in Sophia's mailbox? Right-click the RSS Feeds folder in a different mailbox on your computer.

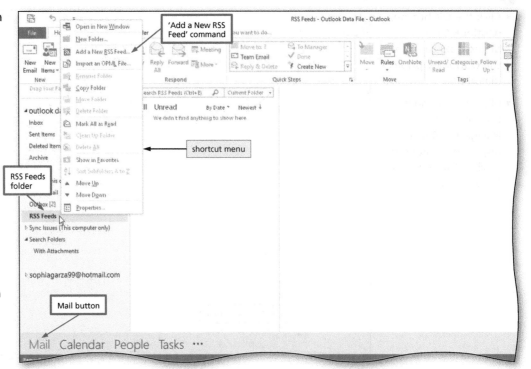

Figure 5–80

2

- Click the Add a New RSS Feed command to display the New RSS Feed dialog box (Figure 5–81).

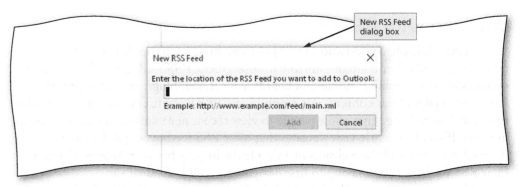

Figure 5–81

3

- Type `http://www.nirmaltv.com/feed/` in the text box to enter the address of an RSS feed (Figure 5–82).

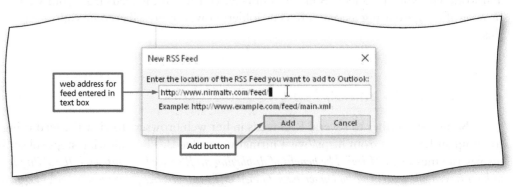

Figure 5–82

4

- Click the Add button (New RSS Feed dialog box) to add the RSS feed to the RSS Feeds folder.
- Click the Yes button (Microsoft Outlook dialog box) to confirm you want to add the RSS feed (Figure 5–83).

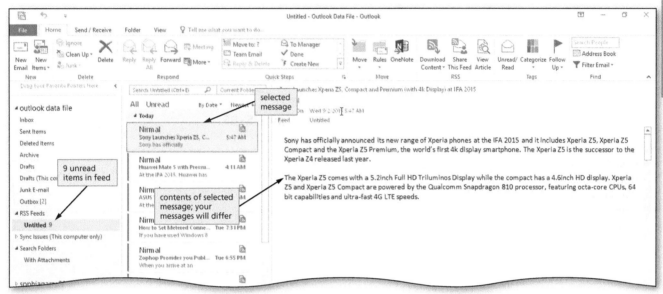

Figure 5–83

Experiment

- Click the different messages to see what has been posted in the RSS Feeds folder.

To Delete an RSS Feed

1 CUSTOMIZE EMAIL MESSAGES | 2 CUSTOMIZE SIGNATURES & STATIONERY | 3 MANAGE JUNK EMAIL FILTERS
4 CONFIGURE RULES | 5 CHANGE CALENDAR OPTIONS | 6 ADD NEWS FEED

Why? *When you no longer need to use an RSS feed, you should delete it so that you do not have unwanted messages in your account.* The following steps delete an RSS feed.

1

- Right-click the Untitled folder below the RSS Feeds folder in the Navigation Pane to display a shortcut menu (Figure 5–84).

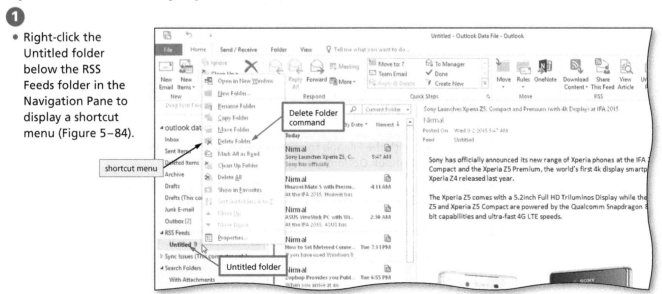

Figure 5–84

- Click the Delete
Folder command to
display the Microsoft
Outlook dialog box
(Figure 5–85).

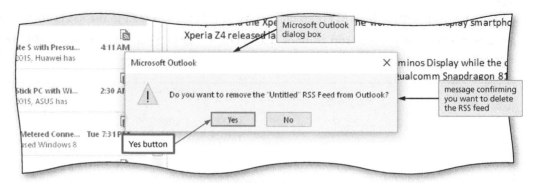

Figure 5–85

- Click the Yes button
(Microsoft Outlook
dialog box) to
delete the RSS Feed
(Figure 5–86).

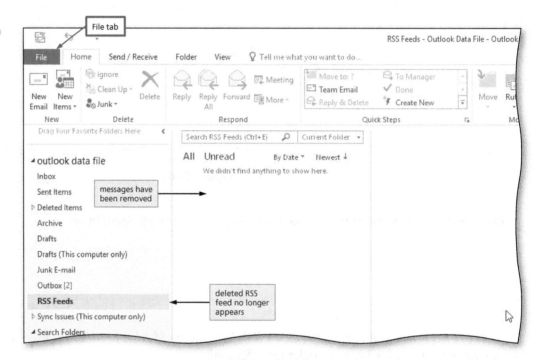

Figure 5–86

To Reset the Time Zone Setting

Why? *You should change the time zone back to your original time zone before quitting Outlook.* The following steps reset the time zone.

1. If necessary, click the File tab to open the Backstage view, and then click Options to display the Outlook Options dialog box.

2. Click Calendar, and then scroll down until the Time zones settings are visible in the Outlook Options dialog box.

3. Click the Time zone box arrow to display a list of time zones.

4. Click your time zone to select the time zone.

5. Exit Outlook.

Summary

In this module, you have learned how to add another email account, customize Outlook options, add signatures and stationery, manage the junk email filter, create rules, customize calendar options, and add RSS Feeds.

CONSIDER THIS: PLAN AHEAD

What future decisions will you need to make when customizing email messages, adding signatures and stationery, managing junk email options, working with rules, customizing the calendar, and adding RSS feeds?

1. Customize Email Messages.

    a) Determine which options you want to customize.

    b) Determine the information to include in your signature.

    c) Determine the layout that you would like for stationery.

2. Managing Junk Email Options.

    a) Determine which domains should be placed on the Safe Senders list.

    b) Determine which specific email addresses should be placed on the Blocked Senders list.

3. Working with Rules.

    a) Plan rules to use with your email messages.

    b) Determine how you would like your email messages to be processed.

4. Customizing the Calendar.

    a) Determine the calendar settings you need.

5. Adding RSS Feeds.

    a) Determine what news feeds you would like to use.

CONSIDER THIS

How should you submit solutions to questions in the assignments identified with a symbol?

Every assignment in this book contains one or more questions with a symbol. These questions require you to think beyond the assigned file. Present your solutions to the question in the format required by your instructor. Possible formats may include one or more of these options: write the answer; create a document that contains the answer; present your answer to the class; discuss your answer in a group; record the answer as audio or video using a webcam, smartphone, or portable media player; or post answers on a blog, wiki, or website.

Apply Your Knowledge

Reinforce the skills and apply the concepts you learned in this module.

Note: To complete this assignment, you will be required to use the Data Files. Please contact your instructor for information about accessing the Data Files.

Creating a Personalized Signature

Instructions: Run Outlook. You will use the Signatures and Stationery dialog box (Figure 5–87) to create a personalized signature to use when you send email messages to others.

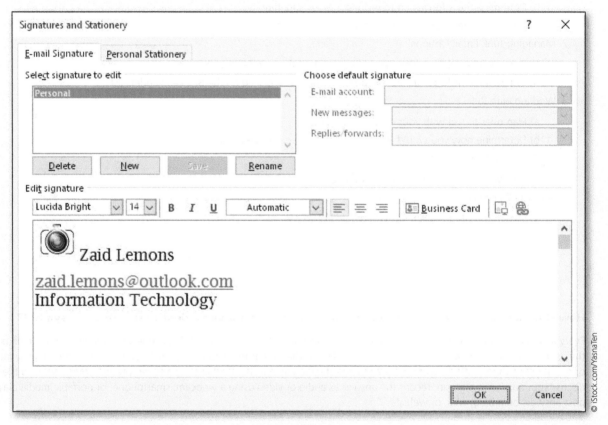

Figure 5–87

Perform the following tasks:

1. Display the Outlook Options dialog box, and then display the Signatures and Stationery dialog box.

2. Create a signature using **Personal** as the name of the signature.

3. From the Data Files, add the image named Camera to the signature.

4. Change the font to Lucida Bright and the font size to 14.

5. On three lines, enter the following information: your name, your email address, and your major.

6. Set the signature to apply to new messages, replies, and forwards.

7. Select the Profile theme as your stationery.

8. Accept the changes in the dialog boxes and then create a new email message addressed to your instructor to display your new signature and stationery.

9. Submit the email message in the format specified by your instructor.

10. ✴ Why is it a good idea to configure Outlook to include a signature in outgoing email messages?

Extend Your Knowledge

Extend the skills you learned in this module and experiment with new skills. You may need to use Help to complete the assignment.

Adding a Second Email Account to Microsoft Outlook

Instructions: Run Outlook. You are going to add a second email account to Microsoft Outlook so that you can send and receive email messages from two accounts. If you do not already have another email account to add to Microsoft Outlook, sign up for a free account using a service such as Outlook.com, Gmail, or Yahoo!. Once you create the account, you will add the email account to Outlook using the Add Account Wizard shown in Figure 5–88, and then send an email to your instructor.

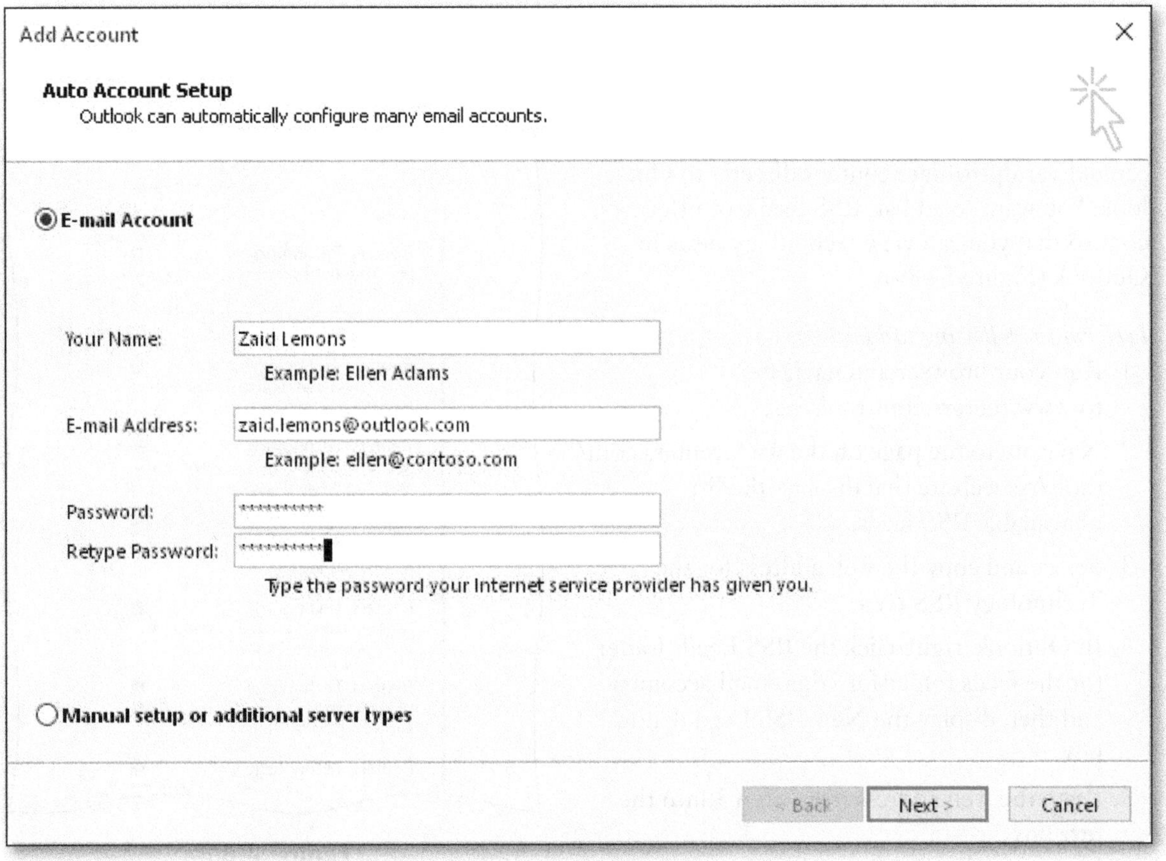

Figure 5–88

Continued >

Extend Your Knowledge *continued*

Perform the following tasks:

1. If necessary, navigate to a free email service and sign up for a free email account.

2. Start Outlook and display the Backstage view.

3. If necessary, click the Info tab to display the Info gallery.

4. Click the Add Account button to display the first dialog box in the Add Account Wizard.

5. Enter the desired information for the email account you are adding, including your name, email address, and password.

6. Click the Next button to instruct Outlook to automatically configure the account. If Outlook is unable to configure the account automatically, you may need to manually configure the account settings.

7. When the account has been configured successfully, click the Finish button.

8. Open a new email message addressed to your instructor stating that you have configured a new email account in Outlook. Send the email message to your instructor using the account you have just configured.

9. ✳ In what circumstances is it helpful to have multiple email accounts configured in Microsoft Outlook?

Expand Your World: Cloud and Web Technologies

Viewing a Tech News RSS Feed in Outlook

Problem: RSS feeds are web technologies that can deliver up-to-date content directly to Outlook. You want to add an RSS feed from Reuters.com so that you can view technology news in Outlook (Figure 5–89).

Perform the following tasks:

1. Run your browser and navigate to www.reuters.com/tools/rss.

2. Navigate to the page on the www.reuters.com/tools/rss website that displays the list of available RSS feeds.

3. Select and copy the web address for the Technology RSS feed.

4. In Outlook, right-click the RSS Feeds folder (or the feeds folder for your email account) and then display the New RSS Feed dialog box.

5. Paste the web address from Step 3 into the text box.

6. Add the feed to Outlook.

7. Open the first RSS message.

8. Print the message and then submit it in the format specified by your instructor.

9. ✳ What other RSS feeds might you find useful to include in Microsoft Outlook?

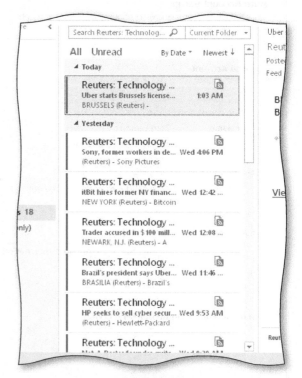

Figure 5–89

In the Labs

Design, create, modify, and/or use files following the guidelines, concepts, and skills presented in this module. Labs 1 and 2, which increase in difficulty, require you to create solutions based on what you learned in the module; Lab 3 requires you to apply your creative thinking and problem-solving skills to design and implement a solution.

Lab 1: **Creating Multiple Signatures**

Problem: You communicate with both instructors and other students via email. Your professors ask students to clearly identify themselves in email messages, but you do not want to include the same information in email messages you send to your friends. Instead, you want to include your nickname and cell phone number in your email signature. You will create two signatures: one to use when you send email messages to your instructors, and another for email messages you send to friends. You will use the Signatures and Stationery dialog box to create the signatures (Figure 5–90).

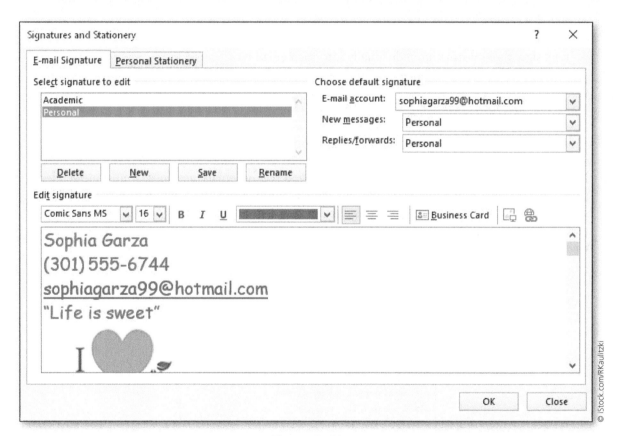

Figure 5–90

Perform the following tasks:

1. Display the Outlook Options dialog box, and then display the Signatures and Stationery dialog box.
2. Create a signature using **Academic** as the name of the signature.
3. Change the font to Cooper Black and the font size to 16.

Continued >

In the Labs continued

4. On three lines, enter the following information: your name, the name of your school, and your email address.

5. Using the Academic signature, send an email message to your instructor. The email message should specify that the signature is the Academic signature.

6. Create another signature using **Personal** as the name of the signature.

7. Change the font to Comic Sans MS, the font size to 16, and the font color to one of your choosing.

8. On four lines, enter the following information: your name, your phone number, your email address, and a life quote in quotation marks.

9. From the Data Files, add the image named Vegan in your signature file or add your own photo for your personal signature.

10. Select a Theme for your Personal signature.

11. Using the Personal signature, send an email message to a friend and a copy to your instructor to tell them what you are learning in this class. The email message should specify that the signature is the Personal signature.

12. ☀ Do you think it is easier to switch back and forth between different signatures or manually type signature information individually into each email message? Why?

Lab 2: **Configuring Junk Email**

Problem: You occasionally find email messages you want to read in the Junk E-mail folder for your Outlook email account. You also receive spam from a certain email address. You want to use the Junk E-mail Options dialog box to make sure you receive email messages from some senders, while blocking email messages from another sender. Set up a rule as shown in Figure 5-91. This lab requires that you capture screen shots during the following steps. Your instructor will provide instructions for how to create a screen shot using the Microsoft Word Screenshot tool or the Microsoft Windows Snipping Tool.

Figure 5–91

Perform the following tasks:

1. In Outlook, display the Junk E-mail Options dialog box.

2. Add @yahoo.com to the Safe Senders list. Take a screen shot of what is displayed in the Safe Senders list.

3. Add eblue179@gmail.com to the Safe Recipients list. Take a screen shot of what is displayed in the Safe Recipients list.

4. Add @worldgames.net to the Blocked Senders list. Take a screen shot of what is displayed in the Blocked Senders list.

5. Create a new rule that flags messages for follow-up from ctirrell@live.com. Flag the message for follow-up today. Take a screen shot of what is displayed in the Rules Wizard setup dialog box after you set up the rule as shown in Figure 5–91.

6. Submit the screen shots in the format specified by your instructor.

7. ⊛ What other domains and email addresses might you add to the Safe Senders list? What are some examples of other domains and email addresses you might add to the Blocked Senders list?

Lab 3: **Consider This: Your Turn**

Apply your creative thinking and problem solving skills to design and implement a solution.

Creating Rules for Email

Problem: This semester you will be receiving emails from many different instructors. To stay organized, create the following folders and rules. This lab requires that you capture screen shots during the following steps. Your instructor will provide instructions for how to create a screen shot using the Microsoft Word Screenshot tool or the Microsoft Windows Snipping Tool.

Part 1: For four of the classes you are currently taking, create email folders for each class and take a screen shot of the four folders. Create four rules to move messages related to the classes to the appropriate class email folder and take a screen shot of each completed rule. Write a rule for the fourth class that flags messages for follow-up for today. Submit the screen shots in the format specified by your instructor.

Part 2: ⊛ You made several decisions when creating the rules in this exercise, such as which folders to create and how to set up the rule to identify to which class an email message belongs. What was the rationale behind each of these decisions?

Index

Note: **Boldfaced** page numbers indicate key terms